April 12–14, 2016
Vienna , Austria

Association for
Computing Machinery

Advancing Computing as a Science & Profession

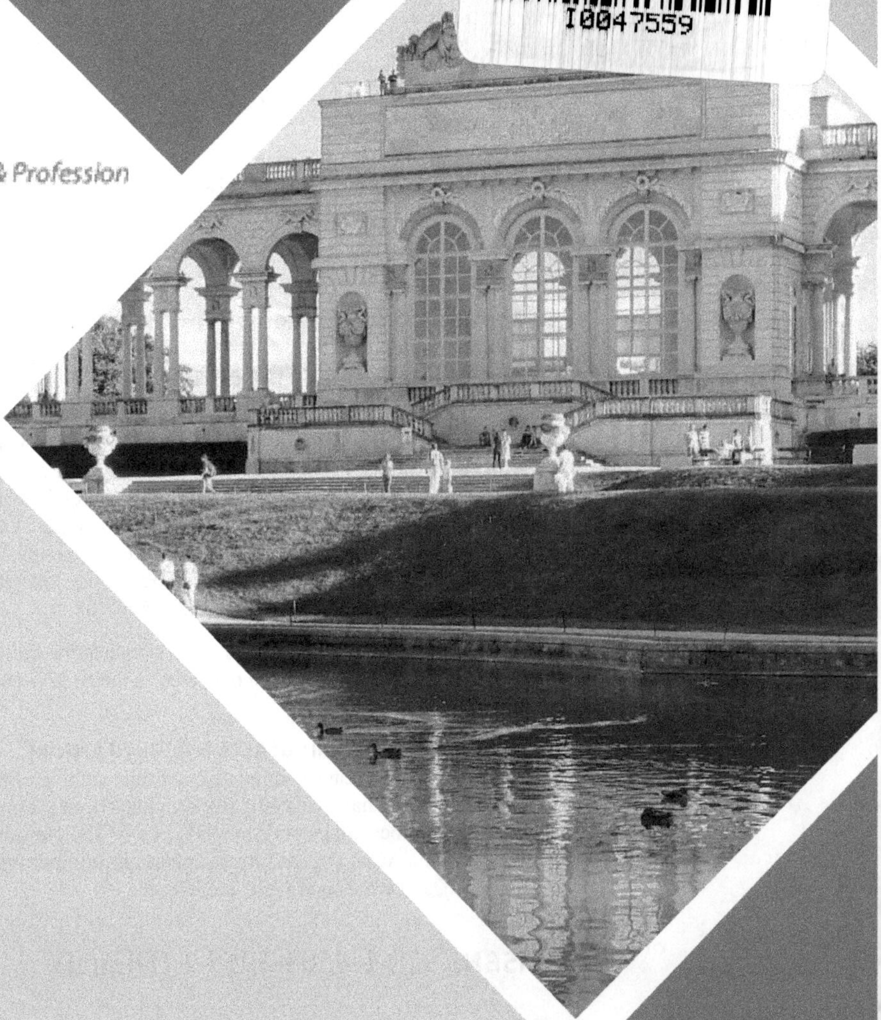

HSCC'16

Proceedings of the 19th International Conference on

Hybrid Systems: Computation and Control

Sponsored by:

ACM SIGBED

Technical co-sponsor:

IEEE Control Systems Society

Supported by:

DENSO Corporation
and Toyota Motor Engineering & Manufacturing North America

Association for
Computing Machinery

Advancing Computing as a Science & Profession

The Association for Computing Machinery
2 Penn Plaza, Suite 701
New York, New York 10121-0701

ISBN: 978-1-4503-3955-1 (Digital)

ISBN: 978-1-4503-4476-0 (Print)

Additional copies may be ordered prepaid from:

ACM Order Department
PO Box 30777
New York, NY 10087-0777, USA

Phone: 1-800-342-6626 (USA and Canada)
+1-212-626-0500 (Global)
Fax: +1-212-944-1318
E-mail: acmhelp@acm.org
Hours of Operation: 8:30 am – 4:30 pm ET

Printed in the USA

HSCC 2016 - Chairs' Welcome

It is our great pleasure to welcome you to the proceedings of the 19th International Conference on "Hybrid Systems: Computation and Control" (HSCC 2016) held in Vienna, Austria, on April 12-14th 2016. HSCC has long been the leading, single-track conference on foundations, techniques, and tools for analysis, verification, control, synthesis, optimization, implementation, and applications of dynamical systems that exhibit continuous and discrete (hybrid) dynamics. Applications at HSCC deal broadly with Cyber-Physical Systems (CPS), and include (but are not limited to) robotics, mixed signal circuits, large-scale infrastructure networks, as well as natural systems such as biochemical and physiological models.

HSCC 2016 is held as part of the 8th Cyber Physical Systems Week (CPS Week), alongside the International Conference on Cyber-Physical Systems (ICCPS), the International Conference on Information Processing in Sensor Networks (IPSN), the Real-Time and Embedded Technology and Applications Symposium (RTAS), and additional CPS-related workshops. Previous editions of the HSCC conferences have been held as a single event since 1998, and in conjunction with CPS Week since 2009. Information on the HSCC conference series can be found at

http://www.hscc-conference.org

Forty-five Program Committee members have helped to provide at least 4 reviews for each of the 65 submitted contributions. Continuing the tradition of HSCC started in 2012, a 7-day rebuttal period has been offered to the authors in order to respond to the comments of the reviewers. Based on the PC discussions following the author rebuttal, 28 high-quality articles have been accepted, to be presented during the thirty-minute single-track sessions at the conference. These contributions appear as full papers in the proceedings. Furthermore, 4 tool and case study articles appear as short papers in the proceedings. The short papers are presented alongside other contributions during the joint CPS Week Poster and Demo session. The Demo and Poster session for HSCC 2016 has been organized by Dr. Jim Kapinski. The overall acceptance rate for the conference was 49%, while specifically for the regular papers the acceptance rate was 47%.

We have decided to strongly promote the Repeatability Evaluation (RE) process, which draws upon several similar efforts at other conferences (SIGMOD, SAS, CAV, ECOOP, OOPSLA, all of them having an emphasis on "artifacts"), and which follows a first experimental run during HSCC 2014. HSCC has a rich history of publishing strong papers emphasizing computational contributions. However, subsequent re-creation of these computational elements is often challenging because details of the implementation are unavoidably absent in the paper. The goal of the HSCC RE process is to improve the reproducibility of computational results in the papers selected for the conference. Prof. Ian Mitchell has led the effort, aided by an RE Committee of 21 junior researchers, providing on average 3 evaluations to each of the 18 submitted RE packages. This year, 14 papers have passed the RE process and they have been recognized in the proceedings by printing an RE stamp on their first page (for further information please see the report below).

The contributions have been bundled in eight thematic single-track sessions, ranging over the following themes: temporal logic applications; analysis of switched systems; safety and stability analysis; methods for reachability analysis; time- and event-based models; control synthesis; models with uncertainty; reachability computation. Furthermore, one session hosts poster and demo (tool papers or RE packages) contributions, as well as the case study papers.

A highlight of HSCC 2016 has been the presence of a high-profile invited speaker, Prof. Sandra Hirche from TU Munich, giving a lecture on the topic of "Optimal Co-Design of Scheduling and Control for Networked Systems." Furthermore, CPS Week has featured plenary talks by two distinguished academic speakers, Prof. Rajeev Alur (University of Pennsylvania) and Prof. Tomaso Poggio (MIT), and from an industrial panel discussion on CPS. The distinguished panelists have been: Ken Butts, Toyota, USA; Rada Rodriguez, Schneider Electric, Germany; Joe Salvo, GE Global Research, USA; Sabine Herlitschka, Infineon, Austria.

HSCC 2016 features three awards: a best student paper award; a best poster/demo award; and a best RE award. These awards have been administered by a selection of colleagues from the PC. Further details on HSCC 2016 are featured on the website:

http://www.cs.ox.ac.uk/conferences/hscc2016

A few words of acknowledgment are due. Especially this year, HSCC was a team effort. First and foremost, we would like to thank the authors for entrusting their best work to the HSCC review process. We would like to thank the members of the HSCC Steering Committee (Rajeev Alur, Werner Damm, John Lygeros, Oded Maler, Paulo Tabuada, and Claire Tomlin), and to the most recent HSCC PC chairs (Antoine Girard and Sriram Sankaranarayanan), for their help and feedback on the organization process. Thanks to Ian Mitchell, Sayan Mitra, and Jim Kapinski for leading the RE process, the publicity, and the organization of the poster/demo session, respectively. We would also like to thank the PC members in the awards committees and the CPS Week organizers for the supportive and can-do attitude. A special thanks goes to Lisa M. Tolles from Sheridan Printing, and to ACM for hosting the HSCC proceedings. We would also like to thank Denso Corporation and Toyota Motor Engineering & Manufacturing North America for supporting HSCC, particularly for the conference awards. Finally, our heartfelt thanks goes to all the PC members and additional reviewers for their hard work in ensuring the quality of the contributions to HSCC 2016, and to all the participants for contributing to this memorable event.

We hope that you find this program interesting and thought provoking, and that the conference provides you with a valuable opportunity to share ideas with other researchers and practitioners from institutions around the world.

Alessandro Abate
HSCC'16 Program Co-Chair,
University of Oxford,
Oxford, UK

Georgios Fainekos
HSCC'16 Program Co-Chair
Arizona State University,
Tempe, Arizona, USA

HSCC 2016 Repeatability Evaluation

Computation is a core part of HSCC, both in the name of the conference and as a significant component of the majority of papers published each year. Unfortunately, it is rarely possible to document the details of these computational results in the constrained space allotted to a paper; therefore, repeating these results at a later date is often a challenge not just for other researchers, but even for the original authors once the details of parameter settings, compilers, toolchains and environments slip from memory.

To help members of the HSCC community address this challenge, we ran a successful repeatability evaluation procedure in 2014. A medical situation lead to the cancellation of the 2015 effort, but with that situation resolved we were able to run the process again this year. Through this process we hope to provide authors an incentive to improve the reproducibility of their computational results, guidance on how to do so, and an opportunity to test whether they have achieved that goal.

For this year's edition, we followed almost the same model as was used in 2014. Full details can be found at the HSCC 2016 repeatability evaluation website:

http://www.cs.ox.ac.uk/conferences/hscc2016/re.html

All authors of accepted papers were invited to submit a *repeatability package* (RP) in late January. The RPs were reviewed by a separate *repeatability evaluation committee* (REC) consisting of junior researchers, postdocs and senior graduate students from the HSCC community. The primary difference this year compared to 2014 was in the timing: the RP submission deadline was several weeks before the final version of the paper was due, so that the REC would have time to complete its evaluations before the proceedings were finalized. We received a total of 18 RPs. Each RP was reviewed by 2–3 members of the REC and judged on three equally weighted criteria: Coverage (fraction of computational results which could be repeated), instructions (difficulty of repeating those results based on the instructions provided by the authors), and quality (documentation and testing of the code). The following 14 RPs were judged to be repeatable (listed in the same order as they appear in the proceedings):

- "A Decision Tree Approach to Data Classification using Signal Temporal Logic" by Giuseppe Bombara, Cristian-Ioan Vasile, Francisco Penedo, Hirotoshi Yasuoka and Calin Belta
- "Temporal Logic as Filtering" by Alena Rodionova, Ezio Bartocci, Dejan Nickovic and Radu Grosu
- "Directed Specifications and Assumption Mining for Monotone Dynamical Systems" by Eric S. Kim, Murat Arcak and Sanjit A. Seshia
- "Diagnosis and Repair for Synthesis from Signal Temporal Logic Specifications" by Shromona Ghosh, Dorsa Sadigh, Pierluigi Nuzzo, Vasumathi Raman, Alexandre Donze, Alberto Sangiovanni-Vincentelli, Shankar Sastry and Sanjit Seshia
- "Generating unstable trajectories for Switched Systems via Dual Sum-Of-Squares techniques" by Benoit Legat, Raphael Jungers and Pablo A. Parrilo
- "SCOTS: A Tool for the Synthesis of Symbolic Controllers" (tool paper) by Matthias Rungger and Majid Zamani

- "Verification and Synthesis of Timing Contracts for Embedded Controllers" by Mohammad Al Khatib, Antoine Girard and Thao Dang
- "Formal Analysis of Robustness at Model and Code Level" by Timothy Wang, Pierre-Loic Garoche, Pierre Roux, Romain Jobredeaux and Eric Feron
- "Scalable Static Hybridization Methods for Analysis of Nonlinear Systems" by Stanley Bak, Sergiy Bogomolov, Thomas Henzinger, Taylor T Johnson and Pradyot Prakash
- "Adaptive Decentralized MAC for Event-triggered Networked Control Systems" by Mikhail Vilgelm, Mohammadhossein Mamduhi, Wolfgang Kellerer and Sandra Hirche
- "Control Synthesis for Large Collections of Systems with Mode-counting Constraints" by Petter Nilsson and Necmiye Ozay
- "Entropy and Minimal Data Rates for State Estimation and Model Detection" by Daniel Liberzon and Sayan Mitra
- "Safety Verification of Piecewise-Deterministic Markov Processes" by Rafael Wisniewski, Christoffer Sloth, Manuela Bujorianu and Nir Piterman
- "Reachset Conformance Testing of Hybrid Automata" by Hendrik Roehm, Jens Oehlerking, Matthias Woehrle and Matthias Althoff

Figure 1. Repeatability Evaluation badge.

The aforementioned papers will feature the HSCC repeatability badge (shown above) on their final submissions. The RPs are considered confidential and there is no requirement to make them publicly available; however, we have encouraged the authors to do so through one or more of the following routes: Submission as auxiliary material for the corresponding paper in the ACM Digital Library, a link from the HSCC 2016 repeatability evaluation website, release on one of the many open source code repository sites and/or through a private web page.

By far the most common reason that RPs were judged not to be repeatable was that the reviewers were unable to perform a successful installation and execution of the software; consequently, the absence of a paper from the list above should not be interpreted as a lack of confidence in that paper's computational conclusions, since every paper appearing at HSCC has passed a competitive standard peer review process.

The HSCC repeatability evaluation process is based on similar efforts at other conferences, and we would particularly like to acknowledge the websites of Shriram Krishnamurthi and Matthias Hauswirth, which provide a wealth of information about the closely related "artifact evaluation" processes being used at many other conferences. We have decided to use the term "repeatability evaluation" for HSCC because at present we are focusing our efforts on software artifacts only, and have consequently been able to develop more detailed (and hopefully calibrated) acceptance criteria; however, we are observing the various processes used at other conferences and look forward to the day when we converge to an approach which is as widely accepted and deployed as is basic peer review of manuscripts.

To conclude, we would like to thank the steering committee and this year's program committee chairs for their ongoing encouragement and support, the 2016 program committee members for their nominations to the REC, and especially the members of the 2016 REC for volunteering their time.

Ian M. Mitchell
Repeatability Evaluation Chair
University of British Columbia
Vancouver, Canada

Table of Contents

Invited Speaker

Session Chair: Alessandro Abate *(University of Oxford)*

Session: Models with Uncertainty

Session Chair: Antoine Girard *(CNRS)*

Session: Reachability Computation

Session Chair: Alex Donze *(University of California, Berkeley)*

Back Matter

HSCC 2016 Conference Organization

Program co-Chairs: Alessandro Abate *(University of Oxford, UK)*
Georgios Fainekos *(Arizona State University, USA)*

Repeatability Evaluation Chair: Ian Mitchell *(University of British Columbia, Canada)*

Publicity Chair: Sayan Mitra *(University of Illinois at Urbana Champaign, USA)*

Poster and Demo Chair: Jim Kapinski *(Toyota Motors, USA)*

Steering Committee: Rajeev Alur *(University of Pennsylvania, USA)*
Werner Damm *(OFFIS, Germany)*
John Lygeros *(ETH Zurich, Switzerland)*
Oded Maler *(Verimag, France)*
Paulo Tabuada *(University of California at Los Angeles, USA)*
Claire Tomlin *(University of California Berkeley, USA)*

Program Committee: Shun-Ichi Azuma *(Kyoto University, Japan)*
Christel Baier *(TU Dresden, Germany)*
Ezio Bartocci *(TU Vienna, Austria)*
Calin Belta *(Boston University, USA)*
Spring Berman *(Arizona State University, USA)*
Mireille Broucke *(University of Toronto, Canada)*
Krishnendu Chatterjee *(Institute of Science and Technology, Austria)*
Alessandro Cimatti *(Fondazione Bruno Kessler, Italy)*
Alessandro D'Innocenzo *(University of L'Aquila, Italy)*
Thao Dang *(VERIMAG, France)*
Jyotirmoy Deshmukh *(Toyota Motors, USA)*
Xu Chu Ding *(United Technologies Research Center, USA)*
Alexandre Donzé *(UC Berkeley, USA)*
Martin Fränzle *(Carl von Ossietzky Universität Oldenburg, Germany)*
Antoine Girard *(CNRS, France)*
Ichiro Hasuo *(University of Tokyo, Japan)*
Jun-Ichi Imura *(Tokyo Institute of Technology, Japan)*
Franjo Ivancic *(Google, USA)*
Taylor T Johnson *(University of Texas at Arlington, USA)*
Agung Julius *(Rensselaer Polytechnic Institute, USA)*
Sertac Karaman *(Massachusetts Institute of Technology, USA)*
Joost-Pieter Katoen *(RWTH Aachen University, Germany)*
Marta Kwiatkowska *(University of Oxford, UK)*
Jun Liu *(University of Waterloo, Canada)*
Daniele Magazzeni *(King's College London, UK)*
Manuel Mazo Jr. *(TU Delft, Netherlands)*
Sayan Mitra *(University of Illinois at Urbana-Champaign, USA)*
Jens Oehlerking *(Robert Bosch GmbH, Germany)*
Meeko Oishi *(University of New Mexico, USA)*
Necmiye Ozay *(University of Michigan, USA)*

Program Committee (continued):

Andreas Podelski *(University of Freiburg, Germany)*
Pavithra Prabhakar *(Kansas State University, USA)*
Maria Prandini *(Politecnico di Milano, Italy)*
Akshay Rajhans *(The MathWorks, USA)*
S Ramesh *(General Motors R&D, India)*
Sriram Sankaranarayanan *(University of Colorado at Boulder, USA)*
Oleg Sokolsky *(University of Pennsylvania, USA)*
Herbert Tanner *(University of Delaware, USA)*
Ufuk Topcu *(University of Texas at Austin, USA)*
Ashutosh Trivedi *(Indian Institute of Technology, Bombay, India)*
Jana Tumova *(KTH, Sweden)*
Verena Wolf *(Saarland University, Germany)*
Majid Zamani *(Technical University of Munich, Germany)*
Naijun Zhan *(Chinese Academy of Sciences, China)*
Paolo Zuliani *(Newcastle University, UK)*

Repeatability Evaluation Program Committee:

Dieky Adzkiya *(Institut Teknologi Sepuluh Nopember, Indonesia)*
Nikos Arechiga *(Toyota InfoTechnology Center, USA)*
Sergiy Bogomolov *(Institute of Science and Technology, Austria)*
Alessandro Borri *(Italian National Research Council, Italy)*
Milan Ceska *(University of Oxford, UK)*
Xin Chen *(University of Colorado at Boulder, USA)*
Tommaso Dreossi *(University of California, Berkeley, USA)*
Meng Guo *(Royal Institute of Technology, Sweden)*
Ernst Moritz Hahn *(Chinese Academy of Sciences, China)*
Bardh Hoxha *(Arizona State University, USA)*
Taylor T Johnson *(University of Texas at Arlington, USA)*
Pablo Nanez *(Universidad de los Andes, Colombia)*
Lars Petter Nilsson *(University of Michigan, USA)*
Alessandro Vittorio Papadopoulos *(Lund University, Sweden)*
Matthias Rungger *(Technical University of Munich, Germany)*
Dorsa Sadigh *(University of California, Berkeley, USA)*
Christoffer Sloth *(Aalborg University, Denmark)*
Sadegh Soudjani *(University of Oxford, UK)*

Additional reviewers:

Santosh Arvind Adimoolam
Dieky Adzkiya
Ilge Akkaya
Derya Aksaray
Nikos Arechiga
Ebru Aydin Gol
Stanley Bak
Laurent Bako
Ayca Balkan
Nicolas Basset
Mohamed Amin Ben Sassi
Sergiy Bogomolov
Alessandro Borri
Luca Bortolussi
Anton Cervin
Milan Ceska
Xin Chen
Jonathan Decastro
Jason Derenick
Soumyajit Dey
Rayna Dimitrova
Jerry Ding
Manoj Dixit
Tijs Donkers

Additional reviewers (continued):

Tommaso Dreossi
Ray Essick
Farhad Farokhi
Lu Feng
Ioannis Filippidis
Vojtech Forejt
Bernhard Fromel
Anqi Fu
Jie Fu
Sicun Gao
Christoph Gladisch
Alexander Graf-Brill
Alberto Griggio
Willem Hagemann
Ernst Moritz Hahn
Zhi Han
Naoki Hayashi
Thomas Heinz
Holger Hermanns
Takayuki Ishizaki
Nils Jansen
Xiaoqing Jin
Aleksandra Jovanovic
Raphael Jungers
Kostas Karydis
Koichi Kobayashi
Kiminao Kogiso
Zhaodan Kong
Daniel Kraehmann
Yinan Li
Yangjia Li
Qiang Ling
Jiang Liu
Scott C. Livingston
Gabriel Lopes
Anna Lukina
Victor Magron
John Martin
Pierre-Jean Meyer
Salar Moarref
Swarup Mohalik
Eike Mohlmann
Sergio Mover
Mauricio Munoz-Arias
Laura Nenzi
Alexandros Nikou
Lars Petter Nilsson
Ali Pakniyat
Simone Paoletti
Nicola Paoletti
Ivan Papusha
Francisco Penedo Alvarez
Vinayak Prabhu
Vasumathi Raman
Denise Ratasich
Hadi Ravanbakhsh
Gunther Reissig
Hendrik Roehm
Matthias Rungger
Dorsa Sadigh
Sadra Sadraddini
Sayan Saha
Soheil Samii
Christian Schilling
Arman Sharifi-Kolarijani
Barys Shyrokau
Sadegh Soudjani
Adam Stager
Ingo Stierand
Aneel Tanwani
Yuichi Tazaki
Ashish Tiwari
Stefano Tonetta
Alphan Ulusoy
Toshimitsu Ushio
Cristian-Ioan Vasile
Matthias Wenzl
Eric Wolff
Guosong Yang
Chengzhi Yuan
Shuo Zhang
Fu Zhang
Hengjun Zhao
Changhong Zhao

HSCC 2016 Sponsors & Supporters

Sponsor: ACM Special Interest Group on Embedded Systems

Technical co-sponsor: IEEE Control Systems Society

Supporters (Alphabetical order):

DENSO Corporation

Toyota Motor Engineering & Manufacturing North America

A Decision Tree Approach to Data Classification using Signal Temporal Logic

Giuseppe Bombara
Boston University
Boston, MA, USA
gbombara@bu.edu

Cristian-Ioan Vasile
Boston University
Boston, MA, USA
cvasile@bu.edu

Francisco Penedo
Boston University
Boston, MA, USA
franp@bu.edu

Hirotoshi Yasuoka
DENSO CORPORATION
Kariya, Aichi, Japan
hirotoshi_yasuoka@denso.co.jp

Calin Belta
Boston University
Boston, MA, USA
cbelta@bu.edu

ABSTRACT

This paper introduces a framework for inference of timed temporal logic properties from data. The dataset is given as a finite set of pairs of finite-time system traces and labels, where the labels indicate whether the traces exhibit some desired behavior (e.g., a ship traveling along a safe route). We propose a decision-tree based approach for learning signal temporal logic classifiers. The method produces binary decision trees that represent the inferred formulae. Each node of the tree contains a test associated with the satisfaction of a simple formula, optimally tuned from a predefined finite set of *primitives*. Optimality is assessed using heuristic *impurity* measures, which capture how well the current primitive splits the data with respect to the traces' labels. We propose extensions of the usual impurity measures from machine learning literature to handle classification of system traces by leveraging upon the *robustness degree* concept. The proposed incremental construction procedure greatly improves the execution time and the accuracy compared to existing algorithms. We present two case studies that illustrate the usefulness and the computational advantages of the algorithms. The first is an anomaly detection problem in a maritime environment. The second is a fault detection problem in an automotive powertrain system.

CCS Concepts

•**Computing methodologies → Logical and relational learning;** *Classification and regression trees;* •**Theory of computation →** *Modal and temporal logics;*

Keywords

Signal Temporal Logic; Logic Inference; Decision Trees; Impurity Measure; Machine Learning; Anomaly Detection; Supervised Learning;

HSCC '16, April 12–14, 2016, Vienna, Austria.

DOI: http://dx.doi.org/10.1145/2883817.2883843

1. INTRODUCTION

Machine learning deals with the construction of algorithms that can learn from data. Such algorithms operate by building a classifier from examples, called training data, in order to make accurate predictions on new data [24]. One of the main problems in machine learning is the so called *two-class classification problem*. In this setting, the goal is to build a classifier that can distinguish objects belonging to one of two possible classes. This problem is of fundamental importance because its solution leads to solving the more general multi-class problem [24]. Furthermore, it can be directly used in the context of anomaly detection, where the objective is to find patterns in data that do not conform to the expected behavior. These non-conforming patterns are often referred to as *anomalies* or *negatives*, whereas the normal working conditions are usually referred to as *targets* or *positives*. Given the importance of this problem and its broad applicability, it has been the topic of several surveys [16, 6].

A specific formulation of the two-class problem is determined by several factors such as the nature of the input data, the availability of labels, as well as the constraints and requirements determined by the application domain [6]. In this paper, we deal with data in form of finite time series, called signals or traces, and we suppose that the labels of these traces are available. That is, the true class of each trace is known, either *positive* or *negative*, and this information is exploited during the classifier construction phase (*supervised learning*). We tackle the two-class classification problem by bringing together concepts and tools from formal methods and machine learning. Our thesis is that a *formal specification* of the normal working conditions can be gleaned directly from execution traces and expressed in the form of Signal Temporal Logic (STL) formulae, a specification language used in the field of formal methods to define the behavior of continuous systems [22]. The inferred formulae can then be applied directly as data classifiers for new traces. In this context, some work has been initially done to optimize the parameters of a formula for a given, fixed, formula structure [17, 1, 26]. Kong et. al. [20, 18] were the first to propose an algorithm to learn *both* the formula structure and its parameters from data and called this approach *temporal logic inference* (TLI). This approach, while retaining many qualities of traditional classifiers, presents several additional advantages. First, STL formulae have precise meaning and allow for a rich specification of the normal behaviour that is easily *interpretable by humans*. Second, anomaly detection methods commonly applied to time series data are often model-based, i.e., they require a *good* model of the system running alongside the physical system [16]. Third, classical machine learning methods are often over specific to the task. That is, they focus exclusively on solving the classification problem but offer no other insight on the system where they have been applied. On the contrary, TLI fits naturally as a step in the system's design workflow and its analysis and results can be employed in other phases.

In this paper, we propose a novel, decision-tree based framework for solving the two-class classification problem involving signals using STL formulae as data classifiers. We refer to it as *framework* because we are not just proposing a single algorithm but a *class* of algorithms. Every algorithm produces a binary decision tree which can be translated to an STL formula and used for classification purposes. Each node of a tree is associated with a simple formula, chosen from a finite set of primitives. Nodes are created by finding the best primitive, along with its optimal parameters, within a greedy growing procedure. The optimality at each step is assessed using *impurity* measures, which capture how well a primitive splits the signals in the training data. The impurity measures described in this paper are modified versions of the usual impurity measures to handle signals, and were obtained by exploiting the *robustness degree* concept [9]. Our novel framework presents several advantages. In particular, the proposed incremental construction procedure requires the optimization of a small and fixed number of primitives at each node. Moreover, the number of objects to be processed decreases at each iteration. These two features greatly improve the execution time and the accuracy compared to the algorithms proposed in [20, 18].

This paper is organized as follows. In Section 2 we briefly survey some previous research efforts related to learning temporal logic formulae. In Section 3, we review the definition of Signal Temporal Logic, and its parameterized version PSTL used in the rest of the paper. The classification problem is formally stated in Section 4, and our decision tree framework is presented in detail in Section 5. Two case studies are introduced in Section 6. In Section 7 we report and discuss the results obtained by applying our temporal logic inference algorithms. We conclude in Section 8 with a summary and an outlook to future research directions.

2. RELATED WORK

Most of the recent research on temporal logical inference has focused on mining only the values of parameters associated with a given temporal logic formula structure [1, 26, 17, 2]. That is, a designer provides a formula template such as "The engine speed settles below v m/s within τ second" and an optimization procedure finds values for v and τ. The given structure reflects the (substantial) domain knowledge of the designer on the system and its properties of interest to be queried. With this approach, it is not possible to acquire new knowledge about the system directly from data, since it requires the designer to be very specific about the form of system properties that are investigated.

In [18, 20], the authors proposed methods for inferring both the formula structure and its parameters from data. They defined a fragment of STL, called inference parametric signal temporal logic (iPSTL), and showed that this fragment admits a partial order among formulae (1) in the sense of language inclusion, and (2) with respect to the robustness degree. This implies that iPSTL formulae can be organized in an infinite directed acyclic graph (DAG) according to how general they are (for any valuation). This result enabled them to formulate the classification problem as an optimization problem, whose objective function involves the robustness degree, and solve it in two cyclic steps: first, optimize the formula structure by exploring the DAG, pruning and growing it, and then, optimize the formula parameters, for a fixed structure, using a nonlinear optimization algorithm. This approach presents two major limitations. First, the parameter optimization routine has high computational cost. This is mostly due to its nonlinear nature. Finding the optimal valuation becomes more and more challenging as the algorithm proceeds, because the dimension of the parameter space grows at each iteration. This leads to long execution times. On the contrary, in our algorithm the dimension of the parameter space is fixed. Second, the DAG is built using an ordering on the language accepted by PSTL formulae. This has adverse effects on the performance. In particular, even though changing the formula structure according to the DAG offers guarantees in terms of the language, it does not imply an improvement in terms of the misclassification rate, which is the metric of interest for a classification problem. In Sec. 7, we show through a case study that our approach is able to obtain 20 times better classification performance with respect to the results in [19].

Recently, [3, 5] also tackled the two-class classification problem for inferring temporal logic formulae. Their approach can be divided in two separate steps. First, they build two generative models, one for each class. The models have to be in the form of stochastic systems and are used to compute the probability of satisfaction of a formula. Second, a discriminative formula is obtained by searching a formula that maximizes the odds of being true for the first model and false for the other model. As with other approaches, the formula structure and parameters are optimized separately. In particular, the formula structure is constructed through heuristics [3] or with a genetic algorithm [5], whereas the parameter space is explored through statistical model checking. This approach present some disadvantages. Primarily, it needs to build models of the system under analysis. This requires a domain expert and a certain amount of data. We do not agree with the authors' statement that model-based methods require less data than direct methods. On the contrary, we believe that more or the same amount of data is needed for the model parameter selection and the model validation. Overall, in the case studies reported, a significant designer intervention was required to guide the procedure to obtain a satisfactory formula. As opposed, our method does not need a model of the system nor an expert to guide the learning process.

To conclude, [12, 11] used a learning procedure for formulae defined in particular spatial superposition logics. These logics were developed for describing patterns in images without a time component. In particular, every image is represented with a multi-resolution format using a fixed height quad-tree data structure (which should not be confused with a decision tree). In this representation, every node contains an attribute describing an area of the image. Nodes that appear at deeper levels provide information about smaller areas. A pattern in an image corresponds to a path [12] or a combination of several paths [11] in the relative quad-tree. Therefore, to describe the patterns, the semantics of these spatial logics are defined over the paths of quad-trees. In these works, formulae are learned from a labeled set of paths [12] or a labeled set of quad-trees [11] by applying off-the-shelf rule-based learning algorithms to the attributes of the nodes.

3. SIGNAL TEMPORAL LOGIC

Let $\mathbb{R}$ be the set of real numbers. For $t \in \mathbb{R}$, we denote the interval $[t, \infty)$ by $\mathbb{R}_{\geq t}$. We use $\mathcal{S} = \{s : \mathbb{R}_{\geq 0} \to \mathbb{R}^n\}$ with $n \in \mathbb{N}$ to denote the set of all continuous parameterized curves in the n-dimensional Euclidean space $\mathbb{R}^n$. In this paper, an element of $\mathcal{S}$ is called a *signal* and its parameter is interpreted as *time*. Given a signal $s \in \mathcal{S}$, the components of s are denoted by s_i, $i \in \{1, \ldots, n\}$. The set $\mathcal{F}$ contains the projection operators from a signal s to one of its components s_i, specifically $\mathcal{F} = \{f_i : \mathbb{R}^n \to \mathbb{R}, f_i(s) = s_i, i = \{1, \ldots, n\}\}$. The *suffix* at time $t \geq 0$ of a signal is denoted by $s[t] \in \mathcal{S}$ and it represents the signal s shifted forward in time by t time units, i.e., $s[t](\tau) = s(\tau + t)$ for all $\tau \in \mathbb{R}_{\geq 0}$.

The syntax of *Signal Temporal Logic* (STL) [22] is defined as follows:

$$\phi ::= \top \mid p_{f(x) \leq \mu} \mid \neg\phi \mid \phi_1 \wedge \phi_2 \mid \phi_1 \mathcal{U}_{[a,b)} \phi_2$$

where $\top$ is the Boolean *true* constant; $p_{f(x) \leq \mu}$ is a predicate over $\mathbb{R}^n$ defined by the function $f \in \mathcal{F}$ and $\mu \in \mathbb{R}$ of the form $p_{f(x) \leq \mu}(x) = f(x) \leq \mu$; $\neg$ and $\wedge$ are the Boolean operators negation and conjunction; and $\mathcal{U}_{[a,b)}$ is the bounded temporal operator *until*. We use $\perp$ to denote the Boolean *false* constant.

The semantics of STL is defined over signals in $\mathcal{S}$ recursively as follows [22]:

$$\begin{array}{lll}
s[t] \models \top & \Leftrightarrow & \top \\
s[t] \models p_{f(x) \leq \mu} & \Leftrightarrow & (f(s(t)) \leq \mu) \\
s[t] \models \neg\phi & \Leftrightarrow & \neg(s[t] \models \phi) \\
s[t] \models (\phi_1 \wedge \phi_2) & \Leftrightarrow & (s[t] \models \phi_1) \wedge (s[t] \models \phi_2) \\
s[t] \models (\phi_1 \mathcal{U}_{[a,b)} \phi_2) & \Leftrightarrow & \exists t_u \in [t+a, t+b) \text{ s.t. } (s[t_u] \models \phi_2) \\
 & & \wedge \left(\forall t_1 \in [t, t_u)\ s[t_1] \models \phi_1\right)
\end{array}$$

A signal $s \in \mathcal{S}$ is said to satisfy an STL formula ϕ if and only if $s[0] \models \phi$. We extend the type of allowed inequality predicates in STL to $s[t] \models p_{f(x) > \mu} \equiv s[t] \models \neg p_{f(x) \leq \mu}$. Thus, predicates are defined in this paper by a function $f \in \mathcal{F}$, a real number $\mu \in \mathbb{R}$ and an order relation $\sim \in \{\leq, >\}$. The other Boolean operations (i.e., disjunction, implication, equivalence) are defined in the usual way. Also, the temporal operators *eventually* and *globally* are defined as $\mathbf{F}_{[a,b)}\phi \equiv \top \mathcal{U}_{[a,b)} \phi$ and $\mathbf{G}_{[a,b)}\phi \equiv \neg \mathbf{F}_{[a,b)} \neg\phi$, respectively.

In addition to Boolean semantics defined above, STL admits *quantitative semantics* [9, 10], which is formalized by the notion of *robustness degree*. The robustness degree of a signal $s \in \mathcal{S}$ with respect to an STL formula ϕ at time t is a function $r(s, \phi, t)$ and is recursively defined as

$$\begin{array}{ll}
r(s, \top, t) & = r_\top \\
r(s, p_{f(x) \leq \mu}, t) & = \mu - f(s(t)) \\
r(s, \neg\phi, t) & = -\, r(s, \phi, t) \\
r(s, \phi_1 \wedge \phi_2, t) & = \min\{r(s, \phi_1, t), r(s, \phi_2, t)\} \\
r(s, \phi_1 \mathcal{U}_{[a,b)} \phi_2, t) & =
\end{array}$$

$$\sup_{t_u \in [t+a, t+b)} \left\{ \min\left\{ r(s, \phi_2, t_u), \inf_{t_1 \in [t, t_u)} \{ r(s, \phi_1, t_1) \} \right\} \right\}$$

where $b > a > 0$ and $r_\top \in \mathbb{R}_{\geq 0} \cup \{\infty\}$ is a large constant representing the maximum value of the robustness. Note that a positive robustness degree $r(s, \phi, 0)$ of a signal s with respect to a formula ϕ implies that s satisfies ϕ (in Boolean semantics). In the following, we denote by $r(s, \phi)$ the robustness degree $r(s, \phi, 0)$ at time 0. Robustness can be extended to the derived predicates and operators as follows:

$$\begin{array}{ll}
r(s, p_{f(x) > \mu}, t) & = f(s(t)) - \mu \\
r(s, \phi_1 \vee \phi_2, t) & = \max\{r(s, \phi_1, t), r(s, \phi_2, t)\} \\
r(s, \mathbf{F}_{[a,b)} \phi, t) & = \sup_{t_f \in [t+a, t+b)} \{ r(s, \phi, t_f) \} \\
r(s, \mathbf{G}_{[a,b)} \phi, t) & = \inf_{t_g \in [t+a, t+b)} \{ r(s, \phi, t_g) \}
\end{array}$$

Moreover, the interpretation of robustness degree as a quantitative measure of satisfaction is justified by the following proposition from [8].

PROPOSITION 3.1. *Let $s \in \mathcal{S}$ be a signal and ϕ an STL formula such that $r(s, \phi) > 0$. All signals $s' \in \mathcal{S}$ such that $\|s - s'\|_\infty < r(s, \phi)$ satisfy the formula ϕ, i.e., $s' \models \phi$.*

Parametric Signal Temporal Logic (PSTL) was introduced in [1] as an extension of STL, where formulae are parameterized. A PSTL formula is similar to an STL formula, however all the time bounds in the time intervals associated with temporal operators and all the constants in the inequality predicates are replaced by free parameters. The two types of parameters are called *time* and *space* parameters, respectively. Specifically, let ψ be a PSTL formula and n_p and n_{TL} be the number of predicates and temporal operators contained in ψ, respectively. The parameter space of ψ is $\Theta = \Pi \times T$, where $\Pi \subseteq \mathbb{R}^{n_p}$ is set of all possible *space* parameters and $T = T_1 \times \ldots T_{n_{TL}}$ is the set of all *time* parameters, where $T_i = \{(a_i, b_i) \in \mathbb{R}^2_{\geq 0} \mid a_i \leq b_i\}$ for all $i \in \{1, \ldots, n_{TL}\}$. Conversely, if ψ is a PSTL formula, then every parameter assignment $\theta \in \Theta$ induces a corresponding STL formula ϕ_θ, where all the space and time parameters of ψ have been fixed according to θ. This assignment is also referred to as a valuation θ of ψ. For example, given $\psi = \mathbf{G}_{[a,b)}(s_1 \leq c)$ and $\theta = [2.5, 0, 1]$, we obtain the STL formula $\phi_\theta = \mathbf{G}_{[0,1)}(s_1 \leq 2.5)$.

4. PROBLEM FORMULATION

We wish to find an STL formula that separates traces produced by a system that exhibit some desired property, such as behaving normally, from other traces of the same system. Formally, let $C = \{C_p, C_n\}$ be the set of classes, with C_p for the positive class and C_n for the negative class. Let s^i be an n-dimensional signal, $s^i : \mathbb{R}_{\geq 0} \to \mathbb{R}^n$, and let $l^i \in C$ be its label. We consider the following problem:

PROBLEM 4.1 (TWO-CLASS CLASSIFICATION). *Given a set of labeled signals* $\{(s^i, l^i)\}_{i=1}^N$, *where* $l^i = C_p$ *if* s^i *exhibits a desired behavior, and* $l^i = C_n$ *if* s^i *does not, find an STL formula* ϕ *such that the misclassification rate* $\mathrm{MCR}(\phi)$ *is minimized, where the misclassification rate is defined as:*

$$\mathrm{MCR}(\phi) := \frac{\left|\{s^i \mid (s^i \models \phi \wedge l^i = C_n) \vee (s^i \not\models \phi \wedge l^i = C_p)\}\right|}{N}$$

In the above formula, $|\cdot|$ denotes the cardinality of a set, and $(s^i \models \phi \wedge l^i = C_n)$ represents a *false positive*, while $(s^i \not\models \phi \wedge l^i = C_p)$ represents a *false negative*.

5. LEARNING DECISION TREES

In our approach, the key insight to tackle Problem 4.1 is that it is possible to build a map between a fragment of STL and decision trees. Therefore, we can exploit the decision trees learning literature [24, 23, 4] to build a decision tree that classifies signals and then map the constructed tree to an STL formula.

A decision tree is a tree-structured sequence of questions about the data used to make predictions about the data's labels. In a tree, we define: the root as the initial node; the depth of a node as the length of the path from the root to that node; the parent of a node as the neighbor whose depth is one less; the children of a node as the neighbors whose depths are one more. A node with no children is called a leaf, all other nodes are called non-terminal nodes. In this paper, we focus on *binary* decision trees, where every non-terminal node splits the data into two children nodes and every leaf node predicts a label.

Unfortunately, the space of all possible decision trees for a given classification problem is very large, and it is known that the problem of learning the optimal decision tree is NP-complete, for various optimality criteria [14]. Therefore, most decision-tree learning algorithms are based on *greedy* approaches, where locally optimal decisions are taken at each node. These greedy growing algorithms can be stated in a simple recursive fashion, starting from the root node, and require three meta-parameters: the first is a list of possible ways to split the data; the second is a criterion to select the best split; and the third is a set of rules for stopping the algorithm.

Several learning algorithms can be created by selecting different meta-parameters. That is, once the meta-parameters have been fixed, a specific learning algorithm is *instantiated.* Since we are not just proposing a single algorithm but a class of algorithms, we refer to this approach as "decision tree learning framework for temporal logic inference". In the next sections, we explain in detail the parameterized algorithm and the choices we propose for the meta-parameters.

5.1 Parameterized learning algorithm

In Alg. 1 we present the parameterized procedure for inferring temporal logic formulae from data. The meta-parameters of Alg. 1 are: (1) a set of PSTL primitives $\mathcal{P}$; (2) an impurity measure J; and (3) a set of stopping criteria *stop.* The algorithm is recursive and takes as input arguments the formula to reach the current node ϕ^{path}, the set of data that reached that node S, and the current depth level h.

At the beginning, the stopping conditions are checked (line 1). If they are met, the algorithm returns a single leaf node marked with the label $c \in C$. The label c is chosen according to the best classification quality (line 2), using $p(S, c; \phi^{path})$ defined in Def. 5.4. If the stopping conditions are not met (line 4), the algorithm proceeds to find the optimal STL formula among all the valuations of PSTL formulae from the set of primitives $\mathcal{P}$ (details in Sec. 5.3). The cost function used in the optimization is the impurity measure J, which assesses the quality of the partition induced by PSTL primitives valuations. See Sec. 5.4 for details. At line 5, a new non-terminal node is created and associated with the optimal STL formula ϕ^*. Next, the partition induced by the formula $\phi^{path} \wedge \phi^*$ is computed (line 6). For each outcome of the split, the *buildTree*() procedure is called recursively to construct the left and right subtrees (lines 7-8). The corresponding formula to reach a subtree and the corresponding data partition are passed. The depth level is increased by one.

Algorithm 1: Parameterized Decision Tree Construction – *buildTree*($\cdot$)

Parameter: $\mathcal{P}$ – set of PSTL primitives
Parameter: J – impurity measure
Parameter: *stop* – set of stopping criteria
Input: ϕ^{path} – formula associated with current path
Input: $S = \{(s^i, l^i)_{i=1}^N\}$ – set of labeled signals
Input: h – the current depth level
Output: a (sub)-tree

1 **if** $stop(\phi^{path}, h, S)$ **then**
2 $\quad t \leftarrow leaf(\arg\max_{c \in C}\{p(S, c; \phi^{path})\})$
3 $\quad$ **return** t
4 $\phi^* = \arg\max_{\psi \in \mathcal{P}, \theta \in \Theta} J(S, partition(S, \phi_\theta \wedge \phi^{path}))$
5 $t \leftarrow non\_terminal(\phi^*)$
6 $S^*_\top, S^*_\bot \leftarrow partition(S, \phi^{path} \wedge \phi^*)$
7 $t.left \leftarrow buildTree(\phi^{path} \wedge \phi^*, S^*_\top, h+1)$
8 $t.right \leftarrow buildTree(\phi^{path} \wedge \neg\phi^*, S^*_\bot, h+1)$
9 **return** t

The parameterized family of algorithms uses three procedures: (a) $leaf(c)$ creates a leaf node marked with the label $c \in C$, (b) *non_terminal*(ϕ) creates a non-terminal node associated with the valuation of a PSTL primitive from $\mathcal{P}$, and (c) *partition*(S, ϕ) splits the set of signals S into satisfying and non-satisfying signals with respect to ϕ, i.e., $S_\top, S_\bot = partition(S, \phi)$, where $S_\top = \{(s^i, l^i) \in S \mid s^i \models \phi\}$ and $S_\bot = \{(s^i, l^i) \in S \mid s^i \not\models \phi\}$.

By fixing the meta-parameters ($\mathcal{P}$, J, *stop*), a particular algorithm is *instantiated.* For each possible instance, a decision tree is obtained by executing *buildTree*($\top, S_{root}, 0$) on the set of labeled signals S_{root}. Clearly, the returned tree depends on both the input data S_{root} and the particular instance chosen.

5.2 Tree to STL formula

A decision tree obtained by an instantiation of Alg. 1 can be used directly for classification or converted to an equivalent STL formula using Alg. 2. The algorithm recursively traverses the subtree t given as input. At each node, the formula is obtained by (1) conjunction of the nodes's formula with its left subtree's formula, (2) conjunction of the negation of the node's formula with its right subtree's formula, (3) disjunction of (1) and (2). During the recursion process, Alg. 2 only keeps track of the paths reaching leaves associated with the positive class C_p. To produce the final

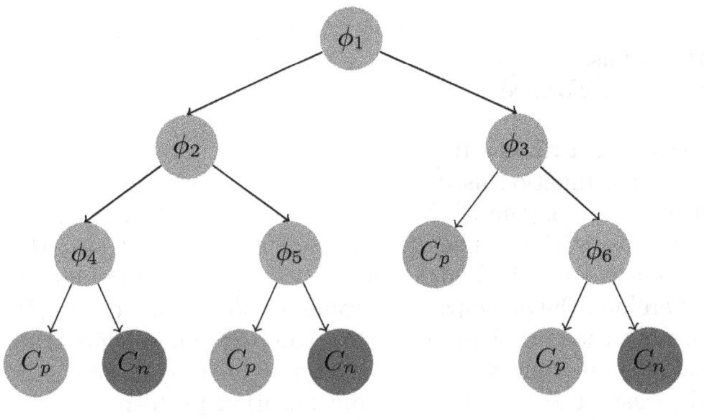

Figure 1: The formula associated with the tree is $\phi_{tree} = \big(\phi_1 \wedge ((\phi_2 \wedge \phi_4) \vee (\neg\phi_2 \wedge \phi_5))\big) \vee \big(\neg\phi_1 \wedge (\phi_3 \vee (\neg\phi_3 \wedge \phi_6))\big)$ and can be obtained algorithmically using Alg. 2, where ϕ_i, $i \in \{1,\dots,6\}$ are valuations of primitive formulae from a set of PSTL formulae $\mathcal{P}$.

formula, the algorithm is executed starting from the root node, i.e., *Tree2STL(root)*. Fig. 1 shows a decision tree and its corresponding formula obtained by applying Alg. 2.

Algorithm 2: Tree to formula – $Tree2STL(\cdot)$

```
Input: t – node of a tree
Output: STL Formula
if t is a leaf and class associated with t is C_p then
  | return ⊤
if t is a leaf and class associated with t is C_n then
  | return ⊥
φ_l = (t.φ ∧ Tree2STL(t.left))
φ_r = (¬t.φ ∧ Tree2STL(t.right))
return φ_l ∨ φ_r
```

5.3 PSTL primitives

To partition the data at each node, a finite list of possible splitting rules is usually considered [24]. We propose to use simple PSTL formulae, called *primitives*, to split the data. In particular, we define two types of primitives:

DEFINITION 5.1 (FIRST-LEVEL PRIMITIVES). *Let $\mathcal{S}$ be the set of signals with values in $\mathbb{R}^n$, $n \geq 1$. We define the set of first-level primitives as follows:*

$$\mathcal{P}_1 = \big\{\mathbf{F}_{[\tau_1,\tau_2)}(x_i \sim \mu) \text{ or } \mathbf{G}_{[\tau_1,\tau_2)}(x_i \sim \mu) \mid i \in \{1,\dots,n\},\ \sim \in \{\leq, >\}\big\}$$

The parameters of $\mathcal{P}_1$ are (μ, τ_1, τ_2) and the space of parameters is $\Theta_1 = \mathbb{R} \times \{(a,b) \mid a < b,\ a,b \in \mathbb{R}_{\geq 0}\}$.

DEFINITION 5.2 (SECOND-LEVEL PRIMITIVES). *Let $\mathcal{S}$ be the set of signals with values in $\mathbb{R}^n$, $n \geq 1$. We define the set of second-level primitives as follows:*

$$\mathcal{P}_2 = \big\{\mathbf{G}_{[\tau_1,\tau_2)}\mathbf{F}_{[0,\tau_3)}(x_i \sim \mu) \text{ or } \mathbf{F}_{[\tau_1,\tau_2)}\mathbf{G}_{[0,\tau_3)}(x_i \sim \mu) \mid i \in \{1,\dots,n\},\ \sim \in \{\leq, >\}\big\}$$

The parameters of $\mathcal{P}_2$ are $(\mu, \tau_1, \tau_2, \tau_3)$ and the space of parameters is $\Theta_2 = \mathbb{R} \times \{(a,b) \mid a < b,\ a,b \in \mathbb{R}_{\geq 0}\} \times \mathbb{R}_{\geq 0}$.

The meaning of first-level primitives is straightforward. The two primitives $\mathbf{F}_{[\tau_1,\tau_2)}(x_i \sim \mu)$ and $\mathbf{G}_{[\tau_1,\tau_2)}(x_i \sim \mu)$ are used to express that the predicate $x_i \sim \mu$ must be true for at least one time instance or for all time instances in the interval $[\tau_1, \tau_2)$, respectively. Similarly, the second-level primitives can be interpreted in natural language as: (a) $\mathbf{F}_{[\tau_1,\tau_2)}\mathbf{G}_{[0,\tau_3)}(x_i \sim \mu)$ specifies that "the predicate $(x_i \sim \mu)$ of duration τ_3 must be performed and its start time must be in the interval $[\tau_1, \tau_2)$"; and (b) $\mathbf{G}_{[\tau_1,\tau_2)}\mathbf{F}_{[0,\tau_3)}(x_i \sim \mu)$ specifies that "at each time instance in the interval $[\tau_1, \tau_2)$, the predicate $(x_i \sim \mu)$ must be true within τ_3 time units". Both first- and second-level primitives may be thought as specifications for bounded reachability and safety with varying degrees of flexibility.

Given a set of primitives $\mathcal{P}$, we denote by $\text{STL}_{\mathcal{P}}$ the STL fragment obtained by Boolean closure from $\mathcal{P}$.

DEFINITION 5.3 (BOOLEAN CLOSURE). *Let $\mathcal{P}$ be a finite set of PSTL formulae. The fragment of STL formulae induced by $\mathcal{P}$ using Boolean closure is defined as:*

$$\phi ::= \top \mid \varphi \mid \neg\phi \mid \phi_1 \wedge \phi_2 \mid \phi_1 \vee \phi_2$$

where φ is a valuation of a PSTL formula from $\mathcal{P}$.

$\text{STL}_{\mathcal{P}}$ is the fragment of STL that is mapped with decision trees. In other terms, each decision tree constructed with the set of primitives $\mathcal{P}$ is mapped to an STL formula belonging to the $\text{STL}_{\mathcal{P}}$ fragment.

Remark 1. Note that $\text{STL}_{\mathcal{P}_1} \subset \text{STL}_{\mathcal{P}_2}$, because $\mathbf{F}_{[\tau_1,\tau_2)}l \equiv \mathbf{F}_{[\tau_1,\tau_2)}\mathbf{G}_{[0,0^+)}l$ and similarly $\mathbf{G}_{[\tau_1,\tau_2)}l \equiv \mathbf{G}_{[\tau_1,\tau_2)}\mathbf{F}_{[0,0^+)}l$, where $l \equiv (x_i \sim \mu)$ is a linear inequality predicate and 0^+ represents the upper limit towards 0.

Remark 2. It is important to stress that the proposed PSTL primitives are not the only possible ones. A user may define other primitives, either generic ones, like the first- and second- level primitives, or specific ones, guided by the particular nature of the learning problem at hand.

5.4 Impurity measures

In the previous section, we defined a list of possible ways to split the data using a set of primitives $\mathcal{P}$. Now, it is necessary to define a criterion to select which primitive best splits the data at each node. Intuitively, a good split leads to children that are *homogeneous*, that is, they contain mostly objects belonging to the same class. This concept has been formalized in literature with *impurity measures*, and the goal of the optimization algorithm is to obtain children purer that their parents. In this section, we first state the canonical impurity measures and then we propose three modified measures, which are more suited to handle signals, using the robustness degree.

DEFINITION 5.4 (IMPURITY MEASURES). *Let S be a finite set of signals, ϕ an STL formula and $S_\top, S_\bot = partition(S, \phi)$. The following partition weights are introduced to describe how the signals s^i are distributed according to their labels l^i and the formula ϕ:*

$$p_\top = \frac{|S_\top|}{|S|},\quad p_\bot = \frac{|S_\bot|}{|S|},\quad p(S, c; \phi) = \frac{|\{(s^i, l^i) \mid l^i = c\}|}{|S|} \tag{1}$$

Particularly, $p_\top$ and $p_\bot$ represent the fraction of signals from S present in $S_\top$ and $S_\bot$, respectively, and $p(S, c; \phi)$ represents the fraction of signals in S that belong to class $c \in C$.

The (canonical) impurity measures are defined as [4, 23]:
- Information gain (IG)

$$IG(S, \{S_\top, S_\bot\}) = H(S) - \sum_{\otimes \in \{\top, \bot\}} p_\otimes \cdot H(S_\otimes)$$

$$H(S) = -\sum_{c \in C} p(S, c; \phi) \log p(S, c; \phi) \quad (2)$$

- Gini gain (GG)

$$GG(S, \{S_\top, S_\bot\}) = Gini(S) - \sum_{\otimes \in \{\top, \bot\}} p_\otimes \cdot Gini(S_\otimes)$$

$$Gini(S) = \sum_{c \in C} p(S, c; \phi)(1 - p(S, c; \phi)) \quad (3)$$

- Misclassification gain (MG)

$$MG(S, \{S_\top, S_\bot\}) = MR(S) - \sum_{\otimes \in \{\top, \bot\}} p_\otimes \cdot MR(S_\otimes)$$

$$MR(S) = \min(p(S, C_p; \phi), p(S, C_n; \phi)) \quad (4)$$

We extend the impurity measures to account for the robustness degrees of the signals to be classified. These extensions are based on the intuition that, according to Prop. 3.1, the robustness degree can be used in the context of learning as a measure of the classification quality of a signal with respect to an STL formula.

DEFINITION 5.5 (EXTENDED IMPURITY MEASURES). *Consider the same setup as in Def. 5.4, and the same impurity measures, we redefine the partition weights as follows:*

$$p_\top = \frac{\sum_{s^i \in S_\top} r(s^i, \phi)}{\sum_{s^i \in S} |r(s^i, \phi)|} \qquad p_\bot = -\frac{\sum_{s^i \in S_\bot} r(s^i, \phi)}{\sum_{s^i \in S} |r(s^i, \phi)|}$$

$$p(S, c; \phi) = \frac{\sum_{s^i \in S_c} |r(s^i, \phi)|}{\sum_{s^i \in S} |r(s^i, \phi)|} \quad (5)$$

where $S_c = \{s^i \in S \mid l^i = c\}$.

We will distinguish between the usual impurity measures and the extended ones by using the subscript r (e.g., IG_r) for the extended impurity measures. The following proposition ensures that the extended impurity measures are well defined.

PROPOSITION 5.1. *The intra-partition weights are bounded within* 0 *and* 1 *and sum to* 1*, i.e.,* $0 \le p_\top, p_\bot \le 1$ *and* $p_\top + p_\bot = 1$*, in both definitions Def. 5.4 and Def. 5.5. The same invariant property is true for the inter-partition weights, i.e.,* $0 \le p(S, C_n; \phi), p(S, C_p; \phi) \le 1$ *and* $\sum_{c \in C} p(S, c; \phi) = 1$.

Remark 3. The advantages of using the extended versions of the impurity measures over the canonical ones are most pertinent in the context of optimizing these over PSTL formulae. The robustness-based impurity functions are better behaved cost functions, because these are less flat over the space parameter than their frequency-based counterparts, i.e., the canonical measures are piecewise constant functions. Also, we argue that the use of robustness makes the computed classifiers better at generalizing, i.e., performance on unseen (test) data. The intuition is that the separation boundaries tend to be as far as possible from signals of the two classes in the sense of robustness. In this sense, the canonical measures are unable to distinguish between formulae which are barely satisfied by some signals from more robust ones. As future work, an empirical comparison of the robustness-based measures against the canonical ones will be performed.

Local optimization

The cost function used in the local node optimization (line 4 of Alg. 1) is one of the impurity measures defined in the previous section. The optimization is performed over the chosen set of PSTL primitives $\mathcal{P}$ and their valuations Θ. Therefore, the optimization problem is decomposed into $|\mathcal{P}|$ optimization problems over a fixed and small number of real-valued parameters. Consider signals of dimension n. In the case of $\mathcal{P}_1$, we have $4n$ optimization problems with 3 parameters each. On the other hand, for $\mathcal{P}_2$ we have $4n$ optimization problems with 4 parameters each.

The local optimization approach presents several advantages. In particular, the computation of the robustness values in the definition of the extended impurity measures (Def. 5.5) can be performed incrementally with respect to the tree data structure according to the following preposition.

PROPOSITION 5.2. (INCREMENTAL COMPUTATION OF ROBUSTNESS) *At each step of the recursion of Alg. 1, the robustness of a signal* s^i *reaching the current node* n_c *can be computed as follows*

$$r(s^i, \phi^{tree}) = r(s^i, \phi^{path} \wedge \phi) = \min\{r(s^i, \phi^{path}), r(s^i, \phi)\} \quad (6)$$

where ϕ^{tree} *corresponds to the currently computed tree,* ϕ^{path} *corresponds to the branch of the tree from the root to the parent of* n_c*, and* ϕ *is a candidate valuation of a PSTL primitive for* n_c.

The first equality in Eq. (6) follows from the construction of the tree, because the robustness of a signal s^i reaching n_c is negative for any other branch of the tree not ending in n_c. The incremental computation can be achieved by taking advantage of the recursion in the second equality in Eq. (6).

Another very important advantage of the proposed approach is that at each iteration of Alg. 1, the data is partitioned between the children of the currently processed node. Thus, the local optimization problems become easier as the depth of the nodes increases.

The local optimization problems may be solved using any global non-linear optimization algorithm, such as Simulated Annealing [15] or Differential Evolution [25]. However, in order to use these numerical optimization algorithms, we need to define finite bounds for the parameters of the primitive formulae. These bounds may easily be inferred from data, but may also be application specific, if expert knowledge is available.

5.5 Stop conditions

Several stopping criteria can be set for Alg. 1. The most common strategy is to just split until the current node contains only signals from a single class or no signals. This strategy is very permissive, that is, it allows the algorithm to run for many iterations. However, it represents the sufficient conditions that guarantee the termination of the algorithm. Other more restrictive conditions are possible. For instance, stop if the vast majority of the signals belong to the same class, either positive or negative, e.g., stop if 99% of signals belong to the same class. Another common strategy is to stop if the algorithm has reached a certain, fixed, depth. These conditions usually provide a faster termination of the algorithm. In general, a set of stopping criteria can be assembled by picking several stopping conditions, as long as the sufficient conditions for the termination of the algorithm are included.

5.6 Complexity

In this section, we provide a worst-case and average-case complexity analysis of Alg. 1 in terms of the complexity of the local optimization procedure (Alg. 1, line 4). This complexity analysis assumes that just the sufficient stopping conditions are set. Let $C(N)$ and $g(N)$ be the complexity of Alg. 1 and of the local optimization algorithm, respectively, where N is the number of signals to be processed by the algorithms. Trivially, we have $g(N) = \Omega(N)$, where $\Omega(\cdot)$ is the asymptotic notation for lower bound [7], because the algorithm must at least check the labels of all signals. The worst-case complexity of Alg. 1 is attained when at each node the optimal partition has size $(1, N-1)$. In this case, the complexity satisfies the recurrence $C(N) = C(N-1) + C(1) + g(N)$, which implies $C(N) = \Theta(N + \sum_{k=2}^{N} g(k))$, where $\Theta(\cdot)$ is the two-sided asymptotic notation for complexity bound [7]. However, the worst case scenario is not likely to occur in large datasets. Therefore, we consider the average case where at least a fraction $\gamma \in (0, 1)$ of the signals are in one set of the partition. The recurrence relation becomes $C(N) = C(\gamma N) + C((1-\gamma)N) + g(N)$, which implies the following complexity bound

$$C(N) = \Theta\left(N \cdot \left(1 + \int_1^x \frac{g(u)}{u^2} \mathrm{d}\, u\right)\right)$$

obtained using the Akra-Bazzi method [7]. Finally, note that the hidden constants in the complexity bounds above depend on the cardinality of the set of primitives considered and the size of their parameterization.

6. CASE STUDIES

In this section, we present two case studies that illustrate the usefulness and the computational advantages of the algorithms. The first is an anomalous trajectory detection problem in a maritime environment. The second is a fault detection problem in an automotive powertrain system. The automotive application is particularly appealing because the systems involved are getting more and more sophisticated. In a modern vehicle, several highly complex dynamical systems are interconnected and the methods present in literature may fail to cope with this complexity.

6.1 Maritime surveillance

This synthetic dataset emulates a maritime surveillance problem, where the goal is to detect suspicious vessels approaching the harbor from sea by looking at their trajectories. It was developed in [19], based on the scenarios described in [21], for evaluating their inference algorithms.

The trajectories are represented with planar coordinates $x(t)$ and $y(t)$ and were generated using a Dubins' vehicle model with additive Gaussian noise. Three types of scenarios, one normal and two anomalous, were considered. In the normal scenario, a vessel approaching from sea heads directly towards the harbor. In the first anomalous scenario, a ship veers to the island and heads to the harbor next. This scenario is compatible with human trafficking. In the second

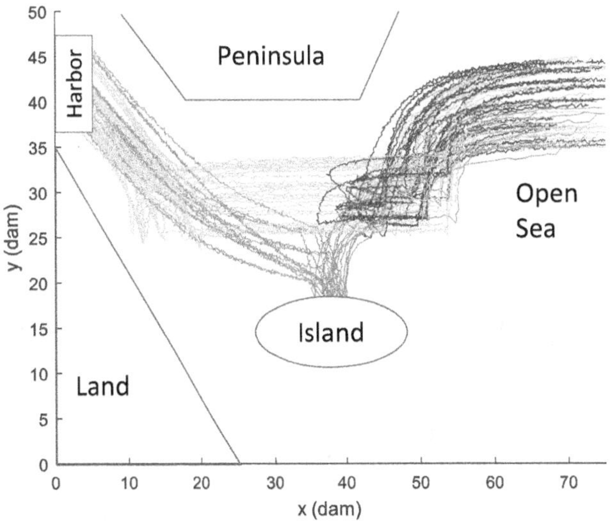

Figure 2: Naval surveillance dataset [19]. The vessels behaving normally are shown in green. The magenta and blue trajectories represent two types of anomalous paths.

anomalous scenario, a boat tries to approach other vessels in the passage between the peninsula and the island and then veers back to the open sea. This scenario is compatible with terrorist activity. Some sample traces are shown in Fig. 2. The dataset is composed of 2000 total traces, with 61 sample points per trace. There are 1000 normal traces and 1000 anomalous.

6.2 Fuel control system

We investigate a fuel control system for a gasoline engine. A model for this system is provided as built-in example in Simulink and we modified it for our purposes. This model was initially used for Bayesian statistical model checking [27] and has been recently proposed as benchmark for the hybrid systems community [13]. We selected this model because it includes all the complexities of real world industrial models, but is still quick to simulate, i.e., it is easy to obtain a large number of traces.

The key quantity in the model is the *air-to-fuel ratio*, that is, the ratio between the mass of air and the mass of fuel in the combustion process. The goal of the control system is to keep it close to the "ideal" stoichiometric value for the combustion process. For this system, the target air-fuel ratio is 14.6, as it provides a good compromise between power, fuel economy, and emissions. The system has one main output, the air-to-fuel ratio, one control variable, the fuel rate, and two inputs, the engine speed and the throttle command. The system estimates the correct fuel rate to achieve the target stoichiometric ratio by taking into account four sensor readings. Two are related directly to the inputs, the engine speed and the throttle angle. The remaining two sensors provide crucial feedback information: the EGO sensor reports the amount of residual oxygen present in the exhaust gas, and the MAP sensor reports the (intake) manifold absolute pressure. The EGO value is related to the air-to-fuel ratio, whereas the MAP value is related to the air mass rate. The Simulink diagram is made of several subsystems with different kinds of blocks, both continuous and discrete,

Instance	Primitives	Impurity	Stopping
I_1	$\mathcal{P}_1$	MG_r	Majority class rate >0.975, Depth >4
I_2	$\mathcal{P}_2$	IG_r	Depth >3

Table 1: Algorithm meta-parameters. Refer to Sec. 5 for details.

among which there are look-up tables and a hybrid automaton. Due to these characteristics, this model can exhibit a rich and diverse number of output traces, thus making it an interesting candidate for our investigation.

The base model, that is, the one included in Simulink, includes a very basic fault detection scheme and fault injection mechanism. The fault detection scheme is a simple threshold crossing test (within a Stateflow chart), and is only able to detect single off range values. For avoiding the overlap of two anomaly detection schemes, the built-in one has been removed. In the base model, the faults are injected by simply reporting an incorrect and fixed value for a sensor's reading. Moreover, these faults are always present from the beginning of the simulation. We replaced this simple fault injection mechanism with a more sophisticated unit. The new subsystem is capable of inducing faults in both the EGO and MAP sensors with a *random* arrival time and with a *random* value. Specifically, the faults can manifest at anytime during the execution (uniformly at random) and the readings of the sensors affected are offset by a value that *varies* at every execution. Finally, independent Gaussian noise signals, with zero mean and variance $\sigma^2 = 0.01$, have been added at the output of the sensors.

For the fuel control system, 1200 total simulations were performed. In all cases, the throttle command provides a periodic triangular input, and the engine speed is kept constant at 300 rad/sec (2865 RPM). The simulation time is 60 seconds. In details, we obtained: 600 traces where the system was working normally; 200 traces with a fault in the EGO sensor; 200 traces with a fault in the MAP sensor; 200 traces with faults in both sensors. For every trace, we collected 200 samples of the EGO and MAP sensors' readings. Some sample traces are shown in Fig. 3. The average simulation time to obtain a single trace was roughly 1 second.

7. IMPLEMENTATION AND RESULTS

We implemented and tested two different instances of Alg.1, I_1 and I_2, defined by the choice of meta-parameters given in Table 1. In the case of I_1, the implementation was done in MATLAB using standard libraries, employing the simulated annealing optimization method [15], and run on a 3.5 GHz processor with 16 GB RAM. As for I_2, we used the SciPy library for Python, solving the optimization problem with its implementation of the differential evolution algorithm [25], and we tested it on similar hardware. [1]

7.1 Maritime surveillance

We tested the I_2 instance using a non stratified 10-fold cross-validation with a random permutation of the data set, obtaining a mean misclassification rate of 0.007 with a standard deviation of 0.008 and a run time of about 4 hours per split. A sample formula learned in one of the cross-validation splits is:

[1]The software is available at http://hyness.bu.edu/Software.html

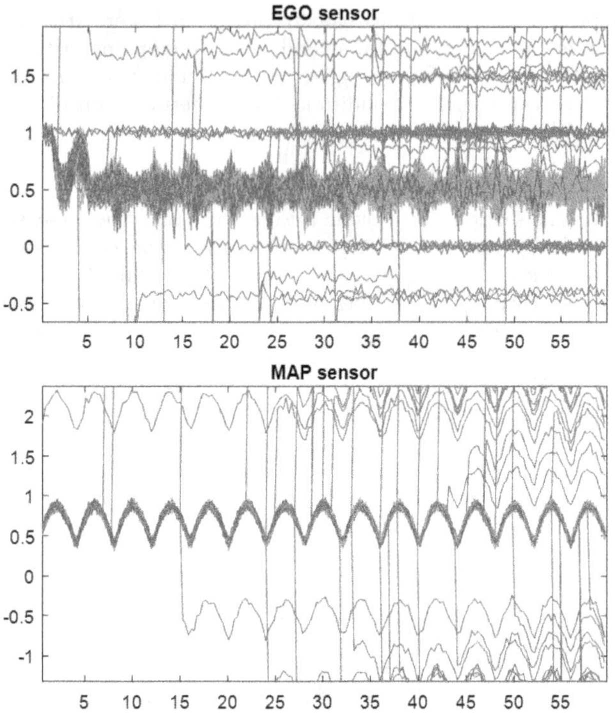

Figure 3: Fuel Control Dataset. Normal traces are shown in green, anomalous traces are shown in red.

$$
\begin{aligned}
\phi^{I_2} &= (\phi_1^{I_2} \wedge (\neg\phi_2^{I_2} \vee (\phi_2^{I_2} \wedge \neg\phi_3^{I_2}))) \\
&\quad \vee (\neg\phi_1^{I_2} \wedge (\phi_4^{I_2} \wedge \phi_5^{I_2})) \\
\phi_1^{I_2} &= \mathbf{G}_{[199.70,297.27)}\mathbf{F}_{[0.00,0.05)}(x \leq 23.60) \\
\phi_2^{I_2} &= \mathbf{G}_{[4.47,16.64)}\mathbf{F}_{[0.00,198.73)}(y \leq 24.20) \\
\phi_3^{I_2} &= \mathbf{G}_{[34.40,52.89)}\mathbf{F}_{[0.00,61.74)}(y \leq 19.62) \\
\phi_4^{I_2} &= \mathbf{G}_{[30.96,37.88)}\mathbf{F}_{[0.00,250.37)}(x \leq 36.60) \\
\phi_5^{I_2} &= \mathbf{G}_{[62.76,253.23)}\mathbf{F}_{[0.00,41.07)}(y \leq 29.90)
\end{aligned} \tag{7}
$$

We can see in Fig. 4 how the thresholds for ϕ_1 and ϕ_2 capture the key features of the data set. Notice also the insight we can gain from their plain English translation: "Normal vessels' x coordinate is below 23.6 during the last 100 seconds, i.e., they approach and remain at the port", and "normal vessels' y coordinate never go below 24.2, i.e., they don't approach the island". It is worth mentioning the second term of the outer disjunction in ϕ^{I_2}, as it highlights a feature of the data set difficult to spot on the figures: some normal vessels don't reach the port (inspecting the data set, some normal traces stop right after crossing the passage). As usual when employing decision trees, deeper formulae focus on finer details of the data set.

In the case of I_1, we tested it using a 5-fold cross-validation, obtaining a mean misclassification rate of 0.0040 and a standard deviation of 0.0029. The run time is about 16 minutes

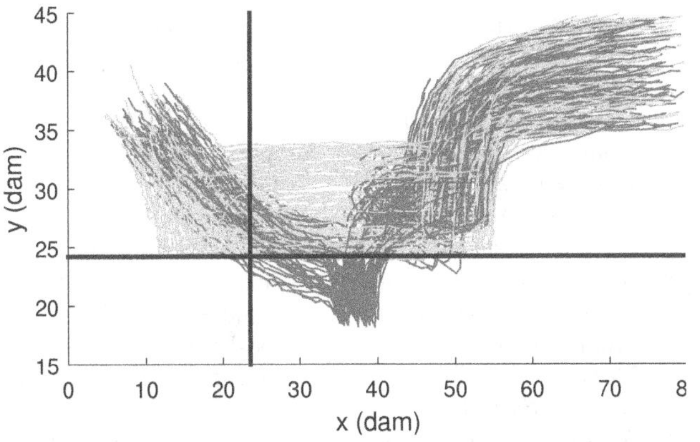

Figure 4: Sample of the naval surveillance dataset. Normal trajectories are green and anomalous trajectories are red. We show in blue the boundaries of $\phi_1^{I_2}$ and $\phi_2^{I_2}$ of Eq. (7).

per split. A sample formula learned in one of the splits is:

$$\begin{aligned}
&\phi^{I_1} = (\phi_1^{I_1} \wedge \phi_2^{I_1}) \vee (\neg\phi_1^{I_1} \wedge ((\phi_3^{I_1} \wedge (\phi_4^{I_1} \wedge \phi_5^{I_1})) \vee (\neg\phi_3^{I_1} \wedge \phi_6^{I_1})))\\
&\phi_1^{I_1} = \mathbf{G}_{[224,280)}(x \leq 18) \qquad \phi_2^{I_1} = \mathbf{G}_{[14.2,125)}(y > 22)\\
&\phi_3^{I_1} = \mathbf{F}_{[109,277)}(y > 30.6) \qquad \phi_4^{I_1} = \mathbf{G}_{[279,293)}(x \leq 19.2)\\
&\phi_5^{I_1} = \mathbf{F}_{[77.8,107)}x > 41) \qquad \phi_6^{I_1} = \mathbf{F}_{[258,283)}(x \leq 29.5)
\end{aligned} \tag{8}$$

This dataset was also used in [19]. Unfortunately, it is not possible to make a formal comparison between the formulae learned by our approach and the ones in [19]. This is due to the fact that iPSTL, defined in [19], and $\text{STL}_{\mathcal{P}_1}$ (or $\text{STL}_{\mathcal{P}_2}$) do not represent the same STL fragment. However, it is always possible to make a comparison in terms of sheer classification performance. In the comparison, it is clear that we improve the misclassification rate by a factor of 20 while spending a similar amount of execution time.

7.2 Fuel control

In this scenario, we tested both instances using the EGO and MAP sensors' readings (variables x_1 and x_2). We performed a similar cross-validation for I_2, resulting in a mean misclassification rate of 0.054 with a standard deviation of 0.025 and a run time of about 15 hours per split. A sample formula, obtained from one of the cross-validation splits, is:

$$\begin{aligned}
&\phi^{I_2} = \neg\phi_1^{I_2} \wedge \phi_2^{I_2} \wedge \phi_3^{I_2}\\
&\phi_1^{I_2} = \mathbf{F}_{[1.85,58.70)}\mathbf{G}_{[0.00,0.57)}(x_1 \leq 0.13)\\
&\phi_2^{I_2} = \mathbf{G}_{[11.35,59.55)}\mathbf{F}_{[0.00,0.03)}(x_1 \leq 0.99)\\
&\phi_3^{I_2} = \mathbf{G}_{[1.65,58.89)}\mathbf{F}_{[0.00,0.44)}(x_2 \leq 0.90)
\end{aligned} \tag{9}$$

Notice in this case how the resulting subformulae are equivalent to first-level primitives, suggesting that $\mathcal{P}_2$ is an overly complicated set of primitives.

Regarding I_1, using a 5-fold cross-validation, we obtained a mean misclassification rate of 0.0350 and a standard deviation of 0.0176. The run time is about 18 minutes per split. A sample formula learned in one of the splits is:

$$\begin{aligned}
&\phi_1 = (\phi_1^{I_1} \wedge (\phi_2^{I_1} \wedge (\phi_3^{I_1} \wedge \phi_4^{I_1}))) \vee (\neg\phi_1^{I_1} \wedge (\phi_5^{I_1} \wedge (\phi_6^{I_1} \wedge \phi_7^{I_1})))\\
&\phi_1^{I_1} = \mathbf{F}_{[22,58.4)}(x_2 > 0.932) \quad \phi_2^{I_1} = \mathbf{G}_{[29.3,59.6)}(x_2 < 0.994)\\
&\phi_3^{I_1} = \mathbf{G}_{[56,58.3)}(x_1 > 0.0979) \quad \phi_4^{I_1} = \mathbf{G}_{[49.9,55.3)}(x_1 < 0.863)\\
&\phi_5^{I_1} = \mathbf{G}_{[39.5,58.4)}(x_2 > 0.193) \quad \phi_6^{I_1} = \mathbf{F}_{[59.4,59.7)}(x_1 > 0.25)\\
&\phi_7^{I_1} = \mathbf{G}_{[2.52,53.3)}(x_1 < 1.05)
\end{aligned} \tag{10}$$

In both case studies, the execution time of I_2 is higher then I_1. This occurs because the instance I_2 involves a more complicated optimization problem. Specifically, I_2 uses primitives from $\mathcal{P}_2$ with 4 free parameters, whereas I_1 uses primitives with only 3 free parameters.

8. CONCLUSION

In this paper, we presented an inference framework of timed temporal logic properties from time series data. The framework defines customizable decision-tree algorithms that output Signal Temporal Logic (STL) formulae as classifiers. This work is in line with recent interest in Temporal Logic Inference (TLI) and is motivated by the need to construct classifiers which provide good performance and can be interpreted over specific application domains. The proposed algorithms are model-free and are suitable for inferring properties from time series data for problems such as anomaly detection, monitoring, and application domains as diverse as the automotive industry and maritime port security.

The proposed framework describes decision-tree learning algorithms which may be customized by providing three components: (a) a set of primitive properties of interest; (b) an impurity measure which captures the node's homogeneity; and (c) stopping conditions for the algorithm. The performance advantage of the proposed procedures is due to the incremental nature of growing STL formulae represented as trees. Moreover, the problem of finding optimal primitives becomes easier as a procedure grows a tree. This follows from the fact that a node's optimization problem has always a fixed number of parameters and the data is partitioned between the two children of the node. Another contribution of the paper is the definition of extended versions of the classical impurity measures such that these take into account the robustness degrees of signals. We argue that the extended versions of the impurity measures increase the generalization capability of the resulting formulae.

In the paper, we test two possible instances of the framework (form a possibly very large set of choices) on two case studies in the maritime security and automotive fields. We show that the algorithms are able to capture relevant timed properties in both cases. The quality of the computed STL formulae is assessed using the misclassification rate averaged over multiple test folds.

Future work includes extending the proposed framework to online mode, where traces are provided incrementally, instead of a single batch of signals available from the beginning of the learning procedure. We plan to perform a comprehensive comparative study of the framework for multiple choices of primitive formulae sets and impurity measures, tested on case studies of varying complexity. Future work will also focus on improving the local optimization procedures, which will boost the overall performance of the framework.

9. ACKNOWLEDGMENTS

This work was partially supported by DENSO CORPORATION and by the Office of Naval Research under grant N00014-14-1-0554.

10. REFERENCES

[1] E. Asarin, A. Donzé, O. Maler, and D. Nickovic. Parametric identification of temporal properties. In *Runtime Verification*, pages 147–160. Springer, 2012.

[2] E. Bartocci, L. Bortolussi, L. Nenzi, and G. Sanguinetti. System design of stochastic models using robustness of temporal properties. *Theoretical Computer Science*, 587:3–25, July 2015.

[3] E. Bartocci, L. Bortolussi, and G. Sanguinetti. Data-driven statistical learning of temporal logic properties. In *Formal Modeling and Analysis of Timed Systems*, pages 23–37. Springer, 2014.

[4] L. Breiman, J. Friedman, C. J. Stone, and R. A. Olshen. *Classification and regression trees*. CRC press, 1984.

[5] S. Bufo, E. Bartocci, G. Sanguinetti, M. Borelli, U. Lucangelo, and L. Bortolussi. Temporal Logic Based Monitoring of Assisted Ventilation in Intensive Care Patients. In *Leveraging Applications of Formal Methods, Verification and Validation*, number 8803 in Lecture Notes in Computer Science, pages 391–403. Springer, Oct. 2014.

[6] V. Chandola, A. Banerjee, and V. Kumar. Anomaly Detection: A Survey. *ACM Comput Surv*, 41(3):15:1–15:58, July 2009.

[7] T. H. Cormen. *Introduction to Algorithms*. MIT Press, third edition, July 2009.

[8] A. Donzé, T. Ferrere, and O. Maler. Efficient robust monitoring for STL. In *Computer Aided Verification*, pages 264–279. Springer, 2013.

[9] A. Donzé and O. Maler. Robust Satisfaction of Temporal Logic over Real-Valued Signals. In K. Chatterjee and T. A. Henzinger, editors, *Formal Modeling and Analysis of Timed Systems*, number 6246 in Lecture Notes in Computer Science, pages 92–106. Springer Berlin Heidelberg, 2010.

[10] G. E. Fainekos and G. J. Pappas. Robustness of temporal logic specifications for continuous-time signals. *Theor. Comput. Sci.*, 410(42):4262–4291, Sept. 2009.

[11] E. A. Gol, E. Bartocci, and C. Belta. A formal methods approach to pattern synthesis in reaction diffusion systems. In *Decision and Control (CDC), 2014 IEEE 53rd Annual Conference on*, pages 108–113. IEEE, 2014.

[12] R. Grosu, S. A. Smolka, F. Corradini, A. Wasilewska, E. Entcheva, and E. Bartocci. Learning and detecting emergent behavior in networks of cardiac myocytes. *Commun. ACM*, 52(3):97–105, 2009.

[13] B. Hoxha, H. Abbas, and G. Fainekos. Benchmarks for temporal logic requirements for automotive systems. *Proc Appl. Verification Contin. Hybrid Syst.*, 2014.

[14] L. Hyafil and R. L. Rivest. Constructing optimal binary decision trees is NP-complete. *Information Processing Letters*, 5(1):15–17, May 1976.

[15] L. Ingber. Adaptive simulated annealing (ASA): Lessons learned. *Control Cybern.*, 25:33–54, 1996.

[16] R. Isermann. *Fault-diagnosis systems*. Springer, 2006.

[17] X. Jin, A. Donzé, J. Deshmukh, and S. A. Seshia. Mining Requirements from Closed-Loop Control Models. *IEEE Trans. Comput.-Aided Des. Integr. Circuits Syst.*, PP(99):1–1, 2015.

[18] A. Jones, Z. Kong, and C. Belta. Anomaly detection in cyber-physical systems: A formal methods approach. In *Decision and Control (CDC), 2014 IEEE 53rd Annual Conference on*, pages 848–853. IEEE, 2014.

[19] Z. Kong, A. Jones, and C. Belta. Temporal Logics for Learning and Detection of Anomalous Behaviors. *IEEE Trans. Autom. Control*, 2016. inpress.

[20] Z. Kong, A. Jones, A. Medina Ayala, E. Aydin Gol, and C. Belta. Temporal Logic Inference for Classification and Prediction from Data. In *Proceedings of the 17th International Conference on Hybrid Systems: Computation and Control*, HSCC '14, pages 273–282, New York, NY, USA, 2014. ACM.

[21] K. Kowalska and L. Peel. Maritime anomaly detection using Gaussian Process active learning. In *2012 15th International Conference on Information Fusion (FUSION)*, pages 1164–1171, July 2012.

[22] O. Maler and D. Nickovic. Monitoring Temporal Properties of Continuous Signals. In Y. Lakhnech and S. Yovine, editors, *Formal Techniques, Modelling and Analysis of Timed and Fault-Tolerant Systems*, number 3253 in Lecture Notes in Computer Science, pages 152–166. Springer Berlin Heidelberg, 2004.

[23] J. R. Quinlan. *C4.5: Programs for Machine Learning*. Elsevier, June 2014.

[24] B. D. Ripley. *Pattern recognition and neural networks*. Cambridge university press, 1996.

[25] R. Storn and K. Price. Differential Evolution – A Simple and Efficient Heuristic for global Optimization over Continuous Spaces. *Journal of Global Optimization*, 11(4):341–359, Dec. 1997.

[26] H. Yang, B. Hoxha, and G. Fainekos. Querying Parametric Temporal Logic Properties on Embedded Systems. In *Testing Software and Systems*, number 7641 in Lecture Notes in Computer Science, pages 136–151. Springer, 2012.

[27] P. Zuliani, A. Platzer, and E. M. Clarke. Bayesian statistical model checking with application to Stateflow/Simulink verification. *Form Methods Syst Des*, 43(2):338–367, Aug. 2013.

Temporal Logic as Filtering

Alena Rodionova
TU Wien
Treitlstrasse 3
Vienna, Austria
alena.rodionova@tuwien.ac.at

Ezio Bartocci
TU Wien
Treitlstrasse 3
Vienna,
Austria
ezio@cps.tuwien.ac.at

Dejan Nickovic
Austrian Institute of
Technology
Donau-City-Strasse 1
Vienna, Austria
dejan.nickovic@ait.ac.at

Radu Grosu
TU Wien
Treitlstrasse 3
Vienna, Austria
radu.grosu@tuwien.ac.at

ABSTRACT

We show that metric temporal logic (MTL) can be viewed as linear time-invariant filtering, by interpreting addition, multiplication, and their neutral elements, over the idempotent dioid (max,min,0,1). Moreover, by interpreting these operators over the field of reals (+,×,0,1), one can associate various quantitative semantics to a metric-temporal-logic formula, depending on the filter's kernel used: square, rounded-square, Gaussian, low-pass, band-pass, or high-pass. This remarkable connection between filtering and metric temporal logic allows us to freely navigate between the two, and to regard signal-feature detection as logical inference. To the best of our knowledge, this connection has not been established before. We prove that our qualitative, filtering semantics is identical to the classical MTL semantics. We also provide a quantitative semantics for MTL, which measures the normalized, maximum number of times a formula is satisfied within its associated kernel, by a given signal. We show that this semantics is sound, in the sense that, if its measure is 0, then the formula is not satisfied, and it is satisfied otherwise. We have implemented both of our semantics in Matlab, and illustrate their properties on various formulas and signals, by plotting their computed measures.

1. INTRODUCTION

Starting with natural sciences, such as, chemistry, physics, and mathematics, and ending with the applied sciences, such as, mechanical engineering, electrical engineering, and computer science, the process of *filtering* plays a central role. In each of the above-mentioned domains, it takes a signal u as input, and it produces a signal y as output, where the components of u satisfying some given property are removed.

HSCC'16, April 12 - 14, 2016, Vienna, Austria

ISBN 978-1-4503-3955-1/16/04...$15.00
DOI: http://dx.doi.org/10.1145/2883817.2883839

For example, in chemistry, a filter f may remove particular molecules from a given solution. In optics (physics) and electrical engineering, f may remove particular frequencies of u, as in a low-pass, high-pass or band-pass filter. Finally, in computer science (eg. in functional programming), f may remove the elements in a list that satisfy a predicate p.

If the relation between u and y is linear, that is, if $f(u)$ is a linear function, the filter is called *linear*, otherwise it is called *nonlinear*. Moreover, if the operation of f depends only on the values of u and not on time, the filter is called *time invariant*. The most commonly used filters, in all of the above areas, are the linear, time-invariant (LTI) filters.

Intuitively, an LTI filter operates by sweeping a *kernel* distribution $k(s)$ over the entire domain of the lagged input signal $u(t-s)$, performing for every s the multiplication $u(t-s)k(s)$, and than summing up (or integrating) the results, in order to obtain the value of the output signal $y(t)$ at time t. One says that $y = u*k = k*u$ is the *convolution* of u and k.

If one interprets $(+, \times, 0, 1)$ over the *field* of reals, then filtering a discrete- or continuous-time {0,1}-valued signal u results in a signal y ranging over the reals. One can speak in this case about a *quantitative semantics* of the LTI filter:

$$y(n) = \sum_{i=0}^{\infty} u(n-i)k(i), \quad y(t) = \int_{0}^{\infty} u(t-s)k(s)\,ds. \qquad (1)$$

An important aspect of an LTI filter f is that, the kernel k is the response $f(\delta(s))$ of the filter to an impulse δ placed at the origin. In discrete time, δ is the Kronecker function, while in continuous time, δ is the Dirac distribution.

If one interprets $(+, \times, 0, 1)$ over the (max,min,0,1) *idempotent dioid* [15], then filtering a discrete- or continuous-time {0,1}-valued signal u, results in a {0,1}-valued signal y. In this case, one can speak about a *qualitative semantics* of the LTI filter. The filter has in this case the following form:

$$y(t) = \sup_{s=0}^{\infty} \min(u(t-s), k(s)). \qquad (2)$$

This qualitative semantics can be readily mapped to either linear temporal logic (LTL), or to *metric temporal logic (MTL)*, by using discrete time for LTL, discrete or continuous time for MTL, and choosing a *rectangular window* distribution k. In particular, (2) will represent the *finally operator.* To the best of our knowledge, this remarkable correspondence between LTI filters and MTL has not been established before. This correspondence allows us to freely navigate between logic and signal processing, and to understand signal analysis, such as, feature detection, as a logical inference. It also allows us to equip MTL with various quantitative semantics, depending on the LTI-filter-kernel k used: From square, to rounded, or to even a Gaussian windows, or from low-pass, to band-pass, or to even high-pass-filter kernel.

We prove that our qualitative, LTI-filtering semantics is identical to the classical MTL semantics. We also provide:

A quantitative semantics for MTL, which measures the normalized, maximum number of times a formula is satisfied within its associated kernel, with respect to a given signal.

We show that this quantitative semantics is sound, in the sense that, if its measure is 0, then the formula is not satisfied, and it is satisfied otherwise. We implemented both of our semantics in Matlab, and illustrate their properties on various formulas and signals by plotting their measures.

It is important to note that an LTI filter is called *causal* if the value of u is known for the entire kernel k at the time the multiplication is performed, and otherwise *not-causal.* This can be easily accomplished for signals with bounded domain. This restriction corresponds to bounded MTL, too. In the rest of the paper we will stick to this restriction.

The rest of the paper is organized as follows. In Section 2 we discuss related work. In Section 3 we revise MTL, and in Section 4 we revise LTI filters. In Section 5 we show that MTL semantics corresponds to a qualitative semantics in terms of LTI filters, and then also provide associated quantitative semantics, depending on the chosen kernel. Finally in Section 6 we draw conclusions and discuss future work.

2. RELATED WORK

Linear temporal logic (LTL) [19], and metric temporal logic (MTL) [16], have proven to be concise and elegant formalisms for rigorously specifying a required temporal behaviour, for a system under investigation. While in LTL real time is not of concern (one speaks about logical time), in MTL all the logical formulas are qualified with a time interval (window), during which the system has to satisfy the corresponding formula. Moreover, while in LTL time is discrete, in MTL time can be either discrete or continuous. In fact, by restricting the windows in MTL to $[0, \infty]$, or the length of the signal, one can obtain LTL or bounded LTL, respectively.

The classical semantics for LTL or MTL is *qualitative*, that is, it provides a true or false answer, to whether a signal satisfies, or violates, a given LTL or MTL formula. Moreover, the signals themselves, are Boolean, too. With the increasing importance of analog- or even mixed digital-analog signals, this classical semantics has been extended to account for real-time, real-valued signals. To this end, the set of atomic propositions has been extended to also include relational propositions of the form $p > \theta$, where θ is a constant value, representing a threshold. By negation and conjunction, one obtains all other relational variations.

When monitoring LTL or MTL properties over real-time, real-valued, possibly noisy signals, the classic, true or false interpretation, has the limitation that, a small perturbation (also called a jitter), in either the temporal- or in the value-domain, may affect the overall verdict. In the last decade, there has been a concerted effort, to provide alternative ways to interpret LTL or MTL, by proposing a so called *quantitative*, or metric semantics for an LTL or MTL specification. This is often referred to as a *measure* of the specification.

In [20], Rizk et. al propose a quantitative semantics for an LTL over the reals (LTL($\mathbb{R}$)) that computes, using a constraint solving algorithm, the domain, that is, all the time points in which the real variables occurring in a formula, make this formula true, for a signal under analysis.

In [14], Fainekos et al. introduce a notion of *space robustness* for MTL, with numeric predicates interpreted over real-valued behaviors. The space robustness measures the degree by which a continuous signal satisfies or violates the specification. The key idea consists in computing for each moment of time the distance $x_p(t) - \theta$, and in using min and max, to summarize these distances. Consequently, min and max replace the Boolean operators and, and or. The temporal operators globally and eventually, had to be replaced accordingly, with inf and sup. This quantitative interpretation of MTL over real-time, real-valued signals, has found a number of applications in the hybrid systems community, for both the identification of the uncertain parameters [4, 11, 12] in a system, and for the falsification analysis of a model [3].

In [13], Donzé et al. define a notion of *time robustness* for MTL interpreted over dense-real-time, real-valued signals. The time robustness of a propositional formula evaluated at time t measures the distance between t and the nearest instant t' in which the proposition switches its value. The other logical and temporal operators are computed using the same rules as in the space robustness. In contrast, as shown in Section 5, we provide within the same filtering framework, both a qualitative and a quantitative semantics for MTL interpreted over real-time, *Boolean-valued* signals. Moreover, our quantitative semantics is different from time robustness. The latter does not allow to integrate the truth value of the formulas over time, and hence reason about the satisfaction rate of a specification.

Other notions of robustness based on accumulation have been in part explored in the discrete time setting, motivated by the goal to equip formal verification and synthesis with quantitative objectives. For example, in [5], Boker et al. investigate the extension of LTL with *prefix-accumulation*, *path-accumulation*, *average* and *infinite average* assertions. However, the interpretation of this extended logic remains in the Boolean domain. Another related approach consists in extending temporal logics with discounting operators [9, 2] weighting the importance of the events according to how late they occur. In the context of real-time, the Duration Calculus (DC) [7] is an interval logic containing the special duration operator. This operator allows to integrate the truth values of state expressions over an interval of time. Recently, Akazaki et al. [1] extend MTL with *average* temporal operators that quantifies the average over time of the space and time robustness previously introduced. The aforementioned logics based on the idea of accumulation share a common aspect – they are all equipped with special syntactic constructs that allow to specify integration of values. This is in contrast to our work, in which we use convolution to provide the power of value accumulation directly to the semantics of MTL without the need to adapt its syntax. Finally, we also note that we are not aware of any previous studies that relate convolution and filtering to the specification formalisms described in this section.

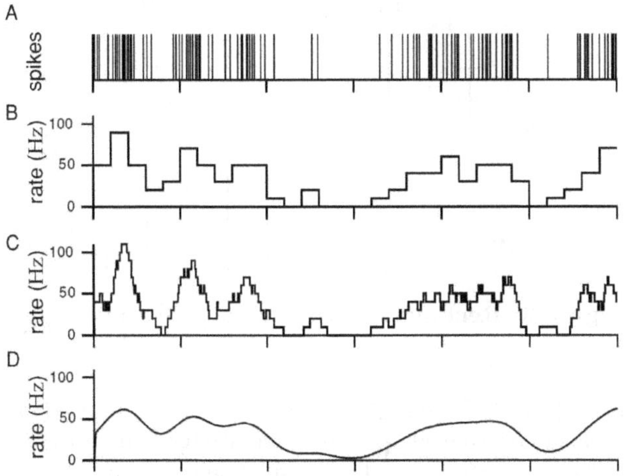

Figure 1: Measuring the spiking rate of a neuron.

3. METRIC TEMPORAL LOGIC

Let $P=\{p_1,\ldots,p_n\}$ be a set of atomic propositions. A *signal* $x:\mathbb{T}\rightarrow 2^P$ over P is a set-valued function, with time domain $\mathbb{T}$. In this paper, we only consider finite-length signals, that is, we restrict their domains to $\mathbb{T}=[0,T]$, for an arbitrary, finite value T. In other words, $\mathbb{T}$ is an interval which is either a subset of non-negative reals $\mathbb{R}_{\geq 0}$ or naturals $\mathbb{N}$. We denote by x_p the projection of x to the proposition p.

Metric Temporal Logic (MTL) [16] is a real-time extension of Linear Temporal Logic (LTL) [19]. We consider a bounded variant of MTL that contains both *future* and *past* temporal operators. Its principal modalities are timed until $\mathcal{U}_I$ and since $\mathcal{S}_I$, where I is a non-empty interval.

We provide a generic definition of MTL which is consistent with both the dense and discrete time interpretation of signals. Formally, the syntax of MTL interpreted over such signals is defined by the following grammar:

$$\varphi := p \mid \neg\varphi \mid \varphi_1 \vee \varphi_2 \mid \varphi_1 \mathcal{U}_I \varphi_2 \mid \varphi_1 \mathcal{S}_I \varphi_2,$$

where $p\in P$ and I is a non-empty interval of the form $\langle a,b\rangle$, such that, the left boundary $\langle$ is either open (or closed [, the right boundary $\rangle$ is either open) or closed], and the boundary values $a,b\in\mathbb{N}$ are natural numbers with $0\leq a\leq b$.

The satisfaction of a given formula φ with respect to a signal x at time point i is a relation denoted by $(x,i)\models\varphi$ and defined inductively as follows:

$$\begin{array}{lcl}
(x,i)\models p & \Longleftrightarrow & x_p[i]=1\\
(x,i)\models \neg\varphi & \Longleftrightarrow & (x,i)\not\models\varphi\\
(x,i)\models \varphi\vee\psi & \Longleftrightarrow & (x,i)\models\varphi \text{ or } (x,i)\models\psi\\
(x,i)\models \varphi\mathcal{U}_I\psi & \Longleftrightarrow & \exists j\in(i+I)\cap\mathbb{T}:(x,j)\models\psi\\
 & & \text{and } \forall k\in(i,\,j),\ (x,k)\models\varphi\\
(x,i)\models \varphi\mathcal{S}_I\psi & \Longleftrightarrow & \exists j\in(i-I)\cap\mathbb{T}:(x,j)\models\psi\\
 & & \text{and } \forall k\in(j,\,i),\ (x,k)\models\varphi.
\end{array}$$

From the basic definition of MTL, we can derive other standard Boolean and temporal operators as follows:

$$\top=p\vee\neg p,\quad \bot=\neg\top,\quad \varphi\wedge\psi=\neg(\neg\varphi\vee\neg\psi),$$
$$\Diamond_I\varphi=\top\mathcal{U}_I\varphi,\quad \Box_I\varphi=\neg\Diamond_I\neg\varphi,$$
$$\diamondminus_I\varphi=\top\mathcal{S}_I\varphi,\quad \boxminus_I\varphi=\neg\diamondminus_I\neg\varphi.$$

The Finally $\Diamond_I$, Globally $\Box_I$, Once $\diamondminus_I$ and Historically $\boxminus_I$ also admit a natural direct definition of their semantics:

$$\begin{array}{lcl}
(x,i)\models\Diamond_I\varphi & \Longleftrightarrow & \exists j\in(i+I)\cap\mathbb{T}:(x,j)\models\varphi\\
(x,i)\models\Box_I\varphi & \Longleftrightarrow & \forall j\in(i+I)\cap\mathbb{T},(x,j)\models\varphi\\
(x,i)\models\diamondminus_I\varphi & \Longleftrightarrow & \exists j\in(i-I)\cap\mathbb{T}:(x,j)\models\varphi\\
(x,i)\models\boxminus_I\varphi & \Longleftrightarrow & \forall j\in(i-I)\cap\mathbb{T},(x,j)\models\varphi.
\end{array}$$

4. LINEAR TIME-INVARIANT FILTERS

One of the most fundamental operations in signal processing is *linear filtering*, that is, the *convolution* of a signal with an appropriately chosen *kernel* or *window*. From audio, to image, and to video processing, linear filtering is used to either transform a signal in an appropriate way (eg. blur, sharpen) or to detect its features (eg. edges, patterns).

In order to understand linear filtering, it is instructive to describe it first in terms of the most fundamental windowing primitives: the Kronecker δ function, for the discrete-time case, and the Dirac δ distribution, for the continuous-time case. This distribution is defined as follows:

$$\delta(n)=\begin{cases}\infty, & \text{if } n=0\\ 0, & \text{otherwise,}\end{cases}\qquad \int_{-\infty}^{+\infty}\delta(s)\,ds=1. \tag{3}$$

It is interesting to note, that Kronecker δ is a function, whereas Dirac δ is not, that is, it makes sense only within an integral. Starting with Cauchy and up to Dirac, it took a long time to properly define this distribution [10, 6].

The main motivation for developing the impulse windowing primitive, was the ability to extract the instantaneous action of a function at a particular moment of time. For example, the impulse provided by a baseball bat when hitting the ball. This fundamental ability, allows to describe any discrete (or continuous) signal x as an infinite summation (or integral):

$$x(n)=\sum_{i=-\infty}^{\infty}x(n-i)\delta(i),\quad x(t)=\int_{-\infty}^{+\infty}x(t-s)\delta(s)\,ds. \tag{4}$$

This infinite sum (or integral) is denoted as $x*\delta$ and it is called the *convolution* of x and δ. Convolution is commutative, that is, $x{*}y=y{*}x$. Since $x=x{*}\delta$, convoluting x with δ is an identity transformation. Its main appeal, is that it allows to express any linear, time-invariant (LTI) function f, as the convolution of its response y to an impulse δ at the origin, with its (lagged) input u. For the discrete-time case (the continuous-time case is analogue), one can write:

$$f(\sum_{i=-\infty}^{\infty}u(n-i)\delta(i))=\sum_{i=-\infty}^{\infty}u(n-i)f(\delta(i)), \tag{5}$$

where $y(i)=f(\delta(i))$ is the response of f to δ at time zero. This response can be seen as the filtering kernel, and therefore f, as a linear, time-invariant filter. The popularity of such filters stems from the fact that the response of f to an impulses δ at the origin is easy to determine experimentally.

In order to motivate the use of various kernels (windows), and to establish a link between LTI-filtering and the semantics of MTL's *finally operator*, we borrow an example from [8]: measuring the firing rate of a spiking neuron.

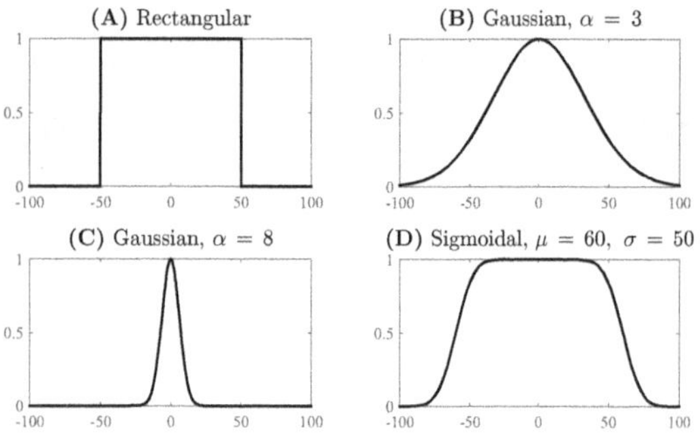

Figure 2: Windowing function types

If one ignores the duration and the pulse-like shape of a spike (also called an action potential), a spike sequence ρ can be simply characterized as a sum of Dirac distributions:

$$\rho(t) = \sum_{i=0}^{n} \delta(t-t_i), \qquad r = \frac{1}{T}\int_{0}^{T} \rho(s)\, ds, \tag{6}$$

where t_i is the time where the neuron generates a spike. The normalized integral r of $\rho(t)$ over an interval [0,T], is called the *spike-count rate* for that interval.

Now suppose one would like to approximate the spike rate of a neuron from an experimentally-obtained spike train. For example, Figure 1(A) shows the spike train obtained from a monkey's inferotemporal-cortex neuron, while watching a movie. There are various ways to computing this rate.

A very simple-minded way is to divide the signal's time domain in a set of disjoint bins, say of length Δt, count the number of spikes in each bin, and divide by Δt. For example, Figure 1(B) shows this approach, for $\Delta t = 100$ms. The result is a discrete (in multiples of $1/\Delta t$), piecewise constant, function. Decreasing Δt increases the temporal resolution, at the expense of the rate resolution. Moreover, the bin placement has an impact on the computed rates, too.

One can avoid an arbitrary bin-placement, by taking only one bin (or window) of duration Δt, slide it along the spike train, and then counting for each position t, the number of spikes within the bin. This approach is shown in Figure 1(C), where the window size is $\Delta t = 100$ms. A centered discrete-time window can be defined as follows:

$$w_{\Delta t}(n) = \frac{1}{\Delta t}\sum_{i=-\Delta t/2}^{+\Delta t/2} \delta(n-i). \tag{7}$$

A centered continuous-time window of size Δt can be defined as follows (this would work in discrete-time, too):

$$w_{\Delta t}(t) = \begin{cases} 1/\Delta t, & \text{if } -\Delta t/2 \le t \le \Delta t/2 \\ 0, & \text{otherwise.} \end{cases} \tag{8}$$

The bin sliding along the spike train, the counting, and the normalization with Δt, can be succinctly expressed in terms of convolution, either in discrete or continuous time:

$$r(n) = \sum_{i=0}^{T} \rho(i) w_{\Delta t}(n-i), \quad r(t) = \int_{0}^{T} \rho(s) w_{\Delta t}(t-s)\, ds, \tag{9}$$

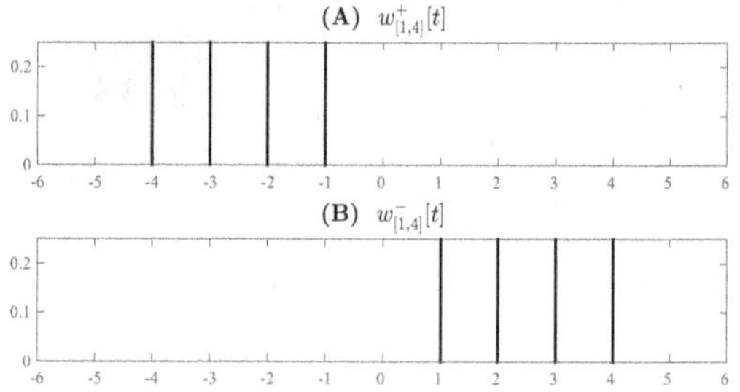

Figure 3: Rectangular windows $w^{+}_{[1,4]}[t]$ and $w^{-}_{[1,4]}[t]$

where $[0, T]$ is the domain of the spike train $\rho(t)$. If $\rho(t)$ is defined to be 0 outside $[0, T]$ one can take the sum (or the integral) over $[-\infty, +\infty]$. The convolution equation defines a discrete (and continuous) *linear filter* with *kernel* $w_{\Delta t}$. Note that the rates $r(t)$ at times less than one bin apart are correlated, because they involve common spikes. Moreover, the discontinuous nature of $r(t)$ is caused by the discontinuous nature of the window $w_{\Delta t}$ at its borders.

One can smoothen $r(t)$ and reduce the correlation between bins, by using a Gaussian window $N(0, \sigma)$ with $\sigma = 100$ms, as shown in Figure 1(D). A Gaussian is defined as follows:

$$N(\mu, \sigma)(t) = \frac{1}{\sigma\sqrt{2\pi}} e^{-\frac{(t-\mu)^2}{2\sigma^2}}. \tag{10}$$

In fact, one could use any windowing function, as long as the area below the window (the integral) is one.

The spike train $\rho(t)$ discussed above could as well represent the truth-values of a discrete-time MTL signal x. Alternatively, connecting equal, successive values in $\rho(t)$, would result in the truth-values of a continuous-time MTL signal x. Hence, the LTI-filters above can be understood as a *quantitative semantics* for the MTL operators finally and once interpreted over x: *The percentage of satisfaction of x within the associated window.* The size and the shape of the windows allow (as shown in the next section) to introduce a *temporal jitter* with respect to a satisfaction. Moreover, considering only square windows, and interpreting $(+, \times, 0, 1)$ over the *idempotent dioid* (max, min, 0, 1) gives a logical, *qualitative* semantics to the LTI-filter as the classic finally operator.

5. MTL AS LTI-FILTERING

As it has already been mentioned before, all LTI-filters are characterized by the particular type of the kernel (window). Although there are a lot of such kernels, the main idea is the same: a kernel function should have a bounded support, that is, a bounded domain where the function is not zero.

General definitions allow such kernels to go sufficiently rapid towards zero. The simplest finite support window is when the function is constant inside of some interval, and zero elsewhere. This function is called a *rectangular window* or "Boxcar" (see Figure 2). A smooth Gaussian window is the second type of a window, because it extends to infinity. So it should be truncated at the ends of the window. The main advantage of such a function is its smooth nature.

Let us start with a rectangular window definition: for a given continuous-time MTL formula with constrained time interval $I = \langle a, b\rangle$, a rectangular window function $w_I(t) : \mathbb{R} \to [0, 1]$ is constructed as follows:

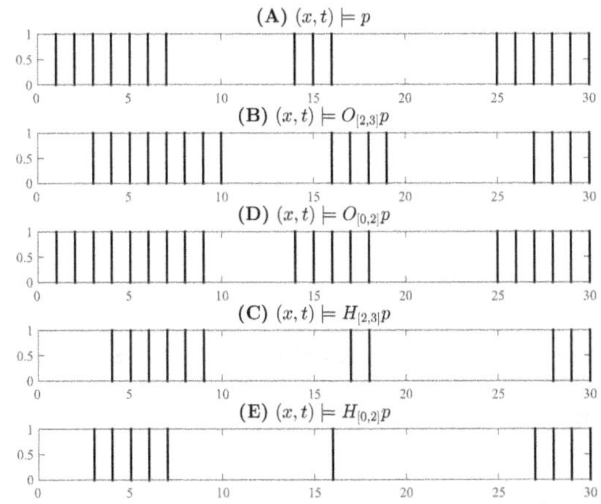

Figure 4: Qualitative discrete-time semantics.

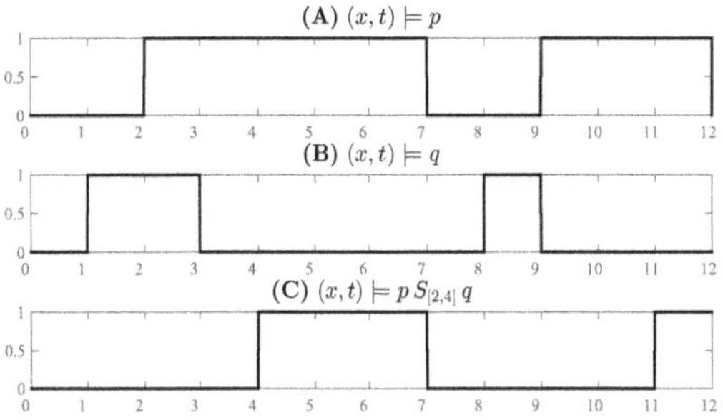

Figure 5: Continuous-time semantics for $p\mathcal{S}_{[2,4]}q$

$$w_I^+(t) = \begin{cases} \frac{1}{|\tilde{I}|}, & \text{if } t \in \tilde{I} \\ 0, & \text{if } t \notin \tilde{I}, \end{cases} \quad w_I^-(t) = \begin{cases} \frac{1}{|I|}, & \text{if } t \in I \\ 0, & \text{if } t \notin I, \end{cases} \tag{11}$$

where $\tilde{I} = \langle -b, -a\rangle$ is used for the future MTL operators $\Diamond_I$ or $\Box_I$ and $I = \langle a, b\rangle$ for the past MTL operators $\diamondminus_I$ or $\boxminus_I$. If $I = [a, a]$ is singular, then $w_{[a,a]}$ is defined as the Dirac-δ distribution. We will denote this window by $w_{\{a\}}$.

For discrete-time, open intervals can always be replaced with closed intervals. Hence we restrict I to closed intervals, only. In this case, we define w_I in terms of Kronecker-δ, as follows:

$$w_I^+[t] = \frac{1}{|I|}\sum_{i\in I}\delta(t+i), \quad w_I^-[t] = \frac{1}{|I|}\sum_{i\in I}\delta(t-i), \tag{12}$$

where the $+$ and the $-$ superscripts correspond to the future and past MTL operators, respectively.

Note that for past MTL operators one needs to delay the kernel, so the sign is negative, and for future MTL operators one has to rush the kernel, so the sign is positive. For instance, consider the discrete-time MTL formulas $\Diamond_{[1,4]}\,p$ and $\diamondminus_{[1,4]}\,p$. The windows used by these formulas:

$$w_{[1,4]}^+[t] = \frac{1}{4}\sum_{i=1}^{4}\delta(t+i), \quad w_{[1,4]}^-[t] = \frac{1}{4}\sum_{i=1}^{4}\delta(t-i), \tag{13}$$

are shown graphically in Figure 3(A) and (B), respectively.

5.1 Qualitative Semantics

In this section, we show that all temporal operators of MTL can be defined in terms of LTI-filtering. For this purpose, we interpret addition, multiplication, and their associated neutral elements over $(\{0,1\}, \max, \min, 0, 1)$ the *max-min idempotent dioid* with value domain $\{0,1\}$. In this dioid one can define the *complement* $\neg v$ of a value v as $1-v$. Moreover, the normalization factor in the definition of the window function $w_I(t)$ should be omitted in order to preserve Boolean values.

5.1.1 Discrete-time semantics

In the discrete-time domain, any signal is bounded (remember that we only consider bounded MTL), and therefore all the intervals of the MTL operators are bounded, too. As a consequence, the number of discrete points in each interval is finite, and we can extend the binary max operator to an *n-ary max operator*, which we can use for the convolution integral. Thus, the discrete-time semantics of MTL can be formulated as below:

$$\begin{aligned}
(x,i) \models p &\iff x_p[i] \\
(x,i) \models \neg\varphi &\iff 1 - (\,(x,i) \models \varphi\,) \\
(x,i) \models \varphi \vee \psi &\iff \max\left((x,i) \models \varphi,\, (x,i) \models \psi\right) \\
(x,i) \models \Diamond_I\varphi &\iff \max_{j\in\mathbb{T}} \min\left((x,j) \models \varphi,\, w_I^+[i-j]\right) \\
(x,i) \models \Box_I\varphi &\iff 1 - (\,(x,i) \models \Diamond_I\neg\varphi\,) \\
(x,i) \models \diamondminus_I\varphi &\iff \max_{j\in\mathbb{T}} \min\left((x,j) \models \varphi,\, w_I^-[i-j]\right) \\
(x,i) \models \boxminus_I\varphi &\iff 1 - (\,(x,i) \models \diamondminus_I\neg\varphi\,) \\
(x,i) \models \varphi\,\mathcal{U}_I\,\psi &\iff \max_{j\in I} \min\Big((x,i) \models \Box_{[1,j-1]}\varphi, \\
&\qquad (x,i) \models \Diamond_{\{j\}}\psi\Big) \\
(x,i) \models \varphi\,\mathcal{S}_I\,\psi &\iff \max_{j\in I} \min\Big((x,i) \models \boxminus_{[1,j-1]}\varphi, \\
&\qquad (x,i) \models \diamondminus_{\{j\}}\psi\Big).
\end{aligned}$$

In fact, we can define the entire semantics of MTL in terms of LTI-filtering, by using the Kronecker-δ kernel:

$$\begin{aligned}
(x,i) \models p &\iff \max_{j\in\mathbb{T}} \min\left(x_p[j],\, \delta(i-j)\right) \\
(x,i) \models \neg\varphi &\iff \max_{j\in\mathbb{T}} \min\left(1 - ((x,j) \models \varphi), \delta(i-j)\right) \\
(x,i) \models \varphi \vee \psi &\iff \max_{j\in\mathbb{T}} \min\Big(\max\big(\\
&\qquad (x,j) \models \varphi,\, (x,j) \models \psi\big),\, \delta(i-j)\Big).
\end{aligned}$$

In order, to illustrate the qualitative, discrete-time semantics for various temporal operators, consider the example shown in Figure 4. In Figure 4(A) we show the values x_p of discrete-time signal x, for which it satisfies proposition p. This signal is defined over the interval $[0, 30]$, with $\Delta t = 1$. In other words, the domain of x is $\{0, 1, \ldots, 30\}$.

In order to interpret the MTL operators $\diamondminus$ and $\boxminus$ over x, we use two indexing windows I, for both: The first is $I = [2, 3]$, and the second is $I = [0, 2]$. To simplify the caption in the Matlab figures, we use the textual representation of the temporal operators: F (finally) for $\Diamond$, G (globally) for $\Box$, O (once) for $\diamondminus$, and H (historically) for $\boxminus$.

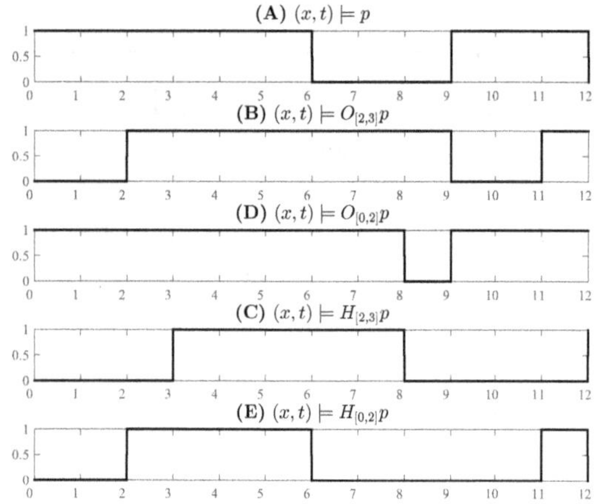

Figure 6: Qualitative continuous-time semantics.

The satisfaction of the MTL formulas $\diamondminus_{[2,3]}p$ and $\diamondminus_{[0,2]}p$ for the signal x_p are shown in Figure 4(B-C). Similarly, the satisfaction of $\boxminus_{[2,3]}p$ and $\boxminus_{[0,2]}p$ for the signal x_p are shown in Figure 4(D-E). The dependence on the length of the interval I is precise: Increasing the length, increases the number of points where the operator $\diamondminus_I p$ is satisfied and $\boxminus_I p$ is not. Moreover, the shift of the interval's beginning point leads to the same shift of the output signal.

For the qualitative, discrete-time semantics of an MTL formula φ with respect to a signal x, it is straight forward to show, that the semantics is sound, in the sense that, if it produces the value 0, then the formula is not satisfied in the classical semantics, and if it produces 1 then it is satisfied. Let us index satisfaction with C as classic semantics, and with L as LTI-filtering semantics in the following theorem.

THEOREM 1 (SOUNDNESS). *For an MTL formula φ and a discrete-time signal x, it holds that x satisfies φ in the LTI-filtering interpretation, if and only if, it satisfies φ in the classic interpretation. More formally one can write:*

$$(x,i) \models_L \varphi \iff (x,i) \models_C \varphi.$$

PROOF. (Sketch) First, observe that the Boolean operators are interpreted the same way, as the max-min dioid provides a logical interpretation for the set $\{0,1\}$: the truth tables for conjunction and min, disjunction and max, and negation and complement, are all the same, respectively. Second, the existential quantifier in the classic interpretation, corresponds to max in the max-min dioid, which leads to the same interpretation for $\Diamond_I$ and $\diamondminus_I$. Through the properties of negation, we immediately establish the same interpretation for $\Box_I$ and $\boxminus_I$. Finally, the definition of $\mathcal{U}_I$ and $\mathcal{S}_I$ can be written solely in terms of the previous temporal operators, as we did in the LTI-filter semantics. □

5.1.2 Continuous-time semantics

In the continuous-time semantics, each bounded interval is going to have an infinite number of points, except for the singular intervals, which contain only a single point. As a consequence, we have to interpret the integral in this case, as the *supremum operator*, which is the proper extension of max over infinite domains.

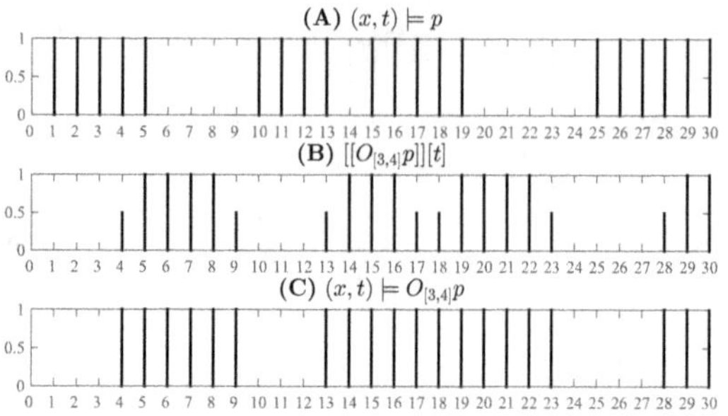

Figure 7: Soundness of discrete-time semantics.

$$\begin{aligned}
(x,i) \models p &\iff x_p(i)\\
(x,i) \models \neg\varphi &\iff 1 - (\,(x,i) \models \varphi\,)\\
(x,i) \models \varphi \vee \psi &\iff \max\left((x,i) \models \varphi,\ (x,i) \models \psi\right)\\
(x,i) \models \Diamond_I \varphi &\iff \sup_{j\,\in\,\mathbb{T}} \min\left((x,j) \models \varphi,\ w_I^{+}(i-j)\right)\\
(x,i) \models \Box_I \varphi &\iff 1 - (\,(x,i) \models \Diamond_I \neg\varphi\,)\\
(x,i) \models \diamondminus_I \varphi &\iff \sup_{j\,\in\,\mathbb{T}} \min\left((x,j) \models \varphi,\ w_I^{-}(i-j)\right)\\
(x,i) \models \boxminus_I \varphi &\iff 1 - (\,(x,i) \models \diamondminus_I \neg\varphi\,)\\
(x,i) \models \varphi\,\mathcal{U}_I\,\psi &\iff \sup_{j\,\in\,I} \min\Big((x,i) \models \Box_{(0,j)}\varphi,\\
&\qquad\qquad (x,i) \models \Diamond_{\{j\}}\psi\Big)\\
(x,i) \models \varphi\,\mathcal{S}_I\,\psi &\iff \sup_{j\,\in\,I} \min\Big((x,i) \models \boxminus_{(0,j)}\varphi,\\
&\qquad\qquad (x,i) \models \diamondminus_{\{j\}}\psi\Big).
\end{aligned}$$

In order to illustrate the qualitative, continuous-time semantics for various temporal operators, consider the example shown in Figure 6. In Figure 6(A) we show x_p, the value of continuous-time signal x, for which proposition p is true. This signal is defined over the interval $[0,12]$. Every subinterval in the plot is left-closed and right-open.

In order to interpret the MTL operators $\diamondminus$ and $\boxminus$ over x, we use, the same indexing windows as before: First, $I = [2,3]$ and next, $I = [0,2]$. The satisfaction of the MTL formulas $\diamondminus_{[2,3]}p$ and $\diamondminus_{[0,2]}p$ for the signal x are shown in Figure 6(B-C). Similarly, the satisfaction of $\boxminus_{[2,3]}p$ and $\boxminus_{[0,2]}p$ for the signal x are shown in Figure 6(D-E).

The qualitative, continuous-time semantics of the since operator $(x,i) \models p\,\mathcal{S}_{[2,4]}q$ is shown in Figure 5. The semantics of $(x,i) \models p$ (signal x_p) is shown in Figure 5(A) and the semantics of $(x,i) \models q$ (signal x_q) shown in Figure 5(B). Finally, the semantics of $(x,i) \models p\,\mathcal{S}_{[2,4]}q$ is shown in Figure 5(C). It should be emphasized that, the obtained qualitative semantics corresponds to a standard MTL semantics.

THEOREM 2 (SOUNDNESS). *For an MTL formula φ and a continuous-time signal x, it holds that x satisfies φ in the LTI-filtering interpretation, if and only if, it satisfies φ in the classic interpretation. More formally one can write:*

$$(x,i) \models_L \varphi \iff (x,i) \models_C \varphi.$$

PROOF. (Sketch) The proof is very similar to the one for the discrete-time, qualitative semantics. The only difference is that we work now with windows having dense (infinite) domain, and max have to be therefore extended to sup, the proper extension on such domains. □

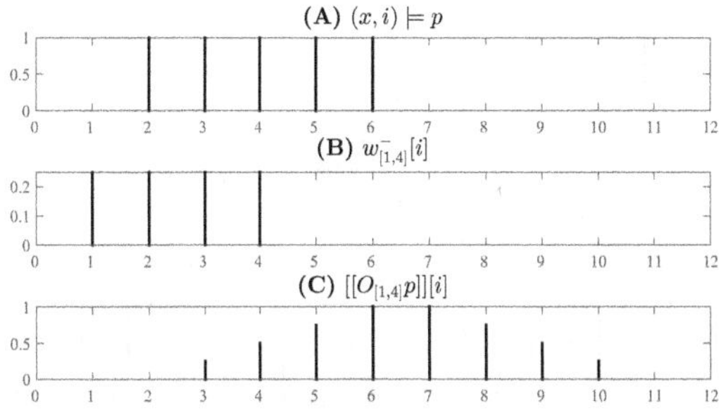

Figure 8: Quantitative discrete-time semantics.

5.2 Quantitative Semantics

If we interpret addition, multiplication, and their associated neutral elements over $([0,1], +, \times, 0, 1)$, the *field of reals* restricted to the interval [0,1], we recover the standard definition of LTI-filtering. This definition allows us to associate a *quantitative semantics* to MTL temporal formulas.

This semantics measures the normalized, maximum number of times the formula is satisfied within its associated window. Since $\Box_I$ and $\boxminus_I$ can be satisfied only once within I, the measure returns 1, in case of satisfaction, and 0, otherwise. However, $\Diamond_I$ and $\diamondminus_I$ are more interesting, as they may be satisfied several times in I. As in Section 5.1, we distinguish between discrete- and continuous-time semantics, and use summations and integrals, respectively. Moreover, we give up the duality property between the $\Box_I$ and $\Diamond_I$ operators (same for past operators $\boxminus_I$ and $\diamondminus_I$). In the rest of the paper we will stick to the *positive normal form* representation of an MTL formula, where negations may only occur in front of atomic propositions [18].

5.2.1 Discrete-time semantics

Assume we are given a discrete signal with $[0,T]$ duration interval. Then the quantitative semantics for MTL can be formulated as follows:

$$
\begin{aligned}
[\![x,p]\!][i] &= x_p[i]\\
[\![x,\neg p]\!][i] &= 1-[\![x,p]\!][i]\\
[\![x,\varphi\vee\psi]\!][i] &= \max([\![x,\varphi]\!][i],\ [\![x,\psi]\!][i])\\
[\![x,\varphi\wedge\psi]\!][i] &= \min([\![x,\varphi]\!][i],\ [\![x,\psi]\!][i])\\
[\![x,\Diamond_I\varphi]\!][i] &= \sum_{j\,\in\,\mathbb{T}} [\![x,\varphi]\!][j]\cdot w_I^{+}[i-j]\\
[\![x,\diamondminus_I\varphi]\!][i] &= \sum_{j\,\in\,\mathbb{T}} [\![x,\varphi]\!][j]\cdot w_I^{-}[i-j]\\
[\![x,\Box_I\varphi]\!][i] &= \min_{j\,\in\,i+I}[\![x,\varphi]\!][j]\\
[\![x,\boxminus_I\varphi]\!][i] &= \min_{j\,\in\,i-I}[\![x,\varphi]\!][j]\\
[\![x,\varphi\,\mathcal{U}_I\,\psi]\!][i] &= \frac{1}{|I|}\sum_{j\,\in\,I}[\![x,\Box_{[1,j-1]}\varphi]\!][i]\cdot[\![x,\Diamond_{\{j\}}\psi]\!][i]\\
[\![x,\varphi\,\mathcal{S}_I\,\psi]\!][i] &= \frac{1}{|I|}\sum_{j\,\in\,I}[\![x,\boxminus_{[1,j-1]}\varphi]\!][i]\cdot[\![x,\diamondminus_{\{j\}}\psi]\!][i],
\end{aligned}
$$

where the window superscripts + and − correspond to the window direction, according to Equations (12).

For example, consider the discrete-time signal x over the interval $[0,12]$, with $\Delta t = 1$, shown in Figure 8. Since it is discrete-time, its domain is $\{0,1,\ldots,12\}$. In order to interpret the MTL operator $\diamondminus_{[1,4]}\,p$, we construct the rectangular windowing function $w^{-}_{[1,4]}[i]$ as shown at the beginning of Section 5. The representation of this window is shown in Figure 3(B). Since the MTL formula, is a past formula, the corresponding window is formally defined as follows:

$$w^{-}_{[1,4]}[i] = \frac{1}{4}\sum_{j=1}^{4}\delta(i-j). \tag{14}$$

Now we are able to evaluate the quantitative semantics of signal x with respect to the Once-formula given below:

$$[\![\diamondminus_{[1,4]}p]\!]\,[i] = \sum_{j=0}^{12} p[j]\cdot w^{-}_{[1,4]}[i-j].$$

The quantitative-values of the result are given in a Table 1, and their graphical representation is shown in Figure 8.

For the quantitative, discrete-time semantics of an MTL formula φ and signal x, it is straight forward to show, that the semantics is sound, in the sense that, it produces a measure greater than 0, if and only if, the formula is satisfied by the discrete-time qualitative semantics, and 0, otherwise.

Table 1: Quantitative semantics values

MTL Formula	Time point							
	3	4	5	6	7	8	9	10
$[\![\diamondminus_{[1,4]}p]\!]$	$\frac{1}{4}$	$\frac{1}{2}$	$\frac{3}{4}$	1	1	$\frac{3}{4}$	$\frac{1}{2}$	$\frac{1}{4}$

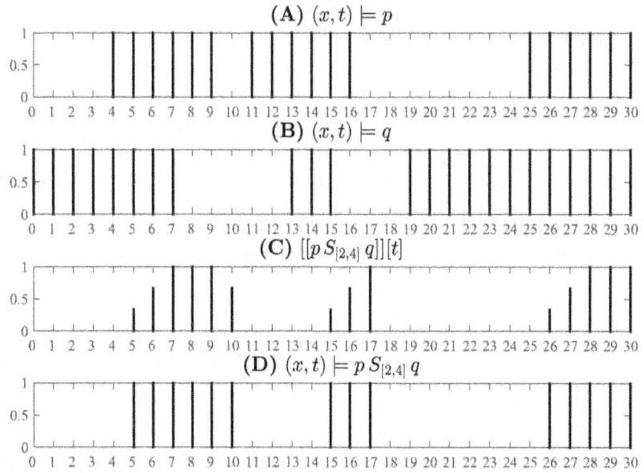

Figure 9: Discrete quantitative semantics for $\mathcal{S}_I$.

THEOREM 3 (SOUNDNESS). *For a positive normal form MTL formula φ and a discrete-time signal x, it holds that x satisfies φ, if and only if, its quantitative semantics is strictly greater than 0. It does not satisfy φ, if and only if, its quantitative semantics is 0:*

$$
\begin{aligned}
(x,i)\models\varphi &\iff [\![x,\varphi]\!][i]>0,\\
(x,i)\not\models\varphi &\iff [\![x,\varphi]\!][i]=0.
\end{aligned}
$$

PROOF. (Sketch) First, as shown in Theorem 1, the qualitative discrete-time semantics in terms of LTI-filtering over the idempotent dioid $(\max,\min,0,1)$, is the same as the classical MTL semantics. Second, the interpretation of Boolean

MTL formulas p, $\neg p$, $\varphi \vee \psi$, and $\varphi \wedge \psi$ over x is the same in both the qualitative and quantitative semantics. Third, the interpretation of the temporal MTL formulas $\Box_I$ and $\boxminus_I$ over x is also the same. Fourth, the interpretation of MTL formulas $\Diamond_I$ and $\diamondminus_I$ ensure that they are strictly positive only if they are satisfied by x and 0, otherwise. Fifth, the interpretation of $\mathcal{U}_I$ and $\mathcal{S}_I$ are properly derived from $\Box_I$ and $\Diamond_I$, $\boxminus_I$ and $\diamondminus_I$, respectively. $\Box$

In order to illustrate the relation between the qualitative and the quantitative, discrete-time semantics, consider the example shown in Figure 7. In Figure 7(A) we show the signal x_p. This signal is defined over the set $\{0, \ldots, 30\}$. In Figure 7(B) we illustrate the quantitative semantics of the formula $\diamondminus_{[3,4]} p$ with respect to x, and in Figure 7(C) we show the qualitative semantics of the same formula with respect to x. As Figures 7(B-C) show, the two are in agreement, that is whenever the quantitative semantics is strictly greater than 0, the formula is satisfied, and whenever the quantitative semantics is 0, the formula is not satisfied.

In Figure 9 we illustrate the interplay between the once and the historically operators as they occur in the definition of the since operator. Note that the outside sum also plays the role of an enclosing temporal operator. In Figure 9(A) and (B) we show the discrete-time signals x_p and x_q, respectively. In Figure 9(C) we show the quantitative semantics of $p\,\mathcal{S}_{[2,4]}\,q$ with respect to x_p and x_q. Finally in Figure 9(D), we show the qualitative semantics of the same formula with respect to x_p and x_q. As one can see from Figure 9(C-D), the quantitative semantics is sound.

5.2.2 *Continuous-time semantics*

In the continuous-time semantics, we restrict ourselves to piecewise constant *cadlag signals* [17]. Such signals are right-continuous and have left limits everywhere. As a consequence, we do not consider signals that may have a distinct value in some isolated point. Since this property has to be preserved by temporal operators, we adopt the MTL fragment from [17], where temporal modalities are restricted to be closed intervals only. Assume we are given a signal x with domain $[0, T)$. Then the quantitative semantics for MTL is defined as follows:

$$\begin{aligned}
[\![x, p]\!](i) &= x_p(i)\\
[\![x, \neg p]\!](i) &= 1 - [\![x, p]\!](i)\\
[\![x, \varphi \vee \psi]\!](i) &= \max([\![x, \varphi]\!](i),\ [\![x, \psi]\!](i))\\
[\![x, \varphi \wedge \psi]\!](i) &= \min([\![x, \varphi]\!](i),\ [\![x, \psi]\!](i))\\
[\![x, \Diamond_I \varphi]\!](i) &= \int_{\mathbb{T}} [\![x, \varphi]\!](j) \cdot w_I^{+}(i{-}j)\ \mathrm{d}j\\
[\![x, \diamondminus_I \varphi]\!](i) &= \int_{\mathbb{T}} [\![x, \varphi]\!](j) \cdot w_I^{-}(i{-}j)\ \mathrm{d}j\\
[\![x, \Box_I \varphi]\!](i) &= \inf_{j\,\in\, i+I} [\![x, \varphi]\!](j)\\
[\![x, \boxminus_I \varphi]\!](i) &= \inf_{j\,\in\, i-I} [\![x, \varphi]\!](j)\\
[\![x, \varphi\, \mathcal{U}_I \psi]\!](i) &= \frac{1}{|I|} \int_I [\![x, \Box_{(0,j)} \varphi]\!](i) \cdot [\![x, \Diamond_{\{j\}} \psi]\!](i) \mathrm{d}j\\
[\![x, \varphi\, \mathcal{S}_I \psi]\!](i) &= \frac{1}{|I|} \int_I [\![x, \boxminus_{(0,j)} \varphi]\!](i) \cdot [\![x, \diamondminus_{\{j\}} \psi]\!](i) \mathrm{d}j,
\end{aligned}$$

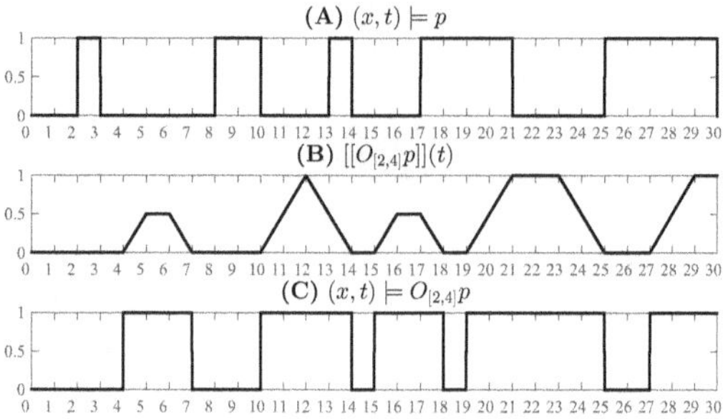

Figure 10: Soundness of continuous-time semantics.

where the window superscripts $+$ and $-$ correspond to the direction of the window according to (12). As usual, the inf operation over an empty set is assumed to be 1.

Like in the discrete-time case, it is relatively straightforward to show that the quantitative semantics of an MTL formula φ with respect to a continuous-time signal x, is sound.

THEOREM 4 (SOUNDNESS). *Let φ be a positive normal form MTL formula and x be a continuous-time signal. Then the following properties hold:*

$$\begin{aligned}
[\![x, \varphi]\!](i) > 0 &\implies (x, i) \models \varphi,\\
(x, i) \not\models \varphi &\implies [\![x, \varphi]\!](i) = 0.
\end{aligned}$$

PROOF. (Sketch) The proof goes along the same lines as the one for the discrete-time semantics, but with a set of complementary remarks. First, one has to observe that inf operator properly extends min and the integral properly extends the sum operator. Second, the Dirac-δ is the proper substitute of the Kronecker-δ within the integral. Third, if the MTL formula is valid only in a punctual interval within the given time constraints, it is not allowed to measure the normalized number of times the formula is satisfied within the window. In this case the quantitative measure is equal to zero and it is essential to drop the contrary claim. $\Box$

In order to illustrate the quantitative, continuous-time semantics for various temporal operators, and their relation to the qualitative, continuous-time semantics, consider the example shown in Figure 10. In Figure 10(A) we show the signal x_p. This signal is defined over the interval $[0, 30)$. In Figure 10(B) we illustrate the quantitative semantics of the formula $\diamondminus_{[2,4]} p$ with respect to x, and in Figure 10(C) we show the qualitative semantics of the same formula with respect to x. As Figures 10(B-C) show, the two are in agreement, that is whenever the quantitative semantics is strictly greater than 0, the formula is satisfied, and whenever formula is not satisfied, the quantitative semantics is 0.

Remark 1. Note that for a singular interval $I = \{a\}$, the semantics of $\Diamond_I \varphi$ or $\diamondminus_I \varphi$ is not necessarily zero (although a point has zero area), because this interval is represented by the Dirac-δ distribution which is an "infinite" value at a:

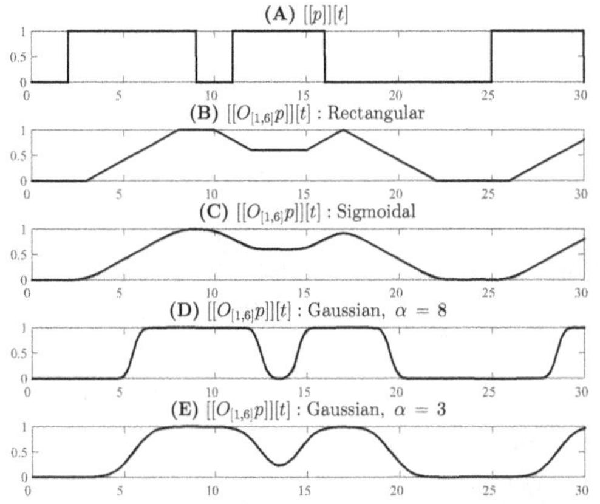

Figure 11: Smooth evaluation of $[\![\diamondminus_{[1,6]}p]\!]\,[t]$.

$$[\![x, \diamondminus_{\{a\}}\varphi]\!](t) = \int_0^T [\![x,\varphi]\!](s) \cdot w^{-}_{\{a\}}(t-s)\;\mathrm{d}s = [\![x,\varphi]\!](t-a),$$

$$[\![x, \Diamond_{\{a\}}\varphi]\!](t) = \int_0^T [\![x,\varphi]\!](s) \cdot w^{+}_{\{a\}}(t-s)\;\mathrm{d}s = [\![x,\varphi]\!](t+a).$$

Moreover, the semantics of $\Box_I$ and $\boxminus_I$ is also not zero, because of the infimum operator over a single point. As a consequence, we have that $\Box_I \equiv \Diamond_I$ and $\boxminus_I \equiv \diamondminus_I$.

In order to illustrate the effect of applying various smooth kernels to a signal x_p, consider the example shown in Figure 11. In Figure 11(A) we show the signal x_p. In Figure 11(B) we illustrate the quantitative semantics with respect to a square kernel. In Figure 11(C) we show the same semantics with respect to a sigmoidal window. This automatically adds tolerance to a time-jitter at the boundaries of the kernel. Finally, in Figures 11(D-E) we show the result of applying Gaussian kernels, with reciprocal of standard deviation 8 and 3, respectively. Note how they influence the domain of satisfaction.

In Figure 12 we illustrate the since operator with respect to continuous-time signals x_p and x_q. In Figures 12(A-B) we show these two signals. In Figure 12(C) we show the quantitative semantics of $p\,\mathcal{S}_{[1,3]}q$ with respect to x_p and x_q. Finally in Figure 12(D), we show the qualitative semantics of the same formula with respect to x_p and x_q. As one can see from Figures 12(C-D), the quantitative semantics is sound.

6. CONCLUSIONS

We have shown that linear, time-invariant (LTI) filtering corresponds to metric temporal logic (MTL) if addition and multiplication are interpreted as max and min, and if true and false are interpreted as one and zero, respectively.

We have also provided a quantitative semantics to temporal MTL formula with respect to a discrete- or continuous-time signal, measuring the normalized, maximum number of times, the formula is satisfied within its associated window. This semantics is sound, in the sense that, if its measure is strictly greater than zero, then the formula is satisfied.

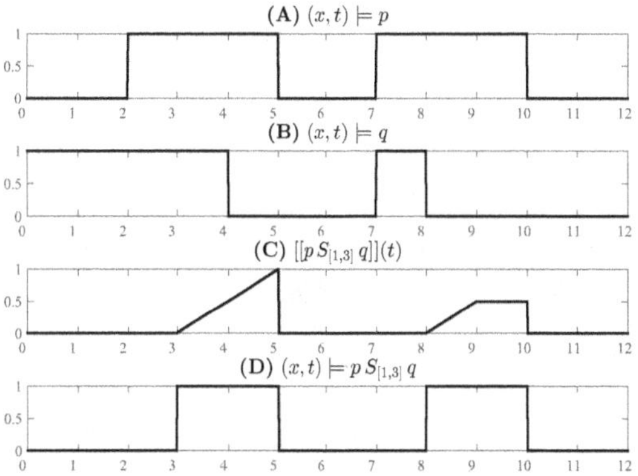

Figure 12: Cont. quantitative semantics for $\mathcal{S}_I$.

In future work we would like to explore alternative quantitative semantics for MTL, which are more informative, in case the MTL formula is not satisfied. We would also like to explore the logical meaning of other types of LTI-filter kernels, such as band-pass and high-pass. Moreover, we would like to investigate how the correspondence between MTL and LTI-filters can be exploited in order to build very efficient MTL monitors, using digital signal processors (DSPs). These are specialized microprocessors, optimized for filtering and compression operations in signal processing.

7. ACKNOWLEDGMENTS

This work was partially supported by the Austrian FFG project HARMONIA (nr. 845631), the Doctoral Program Logical Methods in Computer Science funded by the Austrian FWF, the Austrian National Research Network (nr. S 11405-N23 and S 11412-N23) SHiNE funded by the Austrian Science Fund (FWF), the EU ICT COST Action IC1402 on Runtime Verification beyond Monitoring (ARVI), the US National-Science-Foundation Frontiers project CyberCardia, the MISTRAL project A-1341-RT-GP coordinated by the European Defence Agency (EDA) and funded by the Joint Investment Programme on Second Innovative Concepts and Emerging Technologies (JIP-ICET 2). The authors also would like to acknowledge César Sánchez from IMDEA Software Institute for helpful insight and comments that greatly improved the paper.

8. REFERENCES

[1] T. Akazaki and I. Hasuo. Time robustness in MTL and expressivity in hybrid system falsification. In *Proc. of CAV 2015: the 27th International Conference on Computer Aided Verification, Part II*, volume 9207 of *LNCS*, pages 356–374. Springer, 2015.

[2] S. Almagor, U. Boker, and O. Kupferman. Discounting in LTL. In *Proc. of TACAS 2015: the 20th International Conference on Tools and Algorithms for the Construction and Analysis of System*, volume 8413 of *LNCS*, pages 424–439. Springer, 2014.

[3] Y. S. R. Annapureddy, C. Liu, G. E. Fainekos, and S. Sankaranarayanan. S-taliro: A tool for temporal logic falsification for hybrid systems. In *Proc. of TACAS 2011: the 17th International Conference on*

Tools and Algorithms for the Construction and Analysis of Systems, volume 6605 of *LNCS*, pages 254–257. Springer, 2011.

[4] E. Bartocci, L. Bortolussi, L. Nenzi, and G. Sanguinetti. System design of stochastic models using robustness of temporal properties. *Theor. Comput. Sci.*, 587:3–25, 2015.

[5] U. Boker, K. Chatterjee, T. A. Henzinger, and O. Kupferman. Temporal specifications with accumulative values. *ACM Trans. Comput. Log.*, 15(4):27:1–27:25, 2014.

[6] A.-L. Cauchy. *Théorie de la propagation des ondes à la surface d'un fluide pesant d'une profondeur indéfinie.* Académie des sciences (France), 1815.

[7] Z. Chaochen, C. A. R. Hoare, and A. P. Ravn. A calculus of durations. *Inf. Process. Lett.*, 40(5):269–276, 1991.

[8] P. Dayan and L. F. Abbott. *Theoretical Neuroscience: Computational and Mathematical Modeling of Neural Systems.* The MIT Press, 2001.

[9] L. de Alfaro, M. Faella, T. A. Henzinger, R. Majumdar, and M. Stoelinga. Model checking discounted temporal properties. In *Proc. of TACAS 2004: the 10th International Conference on Tools and Algorithms for the Construction and Analysis of Systems*, volume 2988 of *LNCS*, pages 77–92. Springer, 2004.

[10] P. Dirac. *The Principles of Quantum Mechanics.* Oxford University Press, 1930.

[11] A. Donzé. Breach, a toolbox for verification and parameter synthesis of hybrid systems. In *Proc. of CAV 2010: the 22nd International Conference on Computer Aided Verification*, volume 6174 of *LNCS*, pages 167–170. Springer Berlin, 2010.

[12] A. Donzé, G. Clermont, and C. J. Langmead. Parameter synthesis in nonlinear dynamical systems: Application to systems biology. *Journal of Computational Biology*, 17(3):325–336, 2010.

[13] A. Donzé and O. Maler. Robust satisfaction of temporal logic over real-valued signals. In *Proc. of FORMATS 2010: the 8th International Conference on Formal Modeling and Analysis of Timed Systems*, volume 6246 of *LNCS*, pages 92–106. Springer, 2010.

[14] G. E. Fainekos and G. J. Pappas. Robustness of temporal logic specifications for continuous-time signals. *Theor. Comput. Sci.*, 410(42):4262–4291, 2009.

[15] M. Gondran and M. Minoux. *Graphs, Dioids and Semirings.* Springer, 2008.

[16] R. Koymans. Specifying real-time properties with metric temporal logic. *Real-Time Systems*, 2(4):255–299, 1990.

[17] O. Maler, D. Nickovic, and A. Pnueli. From MITL to timed automata. In *Formal Modeling and Analysis of Timed Systems, 4th International Conference, FORMATS 2006, Paris, France, September 25-27, 2006, Proceedings*, pages 274–289, 2006.

[18] J. Ouaknine and J. Worrell. On the decidability of metric temporal logic. In *Logic in Computer Science, 2005. LICS 2005. Proceedings. 20th Annual IEEE Symposium on*, pages 188–197. IEEE, 2005.

[19] A. Pnueli. The temporal logic of programs. In *18th Annual Symposium on Foundations of Computer Science, Providence, Rhode Island, USA, 31 October - 1 November 1977*, pages 46–57, 1977.

[20] A. Rizk, G. Batt, F. Fages, and S. Soliman. Continuous valuations of temporal logic specifications with applications to parameter optimization and robustness measures. *Theoretical Computer Science*, 412(26):2827–2839, 2011.

Directed Specifications and Assumption Mining for Monotone Dynamical Systems *

Eric S. Kim, Murat Arcak, Sanjit A. Seshia
{eskim, arcak, sseshia}@eecs.berkeley.edu
University of California at Berkeley, Berkeley, CA, USA
Department of Electrical Engineering and Computer Sciences

ABSTRACT

Given a dynamical system and a specification, assumption mining is the problem of identifying the set of admissible disturbance signals and initial states that generate trajectories satisfying the specification. We first introduce the notion of a directed specification, which describes either upper or lower sets in a partially ordered signal space, and show that this notion encompasses an expressive temporal logic fragment. We next show that the order preserving nature of monotone dynamical systems makes them amenable to a systematic form of assumption mining that checks numerical simulations of system trajectories against directed specifications. The assumption set is then located with a multidimensional bisection method that converges to the boundary from above and below. Typical objectives in vehicular traffic control, such as avoiding or clearing congestion, are directed specifications. In an application to a freeway flow model with monotone dynamics, we identify the set of vehicular demand profiles that satisfy a specification that congestion be intermittent.

Keywords

Monotone Dynamical Systems; Temporal Logic; Partially Ordered Sets; Assumption Mining

1. INTRODUCTION

Component-based design and analysis is a common paradigm for managing complexity in large networked systems. Each component is characterized by an input-output relationship, such as a finite input-output gain in control theory or an assume-guarantee contract in the formal methods literature, enabling higher order reasoning about global behavior.

*This work was supported in part by NSF grant CNS-1446145, the NSF Graduate Research Fellowship Program, NSF Expeditions grant CCF-1139138 and by STARnet, a Semiconductor Research Corporation program, sponsored by MARCO and DARPA.

HSCC'16, April 12 - 14, 2016, Vienna, Austria

ISBN 978-1-4503-3955-1/16/04...$15.00

DOI: http://dx.doi.org/10.1145/2883817.2883833

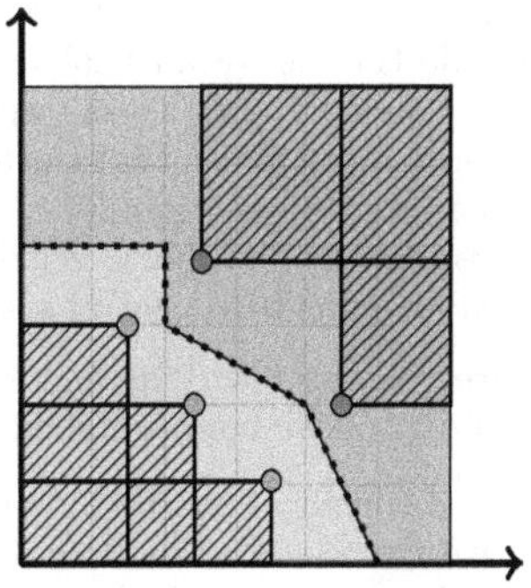

Figure 1: Geometry of a lower set (green), an upper set (red) and their boundary (dotted line). If a point (green dot) is in a lower set, then we can extrapolate that all points below it (patterned box) are also contained in that set.

To develop complex, yet robust, systems through interconnections of simpler components, it is of utmost importance to identify failure modes and to determine the limits for safe system operation. Towards this end, we formulate an assumption mining problem for dynamical systems where, given a deterministic system and a specification encoded as a set of acceptable state trajectories, we seek the largest set of initial states and exogenous disturbances for which the system satisfies the specification. Computing an exact representation of the assumption set for arbitrary specifications and dynamics is impossible. The next best option is to systematically and extensively test the system under a variety of environmental disturbances to construct an approximation of the assumption set.

In this paper, we define directed specifications and show that when paired with monotone dynamical systems, they are well suited to a systematic form of assumption mining. Directed specifications correspond to lower and upper sets in a signal space and thus favor signals with low or high values respectively. For instance, in a traffic network where the state represents number of vehicles, the specification "congestion will never be present" is a directed specification because it encourages state signals with low vehicle counts. As depicted in Fig. 1, lower and upper sets have a convenient geometry that makes it possible to use individual samples to extrapolate information about set membership. We provide a set of syntactic rules that provide a sufficient condition for a temporal logic specification to be directed. This condition is agnostic to timing semantics of the chosen temporal logic specification language and encompasses linear temporal logic [16] and signal temporal logic [11] as long as predicates are over a partially ordered set.

Monotone dynamical systems exhibit order preserving dynamics and provide a clear functional relationship between the space of initial states and disturbance signals with the trajectories they generate. In particular, they preserve the aforementioned directed property, and the assumption set must be lower(upper) if the specification is lower(upper).

To construct a tight approximation of a directed set in Euclidean space, it suffices to converge to its boundary from below and above. For discrete time signals of finite length and spaces of finite dimension, we exploit the extrapolation property of directed sets highlighted in Fig. 1 and converge to the boundary with a variant of multi-dimensional binary search. Our solution uses simulation traces and harnesses a satisfiability modulo theories (SMT) solver [2] to systematically explore the space of initial state and disturbance signals until it provides a certificate that the assumption set is approximated to a desired precision.

To summarize, we make two primary contributions about mining assumptions for monotone control systems:

1. We define directed specifications and show that they encompass an expressive temporal logic fragment.
2. Given a directed specification and a monotone system, we characterize the set of admissible disturbance signals and show how a bisection algorithm exploits the ordering present in the problem.

Section 3 first describes directed specifications geometrically as a subset of the signal space and shows how to construct directed temporal logic specifications. Section 4 reviews monotone dynamical systems, and Section 5 explains how we can exploit both the specification and dynamics via a generalized bisection method.

Related Work

Assumption mining has previously been studied for the synthesis of discrete controllers that realize a temporal logic specification [1][3][15]. Our formulation of the assumption mining problem resembles the problem of computing weakest preconditions but we also compute admissible disturbance profiles [9].

Our work contains a number of parallels to prior work on requirement mining by Jin, Donze, Deshmukh, and Seshia [13] and robust controller synthesis by Topcu, Ozay, Liu, and Murray [18]. Both make use of partial orderings and allude to similar bisection search heuristics, but neither utilize properties of directed sets, and their orderings are over different sets than those found in this paper. Jin et al. use monotonicity of a parametric signal temporal logic (pSTL) template to prune regions of the parameter space and find a tight overapproximation of the system's possible state trajectories. Fundamentally, monotonicity with respect to pSTL parameters is about comparing two different specifications and checking if one implies the other. Directedness, in contrast, is a property that is intrinsic to a single specification. Additionally, in our work monotonicity is a dynamical system property and should not be confused with monotonicity with respect to specification parameters. Topcu et al. seek to synthesize a controller that is robust to the presence of an environmental adversary with varying levels of strength, where a stronger adversary has more available moves in the synthesis game. Our problem is formulated in a way that stronger environments are encoded directly in the partial ordering on disturbance signals, instead of as a larger set of available environment disturbances.

2. PRELIMINARIES

2.1 Notation and Terminology

For a given set $\mathcal{P}$ we let $\mathcal{P}^C$ and $\mathcal{P} \times \mathcal{Q}$ respectively denote its complement (with respect to some universal set) and its Cartesian product with $\mathcal{Q}$. The empty set is $\emptyset$. The symbol $\Rightarrow$ represents the Boolean implication operator while the symbol $\mapsto$ represents a map between a domain and codomain. The *image* $f(\mathcal{M})$ of a set $\mathcal{M} \subseteq \mathcal{P}$ under function $f : \mathcal{P} \mapsto \mathcal{Q}$ is the set of points $\{f(x) : x \in \mathcal{M}\}$ and the *preimage* $f^{-1}(\mathcal{N})$ of the set $\mathcal{N} \subseteq \mathcal{Q}$ is $\{x \in \mathcal{P} : f(x) \in \mathcal{N}\}$.

The sets $\mathbb{R}_{\geq 0}$ and $\mathbb{Z}_{\geq 0}$ are the sets of non-negative real numbers and integers, and the non-negative orthant is represented by $\mathbb{R}^n_{\geq 0}$. A discrete time interval $I = [a, b]$ is a contiguous subset of $\mathbb{Z}_{\geq 0}$ where $a, b \in \mathbb{Z}_{\geq 0} \cup \{\infty\}$ and $a \leq b$. The Boolean domain is denoted $\mathbb{B} = \{\bot, \top\}$ where $\top$ is true and $\bot$ is false.

The sets $\mathcal{X} \subset \mathbb{R}^n$, $\mathcal{D} \subset \mathbb{R}^m$ and $\mathcal{Y} \subset \mathbb{R}^p$ represent state, disturbance, and output spaces for appropriate positive integers n, m, p and $x[k], d[k], y[k]$ respectively denote variables in these spaces at time k. When clear from context, the time index is dropped. For a set $\mathcal{P}$ and an interval I, the space of *signals*, $\mathcal{P}[\cdot]$, is given by a Cartesian product indexed by elements of I:

$$\mathcal{P}[\cdot] = \prod_{k \in I} \mathcal{P}. \tag{1}$$

For instance, a discrete-time real signal of length N can be thought of as a point in $\mathbb{R}^N$. In this paper, the terms signal, trace, and trajectory are synonyms. For notational brevity, the interval I is typically omitted and specified only when necessary. The sets $\mathcal{X}[\cdot], \mathcal{D}[\cdot], \mathcal{Y}[\cdot]$ are the sets of state, disturbance, and output signals.

A specification ϕ can be viewed as the subset of the signal space for which it is true. We signify that a signal $x[\cdot]$ *satisfies* a specification ϕ by $x[\cdot] \models \phi$. One can switch between set theoretic and Boolean views of ϕ by the definition $\phi = \{x[\cdot] \in \mathcal{X}[\cdot] : x[\cdot] \models \phi\}$ and the identity $x[\cdot] \models \phi$ if and only if $x[\cdot] \in \phi$ (using the set theoretic definition of ϕ).

2.2 Assumption Mining

A deterministic dynamical system $\Sigma : \mathcal{X} \times \mathcal{D}[\cdot] \mapsto \mathcal{X}[\cdot]$ is a map from an initial state and disturbance pair to a state trajectory. We formulate assumption mining as the problem of determining which exogenous disturbances and initial conditions are permitted for a system to satisfy a specification.

PROBLEM 1 (ASSUMPTION MINING). *Given a deterministic system $\Sigma : \mathcal{X} \times \mathcal{D}[\cdot] \mapsto \mathcal{X}[\cdot]$ and a specification $\phi \subseteq \mathcal{X}[\cdot]$, what is the subset of initial states and disturbance signals, $\Sigma^{-1}(\phi) \subseteq \mathcal{X} \times \mathcal{D}[\cdot]$, that ensures satisfaction of ϕ?*

By viewing a dynamical system Σ as a mapping $\Sigma : \mathcal{X} \times \mathcal{D}[\cdot] \mapsto \mathcal{X}[\cdot]$, the solution to the assumption mining problem is found by computing the pre-image $\Sigma^{-1}(\phi)$ of specification ϕ. Computation of pre-images is typically intractable for arbitrary specifications ϕ and non-linear dynamics for Σ. We

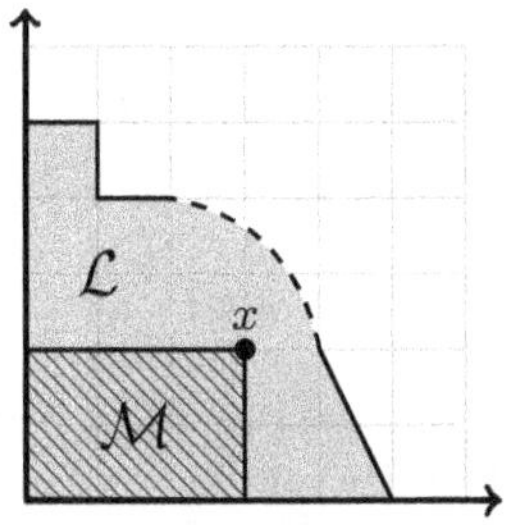

Figure 2: A lower set in $\mathcal{L} \subset \mathbb{R}^2_{\geq 0}$ with the standard ordering. Lower sets are not necessarily convex, open, or closed. The principal lower set $\mathcal{M}$ with associated point x is a subset of $\mathcal{L}$.

focus on monotone dynamical systems and directed specifications and show that this pair is particularly amenable to assumption mining.

2.3 Partially Ordered Sets and Signals

A partially ordered set $\mathcal{P}$ has an associated binary relation $\leq_{\mathcal{P}}$ if all $p_1, p_2, p_3 \in \mathcal{P}$ satisfy 1) $p_1 \leq_{\mathcal{P}} p_1$, 2) if $p_1 \leq_{\mathcal{P}} p_2$ and $p_2 \leq_{\mathcal{P}} p_1$ then $p_1 = p_2$ and, 3) if $p_1 \leq_{\mathcal{P}} p_2$ and $p_2 \leq_{\mathcal{P}} p_3$ then $p_1 \leq_{\mathcal{P}} p_3$. We define $\geq_{\mathcal{P}}$ so that $p_1 \geq_{\mathcal{P}} p_2$ holds if and only if $p_2 \leq_{\mathcal{P}} p_1$. If neither $p_1 \leq_{\mathcal{P}} p_2$ nor $p_1 \geq_{\mathcal{P}} p_2$ hold, we say that p_1 and p_2 are *incomparable*.

Given a collection of partially ordered sets $\mathcal{P}_i$ and relations $\leq_{\mathcal{P}_i}$ indexed by $\mathcal{A}$, let $\mathcal{P} = \prod_{i \in \mathcal{A}} \mathcal{P}_i$, and $\pi_i(p) : \mathcal{P} \mapsto \mathcal{P}_i$ map $p \in \mathcal{P}$ to its i-th component. For $p_1, p_2 \in \mathcal{P}$, the product ordering relation $p_1 \leq_{\mathcal{P}} p_2$ holds if and only if $\pi_i(p_1) \leq_{\mathcal{P}_i} \pi_i(p_2)$ for all $i \in \mathcal{A}$. Time will frequently play the role of the index set as it does in (1).

In this paper, all sets $\mathcal{X}$, $\mathcal{D}$, and $\mathcal{Y}$ are equipped with partial orders $\leq_{\mathcal{X}}$, $\leq_{\mathcal{D}}$, and $\leq_{\mathcal{Y}}$. We also introduce an induced *signal partial ordering* $\leq_{\mathcal{P}[\cdot]}$ over $\mathcal{P}$ and interval $I = [a, b]$ such that for signals $p_1[\cdot], p_2[\cdot]$ the ordering $p_1[\cdot] \leq_{\mathcal{P}[\cdot]} p_2[\cdot]$ signifies that $p_1[k] \leq_{\mathcal{P}} p_2[k]$ for all $k \in [a, b]$.

A function between partially ordered sets $f : \mathcal{P} \mapsto \mathcal{Q}$ is a *monotone function* if $p_1 \leq_{\mathcal{P}} p_2$ implies $f(p_1) \leq_{\mathcal{Q}} f(p_2)$ for all $p_1, p_2 \in \mathcal{P}$. The composition of monotone functions is also a monotone function [6].

3. DIRECTED SPECIFICATIONS

3.1 Lower and Upper Sets

DEFINITION 1. *(Lower Set) Given a partially ordered set $\mathcal{P}$ with relation $\leq_{\mathcal{P}}$, a subset $\mathcal{L} \subseteq \mathcal{P}$ is a lower set if for all $p, q \in \mathcal{P}$:*

$$p \in \mathcal{L} \text{ and } q \leq_{\mathcal{P}} p \Longrightarrow q \in \mathcal{L}. \tag{2}$$

An *upper set* satisfies Definition 1 with the relation $\geq_{\mathcal{P}}$ instead. Common alternative names for lower sets are down sets and downward closed sets [6].

A lower set $\mathcal{M} \subseteq \mathcal{P}$ is a *principal subset* if there exists $x \in \mathcal{P}$ such that $\mathcal{M} = \{y : y \leq x\}$. If $x \in \mathcal{L}$, then $\mathcal{M} \subseteq \mathcal{L}$. With a coordinate-wise ordering, principal sets are rectangles. See Fig. 2 for visualizations of $\mathcal{L}$ and $\mathcal{M}$ in $\mathbb{R}^n_{\geq 0}$.

Lower sets on $\mathcal{P}$ have the following useful properties (the dual properties for upper sets can be obtained by swapping "lower" and "upper") [6]:

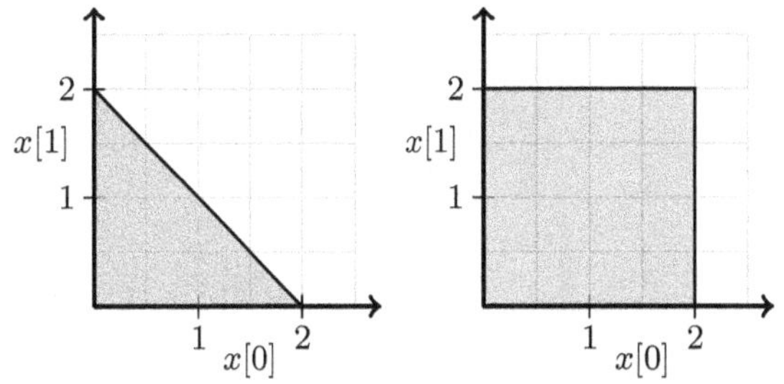

Figure 3: Sets with norm bounds $\{x[\cdot] : ||x[\cdot]||_i \leq 2\}$ for $i \in \{1, \infty\}$ are lower specifications on positive signals $x[\cdot] : [0, 1] \mapsto \mathbb{R}_{\geq 0}$.

PROPERTY 1. *If $\mathcal{L} \subseteq \mathcal{P}$ is a lower set, then $\mathcal{L}^C$ is an upper set.*

PROPERTY 2. *The collection of all lower sets of $\mathcal{P}$ is closed under arbitrary unions and intersections.*

PROPERTY 3. *Let the collection of lower sets $\mathcal{L}_i \subseteq \mathcal{P}_i$ be indexed by a set $\mathcal{A}$ and $\mathcal{P} = \prod_{i \in \mathcal{A}} \mathcal{P}_i$. Their Cartesian product $\prod_{i \in \mathcal{A}} \mathcal{L}_i$ is a lower set with the product ordering $\leq_{\mathcal{P}}$.*

PROPERTY 4. *Sets $\mathcal{P}$ and $\emptyset$ are both upper and lower sets.*

We now define a set of specifications ϕ that are satisfied on lower/upper sets in the signal space.

DEFINITION 2 (LOWER/UPPER SPECIFICATIONS). *A lower specification ϕ on signals $\mathcal{X}[\cdot]$ satisfies*

$$\Big((x_1[\cdot] \leq_{\mathcal{X}[\cdot]} x_2[\cdot]) \wedge (x_2[\cdot] \models \phi)\Big) \Rightarrow (x_1[\cdot] \models \phi). \tag{3}$$

Likewise, an upper specification ϕ on signals $\mathcal{X}[\cdot]$ satisfies

$$\Big((x_1[\cdot] \leq_{\mathcal{X}[\cdot]} x_2[\cdot]) \wedge (x_1[\cdot] \models \phi)\Big) \Rightarrow (x_2[\cdot] \models \phi). \tag{4}$$

A directed specification is one that is either a lower or upper specification.

Common examples of lower specifications in the control theory literature are the set of non-negative signals with upper bounds on some norm, as shown in Fig. 3. However, norms constitute a restrictive subset of directed specifications and do not permit non-convex specifications such as "intermittent spikes in freeway occupancy are permitted as long as they do not last longer than 30 minutes". Lower sets do not need to be convex, open, or closed, and allow specifications like the freeway example above. The following section covers a set of rules that provides a sufficient condition for a temporal logic specification to be directed.

3.2 Constructing Directed Specifications

Temporal logics are logical formalisms for expressing specifications as sets of admissible signals [16]. We restrict our interest to signals over a partially ordered set $\mathcal{X}$. A *predicate* $\mu : \mathcal{X} \mapsto \mathbb{B}$ assigns a truth value to elements in $\mathcal{X}$. As an example, consider a discrete-time variant on signal temporal logic(STL) [11] where specifications can be constructed with the grammar

$$\phi := \top | \mu | \neg\phi | \phi_1 \wedge \phi_2 | \phi_1 \mathbf{U}_I \phi_2 \tag{5}$$

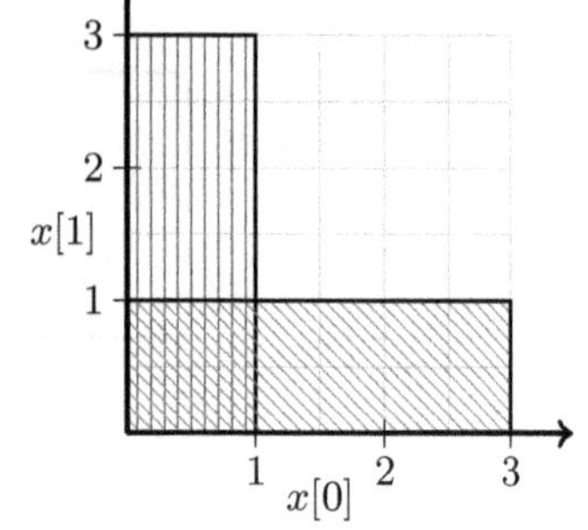

Figure 4: The set of signals $x[\cdot]$ over $\mathcal{X} = [0,3]$ with interval $I = [0,1]$ that satisfy lower specification $\phi = \Diamond_{[0,1]}(x[\cdot] \leq 1)$. Specification ϕ is the union of two clauses $(x[0] \leq 1)$ and $(x[1] \leq 1)$, respectively depicted with vertical and diagonal lines.

where I is an interval, $\neg$ is Boolean negation, and $\wedge$ is a Boolean AND. Specification $\phi_1 \mathbf{U}_I \phi_2$ is true if there exists a time $k \in I$ such that ϕ_2 is true at time k and ϕ_1 is true until k. From the above grammar, one can derive additional temporal operators $\Diamond_I \phi = \top \mathbf{U}_I \phi$ for "ϕ is eventually true in I" and $\Box_I \phi = \neg(\Diamond_I \neg\phi)$ for "ϕ is always true in I". Formally:

$$
\begin{array}{lll}
(x[\cdot],k) \models \mu & \text{iff} & x[\cdot] \text{ satisfies } \mu \text{ at time } k \\
(x[\cdot],k) \models \neg\phi & \text{iff} & (x[\cdot],k) \not\models \phi \\
(x[\cdot],k) \models \phi_1 \wedge \phi_2 & \text{iff} & (x[\cdot],k) \models \phi_1 \text{ and } (x[\cdot],k) \models \phi_2 \\
(x[\cdot],k) \models \phi_1 \mathbf{U}_{[a,b]} \phi_2 & \text{iff} & \exists p \in [k+a, k+b] \text{ such that} \\
& & (x[\cdot],p) \models \phi_2 \text{ and} \\
& & \forall q \in [k+a, p-1], (x[\cdot],q) \models \phi_1
\end{array}
$$

When temporal operators omit the interval I, it is assumed that $I = [0,\infty)$ and $x[\cdot] \models \phi$ is a shorthand for $(x[\cdot],0) \models \phi$.

In this section, we adopt a geometric view of temporal logic formulas with predicates on $\mathbb{R}$ by viewing them as subsets of a Euclidean signal space, just as level sets of l_1, l_2 and l_∞ norms are visualized as high dimensional diamonds, balls and boxes. Fig. 4 depicts a specification consisting of an eventually operator and shows that it can be thought of as a union over different sets in the signal space. The mixed-integer constraints appearing in model predictive control with temporal logic constraints effectively encode unions of polyhedra in a signal space [19] [17].

3.3 Order Preserving Operations

We outline a fragment of the temporal logic over a partially ordered set by restricting the grammar (5) in such a way that all generated specifications are directed.

THEOREM 1. *Let μ^l and μ^u be restricted to predicates that are true on lower and upper sets of $\mathcal{X}$ respectively. Let ϕ^d be constructed with the grammar*

$$\phi^d := \phi^l | \phi^u$$

$$\phi^l := \top | \mu^l | \neg\phi^u | \phi_1^l \wedge \phi_2^l | \phi_1^l \mathbf{U}_I \phi_2^l$$

$$\phi^u := \top | \mu^u | \neg\phi^l | \phi_1^u \wedge \phi_2^u | \phi_1^u \mathbf{U}_I \phi_2^u$$

Any specification ϕ^d respecting the grammar above is a directed specification of $\mathcal{X}[\cdot]$ satisfying (3) or (4).

PROOF. We adopt a syntax directed approach to proving that a specification is directed and only prove the following statements about lower specifications ϕ^l. The dual statements for upper specifications are easily derived.

- Formulas $\phi = \top$ and $\phi = \bot$ are both lower and upper specifications.
  Proof: Follows from Property 4.

- If predicate μ^l is true on a lower set in $\mathcal{X}$, then $\phi = \mu^l$ is a lower specification in $\mathcal{X}[\cdot]$.
  Proof Sketch: Follows from the definition of lower set, Property 3, and the identity:

$$\{x[\cdot] : x[0] \in \mu^l\} \equiv \{x[\cdot] : x[\cdot] \in \left(\mu^l \times \prod_{i \in [1,\infty]} \mathcal{X}\right)\}$$

- If ϕ^l is a lower specification, then $\neg\phi^l$ is an upper specification, as shown using DeMorgan's law:

$$
\begin{aligned}
&(x_1[\cdot] \leq_{\mathcal{X}[\cdot]} x_2[\cdot] \wedge x_2[\cdot] \models \phi^l) \Rightarrow (x_1[\cdot] \models \phi^l) \\
&\equiv \neg(x_1[\cdot] \leq_{\mathcal{X}[\cdot]} x_2[\cdot] \wedge x_2[\cdot] \models \phi^l) \vee x_1[\cdot] \models \phi^l \\
&\equiv x_1[\cdot] \not\leq_{\mathcal{X}[\cdot]} x_2[\cdot] \vee x_2[\cdot] \models \neg\phi^l \vee x_1[\cdot] \models \phi^l \\
&\equiv \neg(x_1[\cdot] \leq_{\mathcal{X}[\cdot]} x_2[\cdot] \wedge x_1[\cdot] \models \neg\phi^l) \vee x_2[\cdot] \models \neg\phi^l \\
&\equiv (x_1[\cdot] \leq_{\mathcal{X}[\cdot]} x_2[\cdot] \wedge x_1[\cdot] \models \neg\phi^l) \Rightarrow x_2[\cdot] \models \neg\phi^l.
\end{aligned}
$$

- If ϕ_1^l and ϕ_2^l are both lower specifications, then $\phi_1^l \wedge \phi_2^l$ also is a lower specification.
  Proof Sketch: Consider two signals $x_1[\cdot], x_2[\cdot]$ where $x_1[\cdot] \leq_{\mathcal{X}[\cdot]} x_2[\cdot]$. If $x_2[\cdot] \models \phi_1^l \wedge \phi_2^l$, then the inequality $x_1[\cdot] \leq_{\mathcal{X}[\cdot]} x_2[\cdot]$ and the definition of lower specification guarantee that $x_1[\cdot] \models \phi_1^l$ and $x_1[\cdot] \models \phi_2^l$.

- If ϕ_1^l and ϕ_2^l are lower specifications, then $\phi_1^l \mathbf{U}_{[a,b]} \phi_2^l$ also is a lower specification.
  Proof Sketch: Consider two signals $x_1[\cdot], x_2[\cdot]$ where $x_1[\cdot] \leq_{\mathcal{X}[\cdot]} x_2[\cdot]$ and $x_2[\cdot] \models \phi_1^l \mathbf{U}_{[a,b]} \phi_2^l$. At some time $p \in [a,b]$, signal $(x_2[\cdot],p) \models \phi_2^l$ and the definition of lower specification guarantees that $(x_1[\cdot],p) \models \phi_2^l$ ($x_1[\cdot]$ may satisfy ϕ_2^l earlier than time p). A similar argument can be made about $x_1[\cdot] \models \phi_1^l$ for all time in $[a, p-1]$.

Although this proof is for discrete-time specifications, the above properties also apply to specifications with continuous-time semantics. □

It is straightforward to prove the above properties about temporal logic operators in a set theoretic context using Properties 1-4 of lower/upper sets. The above are sufficient conditions to determine satisfaction of properties (3) and (4), and allow derivation of similar statements for $\Box\phi$, $\Diamond\phi$, $\phi_1 \vee \phi_2$, and $\phi_1 \Rightarrow \phi_2$.

- $\Box\phi$ and $\Diamond\phi$ are lower specifications if ϕ is a lower specification. Fig. 5 demonstrates how order preserving operators are used to derive $\Box\phi$'s directed property.

- $\phi_1 \vee \phi_2$ is a lower specification if ϕ_1 and ϕ_2 are lower specifications.

- $\phi_1 \Rightarrow \phi_2$ is a lower specification if ϕ_1 is an upper specification and ϕ_2 is a lower specification.

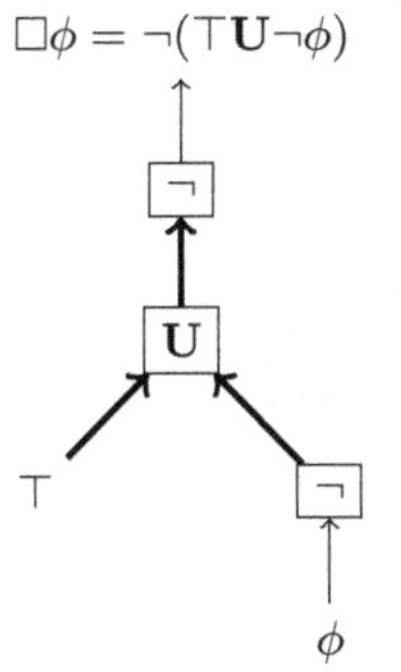

Figure 5: Parse tree that uses order preserving operations to determine that $\Box\phi$ is a lower specification if ϕ is also a lower specification. Thick and thin lines respectively denote upper and lower specifications.

Note that the proof for Theorem 1 only assumes that sets have a partial ordering and makes no restrictions that predicates be over discrete or continuous sets such as $\mathbb{B}^n$ or $\mathbb{R}^n$, respectively.

Curiously, it is possible to generate lower specifications that combine elements of temporal logics and norms that are not expressible in either alone. Consider

$$\Box_{[0,100]}\Diamond_{[0,7]}(\sum_{i=0}^{4} x[i] \leq 3)$$

which encodes that a running average is periodically below a constant. This is a specification that cannot be written in signal temporal logic, yet is still a lower specification.

4. MONOTONE SYSTEM DYNAMICS

Let the discrete time system Σ have an associated update equation $F_\Sigma : \mathcal{X} \times \mathcal{D} \mapsto \mathcal{X}$ such that

$$x[k+1] = F_\Sigma(x[k], d[k]) \tag{6}$$

for all $k \geq 0$.

DEFINITION 3 (MONOTONE SYSTEMS). *A system (6) is monotone with respect to ordering $\leq_\mathcal{X}$ and $\leq_\mathcal{D}$ if*

$$x_1 \leq_\mathcal{X} x_2 \text{ and } d_1 \leq_\mathcal{D} d_2 \Longrightarrow F_\Sigma(x_1, d_1) \leq_\mathcal{X} F_\Sigma(x_2, d_2). \tag{7}$$

The system has a monotone output if the output function $h(\cdot) : \mathcal{X}[\cdot] \mapsto \mathcal{Y}[\cdot]$ is monotone.

To extend the definition of monotone system from a single-step update equation F_Σ to a definition about the signals generated by Σ, consider $d_1[\cdot] \leq_{\mathcal{D}[\cdot]} d_2[\cdot]$ on the interval $[a, b]$ and $x_1[a] \leq_\mathcal{X} x_2[a]$. If the system is monotone, it follows from iterating Definition 3 via (6) that:

$$x_1[\cdot] \leq_{\mathcal{X}[\cdot]} x_2[\cdot] \tag{8}$$

for state signals $x_1[\cdot], x_2[\cdot]$ on the interval $[a, b+1]$.

Thus monotonicity of $F_\Sigma(\cdot,\cdot)$ in (7) implies the monotonicity of $\Sigma : \mathcal{X} \times \mathcal{D}[\cdot] \mapsto \mathcal{X}[\cdot]$.

EXAMPLE 1. *Let $a \geq 0, x \in \mathbb{R}_{\geq 0}, d \in \mathbb{R}$. The system*

$$x[k+1] = \max(0, ax[k] + d[k])$$

is monotone.

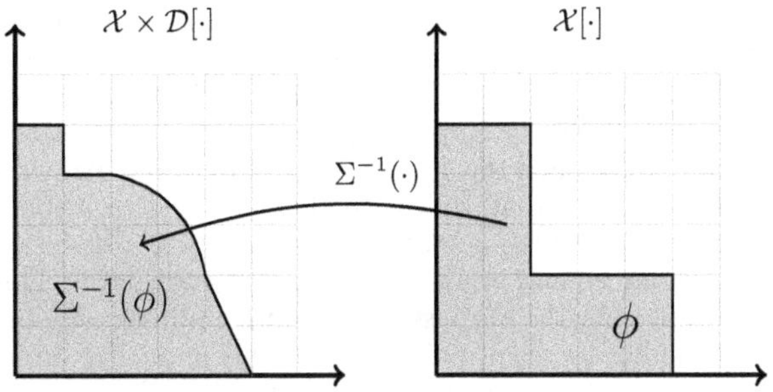

Figure 6: A monotone function's preimage of a lower set is itself a lower set. Therefore, the assumption set $\Sigma^{-1}(\phi) \subseteq \mathcal{X} \times \mathcal{D}[\cdot]$ of the lower specification $\phi \subseteq \mathcal{X}[\cdot]$ is a lower set. Although $\Sigma^{-1}(\phi)$ is unknown, the lower set property is useful for constructing approximations.

Consider the assumption mining problem as formalized in Problem 1, but with the additional information that the system Σ is monotone and the specification ϕ is a lower set. The following property of lower sets and monotone functions lets us deduce that the assumption set is also a lower set as depicted in Fig. 6.

PROPERTY 5. *If $f : \mathcal{P} \mapsto \mathcal{Q}$ is a monotone function, the preimage $f^{-1}(\mathcal{M})$ of a lower(upper) set, $\mathcal{M} \subseteq \mathcal{Q}$, is itself a lower(upper) set.*

PROOF. Consider the case when $\mathcal{M}$ is a lower set. The preimage $f^{-1}(\mathcal{M}) = \{x \in \mathcal{P} | f(x) \in \mathcal{M}\}$ may be the empty set, in which case it satisfies Definition 1. If $f^{-1}(\mathcal{M})$ is nonempty then let there be p_1, p_2 such that $p_2 \in f^{-1}(\mathcal{M})$ and $p_1 \leq_\mathcal{P} p_2$. By monotonicity of f, it follows that $f(p_1) \leq_\mathcal{Q} f(p_2)$ and $f(p_1) \in \mathcal{M}$ because $\mathcal{M}$ is a lower set. Thus, p_1 is an element of the preimage $f^{-1}(\mathcal{M})$, which satisfies the definition of a lower set. A similar argument can be used when $\mathcal{M}$ is an upper set. □

Because Σ is monotone and ϕ is true on a lower set, the assumption set $\Sigma^{-1}(\phi)$ is a lower set and the assumption violation set $\Sigma^{-1}(\neg\phi)$ is an upper set. Because a composition of monotone functions is monotone, if $\phi \subseteq \mathcal{Y}[\cdot]$ is a directed specification on the system's output signals, then the assumption set will also be directed.

5. ASSUMPTION MINING FOR MONOTONE SYSTEMS

5.1 Approximating the Assumption Set

Determining the set of all admissible initial state and disturbance signals that satisfy (or falsify) arbitrary specifications for nonlinear or hybrid systems is intractable. However, when Σ is monotone and ϕ is directed, we can take advantage of $\Sigma^{-1}(\phi)$'s geometric properties.

We assume that a single simulation of Σ with different initial states and disturbance signals induces a trajectory that either satisfies ϕ or $\neg\phi$. To evaluate a trace's satisfaction of a signal temporal logic specification, we would use the Breach toolbox [10]. An initial state and disturbance pair $(x_0, d[\cdot])$ is used to underapproximate $\Sigma^{-1}(\phi)$ if $\Sigma(x_0, d[\cdot]) \models \phi$ and is used to underapproximate $\Sigma^{-1}(\neg\phi)$ if $\Sigma(x_0, d[\cdot]) \models \neg\phi$ (see lines 8-13 of Algorithm 1 and green/red points in Fig. 7a).

Observe that the boundary between a lower and upper set can be under-approximated arbitrarily well by a union of principal sets, which under a coordinate-wise ordering are rectangular. If the assumption space is of finite dimension and is bounded, then the set can be approximated arbitrarily well (in a way that will be made precise) with a finite number of simulations. We impose a practical restriction that disturbance and state signals be of finite length. This assumption is for the purpose of assumption mining only because simulations are of finite length. This implicitly limits the set of specifications that can be mined to those whose satisfaction can be decided for signals of that length. For instance, given a signal $x[\cdot]$ over $I = [0, N]$, the specifications $\Box_{[0,2N]}(x[\cdot] \leq 1)$ and $\Diamond_{[0,2N]}(x[\cdot] \leq 1)$ are disallowed.

Ideally, one would like to represent the lower set as accurately as possible while simulating a minimal number of points in the assumption space. This problem becomes more difficult as the signal length increases because the lower set resides in progressively larger dimension spaces. We provide an algorithm that uses the Z3 satisfiability modulo theories (SMT) solver as an oracle to determine the location of the next query [7]. Legriel, Le Guernic, Cotton, and Maler take a similar approach when tackling the problem of estimating a Pareto front of a multi-criteria optimization problem by making queries to a satisfiability solver [14].

The algorithm is best understood visually by following Fig. 7. If we query a signal in the white region of Fig. 7a, then we are guaranteed to refine our approximation of the ordered set. A rectangle is encoded as an intersection of half planes, and its complement is a union over the opposite half planes. The white region is equivalent to the intersection of the complements of each rectangle, and a logical formula encoding that region is in conjunctive normal form with predicates representing linear inequalities. To find a point in that region, we pose a satisfiability query of the aforementioned logical formula to a SMT solver.

The query may return a point that does not contribute to improving the boundary approximation such as the black dot in Fig. 7b. To explore the signal space effectively, we "bloat" each rectangle along each side by a constant ϵ before sending the query to the SMT solver. The bloating factor is represented by the grey region in Fig. 7b, and this technique serves a similar purpose to tabu search in [8].

A satisfying query will return a point in the white region, whereas unsatisfiability signifies that the white region does not exist and the entire space $\mathcal{X} \times \mathcal{D}[\cdot]$ is covered as in Fig. 7c. Unsatisfiability of the queried formula indicates that the rectangle bloating was too aggressive and covered the entire space; it serves as a convenient certificate for the quality of our approximation of the ordered set. Unsatisfiability with an ϵ bloating indicates that every point on the boundary must lie within ϵ coordinate-wise of a point in either the set of upper or lower points as depicted in Fig. 7c. If a query is unsatisfiable, then we decrease the size of ϵ by multiplying by a learning rate $\alpha \in (0, 1)$ and create another white region by reducing the aggressiveness of the bloating, as in Fig. 7d, until our algorithm reaches a given desired precision ϵ_{final} (see lines 2,4-7 of Algorithm 1) or a timeout.

5.2   Remarks on Tractability

If the assumption space is of finite dimension and is bounded, then a finite number of queries are needed for our algorithm to approximate the set to an arbitrary degree of pre-

---

Algorithm 1 ϵ-approximation of assumption $\Sigma^{-1}(\phi)$

Input: $\Sigma, \phi, \alpha \in (0, 1), \epsilon, \epsilon_{\text{final}}$
Output: $lowerPts, upperPts$
1: $lowerPts = [], upperPts = []$
2: **while** $\epsilon \geq \epsilon_{\text{final}}$ **do**
3:     $(x_0, d[\cdot]) = orderedQuery(lowerPts, upperPts, \epsilon)$
4:     **if** (x_0 is NaN) **then**
5:         $\epsilon = \alpha * \epsilon$
6:         **continue**
7:     **end if**
8:     $x[\cdot] = \Sigma(x_0, d[\cdot])$
9:     **if** ($x[\cdot] \models \phi$) **then**
10:         $lowerPts.append(x_0, d[\cdot])$
11:     **else**
12:         $upperPts.append(x_0, d[\cdot])$
13:     **end if**
14: **end while**
15: **return** $(lowerPts, upperPts)$

Algorithm 2 Ordered Query

Input: $lowerPts, upperPts, \epsilon$
Output: $x, d[\cdot]$
1: smtConstraints $= []$
2: **for all** $(x_i, d_i[\cdot] \in lowerPts)$ **do**
3:     rect = getLowerRect($x_i, d_i[\cdot]$)
4:     bloatedRect = bloatRect(rect,ϵ)
5:     smtConstraints.append(bloatedRect)
6: **end for**
7: **for all** $(x_i, d_i[\cdot] \in upperPts)$ **do**
8:     rect = getUpperRect($x_i, d_i[\cdot]$)
9:     bloatedRect = bloatRect(rect,ϵ)
10:     smtConstraints.append(bloatedRect)
11: **end for**
12: satisfied = smt.solve(smtConstraints)
13: **if** satisfied **then**
14:     **return** $(x, d[\cdot])$ = smt.model()
15: **else**
16:     **return** $(x, d[\cdot])$ = (NaN, NaN)
17: **end if**

---

cision $\epsilon_{\text{final}} > 0$. As a worst case scenario, our algorithm has an upper bound of $(\frac{b}{\epsilon_{\text{final}}})^d$ queries, where d is the dimension of the assumption set and $b = \sup(||x - y||_\infty, x, y \in \mathcal{X} \times \mathcal{D}[\cdot])$ is the diameter of the assumption space. If the assumption space and assumption set are not bounded, it may still be possible for the latter to have a finite ϵ-approximation for all $\epsilon > 0$, but establishing this requires prior knowledge about the assumption set, the very object we are trying to identify.

As highlighted in our freeway example in Section 6 below, the aforementioned upper bound is rather conservative and the number of queries is typically orders of magnitude less. The variable bloating ϵ effectively amounts to a way to vary the grid granularity. Picking a learning rate α requires a delicate tradeoff between exploring the space earlier. A conservative learning rate will result in slower convergence but better coverage of the space, whereas a too aggressive learning rate will rapidly increase the number of grid points.

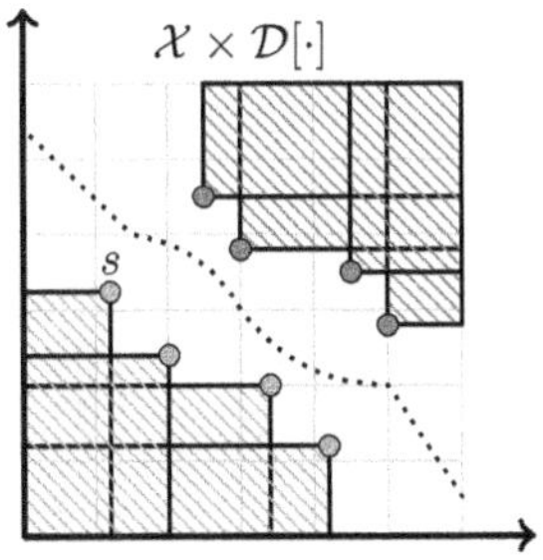

(a) A green point $s = (x[0], d[\cdot])$ generates a state signal $\Sigma(s) \models \phi$ that satisfies ϕ; therefore, $s \in \Sigma^{-1}(\phi)$. Because $\Sigma^{-1}(\phi)$ is known to be a lower set, the patterned principal set $\{t : t \leq s\}$ is a subset of $\Sigma^{-1}(\phi)$. A union of upper and lower rectangles can converge on the lower set's boundary (dotted line).

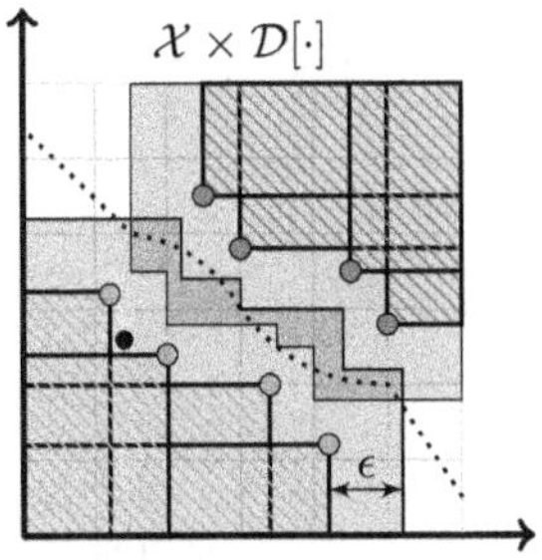

(b) Bloating the set of sampled points by ϵ (grey region) to encourage exploration of the assumption space and avoid new samples like the solid dot. The oracle must return a point in the now smaller white region.

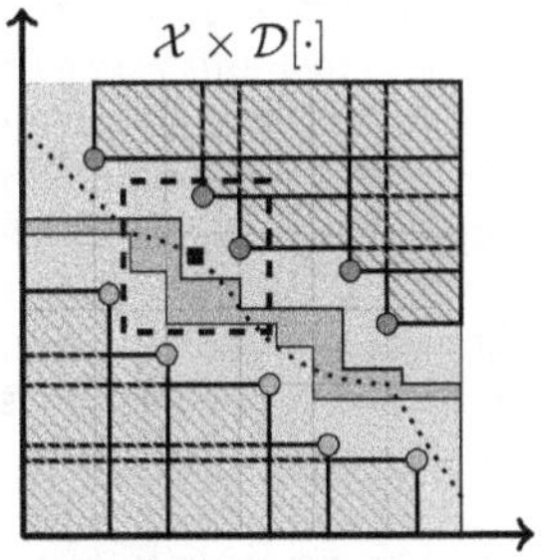

(c) After two more samples are taken, all points on the boundary, e.g. the solid square, have an ϵ neighborhood (dashed box) that contains at least one circular sampled point.

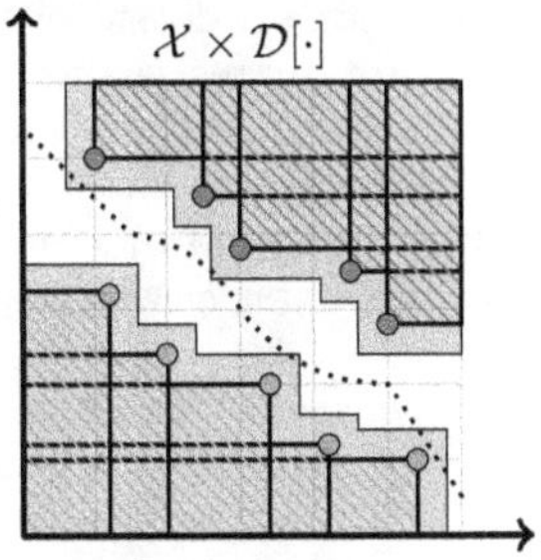

(d) Make the bloating less aggressive by shrinking ϵ. Repeat procedure the starting from Fig. 7b and sample from the new white region.

Figure 7: The assumption mining algorithm consists of generalizing information from simulations (Fig. 7a) and systematic exploration of the assumption space (Fig. 7b). We have a certificate for the approximation's quality when enough samples cover the space (Fig. 7c) and can continue refining our approximation with a more granular cover (Fig. 7d).

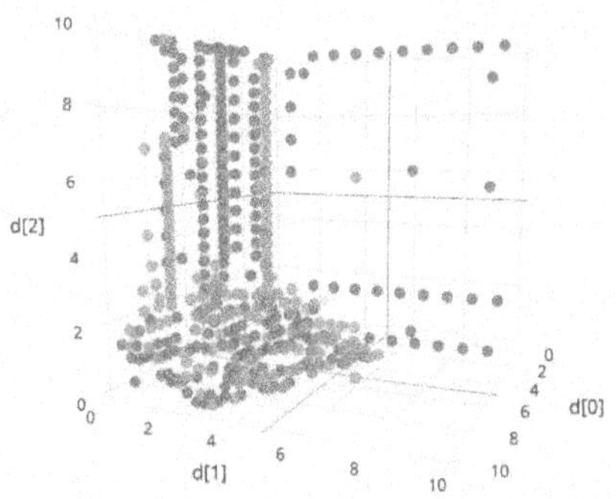

Figure 8: Converging on the boundary of system (9)'s assumption set. Dark blue balls represent points contained within the lower set $\Sigma^{-1}(\phi)$ and lighter red balls are in the upper set $\Sigma^{-1}(\neg\phi)$. We fix the initial state to be zero and only plot the $\mathcal{D}[\cdot]$ component of the assumption set.

6. EXAMPLES

6.1 Monotone Integrator Example

Our first example illustrates the use of our mining algorithm for a simple system and short disturbance signals. Let Σ be a discrete-time system with $x \in \mathbb{R}_{\geq 0}, d \in \mathbb{R}$ and update equations

$$x[k+1] = \max(0, ax[k] + d[k]) \tag{9}$$

where $a = .4$. We let the initial state $x[0] = 0$. This system is monotone with respect to the standard ordering on $\mathbb{R}$. The specification $\phi = \Box_{[0,1]}(\Diamond_{[0,2]}(x(t) \leq 4.0))$ is a lower specification according to the rules outlined in Section 3.3 and it is either satisfied or violated with a state signal on the discrete interval $[0, 3]$, which is generated by a disturbance signal on the interval $[0, 2]$. The signal length was chosen to allow visualization of the assumption set in Fig. 8, which shows a total of 430 sampled points used to approximate the assumption set for ϕ with an absolute precision $\epsilon = .25$.

6.2 Freeway Example

Our second example is of a freeway traffic network, where we seek to determine the limits of the assumption mining algorithm by introducing a large state space and long disturbance signals. Consider the network depicted in Fig. 9, which has a main stretch of three links x_0, x_2, x_4 and two onramps x_1, x_3. The dynamics are taken from the cell transmission model (CTM) [5][12], a macroscopic fluid-like model of freeway dynamics. Individual vehicles are not a component of this model. Each discrete time instant represents a five minute interval. Our state space $\mathcal{X} = \prod_{i=1}^{5}[0, 100] \subset \mathbb{R}^5_{\geq 0}$ represents the average occupancy over the five minute period in each of the five links. We overload notation and refer to links and their occupancy values using the same variable. The state update equations arise from conservation of

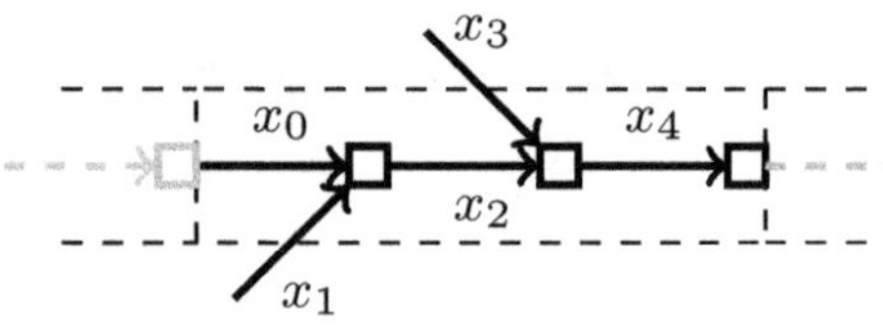

Figure 9: An example network with two on-ramps x_1, x_3. Dashed arrows are exogenous network links

mass:

$$
\begin{aligned}
x_0[k+1] &= \min(100, x_0[k] - f_0^{\text{out}}[k] + 30)\\
x_1[k+1] &= \min(100, x_1[k] - f_1^{\text{out}}[k] + d_1[k])\\
x_2[k+1] &= \min(100, x_2[k] - f_2^{\text{out}}[k] + \sum_{i=\{0,1\}} f_i^{\text{out}}[k])\\
x_3[k+1] &= \min(100, x_3[k] - f_3^{\text{out}}[k] + d_3[k])\\
x_4[k+1] &= \min(100, x_4[k] - f_4^{\text{out}}[k] + \sum_{i=\{2,3\}} f_i^{\text{out}}[k])
\end{aligned}
$$

where $f_i^{\text{out}}[k]$ represents the flow exiting link x_i at time k. The disturbances $d_1[k], d_3[k]$ represent the number of vehicles that would like to enter the network via on-ramps x_1, x_3 and lie within a range $[0, 30]$. We assume link x_0 experiences a constant disturbance of 30 vehicles from the exogenous upstream link. The disturbance space is $\mathcal{D} = \prod_{i=\{1,3\}}[0, 30] \subset \mathbb{R}^2_{\geq 0}$. The minimization terms above prevent the occupancy from exceeding the maximum capacity of the freeway segments.

The flows into and out of a link are determined by *supply* and *demand*. A link's demand is the rate at which it would like to send vehicles to downstream links. The demand $\Phi_i(x_i[k])$ that link x_i exhibits is a non-decreasing function

$$\Phi_i(x_i[k]) = \min(c_i, \alpha_i x_i[k]) \tag{10}$$

where c_i is a saturation rate and $\alpha_i \in [0, 1]$ is the fraction of current vehicles that will leave x_i. The primary links have saturation rates $c_0 = c_2 = c_4 = 40$ and on-ramps have saturation rates $c_1 = c_3 = 30$. Link x_i also exhibits a supply

$$\Psi(x_i[k]) = 100 - x_i[k], \tag{11}$$

which is the rate of incoming vehicles that it can accept from upstream. A link's supply is partitioned among upstream links, with links x_2, x_4 allocating 80% of their supply to an upstream highway link and 20% to on-ramps. The flow out of a link x_i is the minimum between supply available to it and x_i's demand:

$$
\begin{aligned}
f_0^{\text{out}}[k] &= \min(.8(100 - x_2[k]), 40, .5x_0[k])\\
f_1^{\text{out}}[k] &= \min(.2(100 - x_2[k]), 30, x_1[k])\\
f_2^{\text{out}}[k] &= \min(.8(100 - x_4[k]), 40, .5x_2[k])\\
f_3^{\text{out}}[k] &= \min(.2(100 - x_4[k]), 30, x_3[k])\\
f_4^{\text{out}}[k] &= \min(40, x_4[k])
\end{aligned}
$$

The exogenous link that is immediately downstream from x_4 can always accept up to 40 vehicles.

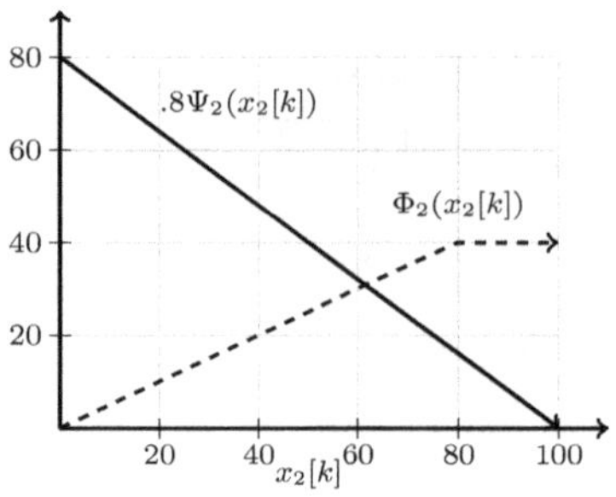

Figure 10: Supply (solid) that link x_2 provides to link x_0 and Demand (dashed) that link x_2 creates for link x_4

Congestion occurs when demand exceeds supply and the left term in the minimization is active; one can verify that congestion occurs on an upper set of the state space because the left term remains active after an increase in any $x_i[k]$. Let the predicate $c(x)$ be true if congestion is present. Our specification, $\phi = \Box_{[0,T]}\Diamond_{[0,1]}(\neg c(x[\cdot]))$, requires that congestion be intermittent. Note that ϕ's satisfaction value can be determined for inputs over $I = [0, T]$ because the generated state trajectories are over $I = [0, T+1]$. Because a maximum rate of 40 vehicles can exit the network but a net rate of 90 vehicles can enter via links x_0, x_1, x_3 at any time step, ϕ can easily be violated with a determined adversary. The network in Fig. 9 was shown to exhibit monotone dynamics in [4].

We consider disturbance signals $I = [0, T-1]$ with signal lengths $T \in \{2, 3, \ldots, 11\}$. The input is two dimensional and the state space has five dimensions, so the dimension of the assumption space is $2T+5$ and the boundary of the assumption set can be as complex as a $2T+4$ dimensional object. Fig. 11 shows how increasing the dimension of the problem presents a tradeoff between granularity and sample points. The precision ϵ is normalized along each axis; for example, $\epsilon = .1$ represents that demand signals $d_1[k], d_3[k] \in [0, 30]$ have a granularity of a rate of three vehicles at each time k and that $x_i[0] \in [0, 100]$ has granularity of ten vehicles. We opted to test our method for higher dimensions and coarser granularity (i.e. higher ϵ_{final}) because obtaining a fine approximation of the assumption set doesn't make sense when traffic model parameters are imprecise and the model does not incorporate higher-order dynamics. The learning rate was $\alpha = .95$ and the initial bloating factor was $\epsilon = .6$. Our algorithm required anywhere from 3 to 12 orders of magnitude less samples than the worst case scenario number of samples $(\frac{1}{\epsilon})^{2T+5}$.

Runtimes for $T = \{2, \ldots, 7\}$ are plotted in Fig 12. Larger dimensions did not achieve the desired precision by a mining algorithm timeout of 10 minutes. Experiments were run on a standard on a laptop with 8 GB memory and 2.4 GHz Intel Core i7 processor. As expected, the main factors that influenced the miner's total run time was dimension and the target ϵ_{final}. However, individual SMT query times depended much more on the presence of "easy solutions" than on problem dimension or the number of constraints. In lower dimensions, M samples provide more comprehensive coverage of the ambient space than M samples in a higher dimension space. Thus, for lower dimension spaces obvious solutions to the SMT queries become sparse sooner than for higher dimensions.

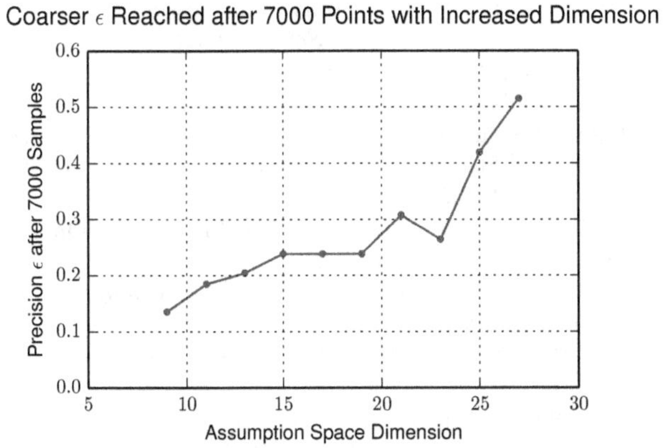

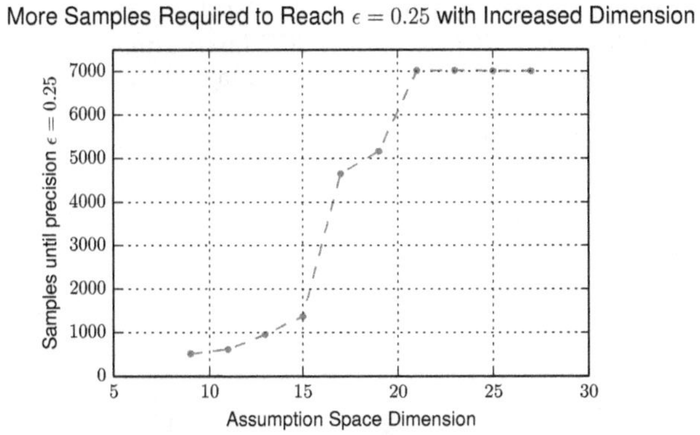

Figure 11: For assumption spaces of varying dimension, precision and number of samples are used as two stopping criteria, with the other criterion plotted after termination. Lower values are better for both plots. The samples plateau in the lower graph appears because of a time out.

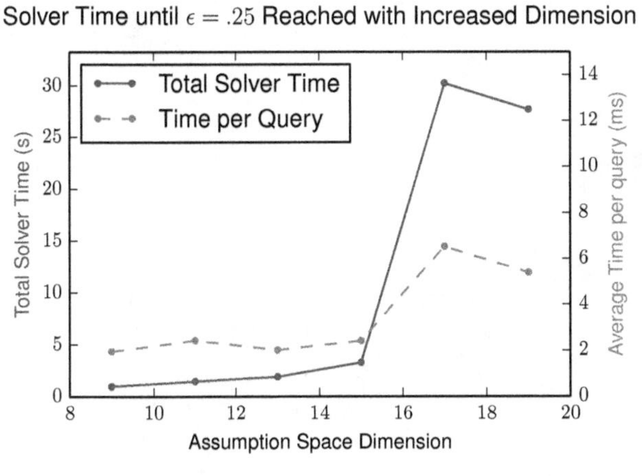

Figure 12: For a fixed $\epsilon_{\text{final}} = .25$, the total solver runtime and average runtime for each SMT query. The increase in total solver time is primarily due to the fact that more points were required to cover the space with an ϵ bloating. The total solver time does not include overhead for declaring constraints and was a variable proportion of total mining time.

7. CONCLUSION

We have introduced directed specifications and shown how their structure can be exploited in the assumption mining problem for monotone dynamical systems. Future work will focus on seeking out other connections between classes of dynamical systems and temporal logic fragments. Viewing temporal logic specifications as geometric objects in a signal space could enable a common language to explore connections between objectives written as temporal logic specifications and traditional control theoretic properties on signals and dynamical systems.

8. REFERENCES

[1] R. Alur, S. Moarref, and U. Topcu. Counter-strategy guided refinement of GR(1) temporal logic specifications. In *Formal Methods in Computer-Aided Design, FMCAD 2013, Portland, OR, USA, October 20-23, 2013*, pages 26–33, 2013.

[2] C. Barrett, R. Sebastiani, S. Seshia, and C. Tinelli. Satisfiability Modulo Theories. In *Handbook of Satisfiability*, volume 185 of *Frontiers in Artificial Intelligence and Applications*, chapter 26, pages 825–885. IOS Press, Feb. 2009.

[3] K. Chatterjee, T. Henzinger, and B. Jobstmann. Environment Assumptions for Synthesis. In *CONCUR 2008 - Concurrency Theory*, volume 5201 of *Lecture Notes in Computer Science*, pages 147–161. Springer Berlin Heidelberg, 2008.

[4] S. Coogan and M. Arcak. Scalable finite abstraction of mixed monotone systems. *Proceedings of the 18th ACM International Conference on Hybrid Systems: Computation and Control*, 2015.

[5] C. F. Daganzo. The cell transmission model: A Dynamic Representation of Highway Traffic Consistent with the Hydrodynamic Theory. *Transportation Research*, 28:269–287, 1994.

[6] B. Davey and H. Priestley. *Introduction to Lattices and Order.* Cambridge University Press, 2nd edition.

[7] L. De Moura and N. Bjørner. Z3: An Efficient SMT Solver. In *Proceedings of the Theory and Practice of Software, 14th International Conference on Tools and Algorithms for the Construction and Analysis of Systems*, TACAS'08/ETAPS'08, pages 337–340, Berlin, Heidelberg, 2008. Springer-Verlag.

[8] J. Deshmukh, X. Jin, J. Kapinski, and O. Maler. Stochastic Local Search for Falsification of Hybrid Systems. In *13th International Symposium on Automated Technology for Verification and Analysis*, 2015.

[9] E. W. Dijkstra. Guarded Commands, Nondeterminacy and Formal Derivation of Programs. *Commun. ACM*, 18(8):453–457, Aug. 1975.

[10] A. Donzé. Breach, a Toolbox for Verification and Parameter Synthesis of Hybrid Systems. In *Proceedings of the 22nd International Conference on Computer Aided Verification*, CAV'10, 2010.

[11] A. Donzé and O. Maler. Robust satisfaction of temporal logic over real-valued signals. In *Proceedings of the 8th International Conference on Formal Modeling and Analysis of Timed Systems*, FORMATS'10, pages 92–106, Berlin, Heidelberg, 2010. Springer-Verlag.

[12] G. Gomes and R. Horowitz. Optimal freeway ramp metering using the asymmetric cell transmission model. *Transportation Research Part C: Emerging Technologies*, 14(4):244 – 262, 2006.

[13] X. Jin, A. Donze, S. A. Seshia, and J. V. Deshmukh. Mining Requirements from Closed-Loop Control Models. In *Hybrid Systems: Computation and Control*, 2013.

[14] J. Legriel, C. Le Guernic, S. Cotton, and O. Maler. Approximating the Pareto Front of Multi-criteria Optimization Problems. In *Tools and Algorithms for the Construction and Analysis of Systems*, volume 6015 of *Lecture Notes in Computer Science*, pages 69–83. Springer Berlin Heidelberg, 2010.

[15] W. Li, L. Dworkin, and S. A. Seshia. Mining assumptions for synthesis. In *In Proc. 9th MEMOCODE*, 2011.

[16] A. Pnueli. The Temporal Logic of Programs. In *Proceedings of the 18th Annual Symposium on Foundations of Computer Science*, pages 46–57, 1977.

[17] V. Raman, A. Donzé, D. Sadigh, R. M. Murray, and S. A. Seshia. Reactive Synthesis from Signal Temporal Logic Specifications. In *18th International Conference on Hybrid Systems: Computation and Control*, HSCC '15, pages 239–248. ACM, 2015.

[18] U. Topcu, N. Ozay, J. Liu, and R. M. Murray. On Synthesizing Robust Discrete Controllers Under Modeling Uncertainty. In *15th ACM International Conference on Hybrid Systems: Computation and Control*, HSCC '12, pages 85–94, New York, NY, USA, 2012. ACM.

[19] E. Wolff, U. Topcu, and R. Murray. Optimization-based trajectory generation with linear temporal logic specifications. In *Robotics and Automation (ICRA), 2014 IEEE International Conference on*, pages 5319–5325, May 2014.

Diagnosis and Repair for Synthesis from Signal Temporal Logic Specifications

Shromona Ghosh[§] Dorsa Sadigh[§] Pierluigi Nuzzo[§]
Vasumathi Raman[†] Alexandre Donzé[§] Alberto Sangiovanni-Vincentelli[§]
S. Shankar Sastry[§] Sanjit A. Seshia[§]
[§]Department of Electrical Engineering and Computer Sciences, University of California, Berkeley, CA
[†]United Technologies Research Center, Berkeley, CA

ABSTRACT

We address the problem of diagnosing and repairing specifications for hybrid systems, formalized in signal temporal logic (STL). Our focus is on automatic synthesis of controllers from specifications using model predictive control. We build on recent approaches that reduce the controller synthesis problem to solving one or more mixed integer linear programs (MILPs), where infeasibility of an MILP usually indicates unrealizability of the controller synthesis problem. Given an infeasible STL synthesis problem, we present algorithms that provide feedback on the reasons for unrealizability, and suggestions for making it realizable. Our algorithms are sound and complete relative to the synthesis algorithm, i. e., they provide a diagnosis that makes the synthesis problem infeasible, and always terminate with a non-trivial specification that is feasible using the chosen synthesis method, when such a solution exists. We demonstrate the effectiveness of our approach on controller synthesis for various cyber-physical systems, including an autonomous driving application and an aircraft electric power system.

1. INTRODUCTION

The automatic synthesis of controllers for hybrid systems from expressive high-level specification languages allows raising the level of abstraction for the designer while ensuring correctness of the resulting controller. In particular, several controller synthesis methods have been proposed for expressive temporal logics and a variety of system dynamics. However, a major challenge to the adoption of these methods in practice is the difficulty of writing formal specifications. Specifications that are poorly stated, incomplete, or inconsistent can produce synthesis problems that are unrealizable (no controller exists for the provided specification), intractable (synthesis is computationally too hard), or lead to solutions that fail to capture the designer's intent. In this paper, we present an algorithmic approach to reduce the specification burden for controller synthesis from temporal logic specifications, focusing on the case when the original specification is unrealizable.

Logical specifications can be provided in multiple ways. One approach is to provide *monolithic* specifications, combining within a single formula constraints on the environment with desired properties of the system under control. However, in many cases, a system specification can be more conveniently provided as a *contract* separating the responsibilities of the system under control (i. e., the guarantees) from the assumptions on the external, possibly adversarial environment [20, 19]. In such a scenario, besides *"weakening" the guarantees*, realizability of a controller can be achieved by *"strengthening" the assumptions.* Indeed, a specification could be unrealizable because the environment assumptions are too weak, the requirements are too strong, or a combination of both. Finding the "problem" with the specification manually can be a tedious and time-consuming process, nullifying the benefits of automatic synthesis. Further, in the *reactive* setting, when the environment is adversarial, finding the right assumptions a priori can be difficult. Thus, given an unrealizable logical specification, there is a need for tools that localize the cause of unrealizability to (hopefully small) parts of the formula, and provide suggestions for repairing the formula in an "optimal" manner.

The problem of diagnosing and repairing formal requirements has received its share of attention in the formal methods community. Ferrère et al. perform diagnosis on faulty executions of systems with specifications expressed in linear temporal logic (LTL) and Metric Temporal Logic (MTL) [9]. They identify the cause of unsatisfiability of these properties in the form of prime implicants, which are conjunctions of literals, and map the failure of a specification to the failure of these prime implicants. Similar syntax tree based definitions of unsatisfiable cores for LTL were presented in [24]. In the context of synthesis from LTL, Raman et al. [22] address the problem of categorizing the causes of unrealizability, and how to detect them in high-level robot control specifications. The use of counter-strategies to derive new environment assumptions for synthesis was first proposed by Li et al. [13] and further explored by others [2, 14]. Our approach, based on exploiting information from optimization solvers, has similarities to these techniques as well as to the work of Nuzzo et al. [18] on extracting unsatisfiable cores for satisfiability modulo theories (SMT) solving.

In this paper, we address the problem of diagnosing and repairing specifications formalized in *signal temporal logic (STL)* [16], a specification language that is well-suited for hybrid systems. Our work is conducted in the setting of automated synthesis from STL via optimization in a model predictive control (MPC) framework [23, 21]. In this approach to synthesis, both the system dynamics and the STL requirements on the system are encoded as mixed integer linear constraints on variables modeling the dynamics of the system and its environment. Controller synthesis is then formulated as an optimization problem to be solved subject to these constraints [23]. In the reactive setting, this approach proceeds by iteratively solving a combination of optimization problems using a *counterexample-guided inductive syn-*

HSCC'16, April 12 - 14, 2016, Vienna, Austria

ISBN 978-1-4503-3955-1/16/04... $15.00
DOI: http://dx.doi.org/10.1145/2883817.2883847

thesis (CEGIS) scheme [21]. In this context, an unrealizable STL specification leads to an infeasible optimization problem. The problem of infeasibility in constrained predictive control schemes has been widely addressed in the literature, e.g., by adopting robust MPC, soft constraints, and penalty functions [12, 25, 4]. Rather than tackling general infeasibility issues in MPC, our focus is on providing tools to help debug the controller specification at design time. However, the deployment of robust or soft-constrained MPC approaches can also benefit from our techniques.

We leverage the ability of existing mixed integer linear programming (MILP) solvers to localize the cause of infeasibility to so-called *irreducibly inconsistent systems* (IIS). Our algorithms use the IIS to localize the cause of unrealizability to the relevant parts of the STL specification. Additionally, we give a method for generating a *minimal set of repairs* to the STL specification such that, after applying those repairs, the resulting specification is realizable. The set of repairs is drawn from a suitably defined space that ensures that we rule out vacuous and other unreasonable adjustments. Specifically, in this paper, we focus on the numerical parameters in a formula, since their specification is often the most tedious and error-prone part.

Our algorithms are sound and complete relative to the synthesis algorithm, i. e., they provide a diagnosis that makes the synthesis problem infeasible, and always terminate with a non-trivial specification that is feasible using the chosen synthesis method, when such a repair exists in the space of possible repairs. Our use of MILP enables us to handle constrained linear and piecewise affine systems, mixed logical dynamical (MLD) systems [3], and certain differentially flat systems. We demonstrate the effectiveness of our approach on the synthesis of controllers for a number of cyber-physical systems, including autonomous driving and aircraft electric power system applications.

The paper is organized as follows. We begin in Sec. 2 and 3 with preliminaries and a running example. We formalize the diagnosis and repair problems in Sec. 4 and describe our algorithms for both monolithic and contract specifications in Sec. 5 and 6. Case studies are presented in Sec. 7.

2. PRELIMINARIES

In this section, we introduce notation and definitions for hybrid dynamical systems, the specification language *Signal Temporal Logic*, and the *Model Predictive Control* framework.

2.1 Hybrid Dynamical Systems

We consider continuous-time hybrid dynamical systems:

$$\dot{x}_t = f(x_t, u_t, w_t), \quad y_t = g(x_t, u_t, w_t), \tag{1}$$

where $x_t \in \mathcal{X} \subseteq (\mathbb{R}^{n_c} \times \{0,1\}^{n_l})$ represents the hybrid (continuous and logical) state at time t, $u_t \in \mathcal{U} \subseteq (\mathbb{R}^{m_c} \times \{0,1\}^{m_l})$ is the hybrid control input, $y_t \in \mathcal{Y} \subseteq (\mathbb{R}^{p_c} \times \{0,1\}^{p_l})$ is the output, and $w_t \in \mathcal{W} \subseteq (\mathbb{R}^{e_c} \times \{0,1\}^{e_l})$ is the hybrid external input, including disturbances and other adversarial inputs from the environment. Using a sampling period $\Delta t > 0$, the continuous-time system (1) lends itself to the following discrete-time approximation:

$$x_{k+1} = f_d(x_k, u_k, w_k), \quad y_k = g_d(x_k, u_k, w_k), \tag{2}$$

where state and output evolve over time steps $k \in \mathbb{N}$, where $x_k = x(\lfloor t/\Delta t \rfloor) \in \mathcal{X}$. Given the initial state of the system $x_0 \in \mathcal{X}$, a *run* of the system is expressed as:

$$\xi = (x_0, y_0, u_0, w_0), (x_1, y_1, u_1, w_1), (x_2, y_2, u_2, w_2), \ldots \tag{3}$$

i. e., as a sequence of assignments over the system variables $V = (x, y, u, w)$. A run is, therefore, a *discrete-time signal.* We define $\xi_k = (x_k, y_k, u_k, w_k)$.

Given an initial state x_0, a finite horizon input sequence $\mathbf{u}^H = u_0, u_1, \ldots, u_{H-1}$, and a finite horizon environment sequence $\mathbf{w}^H = w_0, w_1, \ldots, w_{H-1}$, the finite horizon run of the system modeled by the system dynamics in (2) is uniquely expressed as:

$$\xi^H(x_0, \mathbf{u}^H, \mathbf{w}^H) = \\ (x_0, y_0, u_0, w_0), \ldots, (x_{H-1}, y_{H-1}, u_{H-1}, w_{H-1}),$$

where $x_1, \ldots, x_{H-1}$, $y_0, \ldots, y_{H-1}$ are computed using (2). We finally define a finite-horizon cost function $J(\xi^H)$, mapping H-horizon trajectories $\xi^H \in \Xi$ to costs in $\mathbb{R}^+$.

2.2 Signal Temporal Logic

Signal Temporal Logic (STL) has been largely applied to specify and monitor real-time properties of hybrid systems [8]. Moreover, it offers a robust, quantitative interpretation for the satisfaction of a formula [7, 6].

An STL formula φ is evaluated on a signal ξ at time t: $(\xi, t) \models \varphi$ denotes that φ evaluates to true on ξ at time t. We instead write $\xi \models \varphi$, if ξ satifies φ at time 0. The atomic predicates of STL are defined by inequalities of the form $\mu(\xi(t)) > 0$, where μ is a function of signal ξ at t. Specifically, μ is used to denote both the function of $\xi(t)$ and the predicate. Any STL formula φ consists of Boolean and temporal operations on such predicates. The syntax of STL formulae is defined recursively as follows:

$$\varphi ::= \mu \mid \neg\mu \mid \varphi \wedge \psi \mid \mathbf{G}_{[a,b]}\psi \mid \mathbf{F}_{[a,b]}\psi \mid \varphi\, \mathbf{U}_{[a,b]}\psi, \tag{4}$$

where ψ and φ are STL formulae, $\mathbf{G}$ is the *globally* operator, $\mathbf{F}$ is the *finally* operator and $\mathbf{U}$ is the *until* operator. For example, $\xi \models \mathbf{G}_{[a,b]}\psi$ specifies that ψ must hold for signal ξ at all times of the given interval, i. e., $\forall t \in [a, b], (\xi, t) \models \psi$. Formally, the satisfaction of a formula φ for a signal ξ at time t is defined as:

$$\begin{array}{lcl}
(\xi,t) \models \mu & \Leftrightarrow & \mu(\xi(t)) > 0 \\
(\xi,t) \models \neg\mu & \Leftrightarrow & \neg((\xi,t) \models \mu) \\
(\xi,t) \models \varphi \wedge \psi & \Leftrightarrow & (\xi,t) \models \varphi \wedge (\xi,t) \models \psi \\
(\xi,t) \models \mathbf{F}_{[a,b]}\varphi & \Leftrightarrow & \exists t' \in [t+a, t+b], (\xi,t') \models \varphi \\
(\xi,t) \models \mathbf{G}_{[a,b]}\varphi & \Leftrightarrow & \forall t' \in [t+a, t+b], (\xi,t') \models \varphi \\
(\xi,t) \models \varphi\ \mathbf{U}_{[a,b]}\ \psi & \Leftrightarrow & \exists t' \in [t+a, t+b] \text{ s.t. } (\xi,t') \models \psi \\
 & & \wedge \forall t'' \in [t,t'], (\xi,t'') \models \varphi.
\end{array}$$

A *quantitative* or *robust semantics* is defined for an STL formula φ by associating it with a real-valued function ρ^φ of the signal ξ and time t, which provides a "measure" of the margin by which φ is satisfied [6].

2.3 Model Predictive Control

Model Predictive Control (MPC), or *Receding Horizon Control* (RHC), is a well studied control method for hybrid dynamical systems [17, 10]. In RHC, at any time step, the state of the system is observed and an optimal control problem is solved over a finite time horizon H, for a given set of constraints and a cost function J. When f, as defined in (2), is nonlinear, we assume this optimization is performed at each MPC step after locally linearizing the system dynamics. For example, at time $t = k$, the linearized dynamics around the current state and time are used to compute an optimal strategy $\mathbf{u}_*^H$ over the time interval $[k, k + H - 1]$. Then, only the first component of $\mathbf{u}_*^H$ is applied, and a similar optimization is solved at $k+1$ to compute a new optimal control sequence along the interval $[k + 1, k + H]$ for the model linearized around time step $k + 1$. While the global optimality of MPC is not guaranteed, the technique is widely used and performs well in practice.

In this paper, we use STL to express temporal constraints on the environment and system runs during MPC. We then translate an STL specification into a set of mixed integer linear constraints [23, 21]. Given a formula φ to be satisfied over a finite horizon H, the associated optimization is:

$$\min_{\mathbf{u}^H} J(\xi^H(x_0, \mathbf{u}^H)) \quad \text{s. t.} \quad \xi^H(x_0, \mathbf{u}^H) \models \varphi, \tag{5}$$

which yields a control strategy $\mathbf{u}^H$ that minimizes the cost function $J(\xi^H)$ over the finite-horizon trajectory ξ^H, while satisfying the STL formula φ at time step 0. In a closed-loop setting, we compute a fresh $\mathbf{u}^H$ at every time step $i \in \mathbb{N}$, replacing x_0 with x_i in (5) [23, 21].

While (5) applies to systems without uncontrolled inputs, a more general formulation can be provided to account for an uncontrolled disturbance input $\mathbf{w}^H$ that acts, in general, adversarially [21]. To provide this formulation, we assume the specification is given in the form of an STL *assume-guarantee (A/G) contract* [20, 19] $\mathcal{C} = (V, \varphi_e, \varphi \equiv \varphi_e \rightarrow \varphi_s)$, where V is the set of variables, φ_e captures the assumptions (admitted behaviors) over the (uncontrolled) environment inputs w, and φ_s describes the guarantees (promised behaviors) over all the system variables. A game-theoretic formulation of the controller synthesis problem is then represented as a *minimax* optimization problem:

$$\begin{aligned} &\underset{\mathbf{u}^H}{\text{minimize}} && \underset{\mathbf{w}^H \in \mathcal{W}^e}{\text{maximize}} && J(\xi^H(x_0, \mathbf{u}^H, \mathbf{w}^H)) \\ &\text{subject to} && \forall \mathbf{w}^H \in \mathcal{W}^e && \xi^H(x_0, \mathbf{u}^H, \mathbf{w}^H) \models \varphi, \end{aligned} \tag{6}$$

where we aim to find a strategy $\mathbf{u}^H$ that minimizes the worst case cost $J(\xi^H)$ over the finite horizon trajectory, under the assumption that the disturbance signal $\mathbf{w}^H$ acts adversarially. We use $\mathcal{W}^e$ in (6) to denote the set of disturbances that satisfy the environment specification φ_e, i.e., $\mathcal{W}^e = \{\mathbf{w} \in \mathcal{W}^H | \mathbf{w} \models \varphi_e\}$.

Mixed Integer Linear Program Formulation.

Following [23, 21], we solve the optimization problems in (5) and (6) by translating the STL formula φ into a set of mixed integer constraints, thus reducing the problem to a *Mixed Integer Program* (MIP). In this paper, we consider control problems that are encoded as *Mixed Integer Linear Programs* (MILP).

The MILP constraints are constructed recursively on the structure of the STL specification, and express the robust satisfaction value of the formula. Recall that $(\xi, t) \models \varphi \Leftrightarrow \rho^{\varphi}(\xi, t) > 0$. The robustness value of a formula with temporal or Boolean operators is expressed recursively as the *min* or *max* of the robustness values of the operands over time. These operations can in turn be encoded as mixed integer constraints. For instance, to encode $min(\rho^{\varphi_1}, ..., \rho^{\varphi_n})$, we introduce Boolean variables z^{φ_i} for $i \in \{1, \ldots, n\}$ and a continuous variable p. The resulting MILP constraints are:

$$\begin{aligned} &p \leq \rho^{\varphi_i}, \sum_{i=1\ldots n} z^{\varphi_i} \geq 1 \\ &\rho^{\varphi_i} - (1 - z^{\varphi_i})M \leq p \leq \rho^{\varphi_i} + (1 - z^{\varphi_i})M, \end{aligned} \tag{7}$$

where M is a constant selected to be much larger than $|\rho^{\varphi_i}|$ for all i, and $i \in \{1, \ldots, n\}$. The above constraints ensure that p takes the value of the minimum robustness and $z^{\varphi_i} = 1$ if ρ^{φ_i} is the minimum. To get the constraints for *max*, we replace $\leq$ by $\geq$ in (7).

We solve the MILP with an off-the-shelf solver. If the receding horizon scheme is feasible, then the controller synthesis problem is *realizable*, i.e., the algorithm returns a controller that satisfies the specification and optimizes the objective. However, if the MILP is infeasible, the synthesis problem is *unrealizable*. In this case, the failure to synthesize a controller may well be attributed to just a portion of the STL specification. In the rest of the paper we discuss how infeasibility of the MILP constraints can be used to

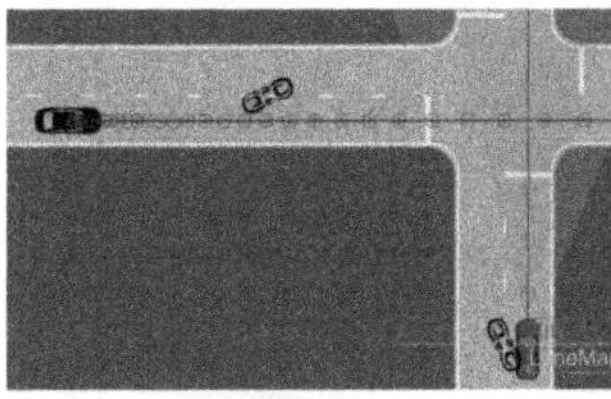

Figure 1: Vehicles crossing an intersection. The red car is the *ego* vehicle, while the black car is part of the environment.

infer the "cause" of failure and, consequently, diagnose and repair the original STL specification.

3. A RUNNING EXAMPLE

To illustrate our approach, we introduce a running example from the autonomous driving domain. As shown in Fig. 1, we consider a scenario in which two moving vehicles approach an intersection. The red car, labeled the *ego* vehicle, is the vehicle under control, while the black car is part of the external environment and may behave, in general, adversarially. The state of the system includes the position and velocity of each vehicle, the control input is the acceleration of the *ego* vehicle, and the environment input is the acceleration of the other vehicle, i.e.,

$$\begin{aligned} &\tilde{x}_t = (x_t^{\text{ego}}, y_t^{\text{ego}}, v_t^{\text{ego}}, x_t^{\text{adv}}, y_t^{\text{adv}}, v_t^{\text{adv}}) \\ &u_t = a_t^{\text{ego}} \quad w_t = a_t^{\text{adv}}. \end{aligned} \tag{8}$$

We assume the dynamics of the system is given by a simple double integrator for each vehicle, e.g.,

$$\begin{bmatrix} \dot{x}^{\text{ego}} \\ \dot{y}^{\text{ego}} \\ \dot{v}^{\text{ego}} \end{bmatrix} = \begin{bmatrix} 0 & 0 & 0 \\ 0 & 0 & 1 \\ 0 & 0 & 0 \end{bmatrix} \begin{bmatrix} x^{\text{ego}} \\ y^{\text{ego}} \\ v^{\text{ego}} \end{bmatrix} + \begin{bmatrix} 0 \\ 0 \\ 1 \end{bmatrix} u. \tag{9}$$

A similar equation holds for the environment vehicle which is, however, constrained to move along the horizontal axis rather than the vertical axis. We assume the *ego* vehicle is initialized at the coordinates $(0, -1)$ and the other vehicle is initialized at $(-1, 0)$. All units in this example follow the metric system. We would like to design a controller for the *ego* vehicle to satisfy an STL specification under some assumptions on the external environment, and provide diagnosis and feedback if the specification is infeasible. We discuss the following three scenarios.

EXAMPLE 1 (COLLISION AVOIDANCE). *We want to avoid a collision between the* ego *and the adversary vehicle. In this example, we assume the environment vehicle's acceleration is fixed at all times, i.e.,* $a_t^{\text{adv}} = 2$*, while the initial velocities are* $v_0^{\text{adv}} = 0$ *and* $v_0^{\text{ego}} = 0$*. We encode our requirements using the formula* $\varphi := \varphi_1 \wedge \varphi_2$*, where* φ_1 *and* φ_2 *are defined as follows:*

$$\begin{aligned} &\varphi_1 = \mathbf{G}_{[0,\infty)} \neg\big((-0.5 \leq y_t^{\text{ego}} \leq 0.5) \wedge (-0.5 \leq x_t^{\text{adv}} \leq 0.5)\big), \\ &\varphi_2 = \mathbf{G}_{[0,\infty)} \big(1.5 \leq a_t^{\text{ego}} \leq 2.5\big). \end{aligned}$$

We prescribe bounds on the system acceleration, and state that both cars should never be confined together within a box of width 1 *around the intersection* $(0, 0)$*, to avoid a collision.*

EXAMPLE 2 (NON-ADVERSARIAL RACE). *In the race scenario, assuming the adversary's velocity always exceeds* 0.5*, the* ego *vehicle must maintain a velocity above* 0.5*. We formalize our requirement as a contract* $(\psi_e, \psi_e \rightarrow \psi_s)$*, where* ψ_e *are the assumptions made on the environment and* ψ_s *are the guarantees of the system provided the environment satisfies the assumptions. Specifically:*

$$\begin{aligned} &\psi_e = \mathbf{G}_{[0,\infty)}(v_t^{\text{adv}} \geq 0.5), \\ &\psi_s = \mathbf{G}_{[0,\infty)}(-1 \leq a_t^{\text{ego}} \leq 1) \wedge (v_t^{\text{ego}} \geq 0.5). \end{aligned} \tag{10}$$

The initial velocities are $v_0^{\text{adv}} = 0.55$ and $v_0^{\text{ego}} = 0$, while the environment vehicle's acceleration is $a_t^{\text{adv}} = 1$ at all times. We require the acceleration to be bounded by 1.

EXAMPLE 3 (ADVERSARIAL RACE). *We discuss another race scenario, in which the environment vehicle acceleration a_t^{adv} is no longer fixed, but varies up to a value of 2. Initially, $v_0^{\text{adv}} = 0$ and $v_0^{\text{ego}} = 0$ hold. Under these assumptions, we would like to guarantee that the velocity of the* ego *vehicle exceeds 0.5 if the speed of the adversary vehicle exceeds 0.5, while maintaining an acceleration in the $[-1, 1]$ range. Altogether, we capture the requirements above via a contract $(\phi_w, \phi_w \to \phi_s)$, where:*

$$\phi_w = \mathbf{G}_{[0,\infty)}\left(0 \le a_t^{\text{adv}} \le 2\right),$$

$$\phi_s = \mathbf{G}_{[0,\infty)}\left((v_t^{\text{adv}} > 0.5) \to (v_t^{\text{ego}} > 0.5)\right) \wedge \left(|a_t^{\text{ego}}| \le 1\right).$$

4. PROBLEM STATEMENT

In this section, we define the problems of specification diagnosis and repair in the context of controller synthesis from STL. We assume the discretized system dynamics f_d and g_d, the initial state x_0, the STL specification φ, and a cost function J are given. The *controller synthesis* problem, denoted $\mathcal{P} = (f_d, g_d, x_0, \varphi, J)$, is to solve (5) (when φ is a monolithic specification of the desired system behaviors) or (6) (when φ represents a contract between the system and the environment).

If synthesis fails, the *diagnosis* problem is, intuitively, to return an explanation in the form of a "subset" of the original problem that is already infeasible when taken alone. The *repair* problem is to return a "minimal" set of changes to the specification that would render the resulting controller synthesis problem feasible. To diagnose and repair an STL formula, we focus on its atomic predicates and the time intervals of its temporal operators. We start by providing a definition of the *support* of a formula's atomic predicates, i.e., the set of times at which the value of a predicate affects satisfiability of the formula. We build on this definition to formalize the set of repairs that we allow.

DEFINITION 1 (SUPPORT). *The* support *of a predicate μ in an STL formula φ is the set of times t such that $\mu(\xi(t))$ appears in φ.*

For example, given $\varphi = \mathbf{G}_{[6,10]}(x_t > 0.2)$, the support of predicate $\mu = (x_t > 0.2)$ is the time interval $[6, 10]$.

DEFINITION 2 (ALLOWED REPAIRS). *Let Φ denote the set of all possible STL formulae. A* repair action *is a relation $\gamma : \Phi \to \Phi$ consisting of the union of the following:*

- *A* predicate repair *returns the original formula after modifying one of its atomic predicates μ to μ^*. We denote this sort of repair by $\varphi[\mu \mapsto \mu^*] \in \gamma(\varphi)$;*
- *A* time interval repair *returns the original formula after replacing the interval of a temporal operator. This is denoted $\varphi[\Delta_{[a,b]} \mapsto \Delta_{[a^*,b^*]}] \in \gamma(\varphi)$ where $\Delta \in \{\mathbf{G}, \mathbf{F}, \mathbf{U}\}$.*

We can compose repair actions to get a *sequence of repairs* $\Gamma = \gamma_n(\gamma_{n-1}(\ldots(\gamma_1(\varphi))\ldots))$. Given an STL formula φ, we denote as $\texttt{REPAIR}(\varphi)$ the set of all possible formulae obtained through allowed sequences of repairs on φ. Further, given a set of atomic predicates $\mathcal{D}$ and a set of time intervals $\mathcal{T}$, let $\texttt{REPAIR}_{\mathcal{T},\mathcal{D}}(\varphi) \subseteq \texttt{REPAIR}(\varphi)$ denote the set of repair actions that act only on predicates in $\mathcal{D}$ or time intervals in $\mathcal{T}$. We are now ready to formulate the problems addressed in this paper, namely that of diagnosis and repair of a *monolithic* specification φ (*general diagnosis and repair*), and of an A/G contract $(\varphi_e, \varphi_e \to \varphi_s)$ (*contract diagnosis and repair*).

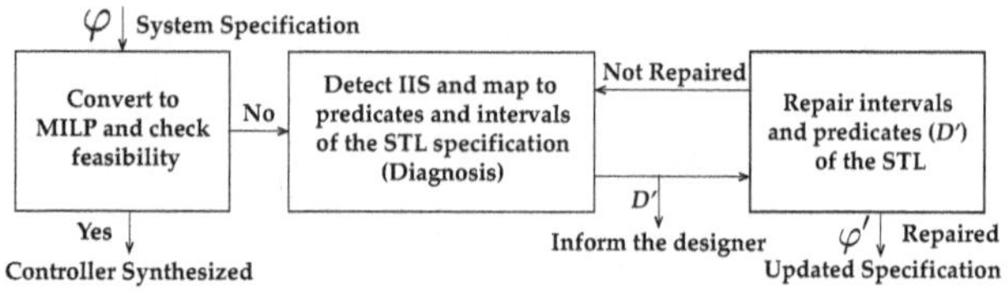

Figure 2: Diagnosis and repair flow diagram.

PROBLEM 1 (GENERAL DIAGNOSIS AND REPAIR). *Given a controller synthesis problem $\mathcal{P} = (f_d, g_d, x_0, \varphi, J)$ such that (5) is infeasible, find:*

- *A set of atomic predicates $\mathcal{D} = \{\mu_1, \ldots, \mu_d\}$ or time intervals $\mathcal{T} = \{\tau_1, \ldots, \tau_d\}$ of the original formula φ,*
- *$\varphi' \in \texttt{REPAIR}_{\mathcal{T},\mathcal{D}}(\varphi)$,*

such that $\mathcal{P}' = (f_d, g_d, x_0, \varphi', J)$ is feasible, and the following minimality conditions hold:

- (predicate minimality) *if φ' is obtained by predicate repair*[1], *$s_i = \mu_i^* - \mu_i$ for $i \in \{1, \ldots, d\}$, $s_{\mathcal{D}} = (s_1, \ldots, s_d)$, and $||\cdot||$ is a norm on $\mathbb{R}^d$, then*

$$\nexists\,(\mathcal{D}', s_{\mathcal{D}'}) \text{ s.t. } ||s_{\mathcal{D}'}|| \le ||s_{\mathcal{D}}|| \wedge \exists\, \varphi'' \in \texttt{REPAIR}_{\mathcal{T},\mathcal{D}'}(\varphi) \text{ s.t. } \mathcal{P}'' = (f_d, g_d, x_0, \varphi'', J) \text{ is feasible.} \tag{11}$$

- (time interval minimality) *if φ' is obtained by time interval repair, $\mathcal{T}^* = \{\tau_1^*, \ldots, \tau_l^*\}$ are the non-empty repaired intervals, and $||\tau||$ is the length of interval τ:*

$$\nexists\, \mathcal{T}' = \{\tau_1', \ldots, \tau_l'\}, \text{ s.t. } \exists i \in \{1, \ldots, l\}, ||\tau_i^*|| \le ||\tau_i'|| \wedge \exists\, \varphi'' \in \texttt{REPAIR}_{\mathcal{T}',\mathcal{D}}(\varphi) \text{ s.t. } \mathcal{P}'' = (f_d, g_d, x_0, \varphi'', J) \text{ is feasible.} \tag{12}$$

PROBLEM 2 (CONTRACT DIAGNOSIS AND REPAIR). *Given a controller synthesis problem $\mathcal{P} = (f_d, g_d, x_0, \varphi \equiv \varphi_e \to \varphi_s, J)$ such that (6) is infeasible, find:*

- *Sets of atomic predicates $\mathcal{D}_e = \{\mu_1^e, \ldots, \mu_d^e\}$, $\mathcal{D}_s = \{\mu_1^s, \ldots, \mu_{\bar{d}}^s\}$ or sets of time intervals $\mathcal{T}_e = \{\tau_1^e, \ldots, \tau_l^e\}, \mathcal{T}_s = \{\tau_1^s, \ldots, \tau_{\bar{l}}^s\}$, respectively, of the original formulas φ_e and φ_s,*
- *$\varphi_e' \in \texttt{REPAIR}_{\mathcal{T}_e,\mathcal{D}_e}(\varphi_e)$, $\varphi_s' \in \texttt{REPAIR}_{\mathcal{T}_s,\mathcal{D}_s}(\varphi_s)$,*

such that $\mathcal{P}' = (f_d, g_d, x_0, \varphi', J)$ is feasible, and $\mathcal{D} = \mathcal{D}_e \cup \mathcal{D}_s$, $\mathcal{T} = \mathcal{T}_e \cup \mathcal{T}_s$, and φ' satisfy the minimality conditions of Problem (1).

5. MONOLITHIC SPECIFICATIONS

Fig. 2 represents the workflow adopted to diagnose inconsistencies in the specification and provide constructive feedback to the designer. In this section, we describe our solution to Prob. 1, as summarized in Alg. 1. Given a problem $\mathcal{P}$, defined as in Sec. 4, the method $\texttt{GenMILP}$ reformulates (5) in terms of the following MILP:

$$\begin{aligned} \underset{u^H}{\text{minimize}} \quad & J(\xi^H) & \\ \text{subject to} \quad & f_i^{\text{dyn}} \le 0 & i \in \{1, \ldots, m_d\} \\ & f_k^{\text{stl}} \le 0 & k \in \{1, \ldots, m_s\}, \end{aligned} \tag{13}$$

where f^{dyn} and f^{stl} are mixed integer linear constraint functions over the states, outputs, and inputs of the finite horizon trajectory ξ^H associated, respectively, with the system

[1] For technical reasons, our minimality conditions are predicated on a single type of repair being applied to obtain φ'.

Algorithm 1 `DiagnoseRepair`

procedure `DiagnoseRepair`
  Input: $\mathcal{P}$
  Output: $\mathbf{u}^H$, $\mathcal{D}$, *repaired*, φ'
  $(J, C) \leftarrow$ `GenMILP(`$\mathcal{P}$`)`, *repaired* $\leftarrow 0$
  $\mathbf{u}^H \leftarrow$ `Solve(`J, C`)`
  if $\mathbf{u}^H = \emptyset$ **then**
    $\mathcal{D} \leftarrow \emptyset$, $\mathcal{S} \leftarrow \emptyset$, $I \leftarrow \emptyset$, $\mathcal{M} \leftarrow (0, C)$
    while *repaired* $= 0$ **do**
      $(\mathcal{D}', \mathcal{S}', I') \leftarrow$ `Diagnosis(`$\mathcal{M}$, $\mathcal{P}$`)`
      $\mathcal{D} \leftarrow \mathcal{D} \cup \mathcal{D}'$, $\mathcal{S} \leftarrow \mathcal{S} \cup \mathcal{S}'$, $I \leftarrow I \cup I'$
      options $\leftarrow$ `UserInput(`$\mathcal{D}'$`)`
      $\lambda \leftarrow$ `ModifyConstraints(`I', *options*`)`
      $(repaired, \mathcal{M}, \varphi') \leftarrow$ `Repair(`$\mathcal{M}, I', \lambda, \mathcal{S}, \varphi$`)`
    $\mathbf{u}^H \leftarrow$ `Solve(`J, $\mathcal{M}.C$`)`

Algorithm 2 `Diagnosis`

procedure `Diagnosis(`$\mathcal{M}$, $\mathcal{P}$`)`
  Input: $\mathcal{M}$, $\mathcal{P}$
  Output: $\mathcal{D}$, $\mathcal{S}$, I'
  $I_C \leftarrow$ `IIS(`$\mathcal{M}$`)`
  $(\mathcal{D}, \mathcal{S}) \leftarrow$ `ExtractPredicates(`I_C,$\mathcal{P}$`)`
  $I' \leftarrow$ `ExtractConstraints(`$\mathcal{M}$,$\mathcal{D}$`)`

dynamics and the STL specification φ. We let (J, C) represent this MILP, where J is the objective, and C is the set of constraints. If Prob. (13) is infeasible, we iterate between diagnosis and repair phases until the repaired feasible specification φ' is obtained. We let $\mathcal{D}$ and I denote, respectively, the set of predicates returned by the diagnosis procedure, and the constraints corresponding to those predicates.

Optionally, we support an interactive repair mechanism, where the designer provides a set of *options* that prioritize which predicates to modify (`UserInput`) and get converted into a set of weights λ (`ModifyConstraints`). The designer can leverage this weighted-cost variant of the problem to define "soft" and "hard" constraints in the controller synthesis problem. In the following, we detail the operation of the `Diagnosis` and `Repair` subroutines.

5.1 Diagnosis

Our diagnosis procedure is summarized in Alg. 2. The method `Diagnosis` receives as inputs the controller synthesis problem $\mathcal{P}$ and an associated MILP formulation $\mathcal{M}$. $\mathcal{M}$ can either be the *feasibility problem* associated with the original problem in Eq. (13), or a relaxation thereof. This feasibility problem has the same (possibly relaxed) constraints as Eq. (13), but zero cost. Formally, we provide the following definition of a *relaxed* constraint and optimization problem.

DEFINITION 3 (RELAXED PROBLEM). *We say that a constraint $f' \leq 0$ is a* relaxed version *of $f \leq 0$ if there exists a slack variable $s \in \mathbb{R}^+$ such that $f' = (f - s)$. In this case, we say that $f \leq 0$ is relaxed into $f' \leq 0$. An optimization problem $\mathcal{O}'$ is a* relaxed version *of another optimization problem $\mathcal{O}$ if it is obtained from $\mathcal{O}$ by relaxing at least one of its constraints.*

When $\mathcal{M}$ is infeasible, we rely on the capability of state-of-the-art MILP solvers to provide an *Irreducibly Inconsistent System* (IIS) [1, 5] of constraints I_C, defined as follows.

DEFINITION 4 (IRREDUCIBLY INCONSISTENT SYSTEM). *Given a feasibility problem $\mathcal{M}$ with constraint set C, an* Irreducibly Inconsistent System *I_C is a subset of constraints $I_C \subseteq C$ such that: (i) the optimization problem $(0, I_C)$ is infeasible; (ii) $\forall\ c \in I_C$, problem $(0, I_C \setminus \{c\})$ is feasible.*

In other words, an IIS is an infeasible subset of constraints that becomes feasible if any single constraint is removed. For each constraint in I_C, `ExtractPredicates` traces back to the

Algorithm 3 `Repair`

procedure `Repair`
  Input: $\mathcal{M}$, I, λ, $\mathcal{S}$, φ
  Output: *repaired*, $\mathcal{M}$, φ
  $\mathcal{M}.J \leftarrow \mathcal{M}.J + \lambda^\top s_I$
  for c in I **do**
    if $\lambda(c) > 0$ **then**
      $\mathcal{M}.C(c) \leftarrow \mathcal{M}.C(c) + s_c$
  $(repaired, \mathbf{s}^*) \leftarrow$ `Solve(`$\mathcal{M}.J$, $\mathcal{M}.C$`)`
  if *repaired* $= 1$ **then**
    $\varphi \leftarrow$ `ExtractFeedback(`$\mathbf{s}^*$,$\mathcal{S}$,φ`)`

set of STL predicates from which it originates, which is then used to construct the set $\mathcal{D} = \{\mu_1, \ldots, \mu_d\}$ in Problem 1, and the corresponding set of support intervals $\mathcal{S} = \{\sigma_1, \ldots, \sigma_d\}$ (adequately truncated to the current horizon H), as obtained from the STL syntax tree. The set $\mathcal{D}$ will be used to produce a relaxed version of $\mathcal{M}$ as further detailed in Sec. 5.2. The procedure also returns the subset I of all the constraints in $\mathcal{M}$ that are associated with predicates in $\mathcal{D}$.

5.2 Repair

The diagnosis procedure isolates a set of STL atomic predicates that jointly produce a source of infeasibility for the synthesis problem. For repair, we are instead interested in how to modify the original formula to make the problem feasible. The repair procedure is summarized in Alg. 3. We formulate relaxed versions of the feasibility problem $\mathcal{M}$ associated with Eq. (13) by using *slack variables.*

Let f_i, $i \in \{1, \ldots, m\}$ denote both categories of constraints f^{dyn} and f^{stl} in the feasibility problem $\mathcal{M}$. We reformulate $\mathcal{M}$ as the following *feasibility problem with slacks*:

$$
\begin{array}{lll}
\underset{\mathbf{s}\in\mathbb{R}^{|I|}}{\text{minimize}} & ||\mathbf{s}|| & \\
\text{subject to} & f_i - s_i \leq 0 & i \in \{1, \ldots, |I|\} \\
& f_i \leq 0 & i \in \{|I|+1, \ldots, m\} \\
& s_i \geq 0 & i \in \{1, \ldots, |I|\},
\end{array}
\tag{14}
$$

where $\mathbf{s} = s_1 \ldots s_{|I|}$ is a vector of slack variables added to the set I obtained after the latest call of `Diagnosis`. Note that not all the constraints in the original optimization Eq. (13) can be modified. For instance, the designer will not be able to arbitrarily modify constraints that can directly affect the dynamics of the system, i. e., constraints encoded in f^{dyn}. Solving Eq. (14) is equivalent to looking for a set of slacks that make the original control problem feasible while minimizing a suitable norm $||\cdot||$ of the slack vector. In most of our applications, we choose the l_1-norm, which tends to provide sparser solutions for $\mathbf{s}$, i.e., nonzero slacks for a smaller number of constraints. However, other norms can be used, including weighted norms based on the set of weights λ. If Problem (14) is feasible, `ExtractFeedback` uses the solution $\mathbf{s}^*$ to repair the original infeasible specification φ. Otherwise, an infeasible problem is returned for another round of diagnosis to retrieve further constraints to relax. Next, we provide details on the implementation of `ExtractFeedback`.

Given a minimum norm solution $\mathbf{s}^*$ to Eq. (14), the slack variables $\mathbf{s}^*$ are mapped to a set of *predicate repairs* $s_{\mathcal{D}}$, as defined in Problem 1, as follows. The slack vector $\mathbf{s}^*$ in Alg. 3 includes the set of slack variables $\{s^*_{\mu_i,t}\}$, where $s^*_{\mu_i,t}$ is the variable added to the optimization constraint associated with an atomic predicate $\mu_i \in \mathcal{D}$ at time t, $i \in \{1, \ldots, d\}$. We then set $\forall\ i \in \{1, \ldots, d\}$,

$$
s_i = \mu_i^* - \mu_i = \max_{t\in\{1,\cdots,H\}} s^*_{\mu_i,t}, \tag{15}
$$

H being the time horizon for (13), and $s_{\mathcal{D}} = \{s_1, \ldots, s_d\}$. To find a set of *time-interval repairs* instead, we proceed as follows:

1. The slack vector $\mathbf{s}^*$ in Alg. 3 includes the set of slack variables $\{s^*_{\mu_i,t}\}$, where $s^*_{\mu_i,t}$ is added to the optimization constraint associated with atomic predicate $\mu_i \in \mathcal{D}$ at time t. For each μ_i, with support interval σ_i, we search for the largest time interval $\sigma'_i \subseteq \sigma_i$ such that $\forall t \in \sigma'_i,\ s^*_{\mu_i,t} = 0$. If $\mu_i \notin \mathcal{D}$, we set $\sigma'_i = \sigma_i$.

2. We convert every temporal operator in φ into a combination of $\mathbf{G}$ (timed or untimed) and untimed $\mathbf{U}$ by using the following transformations:

$$\mathbf{F}_{[a,b]}\psi = \neg\mathbf{G}_{[a,b]}\neg\psi,$$

$$\psi_1\mathbf{U}_{[a,b]}\psi_2 = \mathbf{G}_{[0,a]}(\psi_1\mathbf{U}\ \psi_2) \wedge \mathbf{F}_{[a,b]}\psi_2,$$

where $\mathbf{U}$ is the untimed (unbounded) *until* operator. Let $\hat{\varphi}$ be the formula obtained from φ after these transformations[2].

3. We construct the syntactic parse tree of $\hat{\varphi}$ based on (4): each node is an operator, and the leaves are atomic predicates. The nodes of the parse tree of $\hat{\varphi}$ can be partitioned into three subsets, ν, κ, and δ, respectively associated with the atomic *predicates*, *Boolean operators*, and *temporal operators* $(\mathbf{G}, \mathbf{U})$ in $\hat{\varphi}$. We traverse this parse tree from the leaves (atomic predicates) to the root and recursively define for each node i a new support interval σ^*_i as follows:

$$\sigma^*_i = \begin{cases} \sigma'_i & \text{if } i \in \nu \\ \bigcap_{j\in C(i)} \sigma^*_j & \text{if } i \in \kappa \cup \delta_{\mathbf{U}} \\ \sigma^*_{j\in C(i)} & \text{if } i \in \delta_{\mathbf{G}} \end{cases} \tag{16}$$

where $C(i)$ denotes the children of node i, while $\delta_{\mathbf{G}}$ and $\delta_{\mathbf{U}}$ are, respectively, the subsets of nodes associated with the $\mathbf{G}$ and $\mathbf{U}$ operators. We observe that a $\mathbf{G}$ node has a single child. Therefore, with some abuse of notation, we use $C(i)$ in (16) to denote a single node in the parse tree.

4. We define the interval repair $\hat{\tau}_j$ for each (timed) temporal operator node j in the parse tree of $\hat{\varphi}$ as $\hat{\tau}_j = \sigma^*_j$. If $\hat{\tau}_j$ is empty for any j, no time-interval repair is possible. Otherwise, we map the set of intervals $\{\hat{\tau}_j\}$ to a set of interval repairs $\mathcal{T}^*$ for the original formula φ according to the transformations in step 2 and return $\mathcal{T}^*$. We provide an example of predicate repair below, while time interval repair is demonstrated in Sec. 6.1.

EXAMPLE 4 (COLLISION AVOIDANCE). *We diagnose the specifications introduced in Example 1. To formulate the synthesis problem, we assume a horizon $H = 10$ and a discretization step $\Delta t = 0.2$. The system is found infeasible at the first MPC run, and* `Diagnosis` *detects the infeasibility of $\varphi_1 \wedge \varphi_2$ at time $t = 6$. Intuitively, given the limits on the acceleration of the* ego *vehicle, both the cars end up entering the forbidden box at the same time. Alg. 1 chooses to repair φ_1 by adding slacks to all of its predicates, such that $\varphi'_1 = (-0.5 - s_{l1} \leq y^{\text{ego}}_t \leq 0.5 + s_{u1}) \wedge (-0.5 - s_{l2} \leq x^{\text{adv}}_t \leq 0.5 + s_{u2})$. Table 1 shows the optimal slack values at each t, while s_{u1} and s_{l2} are set to zero at all t. We conclude that the specification replacing φ_1 with φ'_1*

$$\varphi'_1 = \mathbf{G}_{[0,\infty)}\neg((-0.24 \leq y^{\text{ego}}_t \leq 0.5) \wedge (-0.5 \leq x^{\text{adv}}_t \leq 0.43))$$

is feasible, i.e., the cars will not collide, but the original requirement was overly demanding.

Alternatively, the user can choose to run the repair procedure on φ_2 and change its predicate by $(1.5 - s_l \leq a^{\text{ego}}_t \leq 2.5 + s_u)$. In this case, we keep the original requirement on collision avoidance, and tune, instead, the control "effort" to satisfy it. Under the assumption of constant acceleration (and bounds), the slacks will be the same at all t. We then obtain $[s_l, s_u] = [0.82, 0]$, which ultimately gives $\varphi'_2 = \mathbf{G}_{[0,\infty)}(0.68 \leq a^{\text{ego}}_t \leq 2.5)$. The ego *vehicle should then slow down to prevent entering the forbidden box at the same time as the other car.*

time	0	0.2	0.4	0.6	0.8	1	1.2	1.4	1.6	1.8
s_{l1}	0	0	0	0	0	-0.26	0	0	0	0
s_{u2}	0	0	0	0	0	0	-0.07	0	0	0

Table 1: Slack variables for horizon, with $\Delta t = 0.2$, and $H = 10$.

Our algorithm offers the following guarantees, for which a proof sketch is given below. The complete proofs can be found in the extended version of this paper [11].

THEOREM 1 (SOUNDNESS). *Given a controller synthesis problem $\mathcal{P} = (f_d, g_d, x_0, \varphi, J)$, such that (5) is infeasible at time t, let $\varphi' \in$ **REPAIR**$_{\mathcal{D},\mathcal{T}}(\varphi)$ be the repaired formula returned from Alg. 1 for a given set of predicates $\mathcal{D}$ or time interval $\mathcal{T}$. Then, $\mathcal{P}' = (f_d, g_d, x_0, \varphi', J)$ is feasible at time t and $(\varphi', \mathcal{D}, \mathcal{T})$ satisfy the minimality conditions in Prob.1.*

THEOREM 2 (COMPLETENESS). *Assume the controller synthesis problem $\mathcal{P} = (f_d, g_d, x_0, \varphi, J)$ results in (5) being infeasible at time t. If there exist a set of predicates $\mathcal{D}$ or time-intervals $\mathcal{T}$ and $\Phi \subseteq$ **REPAIR**$_{\mathcal{D},\mathcal{T}}(\varphi)$ for which $\forall\ \phi \in \Phi$, $\mathcal{P}' = (f_d, g_d, x_0, \phi, J)$ is feasible at time t and $(\phi, \mathcal{D}, \mathcal{T})$ are minimal in the sense of Problem 1, then Alg. 1 returns a repaired formula φ' in Φ.*

PROOF SKETCH. We start by discussing the case of soundness for *predicate repair*. Let $\mathcal{M}$ be the MILP encoding of $\mathcal{P}$ as defined in (13), $\mathcal{M}'$ be the encoding of $\mathcal{P}'$, and $\mathcal{M}''$ the feasible MILP obtained from Alg. 1, together with the optimal slack set $\{s^*_{\mu,t} | \mu \in \mathcal{D}, t \in \{1, \ldots, H\}\}$. We note that $\mathcal{M}'$ and $\mathcal{M}''$ are both relaxed versions of $\mathcal{M}$. Moreover, each constraint with a nonzero slack variable in $\mathcal{M}''$ is relaxed in $\mathcal{M}'$, and offset by the largest slack value over the horizon H. Since $\mathcal{M}''$ is feasible, $\mathcal{M}'$, and subsequently $\mathcal{P}'$, are feasible. To prove that $(\varphi', \mathcal{D})$ satisfy the predicate minimality condition, by Definition 4, at least one predicate in $\mathcal{D}$ generates a conflicting constraint and must be repaired. Moreover, because Alg. 1 finds all the IISs in the original optimization problem and allows relaxing any constraints in the union of the IISs, repairing any predicate outside of $\mathcal{D}$ is redundant. Therefore, if a formula $\tilde{\varphi}$ is obtained from φ after repairing a set of predicates $\tilde{\mathcal{D}}$, then the associated repair set $s_{\tilde{\mathcal{D}}}$ is seen as a repair set on the same predicate set as $s_{\mathcal{D}}$. Finally, by the norm minimization in (14), we conclude $||s_{\mathcal{D}}|| \leq ||s_{\tilde{\mathcal{D}}}||$.

We now consider the MILP formulation $\mathcal{M}'$ associated with φ' in the case of *time-interval repairs.* For each atomic predicate $\mu_i \in \mathcal{D}$, $\mathcal{M}'$ includes only the associated constraints evaluated over time intervals σ'_i for which the slack variables $\{s^*_{\mu_i,t}\}$ are zero. Such a subset of constraints is trivially feasible. Moreover, because of the structure of the MILP encoding and the manner in which slacks are added, if the constraints corresponding to the atomic predicates in $\mathcal{D}$ have slack zero, so will any constraints enforcing Boolean or temporal combinations of these predicates. Thus, $\mathcal{M}'$ is feasible. To show the satisfaction of the minimality condition, we observe that Alg. 1 selects, for each $\mu_i \in \mathcal{D}$, the largest interval σ'_i such that the associated constraints are feasible, i.e., their slack variables are zero after norm minimization. Because feasible intervals for Boolean combinations of atomic predicates are obtained by intersecting these maximal intervals, and then propagated to the temporal operators, the length of the intervals of each $\mathbf{G}$ operator in $\hat{\varphi}$, and finally of the temporal operators in φ, will be maximal.

To prove completeness, we first observe that Alg. 1 always terminates with a feasible solution since the set of MILP constraints to diagnose and repair is finite. Let $\mathcal{D}$ be the

[2] While the second transformation introduces a new interval $[0, a]$, its parameters are directly linked to the ones of the original interval $[a, b]$ (now inherited by the $\mathbf{F}$ operator) and will be accordingly processed by the repair routine.

set of predicates modified to obtain $\phi \in \Phi$ and $\mathcal{D}'$ the set of diagnosed predicates returned by Alg. 1. Then, because $\mathcal{D}'$ includes all the predicates responsible for inconsistencies, as argued above, we conclude $\mathcal{D} \subseteq \mathcal{D}'$. By Eq. (14), $||s_{\mathcal{D}'}|| \leq ||s_{\mathcal{D}}||$, hence $\varphi' \in \Phi$. Further, if $\phi \in \Phi$ repairs a set of intervals $\mathcal{T} = \{\tau_1, \ldots, \tau_l\}$, then there exists a set of constraints associated with atomic predicates in φ which are consistent in the MILP associated with ϕ and make the overall problem feasible. Then, the relaxed MILP associated with φ after slack norm minimization will include a set of constraints admitting zero slacks over the same set of time intervals, thus terminating with a set of non-empty intervals $\mathcal{T}' = \{\tau_1', \ldots, \tau_l'\}$. Finally, because Alg. 1 finds the longest such intervals, we are guaranteed that $||\tau_i'|| \geq ||\tau_i||$ for all $i \in \{1, \ldots, l\}$, hence $\varphi' \in \Phi$ holds. □

In the worst case, Alg. 1 solves a number of MILP problem instances equal to the number of atomic predicates in the STL formula. While the complexity of solving a MILP is NP-hard, the actual runtime depends on the size of the MILP, which is quadratic in the size (number of predicates and operators) of the STL specification.

6. CONTRACTS

In this section, we consider specifications provided in the form of a contract $(\varphi_e, \varphi_e \rightarrow \varphi_s)$, where φ_e expresses the assumptions and φ_s captures the guarantees. To repair contracts, we capture tradeoffs between assumptions and guarantees in terms of minimization of a weighted norm of slacks. We now describe our results for both non-adversarial and adversarial environments.

6.1 Non-Adversarial Environment

For a contract, we distinguish between controlled inputs u_t and uncontrolled (environment) inputs w_t of the dynamical system. In this section we assume that the environment signal $\mathbf{w}^H$ can be predicted over a finite horizon and set to a known value for which the controller must be synthesized. With $\varphi \equiv \varphi_e \rightarrow \varphi_s$, equation (6) reduces to:

$$\begin{aligned} &\underset{\mathbf{u}^H}{\text{minimize}} && J(\xi^H(x_0, \mathbf{u}^H, \mathbf{w}^H)) \\ &\text{subject to} && \xi^H(x_0, \mathbf{u}^H, \mathbf{w}^H) \models \varphi, \end{aligned} \tag{17}$$

Because of the similarity of Eq. (17) and Eq. (5), we diagnose and repair a contract using the same methodology illustrated in Sec. 5. However, to reflect the different structure of the specification, i.e., its partition into assumption and guarantees, we adopt a weighted sum of the slack variables in Alg. 1, allocating different weights to predicates in the assumption and guarantee formulae. We provide the same guarantees as in Thms. 1 and 2, where $\varphi \equiv \varphi_e \rightarrow \varphi_s$ and the minimality conditions are stated with respect to the weighted norm.

EXAMPLE 5 (NON-ADVERSARIAL RACE). *We consider Example 2 with the same discretization step $\Delta t = 0.2$ and horizon $H = 10$. The MPC scheme results infeasible at time 0. In fact, we observe that ψ_e is always true as $v_0^{\text{adv}} \geq 0.5$ and $a_t^{\text{adv}} = 1 \geq 0$ holds at all times. Since $v_0^{ego} = 0$, the predicate $\psi_{s2} = \mathbf{G}_{[0,\infty)}(v_t^{\text{ego}} \geq 0.5)$ in ψ_s is found to be failing. As in Sec. 5.2, we modify the conflicting predicates in the specification by using slack variables as follows: $v_t^{\text{adv}} + s_e(t) \geq 0.5$ and $v_t^{\text{ego}} + s_s(t) \geq 0.5$. Moreover, we assign weights to the assumption (λ_e) and guarantee (λ_s) predicates, our objective being $\lambda_e|s_e| + \lambda_s|s_s|$. By setting $\lambda_s > \lambda_e$, we encourage modifications in the assumption by falsifying it, which would provide a trivial solution. We instead prefer setting $\lambda_s < \lambda_e$, obtaining the slack values in Table 2, which leads to the following predicate repair: $\psi_{s2}' = \mathbf{G}_{[0,\infty)}(v_t^{\text{ego}} \geq -0.01)$.*

time	0	0.2	0.4	0.6	0.8	1	1.2	1.4	1.6	1.8
s_s	0.51	0.31	0.11	0	0	0	0	0	0	0

Table 2: Slack variables used in Example 2 and 5.

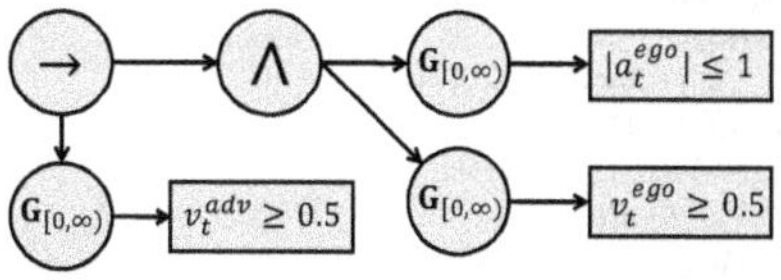

Figure 3: Parse tree of $\psi \equiv \psi_e \rightarrow \psi_s$ used in Example 2 and 5.

We can also modify the time interval of the temporal operator associated with ψ_{s2} to repair the overall specification. Based on the slack values in Table 2, we conclude $\sigma_1' = \sigma_2' = [0, 9]$ (the optimal slack values for these predicates are always zero), while $\sigma_3' = [3, 9]$. For the syntax tree in Fig. 3, we have $\sigma_1^* = \sigma_1'$, $\sigma_2^* = \sigma_2'$, and $\sigma_3^* = \sigma_3'$ for the temporal operator nodes that are parent nodes of μ_1, μ_2, and μ_3. Since none of the above intervals are empty, a time interval repair is indeed possible by modifying the time interval of the parent node of μ_3, thus achieving $\tau_3^* = \sigma_3^*$. This leads to the following proposed sub-formula $\psi_{s2}' = \mathbf{G}_{[0.6,\infty)}(v_t^{\text{ego}} \geq 0.5)$. In this example, repairing the specification over the first horizon is enough to guarantee controller realizability in the future, and we can keep the upper bound of the $\mathbf{G}$ operator at infinity.

6.2 Adversarial Environment

When the environment behaves adversarially, the control synthesis problem assumes the structure in (6). In this paper, we allow w_t to lie in an interval $[w_{\min}, w_{\max}]$ at all times; this corresponds to the STL formula $\varphi_w = \mathbf{G}_{[0,\infty)}(w_{\min} \leq w_t \leq w_{\max})$. We decompose a specification φ of the form $\varphi_w \wedge \varphi_e \rightarrow \varphi_s$, representing the contract, as $\varphi \equiv \varphi_w \rightarrow \psi$, where $\psi \equiv (\varphi_e \rightarrow \varphi_s)$. Our diagnosis and repair method is summarized in Alg. 4.

We first check the satisfiability of the control synthesis problem by examining whether there exists a pair of $\mathbf{u}^H$ and $\mathbf{w}^H$ for which Prob. (6) is feasible (`CheckSAT` routine):

$$\begin{aligned} &\underset{\mathbf{u}^H, \mathbf{w}^H}{\text{minimize}} && J(\xi^H(x_0, \mathbf{u}^H, \mathbf{w}^H)) \\ &\text{subject to} && \xi^H(x_0, \mathbf{u}^H, \mathbf{w}^H) \models \varphi \\ & && \mathbf{w}^H \models \varphi_w \wedge \varphi_e. \end{aligned} \tag{18}$$

If (18) is unsatisfiable, we use the techniques introduced in Sec. 5.2 and 6.1 to diagnose and repair the infeasibility. Therefore, we assume that (18) is satisfiable, hence there exist $\mathbf{u}_0^H$ and $\mathbf{w}_0^H$ that solve (18). To check realizability, we use the following CEGIS loop (`SolveCEGIS` routine). By first fixing the control trajectory to $\mathbf{u}_0^H$, we find the worst case disturbance trajectory $\mathbf{w}_1^H$ that minimizes the robustness value of φ by solving the following problem:

$$\begin{aligned} &\underset{\mathbf{w}^H}{\text{minimize}} && \rho^{\varphi}(\xi^H(x_0, \mathbf{u}^H, \mathbf{w}^H), 0) \\ &\text{subject to} && \mathbf{w}^H \models \varphi_e \wedge \varphi_w \end{aligned} \tag{19}$$

with $\mathbf{u}^H = \mathbf{u}_0^H$. The optimal $\mathbf{w}_1^H$ from (19) will falsify the specification if the resulting robustness value is below zero[3]. If this is the case, we look for a $\mathbf{u}_1^H$ which solves (17) with the additional restriction of $\mathbf{w}^H \in \mathcal{W}_{cand} = \{\mathbf{w}_1^H\}$. If this

[3]A tolerance ρ_{min} is selected to accommodate approximation errors, i.e., $\rho^{\varphi}(\xi^H(x_0, \mathbf{u}_0^H, \mathbf{w}_1^H), 0) < \rho_{min}$.

Algorithm 4 `DiagnoseRepairAdversarial`

procedure `DiagnoseRepairAdversarial`
  Input: $\mathcal{P}$
  Output: $\mathbf{u}^H, \mathcal{P}'$
  $(J, C) \leftarrow$ `GenMILP`$(\mathcal{P})$
  $(\mathbf{u}_0^H, \mathbf{w}_0^H, sat) \leftarrow$ `CheckSAT`(J, C)
  if sat **then**
    $\mathcal{W}^*_{cand} \leftarrow$ `SolveCEGIS`$(\mathbf{u}_0^H, \mathcal{P})$
    $\mathcal{W}_{cand} \leftarrow \mathcal{W}^*_{cand}$
    while $\mathcal{W}_{cand} \neq \emptyset$ **do**
      $\mathcal{P}_w \leftarrow$ `RepairAdversarial`$(\mathcal{W}_{cand}, \mathcal{P})$
      $\mathcal{W}_{cand} \leftarrow$ `SolveCEGIS`$(\mathbf{u}_0^H, \mathcal{P}_w)$
    $\mathcal{W}_{cand} \leftarrow \mathcal{W}^*_{cand}$, $\mathcal{P}_\psi \leftarrow \mathcal{P}$
    while $\mathcal{W}_{cand} \neq \emptyset$ **do**
      $\mathcal{P}_\psi \leftarrow$ `DiagnoseRepair`$(\mathcal{P}_\psi)$
      $\mathcal{W}_{cand} \leftarrow$ `SolveCEGIS`$(\mathbf{u}_0^H, \mathcal{P}_\psi)$
    $\mathcal{P}' \leftarrow$ `FindMin`$(\mathcal{P}_w, \mathcal{P}_\psi)$

step is feasible, we once again attempt to find a worst-case disturbance sequence $\mathbf{w}_2^H$ that solves (19) with $\mathbf{u}^H = \mathbf{u}_1^H$: this is the counterexample-guided inductive step. At each iteration i of this CEGIS loop, the set of candidate disturbance sequences $\mathcal{W}_{cand}$ expands to include $\mathbf{w}_i^H$. If the loop terminates at iteration i with a successful $\mathbf{u}_i^H$ (one for which the worst case disturbance $\mathbf{w}_i^H$ in (19) has positive robustness), we conclude that the formula φ is realizable.

The CEGIS loop may not terminate if the set $\mathcal{W}_{cand}$ is infinite. We, therefore, run it for a maximum number of iterations. If **SolveCEGIS** fails to find a controller sequence prior to the timeout, then (17) is infeasible for the current $\mathcal{W}_{cand}$, i.e., there is no control input that can satisfy φ for all disturbances in $\mathcal{W}_{cand}$. We conclude the specification is not realizable (or, equivalently, the contract is inconsistent). While this infeasibility can be repaired by modifying ψ based on the techniques in Sec. 5.2 and 6.1, an alternative solution is to repair φ_w by minimally pruning the bounds on w_t (**RepairAdversarial** routine). To do so, a basic linear search procedure is implemented as follows. Let:

$$w_u = \max_{\substack{\mathbf{w}_i^H \in \mathcal{W}_{cand} \\ t \in \{1,\ldots,H-1\}}} w_{i,t} \qquad w_l = \min_{\substack{\mathbf{w}_i^H \in \mathcal{W}_{cand} \\ t \in \{1,\ldots,H-1\}}} w_{i,t}, \tag{20}$$

and define $s_u = w_{\max} - w_u$ and $s_l = w_l - w_{\min}$. The differences s_u and s_l are used to update the range for w_t in φ_w to a maximal interval $[w'_{\min}, w'_{\max}] \subseteq [w_{\min}, w_{\max}]$ and such that at least one $\mathbf{w}_i^H \in \mathcal{W}_{cand}$ is excluded. Specifically, if $s_u \leq s_l$, $[w'_{\min}, w'_{\max}]$ is set to $[w_{\min}, w_u - \epsilon]$, $\epsilon \in \mathbb{R}^+$ being a suitable (small) constant; otherwise $[w'_{\min}, w'_{\max}]$ is set $[w_l + \epsilon, w_{\max}]$. We implement an improved version of the above procedure, which allows optimizations over subsets of the time sets in (20) based on the time instants at which an infeasibility occurs. Moreover, we use binary search over the range of w_t for faster convergence. Finally, we use the updated formula φ'_w to run **SolveCEGIS** again until a realizable control sequence $\mathbf{u}^H$ is found. In Alg. 4, for a predicate repair procedure, **FindMin** provides the solution with minimum slack norm over all solutions repairing ψ and φ_w.

EXAMPLE 6 (ADVERSARIAL RACE). *We consider the specification in Example 3. For the same horizon as in the previous examples, after solving the satisfiability problem, for the fixed* $\mathbf{u}_0^H$, *the CEGIS loop returns* $a_t^{\text{adv}} = 2$ *for all* $t \in \{0, \ldots, H-1\}$ *as the single element in* $\mathcal{W}_{cand}$ *for which no controller sequence is found. We then choose to tighten the environment assumptions to make the controller realizable and shrink the bounds on* a_t^{adv} *by using Alg. 4 (with* $\epsilon = 0.01$*). After a few iterations, we finally obtain* $w'_{\min} = 0$ *and* $w'_{\max} = 1.24$, *and therefore* $\phi'_w = \mathbf{G}_{[0,\infty)}(0 \leq a_t^{\text{adv}} \leq 1.24)$.

To account for the error introduced by ϵ, given $\varphi' \in$ **REPAIR**$_{\mathcal{D},\mathcal{T}}(\varphi)$, we say that $(\varphi', \mathcal{D}, \mathcal{T})$ are ϵ-minimal if the magnitudes of the predicate repairs (predicate slacks) or time-interval repairs differ by at most ϵ from a minimal repair in the sense of Problem 2. Assuming that **SolveCEGIS** terminates before reaching the maximum number of iterations[4], the following theorems state the properties of Alg. 4.

THEOREM 3 (SOUNDNESS). *Given a controller synthesis problem* $\mathcal{P} = (f_d, g_d, x_0, \varphi, J)$, *such that (6) is infeasible at time t, let* $\varphi' \in$ ***REPAIR***$_{\mathcal{D},\mathcal{T}}(\varphi)$ *be the repaired formula returned from Alg. 4 for a given set of predicates* $\mathcal{D}$ *or time interval* $\mathcal{T}$. *Then,* $\mathcal{P}' = (f_d, g_d, x_0, \varphi', J)$ *is feasible at time t and* $(\varphi', \mathcal{D}, \mathcal{T})$ *is* ϵ*-minimal.*

THEOREM 4 (COMPLETENESS). *Assume the controller synthesis problem* $\mathcal{P} = (f_d, g_d, x_0, \varphi, J)$ *results in (6) being infeasible at time t. If there exist a set of predicates* $\mathcal{D}$ *and time-intervals* $\mathcal{T}$ *such that there exists* $\Phi \subseteq$ ***REPAIR***$_{\mathcal{D},\mathcal{T}}(\varphi)$ *for which* $\forall\ \phi \in \Phi$, $\mathcal{P}' = (f_d, g_d, x_0, \phi, J)$ *is feasible at time t and* $(\phi, \mathcal{D}, \mathcal{T})$ *is* ϵ*-minimal, then Alg. 4 returns a repaired formula* φ' *in* Φ.

PROOF SKETCH. When $\psi = \varphi_e \rightarrow \varphi_s$ is modified using Alg. 1, soundness and completeness are guaranteed by Thm. 1 and the termination of the CEGIS loop. Assuming Alg. 4 modifies the atomic predicates in ϕ_w, the **RepairAdversarial** routine and (20), together with the termination of the CEGIS loop, assure that φ_w is repaired in such a way that the controller is realizable and ϵ-optimal. This gives us soundness. For completeness, we assume there exists a minimum norm repair for the atomic predicates of φ_w, which returns a maximal interval $[w'_{\min}, w'_{\max}] \subseteq [w_{\min}, w_{\max}]$. Then, given the termination of the CEGIS loop, repeated application of (20) and **RepairAdversarial** will produce a predicate repair such that the corresponding interval $[w''_{\min}, w''_{\max}]$ makes the control synthesis realizable and is maximal within an error bounded by ϵ. Hence, $\varphi' \in \Phi$ holds. □

7. CASE STUDIES

We developed the toolbox DIARY (Diagnosis and Repair for sYnthesis)[5] implementing our algorithms. DIARY uses YALMIP [15] to formulate the optimization problems and GUROBI [1] to solve them. It interfaces to different synthesis tools, e.g., BLUSTL[6] and CRSPRSTL[7]. Here, we summarize some of the results of DiaRY for diagnosis and repair.

7.1 Autonomous Driving

We consider the problem of synthesizing a controller for an autonomous vehicle in a city driving scenario. We analyze the following two tasks: (i) changing lanes on a busy road; (ii) performing an unprotected left turn at a signalized intersection. We use a simple point-mass model for the vehicles on the road. For each vehicle, we define the state as $\mathbf{x} = [x\ y\ \theta\ v]^\top$, where x and y denote the coordinates, and θ and v represent the direction and speed, respectively. Let $\mathbf{u} = [u_1\ u_2]^\top$ be the control input for each vehicle, where u_1 is the steering input and u_2 is the acceleration. Then, the vehicle's state evolves according to the following dynamics:

$$\begin{aligned} \dot{x} &= v\cos\theta & \dot{y} &= v\sin\theta \\ \dot{\theta} &= v \cdot u_1/m & \dot{v} &= u_2, \end{aligned} \tag{21}$$

where m is the vehicle mass. To determine the control strategy, we linearize the overall system dynamics around the initial state at each run of the MPC, which is completed in less

[4]Under failing assumptions, Alg. 4 terminates with UNKNOWN.
[5]https://github.com/shromonag/DiaRY
[6]https://github.com/BluSTL/BluSTL
[7]https://github.com/dsadigh/CrSPrSTL

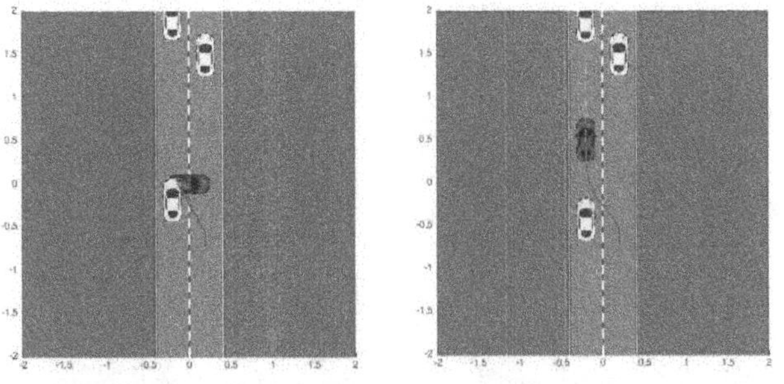

(a) (b)

Figure 4: Lane Change: (a) Infeasible at $t = 1.2$ s, (b) Repaired.

than 2 s on a 2.3-GHz Intel Core i7 processor with 16-GB memory. We further impose the following constraints on the *ego* vehicle (i.e., the vehicle under control): (i) a minimum distance must be established between the *ego* vehicle and other cars on the road to avoid collisions; (ii) the *ego* vehicle must obey the traffic lights; (iii) the *ego* vehicle must stay within its road boundaries.

7.1.1 Lane Change

We consider a lane change scenario on a busy road as shown in Fig. 4a. The *ego* vehicle is in red. *Car 1* is at the back of the left lane, *Car 2* is in the front of the left lane, while *Car 3* is on the right lane. The states of the vehicles are initialized as follows: $x_0^{\text{Car 1}} = [-0.2 \; -1.5 \; \frac{\pi}{2} \; 0.5]^\top$, $x_0^{\text{Car 2}} = [-0.2 \; 1.5 \; \frac{\pi}{2} \; 0.5]^\top$, $x_0^{\text{Car 3}} = [0.2 \; 1.5 \; \frac{\pi}{2} \; 0]^\top$, and $x_0^{\text{ego}} = [0.2 \; -0.7 \; \frac{\pi}{2} \; 0]^\top$. The control inputs are initialized as follows: $u_0^{\text{Car 1}} = [0 \; 1]^\top$, $u_0^{\text{Car 2}} = [0 \; -0.25]^\top$, $u_0^{\text{Car 3}} = [0 \; 0]^\top$ and $u_0^{\text{ego}} = [0 \; 0]^\top$. The objective of *ego* is to safely change lane, while satisfying the following requirements:

$$\begin{aligned} \varphi_{\text{str}} &= \mathbf{G}_{[0,\infty)}(|u_1| \leq 2) && \text{Steering Bounds} \\ \varphi_{\text{acc}} &= \mathbf{G}_{[0,\infty)}(|u_2| \leq 1) && \text{Acceleration Bounds} \\ \varphi_{\text{vel}} &= \mathbf{G}_{[0,\infty)}(|v| \leq 1) && \text{Velocity Bounds} \end{aligned} \quad (22)$$

The solid blue line in Fig. 4 is the trajectory of *ego* as obtained from our MPC scheme, while the dotted green line is the future trajectory pre-computed for a given horizon at a given time. MPC becomes infeasible at time $t = 1.2$ s when the no-collision requirement is violated, and a possible collision is detected between the *ego* vehicle and *Car 1* before the lane change is completed (Fig. 4a). Our solver takes 2 s, out of which 1.4 s are needed to generate all the IISs, consisting of 39 constraints. The run time is negligible with respect to the time needed to encode the original optimization problem, which is typically higher by an order of magnitude. To make the system feasible, the proposed repair increases both the acceleration bounds and the velocity bounds on the *ego* vehicle as follows:

$$\varphi_{\text{acc}}^{\text{new}} = \mathbf{G}_{[0,\infty)}(|u_2| \leq 3.5), \quad \varphi_{\text{vel}}^{\text{new}} = \mathbf{G}_{[0,\infty)}(|v| \leq 1.54).$$

When replacing the initial requirements φ_{acc} and φ_{vel} with the modified ones, the revised MPC scheme allows the vehicle to travel faster and safely complete a lane change maneuver, without risks of collision, as shown in Fig. 4b.

7.1.2 Unprotected Left Turn

In the second scenario, we would like the *ego* vehicle to perform an unprotected left turn at a signalized intersection, where the *ego* vehicle has a green light and is supposed to yield to oncoming traffic, represented by the yellow cars crossing the intersection in Fig. 5. The environment vehicles are initialized at the states $x_0^{\text{Car 1}} = [-0.2 \; 0.7 \; -\frac{\pi}{2} \; 0.5]^\top$ and $x_0^{\text{Car 2}} = [-0.2 \; 1.5 \; -\frac{\pi}{2} \; 0.5]^\top$, while the *ego* vehicle is

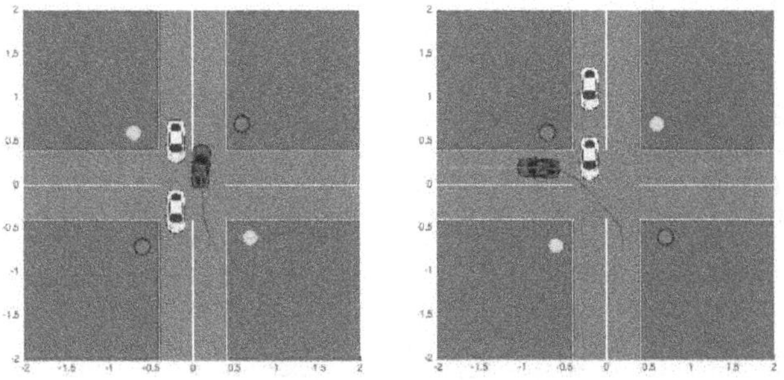

(a) (b)

Figure 5: Left turn becomes infeasible at time $t = 2.1$ s in (a) and is repaired in (b).

=

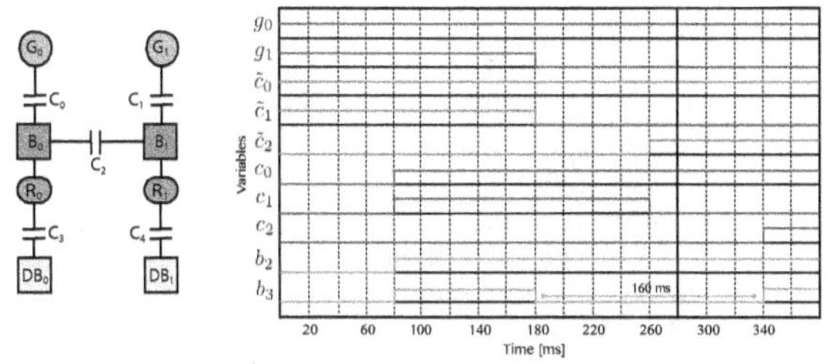

Figure 6: Simplified model of an aircraft electric power system (left) and counterexample trajectory (right). The blue, green and red lines represent environment, state, and controller variables, respectively, for a 380-ms run.

initialized at $x_0^{\text{ego}} = [0.2 \; -0.7 \; \frac{\pi}{2} \; 0]^\top$. The control input for each vehicle is initialized at $[0 \; 0]^\top$. Moreover, we use the same bounds as in (22).

The MPC scheme becomes infeasible at $t = 2.1$ s. The solver takes 5 s, out of which 2.2 s are used to generate the IISs, including 56 constraints. As shown in Fig. 5a, the *ego* vehicle yields in the middle of intersection for the oncoming traffic to pass. However, the traffic signal turns red in the meanwhile, and there is no feasible control input for the *ego* vehicle without breaking the traffic light rules. Since we do not allow modifications to the traffic light rules, the original specification is repaired again by increasing the bounds on acceleration and velocity, thus obtaining:

$$\varphi_{\text{acc}}^{\text{new}} = \mathbf{G}_{[0,\infty)}\big(|u_2| \leq 11.903\big), \quad \varphi_{\text{vel}}^{\text{new}} = \mathbf{G}_{[0,\infty)}\big(|v| \leq 2.42\big).$$

As shown by the trajectory in Fig. 5b, under the assumptions and initial conditions of our scenario, higher allowed velocity and acceleration make the *ego* vehicle turn before the oncoming cars get close or cross the intersection.

7.2 Aircraft Electric Power System

Fig. 6 shows a simplified architecture for the primary power distribution system in a passenger aircraft [20]. Two power sources, the left and right generators G_0 and G_1, deliver power to a set of high-voltage AC and DC buses (B_0, B_1, DB_0, and DB_1) and their loads. AC power from the generators is converted to DC power by rectifier units (R_1 and R_2). A bus power control unit (controller) monitors the availability of power sources and configures a set of electromechanical switches, denoted as contactors ($C_0, \ldots, C_4$), such that essential buses remain powered even in the presence of failures, while satisfying a set of safety, reliability, and real-time performance requirements [20]. Specifically, we assume that only the right DC bus DB_1 is essential, and use our algorithms to check the feasibility of a controller that accommodates a failure in the right generator G_1, by rerouting power from the left generator to the right DC bus in a time interval which is less than or equal to $t_{\max} = 100$ ms. In addition, the controller must satisfy the following set of requirements, all captured by an STL contract.

Assumptions. *When a contactor receives an open (close) signal, it shall become open (closed) in 80 ms or less.* Let the time discretization step $\Delta t = 20$ ms, $\tilde{c}_i$, $i \in \{0, \ldots, 4\}$ be a set of Boolean variables describing the controller signal (where 1 (0) stands for "closed" ("open")), c_i be a set of Boolean variables denoting the state of the contactors. The system assumptions are a conjunction of formulas of the form: $\mathbf{G}_{[0,\infty)}(\tilde{c}_i \rightarrow \mathbf{F}_{[0,4]} c_i)$, providing a model for the discrete-time binary-valued contactor states. The actual delay of each contactor is modeled using an integer (environment) variable k_i for which we require: $\mathbf{G}_{[0,\infty)}(0 \leq k_i \leq 4)$.

Guarantees. *If a generator becomes unavailable (fails), the controller shall disconnect it from the power network in 20 ms or less.* Let g_0 and g_1 be Boolean environment variables representing the state of the generators, where 1 (0) stands for "available" ("failure"). We encode the above guarantees as $\mathbf{G}_{[0,\infty)}(g_i \rightarrow \mathbf{F}_{[0,1]}\tilde{c}_i)$. *A DC bus shall never be disconnected from an AC generator for 100 ms or more,* i.e., $\mathbf{G}_{[0,\infty)}(\neg b_i \rightarrow \mathbf{F}_{[0,5]} b_i)$, where b_i, $i \in \{0, \ldots, 3\}$ is a set of Boolean variables denoting the status of a bus, where 1 (0) stands for "powered" ("unpowered"). Additional guarantees expressed as STL formulas, include: (i) If both AC generators are available, the left (right) AC generator shall power the left (right) AC bus. C_3 and C_4 shall be closed. (ii) If only one generator is available, all buses shall be connected to it. (iii) Two generators must never be directly connected.

We apply the diagnosis and repair procedure in Sec. 6.2 to investigate if there exists a control strategy that satisfies the specification above over all possible values of contactor delays. Fig. 6 shows the controller is unrealizable; a trace of contactor delays equal to 4 at all times provides a counterexample, which leaves DB_1 unpowered for 160 ms, exceeding the maximum allowed delay of 100 ms. In fact, the controller cannot close C_2 until C_1 is tested as being open, to ensure that G_1 is safely isolated from G_2. To guarantee realizability, Alg. 4 suggests to modify our assumptions to $\mathbf{G}_{[0,\infty)}(0 \leq k_i \leq 2)$ for $i \in \{0, \ldots, 4\}$. Alternatively, by interpreting the provided counterexamples, it is possible to relax the guarantee on DB_1 to $\mathbf{G}_{[0,\infty)}(\neg b_3 \rightarrow \mathbf{F}_{[0,8]} b_3)$. The execution time was 326 s, which includes formulating and executing 3 CEGIS loops, requiring 6 optimization problems.

8. CONCLUSION

We presented a set of algorithms for diagnosis and repair of STL specifications in the setting of controller synthesis for hybrid systems using a mixed integer programming approach. Given an unrealizable specification, our algorithms detect possible reasons for infeasibility and suggest repairs to make it realizable. We showed the effectiveness of our approach on the synthesis of controllers for several applications. As future work, we plan to investigate techniques that better leverage the structure of the STL formulas, handle a broader range of environment assumptions, and apply to the control of human-in-the-loop systems as explored in [14].

9. ACKNOWLEDGMENTS

This work was partially supported by IBM and United Technologies Corporation via the iCyPhy consortium, TerraSwarm, one of six centers of STARnet, a Semiconductor Research Corporation program sponsored by MARCO, DARPA, NSF grants CCF-1139138 and CCF-1116993, and NDSEG Fellowship.

10. REFERENCES

[1] Gurobi Optimizer. [Online]: http://www.gurobi.com/.

[2] R. Alur, S. Moarref, and U. Topcu. Counter-strategy guided refinement of GR(1) temporal logic specifications. In *Formal Methods in Computer-Aided Design*, 2013.

[3] A. Bemporad and M. Morari. Control of systems integrating logic, dynamics, and constraints. *Automatica*, 35, 1999.

[4] A. Bemporad and M. Morari. Robust model predictive control: A survey. In *Robustness in identification and control*, pages 207–226. Springer, 1999.

[5] J. W. Chinneck and E. W. Dravnieks. Locating minimal infeasible constraint sets in linear programs. *ORSA Journal on Computing*, 3(2):157–168, 1991.

[6] A. Donzé, T. Ferrère, and O. Maler. Efficient robust monitoring for STL. In *Computer Aided Verification*, 2013.

[7] A. Donzé and O. Maler. Robust satisfaction of temporal logic over real-valued signals. In *FORMATS*, 2010.

[8] A. Donzé, O. Maler, E. Bartocci, D. Nickovic, R. Grosu, and S. Smolka. On temporal logic and signal processing. In *Automated Technology for Verification and Analysis*. 2012.

[9] T. Ferrère, O. Maler, and D. Nickovic. Trace diagnostics using temporal implicants. In *Proc. Int. Symp. Automated Technology for Verification and Analysis*, 2015.

[10] C. E. Garcia, D. M. Prett, and M. Morari. Model predictive control: theory and practice–a survey. *Automatica*, 25, 1989.

[11] S. Ghosh, D. Sadigh, P. Nuzzo, V. Raman, A. Donze, A. Sangiovanni-Vincentelli, S. Sastry, and A. Seshia. Diagnosis and repair for synthesis from signal temporal logic specifications. http://arxiv.org/abs/1602.01883, Feb 2016.

[12] E. C. Kerrigan and J. M. Maciejowski. Soft constraints and exact penalty functions in model predictive control. In *Control 2000 Conference, Cambridge*, 2000.

[13] W. Li, L. Dworkin, and S. A. Seshia. Mining assumptions for synthesis. In *ACM/IEEE Int. Conf. Formal Methods and Models for Codesign*, 2011.

[14] W. Li, D. Sadigh, S. S. Sastry, and S. A. Seshia. Synthesis for human-in-the-loop control systems. In *TACAS*. 2014.

[15] J. Löfberg. Yalmip: A toolbox for modeling and optimization in MATLAB. In *Proceedings of the CACSD Conference*, Taipei, Taiwan, 2004.

[16] O. Maler and D. Nickovic. Monitoring temporal properties of continuous signals. In *Formal Techniques, Modelling and Analysis of Timed and Fault-Tolerant Systems*. 2004.

[17] M. Morari, C. Garcia, J. Lee, and D. Prett. *Model predictive control*. Prentice Hall Englewood Cliffs, NJ, 1993.

[18] P. Nuzzo, A. Puggelli, S. A. Seshia, and A. L. Sangiovanni-Vincentelli. CalCS: SMT solving for non-linear convex constraints. In *IEEE Int. Conf. Formal Methods in Computer-Aided Design*, 2010.

[19] P. Nuzzo, A. Sangiovanni-Vincentelli, D. Bresolin, L. Geretti, and T. Villa. A platform-based design methodology with contracts and related tools for the design of cyber-physical systems. *Proc. IEEE*, 103(11), Nov. 2015.

[20] P. Nuzzo, H. Xu, N. Ozay, J. Finn, A. Sangiovanni-Vincentelli, R. Murray, A. Donzé, and S. Seshia. A contract-based methodology for aircraft electric power system design. *IEEE Access*, 2:1–25, 2014.

[21] V. Raman, A. Donzé, D. Sadigh, R. M. Murray, and S. A. Seshia. Reactive synthesis from signal temporal logic specifications. In *Proc. Int. Conf. Hybrid Systems: Computation and Control*, 2015.

[22] V. Raman and H. Kress-Gazit. Explaining impossible high-level robot behaviors. *IEEE Trans. Robotics*, 29, 2013.

[23] V. Raman, M. Maasoumy, A. Donzé, R. M. Murray, A. Sangiovanni-Vincentelli, and S. A. Seshia. Model predictive control with signal temporal logic specifications. In *IEEE Conf. on Decision and Control*, 2014.

[24] V. Schuppan. Towards a notion of unsatisfiable cores for LTL. In *Fundamentals of Software Engineering*, 2009.

[25] P. O. Scokaert and J. B. Rawlings. Feasibility issues in linear model predictive control. *AIChE Journal*, 45(8):1649–1659, 1999.

Computing the Domain of Attraction of Switching Systems Subject to Non-Convex Constraints*

Nikolaos Athanasopoulos
ICTEAM Institute,
Université Catholique de Louvain
4 Avenue Georges Lemaitre,
nikolaos.athanasopoulos@uclouvain.com

Raphaël M. Jungers†
ICTEAM Institute,
Université Catholique de Louvain
4 Avenue Georges Lemaitre,
raphael.jungers@uclouvain.com

ABSTRACT

We characterize and compute the maximal admissible positively invariant set for asymptotically stable constrained switching linear systems. Motivated by practical problems found, e.g., in obstacle avoidance, power electronics and nonlinear switching systems, in our setting the constraint set is formed by a finite number of polynomial inequalities. First, we observe that the so-called Veronese lifting allows to represent the constraint set as a polyhedral set. Next, by exploiting the fact that the lifted system dynamics remains linear, we establish a method based on reachability computations to characterize and compute the maximal admissible invariant set, which coincides with the domain of attraction when the system is asymptotically stable. After developing the necessary theoretical background, we propose algorithmic procedures for its exact computation, based on linear or semidefinite programs. The approach is illustrated in several numerical examples.

Keywords

semi-algebraic constraints, switching linear systems, domain of attraction, maximal admissible invariant set, algorithms

1. INTRODUCTION

When a set $\mathcal{S} \subset \mathbb{R}^n$ is invariant[1] with respect to a system, all trajectories starting from $\mathcal{S}$ remain in it forever. Since almost every system in practice is subject to some type of constraints on its states or outputs, the notion of invariance becomes extremely relevant in control applications [9]. Specifically, problems related to safety and viability [3] can be addressed by computing sets which possess the invariance property or a variant of it.

*Research supported by the Belgian Interuniversity Attraction Poles, and by the ARC grant 13/18-054 from Communauté francaise de Belgique - Actions de Recherche Concertées.

†R. M. Jungers is a F.R.S.-FNRS Research Associate.

[1]Throughout the paper and for simplicity, we use the terminology 'invariant set' for the concept which is usually referred to as 'positively invariant set' [9].

HSCC'16, April 12 - 14, 2016, Vienna, Austria

ISBN 978-1-4503-3955-1/16/04...$15.00

DOI: http://dx.doi.org/10.1145/2883817.2883823

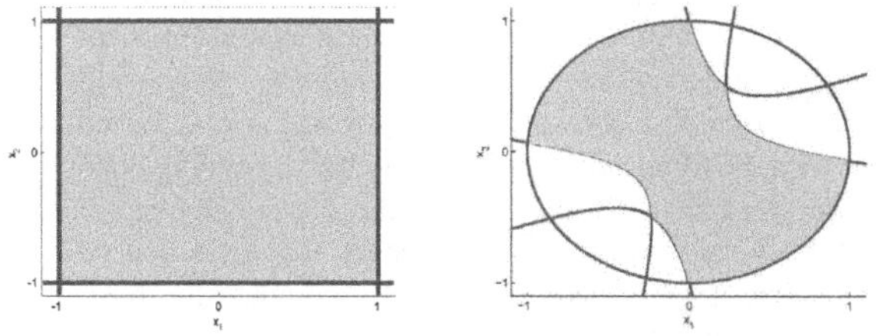

(a) Polytopic set (b) Semi-algebraic set

Figure 1: State constraint sets.

For linear switching systems, there are at least two approaches one can follow to compute invariant sets, namely use dynamic programming or find a Lyapunov function and utilise its sub-level sets [23]. The mechanism behind the first approach consists in iteratively computing elements of a convergent set sequence generated from the pre-image map, starting from an appropriately chosen initial set, [10, Ch. 5], [2,6,16,17]. The second approach consists in first characterizing non-conservative families of candidate Lyapunov functions and (hopefully) in developing a computational methodology for solving the corresponding conditions. For linear switching systems, polytopic [26], piecewise quadratic [20,21] and sum of squares (sos) polynomial functions [22,30] have been identified as universal, while efficient algorithmic procedures have been established using linear or semidefinite programming [13,28].

Apart from few exceptions that include the sub-level sets of min-of-quadratics and sos Lyapunov functions, the available constructions concern invariant sets which are convex. This is not restrictive for the stability analysis problem. Moreover, convex shapes recover the maximal invariant set for systems under polytopic constraints such as in Figure 1(a), since the convex hull of any invariant set preserves invariance.

Nevertheless, the use of convex invariant sets or Lyapunov functions is restrictive in the setting studied in this paper. Indeed, when the constraint set is semi-algebraic, as for example in Figure 1(b), the maximal invariant set does not need to be convex. Furthermore, modifying the standard approaches in order to deal with the non-convex case is not straightforward; it is neither clear how to handle non-polytopic sets efficiently in dynamic programming nor how to identify and optimize over families of Lyapunov functions which capture exactly the maximal invariant set. Additional to the theoretical challenge, the practical motivation for dealing with systems under semi-algebraic constraints comes from a variety of applications found for example in the path planning and obstacle avoidance [5], in power electronics and in non-linear switching systems [1].

In this paper we solve both the problems of characterizing the maximal invariant set and of computing it efficiently. A first helpful observation towards achieving this goal is that semi-algebraic sets are represented by polyhedra in the lifted space induced by the Veronese embedding. Roughly, the Veronese embedding is a nonlinear mapping of a vector $x \in \mathbb{R}^n$ to a higher dimensional space $\mathbb{R}^N$ defined by the monomials $x^\alpha = [x^{\alpha_1} \quad x^{\alpha_2} \dots x^{\alpha_N}]^\top$ that are of order d, where $\alpha_i \in \mathbb{N}^n$ stands for the n-tuples that sum up to d and construct each monomial. This lifting technique has been used with success in the past, see e.g., [29, 38], to deal with problems related to stability analysis and approximation of the joint spectral radius of switching systems.

The lifted system enjoys the same stability property with the original system, and more importantly, it remains a switching linear system. Taking this into account, we are able to establish a relationship between invariant sets in the lifted and original state space. Additionally, we characterize the maximal invariant set by applying a variant of the *backward reachability algorithm* [3, 10] in the lifted space. The corresponding set sequence may be initialized either with the lifted constraint set or with the, possibly unbounded, polyhedral set that is induced from the semi-algebraic constraint set. We address two specific challenges that arise depending on each choice, namely how to efficiently compute the reachability mapping in the former case and how to guarantee convergence in the latter case. We show that the maximal admissible invariant set is well-defined, it can be computed in a finite number of steps and it is expressed as the unit sub-level set of a max-polynomial function consisting of a finite number of pieces. To this end, we establish three possible algorithmic implementations for computing the maximal invariant set based on linear or semidefinite programs. To the best of our knowledge, this is the first time that the exact computation of the domain of attraction under non-convex constraints is possible.

Finally, it is worth to distinguish between the different research objectives set in this work from the ones found in the sos framework, see for example [27], where more complex dynamics and constraints are studied. The problem studied there concerns the assessment of local asymptotic stability in the neighborhood of the equilibrium point, however, no guarantee on the level of the approximation of the domain of attraction is sought or provided. Another distinction should be made with the work in [1], where the focus is restricted to computing convex invariant approximations of the domain of attraction.

In section 2, the basic definitions and the problem setting are presented, together with the technical details regarding the procedure of lifting the system and the constraint set. In section 3, we characterize the maximal admissible invariant set by first associating the invariance properties of sets in the lifted and original space and next by applying a modified version of the backward reachability algorithm. The corresponding algorithms are presented in section 4. In section 5 two numerical examples are presented, whereas conclusions are drawn in section 6. Finally, further details concerning the algorithmic implementation of the results are exposed in the Appendix.

2. PRELIMINARIES

We denote the field of real numbers and the set of non-negative integers with $\mathbb{R}$ and $\mathbb{N}$ respectively. We write vectors x, y with small letters and sets $\mathcal{S}, \mathcal{X}, \mathcal{V}$ with capital letters in italics. The vector in $\mathbb{R}^n$ with all elements equal to one is denoted by 1_n. For matrices and vectors, inequalities hold component-wise.

2.1 Setting and problem formulation

Let $\mathcal{A} := \{A_1, ..., A_M\} \subset \mathbb{R}^{n\times n}$ be a set consisting of M matrices. The system under study is

$$x(t+1) = A_{\sigma(t)}x(t), \tag{2.1}$$

where $x(0) \in \mathbb{R}^n$, $t \in \mathbb{N}$ and the switching signal $\sigma(\cdot) : \mathbb{N} \to \{1, ..., M\}$ assigns at each time instant a matrix from the set $\mathcal{A}$. The System (2.1) is subject to state constraints

$$x(t) \in \mathcal{X}, \quad t \geq 0. \tag{2.2}$$

The state constraint set is of the form

$$\mathcal{X} := \{x \in \mathbb{R}^n : c_i(x) \leq 1, i = 1, ..., p\}, \tag{2.3}$$

where $c_i(\cdot) : \mathbb{R}^n \to \mathbb{R}$, $i = 1, .., p$, are polynomials of maximum degree $d \geq 1$. We are interested in characterizing the domain of attraction for the linear switching System (2.1) subject to constraints (2.2). Throughout the paper, we make the following assumptions.

ASSUMPTION 1. *The System* (2.1) *is asymptotically stable.*

ASSUMPTION 2. *The set* $\mathcal{X} \subset \mathbb{R}^n$ (2.3) *is closed, bounded and contains the origin in its interior.*

Assumption 1 does not affect the generality of the problem since we are interested in computing non-trivial domains of attraction for the switching linear System (2.1). Moreover, under Assumptions 1 and 2, the admissible domain of attraction coincides with the maximal admissible invariant set. The assumption that the origin is in the interior of the constraint set $\mathcal{X}$ in Assumption 2 is a technical one, and it is required in the proofs of Theorems 1-3. It is worth mentioning that this assumption is taken in the standard problem of computing the maximal admissible invariant set for linear switching systems under polytopic constraints [10], while its removal, even when the constraint set is a polyhedron is still being investigated, see e.g., [8].

DEFINITION 1. *A set* $\mathcal{S} \subset \mathbb{R}^n$ *is called* invariant *with respect to the System* (2.1) *if* $x(0) \in \mathcal{S}$ *implies* $x(t) \in \mathcal{S}$ *for all* $t \in \mathbb{N}$ *and any switching signal* $\sigma(\cdot) : \mathbb{N} \to \{1, ..., M\}$. *Moreover, if* $\mathcal{S} \subseteq \mathcal{X}$, *the set* $\mathcal{S}$ *is called an* admissible invariant set *with respect to the System* (2.1) *and the constraints* (2.2).

DEFINITION 2. *The set* $\mathcal{M} \subset \mathbb{R}^n$ *is called the* maximal admissible invariant set *with respect to the System* (2.1) *and the constraints* (2.2) *if it is admissible invariant, and, moreover, for any admissible invariant set* $\mathcal{S} \subseteq \mathcal{X}$, *it holds that* $\mathcal{S} \subseteq \mathcal{M}$.

Thus, the problem investigated in this paper is naturally formulated as follows: Suppose that Assumptions 1 and 2 hold. Compute the maximal admissible invariant set with respect to the System (2.1) and the state constraints (2.2).

2.2 Lifting the system

We now describe formally the algebraic lifting applied to System (2.1), resulting in a dynamical system which enjoys the same stability properties. The broad idea is to construct monomials of x of a certain maximum degree d and infer properties of our dynamical system from the one obtained after this state-space transformation. To this end, given a n-tuple $\alpha \in \mathbb{N}^n$, the α monomial of a vector $x \in \mathbb{R}^n$ is $x^\alpha = x_1^{\alpha_1} \dots x_n^{\alpha_n}$. The degree of the monomial is $d = \sum_{i=1}^n \alpha_i$. We denote by $\alpha!$ the multinomial coefficient $\alpha! = \frac{d!}{\alpha_1! \dots \alpha_n!}$.

DEFINITION 3. [29], [22]. *Given a vector $x \in \mathbb{R}^n$ and an integer $d \geq 1$, the d-lift of x, denoted by $x^{[d]}$, is the vector in $\mathbb{R}^{\binom{n+d-1}{d}}$, having as elements all the exponents α of degree d, i.e,.*

$$x_\alpha = \sqrt{\alpha!}x^\alpha.$$

DEFINITION 4. [29], [22]. *Given $\mathcal{A} \subset \mathbb{R}^{n\times n}$ and an integer $d \geq 1$, the d-lift of the set $\mathcal{A}$ is $\mathcal{A}^{[d]} := \{A_1^{[d]}, \ldots A_M^{[d]}\} \subset \mathbb{R}^{\binom{n+d-1}{d}\times\binom{n+d-1}{d}}$ where each matrix $A_i^{[d]}$, $i = 1, ..., M$, is associated to the linear map[2] $A_i^{[d]} : x^{[d]} \to (A_i x)^{[d]}$.*

In what follows, we define a natural extension of the d-lift which is generated by stacking the l-lifts of a vector, for a set of integers l, in a single augmented vector. To this end, let us consider the ordered set of integers $\mathcal{L} := \{l_1, l_2, ..., l_K\}$, $l_i \in [1, d]$, $i \in [1, K]$, where $K \leq d$.

DEFINITION 5. *Given an integer $d \geq 1$, the set $\mathcal{L} := \{l_1, ..., l_K\}$, $K \leq d$ and a vector $x \in \mathbb{R}^n$, the $\mathcal{L}$-lift of x, denoted by $x^{[\mathcal{L}]} \in \mathbb{R}^N$, $N = \sum_{l_i \in \mathcal{L}} \binom{n+l_i-1}{l_i}$ is*

$$x^{[\mathcal{L}]} := \left[x^{[l_1]\top} \quad x^{[l_2]\top} \ldots x^{[l_K]\top}\right]^\top.$$

Similarly, the $\mathcal{L}$-lift of the set $\mathcal{A}$ is $\mathcal{A}^{[\mathcal{L}]} := \{A_1^{[\mathcal{L}]}, \cdots, A_M^{[\mathcal{L}]}\} \subset \mathbb{R}^{N\times N}$, where

$$A_i^{[\mathcal{L}]} := \mathrm{diag}(A_i^{[l_1]}, \ldots, A_i^{[l_K]}), \quad i = 1, ..., M.$$

We define the $\mathcal{L}$-lifted system

$$y(t+1) = A_{\sigma(t)}^{[\mathcal{L}]} y(t), \tag{2.4}$$

where $y_0 \in \mathbb{R}^N$, $N = \sum_{i=1}^K \binom{n+l_i-1}{l_i}$, $t \in \mathbb{N}$ and $\sigma(\cdot) : \mathbb{N} \to \{1, ..., M\}$ is the switching signal. System (2.4) can simply be considered to be generated by stacking the $[l_i]$-lifts of (2.1) for all $i \in [1, K]$. The properties below follow from the definition of the d-lift.

FACT 1. *Consider an integer $d \geq 1$, the ordered set of integers $\mathcal{L} = \{l_1, ..., l_K\}$, $l_i \in [1, d]$, $K \leq d$ and a matrix $A \in \mathbb{R}^{n\times n}$. Then, for any $x \in \mathbb{R}^n$, it holds that*

$$(Ax)^{[d]} = A^{[d]}x^{[d]},$$
$$(Ax)^{[\mathcal{L}]} = A^{[\mathcal{L}]}x^{[\mathcal{L}]}.$$

We make use of the following notion, which formalizes the stability notion for a linear switching system.

DEFINITION 6. [33], [22]. *The joint spectral radius of a matrix set $\mathcal{A} \subset \mathbb{R}^{n\times n}$ is equal to*

$$\rho(\mathcal{A}) := \lim_{t\to\infty} \max\{\|A\|^{\frac{1}{t}} : A \in \mathcal{A}^t\}. \tag{2.5}$$

The switching System (2.1) is asymptotically stable if and only if $\rho(\mathcal{A}) < 1$ [22].

[2]One can obtain a numerical expression of the entries of $A^{[d]}$ with the formula $A_{\alpha\beta}^{[d]} = \frac{\mathrm{per}(A(\alpha,\beta))}{\sqrt{\mu(\alpha)\mu(\beta)}}$, where $\mu(\alpha)$ is the product of the factorials of the entries of α, the matrix $\overline{A} = A(\alpha, \beta) \in \mathbb{R}^{n\times n}$ has elements $\overline{a}_{ij} := a_{\alpha_i\beta_j}$, $i \in [1, n]$, $j \in [1, m]$ and $\mathrm{per}(A) = \sum_{\pi\in S_n} \cdot \prod_{i=1}^n a_{i,\pi(i)}$ is the permanent of a matrix $A \in \mathbb{R}^{n\times n}$, where S_n is the symmetric group on n elements.

PROPOSITION 1. *The System (2.1) is globally absolutely exponentially stable (GAES) if and only if the System (2.4) is globally absolutely exponentially stable.*

PROOF. For any $j \geq 1$, it holds that $\rho(\mathcal{A})^j = \rho(\mathcal{A}^{[j]})$ [12]. Moreover, since the matrices $\mathcal{A}^{[l_i]}$ are block diagonal, $i \in [1, K]$, it holds [22]

$$\rho(\mathcal{A}^{[\mathcal{L}]}) = \max_{i\in[1,K]}\{\rho(\mathcal{A}^{[l_i]})\} = \max_{i\in[1,K]}\{\rho^{l_i}(\mathcal{A})\}.$$

Consequently, $\rho(\mathcal{A}) < 1$ if and only if $\rho(\mathcal{A}^{[\mathcal{L}]}) < 1$. We finish the proof by recalling the equivalence between asymptotic and exponential stability for homogeneous systems, see e.g., [24, Corollary V.3], of which switching linear systems are a subclass, and that the switching System (2.1) is GAES if and only if $\rho(\mathcal{A}) < 1$ [22]. □

RUNNING EXAMPLE PART 1. *Let us consider a two-dimensional system (2.1) consisting of two modes, i.e., $\mathcal{A} := \{A_1, A_2\}$, with $A_1 = \begin{bmatrix} 1.0425 & 0.3416 \\ -0.5893 & 0.5839 \end{bmatrix}$, $A_2 = \begin{bmatrix} 0 & 0.6500 \\ 0.6500 & 0 \end{bmatrix}$. Let $\mathcal{L} = \{2\}$. Following Definition 5, the $\mathcal{L}$-lift of x is*

$$x^{[\mathcal{L}]} = x^{[2]} = [x_2^2 \quad \sqrt{2}x_2x_1 \quad x_1^2]^\top,$$

while $\mathcal{A}^{[\mathcal{L}]} = \{A_1^{[2]}, A_2^{[2]}\}$, with (rounded up to the second digit)

$$A_1^{[2]} = \begin{bmatrix} 0.34 & -0.49 & 0.35 \\ 0.28 & 0.40 & -0.87 \\ 0.12 & 0.50 & 1.09 \end{bmatrix}, A_2^{[2]} = \begin{bmatrix} 0 & 0 & 0.42 \\ 0 & 0.42 & 0 \\ 0.42 & 0 & 0 \end{bmatrix}.$$

Using the JSR Toolbox [37], we calculate the joint spectral radius of the matrix set $\mathcal{A}$ to be to 0.9 with accuracy $9\cdot 10^{-8}$, thus the system (2.1) is asymptotically stable. As expected from Proposition 1, the joint spectral radius of the set $\mathcal{A}^{[2]}$ is found equal to 0.81 with accuracy $7.64 \cdot 10^{-7}$, thus the system (2.4) is also asymptotically stable.

2.3 Lifting the constraints

We consider the set $\mathcal{X}$ (2.3) and denote with $\mathcal{L}_i \subseteq [1, d]^{K_i}$, $i \in [1, p]$, $K_i \leq d$ the index sets that correspond to the degrees of all monomials appearing in each function $c_i(x)$. Also, we let $\mathcal{L} \subseteq [1, d]^d$ contain all the elements of the index sets $\mathcal{L}_i$, $i = 1, ..., p$. We can write each polynomial function $c_i(x)$, $i \in [1, p]$, as a sum of positively homogeneous polynomials $c_{i,l}(x)$ of degree $l \in \mathcal{L}$, i.e.,

$$c_i(x) = \sum_{l\in\mathcal{L}_i} c_{i,l}(x).$$

In addition, we can express each homogeneous polynomial $c_{i,l}(x)$, $i \in [1, p]$, $l \in \mathcal{L}_i$, as a linear function of the $\mathcal{L}$-lifted vectors $x^{[j]}$, $j \in \mathcal{L}$ as follows

$$c_i(x) := \sum_{l\in\mathcal{L}_i} g_{i,l}^\top x^{[l]} = g_i^\top x^{[\mathcal{L}]}, \quad i \in [1, p], \tag{2.6}$$

where $g_{i,l}^\top x^{[l]} := c_{i,l}(x)$, $l \in \mathcal{L}_i$. Also, we have that $g_i := [g_{i,l_1}^\top \quad \cdots \quad g_{i,l_K}^\top]^\top$, $g_i \in \mathbb{R}^N$, $i = 1, .., p$, where

$$N := \sum_{l\in\mathcal{L}} \binom{n+l-1}{l}. \tag{2.7}$$

We are in a position to define the $\mathcal{L}$-lift of a set $\mathcal{S} \subset \mathbb{R}^n$.

DEFINITION 7. *Consider the set $\mathcal{X} \subset \mathbb{R}^n$ (2.3) that satisfies Assumption 2. Let $\mathcal{L} \subset [1, d]^K$, be the ordered set of integers containing the degrees of all monomials appearing in $c_i(x)$, $i \in$*

$[1,p]$, *and* $g_{i,l}$, $i \in [1,p]$, $l \in \mathcal{L}$ *be vectors satisfying* (2.6). *We define the* $\mathcal{L}$*-lift of the set* $\mathcal{X}$ *as* $\mathcal{X}^{[\mathcal{L}]} \subset \mathbb{R}^N$, *where* N *is given in* (2.7), *as*

$$\mathcal{X}^{[\mathcal{L}]} := \left\{ y \in \mathbb{R}^N : g_i^\top y \le 1, i = 1, ..., p \right\}. \tag{2.8}$$

Moreover, we define the manifold $\mathcal{V} \subset \mathbb{R}^N$ which is an algebraic variety,

$$\mathcal{V} := \left\{ y \in \mathbb{R}^N : \left(\exists x \in \mathbb{R}^n : y = x^{[\mathcal{L}]} \right) \right\}. \tag{2.9}$$

Taking into account Fact 1, we can show that the set $\mathcal{V}$ (2.9) is invariant with respect to the lifted System (2.4).

RUNNING EXAMPLE PART 2. *Let us consider as constraint set* $\mathcal{X}$ (2.3) *the set depicted in Figure 1(b). For this case, the polynomials* $c_i(x)$, $i = 1, 2, 3$ *that define the set are*

$$c_1(x) = x_1^2 + x_2^2,$$
$$c_2(x) = x_2^2 + 6\sqrt{2}x_1x_2 - 4x_1^2,$$
$$c_3(x) = -3x_2^2 + 10\sqrt{2}x_1x_2 + 2x_1^2.$$

We have $\mathcal{L} = \mathcal{L}_1 = \mathcal{L}_2 = \mathcal{L}_3 = \{2\}$, *and consequently,* $\mathcal{X}^{[\mathcal{L}]} \in \mathbb{R}^3$ *is given by* (2.8), *with* $g_1 = [1 \quad 0 \quad 1]^\top$, $g_2 = [1 \quad 6 \quad -4]^\top$, $g_3 = [-3 \quad 10 \quad 2]^\top$. *The set* $\mathcal{X}^{[2]}$ *is an unbounded polyhedron and its defining hyperplanes are depicted in Figure 2 in red. The set* $\mathcal{V} \cap \mathcal{X}^{[2]}$, *i.e., the intersection of the algebraic variety* $\mathcal{V}$ *with the* $\mathcal{L}$*-lift of the constraint set* $\mathcal{X}^{[2]}$, *or in other words the lifted constraint set* $\mathcal{V} \cap \mathcal{X}^{[2]}$, *is also shown in Figure 2 in grey.*

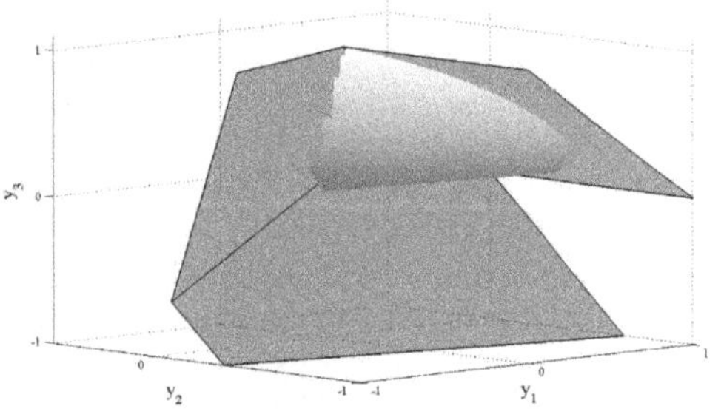

Figure 2: The lifted semi-algebraic set $\mathcal{X}^{[2]} \cap \mathcal{V}$ of Figure 1(b) is depicted in grey. The constraint set is bounded tightly by the polyhedron $\mathcal{X}^{[2]}$, defined by the intersection of three half-spaces and shown in red.

3. CHARACTERIZATION OF THE MAXIMAL ADMISSIBLE INVARIANT SET

The set $\mathcal{X}$ (2.3) is invariant with respect to the System (2.1) if and only if

$$\forall x \in \mathbb{R}^n, \forall j \in [1, M],$$
$$(\forall i \in [1,p], c_i(x) \le 1) \Rightarrow (\forall i \in [1,p], c_i(A_j x) \le 1).$$

If $c_i(\cdot)$, $i \in [1,p]$, are linear functions, it is well known that invariance can be verified by solving a linear program [7]. If the functions $c_i(x)$, $i \in [1,p]$, are positive definite quadratic functions, then invariance can be verified by solving a convex quadratic program [25]. In comparison, in this paper we aim to find a way to verify and compute invariant sets when the functions $c_i(\cdot)$, $i \in [1,p]$, are general polynomial functions.

In what follows we show that the projection of an admissible invariant set $\mathcal{S} \subseteq \mathcal{X}^{[\mathcal{L}]}$ of the $\mathcal{L}$-lifted system on $\mathbb{R}^n$ is invariant for the system under study. To this end, we define the "reverse" operation of lifting.

DEFINITION 8. *Given an index set* $\mathcal{L} \subseteq [1,d]^d$, *and a set in the* $\mathcal{L}$*-lifted space* $\mathcal{S} \subseteq \mathbb{R}^N$, $N = \sum_{l \in \mathcal{L}} \binom{n+l-1}{l}$, *the lowering operation of* $\mathcal{S}$ *to* $\mathbb{R}^n$ *is*

$$\text{lower}(\mathcal{S}) := \left\{ x \in \mathbb{R}^n : \left(\exists y \in \mathcal{S} : y = x^{[\mathcal{L}]} \right) \right\}.$$

Taking into account (2.9), it is not difficult to see that the relation

$$\text{lower}(\mathcal{S}) = \text{lower}(\mathcal{S} \cap \mathcal{V})$$

holds for any set $\mathcal{S} \subset \mathbb{R}^N$.

PROPOSITION 2. *Consider the System* (2.1) *and the constraint set* (2.3). *If* $\mathcal{S} \subseteq \mathcal{X}^{[\mathcal{L}]} \subset \mathbb{R}^N$,

$$\mathcal{S} := \{ y \in \mathbb{R}^N : f_i^\top y \le 1, i = 1, ..., q \}, \tag{3.1}$$

where $N = \sum_{l \in \mathcal{L}} \binom{n+l-1}{l}$, $f_i \in \mathbb{R}^N$, $i \in [1,q]$, *is an admissible invariant set with respect to System* (2.4) *and the constraint set* $\mathcal{X}^{[\mathcal{L}]}$ (2.8) *then the set* lower$(\mathcal{S})$ *is an admissible invariant set with respect to System* (2.1) *and the constraint set* (2.3).

PROOF. Since $\mathcal{S} \subseteq \mathcal{X}^{[\mathcal{L}]}$, it follows that $\mathcal{S} \cap \mathcal{V} \subseteq \mathcal{X}^{[\mathcal{L}]} \cap \mathcal{V}$, and consequently, lower$(\mathcal{S} \cap \mathcal{V}) \subseteq$ lower$(\mathcal{X}^{[\mathcal{L}]} \cap \mathcal{V}) = \mathcal{X}$. Next, we show that lower$(\mathcal{S})$ is invariant. By construction, lower$(\mathcal{S}) = \{x \in \mathbb{R}^n : b_i(x) \le 1\}$, where $b_i(x) := f_i^\top x^{[\mathcal{L}]}$, $i \in [1,q]$. From hypothesis, for all $y \in \mathcal{S}$, relation $f_i^\top y \le 1$, $i \in [1,q]$, implies $f_i^\top A_j^{[\mathcal{L}]} y \le 1$, for all $j \in [1,M]$. By definition, for any $x \in$ lower$(\mathcal{S}) \subseteq \mathcal{X}$, there exists a vector $y \in \mathcal{S} \cap \mathcal{V}$ such that $y := x^{[\mathcal{L}]}$. Thus, we have

$$f_i^\top A_j^{[\mathcal{L}]} y = f_i^\top A_j^{[\mathcal{L}]} x^{[\mathcal{L}]} = f_i^\top (A_j x)^{[\mathcal{L}]} = b_i(A_j x) \le 1.$$

Consequently, $b_i(x) \le 1$ for all $i \in [1,p]$ implies $b_i(A_j x) \le 1$ for all $i \in [1,q]$, for all $j \in [1,M]$, and the set lower$(\mathcal{S})$ is admissible invariant with respect to the System (2.1). □

REMARK 1. *It is worth underlining that the statement of Proposition 2 becomes both necessary and sufficient when* $\mathcal{S} \subseteq \mathcal{X}^{[\mathcal{L}]}$ *is any set lying on* $\mathcal{V}$, *i.e., when* $\mathcal{S} \cap \mathcal{V} = \mathcal{S}$.

REMARK 2. *The lowering operation is straightforward when* $\mathcal{S}$ *is a polyhedron* (3.1), *since in this case* lower$(\mathcal{S}) = \{x \in \mathbb{R}^n : c_i(x) \le 1, i = 1, ..., q\}$, *where* $c_i(x) = f_i^\top x^{[\mathcal{L}]}$, $i \in [1,q]$.

Proposition 2 suggests that in order to compute invariant sets for the original system and constraint set (2.3), one can first compute admissible invariant sets with respect to the $\mathcal{L}$-lifted System (2.4) and the $\mathcal{L}$-lifted constraint set (2.8) and consequently perform a projection on the original space. This observation provides a potential advantage. Indeed, since the System (2.4) is a switching linear system and $\mathcal{X}^{[\mathcal{L}]}$ (2.8) is a polyhedral set, one can apply established results for checking invariance of a given polyhedral set.

PROPOSITION 3. *Consider the System* (2.1) *and the set* $\mathcal{X}$ *defined in* (2.3). *Let* $G \in \mathbb{R}^{p \times N}$ *be the matrix having as rows the vectors* $g_i^\top$, $i \in [1,p]$ *that describe the set* $\mathcal{X}^{[\mathcal{L}]}$, *defined in* (2.8). *Then, the set* $\mathcal{X}$ *is invariant with respect to* (2.1) *if there exist non negative matrices* $H_i \in \mathbb{R}^{p \times p}$, $i \in [1,M]$, *that satisfy the relations*

$$GA_i^{[\mathcal{L}]} = H_i G, \quad i \in [1,M], \tag{3.2}$$
$$H_i 1_p \le 1_p \quad i \in [1,M], \tag{3.3}$$
$$H_i \ge 0, \quad i \in [1,M]. \tag{3.4}$$

PROOF. Conditions (3.2)-(3.4) are necessary and sufficient for the set $\mathcal{X}^{[\mathcal{L}]}$ to be invariant with respect to the System (2.4) [7], [18]. Consequently, from Proposition 2, the set $\mathcal{X} = \text{lower}(\mathcal{X}^{[\mathcal{L}]})$ is invariant with respect to the System (2.1). □

The algebraic relations (3.2)-(3.4) can be solved by linear programming. However, although these conditions are necessary and sufficient for a polyhedral set $\mathcal{X}^{[\mathcal{L}]}$ to be invariant with respect to the lifted System (2.4), they are only sufficient for $\mathcal{X}$ to be invariant w.r.t. the original System (2.1). Additionally, since it is impossible to define a polyhedron $\mathcal{X}^{[\mathcal{L}]}$ lying on the manifold $\mathcal{V}$, we cannot exploit Remark 1 to pose necessary and sufficient conditions of invariance for $\mathcal{X}$ w.r.t. (2.1) via $\mathcal{X}^{[\mathcal{L}]}$. Also, apart from the above observations, it might happen that the set $\mathcal{X}$ is not invariant and consequently the maximal admissible invariant set is a subset of $\mathcal{X}$. Thus, exploiting Proposition 3 to characterize an invariant set is limited.

RUNNING EXAMPLE PART 3. *Let us consider the lifted system and the set $\mathcal{X}^{[\mathcal{L}]}$ calculated in the previous parts of the Running Example. In order to verify if $\mathcal{X}^{[\mathcal{L}]}$ is an invariant set we utilise Proposition 3. To this end, by setting*

$$G = \begin{bmatrix} 1 & 0 & 1 \\ 1 & 6 & -4 \\ -3 & 10 & 2 \end{bmatrix},$$

constructed from the vectors g_i, $i = 1, 2, 3$, that define the set $\mathcal{X}^{[\mathcal{L}]}$, we solve the optimization problem

$$\min_{\varepsilon, H_1, H_2} \varepsilon$$

subject to (3.2),(3.4) *and inequalities $H_1 1_3 \leq \varepsilon 1_3$, $H_2 1_3 \leq \varepsilon 1_3$, The optimization problem is infeasible, thus, the set $\mathcal{X}^{[\mathcal{L}]}$ is not invariant with respect to* (2.4)*, and consequently, we cannot decide if $\mathcal{X}$ is invariant with respect to* (2.1).

For linear switching systems under polytopic constraints, one can apply well known iterative reachability-based procedures to construct the maximal invariant set, see, e.g., [10]. The approach taken in this paper follows a similar path. In specific, in order to recover the maximal admissible invariant set,we would like to characterize the fixed point of a set sequence generated by applying the pre-image map of the $\mathcal{L}$-lifted System (2.4) for two different initial conditions, namely the $\mathcal{L}$-lifted set $\mathcal{X}^{[\mathcal{L}]}$ (2.8) or $\mathcal{X}^{[\mathcal{L}]} \cap \mathcal{V}$. Nevertheless, two issues not present in the standard reachability analysis approach have to be taken into account: On the one hand, as illustrated in the Running Example and Figure 2, the set $\mathcal{X}^{[\mathcal{L}]}$ might be unbounded, thus, convergence to the maximal invariant set cannot be guaranteed when starting from the set $\mathcal{X}^{[\mathcal{L}]}$. On the other hand, when starting from the set $\mathcal{X}^{[\mathcal{L}]} \cap \mathcal{V}$, one has to account for computations of the reachability operations involving non-polytopic sets. We address these two challenges in the remaining of the paper.

DEFINITION 9. *The pre-image map of a set $\mathcal{S} \subset \mathbb{R}^N$, $N = \sum_{l \in \mathcal{L}} \binom{n+l-1}{l}$ with respect to System* (2.4) *is*

$$\mathcal{C}(\mathcal{S}) := \left\{ y \in \mathbb{R}^N : A_i^{[\mathcal{L}]} y \in \mathcal{S}, \forall i \in [1, M] \right\}. \tag{3.5}$$

Next, let us consider the set sequence $\{\mathcal{S}_i\}_{i \geq 0}$ generated by the iteration

$$\mathcal{S}_0 \subset \mathbb{R}^N, \tag{3.6}$$

$$\mathcal{S}_{i+1} := \mathcal{C}(\mathcal{S}_i) \cap \mathcal{S}_0, \tag{3.7}$$

where $N = \sum_{l \in \mathcal{L}} \binom{n+l-1}{l}$ and $\mathcal{X}^{[\mathcal{L}]}$ denotes the $\mathcal{L}$-lift of the set (2.3). In what follows, we will show convergence of the set sequence to the maximal invariant set choosing different initial condition $\mathcal{S}_0$ (3.6).

FACT 2. *Let $\mathcal{X} \subset \mathbb{R}^n$* (2.3) *be a semi-algebraic set satisfying Assumption 2. Then, the set $\mathcal{V} \cap \mathcal{X}^{[\mathcal{L}]}$ is compact.*

PROOF. Since $\mathcal{V} \cap \mathcal{X}^{[\mathcal{L}]} = \{y \in \mathbb{R}^N : (\exists x \in \mathcal{X} : y = x^{[\mathcal{L}]})\}$, the statement follows because the continuous polynomial map of a compact set is compact. □

THEOREM 1. *Consider the System* (2.1)*, the constraint set* (2.3) *and the set sequence $\{\mathcal{S}_i\}_{i \geq 0}$ generated by* (3.7) *with*

$$\mathcal{S}_0 := \mathcal{V} \cap \mathcal{X}^{[\mathcal{L}]}.$$

Then, there exists a finite integer $\overline{k} \geq 1$ such that

$$\mathcal{S}_{\overline{k}} = \mathcal{S}_{\overline{k}+1}$$

and the maximal admissible invariant set $\mathcal{M}$ with respect to the System (2.1) *and the constraints* (2.3) *is $\mathcal{M} = \text{lower}(\mathcal{S}_{\overline{k}})$.*

PROOF. Under Assumption 1 and from Proposition 1, there exist scalars $\Gamma \geq 1$, $\varepsilon \in (0, 1)$ such that $\|y(t)\| \leq \Gamma \varepsilon^t \|y(0)\|$, for all $y(0) \in \mathbb{R}^N$, for all $y(t)$ satisfying (2.4) and for all $t \geq 0$. From Fact 2, there exists a number $R > 0$ such that $\|y(0)\| \leq R$, for all $y \in \mathcal{S}_0$. Consider the set $\mathcal{R} = \{y \in \mathbb{R}^N : \|y\| \leq R\}$, the number $a \in \mathbb{R}$, where

$$a := \max\{\lambda : \lambda\mathcal{R} \cap \mathcal{V} \subseteq \mathcal{S}_0\},$$

and the integer $\overline{k} = \left\lceil \log_\varepsilon \frac{a}{\Gamma} \right\rceil$. Then, $y(0) \in \mathcal{S}_0$ implies $y(t) \in \mathcal{S}_0$, for all $t \geq \overline{k}$. On the other hand, for any $t \geq 0$, the relation $y(t) \in \mathcal{S}_0$ holds for all $y(0) \in \mathcal{S}_0$ for which $y(0) \in \mathcal{S}_t$. Let us assume that there exists a vector $y(0) \in \mathcal{S}_{\overline{k}}$ such that $y(0) \notin \mathcal{S}_{\overline{k}+1}$. This implies that $y(\overline{k}+1) \notin \mathcal{S}_0$ which is a contradiction, thus, $\mathcal{S}_{\overline{k}+1} \supseteq \mathcal{S}_{\overline{k}}$. From (3.7), it holds that $\mathcal{S}_1 \subseteq \mathcal{S}_0$. Suppose that $\mathcal{S}_{i+1} \subseteq \mathcal{S}_i$. Then, we have that $\mathcal{C}(\mathcal{S}_{i+1}) \cap \mathcal{S}_0 \subseteq \mathcal{C}(\mathcal{S}_i) \cap \mathcal{S}_0$, or $\mathcal{S}_{i+2} \subseteq \mathcal{S}_{i+1}$. Consequently, $\mathcal{S}_{\overline{k}+1} \subseteq \mathcal{S}_{\overline{k}}$, thus, $\mathcal{S}_{\overline{k}} = \mathcal{S}_{\overline{k}+1}$.

Next, we show that $\mathcal{M}$ is the maximal invariant set. By construction it holds that $\mathcal{S}_{\overline{k}} \subseteq \mathcal{S}_0$, thus, $\mathcal{M} = \text{lower}(\mathcal{S}_{\overline{k}}) \subseteq \text{lower}(\mathcal{S}_0) = \mathcal{X}$. Moreover, for any $x_0 \in \mathcal{M}$, there exists a $y_0 \in \mathcal{S}_{\overline{k}}$ such that $y_0 = x_0^{[\mathcal{L}]}$. Since $\mathcal{S}_{\overline{k}} = \mathcal{S}_{\overline{k}+1}$, it holds that $A_i^{[\mathcal{L}]} y_0 \in \mathcal{S}_{\overline{k}}$, for all $i \in [1, M]$ or, $(A_i x_0)^{[\mathcal{L}]} \in \mathcal{S}_{\overline{k}}$, which implies $A_i x_0 \in \mathcal{M}$, for all $i \in [1, M]$. Consequently, by time invariance of the dynamics, $\mathcal{M}$ is admissible invariant with respect to (2.1). To show that $\mathcal{M}$ is maximal, we assume that there exists an admissible invariant set $\mathcal{W} \subseteq \mathcal{X}$ satisfying $\mathcal{W} \nsubseteq \mathcal{M}$. Then, the set $\mathcal{W}_\mathcal{L} := \{y \in \mathbb{R}^N : (\exists x \in \mathcal{W} : y := x^{[\mathcal{L}]})\}$, $\mathcal{W}_\mathcal{L} \subseteq \mathcal{V} \cap \mathcal{X}^{[\mathcal{L}]}$, is admissible invariant with respect to (2.4) and moreover there exists a vector $y_0 \in \mathcal{W}_\mathcal{L}$ such that $y_0 \notin \mathcal{S}_{\overline{k}}$. Taking into account that $\mathcal{V}$ is invariant under the dynamics (2.4), the last relation implies that for the vector $x_0 \in \mathcal{W}$, where $y_0 = x_0^{[\mathcal{L}]}$, it holds that $y(\overline{k}) \notin \mathcal{X}^{[\mathcal{L}]} \cap \mathcal{V}$, or, $x(\overline{k}) \notin \mathcal{X}$, thus, the set $\mathcal{W}$ is not admissible invariant and we have reached a contradiction. Consequently, $\mathcal{W} \subseteq \mathcal{M}$ and $\mathcal{M}$ is the maximal admissible invariant set. □

Theorem 1 establishes that the set iteration defined by the pre-image map and initialized with the intersection between the algebraic variety $\mathcal{V}$ and the lifted set $\mathcal{X}$ is convergent. Moreover, the maximal invariant set for the System (2.1) is retrieved directly, by applying the lowering operation on that fixed point.

As discussed and analyzed in the following section, the involved computations at each iteration for the set sequence are linear. However, checking the convergence condition $\mathcal{S}_{\overline{k}} = \mathcal{S}_{\overline{k}+1}$ is equivalent to verifying equivalence between two algebraic varieties, a problem which is known to be NP-hard. The following result establishes that the maximal invariant set has an alternative and equivalent characterization. Moreover, the involved convergence criterion in that case requires checking equivalence between two polytopes, which is known to be equivalent to the solution, at the worst case, of a series of linear programs only. As it is explained below, this alternative approach comes at the cost of possibly introducing redundancies on the description of the maximal invariant set, which however can be removed algorithmically in a post-processing step.

THEOREM 2. *Consider the System* (2.1)*, the constraint set* (2.3)*, the set sequence* $\{\mathcal{S}_i\}_{i\geq 0}$ *generated by* (3.7) *with*

$$\mathcal{S}_0 := \mathcal{X}^{[\mathcal{L}]}$$

and any compact set $\mathcal{B} \subset \mathbb{R}^N$ *satisfying* $\mathcal{V} \cap \mathcal{X}^{[\mathcal{L}]} \subseteq \mathcal{B}$*. Then, there exists a finite integer* $\overline{k} \geq 1$ *such that*

$$\mathcal{S}_{\overline{k}} \cap \mathcal{B} = \mathcal{S}_{\overline{k}+1} \cap \mathcal{B}$$

and the maximal admissible invariant set $\mathcal{M}$ *with respect to the System* (2.1) *and the constraints* (2.3) *is* $\mathcal{M} = \mathrm{lower}(\mathcal{S}_{\overline{k}})$.

PROOF. Under Assumption 1, there exist scalars $\Gamma \geq 1$, $\varepsilon \in (0, 1)$ such that $\|y(t)\| \leq \Gamma\varepsilon^t\|y(0)\|$, for all $y(0) \in \mathbb{R}^N$, $t \geq 0$ and $y(t)$ satisfying (2.4). Moreover, consider the number

$$a := \max\{\lambda : \lambda\mathcal{B} \subseteq \mathcal{B} \cap \mathcal{X}^{[\mathcal{L}]}\},$$

and the integer $\overline{k} = \lceil \log_\varepsilon \frac{a}{\Gamma} \rceil$. Then, $y(0) \in \mathcal{B} \cap \mathcal{X}^{[\mathcal{L}]}$ implies $y(t) \in \mathcal{B} \cap \mathcal{X}^{[\mathcal{L}]}$, for all $t \geq \overline{k}$. The rest of the proof follows the same steps of the proof of Theorem 1. □

It is worth observing that the sets $\mathcal{S}_i$, $i \geq 0$ in Theorem 2 are polyhedral sets.

REMARK 3. *We note that the crucial requirement for this alternative characterization of the maximal admissible invariant set in Theorem 2 is the boundedness of the set* $\mathcal{B}$*, allowing for the criterion* $\mathcal{S}_{\overline{k}} \cap \mathcal{B} = \mathcal{S}_{\overline{k}+1} \cap \mathcal{B}$ *to be verified for a finite integer* $\overline{k} \geq 1$.

The following result applies standard results from the literature to the studied setting, providing a third alternative characterization of the maximal admissible invariant set, possibly at the cost of adding redundancies in the pre-image map computations.

THEOREM 3. *Consider the System* (2.1)*, the constraint set* (2.3)*, the set sequence* $\{\mathcal{S}_i\}_{i\geq 0}$ *generated by* (3.7) *with*

$$\mathcal{S}_0 := \mathcal{B} \cap \mathcal{X}^{[\mathcal{L}]},$$

where $\mathcal{B} \subset \mathbb{R}^N$ *is a compact polytopic set which contains the origin in its interior and satisfies* $\mathcal{V} \cap \mathcal{X}^{[\mathcal{L}]} \subset \mathcal{B}$*. Then, there exists a finite integer* $\overline{k} \geq 1$ *such that*

$$\mathcal{S}_{\overline{k}} = \mathcal{S}_{\overline{k}+1}$$

and the maximal admissible invariant set $\mathcal{M}$ *with respect to the System* (2.1) *and the constraints* (2.3) *is* $\mathcal{M} = \mathrm{lower}(\mathcal{S}_{\overline{k}})$.

PROOF. From Fact 2, the set $\mathcal{X} \cap \mathcal{V}$ is compact, thus, by construction and Assumption 2, the set $\mathcal{S}_0$ is compact and contains the origin in its interior. Consequently, under Assumption 1, from [10, Ch. 5] there exists a finite integer $\overline{k}$ such that $\mathcal{S}_{\overline{k}}$ is the maximal admissible invariant set with respect to $\mathcal{X}^{[\mathcal{L}]}$. Taking into account Proposition 2 and observing that $\mathcal{V} \cap \mathcal{X}^{[\mathcal{L}]} \subset \mathcal{B}$ and that $\mathcal{V}$ is invariant under (2.4), the result follows. □

Theorem / Algorithm	Initial set $\mathcal{S}_0$	Convergence criterion
1	$\mathcal{V} \cap \mathcal{X}^{[\mathcal{L}]}$	$\mathcal{S}_{\overline{k}+1} = \mathcal{S}_{\overline{k}}$
2	$\mathcal{X}^{[\mathcal{L}]}$	$\mathcal{S}_{\overline{k}+1} \cap \mathcal{B} = \mathcal{S}_{\overline{k}} \cap \mathcal{B}$
3	$\mathcal{B} \cap \mathcal{X}^{[\mathcal{L}]}$	$\mathcal{S}_{\overline{k}+1} = \mathcal{S}_{\overline{k}}$

Table 1: Summary of the results of section 3 and section 4: Each set sequence obeys the update relation $\mathcal{S}_{i+1} = \mathcal{C}(\mathcal{S}_i) \cap \mathcal{S}_0$. The sets $\mathcal{V} \subset \mathbb{R}^N$, $\mathcal{X}^{[\mathcal{L}]}$ are defined in (2.9) and (2.8) respectively, the compact set $\mathcal{B} \subset \mathbb{R}^N$ satisfies $\mathcal{B} \supseteq \mathcal{V} \cap \mathcal{X}^{[\mathcal{L}]}$ in Theorem/Algorithm 2, while the compact polytopic set $\mathcal{B} \subset \mathbb{R}^N$ in Theorem/Algorithm 3 contains the origin in its interior and satisfies $\mathcal{B} \supseteq \mathcal{V} \cap \mathcal{X}^{[\mathcal{L}]}$.

REMARK 4. *We can replace boundedness of* $\mathcal{B}$ *in Theorem 3 with requiring* $\mathcal{B}$ *to be a symmetric polyhedron whose defining matrix in the half-space description satisfies an observability condition with at least a member of the set*[3] $\mathrm{conv}(\{A_1^{[\mathcal{L}]}, ..., A_M^{[\mathcal{L}]}\})$*. For more details see, e.g.,* [15].

4. IMPLEMENTATION

In this section, we present three algorithmic procedures for computing the maximal admissible invariant set for the System (2.1) subject to the constraints (2.2). In detail, we present an efficient way to realize the set sequences and verify the convergence criteria of the theoretical results of the previous section. First, we establish the relationship between the set sequences generated in Theorem 1 and Theorem 2.

FACT 3. *Consider any two sets* $\mathcal{Y} \subset \mathbb{R}^N, \mathcal{Z} \subset \mathbb{R}^N$*, the pre-image map* (3.5) *and the Veronese variety* $\mathcal{V}$ (2.9)*. Then, (i)* $\mathcal{C}(\mathcal{Y} \cap \mathcal{Z}) = \mathcal{C}(\mathcal{Y}) \cap \mathcal{C}(\mathcal{Z})$ *,and (ii)* $\mathcal{V} \subseteq \mathcal{C}(\mathcal{V})$.

PROOF. Statement (i) follows from the definition (3.5), while (ii) follows from the fact that $\mathcal{V}$ is invariant with respect to the System (2.4). □

Algorithm 1 Inputs: $\mathcal{A} := \{A_1, ..., A_M\} \subset \mathbb{R}^{n\times n}$, $\mathcal{X} = \{x \in \mathbb{R}^n : c_i(x) \leq 1, i \in [1, p]\}$ **Output:** The maximal admissible invariant set $\mathcal{M}$.

Extract $\mathcal{L} \subseteq \{1, d\}$, $g_i \in \mathbb{R}^N$, satisfying $g_i^\top x^{[\mathcal{L}]} = c_i(x)$, $i \in [1, p]$.
$i \leftarrow 0$, eq$\leftarrow 0$, $\mathcal{Z}_0 \leftarrow \mathcal{X}^{[\mathcal{L}]}$, $\mathcal{Y}_0 \leftarrow \mathcal{Z}_0 \cap \mathcal{V}$
while eq$= 0$ **do**
    $\mathcal{Z}_{i+1} \leftarrow \mathcal{C}(\mathcal{Z}_i)$, as in (4.3), (4.4)
    Compute the minimal description of $\mathcal{Z}_{i+1}$ (Appendix A)
    $\mathcal{Y}_{i+1} \leftarrow \mathcal{Z}_{i+1} \cap \mathcal{V}$
    Compute the minimal description of $\mathcal{Y}_{i+1}$ (Appendix B)
    if $\mathcal{Y}_{i+1} = \mathcal{Y}_i$ **then**
        eq$\leftarrow 1$
    end if
    $i \leftarrow i + 1$
end while
$\mathcal{M} \leftarrow \mathrm{lower}(\mathcal{Z}_i)$

LEMMA 1. *Let* $\{\mathcal{Y}_i\}_{i\geq 0}$*,* $\{\mathcal{Z}_i\}_{i\geq 0}$ *be the set sequences generated by* (3.7) *with initial conditions* $\mathcal{Y}_0 = \mathcal{V} \cap \mathcal{X}^{[\mathcal{L}]}$ *and* $\mathcal{Z}_0 = \mathcal{X}^{[\mathcal{L}]}$ *respectively. Then, for all* $i \geq 0$*, the followng relation holds*

$$\mathcal{Y}_i = \mathcal{Z}_i \cap \mathcal{V}. \quad (4.1)$$

[3] $\mathrm{conv}(\cdot)$ stands for the convex hull.

PROOF. For $i = 0$, (4.1) holds by definition. Suppose that (4.1) holds for $i = k$. Then, for $i = k+1$ and taking into account Fact 3, it follows that

$$\begin{aligned}\mathcal{Y}_{k+1} &= \mathcal{C}(\mathcal{Z}_k \cap \mathcal{V}) \cap \mathcal{V} \cap \mathcal{X}^{[\mathcal{L}]} = \mathcal{C}(\mathcal{Z}_k) \cap \mathcal{C}(\mathcal{V}) \cap \mathcal{V} \cap \mathcal{Z}_0 \\ &= \mathcal{C}(\mathcal{Z}_k) \cap \mathcal{Z}_0 \cap \mathcal{V} = \mathcal{Z}_{k+1} \cap \mathcal{V}.\end{aligned}$$

Thus, the relation (4.1) holds for all $i \geq 0$. □

Lemma 1 states that the set sequence defined in Theorem 1 can be generated in two steps and in specific by computing first the pre-image map of a polyhedral set and consequently its intersection with the manifold $\mathcal{V}$.

REMARK 5. *In Line 4 of Algorithm 1 the computation of the pre-image map of a polyhedral set is required. To this end, let $\mathcal{Z}_i \subset \mathbb{R}^N$ be the polyhedral set computed at iteration i in half-space representation, i.e.,*

$$\mathcal{Z}_i := \{y \in \mathbb{R}^N : G_i y \leq 1_{p_i}\}, \tag{4.2}$$

where $G_i \in \mathbb{R}^p_i \times N$ and $p_i \geq 1$. Then, the pre-image map $\mathcal{C}(\mathcal{S})$ with respect to the System (2.4) *is*

$$\begin{aligned}\mathcal{C}(\mathcal{Z}_i) &= \{y \in \mathbb{R}^N : G_i A_j^{[\mathcal{L}]} y \leq 1_{p_i}, j = 1, ..., M\} \\ &= \{y \in \mathbb{R}^N : G^\star y \leq 1_{p^\star}\},\end{aligned} \tag{4.3}$$

where $p^\star = pM$ and

$$G^\star = \begin{bmatrix} (G_i A_1^{[\mathcal{L}]})^\top & \dots & (G_i A_M^{[\mathcal{L}]})^\top \end{bmatrix}^\top. \tag{4.4}$$

The number of hyperplanes that describe the set $\mathcal{Z}_i$ is bounded by p^M, where p is the number of hyperplanes that describe the set $\mathcal{X}^{[\mathcal{L}]}$ and M is the number of matrices defining the system (2.1)*. However, in practice the number of hyperplanes, or equivalently, the size of the matrices G_i, $i \geq 0$ that are required to describe $\mathcal{Z}_i$ is significantly smaller.*

In Appendix A, a procedure of computing the minimal representation of the set $\mathcal{Z}_i$, required in Line 5 of Algorithm 1 is described.

Algorithm 2 Inputs: $\mathcal{A} := \{A_1, ..., A_M\} \subset \mathbb{R}^{n \times n}$, $\mathcal{X} = \{x \in \mathbb{R}^n : c_i(x) \leq 1, i \in [1, p]\}$, compact polytopic set $\mathcal{B} \supset \mathcal{X}^{[\mathcal{L}]} \cap \mathcal{V}$ (Appendix C) **Output:** The maximal admissible invariant set $\mathcal{M}$.

1: Extract $\mathcal{L} \subseteq \{1, d\}$, $g_i \in \mathbb{R}^N$, satisfying $g_i^\top x^{[\mathcal{L}]} = c_i(x)$, $i \in [1, p]$.
2: $i \leftarrow 0$, eq$\leftarrow 0$, $\mathcal{Z}_0 \leftarrow \mathcal{X}^{[\mathcal{L}]}$
3: **while** eq$= 0$ **do**
4: $\quad\mathcal{Z}_{i+1} \leftarrow \mathcal{C}(\mathcal{Z}_i)$, as in (4.3), (4.4)
5: $\quad$Compute the minimal description of $\mathcal{Z}_{i+1}$ (Appendix A)
6: $\quad$**if** $\mathcal{Y}_{i+1} \cap \mathcal{B} = \mathcal{Y}_i \cap \mathcal{B}$ **then**
7: $\quad\quad$eq$\leftarrow 1$
8: $\quad$**end if**
9: $\quad i \leftarrow i+1$
10: **end while**
11: $\mathcal{M} \leftarrow$ lower$(\mathcal{Y}_i)$
12: (*optional*) Compute the minimal representation of $\mathcal{M}$ (Appendix B)

The set $\mathcal{Y}_i = \mathcal{Z}_i \cap \mathcal{V}$ in Line 6 of Algorithm 1 has a straightforward description. In specific, if $\mathcal{Z}_i$ is described by (4.2), it holds that

$$\mathcal{Y}_i = \{y \in \mathbb{R}^N : (\exists x \in \mathbb{R}^n : y = x^{[\mathcal{L}]}, G_i y \leq 1_{p_i})\}. \tag{4.5}$$

However, computing the minimal description of the set $\mathcal{Y}_{i+1}$ in Algorithm 1, or in other words removing the redundant polynomial inequalities of the set lower$(\mathcal{Y}_i)$, is equivalent to verifying equivalence between two algebraic varieties. The approach taken in this paper is to iteratively check for redundancy of each hyperplane of the set $\mathcal{Y}_i$, or equivalently, to check for redundant polynomial inequalities of the set lower$(\mathcal{Y}_i)$. In Appendix B, a possible approach for tackling this problem, based on a version of the Positivstellensatz [32], [11, Theorem 3.138], is presented.

Algorithm 3 Inputs: $\mathcal{A} := \{A_1, ..., A_M\} \subset \mathbb{R}^{n \times n}$, $\mathcal{X} = \{x \in \mathbb{R}^n : c_i(x) \leq 1, i \in [1, p]\}$, compact polytopic set $\mathcal{B} \supset \mathcal{X}^{[\mathcal{L}]} \cap \mathcal{V}$ containing the origin in its interior (Appendix C) **Output:** The maximal admissible invariant set $\mathcal{M}$.

1: Extract $\mathcal{L} \subseteq \{1, d\}$, $g_i \in \mathbb{R}^N$, satisfying $g_i^\top x^{[\mathcal{L}]} = c_i(x)$, $i \in [1, p]$.
2: $i \leftarrow 0$, eq$\leftarrow 0$, $\mathcal{Z}_0 \leftarrow \mathcal{B} \cap \mathcal{X}^{[\mathcal{L}]}$
3: **while** eq$= 0$ **do**
4: $\quad\mathcal{Z}_{i+1} \leftarrow \mathcal{C}(\mathcal{Z}_i)$, as in (4.3), (4.4)
5: $\quad$Compute the minimal description of $\mathcal{Z}_{i+1}$ (Appendix A)
6: $\quad$**if** $\mathcal{Y}_{i+1} \cap \mathcal{B} = \mathcal{Y}_i \cap \mathcal{B}$ **then**
7: $\quad\quad$eq$\leftarrow 1$
8: $\quad$**end if**
9: $\quad i \leftarrow i+1$
10: **end while**
11: $\mathcal{M} \leftarrow$ lower$(\mathcal{Y}_i)$
12: (*optional*) Compute the minimal representation of $\mathcal{M}$ (Appendix B)

Contrary to Algorithm 1, Algorithms 2 and 3 are based solely on linear operations and on solving linear programs. It is worth observing that the number of iterations needed in Algorithms 2 and 3 to recover the maximal admissible invariant set is lower bounded by the number of iterations needed in Algorithm 1. This is the cost that has to be paid in order to avoid computing the minimal representation of the set $\mathcal{Z}_{i+1} \cap \mathcal{V}$ at each iteration in Algorithm 1. Naturally, if one is interested in the minimal representation of the maximal admissible invariant set $\mathcal{M}$, the approach described in Appendix B can be used in a single post-processing step in Line 12 of Algorithms 2 and 3.

RUNNING EXAMPLE PART 4. *We implement Algorithm 2 in order to compute the maximal admissible invariant set. To this end, we first choose a compact polytopic set*

$$\mathcal{B} = \{y \in \mathbb{R}^3 : -\sqrt{2} \leq y_2 \leq \sqrt{2}, 0 \leq y_i \leq 1, i = 1, 3\}$$

such that $\mathcal{B} \supset \mathcal{V} \cap \mathcal{X}^{[\mathcal{L}]}$. As described above, we set $\mathcal{Z}_0 = \mathcal{X}^{[\mathcal{L}]}$. The Algorithm 2 converges after 8 iterations, i.e., the relation $\mathcal{Z}_8 \cap \mathcal{B} = \mathcal{Z}_7 \cap \mathcal{B}$ is satisfied. In Figure 3 the set $\mathcal{Z}_7$ is shown in blue while the hyperplanes that define the set $\mathcal{X}^{[\mathcal{L}]}$ are also shown in grey. In Figure 4, the maximal invariant set lower$(\mathcal{Z}_7)$ *together with the constraint set $\mathcal{X}$ are shown. It is worth observing that the maximal invariant set is not convex, as expected. The level curves of the polynomial functions that define the maximal invariant set are also shown. In specific, there are 14 polynomials in total which define the set, out of which 5 of them are redundant and have been identified by applying the post-processing step (Line 12 of Algorithm 2).*

Finally, two properties of the maximal invariant set $\mathcal{M}$ which are inherited from the constraint set $\mathcal{X}$ are summarized below.

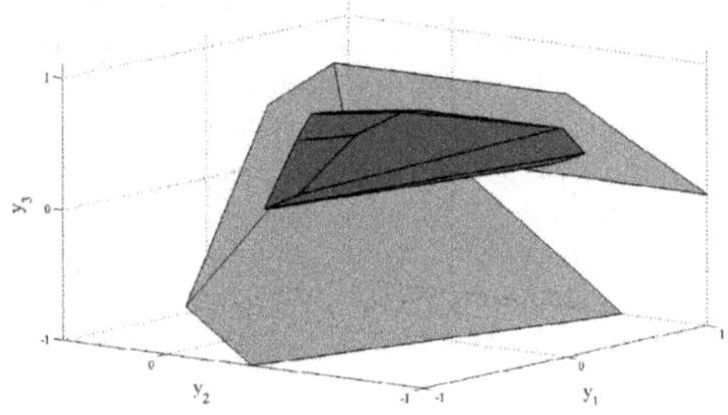

Figure 3: Running example, the set $\mathcal{Z}_7$ (blue) and the hyperplanes that define the set $\mathcal{X}^{[2]}$ (red).

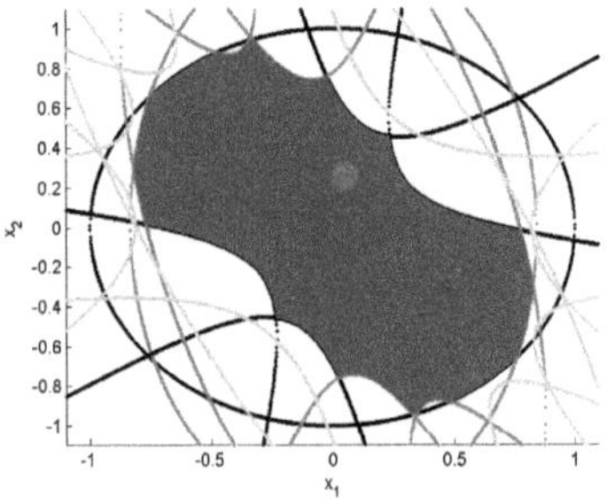

Figure 4: Running example, the maximal admissible invariant set $\text{lower}(\mathcal{Z}_7)$ **(blue) and the level curves of the polynomial inequalities which define** $\text{lower}(\mathcal{Z}_7)$**: The polynomial constraints inherited from $\mathcal{X}$ are in black, the added active constraints are in red, whereas the added redundant constraints are shown in grey.**

PROPOSITION 4. *Consider the System* (2.1) *subject to constraints* (2.3) *and let $\mathcal{M}$ be the maximal admissible invariant set. Then, the following hold:*

(i) $\mathcal{M}$ is the sub-level set of a max-polynomial function of at most degree d, described by a finite number of pieces.

(ii) If $\mathcal{X}$ is convex, then $\mathcal{M}$ is convex.

PROOF. (i) Follows directly from Algorithms 2, 3 and in specific from the facts that the sets $\mathcal{Z}_i$, $i \geq 0$, are polyhedral and that the algorithm terminates in finite time.
(ii) Taking into account Theorem 1, it is enough to show that the pre-image map $\mathcal{C}(\mathcal{S})$ with respect to (2.1) is always convex when $\mathcal{S} := \{x \in \mathbb{R}^n : c_i(x) \leq 1, i = 1, ..., p\} \subset \mathbb{R}^n$ is convex. Since $\mathcal{C}(\mathcal{S}) = \{x \in \mathbb{R}^n : c_i(A_j(x)) \leq 1, i = 1, ..., p, j = 1, ..., M\}$ and taking into account [34, Ch. 3] that the composition of a convex function and a linear function is convex and the maximum of convex functions is convex, it follows that $\mathcal{C}(\mathcal{S})$ is convex, thus, the maximal invariant set is convex. □

5. NUMERICAL EXAMPLES

The algorithms were implemented in Matlab, version 2014a, for the Running Example and all numerical examples of the current section. Additionally, the MPT3 toolbox [19] (Algorithms 1-3, appendix A) and the SOSTOOLS toolbox [31] (Algorithm 1, appendix B) were utilized. A standard desktop computer (Intel Core i7-4790 3.6GHz, RAM 16GB) was used for all computations.

EXAMPLE 1. *We consider a linear time invariant system*

$$x(t+1) = Ax(t), \tag{5.1}$$

with $A = \begin{bmatrix} 1.0216 & 0.3234 \\ -0.6597 & 0.5226 \end{bmatrix}$. *We are interested in computing the maximal admissible invariant set when the constraint set $\mathcal{X} \subset \mathbb{R}^2$ is the unit circle. For all three Algorithms 1-3, the maximal admissible invariant set $\mathcal{M}$ is recovered in 6 iterations. To compare with standard approaches, we compute the maximum invariant ellipsoid $\mathcal{E}_{\max}$ contained in $\mathcal{X}$ by solving a linear matrix inequality problem, (for details see, e.g., [13, Ch. 5]). As expected, we can see in Figure 5 that $\mathcal{E}_{\max} \subset \mathcal{M}$.*

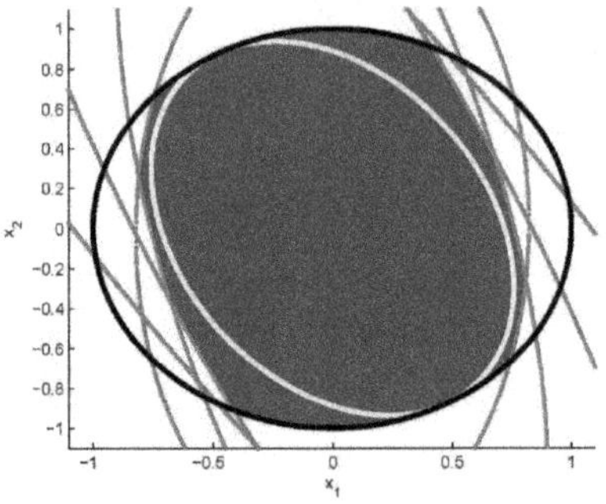

Figure 5: Example 1, the maximal admissible invariant set $\mathcal{M}$ is in blue, the level curves of the polynomial inequalities which define the set $\mathcal{M}$ are in red, while the maximum invariant inscribed ellipsoid $\mathcal{E}_{\max}$ is shown in yellow.

EXAMPLE 2. *We consider the System* (2.1) *with* $\mathcal{A} = \{A_1, A_2\}$, *where* $A_1 = \begin{bmatrix} 0.2137 & 1.2052 \\ -0.2125 & 0.1703 \end{bmatrix}$, $A_2 = \begin{bmatrix} -0.3576 & 1.0351 \\ 0.3290 & 0.3514 \end{bmatrix}$. *The constraint set $\mathcal{X}$ (2.3) is non simply connected and is described by the intersection of the unit circle and the complements of two circles and an ellipse. It is worth noting that in this setting we have $\mathcal{L} = \{1, 2\}$. By applying Algorithm 2, the maximal admissible invariant set $\mathcal{M}$ is retrieved in 5 iterations and is described by 36 polynomial inequalities. The set $\mathcal{M}$ is not connected.*

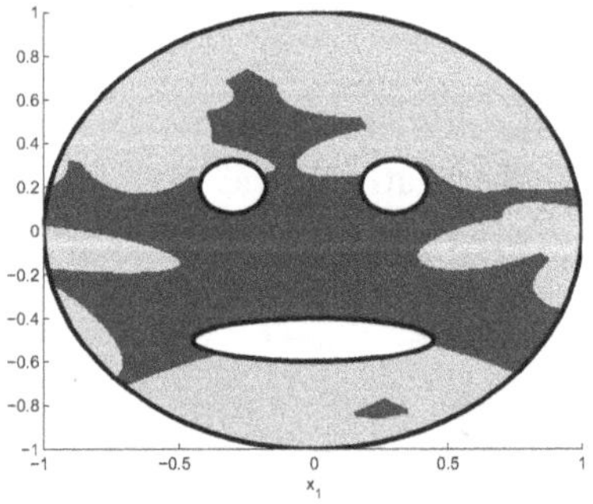

Figure 6: Example 2, the maximal admissible invariant set $\mathcal{M}$ is shown in blue, while the constraint set $\mathcal{X}$ is shown in grey.

REMARK 6. *Algorithms 2 and 3 have significantly smaller runtimes compared to Algorithm 1. In specific, Algorithms 2 and 3 converged within milliseconds for all numerical examples of this paper. Algorithm 1 exhibits longer run-times (range between seconds and tens of seconds). Moreover, since the dimensions of the lifted space depend both on the dimensions of the system and the order of the polynomials that describe the constraint set, we expect the computational times to grow for complex constraint sets and/or high order systems.*

6. CONCLUSIONS AND FUTURE WORK

We studied the computation of the maximal admissible invariant set for switching linear discrete time systems that are subject to semi-algebraic constraints. In this setting, the maximal admissible invariant set might be non-convex, or even non-connected. Nevertheless, we showed that despite the complexity of these constraints, the computation of the maximal admissible invariant set can be reduced to a problem with much simpler linear constraints (i.e., a polytopic constraint set). The approach consists in applying the Veronese embedding and consequently lifting the system and the constraint set in a higher dimensional space, allowing for efficient reachability operations.

This comes at the price of inflating the dimension, and hence, the number of variables, calling for a careful study of the computational burden necessary for computing these invariant sets. In this work, we made a first step in that direction by presenting three different algorithms, with different advantages. Moreover, we suggested several subroutines that are required. We leave for further research the question of precisely comparing the efficiency between the established algorithms and choosing the optimal mathematical tools, e.g., for the removal of redundant constraints. In addition, we plan to investigate how the approach can be applied to systems with inputs, and how it can be utilised for systems where the maximal admissible invariant set is a polytope, but one would like to approximate it with much fewer constraints.

7. REFERENCES

[1] A. A. Ahmadi and R. M. Jungers. Switched stability of nonlinear systems via SOS-convex Lyapunov functions and semidefinite programming . In *American Control Conference*, pages 2686–2700, Boston, MA, USA, 2005.

[2] N. Athanasopoulos, M. Lazar, and G. Bitsoris. Property-preserving convergent sequences of invariant sets for linear discrete-time systems. In *21st International Symposium on Mathematical Theory of Networks and Systems*, pages 1280–1286, Groningen, The Netherlands, 2014.

[3] J. P. Aubin, A. M. Bayen, and P. Saint-Pierre. *Viability Theory: New Directions*. Springer, Heidelber Dordrecht London New York , 2011.

[4] C. B. Barber, D. P. Dobkin, and H. Huhdanpaa. The Quickhull Algorithm for Convex Hulls. *ACM Transactions on Mathematical Software*, 22:469–483, 1996.

[5] C. Belta, V. Isler, and G. J. Pappas. Discrete abstractions for robot motion planning and control in polygonal environments. *IEEE Transactions on Robotics*, 21(5):864–874, 2005.

[6] D. P. Bertsekas. Infinite–Time Reachability of State–Space Regions by Using Feedback Control. *IEEE Transactions on Automatic Control*, 17(5):604–613, 1972.

[7] G. Bitsoris. On the positive invariance of polyhedral sets for discrete-time systems. *Systems and Control Letters*, 11:243–248, 1988.

[8] G. Bitsoris and S. Olaru. Further Results on the Linear Constrained Regulation Problem. In *21st IEEE Mediterranean Conference on Control and Automation*, pages 824–830, Platanias, Greece, 2013.

[9] F. Blanchini. Set Invariance in Control – A Survey. *Automatica*, 35(11):1747–1767, 1999. Survey Paper.

[10] F. Blanchini and S. Miani. *Set-theoretic methods in control*. Systems & Control: Foundations & Applications. Birkhäuser, Boston, MA, 2008.

[11] G. Blekherman, P. A. Parrilo, and R. R. Thomas. *Semidefinite Optimization and Convex Algebraic Geometry*, volume 13 of *MOS-SIAM Series on Optimization*. SIAM, 2012.

[12] V. D. Blondel and Y. Nesterov. Computationally efficient approximations of the joint spectral radius. *SIAM Journal of Matrix Analysis*, 27:256–272, 2005.

[13] S. Boyd, L. E. Ghaoui, E. Feron, and V. Balakrishnan. *Linear Matrix Inequalities in System and Control Theory*. Studies in Applied Mathematics. SIAM, 1994.

[14] K. Fukuda. Frequently asked questions in polyhedral computation. Official website: http://www.ifor.math.ethz.ch/∼fukuda/polyfaq/polyfaq.html.

[15] E. G. Gilbert and K. T. Tan. Linear systems with state and control constraints: the theory and application of maximal output admissible sets. *IEEE Transactions on Automatic Control*, 36(9):1008–1020, 1991.

[16] E. M. Gilbert and K. T. Tan. Linear systems with state and control constraints: The theory and application of maximal output admissible sets. *IEEE Transactions on Automatic Control*, 36(9):1008–1020, 1991.

[17] P. O. Gutman and M. Cwikel. An algorithm to find maximal state constraint sets for discrete-time linear dynamical systems with bounded control and states. *IEEE Transactions on Automatic Control*, 32:251–254, 1987.

[18] J. C. Hennet. Discrete Time Constrained Linear Systems. *Control and Dynamic Systems, Leondes Ed. Academic Press*, 71:157–213, 1995.

[19] M. Herceg, M. Kvasnica, C. N. Jones and M. Morari Multi-parametric toolbox 3.0. In *European Control Conference*, pages 502–510, Zurich, Switzerland, 2013.

[20] T. Hu and Z. Lin. Composite quadratic Lyapunov functions for constrained control systems. *IEEE Transactions on Automatic Control*, 48(3):440–450, 2003.

[21] M. Johansson and A. Rantzer. Computation of piecewise quadratic Lyapunov functions for hybrid systems. *IEEE Transactions on Automatic Control*, 43(4):555–559, 1998.

[22] R. M. Jungers. *The joint spectral radius: theory and applications*, volume 385 of *Lecture Notes in Control and Information Sciences*. Springer, 2008.

[23] H. Khalil. *Nonlinear Systems, Third Edition*. Prentice Hall, 2002.

[24] M. Lazar, A. I. Doban, and N. Athanasopoulos. On stability analysis of discrete–time homogeneous dynamics. In *17th International Conference on System Theory, Control and Computing*, pages 1–8, Sinaia, Romania, 2013.

[25] H. Lin and P. J. Antsaklis. Stability and stabilizability of switched linear systems : a survey of recent results. *IEEE Transactions on Automatic Control*, 54:308–322, 2009.

[26] A. P. Molchanov and Y. S. Pyatnitsky. Criteria of asymptotic stability of differential and difference inclusions encountered in control theory. *Systems and Control Letters*, 13:59–64, 1989.

[27] A. Papachristodoulou and S. Prajna. A tutorial on sum of squares techniques for systems analysis. In *American Control Conference*, pages 2686–2700, Boston, MA, USA, 2005.

[28] P. Parrilo. *Structured Semidefinite Programs and Semialgebraic Geometry Methods in Robustness and Optimization*. PhD thesis, California Institute of Technology, CA, USA, 2000.

[29] P. A. Parrilo and A. Jadbabaie. Approximation of the joint spectral radius using sum of squares. *Linear Algebra and Its Applications*, 428(10):2385–2402, 2008.

[30] S. Prajna and A. Papachristodoulou. Analysis of switched and hybrid systems - beyond piecewise qudratic methods. In *22nd American Control Conference*, pages 2779–2784, Denver, Colorado, 2003.

[31] S. Prajna, A. Papachristodoulou, and P. A. Parillo. Introducing SOSTOOLS: A general purpose sum of squares programming solver. In *41st IEEE Conference on Decision and Control*, pages 741–746, Las Vegas, USA, 2002.

[32] M. Putinar. Positive polynomials on compact semi-algebraic sets. *Indiana University Mathematics Journal*, 42:969–984, 1993.

[33] G. C. Rota and W. G. Strang. A note on the joint spectral radius. *Proceedings of the Netherlands Academy*, 22:379–381, 1960.

[34] S. Boyd and L. Vandenberghe. *Convex Optimization.* Cambridge University Press, Cambridge, England, 2004.

[35] A. Seidenberg. A New Decision Method for Elementary Algebra. *Annals of Mathematics*, 60:365–374, 1954.

[36] A. Tarski. *A decision method for elementary algebra and geometry*. Rand Corporation Publication, 1948.

[37] G. Vankeerberghen, J. Hendrickx, and R. M. Jungers. JSR: A toolbox to compute the joint spectral radius. In *17th International Conference on Hybrid systems: Computation and Control*, pages 151–156, Berlin, Germany, 2014.

[38] A. Zelentsovsky. Nonquadratic Lyapunov Functions for Robust Stability Analysis of Linear Uncertain systems. *IEEE Transactions on Automatic Control*, 39(1):135–138, 1994.

[39] G. M. Ziegler. *Lectures on Polytopes, Updated Seventh Printing*. Springer, 2007.

APPENDIX

A. MINIMAL DESCRIPTION OF POLYHEDRAL SETS

It is generally accepted [14, 39] that the minimal representation problem of a polyhedral set can be solved efficiently in relatively low dimensions N. A simple way to remove a redundant hyperplane in the description of $\mathcal{S}$ is by solving a linear program. To this end, consider the set $\mathcal{S} = \{y \in \mathbb{R}^N : g_i^\top y \leq 1, i = 1, ..., p\}$, $p \geq 2$. Then, $\mathcal{S} = \{y \in \mathbb{R}^N : g_i^\top y \leq 1, i = 1, ..., p, i \neq j\}$ for some $j \in [1, p]$ if and only if the optimal cost of the linear program $\max_x g_j^\top x$ subject to $g_i^\top x \leq 1, \quad \forall i \in [1, p] \setminus \{j\}$ satisfies $g_j^\top x^\star < 1$. It is worth noting that there are methods in which a set of redundant inequalities is removed at each step rather than a single inequality, see e.g., convex hull algorithms [4] which are directly applicable by the duality of the problems.

B. MINIMAL DESCRIPTION OF SEMI-ALGEBRAIC SETS

Finding the minimal representation of a semi-algebraic set is a much more difficult problem when the polynomials defining the set are not linear. Deciding for redundancy of a polynomial inequality in the description of a semi-algebraic set can be performed using the Tarski-Seidenberg elimination theorem [35, 36]. This implies that the redundancy removal problem is decidable. However, despite its generality, the drawback of the corresponding algorithmic method is its computational complexity, which increases at least exponentially with the number of unknowns. In what follows we propose a way to remove a redundant polynomial inequality by transforming the problem in a series of semidefinite programs. It is worth stating that this approach poses sufficient conditions for checking redundancy, however in a computationally efficient manner, see e.g., [28]. To this end, let $\mathcal{S} \subset \mathbb{R}^n$,

$$\mathcal{S} = \text{lower}(\mathcal{Y}_i \cap \mathcal{V}) = \{x \in \mathbb{R}^n : g_i^\top x^{[\mathcal{L}]} \leq 1, i = 1, ..., p\}. \tag{B.1}$$

The next result is an application of Putinar's theorem [32], [11, Theorem 3.138].

Proposition 5. *Consider the set $\mathcal{S} \subset \mathbb{R}^n$ (B.1). Then, there exists an integer $j \in [1, p]$ such that*

$$\mathcal{S} = \{x \in \mathbb{R}^n : g_i^\top x^{[\mathcal{L}]} \leq 1, i = 1, ..., p, i \neq j\} \tag{B.2}$$

if and only if there exist polynomials $s_0(x)$, $s_i(x)$, $i \in [1, p] \setminus \{j\}$, such that

$$1 - g_j^\top x^{[\mathcal{L}]} = s_0^2(x) + \sum_{i=1, i\neq j}^{p} s_i^2(x)(1 - c_i(x)). \tag{B.3}$$

Proposition 5 provides a necessary and sufficient condition of identifying redundant inequalities $g_j^\top x^{[\mathcal{L}]} \leq 1$ in the description of the set $\mathcal{S}$. However, it is not algorithmically implementable, since the degree of the functions $s_0(x)$, $s_i(x)$, $i \in [1, p] \setminus \{j\}$ can be arbitrarily high. Nevertheless, by fixing the maximum degree of the polynomials $s_0(x), s_i(x)$, we can formulate the optimization problem $\min_{s_0(x), s_i(x)} \varepsilon$ subject to $\varepsilon - g_j^\top x^{[\mathcal{L}]} = s_0^2(x) + \sum_{i=1, i\neq j}^{p} s_i^2(x)(1 - c_i(x))$. The optimization problem is equivalent to a semidefinite program, see e.g. [28, 31]. If the optimal cost is $\varepsilon^\star < 1$ for an index j, then the set $\mathcal{S}$ can be described by (B.2).

C. COMPUTATION OF THE SET $\mathcal{B} \subset \mathbb{R}^N$ REQUIRED FOR THE INITIALIZATION OF ALGORITHMS 2 AND 3.

Under Assumption 2, one can always find polytopic sets $\mathcal{B} \subset \mathbb{R}^N$ satisfying the properties in Theorems 2 and 3. In this section we propose one such possible construction. To this end, we first compute a set $\mathcal{B}_1 \subset \mathbb{R}^n$ such that $\mathcal{B}_1 \supseteq \mathcal{X}$, $\mathcal{B}_1 := \{x \in \mathbb{R}^n : x_{\min} \leq x \leq x_{\max}\}$. Next, we define $\mathcal{B}_{l_j}$, $l_j \in \mathcal{L}$, $\mathcal{B}_{l_j} := \{y \in \mathbb{R}^{N_j} : y_{\min}^{l_j} \leq y \leq y_{\max}^{l_j}\}$, where

$$y_{\max,k}^{l_j} := \max\left\{x^{\alpha_k}\sqrt{\alpha_k!} : x_i \in \{x_{\min,i}, x_{\max,i}\}, i \in [1, n]\right\},$$

$$y_{\min,k}^{l_j} := \min\left\{x^{\alpha_k}\sqrt{\alpha_k!} : x_i \in \{x_{\min,i}, x_{\max,i}\}, i \in [1, n]\right\},$$

$k \in [1, N_j]$, $N_j = \binom{n+l_j-1}{l_j}$ while each element y_k, $k \in [1, N_j]$, corresponds to the monomial x^α of the l_j-lift of x. The set $\mathcal{B} := \mathcal{B}_{l_1} \times \mathcal{B}_{l_2} \times \ldots \times \mathcal{B}_{l_K}$ is a polytope, can be used to initialize Algorithm 2 since $\mathcal{B} \supset \mathcal{X}^{[\mathcal{L}]} \cap \mathcal{V}$ and is described by $\mathcal{B} = \{y \in \mathbb{R}^N : R_{\min} \leq y \leq R_{\max}\}$, where $R_{\min} = \begin{bmatrix} y_{\min}^{l_1 \top} & \ldots & y_{\min}^{l_K \top} \end{bmatrix}^\top$, $R_{\max} = \begin{bmatrix} y_{\max}^{l_1 \top} & \ldots & y_{\max}^{l_K \top} \end{bmatrix}^\top$. To recover a set $\mathcal{B} \subset \mathbb{R}^N$ which can be used for initialization in Algorithm 3, it is sufficient to replace $R_{\min}$ with $\hat{R}_{\min,i} = \min\{-\delta, R_{\min,i}\}$, for some positive scalar $\delta > 0$.

Generating Unstable Trajectories for Switched Systems via Dual Sum-Of-Squares Techniques

Benoît Legat[*]
Université catholique de Louvain
4 Av. G. Lemaître,
1348 Louvain-la-Neuve,
Belgium
benoit.legat
@student.uclouvain.be

Raphaël M. Jungers[†]
ICTEAM
Université catholique de Louvain
4 Av. G. Lemaître,
1348 Louvain-la-Neuve,
Belgium
raphael.jungers
@uclouvain.be

Pablo A. Parrilo
Laboratory for Information and Decision Systems
Massachusetts Institute of Technology
77 Massachusetts Avenue
Cambridge MA 02139, USA
parrilo@mit.edu

ABSTRACT

The joint spectral radius (JSR) of a set of matrices characterizes the maximal asymptotic growth rate of an infinite product of matrices of the set. This quantity appears in a number of applications including the stability of switched and hybrid systems. Many algorithms exist for estimating the JSR but not much is known about how to generate an infinite sequence of matrices with an optimal asymptotic growth rate. To the best of our knowledge, the currently known algorithms select a small sequence with large spectral radius using brute force (or branch-and-bound variants) and repeats this sequence infinitely.

In this paper we introduce a new approach to this question, using the dual solution of a sum of squares optimization program for JSR approximation. Our algorithm produces an infinite sequence of matrices with an asymptotic growth rate arbitrarily close to the JSR. The algorithm naturally extends to the case where the allowable switching sequences are determined by a graph or finite automaton. Unlike the brute force approach, we provide a guarantee on the closeness of the asymptotic growth rate to the JSR. This, in turn, provides new bounds on the quality of the JSR approximation. We provide numerical examples illustrating the good performance of the algorithm.

*This research took place in the framework of the MIT-UCL Internship Program supported by the International Lhoist Berghmans Innovation Chair.

†R. M. J. is a F.R.S.-FNRS Research Associate. His research is supported by the Belgian Interuniversity Attraction Poles, and by the ARC grant 13/18-054 from Communauté française de Belgique.

HSCC'16, April 12–14, 2016, Vienna, Austria.

DOI: http://dx.doi.org/10.1145/2883817.2883821

Keywords

Joint spectral radius; Sum of squares programming; Switched Systems; Path-complete Lyapunov functions.

1. INTRODUCTION

In recent years, the study of the stability of hybrid systems has been the subject of extensive research using methods based on classical ideas from Lyapunov theory and modern mathematical optimization techniques. Even for switched linear systems, arguably the simplest class of hybrid systems, determining stability is undecidable and approximating the maximal asymptotic growth rate is NP-hard [5]. Despite these negative results, the vast range of applications has motivated a wealth of algorithms to approximate this quantity.

A switched linear system is characterized by a finite set of matrices $\mathcal{M} \triangleq \{A_1, A_2, \dots, A_m\} \subset \mathbb{R}^{n \times n}$ and the iteration

$$x_k = A_{\sigma_k} x_{k-1}, \quad \sigma_k \in \{1, \dots, m\}.$$

The maximal asymptotic growth rate of this iteration is given by the *joint spectral radius* (JSR). The JSR $\rho(\mathcal{M})$ of a finite set of matrices $\mathcal{M}$ is defined as

$$\rho(\mathcal{M}) = \lim_{k \to \infty} \max_{\sigma \in \{1,\dots,m\}^k} \|A_{\sigma_k} \cdots A_{\sigma_2} A_{\sigma_1}\|^{1/k}.$$

This definition is independent of the norm used.

The JSR was introduced by Rota and Strang [16] and has many other applications such as wavelets, the capacity of some particular codes, zero-order stability of ordinary differential equations, congestion control in computer networks, curve design and networked and delayed control systems; see [10] for a survey on the JSR and its applications. Many algorithms exist for estimating the JSR but not much is known on how to generate an infinite sequence of matrices with an asymptotic growth rate close to the JSR. However generating such sequence can be of particular interest, depending on the application, such as exhibiting unstable trajectories for switched linear systems. To the best of our knowledge, the currently known algorithms select a small sequence of matrices with high spectral radius using brute force (or branch-

and-bound variants) and repeats this sequence infinitely [8, 9, 11].

Parrilo and Jadbabaie [14] give an efficient approximation algorithm for computing the JSR using sum of squares (SOS) programming. In this paper we compute the dual of the corresponding SOS program and give an algorithm that generates an infinite sequence of matrices with an asymptotic growth rate arbitrarily close to the JSR. Unlike the brute force approach, we provide a guarantee on the quality of the asymptotic growth rate. As a by-product of the algorithm, the spectral radius of a finite part of this infinite sequence can be used to give lower bounds on the JSR. We show on numerical examples that the technique works well in practice.

In some applications the values that σ_k can take may depend on $\sigma_{k-1}, \sigma_{k-2}, \ldots$. These constraints are often conveniently represented using a *finite automaton* and the JSR under such constraints is called constrained joint spectral radius (CJSR) [7]; an example of constrained switched system is given by Example 1 and its automaton is illustrated by Figure 1. Philippe et al. generalize the SOS-based approximation algorithm for the CJSR in [15, Section 3]. Our technique is well suited for analysing the more general constrained systems as well.

We provide a new estimate of the accuracy of the SOS-based approximation algorithm for the CJSR which is better than the previously existing one for sufficiently large SOS degree. The existing estimate only depends on the dimension of the matrices while our new one relates the accuracy of the SOS-based approximation algorithm with the combinatorial structure of the automaton representing the constraints.

The automaton representing the constraints can be represented by a strongly connected labelled directed graph $G(V, E)$, possibly with parallel edges. The labels are elements of the set $\{1, \ldots, m\}$ and E is a subset of $V \times V \times \{1, \ldots, m\}$. We say that $(u, v, \sigma) \in E$ if there is an edge between node u and node v with label σ.

The following will serve as a running example.

Example 1 (Running example[1]). We borrow the example of [15, Section 4]. The set of matrices $\mathcal{M}$ is composed of the following four matrices

$$A_1 = A + B\begin{pmatrix}k_1 & k_2\end{pmatrix}, \qquad A_2 = A + B\begin{pmatrix}0 & k_2\end{pmatrix},$$
$$A_3 = A + B\begin{pmatrix}k_1 & 0\end{pmatrix}, \qquad A_4 = A.$$

where $k_1 = -0.49$, $k_2 = 0.27$,

$$A = \begin{pmatrix}0.94 & 0.56\\ 0.14 & 0.46\end{pmatrix} \text{ and } B = \begin{pmatrix}0\\1\end{pmatrix}.$$

The automaton is represented by Figure 1.

In Section 2, we explain the SOS-based approximation algorithm for the CJSR and give our new estimate for its accuracy. The new bounds explicitly depend on the allowable transitions, through the graph $G(V, E)$.

In Section 3, we compute the dual of the corresponding SOS program and we give our algorithm for generating a sequence of matrices with an asymptotic growth rate close to the CJSR.

[1]The source code and instructions are available at the author's web site to reproduce the numerical results obtained for the running example. The switched system considered in Example 2, Example 4 and Example 6 is simpler than the running example and the results given in those examples can be obtained by hand.

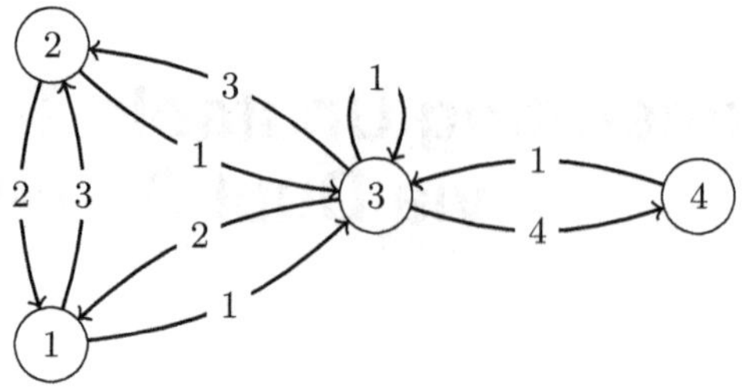

Figure 1: Automaton for the running example. The numbers on the edges are their respective labels.

Notations.

We define the automaton $G^\top(V, E^\top)$ where $E^\top = \{ (v, u, \sigma) : (u, v, \sigma) \in E \}$. We denote as E_k the subset of E^k that represents valid paths of length k. The k-uple $(\sigma_1, \sigma_2, \ldots, \sigma_k)$ is said to be *G-admissible* if $\sigma_1, \ldots, \sigma_k$ are the respective labels of a path of length k. The *arbitrary switching* case, that is, when every tuple is G-admissible, can be seen as the particular case when the automaton has only one node and m self-loops with labels $1, \ldots, m$. We denote the set of all k-uples of $\{1, \ldots, m\}^k$ that are G-admissible as G_k. The sequence $\sigma_1, \sigma_2, \ldots$ is G-admissible (resp. $G^\top$-admissible) if $(\sigma_1, \ldots, \sigma_k)$ (resp. $(\sigma_k, \ldots, \sigma_1)$) is G-admissible for any $k \geq 1$. We denote $A_{\sigma_k} \cdots A_{\sigma_1}$ as A_s where $s = (\sigma_1, \ldots, \sigma_k)$ or s is a path with those respective labels.

We denote the set of homogeneous polynomials of degree $2d$ as $\mathbb{R}_{\mathbf{2d}}[x]$, the cone of homogeneous SOS polynomials of degree $2d$ as $\Sigma_{\mathbf{2d}}$ and the dual of $\Sigma_{\mathbf{2d}}$ as $\Sigma^*_{\mathbf{2d}}$.

2. AUTOMATON-DEPENDENT BOUNDS

The definition of the JSR is generalized as follows for constrained systems.

Definition 1 ([7]). The *constrained joint spectral radius* (CJSR) of a finite set of matrices $\mathcal{M}$ constrained by an automaton G, denoted as $\rho(G, \mathcal{M})$, is

$$\rho(G, \mathcal{M}) = \lim_{k\to\infty} \max\left\{ \|A_s\|^{1/k} : s \in G_k \right\}.$$

2.1 CJSR Approximation via SOS

A key result used in the SOS-based approximation algorithm for the unconstrained JSR [14] is the following:

Proposition 1 ([16, Proposition 1]). Consider a finite set of matrices $\mathcal{M}$. For any $\epsilon > 0$ there exists a norm $\|\cdot\|$ such that

$$\|A_\sigma x\| \leq (\rho(\mathcal{M}) + \epsilon)\|x\|$$

for all $x \in \mathbb{R}^n$ and $\sigma = 1, \ldots, m$.

Philippe et al. recently gave a generalization of that algorithm, relying on the following extension of Proposition 1 to constrained switched systems.

Proposition 2 ([15, Proposition 2.2]). Consider a finite set of matrices $\mathcal{M}$ constrained by an automaton $G(V, E)$. For any $\epsilon > 0$, there exists a set of norms $\{ \|\cdot\|_v : v \in V \}$ such that

$$\|A_\sigma x\|_v \leq (\rho(G, \mathcal{M}) + \epsilon)\|x\|_u$$

holds for all edge $(u, v, \sigma) \in E$.

Strictly positive homogeneous polynomials are not necessarily norms because their sublevel sets may not be convex. However we can provide upper bounds for the CJSR using polynomials instead of norms.

Theorem 1. Consider a finite set of matrices $\mathcal{M}$ constrained by an automaton $G(V, E)$. If there exists a strictly positive homogeneous polynomial $p_v(x)$ of degree $2d$ for all $v \in V$ such that

$$p_v(A_\sigma x) \leq \gamma^{2d} p_u(x)$$

holds for all edge $(u, v, \sigma) \in E$. Then $\rho(G, \mathcal{M}) \leq \gamma$.

Proof. Consider a norm $\|\cdot\|$ of $\mathbb{R}^n$ and its corresponding induced matrix norm of $\mathbb{R}^{n\times n}$. For each $v \in V$, we know by compactness of the unit ball in $\mathbb{R}^n$, continuity and strict positivity of $p_v(x)$ that there exist $0 < \alpha_v \leq \beta_v$ such that

$$\alpha_v \|x\|^{2d} \leq p_v(x) \leq \beta_v \|x\|^{2d}$$

for all $x \in \mathbb{R}^n$. Let $\alpha = \min_{v\in V} \alpha_v$ and $\beta = \max_{v \in V} \beta_v$.

For a G-admissible k-uple $(\sigma_1, \sigma_2, \ldots, \sigma_k)$,

$$\|A_{\sigma_k} \cdots A_{\sigma_1}\| = \sup_{x\neq 0} \frac{\|A_{\sigma_k} \cdots A_{\sigma_1} x\|}{\|x\|}.$$

Consider a path such that the ith edge has label σ_i for $i = 1, \ldots, k$ and denote the intermediary nodes of that path as $v_0, v_1, \ldots, v_k$. For any $x \in \mathbb{R}^n$, we have

$$\begin{aligned}\|A_{\sigma_k} \cdots A_{\sigma_1} x\| &\leq \alpha_{v_k}^{-\frac{1}{2d}} p_{v_k}(A_{\sigma_k} \cdots A_{\sigma_1} x)^{\frac{1}{2d}} \\ &\leq \alpha_{v_k}^{-\frac{1}{2d}} \gamma p_{v_{k-1}}(A_{\sigma_{k-1}} \cdots A_{\sigma_1} x)^{\frac{1}{2d}} \\ &\leq \alpha_{v_k}^{-\frac{1}{2d}} \gamma^k p_{v_0}(x)^{\frac{1}{2d}}\end{aligned}$$

and

$$\|x\| \geq \beta_{v_0}^{-\frac{1}{2d}} p_{v_0}(x)^{\frac{1}{2d}}$$

hence

$$\|A_{\sigma_k} \cdots A_{\sigma_1}\| \leq \left(\frac{\beta_{v_k}}{\alpha_{v_0}}\right)^{\frac{1}{2d}} \gamma^k \leq \left(\frac{\beta}{\alpha}\right)^{\frac{1}{2d}} \gamma^k.$$

Taking the kth root, the limit $k \to \infty$ and using Definition 1 we obtain the result. □

We relax the positivity condition of Theorem 1 by the more tractable sum of squares (SOS) condition and define $\rho_{\mathrm{SOS},2d}(G, \mathcal{M})$ as the solution of the following SOS program:

Program 1 (Primal).

$$\inf_{p_v(x)\in\mathbb{R}_{2d}[x],\gamma\in\mathbb{R}} \gamma$$

$$p_v(x) \text{ is SOS } \quad \forall v \in V \qquad (1)$$

$$p_v(x) \text{ is strictly positive } \quad \forall v \in V \qquad (2)$$

$$\gamma^{2d} p_u(x) - p_v(A_\sigma x) \text{ is SOS } \quad \forall (u, v, \sigma) \in E.$$

Remark 1. In practice we can replace (1) and (2) by "$p_v(x) - \epsilon\|x\|_2^{2d}$ is SOS" for any $\epsilon > 0$. Note that this constrains $p_v(x)$ to be in the interior of the SOS cone, which is sufficient for $p_v(x)$ to be strictly positive. The bounds given in Section 2.2 are valid if $p_v(x)$ is in the interior of the SOS cone.

By Theorem 1, a feasible solution of Program 1 gives an upper bound for $\rho(G, \mathcal{M})$, and thus, for any positive degree $2d$,

$$\rho(G, \mathcal{M}) \leq \rho_{\mathrm{SOS},2d}(G, \mathcal{M}). \qquad (3)$$

Example 2. Consider the unconstrained system [2, Example 2.1] with $m = 3$:

$$\mathcal{M} = \{A_1 = e_1 e_2^\top, A_2 = e_2 e_3^\top, A_3 = e_3 e_1^\top\}$$

where e_i denotes the ith canonical basis vector.

For any d, a solution to Program 1 is given by

$$(p(x), \gamma) = (x_1^{2d} + x_2^{2d} + x_3^{2d}, 1).$$

Indeed, for example, with A_1 we have

$$p(e_1 e_2^\top x) = p(x_2, 0, 0) = x_2^{2d} + 0 + 0 \leq x_1^{2d} + x_2^{2d} + x_3^{2d}.$$

Example 3. Let us reconsider our running example; see Example 1. The optimal solution of Program 1 is represented by Figure 2 for $2d$ = 2, 4, 6, 8, 10 and 12. We can see a big difference between the shape of the sublevel sets for $2d = 2$ and $2d = 4$ while between $2d = 4$ and $2d = 12$, the difference seems to be more subtle.

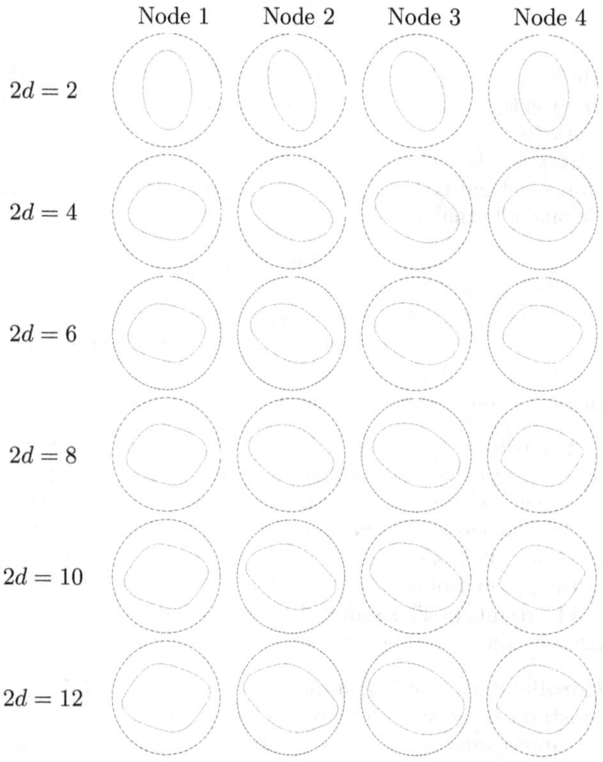

Figure 2: Representation of the solutions to Program 1 with different values of d for the running example. The blue curve represents the boundary of the 1-sublevel set of the optimal solution p_v at each node $v \in V$. The dashed curve is the boundary of the unit circle.

2.2 Approximation guarantees

Philippe et al. show, based on [14], the following accuracy guarantees for Program 1.

Theorem 2 ([15, Theorem 3.6]). Consider a finite set of matrices $\mathcal{M} \subset \mathbb{R}^{n\times n}$ constrained by an automaton G and a positive integer d. The approximation given by Program 1 using homogeneous polynomials of degree $2d$ satisfies:

$$\rho_{\text{SOS},2d}(G,\mathcal{M}) \le \binom{n+d-1}{d}^{\frac{1}{2d}} \rho(G,\mathcal{M}).$$

This guarantee only depends on the dimension of the matrices and neither on the number of matrices nor on the automaton. In this section, we show the following guarantee that relates the accuracy of Program 1 to the evolution of the number of paths in G for increasing length.

Theorem 3. Consider a finite set of matrices $\mathcal{M}$ constrained by an automaton G and a positive integer d. The approximation given by Program 1 using homogeneous polynomials of degree $2d$ satisfies:

$$\rho_{\text{SOS},2d}(G,\mathcal{M}) \le \rho(A(G))^{\frac{1}{2d}} \rho(G,\mathcal{M})$$

where $A(G)$ is the adjacency matrix of G.

Remark 2. Consider the matrix norm $\|\cdot\|_\infty$ on $\mathbb{R}^{n\times n}$ induced by the infinity norm on $\mathbb{R}^n$. It is well known that

$$\|A\|_\infty = \max_{1\le i\le n} \sum_{j=1}^{n} |a_{ij}|$$

where a_{ij} is (i,j) entry of A. It is also well known that the (u,v) entry of $A(G)^k$ gives the number of paths of length k starting at node u and ending at node v in G. Hence $\|A(G)^k\|_\infty$ is the maximum, over all nodes of G, of the number of paths of length k starting at that node. By the Gelfand's formula,

$$\rho(A(G)) = \lim_{k\to\infty} \|A(G)^k\|_\infty^{1/k}.$$

Therefore the spectral radius $\rho(A(G))$ represents the "maximal asymptotic growth rate of the number of paths". This is somewhat related to how constrained the automaton is: the more constrained, the better the approximation.

As a corollary of Theorem 3, in the trivial cases such that $\rho(A(G)) = 1$, the approximation is exact. This corresponds to the case where every node of G has indegree and outdegree 1. In that case, the graph forms a cycle of some length k and the CJSR is simply the kth root of the spectral radius of the product of the matrices along this cycle.

The results of Theorem 2, Theorem 3 and (3) are summarized by the following corollary.

Corollary 1. Consider a finite set of matrices $\mathcal{M} \subset \mathbb{R}^{n\times n}$ constrained by an automaton G and a positive integer d, the approximation given by Program 1 using homogeneous polynomials of degree $2d$ satisfies:

$$\min\left\{\binom{n+d-1}{d}, \rho(A(G))\right\}^{-\frac{1}{2d}} \rho_{\text{SOS},2d}(G,\mathcal{M}) \le \rho(G,\mathcal{M}) \le \rho_{\text{SOS},2d}(G,\mathcal{M}).$$

where $A(G)$ is the adjacency matrix of the automaton G.

We see that we can have arbitrary accuracy by increasing d.

For the arbitrary switching case, $\rho(A(G)) = m$. Theorem 3 was already known in this particular case [14, Theorem 4.3]. This section can thus be seen as a generalization of [14, Section 4].

Our proof technique relies on the analysis of an iteration in the vector space of polynomials of degree $2d$. When this iteration converges, it converges to a feasible solution of Problem 1. By analysing this iteration as affine iterations in this vector space, we derive a sufficient condition for its convergence and thus an upper bound for $\rho_{\text{SOS},2d}(G,\mathcal{M})$.

Consider the iteration

$$P_{v,0}(x) = 0,$$
$$P_{v,k+1}(x) = Q_v(x) + \frac{1}{\beta} \sum_{(u,v,\sigma)\in E} P_{u,k}(A_\sigma x), \quad v \in V \quad (4)$$

for fixed homogeneous polynomial $Q_v(x)$ of degree $2d$ in n variables (not necessarily different) and a constant $\beta > 0$.

When this iteration converges, it converges to a feasible solution of Program 1.

Theorem 4. Consider a constant $\beta > 0$. If there exists homogeneous polynomials $Q_v(x)$ in the interior of the SOS cone such that the iteration (4) converges then

$$\rho_{\text{SOS},2d}(G,\mathcal{M}) \le \beta^{\frac{1}{2d}}.$$

Proof. Suppose the iteration converges to the polynomials $P_{v,\infty}(x)$. It is easy to show by induction that $P_{v,k}(x)$ is SOS for all k. It is trivial for $k = 0$ and if it is true for k then it is also true for $k+1$ by (4). Since the SOS cone is closed, $P_{v,\infty}$ is SOS. Now by (4), for each $v \in V$,

$$P_{v,\infty}(x) = Q_v(x) + \frac{1}{\beta} \sum_{(u,v,\sigma)\in E} P_{u,\infty}(A_\sigma x)$$

so $P_{v,\infty}(x)$ is also in the interior of the SOS cone. For each edge (u,v,σ), by manipulating the above equation, we have

$$\beta P_{v,\infty}(x) - P_{u,\infty}(A_\sigma x) = \beta Q_v(x) + \sum_{\substack{(u',v,\sigma')\in E\\(u',\sigma')\ne(u,\sigma)}} P_{u',\infty}(A_{\sigma'} x)$$

so $\beta P_{v,\infty}(x) - P_{u,\infty}(A_\sigma x)$ is in the interior of the SOS cone. Therefore $(\{P_{v,\infty}(x) : v \in V\}, \beta^{\frac{1}{2d}})$ is a feasible solution of Program 1. □

Remark 3. Before going into the details, we first provide an intuition on how we prove Theorem 3 using the iteration (4). Consider the following iteration (it is not the same as (4) but the sufficient condition of convergence that we develop in Theorem 5 is the same for both iterations)

$$P_{v,0}(x) = Q_v(x),$$
$$P_{v,k+1}(x) = \frac{1}{\beta} \sum_{(u,v,\sigma)\in E} P_{u,k}(A_\sigma x), \quad v \in V.$$

We can see that

$$P_{v,k+1}(x) = \frac{\rho(G,\mathcal{M})^{2dk}}{\beta^k} \sum_{\substack{s\in E_k,\\ s(k+1)=v}} Q_{s(1)}\Big(\frac{A_s}{\rho(G,\mathcal{M})^k} x\Big) \quad (5)$$

where $s(i)$ denotes the ith node of the path s. As $k \to \infty$, $A_s/\rho(G,\mathcal{M})^k$ tends to zero. However, the number of terms in the right-hand side may tend to infinity. It is equal to the number of paths of length k whose last node is v. Therefore $\beta/\rho(G,\mathcal{M})^{2d}$ should be at least the asymptotic value of the kth root of the number of paths of length k. We have seen in Remark 2 that this value is $\rho(A(G))$.

In view of Theorem 4, it is thus natural to analyse under which condition the iteration 4 converges. While we could convert the idea behind Remark 3 into a full proof, we present here a slightly different approach. Recall that iteration 4 is an affine map on the vector space of homogeneous polynomials of degree $2d$. We would like to choose a basis for this vector space to represent the linear operator as a matrix and use a sufficient condition for convergence depending on the spectral radius of the matrix. A simple choice is the monomial basis x^α with α such that $|\alpha| = d$ where x^α denotes $x_1^{\alpha_1} \cdots x_n^{\alpha_n}$ and $|\alpha|$ denotes $\alpha_1 + \cdots + \alpha_n$. We choose instead a basis for which each monomial x^α is scaled by the coefficient $\binom{d}{\alpha} = \frac{d!}{\alpha_1!\alpha_2!\cdots\alpha_n!}$ so that the corresponding lift operation for vectors of $\mathbb{R}^n$ that we define below preserves the Euclidean norm (up to power).

Definition 2 (*d*-lift)**.** Let $N_d = \binom{n+d-1}{d}$. The d-lift of a vector $x \in \mathbb{R}^n$ is the vector $x^{[d]} \in \mathbb{R}^{N_d}$ (indexed by the n-uples $\alpha \in \mathbb{N}^n$ such that $|\alpha| = d$) such that $x^{[d]}_\alpha = \binom{d}{\alpha} x^\alpha$.

For any matrix $A \in \mathbb{R}^{n\times n}$, the d-lift induces an associated map $A^{[d]} \in \mathbb{R}^{N_d \times N_d}$ which is the unique $N_d \times N_d$ matrix that satisfies $(Ax)^{[d]} = A^{[d]}x^{[d]}$. We also denote $\mathcal{M}^{[d]} \triangleq \{A_1^{[d]}, \ldots, A_m^{[d]}\}$.

As mentioned above, we have chosen to scale the monomials so that $\|x^{[d]}\|_2 = \|x\|_2^d$ where $\|\cdot\|_2$ is the Euclidean norm. The purpose of this choice is to have the following lemma for the lift operation.

Lemma 1 ([15, Lemma 3.5])**.** *Consider a finite set of matrices $\mathcal{M}$ constrained by an automaton G and a positive integer d. The following identity holds:*

$$\rho(G, \mathcal{M}^{[d]}) = \rho(G, \mathcal{M})^d.$$

We can now formulate a sufficient condition for the convergence of the iteration 4.

Theorem 5. *Let*

$$B_{2d} = \sum_{(u,v,\sigma)\in E} (e_u e_v^\top) \otimes A_\sigma^{[2d]}$$

where $\otimes$ is the Kronecker product. If $\beta < \rho(B_{2d})$ then the iteration (4) converges for any homogeneous polynomials $Q_v(x)$ of degree $2d$ in the interior of the SOS cone.

Proof. We can rewrite the polynomials in terms of the basis of scaled monomials. For each $v \in V$, we consider the vector $q_v \in \mathbb{R}^{N_{2d}}$ such that $Q_v(x) = \langle q_v, x^{[2d]}\rangle$. We see that $Q_v(A_\sigma x) = \langle q_v, A_\sigma^{[2d]} x^{[2d]}\rangle = \langle (A_\sigma^{[2d]})^\top q_v, x^{[2d]}\rangle$. The iteration (4) is

$$p_{v,0} = 0,$$
$$p_{v,k+1} = q_j + \frac{1}{\beta}\sum_{u\in V}\Big(\sum_{(u,v,\sigma)\in E} A_\sigma^{[2d]}\Big)^\top p_{u,k}, \quad v \in V$$

which can be rewritten as

$$p_0 = 0, \quad p_{k+1} = q + \frac{1}{\beta} B_{2d}^\top p_k. \tag{6}$$

where the vectors $p_k \in \mathbb{R}^{|V|N_{2d}}$ are (resp. $q \in \mathbb{R}^{|V|N_{2d}}$ is) the concatenation of $p_{1,k}, \ldots, p_{|V|,k}$ (resp. $q_1, \ldots, q_{|V|}$).

The iteration in Equation (6) is an affine iteration, and it is well known that it converges if $\rho(B_{2d}) < \beta$, independently of q. □

Remark 4. If $\rho(B_{2d}) < \beta$, $p_\infty \triangleq \lim_{k\to\infty} p_k$ can be computed by solving the linear system $(I - B_{2d}/\beta)^\top p_\infty = q$.

As a corollary of Theorem 4 and Theorem 5,

$$\rho_{\mathrm{SOS},2d}(G, \mathcal{M}) \le \rho(B_{2d})^{\frac{1}{2d}}. \tag{7}$$

To prove Theorem 3, it remains to find a relation between $\rho(B_{2d})$ and $\rho(G, \mathcal{M})$.

Given a sub-multiplicative norm $\|\cdot\|$ on $\mathbb{R}^{n_1\times n_1}$, consider the sub-multiplicative norm $|||\cdot|||$ on $\mathbb{R}^{n_2 n_1 \times n_2 n_1}$ induced by $\|\cdot\|$ defined in [12] as

$$|||M||| \triangleq \max_{1\le i\le N} \sum_{j=1}^{n_2} \|m_{ij}\| \tag{8}$$

for a block $n_2 \times n_2$ matrix $M = (m_{ij})_{i,j=1}^{n_2}$ with $m_{ij} \in \mathbb{R}^{n_1\times n_1}$. We can show that

Lemma 2. *Given a norm $\|\cdot\|$ on $\mathbb{R}^{n_1\times n_1}$ and the norm $|||\cdot|||$ defined by (8), for any matrices $A_1, \ldots, A_m \in \mathbb{R}^{n_1\times n_1}$ and any nonnegative matrices $B_1, \ldots, B_m \in \mathbb{R}^{n_2\times n_2}$, we have*

$$\Big|\Big|\Big|\sum_{k=1}^m B_k \otimes A_k\Big|\Big|\Big| \le \Big\|\sum_{k=1}^m B_k\Big\|_\infty \max_{1\le k\le m} \|A_k\|.$$

Proof. Using (8) and the subadditivity of the norm $\|\cdot\|$,

$$\begin{aligned}
\Big|\Big|\Big|\sum_{k=1}^m B_k \otimes A_k\Big|\Big|\Big| &= \max_{1\le i\le N} \sum_{j=1}^N \Big\|\sum_{k=1}^m (B_k)_{ij} A_k\Big\| \\
&\le \max_{1\le i\le N} \sum_{j=1}^N \sum_{k=1}^m (B_k)_{ij} \|A_k\| \\
&\le \big(\max_{1\le k\le m} \|A_k\|\big) \max_{1\le i\le N} \sum_{j=1}^N \sum_{k=1}^m (B_k)_{ij} \\
&\le \Big\|\sum_{k=1}^m B_k\Big\|_\infty \max_{1\le k\le m} \|A_k\|.
\end{aligned}$$

□

This Lemma allows us to prove the following generalization of [4, Lemma 1].

Lemma 3. *For any finite set of matrices $\mathcal{M} = \{A_1, \ldots, A_m\}$ of $\mathbb{R}^{n_1\times n_1}$, any nonnegative matrices $B_1, \ldots, B_m \in \mathbb{R}^{n_2\times n_2}$ and any automaton $G(V,E)$ such that for each path p that is not G-admissible, $B_p = 0$, we have*

$$\rho(\sum_{i=1}^m B_i \otimes A_i) \le \rho(\sum_{i=1}^m B_i)\rho(G, \mathcal{M}).$$

Proof. By Lemma 2,

$$\begin{aligned}\left\|\left\|\left(\sum_{i=1}^{m} B_i \otimes A_i\right)^k\right\|\right\| &= \left\|\left\|\sum_{s\in E^k} B_p \otimes A_s\right\|\right\| \\ &= \left\|\left\|\sum_{s\in E_k} B_p \otimes A_s\right\|\right\| \\ &\le \left\|\sum_{s\in E_k} B_p\right\|_\infty \max_{s\in E_k} \|A_s\| \\ &= \left\|\left(\sum_{i=1}^{m} B_i\right)^k\right\|_\infty \max_{s\in E_k} \|A_s\|.\end{aligned}$$

Taking the kth root and the limit of $k \to \infty$ we obtain the result. □

We are now ready to prove Theorem 3.

Proof of Theorem 3. We have

$$\begin{aligned}\rho_{\mathrm{SOS},2d}(G,\mathcal{M}) &\le \rho(B_{2d})^{\frac{1}{2d}} \\ &\le \left[\rho\Big(\sum_{(i,j,\sigma)\in E} e_i e_j^\top\Big)\rho(G,\mathcal{M}^{[2d]})\right]^{\frac{1}{2d}} \\ &= [\rho(A(G))\rho(G,\mathcal{M}^{[2d]})]^{\frac{1}{2d}} \\ &= \rho(A(G))^{\frac{1}{2d}}\rho(G,\mathcal{M}).\end{aligned}$$

where the first inequality is (7), the second is given by Lemma 3, the first equality is given by the fact that

$$\sum_{(i,j,\sigma)\in E} e_i e_j^\top = A(G)$$

and the second equality is given by Lemma 1. □

3. FINDING HIGH-GROWTH SEQUENCES

3.1 Dual SOS program

Consider the feasibility version of Program 1, i.e. γ is fixed and we want to find polynomials such that the constraints hold.

The dual variables are in the dual of the SOS cones, i.e. they are linear functionals over homogeneous polynomials of degree $2d$ that gives a positive value when applied to a SOS polynomials. Barak et al. [3] introduced the *pseudo-expectation* $\widetilde{\mathbb{E}}$ as a way to interpret those linear functionals. It can be seen as the expectation of a *pseudo-distribution* $\widetilde{\mu}$. That is,

$$\langle \widetilde{\mathbb{E}}, p(x)\rangle = \widetilde{\mathbb{E}}[p(x)] = \int_{\mathbb{S}^{n-1}} p(x)\,\mathrm{d}\widetilde{\mu}. \quad (9)$$

We say that $\widetilde{\mu}$ is only a 'pseudo-distribution' (and not a classical distribution) in the sense that it is not necessarily a positive measure, it might be possible that $\widetilde{\mathbb{E}}[p(x)] < 0$ while $p(x)$ is nonnegative. However, if $p(x)$ is an homogeneous SOS polynomial of degree $2d$ then $\widetilde{\mathbb{E}}[p(x)] \ge 0$ since $\widetilde{\mathbb{E}}$ belongs to the dual of the SOS cone.

Note that for any matrix $A \in \mathbb{R}^{n\times n}$, the polynomial $p(Ax)$ depends linearly on $p(x)$. Let $\mathcal{A}$ be the linear map such that $\mathcal{A}(p(x)) = p(Ax)$ for all $p(x) \in \mathbb{R}[x]_{\mathbf{2d}}$. We define the adjoint map $\mathcal{A}^*$, the linear map such that $\langle \mathcal{A}^*\widetilde{\mathbb{E}}, p(x)\rangle = \langle \widetilde{\mathbb{E}}, \mathcal{A}(p(x))\rangle$ for all $\widetilde{\mathbb{E}} \in (\mathbb{R}[x]_{\mathbf{2d}})^*$ and $p(x) \in \mathbb{R}[x]_{\mathbf{2d}}$.

The dual of the feasibility version of the primal is given by

Program 2 (Dual).

$$\sum_{(u,v,\sigma)\in E} \mathcal{A}_\sigma^*\widetilde{\mathbb{E}}_{uv\sigma} \succeq \gamma^{2d} \sum_{(v,w,\sigma)\in E} \widetilde{\mathbb{E}}_{vw\sigma}, \forall v \in V, \quad (10)$$

$$\widetilde{\mathbb{E}}_{uv\sigma} \in \Sigma_{\mathbf{2d}}^*, \qquad \forall (u,v,\sigma) \in E,$$

$$\sum_{(u,v,\sigma)\in E} \widetilde{\mathbb{E}}_{uv\sigma}\Big[\sum_{i=1}^{n} x_i^{2d}\Big] = 1. \quad (11)$$

Note that the dual constraint (10) is equivalent to:

$$\sum_{(u,v,\sigma)\in E} \widetilde{\mathbb{E}}_{uv\sigma}[p(A_\sigma x)] \ge \gamma^{2d} \sum_{(v,w,\sigma)\in E} \widetilde{\mathbb{E}}_{vw\sigma}[p(x)] \quad (12)$$

for all $v \in V$ and for all $p(x) \in \Sigma_{\mathbf{2d}}$.

Example 4. Consider Example 2. For $i = 1, 2, 3$, let $\widetilde{\mathbb{E}}_i$ be the dual solution at the edge corresponding to the matrix A_i. For any d, we can see that the dual solution for $\gamma = 1$ is such that the only monomial x^α such that $\widetilde{\mathbb{E}}_1[x^\alpha]$ (resp. $\widetilde{\mathbb{E}}_2[x^\alpha]$, $\widetilde{\mathbb{E}}_3[x^\alpha]$) is non-zero is x_1^{2d} (resp. x_2^{2d}, x_3^{2d}) and $\widetilde{\mathbb{E}}_1[x_1^{2d}] = \widetilde{\mathbb{E}}_2[x_2^{2d}] = \widetilde{\mathbb{E}}_3[x_3^{2d}] = 1/3$. Note that it means that $\widetilde{\mu}_1 = \delta_{(1,0,0)}/3$, $\widetilde{\mu}_2 = \delta_{(0,1,0)}/3$ and $\widetilde{\mu}_3 = \delta_{(0,0,1)}/3$ where δ_x is the Dirac measure centered on x. Since there also exists a primal solution for $\gamma = 1$ (see Example 2) we have $\rho_{\mathrm{SOS},2d}(G,\mathcal{M}) = 1$ for any d.

Example 5. We continue the running example; see Example 1 and Example 3.

For all d, $\widetilde{\mathbb{E}}_{212} = \widetilde{\mathbb{E}}_{323} = \widetilde{\mathbb{E}}_{344} = \widetilde{\mathbb{E}}_{431} = 0$ hence the node 4 is "unused" by the dual. For $2d = 2, 4, 6, 8$, $\widetilde{\mathbb{E}}_{123} = \widetilde{\mathbb{E}}_{231} = 0$ so the node 2 is "unused" for low degree.

At first, one could think that the dual variables can be used to reduce the systems, e.g. remove nodes or edges. However, as we will see, it would be a mistake to remove the node 2.

For $2d = 10$, $\widetilde{\mathbb{E}}_{123}$ and $\widetilde{\mathbb{E}}_{231}$ are not zero and are of the "same order or magnitude" than $\widetilde{\mathbb{E}}_{131}$ and $\widetilde{\mathbb{E}}_{312}$. Then for $2d = 12$, $\widetilde{\mathbb{E}}_{123}$ and $\widetilde{\mathbb{E}}_{231}$ have "larger magnitude" than $\widetilde{\mathbb{E}}_{131}$ and $\widetilde{\mathbb{E}}_{312}$. This observation will be useful for Example 7.

We can see that while the shape of the primal variables change a lot between $2d = 2$ and $2d = 4$ as mentioned in Example 3, the "important" change for the dual variables happens around $2d = 10$.

It is also interesting to notice that the matrices corresponding to the dual variables have low rank. For example, for $2d = 2$, the measure corresponding to the dual variable $\widetilde{\mathbb{E}}_{131}$ (resp. $\widetilde{\mathbb{E}}_{312}$, $\widetilde{\mathbb{E}}_{331}$) is the Dirac measure $0.324 \times \delta_{(0.917,0.399)}$ (resp. $0.229\times\delta_{(0.875,0.485)}$, $0.447\times\delta_{(0.757,-0.653)}$).

3.2 Basic algorithm

In this section we give an algorithm that generates an infinite sequence of matrices such that the asymptotic value of the norm of the product of the matrices is arbitrarily close to the CJSR. Note that by Definition 1, this asymptotic value must be smaller than the CJSR.

Remark 5. The algorithm generates the sequence of matrices in the *reverse order*. We can either see the sequence as G-admissible and left infinite or $G^\top$-admissible and right infinite.

Denote the indegree of a node $v \in V$ as $d^-(v)$ and the maximum indegree of G as $\Delta^-(G) = \max_{v\in V} d^-(v)$. Suppose that we are given a polynomial $p_0(x) \in \text{int}(\Sigma_{\mathbf{2d}})$, i.e. in the interior of the cone of SOS homogeneous polynomials of degree $2d$. Since it is in the interior, $\widetilde{\mathbb{E}}_{uv\sigma}[p_0(x)] > 0$ for all $(u, v, \sigma) \in E$ such that $\widetilde{\mathbb{E}}_{uv\sigma}$ is not zero. By (11), at least one dual variable is nonzero and we can choose one of such edges, say (v_1, v_0, σ_0).

The design of the algorithm is to build a $G^\top$-admissible sequence $(v_1, v_0, \sigma_0), (v_2, v_1, \sigma_1), \dots$ such that

$$\theta_k \triangleq \widetilde{\mathbb{E}}_{v_{k+1}v_k\sigma_k}[p_0(A_{\sigma_1}\cdots A_{\sigma_k}x)]$$

remains large for increasing k. Indeed, this would suggest that the product $A_{\sigma_1}\cdots A_{\sigma_k}$ has a large norm. The key idea is that maintaining a large value for θ_k is possible thanks to (12).

Algorithm 1 Producing a sequence of matrices with an asymptotic growth rate close to the CJSR.

Pick an arbitrary polynomial $p_0(x) \in \text{int}(\Sigma_{\mathbf{2d}})$
Pick an edge $(v_1, v_0, \sigma_0) \in E$ such that $\widetilde{\mathbb{E}}_{v_1v_0\sigma_0}[p_0(x)] > 0$
Set $p_1(x) \leftarrow p_0(x)$
for $k = 1, 2, \dots$ **do**
  $(v_{k+1}, v_k, \sigma_k) \leftarrow \arg\max_{(u,v_k,\sigma)\in E} \widetilde{\mathbb{E}}_{uv_k\sigma}[p_k(A_\sigma x)]$
  $p_{k+1} \leftarrow p_k(A_{\sigma_k}x)$
end for

Expanding $p_{k+1}(x)$, we obtain

$$p_{k+1}(x) = p_0(A_{\sigma_1}A_{\sigma_2}\cdots A_{\sigma_k}x).$$

The dual constraint (12) enables us to guarantee the following.

Lemma 4. Consider a finite set of matrices $\mathcal{M}$ constrained by an automaton $G(V, E)$. For any positive integer d, using Program 2 with any $\gamma < \rho_{\text{SOS},2d}(G, \mathcal{M})$, Algorithm 1 produces a $G^\top$-admissible sequence $(v_1, v_0, \sigma_0), (v_2, v_1, \sigma_1), \dots$ that satisfies the following inequality for all $k \geq 1$:

$$\theta_k \geq \frac{\gamma^{2d}}{d^-(v_k)}\theta_{k-1}.$$

Proof. For any integer $k \geq 1$, since $p_0(x)$ is SOS,

$$p_0(A_{\sigma_1}\cdots A_{\sigma_{k-1}}x) \text{ is SOS.}$$

Therefore, by (12),

$$\sum_{(u,v_k,\sigma)\in E} \widetilde{\mathbb{E}}_{uv_k\sigma}[p_0(A_{\sigma_1}\cdots A_{\sigma_{k-1}}A_\sigma x)] \geq \gamma^{2d} \sum_{(v_k,w,\sigma)\in E} \widetilde{\mathbb{E}}_{v_kw\sigma}[p_0(A_{\sigma_1}\cdots A_{\sigma_{k-1}}x)]$$

Since the dual variables $\widetilde{\mathbb{E}}_{v_kw\sigma}$ of the right-hand side are in the dual of the SOS cone, all the terms of the right-hand side are positive. Since one of them is θ_{k-1},

$$\sum_{(u,v_k,\sigma)\in E} \widetilde{\mathbb{E}}_{uv_k\sigma}[p_0(A_{\sigma_1}\cdots A_{\sigma_{k-1}}A_\sigma x)] \geq \gamma^{2d}\theta_{k-1}.$$

Since the left-hand side has $d^-(v_k)$ positive terms and Algorithm 1 picks the term with highest value, the result follows. □

To give a guarantee for the norm of the product of the matrices of the sequence, we introduce the following two Lemmas.

Lemma 5. For any matrix $A \in \mathbb{R}^{n\times n}$ and symmetric positive semidefinite matrix Q, the following inequality holds

$$\rho(A^\top QA) \leq \rho(Q)\rho(A^\top A).$$

Lemma 6. For any polynomial $p(x) \in \text{int}(\Sigma_{\mathbf{2d}})$ and any matrix $A \in \mathbb{R}^{n\times n}$, there exists a constant β that does not depend on A such that

$$\beta\|A\|_2^{2d}p(x) - p(Ax) \quad \text{is SOS.}$$

Moreover we can choose $\beta = \kappa(Q)$ where $Q \in \mathcal{S}^{\binom{n+d}{d}}$ is the symmetric matrix such that $p(x) = (x^{[d]})^\top Qx^{[d]}$ and $\kappa(Q) = \rho(Q)\rho(Q^{-1})$ is the condition number of Q.

Proof. Consider the matrix Q defined in the statement of the lemma. Note that since $p(x) \in \text{int}(\Sigma_{\mathbf{2d}})$, Q is positive definite. We can see that

$$((Ax)^{[d]})^\top Q(Ax)^{[d]} = (x^{[d]})^\top(A^{[d]})^\top QA^{[d]}x^{[d]}.$$

Moreover, for all $x \in \mathbb{R}^n$,

$$(x^{[d]})^\top Qx^{[d]} \geq \|x^{[d]}\|_2/\rho(Q^{-1})$$

and by Lemma 5,

$$(x^{[d]})^\top(A^{[d]})^\top QA^{[d]}x^{[d]} \leq \rho(Q)\rho((A^{[d]})^\top A^{[d]})\|x^{[d]}\|_2.$$

Using the fact that $\rho(A^{[d]}) = \rho(A)^d$ and $(AB)^{[d]} = A^{[d]}B^{[d]}$ for any matrix A and B, we have

$$\kappa(Q)\rho(A^\top A)^dQ - (A^{[d]})^\top QA^{[d]} \succeq 0.$$

□

Theorem 6. Consider a finite set of invertible matrices $\mathcal{M}$ constrained by an automaton $G(V, E)$. For any positive integer d, using Program 2 with any $\gamma < \rho_{\text{SOS},2d}(G, \mathcal{M})$, Algorithm 1 produces a $G^\top$-admissible sequence (v_1, v_0, σ_0), $(v_2, v_1, \sigma_1), \dots$ such that

$$\lim_{k\to\infty} \|A_{\sigma_1}\cdots A_{\sigma_k}\|_2^{\frac{1}{k}} \geq \frac{\gamma}{[\Delta^-]^{\frac{1}{2d}}}. \tag{13}$$

Proof. Consider the sequence produced by Algorithm 1. Since the set of edges E is finite, there must be an edge $(\bar{u}, \bar{v}, \bar{\sigma}) \in E$ that appears infinitely many times in the sequence. Let k_1 be the smallest integer such that $(v_{k_1+1}, v_{k_1}, \sigma_{k_1}) = (\bar{u}, \bar{v}, \bar{\sigma})$ and let $q(x) = p_{k_1+1}(x)$. Since the matrices of $\mathcal{M}$ are invertible and $p_0(x) \in \text{int}(\Sigma_{\mathbf{2d}})$, we know that $q(x) \in \text{int}(\Sigma_{\mathbf{2d}})$.

For an arbitrarily large integer K, there exists an integer $k \geq K$ such that $(v_{k_1+k+1}, v_{k_1+k}, \sigma_{k_1+k}) = (\bar{u}, \bar{v}, \bar{\sigma})$. Let $s_K = (\sigma_{k_1+k}, \dots, \sigma_{k_1+1})$. By Lemma 4, we have

$$\widetilde{\mathbb{E}}_{\bar{u}\bar{v}\bar{\sigma}}[q(A_{s_K}x)] \geq \frac{\gamma^{2dk}}{[\Delta^-]^k}\widetilde{\mathbb{E}}_{\bar{u}\bar{v}\bar{\sigma}}[q(x)]. \tag{14}$$

By Lemma 6, there exists a constant β that does not depend on A_{s_K} such that

$$\beta\|A_{s_K}\|_2^{2d}q(x) - q(A_{s_K}x) \text{ is SOS.}$$

Therefore,

$$\widetilde{\mathbb{E}}_{\bar{u}\bar{v}\bar{\sigma}}[\beta\|A_{s_K}\|_2^{2d}q(x)] \geq \widetilde{\mathbb{E}}_{\bar{u}\bar{v}\bar{\sigma}}[q(A_{s_K}x)]$$

and by (14),

$$\beta\|A_{s_K}\|_2^{2d}\widetilde{\mathbb{E}}_{\bar{u}\bar{v}\bar{\sigma}}[q(x)] \geq \frac{\gamma^{2dk}}{[\Delta^-]^k}\widetilde{\mathbb{E}}_{\bar{u}\bar{v}\bar{\sigma}}[q(x)].$$

Since $\widetilde{\mathbb{E}}_{\bar{u}\bar{v}\bar{\sigma}}[q(x)] > 0$,

$$\frac{\gamma^{2dk}}{[\Delta^-]^k} \leq \beta\|A_{s_K}\|_2^{2d}$$

or equivalently

$$\frac{\gamma}{[\beta^{\frac{1}{k}}\Delta^-]^{\frac{1}{2d}}} \leq \|A_{s_K}\|_2^{\frac{1}{k}}.$$

Taking the limit of K to ∞ we obtain the result. □

Example 6. Suppose we apply Algorithm 1 to Example 4 and the algorithm chooses $p_0(x) = \sum_\alpha c_\alpha x^\alpha$. The start of the sequence produced depends on the order between the coefficients $c_{(2d,0,0)}, c_{(0,2d,0)}, c_{(0,0,2d)}$. If $c_{(2d,0,0)}$ is the largest then the G-admissible left-infinite sequence found is

$$\ldots, 1, 2, 3, 1, 2, 3, 1, 2, 3.$$

The product $A_{\sigma_1}A_{\sigma_2}A_{\sigma_3}\cdots = A_3A_2A_1A_3A_2A_1\cdots$ is periodic and has an asymptotic growth rate $\rho(A_{\sigma_1}A_{\sigma_2}A_{\sigma_3})^{1/3} = 1$. Hence $1 \leq \rho(G, \mathcal{M})$. We saw in Example 4 that $\rho_{\text{SOS},2d}(G, \mathcal{M}) = 1$ for any d. Therefore $\rho(G, \mathcal{M}) = 1$.

3.3 Refinement of the algorithm

As a consequence of Theorem 6 and Definition 1,

$$\rho_{\text{SOS},2d}(G, \mathcal{M}) \leq [\Delta^-]^{\frac{1}{2d}}\rho(G, \mathcal{M}).$$

However it is easy to see that $\Delta^- \geq \rho(A(G))$ so Theorem 3 is a stronger statement. This is somewhat surprising, since Algorithm 1 uses more information than the power iteration of Section (2.2) (i.e., the dual solution of the SOS program), so we should be able to improve on it.

Indeed, we give now a generalization of Algorithm 1. The generalized algorithm has an integer parameter l. When $l = 1$, it reduces to Algorithm 1 which has a guarantee of accuracy with Δ^- given by Theorem 6. Increasing l increases the computation time of the generalized algorithm to produce a sequence of the same length but it also improves the guarantee. With $l \to \infty$, it has the same guarantee except that $\rho(A(G))$ replaces Δ^-; see Theorem 7. This section therefore provides an alternative proof of Theorem 3.

Consider the example illustrated by Figure 3. Algorithm 1 considers all the edges ending at v_1 and chooses one of them. This is what is illustrated by Figure 3a. Then it denotes the start of the chosen edge as v_2 and considers all the edges ending at v_2. Instead of doing so, the algorithm could postpone the choice of v_2 and look at all the pairs $(v_3, v_2, \sigma_2), (v_2, v_1, \sigma_1)$ or equivalently, all the paths of length 2 whose last node is v_1 and choose one of them based on the dual variables of the edges (v_3, v_2, σ_2) ignoring the dual variables of the edges (v_2, v_1, σ_1). The intuition behind this is that even if for large enough d the accuracy is arbitrarily good, for small d, we should not follow the dual variables "blindly". Building the sequence with a "larger horizon" is a way to be less affected by the possible imprecision of the dual variables.

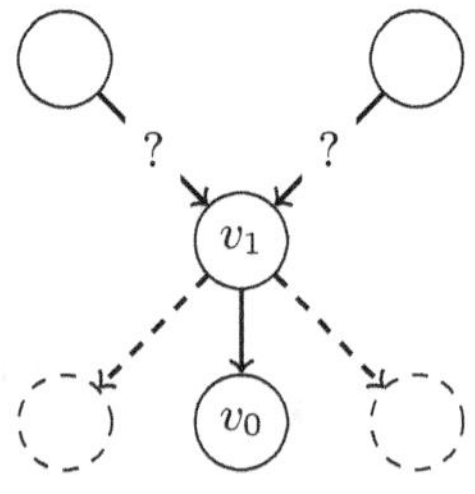

(a) One iteration of Algorithm 1.

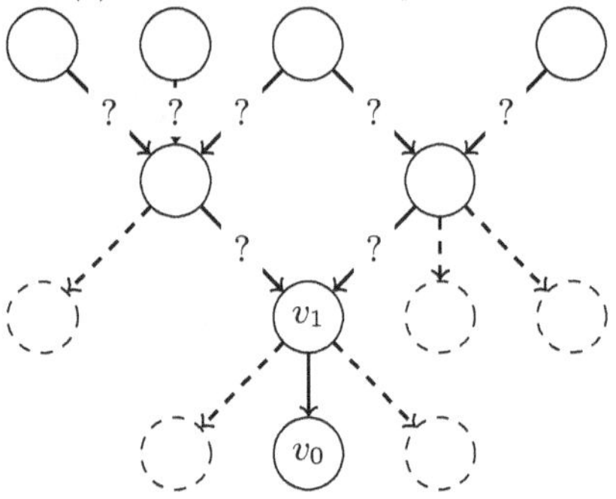

(b) One iteration of Algorithm 2 with $l = 2$.

Figure 3: Comparison between Algorithm 1 and Algorithm 2

This idea can be generalized for any length l. To shorten the notation we denote the ith node of a path s as $s(i)$ and the ith label as $s[i]$.

Algorithm 2 Generates sequences of large asymptotic growth using paths of length l.

Pick an arbitrary polynomial $p_0(x) \in \text{int}(\Sigma_{\mathbf{2d}})$
Pick an edge $(v_1, v_0, \sigma_0) \in E$ such that $\widetilde{\mathbb{E}}_{v_1v_0\sigma_0}[p_0(x)] > 0$
Set $p_1(x) \leftarrow p_0(x)$
for $k = 1, 2, \ldots$ **do**
  $(v_{k+l}, \sigma_{k+l-1}, \ldots, \sigma_k, v_k) \leftarrow$
    $\arg\max_{s \in E_l, s(l+1)=v_k} \widetilde{\mathbb{E}}_{s(1)s(2)s[1]}[p_k(A_s x)]$
  $p_{k+1} \leftarrow p_k(A_{\sigma_k}\cdots A_{\sigma_{k+l-1}}x)$
end for

Lemma 4 is generalized into the following Lemma.

Lemma 7. Consider a finite set of matrices $\mathcal{M}$ constrained by an automaton $G(V, E)$. For any positive integer d and l, using Program 2 with any $\gamma < \rho_{\text{SOS},2d}(G, \mathcal{M})$, Algorithm 2 with paths of length l produces a $G^\top$-admissible sequence $(v_1, v_0, \sigma_0), (v_2, v_1, \sigma_1), \ldots$ that satisfies the following inequality for all $k \geq 1$ that is a multiple of l:

$$\theta_k \geq \frac{\gamma^{2dl}}{d_l^-(v_{k-l+1})}\theta_{k-l}.$$

where for a node $v \in V$, $d_l^-(v)$ is the number of paths of length l ending at v.

Proof. For any integer $k \geq 1$ multiple of l, since $p_0(x)$ is SOS, $p_{k-l+1}(x), \ldots, p_k(x)$ are all SOS. Therefore, by (12),

$$\sum_{\substack{s \in E_l,\\ s(l+1)=v_{k-l+1}}} \widetilde{\mathbb{E}}_{s(1)s(2)s[1]}[p_{k-l+1}(A_s x)]$$

$$\geq \gamma^{2d} \sum_{\substack{s \in E_{l-1}, \\ s(l)=v_{k-l+1}}} \widetilde{\mathbb{E}}_{s(1)s(2)s[1]}[p_{k-l+1}(A_s x)]$$

$$\vdots$$

$$\geq \gamma^{2dl} \theta_{k-l}$$

Since the first expression has $d_l^-(v_{k-l+1})$ positive terms and Algorithm 2 picks the term with highest value, the result follows. □

Theorem 6 is generalized in the following Theorem.

Theorem 7. Consider a finite set of invertible matrices $\mathcal{M}$ constrained by an automaton $G(V, E)$. For any positive integers d and l and any $\epsilon > 0$, using Program 2 with any $\gamma < \rho_{\mathrm{SOS},2d}(G, \mathcal{M})$, Algorithm 2 with paths of length l produces a $G^\top$-admissible sequence $(v_1, v_0, \sigma_0), (v_2, v_1, \sigma_1), \ldots$ such that

$$\lim_{k\to\infty} \|A_{\sigma_1} \cdots A_{\sigma_k}\|_2^{\frac{1}{k}} \geq \frac{\gamma}{\|[A(G)^\top]^l\|_\infty^{\frac{1}{2dl}}}. \tag{15}$$

Proof. Consider the sequence produced by Algorithm 2. Since the set of edges E is finite, there must be an edge $(\bar{u}, \bar{v}, \bar{\sigma}) \in E$ that appears infinitely many times in the sequence at multiples of l. Let k_1 be the smallest multiple of l such that $(v_{k_1+1}, v_{k_1}, \sigma_{k_1}) = (\bar{u}, \bar{v}, \bar{\sigma})$ and let $q(x) = p_{k_1+1}(x)$. Since the matrices of $\mathcal{M}$ are invertible and $p_0(x) \in \mathrm{int}(\Sigma_{\mathbf{2d}})$, we know that $q(x) \in \mathrm{int}(\Sigma_{\mathbf{2d}})$.

For an arbitrarily large integer K, there exists an multiple of l $k \geq K$ such that $(v_{k_1+k+1}, v_{k_1+k}, \sigma_{k_1+k}) = (\bar{u}, \bar{v}, \bar{\sigma})$. Let $s_K = (\sigma_{k_1+k}, \ldots, \sigma_{k_1+1})$. By the definition of the matrix norm $\|\cdot\|_\infty$, $\max_{v\in V} d_l^-(v) = \|[A(G)^\top]^l\|_\infty$. Theorefore, by Lemma 7, we have

$$\widetilde{\mathbb{E}}_{\bar{u}\bar{v}\bar{\sigma}}[q(A_{s_K} x)] \geq \frac{\gamma^{2dk}}{\|[A(G)^\top]^l\|_\infty^{k/l}} \widetilde{\mathbb{E}}_{\bar{u}\bar{v}\bar{\sigma}}[q(x)]. \tag{16}$$

By Lemma 6, there exists a constant β that does not depend on A_{s_K} such that

$$\beta\|A_{s_K}\|_2^{2d} q(x) - q(A_{s_K} x) \text{ is SOS.}$$

Therefore by (16),

$$\beta\|A_{s_K}\|_2^{2d} \widetilde{\mathbb{E}}_{\bar{u}\bar{v}\bar{\sigma}}[q(x)] \geq \frac{\gamma^{2dk}}{\|[A(G)^\top]^l\|_\infty^{k/l}} \widetilde{\mathbb{E}}_{\bar{u}\bar{v}\bar{\sigma}}[q(x)].$$

Hence,

$$\frac{\gamma}{[\beta^{\frac{1}{k}} \|[A(G)^\top]^l\|_\infty^{1/l}]^{\frac{1}{2d}}} \leq \|A_{s_K}\|_2^{\frac{1}{k}}.$$

Taking the limit of K to ∞ we obtain the result. □

Since $\lim_{l\to\infty} \|[A(G)^\top]^l\|_\infty^{\frac{1}{l}} = \rho(A(G)^\top) = \rho(A(G))$, Theorem 3 is a consequence of Theorem 7.

3.4 Producing lower bounds

By definition of the CJSR, the asymptotic growth rate of the norm of the product of any G-admissible (or $G^\top$-admissible) sequence of matrices gives a lower bound for the CJSR. In particular the sequence produced by Algorithm 2 provides a lower bound for the CJSR.

If there are two integers $\bar{k}, k$ such that the sequence after $\bar{k}$ is periodic of period k, the asymptotic growth rate of the norm is equal to the kth root of the spectral radius of the product of the matrices of one period. This is due to the Gelfand's formula $\rho(A) = \lim_{k\to\infty} \|A^k\|^{1/k}$. From the same identity, we see that the spectral radius of the product of the matrices of one G-admissible cycle gives a lower bound for the CJSR.

More formally, for any natural k, we have

$$\rho_k(G, \mathcal{M}) \leq \rho(G, \mathcal{M})$$

where

$$\rho_k(G, \mathcal{M}) = \max\left\{ \rho(A_c)^{1/k} : c \in G_k, c \text{ is a cycle} \right\}.$$

This is the generalization to the constrained case of the first inequality of the three members inequalities; see [10, Section 1.2.2.6].

To find lower bounds for the CJSR, one could generate all the cycles of length smaller than some maximum length and compute the spectral radius for all of them. This brute force approach is not scalable because the number of paths considered grows exponentially with the maximum length. The exponential growth of the brute force approach is the reason why one should choose small l for Algorithm 2.

Gripenberg [8] proposes a branch-and-bound algorithm that prunes the search using an a priori fixed absolute error. Two other branch-and-bound variant exists: the balanced complex polytope algorithm [9] and the invariant conitope algorithm [11].

These algorithms can also be used to produce a G-admissible sequence of matrices of high asymptotic growth rate by reproducing the cycles of high spectral radius infinitely. The advantage of Algorithm 2 is that it provides a guarantee of accuracy given in Theorem 7. Algorithm 2 provides at the same time unstable trajectories and lower bounds of guaranteed accuracy.

We can compute lower bounds using the upper bound provided by Program 1 and Corollary 1 but in practice the trajectories are periodic after some time $\bar{k}$ so we are able to compute much better lower bounds than the pessimistic bound provided by Corollary 1. This is shown by the following example.

Example 7. We first analyse the behaviour of Algorithm 1 on our running example; see Example 1, Example 3 and Example 5. We use the recent CSSystem toolbox [6]. For $2d = 2, 4, 6, 8$, the sequence can only contain the edges $(1, 3, 1)$, $(3, 1, 2)$ and $(3, 3, 1)$ since the other edges have a dual variables of value 0.

To find a cycle with good spectral radius, we generate the sequence for a fixed length and then look through all the cycles of the sequence. The G-admissible cycle found depends on $p_0(x)$, but most of the time, it is

$$(3, 1, 2), (1, 3, 1), (3, 1, 2), (1, 3, 1), (3, 3, 1)^4$$

where the k in exponent means that the edges is taken k times. The 8th root of the corresponding spectral radius is 0.97289.

Using Algorithm 2 with $l = 3$, the produced sequence may include two consecutive edges that have a dual variables of value 0. Even for $2d = 2$, the Algorithm 2 with $l = 3$ finds the G-admissible cycle

$$(3, 1, 2), (1, 3, 1), (3, 1, 2), (1, 2, 3), (2, 3, 1), (3, 3, 1)^3$$

for which the 8th root of the corresponding spectral radius is

0.97482. We can show that it is equal to the CJSR, e.g. using [9]. That is, it is a *spectrum maximizing product* (s.m.p.).

With $2d = 10$ and $2d = 12$, we have seen in Example 5 that $\widetilde{\mathbb{E}}_{123}$ and $\widetilde{\mathbb{E}}_{231}$ are not zero. For $2d = 12$, the s.m.p. is found for any l, initial node and $p_0(x)$. For $2d = 10$, despite the fact that $\widetilde{\mathbb{E}}_{123}$ and $\widetilde{\mathbb{E}}_{231}$ are not zero, the s.m.p. seems to be never found for $l = 1$.

For $2d = 10$ and $l = 2$, it is found from the node 1 and 4[2] with high probability from a random $p_0(x)$ or from $p_0(x)$ equal to the primal solution at this node. From node 3, it is not found using the primal solution of node 3 but it is sometimes found using a random $p_0(x)$. This shows that choosing the primal solution as $p_0(x)$ may not be the best choice. From node 2, it does not seem to be found for any $p_0(x)$.

Instead of increasing l and d, path-complete techniques [1] can be used to improve the lower bounds provided by Algorithm 2 and the upper bounds provided by Program 1. The idea is to replace the automaton G and the matrices of $\mathcal{M}$ by another automaton G' and other matrices $\mathcal{M}'$ but without changing the set of admissible products of matrices. Typically, the new set $\mathcal{M}'$ contains products of the matrices of the initial set $\mathcal{M}$ and the automaton G' is designed so as to maintain the same set of admissible products.

We tried two examples: The T-product lift [15] and M-path-dependent lift [13]. Using the 2-product lift, the s.m.p. is found using $2d = 6$ and $l = 1$ and using the 2-path-dependent lift, the s.m.p. is found using $2d = 4$ and $l = 1$. This is concordant with the empirical observation reported in [15].

4. CONCLUSIONS

We have introduced a new technique, based on the dual solution of the SOS approximation, to generate a sequence of matrices with asymptotic growth rate close to the CJSR. In Theorem 7, we gave an estimate of its performance. However, in practical examples, the sequence produced achieves a growth rate which is often better than this estimate. This gives rise to the following question: Is it possible to improve the guarantee both for the upper bounds and the lower bounds? To the best of our knowledge, there are currently two bounds, Theorem 2 only depending on the dimension of the matrices and Theorem 3 only depending on the automaton. Is there a bound that combines both in a more sophisticated way than Corollary 1?

Our algorithm seems to always produce periodic sequences so in practice we can compute an asymptotic growth rate bound better than what is provided by Corollary 1. This motivates other questions with important algorithmic consequences: Does Algorithm 2 always produce a sequence that is periodic after some $\bar{k}$? Can we give a bound for $\bar{k}$ and the size of the period depending on the dimension of the matrices and on the automaton?

More generally, the techniques developed in this work, based on generating "bad" trajectories for a dynamical system via the dual solution of the natural convex problems used for analysis, naturally extend to many other problems in systems theory. We are currently exploring such possibilities.

[2]In practice, the dual variables of the edges $(3, 4, 4)$ and $(4, 3, 1)$ are close to zero but not zero. It is possible to start in node 4 even if the sequence will never go back in node 4.

5. REFERENCES

[1] A. A. Ahmadi, R. M. Jungers, P. A. Parrilo, and M. Roozbehani. Joint spectral radius and path-complete graph Lyapunov functions. *SIAM Journal on Control and Optimization*, 52(1):687–717, 2014.

[2] A. A. Ahmadi and P. A. Parrilo. Joint spectral radius of rank one matrices and the maximum cycle mean problem. In *CDC*, pages 731–733, 2012.

[3] B. Barak, F. G. Brandao, A. W. Harrow, J. Kelner, D. Steurer, and Y. Zhou. Hypercontractivity, sum-of-squares proofs, and their applications. In *Proceedings of the forty-fourth annual ACM Symposium on Theory of Computing*, pages 307–326. ACM, 2012.

[4] V. D. Blondel and Y. Nesterov. Computationally efficient approximations of the joint spectral radius. *SIAM Journal on Matrix Analysis and Applications*, 27(1):256–272, 2005.

[5] V. D. Blondel and J. N. Tsitsiklis. The boundedness of all products of a pair of matrices is undecidable. *Systems & Control Letters*, 41(2):135–140, 2000.

[6] L. Cambier, M. Philippe, and R. Jungers. The CSSystem toolbox. http://www.mathworks.com/matlabcentral/fileexchange/52723-the-cssystem-toolbox, August 2015.

[7] X. Dai. A Gel'fand-type spectral radius formula and stability of linear constrained switching systems. *Linear Algebra and its Applications*, 436(5):1099–1113, 2012.

[8] G. Gripenberg. Computing the joint spectral radius. *Linear Algebra and its Applications*, 234:43–60, 1996.

[9] N. Guglielmi and M. Zennaro. An algorithm for finding extremal polytope norms of matrix families. *Linear Algebra and its Applications*, 428(10):2265–2282, 2008.

[10] R. Jungers. *The joint spectral radius: theory and applications*, volume 385. Springer Science & Business Media, 2009.

[11] R. M. Jungers, A. Cicone, and N. Guglielmi. Lifted polytope methods for computing the joint spectral radius. *SIAM Journal on Matrix Analysis and Applications*, 35(2):391–410, 2014.

[12] V. Kozyakin. The Berger–Wang formula for the Markovian joint spectral radius. *Linear Algebra and its Applications*, 448:315–328, 2014.

[13] J.-W. Lee and G. E. Dullerud. Uniform stabilization of discrete-time switched and Markovian jump linear systems. *Automatica*, 42(2):205–218, 2006.

[14] P. A. Parrilo and A. Jadbabaie. Approximation of the joint spectral radius using sum of squares. *Linear Algebra and its Applications*, 428(10):2385–2402, 2008.

[15] M. Philippe, R. Essick, G. Dullerud, and R. M. Jungers. Stability of discrete-time switching systems with constrained switching sequences. *arXiv preprint arXiv:1503.06984*, 2015.

[16] G.-C. Rota and W. Strang. A note on the joint spectral radius. *Proceedings of the Netherlands Academy*, 1960. 22:379–381.

A Topological Method for Finding Invariant Sets of Switched Systems

Laurent Fribourg
LSV, ENS Cachan, CNRS
Université Paris-Saclay
France
fribourg@lsv.fr

Eric Goubault
Sylvie Putot
LIX, Ecole Polytechnique,
CNRS, Université Paris-Saclay
France
{goubault,putot}@lix.polytechnique.fr

Sameh Mohamed
LSV, ENS Cachan, CNRS
LIX, Ecole Polytechnique
Université Paris-Saclay
France
mohamed@lsv.fr

ABSTRACT

We revisit the problem of finding controlled invariants sets (viability), for a class of differential inclusions, using topological methods based on Ważewski property. In many ways, this generalizes the Viability Theorem approach, which is itself a generalization of the Lyapunov function approach for systems described by ordinary differential equations. We give a computable criterion based on SoS methods for a class of differential inclusions to have a non-empty viability kernel within some given region. We use this method to prove the existence of (controlled) invariant sets of switched systems inside a region described by a polynomial template, both with time-dependent switching and with state-based switching through a finite set of hypersurfaces. A Matlab implementation allows us to demonstrate its use.

Keywords

control; differential inclusion; viability; cyber-physical systems

1. INTRODUCTION

In order to understand and control the dynamics of systems ruled by differential equations, it is important to locate regions of the phase space that contain "invariant sets", i.e., sets of points that are invariant under the action of the dynamical system. Topological methods, based on Ważewski property and Conley index [20], have been used with success in order to find such invariant sets, within prescribed semi-algebraic sets (or "templates") and give their qualitative behavior: periodic orbits, attractors, repellers, chaos, ... (see, e.g., [21]). The boundary of these templates are decomposed into "exit sets" and "entrance sets" according to the directions of the flow at these points. It is well-known, for example, that if all the flows are either entering into or exiting from the template, then there exists an invariant inside the template. The Ważewski property, in particular, gives criteria for guaranteeing the existence of invariants, in more general cases with both entering and exiting flows at the boundary. This method has been used in our previous work on continuous systems [8]. We extend here this work by considering the case of *switched systems*. Switched systems are dynamical hybrid systems that combine continuous and discrete dynamics. These systems are more and more used in industrial applications, such as power electronics, due to their versatility and ease of implementation. A switched system is defined by a family of continuous dynamics, and by a switching signal that changes the operating mode of the system from one dynamics of the family to another. We use here topological methods (in the sense of topological dynamics : we are concentrating on closedness and non-connectedness of the exit set) in order to guarantee the presence of invariants inside templates for different classes of switching signal: time-dependent or state-dependent.

Related work.

Similar problems have been investigated in the literature. For example, in [2, 19, 25, 15, 14], authors calculate a controlled invariant set contained in K via an *iterative algorithm*. The algorithm is initialized with K and iteratively removes trajectories that may be forced to exit the set due to system dynamics. If the algorithm terminates at a fixed point, this final set is the maximal controlled invariant set (MCIS) contained in K. In general, the algorithm does not terminate, and only an approximation of the MCIS is found, which is still invariant but not maximal.

An alternative approach is to synthesize guards or tuning the parameter values of switching surfaces in order to minimize an integral cost function (see, e.g. [4, 23]). In [12, 10], the authors create a transition system from the hybrid dynamics by partitioning the state-space and introducing transitions between partitions which reflect the dynamics and invariance properties of the hybrid system model. The relation between the hybrid system and the new transition system is called a *bisimulation*, and a controller for the original system can be synthesized from this bisimulation.

In [6], the authors use sum of squares (SOS) programming to synthesize switching laws that are guaranteed to satisfy a state-based safety constraint. They consider hybrid systems with a finite number of modes in which the state evolution is governed by a differential inclusion, and they synthesize guards that trigger transitions between modes. Guards are assumed to be semialgebraic sets, i.e. a guard is a subset of the continuous state space which satisfies a collection of polynomial inequalities and equalities.

HSCC'16, April 12–14, 2016, Vienna, Austria.

© 2016 Copyright held by the owner/author(s). Publication rights licensed to ACM.
ISBN 978-1-4503-3955-1/16/04...$15.00

DOI: http://dx.doi.org/2883817.2883822

Although all these works pursue an objective similar to ours, they use techniques such as Lyapunov function calculation, bisimulation, fix-point iteration, which differ from our topological approach. Besides they generally treat only linear or affine modes while our method is suitable to switched systems with *polynomial* modes. Note also that, as mentioned above, our method is based on the Ważewski property which generalizes the Lyapunov approach, and can treat examples that would have been very difficult to obtain with Lyapunov functions (see [8] for examples).

2. DIFFERENTIAL INCLUSIONS AND VIABILITY

2.1 Basic facts

Consider the general differential inclusion

$$\dot{x} \in F(x) \tag{1}$$

where F is a map from $\mathbb{R}^n$ to $\wp(R^n)$, the set of subsets of $\mathbb{R}^n$. A function $x(\cdot) : \mathbb{R}^+ \to \mathbb{R}^n$ is a *solution* of Equation (1) if x is an absolutely continuous function and satisfies for almost all $t \in \mathbb{R}$, $\dot{x}(t) \in F(x(t))$ (see [3]). In general, there can be many solutions to a differential inclusion. Throughout the paper we note $S_F(x_0)$ the set of all (absolutely continuous) solutions to the Equation (1).

DEFINITION 1. *[3] The set-valued map $F : \mathbb{R}^n \rightsquigarrow \mathbb{R}^n$ is a* Marchaud map *if F is upper semicontinuous (in short: u.s.c.) with compact convex values and linear growth (that is, there is a constant $c > 0$ such that $|F(x)| := sup\{|y| \mid y \in F(x)\} \leq c(1 + |x|)$, for every x).*

We know from [3] that when F is a Marchaud map, then the inclusion (1) has a solution such that $x(t_0) = x_0$ (for all x_0) and for a sufficiently small time interval $[t_0, t_0 + \varepsilon)$, $\varepsilon > 0$. Global existence, for all $t \in \mathbb{R}$ can be shown provided F does not allow "blow-up" ($\|x(t)\| \to \infty$ as $t \to t^*$ for a finite t^*).

DEFINITION 2. *[3] Let K be a closed subset of $\mathbb{R}^n$. A trajectory of the differential inclusion (1), $t \to x(t)$, is said to be viable (in K) when for all t, $x(t) \in K$. The viability kernel of Equation (1) in K is $Viab_K(F)$, the set of initial conditions $x_0 \in K$ such that there exists a solution of $S_F(x_0)$ staying forever in K.*

A closed set $K \subset \mathbb{R}^n$ being given, we study the following problem of the existence of trajectories for the differential inclusion (1) remaining in K: is $Viab_F(K)$ not empty? That is, does there exist x_0 in K and $x(\cdot) \in S_F(x_0)$ such that $\forall t \geq 0, x(t) \in K$? It is well known that the problem has a positive answer for any $x_0 \in K$, and all trajectories, when the boundary of K is the level set of a Lyapunov function associated with the differential inclusion [9]. But finding such Lyapunov functions is generally difficult. The Viability Theorem is a slight relaxation of this approach, to prove that there exists a trajectory staying inside K, whereas all trajectories may not stay inside K. Let us denote by $C_K(x)$ the Bouligant contingent cone of K at x [3], which, in the case where K is a closed convex subset of $\mathbb{R}^n$ is just the closure of the tangent cone of K at x, $\bigcup_{h>0} \{\frac{k-x}{h} | k \in K\}$.

THEOREM 1. *[3] Consider a Marchaud map $F : \mathbb{R}^n \to \wp(\mathbb{R}^n)$ and a closed convex $K \subseteq \mathbb{R}^n$. Suppose that $\forall x \in K$, $F(x) \cap C_K(x) \neq \emptyset$, then $Viab_K(F) = K$, i.e. there always exists a trajectory for the differential inclusion (1) from any point of K, staying in K.*

The idea behind this theorem is that if there is always a vector field which points inside K in $F(x)$, for all $x \in K$, then there is a way to follow it to stay inside K. In this paper, we are going to generalize this approach using a finer characterization of the *exit set* of the differential inclusion F. Let $K^S(F) := \{x_0 \in \partial K \mid \forall x \in S_F(x_0) :$ x leaves K immediately$\}$, be the exit set for the differential inclusion F. Here, "immediately" means that for every $\varepsilon > 0$ there is $0 < t < \varepsilon$ such that $x(t) \notin K$. We now have the following result, which is a Ważewski property for differential inclusions :

PROPOSITION 1. *[5] Let K be a closed convex subset of $\mathbb{R}^n$ and F a Marchaud map. If the set $K^S(F)$ is closed and not connected[1], then $Viab_F(K) \neq \emptyset$.*

This provides us indeed with a generalization of Theorem 1 in that the former deals with the case where $K^S(F)$ is empty, and hence, is closed and not connected. In the sequel, we focus on deriving conditions on differential inclusions to get closed and disconnected exit sets. We then apply these characterizations to prove the existence of switching modes that make a switched system's trajectory stay within some prescribed region of space.

Viability is a generalization of invariance properties, that can be used to verify properties of dynamical systems under uncertainties (Section 6.1) or controlled systems (e.g. Section 8), but few methods are available to compute the viability kernel, and they are not tractable. Our goal is thus only to prove non-emptyness of the viability kernel within some fixed region. As an application of this, for instance, knowing that a parameterized (with uncertain parameters in U) dynamical system is viable inside K means that the system is controllable with parameters in U. Similarly for arbitrary switching systems : if we prove that the viability kernel is not empty within K, then we know that there is a switching strategy to stabilize it, i.e. the system is controllable. For those switched systems which have unique solutions within K (which include a large class of practically meaningful systems), our method will prove that there exists a maximal positive invariant set within K, which allows for spotting areas in space where the system is stable (and by way of complement, unstable), if K can be made sufficiently small.

[1]With the convention here that the empty set has no connected component, hence is not connected.

2.2 Convex polynomial differential inclusions, in convex compact semi-algebraic sets

2.2.1 *Convex polynomial differential inclusions*

For the rest of the article, we will restrict to the case where F is given as the closed convexification of a finite set of polynomial vector fields $f_1, \ldots, f_q$:

$$F(x) = \overline{co}(f_1, \ldots, f_q) \tag{2}$$

where $co(y_1, \ldots, y_q)$ is the convex combination of the q vectors $y_1, \ldots, y_q$ in $\mathbb{R}^n$ and $\overline{A}$ is the topological closure of A in $\mathbb{R}^n$. For every such $\lambda = (\lambda_1, \ldots, \lambda_q)$ we will write $f_\lambda = \sum_{i=1}^{q} \lambda_i f_i$ so that $F(x)$ can be identified with the set of all such $f_{\lambda(x)}$, where λ is a continuous function. Such differential inclusions are very well behaved and we will be allowed to apply the results that we recapped in Section 2.1 :

LEMMA 1. *Set functions F of the form given at Equation (2) are Marchaud maps.*

2.2.2 *Convex compact semi-algebraic sets*

We will also restrict ourselves further by looking for viable solutions in closed convex sets $K \subset \mathbb{R}^n$, which are defined, for some vector $c = (c_1, \ldots, c_m) \in \mathbb{R}^m$, by the m polynomials inequalities:

$$(P) \left\{ \begin{array}{lcl} p_1(x_1, \ldots, x_n) & \leq & c_1 \\ & \cdots & \\ p_m(x_1, \ldots, x_n) & \leq & c_m \end{array} \right.$$

We say that K is a *(polynomial) template.* We call *minimal polynomial templates*, the templates K which border ∂K is equal (and not just included as would be generally the case) to $\bigcup_{i=1}^{m} \{x \mid p_i(x) = c_i, p_j(x) \leq c_j \ \forall j \neq i\}$.

2.2.3 *Lie derivatives*

Before stating results about the viability kernel of the corresponding differential inclusion, we need to introduce some notions that will be necessary, on polynomial differential equations. $\mathbb{R}[x]$ is the ring of polynomials in x.

DEFINITION 3. *(Lie derivative and higher-order Lie derivatives). The Lie derivative of $h \in \mathbb{R}[x]$ along the vector field $f = (f^1, \ldots, f^n)$ is defined by $\mathcal{L}_f(h) = \sum_{i=1}^{n} \frac{\partial h}{\partial x_i} f^i = \langle f, \nabla h \rangle$. Higher-order derivatives are defined by $\mathcal{L}_f^{(k+1)}(h) = \mathcal{L}_f(\mathcal{L}_f^{(k)}(h))$ with $\mathcal{L}_f^0(h) = h$.*

For polynomial dynamical systems, only a finite number of Lie derivatives are necessary to generate all higher-order Lie derivatives. Indeed, let $h \in \mathbb{R}[x_1, \ldots, x_n]$, we recursively construct an ascending chain of ideals of $\mathbb{R}[x_1, \ldots, x_n]$ by appending successive Lie derivatives of h to the list of generators : $\langle h \rangle \subseteq \langle h, \mathcal{L}_f^1(h) \rangle \subseteq \cdots \subseteq \langle h, \mathcal{L}_f^1(h), \ldots, \mathcal{L}_f^{(N)}(h) \rangle$. Since the ring $\mathbb{R}[x]$ is Noetherian [16], this increasing chain of ideals has necessarily a finite length: the maximal element of the chain is called the differential radical ideal of h and will be noted $\sqrt[\mathcal{L}]{\langle h \rangle}$. Its order is the smallest N such that:

$$\mathcal{L}_f^{(N)}(h) \in \langle h, \mathcal{L}_f^{(1)}(h), \ldots, \mathcal{L}_f^{(N-1)}(h) \rangle \tag{3}$$

This N is computationally tractable. If we note N_i the order of the ideal $\sqrt[\mathcal{L}]{\langle p_i \rangle}$, then for face i we should compute the successive Lie derivatives until N_i. This can be done by testing if the *Gröbner basis* spanned by the derivatives changes. Indeed, two ideals are equal if they have the same reduced Gröbner basis [1]. If we denote by $\mathcal{G}(\{g_1, \cdots, g_n\})$ the Gröbner basis of $\{g_1, \cdots, g_n\}$, the first n s.t. $\mathcal{G}(\{\mathcal{L}_f^{(0)}(p_i), \cdots, \mathcal{L}_f^{(n)}(p_i)\}) = \mathcal{G}(\{\mathcal{L}_f^{(1)}(p_i), \cdots, \mathcal{L}_f^{(n+1)}(p_i)\})$ is equal to N_i.

3. VIABILITY OF CONVEX DIFFERENTIAL INCLUSIONS IN TEMPLATES

3.1 Viability: a first topological approach

There is first a simple characterization of $K^S(F)$ for differential inclusions of the form we consider in this section, along the lines of [8]:

THEOREM 2. *Consider the differential inclusion (2). Let K be a compact minimal polynomial template defined by the set of inequalities (P) and let N_i^j be the order of the differential ideal $\sqrt[\mathcal{L}]{\langle p_i \rangle}$ along f_j. If for each face K_i of template K we have (H_i):*

- *for all $k \in \{1, \ldots, N_i^j - 2\}$, for all $\lambda \in \mathbb{R}^q$, for all (x, λ),* $\Big(p_i(x) = c_i, \forall j \neq i,\ p_j(x) \leq c_j \ \&\ \sum_{u=1}^{q} \lambda_u = 1,\ \lambda_1, \ldots, \lambda_q \geq 0 \ \&\ \mathcal{L}_{f_\lambda}^{(1)}(p_i)(x) = 0, \ldots, \mathcal{L}_{f_\lambda}^{(k)}(p_i)(x) = 0\Big) \Longrightarrow \mathcal{L}_{f_\lambda}^{(k+1)}(p_i)(x) \geq 0$
- $\Big\{(x, \lambda) \mid p_i(x) = c_i, \forall j \neq i\ p_j(x) \leq c_j \ \&\ \sum_{u=1}^{q} \lambda_u = 1,\ \forall u,\ \lambda_u \geq 0 \ \&\ \mathcal{L}_{f_\lambda}^{(1)}(p_i)(x) = \cdots = \mathcal{L}_{f_\lambda}^{(N_i^j - 1)}(p_i)(x) = 0\Big\}$ *is empty.*

Then $K^S(F)$ is closed and equal to

$$\bigcup_{i=1}^{m} \bigcap_{\sum_{u=1}^{q} \lambda_u = 1,\ \lambda_1, \ldots, \lambda_q \geq 0} \{x \in K_i \mid \mathcal{L}_{f_\lambda}(p_i)(x) \geq 0\}$$

If furthermore $K^S(F)$ is disconnected, then $Viab_K(F) \neq \emptyset$.

Note that (H_i) can be checked by SoS relaxation [17] in the ring of multivariate polynomials $\mathbb{R}[\lambda_1, \ldots, \lambda_q, x_1, \ldots, x_n]$, as in [8]. As a matter of fact, $\mathcal{L}_{f_\lambda}^{(v)}(p_i)$ is a polynomial in $\mathbb{R}[\lambda_1, \ldots, \lambda_q, x_1, \ldots, x_n]$, as easily shown by induction on v. But this is both an expensive way to solve our problem and a fairly weak condition for solving problem (P). What the theorem says is that $K^S(F)$ is closed when $K^S(\{f_\lambda\})$ is closed for all λ. As the example below shows, this is far too strict a condition in general, to be applicable.

EXAMPLE 1 (EXAMPLE 2.7 OF [24]). *Consider the switched system defined by :*

$$f_1(x, y) = \begin{pmatrix} -y \\ x - y^3 \end{pmatrix} \quad f_2(x, y) = \begin{pmatrix} y \\ -x - y^3 \end{pmatrix}$$

We consider the differential inclusion in $\mathbb{R}^2$, $F(x, y) = \overline{co}(f_1, f_2)$ and the template $K = [-0.5, 0.5] \times [-0.5, 0.5]$ given by $p_1 = -x$, $p_2 = x$, $p_3 = -y$, $p_4 = y$ and $c_1 = c_2 = c_3 = c_4 = 0.5$. We have:

$$\begin{array}{lcl} \mathcal{L}_{f_1}(p_1) & = & y \\ \mathcal{L}_{f_1}(p_2) & = & -y \\ \mathcal{L}_{f_1}(p_3) & = & -x + y^3 \\ \mathcal{L}_{f_1}(p_4) & = & x - y^3 \end{array} \qquad \begin{array}{lcl} \mathcal{L}_{f_2}(p_1) & = & -y \\ \mathcal{L}_{f_2}(p_2) & = & y \\ \mathcal{L}_{f_2}(p_3) & = & x + y^3 \\ \mathcal{L}_{f_2}(p_4) & = & -x - y^3 \end{array}$$

For instance, for $p_1(x) = c_1$, $\lambda_1 + \lambda_2 = 1$, *we get* $\mathcal{L}_{f_\lambda}(p_1) = (\lambda_1 - \lambda_2)y = (1-2\lambda_2)y$ *which is zero for* $y = 0$ *or* $\lambda_2 = \frac{1}{2}$. *In the first case,* $\mathcal{L}^{(2)}_{f_\lambda}(p_1) = \frac{1}{2}(1-2\lambda_2)^2$ *and in the second case* $\mathcal{L}^{(2)}_{f_\lambda}(p_1) = (1-2\lambda_2)y^3 = 0$. *Therefore, the 2nd criterion of* (H_i) *for* $i = 1$ *in Theorem 2 is not satisfied. But it can be verified that* $V(x, y) = x^2 + y^2$ *is a common weak Lyapunov function, so that the system is uniformly stable [24]. We will show later on that more refined topological methods can prove the existence of viable trajectories within* K.

3.2 Viability in templates with one face

In this section, we further characterize $K^S(F)$ for F of the form given by Equation (1), when K is defined by one face only (for example, when K is an ellipsoid).

LEMMA 2.

$$K^S(F) = \bigcap_{\lambda_1,\ldots,\lambda_q \geq 0,\ \sum_{i=1}^{q} \lambda_i = 1} K^S(\{f_\lambda\})$$

Furthermore, if the template K *is defined by a unique polynomial* p_1, $K^S(F) = \bigcap_{i=1}^{q} K^S(\{f_i\})$

In the case of a one-face template K, we can refine Theorem 2 to the following result:

THEOREM 3. *Consider the differential inclusion (2). Let* K *be a convex compact minimal polynomial template defined by the set of inequalities* (P) *and let* N_1^j *be the order of the differential ideal* $\sqrt[\mathcal{L}]{\langle p_1 \rangle}$ *along* f_j. *If for the only face* K_1 *of template* K, *for all* $j = 1, \ldots, q$ *we have* (H_j):

- *for all* $k \in \{1, \ldots, N_1^j - 2\}$,

$$\{x \in K_1 \mid \mathcal{L}^{(1)}_{f_j}(p_1)(x) = 0, \ldots, \mathcal{L}^{(k)}_{f_j}(p_1)(x) = 0, \\ \forall i \neq j,\ \mathcal{L}^{(1)}_{f_i}(p_1) \geq 0,\ \mathcal{L}^{(k+1)}_{f_j}(p_1)(x) < 0\}$$

  is empty.

- $$\{x \in K_1 \mid \forall i \neq j,\ \mathcal{L}^{(1)}_{f_i}(p_1) \geq 0\ \& \\ \mathcal{L}^{(1)}_{f_j}(p_1)(x) = 0, \ldots, \mathcal{L}^{(N_1^j - 1)}_{f_j}(p_1)(x) = 0\}$$

  is empty

Then $K^S(F)$ *is closed and equal to*

$$\{x \in K_1 \mid \bigwedge_{j=1}^{q} \mathcal{L}^{(1)}_{f_j}(p_1)(x) \geq 0\}$$

If furthermore $K^S(F)$ *is disconnected, then* $Viab_F(K) \neq \emptyset$.

Algorithm (A).

We can check the conditions of Theorem 3, in a similar way as what was developed in [8], using Sum of Squares optimization [17] and Stengle's nichtnegativstellensatz, for increasing k from 1 to $N_1^j - 2$, for each vector field f_j. We determine polynomials α_n ($n = 0, \ldots, k$), SoS polynomials $\beta_{S,\mu}$ ($S \subseteq \{1, \ldots, j-1, j+1, \ldots, q\}, \mu \in \{0, 1\}$) and an integer l, such that

$$\sum_{n=0}^{k} \alpha_n \mathcal{L}^{(n)}_{f_j} + \sum_{\substack{S \subseteq \{1,\ldots,j-1,j+1,\ldots,q\} \\ \mu \in \{0,1\}}} \beta_{S,\mu} G_{S,\mu} + \left(\mathcal{L}^{(k+1)}_{f_j}\right)^{2l} = 0 \tag{4}$$

where $G_{S,\mu} = (-\mathcal{L}^{(k+1)}_{f_j})^\mu \prod_{s \in S} \mathcal{L}^{(1)}_{f_s}$ for any $S \subseteq \{1, \ldots, j-1, j+1, \ldots, q\}$, $\mu \in \{0, 1\}$ and the convention that $\mathcal{L}^0_{f_j}(p_1) = c_1 - p_1$. Practically, this is done by bounding the degrees of the polynomials α_n and $\beta_{S,\mu}$ we are looking for, and taking low values for l (in all our examples, we took $l = 1$), the problem can thus be tested by semidefinite programming. An example of application of Theorem 3 to compute the exit set of a one-face template (ball) is given in Section 6.4.

3.3 Viability for general templates

In general, we do not have the same results when the boundary of K is defined by several template polynomials p_i, as illustrated in the following example.

EXAMPLE 2. *We carry on with Example 1. We have:* $K^S(\{f_1\}) = [-0.5, 0[\times \{-0.5\} \cup [0, 0.5[\times \{0.5\} \cup \{0.5\} \times [-0.5, 0[\cup \{-0.5\} \times]0, 0.5]$ *and* $K^S(\{f_2\}) = [-0.5, 0[\times \{0.5\} \cup]0, 0.5] \times \{-0.5\} \cup \{-0.5\} \times [-0.5, 0[\cup \{0.5\} \times]0, 0.5]$

Hence $K^S(\{f_1\}) \cap K^S(\{f_2\})$ *is* $\{(-0.5, -0.5), (-0.5, 0.5), (0.5, 0.5), (0.5, -0.5)\}$. *But at any of the four points above, there is always a vector field within* $F(x, y) = \overline{co}(f_1(x, y), f_2(x, y))$ *which points strictly inside template* K. *For instance, for point* $(0.5, 0.5)$, *we have:*

$$\mathcal{L}_{f_\lambda}(p_2) = 0.5(\lambda_2 - \lambda_1) \quad \mathcal{L}_{f_\lambda}(p_4) = 0.5(\lambda_1 - \lambda_2)x - \tfrac{1}{8}$$

Take for instance $\lambda_1 = \frac{9}{16}$, $\lambda_2 = \frac{7}{16}$, *the solutions for* $\frac{9}{16} f_1 + \frac{7}{16} f_2$ *are entering* K. *The same occurs for the other three points: this is pictured in Figure 2. It follows that* $K^S(\{f_\lambda\})$ *is empty for* $\lambda = (\frac{9}{16}, \frac{7}{16})$, *hence* $K^S(F)$ *is empty (by Lemma 2), hence* $K^S(F) \neq K^S(\{f_1\}) \cap K^S(\{f_2\})$.

Let K now be a convex compact minimal polynomial templates. It is a stratified space. We call K_i the face of the template K given by $\{(x_1, \ldots, x_n) \mid p_i(x_1, \ldots, x_n) = c_i\} \cap K$, and, for all multi-indices $\mathbf{k} \in \{(k_1, \ldots, k_i) \mid 1 \leq k_1 < \ldots < k_i \leq m\}$, $K_\mathbf{k}$ the $\mathbf{k}$-face of K given by $K_\mathbf{k} = \{x \mid p_{k_1}(x) = c_{k_1}, \ldots, p_{k_i}(x) = c_{k_i}\}$. We write $\overset{\circ}{K}_i$ for the interior of the i-face, given by $\overset{\circ}{K}_i = \{x \mid p_i(x) = c_i\ \&\ \forall j \neq i, p_j(x) < c_j\}$ and for all multi-indices $\mathbf{k} \in \{(k_1, \ldots, k_i) \mid 1 \leq k_1 < \ldots < k_i \leq m\}$, $\overset{\circ}{K}_\mathbf{k}$ is the interior of the $\mathbf{k}$-face of K given by $\overset{\circ}{K}_\mathbf{k} = \{x \mid p_{k_1}(x) = c_{k_1}, \ldots, p_{k_i}(x) = c_{k_i}\ \&\ \forall j \notin \mathbf{k}, p_j(x) < c_j\}$

EXAMPLE 3. *Consider template* K *in* $\mathbb{R}^3$ *given by* $p_1(x) = -x_1$, $p_2(x) = x_1$, $p_3(x) = -x_2$, $p_4(x) = x_2$, $p_5(x) = -x_3$, $p_6(x) = x_3$ *and* $c_1 = c_2 = c_3 = c_4 = c_5 = c_6 = 1$. *Geometrically,* K *is the cube* $[-1, 1] \times [-1, 1] \times [-1, 1]$, *stratified by its 6 faces, 12 edges and 8 extremal points as depicted in Figure 1.*

We have a full characterization of the exit set for F in K, which is indeed more involved than Lemma 2. We note $\mathcal{K}^S_\mathbf{k}(F) = K^S(F) \cap \overset{\circ}{K}_\mathbf{k}$ the intersection of $K^S(F)$ with the interior of face $K_\mathbf{k}$.

PROPOSITION 2. *Suppose we have a convex compact minimal polynomial template* K *defined by the set of inequalities* (P), *and consider the differential inclusion for (1).* $K^S(F)$ *is defined by its intersections with all (iterated) faces of* K :

- *for all* $i = 1, \ldots, m$, $\mathcal{K}^S_i(F) = \bigcap_{j=1}^{q} \mathcal{K}^S_i(\{f_j\})$

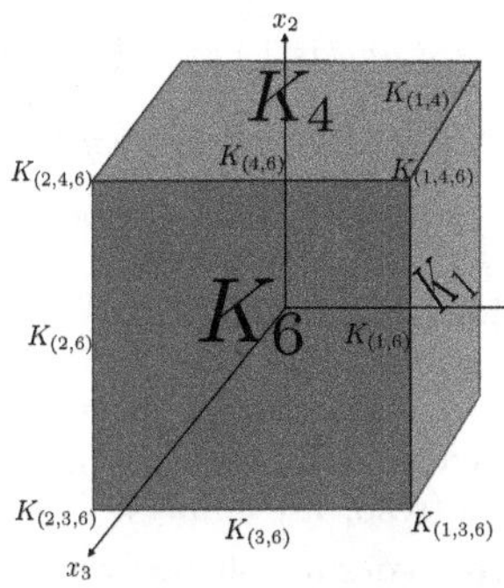

Figure 1: Stratification of a parallellepipedic template.

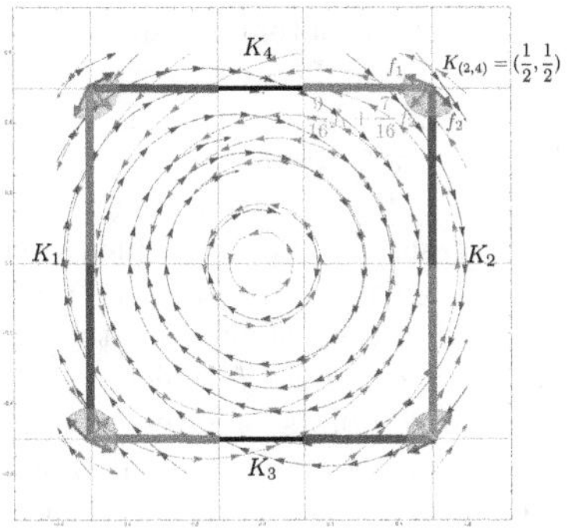

Figure 2: Field $\lambda_1 f_1 + \lambda_2 f_2$ is entrant at $K_{(2,4)}$.

- *for all multi-indices* $\mathbf{k} = (k_1, \ldots, k_i)$ *of cardinality at least 2*
$\mathcal{K}^S_{\mathbf{k}}(F) = \bigcap_{\lambda_1,\ldots,\lambda_q \geq 0,\ \sum_{i=1}^q \lambda_i = 1} \mathcal{K}^S_{\mathbf{k}}(\{f_\lambda\})$.

EXAMPLE 4. *We carry on with Example 2. We derive from the calculations of the Lie derivative made in Example 1 that* $\mathcal{K}^S_2(\{f_1\}) = \{0.5\} \times [-0.5, 0[$ *and* $\mathcal{K}^S_2(\{f_2\}) = \{0.5\} \times]0, 0.5]$. *By Proposition 2, we have then:*

$$\mathcal{K}^S_2(F) = \mathcal{K}^S_2(\{f_1\}) \cap \mathcal{K}^S_2(\{f_2\}) = \emptyset \quad \textit{and}$$

$$\mathcal{K}^S_{(2,4)}(F) = \bigcap_{\lambda_1,\lambda_2 \geq 0, \lambda_1+\lambda_2=1} \mathcal{K}^S_{(2,4)}(\{\lambda_1 f_1 + \lambda_2 f_2\}) = \emptyset$$

because of the pair $(\lambda_1, \lambda_2) = (\frac{9}{16}, \frac{7}{16})$ *found out in Example 2 that makes the vector field* $\lambda_1 f_1 + \lambda_2 f_2$ *entrant in* K *in the face* $K_{(2,4)} = (0.5, 0.5)$. *The three other extremal points of* K *can be treated in a similar manner, and we conclude that* $K^S(F) = \emptyset$. *Figure 2 illustrates the entrant field* $\lambda_1 f_1 + \lambda_2 f_2$ *at* $K_{(2,4)}$.

Unfortunately, the formula for $K^S(F)$ given in Proposition 2 is still highly inconvenient, for two reasons. First, although it is simple to characterize $\mathcal{K}^S_i(F)$ (for all $i = 1, \ldots, m$) in the style of [8], it is hard to characterize $\mathcal{K}^S_{\mathbf{k}}(F)$ as soon as the cardinal of $\mathbf{k}$ is greater than 2. Second, we have to prove that $K^S(F)$ is closed in order to be able to apply Proposition 1 and prove that $Viab_F(K) \neq \emptyset$. The only simple characterization we have at hand is weak: if for all multi-indices $\mathbf{k}$, $\mathcal{K}^S_{\mathbf{k}}(F)$ is closed *in* $\mathbb{R}^n$, then $K^S(F)$ is closed.

We now give a simple criterion for the closedness of $K^S(F)$. The idea is to test closedness of the exit sets on all faces

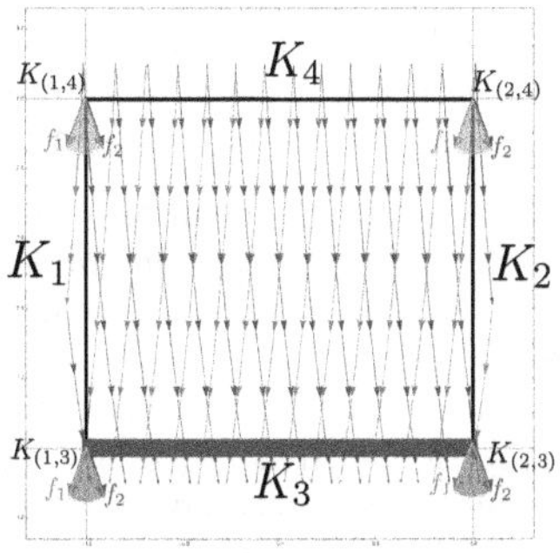

Figure 3: Illustration of Lemmas 3, 4 on Examples 5, 6

similarly to Proposition 2 and to test whether intersections of faces are entirely exiting or entirely non-exiting (this is called an entrance set or face). In this case, we can easily test whether the exit set is closed by looking only at intersections with each closure of faces K_i. Then we will use simple criteria for deciding whether intersections of faces are entirely exiting or entirely non-exiting in Lemmas 3 and 4. Finally, these will have a simple translation in terms of positivstellensatz conditions for some Lie derivative in Theorem 4.

For all multi-indices $\mathbf{k} = (k_1, \ldots, k_j)$, let us write $K^S_{\mathbf{k}}(\{f_i\})$ for the exit set of the (not necessarily compact) set $\{x \in \mathbb{R}^n \mid p_{k_1}(x) \leq c_{k_1}, \ldots, p_{k_j}(x) \leq c_{k_j}\}$ under flow f_i, intersected with $K_{\mathbf{k}}$.

PROPOSITION 3. *A sufficient condition for* $K^S(F)$ *to be closed is:*

- *For all* $i = 1, \ldots, m$, $\bigcap_{j=1}^q K^S_i(\{f_j\})$ *is closed in* $\mathbb{R}^n$
- *For all* $\mathbf{k}$ *multi-index of cardinality at least 2,*

$$\bigcap_{\lambda_1,\ldots,\lambda_q \geq 0,\ \sum_{i=1}^q \lambda_i = 1} K^S_{\mathbf{k}}(\{f_\lambda\})$$

is either empty or the full (iterated) face $K_{\mathbf{k}}$.

Deciding the second condition of Proposition 3 can be done combinatorially, in simple cases:

LEMMA 3. *Consider a point* $x \in \overset{\circ}{K}_{\mathbf{k}}$ *for some multi-index* $\mathbf{k} = (1 \leq k_1 < \ldots < k_i \leq m)$. *Suppose that there exists* j *in* $\{1, \ldots, i\}$ *such that for all* u *in* $\{1, \ldots, q\}$, $x \in K^S_{k_j}(\{f_u\})$. *Then* x *is in the exit set for* F, *in face* $K_{\mathbf{k}}$*:* $x \in \bigcap_{\lambda_1,\ldots,\lambda_q \geq 0,\ \sum_{i=1}^q \lambda_i = 1} K^S_{\mathbf{k}}(\{f_\lambda\})$.

EXAMPLE 5. *Consider again Example 1, with the box* $K' = [-1, 1] \times [2, 3]$. *Simple computations using the corresponding Lie derivatives show that:*
$K^S_3(\{f_1\}) = [-1, 1] \times \{2\}$ $\quad K^S_3(\{f_2\}) = [-1, 1] \times \{2\}$
$\mathcal{K}^S_j(\{f_i\}) = \emptyset$ $\quad$ *for all* $i = 1, 2$ $j \neq 3$

Figure 3 illustrates this example, where $K^S(F) = [-1, 1] \times \{2\}$ *is represented as a thick line. Since* $\overset{\circ}{K}_{(1,3)} = \{(-1, 2)\} \in K^S_3(\{f_1\}) \cap K^S_3(\{f_2\})$ *and* $\overset{\circ}{K}_{(2,3)} = \{(1, 2)\} \in K^S_3(\{f_1\}) \cap K^S_3(\{f_2\})$, *Lemma 3 applies and we know that* $K^S_{(1,3)}(F) = \{(-1, 2)\}$, $K^S_{(2,3)}(F) = \{(1, 2)\}$. *To apply Proposition 3, we need also to sort out whether the 2 other (iterated) faces* $K_{(1,4)} = \{(-1,3)\}$ *and* $K_{(2,4)} = \{(1,3)\}$ *are entrant or exit faces. This is the objective of the following Lemma.*

We note hereafter $K^T(F)$, the subset of the boundary of template K for which *there exists a solution* to the differential inclusion for (1) which *enters* K immediately. Note that $K^T(F)$ is in the complement of $K^S(F)$. For all multi-indices $\mathbf{k} = (k_1, \ldots, k_i)$, in a similar way as we did for $K^S(F)$, we also note $K^T_{\mathbf{k}}(\{f_i\})$ for such an entrance set for the template $\{x \in \mathbb{R}^n \mid p_{k_1}(x) \le c_{k_1}, \ldots, p_{k_i}(x) \le c_{k_i}\}$ under flow f_i, intersected with $K_{\mathbf{k}}$. We then have somehow a dual to Lemma 3, with similar proof:

LEMMA 4. *Consider a point* $x \in \overset{\circ}{K}_{\mathbf{k}}$ *for some multi-index* $\mathbf{k} = (1 \le k_1 < \ldots < k_i \le m)$. *Suppose that there exists* u *in* $\{1, \ldots, q\}$ *such that for all* j *in* $\{1, \ldots, i\}$, $x \in K^T_{k_j}(\{f_u\})$. *Then* $x \in K^T(F)$: $x \in \bigcap_{\lambda_1, \ldots, \lambda_q \ge 0,\ \sum_{i=1}^{q} \lambda_i = 1} K^T_{\mathbf{k}}(\{f_\lambda\})$.

EXAMPLE 6. *We carry on with Example 5. Let us look at face* $K_{(1,4)} = \{(-1,3)\}$. *We see that* $\mathcal{L}_{f_2}(p_1)(-1,3) = -3 < 0$ *and* $\mathcal{L}_{f_2}(p_4)(-1,3) = -26 < 0$, *hence* $(-1,3) \in K^T_{(1,4)}(\{f_1, f_2\})$. *By Lemma 4,* $K_{(1,4)} = (-1,3)$ *is entrant and* $K^S_{(1,4)}(F) = \emptyset$. *Similarly, we would find* $K^S_{(2,4)}(F) = \emptyset$ *so now Proposition 3 applies and* $K^S(F) = [-1,1] \times \{2\}$ *is closed. This situation is illustrated on Figure 3, where at the corners, always exiting flows (at* $K_{(1,3)}$ *and* $K_{(2,3)}$*) are represented in orange, whereas the flows that can possibly enter the template (at* $K_{(1,4)}$ *and* $K_{(2,4)}$*) are in green.*

Proposition 3, Lemmas 3, 4, translate into polynomial decision problems, as the theorem below expresses. These polynomial problems derive from similar conditions given for ordinary flows in [8] as we explain below.

THEOREM 4. *Consider the differential inclusion for (2). Let* K *be a convex compact minimal polynomial template defined by the set of inequalities* (P) *and let* N_i^j *be the order of the differential ideal* $\sqrt[\mathcal{L}]{\langle p_i \rangle}$ *along* f_j. *Suppose we have:*

- *For all faces* i, *all* $j = 1, \ldots, q$, *and all* $l = 1, \ldots, N_i^j - 2$, *we have* $(H_{i,j,l})$:

$$\Big(p_i(x) = c_i \;\&\; \forall k \neq i,\ p_k(x) \le c_k \;\&\; \mathcal{L}_{f_j}(p_i) = 0, \ldots, \mathcal{L}^{(l)}_{f_j}(p_i) = 0 \;\&\; \forall v \neq j,\ \mathcal{L}_{f_v}(p_i) \ge 0\Big) \Rightarrow \mathcal{L}^{(l+1)}_{f_j}(p_i)(x) \ge 0$$

  and (H_{i,j,N_i^j-1}): *the following set is empty*

$$\{x \in K_i \mid \quad \forall k \neq i,\ \mathcal{L}^{(1)}_{f_k}(p_i) \ge 0 \;\&\; \mathcal{L}^{(1)}_{f_j}(p_i)(x) = 0, \ldots, \mathcal{L}^{(N_i^j-1)}_{f_j}(p_i)(x) = 0\}$$

- *For all multi-indices* $\mathbf{k}$ *in* $\{1, \ldots, m\}$, *of cardinality greater or equal than 2,*

  - *there exists* $l = 1, \ldots, i$ *s.t. we have* $(H^+_{l,\mathbf{k}})$:

$$\begin{aligned}&(p_{k_1}(x) = c_{k_1} \;\&\; \ldots \;\&\; p_{k_i}(x) = c_{k_i} \&\\ &\forall k \neq \{k_1, \ldots, k_i\},\ p_k(x) \le c_k)\\ &\Longrightarrow (\mathcal{L}_{f_1}(p_{k_l})(x) > 0 \;\&\; \ldots \;\&\; \mathcal{L}_{f_q}(p_{k_l}(x) > 0)\end{aligned}$$

  - *Or there exists* $j = 1, \ldots, q$ *such that* $(H^-_{j,\mathbf{k}})$:

$$\begin{aligned}&(p_{k_1}(x) = c_{k_1} \;\&\; \ldots \;\&\; p_{k_i}(x) = c_{k_i} \&\\ &\forall k \neq \{k_1, \ldots, k_i\},\ p_k(x) \le c_k)\\ &\Longrightarrow (\mathcal{L}_{f_j}(p_{k_1})(x) < 0 \;\&\; \ldots \;\&\; \mathcal{L}_{f_j}(p_{k_i})(x) < 0)\end{aligned}$$

Then $K^S(F)$ *is closed and is* $\bigcup_{i=1}^{m} \{x \in K_i \mid \bigwedge_{j=1}^{q} \mathcal{L}^{(1)}_{f_j}(p_i)(x) \ge 0\}$. *Also, if* $K^S(F)$ *is disconnected, then* $Viab_K(F) \neq \emptyset$.

Conditions $(H_{i,j,l})$ ensure that at a point of tangency of flow f_j, on face K_i, of order l, which is also in the exit set of the other flows f_v, a certain $(l+1)$th Lie derivative is non-negative, meaning that flow f_j at that point is still exiting – this ensures closedness of the exit set on this face. Conditions $(H^+_{l,k})$ (resp. $(H^-_{l,k})$ ensure that the exit sets on $K_{\mathbf{k}}$ are the full face (resp. are empty).

PROOF. The proof goes as follows: we know that $K^S(F)$ is closed under the conditions of Proposition 3. For the first item of the hypotheses of Proposition 3, we use the characterization of [8], to get conditions $(H_{i,j,l})$ at each order l, for each face i and all potential tangencies for vector field f_j. Furthermore, using Lemma 3 we can decide whether a face $K_{\mathbf{k}}$ is entirely exiting, and this translates to $(H^+_{l,\mathbf{k}})$: all vector fields f_1 to f_q are exiting with respect to face K_l which contains $K_{\mathbf{k}}$. Finally, using Lemma 4 we can decide whether a face $K_{\mathbf{k}}$ has all its points which are non-exiting, by imposing that it is entirely within $K^T(F)$. Condition $(H^-_{j,k})$ translates the second item of the hypotheses of Proposition 3: if there exists a vector field f_j which is entrant on all faces K_{k_1} to K_{k_i} at their points of intersection, then $K_{\mathbf{k}}$ does not contain any exiting point for differential inclusion F. Finally, $K^S(F)$ is given as the union on all closed faces K_i of the intersections of the exit sets for the template given by p_i of all vector fields $f_1, \ldots, f_q$ since, on iterated faces $K_{\mathbf{k}}$ of face K_i, if the exit sets (for all $j = 1, \ldots, q$) $K^S_i(\{f_j\})$ intersect $K_{\mathbf{k}}$ then $K^S_{\mathbf{k}}(\{f_j\})$ is the whole face $K_{\mathbf{k}}$ and by Lemma 3 this is equal to $K^S_{\mathbf{k}}(F)$. □

Algorithm (B).
In the same way as with the algorithm of Theorem 3, we can check the conditions of Theorem 4 by using Sum of Squares optimization [17] and Stengle's nichtnegativstellensatz, for increasing k from 1 to $N_i^j - 2$ and j from 1 to q. In practice, as in [8], we generally use only a sufficient condition $(H_{i,j})$, which implies all $(H_{i,j,l})$:

$$\begin{aligned}&(p_i(x) = c_i \;\&\; \forall k \neq i,\ p_k(x) \le c_k \;\&\; \mathcal{L}_{f_j}(p_i) = 0 \;\&\\ &\forall l \neq j,\ \mathcal{L}_{f_l}(p_i) \ge 0) \Longrightarrow \mathcal{L}^{(2)}_{f_j}(p_i)(x) > 0\end{aligned}$$

and which can be checked using the much less computationally demanding Putinar positivstellensatz. When conditions $(H^+_{l,k})$ or $(H^-_{l,k})$ are not satisfied, we use the characterization of Proposition 3 translated as in Theorem 2, as a polynomial decision problem on variables (x, λ). This will be exemplified in Example 8.

We are now going to explain how Theorem 4 can be applied for proving the existence of viable solutions for time-dependent switched systems (Section 4) and state-dependent switched systems (Section 5).

4. VIABILITY AND INVARIANTS OF TIME-DEPENDENT SWITCHED SYSTEMS

Let us recall the notions related to *time-dependent switched system* (see, e.g., [18]). Suppose that we are given a family f_i, $i \in Q = \{1, \ldots, q\}$ of functions from $\mathbb{R}^n$ to $\mathbb{R}^n$. The set Q is called the set of *modes*. We still assume here that the functions are polynomials (hence locally Lipschitz). Let G defined on every point x of $\mathbb{R}^n$ by $G(x) = \{f_1(x), \ldots, f_q(x)\}$. It has closed, non-empty values, and is locally-Lipschitz, hence [3], the corresponding differential inclusion

$$\dot{x} \in G(x) \tag{5}$$

has solutions over finite time intervals. A solution of such a differential inclusion is any absolutely continuous functions satisfying $\dot{x}(t) \in G(x(t))$ almost everywhere. Such functions define time-dependent trajectories of the switched systems with the q modes $f_1, \ldots, f_q$.

A classical way to study the switched system (5) is to consider instead the differential inclusion equation $\dot{x} \in F(x)$ where F is defined by (2). Indeed, the Filippov-Ważewski theorem, which is basically a generalisation of the bang-bang control in ordinary linear control, states that all solutions of the convexified equation (2) can be approximated by solutions of Equation (5) with the same initial value, at least over a compact time interval, and under some simple hypotheses.

But we will actually need a little more than this classical theorem if we want to use the results of the previous section for switched systems with time-dependent switching. There are ways to extend it to infinite time horizon, still keeping some control over the switched trajectories, with respect to the trajectories of the corresponding differential inclusion, at the expense of possibly having to slightly perturbate the initial condition [13]. We restrict this version of Filippov-Ważewski "in infinite horizon" to our case, where we study differential inclusions $F = \overline{co}(f_1, \ldots, f_q)$ over $\mathbb{R}^n$, which are autonomous (they do not depend on time). In what follows, let $B(x, R)$ be the Euclidean ball in $\mathbb{R}^n$ of center x and radius R, and d_H the Hausdorff distance.

THEOREM 5. *[13] Let $0 < T \leq \infty$. Suppose the set-valued map $G : \mathbb{R}^n \to \wp(\mathbb{R}^n)$ is measurable with respect to the Borel subsets of $\mathbb{R}^n$. Suppose also that for all $R > 0$ there exists $k_R \in \mathbb{R}$ such that for any $\xi, \eta \in B(0, R)$,*

$$d_H(G(\xi), G(\eta)) \leq k_R|\xi - \eta|$$

and that there exists $\alpha_R \in \mathbb{R}$ such that for each $\xi \in B(0, R)$,

$$\sup\{|\zeta| : \zeta \in G(\xi)\} \leq \alpha_R$$

Fix $\xi \in X$ and let $z \in [0, T) \to X$ be a solution of $\dot{x} \in \overline{co}(G(x))$, $x(0) = \xi$. Let $r = [0, T) \to \mathbb{R}$ be a continuous function satisfying $r(t) > 0$ for all $t \in [0, T]$.

Then there exists $\eta^0 \in B(\xi, r(0))$ and a solution $x = [0, T) \to X$ of $\dot{x} \in G(x)$, $x(0) = \eta^0$ which satisfies

$$|z(t) - x(t)| \leq r(t) \;\forall t \in [0, T)$$

LEMMA 5. *The switched system (5) satisfies the hypotheses of Theorem 5.*

We are now in a position to use Theorem 5 for the differential inclusion $\overline{co}(f_1, \ldots, f_q)$. We can prove the following adaptation of Theorem 4 to time-dependent switched systems:

THEOREM 6. *Consider the time-dependent switched system of Equation (5). Let K be a compact minimal polynomial template defined by the set of inequalities (P) and let N_i^j be the order of the differential ideal $\sqrt[\mathcal{L}]{\langle p_i \rangle}$ along f_j.*

Under the same conditions as those of Theorem 4, $K^S(F)$ is closed and equal to

$$\bigcup_{i=1}^{m} \{x \in K_i \mid \bigwedge_{j=1}^{q} \mathcal{L}_{f_j}^{(1)}(p_i)(x) \geq 0\}$$

If furthermore $K^S(F)$ is disconnected, then for any open set $\hat{K}$ strictly containing K, $Viab_G(\hat{K}) \neq \emptyset$, i.e.: there exists a viable solution of (5) within $\hat{K}$.

PROOF. By Theorem 4 we know that there exists at least a trajectory δ of $\dot{x} \in \overline{co}(G(x))$ which is included in K. By Lemma 5 and Theorem 5 we know that for any $r > 0$ there is a trajectory δ_r of $\dot{x} \in G(x)$ at distance at most r of δ. Let $\hat{K}$ be any open set strictly containing K, by compactness of K, there exists $r > 0$ such that $\bigcup_{x \in K} B(x, r) \subseteq \hat{K}$, hence $\delta_r \subseteq \hat{K}$ and $Viab_G(\hat{K}) \neq \emptyset$. □

EXAMPLE 7. *Consider again the switched system of Example 1. >From Example 5, we know that for template $K' = [-1, 1] \times [2, 3]$, $K^S(F) = [-1, 1] \times \{2\}$. But this exit set is connected, and Theorem 6 does not apply. It is actually clear that there is no switching that can stabilize F within K': any infinite trajectory of the convexified flow of f_1 and f_2 either does not intersect with K', or traverses K' (i.e., enters into K' then exits from it), as shown in Figure 3.*

We consider now the same switched system, but with the box $K = [-0.5, 0.5] \times [-0.5, 0.5]$. We know from Example 4 that $K^S(F) = \emptyset$ and Theorem 6 applies. We can then conclude that there exists a time-dependent switching which stabilizes F within e.g. any square $K_\epsilon =]-0.5 - \epsilon, 0.5 + \epsilon[\times]-0.5 - \epsilon, 0.5 + \epsilon[$ $(\epsilon > 0)$, by choosing appropriately f_1 or f_2 for some amount of time. Actually, there is a trivial switching: both systems f_1 and f_2 stabilize within K (this is clear from Figure 2). Note however that the topological criterion given in [8] is too weak to conclude, as both exit sets $K^S(\{f_1\})$ and $K^S(\{f_2\})$ are non-closed.

5. VIABILITY AND INVARIANTS OF STATE-DEPENDENT SWITCHED SYSTEMS

Switching events often depend not only on time, but also on the current state of the system (see [18]). Suppose we are given a partition of $\mathbb{R}^n$ as a finite or infinite number of *operating regions* by means of a family of *switching surfaces*, or *guards*. A *state-dependent switched system* is defined by these operating regions, and in the interior of each of these regions a continuous dynamical system. Whenever the system trajectory hits a switching surface, the continuous state changes its *mode*. For simplicity, we suppose hereafter that there are only 2 modes and 1 switching surface. The generalization is easy.

Consider a state-dependent switched system, described by a $\mathcal{C}^1$ switching surface $\mathcal{S}$, given by equation $s(x) = 0$ separating $\mathbb{R}^n$ into two open components $\mathcal{S}_+ = \{x \in \mathbb{R}^n \mid s(x) > 0\}$ and $\mathcal{S}_- = \{x \in \mathbb{R}^n \mid s(x) < 0\}$, and two subsystems $\dot{x} = f_i(x)$, $i = +, -$, one on each side of each element of $\mathcal{S}$:

$$\dot{x} = \begin{cases} f_+(x) & \text{if } s(x) > 0 \\ f_-(x) & \text{if } s(x) < 0 \end{cases} \tag{6}$$

We rely on Filippov's definition of a solution to such systems :

DEFINITION 4. *[18] Given a state-dependent switched system $\mathcal{H}$ defined by Equation 6, a function $x(\cdot) : \mathbb{R}^+ \to \mathbb{R}^n$ is a solution of $\mathcal{H}$ if it is absolutely continuous and satisfies the differential inclusion $\dot{x}(t) \in F(x(t))$ for almost all $t \in \mathbb{R}^+$,* *where F is a multi-valued function defined as follows:*

$$F(x) \quad = \quad \begin{cases} \{f_-(x)\} & \textit{if } x \in \mathcal{S}_- \\ \{f_+(x)\} & \textit{if } x \in \mathcal{S}_+ \\ \overline{co}\{f_+(x), f_-(x)\} & \textit{if } x \in \mathcal{S} \end{cases}$$

Similarly to Lemma 1, function F from Definition 4 is a Lipschitzean Marchaud map, hence admits solutions on finite time intervals (see [7], Chapter 2). We apply again Theorem 5 and get a theorem similar to Theorem 6 :

THEOREM 7. *Consider the state-dependent switched system defined by Equation (6). Let K be a compact minimal polynomial template defined by the set of inequalities (P). Suppose the switching surface $\mathcal{S}$ intersects K only at intersections of faces defining K, i.e. is entirely within* **k***-faces (with $|\mathbf{k}| \geq 2$) of K.*

Suppose, up to a reordering of faces, that $\{p_i \mid i = 1, \ldots, l\}$ (resp. $\{p_j \mid j = l+1, \ldots, m\}$) are the polynomials defining the faces of K whose interior are in $\mathcal{S}^+$ (resp. $\mathcal{S}^-$) and let N_i^j be the order of the differential ideal $\sqrt[\mathcal{L}]{\langle p_i \rangle}$ along f_j.

Under the same conditions as those of Theorem 4, $K^S(F)$ is closed and equal to

$$\bigcup_{i=1}^{l} \{x \in K_i | \mathcal{L}_{f_+}^{(1)}(p_i)(x) \geq 0\} \cup \bigcup_{j=l+1}^{m} \{x \in K_j | \mathcal{L}_{f_-}^{(1)}(p_j)(x) \geq 0\}$$

If furthermore $K^S(F)$ is disconnected, then $Viab_F(\hat{K}) \neq \emptyset$ ($\hat{K}$ is any open set strictly containing K), i.e.: there exists a state-dependent switching signal for which there is a viable solution of (6) within $\hat{K}$.

6. EXPERIMENTS

6.1 An uncertain differential system

We consider a perturbation of the system discussed in [8] :

$$f_\epsilon \begin{pmatrix} x \\ y \\ z \end{pmatrix} = \begin{pmatrix} x^3 + y - x/10 + \varepsilon \\ -x - y/10 + \varepsilon \\ 5z + \varepsilon \end{pmatrix}$$

and we take as differential inclusion $F(x, y, z) = \{f_\epsilon \mid -0.05 \leq \varepsilon \leq 0.05\}$. We consider the template given by the unique face $p_1 = x_1^2 + (x_2 - 1)^2 + (x_3 + 1)^2$ and $c_1 = 1/25$. We use Theorem 2 and its implementation as Algorithm (A). With our Matlab implementation, the exit set for the differential inclusion is proved closed in 348 seconds. It has two connected components hence there is a viable trajectory within the template considered.

6.2 Boost DC-DC Converter

EXAMPLE 8. *The boost DC-DC converter is an example from power electronic, where the state of the system is $x(t) = [i_l(t)\ v_c(t)]^T$ with i_l the current intensity in an inductor, and $v_c(t)$ the voltage of a capacitor. The aim of the control is to maintain the system inside a given zone K (while the output voltage stabilizes around a desired value). The dynamics associated with mode u is given by $\dot{x}(t) = f_u(x) = A_u x(t) + b$ ($u = 1, 2$).*

We use in the experiments the numerical values of [11] for A_1 and A_2, $x_c = 70$, $x_l = 3$, $r_c = 0.005$, $r_l = 0.05$, $r_0 = 1$, $v_s = 1$. We instantiate to $b = (\frac{1}{3}\ 0)^T$,

$$A_1 = \begin{pmatrix} -0.0167 & 0 \\ 0 & -0.0142 \end{pmatrix}, A_2 = \begin{pmatrix} -0.0183 & -0.3317 \\ 0.0142 & -0.0142 \end{pmatrix}$$

and study the system in the rectangle $K = [1.55, 2.15] \times [1.0, 1.4]$, which corresponds to the template $p_1 = x$, $p_2 = -x$, $p_3 = y$, $p_4 = -y$ with $c_1 = 2.15, c_2 = -1.55, c_3 = 1.4, c_4 = -1$.

Time-dependent switching.

The Lie derivatives for each dynamic and each face, instantiated for the chosen parameters and template K, are given below :

$$\begin{array}{llll} \mathcal{L}_{f_1}(p_1) = & -.017x + .3 & \mathcal{L}_{f_2}(p_1) = & -.018x - .33y + .3 \\ & > 0 & & < 0 \\ \mathcal{L}_{f_1}(p_2) = & -L_{f_1}(p_1) < 0 & \mathcal{L}_{f_2}(p_2) = & -\mathcal{L}_{f_2}(p_1) > 0 \\ \mathcal{L}_{f_1}(p_3) = & -.014y < 0 & \mathcal{L}_{f_2}(p_3) = & .014x - .014y > 0 \\ \mathcal{L}_{f_1}(p_4) = & -L_{f_1}(p_3) > 0 & \mathcal{L}_{f_2}(p_4) = & -\mathcal{L}_{f_2}(p_3) < 0 \end{array}$$

The conditions of Theorem 6 are satisfied, using the simpler version of Algorithm B, for all faces K_i: actually all first-order Lie derivatives are strictly positive on the faces. This is checked in 12.22 seconds using our Matlab implementation. The conditions of Theorem 6 are not satisfied on the two extremal points $K_{(1,3)} = (1.55, 1.0)$ and $K_{(2,4)} = (2.15, 1.4)$ where we use the more complex characterization of Proposition 3 as explained in Algorithm (B), showing the these two points are not part of the exit set (see also Figure 4). Therefore $K^S(F) = \emptyset$ and there exists a viable solution in any open set containing K.

State-dependent switching.

We now consider the same system with a switching surface S given by the affine function going through the corners (1.55, 1.0) and (2.15, 1.4) i.e. $\{s(x) = y - ax - b = 0\}$ where $a = 2/3$ and $b = -1/30$, and f_1 is applied in $\{s(x) > 0\}$ and f_2 in $\{s(x) < 0\}$ (see Figure 4).

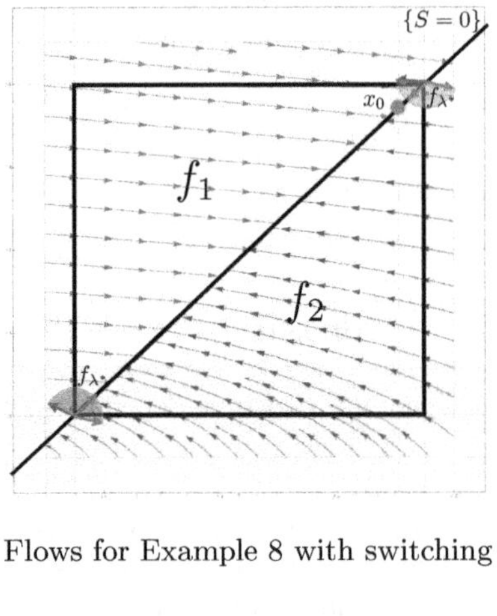

Figure 4: Flows for Example 8 with switching surface S

Here again, we can show that $K^S(F)$ is empty using Theorem 7. It is clear indeed that all the points of $\mathcal{S}_- \cap \partial K$ and $\mathcal{S}_+ \cap \partial K$ are entrant and satisfy the conditions of Theorem 7 (i.e., those of Theorem 4). For the corners located on $\mathcal{S}$, this is less trivial (similarly to what happens in the time-

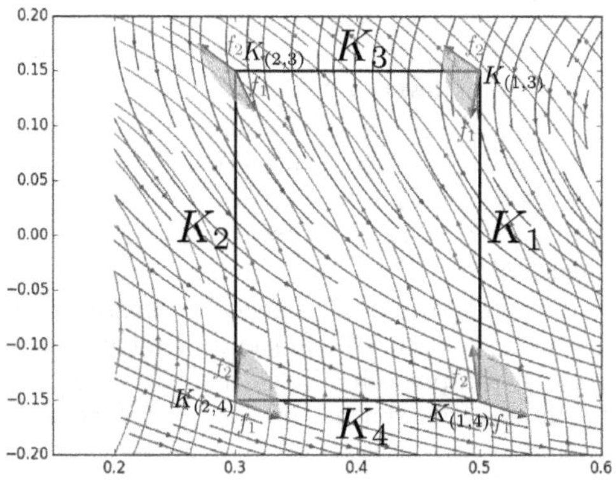

Figure 5: $K^S = \emptyset$ for template $(c_0, \delta_1, \delta_2) = (0.4, 0.1, 0.15)$.

dependent switching case) since f_1 and f_2 are both exiting. But there are values of λ for which flow f_λ is entrant. [2]

6.3 Defocused switched systems

EXAMPLE 9. *Let us consider the defocused switched system defined by*

$$f_1 \begin{pmatrix} x \\ y \end{pmatrix} = \begin{pmatrix} -\rho_A & -1/E \\ E & -\rho_A \end{pmatrix} \begin{pmatrix} x - x_c \\ y - y_c \end{pmatrix} \quad (7)$$

$$f_2 \begin{pmatrix} x \\ y \end{pmatrix} = \begin{pmatrix} -\rho_B & -1 \\ 1 & -\rho_B \end{pmatrix} \begin{pmatrix} x \\ y \end{pmatrix} \quad (8)$$

The invariant sets of such systems are studied in [22]. We consider here the case $(x_c, y_c) = (cos(\phi), sin(\phi))$, $\rho_A = 0.5, \rho_B = 0.4, E = 0.5, \phi = 0$. *The flows for the two systems are represented in Figure 6.*

We choose box templates centered on the x axis, defined by $p_1 = x$, $p_2 = -x$, $p_3 = y$, $p_4 = -y$ and $c_1 = c_0 + \delta_1$, $c_2 = -c_0 + \delta_1$, $c_3 = c_4 = \delta_2$ (see Figure 6). Calculating the first-order Lie derivative for each dynamic and face, we see that the boxes have an empty exit set $K_S(F)$, and it follows from Theorem 6 that the state of the system can be maintained inside any box using an appropriate switching law. For example the system can be controlled inside the box defined by $(c_0 = 0.4, \delta_1 = 0.1, \delta_2 = 0.15)$ (see Figure 5) and $(c_0 = 0.55, \delta_1 = 0.05, \delta_2 = 0.15)$, hence fairly accurately.

6.4 Disconnected exit sets

EXAMPLE 10. *We consider the switched system defined by*

$$f_1 \begin{pmatrix} x \\ y \end{pmatrix} = \begin{pmatrix} 1 + y^2 \\ y \end{pmatrix} \text{ and } f_2 \begin{pmatrix} x \\ y \end{pmatrix} = \begin{pmatrix} -1 - y^2 \\ y \end{pmatrix}$$

Box template.

We consider the template $p_1 = -x$, $p_2 = x$, $p_3 = -y$, $p_4 = y$ and $c_1 = c_2 = c_3 = c_4 = 1$. Calculating the Lie

[2]Actually, the surface $\mathcal{S}$ can be seen as a *sliding* surface, i.e. there exists a solution which stays indefinitely on it: the sliding strategy makes all the trajectories starting from K converge to an equilibrium point $(2.10648, 1.37098)$, represented as a green bullet point on Figure 4.

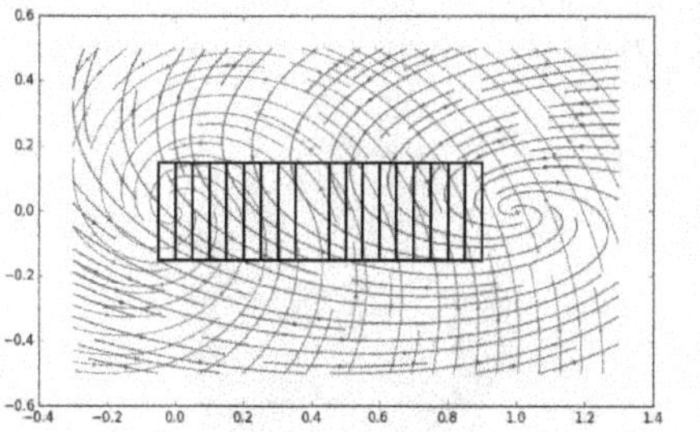

Figure 6: Box templates between the equilibrium points of the defocused switched system.

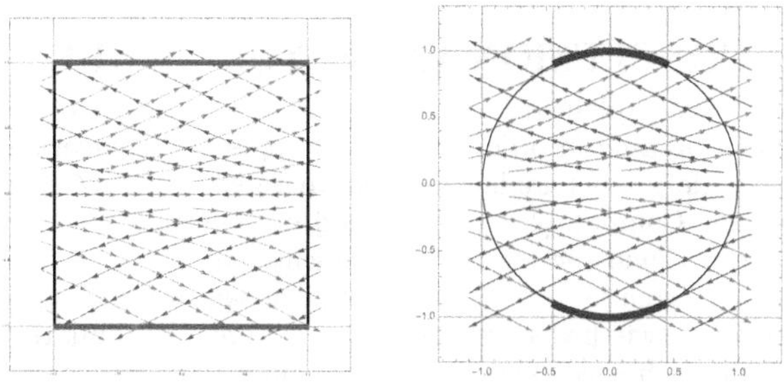

Figure 7: Flows f_1 and f_2, with $K^S(F)$ in thick line.

derivative of the template, we can deduce closedness of the exit set by Theorem 6, and, by Algorithm (B), in 22 seconds in Matlab, $K^S(F) = [-1, 1] \times \{-1\} \cup [-1, 1] \times \{1\}$, which is closed and disconnected (left of Figure 7).

Ball template.

Let us now take a unit ball template: $p = x^2 + y^2$ and $c = 1$. Calculating the Lie derivatives on this template we can deduce, using Theorem 6 and Algorithm (B), in 8.6 seconds using our Matlab implementation that $K^S(F) = \{(x, y) \in [-0.445042, 0.445\,042] \times [-1, 1] \mid x^2 + y^2 = 1\}$, which is closed and disconnected (right of Figure 7). Hence the ball as well as the box contain a viable trajectory for some time-dependent switching strategy.

EXAMPLE 11. *Consider now the following generalization of the previous system, to dimension 3 :*

$$f_1 \begin{pmatrix} x \\ y \\ z \end{pmatrix} = \begin{pmatrix} 1 + y^2 + z^2 \\ y \\ z \end{pmatrix}, f_2 \begin{pmatrix} x \\ y \\ z \end{pmatrix} = \begin{pmatrix} -1 - y^2 - z^2 \\ y \\ z \end{pmatrix},$$

$$f_3 \begin{pmatrix} x \\ y \\ z \end{pmatrix} = \begin{pmatrix} x \\ 1 + x^2 + z^2 \\ z \end{pmatrix}, f_4 \begin{pmatrix} x \\ y \\ z \end{pmatrix} = \begin{pmatrix} x \\ -1 - x^2 - z^2 \\ z \end{pmatrix}$$

Ball template.

We use a ball template defined by $p = x^2 + y^2 + z^2$ and $c = 1$. By application of Theorem 6, with just the first two Lie derivatives as in Algorithm (B), we find in 68.5 seconds using our Matlab implementation that the exit set is closed. It is made of two components (see Figure 8, the components are in red) $K^S(F) = \{(x, y, z) \in [-0.445042, 0.445042] \times [-0.445042, 0.445042] \times [-1, 1] \mid x^2 + y^2 + z^2 = 1\}$: there exists a time-dependent switch stabilizing this system of four non-linear ODEs in the unit ball of dimension 3.

Figure 8: The two components of the exit set, Example 11

7. CONCLUSION AND FUTURE WORK

We have explained in this paper how topological methods can be used in order to show the presence of invariant sets inside given templates of the phase space of switched systems. Computable criteria based on SoS methods have been given, and successfully experimented on various examples of differential inclusions and time-dependent and state-dependent switched systems of the literature. We think that our approach sheds new light on the important problem of locating invariants of switched systems. It is now natural to consider *parametric* templates of a given form, and determine the values of the parameters which satisfy our criteria: this will allows us to *synthesize* templates containing invariants. As future work, we plan to apply more refined topological methods based on the Conley index, in order to determine the dynamical nature of located invariants (stable or unstable equilibrium point, limit cycle, chaos,...).

Acknowledgments..

The authors were partially supported by Digiteo Project SIMS 2013-0544D, by ANR projects CAFEIN, ANR-12-INSE-0007 and MALTHY, ANR-13-INSE-0003, by iCODE and by the academic chair "Complex Systems Engineering" of Ecole polytechnique-ENSTA-Télécom-Thalès-Dassault Aviation-DCNS-DGA-FX-Fondation ParisTech-FDO ENSTA.

8. REFERENCES

[1] W. W. Adams and P. Loustaunau. *An introduction to Grobner bases.* Graduate studies in mathematics. American mathematical society, 1994.

[2] E. Asarin, O. Bournez, D. Thao, O. Maler, and A. Pnueli. Effective synthesis of switching controllers for linear systems. *Proc. of the IEEE*, 88(7):1011–1025, July 2000.

[3] J.-P. Aubin and A. Cellina. *Differential Inclusions, Set-Valued Maps And Viability Theory.* Number 264 in Grundl. der Math. Wiss. Springer, 1984.

[4] M. Boccadoro, Y. Wardi, M. Egerstedt, and E. Verriest. Optimal control of switching surfaces in hybrid dynamical systems. *Discrete Event Dynamical Systems*, 15:433–448, 2005.

[5] P. Cardaliaguet. Conditions suffisantes de non-vacuité du noyau de viabilité. *C. R. Acad. Sci. Paris Ser. I*, 314:797–800, 1992.

[6] S. Coogan and M. Arcak. Guard synthesis of hybrid systems using sum of squares programming. In *Conference on Decision and Control*, 2012.

[7] A. F. Filippov. *Differential equations with discontinuous righthand sides.* Mathematics and its applications. Kluwer, 1988.

[8] L. Fribourg, É. Goubault, S. Mohamed, M. Mrozek, and S. Putot. A topological method for finding invariants of continuous systems. In *Workshop on Reachability Problems*, volume 9328 of *LNCS*. Springer, 2015.

[9] G. Gabor and M. Quincampoix. On existence of solutions to differential equations or inclusions remaining in a prescribed closed subset of a finite-dimensional space. *Journal of Differential Equations*, 185:483–512, 2002.

[10] A. Girard and G. Pappas. Approximated bisimulation relations for constrained linear systems. *Automatica*, 43:1307–1317, 2007.

[11] A. Girard, G. Pola, and P. Tabuada. Approximately bisimilar symbolic models for incrementally stable switched systems. *IEEE Transactions on Automatic Control*, 55:116–126, 2010.

[12] E. Haghverdi, P. Tabuada, and G. Pappas. Bisimulation relations for dynamical, control, and hybrid systems. *Theor. Comput. Sci.*, 342, 2005.

[13] B. Ingalls, E. D. Sontag, and Y. Wang. An infinite-time relaxation theorem for differential inclusions. *Proceedings of the AMS*, 131(2), 2002.

[14] S. Jha, S. Gulwani, S. Seshia, and A. Tiwari. Synthesizing switching logic for safety and dwell-time requirements. In *ACM/IEEE Int. Conf. on Cyber-Physical Systems*, 2010.

[15] A. Julius and A. van der Schaft. The maximal controlled invariant set of switched linear systems. In *Conference on Decision and Control*. IEEE, 2002.

[16] S. Lang. *Algebra.* Graduate Texts in Mathematics. Springer New York, 2002.

[17] J.-B. Lasserre. *Moments, positive polynomials and their applications*, volume 1. World Scientific, 2009.

[18] D. Liberzon. *Switching in Systems and Control.* Systems and Control: Foundations and Applications. Birkhauser, 2003.

[19] J. Lygeros, C. Tomlin, and S. Sastry. Controllers for reachability specifications for hybrid systems. *Automatica*, 35:349–370, 1999.

[20] K. Mischaikow and M. Mrozek. Conley index theory. *Handbook of Dynamical Systems II*, 2002.

[21] R. Moeckel. Sturm's algorithm and isolating blocks. *Journal of Symbolic Computation*, 40:1242–1255, 2005.

[22] P. Nilsson, U. Boscain, M. Sigalotti, and J. Newling. Invariant sets of defocused switched systems. In *Conference of Decision and Control*, 2013.

[23] N. Ozay, J. Liu, P. Prabhakar, and R. M. Murray. Computing augmented finite transition systems to synthesize switching protocols for polynomial switched systems. In *American Control Conference, ACC 2013, Washington, DC, USA, June 17-19, 2013*, pages 6237–6244, 2013.

[24] Z. Sun and S. S. Ge. *Stability Theory of Switched Dynamical Systems.* Springer, 2011.

[25] C. Tomlin, J. Lygeros, and S. Sastry. A game theoretic approach to controller design for hybrid systems. In *Proceedings of the IEEE*, 2000.

Hybridization for Stability Analysis of Switched Linear Systems

Pavithra Prabhakar *
Kansas State University, Manhattan, KS
pprabhakar@ksu.edu

Miriam García Soto
IMDEA Software Institute, Madrid, Spain
miriam.garcia@imdea.org

ABSTRACT

In this paper, we present a hybridization method for stability analysis of switched linear hybrid system (*LHS*), that constructs a switched system with polyhedral inclusion dynamics (*PHS*) using a state-space partition that is specific to stability analysis. We use a previous result based on quantitative predicate abstraction to analyse the stability of *PHS*. We show completeness of the hybridization based verification technique for the class of asymptotically stable linear system and a subclass of switched linear systems whose dynamics are pairwise Lipschitz continuous on the state-space and uniformly converging in time. For this class of systems, we show that by increasing the granularity of the region partition, we eventually reach an abstract switched system with polyhedral inclusion dynamics that is asymptotically stable. On the practical side, we implemented our approach in the tool `Averist`, and experimentally compared our approach with a state-of-the-art tool for stability analysis of hybrid systems based on Lyapunov functions. Our experimental results illustrate that our method is less prone to numerical errors and scales better than the traditional approaches. In addition, our tool returns a counterexample in the event that it fails to prove stability, providing feedback regarding the potential reason for instability. We also examined heuristics for the choice of state-space partition during refinement.

1. INTRODUCTION

Stability is a fundamental property in the design of cyber-physical systems that ensures robustness of these systems with respect to perturbations in the initial states or inputs. Linear hybrid systems (*LHS*) are an important class of cyber-physical systems, that manifest in several embedded control systems. In addition, more often than not, the design and analysis of non-linear control systems is conducted by considering linearizations of these systems at different operating points. Hence, linear hybrid systems have been extensively studied in the literature; see, for instance, [10] for a survey of methods for stability analysis.

Stability analysis is a challenging problem, especially, for hybrid systems. For instance, while it is well-known that the stability of a purely continuous linear dynamical system can be inferred solely based on analyzing its eigenvalues, the same is not true when switching is allowed between these systems [4]. Hence, alternate methods based on exhibiting Lyapunov functions, which provide a certificate of stability, and their extensions to common and multiple Lyapunov functions for switched system analysis have gained prominence [9].

Computational methods for stability analysis essentially consist of a template based search for a Lyapunov function [3, 12]. Here, a template, for instance, a polynomial with coefficients as parameters, is chosen. The conditions on the Lyapunov functions, such as, non-negativity, are encoded in a constraint solving formalism. For instance, a sufficient condition for a polynomial to be non-negative is to be expressible as a sum of squares of terms. Efficient tools for semi-definite programming and sum-of-squares optimization are employed to solve for the parameters in the templates.

While the template based search has gained popularity due to the advances in convex optimization tools over the last decade, there are some fundamental difficulties with the approach which have not been adequately addressed. First, finding the right template requires user ingenuity, and the alternative of exhaustively iterating over all possible templates is highly inefficient. Next, the stability analysis tools provide no insights into the reason for instability or guide the choice of better templates, when the solvers fail to instantiate the template.

To overcome the difficulties with the template based search, an alternate approach based on abstraction-refinement was proposed by the authors in their previous work [14, 15] for stability analysis of hybrid systems with piecewise constant and polyhedral inclusion dynamics. Here, a quantitative predicate abstraction (QPA) for stability analysis was presented, which extends the standard finite state graph construction of predicate abstraction [7], by annotating the edges with weights which capture information about the distance of the state to the equilibrium point during evolution along a trajectory. This approach returned a counterexample when the abstraction failed to prove stability.

One of the main difficulties in extending QPA to linear hybrid systems, is the computation of the edges and their

*Pavithra Prabhakar is partially supported by EU FP7 Marie Curie Career Integration Grant no. 631622 and NSF CAREER award no. 1552668.

HSCC '16, April 12–14, 2016, Vienna, Austria.
© 2016 ACM. ISBN 978-1-4503-3955-1/16/04...$15.00
DOI: http://dx.doi.org/10.1145/2883817.2883840

weights, which require computing a reachability relation to the linear hybrid systems. This is a challenging problem, especially, when the number of edge switchings is not bounded. Hence, we propose to abstract the linear hybrid system to a polyhedral hybrid system for which the edge relation and weights can be efficiently computed (even in the presence of unbounded number of mode switches [15]).

Our main result is a novel application of the hybridization approach [1, 5] for stability analysis. Broadly, hybridization consist of splitting the state-space into a finite number of regions and approximating the dynamics in each of the regions by a simpler dynamics. Our hybridization is specialized for stability analysis, and differs from those used for safety analysis, in the class of partitions considered for hybridization. We use partitions that split the state-space into conic polyhedral sets. The linear dynamics in each of the regions is overapproximated by a polyhedral inclusion dynamics. Our partitioning is fine tuned for stability analysis, since, it guarantees a bound on the "scaling" in a region, ratio of the distance to the origin at the end of the execution to that at the beginning. Hybridization techniques for safety analysis instead seek a bound on the approximation error in the reach set [1, 5].

Our main theoretical result is the completeness of the hybridization technique for the class of asymptotically stable switched linear systems that are "uniformly converging in time" and Lipschitz continuous. For this class of systems, we show that by increasing the granularity of the region partition, we eventually reach a polyhedral switched system abstraction that is asymptotically stable.

We have implemented our approach in the tool `Averist`. We experimentally compared our approach with the state-of-the-art tool for stability analysis of hybrid systems based on Lyapunov functions, `Stabhyli`. Our experimental results illustrate that our method is less prone to numerical errors and scales better than the traditional approaches. In addition, our tool returns a potential counterexample in the event that it fails to prove stability, providing feedback regarding the potential reason for instability. This is a result of the quantitative algorithmic method that we use in the back-end for analyzing polyhedral switched systems. We also investigate some heuristics for partitioning the state-space in a more efficient manner.

2. HYBRID AUTOMATA

In this section, we define hybrid automata, which are a popular formalism for capturing the mixed discrete-continuous behaviors of cyber-physical systems. We consider switched systems that do not allow instantaneous jumps in the continuous state of the system. Below, we define a subclass of switched hybrid systems. Let *Poly*(n) denote the set of all convex polyhedra in the n-dimensional state-space. In the sequel, by a polyhedral set, we always mean a convex polyhedral set.

Definition. A *hybrid automaton* (*HA*) is a tuple $\mathcal{H} =$ (*Loc*, *Edges*, *Cont*, *Flow*, *Inv*, *Guard*), where:

- *Loc* is a finite set of control modes or locations;
- *Edges* $\subseteq$ *Loc* $\times$ *Loc* is a finite set of edges;
- *Cont* $= \mathbb{R}^n$, for some n, is the continuous state-space;

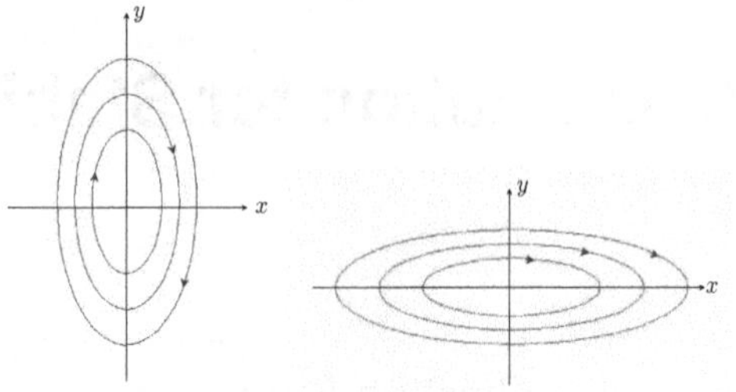

(a) $\dot{x} = A_1 x$ (b) $\dot{x} = A_2 x$

Figure 1: Linear systems

- *Flow* : *Loc* $\rightarrow (\mathbb{R}^n \mapsto 2^{\mathbb{R}^n})$ is the vector field function;
- *Inv* : *Loc* $\rightarrow$ *Poly*(n) is the invariant function; and
- *Guard* : *Edges* $\rightarrow$ *Poly*(n) is the guard function.

We call n, the dimension of $\mathcal{H}$.

The hybrid automaton evolves continuously by following the vector field function at each location. It executes starting in a mode q and a continuous state x. For every location $q \in$ *Loc* the state follows the vector field *Flow*(q) while being inside the invariant *Inv*(q). The continuous state switches from one location to other when it satisfies the guard between these locations. The vector field function is typically represented as a differential inclusion $\dot{x} \in F(x)$ or a linear differential equation $\dot{x} = Ax$, where $F(x)$ represents a polyhedron and A is a real matrix.

We say that a hybrid automaton is *linear* if in every mode q the behaviour of the system is determined by a linear dynamical system of the form $\dot{x} = A_q x$. Hence, for every $q \in$ *Loc* and $x \in$ *Inv*(q), the flow in the hybrid automaton is given by *Flow*(q)(x) $= \{A_q x\}$. And we say that a hybrid automaton is *polyhedral*, when, for every mode q, the dynamics is defined by a polyhedral inclusion of the form $\dot{x} \in P_q$ where P_q is a polyhedron. Here, the flow is specified as *Flow*(q)(x) $= P_q$ for every $q \in$ *Loc* and $x \in$ *Inv*(q).

Let $\mathcal{I}$ denote the set of all closed intervals over $\mathbb{R}$. Given an interval $I \in \mathcal{I}$, let *first*(I) and *last*(I) denote the greatest lower bound and the least upper bound of I. Let $F\lfloor_X$ denote the restriction of the function F to the set X as its domain.

Definition. An *execution* of a *HA* $\mathcal{H} =$ (*Loc*, *Edges*, *Cont*, *Flow*, *Inv*, *Guard*) is a function $\sigma : I \rightarrow \mathbb{R}^n$, where $I = [0, T]$ or $I = [0, \infty)$, such that there exists a finite or infinite sequence $(q_0, I_0), (q_1, I_1), (q_2, I_2) \ldots$ satisfying for all $i \geq 0$:

- $(q_i, I_i) \in$ *Loc* $\times \mathcal{I}$, such that $\cup_i I_i = I$ and *last*(I_i) $=$ *first*(I_{i+1});
- $\sigma\lfloor_{I_i}$ is a solution of $\dot{x} \in$ *Flow*(q_i)(x), that is, $\frac{d}{dt}\sigma\lfloor_{I_i}$ (t) $\in$ *Flow*(q_i)($\sigma\lfloor_{I_i}$ (t)) and satisfies $\sigma\lfloor_{I_i}$ (t) $\in$ *Inv*(q_i) for all $t \in I_i$ and σ(*last*(I_i)) $\in$ *Guard*(q_i, q_{i+1}).

Let *Exec*($\mathcal{H}$) denote the set of all executions of $\mathcal{H}$.

The evolution of a linear dynamical system is determined by the equation $\dot{x} = Ax$ where A is a real square matrix. Consider two linear dynamical systems of the form $\dot{x} = A_1 x$ and $\dot{x} = A_2 x$, where the matrices are given as follows

$$A_1 = \begin{pmatrix} 0 & 1 \\ -4 & 0 \end{pmatrix} \qquad A_2 = \begin{pmatrix} 0 & 1 \\ -0.1 & 0 \end{pmatrix}$$

The phase portraits showing the solutions for each of these systems are depicted in Figure 1. A linear dynamical system defines the evolution of a linear hybrid automaton at each location. A linear hybrid automaton model is depicted in Figure 2. Observe this system consists of four modes, q_1, q_2, q_3 and q_4, with associated invariants R_1, R_2, R_3 and R_4, which correspond to the first, second, third and fourth quadrants of the two dimensional plane, respectively. The dynamics A_1 and A_2 are as given in Figure 6. Hence, the system evolves in the first and third quadrants following a solution of the dynamical system $\dot{x} = A_1 x$ and in the other two quadrants following one of $\dot{x} = A_2 x$. The switching condition is along the common boundaries, and is specified by the guard annotations on the edges. A sample execution of the system is given in Figure 3.

A polyhedral hybrid automaton is shown in Figure 4, analogous to the linear one but with dynamics determined by the differential inclusion $\dot{x} \in P_i$ for each mode q_i. A sample execution of the polyhedral system is depicted in Figure 5.

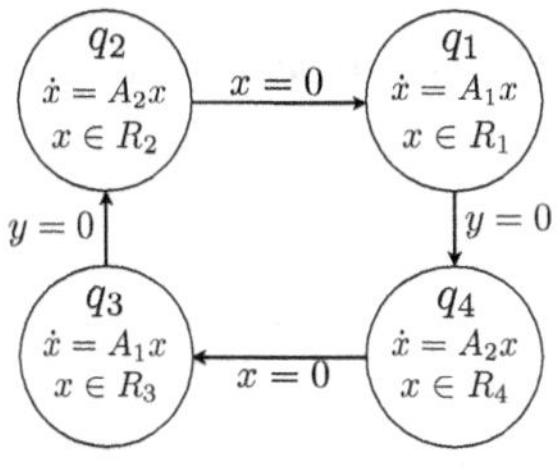

Figure 2: Linear hybrid automaton $\mathcal{H}$

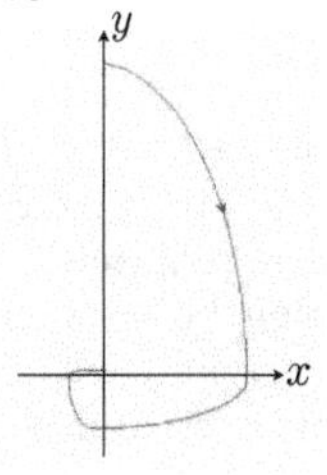

Figure 3: A sample execution of $\mathcal{H}$

3. STABILITY

Stability is a fundamental property in control system design. We consider two classical notions of stability in control theory, namely, Lyapunov and asymptotic stability. An *equilibrium point* is a state of the system such that an execution starting from it remains there. Origin $\bar{0}$ will be an equilibrium point in the systems we consider, and we define stability with respect to the origin. A system is said to be *Lyapunov stable* if small perturbations in the initial state lead to small deviations in the executions with respect to the equilibrium point. Further, it is said to be *asymptotically stable* if the executions starting in a small neighborhood of the equilibrium point converge to the point. In the following $B_r(\bar{0})$ refers to a ball of radius r around $\bar{0}$.

Definition. A hybrid system $\mathcal{H}$ is said to be *Lyapunov stable* if for every $\epsilon > 0$, $\exists \delta > 0$ such that for every $\sigma \in$ *Exec*$(\mathcal{H})$ $[(\sigma(0) \in B_\delta(\bar{0})) \Rightarrow (\forall t \in dom(\sigma), \sigma(t) \in B_\epsilon(\bar{0}))]$.

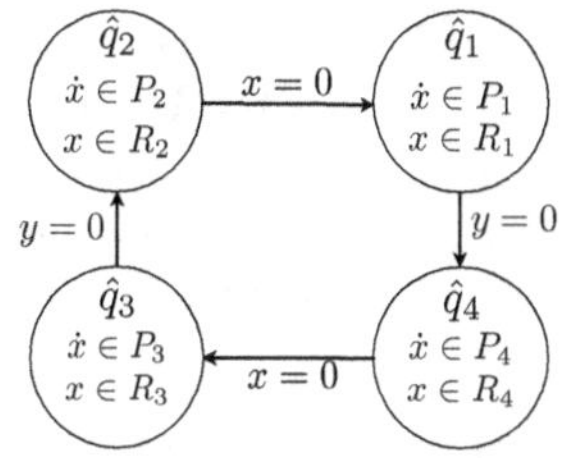

Figure 4: Polyhedral hybrid automaton $\widehat{\mathcal{H}}$

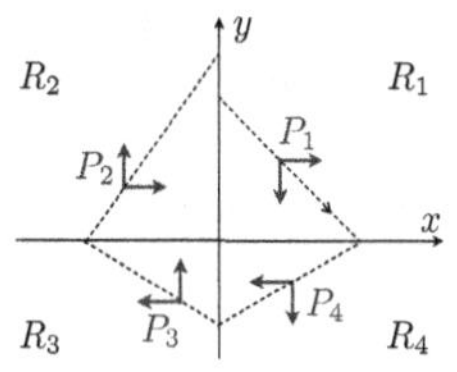

Figure 5: A sample execution of $\widehat{\mathcal{H}}$

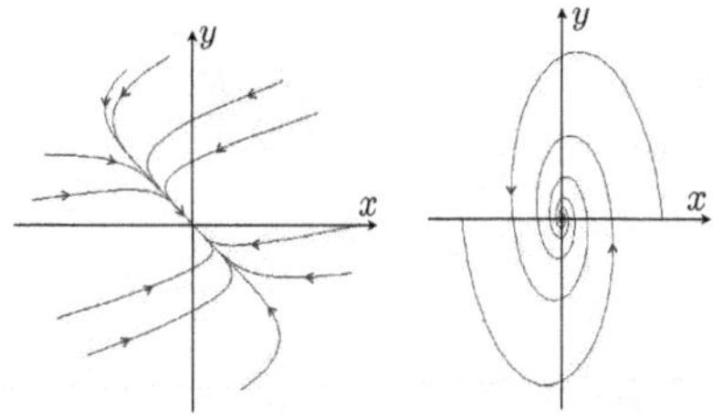

(a) $\dot{x} = A_3 x$ (b) $\dot{x} = A_4 x$

Figure 6: Sample Executions

Definition. A hybrid system $\mathcal{H}$ is said to be *asymptotically stable* if it is Lyapunov stable and

$$\exists \gamma > 0 \, \forall \sigma \in Exec(\mathcal{H}) \, [(\sigma(0) \in B_\gamma(\bar{0})) \Rightarrow Conv(\sigma, \bar{0})].$$

$$Conv(\sigma, \bar{0}) := \forall \epsilon > 0 \, \exists T \geq 0 \, \forall t \geq T \, \sigma(t) \in B_\epsilon(\bar{0}).$$

In fact, for the purpose of stability analysis,we can assume that the invariants and guards of the linear hybrid system are closed under positive scaling. A polyhedral set P is *closed under positive scaling* if for every $x \in P$, $\alpha x \in P$ for all $\alpha \geq 0$. Note that the Lyapunov and asymptotic stability analysis with respect to origin depend on the behavior of the system in a small neighborhood of the equilibrium point. Hence, the stability of every hybrid system is equivalent to the stability of a hybrid system constructed by removing constraints which do not pass through $\bar{0}$ (or equivalently, replacing all the invariants and guards by their positive scaling closure.)

Observe that the executions of linear systems depicted in Figure 1 determine both systems to be Lyapunov stable. The systems shown in Figure 6 correspond to asymptotically stable systems, while if the executions were pointing out they would be unstable.

4. HYBRIDIZATION FOR STABILITY ANALYSIS OF LINEAR HYBRID AUTOMATA

In this section, we formally present the hybridization procedure for constructing a polyhedral hybrid automaton from a linear hybrid automaton, and provide soundness and completeness results.

4.1 Hybridization construction

The basic construct in the hybridization procedure is the abstraction of the linear vector field in a region by a polyhedron. This is done by the function *CPoly*. Given $F : \mathbb{R}^n \to 2^{\mathbb{R}^n}$ and $P \subseteq \mathbb{R}^n$, let $\mathit{CPoly}(F, P) = \cup_{x \in P} F(x)$. Next, we present the formal definition of hybridizing a system $\mathcal{H}$ with respect to a partition $\mathcal{R}$.

A partition $\mathcal{R}$ of the state space $\mathbb{R}^n$ is a finite set of polyhedra $\{R_1, \ldots, R_k\}$ such that $\mathbb{R}^n = \cup_{i=1}^k R_i$ and for every pair of different indices i, j, $R_i \cap R_j$ has affine dimension smaller than n. Two polyhedra $P, Q \subseteq \mathbb{R}^n$ are adjacent in case of $P \cap Q$ has affine dimension $n - 1$, and we denote as $P \mathit{adj}\, Q$.

Definition.[Hybridization] Given an n-dimensional linear hybrid system $\mathcal{H} = (\mathit{Loc}, \mathit{Edges}, \mathit{Cont}, \mathit{Flow}, \mathit{Inv}, \mathit{Guard})$ and a polyhedral partition $\mathcal{R} = \{R_1, \ldots, R_k\}$, we define the hybridization of $\mathcal{H}$ with respect to $\mathcal{R}$, as $\mathit{PolyH}(\mathcal{H}, \mathcal{R}) = (\widehat{\mathit{Loc}}, \widehat{\mathit{Edges}}, \mathit{Cont}, \widehat{\mathit{Flow}}, \widehat{\mathit{Inv}}, \widehat{\mathit{Guard}})$, where:

- $\widehat{\mathit{Loc}} = \{(q, R) : q \in \mathit{Loc}, R \in \mathcal{R} \text{ and } R \subseteq \mathit{Inv}(q)\}$
- $\widehat{\mathit{Edges}} = \{((q_i, R_i), (q_j, R_j)) \in \widehat{\mathit{Loc}} \times \widehat{\mathit{Loc}} : q_i = q_j$ or $(q_i, q_j) \in \mathit{Edges}$ and $R_i \,\mathit{adj}\, R_j\}$
- $\widehat{\mathit{Flow}}((q, R))(x) = \mathit{CPoly}(\mathit{Flow}(q), R)$.
- $\widehat{\mathit{Inv}}(q, R) = \mathit{Inv}(q) \cap R$.
- $\widehat{\mathit{Guard}}((q_i, R_i), (q_j, R_j)) = \mathbb{R}^n$ if $q_i = q_j$ and $\mathit{Guard}((q_i, q_j))$, otherwise.

Note that for every $q \in \mathit{Loc}$ and $R \in \mathcal{R}$, $\mathit{CPoly}(\mathit{Flow}(q), R)$ is a polyhedral set. Hence, the polyhedral differential inclusion $\dot{x} \in \mathit{CPoly}(\mathit{Flow}(q), R)$ over-approximates the dynamical system $\dot{x} \in \mathit{Flow}(q)(x)$ in the polyhedral region R. Then, it follows that $\mathit{PolyH}(\mathcal{H}, \mathcal{R})$ is a polyhedral hybrid automaton.

Remark. We will assume from now on that the partition $\mathcal{R}$ used in the hybridization only consists of conic polyhedral sets, that is, those that are positive scaling closed. Our hybridization is similar to that in the literature [17, 6], where rectangular/polyhedral abstractions are considered, except that we consider a partition of the state-space specific to stability analysis.

4.1.1 Illustration

We explain in detail the hybridization process for a particular 2-dimensional linear hybrid system example. The dynamical behaviour of the example is determined by the linear switched system explained in Section 2.

To perform hybridization, we choose a polyhedral partition of the continuous state-space. Consider the polyhedral partition $\mathcal{R} = \{R_1, R_2, R_3, R_4\}$, formed by the planar quadrants, where R_i corresponds to the i-th one. This choice determines a polyhedral hybrid system with the same number of modes as in the linear automaton, with the same associated invariants, and the same edges labelled with the same guards. The polyhedral dynamics in the four modes are given by $\dot{x} \in P_1$, $\dot{x} \in P_2$, $\dot{x} \in P_3$ and $\dot{x} \in P_4$, respectively, where $P_1 = \mathit{CPoly}(A_1, R_1)$, $P_2 = \mathit{CPoly}(A_2, R_2)$, $P_3 = \mathit{CPoly}(A_1, R_3)$ and $P_4 = \mathit{CPoly}(A_2, R_4)$. For instance, in the first quadrant all the flow vectors of the linear hybrid system are between $(1, 0)$ and $(0, -1)$, therefore P_1 is determined by the constraints $x > 0$ and $y < 0$, as we observe in Figure 5. The polyhedral hybrid system is shown in Figure 4. However, this polyhedral hybrid automaton is not stable. To obtain a stable one, we need to use a finer partition.

4.2 Stability preservation theorem

Next, we show that our hybridization procedure is sound, in that, the stability of the polyhedral hybrid system output by the hybridization procedure implies the stability of the linear hybrid system. This is formalized below.

Theorem 1. *Given a linear hybrid automaton $\mathcal{H}$ and a polyhedral partition $\mathcal{R}$, the following hold:*

1. *$\mathit{PolyH}(\mathcal{H}, \mathcal{R})$ is Lyapunov stable implies $\mathcal{H}$ is Lyapunov stable.*
2. *$\mathit{PolyH}(\mathcal{H}, \mathcal{R})$ is asymptotically stable implies $\mathcal{H}$ is asymptotically stable.*

PROOF. This follows from the fact that $\mathit{Exec}(\mathcal{H}) \subseteq \mathit{Exec}(\mathit{PolyH}(\mathcal{H}, \mathcal{R}))$, which in turn follows from the fact that the polyhedral differential inclusion $\dot{x} \in \mathit{CPoly}(F, R)$ over-approximates the dynamical system $\dot{x} = F(x)$ in the polyhedral region R. □

Remark. It has been observed in [13] that simulations do not preserve stability and the stronger notion of uniformly continuous simulations is required. Note that in Theorem 1, the simulation relation between the two systems is the identity relation which trivially satisfies the additional constraints of uniform continuity imposed by [13].

4.3 Completeness results for hybridization

In this section, we identify a subclass of switched linear hybrid systems for which the hybridization procedure is complete, that is, for every asymptotically stable system in this class, by iteratively choosing finer and finer partitions for the hybridization, we will arrive at an abstract polyhedral hybrid system that is asymptotically stable.

Before identifying the subclass of systems referred above, we provide a detailed proof for the class of linear dynamical systems. We then sketch how this proof can be extended for the class that we define. Let $\mathcal{H}_A$ denote the linear hybrid automaton (with one mode) corresponding to the dynamical system $\dot{x} = Ax$.

Theorem 2. *Let $\mathcal{H}_A$ be a linear hybrid automaton corresponding to the dynamical system $\dot{x} = Ax$ which is asymptotically stable. Then, there exists a polyhedral partition $\mathcal{R}$ such that the polyhedral hybrid system $\mathit{PolyH}(\mathcal{H}_A, \mathcal{R})$ is asymptotically stable with respect to $\bar{0}$.*

The hybridization techniques for safety analysis ensure a bounded error in the executions of the original and approximate systems over a bounded time. They rely on the fact that error between the concrete and the abstract vector fields is bounded. However, this is no more true in our setting. More precisely, the Hausdorff distance between Ax (the value of the concrete vector field) and $P = \{Ax \mid x \in R\}$, the abstract vector field in a region R (positively closed) is infinity. Hence, our proof of completeness is bit more involved. We construct an intermediate system which is equivalent to the abstract system. In this new system, though we cannot bound the distance between the vector fields of the concrete system and that of the intermediate system at state x by some ϵ, we can bound it by $\epsilon||x||$.

Observe that the scaling in a region R is determined by the vector field restricted to the state-space with norm 1. Let $CUPoly(A, R) = \{Ax \mid x \in R, ||x|| = 1\}$.

Definition. We define the scaled hybridization of $\mathcal{H}$ with respect to $\mathcal{R}$, as $SPolyH(\mathcal{H}, \mathcal{R}) = (\widehat{Loc}, \widehat{Edges}, Cont, \widehat{Flow}, \widehat{Inv}, \widehat{Guard})$, where all the elements in the tuple are the same as for the hybrid system $PolyH(\mathcal{H}, \mathcal{R})$ but for the vector field function, which for every $(q, R) \in \widehat{Loc}$, $\widehat{Flow}((q, R))(x) = CUPoly(Flow(q), R)||x||$.

The following lemmas comprise the proof for Theorem 2.

Lemma 1. *$SPolyH(\mathcal{H}, \mathcal{R})$ is asymptotically stable if and only if $PolyH(\mathcal{H}, \mathcal{R})$ is asymptotically stable.*

Lemma 2. *Let A be an $n \times n$ matrix and let $\mathcal{H}_A$ be the hybrid system associated to the matrix. Let $\mathcal{H}_A$ be asymptotically stable with respect to $\bar{0}$. Then, there exists a partition $\mathcal{R}$ such that the polyhedral system $SPolyH(\mathcal{H}_A, \mathcal{R})$ is asymptotically stable with respect to $\bar{0}$.*

Definition. Given a polyhedral set P and a scalar a, let $Pa = \{xa : x \in P\}$. The *norm of a polyhedral set P* is $||P|| = \max\{||p|| \mid p \in P\}$.

The Lemma 2 depends on the following two propositions.

Proposition 1. *Consider a polyhedral partition $\mathcal{R} = \{R_1, \ldots, R_k\}$ and a finite set of bounded polyhedral sets $\{P_1, \ldots, P_k\}$. Consider two differential inclusions,*

$$\dot{x} \in \{Ax\} \tag{1}$$

$$\dot{x} \in F(x) \tag{2}$$

where $F(x) = P_i||x||$ for $x \in R_i$ and for every $0 \leqslant i \leqslant k$. Let $d_H(Ax, F(x)) \leqslant \epsilon||x||$ for every x. Let x and y be solutions of 1 and 2 respectively, such that $x(0) = y(0)$. Then,

$$||x(t) - y(t)|| \leqslant \frac{\epsilon||y(0)||}{m - ||A||}(e^{mt} - e^{||A||t})$$

for every $t \geqslant 0$ with $m = \max_{0 \leqslant i \leqslant k} ||P_i||$.

Proof. Consider x and y be solutions of 1 and 2 respectively, such that $x(0) = y(0)$. Define the error function $z(t) = ||x(t) - y(t)||$ for $t \in [0, \infty)$. For infinity norm we know that $\frac{d}{dt}||f(t)|| \leqslant ||\frac{d}{dt}f(t)||$. Then, $\dot{z} \leq ||\dot{x} - \dot{y}||$, which is equal, for some $y' \in F(y)$, to $||Ax - y'|| = ||Ax - Ay + Ay - y'|| \leqslant ||Ax - Ay|| + ||Ay - y'||$, and since $||Ay - y'|| \leqslant \epsilon||y'||$, We obtain the differential system

$$\begin{cases} \dot{z}(t) \leqslant ||A||z(t) + \epsilon||y'|| \\ \dot{y} \in F(y) \end{cases}$$

Let us first solve the inclusion in the system. Consider $y \in R_i$. Then we have $\dot{y} \in P_i||y||$, therefore $||\dot{y}|| \in ||P_i||y|| \, || = ||P_i|| \, ||y||$. Define $m = \max_{0 \leqslant i \leqslant k} ||P_i||$. Therefore, $||\dot{y}|| \leqslant m||y||$. Denote $||y(t)|| = r(t)$. Since $\frac{d}{dt}||y|| \leqslant ||\dot{y}||$, we get the inequality $\dot{r}(t) \leqslant mr(t)$. Since infinity norm is differentiable everywhere except at the origin, and there is no time such that we get zero norm, we can apply Grönwall's lemma, which states that the inequality solution is bounded by the correspondent differential equation. We get the solution $r(t) \leqslant r(0)e^{mt}$. Plug the solution to the first equation in the system, $\dot{z}(t) \leqslant ||A||z(t) + \epsilon e^{mt} r(0)$ where $z(t)$ is differentiable everywhere but in the origin and by applying also the Grönwall's lemma and solving the differential equation, we obtain

$$z(t) \leqslant e^{||A||t} z(0) + \frac{\epsilon r(0)}{m - ||A||}(e^{mt} - e^{||A||t}) \tag{3}$$

Since $z(0) = 0$, the inequality is just

$$z(t) \leqslant \frac{\epsilon r(0)}{m - ||A||}(e^{mt} - e^{||A||t}) \tag{4}$$

□

Proposition 2. *Let A be an $n \times n$ matrix and $\mathcal{H}_A$ be the hybrid system associated to the matrix. Consider $\epsilon > 0$. Then, there exists a partition $\mathcal{R} = \{R_1, \ldots, R_k\}$ such that $d_H(Ax, P_i||x||) \leqslant \epsilon||x||$ for every $x \in R_i$ where $P_i = CUPoly(A, R_i)$.*

Proof. Ax is a continuous function and the state-space with norm 1 is compact. Hence, Ax restricted to the state-space of norm 1 is a uniformly continuous function. Therefore, given any ϵ, there exists a δ, such that for every x, y with $||x - y|| \leqslant \delta$, $||Ax - Ay|| \leqslant \epsilon$. We can choose a polyhedral partition such that each of the regions restricted to norm 1 is contained in a δ ball. Consider a region R_i, we want to prove that $d_H(Ax, P_i||x||) \leqslant \epsilon||x||$. We know $d_H(Ax, P_i||x||) = ||Ax - Ay||x|| \, ||$ for some $y \in R_i$ such that $||y|| = 1$. Then, $||Ax - Ay||x|| \, || = ||Ax - Ay'||$ where $y' \in R_i$ and $||y'|| = ||x||$, so we can rewrite as $||(A\frac{x}{||x||} - A\frac{y'}{||y'||})||x|| \, ||$. Since $||\frac{x}{||x||} - \frac{y'}{||y'||}|| \leqslant \delta$ by the partition construction, we get $||A\frac{x}{||x||} - A\frac{y'}{||y'||}|| \leqslant \epsilon$ and finally, by substituting, $d_H(Ax, P_i||x||) \leqslant \epsilon||x||$. □

Theorem 1 states that our hybridization based analysis approach is sound in that if the polyhedral abstraction is stable, then so is the linear hybrid system. Here, we show that our analysis method is complete for linear dynamical systems with respect to asymptotic stability, that is, given a linear dynamical system which is aymptotically stable, one can construct a polyhedral abstraction which is stable.

Proposition 3. *Let $\dot{x} = Ax$ be a dynamical system in $\mathbb{R}^n$ which is asymptotically stable. Then, for every $\gamma > 0$ there exists a value $T_\gamma \geqslant 0$ such that for every solution $x(t)$ with $||x(0)|| = \gamma$, $||x(t)|| \leqslant \frac{\gamma}{2}$ holds for every $t \geqslant T_\gamma$.*

Proof. Let $\dot{x} = Ax$ be asymptotically stable. Then A can be written as PJP^{-1}, where P is a real invertible matrix and J is the real Jordan matrix [8]. A solution $x(t)$ of the system can be expressed as $e^{At}x(0) = e^{PAP^{-1}t}x(0)$, which is equal to $Pe^{Jt}P^{-1}x(0)$ by definition of matrix exponential. Because of norm matrix properties, we get $||x(t)|| \leqslant ||P|| \, ||e^{Jt}|| \, ||P^{-1}||\gamma$. The asymptotic stability implies that

A is Hurtwitz, and therefore the matrix e^{Jt} is also Hurwitz, which means that every term in it is of the form $e^{\lambda t}p(t)$ where $\lambda < 0$ and $p(t)$ is a polynomial function. Then, every term in $Pe^{Jt}P^{-1}x(0)$ is equal to $e^{\lambda t}p'(t)$ where $p'(t)$ is a different polynomial and the values will be dominated by the exponentials. Hence, for every row, $x_i(t)$, there exists $T^i_\gamma > 0$ such that $||x_i(t)|| \leqslant \frac{\gamma}{2}$ for every $t \geqslant T^i_\gamma$. So it is enough to choose $T_\gamma = \max_{0 \leqslant i < n}(T^i_\gamma)$. □

Proof of Lemma 2.

Suppose $\mathcal{H}_A$ to be asymptotically stable. Fix $\gamma \geqslant 0$. We know by Proposition 3 that there exists $T_\gamma \geqslant 0$ such that for every $\sigma \in Exec(\mathcal{H}_A)$ with $||\sigma(0)|| = \gamma$, $||\sigma(t)|| \leqslant \frac{\gamma}{2}$ for every $t \geqslant T_\gamma$. Fix $\epsilon = \dfrac{\gamma(m - ||A||)}{4||\sigma'(0)||(e^{mT_\gamma} - e^{||A||T_\gamma})}$. By Proposition 2 we know there exists a partition $\mathcal{R}$ such that $d_H(Ax, CUPoly(A, \mathcal{R})) \leqslant \epsilon||x||$. Consider $\sigma \in Exec(\mathcal{H}_A)$ and $\sigma' \in Exec(SPolyH(\mathcal{H}_A, \mathcal{R}))$ with $\sigma(0) = \sigma'(0)$. Then, by Proposition 1 $||\sigma(t) - \sigma'(t)|| \leqslant \frac{\gamma}{4}$. Since we also know that $||\sigma(T_\gamma)|| \leqslant \frac{\gamma}{2}$, we get $\sigma'(T_\gamma) \leqslant \frac{3\gamma}{4}$. It is possible to iterate such construction for values of γ smaller and smaller, obtaining $\sigma' \in SPolyH(\mathcal{H}_A, \mathcal{R})$ closer and closer to zero for some time values.

Definition. A linear hybrid system $\mathcal{H}$ is Lipschitz continuous if there exists a constant L such that for every $x, y \in Cont_{\mathcal{H}}$ with $x \in Inv(q_1)$ and $y \in Inv(q_2)$ the following holds $||A_{q_1}x - A_{q_2}y|| \leqslant L||x - y||$. We say that $\mathcal{H}$ is uniformly converging if for every $\gamma > 0$, there exists $T_\gamma \geq 0$ such that for every execution σ of $\mathcal{H}$, $||\sigma(0)|| = \gamma$ implies $||\sigma(t)|| \leq \gamma/2$ for all $t \geq T_\gamma$.

Theorem 3. *Let $\mathcal{H}$ be a linear hybrid system that is Lipschitz continuous and uniformly converging. Then, there exists a polyhedral partition $\mathcal{R}$ such that the polyhedral hybrid system $PolyH(\mathcal{H}, \mathcal{R})$ is asymptotically stable with respect to $\bar{0}$.*

PROOF. Here we sketch the proof of the theorem, which is similar to that of the proof of Theorem 2. Proposition 1 can be extended to linear switched systems which are Lipschitz continuous. The error between the solution of $\mathcal{H}$ and some approximation whose vector field is at most ϵ far from $\mathcal{H}$ can be analyzed as follows. $\dot{z} \leq ||\dot{x} - \dot{y}|| = ||A_i x - y'|| = ||A_i x - A_j y + A_j y - y'|| \leqslant ||A_i x - A_j y|| + ||A_j y - y'||$ for some $y' \in F_j(y)$. Then, we obtain a new differential system

$$\begin{cases} \dot{z}(t) \leqslant Lz(t) + \epsilon||y'|| \\ \dot{y} \in F_j(y) \end{cases}$$

The rest of the proof is similar to that of Proposition 1. Propostion 2 requires to choose a partition such that the difference in the vector fields between $\mathcal{H}$ and the polyhedral inclusion induced by it is bounded by ϵ. This can be done by choosing a partition which ensures the ϵ bound for every A_i in $\mathcal{H}$. Propositon 3 is in fact captured using the uniformly converging condition in the theorem. □

5. HEURISTICS FOR NON UNIFORM PREDICATE CONSTRUCTION

Next, we explore certain heuristics to construct the polyhedral partition for the hybridization procedure. A naive algorithm is to uniformly partition the state-space and gradually increase the granularity of the partitions. This ignores the dynamics of the system in the selection of the partition. Instead, we propose a heuristic to refine the partition, such that the size of the resulting polyhedral inclusions are similar.

Here, we explain the heuristics for defining a non uniform predicate construction. Consider a polyhedral switched system $PolyH(\mathcal{H}, \mathcal{R})$, obtained by hybridization of the linear switched system $\mathcal{H}$ with an initial set of predicates. We want to partition the state space in order to obtain a more accurate polyhedral hybrid system. For constructing a finer partition, we choose a location, (q, R), in $PolyH(\mathcal{H}, R)$ and the polyhedral inclusion associated to such location, $P = CPoly(Flow(q), R)$. The target is to split region R. To split this region, we first compute the diameter of P, d_P, which corresponds to the maximum of $||x - y||$ while $x, y \in P$ and $||x|| = ||y|| = 1$. The solution to the optimization problem returns the diameter value d_P and the two points x_P, y_P. We construct a vector v_P starting at x_P and finishing at y_P. This vector determines the direction in the dynamical polyhedron P where the longest error on approximating the linear dynamics arises. To overcome this problem, we construct a hyperplane which splits the dynamical polyhedron and it is perpendicular to that direction. The hyperplane is the set $\{x \in \mathbb{R}^n : v_P \cdot x = 0\}$. Observe that this hyperplane is not partitioning the state space but the polyhedral dynamics. Then, the hyperplane is transformed into a hyperplane in region R which will result in the polyhedral dynamics splitting. This hyperplane is the set $\{x \in R : v_P Ax = 0\}$, where A is the matrix for the linear dynamical system defining the vector field of location q in the initial linear hybrid system.

We need to split just regions that generate a coarse polyhedral inclusion dynamics. For choosing such regions we compare the diameter of each dynamical polyhedra with a diameter bound. This diameter bound is computed by considering every location (q, R) in $PolyH(\mathcal{H}, R)$ and the polyhedra $CUPoly(Flow(q), R)$, and it is defined as

$$D = \max_{(q,R) \in \widetilde{Loc}} d_{CUPoly(Flow(q),R)}$$

The regions chosen are those with polyhedral inclusion dynamics whose polyhedral diameter is greater or equal to D or to some percentage of D. The higher the percentage, the less predicates will be added for partitioning the state space.

Example 1. *We illustrate the hybridization process for a 2-dimensional linear hybrid system $\mathcal{H}$. The dynamical behaviour of the system is determined by two linear dynamical systems, $\dot{x} = A_1 x$ and $\dot{x} = A_2 x$, defined by the following matrices:*

$$A_1 = \begin{pmatrix} 0 & 1 \\ -4 & 2 \end{pmatrix} \qquad A_2 = \begin{pmatrix} 0 & 1 \\ -3 & 2 \end{pmatrix}$$

We evaluate the difference between uniform and non uniform predicate construction methods. In the case of the uniform method, 64 predicates are needed to obtain stability answer for the polyhedral hybrid system $PolyH(\mathcal{H})$, while with the non uniform method, stability is verified by considering 40 predicates for the polyhedral hybrid system construction. We observe that the non uniform method provides a less

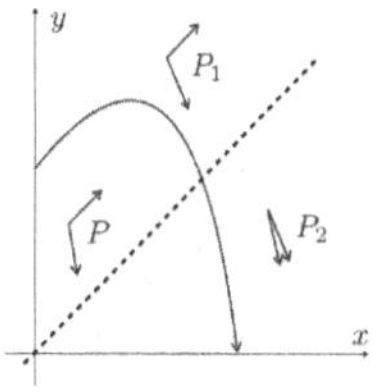

(a) Uniform

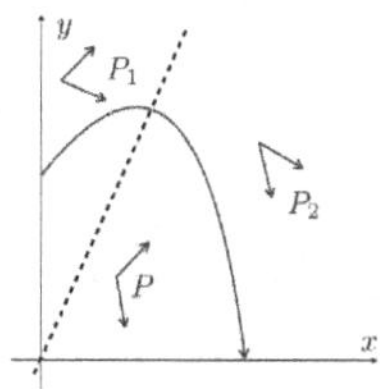

(b) Non uniform

Figure 7: Predicate construction

number of predicates for verifying stability. The fewer quantity of predicates in comparison with the uniform predicate construction is because the choice for new predicates in the non uniform methods implies an homogeneous division of the dynamical polyhedra.

Let us consider the linear dynamical system defined by the matrix A_1 and restrict it to the polyhedral region $R = \{(x, y) \in \mathbb{R} : x \geq 0, y \geq 0\}$ which coincides with the first quadrant. We observe in Figure 7 a sample execution in R of the linear system $\dot{x} = A_1 x$, and the dynamical polyhedron defined for such region and linear dynamics, denoted as P. For the case of uniform predicate construction we observe in Figure 7(a) the addition of the hyperplane $\{(x, y) \in \mathbb{R} : x - y = 0\}$, which results in a new partition with two regions, $\mathcal{R} \cap \{(x, y) \in \mathbb{R} : x - y <= 0\}$ and $\mathcal{R} \cap \{(x, y) \in \mathbb{R} : x - y >= 0\}$. For the first region we get a new dynamical polyhedron P_1 with diameter 2 while in the second region the new dynamical polyhedron P_2 has diameter 0.05. In the case of applying the heuristics explained above, we obtain the hyperplane $\{(x, y) \in \mathbb{R} : 2x - y = 0\}$ which partition R into two new subregions in an analogous manner to the uniform case. These subregions determine two new dynamical polyhedra, P_1 and P_2 with 1 as diameter value for both as shown in Figure 7(b). Observe that the case of non uniform partition results in a more homogeneous distribution of the error between linear and polyhedral dynamics.

6. EXPERIMENTAL RESULTS

In this section, we provide details regarding the implementation of the presented hybridization method, its integration into an abstraction based stability analysis approach for polyhedral hybrid systems, experimental set up, experimental evaluation and comparison with another stability verification tool based on Lyapunov function proofs.

The hybridization procedure is implemented in `Averist` [15]. `Averist` is a stability verification tool based on quantitative predicate abstraction. It has been implemented in Python and uses Parma Polyhedra Library (PPL) to deal with polyhedral operations and NetworkX Python package to manage graphs and their analysis. It performs stability analysis of polyhedral switched systems by constructing weighted graph abstractions, and returns a counterexample, a cycle with product of weights > 1, in case it cannot establish stability.

The hybridization technique has been implemented in Python 2.7 and it uses the Parma Polyhedral Library (PPL) [2] for computing *CPoly*(A, R) and the NetworkX Python package to represent the underlying graphs in linear and polyhedral hybrid automata. The experiments have been performed on a virtual machine with OS Ubuntu 14.04, processor equivalent to 4 virtual CPUs and 4.68 GB of memory, installed on Mac OS X 10.10 with processor 2.8 GHz Intel Core i5 and 8GB 1600 MHz DDR3 memory.

These experiments are performed, first, to evaluate the scalability of `Averist`, in terms of state-space dimension, number of modes in the input hybrid automaton and predicates involved in hybridization, and second, to compare our general approach with a stability verification tool based on searching for Lyapunov functions.

6.1 Averists evaluation

We have constructed two kinds of input linear hybrid systems, those with arbitrary switching represented as AS_i and those with state based switching represented as SSi_j. The AS_i examples are chosen from [16] (Example 2) and the SSj_i examples are constructed from AS_i examples by restricting the switchings to happen at the boundaries of a partition with j regions. In particular, the set of executions of $SS8\_i$ is a subset of the executions of $SS4\_i$ which is a subset of the executions of AS_i. The 4 and 8 refer to the number of locations in the hybrid system.

The initial linear predicates used in partitioning the state-space for hybridization are taken to be the linear expressions extracted from the input system definition, the ones delimiting the invariants and guards. `Averist` runs iteratively with increasing number of linear predicates. We have implemented a function to choose the subsequent predicates, the predicates split the state-space into uniform sized chunks. For instance, for a two dimensional system, in addition to the constraints in the hybrid system, after the first iteration the predicates $x = 0$ and $y = 0$ are added, after the second iteration $x = y$ and $x = -y$ are added and so on.

A summary of experimental results is presented in Table 1. Every experiment has been run for a maximum time of 25 minutes as the time out. The first 6 columns consist of the `Averist` experiments. In addition to the dimension (number of continuous variables) and the experiment name, we report the number of iterations of the hybridization procedure that were run until stability was proven or the tool timed out, the number of linear expressions and the regions in the corresponding partition in the final hybridization, and the total time taken to infer Lyapunov stability. The total time includes the time taken by the underlying quantitative predicate abstraction technique to analyse the polyhedral hybrid system as well.

The experimental results in Table 1 demonstrate the feasibility of our approach for stability analysis of linear hybrid systems. Note that our tool was able to prove stability on almost all the 2D, 3D and 4D examples that we considered. The time for analysis increases reasonably slowly with the increase in the number of modes, for instance, consider the 4D systems $SS4\_7$ and $SS8\_7$ with 4 and 8 modes and with similar dynamics. However, the time increase with respect to increase in dimensions is steeper. This is expected because of the large number of regions in the partition as the dimension increases. We intend to explore compositional analysis methods to deal with the curse of dimensionality.

Also, note that since the running time depends on the number of regions, which in turn depends in an exponential manner on the number of linear expressions used in the partitioning, it is crucial to develop methods which are clever in the choice of the linear expressions. We will explore tech-

		Averist				Stabhyli		
Dimension/name		*Iterations*	*Expressions*	*Region*	*Time*	*Degree*	*LF found*	*Time*
$2D$	AS_1	5	32	129	31	6	Y	8
	$SS4\_1$	1	2	9	< 1	8	–	452
	$SS8\_1$	1	4	17	< 1	6	–	443
	$SS16\_1$	1	8	33	1	4	–	177
	AS_2	5	32	129	34	6	Y	9
	$SS4\_2$	1	2	9	< 1	8	–	418
	$SS8\_2$	1	4	17	< 1	6	–	451
	AS_3	4	16	65	16	2	Y	< 1
	$SS4\_3$	1	2	9	< 1	4	Y	7
	$SS8\_3$	1	4	17	1	6	–	417
$3D$	AS_4	2	9	147	194	6	–	410
	$SS4\_4$	3	21	771	484	2	Y	75
	$SS8\_4$	3	21	771	470	2	Y	15
	$SS16\_4$	3	21	771	568	2	Y	138
	AS_5	2	9	147	235	6	–	1254
	$SS4\_5$	3	21	771	418	2	Y	2
	$SS8\_5$	3	21	771	484	2	Y	18
	AS_6	2	9	147	220	6	–	1237
	$SS4\_6$	3	21	771	463	2	Y	2
	$SS8\_6$	3	21	771	489	2	Y	17
$4D$	AS_7	1	4	81	625	2	–	12
	$SS4\_7$	1	4	81	119	2	–	101
	$SS8\_7$	1	6	153	234	2	–	1071
	$SS16\_7$	1	10	297	533	2	–	339
	AS_8	1	4	81	591	4	–	34
	$SS4\_8$	1	4	81	117	4	–	397
	$SS8\_8$	1	6	153	234	2	–	17
	AS_9	1	–	–	out	4	Y	34
	$SS4\_9$	1	4	81	125	4	–	105
	$SS8\_9$	1	6	153	247	2	–	16

Table 1: Comparison of `Averist` and `Stabhyli`

niques which dynamically partition the state-space in a non-uniform manner to circumvent this problem. Some ideas are presented in Section 5.

6.2 Comparison with Stabhyli

Next, we compare our method in **`Averist`** with **`Stabhyli`** [11], which is a tool for global stability verification based on Lyapunov function search that can handle the class of switched linear systems. Broadly, it searches iteratively with increasing degree of polynomial templates until it finds a solution. It only iterates over even degree polynomials, since the Lyapunov functions are required to be non-negative everywhere. In addition, it has the option for finding either common or multiple Lyapunov functions. We ran **`Stabhyli`** on our example set with both common or piecewise Lyapunov function options, in turn, and set a time out of 25 minutes as before. The experimental results of **`Stabhyli`** are summarized in the last three columns of Table 1. The second column from the end indicates whether the system proved stability (Y) or that it timed out (-) with the common Lyapunov function option. The third column from the end shows the maximum degree of the Lyapunov function in the common Lyapunov function case that **`Stabhyli`** successfully analyzed before the time out in the case of (-), or the degree of the polynomial Lyapunov function returned in the case of (Y). The last column shows the total time taken for solving the templates up to the degree indicated in the first column. We were not able to prove stability on any of the examples with the multiple Lyapunov function option, hence, we do not report the details.

First, note that **`Stabhyli`** fails to prove stability on several examples, on which **`Averist`** succeeded. On AS_9, **`Stabhyli`** succeeded, where as **`Averist`** timed out. While we do not claim that the set of benchmarks here is representative, we observed several numerical issues with **`Stabhyli`** with respect to which we claim that our method and tool are well behaved. For instance, in AS_1, **`Stabhyli`** returned with a 6th degree Lyapunov function. We ran **`Stabhyli`** again with the same example by fixing the degree of the polynomial to be 8, and it returned with an answer that stability could not be proved. This is surprising, and we expect it to be a result of numerical issues which cannot set the coefficient of degree 8 term in the polynomial to 0 exactly. Note that this implies that the iteration over the templates needs to be done in a linear fashion. Next, while it found a common Lyapunov function, it did not succeed in finding a multiple Lyapunov function (note that the same Lyapunov function in each mode is a multiple Lyapunov function). In addition, on the systems $SS4\_1$ and $SS8\_1$, **`Stabhyli`** did not succeed in proving stability which consist of fewer executions than AS_1.

On the examples, where **`Stabhyli`** finds a Lyapunov function, it does so quickly. On all examples, except $SS4\_3$,

`Stabhyli` performs better. However, the time required in checking whether a template is a Lyapunov function, increases much faster with the increase in the degree, as compared to, for instance, with the increase in the number of predicates for `Averist`. For instance, in the $4D$ example AS_7, it took 12 seconds to check the polynomial of degree 2, but timed out for the polynomial with degree 4.

To summarize, we believe that the strength of our approach and our tool is that it is less prone to numerical problems, since the tool mainly uses a linear optimization solver at the backend with rational arithmetic. In addition, our tool behaves in a monotonic manner with respect to simpler systems. Finally, it returns counterexamples when it fails to prove stability. We plan to utilize this to devise smarter refinement algorithms in the future.

7. CONCLUSION

In this paper, we proposed a new hybridization approach for stability verification of linear hybrid automata. Our experimental results show the practical feasibility of our approach and exhibit the merits in comparison to existing approaches. Also, our approach returns a counterexample which provides information on the possible cause of instability, that can be used to guide the choice of subsequent partitions. There are several interesting future directions. One direction is to perform an indepth analysis of the class of systems for which the methods is complete, that is, will eventually prove stability if the system is stable. The other direction is to explore this approach for non-linear hybrid systems. While theoretically, extending the approach to the general class of hybrid systems is straightforward, the practical challenge is in finding the right class of partitions to consider for hybridization.

8. REFERENCES

[1] E. Asarin, T. Dang, and A. Girard. Hybridization methods for the analysis of nonlinear systems. *Acta Informatica*, 43(7):451–476, 2007.

[2] R. Bagnara, P. M. Hill, and E. Zaffanella. The Parma Polyhedra Library: Toward a complete set of numerical abstractions for the analysis and verification of hardware and software systems. *Science of Computer Programming*, 72(1–2):3–21, 2008.

[3] S. Boyd, L. El Ghaoui, E. Feron, and V. Balakrishnan. *Linear Matrix Inequalities in System and Control Theory*, volume 15 of *Studies in Applied Mathematics*. SIAM, Philadelphia, PA, June 1994.

[4] M.S. Branicky. Stability of hybrid systems. In H. Unbehauen, editor, *Encylopedia of Life Support Systems*, volume Theme 6.43:Control Sytems, Robotics and Automation, chapter Article 6.43.28.3. UNESCO Publishing, 2004.

[5] T. Dang, O. Maler, and R. Testylier. Accurate hybridization of nonlinear systems. In *Proceedings of the International Conference on Hybrid Systems: Computation and Control*, pages 11–20, 2010.

[6] Laurent Doyen, Thomas A. Henzinger, and Jean françois Raskin. Automatic rectangular refinement of affine hybrid systems. In *Proceedings of Formal Modeling and Analysis of Timed Systems*, pages 144–161. Springer, 2005.

[7] S. Graf and H. Saidi. Construction of abstact state graphs with PVS. In *Proceedings of the International Conference on Computer Aided Verification*, pages 72–83, 1997.

[8] Morris William Hirsch, Stephen Smale, and Robert Luke Devaney. *Differential equations, dynamical systems, and an introduction to chaos.* Academic Press, Waltham (Mass.), 2013.

[9] Daniel Liberzon, Jo ao P. Hespanha, and A. Stephen Morse. Stability of switched systems: a lie-algebraic condition. *Systems Control Lett*, 37:117–122, 1999.

[10] Hai Lin and Panos J. Antsaklis. Stability and stabilizability of switched linear systems: A survey of recent results. *IEEE Transactions on Automatic Control*, 54(2):308–322, 2009.

[11] Eike Möhlmann and Oliver E. Theel. Stabhyli: a tool for automatic stability verification of non-linear hybrid systems. In *HSCC*, pages 107–112, 2013.

[12] P. A. Parrilo. *Structure Semidefinite Programs and Semialgebraic Geometry Methods in Robustness and Optimization.* PhD thesis, California Institute of Technology, Pasadena, CA, May 2000., 2000.

[13] Pavithra Prabhakar, Geir E. Dullerud, and Mahesh Viswanathan. Pre-orders for reasoning about stability. In *Proceedings of the International Conference on Hybrid Systems: Computation and Control*, pages 197–206, 2012.

[14] Pavithra Prabhakar and Miriam Garcia Soto. Abstraction based model-checking of stability of hybrid systems. In *CAV*, pages 280–295, 2013.

[15] Pavithra Prabhakar and Miriam Garcia Soto. An algorithmic approach to stability verification of polyhedral switched system. In *American Control Conference*, 2014.

[16] S. Prajna and A. Papachristodoulou. Analysis of switched and hybrid systems - beyond piecewise quadratic methods. In *American Control Conference, 2003. Proceedings of the 2003*, volume 4, pages 2779–2784 vol.4, June 2003.

[17] A. Puri, V.S. Borkar, and P. Varaiya. ϵ-approximation of differential inclusions. In *Proceedings of the International Conference on Hybrid Systems: Computation and Control*, pages 362–376, 1995.

Case Studies in Data-Driven Verification of Dynamical Systems*

Alexandar Kozarev
Metron, Inc.
San Diego, CA
kozareva@ca.metsci.com

John Quindlen and Jonathan How
Aerospace Controls Lab
MIT, Cambridge, MA
{quindlen,jhow}@mit.edu

Ufuk Topcu
Dept. of Aerospace Eng.
Univ of Texas, Austin, TX
utopcu@utexas.edu

ABSTRACT

We interpret several dynamical system verification questions, e.g., region of attraction and reachability analyses, as data classification problems. We discuss some of the tradeoffs between conventional optimization-based certificate constructions with certainty in the outcomes and this new date-driven approach with quantified confidence in the outcomes. The new methodology is aligned with emerging computing paradigms and has the potential to extend systematic verification to systems that do not necessarily admit closed-form models from certain specialized families. We demonstrate its effectiveness on a collection of both conventional and unconventional case studies including model reference adaptive control systems, nonlinear aircraft models, and reinforcement learning problems.

1. INTRODUCTION

Certification of safety-critical systems is the procedure of demonstrating compliance with often a large collection of criteria to an authority. For example, MilSpecs [1] and DO-178 [2] provide guidelines for flight control applications. While linear stability, performance and robustness metrics have been regarded as satisfactory certification criteria in these guidelines for relatively conventional applications, increasingly adaptable and autonomous systems necessitate new quantitative criteria.

Consider an example in which the system operates at a nominal condition x_{nom} (e.g., a trim condition of an aircraft) in a state space $X \subseteq \mathbb{R}^n$. For simplicity, assume that the system is stationary at this nominal condition x_{nom}. An analyst, who has identified a set G of perturbations to which the system may be subject while operating at x_{nom}, *queries* whether the system can recover (i.e., returns to x_{nom}) from all possible perturbed configurations in G. Given a mathematical model of the system, a number of methods seek answers to similar analysis queries. We consider two of them: extensive simulations (or testing) and deductive methods.

Extensive simulations emanating from initial conditions sampled from G constitute a *data-driven* approach which is widely applicable as long as there exist a simulation model and an oracle that labels the sampled initial conditions as "yes, the nominal condition is recovered from the sampled initial condition" or "no, it is not." Such simulations are informative yet unable to cover all possible perturbations.

If a model is given in a closed-form as differential (or difference) equations, then it may be possible to construct certificates that witness affirmative answers to the queries. Examples of such certificates include the so-called Lyapunov, barrier and storage functions. For example and quite roughly speaking, consider a smooth and positive definite function V that decreases along all trajectories—except for the stationary trajectory at x_{nom}—emanating from the set Ω in which V is less than or equal to 1 and attains its minimum value at x_{nom} [3]. If such a V exists, then an affirmative answer to the above query can be predicted by checking whether $G \subseteq \Omega$. Essentially, the boundary of the set Ω *separates* the states in X into two categories: the initial conditions from which the system is known to recover to x_{nom} and those initial conditions from which the system is *not known* to recover. Equipped with a certificate V and the corresponding set Ω, responding to the above query boils down to *predicting* to which side of the boundary of Ω the set G belongs.

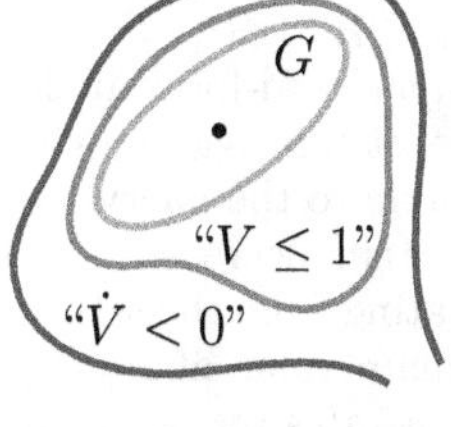

Figure 1: Schematic of a Lyapunov-type proof of G is contained in Ω.

While existence of certificates provides unambiguous answers to system analysis queries, their applicability is limited by whether such certificates can be automatically constructed for given system models. While system models expressed as differential equations that are linear or polynomial in the state variables—though only in modestly sized state spaces—are amenable to automated construction [4, 5, 6], deductive methods cannot be directly applied to a broad range of practically interesting models utilized in simulation-based analysis.

We showcase a data-driven approach to respond to a large collection of system analysis queries. This approach combines the applicability and scalability of simulation-based

*This work has been partly funded by the awards AFRL FA8650-15-C-2546, ONR N000141310778, ARO W911NF-15-1-0592, NSF 1550212 and DARPA W911NF-16-1-0001.

HSCC'16, April 12-14, 2016, Vienna, Austria

DOI: http://dx.doi.org/10.1145/2883817.2883846

analysis[1] with the end use of a certificate to conveniently predict answers to queries. Specifically, we interpret system analysis queries as *data classification* problems [7]. The constructed classifier—as appropriate sublevel sets of Lyapunov-like functions do—separates the set of initial conditions into two categories. It can be used to predict which category a priori unseen (sets of) initial conditions belong along with quantified confidence in the form of generalization errors.

We present a candidate setup for interpreting a sample of system analysis queries as data classification problems. This interpretation in turn opens up dynamical system verification to a wide range of methods from statistical learning theory [7]. We overview a particular classification method and demonstrate the effectiveness of the approach on conventional examples (for comparison with optimization-based proof construction techniques) as well as on systems including those for which the loop is closed by an adaptive controller and by a logic obtained through a prior reinforcement learning phase, hence with no closed-form models.

2. TECHNICAL APPROACH

We now discuss a candidate setup for data-driven verification. For ease of presentation, we focus on *region of attraction* analysis around a stationary trajectory of an autonomous system. That is, we are interested in characterizing the extent of the set of initial conditions from which the system approaches a fixed stationary trajectory.

2.1 Setup

Suppose that the system is represented by a finite collection S of signals (or sequences) $\phi(\cdot; x_0)$ over the time horizon $[0, T_{x_0}]$ and set $X \subseteq \mathbb{R}^n$ parametrized by the initial condition $x_0 \in X$. The signal $\phi(\cdot; x_0)$ may represent the evolution of the state, if evident from the underlying model, of a dynamical system from the initial state x_0. If the state of the system is not evident, then $\phi(\cdot; x_0)$ may simply represent the evolution of the variables in the model that can be monitored by an observer. The latter is often the case for software-based simulation models (e.g., those in Simulink).

Suppose that x_{nom} is a stationary signal, and we are interested in estimating the extent of the region of attraction $\{x \in \mathbb{R}^n : \phi(t; x) \to x_{\text{nom}} \text{ as } t \to \infty\}$ of x_{nom}. If x is the state in a closed-form model for the system, it may be possible to construct Lyapunov certificates that witness affirmative answers to the query. Roughly speaking, a Lyapunov function V that decreases along all nonstationary trajectories emanating from the set $\{x \in \mathbb{R}^n : V(x) \leq 1\}$ and attains its minimum value at x_{nom} [3]. Essentially, $\{x \in \mathbb{R}^n : V(x) = 1\}$ *separates* the states in X (Figure 1): the initial conditions from which the system is *known* to recover to x_{nom} and those from which the system is *not known* to recover. While the existence of certificates provides unambiguous answers, automated construction is possible only for limited family of models with a small-to-modest number of states.

In order to combine the scalability of simulations and the end-use flexibility of analytical certificates, we now interpret the system analysis query as a *data classification* problem. To this end, consider that we are equipped with an *oracle* that labels a given initial condition (more specifically the trajectory through the initial condition) as *converging* (i.e., the trajectory through the initial condition converges to $x = 0$) vs. *non-converging* (i.e., the trajectory through the initial condition does not converge to $x = 0$). Call the set of initial conditions labeled as *converging* as S_C and those labeled as *non-converging* as S_D. Given a collection of converging and non-converging initial conditions, computation of a classifier can be formulated as a supervised learning problem [7].

REMARK 1. *The collection $S_C \cup S_D$ of initial conditions (possibly in the space of observed variables) may be obtained through simulations or come from the monitoring of the actual system operation. The sets S_C and S_D may be extended by including finitely many points along the trajectories emanating from the initial conditions in the corresponding set.*

REMARK 2. *The construction of an oracle is beyond the scope of the paper. In most cases, an oracle will be based on an expert's judgment or a somewhat automated version of such judgment. For example, by limiting the execution over finite windows, one can label the executions that result in undesirable behavior within the window as -1 and all other executions as "practically" $+1$. We also refer the reader to [6] for preliminary ideas in the context of simulation-based proof construction.*

2.2 Classification

Naively, consider the classifier with an affine form $w^T x + b$ such that $w^T \bar{x} + b > 0$ for all initial conditions $\bar{x} \in S_C$ and $w^T \bar{x} + b < 0$ for all $\bar{x} \in S_D$. Then one can efficiently compute w and b that satisfy the conditions imposed at the given initial conditions, for example, by forming a linear program. While the utility of this naive approach vanishes if the data sets are not separable by the level sets of affine functions, richer parameterizations with nonlinear basis functions can be used instead. Given a vector $\Phi(x) \in \mathbb{R}^m$ of basis functions, note that the constraints $w^T \Phi(\bar{x}) + b > 0$ for all $\bar{x} \in S_C$ and $w^T \Phi(\bar{x}) + b < 0$ for all $\bar{x} \in S_D$ remain affine in the parameters w and b. Therefore, the search for a classifier of the form of $w^T \Phi(x) + b$ admits an encoding similar to an affine classifier. Note that depending on the expressivity of the basis functions in Φ, the hyperplane $\{x \in \mathbb{R}^n : w^T \Phi(x) + b = 0\}$ (for fixed w and b) may still be quite complicated. Due to this modest increase (note that typically $m > n$) in computational cost yet potentially enhanced expressivity, this transformation of the search for classifiers from the data space $\mathbb{R}^n$ to the feature space $\mathbb{R}^m$ of Φ is often used in the machine learning literature [7].

The support vector machine (SVM) algorithm computes an optimal, separating linear hyperplane in the feature space $\mathbb{R}^m$ to separate the sample data [7]. Suppose that the points in one set, say S_C, are labeled as -1 and those in the other set S_D as 1. Let $\bar{y}$ denote the label for $\bar{x} \in S_C \cup S_D$ and enumerate the points by $1, \ldots, N$. Then, the soft-margin SVM algorithm solves the following quadratic program for fixed integer $k \geq 1$ and positive constant $C > 0$:

$$
\begin{array}{ll}
\text{minimize}_{w,b} & \frac{1}{2}\|w\|^2 + C(\sum_{i=1}^{N} \xi_i)^k \\
\text{subject to} & y_i(w^T \Phi(x_i) + b) \geq 1 - \xi_i, \; i = 1, \cdots, N. \\
& \xi_i \geq 0, \; i = 1, \cdots, N
\end{array}
\tag{1}
$$

Here, the non-negative slack variables ξ_i are introduced to accommodate possible inseparability of the dataset while minimizing the degree of misclassification.

[1]That is, conducting numerical simulations with a dynamical system model is typically computationally less demanding than constructing algebraic proof certificates using the same model.

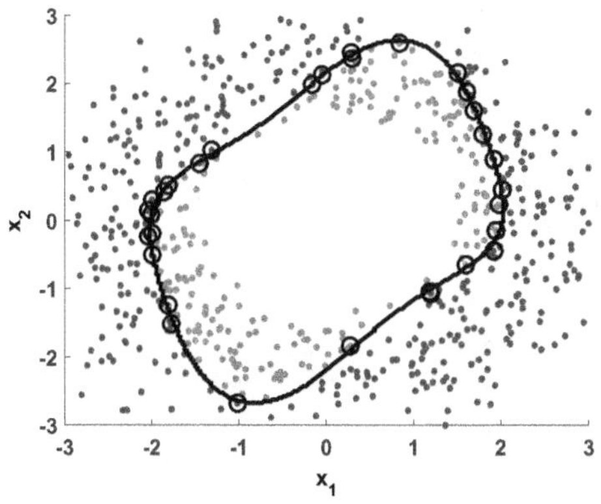

Figure 2: Data samples (S_C – red; S_D – blue), a classifier, and the contour of the decision surface with the support vectors circled.

If m is too large, then computing the map $w^T\Phi(x)+b$ (and solving for w using the formulation in (1)) becomes computationally demanding. In such cases, the so-called "kernel trick" is used to avoid the computation of the map $w^T\Phi(x)+b$. To this end, consider the Lagrangian dual of (1) for $k=1$ (for simplicity):

$$\begin{array}{ll} \text{maximize}_\alpha & \sum_{i=1}^N \alpha_i - \sum_{i,j=1}^N \alpha_i\alpha_j y_i y_j (\Phi(x_i)^T\Phi(x_j)) \\ \text{subject to} & \sum_{i=1}^N \alpha_i y_i = 0 \\ & 0 \le \alpha_i \le C \quad i=1,\cdots,N. \end{array} \tag{2}$$

Now define a kernel function $k:\mathbb{R}^n\times\mathbb{R}^n\to\mathbb{R}$ such that $k(x,\bar{x})=\Phi(x)^T\Phi(\bar{x})$. The dual problem and introduction of the kernel function allow the solution of the dual problem without having to evaluate map Φ with potentially high dimensional feature space. For example, while $k(x,\bar{x}) = (x^T\bar{x}+1)^2$ is a compact representation of a kernel function, the corresponding basis function vector $\Phi(x_1,x_2) = [x_1^2, x_2^2, \sqrt{2}x_1x_2, \sqrt{2}x_1,\ x_2, 1]^T$ requires a larger representation.

Finally, a classifier can be constructed from the solution of the dual problem in the following manner. At the optimal solution, a dual variable α_i is non-zero only when the corresponding primal constraint $y_i(w^T\Phi(x_i)+b)\ge 1-\xi_i$ holds with equality. Similarly, the slack variable ξ_i of the primal problem is zero when α_i is strictly less than then upper bound C [8]. The solution to the primal problem, i.e., a classier, can be constructed as

$$\sum_{j=1}^N \alpha_j y_j k(x_j,x)+b. \tag{3}$$

The elements x_j with non-zero α_j are the "support vectors". In practice, often only a small number of α_i's are non-zero and the classifier admits a simple representation. Figure 2 shows a trained classifier with the training data where the support vectors are emphasized.

2.3 Error Analysis

Once a classifier is constructed, it can be used to respond to verification inquiries. However, it is constructed based on only a finite set of randomly selected data points that represent the underlying dynamical system over a continuous (or partly continuous) state space. Therefore, it is critical to provide an assessment of how correctly it would predict the responses of verification inquiries that involve a priori unseen configurations of the system. Statistical learning theory offers a number of metrics to evaluate the potential errors in classification.

Generalization error describes a classifier's accuracy when applied to arbitrary test data. It represents the expected probability of misclassification and is commonly used as a performance measure for classification algorithms. We use two approaches to calculate the generalization error in the case studies in Section 3.

The first error metric is empirical: construct a grid of fixed spacing across the set of state or observed variables, determine the true class of each sample, and compare that to the class predicted by the classifier. The generalization error is taken as the fraction of samples for which the two differ out of all samples. The level of accuracy of this error metric depends on the granularity of the discrete grid.

The second error metric in based on so-called κ-fold cross-validation, which is a commonly practiced approximation to leave-one-out cross-validation [9, 10]. Leave-one-out procedure removes an element from the training set and attempts to classify the removed element with a classifier trained on the incomplete set. This procedure is repeated for each element and the fraction of misclassified samples estimates the expected probability of error. The complete leave-one-out cross-validation is computationally intensive with large data sets. κ-fold cross-validation is an abbreviated approach. The training data $S=S_c\cup S_D$ is separated into κ disjoint sets $S_1,S_2,\cdots,S_\kappa$. For each $i\in\{1,2,\cdots,\kappa\}$, a classifier is trained on $S\setminus S_i$ and tested on S_i. The accuracy of each iteration is the number of classification errors over the size of the training set. The generalization error is obtained by taking the average iteration accuracy.

REMARK 3. *The soft-margin SVM formulation allows misclassification errors. On the other hand, depending on the application, false positives (e.g., classified as safe while not) and false negatives (e.g., classified as unsafe while safe) may not be equally critical. For example, for verification in safety-critical applications, one may prefer reduce the possibility of false positives at the expense of larger number of false negatives (i.e., safe yet possibly conservative classification). This effect can be achieved by using non-homogenous weights instead of the same weight C in the penalization of possible classification errors in (1)[11].*

3. CASE STUDIES

We now demonstrate the method on several case studies ranging from the commonly used Van der Pol oscillator to multi-dimensional aircraft controllers and reinforcement-learning-based controllers. These cases cover a wide range of dynamics and evaluation criteria. For instance, an unstable oscillator is judged as "safe" if the system reaches the stable equilibrium point while an adaptive control system is concerned with minimizing deviation from a separate reference trajectory. We use the Matlab Machine Learning library for the SVM implementation and a 3.4 GHz dual-core/8GB RAM Windows machine. The implementations for the case studies are available at `http://tinyurl.com/z8hyfrf`. In the case studies, we refer to certain Lyapunov-like functions that we either draw from literature (e.g., from [5, 6, 12]) or compute using sum-of-squares optimization for comparison of the results. We use the sampling method discussed in

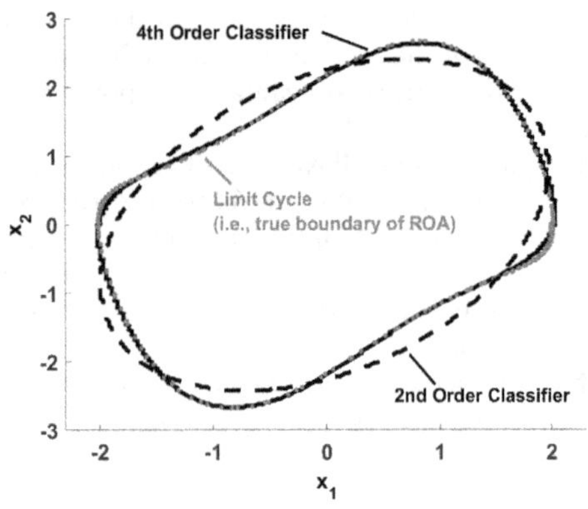

Figure 3: 2nd(dashed) and 4th(solid) order classifiers for Van der Pol dynamics.

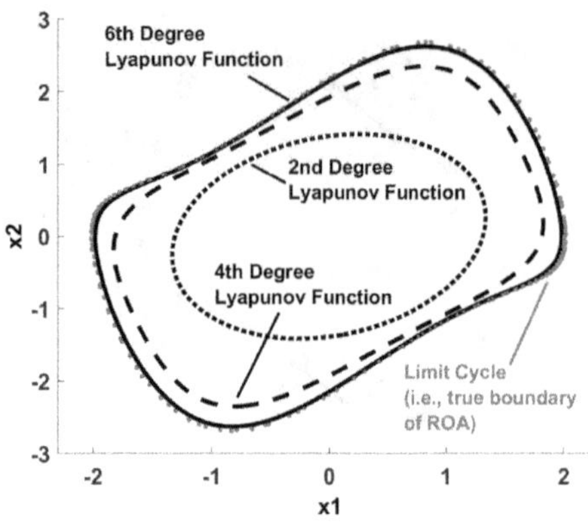

Figure 4: 2nd, 4th, and 6th order Lyapunov-based estimates [6] for Van der Pol dynamics.

[6] in the context of simulation-based search for polynomial Lyapunov functions. For ease of comparison, we often use polynomial kernels in classification unless noted otherwise.

3.1 Van der Pol Oscillator

The first test case is a Van der Pol oscillator $\dot{x}_1 = -x_2$ and $\dot{x}_2 = x_1 + (x_1^2 - 1)x_2$ with an unstable limit cycle and an asymptotically stable equilibrium at the origin. This problem has been widely used in previous nonlinear analysis and verification procedures [6, 13]. As such, the Van der Pol dynamics provide a baseline for data-driven verification as its region of attraction.

We trained two classifiers usingsimulated data (600 samples) with 2nd- and 4th-order polynomial kernels and both with homogenous misclassification costs. The results are shown in Figure 3. The 4th-order classifier separates the training data with 3 errors (2 false positives) and closely follows the limit cycle. The generalization error is calculated empirically as 0.48% on a test set of 75,000 samples. κ-fold cross-validation with 10 folds estimates the expected probability of error at 0.015. Average runtimes for sampling, training, and cross-validation in both cases were 27.78, 0.6, and 1.1 seconds respectively. The test set was generated in 14 minutes.

When compared to the results from traditional Lyapunov-based methods [6] shown in Figure 4, the classification-based results offer an improvement. The coverage provided by the estimate from the classifier using basis functions up to 4th-degree polynomials is comparable with that from the 6th-degree Lyapunov function. This example demonstrates the flexibility of the classification-based method, though it is critical to emphasize that this flexibility is at a cost. While the Lyapunov-based estimate comes with certainty, the classification-based estimate allows classification errors. Therefore, the results from the classification-based method must be interpreted with their quantified confidence.

3.2 Adaptive Controllers

We now apply the method to estimate the region of attraction for multiple systems with recently developed adaptive controllers [14] that challenge the conventional Lyapunov-based barrier certificate methods. First, consider the following second order uncertain system with unknown parameters W_1^*, W_2^* and initial conditions $x_1(0)$, $x_2(0)$:

$$\begin{aligned} \dot{x}_1 &= x_2, \\ \dot{x}_2 &= (-0.2 + W_1^*)x_1 + (-0.2 + W_2^*)x_2 + u. \end{aligned} \tag{4}$$

A concurrent learning model reference adaptive controller is used to estimate the unknown parameters and compute control inputs u to force the system to track a desired reference system $\dot{x}_m(t) = A_m x_m(t) + Br(t)$, where A_m is a Hurwitz matrix [14]. Because of online parameter estimation, the adaptive system has 4 states covering x_1, x_2, W_1^*, W_2^*. For ease of discussion, we fixed the initial values $x_1(0)$ and $x_2(0)$, resulting in a 2-dimensional problem over W_1^*, W_2^*. The success or failure of the system (i.e., the classification criterion) is based upon the ability of the controller to maintain $x_1(t)$ within ± 1.0 of $x_{m1}(t)$ for all $t \geq 0$.

We generated a training dataset of 10000 different (W_1^*, W_2^*) pairs in roughly 2.9 hours. We trained a set of 8th-order polynomial classifiers. In order to observe the effect of non-homogenous weighting on the decrease in unsafe errors, we swept the false-negative to false-positive ratio from 1:1 to 100:1 and evaluated on an independent testing set of over 30000 data points that span the entire feasible (W_1^*, W_2^*) space. The average time required for training and testing the classifiers were 164.17 and 0.229 seconds, respectively. The results are shown in Figure 5 and in Table 1. Note that Figure 5 also includes an independently obtained barrier certificate [12], labeled as "Lyapunov".

Table 1: Error rates for the system in (4). The weighting ratio of false negatives to false positives is increased from 1:1 to 100:1.

Data Set	Error (frac.)	False Neg.	False Pos.
Training	0.0402	54 of 3000	357 of 7222
Testing	0.0332	90 of 13263	986 of 19098
Training	0.0826	844 of 3000	0 of 7222
Testing	0.0704	2275 of 13263	3 of 19098

As seen in Figure 5, the SVM classifiers are able to much less conservatively estimate the ROA than previous Lyapunov-based barrier certificate methods [6]. If the lack of false-positive errors is important, the cost weighting in Remark 3 offers a viable way of reducing unsafe errors, as seen for the 100:1 training and testing data. While the total number of false negatives increases, the weighting does reduce

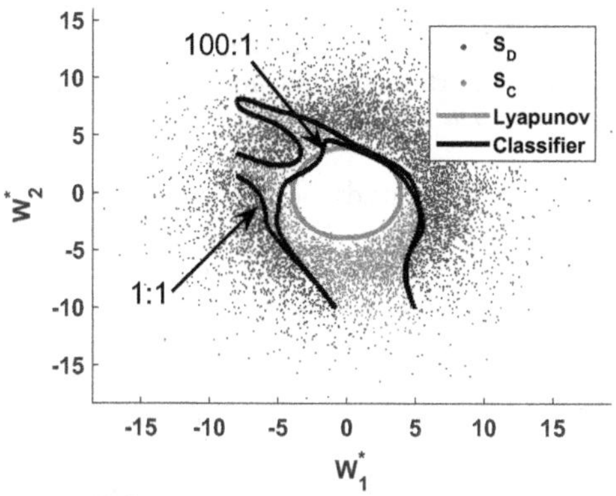

Figure 5: Classifiers for the system in (4) are compared against each other and the ROA estimate from a Lyapunov-based analysis.

probability of unsafe false positives to 1.57×10^{-4}.

As the number of variables considered increases, the sampling, training, and testing times will increase. We provide an additional, more complex example along with the implementation details at `http://tinyurl.com/z8hyfrf`.

3.3 Aircraft Reversionary Safety Controller

Another example is on an aircraft reversionary controller.[2] The reversionary control is intended as a safety check that takes over for the advanced controller in the case of failure. We are interested in estimating the set of perturbed states from which the reversionary controller can recover to a particular nominal condition. The underlying simulation model has 10 states and is highly nonlinear. While the simulations are performed on this 10-dimensional model, the verification inquiry (hence the classification) involves only a 3-dimensional subspace (i.e., the system behavior is monitored in these 3 dimensions).

We trained two 4th-order polynomial classifiers with 4000 and 16000 data points. As this reversionary controller is used as a safety-critical component of the flight control system, the classifier should feature a smaller rate of false-positive predictions (unsafe states labeled as safe) potentially at the cost of an increased number of false-negative predictions. To this end, we increased the weighting ratio of false positives to false negatives gradually from 1:1 to 100:1 with false positive errors going to zero.

Table 2: Error rates for the example in section 3.3 with 100:1 weight ratio.

Data Set	Error (%)	False Pos.	False Neg.
N = 4000	7.90	0 of 1604	316 of 2396
N = 16000	7.74	0 of 6497	1238 of 9503

Table 2 summarizes the results. A 10-fold cross-validation estimates the mean probability of error at 3.4×10^{-3} for the small set and 2.6×10^{-3} for the large test dataset. Observed runtimes for sampling, training, and cross-validation were 222, 13, 137 seconds with 4000 samples and 884, 174, 1818 seconds with 16000 samples. The weighted classifiers show better optimized estimates of the safety region by allowing no false-positives while correctly classifying a greater number of safe samples.

[2]Obtained based on personal communication with J. Schierman and M. Devore of Barron Associates.

3.4 Reinforcement Learning-Based Controller

We now consider an example in which a two-link robot, the *acrobot*, is controlled by a logic from a prior reinforcement learning step using Sarsa(λ) [15]. The controller determines the torque applied at the second joint which is most efficient at achieving the goal of raising the end of the second link a full link length above the top of the first link, simulating a gymnast swinging on a high bar. The system dynamics [15] are

$$\begin{aligned}
\ddot{\theta}_1 &= -d_1^{-1}(d_2\ddot{\theta}_2 + \phi_1)\\
\ddot{\theta}_2 &= (\frac{5}{4} - \frac{d_2^2}{d_1})^{-1}(\tau + \frac{d_2}{d_1}\phi_1 - \frac{1}{2}\dot{\theta}_1^2 \sin\theta_2 - \phi_2)\\
d_1 &= \frac{7}{2} + \cos\theta_2\\
d_2 &= \frac{5}{4} + \frac{1}{2}\cos\theta_2 \qquad (5)\\
\phi_1 &= -\frac{1}{2}\dot{\theta}_2 \sin\theta_2(\dot{\theta}_2 - 2\dot{\theta}_1) + \frac{3}{2}g\cos(\theta_1 - \pi/2) + \phi_2\\
\phi_2 &= \frac{1}{2}g\cos(\theta_1 + \theta_2 - \pi/2),
\end{aligned}$$

where g is gravity. The velocities are limited to $\dot{\theta}_1 \in [-4\pi, 4\pi]$ and $\dot{\theta}_2 \in [-9\pi, 9\pi]$ while the positions are not bounded. The learning process refines an eligibility trace and converges to a sequence of torque selections ($\tau \in \{-1, 0, 1\}$) that guides the controller toward its goal from the current state.

The controller is trained from a single initial condition over a finite grid of the state space and the control inputs applied at points other than these finitely many grid points are determined through interpolation. At the initial conditions, the robot is stationary with its links fully extended as a pendulum, $(\theta_1, \theta_2) = (\dot{\theta}_1, \dot{\theta}_2) = (0, 0)$. Hence, the question of interest here analogous to stability is for which initial conditions will the trained controller still accomplish its objective. The criterion for a successful sample is that the robot achieves the goal in less than 1000 simulation steps (in integration with a uniform increment of 0.05 units of time) after which the episode terminates as a failed attempt. Initial conditions are sampled from the state subspace: $\theta_1 \in [-\pi/2, \pi/2]$, $\theta_2 \in [-\pi/2, \pi/2]$, $\dot{\theta}_1 \in [-2\pi, 2\pi]$, and $\dot{\theta}_2 \in [-2\pi, 2\pi]$.

Table 3 shows the observed classifier results with 4000 samples using 4th order polynomial kernel. The expected probability of error is estimated at 0.075 by 10-fold cross-validation. Runtimes for initial learning, SVM training, and cross-validation are 208, 3.6, and 26.5 seconds respectively.

Table 3: Error rates for the example in section 3.4.

Data Set	Error (%)	False Pos.	False Neg.
Training	0.75	0 of 134	30 of 3866
Testing	1.35	12 of 118	42 of 3882

4. CRITIQUE

The data-driven verification approach connects the classical systems analysis questions to a vast range of concepts and techniques: (i) The method requires only a notion of *observable variables* and an *oracle that generates labels*. Hence, it can be directly applied on datasets without even a model or with high-fidelity simulation models for a range of system analysis questions, including safety, reachability, and more sophisticated temporal logic verification [16]. (ii) Statistical learning literature offers metrics to quantify the possibility of error in predictions (i.e., our confidence in the results) with respect to the amount of data used in classification. It remains open to understand the utility of these metrics in informing system designers. (iii) Regardless of the system representation, classification can be formulated as convex optimization. Rigorous sensitivity analysis and different weights used in the underlying optimization can guide subsequent, informative data collection (or generation) and help adjust the relative levels of prediction errors to meet certain criteria, e.g., *false positives* may be more tolerable than *false negatives* in safety-critical systems.

Though the method we presented makes, for the first time (to the best of our knowledge), connections between deductive dynamical system verification and statistical learning theory, it has similarities with several other methods discussed in the literature. The closest connection is perhaps with statistical model checking [17] of finite-state models. Smoothed model checking [18], a variation on statistical model checking, fits Gaussian process models to sampled data based on probabilistic results. Simulations—or signal-based view—have also been central in the verification techniques in [12, 19, 20, 21] and in the complementing view of falsification [22]. Finally, unlike Monte-Carlo-based approaches, the proposed method computes an algebraic map that can be used for future predictions of set membership and inclusion (e.g., prediction of the label for a new, unseen set of initial conditions).

5. REFERENCES

[1] Department of Defense. *Department of Defense Standard Practice System Safety*, May 2012.

[2] Vance Hilderman and Tony Baghi. *Avionics certification: a complete guide to DO-178 (software), DO-254 (hardware)*. Avionics Communications, 2007.

[3] Hassan K. Khalil. *Nonlinear Systems*. Prentice Hall, 3rd edition edition, 2002.

[4] Stephen Boyd, Laurent El Ghaoui, E. Feron, and V. Balakrishnan. *Linear Matrix Inequalities in System and Control Theory*, volume 15 of *Studies in Applied Mathematics*. Society for Industrial and Applied Mathematics, 1994.

[5] Pablo A. Parrilo. *Structured Semidefinite Programs and Semialgebraic Geometry Methods in Robustness and Optimization*. PhD thesis, California Institute of Technology, 2000.

[6] Ufuk Topcu, Andrew Packard, and Peter Seiler. Local stability analysis using simulations and sum-of-squares programming. *Automatica*, 44(10):2669–2675, 2008.

[7] Vladimir Naumovich Vapnik and Vlamimir Vapnik. *Statistical learning theory*. Wiley New York, 1998.

[8] B Scholkopf. Statistical learning and kernel methods. Technical report, Microsoft Research, 2000.

[9] Davide Anguita, Alessandro Ghio, Sandro Ridella, and Dario Sterpi. K-fold cross validation for error rate estimate in support vector machines. In *International Conference on Data Mining (DMIN)*, pages 291–297, 2009.

[10] Ron Kohavi et al. A study of cross-validation and bootstrap for accuracy estimation and model selection. In *International Joint Conference on Artificial Intelligence*, volume 2, pages 1137–1145, 1995.

[11] Xulei Yang, Qing Song, and Yue Wang. A weighted support vector machine for data classification. *International Journal of Pattern Recognition and Artificial Intelligence*, 21(05):961–976, 2007.

[12] James Kapinski, Jyotirmoy Deshmukh, Sriram Sankaranarayanan, and Nikos Arechiga. Simulation-guided lyapunov analysis for hybrid dynamical systems. In *Hybrid Systems: Computation and Control*, 2014.

[13] Ufuk Topcu, Andrew K. Packard, Peter Seiler, and Gary J. Balas. Robust region-of-attraction estimation. *IEEE Transactions on Automatic Control*, 55(1):137–142, January 2010.

[14] Girish Chowdhary, Hassan A. Kingravi, Jonathan How, and Patricio A. Vela. Bayesian nonparametric adaptive control using gaussian processes. *IEEE Transactions on Neural Networks and Learning Systems*, 26(3):537–550, March 2015.

[15] A. Barto and R. Sutton. *Reinforcement Learning: An Introduction*. MIT Press, 1998.

[16] Christel Baier and Joost-Pieter Katoen. *Principles of Model Checking*. MIT Press, 2008.

[17] Koushik Sen, Mahesh Viswanathan, and Gul Agha. Statistical model checking of black-box probabilistic systems. In *Computer Aided Verification*, pages 202–215, 2004.

[18] Luca Bortolussi, Dimitrios Milios, and Guido Sanguinetti. Smoothed model checking for uncertain continuous time markov chains. Technical report, University of Trieste/University of Edinburgh, 2014.

[19] Alexandre Donze and Oded Maler. Robust satisfaction of temporal logic over real-valued signals. In *Formal Modeling and Analysis of Timed Systems*, pages 92–106. 2010.

[20] Zhenqi Huang and Sayan Mitra. Computing bounded reach sets from sampled simulation traces. In *Hybrid Systems: Computation and Control*, pages 291–294, 2012.

[21] Yi Deng, Akshay Rajhans, and A Agung Julius. Strong: A trajectory-based verification toolbox for hybrid systems. In *Quantitative Evaluation of Systems*, pages 165–168. 2013.

[22] Sriram Sankaranarayanan and Georgios Fainekos. Falsification of temporal properties of hybrid systems using the cross-entropy method. In *Hybrid Systems: Computation and Control*, pages 125–134, 2012.

Towards Model Checking of Implantable Cardioverter Defibrillators

Houssam Abbas, Kuk Jin Jang, Zhihao Jiang, Rahul Mangharam
Department of Electrical and Systems Engineering
University of Pennsylvania, Philadelphia, PA, USA
{habbas, jangkj, zhihaoj, rahulm}@seas.upenn.edu

ABSTRACT

Ventricular Fibrillation is a disorganized electrical excitation of the heart that results in inadequate blood flow to the body. It usually ends in death within a minute. A common way to treat the symptoms of fibrillation is to implant a medical device, known as an *Implantable Cardioverter Defibrillator* (ICD), in the patient's body. Model-based verification can supply rigorous proofs of safety and efficacy. In this paper, we build a hybrid system model of the human heart+ICD closed loop, and show it to be a STORMED system, a class of o-minimal hybrid systems that admit finite bisimulations. In general, it may not be possible to compute the bisimulation. We show that approximate reachability can yield a finite *simulation* for STORMED systems, and that certain compositions respect the STORMED property. The results of this paper are theoretical and motivate the creation of concrete model checking procedures for STORMED systems.

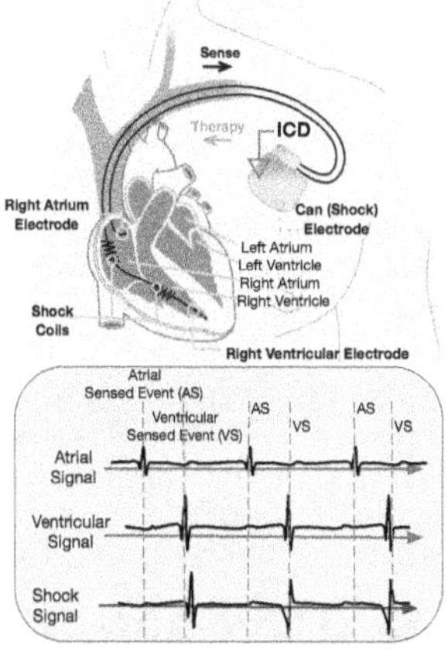

Figure 1: ICD connected to a human heart via two electrodes. The ICD monitors three electrical signals (known as electrograms) traversing the heart muscle.

1. INTRODUCTION

Implantable Cardioverter Defibrillators (ICDs) are life-saving medical devices. An ICD is implanted under the shoulder, and connects directly to the heart muscle though two electrodes and continuously measures the heart's rhythm (Fig. 1). If it detects a potentially fatal accelerated rhythm known as Ventricular Tachycardia (VT), the ICD delivers a high-energy electric shock or sequence of pulses through the electrodes to reset the heart's electrical activity. Without this therapy, the VT can be fatal within seconds of onset. In the US alone, 10,000 people receive an ICD every month. Studies have presented evidence that patients implanted with ICDs have a mortality rate reduced by up to 31%.

Unfortunately, ICDs suffer from a high rate of *inappropriate therapy* due to poor detection of the current rhythm on the part of the ICD. In particular, a class of rhythms known as SupraVentricular Tachycardias (SVTs) can fool the detection algorithms. Inappropriate shocks increase patient stress, reduce their quality of life, and are linked to increased morbidity. Depending on the particular ICD and its settings, the rates of inappropriate therapy can range from 46% to 62% of all delivered therapy episodes. Current practice for ICD verification relies heavily on testing and software cycle reviews. With the advent of computer models of the human heart, *Model-Based Design* (MBD) can supply rigorous evidence of safety and efficacy. This paper presents hybrid system models of the human heart and of the common modules of ICDs currently on the market, and shows that the closed loop formed by these models admits a finite bisimulation. The objective is to develop model checkers for ICDs to further their MBD process.

No work exists on ICD verification. Earlier work on verification of medical devices (formal or otherwise) focuses on pacemakers, which measure the timing of heart events. ICD algorithms are more complex than a pacemaker's, because an ICD also measures and processes the *morphology* of the electrical signal to distinguish many types of arrhythmias. This takes the model out of the realm of timed automata and into hybrid automata proper. Previous work on biological hybrid and/or nonlinear systems uses approximate reachability techniques to verify system invariants [7, 8], and demonstrates success in parameter space exploration.

The first contribution of this paper is to develop a hybrid system model of the heart and ICD measurement process (Section 3), of the ICD sensing process (Section 4), and of the algorithmic components of ICDs from most major manufacturers on the market (Section 5, see Fig. 2). We show that the composition of these three models admits a finite

HSCC '16, April 12–14, 2016, Vienna, Austria.

DOI: http://dx.doi.org/10.1145/2883817.2883841

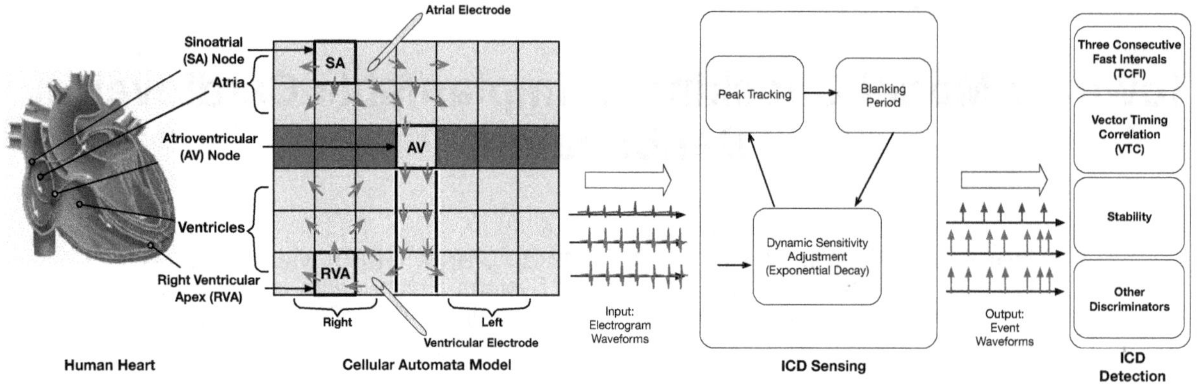

Figure 2: The whole heart is modeled as a 2D mesh of cells (Section 3). The ICD electrodes are shown in the right atrium and ventricle. The electrogram signals measured through the electrodes are processed by the sensing module (see Section 4). The detection algorithm determines the current rhythm using the processed signal (Section 5).

bisimulation. The models presented here are the first formalization of ICD operation. To establish this result we use the theory of STORMED systems [15], a class of hybrid systems that have finite bisimulations. Our second contribution is two general results for STORMED systems. First we prove that parallel compositions of STORMED systems yield STORMED systems (Section 6). Secondly, we show that any definable over-approximate reach tubes can replace the exact trajectories of a STORMED system, yielding a system that still admits a finite *simulation* (Section 7). All proofs are in the online report [1].

2. HYBRID SYSTEMS AND SIMULATIONS

Definition 2.1. *A* hybrid automaton *is a tuple*

$$\mathcal{H} = (X, L, H_0, \{f_\ell\}, Inv, E, \{R_{ij}\}_{(i,j)\in E}, \{G_{ij}\}_{(i,j)\in E})$$

where $X \subset \mathbb{R}^n$ is the continuous state space equipped with the Euclidian norm $\|\cdot\|$, $L \subset \mathbb{N}$ is a finite set of modes, $H_0 \subset X \times L$ is an initial set, $\{f_\ell\}_{\ell\in L}$ determine the continuous evolutions with unique solutions, $Inv : L \to 2^X$ defines the invariants for every mode, $E \subset L^2$ is a set of discrete transitions, $G_{ij} \subset X$ is guard set for the transitions (so $\mathcal{H}$ transitions $i \to j$ when $x \in G_{ij}$), $R_{ij} : X \to X$ is an edge-specific reset function.
Set $H = L \times X$. Given $(\ell, x_0) \in H$, the flow $\theta_\ell(;x_0) : \mathbb{R}_+ \to \mathbb{R}^n$ is the solution to the IVP $\dot{x}(t) = f_\ell(x(t))$, $x(0) = x_0$.

The associated *transition system* is $T_\mathcal{H} = (H, E \cup \{\tau\}, \to, H_0)$ where H is the state set, $E \cup \{\tau\}$ is the label set for transitions, H_0 is the set of initial states, and $\to = (\bigcup_{e\in E} \xrightarrow{e}) \cup \xrightarrow{\tau}$ where $(i,x) \xrightarrow{e} (j,y)$ iff $e = (i,j), x \in G_{ij}, y = R_{ij}(x)$ and $(i,x) \xrightarrow{\tau} (j,y)$ iff $i = j$ and there exists a flow $\theta_i(\cdot;x)$ of $\mathcal{H}$ and $t \geq 0$ s.t. $\theta_i(t;x) = y$ and $\forall t' \leq t$, $\theta_i(t';x) \in Inv(i)$. Let $\sim$ be an equivalence relation on H and $H/\sim$ the corresponding partition. Let $\mathcal{F}_t(H/\sim)$ be the coarsest bisimulation with respect to $\xrightarrow{\tau}$[1] respecting the partition $H/\sim$, and $\mathcal{F}_d(H/\sim) := \{(h_1,h_2) \mid (h_1 \xrightarrow{e} h_1') \implies (\exists e' \in E, h_2'.h_2 \xrightarrow{e'} h_2' \wedge h_1' \sim h_2')\} \cap H/\sim$ [15]. The iteration

$$W_0 = \mathcal{F}_t(H/\sim), \quad \forall i \geq 0, W_{i+1} = \mathcal{F}_t(\mathcal{F}_d(W_i)) \qquad (1)$$

computes a bisimulation of $\mathcal{H}$. However it does not necessarily terminate for hybrid systems because the system's reach set might intersect a given block of $H/\sim$ an infinite number of times (see [11] for an example). The class of systems introduced in the next section has the property that the iteration does terminate for it and returns a finite $\mathcal{S}$.

Given a set of atomic propositions, if $\sim$ is s.t. $\eta \sim \eta'$ iff both states satisfy exactly the same atomic propositions, then model checking temporal logic properties can be done on the finite bisimulation instead of the possibly infinite $\mathcal{H}$.

2.1 O-minimality and STORMED systems

We give a very brief introduction to o-minimal structures. A more detailed introduction can be found in [11] and references therein. We are interested in sets and functions in $\mathbb{R}^n$ that enjoy certain finiteness properties, called order-minimal sets (o-minimal). These are defined inside *structures* $\mathcal{A} = (\mathbb{R}, <, +, -, \cdot, \exp, \ldots)$. The subsets $Y \subset \mathbb{R}^n$ we are interested in are those that are *definable* using first-order formulas φ: $Y = \{(a_1, \ldots, a_n) \in \mathbb{R}^n \mid \varphi(a_1, \ldots, a_n)\}$. (First-order formulas use the boolean connectives and the quantifiers $\exists, \forall$). The atomic propositions from which the formulas are recursively built allow only the operations of the structure $\mathcal{A}$ on the real variables and constants, and the relations of $\mathcal{A}$ and equality. For example $2x - 3.6y < 3z$ and $x = y$ are valid atomic propositions of the structure $\mathcal{L}_\mathbb{R} = (\mathbb{R}, <, +, -, \cdot)$, while $cosh(x) < 3z$ is not because $cosh$ is not in the structure. These structures are already sufficient to describe a set of dynamics rich enough for our purposes and for various classes of linear systems.

Definition 2.2. *A theory of* $(\mathbb{R}, \ldots)$ *is* o-minimal *if the only definable subsets of $\mathbb{R}$ are finite unions of points and (possibly unbounded) intervals. A function $f : x \mapsto f(x)$ is o-minimal if its graph $\{(x,y) \mid y = f(x)\}$ is a definable set.*

We use the terms o-minimal and definable interchangeably, and they refer to $\mathcal{L}_{\exp} = (\mathbb{R}, <, +, -, \cdot, \exp)$ which is known to be o-minimal. The dot product between $x, y \in \mathbb{R}^n$ is denoted $x \cdot y$, and $d(Y,S) = \inf\{\|y - s\| \mid (y,s) \in Y \times S\}$.

Definition 2.3. *[15]. A* STORMED hybrid system *(SHS) Σ is a tuple $(\mathcal{H}, \mathcal{A}, \phi, b_-, b_+, d_{min}, \epsilon, \zeta)$ where $\mathcal{H}$ is a hybrid automaton, $\mathcal{A}$ is an o-minimal structure, d_{min}, ϵ, ζ are positive reals, $b_-, b_+ \in \mathbb{R}$ and $\phi \in X$ such that:*
(S) *The system is d_{min}-separable, meaning that for any $e = (\ell, \ell') \in E$ and $\ell'' \neq \ell'$, $d(R_e(G_{(\ell,\ell')}), G_{(\ell',\ell'')}) > d_{min}$* [2]

[1] I.e., $\mathcal{F}_t$ only considers the continuous transition relation: it is a bisimulation of $T^c_\mathcal{H} := (H/\sim, \{*\}, \xrightarrow{\tau}, H_0/\sim)$.

[2] The original definition of separability [15] required the guards themselves to be separated, which is insufficient to guarantee that if $\mathcal{H}$ flows, it flows a uniform minimum dis-

(T) The flows (i.e., the solutions of the ODEs) are Time-Independent with the Semi-Group property (TISG), meaning that for any $\ell \in L, x \in X$, the flow θ_ℓ starting at (ℓ, x) satisfies: 1) $\theta_\ell(0; x) = x$, 2) for every $t, t' \geq 0$, $\theta_\ell(t + t'; x) = \theta_\ell(t'; \theta_\ell(t; x))$
***(O)** All the sets and functions of $\mathcal{H}$ are definable in the o-minimal structure $\mathcal{A}$*
***(RM)** The resets and flows are monotonic with respect to the same vector ϕ, meaning that*
1) (Flow monotonicity) for all $\ell \in L$, $x \in X$ and $t, \tau \geq 0$, $\phi \cdot (\theta_\ell(t + \tau; x) - \theta_\ell(t; x)) \geq \epsilon||\theta_\ell(t + \tau; x) - \theta_\ell(t; x)||$, and
2) (Reset monotonicity) for any edge $(\ell, \ell') \in E$ and any $x^-, x^+ \in X$ s.t. $x^+ = R_{\ell,\ell'}(x^-)$,

1. *if $\ell = \ell'$, then either $x^- = x^+$ or $\phi \cdot (x^+ - x^-) \geq \zeta$*
2. *if $\ell \neq \ell'$, then $\phi \cdot (x^+ - x^-) \geq \epsilon||x^+ - x^-||$*

***(ED)** Ends are Delimited: for all $e \in E$ we have $\phi \cdot x \in (b_-, b_+)$ for all $x \in G_e$*

Intuitively, the above conditions imply the trajectories of the system always move a minimum distance along ϕ whether flowing or jumping, which guarantees that no area of the state space will be visited infinitely often. This is at the root of the finiteness properties of STORMED systems.

Theorem 2.1. *[15] Let $\mathcal{H}$ be a STORMED hybrid system, and let $\mathcal{P}$ be an o-minimal partition of its hybrid state space. Then $\mathcal{H}$ admits a finite bisimulation that respects $\mathcal{P}$.*

3. HEART MODEL

For the verification of ICDs, we adopt the cellular automata (CA)-based heart model developed in [14],[5]. This model lies in-between high spatial fidelity but slow to compute PDE-based whole heart models, and low spatial fidelity but very fast-to-compute automata-based models [12]. Ionic currents [9] and PDE-based models may be more accurate but are not currently amenable to formal verification (however see [7] for reachability analysis of discretized PDEs). CA-based models were used in [2] and [4]. This paper's model also has the important advantage of forming the basis of software used to train electrophysiologists, and allows interactive simulation of surgical procedures like ablation [13]. In particular, it can simulate tachycardias.

This paper's automata: All hybrid automata in this paper have the whole state space as invariants and transitions are urgent (taken immediately when the guard is enabled). The electrogram (EGM) voltage signal s has upper and lower bounds. We also observe that, as will be seen in Section 5, i) while observing a rhythm, the ICD will always reach a decision of VT or SVT in finite time ii) at which point it resets its controlled (software) variables so new values are computed for the next arrhythmia episode. So while the heart can beat indefinitely, for the purposes of ICD verification, there's a uniform upper bound on the length of time of any execution. Let $D \geq 0$ be this duration (D is on the order of 30sec depending on device settings. More recent ICD models might wait for longer for self-termination). Therefore, every mode of every automaton in what follows has a transition to mode End in which

tance along ϕ. Indeed assume the guards are separated. If $x \in G_{(\ell,\ell')}$ and $y = R_{(\ell,\ell')}(x)$, it can be that $y \in G_{(\ell',\ell'')}$ and thus a jump happens, even though $G_{(\ell,\ell')}$ and $G_{(\ell',\ell'')}$ are separated. Therefore we need $d(y, G_{\ell',\ell''}) > d_{min}$ for all $y \in R_e(G_e)$, which is the condition we use in Def. 2.3. The properties of SHS, in particular the existence of finite bisimulation, are therefore preserved by this change.

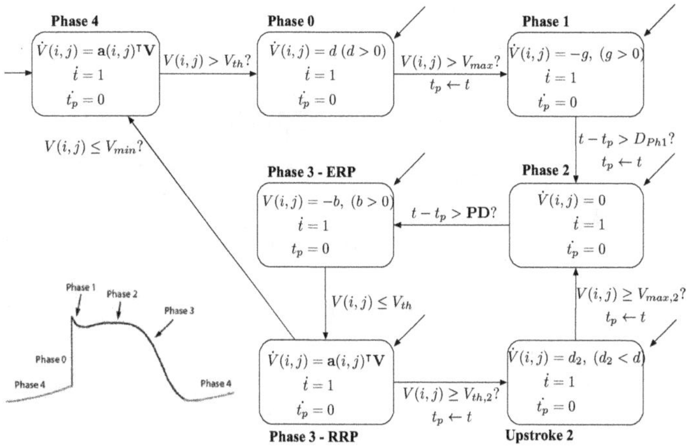

Figure 3: Hybrid model $\mathcal{H}_c$ of one cell of the heart model. AP figure from [6]. $V_{th,2} > V_{th}$, $V_{max,2} < V_{max}$

time does not progress. We don't show these transitions in the automata figures of this paper to avoid congestion.

3.1 Cellular automata model

The heart has two upper chambers called the *atria* and two lower chambers called the *ventricles* (Fig. 1) The synchronized contractions of the heart are driven by electrical activity. Under normal conditions, the SinoAtrial (SA) node (a tissue in the right atrium) spontaneously *depolarizes*, producing an electrical wave that propagates to the atria and then down to the ventricles (Fig.2) In this model, the myocardium (heart's muscle) is treated as a 2D surface (so it has no depth), and discretized into *cells*, which are simply regions of the myocardium (Fig. 2). Thus we end up with N^2 cells in a square N-by-N grid. A cell's voltage changes in reaction to current flow from neighboring cells, and in response to its own ion movements across the cell membrane. This results in an *Action Potential (AP)*.

Fig. 3 shows how the AP is generated by a given cell [10]: in its quiescent mode (Phase 4), a cell (i, j) in the grid has a cross-membrane voltage $V(i, j, t)$ equal to $V_{min} < 0$. As it gathers charge, $V(i, j, t)$ increases until it exceeds a threshold voltage V_{th}. In Phase 0, the voltage then experiences a very fast increase (Phase 0), called the upstroke, to a level $V_{max} > 0$, after which it decreases (Phase 1) to a plateau (Phase 2). It stays at the plateau level for a certain amount of time **PD** then decreases linearly to below V_{th} (Phase 3 - ERP). Once below V_{th} it is said to be in the Relative Refractory Period (Phase 3 - RRP) . In Phase 3 - RRP, the cell can be depolarized a second time, albeit at a higher threshold $V_{th,2}$, slower and to a lower plateau level $V_{max,2} < V_{max}$ (Upstroke 2). Otherwise, when the voltage reaches V_{min} again, the cell enters the quiescent stage again. This model is suitable for both pacemaker and non-pacemaker cells, the main differences being in the duration of the plateau (virtually non-existent for pacemaker cells), and the duration of phases 0 and 4 (both are shorter for pacemaker cells). In Fig. 3, $V(i, j) \in \mathbb{R}$ denotes the voltage in cell (i, j) of the grid, and $V = (V(1, 1), \ldots, V(N, N))^T$ in $\mathbb{R}^{N^2}$ groups the cross-membrane voltages of all cells in the heart. The whole heart model $\mathcal{H}_{CA}$ is the parallel composition of these N^2 single-cell models. The $(i, j)^{th}$ cell's voltage at time t

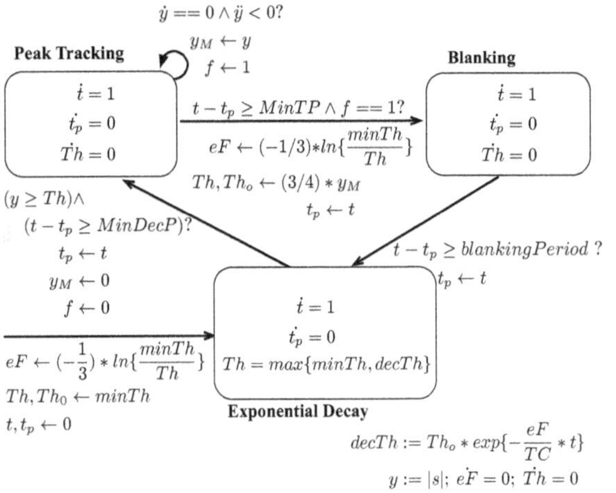

Figure 4: $\mathcal{H}_{Sense}$. States not shown in a mode have a 0 derivative, e.g., $\dot{eF} = 0$ in all modes.

in Phase 4 depends on that of its neighbors and its own as follows [14]

$$\begin{aligned}\dot{V}(i,j,t) &= \frac{[V(i-1,j,t)+V(i+1,j,t)-2V(i,j,t)]}{R_h(i,j)} \\ &+ \frac{[V(i,j-1,t)+V(i,j+1,t)-2V(i,j,t)]}{R_v(i,j)} \\ &= a(i,j)^T V(t),\ a(i,j) \in \mathbb{R}^{N^2} \qquad (2)\end{aligned}$$

where R_h, R_v are conduction constants that can vary across the myocardium. Thus V evolves according to a linear ODE $\dot{V} = AV$ where A is the matrix whose rows are the $a(i,j)$. The two states t and t_p are clocks. Clock t_p keeps track of the value of the last discrete jump. We will use this arrangement in all our models: it avoids resetting the clocks which preserves Reset Monotonicity.

ICDs observe the electrical activity through three channels (Fig. 1). Each signal is called an electrogram (EGM) signal. The signal read on a channel is given by [5]:

$$s(t) = \frac{1}{K}\sum_{i,j}\left(\frac{1}{||p_{i,j}-p_0||} - \frac{1}{||p_{i,j}-p_1||}\right)\dot{V}(i,j,t) \qquad (3)$$

where $||\cdot||$ is the Euclidian norm, p_0 and p_1 are the electrodes' positions and $p_{i,j}$ is the position of the $(i,j)^{th}$ cell on the 2D myocardium ($p_0, p_1, p_{i,j} \in \mathbb{R}^2$). Positions p_0, p_1 should be chosen different from $p_{i,j}$ to avoid infinities.

Extensions. The Action Potential Duration (APD) restitution mechanism as modeled in [14] can be included in this model without changing its formal properties.

We now state the main result of this section.

Theorem 3.1. *Let $\mathcal{H}_{CA}$ be the whole heart cellular automaton model obtained by parallel composition of N^2 models $\mathcal{H}_c$ with state vector $x = [V, t, t_p, s] \in \mathbb{R}^{N^2} \times \mathbb{R}^3$. Assume that all executions of the system have a duration of $D \geq 0$. Then $\mathcal{H}_{CA}$ is STORMED.*

4. ICD SENSING

Sensing is the process by which cardiac signals s measured through the leads of the ICD are converted to timing events. The ICD declares events when the signal exceeds a dynamically-adjusted threshold Th.

Fig. 4 shows the model $\mathcal{H}_{Sense}$ of the sensing algorithm, and Fig. 5 illustrates its operation. The sensing takes place

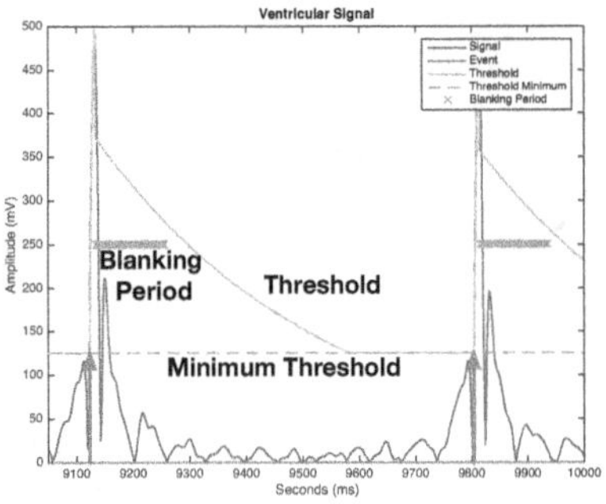

Figure 5: Example of dynamic threshold adjustment in ICD sensing algorithm. The shown signal is rectified.

on the rectified EGM signal $y = |s|$. After an event is declared at the current threshold value ($y(t) \geq Th(t)$ in Fig. 4), the algorithm tracks the signal in order to measure the next peak's amplitude (Peak Tracking). For a duration $MinTP$ (min tracking period) the latest peak is saved in y_M. A variable f indicates that a peak was found. After a peak is found ($f == 1$) and after the end of the tracking period, the algorithm enters a fixed *Blanking Period* (Blanking), during which additional events are ignored. On the transition to Blanking, Th, Th_0 and the exponential factor of decay eF are updated. At the end of the blanking period, the algorithm transitions to the Exponential Decay mode in which Th decays exponentially from Th_0 to a minimum level (Exponential Decay), and stays there for at least a sampling period of $MinDecP$. Different manufacturers may use a stepwise decay instead of exponential, but the principle is the same. Local peak detection is modeled via the $\dot{y} = 0 \wedge \ddot{y} < 0$ transition. While $y = |s|$ is non-differentiable at 0, the peak will occur away from 0, as shown in Fig. 5. States t, t_p are clocks and $minTh$ and TC are constant parameters.

Theorem 4.1. *$\mathcal{H}_{Sense}$ is STORMED.*

5. ARRHYTHMIA DETECTION

A sustained Ventricular Tachycardia (VT) (or Ventricular Fibrillation (VF)) can be fatal whereas a SupraVentricular Tachycardia (SVT) is usually not fatal, so *the ICD's main task is to discriminate VT from SVT and deliver therapy to the former only* [3]. Most VT/SVT detection algorithms found in ICDs today are composed of individual *discriminators*. A discriminator is a software function whose task is to decide whether the current arrhythmia is SVT or VT. No one discriminator can fully distinguish between SVT and VT. Thus a detection algorithm is often a decision tree built using a number of discriminators *running in parallel*. We have modeled each discriminator in Boston Scientific's detection algorithm as a hybrid automaton. **The ICD system is thus $\mathcal{H}_{ICD} = \mathcal{H}_{Sense}||\mathcal{H}_{Detection-Algo}$ where $\mathcal{H}_{Detection-Algo}$ is the parallel composition of the discriminator automata.** We now illustrate the models we created with three discriminators and prove they are SHS.

5.1 Three Consecutive Fast Intervals

Our first module simply detects whether three consecutive fast intervals have occurred, where 'fast' means the interval length, measured between 2 consecutive peaks on the EGM signal, is shorter than some pre-set amount. See Fig. 6. States t and t_p are clocks as before. The vector L_3 is three-dimensional, and stores the values of the last three intervals. The event VEvent? is shorthand for the transition $y(t) \geq Th$

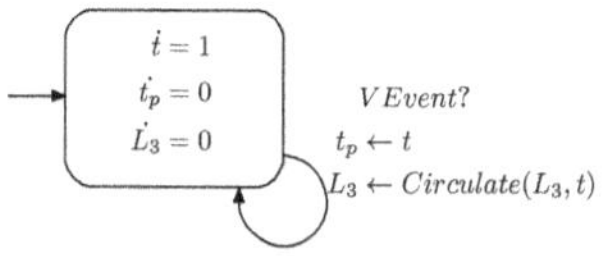

Figure 6: Three Consecutive Fast Intervals $\mathcal{H}_{TCFI}$

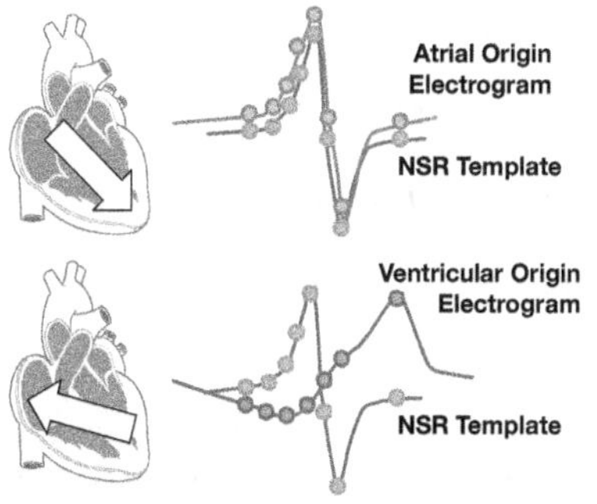

Figure 7: EGMs of different origin have different morphologies, while EGMs of similar origins have very similar morphologies.

being taken by the $\mathcal{H}_{Sense}$ automaton. In other words, it indicates a ventricular event. Then L_3 gets reset to $L_3^+ = (z_1, z_2, z_3)^+ :=$ Circulate$(L_3, t - t_p)$ where

$$L_3^+ = \begin{pmatrix} z_2 \\ z_3 \\ t - t_p \end{pmatrix} = \begin{pmatrix} 0 & 1 & 0 \\ 0 & 0 & 1 \\ 0 & 0 & 0 \end{pmatrix} L_3 + \begin{pmatrix} 0 \\ 0 \\ t - t_p \end{pmatrix} \quad (4)$$

Lemma 5.1. *$\mathcal{H}_{TCFI}$ is STORMED.*

5.2 Vector Timing Correlation

It has been clinically observed that a depolarization wave originating in the ventricles (as produced during VT for example) will in general produce a different EGM morphology than a wave originating in the atria (as produced during SVT) [3]. See Fig. 7. A morphology discriminator measures the correlation between the morphology of the current EGM and that of a stored *template* EGM acquired during normal sinus rhythm. If the correlation is above a pre-set threshold for a minimum number of beats, then this is an indication that the current arrhythmia is supraventricular in origin. Otherwise, it might be of ventricular origin.

Boston Scientific's implementation of a morphology discriminator is called Vector and Timing Correlation (VTC). VTC first samples 8 *fiducial* points $s_i, i = 1, \ldots, 8$ on the current EGM s at pre-defined time instants. Let $s_{m,i}$ be the corresponding points on the template EGM. A simple 0-shift correlation ρ_{new} is calculated between the two sequences. If 3 out of the last 10 calculated correlation values exceed the threshold, then SVT is decided and therapy is withheld.

The system of Fig. 8 implements the VTC discriminator. As before, t is a local clock. μ accumulates the values of the current EGM, α accumulates the product $s_i s_{m,i}$, β accumulates s_i^2. State w is an auxiliary state we need to establish the STORMED property. $\vec{\nu}$ is a 10D binary vector: $\nu_i = -1$ if the ith correlation value fell below the threshold, and is $+1$ otherwise. L_3 is the state of $\mathcal{H}_{TCFI}$: the guard condition $L_3 \leq th$ indicates that all its entries have values less than the tachycardia threshold, which is when $\mathcal{H}_{VTC}$ starts computing. $WindowEnds$ indicates the 'end' of an EGM, measured as a window around the peak sensed by $\mathcal{H}_{Sense}$.

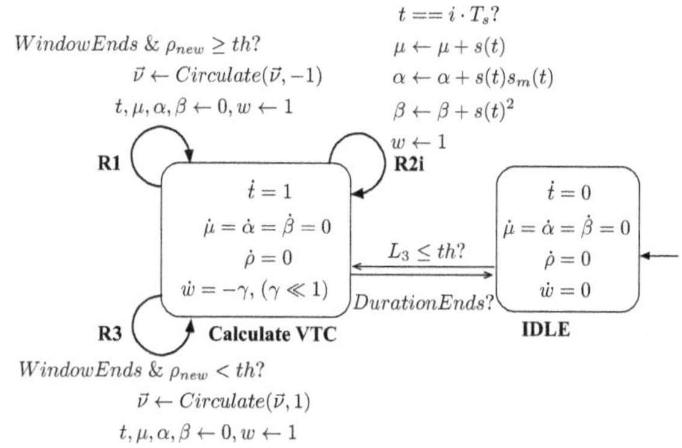

Figure 8: VTC calculation. iT_s is the sampling time for the ith fiducial point, $i = 1, \ldots, 8$. $R2_1, \ldots, R2_8$ are the corresponding resets. For clarity of the figure, 8 transitions are represented on the same edge R2i.

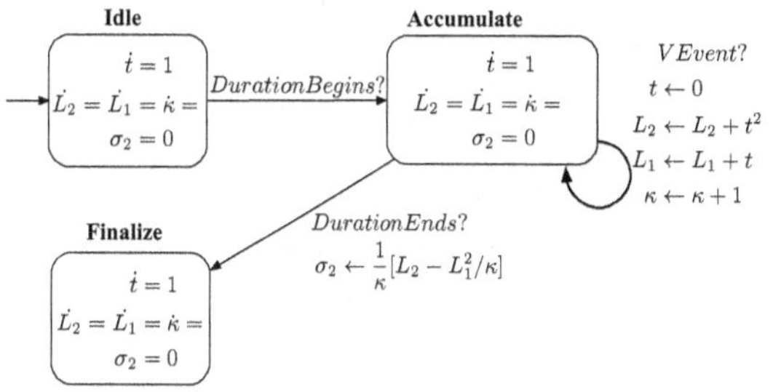

Figure 9: Stability discriminator.

Lemma 5.2. *$\mathcal{H}_{VTC}$ is STORMED.*

5.3 Stability discrimination

Stability refers to the variability of the peak-to-peak cycle length. A rhythm with large variability (above a pre-defined threshold) is said to be *unstable*. The Stability discriminator is used to distinguish between atrial fibrillation, which is usually unstable, and VT, which is usually stable.

The Stability discriminator shown in Fig. 9 simply calculates the variance of the cycle length over a fixed period called a Duration (measured in seconds). Let $DL \geq 0$ be the Duration length. The events *DurationBegins?* and *DurationEnds?* indicate the transitions of a simple system that measures the lapse of one Duration (not shown here). State t is a clock, L_1 accumulates the sum of interval lengths (and will be used to compute the average length), L_2 accumulates the squares of interval lengths, and κ is a counter that counts the number of accumulated beats. σ_2 is assigned the value of the variance given by $\frac{1}{\kappa}[L_2 - L_1^2/\kappa]$

Lemma 5.3. *$\mathcal{H}_{Stab}$ is STORMED.*

Now that each system was shown to be STORMED, it remains to establish that their parallel composition is STORMED. This result does not hold in general - Thm. 6.1 gives conditions under which parallel composition respects the STORMED property. Intuitively, we require that whenever a sub-collection of the systems jumps, the remaining systems that did not jump are separated from all of their respective guards by a uniform distance. This is a requirement that can be shown to hold for our systems by modeling various minimal delays in the systems' operation. We may now state:

Theorem 5.1. *Consider the collection of systems $\mathcal{H}_{CA}$,*

$\mathcal{H}_{ICD} = \mathcal{H}_{Sense}||\mathcal{H}_{Detection-Algo}$ *where the latter is the parallel composition of the discriminator systems. This collection satisfies the hypotheses of Thm. 6.1 (Section 6) and therefore the parallel system* $\mathcal{H}_{CA}||\mathcal{H}_{ICD}$ *is STORMED and has a finite bisimulation.*

6. COMPOSING STORMED SYSTEMS

The results in this section and the next apply to SHS in general, including those with time-unbounded operation. We write $[m] = \{1, \ldots, m\}$. In this section given hybrid systems $\mathcal{H}_1, \ldots, \mathcal{H}_m$, $x^i, G^i, \theta^i, \ldots$ etc refer to a state, guard, flow ... of system $\mathcal{H}_i$. Recall that $\theta_\ell(t;x)$ is the flow starting at (ℓ, x). The parallel composition $\mathcal{H} = \mathcal{H}_1|| \ldots ||\mathcal{H}_m$ is defined in the usual way: $\mathcal{H}.X = \Pi_i X^i$, $\mathcal{H}.L = \Pi_i L^i$, $\mathcal{H}.H_0 = \Pi_i H_0^i$, $Inv(\ell) = \Pi_i Inv^i(\ell^i)$, and the flow $\theta_\ell(x,t) = [\theta^1_{\ell^1}(x^1,t), \ldots, \theta^m_{\ell^m}(x^m,t)]^T$. The system jumps if any of its subsystems jumps. When a guard of a subsystem is satisfied, the state of that subsystem is reset according to its reset map. The guards are disjoint to avoid non-determinism.

We show that the parallel composition of SHS is still a SHS. In general $\mathcal{H}$ is not separable: indeed for any candidate value of d_{min}, one could find a transition (i,j) of $\mathcal{H}$ due to, say, a jump of $\mathcal{H}_1$, s.t. at that moment x^2 is closer than d_{min} to one of its own guards, say $G^2_{(j^2,k^2)}$. This causes $\mathcal{H}$ to further jump $j \to k$ without having traveled the requisite minimum distance, thus violating the separability of $R_{ij}(G_{ij})$ and G_{jk}. Therefore we need to impose an extra condition on minimum separability *across* sub-systems.

Theorem 6.1. *Let* $\Sigma_i = (\mathcal{H}_i, \mathcal{A}, \phi^i, b^{i,-}, b^{i,+}, d^i_{min}, \varepsilon^i, \zeta^i)$, $i = 1, \ldots, m$ *be deterministic SHS defined using the same underlying o-minimal structure, and where each state space* X^i *is bounded by* B_{X^i}.
Define parallel composition $\Sigma = (\mathcal{H}, \mathcal{A}, \phi, b^-, b^+, d_{min}, \varepsilon, \zeta)$ *where* $\mathcal{H} = \mathcal{H}_1|| \ldots ||\mathcal{H}_m$, $\phi = (\phi^1, \ldots, \phi^m)^T \in \mathbb{R}^{mn}$, $b^{i,-} = \inf_{x \in X} \phi \cdot x$, $b^{i,+} = \sup_{x\in X} \phi \cdot x$, $\varepsilon = \min(\min_i \varepsilon^i, \min_i \frac{\zeta^i}{B_{X^i}})$, $\zeta = \min_i \zeta^i$ *and*

$$d_{min} = \min_{I \subset [m]} (\min_{i \in I} d^i_{min}, \min_{i\in I, j \in [m]\setminus I} d^{ij}_{min})$$

Assume that the following **Collection Separability** *condition holds: for all* $i,j \leq m, \neq j$ *there exists* $d^{ij}_{min} > 0$ *s.t. if* $x \in X$ *is in the reachable set of* $\mathcal{H}$ *and* $x^i \in G^i_e \wedge x^j \notin G^j_{e'} \forall e' \in E^j$ *then* $d(x^j, G^j_{e'})) > d^{ij}_{min}$ *for all* $e' \in E^j$ *where* E^j *is the edge set of* Σ_j *and* $G^j_{e'}$ *is a guard of* Σ_j *on edge* $e' \in E^j$. *Then* Σ *is STORMED.*

7. FINITE STORMED SIMULATION

In general it is not possible to compute the reach sets required by the iteration (1) exactly unless the underlying theory is decidable. The $\mathcal{H}_{ICD}||\mathcal{H}_{CA}$ closed loop is definable in $\mathcal{L}_{\exp}$, and the latter is not known to be decidable. Here we show that if an approximate reachability tool with definable over-approximations is available for the continuous dynamics, it can be used in (1) to yield a finite *simulation*. Since we only have a simulation, counter-examples on the abstraction should be validated in a CEGAR-like fashion.

Lemma 7.1. *Let* $\Sigma = (\mathcal{H}, \ldots)$ *be a SHS and* $\sim$ *an equivalence relation on* X. *For any mode* ℓ *of* $\mathcal{H}$, *the dynamical system* $\mathcal{D}$ *with state space* $X = \mathcal{H}.X$ *and set-valued flow* $\Theta(t;x) = \{y \in \mathbb{R}^n \mid ||y - \theta_\ell(t;x)||^2 \leq \epsilon^2\}$ *admits a finite simulation* $\mathcal{S}_\ell$ *that respects* $\sim$.

Let $\mathcal{F}^\epsilon_t(\mathcal{P}) := \cap_\ell \mathcal{S}_{\ell \in L}$ where $\mathcal{P} = X/\sim$. $\mathcal{F}^\epsilon_t$ refines all the $\mathcal{S}_\ell$'s, and it is a finite simulation of $\mathcal{H}$ by itself w.r.t. the continuous transition $\xrightarrow{\tau}$.

Theorem 7.1. *Let* $\mathcal{H}$ *be a STORMED hybrid system, and* $\mathcal{P}$ *be a finite definable partition of its state space. Define*

$$W_0 = \mathcal{F}^\epsilon_t(\mathcal{P}), \quad \forall i \geq 0, W_{i+1} = \mathcal{F}^\epsilon_t(\mathcal{F}_d(W_i)) \qquad (5)$$

Then there exists $U \in \mathbb{N}$ *s.t.* $W_{U+1} = W_U$ *and* $\mathcal{F}^\epsilon_t(W_U)$ *is a simulation of* $\mathcal{H}$ *by itself.*

This paper has presented the first formal models of ICD operation and shown that they admit finite bisimulations by proving new results in the theory of STORMED systems.

8. REFERENCES

[1] H. Abbas, K. J. Jang, Z. Jiang, and R. Mangharam. Model checking implantable cardioverter defibrillators. 2016. Arxiv 1512.08083.

[2] E. Bartocci, F. Corradini, M. D. Berardini, E. Entcheva, S. Smolka, and R. Grosu. Modeling and simulation of cardiac tissue using hybrid I/O automata. *Th. Com. Sci.*, 410(33), 2009.

[3] Boston Scientific Corporation. The Compass - Technical Guide to Boston Scientific Cardiac Rhythm Management Products. *Device Documentation*, 2007.

[4] T. Chen, M. Diciolla, M. Kwiatkowska, and A. Mereacre. Quantitative verification of implantable cardiac pacemakers over hybrid heart models. *Information and Computation*, 236:87 – 101, 2014.

[5] D. D. Correa de Sa, N. Thompson, J. Stinnett-Donnelly, P. Znojkiewicz, N. Habel, J. G. Muller, J. H. Bates, J. S. Buzas, and P. S. Spector. Electrogram fractionation. *Circ Arrhythm Electrophysiol*, 55:909 – 916, Dec 2011.

[6] R. Hood. The EP Lab. Accessed 10/20/2015.

[7] Z. Huang, C. Fan, A. Mereacre, S. Mitra, and M. Kwiatkowska. Invariant verification of nonlinear hybrid automata networks of cardiac cells. In A. Biere and R. Bloem, editors, *CAV*. 2014.

[8] M. A. Islam, R. DeFrancisco, C. Fan, R. Grosu, S. Mitra, and S. Smolka. Model checking tap withdrawal in c. elegans. In *HSB*. 2015.

[9] M. A. Islam, A. Murthy, A. Girard, S. A. Smolka, and R. Grosu. Compositionality results for cardiac cell dynamics. HSCC, 2014.

[10] R. Klabunde. *Cardiovascular electrophysiology concepts*. Lippincott-Williams, 2 edition, 2011.

[11] G. Lafferriere, G. J. Pappas, and S. Sastry. O-minimal hybrid systems. *Mathematics of Control, Signals and Systems*, 13(1):1–21, 2000.

[12] M. Pajic, Z. Jiang, I. Lee, O. Sokolsky, and R. Mangharam. Safety-critical medical device development using the upp2sf model translation tool. *ACM Trans. Embed. Comput. Syst.*, 13(4), 2014.

[13] P. S. Spector. Visible EP. Accessed 10/20/2015.

[14] P. S. Spector, N. Habel, B. E. Sobel, and J. H. Bates. Emergence of complex behavior: An interactive model of cardiac excitation provides a powerful tool for understanding electric propagation. *Circulation: Arrhythmia and Electrophysiology*, 4(4):586–591, 2011.

[15] V. Vladimerou, P. Prabhakar, M. Viswanathan, and G. Dullerud. Stormed hybrid systems. In *Automata, Languages and Programming*. 2008.

SL2SX Translator: From Simulink to SpaceEx Models *

Stefano Minopoli
Univ. Grenoble Alpes, VERIMAG
Centre Équation - 2, avenue de Vignate
38610 GIÉRES
stefano.minopoli@imag.fr

Goran Frehse
Univ. Grenoble Alpes, VERIMAG
Centre Équation - 2, avenue de Vignate
38610 GIÉRES
goran.frehse@imag.fr

ABSTRACT

The tool Matlab/Simulink is a numerical simulation environment that is widely used in industry for model-based design. Numerical simulation scales well and can be applied to systems with highly complex dynamics, but it is also inherently incomplete in the sense that critical events or behavior may be overlooked. The application of formal verification techniques to Simulink models could help to overcome this limitation. Set-based verification tools such as *SpaceEx* use as underlying formalism hybrid automata, which are semantically and structurally different from Simulink models. To address this issue, we are building the tool *SL2SX* for transforming a subset of the Simulink modeling language into a corresponding SpaceEx model. Our method is designed to preserve the syntactic aspects of a given Simulink diagram: the resulting SpaceEx model shows the same hierarchical structure and preserves the names of components and variables. Placeholders with the correct interface are provided for unsupported Simulink blocks, which can then be translated manually. We illustrate the tool *SL2SX* and the verification of the transformed models in SpaceEx on two examples provided by the Mathworks example library.

Keywords

Hybrid Systems; Hybrid Automata; Reachability Analysis; Numerical Analysis; Urgency; Simulink; SpaceEx

1. INTRODUCTION

Matlab/Simulink [18] is a software tool widely used in industry to model and simulate physical systems. For modeling, it provides a set of standard blocks from which one can hierarchically create a block diagram of the system. For simulating, it provides an extensive library of solvers, each of which determines the time of the next simulation step and applies a numerical method to solve the set of ordinary differential equations arising from the model. Different from simulation, formal verification can provide complete coverage, and hence it can be used to ensure whether or not a model meets a requirement. To apply formal verification techniques, it is necessary to switch from a *simulation model* to a *verification model*. Such a transformation needs to take into account the inherent differences between the two classes of models. Typically, a simulation model contains details that need to be abstracted away for the verification model. A verification model can be enriched with nondeterminism to check the system behavior for a whole range of parameters, disturbances, user inputs, etc. Simulink uses *must semantics*, also called *urgent* or *ASAP* semantics, meaning that a transition must be taken as soon as its guard is satisfied. Verification models, such as hybrid automata (HA), are typically defined with *may semantics*, in which the system can delay the transition as long as the invariant (staying condition) is satisfied. This may affect the quality of the model transformation, resulting in overapproximations, and the complexity of the model, resulting in state space explosion. Simulink lacks an actual formal description of its semantics. For the basic blocks one can resort to their ideal mathematical interpretation, but a wide variety of complex blocks is included in the standard Simulink library, many of which are beyond direct translation to functional models such as hybrid automata. Clearly, the process of translating a Simulink diagram into a verification model is not an easy task, and a fully automatic approach seems to be not plausible.

Verification tools like SpaceEx [10] use *Hybrid Automata (HA)* [11] as models and check safety properties using reachability algorithms. Our goal is to make the tool SpaceEx applicable to Matlab/Simulink models. The SpaceEx verification language is able to preserve the structure and the hierarchy of a Simulink diagram, using *basic* and *network* components (a single hybrid automaton and a network of them, respectively). Preserving the structure of the simulation model is not just a secondary aspect because, as described in [27], the structure has a profound impact on several aspects of safety-critical model development. In this paper, we present the tool *Simulink to SpaceEx Translator (SL2SX)* that takes a Simulink model (in xml format) as input, and generates a network of hybrid automata in a format compatible with *SpaceEx* verification tool. Since the SX format closely resembles the mathematical definition of hybrid automata (modulo template and parameter instantiations), SX models can be automatically translated

*The authors gratefully acknowledge financial support by the European Commission project UnCoVerCPS under grant number 643921.

HSCC '16, April 12–14, 2016, Vienna, Austria.
© 2016 ACM. ISBN 978-1-4503-3955-1/16/04. . . $15.00
DOI: http://dx doi org/10 1145/2883817 2883826

for other verification tools based on hybrid automata. The HyST translation tool [4] provides translations from SX to the verification tools Flow* [7], dReach [12], HyCreate [3], and HyComp / HyDI [9].

Our translation is based on the ideal interpretation of Simulink semantics [14]. The translation preserves all structural aspects of the Simulink diagram. Moreover, the translator preserves the names of blocks, variables, and components, as well as the graphical positions and dimensions of blocks. A restriction of our approach is that SpaceEx is currently limited to piecewise constant and piecewise affine dynamics. A theoretical discussion of handling Simulink must semantics can be found in [21, 22].

The translation process of *SL2SX* is not fully automatic, meaning that the SpaceEx model needs to be completed manually by adding hybrid automata to model blocks for which no translation is given. The list for supported blocks is continuously being extended and can be found in [19]. Currently it consists of practically all fundamental continuous-time, logical and arithmetical blocks and several blocks with discontinuous dynamics. The tool aids in the completion process by adding placeholders with proper interface for the missing blocks. Having the mechanical aspects of the model transformation being carried out by a tool reduces errors and results in a model that can be easily compared with the Simulink diagram, due to the preservation of structure and names of blocks and variables. The tool *SL2SX* together with models in this paper are available online [20].

A variety of different approaches to verify Simulink models have been reported in literature. The tools *HyLink* [15] and *GreAT* [1] translate a Simulink diagram into hybrid automaton expressed by intermediate formats (i.e. *hybrid input/output automata (HIOA)* [23] and *hybrid system interchange format (HSIF)* [24], respectively). Both formalisms are not able to model hierarchy and must semantics. The tool *Checkmate* [25] provides a Simulink toolbox containing additional blocks that the designer is allowed to use. A Simulink model thus obtained is then translated into the special class of *Polyhedra Invariant Hybrid Automata (PIHA)* [8]. The PIHA formalism uses ordinary differential equations (ODE) to express the dynamics, hyperplanes for guard transitions and only identity as update functions. Hierarchy can not be handled, and moreover the PIHA may semantics cause overapproximation when modeling must transitions. Other formalisms than hybrid automata are also used. In [26], the discrete part of a Simulink model is translated to a pushdown automaton defined by the *SAL transition system language* [5], while the differential equations arising from the Simulink component are converted into difference equations. The resulting model is a discretization of the original. The tool *S2H* [29] translates Simulink models into the *Hybrid CSP (HCSP)* formalism [13], based on the separation of variable definitions, process definitions, assertion definitions and goals to be proved. This results in a loss of compositional properties and the obtained model may be hard to compare with the original. The tool *HySon* [6], performs set-based simulation with "imprecise" or "uncertain" inputs directly on a Simulink model. The aim is to compute a good approximation of the set of all possible Simulink executions. Being based on numerical simulation methods, HySon is able to handle systems with both nonlinear dynamics and guards, and zero-crossing events are properly treated. We expect that for certain classes of systems, SpaceEx, whose algorithms are highly optimized for piecewise affine dynamics, can outperform the more general algorithm of HySon. A direct comparison is not possible since HySon is not publicly available.

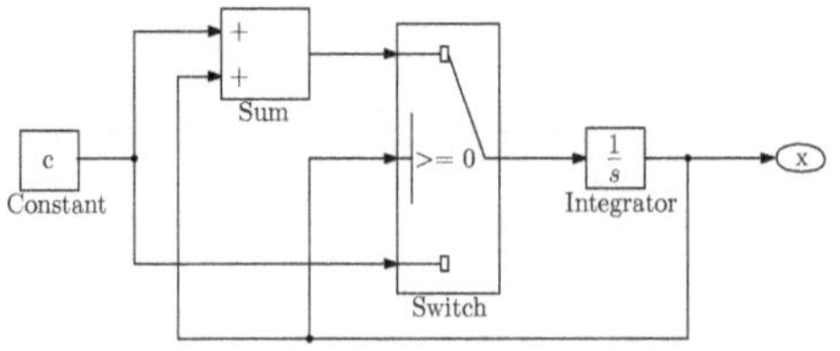

Figure 1: A Matlab/Simulink block diagram

2. SIMULINK, HYBRID AUTOMATA AND SPACEEX

We briefly introduce the modeling language of Simulink, the formalism of hybrid automata and the SpaceEx verification tool, highlighting the features relevant to the translation process.

2.1 Simulink Models

Simulink is an environment for simulation and model-based design for dynamic and embedded systems. It provides an interactive graphical environment and a customizable set of blocks that let one design, simulate, implement, and test a variety of time-varying systems. The modeling language lacks a formal and rigorous definition of its semantics, usually estimated by either the ideal or the numerical simulation interpretation [14]. A Simulink design is represented graphically as a diagram consisting of inter-connected Simulink blocks. It represents the time-dependent mathematical relationship between the inputs, states, and outputs of the design. Figure 1 depicts an example of Simulink diagram, whose signal that drives the switch blocks is modeled by the hybrid dynamics $\dot{x} = c + x$, when $x > 0$, and $\dot{x} = c$ otherwise.

The follows definition derives from [2]. A Simulink model $SL = \langle D, B, C\rangle$ consists of the following components:

- A set D of *variables*, partitioned into input variables D_I and output variables D_O.
- A set B of Simulink *blocks*. Each block $b \in B$ has inputs, outputs, and parameters. The input and output variables are associated with input and output ports. A Simulink block can be itself a Simulink Diagram; such a block is called a *subsystem*.
- An ordered relation $C \subseteq B \times B$ represents *connections* between blocks. A connection $c = \langle b, b'\rangle \in C$ connects an outport of b with an inport of b' and represent the flow of the data between the corresponding variables of b and b'.

Simulink uses *must semantics*, meaning that discrete events happen as soon as possible a given condition (guard) is satisfied (also referred as *urgent* or *as-soon-as-possible (ASAP)* semantics).

2.2 Hybrid Automata

Hybrid automata [11] are a verification modeling formalism that combines discrete states (modeled by locations)

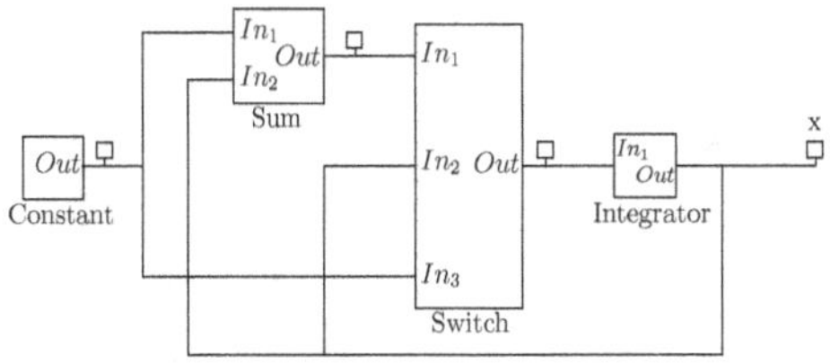

(a) network component

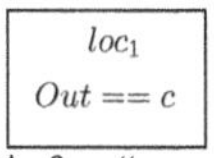

(b) HA for "constant"

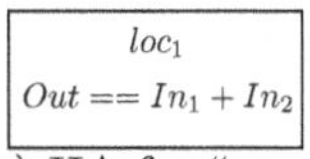

(c) HA for "sum"

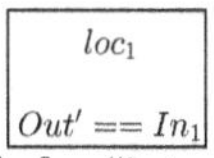

(d) HA for "integrator"

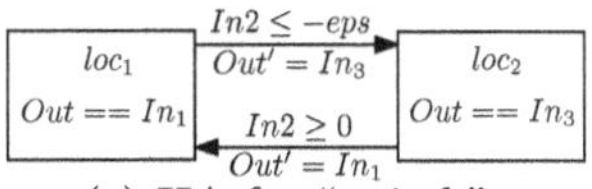

(e) HA for "switch"

Figure 2: SpaceEx model for the Simulink diagram in Figure 1

with continuously evolving, real-valued variables. The discrete states and the transitions from one state to another are described with a finite state-transition system. A change in discrete state can update the continuous variables and modify the set of differential equations that describes how variables evolve with time. Hybrid automata are nondeterministic, which means that different futures may be available from any given state. Rates of change or variable updates can be described by providing bounds instead of fixed numbers. Incomplete knowledge about initial conditions, perturbations, parameters, etc. can easily be captured in this way. A specific source of nondeterminism is due to the *may semantics.* This means that a transition may happen at any time the associated guard is satisfied, but it may also be delayed as long as the invariant (staying condition) of the discrete state is satisfied. Hybrid automata with urgency conditions allow the definition of a urgency condition for each location. A must transition can be easily encoded by adding its guard as urgent condition to the source location. For the class of LHA, an exact reachability algorithm is available [21].

2.3 SpaceEx

SpaceEx is a development platform for verification algorithms based on hybrid automata. The SpaceEx verification engine provides specific reachability algorithms, called *scenarios*, and each of them may come with its own set representation, apply to its own class of models, and produce a different kind of output. The scenarios include a formally exact algorithm for piecewise constant dynamics (PHAVer), two variations of template-based approximate reachability algorithms for piecewise affine dynamics (LGG and STC), and a simulation algorithm that mimics reachability analysis by random sampling of the initial states.

A SpaceEx model is similar to the standard hybrid automata, syntactically extended with hierarchy and templates. A SpaceEx model consists of one or more *components*. Each component has a set of *formal parameters*, like *continuous variables*, *constants*, and synchronization labels. A formal parameter is part of the *interface* of a component, unless it is declared as *local* to the component. There are two types of components: *Base Components* correspond to a single hybrid automaton, and *Network Components* allow the instantiation one or more components (base or other network components), possibly assigning values to their constants. A network component is a parallel composition of its subcomponents. When instantiating a component A in network B, one must specify what happens to each of the formal parameters in its interface. This is called a *bind.* Every formal parameter of A must be bound to either a formal parameter of B or to a numeric value. Components inside B can be connected by binding their variables to the same symbols in B. Because of the acausal semantics, the variables binding does not distinguish source and destination (non-oriented connection). Figure 2(a) depicts a SpaceEx model of the Simulink model in Figure 1, whose components are the hybrid automata in Figures 2(b)–2(e).

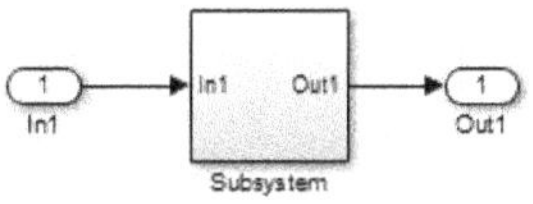

(a) Simulink subsystem

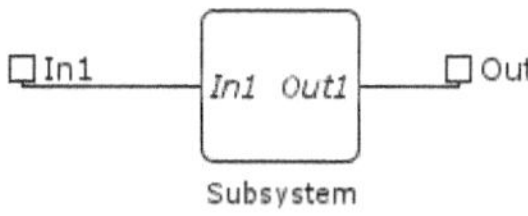

(b) SX component

Figure 3: The translation from a Simulink subsystem to an SX component preserves the interface

Formally, a SpaceEx model $SX = (Comp, Bind)$ has

- a set $Comp$ of SpaceEx *components*, partitioned into the set $Comp_b$ of basic components and the set $Comp_n$ of network components. Each component $b \in Comp$ has a set of formal parameters, including a set of variables Var_b. For lack of space, we omit the discussion about synchronization labels and local variables.
- a relation $Bind \subseteq Comp_n \times Comp$ that associates each network component with a set of components (including other networks components). Each variable of a component associated to a network, is also a variable of the network. For each $(n, c) \in Bind$, a mapping $Map_{n,c} : Var_c \to Var_n$ associates to each basic variable a network variable.

3. FROM SIMULINK TO SPACEEX

The translator analyzes a Simulink model $SL = \langle D, B, C \rangle$ and produces a SpaceEx model $SX = (Comp, Bind)$. B is the set of Simulink blocks and C the set of connections between blocks. Each basic Simulink block (i.e., not a subsystem) is associated to a SpaceEx basic component, while each subsystem is modeled by a network component. Simulink connections are expressed by mapping related variables. Because Simulink connections are oriented, while SpaceEx mappings are not, this task requires some additional considerations as explained in Section 3.3.

An unsupported block is represented by a placeholder with the correct interface. The placeholder is a basic component, with all the necessary variables and mappings, consisting of an empty hybrid automaton.

3.1 Translating Blocks

For each block $b_i \in B$, such that b_i is not a subsystem, an inport or an outport, the translator adds to the set $Comp_b$ the corresponding SpaceEx basic component (an hybrid automaton) with the same name of b_i. For each input and output of b_i a variable is added to Var_b. If b_i is an inport or an outport, then the translator adds to the network component containing b_i a corresponding variable with the same name.

A continuous Simulink block is represented by a hybrid automaton with a single location, where the algebraic constraints are included in the invariant and any ODEs are included in the flow. If the Simulink block contains different modes, e.g., the switch block, each mode is represented by a location, and urgent transitions with appropriate guard conditions model the switching. SpaceEx allows only nonstrict guards for urgent transitions, since strict urgent guards are ill defined in continuous time. For example, consider the trajectory $x(t) = t$. A transition that must be taken as soon as $x(t) > 0$ makes sense in the discrete time steps taken by a simulator, but in dense time there is no earliest point at which $x(t) > 0$. We use the numerical interpretation of the Simulink semantics, which corresponds to the set of traces generated by the simulation engine through numerical interpretation. Under this interpretation, similarly to the *guard enlargement* considered by *Almost ASAP* semantics [28], a strict guard can be relaxed and scaled according to the minimum difference d between the values that variables may assume before and after an integration step. Clearly, d depends on the time step δ. Theorem 1 in [14] guarantees that as δ approaches to zero, the numerical interpretation converges to the ideal interpretation. Moreover, d converges to the machine epsilon *eps*. A strict guard of the form $x > 0$ (resp., $x < 0$) is translated into a nonstrict guard of the form $x \geq eps$ (resp., $x \leq -eps$).

3.2 Translating Subsystems

For each subsystem block $b \in B$, we add to the set $Comp_n$ a network component with the same name. In this case, the translator keeps track of the Simulink blocks b_i that belong to b. Then, for each b_i that is not an inport or an outport, the bind (b, b_i) is added to the set *Bind*. Semantically, the block is translated to the parallel composition of the hybrid automata from its subcomponents. Note that SpaceEx carries out the parallel composition on the fly, so that only reachable locations are instantiated. This typically avoids the construction of the full product automaton, which can be prohibitively large.

3.3 Translating Block Connections

Once components are added to the network, it is necessary to decode the set of block connections C. The main issue for this task is due to the acausal semantics of SpaceEx, where connections among variables are not oriented. Let $c_{ij} = (b_i, b_j) \in C$ be a Simulink connection that links the output of the *source* block b_i to the input of the *destination* block b_j, inside subsystem b_s and let b'_i, b'_j and b_n be the SpaceEx components used to model b_i, b_j and b_s, respectively, and Out_i and In_j be the variables used to model source and destination of c_{ij}. By definition of SpaceEx model, $Map_{n,i}$ contains the mapping between Out_i of b'_i and Out_i of b_n, while $Map_{n,j}$ contains the mapping between In_j of b'_j and In_j of b_n. To model c_{ij} it is necessary to map Out_i and In_j to the same variable. This is done by mapping the destination variable to the source variable. If the source Out_i is connected to many destinations In_z (i.e. there exists at least another $c_{iz} = (b_i, b_z) \in C$), the translator replaces each mapping in Map_{nz} that involves variable In_z,

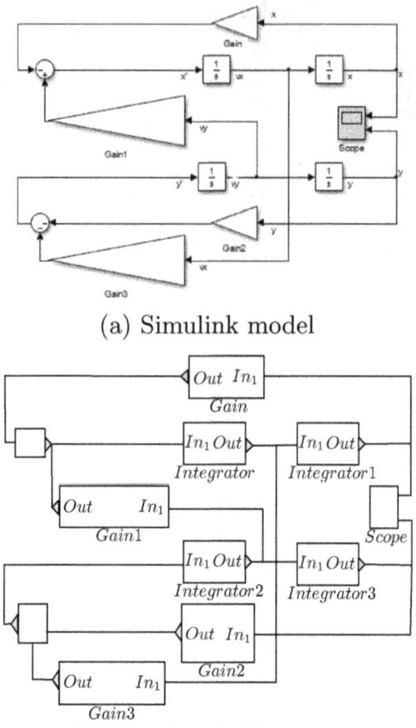

(a) Simulink model

(b) translated SX model

Figure 4: Models for the Foucault pendulum.

by the mapping between In_z and Out_i. This technique does not preserve the names of variables that model outports, which is one of our goals. An outport can be only a destination, and hence the corresponding variable will be replaced by the variable that corresponds to the source. In order to fix this issue, an additional step replaces, for each mapping $Map_{n,i}(Out_i) = Out_j$ such that Out_i is an outport, all the mappings $Map_{n,z}(x) = Out_j$ by $Map_{n,z}(In_z) = Out_i$, where x is a variable that models a source. At the end of this task, all variables Out_i modeling outports appear in the network interface. The block interface is therefore preserved, as illustrated in Figure 3.

4. CASE STUDIES

We illustrate the translation with two Simulink models from the Mathworks examples library. The obtained SpaceEx models are then verified with respect to certain properties by using a standard laptop. Initial states are not shown in related figures, but they are part of configuration files produced by the tool.

4.1 Foucault Pendulum

Figure 4(a) shows a Simulink model of a Foucault pendulum, taken from the Mathworks examples library [16]. The *SL2SX* translator produces a complete SpaceEx model, shown in Figure 4(b), without manual intervention.

The translator also extracts simulation parameters from the Simulink file and stores them in a configuration file for SpaceEx. Figures 5(a) and 5(b) show simulation runs obtained by Simulink and SpaceEx, starting from an initial pendulum length of $x = 0.67$.

To demonstrate the results of a reachability analysis with SpaceEx, we relax the initial condition to the interval $x \in$

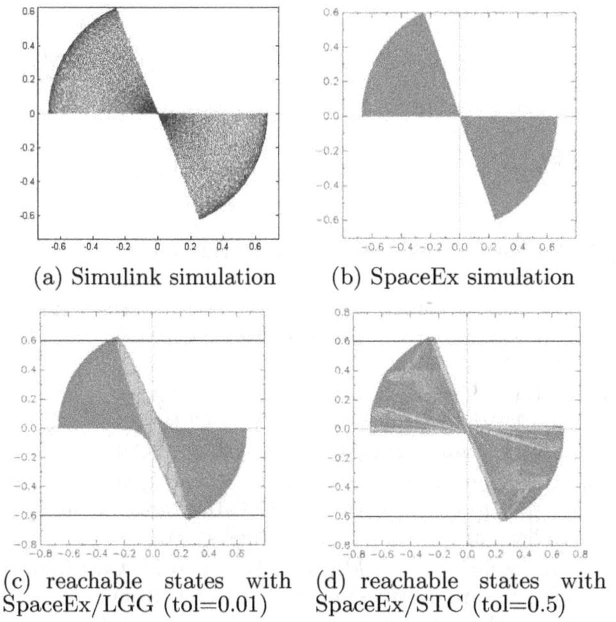

(a) Simulink simulation (b) SpaceEx simulation

(c) reachable states with SpaceEx/LGG (tol=0.01) (d) reachable states with SpaceEx/STC (tol=0.5)

Figure 5: Simulation and reachability analysis for the position of the Foucault Pendulum

[0.669, 0.671]. We show the overapproximation obtained by running two different analysis algorithms of SpaceEx. Figure 5(c) shows the output of the LGG algorithm for a flowpipe tolerance of 0.01, and Figure 5(d) shows the result of the STC algorithm for a flowpipe tolerance of 0.5. Both sets are obtained with bounding box template directions and bounding the time horizon in the model to 6 hours. The LGG scenario takes 8.1 seconds, while the STC scenario takes 5.4 seconds.

4.2 Automotive Suspension

Figure 6 shows a simplified half car model for Simulink, taken from [16]. The model is a hybrid system, since it includes two step blocks. Figure 6(a) shows the main Simulink diagram, while Figure 6(b) depicts the Simulink subsystem that models the suspension.

The *SL2SX* translator produces an incomplete SX model, since the Simulink model includes blocks that are currently unsupported (i.e. step, mux and demux). The user needs to remove the components for mux and demux, and directly map the involved variables. This requires the introduction of an input variable for all components connected to the mux input. Then these variables are mapped to the variables that model the source connection of the mux. Figure 6(c) shows the SX main system after modeling (removing and variables mapping) the mux/demux blocks. The user also needs to build a hybrid automaton to model the unsupported step block. Such manual completions are not necessarily very involved; a simple model for the step block is shown in Figure 9.

Figure 7 shows simulations from Simulink and SpaceEx, with step time set to 0.01 and with the front pitch initially at zero. Figure 8 shows the reachable states for the vertical bounce over a time horizon of 10 seconds, starting with a front pitch in the interval [0, 0.3]. The LGG algorithm takes 0.55 sec and the STC algorithm 0.41 sec.

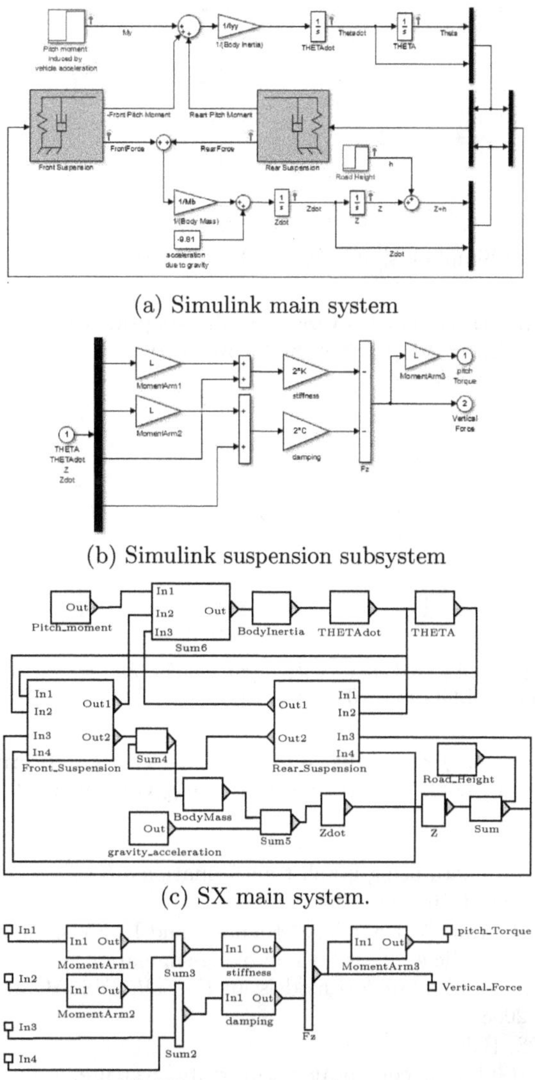

(a) Simulink main system

(b) Simulink suspension subsystem

(c) SX main system.

(d) SX suspension subsystem

Figure 6: A half car model

5. CONCLUSIONS AND FUTURE WORK

The *SL2SX* translation tool takes care of the mechanical, but error-prone, aspects of constructing a hybrid automaton model from a Simulink source. The resulting model preserves the structure and basic graphics, and provides placeholders for components that need to be completed manually. The SX model format closely resembles the standard hybrid automaton formalism. It can be read directly by the verification platform SpaceEx, and fully automatic translations to a variety of tools are already available via the translation tool HyST [4].

Future work will be directed at providing support for more blocks from various Simulink libraries, as well as translating Stateflow components [17].

6. REFERENCES

[1] A. Agrawal, G. Simon, and G. Karsai. Semantic translation of simulink/stateflow models to hybrid

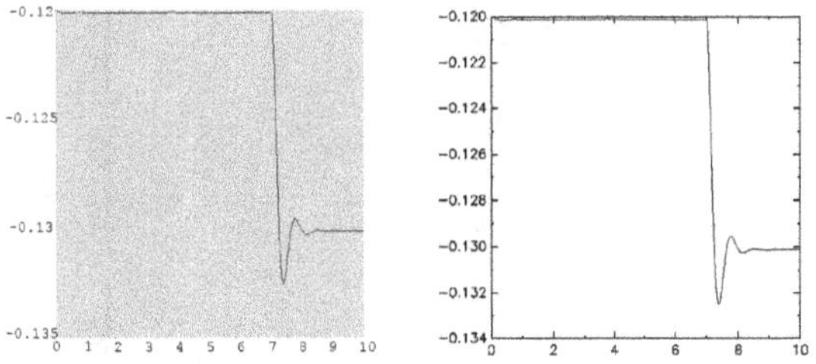

(a) Simulink simulation. (b) SpaceEx simulation.

Figure 7: Vertical bounce for the suspension models, with the front pitch initially at zero

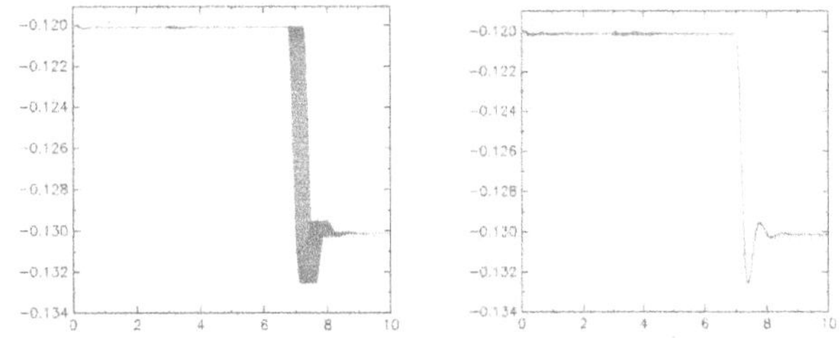

(a) reachable states with SpaceEx/LGG (tol=0.001) (b) reachable states with SpaceEx/STC (tol=0.001)

Figure 8: Reachable states of the vertical bounce, starting with the front pitch in a given interval

automata using graph transformations. *ENTCS*, 109:43–56, Dec. 2004.

[2] R. Alur, A. Kanade, S. Ramesh, and K. Shashidhar. Symbolic analysis for improving simulation coverage of simulink/stateflow models. In *EMSOFT'08*. ACM, 2008.

[3] S. Bak. stanleybak.com/projects/hycreate/hycreate.html.

[4] S. Bak, S. Bogomolov, and T. T. Johnson. HYST: a source transformation and translation tool for hybrid automaton models. In *HSCC'15*, 2015.

[5] S. Bensalem, V. Ganesh, Y. Lakhnech, C. Muñoz, S. Owre, H. Rueß, J. Rushby, V. Rusu, H. Saïdi, N. Shankar, E. Singerman, and A. Tiwari. An overview of SAL. In *LFM'00*. NASA Langley Research Center, 2000.

[6] O. Bouissou, S. Mimram, and A. Chapoutot. Hyson: Set-based simulation of hybrid systems. In *Rapid System Prototyping (RSP'12)*, 2012.

[7] X. Chen, E. Ábrahám, and S. Sankaranarayanan. Flow*: An analyzer for non-linear hybrid systems. In *CAV'13*, 2013.

[8] A. Chutinan and B. Krogh. Verification of polyhedral-invariant hybrid automata using polygonal flow pipe approximations. In *HSCC'99*. 1999.

[9] A. Cimatti, A. Griggio, S. Mover, and S. Tonetta. HyComp: An SMT-based model checker for hybrid systems. In *TACAS'15*, 2015.

[10] G. Frehse, C. L. Guernic, A. Donzé, S. Cotton, R. Ray, O. Lebeltel, R. Ripado, A. Girard, T. Dang, and O. Maler. SpaceEx: Scalable verification of hybrid systems. In *CAV'11*, 2011.

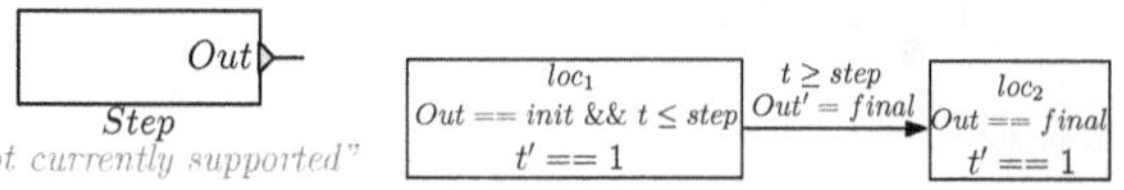

(a) placeholder (b) manually completed HA model

Figure 9: Example unsupported block: Step

[11] T. Henzinger. The theory of hybrid automata. In *LICS'96*, 1996.

[12] S. Kong, S. Gao, W. Chen, and E. M. Clarke. dReach: δ-reachability analysis for hybrid systems. In *TACAS'15*, 2015.

[13] J. Liu, J. Lv, Z. Quan, N. Zhan, H. Zhao, C. Zhou, and L. Zou. A calculus for hybrid CSP. In *Programming Languages and Systems*. 2010.

[14] K. Manamcheri. *Translation of Simulink/Stateflow models to hybrid automata*. PhD thesis, Graduate College of the University of Illinois, 2011.

[15] K. Manamcheri, S. Mitra, S. Bak, and M. Caccamo. A step towards verification and synthesis from simulink/stateflow models. In *HSCC '11*, 2011.

[16] Mathworks. Simulink examples library. mathworks.com/help/simulink/examples/.

[17] MathWorks. Mathworks stateflow: Design and simulate state machines, Sept. 2012. mathworks.fr/products/stateflow/.

[18] MathWorks. Mathworks simulink: Simulation et model-based design, Mar. 2014. www.mathworks.fr/products/simulink.

[19] S. Minopoli. SL2SX tool. http://www-verimag.imag.fr/~minopoli/sl2sx.html.

[20] S. Minopoli and G. Frehse. SL2SX tool and case study. www-verimag.imag.fr/~minopoli/SL2SXdemo.zip.

[21] S. Minopoli and G. Frehse. Non-convex invariants and urgency conditions on linear hybrid automata. In *FORMATS'14*, 2014.

[22] S. Minopoli and G. Frehse. From simulation models to hybrid automata using urgency and relaxation. In *HSCC'16*, 2016.

[23] S. Mitra. *A verification framework for hybrid systems*. PhD thesis, Massachusetts Institute of Technology, Cambridge, September 2007.

[24] MoBIES-team. HSIF semantics. Technical report, University of Pennsylvania, 2002.

[25] B. Silva, K. Richeson, B. H. Krogh, and A. Chutinan. Modeling and verification of hybrid dynamical system using checkmate. In *ADPM*, 2000.

[26] A. Tiwari. Formal semantics and analysis methods for Simulink Stateflow models. Technical report, SRI International, 2002.

[27] M. W. Whalen, A. Murugesan, S. Rayadurgam, and M. P. E. Heimdahl. Structuring simulink models for verification and reuse. In *MiSE'14*, 2014.

[28] M. Wulf, L. Doyen, and J.-F. Raskin. Almost asap semantics: From timed models to timed implementations. In *HSCC'04*. 2004.

[29] L. Zou, N. Zhany, S. Wang, M. Franzle, and S. Qin. Verifying simulink diagrams via a hybrid hoare logic prover. In *EMSOFT'13*, 2013.

SCOTS: A Tool for the Synthesis of Symbolic Controllers

Matthias Rungger
Hybrid Control Systems Group
Technical University of Munich
matthias.rungger@tum.de

Majid Zamani
Hybrid Control Systems Group
Technical University of Munich
zamani@tum.de

ABSTRACT

We introduce SCOTS a software tool for the automatic controller synthesis for nonlinear control systems based on symbolic models, also known as discrete abstractions. The tool accepts a differential equation as the description of a nonlinear control system. It uses a Lipschitz type estimate on the right-hand-side of the differential equation together with a number of discretization parameters to compute a symbolic model that is related with the original control system via a feedback refinement relation. The tool supports the computation of minimal and maximal fixed points and thus natively provides algorithms to synthesize controllers with respect to invariance and reachability specifications. The atomic propositions, which are used to formulate the specifications, are allowed to be defined in terms of finite unions and intersections of polytopes as well as ellipsoids. While the main computations are done in C++, the tool contains a Matlab interface to simulate the closed loop system and to visualize the abstract state space together with the atomic propositions. We illustrate the performance of the tool with two examples from the literature. The tool and all conducted experiments are available at www.hcs.ei.tum.de

Keywords

Symbolic Models; Discrete Abstractions; Feedback Refinement Relations; C++/Matlab Toolbox

1. INTRODUCTION

In recent years, controller synthesis techniques based on so-called *symbolic models* or *discrete abstractions* have received considerable attention within the control systems community, see e.g. [1–13]. Following those methods, it is possible to synthesize correct-by-construction controllers for general nonlinear systems to enforce complex specifications formulated for example in linear temporal logic (LTL).

This work was supported in part by the German Research Foundation (DFG) grant ZA 873/1-1.

HSCC'16, April 12 - 14, 2016, Vienna, Austria

ISBN 978-1-4503-3955-1/16/04...$15.00

DOI: http://dx.doi.org/10.1145/2883817.2883834

There exist numerous theories [1–13] that account for a great variety of different control system dynamics as well as specifications. The dynamics range from simple double integrators [5], over linear [1, 3, 8, 11] and piecewise affine systems [10] to nonlinear [4, 6, 7, 9, 12] and stochastic control systems [2, 13]. The specifications range from reach-avoid specifications [2, 4, 6, 7, 9, 13] and safety [4, 7, 11] specification, over reactivity fragments of LTL [5, 8, 12] to full LTL [1, 3, 10]. Additionally, there exist various software tools such as Pessoa [14], CoSyMA [15], LTLMoP [16], and TuLiP [17] were some of the previously mentioned theories are implemented.

In this paper, we introduce SCOTS, yet another software tool for the synthesis of symbolic controllers, i.e. controllers based on symbolic models. Similar to Pessoa and CoSyMA the tool supports the computation of abstractions of nonlinear control systems. LTLMoP and TuLiP are more restrictive in that respect and accept merely simple integrator dynamics and piecewise affine control systems, respectively. Moreover, the tool provides algorithms for the computation of minimal and maximal fixed points and thus, again similar to Pessoa and CoSyMA, natively supports the controller design to enforce invariance and reachability (time-bounded reachability for CoSyMA) specifications. More complex specifications like GR(1) [18], which are supported by LTLMoP and TuLiP, are currently not natively available in SCOTS.

The differences between Pessoa, CoSyMA, and SCOTS become apparent in terms of the *type* of symbolic model which is used to solve the synthesis problem. CoSyMA requires the original system to be incrementally stable [19] and computes symbolic models that are *approximately bisimilar* to the original system. Pessoa, additionally to approximately bisimilar symbolic models, supports the computation of *approximately alternatingly similar* symbolic models [4]. Approximate alternating simulation relations, compared to approximate bisimulation relations, are a one-sided notion of system relations and the symbolic model can be constructed without stability assumptions [9]. The symbolic models created by SCOTS are based on *feedback refinement relations*, a novel notion of system relation that was recently introduced in [20]. Although the computation of symbolic models based on approximate alternating simulation relations and feedback refinement relations are similar cf. [20, Chapter VIII] and [9], the controller refinement procedure differs. Specifically, the controller based on feedback refinement relations requires quantized state information only, as opposed to exact state information. Moreover, the controller does not require to include the abstraction as a building block [20].

Both properties are essential for a practical implementation of the controller.

From an implementation point of view `SCOTS` is close to `Pessoa` and `CoSyMA`. All three tools use boolean functions to represent the atomic propositions as well as the transition relations of the symbolic models and employ binary decision diagrams [21] as underlying data structures to store and manipulate the boolean functions. Specifically, all three tools use the `CUDD` binary decision diagram library [22]. Even though binary decision diagrams provide a memory efficient way to represent symbolic models, they result in a considerable computation-time overhead when it comes to the construction of the boolean functions. A similar observation is reported in [15] and `CoSyMA` offers hash tables as an alternative data structure.

2. SYMBOLIC CONTROLLER SYNTHESIS

We provide a short introduction to the solution of control problems based on symbolic models as developed in [20]. In general the notation should be self-explanatory. However, in case of any ambiguity, the reader is referred to [20, Sec. II].

In our framework, a system is defined as *simple system*, which is a triple $S = (X, U, F)$, where the *state alphabet* X and *input alphabet* U are non-empty sets and the *transition function* $F : X \times U \rightrightarrows X$ is a set-valued map [23]. The behavior $\mathcal{B}(S)$ consists of the set of the signals (x, u), with *state signal* $x : [0; T[\to X$ and *input signal* $u : [0; T[\to U$, that satisfy the transition function F for all $t \in [0; T-1[$. If T is finite then $F(x(T-1), u(T-1)) = \varnothing$ must hold. Any subset $\Sigma \subseteq (X \times U)^{[0;T[}$, $T \in \mathbb{N} \cup \{\infty\}$ constitutes a *specification* for S. Subsequently, we focus mostly on specifications on state signals, in which case we omit the input signals and consider $\mathcal{B}(S)$ and Σ as subsets of $X^{[0;T[}$, $T \in \mathbb{N} \cup \{\infty\}$. A system S and a specification Σ (for S) constitute a *control problem* (S, Σ). A *controller* C, which is itself a system that is *feedback composable* with S, *solves* the control problem (S, Σ) if the closed loop behavior satisfies $\mathcal{B}(C \times S) \subseteq \Sigma$. We use $U_S(x) = \{u \in U \mid F(x, u) \neq \varnothing\}$ to denote the set of *admissible inputs*. The interested reader is referred to [20] for the precise definitions of the various terms and objects.

A symbolic controller synthesis scheme as it is implemented in `SCOTS` proceeds, roughly speaking, in three steps. First, given a control problem (S_1, Σ_1), a finite simple system S_2 as a substitute of S_1, together with an *abstract specification* Σ_2 is computed. In this context S_1 and S_2 are often referred to as *plant* and *symbolic model*, respectively. In the second step, a *controller* C_2, i.e., system that is feedback composable with S_2, which solves the control problem (S_2, Σ_2) is computed. Provided that the synthesis process of C_2 is successful, the controller C_2 is *refined* to a controller C_1 that solves the original problem (S_1, Σ_1) in the third step.

The correctness of this approach is guaranteed by relating the plant $S_1 = (X_1, U_1, F_1)$ with its symbolic model $S_2 = (X_2, U_2, F_2)$ via a *feedback refinement relation* $Q \subseteq X_1 \times X_2$. Here it is assumed that $U_2 \subseteq U_1$ and every pair $(x_1, x_2) \in Q$ satisfies two conditions (see [20, Def. V.2] for details):

1. $U_{S_2}(x_2) \subseteq U_{S_1}(x_1)$ and
2. $u \in U_{S_2}(x_2) \implies Q(F_1(x_1, u)) \subseteq F_2(x_2, u)$ holds.

A distinct feature of the utilization of feedback refinement relations in a symbolic controller synthesis scheme is the particular simple refinement step, in which the refined controller C_1 for the plant S_1 is naturally obtained from the abstract controller C_2 by using the relation Q as *quantizer* to map the plant states x_1 to abstract states $x_2 \in Q(x_1)$. The refinement scheme is illustrated in Fig. 1.

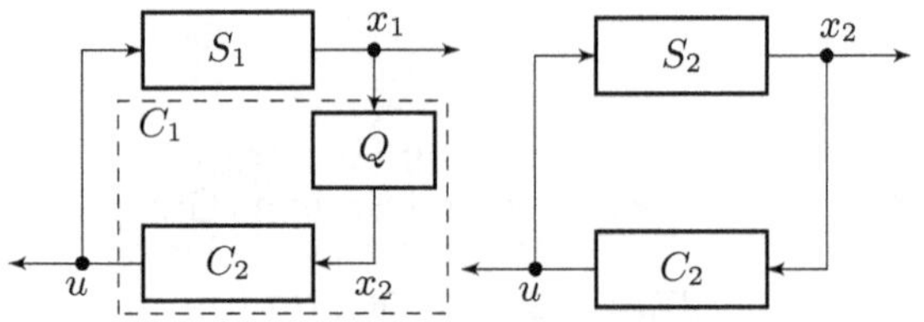

Figure 1: Refined closed loop (left) and abstract closed loop (right).

2.1 Computation of symbolic models

`SCOTS` supports the computation of symbolic models of the sampled behavior of perturbed control systems of the form

$$\dot{\xi}(t) \in f(\xi(t), u) + [\![-w, w]\!] \tag{1}$$

where f is given by $f : \mathbb{R}^n \times U \to \mathbb{R}^n$ and $U \subseteq \mathbb{R}^m$. We assume that the set U is non-empty and $f(\cdot, u)$ is continuously differentiable for every $u \in U$. The vector $w = [w_1, \ldots, w_n] \in \mathbb{R}^n_+$ is a perturbation bound and $[\![-w, w]\!]$ denotes the hyper-interval $[-w_1, w_1] \times \ldots \times [-w_n, w_n]$. Additionally to the perturbations on the right-hand-side of (1), we consider measurement errors, with bound $z \in \mathbb{R}^n_+$, which we model by a set-valued map $P \colon \mathbb{R}^n \rightrightarrows \mathbb{R}^n$,

$$P(x) = x + [\![-z, z]\!]. \tag{2}$$

Let $\tau > 0$ be the sampling time. Formally, we represent the τ-sampled behavior of the control system (1) as simple system $S_1 = (X_1, U_1, F_1)$, with $X_1 = \mathbb{R}^n$, $U_1 = U$ and F_1 is implicitly defined by $x' \in F_1(x, u)$ iff there exists a solution ξ of (1) under input $u \in U$ so that $\xi(0) = x$ and $x' = \xi(\tau)$.

The construction of a symbolic model of S_1 is based on the over-approximation of attainable sets. To this end, we use the notion of a growth bound introduced in [20]. A *growth bound* of (1) is a function $\beta \colon \mathbb{R}^n_+ \times U' \to \mathbb{R}^n_+$, which is defined with respect to a sampling time $\tau > 0$, a set $K \subseteq \mathbb{R}^n$ and a set $U' \subseteq U$. Basically, it provides an upper bound on the deviation of solutions ξ of (1) from *nominal solutions*[1] φ of (1), i.e., for every solution ξ of (1) on $[0, \tau]$ with input $u \in U'$ and $\xi(0), p \in K$, we have

$$|\xi(\tau) - \varphi(\tau, p, u)| \leq \beta(|\xi(0) - p|, u). \tag{3}$$

Here, $|x|$ for $x \in \mathbb{R}^n$, denotes the component-wise absolute value. A growth bound can be obtained essentially by bounding the Jacobian of f. Let $L \colon U' \to \mathbb{R}^{n \times n}$ satisfy

$$L_{i,j}(u) \geq \begin{cases} D_j f_i(x, u) & \text{if } i = j, \\ |D_j f_i(x, u)| & \text{otherwise} \end{cases} \tag{4}$$

for all $x \in K' \subseteq \mathbb{R}^n$ and $u \in U' \subseteq U$. Then

$$\beta(r, u) = e^{L(u)\tau} r + \int_0^\tau e^{L(u)s} w \, ds,$$

is a growth bound on $[0, \tau]$, K, U' associated with (1). The domain K' on which (4) needs to hold, is assumed to be convex and contain any solution ξ on $[0, \tau]$ of (1) with $u \in U'$

[1]A nominal solution $\varphi(\cdot, p, u)$ of (1) is defined as solution of the initial value problem $\dot{x} = f(x, u)$, $x(0) = p$.

and $\xi(0) \in K$, see [20, Thm. VIII.5]. Note that β is obtained by evaluating the solution of the initial value problem

$$\dot{\zeta}(t) = L(u)\zeta(t) + w, \quad \zeta(0) = r. \tag{5}$$

In the computation of a symbolic model S_2 of S_1 we restrict our attention to the case in which X_2 forms a cover of the state alphabet X_1 where the elements of the cover X_2 are non-empty, closed hyper-intervals, subsequently, referred to as *cells*. Specifically, we work with a subset $\bar{X}_2 \subseteq X_2$ of congruent cells that are aligned on a uniform grid

$$\eta\mathbb{Z}^n = \{c \in \mathbb{R}^n \mid \exists_{k\in\mathbb{Z}^n} \forall_{i\in[1;n]}\ c_i = k_i\eta_i\} \tag{6}$$

with *grid parameter* $\eta \in (\mathbb{R}_+ \smallsetminus \{0\})^n$, i.e.,

$$x_2 \in \bar{X}_2 \implies \exists_{c\in\eta\mathbb{Z}^n}\ x_2 = c + [\![-\eta/2, \eta/2]\!]. \tag{7}$$

The remaining cells $X_2 \smallsetminus \bar{X}_2$ are considered as "overflow" symbols, see [6, Sect III.A]. The symbolic model of S_1 is given by $S_2 = (X_2, U_2, F_2)$ where U_2 is a finite subset of U_1 and $F_2(x_2, u) = \varnothing$ for all $x_2 \in X_2 \smallsetminus \bar{X}_2$. For the remaining cells $x_2 \in \bar{X}_2$, the transition function is computed according to Alg. 1. For a correct implementation, the growth bound β needs to be defined w.r.t. $\tau > 0$, $\cup_{x_2\in\bar{X}_2} P(x_2)$, and U_2.

Algorithm 1 Computation of $F_2 : \bar{X}_2 \times U_2 \rightrightarrows \bar{X}_2$

Require: $\bar{X}_2$, U_2, β, φ, z, $r = \eta/2$, τ
for all $c + [\![-r, r]\!] \in \bar{X}_2$ and $u \in U_2$ **do**
  $r' := \beta(r + z, u)$
  $c' := \varphi(\tau, c, u)$
  $A := \{x_2' \in X_2 \mid (c' + [\![-r' - z, r' + z]\!]) \cap x_2' \neq \varnothing\}$
  if $A \subseteq \bar{X}_2$ **then**
    $F_2(x_2, u) := A$
  else
    $F_2(x_2, u) := \varnothing$

Using a similar line of reasoning as in [20, Thm. VIII.4], we can show that $Q' = Q \circ P$ with $Q \subseteq X_1 \times X_2$ defined by $(x_1, x_2) \in Q$ iff $x_1 \in x_2$, is a feedback refinement relation from S_1 to S_2. It follows that a refined controller from an abstract controller is robust w.r.t. the measurement errors P, see [20, Thm. VI.4].

2.2 (Abstract) Specifications

Currently, SCOTS supports the synthesis of controllers to enforce reachability and invariance (often referred to safety) specifications [4]. Given a simple system $S_1 = (X_1, U_1, F_1)$ let $X_1^\infty = \cup_{T\in\mathbb{N}\cup\{\infty\}} X_1^{[0;T[}$. A *reachability* specification associated with $I_1, Z_1 \subseteq X_1$ is defined by

$$\Sigma_1 = \{x_1 \in X_1^\infty \mid x_1(0) \in I_1 \implies \exists_{t\in[0;T[} : x_1(t) \in Z_1\}.$$

An *invariance* specification associated with I_1, Z_1 follows by

$$\Sigma_1 = \{x_1 \in X_1^{[0;\infty[} \mid x_1(0) \in I_1 \implies \forall_{t\in[0;\infty[} : x_1(t) \in Z_1\}.$$

SCOTS supports two classes of sets to define I_1 and Z_1:

- polytopes $R = \{x \in \mathbb{R}^n \mid Hx \leq h\}$ parameterized by $H \in \mathbb{R}^{q\times n}$, $h \in \mathbb{R}^q$, and
- ellipsoids $E = \{x \in \mathbb{R}^n \mid |L(x - y)|_2 \leq 1\}$ parameterized by $L \in \mathbb{R}^{n\times n}$ and $y \in \mathbb{R}^n$, where $|\cdot|_2$ denotes the Euclidean norm.

Consider the plant S_1, the symbolic model S_2 and the relations Q, P as defined in the previous subsections. Let Σ_1 be a reachability (invariant) specification associated with I_1 and Z_1. An abstract specification Σ_2 for S_2 is simply obtained as reachability (invariant) specification associated with I_2 and Z_2, where I_2 is an outer approximation of I_1, i.e., $x_1 \in I_1$ implies $Q \circ P(x_1) \subseteq I_2$ and Z_2 is an inner approximation, i.e., $x_2 \in Z_2$ implies $P^{-1} \circ Q^{-1}(x_2) \subseteq Z_1$.

2.3 Synthesis via fixed point computations

For the synthesis of controllers C to enforce reachability, respectively, invariance specifications, SCOTS provides two fixed point algorithms. Consider $S_2 = (X_2, U_2, F_2)$ with X_2 finite and $I_2, Z_2 \in X_2$. For $Y_2 \subseteq X_2$, we define the map

$$\text{pre}(Y_2) = \{x_2 \in X_2 \mid \exists_{u\in U_{S_2}(x_2)} F_2(x_2, u_2) \subseteq Y_2\}.$$

Consider the functions

$$\check{G}(Y) = \text{pre}(Y) \cup Z_2 \quad \text{and} \quad \hat{G}(Y) = \text{pre}(Y) \cap Z_2.$$

SCOTS supports the minimal fixed point computation of $\check{G}$ and the maximal fixed point computation of $\hat{G}$. Let us shortly recall how we can extract a controller from a fixed point computation.

Suppose we are given a reachability problem (S_2, Σ_2), i.e., Σ_2 is a reachability specification for S_2 associated with I_2 and Z_2. Let Y_∞ denote the minimal fixed point of $\check{G}$ and consider the sets $Y_0 = \varnothing$, $Y_{i+1} = \check{G}(Y_i)$ obtained in the fixed point iteration. Let $j(x) = \inf\{i \in \mathbb{N} \mid x \in Y_i\}$. Then we derive a controller as a system according to [20, Def. III.1] (ver. 2) by $C = (\{q\}, \{q\}, X_2, X_2, U_2, F_c, H_c)$ with

$$H_c(q, x_2) = \begin{cases} H_c'(x_2) \times \{x_2\} & \text{if } x_2 \in Y_\infty \\ U_2 \times \{x_2\} & \text{otherwise} \end{cases}$$

$$F_c(q, x_2) = \begin{cases} \{q\} & \text{if } x_2 \in Y_\infty \\ \varnothing & \text{otherwise} \end{cases}$$

where $H_c'(x_2) = \{u \in U_{S_2}(x_2) \mid F_2(x_2, u) \subseteq Y_{j(x_2)-1}\}$.

To solve an invariance problem (S_2, Σ_2), i.e., Σ_2 is in an invariance specification associated with I_2 and Y_2, we compute the maximal fixed point Y_∞ of $\hat{G}(\cdot)$. The controller is identical to the reachability controller with the difference that H_c' is set to $H_c'(x_2) = \{u \in U_{S_2}(x_2) \mid F_2(x_2, u) \subseteq Y_\infty\}$ if $x_2 \in Y_\infty$ and otherwise to $H_c'(x_2) = U_2$.

For both cases, it is well known that C_2 solves the control problem (S_2, Σ_2) iff $I_2 \subseteq Y_\infty$, see e.g. [4]. Also for both types of specifications the controller is *memoryless* or *static*.

3. TOOL DETAILS

In this section we describe the architecture of SCOTS. The C++ part of the software tool provides the algorithms to compute the symbolic model and to compute the minimal and maximal fixed points. The algorithms are basically distributed across three classes:

- `SymbolicSet`
- `SymbolicModel > SymbolicModelGrowthBound`
- `FixedPoint`

3.1 SymbolicSet

The class `SymbolicSet` is used to define the symbolic state space $\bar{X}_2$ (excluding the overflow symbols), the symbolic input space U_2, and the atomic propositions such as the target set or safe set $Z_2 \subseteq \bar{X}_2$. It accepts the state space dimension n, the grid parameter $\eta \in \mathbb{R}_+^n$ and a compact hyper-rectangle $[\![a, b]\!]$, $a, b \in \mathbb{R}^n$, $a \leq b$ as input. Optionally, the measurement error bound $z \in \mathbb{R}_+^n$ as given in (2) can be provided. The default value is set to $z = 0$. We use the `SymbolicSet` to represent a subset of the grid points in $[\![a, b]\!] \cap \eta\mathbb{Z}^n$. Initially, the set is empty and one should use the various methods of the `SymbolicSet` like `addGridPoints`, `addPolytope`, `remPolytope`, `addEllipsoid` or `remEllipsoid` to add and remove grid points to the symbolic set. Each command (except the `addGridPoints`) accepts the option `INNER` and `OUTER` whose usage is as follows.

Suppose we want to add grid points associated with the set $R = \{x \in \mathbb{R}^n \mid Hx \leq h\}$. In order to add the set $\{p \in [\![a, b]\!] \cap \eta\mathbb{Z}^n \mid p + [\![-\eta/2 - z, \eta/2 + z]\!] \cap R \neq \varnothing\}$ we pick `OUTER` as option in `addPolytope`. If we pick `INNER`, the set $\{p \in [\![a, b]\!] \cap \eta\mathbb{Z}^n \mid p + [\![-\eta/2 - z, \eta/2 + z]\!] \subseteq R\}$ is added. Similarly, for an ellipsoid $\{x \in \mathbb{R}^n \mid |L(x - y)|_2 \leq 1\}$ with $L \in \mathbb{R}^{n \times n}$ and $y \in \mathbb{R}^n$, the outer and inner approximations are determined by $\{p \in [\![a, b]\!] \cap \eta\mathbb{Z}^n \mid |L(p - y)|_2 \leq 1 + r\}$ and $\{p \in [\![a, b]\!] \cap \eta\mathbb{Z}^n \mid |L(p - y)|_2 \leq 1 - r\}$, respectively, where $r = \max_{x \in [\![-\eta/2 - z, \eta/2 + z]\!]} |Lx|_2$.

Technically, we interpret the map $H'_c : Z_\infty \rightrightarrows U_2$ as a subset of $\bar{X}_2 \times U_2$ and represent the controller function H'_c also as `SymbolicSet`. To this end, we can instantiate a `SymbolicSet` with two instances of a `SymbolicSet` with parameters $n, \eta, [\![a, b]\!]$ and $m, \mu, [\![c, d]\!]$, where $n, \eta, [\![a, b]\!]$ and $m, \mu, [\![c, d]\!]$ are the parameters associated with $\bar{X}_2$ and U_2. respectively.

Any instance of a `SymbolicSet` set can be written with all the relevant information to a file. Such a file can be loaded within the C++ library as well as within Matlab. In that way one can use Matlab's build-in functions not only to visualize various entities like atomic propositions and the domain of the controller, but also to simulate the closed loop.

We use binary decision diagrams (BDDs) [21] as underlying data structure. Specifically we use the object oriented wrapper to the `CUDD` library [22].

3.2 SymbolicModel

The class `SymbolicModel` is the base class of `SymbolicModelGrowthBound`. The base class manages BDD related information, such as number and indices of BDD variables. Alg. 1 to compute $S_2 = (X_2, U_2, F_2)$ using growth bounds is implemented in the class `SymbolicModelGrowthBound` which requires the ordinary differential equations (1) and (5) as inputs. In our case studies, we use a Runge-Kutta scheme.

3.3 FixedPoint

The `FixedPoint` class is instantiated with an instance of a `SymbolicModel` and provides two methods `minimalFixedPoint` and `maximalFixedPoint` for the fixed point computation of $\check{G}$ and $\hat{G}$. The input to those methods is a BDD that represents the set Z_2. The outputs are two BDDs, one represents the fixed point and one the map H'_c. The results can be stored to file by first, adding the BDDs to the appropriate instances of a `SymbolicSet` and second, using the `writeToFile` method provided by `SymbolicSet`.

The general work flow with the different user inputs and the possible tool output is illustrated in Fig. 2.

4. NUMERICAL EXPERIMENTS

The tool and all details of the conducted experiments can be found at www.hcs.ei.tum.de

4.1 A path planning problem

As a first example we consider a path planning problem, also considered in [20] and [9], for the bicycle dynamics of a

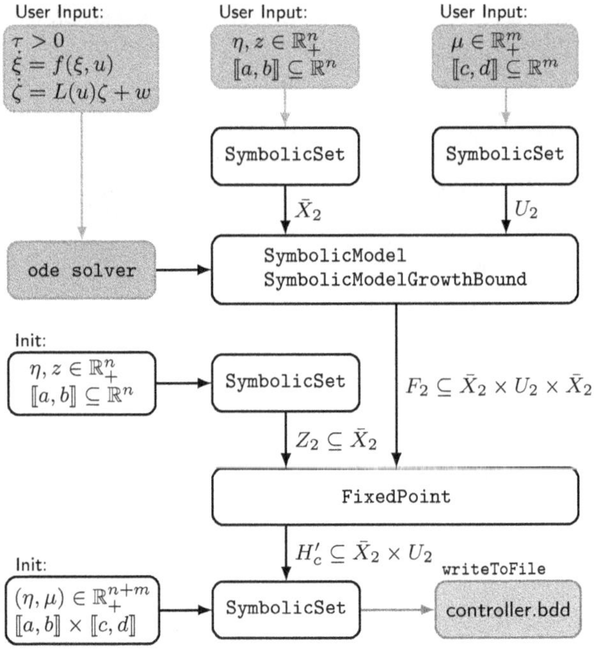

Figure 2: The work flow in SCOTS to compute a symbolic model $S_2 = (X_2, U_2, F_2)$ of the sampled system S_1 associated with (1) and to synthesize a controller to enforce an invariance (reachability) specification where $Z_2 \subseteq \bar{X}_2$ is the safe (target) set.

vehicle. The control system consists of a 3-dimensional state space and a 2-dimensional input space. The states (x_1, x_2) and x_3 correspond to the position, respectively, orientation of the vehicle in the 2-dimensional plane. The inputs are given by the velocity and steering angle. There are no measurement errors or perturbations present. The objective is to steer the robot from a given initial position (green dot) to a target set (red rectangle) while avoiding the obstacles (blue rectangles), see Fig. 3. The precise control problem can be found in [20].

In order to use `SCOTS` we create a C++ file `vehicle.cc` in which we include, among other, the cudd library `cuddObj.hh` and the header-only classes `SymbolicSet.hh`, `SymbolicModelGrowthBound.hh` and `FixedPoint.hh`. We begin with the definition of the dynamics and the growth bound. For example, to provide the nominal solution φ for Alg. 1 we write

```
typedef std::array<double,3> state_t; /* state type */
typedef std::array<double,2> input_t; /* input type */
auto vehicle_post = [](state_t &x, input_t &u) {
  /* the ode describing the vehicle dynamics */
  auto rhs =[](state_t& xx, const state_t &x, const input_t &u) {
    double alpha=std::atan(std::tan(u[1])/2.0);
    xx[0] = u[0]*std::cos(alpha+x[2])/std::cos(alpha);
    xx[1] = u[0]*std::sin(alpha+x[2])/std::cos(alpha);
    xx[2] = u[0]*std::tan(u[1]);
  };
  size_t nint=5; /* number of intermediate steps */
  double h=0.06; /* h*nint = sampling time */
  ode_solver(rhs,x,u,nint,h); /* runge kutte solver */
};
```

Subsequently, we define the uniform grids for the sets $\bar{X}_2$ and U_2 as `SymbolicSet`. To define $\bar{X}_2$ on the hyper-rectangle $[\![lb, ub]\!]$ with grid parameter η we write

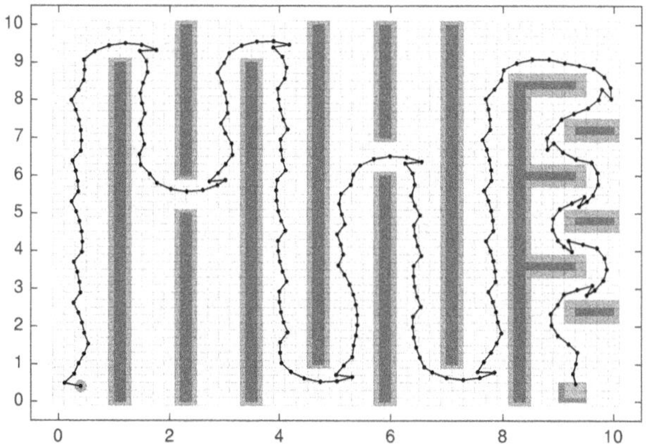

Figure 3: The green dot, the dark blue, and dark red rectangles correspond to the original specifications. The light blue cells are added to the overflow symbols in X_2 and the light red cells are used to define the abstract reachability specification.

```
double lb[3]={0,0,-M_PI-0.4}; /* lower bounds */
double ub[3]={10,10,M_PI+0.4}; /* upper bounds */
double eta[3]={.2,.2,.2}; /* grid parameter */
scots::SymbolicSet ss(mgr,3,lb,ub,eta); /* the uniform grid */
ss.addGridPoints(); /* fill the SymbolicSet */
```

At first the **SymbolicSet** is empty. In the last line we add all grid points contained in $[\![lb, ub]\!]$ to **ss**. It is possible to account for the obstacles by adding them to the overflow symbols, i.e., we remove an outer approximation from **ss**. To remove an obstacle we write, for appropriately defined $H \in \mathbb{R}^{4\times 3}$ and $h \in \mathbb{R}^4$

```
/* remove outer approximation of P={ x | H x <= h } from ss */
ss.remPolytope(4,H,h,scots::OUTER);
```

Similarly, we remove all the other obstacles and define a **SymbolicSet ts** to represent the target Z_2. The computation of the transition function F_2 is implemented by

```
scots::SymbolicModelGrowthBound<state_t,input_t> abs(&ss, &is);
abs.computeTransitionRelation(vehicle_post, radius_post);
```

and the minimal fixed point is computed by

```
scots::FixedPoint reach(&abs);
/* the fixed point algorithm operates directely on BDD's */
BDD target = ts.getSymbolicSet(); /* extract the BDD from ts */
BDD fp; /* the fixed point is stored in fp */
BDD con; /* the controller is stored in con */
reach.minimalFixedPoint(target, fp, con);
```

We store the controller to **vehicle_controller.bdd** by

```
scots::SymbolicSet controller(ss,is);
controller.setSymbolicSet(con);
controller.writeToFile("vehicle_controller.bdd");
```

In order to load the controller in Matlab and to get the inputs associated with a state x we use

```
>> con=SymbolicSet('vehicle_controller.bdd');
>> u=controller.getInputs(x);
```

After we compiled and executed the C++ program, we simulated the controlled vehicle in Matlab. A closed loop trajectory is illustrated in Fig. 3.

A comparison of **SCOTS** with **Pessoa** and the tool developed at the University of Federal Armed Force (UniBW) in Munich (*which is not publicly available*), is listed in Tab. 1. The table contains (apart from the CPU type) the number $\#F_2$ of elements in the transition relation F_2, the time t_{abs} spent to compute the symbolic model and the time t_{syn} spent to solve the abstract synthesis problem. We conducted two experiments. In **SCOTS** #1, we accounted for the obstacles in the synthesis part. To this end, we implemented a modified minimal fixed point computation so that we can solve reach-avoid problems. In this case $\bar{X}_2$ also contains the obstacles. While in **SCOTS** #2, we added an outer approximation of the obstacles (as described above) to the overflow symbols in X_2, which results in a smaller $\bar{X}_2$ and, hence, a smaller number of transitions.

	CPU [GHz]	$\#F_2$	t_{abs}[sec]	t_{syn}[sec]
Pessoa	Core2Duo 2.4	34020088	13509	535
SCOTS #1	i7 3.5	37316812	100	413
UniBW	i7 2.9	28398299	2.33	0.22
SCOTS #2	i7 3.5	18991758	53	210

Table 1: Comparison of SCOTS with numbers reported in [9] and [20].

Unsurprisingly, **SCOTS** outperforms **Pessoa** in terms of the computation times for the symbolic model. This stems from the fact that in **Pessoa** (at least for the nonlinear case) the computation is partly implemented in C/C++ and partly implemented in Matlab, which causes a large overhead. While the difference in the synthesis times is explainable by the different CPUs. The UniBW tool outperforms both **Pessoa** and **SCOTS** with respect to both computation times. We believe that the difference in t_{abs} is mainly due to the large overhead that the management (accessing, iterating over, adding, and removing elements) of the BDD data structure requires, see also [15] for a similar observation. Additionally to the efficient data structure and contrary to the iterative implementation of the minimal fixed point in **SCOTS** and **Pessoa**, the UniBW tool uses a Dijkstra like algorithm [24] and is therefore able to drastically reduce t_{syn}.

4.2 DC-DC boost converter

In this case study, we synthesize a controller for a DC-DC boost converter to enforce a invariance specification. The DC-DC boost converter is modeled by a switched system with two modes, with a 2-dimensional linear dynamics in each mode. The system is incrementally stable and therefore, amenable to the construction of approximately bisimilar symbolic models, see [19] for details. We solve the synthesis problem using **SCOTS** as well as **Pessoa**. The domain of the controller, synthesized using **SCOTS**, together with a closed trajectory is illustrated in Fig. 4. We run **Pessoa** with two option #1 and #2. For option #1 we computed an approximately bisimilar symbolic model, which results in a deterministic transition function. For option #2, we computed an approximately alternatingly similar symbolic model, whose computation is based on attainable sets and therefore closer to the symbolic model obtained with **SCOTS**. The run times of various computations are listed in Tab. 2. Surprisingly, **SCOTS** outperforms **Pessoa** in terms of the construction of the symbolic model, even though, contrary to the nonlinear case, all the computations are implemented in C. In the last row of Tab. 2 we list the numbers reported in [15] (t_{abs} is not listed in [15]). Again we can observe the substantial overhead induced by the BDD usage compared

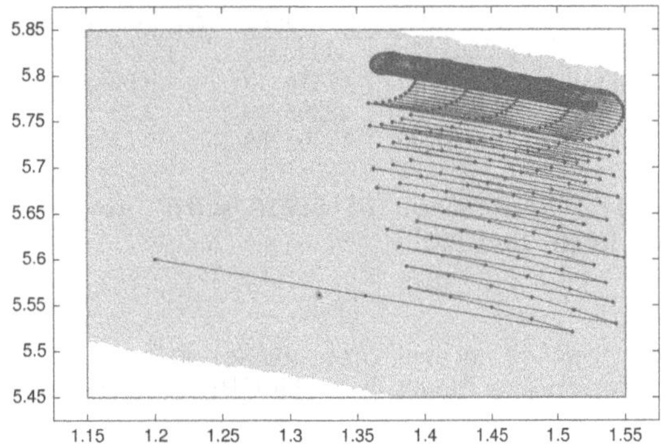

Figure 4: The domain of the invariance controller.

	CPU [GHz]	t_{abs}[sec]	t_{syn}[sec]
Pessoa #1	i7 3.5	478.7	65.2
Pessoa #2	i7 3.5	934.4	91.1
SCOTS	i7 3.5	18.1	75.4
CoSyMA	–	–	8.32

Table 2: Comparison of SCOTS, Pessoa and [15].

to the hash tables in CoSyMA.

5. CONCLUSION

In this paper we introduced SCOTS, a software tool to synthesize controllers for nonlinear control systems based on symbolic models. Contrary to other available tools, it supports the construction of symbolic models in the framework of feedback refinement relations and therefore facilitates a rather straightforward controller refinement procedure [20]. We illustrated by two examples from the literature the effectiveness of the tool by synthesizing controllers for invariance and reachability problems. For those experiments, we could observe a reduction of the time complexity compared to Pessoa, whose implementation similar to SCOTS is based on BDDs. On the other hand, we observed substantial longer run times compared to tools that uses alternative data structures, e.g. hash tables in CoSyMA. Hence, for the future we plan to incorporate such alternatives in SCOTS and investigate the various approaches not only in terms of time complexity but also with respect to memory usage. Additionally, we plan to exploit symbolic and/or automatic differentiation and nonlinear optimization methods to support the user in finding tight Lipschitz matrices that are needed in the computation of growth bounds.

6. REFERENCES

[1] P. Tabuada and G. J. Pappas. "Linear Time Logic Control of Discrete-Time Linear Systems". In: *IEEE TAC* 51 (2006), pp. 1862–1877.

[2] A. Abate et al. "Computational approaches to reachability analysis of stochastic hybrid systems". In: *HSCC*. Springer, 2007, pp. 4–17.

[3] M. Kloetzer and C. Belta. "A fully automated framework for control of linear systems from temporal logic specifications". In: *IEEE TAC* 53 (2008), pp. 287–297.

[4] P. Tabuada. *Verification and Control of Hybrid Systems – A Symbolic Approach.* Springer, 2009.

[5] G. E. Fainekos et al. "Temporal logic motion planning for dynamic robots". In: *Automatica* 45 (2009), pp. 343–352.

[6] G. Reißig. "Computing abstractions of nonlinear systems". In: *IEEE TAC* 56 (2011), pp. 2583–2598.

[7] A. Girard. "Controller synthesis for safety and reachability via approximate bisimulation". In: *Automatica* 48 (2012), pp. 947–953.

[8] T. Wongpiromsarn, U. Topcu, and R. M. Murray. "Receding Horizon Temporal Logic Planning". In: *IEEE TAC* 57 (2012), pp. 2817–2830.

[9] M. Zamani et al. "Symbolic Models for Nonlinear Control Systems Without Stability Assumptions". In: *IEEE TAC* 57 (2012), pp. 1804–1809.

[10] B. Yordanov et al. "Temporal logic control of discrete-time piecewise affine systems". In: *IEEE TAC* 57 (2012), pp. 1491–1504.

[11] M. Rungger, M. Jr. Mazo, and P. Tabuada. "Specification-Guided Controller Synthesis for Linear Systems and Safe Linear-Time Temporal Logic". In: *HSCC*. ACM, 2013, pp. 333–342.

[12] J. Liu et al. "Synthesis of Reactive Switching Protocols From Temporal Logic Specifications". In: *IEEE TAC* 58 (2013), pp. 1771–1785.

[13] M. Zamani et al. "Symbolic control of stochastic systems via approximately bisimilar finite abstractions". In: *IEEE TAC* 59.12 (2014).

[14] M. Jr. Mazo, A. Davitian, and P. Tabuada. "Pessoa: A tool for embedded controller synthesis". In: *Computer Aided Verification*. Springer. 2010, pp. 566–569.

[15] S. Mouelhi, A. Girard, and G. Gössler. "CoSyMA: a tool for controller synthesis using multi-scale abstractions". In: *HSCC*. ACM. 2013, pp. 83–88.

[16] C. Finucane, G. Jing, and H. Kress-Gazit. "LTLMoP: Experimenting with language, temporal logic and robot control". In: *IROS*. IEEE. 2010, pp. 1988–1993.

[17] T. Wongpiromsarn et al. "TuLiP: a software toolbox for receding horizon temporal logic planning". In: *HSCC*. ACM. 2011, pp. 313–314.

[18] N. Piterman, A. Pnueli, and Y. Saár. "Synthesis of reactive (1) designs". In: *Verification, Model Checking, and Abstract Interpretation*. 2006.

[19] A. Girard, G. Pola, and P. Tabuada. "Approximately bisimilar symbolic models for incrementally stable switched systems". In: *IEEE TAC* 55.1 (2010), pp. 116–126.

[20] G. Reißig, A. Weber, and M. Rungger. *Feedback Refinement Relations for the Synthesis of Symbolic Controllers*. 2015. arXiv: 1503.03715v1.

[21] R. E. Bryant. "Symbolic Boolean manipulation with ordered binary-decision diagrams". In: *ACM Computing Surveys* 24.3 (1992), pp. 293–318.

[22] F. Somenzi. "CUDD: CU decision diagram package". In: *University of Colorado at Boulder* (1998).

[23] R. T. Rockafellar and R. J.-B. Wets. *Variational analysis*. Vol. 317. 3rd corr printing 2009. Springer, 1998.

[24] G. Gallo et al. "Directed hypergraphs and applications". In: *Discrete Applied Mathematics* 42 (1993), pp. 177–201.

Safety Analysis of Automotive Control Systems Using Multi-Modal Port-Hamiltonian Systems

Siyuan Dai
Institute for Software-Integrated Systems
Vanderbilt University
Nashville, TN, USA
siyuan.dai@vanderbilt.edu

Xenofon Koutsoukos
Institute for Software-Integrated Systems
Vanderbilt University
Nashville, TN, USA
xenofon.koutsoukos@vanderbilt.edu

ABSTRACT

Safety analysis is important when designing and developing cyber-physical systems (CPS). An autonomous vehicle can be described as a complex CPS where the physical dynamics of the vehicle interact with the control systems. The challenge is ensuring safety despite nonlinearities, hybrid dynamics, and disturbances as well as complex cyber-physical interactions. In this paper, we present an approach for the safety analysis of automotive control systems using multi-modal port-Hamiltonian systems (PHS). The approach uses the Hamiltonian function to represent the energy of the safe and unsafe states and employs passivity to prove that trajectories that begin in safe regions cannot enter unsafe regions. We first apply the approach to the safety analysis of a longitudinal vehicle dynamics composed with an adaptive cruise control (ACC) system. We then extend the results to the safety analysis of a combined longitudinal and lateral vehicle dynamics composed with an ACC and lane keeping control (LKC) system. Simulation results are presented to demonstrate the approach.

1. INTRODUCTION

An autonomous vehicle is an example of a complex cyber-physical system (CPS) containing physical dynamics and controllers controlling the speed and steering of the vehicle [17]. An adaptive cruise control (ACC) system controls the speed of the vehicle and is a hybrid system operating in two modes, throttle control mode where the throttle angle is determined and brake control mode where the brake pressure is determined. A lane keeping control (LKC) system controls the angle of the steering wheel in order to maintain a desired position on the road. Safe operation is an important requirement for a vehicle equipped with an ACC and LKC system.

The design of the ACC and LKC systems must ensure that the host vehicle can safely navigate roads. The appearance of a lead vehicle provides an additional constraint for the ACC in that the host vehicle maintains a desired speed depending on the behavior of the lead vehicle. A lead vehicle which suddenly decelerates creates a safety problem for the host vehicle. The ACC design on the host vehicle must guarantee that the distance between the lead and host vehicle stay above a minimum threshold. Turns and curves provide constraints for the LKC in that the host vehicle must maintain a position in the center of the road. Large road curvatures create skidding problems for the host vehicle. The ACC and LKC design on the host vehicle must guarantee that the lateral acceleration does not exceed a maximum threshold. The challenge considered in this paper is to prove the safety of an automotive control system consisting of ACC and LKC despite the nonlinearities, hybrid dynamics, and disturbances present in the system.

The contribution of this paper is an approach for the safety analysis of CPS such as automotive control systems. The dynamics of the vehicle and the control systems are described using port-Hamiltonian systems (PHS) which gives the approach the benefit of compositionality. Hybrid behavior is characterized using multi-modal PHS. The approach represents the safe states of the system using a bounded from above energy level of the Hamiltonian function. Similarly, the unsafe states of the system are represented using a bounded from below energy level of the Hamiltonian function. Passivity is used to prove that as long as the safe and unsafe energy regions do not overlap, trajectories that begin within a lower energy level (safe states) cannot terminate within a higher energy level (unsafe states). The approach can be applied to any system described as a multi-modal PHS.

We evaluate the approach by analyzing the safety conditions for two systems. First, we assume a straight road and consider the longitudinal dynamics and the ACC. We derive safety conditions for the ACC which ensure that the host vehicle does not collide with a lead vehicle. Second, we assume a curved road and consider the interactions between the longitudinal dynamics, lateral dynamics, ACC, and LKC. We derive safety conditions for the ACC and LKC which ensure that the host vehicle does not collide with a lead vehicle and skid off of the road. We use the vehicle parameters, disturbances, and safety conditions to select control parameters so that the closed-loop system is safe. In order to validate the approach, we present simulation results by implementing the closed-loop system using Simulink [9] and CarSim [2].

The rest of the paper is organized as follows. Section 2 presents the related work. Section 3 presents the energy-based safety analysis approach applied to multi-modal PHS. Section 4 applies the safety analysis approach to the longi-

HSCC'16, April 12-14, 2016, Vienna, Austria
© 2016 ACM. ISBN 978-1-4503-3955-1/16/04...$15.00
DOI: http://dx.doi.org/10.1145/2883817.2883845

tudinal dynamics of the vehicle composed with the ACC system. Section 5 extends the results of Section 4 by including the lateral dynamics and LKC system. Section 6 presents the simulation results which show that the closed-loop system is safe. The paper is concluded in Section 7.

2. RELATED WORK

The theory of PHS is presented in detail in [5]. A PHS consists of a set of ports (control, interaction, resistive, and storage) interconnected through a power-conserving Dirac structure [18]. PHS have significant implications for passivity, which has been studied extensively for control design and analysis of nonlinear systems [8]. An important property of PHS is compositionality, where component PHS compose with each other through the interaction ports of their respective Dirac structures. PHS provide a compositional framework for modeling complex physical lumped-parameter systems [3].

Barrier certificates, which are similar in structure to Lyapunov functions, are typically used for the purpose of validating nonlinear systems with uncertainties [10]. The use of barrier certificates allows for the validation of a larger class of continuous-time nonlinear models, including differential-algebraic systems with uncertain inputs [16]. Barrier certificates are functions which denote that there are no state trajectories starting from a given set of initial conditions that end up in an unsafe region [14].

Barrier certificates are also extended to guarantee safety of hybrid systems [11]. These barrier certificates are functions of both continuous and discrete states. To prove the safety of a hybrid system, a barrier certificate is constructed from a set of continuous state functions where each function corresponds to a discrete state. Each continuous state function needs to satisfy the barrier certificate inequalities in the invariant of the corresponding discrete mode in order to guarantee the safety of the hybrid system. The work presented in this paper is inspired by the concept of barrier certificates, using the Hamiltonian function as a barrier between safe and unsafe states. In contrast to a barrier certificate, the Hamiltonian function is derived from the model.

As the number of controllers added to automobiles increase, automotive CPS become more complex and rigorous engineering methods are needed to ensure safety [15]. Control barrier functions have been used in a control design approach demonstrated for ACC and place constraints on the host vehicle's acceleration and deceleration [1]. They balance the objectives of maintaining a desired host vehicle velocity and a relative distance above a minimum threshold.

The computation of barrier certificates is challenging and often computationally expensive [12]. If the dynamic equations of the system are described as polynomial functions, a sum of squares programming method can be used to approximate the barrier certificates by characterizing state regions as semi-algebraic sets and using semi-definite programming to obtain the optimal solution [13]. The method is restrictive because the dynamic equations of many physical systems cannot be described as polynomial functions.

The approach presented in this paper can be applied to systems with nonlinearities and hybrid dynamics because safety is characterized by the Hamiltonian function and the PHS structure. The inherent passive property of PHS yields the safety conditions and allows the Hamiltonian function to function as a barrier certificate.

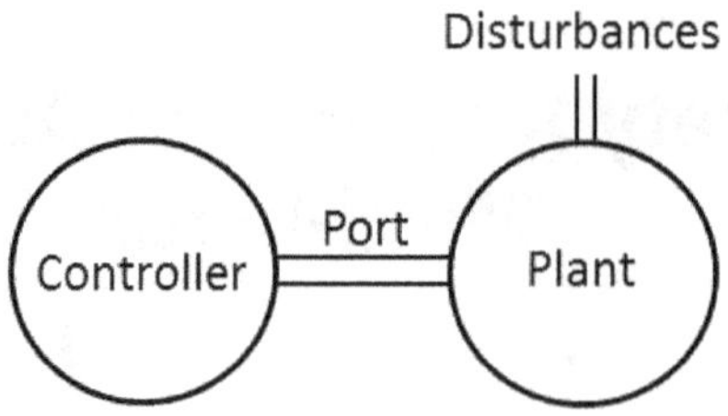

Figure 1: Generic plant system (with disturbances) and control system

3. SAFETY ANALYSIS APPROACH

The idea of the approach is to use the energy of the system as conditions and constraints in order to show the safety property of the system. We consider the plant and controller dynamics described by multi-modal PHS. We use the dynamic equations and Hamiltonian functions to derive the dynamic equations and Hamiltonian function of the closed-loop system. We characterize the initial and unsafe regions using the energy of the Hamiltonian function and show that the system trajectory cannot enter the unsafe region.

3.1 Multi-Modal PHS

Figure 1 provides a diagram of a generic multi-modal PHS of a plant system with disturbances connected to a control system via power ports. Given a plant system with a Hamiltonian function $H_p(x_p)$, continuous states $x_p \in X_p \subseteq \mathbb{R}^{n_p}$, discrete states $s_p \in S_p$, disturbances $\delta \in \mathbb{R}^o$, and a control system a Hamiltonian function $H_c(x_c)$, continuous states $x_c \in X_c \subseteq \mathbb{R}^{n_c}$, and discrete states $s_c \in S_c$, where $\{n_p, n_c, o\} \in \mathbb{N}^4$, we can write the set of dynamic equations of the closed-loop system as an input-state-output multi-modal PHS with Hamiltonian function $H(x) = H_p(x_p) + H_c(x_c)$, continuous states $x = \begin{bmatrix} x_p & x_c \end{bmatrix}^\mathsf{T} \in X = X_p \times X_c$, discrete states $s = \begin{bmatrix} s_p & s_c \end{bmatrix}^\mathsf{T} \in S = S_p \times S_c$, initial states $X_0 = X_{p0} \times S_{p0} \times X_{c0} \times S_{c0}$, and discrete transitions $\mathbb{T} \subseteq (X \times S) \to (X \times S)$:

$$\begin{cases} \dot{x} & = [J(x,s) - R(x,s)]\frac{\partial H}{\partial x} + \begin{bmatrix} L_p(x_p, s_p) \\ 0 \end{bmatrix} \delta \\ \zeta & = \begin{bmatrix} L_p^\mathsf{T}(x_p, s_p) & 0 \end{bmatrix} \frac{\partial H}{\partial x} \end{cases} \tag{1}$$

$$J(x,s) = \begin{bmatrix} J_p(x_p, s_p) & -G_p(x_p, s_p)G_c^\mathsf{T}(x_c, s_c) \\ G_c(x_c, s_c)G_p^\mathsf{T}(x_p, s_p) & J_c(x_c, s_c) \end{bmatrix},$$

$$R(x,s) = \begin{bmatrix} R_p(x_p, s_p) & 0 \\ 0 & R_c(x_c, s_c) \end{bmatrix},$$

where $J_p(x_p, s_p) \in \mathbb{R}^{n_p \times n_p}$ and $J_c(x_c, s_c) \in \mathbb{R}^{n_c \times n_c}$ are skew-symmetric interconnection matrices, $R_p(x_p, s_p) \in \mathbb{R}^{n_p \times n_p}$ and $R_c(x_c, s_c) \in \mathbb{R}^{n_c \times n_c}$ are symmetric positive semi-definite damping matrices, $G_p(x_p, s_p) \in \mathbb{R}^{n_p \times m}$, $G_c(x_c, s_c) \in \mathbb{R}^{n_c \times m}$, $L_p(x_p, s_p) \in \mathbb{R}^{n_p \times o}$, and (δ, ζ) are the input-output pairs corresponding to the disturbance port.

3.2 Safety Problem

Given a hybrid system represented as (1) with Hamiltonian function $H(x)$ and bounded disturbances, the safety problem is to show that there are no trajectories of the closed-loop system that reach an unsafe region of the state space.

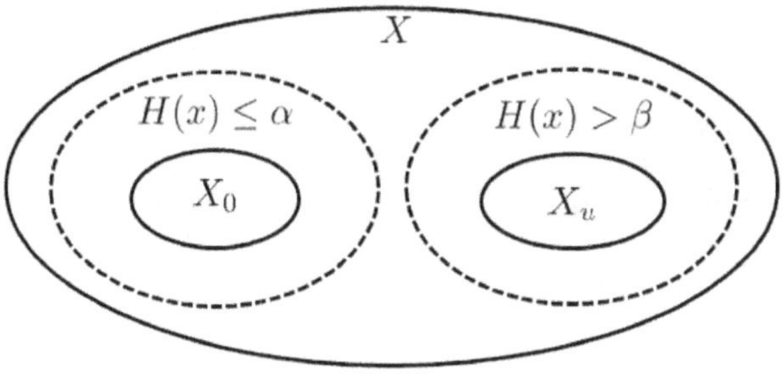

Figure 2: The Hamiltonian function prevents the trajectory from reaching the unsafe set X_u.

DEFINITION 1. *Given a multi-modal PHS (1) and $H(x)$ with continuous states $X = X_p \times X_c \subseteq \mathbb{R}^{n_p+n_c}$, discrete states $S = S_p \times S_c$, initial states $X_{p0} \times X_{c0} \times S_{p0} \times S_{c0} \subseteq X \times S$, unsafe states $X_{pu} \times X_{cu} \times S_{pu} \times S_{cu} \subseteq X \times S$, and disturbances $\Delta \subset \mathbb{R}^o$, a system trajectory $\Gamma(x(t), s(t)) : [0, T] \to X \times S$ is unsafe if there exists a positive time instant T and a finite sequence of discrete transition times $0 \le t_1 \le \cdots \le t_N \le T$ such that $\Gamma(x(0), s(0)) \in X_{p0} \times X_{c0} \times S_{p0} \times S_{c0}$ and $\Gamma(x(T), s(T)) \in X_{pu} \times X_{cu} \times S_{pu} \times S_{cu}$. The system is safe if there are no unsafe state trajectories.*

3.3 Safety Analysis

We consider the following definitions for initial states, unsafe states, and guard conditions that specify discrete mode transitions. For each discrete state $s \in S$, the initial continuous states are defined as $\text{Init}(s) = \{x \in X : (x, s) \in X_{p0} \times X_{c0} \times S_{p0} \times S_{c0}\}$ and the unsafe continuous states are defined as $\text{Unsafe}(s) = \{x \in X : (x, s) \in X_{pu} \times X_{cu} \times S_{pu} \times S_{cu}\}$. Each transition of discrete states from $s \in S$ to $s' \in S$ is associated with the guard condition $\text{Guard}(s, s') = \{x, x' \in X : \{x, s\} \to \{x', s'\} \in \mathbb{T}\}$.

Similar to safety analysis using barrier certificates, the method in this paper shows that trajectories beginning from the safe region cannot reach the unsafe region. However, the barrier certificate typically separates the initial and unsafe states using its zero level set, while the Hamiltonian function characterizes the initial and unsafe states using two energy levels. A canonical coordinate transform Φ is needed to convert the dynamic equations and Hamiltonian function of the system into a form which shows the actual minimum energy. Technical details regarding canonical coordinate transformation of PHS can be found in [7]. The passivity condition prevents trajectories starting in the safe region from reaching the unsafe region. Figure 2 provides a visual illustration of the method.

THEOREM 1. *A multi-modal PHS described by (1) and $H(x)$, with continuous states $x \in X$, discrete states $s \in S$, initial states Init(s), unsafe states Unsafe(s), and bounded disturbances $\delta \in \Delta$ is safe if the canonical coordinate transformation $\overline{x} = \Phi(x)$ and transformed Hamiltonian function $H(\Phi^{-1}(\overline{x}))$ satisfy the following four conditions with $\alpha \le \beta$*

1. $H(\Phi^{-1}(\overline{x})) \le \alpha, \forall x \in \text{Init}(s)$

2. $H(\Phi^{-1}(\overline{x})) > \beta, \forall x \in \text{Unsafe}(s)$

3. $\zeta^{\mathsf{T}}\delta \le \frac{\partial H(\Phi^{-1}(\overline{x}))}{\partial \overline{x}}^{\mathsf{T}} \overline{R}(\overline{x}, s) \frac{\partial H(\Phi^{-1}(\overline{x}))}{\partial \overline{x}}, \forall \{x, \delta\} \in X \times \Delta$

4. $H(\Phi^{-1}(\overline{x})) \le \alpha, \forall x \in \text{Guard}(s, s')$

PROOF. Assuming that the Hamiltonian function $H(x)$ satisfy the four conditions in Theorem 1, yet there exists a time $T \ge 0$, an input δ, and initial states Init(s), and a trajectory $\Gamma(x(t), s(t))$ such that $\Gamma(x(T), s(T)) \in \text{Unsafe}(s)$. We show that the Hamiltonian function cannot simultaneously satisfy the four condition and reach the unsafe region, thus proving safety by contradiction. The time derivative of the Hamiltonian functions $\frac{dH}{dt}$ can be written as:

$$\begin{aligned}
\frac{\partial H(x)}{\partial x}^{\mathsf{T}} \dot{x} &= \frac{\partial H(x)}{\partial x}^{\mathsf{T}} [J(x, s) - R(x, s)] \frac{\partial H(x)}{\partial x} \\
&\quad + \frac{\partial H(x)}{\partial x}^{\mathsf{T}} L(x, s)\delta \\
&= \frac{\partial H(\Phi^{-1}(\overline{x}))}{\partial \overline{x}}^{\mathsf{T}} [\overline{J}(\overline{x}, s) - \overline{R}(\overline{x}, s)] \frac{\partial H(\Phi^{-1}(\overline{x}))}{\partial \overline{x}} \\
&\quad + \frac{\partial H(\Phi^{-1}(\overline{x}))}{\partial \overline{x}}^{\mathsf{T}} \overline{L}(\overline{x}, s)\delta \\
&= -\frac{\partial H(\Phi^{-1}(\overline{x}))}{\partial \overline{x}}^{\mathsf{T}} \overline{R}(\overline{x}, s) \frac{\partial H(\Phi^{-1}(\overline{x}))}{\partial \overline{x}} + \zeta\delta
\end{aligned}$$

$$\overline{J}(\overline{x}, s) = \frac{\partial \Phi}{\partial x} J(x, s) \frac{\partial \Phi}{\partial x}^{\mathsf{T}} \Bigg|_{x=\Phi^{-1}(\overline{x})}$$

$$\overline{R}(\overline{x}, s) = \frac{\partial \Phi}{\partial x} R(x, s) \frac{\partial \Phi}{\partial x}^{\mathsf{T}} \Bigg|_{x=\Phi^{-1}(\overline{x})}$$

$$\overline{L}(\overline{x}, s) = \frac{\partial \Phi}{\partial x} L(x, s) \Bigg|_{x=\Phi^{-1}(\overline{x})}$$

Condition (3) shows that the system trajectory on the time interval of $[0, T]$ is non-increasing, which indicates that $H(x(T)) \le H(x(0))$. Additionally, condition (4) asserts that during a discrete transition, the Hamiltonian function will not jump to an increasing value. These statements, however, contradict the original assumption that the system states start at Init(s) and end at Unsafe(s). As a result, we can conclude that the system is safe. □

4. COLLISION AVOIDANCE

In this section, we consider the safety analysis of a vehicle with ACC following a lead car and maintaining a safe distance between the vehicles. The goal for the ACC is to prevent the host car from colliding into the lead car in the event of rapid deceleration. For simplicity, we consider the case shown in Figure 3 in which the vehicles are driving on a straight road, which allows us to omit the lateral dynamics.

4.1 Multi-Modal PHS

Figure 4 shows the multi-modal PHS of the longitudinal vehicle dynamics connected to the ACC system via power ports. Disturbances from wind and slope of the road are modeled as ports attached to the longitudinal vehicle dynamics. The longitudinal dynamics contain state variables of longitudinal momentum p_x and longitudinal displacement q_x and two control ports (T_a, y_1) and (T_b, y_2). The longitudinal input force from the throttle, T_a, is a function of the throttle valve angle θ_a, $T_a = C_a\theta_a$, where C_a is the experimental throttle constant. The longitudinal input force from the brakes, T_b, is a function of the braking pressure P_b, $T_b = C_bP_b$, where C_b is the experimental braking constant. The outputs of the control ports y_1 and y_2 are V_x and $-V_x$, respectively. The longitudinal dynamics contain two disturbance ports whose inputs, δ_g and δ_{wx} are the disturbance

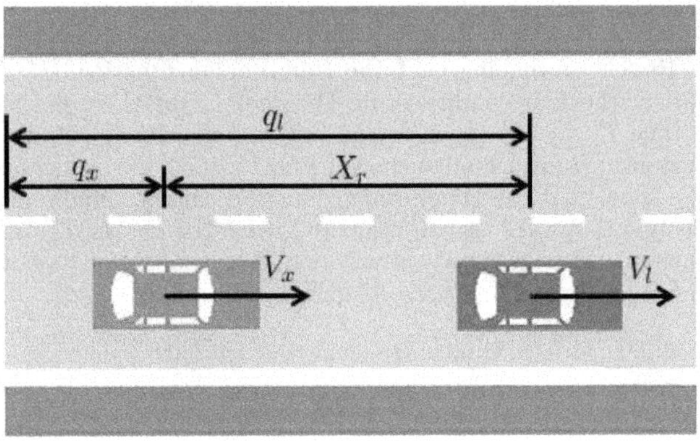

Figure 3: Lead vehicle and host vehicle on a straight road

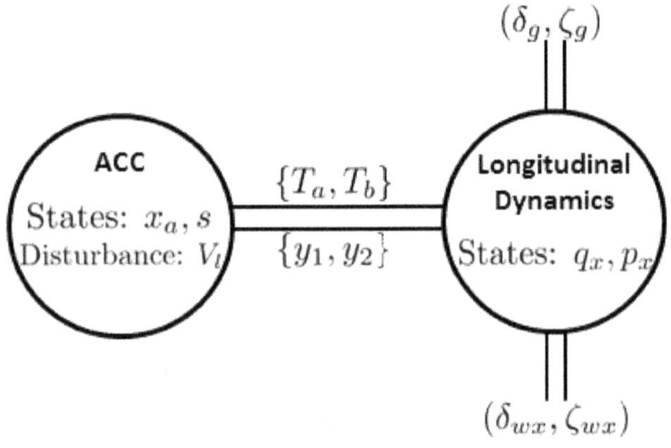

Figure 4: Longitudinal vehicle dynamics and ACC

forces resulting from the slope of the road and longitudinal wind, respectively. The outputs of the disturbance ports, ζ_g and ζ_{wx}, are the corresponding power conjugate values. The longitudinal dynamics has the following Hamiltonian function:

$$H_x(q_x, p_x) = \frac{1}{2m} p_x^2 + U_x(q_x),$$

where m represents the mass of the vehicle and $U_x(q_x)$ represents the potential energy. The longitudinal dynamics contain the continuous states $\{q_x, p_x\} \in X_k \subseteq \mathbb{R}^2$, initial states $X_{k0} \subseteq X_k$, inputs $\{T_a, T_b\}$, and disturbances $\{\delta_g, \delta_{wx}\}$.

$$\begin{cases} \begin{bmatrix} \dot{q}_x \\ \dot{p}_x \end{bmatrix} = \begin{bmatrix} 0 & 1 \\ -1 & -R_x \end{bmatrix} \begin{bmatrix} \frac{\partial H_x}{\partial q_x} \\ \frac{\partial H_x}{\partial p_x} \end{bmatrix} + \begin{bmatrix} 0 \\ G_x \end{bmatrix} \begin{bmatrix} T_a \\ T_b \end{bmatrix} + \begin{bmatrix} 0 & 0 \\ 1 & 1 \end{bmatrix} \begin{bmatrix} \delta_g \\ \delta_{wx} \end{bmatrix} \\ \begin{bmatrix} y_1 \\ y_2 \end{bmatrix} = \begin{bmatrix} 0 & G_x^{\mathsf{T}} \end{bmatrix} \begin{bmatrix} \frac{\partial H_x}{\partial q_x} & \frac{\partial H_x}{\partial p_x} \end{bmatrix}^{\mathsf{T}} \\ \zeta_x = \begin{bmatrix} 0 & L_x^{\mathsf{T}} \end{bmatrix} \begin{bmatrix} \frac{\partial H_x}{\partial q_x} & \frac{\partial H_x}{\partial p_x} \end{bmatrix} \end{cases} \tag{2}$$

where $G_x = \begin{bmatrix} 1 & -1 \end{bmatrix}$, $R_x = a + \frac{bp_x}{m} + \frac{cm}{p_x}$, a represents the tire rolling friction constant, b represents the air resistance constant, and c represents the static friction constant.

The ACC is connected to the longitudinal vehicle dynamics through the control ports and allows for autonomous driving by controlling T_a and T_b. The objective of the ACC is to maintain a desired speed depending on the lead vehicle velocity V_l, which is modeled as a disturbance. If a lead vehicle is not detected, the desired vehicle velocity is the driver's set speed which makes the system behave as a conventional cruise control system. Assuming that there is a lead vehicle, the host vehicle's radar system determines the speed of the lead vehicle. Figure 3 shows that the relative distance between the two vehicles is computed using the lead vehicle velocity, the host vehicle velocity, and the initial relative distance $X_r(0)$.

$$\begin{aligned} X_r(t) &= \int_0^t (V_l - V_x) d\tau + X_r(0) \\ &= \int_0^t \left(V_l(\tau) - \tfrac{1}{m} p_x(\tau)\right) d\tau + X_r(0). \end{aligned}$$

The state variables of the ACC are derived using the lead vehicle velocity and the desired relative distance $X_d = hV_l + S_0$, where h is the time headway and S_0 is the static distance constant. We compile the state variables into a vector $x_a = \begin{bmatrix} x_{at} & x_{ab} \end{bmatrix}^{\mathsf{T}}$, where $x_{at} = \int_0^t ((1 + \gamma \frac{X_r - X_d}{X_d}) V_l - V_x) d\tau$ and $x_{ab} = \int_0^t (V_x - (1 + \gamma \frac{X_r - X_d}{X_d}) V_l) d\tau$ (γ is a constant).

The ACC has hybrid dynamics which is modeled using discrete variables s_t and s_b, where s_t is associated with the throttle control mode and s_b is associated with the brake control mode. The throttle control and brake control modes cannot be active simultaneously, which eliminates the case in which both s_t and s_b are active. We also make the assumption that the throttle control and brake control modes cannot be inactive simultaneously. The guards of the discrete transitions are defined in (3), where h_+ and h_- are hysteresis constants introduced to prevent the system from rapidly alternating between accelerating and decelerating:

$$\begin{cases} (s_t, s_b) = (1, 0) \text{ if } (1 + \gamma \frac{X_r - X_d}{X_d}) V_l - V_x \geq 0, X_r \geq h_+ X_d \\ (s_t, s_b) = (0, 1) \text{ if } (1 + \gamma \frac{X_r - X_d}{X_d}) V_l - V_x < 0, X_r < h_- X_d \end{cases} \tag{3}$$

We design the ACC to have the following Hamiltonian function:

$$H_a(x_a, s) = \frac{1}{2}(k_{ti} x_{at}^2 + k_{bi} x_{ab}^2),$$

where k_{ti} and k_{bi} are the gains of the Hamiltonian. The ACC system has continuous states $x_a \in X_a \subseteq \mathbb{R}^2$, discrete states $\{s_t, s_b\} \in S_a$, initial states $X_{a0} \times S_{a0} \subseteq X_a \times S_a$, and discrete transitions $\mathbb{T}_a \subseteq (X_a \times S_a) \rightarrow (X_a \times S_a)$. Its input-state-output PHS is described by:

$$\begin{cases} \dot{x}_a = -R_a \frac{\partial H_a}{\partial x_a} + G_a u_a \\ y_a = G_a^{\mathsf{T}} \frac{\partial H_a}{\partial x_a} + M_a u_a \end{cases} \tag{4}$$

where (u_a, y_a) are the input-output pairs corresponding to the control port. The parameter matrices are:

$$R_a = \begin{bmatrix} s_t k_t & 0 \\ 0 & s_b k_b \end{bmatrix}, G_a = \begin{bmatrix} s_t P & 0 \\ 0 & s_b \end{bmatrix},$$

$$M_a = \begin{bmatrix} s_t k_{td} & 0 \\ 0 & s_b k_{bd} \end{bmatrix}.$$

where k_t and k_{td} are throttle control gains, and k_b and k_{bd} are brake control gains. P is derived from the inverse engine map of the vehicle and is a mapping of the ratio of the acceleration force to V_x.

The standard feedback interconnection of the longitudinal vehicle dynamics with the ACC system is described using the power-conserving interconnection $u_x = -y_a$ and $y_x = u_a$.

The closed-loop system has a Hamiltonian function $H_k = H_a(x_a, s) + H_x(q_x, p_x)$, initial states $X_0 = X_{k0} \times X_{a0} \times S_{a0}$, discrete transitions $\mathbb{T}_k \subseteq (X \times S_a) \to (X \times S_a)$, and disturbances $\{\delta_g, \delta_{wx}\} \in \Delta_g \times \Delta_{wx}$. Its input-state-output PHS is described by:

$$\begin{cases} \begin{bmatrix} \dot{q}_x \\ \dot{\tilde{p}}_x \\ \dot{x}_{at} \\ \dot{x}_{ab} \end{bmatrix} = [\tilde{J}_x - \tilde{R}_x] \begin{bmatrix} \frac{\partial \tilde{H}_x}{\partial q_x} \\ \frac{\partial \tilde{H}_x}{\partial \tilde{p}_x} \\ \frac{\partial \tilde{H}_x}{\partial x_{at}} \\ \frac{\partial \tilde{H}_x}{\partial x_{ab}} \end{bmatrix} + \begin{bmatrix} 0 & 0 \\ 1 & 1 \\ 0 & 0 \\ 0 & 0 \end{bmatrix} \begin{bmatrix} \delta_g \\ \delta_{wx} \end{bmatrix} \\ \begin{bmatrix} \zeta_g \\ \zeta_{wx} \end{bmatrix} = \begin{bmatrix} 0 & 1 & 0 & 0 \\ 0 & 1 & 0 & 0 \end{bmatrix} \begin{bmatrix} \frac{\partial \tilde{H}_x}{\partial q_x} & \frac{\partial \tilde{H}_x}{\partial \tilde{p}_x} & \frac{\partial \tilde{H}_x}{\partial x_{at}} & \frac{\partial \tilde{H}_x}{\partial x_{ab}} \end{bmatrix}^{\mathsf{T}} \end{cases} \tag{5}$$

$$\tilde{J}_x = \begin{bmatrix} 0 & 1 & 0 & 0 \\ -1 & 0 & -s_t P & s_b \\ 0 & s_t P & 0 & 0 \\ 0 & -s_b & 0 & 0 \end{bmatrix},$$

$$\tilde{R}_x = \begin{bmatrix} 0 & 0 & 0 & 0 \\ 0 & R_x + s_t k_{td} + s_b k_{bd} & 0 & 0 \\ 0 & 0 & s_t k_t & 0 \\ 0 & 0 & 0 & s_b k_b \end{bmatrix}.$$

4.2 Safety Problem

The control gains can be selected to stabilize the host vehicle velocity to $V_l + \gamma \frac{(X_r - X_d)V_l}{X_d}$ [4]. However, stability does not imply safety. We do not consider the scenario in which a lead vehicle appears in front of the host vehicle driving faster than or equal to the host vehicle set speed because the safety property is trivial since the controller stabilizes the host vehicle velocity to the set speed indicating that the relative distance between the two vehicles will not be less than the initial relative distance. We consider the scenario in which a lead vehicle appears in front of the host vehicle driving slower than the host vehicle set speed. In this scenario, the safety property needs to be validated because if the ACC does not react accordingly and slow the host vehicle to a reasonable speed, a collision may occur. The safety condition for the longitudinal dynamics asserts that the relative distance between the two vehicles will never reach a minimum distance q_m. We can represent the unsafe host vehicle displacement as the set of:

$$X_{ku} = \left\{ q_x \in \mathbb{R} : q_x \geq \int_0^t V_l d\tau + q_l(0) + q_m \right\}, \tag{6}$$

where $q_l(0)$ is the initial displacement value of the lead vehicle. Given (5), the safety condition for the longitudinal vehicle dynamics and ACC system states that that all possible trajectories cannot reach the unsafe region described by (6).

4.3 Safety Analysis

In order to show safety, we make some assumptions regarding the parameters of the lead and host vehicle. The first assumption is that the initial velocity of the lead vehicle is greater than a minimum velocity which depends on the deceleration of the lead vehicle (a_l) and the relative distance between the vehicles. The second assumption is that the initial relative distance between the vehicles is greater than a minimum distance which depends on the deceleration and velocity of the lead vehicle. If the initial velocity of the vehicle is high compared to the host vehicle velocity, then the initial relative displacement can be low because the host vehicle does not need a large distance to react to the lead vehicle velocity. However, if the initial velocity of the vehicle is low compared to the host vehicle velocity, then the initial relative displacement must be high because the host vehicle needs a larger distance to react to the low lead vehicle velocity. The relationship between the initial relative distance and the initial vehicle velocities is described in (7).

$$X_r(0) = \frac{V_l^2(0)}{2a_l} - \frac{V_x^2(0)}{2\dot{V}_x}. \tag{7}$$

We need the following definitions for initial states, unsafe states, and guard sets. For each discrete state $s_a \in S_a$, the initial continuous states are defined as $\text{Init}(s_a) = \{ (q_x, p_x, x_a) \in X : (q_x, p_x, x_a, s_a) \in X_0 \}$ and the unsafe continuous states are defined as $\text{Unsafe}(s_a) = \{ (q_x, p_x, x_a) \in X : q_x \in X_{ku} \}$. Each transition of discrete states from $s_a \in S_a$ to $s_a' \in S_a$ is defined using the guard condition $\text{Guard}(s_a, s_a') = \{ (q_x, p_x, x_a), (q_x, p_x, x_a)' \in X : (q_x, p_x, x_a, s_a) \to (q_x', p_x', x_a', s_a') \}$. Safety analysis of the longitudinal dynamics uses $\overline{p}_x = \Phi(p_x) = p_x - m(1 + \gamma \frac{X_r - X_d}{X_d})V_l$ as the canonical coordinate transformation on the longitudinal momentum.

We apply Theorem 1 to the composed longitudinal dynamics and ACC system. Given initial conditions $\text{Init}(s_a)$, we derive the energy bound α as a function of the initial host vehicle velocity $V_x(0)$, initial relative distance $X_r(0)$, and initial lead vehicle velocity $V_l(0)$. The initial relative distance must be greater than or equal to $\frac{V_l^2(0)}{2a_l} - \frac{V_x^2(0)}{2a_l}$ where a_l is the bounded lead vehicle deceleration. Consequently, we restate the first condition of Theorem 1 as $H_k(\Phi^{-1}(\overline{p}_x)) \leq \alpha, \forall x \in \text{Init}(s_a)$, where

$$\alpha = m\frac{k_{td} + k_{bd}}{2}(V_x(0) - (1 + \gamma\frac{X_r(0) - hV_l(0) - S_0}{hV_l(0) + S_0})V_l(0))^2.$$

Given the unsafe states $\text{Unsafe}(s_a)$, we derive the energy bound β as a function of host vehicle velocity V_x and lead vehicle velocity V_l. The energy of the transformed Hamiltonian function has a maximum value which indicates that the minimum relative distance has been reached. Consequently, we restate the second condition of Theorem 1 as $H_k(\Phi^{-1}(\overline{p}_x)) > \beta, \forall x \in \text{Unsafe}(s_a)$, where

$$\beta = m\frac{k_{td} + k_{bd}}{2}(V_x - (1 - \gamma)V_l)^2.$$

Given an initial relative distance greater than q_m, α is less than β, which validates the first two conditions. Given the disturbances $\{\delta_g, \delta_{wx}\} \in \Delta$, we must guarantee that the system trajectory will never begin in $\text{Init}(s_a)$ and end in $\text{Unsafe}(s_a)$. Consequently, we restate the third condition of Theorem 1 as

$$\zeta_g \delta_g + \zeta_{wx} \delta_{wx} \leq$$

$$\frac{\partial H_k(\Phi^{-1}(\overline{p}_x))}{\partial \overline{p}_x}^{\mathsf{T}} \frac{\partial \Phi}{\partial p_x} R_x(\Phi^{-1}(\overline{p}_x)) \frac{\partial \Phi}{\partial p_x}^{\mathsf{T}} \frac{\partial H_k(\Phi^{-1}(\overline{p}_x))}{\partial \overline{p}_x}$$

$$\forall (q_x, p_x, x_a, \delta_g, \delta_{wx}) \in X \times \Delta.$$

Discrete transitions between the throttle and brake control mode must also be taken into account in order to guarantee that the system will not transition into Unsafe(s_a). We restate the fourth condition of Theorem 1 as $H_k(\Phi^{-1}(\overline{p}_x)) \leq \alpha$, $\forall(q_x, p_x, x_a) \in$ Guard(s_t, s_b). In Section 6, the ACC is designed by selecting control parameters that satisfy these safety conditions.

5. SKIDDING AVOIDANCE

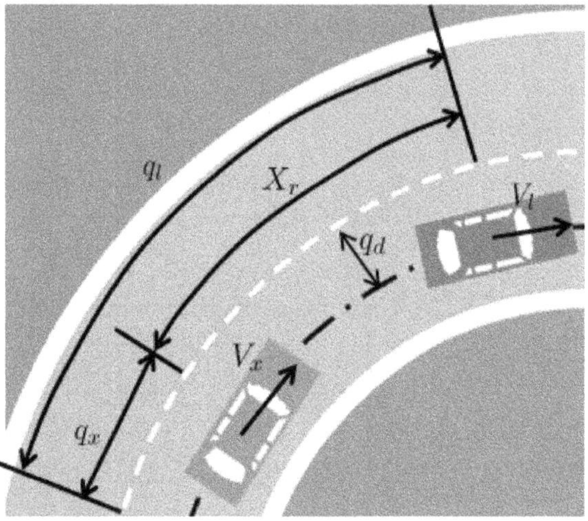

Figure 5: Diagram of lead vehicle and host vehicle on a curved road

In this section, we consider the safety problem of a vehicle with both ACC and LKC following a lead car around a curved road (Figure 5). In addition to maintaining a safe distance between the vehicles, the host car must also maintain a lateral acceleration as to not skid off the road. Interactions between the lateral and longitudinal dynamics, which can be characterized as an interaction structure, contribute to the lateral acceleration.

5.1 Multi-Modal PHS

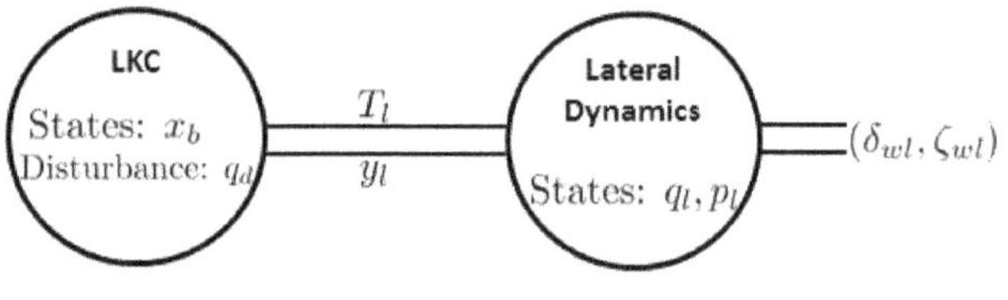

Figure 6: Lateral vehicle dynamics and LKC

Figure 6 shows the multi-modal PHS of the lateral vehicle dynamics connected to the LKC system via power ports. Disturbance from wind is modeled as a port attached to the lateral vehicle dynamics. The lateral dynamics contain state variables $q_l = \begin{bmatrix} q_y & q_r \end{bmatrix}^\mathsf{T}$ and $p_l = \begin{bmatrix} p_y & p_r \end{bmatrix}^\mathsf{T}$, where p_y is the lateral momentum, p_r is the angular momentum, q_y is the lateral displacement, and q_r is the angular displacement. The lateral dynamics contain a control port (T_l, y_l), where the output of the control port y_l is $V_y + l_f r$ (l_f represents the length of the vehicle center to the front wheels). The lateral input force from the steering, T_l, is a function of the steering angle θ_s, $T_l = 2C_f\theta_s$, where C_f is the cornering stiffness of the front wheels. The lateral dynamics contains a disturbance port whose input, δ_{wy}, represents a disturbance force resulting from lateral wind. The output of the disturbance ports, ζ_{wy}, is the corresponding power conjugate value. The lateral velocity, and yaw rate, are represented by V_x, V_y, and r, respectively. The lateral dynamics has the following Hamiltonian function:

$$H_l(q_y, q_r, p_y, p_r) = \frac{1}{2m}p_y^2 + \frac{1}{2I}p_r^2 + U_l(q_y, q_r),$$

where I represents the moment of inertia of the vehicle and $U_l(q_y, q_r)$ represents the potential energy. The lateral dynamics contain the continuous states $\{q_l, p_l\} \in X_l \subseteq \mathbb{R}^4$, initial states $X_{l0} \subseteq X_l$, input T_l, and disturbance δ_{wy}.

$$\begin{cases} \begin{bmatrix} \dot{q}_l \\ \dot{p}_l \end{bmatrix} &= \begin{bmatrix} 0 & I \\ -I & -R_l \end{bmatrix} \begin{bmatrix} \frac{\partial H_l}{\partial q_l} \\ \frac{\partial H_l}{\partial p_l} \end{bmatrix} + \begin{bmatrix} 0 \\ G_l \end{bmatrix} T_l + \begin{bmatrix} 0 \\ L_l \end{bmatrix} \delta_{wl} \\ y_l &= \begin{bmatrix} 0 & G_l^\mathsf{T} \end{bmatrix} \begin{bmatrix} \frac{\partial H_l}{\partial q_l} & \frac{\partial H_l}{\partial p_l} \end{bmatrix}^\mathsf{T} \\ \zeta_{wl} &= \begin{bmatrix} 0 & L_l^\mathsf{T} \end{bmatrix} \begin{bmatrix} \frac{\partial H_l}{\partial q_l} & \frac{\partial H_l}{\partial p_l} \end{bmatrix}^\mathsf{T} \end{cases} \tag{8}$$

$$R_l = \begin{bmatrix} \frac{W_1}{V_x} & \frac{W_2}{V_x} \\ \frac{W_2}{V_x} & \frac{W_3}{V_x} \end{bmatrix},$$

where $G_l = \begin{bmatrix} 1 & l_f \end{bmatrix}^\mathsf{T}$ and $L_l = \begin{bmatrix} 1 & 0 \end{bmatrix}^\mathsf{T}$. The parameter constants of R_l are $W_1 = 2C_f + 2C_r$, $W_2 = 2C_f l_f - 2C_r l_r$, and $W_3 = 2C_f l_f^2 + 2C_r l_r^2$, where C_r is the cornering stiffness of the rear wheels, l_f is the length of the vehicle center to the front wheels, and l_r is the length of the vehicle center to the rear wheels.

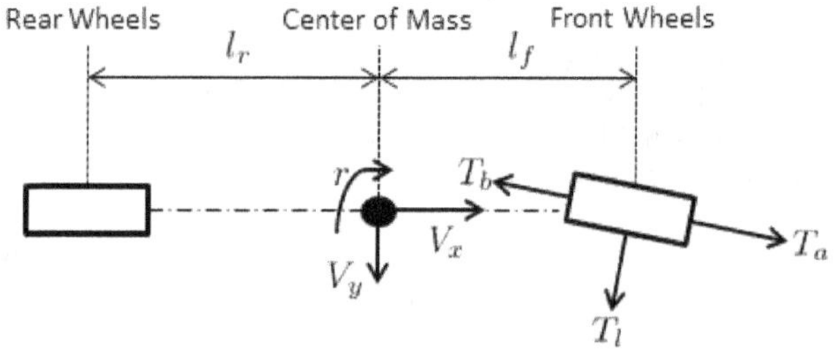

Figure 7: Free-body diagram of the vehicle dynamics

Interactions between the longitudinal and lateral dynamics are a result of the vehicle heading angle being affected by longitudinal velocity and can be derived by analysis of the free-body diagram in Figure 7 [15]. The x-component of the lateral force affecting the longitudinal motion is represented by d_x and its power-conjugate velocity is represented by z_x. The y-component of the longitudinal force affecting the lateral motion is represented by d_l and its power-conjugate velocity is represented by z_l.

Figure 8 shows a diagram of the interacting vehicle dynamics and the two control systems. The altered equations (2) and (8), which include the interaction ports (d_x, z_x) and

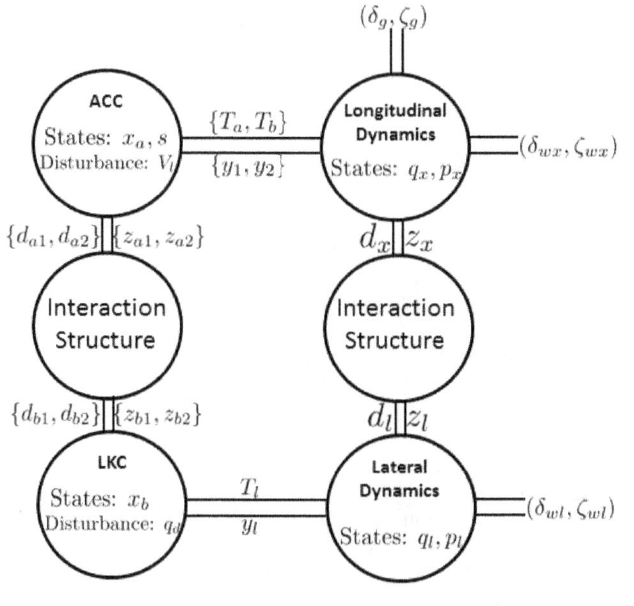

Figure 8: Closed-loop system

(d_l, z_l), are described by:

$$\begin{cases} \begin{bmatrix} \dot{q}_x \\ \dot{p}_x \end{bmatrix} = \begin{bmatrix} 0 & 1 \\ -1 & -R_x \end{bmatrix} \begin{bmatrix} \frac{\partial H_x}{\partial q_x} \\ \frac{\partial H_x}{\partial p_x} \end{bmatrix} + \begin{bmatrix} 0 \\ G_x \end{bmatrix} u_x + \begin{bmatrix} 0 \\ 1 \end{bmatrix} d_x \\ \qquad + \begin{bmatrix} \delta_g \\ \delta_{wx} \end{bmatrix} \\ y_x = \begin{bmatrix} 0 & G_x^\mathsf{T} \end{bmatrix} \begin{bmatrix} \frac{\partial H_x}{\partial q_x} & \frac{\partial H_x}{\partial p_x} \end{bmatrix}^\mathsf{T} \\ z_x = \begin{bmatrix} 0 & 1 \end{bmatrix} \begin{bmatrix} \frac{\partial H_x}{\partial q_x} & \frac{\partial H_x}{\partial p_x} \end{bmatrix}^\mathsf{T} \\ \begin{bmatrix} \varsigma_g \\ \varsigma_{wx} \end{bmatrix} = \begin{bmatrix} 0 & L_x^\mathsf{T} \end{bmatrix} \begin{bmatrix} \frac{\partial H_x}{\partial q_x} & \frac{\partial H_x}{\partial p_x} \end{bmatrix}^\mathsf{T} \end{cases} \tag{9}$$

$$\begin{cases} \begin{bmatrix} \dot{q}_l \\ \dot{p}_l \end{bmatrix} = \begin{bmatrix} 0 & I \\ -I & -R_l \end{bmatrix} \begin{bmatrix} \frac{\partial H_l}{\partial q_l} \\ \frac{\partial H_l}{\partial p_l} \end{bmatrix} + \begin{bmatrix} 0 \\ G_l \end{bmatrix} T_l + \begin{bmatrix} 0 \\ K_l \end{bmatrix} d_l \\ \qquad + \begin{bmatrix} 0 \\ L_l \end{bmatrix} \delta_{wl} \\ y_l = \begin{bmatrix} 0 & G_l^\mathsf{T} \end{bmatrix} \begin{bmatrix} \frac{\partial H_l}{\partial q_l} & \frac{\partial H_l}{\partial p_l} \end{bmatrix}^\mathsf{T} \\ z_l = \begin{bmatrix} 0 & K_l^\mathsf{T} \end{bmatrix} \begin{bmatrix} \frac{\partial H_l}{\partial q_l} & \frac{\partial H_l}{\partial p_l} \end{bmatrix}^\mathsf{T} \\ \varsigma_{wl} = \begin{bmatrix} 0 & L_l^\mathsf{T} \end{bmatrix} \begin{bmatrix} \frac{\partial H_l}{\partial q_l} & \frac{\partial H_l}{\partial p_l} \end{bmatrix}^\mathsf{T} \end{cases} \tag{10}$$

where $K_l = \begin{bmatrix} 1 & 0 \end{bmatrix}^\mathsf{T}$. The interaction between the longitudinal and lateral dynamics is a mapping of velocity to force, which indicates a gyrator relationship. The gyrator ratio has units of kg/s which is represented by multiplying the mass of the vehicle with the yaw rate. The interaction structure is modeled as a Dirac structure modulated by the yaw momentum p_r:

$$\begin{bmatrix} d_x \\ d_l \end{bmatrix} = \begin{bmatrix} 0 & -\frac{mp_r}{I} \\ \frac{mp_r}{I} & 0 \end{bmatrix} \begin{bmatrix} z_x \\ z_l \end{bmatrix}. \tag{11}$$

The LKC connects with the lateral vehicle dynamics via the control ports and allows for autonomous driving by controlling T_l. The objective of the LKC is to maintain a desired lateral displacement q_d. The control system consists of ACC, LKC, and an interaction structure. The LKC shares the control port with the lateral dynamics and its state variable $x_b = q_y - q_d$ is derived using the desired lateral displacement. We design the LKC to have the following Hamiltonian function:

$$H_b(x_b) = \frac{1}{2} k_{si} x_b^2,$$

where k_{si} is the gain associated with the integrator. The LKC system has continuous states $x_b \in X_b \subseteq \mathbb{R}$ and initial states X_{b0}, with dynamic equations as an input-state-output PHS with direct-feedthrough:

$$\begin{cases} \dot{x}_b = u_b \\ y_b = \frac{\partial H_b}{\partial x_b} + k_{sd} u_b, \end{cases} \tag{12}$$

where (u_b, y_b) are the input-output pairs corresponding to the control port and k_{sd} is the gain associated with the steering control. We connect the ACC and LKC using an interaction structure, which alters (4) and (12), so that the state variables and outputs of the speed control are affected by the state variable of the steering control, and vice versa. The purpose of the interaction structure is to lower the speed of the vehicle in the event of a turn by transferring energy from the ACC to the LKC.

$$\begin{cases} \dot{x}_a = -R_a \frac{\partial H_a}{\partial x_a} + G_a y_x + K_{a1} d_{a1} \\ u_x = G_a^\mathsf{T} \frac{\partial H_a}{\partial x_a} + M_a y_x + K_{a2} d_{a2} \\ \begin{bmatrix} z_{a1} \\ z_{a2} \end{bmatrix} = \begin{bmatrix} K_{a1}^\mathsf{T} & 0 \\ 0 & K_{a2}^\mathsf{T} \end{bmatrix} \begin{bmatrix} \frac{\partial H_a}{\partial x_a} \\ y_x \end{bmatrix} \end{cases} \tag{13}$$

$$\begin{cases} \dot{x}_b = y_l + d_{b1} \\ T_l = \frac{\partial H_b}{\partial x_b} + k_{sd} y_l + d_{b2} \\ \begin{bmatrix} z_{b1} \\ z_{b2} \end{bmatrix} = \begin{bmatrix} 1 & 0 \\ 0 & 1 \end{bmatrix} \begin{bmatrix} \frac{\partial H_b}{\partial x_b} \\ y_l \end{bmatrix} \end{cases} \tag{14}$$

The interaction structure of the control system is represented by the following Dirac structure:

$$\begin{bmatrix} d_{a1} \\ d_{a2} \\ d_{b1} \\ d_{b2} \end{bmatrix} = \begin{bmatrix} 0 & 0 & J_c & 0 \\ 0 & 0 & 0 & M_c \\ -J_c^\mathsf{T} & 0 & 0 & 0 \\ 0 & -M_c^\mathsf{T} & 0 & 0 \end{bmatrix} \begin{bmatrix} z_{a1} \\ z_{a2} \\ z_{b1} \\ z_{b2} \end{bmatrix}. \tag{15}$$

The parameters J_c and M_c define how the speed control and the steering control interact. In order to derive the closed-loop system, we define the variables $q = \begin{bmatrix} q_x & q_l \end{bmatrix}^\mathsf{T}$, $p = \begin{bmatrix} p_x & p_l \end{bmatrix}^\mathsf{T}$, $x = \begin{bmatrix} x_{at} & x_{ab} & x_b \end{bmatrix}^\mathsf{T}$, $\delta = \begin{bmatrix} \delta_g & \delta_{wx} & \delta_l \end{bmatrix}^\mathsf{T}$, and $\zeta = \begin{bmatrix} \zeta_g & \zeta_{wx} & \zeta_l \end{bmatrix}^\mathsf{T}$. The closed-loop system has a Hamiltonian function $\tilde{H}(q, p, z) = H_x + H_l + H_a + H_b$, continuous states $\{q, p, x\} \in \tilde{X}$, initial states $\tilde{X}_0 = \tilde{X}_{p0} \times \tilde{X}_{c0} \times S_a$, discrete transitions $\tilde{\mathbb{T}} \subseteq (\tilde{X} \times S_a) \to (\tilde{X} \times S_a)$, and disturbances $\delta = \{\delta_g, \delta_{wx}, \delta_{wy}\} \in \Delta_g \times \Delta_{wx} \times \Delta_{wy}$.

$$\begin{cases} \begin{bmatrix} \dot{q} \\ \dot{p} \\ \dot{x} \end{bmatrix} = \begin{bmatrix} 0 & I & 0 \\ -I & \tilde{J} - \tilde{R} & \tilde{K} \\ 0 & -\tilde{K}^\mathsf{T} & -\tilde{Q} \end{bmatrix} \begin{bmatrix} \frac{\partial \tilde{H}}{\partial q} \\ \frac{\partial \tilde{H}}{\partial p} \\ \frac{\partial \tilde{H}}{\partial x} \end{bmatrix} + \begin{bmatrix} 0 \\ \tilde{L} \\ 0 \end{bmatrix} \delta \\ \zeta = \begin{bmatrix} 0 & \tilde{L} & 0 \end{bmatrix} \begin{bmatrix} \frac{\partial \tilde{H}}{\partial q} & \frac{\partial \tilde{H}}{\partial p} & \frac{\partial \tilde{H}}{\partial x} \end{bmatrix}^\mathsf{T} \end{cases} \tag{16}$$

where $\tilde{J}$, $\tilde{L}$, $\tilde{R}$, $\tilde{K}$, and $\tilde{Q}$ are defined as:

$$\tilde{J} = \begin{bmatrix} 0 & \frac{mp_r}{I} - M_c & -l_f M_c \\ -\frac{mp_r}{I} + M_c & 0 & 0 \\ l_f M_c & 0 & 0 \end{bmatrix}, \tilde{L} = \begin{bmatrix} 1 & 1 & 0 \\ 0 & 0 & 1 \\ 0 & 0 & 0 \end{bmatrix},$$

$$\tilde{R} = \begin{bmatrix} R_x + s_t k_{td} + s_b k_{bd} & 0 & 0 \\ 0 & \frac{mW_1}{p_x} + k_{sd} & \frac{mW_2}{p_x} + l_f k_{sd} \\ 0 & \frac{mW_2}{p_x} + l_f k_{sd} & \frac{mW_3}{p_x} + l_f^2 k_{sd} \end{bmatrix},$$

$$\tilde{K} = \begin{bmatrix} s_t P & s_b & 0 \\ 0 & 0 & -1 \\ 0 & 0 & -l_f \end{bmatrix}, \tilde{Q} = \begin{bmatrix} s_t k_t & 0 & -J_c \\ 0 & s_b k_b & 0 \\ J_c & 0 & 0 \end{bmatrix}.$$

5.2 Safety Problem

The control gains can be selected to stabilize the host vehicle velocity to $V_l + \gamma\frac{(X_r - X_d)V_l}{X_d}$ and the lateral displacement to q_d [4]. However, stability does not imply safety. The unsafe states for the lateral momentum are related to that of the longitudinal momentum because of the interactions between the longitudinal and lateral dynamics. The inputs to the longitudinal dynamics (T_a and T_b) affect the lateral dynamics. Similarly, the input to the lateral dynamics (T_l) affects the longitudinal dynamics. This introduces an additional safety constraint on the system. In order for the vehicle to operate safely on the road, its lateral acceleration must not exceed a maximum value A_m. If the lateral acceleration exceeds A_m, the vehicle will skid. This lateral acceleration value of the vehicle is affected by the yaw rate and longitudinal velocity of the vehicle. This interaction between lateral and longitudinal motion results in an unsafe region characterized by a set defined as:

$$X_{lu} = \{p_x \in \mathbb{R}, p_r \in \mathbb{R} : p_x p_r \geq m^2 I A_m\}. \tag{17}$$

This safety condition indicates that longitudinal and lateral motion are bounded by a hyperbolic relationship. A large longitudinal momentum results in a lower bound for the lateral and yaw momentum, and a large lateral and yaw momentum results in a lower bound for the longitudinal momentum. Using this safety constraint we must verify that the product of longitudinal momentum and yaw rate does not exceed a maximum threshold. Given (16) and $\tilde{H}(q,p,z)$, the safety condition for the vehicle dynamics, ACC system, and LKC system states that that all possible trajectories cannot reach the unsafe region described by (6) and (17).

5.3 Safety Analysis

A road can be divided into segments consisting of four types of road profiles: straight road, decreasing curvature, constant curvature, and increasing curvature. Of the four cases the lateral acceleration safety problem is trivial for the straight road and decreasing curvature cases. A straight road nullifies the unsafe state set X_{lu} and a decreasing road curvature relaxes the safety condition. In order to safely navigate a curved section of the road, the vehicle must avoid the unsafe regions of X_{ku} and X_{lu}. Given a road curvature of ρ, the yaw momentum required is calculated as $p_r = \frac{Ip_x}{m}\rho$, which shows the direct relationship between the yaw momentum and the longitudinal momentum. Additionally, the road curvature is related to the vehicle slip angle ω and steering angle θ_s:

$$\rho = \frac{\cos(\omega)\tan(\theta_s)}{l_f + l_r},$$

$$\omega = \arctan(\frac{l_r}{l_f + l_r}\tan(\theta_s)).$$

The lateral momentum depends on the longitudinal momentum, the yaw momentum, and the vehicle slip angle:

$$p_y = p_x \sin(\frac{p_r}{I} + \omega).$$

Given that ω and p_r are directly proportional to ρ, we can represent the state variable p_y as a function directly proportional to p_x and ρ. We need the following definitions for initial states, unsafe states, and guard sets. For each discrete state $s_a \in S_a$, the initial continuous states are defined as $\overline{\text{Init}}(s_a) = \{(q,p,x) \in \tilde{X} : (q,p,x,s_a) \in \tilde{X}_0\}$ and the unsafe continuous states are defined as $\overline{\text{Unsafe}}(s_a) = \{(q,p,x) \in \tilde{X} : (q_x, p_x, p_r) \in X_{ku} \times X_{lu}$. Each transition of discrete states from $s_a \in S_a$ to $s_a' \in S_a$ is associated with the guard set $\overline{\text{Guard}}(s_a, s_a') = \{(q,p,x),(q,p,x)' \in \tilde{X} : (q,p,x,s_a) \to (q',p',x',s_a')\}$. Safety analysis of the vehicle dynamics uses $\tilde{\Phi}$ as the canonical coordinate transformation for the momentum variables.

$$\begin{bmatrix} \overline{p}_x \\ \overline{p}_y \\ \overline{p}_r \end{bmatrix} = \begin{bmatrix} \tilde{\Phi}_x(p_x) \\ \tilde{\Phi}_y(p_y) \\ \tilde{\Phi}_r(p_r) \end{bmatrix} = \begin{bmatrix} p_x - m(1 + \gamma\frac{X_r - X_d}{X_d})V_l - M_c x_b \\ p_y + k_{si}(q_y - q_d) + M_c(x_{at} + x_{ab}) \\ p_r + k_{si}(q_r - \frac{q_d}{l_f}) + M_c\frac{x_{at} + x_{ab}}{l_f} \end{bmatrix}.$$

We apply Theorem 1 to the composed longitudinal dynamics, lateral dynamics, ACC, and LKC system. Given initial conditions $\overline{\text{Init}}(s_a)$, we derive the energy bound $\tilde{\alpha}$ as a function of the initial host vehicle velocity $V_x(0)$, initial relative distance $X_r(0)$, initial lead vehicle velocity $V_l(0)$, and initial road curvature $\rho(0)$. Consequently, we restate the first condition of Theorem 1 as $\tilde{H}(\tilde{\Phi}^{-1}(\overline{p})) \leq \tilde{\alpha}, \forall (q,p,x) \in \overline{\text{Init}}(s_a)$, where

$$\begin{aligned} \tilde{\alpha} &= m\tfrac{k_{td}+k_{bd}}{2}(V_x(0) - (1 + \gamma\tfrac{X_r(0) - hV_l(0) - S_0}{hV_l(0) + S_0})V_l(0))^2 \\ &\quad + \tfrac{m}{2}V_x^2(0)\sin^2(\rho(0)V_x(0) + \omega(0)) + \tfrac{I}{2}\rho^2(0)V_x^2(0). \end{aligned}$$

Given the unsafe states $\overline{\text{Unsafe}}(s_a)$, we derive the energy bound $\tilde{\beta}$ as a function of host vehicle velocity V_x, relative distance X_r, lead vehicle velocity V_l, and road curvature ρ. The energy of the transformed Hamiltonian function has a maximum value which indicates that the maximum lateral acceleration has been reached. Consequently, we restate the second condition of Theorem 1 as $\tilde{H}(\tilde{\Phi}^{-1}(\overline{p})) > \tilde{\beta}, \forall (q,p,x) \in \overline{\text{Unsafe}}(s_a)$, where

$$\begin{aligned} \tilde{\beta} &= m\tfrac{k_{td}+k_{bd}}{2}(V_x - (1-\gamma)V_l - \tfrac{M_c}{m}(q_y - q_d))^2 \\ &\quad + \tfrac{m}{2}(V_x\sin(\rho V_x + \omega) + k_{si}(q_y - q_d))^2 \\ &\quad + \tfrac{I}{2}(\rho V_x + k_{si}(q_y - \tfrac{q_d}{l_f}))^2. \end{aligned}$$

Given the disturbances $\{\delta_g, \delta_{wx}, \delta_{wy}\} \in \Delta$, we must guarantee that the system trajectory will never begin in $\overline{\text{Init}}(s_a)$ and end in $\overline{\text{Unsafe}}(s_a)$. Consequently, we restate the third condition of Theorem 1 as

$$\zeta_g\delta_g + \zeta_{wx}\delta_{wx} + \zeta_{wy}\delta_{wy} \leq$$

$$\frac{\partial\tilde{H}(\tilde{\Phi}^{-1}(\overline{p}))}{\partial(q,\overline{p})}^{\mathsf{T}}\frac{\partial\tilde{\Phi}}{\partial p}\tilde{R}(\tilde{\Phi}^{-1}(\overline{p}))\frac{\partial\tilde{\Phi}}{\partial p}^{\mathsf{T}}\frac{\partial\tilde{H}(\tilde{\Phi}^{-1}(\overline{p}))}{\partial(q,\overline{p})},$$

$$\forall(q,p,x,\delta_g,\delta_{wx},\delta_{wy}) \in \tilde{X}\times\tilde{\Delta}.$$

Discrete transitions between throttle and brake control mode must also be taken into account in order to guarantee that the system will not transition into $\overline{\text{Unsafe}}(s_a)$. Consequently, we restate the fourth condition of Theorem 1 as $\tilde{H}(\tilde{\Phi}^{-1}(\overline{p})) \le \tilde{\alpha}, \forall(q,p,x) \in \overline{\text{Guard}}(s_t,s_b) \cup \overline{\text{Guard}}(s_b,s_t)$. In Section 6, the ACC and LKC are designed by selecting control parameters that satisfy these safety conditions.

6. SIMULATION RESULTS

In this section, we present simulation results to illustrate the approach. For validation of the PHS model we use a standard E-class sedan model in CarSim as a reference [2]. We select parameters for the vehicle dynamics so that its passivity index values match that of the CarSim model [19]. We determine that the parameters of the vehicle dynamics are $a = 0.1\ \text{s}^{-1}$, $b = 0.06\ \text{m}^{-1}$, $c = 10\ \text{m/s}^2$, $C_f = 300$ N, $l_f = 1.4$ m, $C_r = 200$ N, $l_r = 1.4$ m, $m = 1650$ kg, and $I = 3234\ \text{kg m}^2$ [4]. The inverse engine map of the vehicle, P, can be found in [6]. We then use the vehicle dynamics parameters along with the safety conditions to choose control parameters (Table 1) so that the vehicle dynamics will not reach the unsafe regions (6) and (17). The safety conditions derived in Sections 4 and 5 are valid for vehicle velocities given a maximum road decline angle of 15 degrees which corresponds to $\delta_g = 4200$ N and a maximum lead vehicle deceleration of 5 m/s^2 which corresponds to a braking distance of 50 m from 80 km/hr to 0 km/hr.

Table 1: Table of controller gains

k_{ti}	k_{bi}	k_t	k_{td}	k_b
0.05	0.01	0.1	0.02	0.2
k_{bd}	k_{si}	k_{sd}	J_c	M_c
0.02	40	15	0.2	0.5

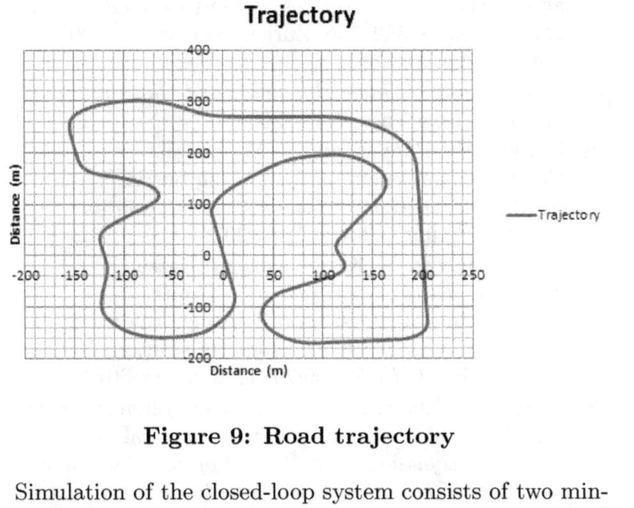

Figure 9: Road trajectory

Simulation of the closed-loop system consists of two minutes of running time in which the host vehicle follows a lead vehicle on the road featured in Figure 9. Figure 10 shows the time range of 0 to 5 s, which is a straight segment of the road with a zero degree decline. The simulation results show that the system is safe since the relative distance is greater than $q_m = 24$ m. The curve radius is large because

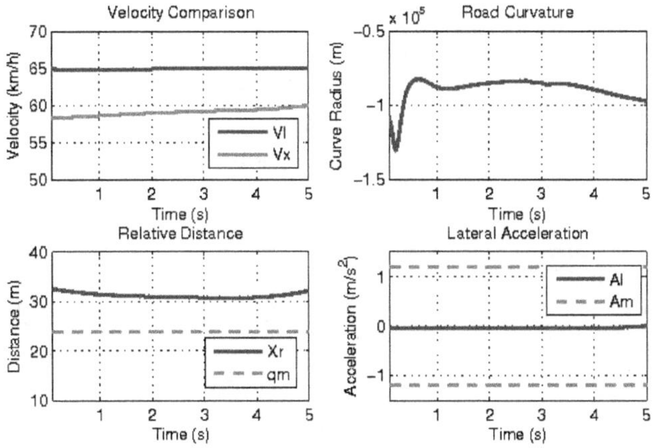

Figure 10: Zero degree decline and straight road

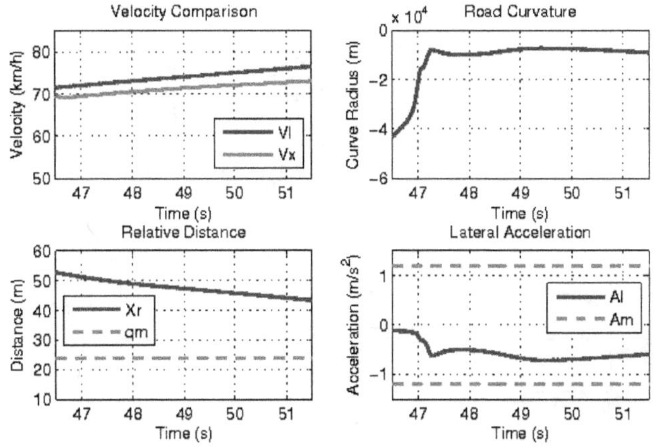

Figure 11: Zero degree decline and curved road

the road is relatively straight, so the lateral acceleration is near zero. Figure 11 shows the time range of 46.5 to 51.5 s, which is a curved segment of the road with a zero degree decline. The curve radius during this time period decreases, which corresponds to a non-zero lateral acceleration value. Safety is ensured because the lateral acceleration is bounded by $A_m = 1.2\ \text{m/s}^2$.

Figure 12 shows the time range of 54 to 58 s, which is a straight segment of the road with a fifteen degree decline. The control parameters of the ACC system are designed to compensate for disturbances such as road decline, and the system is safe since the relative distance is greater than q_m. Similar to the time range of 0 to 5 s, the curve radius is large because the road is relatively straight, so the lateral acceleration is near zero. Figure 13 shows the time range of 70 to 75 s, which is a curved segment of the road with a fifteen degree decline. The simulation results show that safety conditions are satisfied.

7. CONCLUSION

The approach in this paper addresses the safety problem for multi-modal PHS given complex interactions, nonlinearities, and hybrid dynamics. The approach ensures the safety of the system by characterizing safe and unsafe regions using

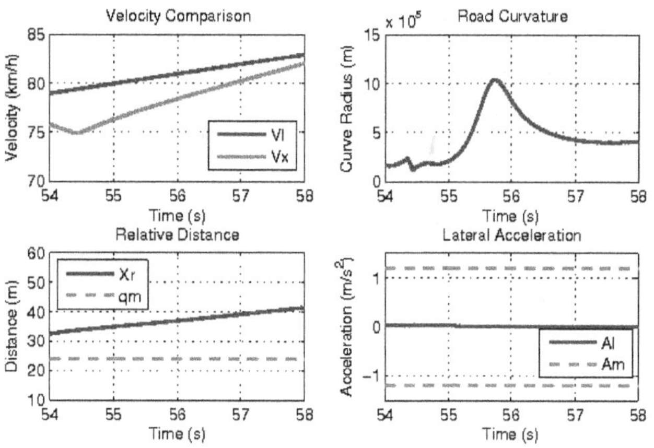

Figure 12: Fifteen degree decline and straight road

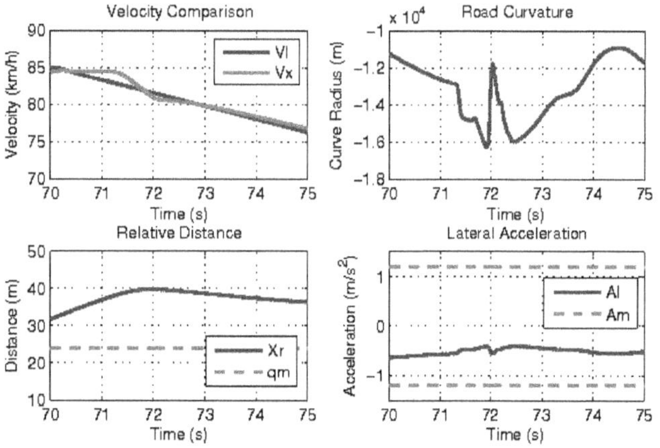

Figure 13: Fifteen degree decline and curved road

energy levels of the Hamiltonian function and deriving conditions on model and control parameters. We demonstrate the approach by analyzing the safety conditions of an automotive control system to prevent collision and skidding. Simulation results from an automotive control system are recorded and show the effectiveness of the safety analysis approach.

ACKNOWLEDGEMENT

This work is supported in part by the National Science Foundation (CNS-1035655).

8. REFERENCES

[1] A. Ames, J. Grizzle, and P. Tabuada. Control barrier function based quadratic programs with application to adaptive cruise control. In *Proceedings of the 53rd IEEE Conference of Decision and Control*, Los Angeles, CA, USA, December 2014.

[2] CarSim. *http://www.carsim.com.* Mechanical Simulation Corporation, Ann Arbor, MI, USA, 2013.

[3] J. Cervera, A. van der Schaft, and A. Banos. Interconnection of port-hamiltonian systems and composition of dirac structures. *Automatica*, 43(2), February 2007.

[4] S. Dai and X. Koutsoukos. Model-based automotive control design using port-hamiltonian systems. In *International Conference on Complex Systems Engineering*, Storrs, CT, USA, November 2015.

[5] V. Duindam, A. Macchelli, S. Stramigioli, and H. Bruyninckx. *Modeling and Control of Complex Physical Systems: The Port-Hamiltonian Approach.* Springer, New York, NY, 2009.

[6] E. Eyisi, Z. Zhang, X. Koutsoukos, J. Porter, G. Karsai, and J. Sztipanovits. Model-based control design and integration of cyberphysical system: An adaptive cruise control case study. *Journal of Control Science and Engineering, Special Issue on Embedded Model-Based Control*, 2013.

[7] K. Fujimoto and T. Sugie. Canonical transformation and stabilization of generalized hamiltonian systems. *Systems and Control Letters*, 42:217–227, 2001.

[8] H. Khalil. *Nonlinear Systems, 3rd Edition.* Prentice Hall, Upper Saddle River, NJ, 2002.

[9] MATLAB. *Version R2012a, http://www.mathworks.com.* The Mathworks, Inc., Natick, MA, USA, 2012.

[10] S. Prajna. Barrier certificates for nonlinear model validation. *Automatica*, 42:117–126, 2006.

[11] S. Prajna and A. Jadbabaie. Safety verification of hybrid systems using barrier certificates. In *Hybrid Systems Computation and Control*, pages 477–492, Philadelphia, PA, USA, 2004. Springer-Verlag.

[12] S. Prajna, A. Jadbabaie, and G. Pappas. A framework for worst-case and stochastic safety verification using barrier certificates. *IEEE Transactions on Automatic Control*, 52(8):1415–1428, August 2007.

[13] S. Prajna, A. Papachristodoulou, and P. Parrilo. Introducing sostools: A general purpose sum of squares programming solver. In *Proceedings of the IEEE Conference on Decision and Control*, Las Vegas, NV, USA, 2002.

[14] S. Prajna and A. Rantzer. Primal-dual tests for safety and reachability. In *Hybrid Systems Computation and Control*, pages 542–556, Zurich, Switzerland, 2005. Springer-Verlag.

[15] R. Rajamani. *Vehicle Dynamics and Control.* Springer, New York, NY, 2006.

[16] C. Sloth, G. Pappas, and R. Wisniewski. Compositional safety analysis using barrier certificates. In *Hybrid System Computation and Control*, Beijing, China, April 2012.

[17] J. Sztipanovits, X. Koutsoukos, G. Karsai, N. Kottenstette, P. Antsaklis, V. Gupta, B. Goodwine, J. Baras, and S. Wang. Toward a science of cyber-physical system integration. *Proceedings of IEEE*, 100:29–44, January 2012.

[18] A. van der Schaft. Port-hamiltonian systems: Network modeling and control of nonlinear physical systems. In *Advanced Dynamics and Control of Structures and Machines. CISM Courses and Lectures No. 444, CISM International Centre for Mechanical Sciences*, pages 127–168, New York, NY, USA, 2004. Springer.

[19] P. Wu, M. McCourt, and P. Antsaklis. Experimentally determining passivity indices: Theory and simulation. In *ISIS Technical Report ISIS-2013-002*, University of Notre Dame, April 2013.

Verification and Synthesis of Timing Contracts for Embedded Controllers *

Mohammad Al Khatib
L2S, CNRS
CentraleSupélec
Université Paris-Sud
Université Paris-Saclay
F-91192 Gif-sur-Yvette
mohammad.alkhatib
@l2s.centralesupelec.fr

Antoine Girard
L2S, CNRS
CentraleSupélec
Université Paris-Sud
Université Paris-Saclay
F-91192 Gif-sur-Yvette
antoine.girard
@l2s.centralesupelec.fr

Thao Dang
Univ. Grenoble Alpes-CNRS
Verimag
F-38000 Grenoble
thao.dang@imag.fr

ABSTRACT

Timing contracts for embedded controller implementation specify the constraints on the time instants at which certain operations are performed such as sampling, actuation, computation, etc. In this paper, we consider the problem of verifying the stability of embedded control systems under such timing contracts. Reformulating the problem in the framework of impulsive linear systems, we provide theoretical conditions for stability and a verification algorithm based on reachability analysis. In the second part of the paper, given a model of the plant and of the controller we propose an approach to synthesize timing contracts that guarantee stability.

Keywords

Stability; Reachability; Impulsive linear systems; Sampled-data systems

1. INTRODUCTION

Physical systems equipped with embedded controllers are becoming pervasive (smart buildings, intelligent cars, drones, robots, etc.), thus increasing the need for high-confidence analysis and design tools that are able to handle tight interactions between the physical and digital worlds. In this context, contract-based approaches have been identified as a promising direction for cyber-physical systems design [28]. For instance, for embedded controller implementation, [11] proposed the use of timing contracts which specify the constraints on the time instants at which certain operations are performed such as sampling, actuation or computation. Under such contracts, the control engineers are responsible for designing a control law that is robust to all possible timing variation specified in the contract while the software engineers can focus on implementing the proposed control law so as to satisfy the timing contract. In this paper, we propose techniques that are useful within this framework. We first consider the problem of stability verification: given models of the physical plant and of the controller and a timing contract, verify that the resulting dynamical system is stable. We then tackle the problem of timing contract synthesis: given models of the physical plant and of the controller, determine a set of timing contracts that guarantee stability of the resulting system.

We adopt the impulsive linear dynamical system framework to model the overall system. Such systems form a class of hybrid systems which describe processes that evolve continuously and undergo instantaneous changes at discrete time instants. Applications of impulsive dynamical systems include sampled-data control systems [9], networked control systems [12], multi-agent systems [8], etc. In the present work, instantaneous changes occur at sampling and actuation times, t_k^s and t_k^a, $k \in \mathbb{N}$, which are assumed to be non-deterministic. More precisely, we assume that some uncertainty lies in each of the kth sampling-to-actuation delay $\tau_k = t_k^a - t_k^s$ and sampling period $h_k = t_{k+1}^s - t_k^s$.

For the stability verification problem, we propose an approach based on the notion of reachable set. In the last decade, hybrid system reachability has had an important breakthrough in computing the reachable set corresponding to a linear continuous dynamics where the developed algorithms are based on representing the reachable sets by ellipsoids [22, 7], zonotopes [17, 2] or by support functions [24, 14]. In general, such algorithms handle time based switching by introducing auxiliary variables (clocks). In the following, we provide a specific approximation scheme for the reachable set at the sampling times to develop an effective stability verification approach. Then, we use this approach to tackle the timing contract synthesis problem. We propose a re-parametrization which provides some monotonicity property to the problem and allows us to develop an effective synthesis method based on guided sampling of the timing parameter space.

In all, we contribute in enriching our stability verification approach initiated in [1] by stating the proofs of the necessary and sufficient theoretical conditions for the stability of the impulsive linear system and by considering more complex timing contracts which require dedicated reachability

*This work was supported by the Agence Nationale de la Recherche (COMPACS project ANR-13-BS03-0004).

HSCC'16, April 12-14, 2016, Vienna, Austria
© 2016 ACM. ISBN 978-1-4503-3955-1/16/04...$15.00
DOI: http://dx.doi.org/10.1145/2883817.2883827

algorithms for stability verification and more involved techniques for timing contract synthesis.

The paper is organized as follows. First, some preliminary notations are defined before formulating the stability verification and timing contract synthesis problems in Section 2. Stability conditions are provided in Section 3. Section 4 presents the reachable set approximation scheme and an algorithm for stability verification. In Section 5, we propose a solution to the timing contract synthesis problem. In Section 6, examples, some of which are used to compare our results with existing ones, are then discussed before concluding our work.

Notations. Let $\mathbb{R}$, $\mathbb{R}_0^+$, $\mathbb{R}^+$, $\mathbb{R}_0^-$, $\mathbb{R}^-$, $\mathbb{N}$, $\mathbb{N}^+$ denote the sets of reals, nonnegative reals, positive reals, nonpositive reals, negative reals, nonnegative integers and positive integers, respectively. For $I \subseteq \mathbb{R}_0^+$, let $\mathbb{N}_I = \mathbb{N} \cap I$. Given a real matrix $A \in \mathbb{R}^{n \times n}$, $|A|$ is the matrix whose elements are the absolute values of the elements of A. Given $\mathcal{S} \subseteq \mathbb{R}^n$ and a real matrix $A \in \mathbb{R}^{n \times n}$, the set $A\mathcal{S} = \{x \in \mathbb{R}^n : (\exists y \in \mathcal{S} : x = Ay)\}$; for $a \in \mathbb{R}$, $a\mathcal{S} = (aI_n)\mathcal{S}$ where I_n is the $n \times n$ identity matrix. The interior of $\mathcal{S}$ is denoted by $\text{int}(\mathcal{S})$. The convex hull of $\mathcal{S}$ is denoted by $\text{ch}(\mathcal{S})$. The interval hull of $\mathcal{S}$ is the smallest n-dimensional interval containing the set $\mathcal{S}$ and is denoted by $\square(\mathcal{S})$. The symmetric interval hull of $\mathcal{S}$ is the smallest symmetric (with respect to 0) n-dimensional interval containing $\mathcal{S}$ and is denoted by $\boxdot(\mathcal{S})$. Given $\mathcal{S}, \mathcal{S}' \subseteq \mathbb{R}^n$, the Minkowski sum of $\mathcal{S}$ and $\mathcal{S}'$ is $\mathcal{S} \oplus \mathcal{S}' = \{x + x' : x \in \mathcal{S}, x' \in \mathcal{S}'\}$. A polytope $\mathcal{P}$ is the intersection of a finite number of closed half-spaces, that is $\mathcal{P} = \{x \in \mathbb{R}^n : Hx \leq b\}$ where $H \in \mathbb{R}^{m \times n}$, $b \in \mathbb{R}^m$ and the vector of inequalities is interpreted component-wise. Let H_i, $i \in \mathbb{N}_{[1,m]}$ denote the row vectors of H, then if $0 \in \text{int}(\text{ch}(\{H_1, \ldots, H_m\}))$, then $\mathcal{P}$ is compact. Given a template matrix $H \in \mathbb{R}^{m \times n}$ and a compact set $\mathcal{S} \subseteq \mathbb{R}^n$, let us define the polytope $\Gamma_H(\mathcal{S}) = \{x \in \mathbb{R}^n : Hx \leq b\}$ where $b_i = \max_{x \in \mathcal{S}} H_i x$, $i \in \mathbb{N}_{[1,m]}$. In other words, $\Gamma_H(\mathcal{S})$ is the smallest polytope whose facets directions are given by H and containing $\mathcal{S}$. We denote the set of all subsets of $\mathbb{R}^n$ by $2^{\mathbb{R}^n}$. We denote by $\mathcal{K}(\mathbb{R}^n)$ the set of compact subsets of $\mathbb{R}^n$ and by $\mathcal{K}_0(\mathbb{R}^n)$ the set of compact subsets of $\mathbb{R}^n$ containing 0 in their interior. For $x \in \mathbb{R}$, $\lceil x \rceil$ is the smallest integer not less than x, and for $c, c' \in \mathbb{R}^n$, $c \leq c'$ if and only if $c_i \leq c'_i$, $i = 1, \ldots, n$.

2. PROBLEM FORMULATION

2.1 Timing contracts for embedded control

In this work, we consider embedded control systems given under the form of general linear sampled-data control systems that take into account the sequences of sampling and actuation instants $(t_k^s)_{k \in \mathbb{N}}$ and $(t_k^a)_{k \in \mathbb{N}}$:

$$\begin{aligned} \dot{z}(t) &= Az(t) + Bu(t), \quad && \forall t \in \mathbb{R}^+ \\ u(t) &= Kz(t_k^s), && t_k^a < t \leq t_{k+1}^a \end{aligned} \tag{1}$$

where $z(t) \in \mathbb{R}^p$ is the state of the system, $u(t) \in \mathbb{R}^m$ is the control input, and $k \in \mathbb{N}$. For $t \in [0, t_0^a]$, $u(t)$ can be any constant value in $\mathbb{R}^m$.

We assume that the sequence of sampling and actuation instants (t_k^s) and (t_k^a) satisfy a *timing contract* given by

$$\begin{aligned} &t_0^s = 0, \ \tau_k = t_k^a - t_k^s \in [\underline{\tau}, \overline{\tau}], \\ &h_k = t_{k+1}^s - t_k^s \in [\max(\underline{h}, \tau_k), \overline{h}], \ \ k \in \mathbb{N} \end{aligned} \tag{2}$$

where $\underline{\tau} \in \mathbb{R}_0^+$, $\overline{\tau} \in \mathbb{R}_0^+$, $\underline{h} \in \mathbb{R}^+$, and $\overline{h} \in \mathbb{R}^+$ provide bounds on the sampling-to-actuation delays (which includes time for computation of the control law) and sampling periods provided that $t_k^s \leq t_k^a \leq t_{k+1}^s$ for all $k \in \mathbb{N}$. Note that we impose $\underline{h} \neq 0$ to prevent Zeno behavior. Moreover, these parameters must belong to the following set so that the time intervals given in (2) are always non-empty:

$$\mathcal{C} = \left\{(\underline{\tau}, \overline{\tau}, \underline{h}, \overline{h}) \in \mathbb{R}_0^+ \times \mathbb{R}_0^+ \times \mathbb{R}^+ \times \mathbb{R}^+ : \underline{\tau} \leq \overline{\tau} \leq \overline{h}, \underline{h} \leq \overline{h}\right\}$$

Contract (2) is a general timing contract which includes or over-approximates the different contracts introduced in [11]. Their relation to the timing contract (2) is described as follows:

1. **ZET Contract**: The Zero Execution Time contract is given by (2) with $\underline{\tau} = \overline{\tau} = 0$ and $\underline{h} = \overline{h} = h \in \mathbb{R}^+$. In other words, the contract states that the sampling and actuation instants are periodic and simultaneous such that $t_k^s = t_k^a = kh$ for $k \in \mathbb{N}$. As mentioned in [11], this contract is hardly achievable in practice since computation always takes time in between the sampling and actuation instants.
2. **LET Contract**: The Logical Execution Time contract is given by (2) with $\underline{\tau} = \overline{\tau} = \underline{h} = \overline{h} = h \in \mathbb{R}^+$. The contract states that the sampling and actuation instants are periodic such that $t_0^s = 0$ and $t_k^s = t_{k-1}^a = kh$ for $k \in \mathbb{N}^+$.
3. **DET Contract**: The Deadline Execution Time contract is given by (2) with $\underline{\tau} = 0$ and $\underline{h} = \overline{h} = h \in \mathbb{R}^+$. The contract states that the sampling instants are periodic, or $t_k^s = kh$ for $k \in \mathbb{N}$, and actuation instants are at some point t_k^a in the interval $[t_k^s, t_k^s + \overline{\tau}]$, with $\overline{\tau} \leq h$.
4. **TOL Contract**: The Timing Tolerance contract is defined by a nominal sampling period $h \in \mathbb{R}^+$, nominal sampling to actuation delay $\tau \in \mathbb{R}_0^+$, and two jitters $J^h, J^\delta \in \mathbb{R}_0^+$ with $J^\tau \leq \tau$ and $J^h + J^\tau + \tau \leq h$, such that $t_k^s \in [kh, kh + J^h]$ and $t_k^a \in [t_k^s + \tau - J^\tau, t_k^s + \tau + J^\tau]$, for $k \in \mathbb{N}$ (refer to Figure 1). We cannot exactly model this contract using (2). However we can over-approximate it using (2) with $\underline{\tau} = \tau - J^\tau$, $\overline{\tau} = \tau + J^\tau$, $\underline{h} = h - J^h$, and $\overline{h} = h + J^h$. Thus stability of system (1) under this latter contract guarantees also its stability under the TOL contract.

It is noteworthy that system (1) has deterministic dynamics under any of the ZET or LET contracts, unlike the case of the DET or TOL contracts where at least one of the sampling-to-actuation delays or sampling period is time-varying. In our previous work [1] we considered the special case of nearly periodic linear impulsive systems (NPILS)

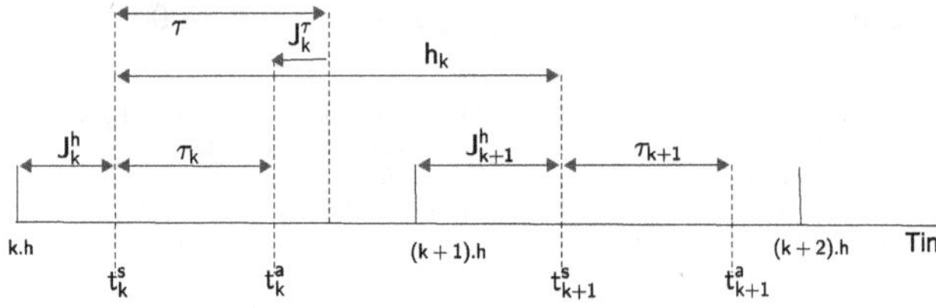

Figure 1: Time variables included in a *TOL* contract. $J_k^h \in [0, J^h]$ **and** $J_k^\tau \in [-J^\tau, J^\tau]$**.**

Table 1: Methods that can solve instances of Problem 1 with description of the modeling and computational approaches, list of restrictions and possible extensions.

	Models	Algorithm	Restrictions	Extensions
[10]	difference inclusion	LMI	–	$\tau_k > h_k$; controller synthesis
[12]		LMI	–	scheduling protocols
[20]		LMI	$\underline{\tau} = \overline{\tau} = 0$	controller synthesis
[21]		LMI	$\underline{\tau} = \overline{\tau} = 0$	–
[29]		SOS	$\underline{\tau} = \overline{\tau} = 0$	–
[13]		Invariant sets	$\underline{\tau} = \overline{\tau} = 0$	–
[1]		Reachability analysis	$\underline{\tau} = \overline{\tau} = 0$	stochastic timing uncertainty
[26]	time-delay systems	LMI	$\underline{h} = 0$	$\tau_k > h_k$; scheduling protocols
[16]		LMI	$\underline{h} = \overline{h}$, $\underline{\tau} = 0$	controller synthesis; quantization
[27]		LMI	$\underline{\tau} = \overline{\tau} = 0$	–
[15]		LMI	$\underline{h} = \underline{\tau} = \overline{\tau} = 0$	–
[4]	hybrid systems	SOS	–	nonlinear dynamics; scheduling protocols
[18]		LMI	$\underline{\tau} = 0$, $\underline{h} = 0$	scheduling protocols

which are modeled by (1) and (2) with $\underline{\tau} = \overline{\tau} = 0$. In other words, the sampling and actuation instants are simultaneous or $t_k^s = t_k^a$, and the duration in between two successive sampling instants is bounded in the interval $[\underline{h}, \overline{h}]$. Therefore, it is clear that we are dealing in this work with a more general timing contract which is more complex than the simple NPILS case.

2.2 Reformulation using impulsive systems

In our analysis it is more practical to transform equation (1) into an impulsive system with two types of resets each referring to a sampling or actuation instant. Such a reformulation is convenient to develop stability conditions based on reachability analysis. The system is thus given by:

$$\begin{aligned} \dot{x}(t) &= A_c x(t), t \neq t_k^s, t \neq t_k^a \\ x(t_k^{s+}) &= A_s x(t_k^s) \\ x(t_k^{a+}) &= A_a x(t_k^a) \end{aligned} \tag{3}$$

where $x(t) \in \mathbb{R}^n$ is the state of the system with $n = p + 2m$, (t_k^s) and (t_k^a) are given by (2), $x(t^+) = \lim_{\tau \to 0, \tau > 0} x(t + \tau)$, and

$$\begin{aligned} A_c &= \begin{pmatrix} A & 0 & B \\ 0 & 0 & 0 \\ 0 & 0 & 0 \end{pmatrix}, \; A_s = \begin{pmatrix} I_p & 0 & 0 \\ K & 0 & 0 \\ 0 & 0 & I_m \end{pmatrix}, \\ A_a &= \begin{pmatrix} I_p & 0 & 0 \\ 0 & I_m & 0 \\ 0 & I_m & 0 \end{pmatrix}, \; x(t) = \begin{pmatrix} z(t) \\ K z(\theta^s(t)) \\ u(t) \end{pmatrix}, \end{aligned} \tag{4}$$

with $\theta^s(t) = t_k^s$ for $t \in (t_k^s, t_{k+1}^s]$.

In this paper, we consider stability in the following sense:

Definition 1. The system (2-3) is *globally uniformly exponentially stable* (GUES) if there exist $\lambda \in \mathbb{R}^+$ and $C \in \mathbb{R}^+$ such that, for all sequences $(t_k^s)_{k \in \mathbb{N}}$ and $(t_k^a)_{k \in \mathbb{N}}$ verifying (2) the solutions of (3) verify

$$\|x(t)\| \leq C e^{-\lambda t} \|x(0)\|, \; \forall t \in \mathbb{R}^+.$$

We are now interested in verifying stability of embedded control systems in the form given by (1) under one of the general timing contracts defined previously. It is noteworthy that we can easily show that system (1) under the ZET and LET contracts is stable if and only if the eigenvalues of the matrix $e^{hA_c} A_a A_s$ and $A_a e^{hA_c} A_s$ are inside the unit circle respectively. As for the DET or TOL contracts, we have that stability of system (1) is guaranteed by the stability of (2-3) with an adequate choice of the timing contract parameters. Consequently, in this work, we consider the following problem:

Problem 1 (Stability verification). *Given A_c, A_s, $A_a \in \mathbb{R}^{n \times n}$, $(\underline{\tau}, \overline{\tau}, \underline{h}, \overline{h}) \in \mathcal{C}$, verify that (2-3) is GUES.*

This problem will be considered in the following section. Afterwards, we shall consider the problem of synthesizing timing contract parameters that guarantee the stability of the system. Given bounds on the parameters $0 \leq \tau_{min} \leq \tau_{max}$, $0 < h_{min} \leq h_{max}$, with $\tau_{min} \leq h_{min}$, $\tau_{max} \leq h_{max}$, let $\mathcal{D} = [\tau_{min}, \tau_{max}]^2 \times [h_{min}, h_{max}]^2$, the problem is formalized as follows:

Problem 2 (Timing contract synthesis). *Given A_c, A_s, $A_a \in \mathbb{R}^{n \times n}$ and $\mathcal{D}$, synthesize a set $\mathcal{C}^* \subseteq \mathcal{C} \cap \mathcal{D}$ such that for all $(\underline{\tau}, \overline{\tau}, \underline{h}, \overline{h}) \in \mathcal{C}^*$, (2-3) is GUES.*

Related work. Several approaches are developed in the literature to solve instances of Problem 1. A non-exhaustive list is given in Table 1. From the modeling perspective, the problem can be tackled using difference inclusions, time-delay systems or hybrid systems. On the computational side, most of the approaches are based on semi-definite programming using either Linear Matrix Inequalities (LMI) or Sum Of Squares (SOS) formulations. This makes a clear distinction with our approach which relies on reachability analysis. Let us remark that only a few approaches [10, 12, 4] appear to be able to address all instances of Problem 1. It is noticeable that [10, 12] have been implemented in the Networked Control Systems (NCS) toolbox [5] whose results will be compared to those of our approach. We should also acknowledge that some of these approaches are able to handle problems that we do not consider in the present work (possibility of having $\tau_k > h_k$, controller synthesis, scheduling protocols, quantization, nonlinear dynamics, stochastic timing uncertainties). Finally, as far as we know, there is no available approach for addressing Problem 2 besides our preliminary work [1] where we impose $\underline{\tau} = \overline{\tau} = 0$.

3. STABILITY CONDITIONS

In this section we state necessary and sufficient theoretical conditions for system (2-3) to be GUES. In addition, we derive practical sufficient conditions that can be used to develop an algorithm for solving Problem 1.

3.1 Necessary and sufficient conditions

Our stability conditions are based on the notion of reachable set defined as follows:

Definition 2. Given a continuous-time dynamical system

$$\dot{x}(t) = Ax(t),\ t \in \mathbb{R}_0^+,\ x(t) \in \mathbb{R}^n$$

the *reachable set* on $[t, t'] \subseteq \mathbb{R}_0^+$ from the set $\mathcal{S} \subseteq \mathbb{R}^n$ is

$$\mathcal{R}^A_{[t,t']}(\mathcal{S}) = \bigcup_{\tau \in [t,t']} e^{\tau A}\mathcal{S}. \tag{5}$$

We also define the map: $\Phi : 2^{\mathbb{R}^n} \to 2^{\mathbb{R}^n}$, given for all $\mathcal{S} \subseteq \mathbb{R}^n$ by

$$\Phi(\mathcal{S}) = \bigcup_{\tau \in [\underline{\tau},\overline{\tau}]} \bigcup_{w \in [\max(0,\underline{h}-\tau),\overline{h}-\tau]} e^{wA_c}A_a e^{\tau A_c} A_s \mathcal{S} \tag{6}$$

It is easy to see that if $\mathcal{S}$ is compact then so is $\Phi(\mathcal{S})$. It is clear that for two sets $\mathcal{S}$, $\mathcal{S}' \subseteq \mathbb{R}^n$ and $a \in \mathbb{R}$, we have $\Phi(\mathcal{S} \cup \mathcal{S}') = \Phi(\mathcal{S}) \cup \Phi(\mathcal{S}')$ and $\Phi(a\mathcal{S}) = a\Phi(\mathcal{S})$.

The interpretation of Φ is as follows. If $\mathcal{S}$ is the set of all states that are reachable by (2-3) at time t_k^s then $\Phi(\mathcal{S})$ is the set of reachable states at time t_{k+1}^s. We define the iterations of Φ as $\Phi^0(\mathcal{S}) = \mathcal{S}$ for all $\mathcal{S} \subseteq \mathbb{R}^n$, and $\Phi^{k+1} = \Phi \circ \Phi^k$ for all $k \in \mathbb{N}$. Then, for all $k \in \mathbb{N}$, $\Phi^k(\mathcal{S})$ is the set of reachable states by (2-3) at time t_k^s for initial states belonging to $\mathcal{S}$.

Next, we state the theoretical conditions on the stability of system (2-3) in terms of the map Φ. Similar results have been stated in [3] for discrete-time switched systems and in [1] for NPILS.

THEOREM 1. *Let $\mathcal{S} \in \mathcal{K}_0(\mathbb{R}^n)$, the following statements are equivalent:*

(a) System (2-3) is GUES,

(b) There exists a triplet $(k, j, \rho) \in \mathbb{N}^+ \times \mathbb{N}_{[0,k-1]} \times (0, 1)$ such that $\Phi^k(\mathcal{S}) \subseteq \rho\Phi^j(\mathcal{S})$,

(c) There exists a pair $(k, \rho) \in \mathbb{N}^+ \times (0, 1)$ such that $\Phi^k(\mathcal{S}) \subseteq \rho \bigcup_{j=0}^{k-1} \Phi^j(\mathcal{S})$.

PROOF. It is obvious that $(b) \implies (c)$. Hence, it is sufficient to prove that $(a) \implies (b)$ and $(c) \implies (a)$.

$(a) \implies (b)$: We will prove that there exists $(k, \rho) \in \mathbb{N}^+ \times (0, 1)$ such that $\Phi^k(\mathcal{S}) \subseteq \rho\mathcal{S}$. This implies (b) with $j = 0$. Let $x(0) \in \mathcal{S}$, then $\Phi^k(\mathcal{S})$ represents all the possible values of $x(t_k^s)$. Since (2-3) is GUES, there exist $C \in \mathbb{R}^+$ and $\lambda \in \mathbb{R}^+$ such that

$$\|x(t_k^s)\| \leq Ce^{-\lambda t_k^s}\|x(0)\| \leq Ce^{-\lambda k \underline{h}}\|x(0)\|$$

which can be rewritten as

$$\Phi^k(\mathcal{S}) \subseteq Ce^{-\lambda k \underline{h}}\|x(0)\|\mathcal{B} \tag{7}$$

where $\mathcal{B}$ is the unit ball. Since $\mathcal{S} \in \mathcal{K}_0(\mathbb{R}^n)$, then there exist $\underline{c} \in \mathbb{R}^+$, $\overline{c} \in \mathbb{R}^+$ such that $\underline{c}\mathcal{B} \subseteq \mathcal{S} \subseteq \overline{c}\mathcal{B}$. Then, (7) and $x(0) \in \mathcal{S}$ give

$$\Phi^k(\mathcal{S}) \subseteq Ce^{-\lambda k \underline{h}}\overline{c}\mathcal{B} \subseteq \frac{Ce^{-\lambda k \underline{h}}\overline{c}}{\underline{c}}\mathcal{S}.$$

For k sufficiently large, $Ce^{-\lambda k \underline{h}}\overline{c} < \underline{c}$ and therefore (b) holds.

$(c) \implies (a)$: Let $\gamma = \rho^{\frac{1}{k}}$; since $\rho \in (0, 1)$ then for all $j \in \mathbb{N}_{[0,k-1]}$, $\rho \leq \gamma^{k-j}$ and

$$\Phi^k(\mathcal{S}) \subseteq \rho \bigcup_{j=0}^{k-1} \Phi^j(\mathcal{S}) \subseteq \bigcup_{j=0}^{k-1} \gamma^{k-j}\Phi^j(\mathcal{S}). \tag{8}$$

Let $\mathcal{S}' = \bigcup_{j=0}^{k-1} \gamma^{-j}\Phi^j(\mathcal{S})$, then using properties of Φ:

$$\begin{aligned}\Phi(\mathcal{S}') &= \Phi\left(\bigcup_{j=0}^{k-1} \gamma^{-j}\Phi^j(\mathcal{S})\right) = \bigcup_{j=0}^{k-1} \gamma^{-j}\Phi^{j+1}(\mathcal{S}) \\ &= \left(\bigcup_{j=0}^{k-2} \gamma^{-j}\Phi^{j+1}(\mathcal{S})\right) \cup \gamma^{-k+1}\Phi^k(\mathcal{S})\end{aligned}$$

Making a change of index in the union and using (8) yield

$$\begin{aligned}\Phi(\mathcal{S}') &\subseteq \left(\bigcup_{j=1}^{k-1} \gamma^{-j+1}\Phi^j(\mathcal{S})\right) \cup \gamma^{-k+1}\left(\bigcup_{j=0}^{k-1} \gamma^{k-j}\Phi^j(\mathcal{S})\right) \\ &\subseteq \gamma\left(\bigcup_{j=0}^{k-1} \gamma^{-j}\Phi^j(\mathcal{S})\right) = \gamma\mathcal{S}'. \end{aligned} \tag{9}$$

Since $\mathcal{S} \in \mathcal{K}_0(\mathbb{R}^n)$, then $\mathcal{S}'$ is compact. Moreover, since it contains $\mathcal{S}$, then $\mathcal{S}' \in \mathcal{K}_0(\mathbb{R}^n)$. Then, there exist $\underline{c}' \in \mathbb{R}^+$, $\overline{c}' \in \mathbb{R}^+$ such that $\underline{c}'\mathcal{B} \subseteq \mathcal{S}' \subseteq \overline{c}'\mathcal{B}$. Now consider a trajectory x of (2-3), then $x(0) \in \|x(0)\|\mathcal{B} \subseteq \frac{\|x(0)\|}{\underline{c}'}\mathcal{S}'$ and (9) gives for all $i \in \mathbb{N}$

$$x(t_i^s) \in \Phi^i\left(\frac{\|x(0)\|}{\underline{c}'}\mathcal{S}'\right) \subseteq \frac{\|x(0)\|\gamma^i}{\underline{c}'}\mathcal{S}' \subseteq \frac{\|x(0)\|\gamma^i\overline{c}'}{\underline{c}'}\mathcal{B}.$$

In other words, it holds for all $i \in \mathbb{N}$,

$$\|x(t_i^s)\| \leq \frac{\gamma^i\overline{c}'}{\underline{c}'}\|x(0)\|.$$

Now, let $t \in \mathbb{R}^+$, let $i \in \mathbb{N}$ be such that $t \in (t_i^s, t_{i+1}^s]$, then $t - t_i^s \leq \overline{h}$. Moreover, if $t \in (t_i^s, t_i^a]$, then

$$\|x(t)\| \leq e^{\|A_c\|\overline{h}}\|A_s\|\frac{\gamma^i\overline{c}'}{\underline{c}'}\|x(0)\|$$

and if $t \in (t_i^a, t_{i+1}^s]$, then

$$\|x(t)\| \leq e^{\|A_c\|\overline{h}}\|A_a\|\|A_s\|\frac{\gamma^i\overline{c}'}{\underline{c}'}\|x(0)\|.$$

In addition, we have $i \geq t/\overline{h}$ and since $\gamma \in (0, 1)$ it follows that for all $t \in \mathbb{R}^+$

$$\begin{aligned}\|x(t)\| &\leq \frac{e^{\|A_c\|\overline{h}}\max(\|A_a\|, 1)\|A_s\|\overline{c}'}{\underline{c}'}\gamma^{(t/\overline{h})}\|x(0)\| \\ &\leq \frac{e^{\|A_c\|\overline{h}}\max(\|A_a\|, 1)\|A_s\|\overline{c}'}{\underline{c}'}e^{\frac{\ln(\gamma)}{\overline{h}}t}\|x(0)\|.\end{aligned}$$

Since $\gamma \in (0, 1)$, (2-3) is GUES. □

3.2 Sufficient conditions

The map Φ involved in Theorem 1 is in general impossible to compute exactly. Then, we may use an over-approximation $\overline{\Phi} : \mathcal{K}(\mathbb{R}^n) \to \mathcal{K}(\mathbb{R}^n)$ satisfying the following assumption:

ASSUMPTION 1. *For all $\mathcal{S} \in \mathcal{K}(\mathbb{R}^n)$, $\Phi(\mathcal{S}) \subseteq \overline{\Phi}(\mathcal{S})$.*

We compute the map $\overline{\Phi}$ instead of Φ in order to derive the practical condition on stability used in the stability verification algorithm later on to solve Problem 1. Section 4 discusses on the effective computation of the map $\overline{\Phi}$. We now derive sufficient conditions for stability based on $\overline{\Phi}$.

COROLLARY 1. *Under Assumption 1, if there exist a set* $\mathcal{S} \in \mathcal{K}_0(\mathbb{R}^n)$ *and a triplet* $(k,i,\rho) \in \mathbb{N}^+ \times \mathbb{N}_{[0,k-1]} \times (0,1)$ *such that* $\overline{\Phi}^k(\mathcal{S}) \subseteq \rho\overline{\Phi}^i(\mathcal{S})$, *then system (2-3) is GUES.*

PROOF. $\overline{\Phi}^k(\mathcal{S}) \subseteq \rho\overline{\Phi}^i(\mathcal{S}) \subseteq \rho\bigcup_{j=0}^{k-1}\overline{\Phi}^j(\mathcal{S})$. Then similar to the second part of the proof of Theorem 1, let $\mathcal{S}' = \bigcup_{j=0}^{k-1}\gamma^{-j}\overline{\Phi}^j(\mathcal{S})$ where $\gamma = \rho^{\frac{1}{k}}$. Then

$$\begin{aligned}\Phi(\mathcal{S}') &= \Phi\left(\bigcup_{j=0}^{k-1}\gamma^{-j}\overline{\Phi}^j(\mathcal{S})\right) = \bigcup_{j=0}^{k-1}\gamma^{-j}\Phi(\overline{\Phi}^j(\mathcal{S}))\\ &\subseteq \bigcup_{j=0}^{k-1}\gamma^{-j}\overline{\Phi}(\overline{\Phi}^j(\mathcal{S})) = \bigcup_{j=0}^{k-1}\gamma^{-j}\overline{\Phi}^{j+1}(\mathcal{S}).\end{aligned}$$

Then, following the same steps as in (9), we can show that $\Phi(\mathcal{S}') \subseteq \gamma\mathcal{S}'$. Following the same line as in the proof of Theorem 1, one concludes that (2-3) is GUES. □

The previous corollary provides the background for designing a solution to Problem 1 in the next section.

4. OVER-APPROXIMATION SCHEME AND STABILITY VERIFICATION

In this section, we present an approach for computing an over-approximation of Φ. Furthermore, we develop an algorithm providing a solution to Problem 1.

4.1 Over-approximation

We first state the following result from [23] which gives an over-approximation scheme for the reachable set given by (5).

THEOREM 2. *[23] Let* $T \in \mathbb{R}^+$, $A \in \mathbb{R}^{n\times n}$, $\mathcal{S} \in \mathcal{K}(\mathbb{R}^n)$ *and* $N \in \mathbb{N}^+$, *let*

$$\overline{\mathcal{R}}^A_{[0,T]}(\mathcal{S}) = \bigcup_{i=1}^{N}\overline{\mathcal{R}}^A_{[(i-1)\delta,i\delta]}(\mathcal{S})$$

where $\delta = T/N$ *is the time step, and* $\overline{\mathcal{R}}^A_{[(i-1)\delta,i\delta]}(\mathcal{S})$ *is defined by the recurrence equation:*

$$\begin{aligned}\overline{\mathcal{R}}^A_{[0,\delta]}(\mathcal{S}) &= ch(\mathcal{S}, e^{\delta A}\,\mathcal{S}) \oplus 1/4\,\epsilon_\delta(\mathcal{S}), \quad (10)\\ \overline{\mathcal{R}}^A_{[i\delta,(i+1)\delta]}(\mathcal{S}) &= e^{\delta A}\,\overline{\mathcal{R}}^A_{[(i-1)\delta,i\delta]}(\mathcal{S}),\ i \in \mathbb{N}_{[1,N-1]}\end{aligned}$$

with

$$\begin{aligned}\epsilon_\delta(\mathcal{S}) = &\ \square(|A|^{-1}(e^{\delta|A|} - I)\boxdot(A(I - e^{\delta A})\mathcal{S}))\oplus\\ &\ \square(|A|^{-2}(e^{\delta|A|} - I - \delta|A|)\boxdot(A^2e^{\delta A}\mathcal{S})).\end{aligned}$$

Then, $\mathcal{R}^A_{[(i-1)\delta,i\delta]}(\mathcal{S}) \subseteq \overline{\mathcal{R}}^A_{[(i-1)\delta,i\delta]}(\mathcal{S})$, *for all* $i \in \mathbb{N}_{[1,N]}$ *and* $\mathcal{R}^A_{[0,T]}(\mathcal{S}) \subseteq \overline{\mathcal{R}}^A_{[0,T]}(\mathcal{S})$.

The previous theorem can serve to compute an over-approximation of Φ. Indeed, from (6), one can easily check that

$$\begin{aligned}\Phi(\mathcal{S}) &\subseteq \mathcal{R}^{A_c}_{[\max(0,\underline{h}-\overline{\tau}),\overline{h}-\underline{\tau}]}\left(A_a\mathcal{R}^{A_c}_{[\underline{\tau},\overline{\tau}]}(A_s\mathcal{S})\right)\\ &\subseteq e^{\max(0,\underline{h}-\overline{\tau})A_c}\mathcal{R}^{A_c}_{[0,\min(\overline{h}-\underline{\tau},\overline{h}-\underline{h}+\overline{\tau}-\underline{\tau})]}\Big(\\ &\qquad A_ae^{\underline{\tau}A_c}\mathcal{R}^{A_c}_{[0,\overline{\tau}-\underline{\tau}]}(A_s\mathcal{S})\Big) \quad (11)\end{aligned}$$

with in turn can easily be over-approximated using the result of Theorem 2. In the case of NPILS, the previous inclusion becomes an equality. This is the approach followed in our previous work [1]. However, for the general timing contract (2), the coupling in the timing uncertainties w and τ in (6) is totally disregarded in (11) and therefore leads to conservatism. Therefore, in this paper, to reduce conservatism, we present a specific approximation scheme for Φ, that takes into consideration the coupling in the timing uncertainties. It is based on the following result:

LEMMA 1. *Let* $\mathcal{S} \in \mathcal{K}(\mathbb{R}^n)$, *let* $N_1, N_2 \in \mathbb{N}^+$, *then*

$$\begin{aligned}\Phi(\mathcal{S}) \subseteq &\bigcup_{j_1=1}^{N_1}\bigcup_{j_2=1}^{n_2(j_1)} e^{(\theta(j_1)+(j_2-1)\delta_2)A_c}\mathcal{R}^{A_c}_{[0,\delta_2]}\Big(\\ &\qquad A_ae^{(\underline{\tau}+(j_1-1)\delta_1)A_c}\mathcal{R}^{A_c}_{[0,\delta_1]}(A_s\mathcal{S})\Big) \quad (12)\end{aligned}$$

where for $j_1 \in \mathbb{N}_{[1,N_1]}$

$$\begin{aligned}\delta_1 &= (\overline{\tau} - \underline{\tau})/N_1\\ \delta_2 &= \min(\overline{h} - \underline{\tau}, \overline{h} - \underline{h} + \delta_1)/N_2\\ \theta(j_1) &= \max(0, \underline{h} - \underline{\tau} - j_1\delta_1)\\ n_2(j_1) &= \lceil\min(\overline{h} - \underline{\tau} - (j_1 - 1)\delta_1, \overline{h} - \underline{h} + \delta_1)/\delta_2\rceil. \quad (13)\end{aligned}$$

PROOF. From (6), it follows that

$$\begin{aligned}\Phi(\mathcal{S}) &= \bigcup_{j_1=1}^{N_1}\bigcup_{\tau\in[\underline{\tau}+(j_1-1)\delta_1,\underline{\tau}+j_1\delta_1]}\\ &\qquad\bigcup_{w\in[\max(0,\underline{h}-\tau),\overline{h}-\tau]} e^{wA_c}A_ae^{\tau A_c}A_s\mathcal{S}\\ &\subseteq \bigcup_{j_1=1}^{N_1}\mathcal{R}^{A_c}_{[\theta(j_1),\overline{h}-\underline{\tau}-(j_1-1)\delta_1]}\Big(\\ &\qquad A_a\mathcal{R}^{A_c}_{[\underline{\tau}+(j_1-1)\delta_1,\underline{\tau}+j_1\delta_1]}(A_s\mathcal{S})\Big)\\ &\subseteq \bigcup_{j_1=1}^{N_1}e^{\theta(j_1)A_c}\mathcal{R}^{A_c}_{[0,\overline{h}-\underline{\tau}-(j_1-1)\delta_1-\theta(j_1)]}\Big(\\ &\qquad A_ae^{(\underline{\tau}+(j_1-1)\delta_1)A_c}\mathcal{R}^{A_c}_{[0,\delta_1]}(A_s\mathcal{S})\Big).\end{aligned}$$

Remarking that

$$\overline{h} - \underline{\tau} - (j_1 - 1)\delta_1 - \theta(j_1) = \min(\overline{h} - \underline{\tau} - (j_1 - 1)\delta_1, \overline{h} - \underline{h} + \delta_1)$$

one gets

$$\begin{aligned}\Phi(\mathcal{S}) \subseteq &\bigcup_{j_1=1}^{N_1}\bigcup_{j_2=1}^{n_2(j_1)} e^{\theta(j_1)A_c}\mathcal{R}^{A_c}_{[(j_2-1)\delta_2,j_2\delta_2]}\Big(\\ &\qquad A_ae^{(\underline{\tau}+(j_1-1)\delta_1)A_c}\mathcal{R}^{A_c}_{[0,\delta_1]}(A_s\mathcal{S})\Big)\end{aligned}$$

which leads to (12). □

REMARK 1. N_1 *and* N_2 *are parameters used to discretize time intervals. For* $N_1 = N_2 = 1$, *the over-approximation given by (12) is the same as the one in (11).*

We now present our over-approximation scheme for Φ:

THEOREM 3. *Let* $\mathcal{S} \in \mathcal{K}(\mathbb{R}^n)$, $N_1, N_2 \in \mathbb{N}^+$, *and* $H \in \mathbb{R}^{m\times n}$, *such that* $0 \in int(ch(\{H_1, \ldots, H_m\}))$, *let* $\overline{\Phi} : \mathcal{K}(\mathbb{R}^n) \to$

$\mathcal{K}(\mathbb{R}^n)$ *be given by*

$$\overline{\Phi}(\mathcal{S}) = \Gamma_H \left(\bigcup_{j_1=1}^{N_1} \bigcup_{j_2=1}^{n_2(j_1)} e^{(\theta(j_1)+(j_2-1)\delta_2)A_c}\overline{\Phi}_{j_1}(\mathcal{S}) \right)$$

where for $j_1 \in \mathbb{N}_{[1,N_1]}$,

$$\overline{\Phi}_{j_1}(\mathcal{S}) = \overline{\mathcal{R}}^{A_c}_{[0,\delta_2]}\left(A_a e^{(\underline{\tau}+(j_1-1)\delta_1)A_c}\overline{\mathcal{R}}^{A_c}_{[0,\delta_1]}(A_s\mathcal{S})\right)$$

with δ_1, δ_2, $\theta(j_1)$, $n_2(j_1)$ *given by (13) , and* $\overline{\mathcal{R}}^{A_c}_{[0,\delta_1]}$, $\overline{\mathcal{R}}^{A_c}_{[0,\delta_2]}$ *computed as in (10). Then,* $\Phi(\mathcal{S}) \subseteq \overline{\Phi}(\mathcal{S})$.

PROOF. The proof is straightforward from Theorem 2 and Lemma 1. □

REMARK 2. *In the previous result, the operation* Γ_H *is not necessary to guarantee over-approximation of* Φ. *On the other hand, without this operation, the over-approximation of* Φ *would be given by the union of possibly numerous sets which may be quite impractical for subsequent manipulations. For that reason, this union is over-approximated by the smallest enclosing polytope whose facets direction are given by a matrix* H. *Moreover, if* $\mathcal{S}$ *is a polytope, then using the properties of support functions [24], the computation of* $\overline{\Phi}(\mathcal{S})$ *reduces to solving a set of linear programs.*

We illustrate the tightness of our new approximation scheme using system (16) (see Section 6) with the timing contract given by $\underline{\tau} = 0$, $\overline{\tau} = 0.4$, $\underline{h} = 0.2$, $\overline{h} = 1.2$. We consider a polytope $\mathcal{S}$ defined by a matrix H with 44 rows. Figure 2 shows sampled points (in grey) from $\Phi(\mathcal{S})$. The white polytope corresponds to the over-approximation $\overline{\Phi}(\mathcal{S})$ given in Theorem 3 with $N_1 = 20$ and $N_2 = 50$. The black polytope is given by (11) over-approximated using Theorem 2 where $\overline{\mathcal{R}}^{A_c}_{[0,\overline{\tau}-\underline{\tau}]}$ and $\overline{\mathcal{R}}^{A_c}_{[0,\min(\overline{h}-\underline{\tau},\overline{h}-\underline{h}+\overline{\tau}-\underline{\tau})]}$ are computed with $N = 20$ and $N = 50$ respectively. One can check that the over-approximation given by Theorem 3 is quite tight and much less conservative than that given by (11).

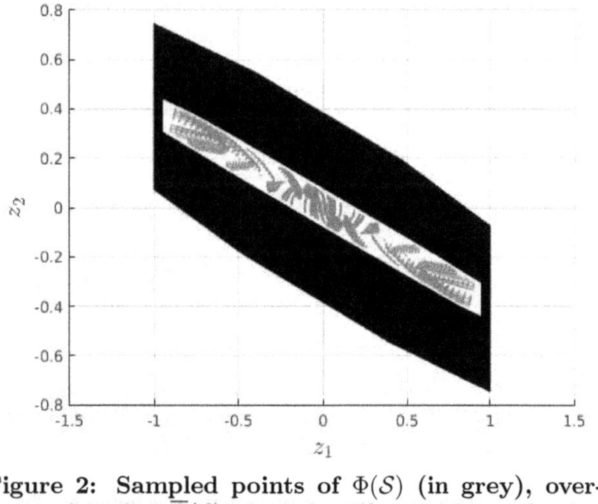

Figure 2: Sampled points of $\Phi(\mathcal{S})$ (in grey), over-approximation $\overline{\Phi}(\mathcal{S})$ given by Theorem 3 and over-approximation of (11) computed using Theorem 2 (in black).

4.2 Stability verification algorithm

We now present our stability verification algorithm which consists of two main steps: an initialization step where an initial set $\mathcal{P}_0$ is computed and a main loop which tries to verify the sufficient stability condition given in Corollary 1 by iterating the map $\overline{\Phi}$ given by Theorem 3 from the set $\mathcal{P}_0$.

4.2.1 Initialization

The choice of the initial set $\mathcal{P}_0$ is crucial as it may impact significantly the number of iterations of $\overline{\Phi}$ that are necessary to check the condition of Corollary 1. Intuitively, in order to minimize this number of iterations, $\mathcal{P}_0$ should be already close to an invariant set. Indeed, if $\overline{\Phi}(\mathcal{P}_0) \subseteq \mathcal{P}_0$, the stability condition holds after only one iterate of $\overline{\Phi}$. One way to choose $\mathcal{P}_0$ close to an invariant set is to define $\mathcal{P}_0$ as a common contracting polytope to $L \in \mathbb{N}^+$ linear discrete-time systems, such that

$$\forall j \in \mathbb{N}_{[1,L]},\ e^{(h_j-\tau_j)A_c}A_a e^{\tau_j A_c}A_s\mathcal{P}_0 \subseteq \mathrm{int}(\mathcal{P}_0),$$

where the couples (τ_j, h_j) satisfy timing contract (2) for all $j \in \mathbb{N}_{[1,L]}$. Then, $\mathcal{P}_0$ can be computed either using a backward iterative method as in [6] and [13] or using a forward iterative method as in [3]. We denote the function computing $\mathcal{P}_0$ by $\mathsf{init}(A_c, A_d, A_s, \underline{\tau}, \overline{\tau}, \underline{h}, \overline{h}, L)$. Then, $\mathcal{P}_0 = \{x \in \mathbb{R}^n : Hx \leq b_0\}$. The matrix H defining $\mathcal{P}_0$ is used in the main loop of the algorithm in the computation of the map $\overline{\Phi}$.

4.2.2 Main loop

The initial set is propagated using the map $\overline{\Phi}$ given by Theorem 3. Then if the stability condition given by Corollary 1 is verified, system (2-3) is GUES and the algorithm returns true. Otherwise, if a maximum number of iterations, k_{max}, is reached then the algorithm fails to prove stability and returns unknown. The algorithm that solves Problem 1 is given as follows:

ALGORITHM 1. *Stability verification*

function *is_GUES*(A_c,A_a,A_s,$\underline{\tau}$,$\overline{\tau}$,$\underline{h}$,$\overline{h}$)
input: A_c, A_a, $A_s \in \mathbb{R}^{n\times n}$, $(\underline{\tau}, \overline{\tau}, \underline{h}, \overline{h}) \in \mathcal{C}$
output: *true if system (2-3) is proved GUES, unknown otherwise*
parameter: N_1,N_2,L, $k_{max} \in \mathbb{N}^+$
1: $\mathcal{P}_0$:=*init*(A_c, A_d, A_s, $\underline{\tau}$, $\overline{\tau}$, $\underline{h}$, $\overline{h}$, L); ▷ *compute initial set*
2: ***for*** $k = 1$ *to* k_{max} ***do***
3: $\mathcal{P}_k$:=$\overline{\Phi}(\mathcal{P}_{k-1})$; ▷ *set propagation*
4: ***if*** $\exists i \in \mathbb{N}_{[0,k-1]}$, $\mathcal{P}_k \subseteq$ *int*($\mathcal{P}_i$) ***then***
5: *return true;* ▷ *system (2-3) is GUES*
6: ***end if***
7: ***end for***
8: *return unknown;*

Note that all polytopes $\mathcal{P}_k$ are of the form $\mathcal{P}_k = \{x \in \mathbb{R}^n : Hx \leq b_k\}$, then the inclusion test at line 4 only consists in checking $b_k \leq b_i$. Although Algorithm 1 is only based on sufficient conditions for the stability of system (2-3), its effectiveness will be demonstrated on numerical examples in Section 6.

5. TIMING CONTRACT SYNTHESIS

In this section, we propose a solution to Problem 2. We first define a re-parametrization of the timing-contract such that stability of system (2-3) becomes monotone with respect to the new parameters. Monotonicity is a very attractive property for designing efficient heuristics for timing contract synthesis since stability is preserved when the parameter values increase. This allows us to tackle the timing contract synthesis by sampling the parameter space.

5.1 Re-parametrization

Let us denote the vector of timing contract parameters $\alpha = (\underline{\tau}, \overline{\tau}, \underline{h}, \overline{h}) \in \mathcal{D} = [\tau_{min}, \tau_{max}]^2 \times [h_{min}, h_{max}]^2$, where $0 \leq \tau_{min} \leq \tau_{max}$, $0 < h_{min} \leq h_{max}$, $\tau_{min} \leq h_{min}$, $\tau_{max} \leq h_{max}$. For $\alpha \in \mathcal{C} \cap \mathcal{D}$ we denote the property:

$$\mathsf{Stab}(\alpha) \equiv \text{(2-3) is GUES with parameters } \alpha.$$

Solving Problem 2 is equivalent to computing (a subset of) the set $\mathcal{C}_o$ defined by

$$\mathcal{C}_o = \{\alpha \in \mathcal{C} \cap \mathcal{D} : \mathsf{Stab}(\alpha)\}.$$

Let us define a new parameter $\beta = (\beta_1, \beta_2, \beta_3, \beta_4) \in \mathcal{D}'$ where $\mathcal{D}' = [\tau_{min}, \tau_{max}] \times [-\tau_{max}, -\tau_{min}] \times [h_{min}, h_{max}] \times [-h_{max}, -h_{min}]$ and the map $f : \mathcal{D}' \to \mathcal{D}$ such that $f(\beta) = \alpha = (\underline{\tau}, \overline{\tau}, \underline{h}, \overline{h})$ where

$$\underline{\tau} = \beta_1,\ \overline{\tau} = \min(-\beta_2, -\beta_4),\ \underline{h} = \beta_3,\ \overline{h} = -\beta_4.$$

We define the following constraint set for the parameter β:

$$\mathcal{C}' = \left\{ \beta \in \mathbb{R}_0^+ \times \mathbb{R}_0^- \times \mathbb{R}^+ \times \mathbb{R}^- : \begin{array}{l} \beta_1 \leq \min(-\beta_2, -\beta_4) \\ \beta_3 \leq -\beta_4 \end{array} \right\}.$$

The following result holds:

LEMMA 2. *Let $\mathcal{C}'_o$ be given by*

$$\mathcal{C}'_o = \{\beta \in \mathcal{C}' \cap \mathcal{D}' : \mathsf{Stab}(f(\beta))\}.$$

Then, $f(\mathcal{C}' \cap \mathcal{D}') = \mathcal{C} \cap \mathcal{D}$ and $f(\mathcal{C}'_o) = \mathcal{C}_o$.

PROOF. Let us first show that $f(\mathcal{C}' \cap \mathcal{D}') \subseteq \mathcal{C} \cap \mathcal{D}$ and $f(\mathcal{C}'_o) \subseteq \mathcal{C}_o$. Let $\beta \in \mathcal{C}' \cap \mathcal{D}'$ and $\alpha = f(\beta) = (\underline{\tau}, \overline{\tau}, \underline{h}, \overline{h})$. Then, $\beta \in \mathcal{D}'$ implies that $\alpha \in \mathcal{D}$, using the fact that $\tau_{min} \leq h_{min}$, $\tau_{max} \leq h_{max}$. Also, $\beta \in \mathcal{C}'$ implies that $\underline{\tau} \leq \overline{\tau}$ and $\underline{h} \leq \overline{h}$. Moreover, $\overline{\tau} = \min(-\beta_2, -\beta_4) \leq -\beta_4 = \overline{h}$. Hence, $\alpha \in \mathcal{C}$. Thus, $\alpha \in \mathcal{C} \cap \mathcal{D}$. Moreover, if $\beta \in \mathcal{C}'_o$ then $\beta \in \mathcal{C}' \cap \mathcal{D}'$ and $\mathsf{Stab}(f(\beta))$ gives $\alpha \in \mathcal{C} \cap \mathcal{D}$ and $\mathsf{Stab}(\alpha)$. Thus, $\alpha \in \mathcal{C}_o$. We now show that $\mathcal{C} \cap \mathcal{D} \subseteq f(\mathcal{C}' \cap \mathcal{D}')$ and $\mathcal{C}_o \subseteq f(\mathcal{C}'_o)$. Let $\alpha = (\underline{\tau}, \overline{\tau}, \underline{h}, \overline{h}) \in \mathcal{C} \cap \mathcal{D}$ and let $\beta = (\underline{\tau}, -\overline{\tau}, \underline{h}, -\overline{h})$. Then, $f(\beta) = (\underline{\tau}, \min(\overline{\tau}, \overline{h}), \underline{h}, \overline{h})$. Since $\alpha \in \mathcal{C}$, it follows that $\min(\overline{\tau}, \overline{h}) = \overline{\tau}$ and $f(\beta) = \alpha$. Moreover, it is straightforward to verify that $\alpha \in \mathcal{C} \cap \mathcal{D}$ implies $\beta \in \mathcal{C}' \cap \mathcal{D}'$ and that $\alpha \in \mathcal{C}_o$ implies $\beta \in \mathcal{C}'_o$. □

The previous result has two important implications. The first one is that the proposed re-parametrization does not introduce any conservatism in the solution to Problem 2 since the set $\mathcal{C}_o$ of admissible parameters α can be obtained by computing the set $\mathcal{C}'_o$ of admissible parameters β, despite the fact that the map f is not injective nor surjective. The second one is stated in the following lemma:

LEMMA 3. *Let $\mathcal{C}'^* \subseteq \mathcal{C}'_o$, then $\mathcal{C}^* = f(\mathcal{C}'^*)$ is a solution to Problem 2.*

PROOF. It holds that $\mathcal{C}^* = f(\mathcal{C}'^*) \subseteq f(\mathcal{C}'_o) = \mathcal{C}_o$. □

We further define the following set

$$\mathcal{E}'_o = \{\beta \in \mathcal{D}' : (\beta \notin \mathcal{C}') \vee ((\beta \in \mathcal{C}') \wedge \mathsf{Stab}(f(\beta)))\}.$$

One can easily check that the following relation holds:

$$\mathcal{C}'_o = \mathcal{C}' \cap \mathcal{E}'_o. \tag{14}$$

Hence, from the previous equality and Lemma 3, we can solve Problem 2 by computing (a subset of) the set $\mathcal{E}'_o$. Moreover, $\mathcal{E}'_o$ satisfies the following monotonicity property:

PROPOSITION 1. *For all $\beta, \beta' \in \mathcal{D}'$, the following implications hold:*

$$((\beta \leq \beta') \wedge (\beta \in \mathcal{E}'_o)) \implies \beta' \in \mathcal{E}'_o.$$

$$((\beta \leq \beta') \wedge (\beta' \notin \mathcal{E}'_o)) \implies \beta \notin \mathcal{E}'_o.$$

PROOF. Let us assume $\beta \leq \beta'$ and $\beta \in \mathcal{E}'_o$. There are two cases:

1. If $\beta \notin \mathcal{C}'$, then either $-\beta'_4 \leq -\beta_4 < \beta_3 \leq \beta'_3$, or $-\beta'_2 \leq -\beta_2 < \beta_1 \leq \beta'_1$, or $-\beta'_4 \leq -\beta_4 < \beta_1 \leq \beta'_1$. In all three cases $\beta' \notin \mathcal{C}'$ and therefore $\beta' \in \mathcal{E}'_o$.
2. If $\beta \in \mathcal{C}'$ and $\mathsf{Stab}(f(\beta))$, then either $\beta' \notin \mathcal{C}'$ which implies $\beta' \in \mathcal{E}'_o$, or $\beta' \in \mathcal{C}'$. In this latter case, $\alpha = (\underline{\tau}, \overline{\tau}, \underline{h}, \overline{h}) = f(\beta)$ and $\alpha' = (\underline{\tau}', \overline{\tau}', \underline{h}', \overline{h}') = f(\beta')$ satisfy $\alpha \in \mathcal{C}$, $\alpha' \in \mathcal{C}$ and
$$\underline{\tau}' \geq \underline{\tau},\ \overline{\tau}' \leq \overline{\tau},\ \underline{h}' \geq \underline{h},\ \overline{h}' \leq \overline{h}. \tag{15}$$
It is straightforward to check that if (2-3) is GUES for $(\underline{\tau}, \overline{\tau}, \underline{h}, \overline{h}) \in \mathcal{C}$ then (2-3) is GUES for all $(\underline{\tau}', \overline{\tau}', \underline{h}', \overline{h}') \in \mathcal{C}$ satisfying (15). Thus, $\mathsf{Stab}(f(\beta'))$ holds and $\beta' \in \mathcal{E}'_o$.

This proves the first implication. For the second implication, it is sufficient to check that

$$\begin{aligned} & ((\beta \leq \beta') \wedge (\beta \in \mathcal{E}'_o)) \implies \beta' \in \mathcal{E}'_o \\ \equiv\ & \neg(\beta \leq \beta') \vee (\beta \notin \mathcal{E}'_o) \vee (\beta' \in \mathcal{E}'_o) \\ \equiv\ & ((\beta \leq \beta') \wedge (\beta' \notin \mathcal{E}'_o)) \implies \beta \notin \mathcal{E}'_o. \end{aligned}$$

□

The previous property is instrumental for computing a subset of $\mathcal{E}'_o$ since it allows us to state the following theorem:

THEOREM 4. *Let $\underline{\beta}^1, \dots, \underline{\beta}^{M_1} \in \mathcal{E}'_o$, and $\overline{\beta}^1, \dots, \overline{\beta}^{M_2} \in \mathcal{D}' \setminus \mathcal{E}'_o$ and let*

$$\underline{\mathcal{E}}' = \bigcup_{j=1}^{M_1} \{\beta \in \mathcal{D}' : \underline{\beta}^j \leq \beta\},\ \overline{\mathcal{E}}' = \mathcal{D}' \setminus \bigcup_{j=1}^{M_2} \{\beta \in \mathcal{D}' : \beta \leq \overline{\beta}^j\}.$$

Then, $\underline{\mathcal{E}}' \subseteq \mathcal{E}'_o \subseteq \overline{\mathcal{E}}'$. Moreover, $\mathcal{C}^* = f(\mathcal{C}' \cap \underline{\mathcal{E}}')$ is a solution to Problem 2 and $\mathcal{C}_o \subseteq f(\mathcal{C}' \cap \overline{\mathcal{E}}')$.

PROOF. $\underline{\mathcal{E}}' \subseteq \mathcal{E}'_o \subseteq \overline{\mathcal{E}}'$ is a direct consequence of Proposition 1. Then, from (14) and Lemmas 2 and 3, it follows that $\mathcal{C}^*$ is a solution to Problem 2 and $\mathcal{C}_o \subseteq f(\mathcal{C}' \cap \overline{\mathcal{E}}')$. □

5.2 Timing contract synthesis algorithm

The previous theorem shows that it is possible to compute under and over-approximations of the set $\mathcal{E}'_o$ by sampling the parameter space $\mathcal{D}'$. In this section, we use this property to design a synthesis algorithm. Similar algorithms have been used in [25, 30] for computing an approximation of the Pareto front of a monotone multi-criteria optimization problem. Indeed, this latter problem can be tackled by computing an under and over-approximation of a set satisfying a monotonicity property similar to that of Proposition 1.

ALGORITHM 2. *Timing contract synthesis*

function *TC_Synth*$(A_c, A_a, A_s, \mathcal{D})$
input: $A_c,\ A_a,\ A_s \in \mathbb{R}^{n\times n}$, $\mathcal{D} = [\tau_{min}, \tau_{max}]^2 \times [h_{min}, h_{max}]^2$
output: $\mathcal{C}^* \subseteq \mathcal{C} \cap \mathcal{D}$ *such that for all* $(\underline{\tau}, \overline{\tau}, \underline{h}, \overline{h}) \in \mathcal{C}^*$, *(2-3) is GUES.*
parameter: $\varepsilon \in \mathbb{R}^+$
1: ***if*** $\beta_{min} = (\tau_{min}, -\tau_{max}, h_{min}, -h_{max}) \in \mathcal{E}'_o$ ***then***
2: *return* $\mathcal{C} \cap \mathcal{D}$;
3: ***else*** $\overline{\mathcal{E}}' := \mathcal{D}' \setminus \{\beta_{min}\}$;
4: ***end if***
5: ***if*** $\beta_{max} = (\tau_{max}, -\tau_{min}, h_{max}, -h_{min}) \notin \mathcal{E}'_o$ ***then***
6: *return* $\emptyset$;
7: ***else*** $\underline{\mathcal{E}}' := \{\beta_{max}\}$;
8: ***end if***
9: ***while*** $d(\underline{\mathcal{E}}', \overline{\mathcal{E}}') > \varepsilon$ ***do*** ▷ *main loop*
10: *Pick* $\beta \in \overline{\mathcal{E}}' \setminus \underline{\mathcal{E}}'$; ▷ *select next sample*
11: ***if*** $\beta \in \mathcal{E}'_o$ ***then*** $\underline{\mathcal{E}}' := \underline{\mathcal{E}}' \cup \{\beta' \in \mathcal{D}' : \beta \leq \beta'\}$;
12: ***else*** $\overline{\mathcal{E}}' := \overline{\mathcal{E}}' \setminus \{\beta' \in \mathcal{D}' : \beta' \leq \beta\}$;
13: ***end if***
14: ***end while***
15: *return* $f(\mathcal{C}' \cap \underline{\mathcal{E}}')$;

Algorithm 2 computes an under-approximation $\underline{\mathcal{E}}'$ and an over-approximation $\overline{\mathcal{E}}'$ of the set $\mathcal{E}'_o$ by sampling iteratively the parameter space $\mathcal{D}'$.

Lines 1 to 8 correspond to the initialization of these approximations by testing the lower bound β_{min} and the upper bound β_{max} of the set $\mathcal{D}'$. If $\beta_{min} \in \mathcal{E}'_o$, then by Theorem 4, $f(\mathcal{C}' \cap \mathcal{D}') = \mathcal{C} \cap \mathcal{D}$ is a solution to Problem 2. Note that in that case, all timing-contract parameters in $\mathcal{C} \cap \mathcal{D}$ guarantee the stability of (2-3). If $\beta_{min} \notin \mathcal{E}'_o$, then $\mathcal{D}' \setminus \{\beta_{min}\}$ is an over-approximation of $\mathcal{E}'_o$. Similarly, if $\beta_{max} \notin \mathcal{E}'_o$, then by Theorem 4, $\mathcal{E}'_o = \emptyset$. Note that in that case, no timing-contract parameters in $\mathcal{C} \cap \mathcal{D}$ can guarantee the stability of (2-3). If $\beta_{max} \in \mathcal{E}'_o$, then $\{\beta_{max}\}$ is an under-approximation of $\mathcal{E}'_o$.

Lines 9 to 14 describe the main loop of the timing contract synthesis algorithm. At any time of the execution, $\underline{\mathcal{E}}' \subseteq \mathcal{E}'_o \subseteq \overline{\mathcal{E}}'$ holds. We pick a sample $\beta \in \overline{\mathcal{E}}' \setminus \underline{\mathcal{E}}'$ which is the unexplored parameter region lying in the over-approximation of $\mathcal{E}'_o$ but not in its under-approximation. If $\beta \in \mathcal{E}'_o$ (or if $\beta \notin \mathcal{E}'_o$), then we update the under-approximation $\underline{\mathcal{E}}'$ (or the over-approximation $\overline{\mathcal{E}}'$) according to Theorem 4. The algorithm stops when the Hausdorff distance between the $\underline{\mathcal{E}}'$ and $\overline{\mathcal{E}}'$ becomes smaller than ε. Of course, the choice of the sample $\beta \in \overline{\mathcal{E}}' \setminus \underline{\mathcal{E}}'$, at line 10, is crucial for the efficiency of the algorithm. In our implementation of the algorithm, we use the selection criteria proposed in [25] which consists in choosing the sample that will produce the fastest decrease of the Hausdorff distance $d(\underline{\mathcal{E}}', \overline{\mathcal{E}}')$. In [30] an alternative selection criteria based on multiscale grid exploration was proposed.

Finally, it is important to note that Algorithm 2 needs testing if the samples $\beta \in \mathcal{E}'_o$ which require checking the condition $\mathsf{Stab}(f(\beta))$. In our implementation, this is done using Algorithm 1. If it returns true, then we can consider that $\mathsf{Stab}(f(\beta))$ holds. If it returns $\mathsf{unknown}$, we treat the sample as if $\mathsf{Stab}(f(\beta))$ is false. As a consequence, in practice it may be the case that $\overline{\mathcal{E}}'$ is not an over-approximation of $\mathcal{E}'_o$. However, it always holds that $\underline{\mathcal{E}}' \subseteq \mathcal{E}'_o$ and therefore the set returned by Algorithm 2 is always a valid solution to Problem 2. Note that the property $\mathsf{Stab}(f(\beta))$ need not be checked using Algorithm 1 but one can use any of the algorithms mentioned in Table 1.

6. ILLUSTRATIVE EXAMPLES

In this section, we first compare our approach for stability verification to that implemented within the NCS toolbox [5]. Then, we show an application of the timing contract synthesis algorithm. We implemented Algorithm 1 and Algorithm 2 in Matlab using the Multi-Parametric Toolbox [19]. All reported experiments are realized on a desktop with i7 4790 processor of frequency 3.6 GHz and a 8 GB RAM.

6.1 Stability Verification

We consider two systems taken from [9], given by (1) with the following matrices:

$$A = \begin{pmatrix} 0 & 1 \\ 0 & -0.1 \end{pmatrix},\ B = \begin{pmatrix} 0 \\ 0.1 \end{pmatrix},\ K = \begin{pmatrix} -3.75 & -11.5 \end{pmatrix}. \quad (16)$$

$$A = \begin{pmatrix} 0 & 1 \\ -2 & 0.1 \end{pmatrix},\ B = \begin{pmatrix} 0 \\ 1 \end{pmatrix},\ K = \begin{pmatrix} 1 & 0 \end{pmatrix}. \quad (17)$$

We consider the stability verification problem for these two 2-dimensional systems. First, we write the systems into 4-dimensional impulsive systems (3). Then, we apply Algorithm 1 to check stability of the impulsive system under several timing contracts. We compare our results to those obtained using the NCS toolbox [5] in Table 2. For the DET timing contract ($\underline{\tau} = 0$, $\underline{h} = \overline{h} = h$), we fix parameter h and report the maximal value of $\overline{\tau}$ for which stability has been verified. For the timing contract that corresponds to NPILS ($\underline{\tau} = \overline{\tau} = 0$), we fix $\underline{h}$ and report the maximal value of $\overline{h}$ for which stability has been verified. Finally, for the general timing contract given by (2), we fix parameters $\underline{\tau}$, $\overline{\tau}$, $\underline{h}$ and report the maximal value of $\overline{h}$ for which stability has been verified. Note that we conducted extra experiments labelled "Algorithm 1 (exp1)" to compare the results in terms of CPU time after fixing the same parameters as those used with the NCS toolbox.

The experiments conducted using the NCS toolbox are done in a particular manner since it uses three different approximation methods to embed the timing uncertainty (Jordan Normal Form (JNF), Cayley Hamilton, and Gridding and Norm Bounding (GNB)): we search for the maximum value of the free timing parameter that guarantees stability by running experiments using the three approximation methods. Then we report the computation time for the experiment in which we obtained this bound. In case the maximum bound could be obtained by more than one experiment, we report the CPU time corresponding to the fastest in terms of computation.Stability for system (16) is guaranteed using the GNB approximation for the DET, NPILS and general contracts, with 50, 35, and 50 gridpoints respectively. As for system (17), stability is guaranteed using the JNF approximation for all three contracts. Parameter setups used by Algorithm 1, for the different experiments, are summarized by Table 3. Note that for the NPILS contract, the parameter N_1 has no effect. It is clear, for the two systems at hand, that our method gives better results than the NCS toolbox in terms of CPU time and tightness.

6.2 Contract Synthesis

We now consider the timing contract synthesis problem for system (17). We rewrite the system in the form of im-

Table 2: Results of Algorithm 1 for systems (16) and (17) under several timing contracts. T_{CPU} is the computation time in seconds.

		DET ($\underline{\tau}=0$, $\underline{h}=\overline{h}=h$)			NPILS ($\underline{\tau}=\overline{\tau}=0$)			General contract (2)				
		$\overline{\tau}$	h	T_{CPU}	$\underline{h}$	$\overline{h}$	T_{CPU}	$\underline{\tau}$	$\overline{\tau}$	$\underline{h}$	$\overline{h}$	T_{CPU}
System (16)	NCS toolbox (GNB)	0.63	1	3.42	10^{-3}	1.7291	3.30	0	0.4	0.2	1.13	9.17
	Algorithm 1(exp1)	0.63	1	0.18	10^{-3}	1.7291	0.20	0	0.4	0.2	1.13	4.49
	Algorithm 1(exp2)	0.67	1	1.16	10^{-3}	1.7294	0.20	0	0.4	0.2	1.23	9.95
System (17)	NCS toolbox (JNF)	0.78	1	2.07	0.4	0.45	1.91	0	0.1	0.4	0.44	3.62
	Algorithm 1(exp1)	0.78	1	0.41	0.4	0.45	0.21	0	0.1	0.4	0.44	1.13
	Algorithm 1(exp2)	1	1	2.97	0.4	1.88	1.22	0	0.1	0.4	1.71	5.15

Table 3: Parameter setup for Algorithm 1 for systems (16) and (17) under several timing contracts.

	DET ($\underline{\tau}=0$, $\underline{h}=\overline{h}=h$)				NPILS ($\underline{\tau}=\overline{\tau}=0$)			General contract (2)			
	k_{max}	N_1	N_2	L	k_{max}	N_2	L	k_{max}	N_1	N_2	L
System (16)(exp1)	30	30	1	2	30	100	2	30	10	10	4
System (16)(exp2)	30	100	1	2	30	1000	2	30	20	50	4
System (17)(exp1)	30	15	1	2	30	1	2	30	10	1	4
System (17)(exp2)	30	150	1	2	30	100	2	30	20	60	4

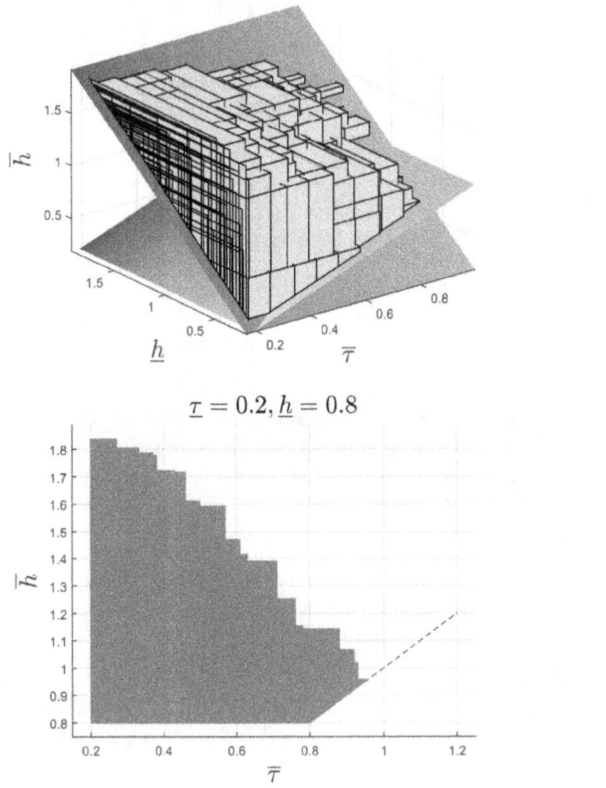

Figure 3: (top) Timing contract synthesis for system (17) in the $(0.2, \overline{\tau}, \underline{h}, \overline{h})$ space where the visualized section of $\mathcal{C}^*$ is in the domain region $\mathcal{C}$ defined above the planes $\overline{h} \geq \overline{\tau}$ and $\overline{h} \geq \underline{h}$. (bottom) The section of $\mathcal{C}^*$ in the $(\overline{\tau}, \overline{h})$ plane such that $\underline{\tau} = 0.2$ and $\underline{h} = 0.8$.

pulsive system (3). We search for a set $\mathcal{C}^* \subseteq \mathcal{C} \cap \mathcal{D}$, where $\mathcal{D} = [0, 1.16]^2 \times [0.21, 2.02]^2$, such that for all $(\underline{\tau}, \overline{\tau}, \underline{h}, \overline{h}) \in \mathcal{C}^*$ the system (2-3) is guaranteed to be GUES. We set the parameter $\varepsilon = 0.07$, and apply Algorithm 2. The output of the latter is a set $\mathcal{C}^* \subset \mathbb{R}^4$. Figure 3 shows a 3D section of $\mathcal{C}^*$ by setting $\underline{\tau} = 0.2$, and a 2D section by setting $\underline{\tau} = 0.2$ and $\underline{h} = 0.8$. Algorithm 2 used 2742 samples in the 4 dimensional parameter space with a total computation time of $T_{CPU} = 200$ minutes. Parameters of Algorithm 1 used in Algorithm 2 are $L = 4$, $k_{max} = 5$ and the numbers of time steps used for the over-approximation of the reachable set are $N_1 = 20$ and $N_2 = 50$.

7. CONCLUSION

In this work, we proposed useful tools for contract-based design of embedded control systems under the form of algorithms for stability verification and timing contract synthesis. These algorithms can be used by control and software engineers to derive requirements that must be met by the real-time implementation of a control law. The effectiveness of our approach has been shown on examples. As future work, it would be interesting to handle the problem of controller synthesis given a timing contract, and to co-synthesize the controller and the timing contract parameters. Also more work is required for the stability verification problem as long as the solutions at hand gives only sufficient conditions.

References

[1] M. Al Khatib, A. Girard, and T. Dang. Stability verification of nearly periodic impulsive linear systems using reachability analysis. In *IFAC Conference on Analysis and Design of Hybrid Systems*, pages 358–363, 2015.

[2] M. Althoff, O. Stursberg, and M. Buss. Computing reachable sets of hybrid systems using a combination of zonotopes and polytopes. *Nonlinear Analysis: Hybrid Systems*, 4(2):233–249, 2010.

[3] N. Athanasopoulos and M. Lazar. Alternative stability conditions for switched discrete time linear systems. In *IFAC World Congress*, pages 6007–6012, 2014.

[4] N. W. Bauer, P. J. H. Maas, and W. P. M. H. Heemels. Stability analysis of networked control

systems: A sum of squares approach. *Automatica*, 48(8):1514–1524, 2012.

[5] N. W. Bauer, S. J. L. M. van Loon, M. C. F. Donkers, N. van de Wouw, and W. P. M. H. Heemels. Networked control systems toolbox: Robust stability analysis made easy. In *IFAC Workshop on Distributed Estimation and Control in Networked Systems*, pages 55–60, 2012.

[6] F. Blanchini. Ultimate boundedness control for uncertain discrete-time systems via set-induced lyapunov functions. In *IEEE Conference on Decision and Control*, pages 1755–1760, 1991.

[7] O. Botchkarev and S. Tripakis. Verification of hybrid systems with linear differential inclusions using ellipsoidal approximations. In *Hybrid Systems: Computation and Control*, pages 73–88. Springer, 2000.

[8] M. C. Bragagnolo, I.-C. Morarescu, J. Daafouz, and P. Riedinger. LMI sufficient conditions for the consensus of linear agents with nearly-periodic resets. In *American Control Conference*, pages 2575–2580. IEEE, 2014.

[9] C. Briat. Convex conditions for robust stability analysis and stabilization of linear aperiodic impulsive and sampled-data systems under dwell-time constraints. *Automatica*, 49(11):3449–3457, 2013.

[10] M. B. G. Cloosterman, L. Hetel, N. Van De Wouw, W. P. M. H. Heemels, J. Daafouz, and H. Nijmeijer. Controller synthesis for networked control systems. *Automatica*, 46(10):1584–1594, 2010.

[11] P. Derler, E. A. Lee, S. Tripakis, and M. Törngren. Cyber-physical system design contracts. In *ACM/IEEE International Conference on Cyber-Physical Systems*, pages 109–118, 2013.

[12] M. C. F. Donkers, W. P. M. H. Heemels, N. Van De Wouw, and L. Hetel. Stability analysis of networked control systems using a switched linear systems approach. *IEEE Transactions on Automatic Control*, 56(9):2101–2115, 2011.

[13] M. Fiacchini and I.-C. Morarescu. Set theory conditions for stability of linear impulsive systems. In *IEEE Conference on Decision and Control*, pages 1527–1532, 2014.

[14] G. Frehse, C. Le Guernic, A. Donzé, S. Cotton, R. Ray, O. Lebeltel, R. Ripado, A. Girard, T. Dang, and O. Maler. SpaceEx: Scalable verification of hybrid systems. In *Computer Aided Verification*, pages 379–395. Springer, 2011.

[15] H. Fujioka. Stability analysis of systems with aperiodic sample-and-hold devices. *Automatica*, 45(3):771–775, 2009.

[16] H. Gao, X. Meng, T. Chen, and J. Lam. Stabilization of networked control systems via dynamic output-feedback controllers. *SIAM Journal on Control and Optimization*, 48(5):3643–3658, 2010.

[17] A. Girard. Reachability of uncertain linear systems using zonotopes. In *Hybrid Systems: Computation and Control*, pages 291–305. Springer, 2005.

[18] W. P. M. H. Heemels, A. R. Teel, N. Van de Wouw, and D. Nešić. Networked control systems with communication constraints: Tradeoffs between transmission intervals, delays and performance. *IEEE Transactions on Automatic Control*, 55(8):1781–1796, 2010.

[19] M. Herceg, M. Kvasnica, C. Jones, and M. Morari. Multi-Parametric Toolbox 3.0. In *European Control Conference*, pages 502–510, 2013.

[20] L. Hetel, J. Daafouz, S. Tarbouriech, and C. Prieur. Stabilization of linear impulsive systems through a nearly-periodic reset. *Nonlinear Analysis: Hybrid Systems*, 7(1):4–15, 2013.

[21] L. Hetel, A. Kruszewski, W. Perruquetti, and J.-P. Richard. Discrete and intersample analysis of systems with aperiodic sampling. *IEEE Transactions on Automatic Control*, 56(7):1696–1701, 2011.

[22] A. B. Kurzhanski and P. Varaiya. Ellipsoidal techniques for reachability analysis: internal approximation. *Systems & Control Letters*, 41(3):201–211, 2000.

[23] C. Le Guernic. *Reachability analysis of hybrid systems with linear continuous dynamics.* PhD thesis, Université Joseph-Fourier-Grenoble I, 2009.

[24] C. Le Guernic and A. Girard. Reachability analysis of linear systems using support functions. *Nonlinear Analysis: Hybrid Systems*, 4(2):250–262, 2010.

[25] J. Legriel, C. Le Guernic, S. Cotton, and O. Maler. Approximating the pareto front of multi-criteria optimization problems. In *Tools and Algorithms for the Construction and Analysis of Systems*, pages 69–83. Springer, 2010.

[26] K. Liu, E. Fridman, and L. Hetel. Networked control systems in the presence of scheduling protocols and communication delays. *SIAM Journal on Control and Optimization*, 53(4):1768–1788, 2015.

[27] K. Liu, V. Suplin, and E. Fridman. Stability of linear systems with general sawtooth delay. *IMA Journal of Mathematical Control and Information*, 27(4):419–436, 2010.

[28] A. Sangiovanni-Vincentelli, W. Damm, and R. Passerone. Taming dr. frankenstein: Contract-based design for cyber-physical systems. *European journal of control*, 18(3):217–238, 2012.

[29] A. Seuret and M. Peet. Stability analysis of sampled-data systems using sum of squares. *IEEE Transactions on Automatic Control*, 58(6):1620–1625, 2013.

[30] P. Tendulkar. *Mapping and Scheduling on Multi-core Processors using SMT Solvers.* PhD thesis, Universite de Grenoble I-Joseph Fourier, 2014.

Formal Analysis of Robustness at Model and Code Level*

Timothy Wang[†]
Georgia Tech
Atlanta, Georgia, USA
first.last@gatech.edu

Pierre-Loïc Garoche
ONERA – The French Aerospace Lab
Toulouse, FRANCE
first.last@onera.fr

Pierre Roux
ONERA – The French Aerospace Lab
Toulouse, FRANCE
first.last@onera.fr

Romain Jobredeaux
Georgia Tech
Atlanta, Georgia, USA
jobredeaux@gatech.edu

Éric Féron
Georgia Tech
Atlanta, Georgia, USA
first.last@gatech.edu

ABSTRACT

Robustness analyses play a major role in the synthesis and analysis of controllers. For control systems, robustness is a measure of the maximum tolerable model inaccuracies or perturbations that do not destabilize the system. Analyzing the robustness of a closed-loop system can be performed with multiple approaches: gain and phase margin computation for single-input single-output (SISO) linear systems, mu analysis, IQC computations, etc. However, none of these techniques consider the actual code in their analyses.

The approach presented here relies on an invariant computation on the discrete system dynamics. Using semi-definite programming (SDP) solvers, a Lyapunov-based function is synthesized that captures the vector margins of the closed-loop linear system considered. This numerical invariant expressed over the state variables of the system is compatible with code analysis and enables its validation on the code artifact.

This automatic analysis extends verification techniques focused on controller implementation, addressing validation of robustness at model and code level. It has been implemented in a tool analyzing discrete SISO systems and generating over-approximations of phase and gain margins. The analysis will be integrated in our toolchain for Simulink and Lustre models autocoding and formal analysis.

1. ANALYSIS OF CLOSED LOOP SYSTEMS

The typical development of control systems is often performed in two steps. First, control experts design the controller using a model of the plant, i.e., the system to be controlled. This design phase is supported by analyses and eventually lead to a discrete controller description to be embedded in the final hardware.

A second phase focuses on the discrete controller artifact produced by the first phase and addresses its implementation in the target embedded language. This phase is now often supported by the use of dedicated models, typically synchronous dataflow languages such as Matlab Simulink, ANSYS Scade or Lustre, and by the use of associated code generators.

In terms of analyses, the classical system level properties addressed are stability, robustness and performance.

Stability.

A stable system guarantees that a small change in the input will not produce a large change in the output. Mathematically speaking, the notion of asymptotic stability ensures that with a null input, the system converges to zero. This stability can be studied in two ways: open loop stability and closed loop stability. In the open loop setting the stability of the controller itself is studied while in the closed loop setting the complete system integrating the feedback interconnection of controller and plant is addressed.

While closed-loop stability is the main stability property of interest – that is, the controlled system will have a stable behavior – ensuring open-loop stability avoids the undesirable situation where the feedback interconnection is stable, while the controller alone is intrinsically unstable. In terms of system implementation, an open-loop stable controller has a reasonable behavior on its own, e.g., assuming only bounded input, it will provide a bounded output. This is called the bounded input bounded output (BIBO) property.

Stability properties can be assessed in different ways. A system's dynamics are expressed as transfer functions mapping inputs to outputs. These are obtained by taking the Fourier or Laplace transform of the impulse response of a system. This so-called frequency domain approach is commonly used for linear systems, along with graphical tools such as Bode plots or Nyquist diagrams. An alternative approach, temporal domain analysis, is performed on the state-space representation, and is based on Lyapunov functions. Lyapunov functions express a notion of positive energy that decreases along the trajectories of the system and captures its asymptotic stability. For linear systems, such functions

*This work has been partially supported by the following grants: ANR-INSE-2012-CAFEIN, NSF CrAVES (1135955), ARO MURI W911NF-11-1-0046, and NSF SORTIES (1446758).

†The author is currently with United Technologies Research Center.

HSCC'16, April 12 - 14, 2016, Vienna, Austria

ISBN 978-1-4503-3955-1/16/04. . . $15.00

DOI: http://dx.doi.org/10.1145/2883817.2883824

are usually defined using a positive definite matrix $P \succeq 0$ such that:

$$A^\intercal PA - P \prec 0, \tag{1}$$

where A is the state matrix of the system.

Code Analyses.

The Verification and Validation (V&V) of controllers is a major part of the cost of the development process for such systems. Since about a decade, the formal analysis of these control software has been the main application of formal methods in the industry [23]. However, most properties addressed, either exhaustively with formal methods or with tests, are focused on low level functionalities and hardly capture the real intended behavior of the controller and the controlled system. For example a famous application of static analysis on control software, the Astrée analyzer [7], only focused on language-related properties such as the absence of runtime errors, *i.e.*, overflow, null pointer dereferencing, division by zero, etc. These low level properties can depend on the BIBO property associated to stable systems. Therefore Astrée relies on analyses specialized for digital filters [11].

Regarding control-level properties evaluated on the implementation, the expression of stability properties using Lyapunov function requires either to be provided with the Lyapunov function or to be computed automatically. Note that, in general, the plant dynamics are no longer available at code level. However, it is important to be able to validate the actual implementation with respect to its high level system properties, such as stability.

This line of work has been developed recently, addressing either the annotation of code with a provided Lyapunov function [15] and the proof of those annotations or their computation using SDP solvers [21]. In order to express the stability of the closed-loop system, a discrete encoding of the plant dynamics is expressed along the code and enables to reason on the extended state space, which includes both controller and plant state variables. Both the Lyapunov annotations scheme [25] and the automatic computation [21] approaches have been extended to closed-loop systems [20].

Expressing Lyapunov functions at code level not only enables the expression of high level properties on code artifacts, but also provides bounds on reachable states. Indeed, stable systems with bounded inputs admit bounded outputs. The Lyapunov function characterized by the matrix $P \succ 0$ also bounds reachable states: for some α,

$$\forall x, \qquad x^\intercal P x \leq \alpha.$$

Systems Considered and Notations.

In the following we focus on linear systems, *i.e.*, a linear plant with a linear controller feedback. We also focus specifically on the discrete model artifact that represents the implementation. In order to enable the analysis of the closed-loop system, we consider a discrete version of the plant dynamics. Therefore both the controller and the plant dynamics are expressed as discrete linear systems. Without loss of generality, we denote, in the following, (A^c, B^c, C^c, D^c) and (A^p, B^p, C^p) the matrices defining the controller and plant dynamics, respectively; e denotes the input of the controller, often referred to as the error, *i.e.*, the distance to the target reference in; u denotes both the output of the controller and the input of the plant, such as the effect of actuator commands; y denotes the measure of the plant state, *i.e.*, the feedback, e.g., as obtained by sensors:

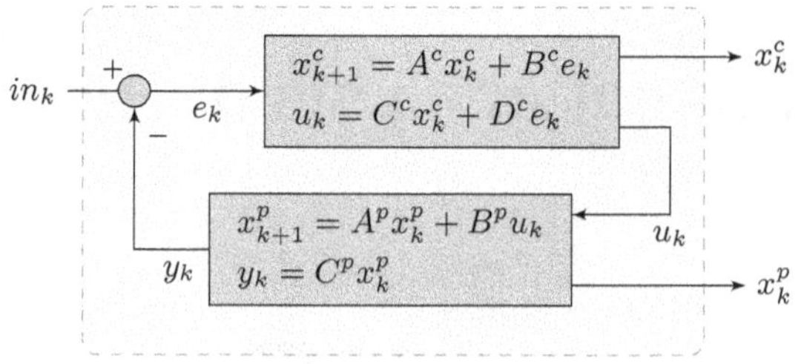

Figure 1: Closed-loop system.

$$\begin{cases} x^c_{k+1} &= A^c x^c_k + B^c e_k \\ u_k &= C^c x^c_k + D^c e_k \end{cases} \quad \begin{cases} x^p_{k+1} &= A^p x^p_k + B^p u_k \\ y_k &= C^p x^p_k \end{cases} \tag{2}$$

A closed-loop representation of the system is given in Fig. 1; it is expressed over the state space defined by vectors $\begin{pmatrix} x^c & x^p \end{pmatrix}^\intercal$. Let $\mathbf{x}$ be such vectors. The error e is computed using a reference command in and the feedback y obtained from the plant.

$$e_k = in_k - y_k$$

One can consider in as the input of the closed-loop system, and $\mathbf{x}$ as its output.

Open-loop and closed-loop stability analyses performed in [20, 21], compute, respectively, positive definite matrices P^o and P^c denoting Lyapunov functions for these open- and closed-loop systems. In terms of static analysis, that is, the exhaustive analysis of the system behavior, considering actual implementation, these stability properties can be expressed as inductive invariants.

For the open-loop system, the Lyapunov function P^o is used to express a BIBO property of the controller alone: to bound reachable states x^c assuming a bounded input e:

$$\|e\|_\infty \leq 1 \implies x^{c\intercal} P^o x^c \leq 1$$

For the closed-loop system, integrating the feedback of the plant in the controller input,a similar property is expressed. For a bounded target reference in, the closed-loop system will admit only bounded reachable states $\mathbf{x}$:

$$\|in\|_\infty \leq 1 \implies \mathbf{x}^\intercal P^c \mathbf{x} \leq 1$$

These boundedness properties may seem weak to control engineers compared to the asymptotic stability properties expressed by the Lyapunov functions. However they are of extreme importance to guarantee that the implementation will behave properly, without diverging and causing runtime errors, e.g., producing numerical overflows. Once provided with a quadratic bound on reachable states using the Lyapunov function characterizing the stability of the controller, static analyses of the discrete model and the code can rely on policy iterations [12] to infer bounds on x^c and $\mathbf{x}$.

Robustness.

A robustness analysis, like a closed-loop stability analysis, requires a plant description. This system-level property evaluates "how much" the closed-loop system is stable and which kind of perturbations or uncertainty can be sustained without losing stability.

Again, this property is classical in control and part of any curriculum in an engineering degree. Bode plots or Nyquist diagrams can be used to characterize these measures depending on frequency related properties. These margins are required in the development process as a quality measure of the proposed controlled system.

However, theses margins are never analyzed or computed on the code artifact, taking into account the real implementation using floating-point arithmetic.

Goal: Hypotheses, Contributions.

The goal of this paper is therefore to continue introducing control-level concepts into the computer science community and, more specifically, the formal verification community. It addresses the automatic expression and computation of robustness properties for SISO (single-input single-output) systems over the code artifact. This class of systems is well studied and is representative enough of the realistic-size systems we are targeting, such as the NASA Transport Class Model [5], the ROSACE usecase [17], or industry-level Full Authority Digital Engine Control (FADEC).

Extending the state of the art of static analyses, this paper makes the following contributions:

- provide a computable algorithm to evaluate robustness margins of a discrete SISO system;
- compute the result automatically on the code artifact;
- take into account the floating-point semantics and its associated numerical errors;
- and validate the output of the SDP solvers used to compute the results.

Our approach has been implemented in a prototype and the approach is extensible to the MIMO (multiple-inputs multiple-outputs) setting.

Paper Organization.

The paper is structured as follows: the next section, Section 2 presents the key concepts behind margin computations for linear systems using frequency domain analyses including phase and gain margin computation. Section 3 proposes an alternate approach based on vector margin computation and presents an automated approach to margin computation. As for our past work on Lyapunov functions on code artifacts, we claim that vector margins are compatible with code level analyses. Section 4 addresses the soundness of the approach with respect to floating-point computations. Section 5 presents the application of our tooled approach to representative example of the literature. Last, Section 6 outlines an integration of the approach in a development process including margins computation and validation on model and code.

2. CLASSICAL ROBUSTNESS ANALYSIS

Beyond stability, an important property which needs to be verified is the robustness of the controller. The property of robustness is necessary in practice as there are many sources of imperfection in the feedback loop. They can include errors in modeling the plant, uncertainties in the plant that cannot be captured by the model, noises in the sensors and actuators, limitations of the controller design, i.e., not accounting for the complete range of behaviors of the system, non-linearities in the actuators, faulty actuators, etc.

The standard metric used in the industry to gauge the robustness of linear SISO controllers consists of phase and gain margins. A way to measure the phase and gain margins of a control system is by constructing a Nyquist plot. Before we describe the Nyquist plot, we introduce the following preliminaries.

2.1 Preliminaries

Consider the z-transform which maps a discrete-time signal $(x_k)_{k\in\mathbb{N}}$ to a function $X(z)$ over the complex field or the z-domain. The z-transform is the discrete-time analogue of the Laplace transform and is defined as

$$\mathcal{Z} : x \mapsto \sum_{k=0}^{\infty} x_k z^{-k}. \tag{3}$$

Consider the feedback system in Fig. 1. Let C be the controller, which has input e and output u. Let P be the plant, which has input u and output y. Applying z-transform on e and u results in a pair of functions $E(z)$ and $U(z)$. Let the ratio of $U(z)$ and $E(z)$ be $C(z)$ i.e. $C(z) := \frac{U(z)}{E(z)}$. The function $C(z)$ is a transfer function representation of the state-space system C. Likewise $P(z) := \frac{Y(z)}{U(z)}$ is the transfer function representation of P. To compute the transfer function of a linear state-space model parameterized by the matrices $A \in \mathbb{R}^{n\times n}, B \in \mathbb{R}^{n\times m}, C \in \mathbb{R}^{k\times n}, D \in \mathbb{R}^{k\times m}$, the algebraic formula

$$C\left(zI_{n\times n} - A\right)^{-1} B + D \tag{4}$$

is used. The formula in (4) can be obtained from applying the z-transform in (3) to the linear state-space system. For $m = 1$ and $k = 1$, *i.e.*, a SISO system, evaluating (4) results in a rational transfer function $G(z)$ with a number of zeros and poles. A simple example of a rational transfer function is the unit-delay function $\frac{1}{z}$, which has only one pole located at 0.

In the transfer function form, the composition of linear state-space systems can be computed using algebraic operations only. For example, the transfer function from $E(z)$ to $Y(z)$ or the loop transfer function is $L(z) := \frac{Y(z)}{E(z)} = \frac{Y(z)}{U(z)}\frac{U(z)}{E(z)} = P(z)C(z)$. Another example would be the closed-loop transfer function from $In(z) := \mathcal{Z}(in)$ to $Y(z)$ which is

$$\tilde{G}(z) = \frac{L(z)}{1 + L(z)}. \tag{5}$$

The formula in (5) can be deduced by noting that

$$Y(z) = L(z)\left(In(z) - Y(z)\right) \implies Y(z)\left(1 + L(z)\right) = L(z)In(z)$$
$$\implies \frac{Y(z)}{In(z)} = \frac{L(z)}{1 + L(z)}. \tag{6}$$

2.2 Nyquist Plot and Stability Criterion

The Nyquist plot is the frequency response (magnitude and phase) of the loop transfer function to a sinusoidal input displayed using a polar coordinate system. To construct the Nyquist plot, the loop transfer function $L(z)$ is evaluated along the Nyquist contour Γ. The Nyquist contour, shown in Fig. 2, encircles the region outside of the unit disk (OUD)

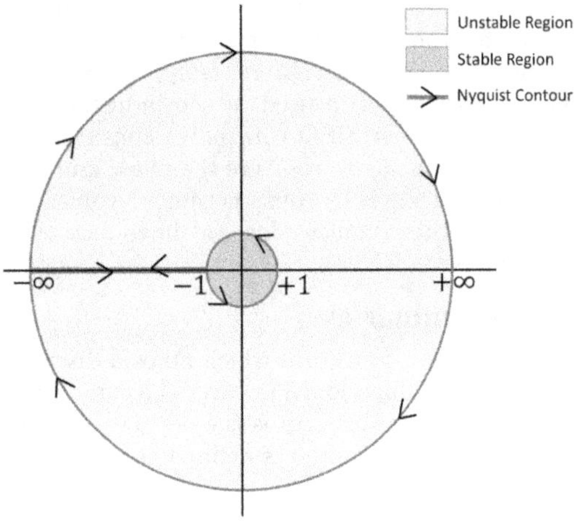

Figure 2: Nyquist contour in discrete-time.

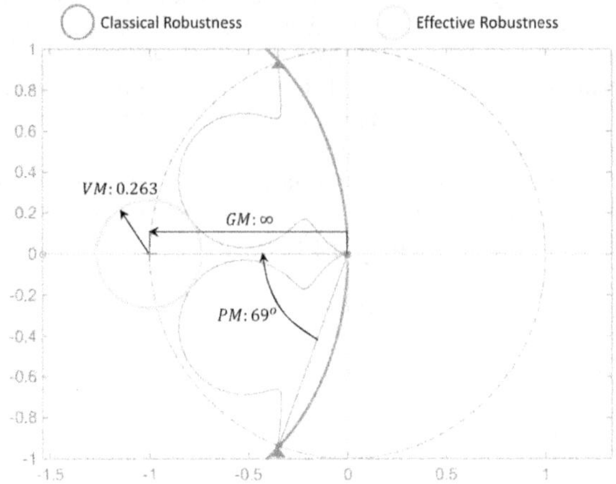

Figure 3: Classical margins versus vector margin shown on the Nyquist plot of (7).

centered at the origin. An example Nyquist plot for the loop transfer function

$$L(z) := \frac{7.552 \times 10^{-5} z^3 - 7.583 \times 10^{-5} z^2 - 7.454 \times 10^{-5} z + 7.488 \times 10^{-5}}{z^4 - 3.979z^3 + 5.937z^2 - 3.937z + 0.979} \tag{7}$$

is shown in Fig. 3.

We now introduce the Nyquist stability criterion which uses the Nyquist plot to determine the closed-loop stability of the system. Let Z_i be the number of OUD zeros of $L(z)+1$ and let P_i be the number of OUD poles of $L(z)+1$. By Cauchy's principle of argument, the Nyquist plot should encircle clockwise[1] the $-1+0j$ point N_i number of times where

$$N_i = Z_i - P_i. \tag{8}$$

Using (8) and the Nyquist plot in Fig. 3, we can conclude the stability of the closed-loop system $\frac{L(z)}{1+L(z)}$ in the following way. First we know the loop transfer function $L(z)$ in (7) is stable, *i.e.*, $L(z)+1$ has 0 OUD poles, which means $P_i = 0$. Since the Nyquist plot in Fig. 3 does not encircle $-1+0j$, *i.e.*, the critical point, we can conclude that Z_i or the number of OUD zeros of $L(z)+1$ is also 0. Since OUD zeros of $L(z)+1$ are also the OUD poles of the closed-loop transfer function, we can conclude that the closed-loop system is also stable.

2.3 Phase and Gain Margins

From the Nyquist stability criterion, one can infer that a possible robustness metric would be the size of the gap between the Nyquist plot and the $-1+0j$ point. In fact, phase and gain margins are two different approximations of the "distance" from the Nyquist plot to the critical point.

The first approximation, phase margin, measures how much phase lag the system can tolerate. A phase lag of $\frac{\pi}{2}$ or 90° corresponds to a delay of a quarter of a period. Geometrically speaking, introducing a phase lag of Δ_ω in the feedback loop results in the original Nyquist plot rotated clockwise by Δ_ω i.e. $L(z) \to e^{j\Delta_\omega} L(z)$. The phase margin represents the amount of clockwise rotation that can be applied to the Nyquist plot before it hits the critical point. As shown in Fig. 3, the phase margin (PM) is precisely the clockwise angle between the point where the unit circle, centered at the origin, intersects with the Nyquist plot and $-1+0j$.

The second approximation, gain margin, measures how much feedback gain the system can tolerate, *i.e.*, how much one can scale up the Nyquist plot radially before it intersects with the $-1+0j$ point. As shown in Fig. 3, the gain margin (GM) is precisely $20\log_{10}\frac{1}{x}$ where x is the magnitude of the Nyquist plot at the phase angle of π. For good robustness, a typical requirement is a phase margin of at least 30° and a gain margin of at least 3db.

3. VECTOR MARGINS

Uncertainties in the feedback loop can introduce simultaneous phase lags and increases in the feedback gain. In those cases, interpreting the phase and gain margins could produce an overly optimistic view of the robustness of the feedback system. For example, a small phase lag combined with a small gain change would destabilize the system in Fig. 3, while a pure increase in gain would never do so and it would take a large phase lag alone to destabilize the system. To give a better indication of the robustness of the system, we look at the distance between $-1+0j$ and the Nyquist plot induced by the complex modulus, *i.e.*, $\min_{z\in\Gamma}|L(z)+1|$. In this paper, we call this robustness measure the vector margin. By plotting a circle of radius equal to the vector margin centered at the $-1+0j$ point, we get the effective robustness envelope in Fig. 3, which for this example, is far more pessimistic than the robustness envelope formed by the classical measures. There are several advantages to using the vector margin.

1. It is a more faithful measure of the robustness.
2. It can be translated into the time-domain and then expressed on the code as a quadratic invariant.
3. It readily extends to MIMO systems [13, 24].

3.1 Computing the Vector Margin

The vector margin can be computed by finding the inverse of the maximum modulus of the sensitivity function $S(z) := \frac{1}{1+L(z)}$ over the Nyquist contour Γ. This can be seen by

[1]Counter-clockwise encirclement counts as negative.

noting that

$$\min_{z\in\Gamma} |L(z)+1| = \frac{1}{\max_{z\in\Gamma} \frac{1}{|L(z)+1|}} = \frac{1}{\max_{z\in\Gamma} \left|\frac{1}{L(z)+1}\right|}.$$

The sensitivity function is a first-order approximation of the change in the output over the change in the input for the closed-loop system. The state-space representation of the sensitivity function $S(z) := \frac{1}{1+L(z)}$ where $L(z) := P(z)C(z)$ can be expressed in terms of the matrices which form the state-space realization of the plant $P(z)$ and the controller $C(z)$. For the example in Fig. 1, the sensitivity transfer function has the following state-space realization

$$\begin{aligned} x_{k+1} &= A_s x_k + B_s in_k \\ e_k &= C_s x_k + D_s in_k \end{aligned} \tag{9}$$

where

$$A_s := \begin{bmatrix} A_c & -B_c C_p \\ B_p C_c & A_p - B_p D_c C_p \end{bmatrix} \quad B_s := \begin{bmatrix} B_c \\ B_p D_c \end{bmatrix} \quad C_s := \begin{bmatrix} 0 & -C_p \end{bmatrix} \quad D_s := \begin{bmatrix} I \end{bmatrix}. \tag{10}$$

By the application of the bounded real lemma [14, pg.821], we have the following result.

Proposition 3.1 If there exists a positive-definite matrix P and $\gamma > 0$, such that

$$x_{k+1}^{\mathsf{T}} P x_{k+1} - x_k^{\mathsf{T}} P x_k \leq \gamma^2 \|in_k\|_2^2 - \|e_k\|_2^2 \tag{11}$$

then $\max_{z\in\Gamma} |S(z)| \leq \gamma$.

The inequality in (11) is a dissipativity condition [26] and can be checked efficiently by solving a lineat matrix inequality (LMI) [4]. We have the following proposition.

Proposition 3.2 The previous inequality (11) can be written as the following LMI

$$\begin{pmatrix} A_s{}^{\mathsf{T}} P A_s - P + C_s{}^{\mathsf{T}} C_s & A_s{}^{\mathsf{T}} P B_s + C_s{}^{\mathsf{T}} D_s \\ B_s{}^{\mathsf{T}} P A_s + D_s{}^{\mathsf{T}} C_s & D_s{}^{\mathsf{T}} D_s + B_s{}^{\mathsf{T}} P B_s - \gamma^2 I \end{pmatrix} \prec 0. \tag{12}$$

By Proposition 3.2, for any $P \succ 0$ and $\gamma > 0$ satisfying (12), we have $\max_{z\in\Gamma} |S(z)| \leq \gamma$. By minimizing γ in (12), we get the vector margin $\delta = \frac{1}{\gamma}$.

Thus, summing (11) from time 0 to any time T, we get

$$x_{T+1}^{\mathsf{T}} P x_{T+1} - x_0^{\mathsf{T}} P x_0 \leq \gamma^2 \left(\sum_{k=0}^{T} \|in_k\|_2^2\right) - \sum_{k=0}^{T} \|e_k\|_2^2$$

and since P is positive definite, assuming $x_0 = 0$

$$\sum_{k=0}^{T} \|e_k\|_2^2 \leq \gamma^2 \left(\sum_{k=0}^{T} \|in_k\|_2^2\right). \tag{13}$$

3.2 Relationship with Phase and Gain Margins

While vector margins could be computed automatically on the linear system, including its implementation, the use of phase and gain margins is often required to interact with control engineers. We propose here classical projections of vector margins onto a safe approximation of their associated phase and gain margins.

Phase margins.

As explained in Sec 2, the phase margin denotes the angle between the intersection of the Nyquist plot of the transfer function with the unit circle and the point $-1 + 0j$.

This angle is necessary larger than the angle between the intersection of the computed safe circle of radius δ with the unit circle and the point $-1 + 0j$ (c.f., Fig. 3, where $\delta = VM$).

In that case a direct projection of vector margins to phase margins is

$$\phi_\delta = 2\ arcsin(\delta/2)$$

Gain margins.

Similarly a safe gain margin can be obtained by projecting the vector margin. Gain margin denotes the acceptable scale of the Nyquist plot to avoid intersection with the point $-1 + 0j$.

We can approximate the gain margin associated to the vector margin δ:

$$\Theta_\delta = \frac{1}{1-\delta}$$

This gain is usually reported in dB:

$$\Theta_\delta = 20 \cdot log10\left(\frac{1}{1-\delta}\right)$$

4. FLOATING POINT ARITHMETIC

Up to now, we considered that every computation could be performed in the real field $\mathbb{R}$. In practice, for the sake of efficiency, all these computations will be performed using some sort of finite precision arithmetic. The most common one, floating-point arithmetic, is considered here.

We have to distinguish two fundamentally different issues regarding the use of floating-point arithmetic:

the analysis itself is performed in floating-point arithmetic, in particular the LMI (12) is solved using approximate SDP solvers, see Section 4.1;

the analyzed controller performs its computations using floating-point arithmetic rather than real numbers, this is discussed in Section 4.2.

4.1 Floating-Point Arithmetic in the Analysis

The analysis is performed by solving the LMI (12) thanks to an SDP solver. These solvers, due both to the algorithms they implement and their implementation using floating-point arithmetic, provide only approximate solutions. This means that for the returned values of P and γ^2, (12) is usually slightly not negative definite.

A simple solution is to slightly pad the LMI, replacing $M \prec 0$ by $M+\epsilon I \prec 0$. ϵ must be greater than the precision of the solver, for instance $\epsilon := 10^{-7}$ is a reasonable choice. This enables to get values of P and γ^2 actually satisfying (12) while remaining close from the optimal values.

Although, in practice, SDP solver return results satisfying the required precision ϵ, they perform all their computations using floating-point arithmetic and cannot be formally trusted. It then remains to formally check that the computed values of P and γ^2 indeed satisfy (12). This can be done by computing the matrix in (12), for instance with exact rational arithmetic, and then checking that the result is negative definite. This last check can be performed using a Cholesky decomposition. For the sake of efficiency, this decomposition can itself be performed using floating-point arithmetic by carefully bounding the rounding errors [22]. The resulting algorithm being non trivial, it has been proved using the proof assistant Coq [18].

4.2 Floating-point Arithmetic in the Controller

The computations of the controller being performed using floating-point arithmetic, rounding errors unavoidably occur and x^c_{k+1} is not exactly equal to $A_c x^c_k + B_c e_k$.

Definition 1 *$\mathbb{F} \subset \mathbb{R}$ denotes the set of floating-point values and $\mathrm{fl}(e) \in \mathbb{F}$ the floating-point evaluation of expression e from left to right*[2].

In practice, a floating-point value $f \in \mathbb{F}$ is encoded as a mantissa $m \in \mathbb{Z}$ and an exponent $e \in \mathbb{Z}$ such that $f = m\beta^e$ where β is the radix (commonly 2). Since f is encoded with a constant number of figures[3], m lies in a bounded range. More precisely, if the mantissa m is encoded with a precision of *prec* figures: $|m| < \beta^{prec}$. To fully exploit the available precision, m and e can be chosen such that $|m| \geq \beta^{prec-1}$.

First Ignoring Over- and Underflows.

The exponent e also lies in a bounded range. When e becomes too large, an overflow occurs whereas e too small implies an underflow. We will first ignore both overflows and underflows as they only rarely happen in practice.

Thus, a real number $x \in \mathbb{R}$ can be represented by a floating-point value $f_x \in \mathbb{F}$ such that $|x - f_x| \leq \beta^{1-prec}|x|$ (or $\left(\beta^{1-prec}/2\right)|x|$ with a rounding to nearest).

Definition 2 $\mathsf{eps} \in \mathbb{R}$ *is a constant, depending on the floating-point format used, such that for all $x \in \mathbb{R}$, $f_x \in \mathbb{F}$ satisfies $|x - f_x| \leq \mathsf{eps}\,|x|$.*

Example 3 *For the IEEE754 [16] binary64 format*[4] *with rounding to nearest, we have* $\mathsf{eps} = 2^{-53}$ $(\simeq 10^{-16})$.

This constant allows to bound the rounding errors of the basic arithmetic operations.

Property 4 *For all $x, y \in \mathbb{F}$ and $\diamond \in \{+, -, \times\}$*

$$\exists \delta \in \mathbb{R},\ |\delta| \leq \mathsf{eps} \wedge \mathrm{fl}(x \diamond y) = (1 + \delta)(x \diamond y).$$

This property is a direct consequence of Definition 2.

Back to our vector margins, what we need is not exactly the inequality (11) but rather[5]

$$\mathrm{fl}(x_{k+1})^\intercal P\,\mathrm{fl}(x_{k+1}) - x_k^T P x_k \leq \gamma^2 \|in_k\|_2^2 - \|\mathrm{fl}(e_k)\|_2^2.$$

The following theorem gives a link between this and (11).

Theorem 5 *If $n' := \mathrm{sz}(x^c) + \mathrm{sz}(in) + 3$, with $\mathrm{sz}(x)$ denoting the size of the vector x, satisfies $2(n' - 2)\mathsf{eps} < 1$ and*

$$x_{k+1}^T P x_{k+1} - x_k^T P x_k + \epsilon\left(\|x_k\|_2^2 + \|in\|_2^2\right) \leq \gamma^2 \|in_k\|_2^2 - \|e_k\|_2^2$$

then

$$\mathrm{fl}(x_{k+1})^T P\,\mathrm{fl}(x_{k+1}) - x_k^T P x_k \leq \gamma^2 \|in_k\|_2^2 - \|\mathrm{fl}(e_k)\|_2^2$$

where $\epsilon := n^2\left(3\gamma_2 m''^2 + s\gamma_{n'} m'\left(2m + \gamma_{n'} m'\right)\right)$ *where $s \in \mathbb{R}$ is such that $P \preceq sI$, $n := \mathrm{sz}(x) + \mathrm{sz}(in)$,*
$\gamma_k = \frac{k\,\mathsf{eps}}{1 - k\,\mathsf{eps}}$, $m := \max_{i,j}\left(|A_s|_{i,j}, |B_s|_{i,j}\right)$,
$m'' := \max_{i,j}\left(1, |C_p|_{i,j}\right)$ *and* $m' := \max(m_1', m_2')$ *with*
$m_1' := \max_{i,j}\left(|A_c|_{i,j}, |B_c|_{i,j}, (|B_c|\,|C_p|)_{i,j}\right)$ *and*
$m_2' := \max_{i,j}\left((|B_p|\,|C_c|)_{i,j}, (|B_p|\,|D_c|)_{i,j}, (|B_p|\,|D_c|\,|C_p|)_{i,j}\right)$.

Thus, instead of checking (12), we just have to check

$$\begin{pmatrix} A_s{}^\intercal P A_s - P + C_s{}^\intercal C_s + \epsilon I & A_s{}^\intercal P B_s + C_s{}^\intercal D_s \\ B_s{}^\intercal P A_s + D_s{}^\intercal C_s & D_s{}^\intercal D_s + B_s{}^\intercal P B_s - \gamma^2 I + \epsilon I \end{pmatrix} \prec 0.$$

In practice, $\epsilon \simeq 10^{-9}$ is small with respect to the ϵ already needed in Section 4.1 to compensate for the SDP solver precision. Thus the new condition is quite easy to satisfy.

Taking Over- and Underflows into Account.

To handle overflows, one has to prove their absence. This can be done by proving that x and e remain bounded. According to the upper left corner of the LMI (12), $x \mapsto x^\intercal P x$ is a Lyapunov function for the closed loop system (c.f., (1)). This means that as soon as the input in is bounded, x and e will remain bounded. Proving the absence of overflows then amounts to computing such an upper bound on the values of x and e and check that it is smaller than the largest representable floating-point value.

Handling underflows is much more tricky. Indeed, the error they induce is no longer relative but absolute and we can only prove

$$\mathrm{fl}(x_{k+1})^\intercal P\,\mathrm{fl}(x_{k+1}) - x_k^T P x_k \leq \gamma^2 \|in_k\|_2^2 - \|\mathrm{fl}(e_k)\|_2^2 + \eta$$

where η is a constant, depending neither on x, nor on in. Thus, instead of (13), we get

$$\sum_{k=0}^{T} \|e_k\|_2^2 \leq \gamma^2 \left(\sum_{k=0}^{T} \|in_k\|_2^2\right) + (T+1)\eta.$$

However, in practice η is tiny ($\eta \simeq 10^{-300}$) so that it can remain negligible in front of the input in as long as the number T of iterations of the system remains bounded (for instance, the flight commands of a plane typically operate at 100Hz and certainly no longer that 100 hours [7], meaning less than $T := 100 \times 3600 \times 100 \simeq 10^8$ iterations).

5. EXPERIMENTS

We illustrate here the proposed approach on simple examples of the literature. A first one is a linearized model of a cruise control presented in [1, §5.11 and §10.3] while a second one is a spring-mass-damper on which we applied our previous code analyses for open and closed loop stability, applied on model and code artifacts [15, 20, 21, 25].

The method has been implemented in a backend of our Lustre and imperative code analyzer [19] for controllers, implemented in Ocaml. Considering the discrete code of the controller and a discrete version of the plant, the sensitivity system is automatically computed and the LMI synthesized. We rely on OSDP – the Ocaml SDP library – our sound in-

[2]Order of evaluation matters since floating-point operations are not associative.

[3]Bits for radix $\beta = 2$ or digits for $\beta = 10$ for instance.

[4]Usual implementation of the type `double` in C.

[5]x_{k+1} and e_k both incur floating-point computations in the controller (c.f., (9)) whereas in_k is just a real number.

terface to SDP solvers such as CSDP, Mosek or SDPA, to solve the optimization problem. Thanks to OSDP, LMI expressions are checked as seen in Section 4.1.

OSDP is available at https://cavale.enseeiht.fr/osdp/ while the following examples with automatic analyses are available at https://cavale.enseeiht.fr/robustness15/.

5.1 Cruise Control

Let us first focus on a classical example of the literature as presented in [1]. A non-linear dynamical model for the car accounting for rolling friction, aerodynamic drag and gravitational disturbance force is linearized around the equilibrium, where the force applied by the engine, balances the disturbance forces.

The resulting first order linear system is defined as

$$\frac{d(v - v_e)}{dt} = a(v - v_e) + b(u - u_e)$$

with $a := -0.0101$ and $b := 1.32$. v is the car velocity and u the throttle input.

A discrete-time version of the plant dynamics, with time step of $0.2s$ is

$$\begin{cases} x^p_{k+1} = 0.9998 * x^p_k + u_k \\ y_k = 0.0264 * x^p_k \end{cases}$$

It corresponds to the following z-expression:

$$P(z) := \frac{0.0264}{z - 0.9998}.$$

A first controller.

According to [1], a PI controller for this system with $\omega_0 = 1$ and $\zeta = 1$, the undamped natural frequency and the damping ratio of the dominant mode, is defined as

$$C_1(z) := 1.51 + 0.757\frac{0.2}{z-1}.$$

From that z-expression, it is possible to extract the associated linear system:

$$\begin{cases} x^c_{k+1} = x^c_k + u_k \\ u_k = 0.0150 x^c_k + 1.5070 u_k. \end{cases}$$

The phase and gain margins computation of the closed loop system $L(z) = C_1(z)P(z)$ gives $\Theta = 34dB$ and $\phi = 75°$.

The sensitivity system is automatically built using Eq. (9):

$$\begin{pmatrix} x^c_{k+1} \\ x^p_{k+1} \end{pmatrix} = \begin{bmatrix} 1.0000 & -0.0264 \\ 0.0150 & 0.9600 \end{bmatrix} \begin{pmatrix} x^p_k \\ x^c_k \end{pmatrix} + \begin{bmatrix} 1.0000 \\ 1.5070 \end{bmatrix} in_k$$
$$e_k = in_k - 0.0264 x^p.$$

And its vector margin computed using the LMI (12):

$$P = \begin{bmatrix} 0.1865 & -0.1245 \\ -0.1245 & 0.1010 \end{bmatrix} \qquad \gamma = 1.0202.$$

We obtain $\delta = 0.9802$.

The projection of this vector margin to conservative gain and phase margins returns:

$$\Theta_\delta = 34dB, \qquad \phi_\delta = 59°.$$

Fig. 4 presents the Nyquist plot and the vector margin.

A second controller.

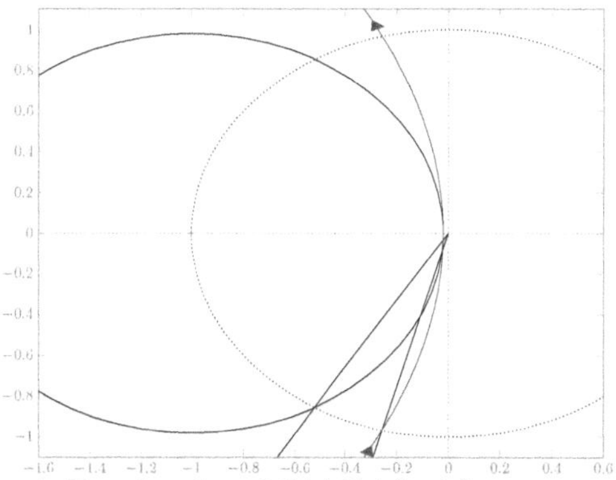

Figure 4: Nyquist plot of $P(z)C_1(z)$ with vector margin.

This PI controller is extremely stable but has low performances. Using an optimization tool, we can also design a second, higher performance controller. This process characterizes the following z-expression for the improved controller:

$$C_2(z) := \frac{2.72z^2 - 4.153z + 1.896}{z^2 - 1.844z + 0.8496}.$$

Again, its associated linear system can be expressed:

$$\begin{cases} x^c_{k+1} = \begin{bmatrix} 1.8440 & -0.8496 \\ 1.0 & 0.0 \end{bmatrix} x^c_k + \begin{bmatrix} 1.0 \\ 0.0 \end{bmatrix} u_k \\ u_k = \begin{bmatrix} 0.0366 & -0.0343 \end{bmatrix} x^c_k + \begin{bmatrix} 2.2720 \end{bmatrix} u_k. \end{cases}$$

The classical phase and gain margins of the feedback system are $\Theta = 31dB$ and $\phi = 84°$.

The sensitivity system is automatically built

$$\begin{pmatrix} x^c_{k+1} \\ x^p_{k+1} \end{pmatrix} = \begin{bmatrix} 1.8440 & -0.84 & -0.0264 \\ 1.0 & 0.0 & 0.0 \\ 0.0366 & -0.0343 & 0.9398 \end{bmatrix} \begin{pmatrix} x^p_k \\ x^c_k \end{pmatrix} + \begin{bmatrix} 1.0000 \\ 0.0 \\ 2.2720 \end{bmatrix} in_k$$
$$e_k = in_k - 0.0264 x^p.$$

And its vector margin computed using the LMI provided in Eq. (3.2):

$$P = \begin{bmatrix} 0.1189 & -0.1002 & -0.0529 \\ -0.1002 & 0.0849 & 0.0447 \\ -0.0529 & 0.0447 & 0.0355 \end{bmatrix}, \qquad \gamma = 1.0307.$$

We obtain $\delta = 0.9703$.

The projection of this vector margin to conservative gain and phase margins returns:

$$\Theta_\delta = 31dB \qquad \phi_\delta = 58°$$

Fig. 5 presents the Nyquist plot and the vector margin.

5.2 Spring Mass Damper

We focus now on a more representative example, already analyzed in previous publications [15, 20, 21, 25]. The interested reader may refer to these to obtain more details on the system. We recall here its definition in a compact way.

The system consists in a simple spring-mass damper. Both the discrete controller and the discrete plant dynamics are expressed as linear systems.

For the sake of completeness we provide the matrices defin-

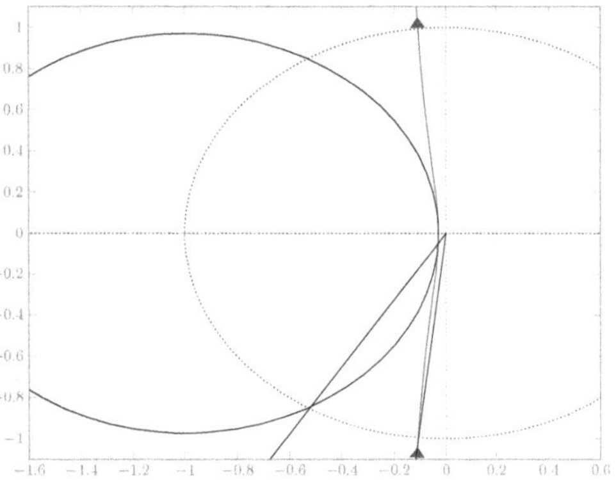

Figure 5: Nyquist plot of $P(z)C_2(z)$ with vector margin

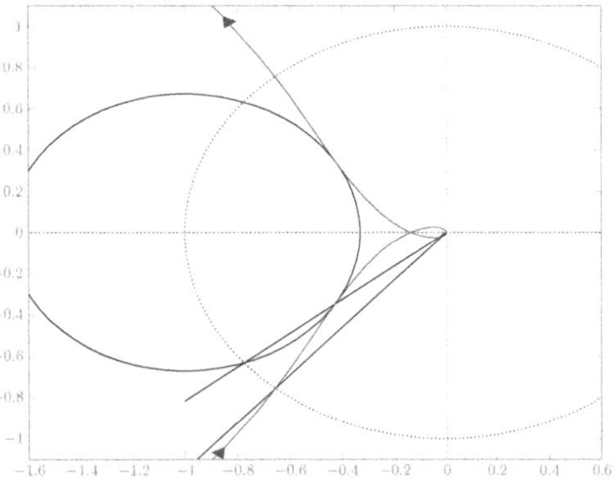

Figure 6: Nyquist plot of the spring mass damper system with vector margin

ing these system:

$$A^p := \begin{bmatrix} 1 & 0.01 \\ -0.01 & 1 \end{bmatrix}, \quad B^p := \begin{bmatrix} 0.00005 \\ 0.01 \end{bmatrix}, \quad C^p := \begin{bmatrix} 1 & 0 \end{bmatrix},$$

$$A^c := \begin{bmatrix} 0.4990 & -0.05 \\ 0.01 & 1 \end{bmatrix}, \qquad B^c := \begin{bmatrix} 1 \\ 0 \end{bmatrix},$$

$$C^c := \begin{bmatrix} 564.48 & 0 \end{bmatrix}, \qquad D^c := 1280.$$

The phase and gain margins computation of the closed loop system gives $\Theta = 17dB$ and $\phi = 49°$.

From the discrete plant and controller description, the sensitivity system is automatically built and analyzed with the LMI (12), we obtain $\gamma = 1.4914$ and

$$P = \begin{bmatrix} 111.8330 & 88.4842 & -48.4990 & 8.8432 \\ 88.4842 & 278.5963 & -20.2482 & 6.9605 \\ -48.4990 & -20.2482 & 28.7964 & -3.7961 \\ 8.8432 & 6.9605 & -3.7961 & 0.7013 \end{bmatrix}.$$

The resulting vector margin is $\delta = 1/\gamma = 0.6705$. And its projection to conservative gain and phase margins returns:

$$\Theta_\delta = 10dB \qquad \phi_\delta = 39°$$

Fig. 6 presents the Nyquist plot and the vector margin.

6. INTEGRATION IN A DEVELOPMENT PROCESS

In order to support the end-to-end formal verification of controller properties on the development artifacts, models and code, along the development process, we setup a representative toolchain, based on autocoders, to compile Simulink models into Lustre models and then C code [10,25]. It is illustrated in Fig. 7.

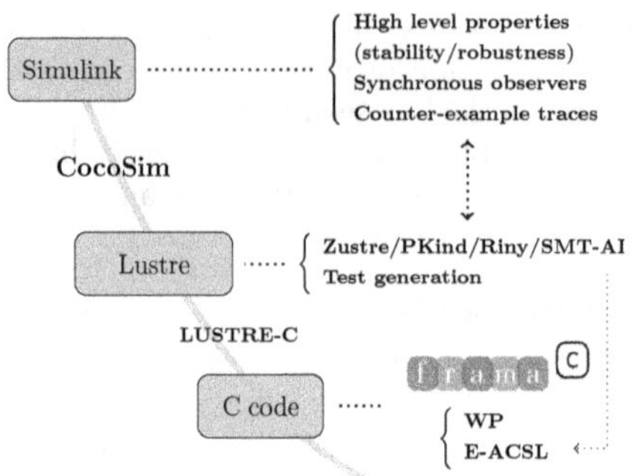

Figure 7: Process cycle with autocoders

This process is representative of industry standards [23] which largely rely on code generation for synchronous dataflow languages. The extraction from the discrete Simulink subset into Lustre is a one-to-one mapping of Simulink subsystems to Lustre nodes, the unit delay operator becoming a `pre` construct. Once the Lustre is obtained, it is compiled into C using the modular compilation scheme [3] used in Scade KCG compiler.

On the verification side, efficient analyses are performed at the Lustre level. Model-checking algorithms based on k-induction or property-directed reachability (PDR aka IC3) are used to address the verification of synchronous observers for safety nodes, while more advanced numerical analyses based on abstract interpretation, policy iteration and Lyapunov function based template synthesis, are focused on the controller core. These numerical analyses work on the model level representation of the systems, *i.e.*, without complex pointers and memory issues, but they consider floating-point semantics. A more detailed explanation of these interactions between solvers is presented in [6].

At the code level, state of the art analyzers are used, such as the open source Frama-C platform [8], a framework for the modular analysis of C code, that integrates a deductive method analysis based on weakest precondition computation.

We sketch here a possible use of the proposed approach within this framework. First, the controller and plant are described in Lustre (c.f., Fig 8).

The `plant` annotation enables the margin analysis which extracts the linear representation of the controller and the plant to build the sensitivity system and analyze it. The Lustre model is enriched with analysis results (c.f., Fig 9).

When generating the final C code, the code is annotated with ACSL predicates [2] relying on our linear algebra library [25]. An additional predicate encodes the dissipativity property (11). The `struct` definitions represent the internal state of each node in our modular compilation scheme. The plant internal state is declared as a ghost `struct` field within the controller own memory. This is presented in Fig. 10.

Finally the controller function is associated to an assert statement ensuring the dissipativity property after each iteration of the system dynamics, as presented in Fig. 11. It is worth noting that the plant code was introduced as ghost C code within the controller code, following the approach we developped in [25].

```
node spring (u:real) returns (y:real);
var xp0, xp1: real ;
let
 xp0 = 0. -> pre xp0 + 0.01 * pre xp1
     + 0.00005 * u;
 xp1 = 0. -> -0.01 * pre xp0 + pre xp1
      + 0.01 * u;
 y = xp0;
tel

--@ plant: spring
node ctl (in,y:real) returns (u:real);
var e, xc0, xc1: real ;
let
 e = in - y;
 xc0 = 0. -> 0.4990 * pre xc0 - 0.05 *
      pre xc1 - e;
 xc1 = 0. -> 0.01 * pre xc0 + pre xc1;
 u = 564.48 * xc0 + 1280. * e;
tel
```

Figure 8: Lustre model including discrete plant description, for the example of Section 5.2.

```
--@ plant: spring
node ctl (in, y: real) returns (u:
    real);
--@ robustness/gamma: 1.4914;
--@ robustness/P: (computed P value);
```

Figure 9: Enriched model with computed properties.

```
#include "acsl_matrices.h"

/*@logic matrix P = mat_of_4x4_scalar(
111.8330,  88.4842, -48.4990,  8.8432,
 88.4842, 278.5963, -20.2482,  6.9605,
-48.4990, -20.2482,  28.7964, -3.7961,
  8.8432,   6.9605,  -3.7961,  0.7013);
    logic real gamma = 1.4914; */

/*@ logic vector state(struct ctl_mem
    self) =
  vector_of_4_scalar (
    self->_reg.__ctl_3,
    self->_reg.__ctl_2,
    self->spec.plant._reg.__plant_3,
    self->spec.plant._reg.__plant_2);*/

/*@ predicate dissip(vector snxt,
    vector s, real in, real e, matrix
    P, real gamma) =
     normP(snxt, P) - normP(s, P) <=
        gamma**2 * in**2 - e**2; */

struct plant_mem {
  struct plant_reg {double __plant_2;
            double __plant_3; } _reg;
  struct _arrow_mem *ni_1; };
struct ctl_mem {
  struct ctl_reg {double __ctl_2;
          double __ctl_3; } _reg;
  struct _arrow_mem *ni_0;
  /*@ghost struct spec {
  struct plant_mem plant; } spec; */};
```

Figure 10: Header of the generated C code including node state description.

We only sketched the global approach; concerning the proof of this property at the code level, we already analyzed similar properties in PVS [15]. Furthermore the current property is simpler since it only involves the positivity of a quadratic form. State of the art SMT solvers such as Z3 [9] should be able to discharge the generated proof objectives without requiring the use of proof assistants.

7. CONCLUSION

This paper had two targets: verification engineers interested in the formal analysis of controller implementations on the one hand, and control engineers on the other hand.

For the first target, this paper provides a gentle introduction to robustness analyses of discrete dynamical SISO systems. It covers the classical definition of stability, phase and gain margin computation and their vector margin counterpart. The method proposed could be used by computer scientists and would enable the generation of conservative phase and gain margins on the code artifact.

For the second target, control engineers, this paper illustrates the fact that the notion of vector margin and its associated LMI characterization is compatible with implementation analysis and should be used instead of frequency based analyses. It also emphasizes the usually forgotten aspect of floating-point imprecision.

Apart from these pedagogical aspects, this paper provides the first automatic tool that analyses robustness of discrete closed-loop systems. It is compatible with analyses such as [19] that extract from the code the linear dynamics and enable its analysis. Our approach instruments the vector margin computation and extends its definition by taking into account floating-point semantics. It also addresses the unsoundness of the SDP solvers implemented with floats by checking *a posteriori* the soundness of the results.

In terms of perspectives, the integration of the approach in our toolchain and its application on more general systems is our next target. As opposed to phase and gain margins, vector margins are also more suited to be extended to evaluate robustness of MIMO systems. Another possibility would be to combine the current robustness characterization on more complex controllers including non- linear ones, *i.e.*, saturated controllers, piecewise systems or LPV controllers.

8. REFERENCES

[1] Astrom, K. J., and Murray, R. M. *Feedback Systems: An Introduction for Scientists and Engineers.* Princeton University Press, Princeton, NJ, USA, 2008.

[2] Baudin, P., Filliâtre, J.-C., Marché, C., Monate, B., Moy, Y., and Prevosto, V. Acsl: Ansi/iso c specification language. version 1.7. http://frama-c.com/download/acsl.pdf.

[3] Biernacki, D., Colaço, J.-L., Hamon, G., and Pouzet, M. Clock-directed modular code generation

C+ACSL

```
void ctl_step (double in, double y,
               double (*u),
               struct ctl_mem *self) {
_Bool __ctl_1;
double e; double xc0; double xc1;
_arrow_step(1,0,&__ctl_1,self->ni_0);
if (__ctl_1) { xc1 = 0.; } else {
  xc1 = ((0.01 * self->_reg.__ctl_3) +
       self->_reg.__ctl_2); }
e = (in - y);
if (__ctl_1) { xc0 = 0.; } else {
  xc0 = (((0.499 * self->_reg.__ctl_3)
       - (0.05 * self->_reg.__ctl_2))
       - e); }
*u = ((564.48 * xc0) + (1280. * e));
self->_reg.__ctl_3 = xc0;
self->_reg.__ctl_2 = xc1;
/*@ghost
_Bool __plant_1;
double xp0; double xp1;
//plant - restricted to state update
_arrow_step (1, 0, &__plant_1,
    self->spec.plant.ni_1);
if (__plant_1) { xp0 = 0.; } else {
  xp0 = ((self->spec.plant._reg.
       __plant_3 + (0.01 * self->spec.
       plant._reg.__plant_2)) + (5e-05
       * *u)); }
if (__plant_1) { xp1 = 0.; } else {
  xp1 = ((((- 0.01) * self->spec.plant
       ._reg.__plant_3) + self->spec.
       plant._reg.__plant_2) + (0.01 *
       *u)); }
self->spec.plant._reg.__plant_3 = xp0;
self->spec.plant._reg.__plant_2 = xp1;
*/
//@assert dissip(state(self), \old(
    state(self)), in, e, P, gamma);
return;
}
```

Figure 11: Transfer function of the controller, including the plant description as annotation and the dissipativity property as function contract.

for synchronous data-flow languages. In *LCTES* (2008).

[4] Boyd, S., El Ghaoui, L., Feron, E., and Balakrishnan, V. *Linear Matrix Inequalities in System and Control Theory.* SIAM, 1994.

[5] Brat, G., Bushnell, D., Davies, M., Giannakopoulou, D., Howar, F., and Kahsai, T. Verifying the safety of a flight-critical system. In *FM* (2015).

[6] Champion, A., Delmas, R., Dierkes, M., Garoche, P., Jobredeaux, R., and Roux, P. Formal methods for the analysis of critical control systems models: Combining non-linear and linear analyses. In *FMICS* (2013).

[7] Cousot, P., Cousot, R., Feret, J., Mauborgne, L., Miné, A., Monniaux, D., and Rival, X. The Astrée analyzer. In *ESOP* (2005).

[8] Cuoq, P., Kirchner, F., Kosmatov, N., Prevosto, V., Signoles, J., and Yakobowski, B. Frama-C: A software analysis perspective. SEFM.

[9] De Moura, L., and Bjørner, N. Z3: An efficient smt solver. In *TACAS* (2008).

[10] Dieumegard, A., Garoche, P., Kahsai, T., Taillar, A., and Thirioux, X. Compilation of synchronous observers as code contracts. In *SAC* (2015).

[11] Feret, J. Static analysis of digital filters. In *ESOP* (2004).

[12] Gawlitza, T., Seidl, H., Adjé, A., Gaubert, S., and Goubault, E. Abstract interpretation meets convex optimization. *J. Symb. Comput.* (2012).

[13] Glover, K., Vinnicombe, G., and Papageorgiou, G. Guaranteed multi-loop stability margins and the gap metric. In *CDC* (2000).

[14] Haddad, W. M., and Chellaboina, V. *Nonlinear Dynamical Systems and Control: A Lyapunov-based Appr.* Princeton University Press, 2008.

[15] Herencia-Zapana, H., Jobredeaux, R., Owre, S., Garoche, P.-L., Feron, E., Perez, G., and Ascariz, P. Pvs linear algebra libraries for verification of control software algorithms in C/ACSL. In *NFM* (2012).

[16] IEEE. Standard for Floating-Point Arithmetic. *IEEE Standard 754-2008* (2008).

[17] Pagetti, C., Saussié, D., Gratia, R., Noulard, E., and Siron, P. The ROSACE case study: From simulink specification to multi/many-core execution. In *RTAS* (2014).

[18] Roux, P. Formal proofs of rounding error bounds. *Journal of Automated Reasoning* (2015).

[19] Roux, P., and Garoche, P.-L. Integrating policy iterations in abstract interpreters. In *ATVA* (2013).

[20] Roux, P., Jobredeaux, R., and Garoche, P.-L. Closed loop analysis of control command software. In *HSCC* (2015).

[21] Roux, P., Jobredeaux, R., Garoche, P.-L., and Féron, E. A generic ellipsoid abstract domain for linear time invariant systems. In *HSCC* (2012).

[22] Rump, S. M. Verification of positive definiteness. *BIT Numerical Mathematics* (2006).

[23] Souyris, J., Wiels, V., Delmas, D., and Delseny, H. Formal verification of avionics software products. In *FM* (2009).

[24] Vinnicombe, G. *Uncertainty and Feedback: H [infinity] Loop-shaping and the [nu]-gap Metric.* World Scientific, 2001.

[25] Wang, T., Jobredeaux, R., Herencia, H., Garoche, P.-L., Dieumegard, A., Feron, E., and Pantel, M. From design to implementation: An automated, credible autocoding chain for control systems. In *Advances in Control System Technology for Aerospace Applications.* 2016.

[26] Willems, J. C. Dissipative dynamical systems part i: General theory. *Archive for rational mechanics and analysis 45*, 5 (1972), 321–351.

Symbolic-Numeric Reachability Analysis of Closed-Loop Control Software

Aditya Zutshi Sriram Sankaranarayanan
University of Colorado, Boulder
aditya.zutshi,srirams@colorado.edu

Jyotirmoy V. Deshmukh and Xiaoqing Jin
Toyota Technical Center, USA
firstname.lastname@tema.toyota.com

ABSTRACT

We study the problem of falsifying reachability properties of real-time control software acting in a closed-loop with a given model of the plant dynamics. Our approach employs numerical techniques to simulate a plant model, which may be highly nonlinear and hybrid, in combination with symbolic simulation of the controller software. The state-space and input-space of the plant are systematically searched using a plant abstraction that is implicitly defined by "quantization" of the plant state, but never explicitly constructed. Simultaneously, the controller behaviors are explored using a symbolic execution of the control software. On-the-fly exploration of the overall closed-loop abstraction results in abstract counterexamples, which are used to refine the plant abstraction iteratively until a concrete violation is found. Empirical evaluation of our approach shows its promise in treating controller software that has precise, formal semantics, using an exact method such as symbolic execution, while using numerical simulations to produce abstractions of the underlying plant model that is often an approximation of the actual plant. We also discuss a preliminary comparison of our approach with techniques that are primarily simulation-based.

Keywords

Reachability; Hybrid Systems; Falsification; Program Analyses

1. INTRODUCTION

In this paper, we study the problem of searching for potential safety violations in real-time controller software by performing a closed-loop symbolic execution of the software in conjunction with a model of the plant dynamics being controlled. Such a closed-loop exploration is quite valuable as it incorporates controller software implementations rather than abstract, hybrid-automata-based models commonly used in formal reachability analysis tools. This allows us to model software centric issues such as fixed point arithmetic, overflows, division by zero and buffer overflows. At the same time, our approach uses a model of the plant dynamics that assures us that bugs found in this process are potentially realizable when deploying the control system.

However, closed-loop symbolic exploration of a controller with its accompanying plant model is quite challenging. Plant models are often nonlinear, and may exhibit hybrid behaviors due to discrete changes in the operating mode. Most modern controller software systems have different control regimes that are chosen based on the environmental conditions, which leads to several control-flow paths in the control code. Exhaustive exploration of all possible combinations of control-flow paths in the controller and plant dynamics can become prohibitively complex. Furthermore, in the control system development process, the control software is an artifact that is deployed in the final system. The plant model, on the other hand, is typically an (unsound) approximation of the actual physical environment, which is hard to characterize exactly. Plant models are often created for the purposes of evaluation and testing of specific aspects of the closed-loop system. Therefore, a precise treatment of the controller semantics is a desirable goal in control verification. However, a similar precise approach to the plant semantics is often prohibitively expensive. Finally, our approach focuses primarily on *falsification*– a best effort search for counterexamples, rather than proving the correctness of closed loop systems.

In this work, we consider the control software to be architected as a set of tasks operating at a fixed rate, where, in each run, the controller reads inputs from the sensors, computes a control value and outputs this to the plant. We call the period at which the controller software runs as the controller sampling period. The value output by the controller is held constant (zero-order hold) for the controller sampling period, before the controller updates it. The plant model is provided as a *black box* specified as a function $\text{SIM}(\mathbf{x}, \mathbf{u}, \tau)$ that simulates the plant model for time $\tau > 0$ starting from a current state $\mathbf{x}$ and under an input $\mathbf{u}$. The underlying plant itself can be a nonlinear hybrid system, or even a data-driven model such as a *neural network* that maps a current state to a next state. We assume that the n-dimensional state of the plant is fully observable by our testing framework. We propose an abstraction of the closed-loop system where: (a) the set of states of the controller is represented by a formula in a suitable logical theory (such as real arithmetic with linear constraints), and (b) the plant is abstracted using a cell-to-cell mapping defined by quantizing real-valued plant states into a finite representation obtained by a *quantization operator* [30]. The plant abstraction is defined as a standard existential abstraction between quantized states and explored using numerical simulations. The controller abstraction is exact, as the operation of the controller is modeled as symbolic execution on the given set of controller states. As a result, our approach treats the controller semantics precisely while potentially missing out on possible plant behaviors. However, any "robust" behavior of the plant can be discovered by increasing the number of simulations used to build the plant abstraction [30].

The overall approach then explores the joint abstractions of the controller and plant using a depth-first search or breadth-first search strategy up to a given time horizon. If the process produces a violation of the time bounded safety property, we discover an abstract counterexample trace. A simplistic refinement scheme that increases

HSCC'16, April 12-14, 2016, Vienna, Austria

DOI: http://dx.doi.org/10.1145/2883817.2883819

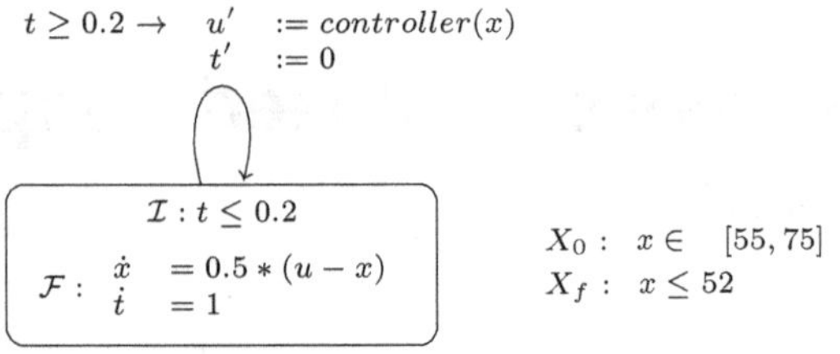

Figure 1: The hybrid automaton for the room-heater-thermostat sampled data system with initial set X_0 and unsafe set X_f.

the number of bits retained by the quantization operator is then used to refine these abstract counterexample further to produce concrete counterexamples.

We implement the overall approach through the combination of the symbolic execution tool Pathcrawler [29] with a simulation infrastructure that can handle plant specifications in a variety of formats including Simulink™ /Stateflow™ models. Using Pathcrawler allows us to treat the control software *as is*, including the ability to handle fixed point arithmetic that is commonly used in embedded controllers. We compare our approach with simulation-based approaches on a few challenging controller benchmarks. By comparing our approach to the standard practice of performing Monte Carlo simulations with uniform random sampling of the initial states and inputs, we hope to highlight the underlying difficulty of arriving at an undesirable behavior purely by chance. We also compare our approach with S-Taliro, a falsification tool that uses simulations guided by an optimizer attempting to minimize the "distance" to a bug; where buggy behavior is specified using Metric Temporal Logic (MTL), and the distance to bug is defined using robust satisfaction semantics for MTL. We also compare with an earlier version of our tool, called S3CAM, that is based on an abstraction-refinement based approach where both the plant and controller abstractions are constructed using simulations.

On one hand, we find that simulation-based approaches are often much faster. This is because of the high overhead of symbolic executions, especially as symbolic execution tools typically use bitvector theories to reason about arithmetic. On the other, we find examples where corner-case behaviors in the controller software trigger reachability violations that cannot be found by the other simulation-based approaches. In doing so, we demonstrate preliminary evidence that despite the high cost of our approach, it can be potentially valuable in detecting corner-case violations that can be missed by approaches primarily based on simulations.

1.1 Motivating Example

Consider the example of a room heating system regulated by a thermostat that controls the operating mode of the heater. The plant dynamics are modeled as a single-mode hybrid automaton with linear dynamics as shown in Fig. 1. The controller action encapsulated inside the reset map of this automaton, can be one of three kinds: OFF, REGULAR HEATING, or FAST HEATING. The control software is a C program shown in Figure 3. This code incorporates extra control logic to prevent the heater from being switched between different modes frequently. The controller is run at 5 Hz (i.e, a controller time-step of 0.2 seconds). Assuming the initial temperature of the room to be $x \in [55, 75]^\circ$ F, we try to find a scenario where the temperature dips too low ($x < 52^\circ$ F) within 10s of system operation. Our implementation runs for about 9 seconds before discovering a violation. A setting where the initial room temperature is set to a small range around $69.9^\circ F$ exposes the poorly coded chatter protection. The system chatters, and the thermostat forces the heater to be non-responsive for too long, causing the room temperature dip too low. Using 100,000 random simulations running for 20 minutes (about 130x longer than our approach), we find 45 violations (instances where temperature dips below 52°F). This corresponds to roughly a one in 1000 chance of discovering this violation by Monte Carlo simulations with uniform random sampling of the initial state.

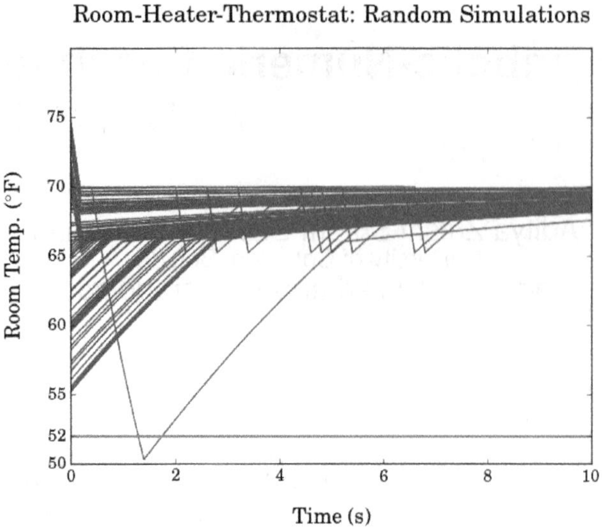

Figure 2: A plot showing around 100 biased random simulations with $T = 10s$. The unsafe regions is below red line at $(52^\circ F)$. Biasing towards $x \in [69.9, 70]$ helps magnify the unsafe behaviors.

2. RELATED WORK

Falsification for Hybrid Systems. In industrial-scale hybrid systems, tools based on falsification of formal safety requirements have recently emerged as a practical alternative to verification approaches which seldom scale well for complex systems. A key factor in this change is that falsification techniques are typically simulation-based and usually best-effort in nature, often providing only asymptotic or probabilistic correctness guarantees. S-Taliro [1] and Breach [10] are tools based on single-shooting based optimization techniques. These tools use the robust satisfaction semantics of a given temporal logic requirement as a cost function to guide the underlying optimizer to find initial states and a parameterized input signal that leads the system to a violation. The term "single shooting" refers to the fact that the optimizer picks a single initial state and an input signal, and then computes the cost of the objective function on the resulting output signal. These tools use a plethora of global optimizers with powerful heuristics to get around the problem that the cost surface is typically highly nonlinear, and occasionally discontinuous. In industrial-scale models, cost surfaces are a challenge for global optimizers, as they can be "flat," *i.e.*, lacking any gradient information to suggest a search-direction for the optimizer. In our experience, such scenarios are often encountered when the controller code has complex Boolean conditions over the continuous state variables or discrete state variables representing operating modes, as they result in mixed discrete-continuous optimization problems. Another dependency of the extant falsification tools is a good distance metric quantifying the distance to bug, which is a challenge to define in the presence of discrete state variables or operating modes, without deep internal knowledge of the model structure [24].

Some of the above challenges are mitigated in our previous work [30]. This technique uses a multiple shooting-based optimization technique, that does not depend on a distance metric on a hybrid state-space. Unlike most simulation based methods, multiple shooting utilizes multiple short simulation traces to search for a falsification. However, this work still treats the entire closed-loop system as a black-box.

```c
#define MAX_TEMP (70.0)
#define MIN_TEMP (66.0)
#define CHATTER_LIMIT (2)

int controller(double room_temp){
  //*************************************************
  // on_ctr, off_ctr       :counters to track on/off cycles
  // chatter_detect_ctr    :counter to track chattering
  // previous_command      :previous command
  // command               :current command
  // u                     :control input to the heater
  //*************************************************
  static int on_ctr, off_ctr, chatter_detect_ctr;
  static int previous_command, command, u;

  // Compute command to heater based on room temperature
  if(room_temp >= MIN_TEMP && room_temp < MAX_TEMP)
    command = NORMAL_HEAT;
  else if(room_temp >= MAX_TEMP)
    command = NO_HEAT;
  else if(room_temp < MIN_TEMP)
    command = FAST_HEAT;
  else
    command = previous_command;

  // Chattering absent, reset the counter
  if(off_ctr >= 5 || on_ctr >= 5)
    chatter_detect_ctr = 0;

  // New command != previous command. Possible chattering
  if(command != previous_command)
    chatter_detect_ctr++;

  // Chattering detected, hold previous command
  if(chatter_detect_ctr > CHATTER_LIMIT)
    command = previous_command;

  // Increment counters
  if(command == NO_HEAT){
    on_ctr = 0;
    off_ctr++;
  }else{
    on_ctr++;
    off_ctr = 0;
  }

  // Translate command to control input
  if(command == NO_HEAT)      u = 20;
  if(command == FAST_HEAT)    u = 100;
  if(command == NORMAL_HEAT)  u = 70;

  return u;
}
```

Figure 3: C code for the Thermostat. All initial control states are 0.

Rapidly exploring Random Trees [19] (RRTs) have also been used to falsify safety properties for hybrid systems [2,11,17,23]. RRTs use a randomized tree-based algorithm to search for a finite sequence of discrete inputs which can lead to unsafe system states. Recent advances in the context of falsification include using a combination of sophisticated heuristics to maximize the exploration of reachable state-space (coverage), and biasing of the tree towards the goal using robust satisfaction measures over partial traces, Even though RRTs have been widely successful in planning, they are not as efficient in finding a violating trajectory of high dimensional search space with a highly constrained reachable space (as is the case with under-actuated systems). They too, operate on a black box assumption.

Symbolic Execution of Programs. Symbolic execution was first formally proposed in [18]. Since then, with increasingly powerful constraint solvers, it has evolved into an efficient code analysis technique, forming the basis for tools such as CUTE [28], KLEE [3], and Pathcrawler [29]. These tools are usually employed to generate inputs that maximize the coverage of control-flow paths in the program. For large programs, a purely symbolic approach can be quite inefficient, and a modified version of symbolic execution, where concrete states are maintained alongside symbolic states is usually preferred. This enables program analyses in the presence of complex constraints that the constraint solvers can not handle, and efficient generation of test cases for path coverage, when 100% coverage is infeasible. Due to their symbolic nature, such techniques can be fused easily with CEGAR-like techniques [6], which we propose in this presentation. Recent surveys on symbolic execution can be found at [4,5].

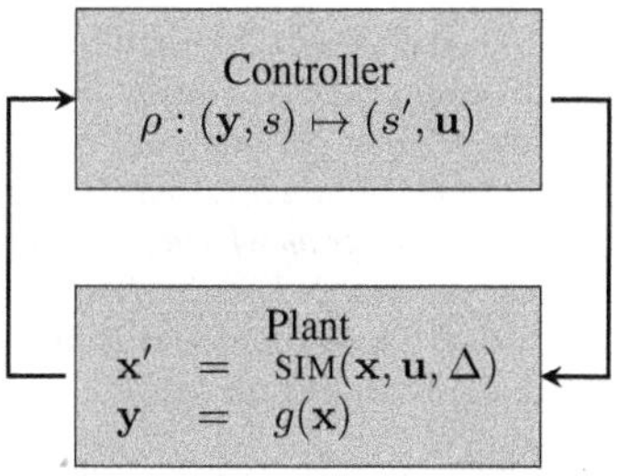

Figure 4: Closed loop composition of a plant and a controller model with controller sampling period Δ.

Closed Loop Analyses Techniques. Closed loop falsification was first proposed by Lerda et al. [20, 21], where model checking of the software was combined with simulation-based systematic exploration of the physical system. Majumdar et al. [22] proposed a verification mechanism for linear dynamical systems using symbolic execution of both the controller code and the plant (using over-approximation of reachable states). In contrast, we provide a more efficient but best effort approach where the physical dynamics are treated as a black-box.

3. SAMPLED DATA CONTROL SYSTEM

In this section, we provide useful definitions, including the problem setup along with the basic abstractions for the controller and the plant. We are interested in analyzing closed-loop systems consisting of a *plant* and a *controller*, wherein the plant is a physical process modeled as a dynamical system and the controller is implemented as a set of software tasks that execute repeatedly with a fixed period known as the *sampling period*.

DEFINITION 3.1 (PLANT MODEL). *The plant model is described by a set of plant states $\mathcal{X}$, plant inputs $\mathcal{U}$ and plant outputs $\mathcal{Y}$ along with two functions:*

- *A simulation function* $\text{SIM} : \mathcal{X} \times \mathcal{U} \times \mathbb{R}_{\geq 0} \mapsto \mathcal{X}$, *where* $\text{SIM}(\mathbf{x}, \mathbf{u}, \tau)$ *maps the current state* $\mathbf{x}$ *at time* t *to the next state* $\mathbf{x}'$ *at time* $t + \tau$ *(where* $\tau \geq 0$*) with the assumption that the input signal* $u(t)$ *is a constant* $\mathbf{u} \in \mathcal{U}$ *for* $t \in [0, \tau)$.
- *An observation function* $g : \mathcal{X} \mapsto \mathcal{Y}$ *that maps the current state* $\mathbf{x}$ *to the observable output* $\mathbf{y} = g(\mathbf{x})$.

The SIM function satisfies the property that $\text{SIM}(\mathbf{x}, \mathbf{u}, 0) = \mathbf{x}$ for all $\mathbf{x} \in \mathcal{X}$ and $\mathbf{u} \in \mathcal{U}$.

The controller samples the output $\mathbf{y}$ of the plant at regular time instants, and updates the control input $\mathbf{u}$ before the next time instant. Controllers are assumed to have an internal state s that is updated by the execution of the controller.

DEFINITION 3.2 (CONTROLLER MODEL). *A controller is specified in terms of its input space $\mathcal{Y}$, its internal state space $\mathcal{S}$, and the controller sampling period Δ. Its semantics are provided by a function $\rho : \mathcal{Y} \times \mathcal{S} \mapsto \mathcal{U} \times \mathcal{S}$, where the function $\rho(\mathbf{y}, s)$ maps the controller input $\mathbf{y}$ (which is the plant output at time t) and internal state s (at time t) to $(s', \mathbf{u})$, where s' and $\mathbf{u}$ are the updated controller state and the input to the plant at time $t + \Delta$, respectively.*

The above mentioned parallel composition of a plant and a controller (Figure 4) is called a *Sampled Data Control System (SDCS)*.

DEFINITION 3.3 (SAMPLED DATA CONTROL SYSTEM). *A sampled data control system (SDCS) consists of two components, as illustrated in Figure 4. (a) A plant model P described by two functions* SIM *and g as in Definition 3.1, and (b) a controller implementation C described by a program whose semantics are described by a function ρ as in Definition 3.2. Finally, the closed-loop parallel composition assumes that the function* SIM *is always called with $\tau = \Delta$, i.e., the controller sampling period.*

In practice, sampled data control systems include A/D (analog-to-digital) and D/A converters for interfacing between the analog plant and the digital controller. Errors are often introduced due to the presence of measurement noise and the quantization of the A/D and D/A converters. Though we allow our models to have an exogenous input modeling a bounded controller disturbance, and allow searching over the disturbance-space during the falsification process, for simplicity of presentation, we omit this from the formalization.

The state of the closed-loop system is given by $(\mathbf{x}, s, \mathbf{u})$ where $\mathbf{x} \in \mathcal{X}$ denotes the plant state, $s \in S$ denotes the internal control state and $\mathbf{u} \in \mathcal{U}$ the plant input. Let $\mathbf{x}_0$ be the initial plant state at $t = 0$, s_0 be the initial controller state and u_0 be the initial plant input or controller output. Given a controller sampling period Δ, the operational semantics of the closed-loop model can be described as a countable sequence of plant and controller moves as follows:

$$\begin{aligned}(\mathbf{x}_0, s_0, \mathbf{u}_0) \rightsquigarrow\ & (\mathbf{x}_1, s_0, \mathbf{u}_0) \rightarrow (\mathbf{x}_1, s_1, \mathbf{u}_1) \rightsquigarrow \\ & (\mathbf{x}_2, s_1, \mathbf{u}_1) \rightarrow (\mathbf{x}_2, s_2, \mathbf{u}_2) \cdots\end{aligned}$$

In each of the above states, the index i denotes the real time $i\Delta$. The closed-loop model interleaves two types of moves:

- *Plant Moves:* $(\mathbf{x}_i, s_i, \mathbf{u}_i) \rightsquigarrow (\mathbf{x}_{i+1}, s_i, \mathbf{u}_i)$, where $\mathbf{x}_{i+1} = \text{SIM}(\mathbf{x}_i, \mathbf{u}_i, \Delta)$ is the next state of the plant after time Δ has elapsed with input $\mathbf{u}_i$. The move has no effect on the controller state, or the control input to the plant that is held constant (zero-order hold).
- *Control Moves:* $(\mathbf{x}_{i+1}, s_i, \mathbf{u}_i) \rightarrow (\mathbf{x}_{i+1}, s_{i+1}, \mathbf{u}_{i+1})$ describes a move by the controller that denotes an instantaneous execution of the control program to yield $(s_{i+1}, \mathbf{u}_{i+1}) = \rho(g(\mathbf{x}_{i+1}), s_i)$. In our idealized semantics, no time elapse occurs during this computation.

Note: The idealized semantics ignores the time taken by the controller code to execute. However, when this time is assumed to be much smaller when compared to the overall time period Δ and the plant's dynamics are assumed to be "slow" enough, the idealized semantics can be justified due to their simplicity. Failing this, we may assume a small but known execution time $\hat{\Delta}$ for the controller and define the controller move to also allow the plant state to change while the controller finishes its computation:

$$(\mathbf{x}, s, \mathbf{u}) \rightarrow (\hat{\mathbf{x}}, \hat{s}, \hat{\mathbf{u}})$$

wherein $\hat{\mathbf{x}} = \text{SIM}(\mathbf{x}, \mathbf{u}, \hat{\Delta})$ and the remaining parts of the definition remain intact.

3.1 Software-Centric View of the Controller

So far, we have used a map ρ to describe the controller. In most industrial embedded systems, implementations of controllers use imperative programming languages such as `C`. For the purpose of our analysis, we present the controller software as a control-flow graph (CFG), a structure that focusses on the structural organization of the execution paths in the controller software.

In the following presentation, we omit any discussion on features such as function calls, arrays, and pointers, but remark that as our technique uses off-the-shelf analysis tools, such features can be handled by our implementation. On the other hand, a programming language like `C`, allows dynamic memory allocation, recursive execution without known termination bounds, pointer arithmetic, and complex data structures. Such features are rarely found in real-time embedded control software, and we can safely assume that we do not encounter these in the controllers to be analyzed. We now formalize the control software as a CFG.

DEFINITION 3.4 (CONTROL-FLOW GRAPH). *A control-flow graph is defined as a tuple $\langle \mathcal{V}, \mathcal{V}_i, \mathcal{V}_o, L, E, \Phi, l_0, l_f \rangle$, where $\mathcal{V}$ is a set of variables, $\mathcal{V}_i \in \mathcal{V}$ and $\mathcal{V}_o \in \mathcal{V}$ are the input and output subset*[1]*. L is a set of nodes (control locations), l_0, l_f are unique start and end locations, representing entry and exit points of the given program respectively. $E \subseteq l \times l$ is a finite set of directed edges, Φ is a function labeling each edge$(l, l') \in E$ with two kinds of constraints:*

1. *An assignment constraint has the following form:*

   $$(v_{l'} = e(\mathcal{V}_l)) \wedge \bigwedge_{w \in \mathcal{V} \setminus \{v\}} (w_{l'} = w_l).$$

   It arises from an assignment statement $v := e$ in the program, where e is the symbolic expression signifying a function over some subset of variables in $\mathcal{V}$. The constraint itself relates the value of the modified variable v at location l' to the values of the variables at location l through the function e, and asserts that all other variables remain unchanged.

2. *A conditional constraint has one of the following forms:*

   $$1.assume(b(\mathcal{V}_l)) \qquad 2.assume(\neg b(\mathcal{V}_l)).$$

   It arises from a conditional statement of the form `if(b) then` *l'* `else` *l''. Here b is a Boolean-valued symbolic expression*[2] *over the variables. For the edge(l, l'), the first label is used, wheres for the edge(l, l''), the second label is used.*

DEFINITION 3.5 (CONTROL-FLOW PATH). *An entry-exit control-flow path π is a sequence of nodes, $l_0, \ldots, l_i, \ldots, l_f$, beginning with l_0 and ending in l_f, such that each location pair $(l_i, l_{i+1}) \in E$.*

During program execution an *edge(l, l')* is taken if its label evaluates to *true*. The *conditional* label is assigned the valuation of its expression b or $\neg b$. The sequence of edges naturally partitions a program into a set of paths $\Pi = \{\pi_1, \ldots, \pi_N\}$. Let each path π_i be described by a path constraint $\rho_i(\mathcal{V}_i, \mathcal{V}_o)$ which sequentially composes the constraints along π_i. The path constraint ρ_i can be understood intuitively as a combination of (a) a path condition $\xi(\mathcal{V}_i)$ on the program inputs which decides if the path is feasible and (b) a path function $\mathcal{V}_o := f_i(\mathcal{V}_i)$ that describes the updates through the assignment statements along the path.

We can now summarize the program as the union of all possible control-flow paths $\rho = \bigcup_{i=1}^{N} \rho_i$. It can be easily shown that this union of path constraints exhaustively covers the entire set of values for $\mathcal{V}_i$, and thus, $\rho(\mathcal{V}_i, \mathcal{V}_o)$ can be written as a function on program inputs $\mathcal{V}_i := \rho_i(\mathcal{V}_i)$. In the present context, we can formulate the piecewise function which computes the controller move for a controller with N paths as follows:

$$\rho(\mathbf{y}, s) = \begin{cases} f_1(\mathbf{y}, s) & \text{if } \xi_1(\mathbf{y}, s) \\ \cdots & \\ f_N(\mathbf{y}, s) & \text{if } \xi_N(\mathbf{y}, s) \end{cases} \tag{1}$$

[1]Note that some of these variables represent the internal state of the controller.

[2]It is assumed that b is side-effect free, i.e., it does not modify the values of the program variables.

This is accomplished by using symbolic execution to find the path condition ξ_i and path function f_i for every path π. In general, a software program might not terminate due to the presence of an infinite path. Additionally, the number of paths in a program can be infinite. It is also non-trivial to determine such cases. Fortunately, best practices in embedded control software discourage the use of jump statements and unbounded loops. Most loops have specified, fixed bounds, and we assume that the same rule is true for the controllers that we encounter. Under this assumption, there is a finite number of finite length control paths in the controller software.

4. IMPLICIT QUANTIZED ABSTRACTION

We now consider the abstraction of the closed loop system by defining abstractions of the plant and the controller state spaces.

4.1 Plant Abstraction

The abstraction of the plant is defined by a *tiling* of the state-state and the control-input space[3] $\mathcal{X} \times \mathcal{U}$ into a set of cells $\mathcal{C}$: $\{C_1, C_2, \ldots\}$. The set $\mathcal{C}$ is a partition on $\mathcal{X} \times \mathcal{U}$, i.e., the cells are pairwise disjoint $C_i \cap C_j \neq \emptyset$ if $i \neq j$, and their union $\bigcup_{C_j \in C} C_j$ is equal to $\mathcal{X} \times \mathcal{U}$. Rather than performing an explicit construction of a tiling of $\mathcal{X} \times \mathcal{U}$, we define the tiling implicitly through *quantization*.

We introduce a quantization function which essentially truncates the decimal representation of the state and control-input to a given level of precision d (i.e., digits after the decimal point).

DEFINITION 4.1 (d-PRECISE QUANTIZATION). *A d-precise quantization is a function* QUANT_d *that maps a state-input pair* $(\mathbf{x}, \mathbf{u})$ *to a* quantized *pair* $(\hat{\mathbf{x}}, \hat{\mathbf{u}})$ *such that:*

$$\text{QUANT}_d(\mathbf{x}, \mathbf{u}) = \frac{1}{10^d}\left(\lfloor 10^d \mathbf{x} \rfloor, \lfloor 10^d \mathbf{u} \rfloor\right) \tag{2}$$

It is easy to see that the d-precise quantization function induces an equivalence relation $\equiv_d$, such that:

$$(\mathbf{x}_1, \mathbf{u}_1) \equiv_d (\mathbf{x}_2, \mathbf{u}_2) \text{ iff } \text{QUANT}_d(\mathbf{x}_1, \mathbf{u}_1) = \text{QUANT}_d(\mathbf{x}_2, \mathbf{u}_2).$$

We observe that the quotient set $(\mathcal{X} \times \mathcal{U})/_{\equiv_d}$ is a set of cells defined as follows. Let $\mathbf{j}$ be a vector of integers, with dimension of $\mathbf{j}$ equal to the sum of dimensions of $\mathcal{X}$ and $\mathcal{U}$. Let $C_{\mathbf{j}}$ be defined as:

$$C_{\mathbf{j}} = \{(\mathbf{x}, \mathbf{u}) \mid \text{QUANT}_d(\mathbf{x}, \mathbf{u}) = \frac{\mathbf{j}}{10^d}\} \tag{3}$$

Then, the set $C_{\mathbf{j}}$ is an element of the quotient set $(\mathcal{X} \times \mathcal{U})/_{\equiv_d}$, with the representative element being $\frac{\mathbf{j}}{10^d}$. It is easy to see that the set of cells $C_{\mathbf{j}}$ forms a tiling; we call this *d-quantized tiling*, with $\equiv_d$ as the cell-equivalence relation. In simple terms, given a d, for any state-input pair $(\mathbf{x}, \mathbf{u})$, the index of the cell to which $(\mathbf{x}, \mathbf{u})$ belongs can be obtained by simply truncating the decimal representation of $(\mathbf{x}, \mathbf{u})$ to d digits and multiplying the result by 10^d. For a given d-quantized tiling, checking if two states belong to the same cell, simply involves checking if their first d digits in decimal notation are the same.

DEFINITION 4.2 (d-SAMPLING). *Given a d-quantized tiling $\mathcal{C}$ and a cell $C_{\mathbf{j}}$ in the tiling, a d-sampling is defined as a random sample of elements of $C_{\mathbf{j}}$.*

We observe that d-sampling is fairly trivial to obtain. If the number of dimensions of the representative element of $C_{\mathbf{j}}$ is $(n+m)$, then we take $(n+m)$ random strings of numbers and append them to each dimension in $\frac{\mathbf{j}}{10^d}$ to get one new random sample. We repeat this process till we get a set of desired size. If each random string generation uses a uniform random sampling, the resulting set contains points that have uniform distribution.

Given a tiling, the plant abstraction is now defined as an existential abstraction that connects two cells. We formally define this below:

DEFINITION 4.3. *Let $\mathcal{C}$ be a d-quantized tiling. The d-quantized tiling-based plant abstraction (denoted $\mathcal{P}_d$) is given by a graph (V, E), where $V = \mathcal{C}$, and the set of edges E is defined such that $(C_{\mathbf{j}}, C_{\mathbf{k}}) \in E$ iff: there is a state-input pair $(\mathbf{x}, \mathbf{u}) \in C_{\mathbf{j}}$ and a state-input pair $(\mathbf{x}', \mathbf{u}) \in C_{\mathbf{k}}$ such that $\mathbf{x}' = \text{SIM}(\mathbf{x}, \mathbf{u}, \tau)$.*

In other words, cells $C_{\mathbf{j}}$ and $C_{\mathbf{k}}$ are connected if there is some source state and source input such that the destination state can be reached from the source state using simulation under the action of the source input. It is easy to show that the abstraction $\mathcal{P}_{d'}$ refines $\mathcal{P}_d$ whenever $d' > d$. I.e, keeping more digits around produces a finer abstraction of the system.

So far, we have implicitly defined the abstraction of the plant. However, we have not yet provided the means to construct these abstractions for a given plant model. We now present the use of numerical simulations to explore $\mathcal{P}_d$.

On-the-fly exploration of the Plant Abstraction: A primitive operation involved in the exploration is to check for a given pair of cells $C_{\mathbf{j}}$ and $C_{\mathbf{k}}$ whether the edge from $C_{\mathbf{j}}$ to $C_{\mathbf{k}}$ exists in the abstraction. In the absence of simplifying assumptions about the nature of the plant model, this problem is equivalent to the general nonlinear reachability problem, and is undecidable in general. In our setup, we have made no assumptions beyond the efficient computation of the SIM function that defines the plant's discrete time behavior. Therefore, we resort to a numerical approach called *scatter-and-simulate*, first introduced in previous work by some of the authors [30]:

1. Obtain a d-sampling of $C_{\mathbf{j}}$ of size $\mathcal{N}, \mathcal{N} > 0$.
2. For each sampled state $\mathbf{x}_\ell$ in the d-sampling, compute $\mathbf{x}'_\ell = \text{SIM}(\mathbf{x}_\ell, \mathbf{u}_\ell, \tau)$.
3. Check if $(\mathbf{x}'_\ell, \mathbf{u}_\ell) \in C_{\mathbf{k}}$ for any $\ell \in [1, \mathcal{N}]$. If yes, then $C_{\mathbf{j}}$ *must* have an edge to $C_{\mathbf{k}}$ in $\mathcal{P}_d$. Otherwise, $C_{\mathbf{j}}$ *may not* have an edge to $C_{\mathbf{k}}$.

In practice, the sampling of $\mathcal{N}$ states can either use a deterministic sampling scheme or the samples can be drawn uniformly at random from C_i. The value of $\mathcal{N}$ itself is a parameter that can be adjusted to achieve a tradeoff between time and precision.

An abstract edge from $C_{\mathbf{j}}$ to $C_{\mathbf{k}}$ is *robust* iff there exist a connected subset $C \subsetneq C_{\mathbf{j}}$ of nonzero volume such that every state $(\mathbf{x}, \mathbf{u}) \in C$ leads to a state in $C_{\mathbf{k}}$ upon the application of the SIM function.

It is shown in our previous work (and elsewhere) that for uniform sampling of $C_{\mathbf{j}}$, as $\mathcal{N}$ increases all robust edges are found with probability 1. However, there may be non-robust plant edges that cannot be discovered by the procedure no matter how large $\mathcal{N}$ is. This is a key theoretical limitation caused by our reliance on black-box models and simulations. In practice, however, non-robust plant edges seldom exist. For instance, the problem of simulating a plant model with such non-robust edges is already nontrivial in the presence of numerical errors.

Another operation of interest over the d-quantized tiling is to find all neighbors $C_{\mathbf{k}} \in \mathcal{C}$ of a given cell $C_{\mathbf{j}}$ such that $(C_{\mathbf{j}}, C_{\mathbf{k}}) \in E$. The process of scatter and simulate is trivially modified to collect all the reached cells $C_{\mathbf{k}}$.

To define the controller abstraction, we need to similarly define a quantization function on the plant output $\mathbf{y}$, such that $C^y = \text{QUANT}_d(y)$. This will allow us to reason over abstract plant outputs in the same way as abstract plant states C.

[3]The quantization is performed only for continuous values and discrete values are treated as is.

4.2 Controller Abstraction

Given a CFG with N control-flow paths $\pi_1, \ldots, \pi_N$, recall that we have a set of concrete partial path functions $\rho_1, \ldots, \rho_N$ whose union yields the overall semantics ρ of the program as in Eq. (1).

Most real-world controllers use nonlinear expressions and conditions in assignment and conditional statements respectively. Performing analyses over such controller software (e.g. to perform symbolic execution), requires solvers capable of reasoning over such theories. Unfortunately, reasoning about non-polynomial arithmetic (such as transcendentals) is undecidable [26], while reasoning about polynomial arithmetic, while decidable, is computationally expensive. A common approach taken in traditional software verification (such as in abstract interpretation [7]) is to have conservative over-approximation of such operations using efficient logical theories (such as linear arithmetic). In this context, we need to over-approximate each path constraint ρ_i to obtain path constraint $\hat{\rho}_i$ that is expressible using the theory of linear arithmetic.

This is typically formalized using an abstraction function α that maps path constraints ρ_j into abstraction path constraints $\hat{\rho}_j : \alpha(\rho_j)$ that satisfy the following property: $\rho_j(\mathbf{y}, s) \subseteq \hat{\rho}_j(\mathbf{y}, s)$. The overall abstract controller relation $\hat{\rho}$ is simply the union of $\hat{\rho}_j$ for each path π_j in the control code. We can abuse notation and use $\hat{\rho}(C^y, \varphi)$ to denote the action of the (abstract) controller on a given cell C^y from the tiling-based plant abstraction, and an abstract set of controller states φ. The result yields a set of control inputs U and updated controller states ψ; we formalize the soundness of the abstraction in the following assumption:

ASSUMPTION 4.1 (CONTROLLER ABSTRACTION SOUNDNESS). *Suppose in the abstract semantics, we have* $(U, \psi) = \hat{\rho}(C^y, \varphi)$, *then for all plant outputs* $\mathbf{y} \in C^y$ *and all controller states* $s \in \varphi$, *the concrete values* $(\mathbf{u}', s') = \rho(\mathbf{y}, s)$ *are contained in their respective abstract states:* $\mathbf{u}' \in U$ *and* $s' \in \psi$.

Having defined an abstraction of the controller semantics, the goal is to compute $(U, \psi) = \hat{\rho}(C^y, \varphi)$. This is achieved through an abstract symbolic execution of the program. One way to achieve this is by precomputing each relation $\hat{\rho}_j$ for path π_j as a tuple of assertions (ξ_j, R_j, T_j), where ξ_j encodes the abstract path condition on C^y and φ, and R_j and T_j are projections of $\hat{\rho}(C^y, \varphi)$ on the controller states and controller outputs (i.e. plant inputs) respectively.

5. CLOSED LOOP FALSIFICATION

Having defined the plant and controller abstractions, we now explore a series of abstract states to analyze the safety of a plant and controller state combinations. The approach presented here can extend to more complex bounded-time temporal logic properties by instrumenting the system with a temporal logic monitor [13–15], and searching for the reachability of a target state in the monitor.

DEFINITION 5.1 (CLOSED LOOP ABSTRACT STATE). *The abstract state of the overall closed-loop system is a combination* (C, φ), *where* C *is an abstract plant cell and* φ *is an abstract controller state, i.e., a logical predicate specifying a set of controller states.*

The closed-loop system abstraction is explored in two phases:

- We consider an abstract plant move $(C, \varphi) \rightsquigarrow_A (C', \varphi)$ wherein $(C, C') \in E_A$ belongs to the abstract edge relation between cells. The new cell C' is generated using the simulate-and-scatter procedure that samples cell C and performs a concrete simulation using the plant's SIM function.
- Next, we consider a controller move $(C', \varphi) \rightarrow_A (C'', \psi)$ wherein we compute $(U, \psi) = \hat{\rho}(C^y, \varphi)$ and obtain a new cell $C'' = \text{QUANT}_d(\mathbf{x}', \mathbf{u}')$ for some $\mathbf{x}' \in C'$, and some $\mathbf{u}' \in U$ by quantizing the new control inputs with the plant states. The updated controller states are now represented by ψ. Also, $C^y = \text{QUANT}_d(g(x'))$.

The two moves combine to give a closed loop move of the system: $(C, \varphi) \xrightarrow{\Delta}_A (C'', \varphi')$.This can now be used for computing the set of reachable abstract states $R_\Delta : \{(C'', \varphi') \mid (C, \varphi) \xrightarrow{\Delta}_A (C'', \varphi')\}$ a one timestep ($\tau = \Delta$). We now present this combined closed loop step as an algorithm.

Algorithm 1: Closed Loop Execution on Abstract States

Input: Abstract states (C, φ), plant input $\mathbf{u}$, abstract plant output C_y, plant simulator SIM, controller summary ρ
Output: Reachable abstract states R_Δ

$X_u := \{(\mathbf{x}_1, \mathbf{u}_1), \ldots, (\mathbf{x}_\mathcal{N}, \mathbf{u}_\mathcal{N})\} = \text{d\_sample}(C, \mathcal{N})$
$X'_u := \{\mathbf{x}' \mid \mathbf{x}' = \text{SIM}(\mathbf{x}, \mathbf{u}, \Delta) \wedge (\mathbf{x}, \mathbf{u}) \in X_u\}$
$Y := \{C^y \mid C^y = \text{QUANT}_d(g(\mathbf{x}')) \wedge \mathbf{x}' \in X'_u\}$
$S_{\varphi Y} := \{(U, \psi) \mid (U, \psi) = \hat{\rho}(C^y, \varphi) \ \wedge \ C^y \in Y\}$
$R_\Delta := \{(C'', \psi) \mid C'' = \text{QUANT}_d(\mathbf{x}', \mathbf{u}') \wedge \mathbf{u}' = \mathit{sample}(U) \wedge (U, \psi) \in S_{\varphi Y} \wedge \mathbf{x}' \in X'_u\}$

To compute the plant step, first d-sampling is used to obtain $\mathcal{N}$ state-input pairs which are then supplied to SIM to compute a representative set of next plant states X'_u . The corresponding set of representative plant outputs are also computed using $g()$ and are then quantized to get Y. Using this set of abstract plant outputs, and controller function $\hat{\rho}$ new abstract controller states and outputs are computed. The controller inputs u are then sampled (using a constraint solver, as discussed in Sec. 6). Finally, R_Δ is built by quantizing plant state-input $(\mathbf{x}', \mathbf{u}')$ pair. The overall search algorithm scatter-and-simulate remains the same as explained in [30].

Thus, in practice, exploring the abstraction is a combination of exploring the plant abstraction through a numerical simulation procedure to compute the resulting cells and then running an abstract symbolic execution of the controller code. In doing so, the robust edges in the plant are captured whereas all possible moves by the controller are taken into account.

6. IMPLEMENTATION

We have prototyped the presented falsification technique as S3CAMX, a falsification tool which uses *scatter-and-simulate* combined with symbolic execution. The primary objective of S3CAMX is to demonstrate the feasibility of testing closed loop controller models designed in popular industrial frameworks like Matlab™ and Simulink™ , as well as legacy control systems.

S3CAMX takes in the controller source code in `C`, a SIM function representing the plant model, and the test description. The test description specifies the initial states and error states (safety property) for the system under test, its sampling period Δ and the time horizon for the test. It also specifies the initial abstraction parameters, a detailed discussion on their description and selection can be found in our previous work [30].

6.1 Controller Description

We assume a controller architecture where the interface to the controller is through a function with signature `controller_step(input, output)`, corresponding to the controller execution on a set of plant outputs. *input* to the controller encapsulates the (a) plant output $\mathbf{y}$, (b) previous controller state s and (c) exogenous controller input $\mathbf{w}$ (disturbances/exogenous inputs). The controller returns a structured *output* consisting of (a) controller's next state and (b) control input (to the plant). This setup is quite generic, and follows a similar format used

```c
int controller(){
    static int var;
    var += 1;
    return 0;
}
```

Listing 1: Present

```c
int controller(int var){
    int var;
    var += 1;
    return var;
}
```

Listing 2: Absent

Figure 5: Listing with and without persistent variables.

by Embedded Coder^{TM} , Matlab^{TM} 's automatic code generation toolbox to generate C code.

We make a special distinction between the persistent ('global') state variables of the controller and 'local' variables that are *reinitialized* each time the controller is invoked. In typical C software, persistent variables are usually easy to identify as their declaration is qualified by *global* or *static*. In a Simulink^{TM} model, persistent variables are associated with data-store blocks with dedicated read and write blocks to access their values. Given a control software with persistent states, it can be transformed to one without them by converting the persistent variables into function parameters. The above C code snippets in Fig. 5 illustrate the transformation of a function with persistent variables to an equivalent function with only local variables.

6.2 Controller Preprocessing

Before beginning the analyses, S3CAMX transforms the controller using a symbolic execution engine to a set of all possible control-flow paths in the controller. The paths are represented by their associated path constraints and update functions. This enumeration is expensive and carried only once for a given controller. Once pre-processed, a controller move involves checking the feasibility of each path constraint and if feasible, computing the valuations of updated state and output. We use Z3 [8], an SMT solver to check feasibility and compute a concrete satisfying assignment on the controller's input $(\mathbf{y}, s)$. The update function is then used to compute $(s', \mathbf{u})$. Multiple satisfying assignments can be obtained by adding blocking constraints.

Pathcrawler [29] is used as the symbolic executor of choice. It can work with constraints over floating points in C programs and uses ECLiPSe [27] as its constraint solver. At the time of implementation, Z3 did not support floating point arithmetic and the theory of reals was used instead. Pathcrawler and Z3 provide for efficient linear constraint solving, but limit the kind of non-linear constraints which can be handled in the controller. Using symbolic execution, we can extend the current implementation to catch program bugs like **division by zero**, **out of bounds access**, and other common programming bugs in the controller. As a remark, we also tried KLEE [3], but unlike Pathcrawler it uses bitvector theories to model C programs. This implies that it can not handle floating point arithmetic, and results in bitvector constraints which are comparatively inefficient to solve.

We note that static generation of *all* controller paths is not always efficient. In practice, controller code base can be quite large and enumerating all paths is an expensive and potentially wasteful process. This can be in part remedied by not doing a plant agnostic path enumeration which can result infeasible paths. Instead, the domain of the inputs to the controller can be constrained appropriately using knowledge about the relevant plant model, thus reducing the number of generated controller paths. A better solution will be a tighter integration of the symbolic execution engine to enable a budget constrained dynamic path exploration using suitable heuristics.

6.3 Plant Description

The current version of the prototype can directly use plants modeled in Python or Matlab^{TM} by using the provided interface. Other frameworks can be easily accommodated by wrapping their respective simulation functionality within a layer of Python. The signature

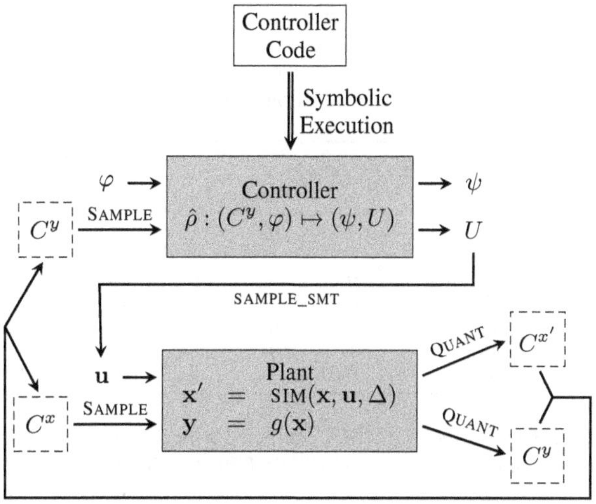

Figure 6: Closed loop symbolic execution.

of the SIM function is of the form $\mathbf{x}' = \text{SIM}(\mathbf{x}, \mathbf{u}, t)$ with $t, \mathbf{x}, \mathbf{u}, \mathbf{x}'$ as defined. The implementation details of the algorithm used to compute the plant abstraction can be found in our previous work [30].

6.4 Closed Loop Execution

The closed loop analyses involves computing the controller and the plant move in lock step Fig. 6. The controller code is first abstracted using symbolic execution to obtain controller $\hat{\rho}$. Given a set of abstract plant states C^x and inputs $\mathbf{u}$ and controller state φ, the closed loop step proceeds with the plant step. C^x is sampled and along with $\mathbf{u}$ simulated to obtain $\mathbf{x}'$ and $\mathbf{y}$, which are then quantized to get $C^{x'}$ and C^y respectively. Next, the controller step takes in C^y and the given φ to compute ψ and U. Using an SMT solver, we find satisfying assignments to the constraints and in essence, compute representative samples for U as $\mathbf{u}$. The implementation differs from the theory here, where we quantize the samples $\mathbf{u}$ and then sample again to get additional samples. This repeats for n steps, where $n = \lceil \frac{T}{\Delta} \rceil$ and T is the time horizon specified by the given property.

6.5 Constraint Blowup

The symbolic treatment of the controller code has benefits of being precise, but as the case with similar methodologies like bounded model checking, automatic test generation, and more, suffers from 'constraint blowup'. Each controller move requires an 'unrolling' of the controller in time, tracking the associated constraints. The constraints accumulate width each time step and become very inefficient to solve. Even though SMT solvers are quite efficient, large constraints can make the entire analyses unusable. We address this by providing an option of selecting the 'history depth' in S3CAMX. Once the given depth is exceeded, the symbolic controller states are concretized, and the accumulated symbolic constraints (history) are purged. This is done by selecting some representative concrete controller states instead of maintaining complex symbolic representation of all reachable controller states. To clarify, it does not limit the length of the abstract trajectories which can be discovered. For all the presented benchmarks, a depth of 1 was used.

7. EXPERIMENTAL RESULTS

We compare our tool S3CAMX in Table 2 against S-Taliro and our previous approach S3CAM which considers the entire composed sampled data controller system as a black-box. As in our previous work [30], we also provide a reference for the difficulty of falsification using random testing. As before, random testing uses 100,000 simulations on most benchmarks (except for AFC). Every time bounded property was tested to the time horizon specified next

Table 1: Summary of benchmarks. Each benchmark mentions the sampling period of the controller Δ and its description is split into constituent controller and plant. The controller is described by number of *States*, exogenous inputs (*Ex. Ip*), lines of code (*LOC*), symbolic paths in the (*Paths*) and time taken to generate them (*SymEx Time*) in minutes. The plant is described by the language used to implement its model (*Impl.*), number of modes if its a hybrid automaton or the number of blocks if its a Simulink™ model (*Modes/Blocks*), continuous states (*C. States*)

Benchmark	Δ(s)	Controller					Plant		
		States	Ex. Ip	LOC	Paths	SymEx Time	Impl.	Plant Modes/Blocks	C. States
SPI	1	0	1	13	3	0	Python	1	1
Heater	0.2	4	0	59	26	0	Python	3	1
Heat	0.5	3	0	37	312	1	Python	6	3
DC Motor	0.02	1	1	29	3	0	Python	0	2
FuzzyC	0.01	0	0	218	208	236	Python	0	3
MRS	1	0	8	29	9	0	Python	0	4
AFC	0.01	7	0	243	120	40	Simulink	170	12

Table 2: Current tool *S3CAMX*, compared with *S-Taliro* and our previous tool *S3CAM*. All processes were run as single threaded on Ubuntu 12.04, running on an Intel i7-2820QM CPU @2.30GHz with 8GB RAM. **All times are in minutes unless mentioned as seconds(s).**

Benchmark	Time Horizon T (s)	Random Testing		S-Taliro		S3CAM		S3CAMX	
		Num. Vio	T	Num. Succ	T_{avg}	Num. Succ	T_{avg}	Num. Succ	T_{avg}
SPI($\mathcal{P}1$)	50	348/100k	17.5	10	0.36	10	0.01	10	0.22
SPI($\mathcal{P}2$)	200	33 /100k	60.9	10	19.59	10	0.03	10	1.31
SPI($\mathcal{P}3$)	500	0 /100k	154.4	0	TO	10	0.08	10	8.39
Heater	2	47 /100k	3.9	10	0.48	10	0.22	10	0.06
Heat	10	156/100k	39.0	10	11.78	10	0.06	10	0.16
DC Motor	1	0 /100k	45.0	0	TO	0	TO	10	0.63
FuzzyC	0.1	6 /100k	10.1	10	0.27	10	0.03	10	1.59
MRS 1	2	0 /100k	0.6	0	TO	0	TO	10	0.18
MRS 2	2	0 /100k	0.4	0	TO	0	TO	10	0.11
MRS 3	2	0 /100k	0.4	0	TO	0	TO	10	0.43
AFC	12	1 /100	238.7	10	0.25	10	16.15	10	13.45

to the benchmark. It should be noted that S3CAMX is a prototype in early stages and optimization and parallelization have been deferred to future releases.

To compare against random testing we used a fixed number of random simulations (ns) and recorded the number of violating (nv) traces. This is mentioned as (nv/ns) along with the time taken to run the simulations. Next to it, is the average time taken for 10 runs by S-Taliro, S3CAM and S3CAMX to find a falsification. This is required due to the randomized nature of all three. The run of the tools is defined as the time to find a falsification, permitting internal restart (multi start strategy is often combined with random search). If a run takes more than 1 hour to finish, we consider it as a time out. If all 10 runs time out, we mention TO as the time taken and 0 as the number of successful runs.

The implementation was benchmarked on several examples mentioned in Table 1, ranging from a simple PI controlled DC Motor to a complex air fuel controller for a powertrain described in Simulink™ . Against each system tested, we mention its sampling period Δ and the controller and plant characteristics. For the former, this includes the number of states, exogenous inputs, lines of code, symbolic controller paths statically discovered by Pathcrawler and the time taken to do so. The plant is characterized by the implementation language for the simulator (Python or Simulink™), the number of discrete modes if the plant is a hybrid system, otherwise the number of Simulink™ blocks, and lastly, the number of continuous states (plants can also have exogenous inputs [30]. A detailed description for each of the benchmark follows.

7.1 Sampled Polarity Integrator System

The SPI benchmark was used in [11] to highlight the difficulty faced by Markov-chain Monte-Carlo based random testing techniques, and optimization-guided techniques such as RRT-REX and S-TaLiRo. The system has an exogenous input w, and a single continuous state x which after every $\Delta = 1$ seconds gets reset to either -1, 0, or 1 if the input $w < 0$, $w = 0$ or $w > 0$ respectively. We split this system into a plant and a controller, where the controller computes $u = -1, 0, 1$ based upon its exogenous input w as $u = sign(w)$. The continuous state of the plant evolves as $\dot{x} = u$. We then check the three properties $\mathcal{P}1 : x < 20$, $\mathcal{P}2 : x < 50$ and $\mathcal{P}3 : x < 150$ for time horizons 50, 200, and 500 respectively. For all properties S3CAM takes only a few seconds. S3CAMX takes a bit longer due constraint solving, but, S-Taliro takes significantly longer and times out for $\mathcal{P}3$. Similar difficulty is faced by RRT-Rex [11]. This example brings out the difference in our iterative approach when compared to directed random search.

7.2 Heater

The heater system introduced in Sec. 1.1 consists of a room, and a heater controlled by a thermostat. The heater has 3 operating modes; *off*, *regular heating*, and *fast heating*. It can be switched between modes by the thermostat in order to reach and maintain a comfortable temperature in the room. Specifically, the thermostat is designed to sense the room temperature after every $\Delta = 0.2s$ and maintain a temperature of around $70°F$. It also has built-in logic to prevent chattering, i.e., avoiding rapid switching of the heater between modes. The heater is modeled as a hybrid system with linear dynamics, with 1 continuous state and three modes. The thermostat's software controller has 26 control-flow paths with 4 states which keep track of recent mode switchings. The property we seek to falsify is that the room-temperature T_F is always greater than $52°F$. We are able to find the falsification trace, which upon investigation indicates the failure of the chatter-prevention logic in a very narrow range of possible initial settings for the ambient room temperature (approx.) $T_{F0} \in [69.9, 70.0]$. Though all tools find the falsification in less than half a minute, S3CAMX is an order of magnitude faster than both S3CAM and S-Taliro.

7.3 Heat benchmarks

The heat benchmarks were proposed in [12], and describe a scenario where a limited number of heaters h are being used to heat r rooms, where $h < r$. The control system can shuffle the heaters or turn them on/off in order to maintain a comfortable temperature in all rooms. We are interested in finding scenarios where the controller fails and the temperature of any room dips below a certain threshold. We choose the first instance in the suite of heat benchmarks for case study; this instance has 3 rooms and 1 heater. The controller software has 312 control-flow paths and 3 states tracking each room's temperature. Correspondingly, the plant has 3 continuous states and 6 modes. Each mode is characterized by the heater's location and it's discrete state (on/off). We try to falsify the property that temperature of the first room does not drop below $17.23°C$. Interestingly, S3CAMX performs comparably to S3CAM even though the control software has 312 paths. Both tools are faster than S-Taliro and finish in a few seconds, where as S-Taliro requires a few minutes for falsification.

7.4 DC Motor

This example illustrates the search for errors in the presence of controller disturbance. The DC motor is a linear continuous system with armature current i and angular velocity $\dot{\theta}$. It is controlled by PI controller with saturation which results in 3 control-flow paths. The bounded additive disturbance in the controller induces error in the sensed plant outputs. We parameterize the disturbance as a piecewise constant signal. We wish the system to never enter the following region of the state-space: $i \in [1, 1.2], \dot{\theta} \in [10, 11]$. We choose this set by design; it is designed to be very hard to reach using random simulations. S3CAMX can, however, find a falsification, demonstrating the effectiveness of symbolic execution in finding a sequence of inputs that lead to a violation. In comparison, S-Taliro and our previous technique S3CAM fail to find a violation.

7.5 Fuzzy Control of Inverted Pendulum

Rule based controllers, such as ones implemented using fuzzy logic, are an interesting challenge for symbolic execution based analyses as they typically have a large number of control-flow paths. We consider an example from [25], where the controller tries to stabilize a nonlinear inverted pendulum balanced on a cart using a 5X5 rule matrix. The C code [4] has 218 lines describing 208 control-flow paths. The controller is stateless and computes the actuation force by classifying the current plant state (θ and $\dot{\theta}$) and selecting a corresponding control output from a lookup table. The safety property defines bounds on states, which when exceeded, indicate undesirable transients or possible unstable behaviors. S-Taliro finds a falsifying trajectory faster than S3CAMX, but not as fast as S3CAM. This result is nevertheless encouraging as it shows the ability of S3CAMX to analyze a large number of control-flow paths and yet be successful at finding a falsifying trajectory.

7.6 Mode-Specific Reference Selection (MRS)

These are a set of 3 benchmarks from [9, 11]. The benchmarks represent distinctive features from proprietary models of automotive controllers, and they highlight issues faced by optimization-guided methods. The systems have simple nonlinear dynamics but complex combinatorial Boolean logic over 8 exogenous inputs. To make the system amenable to S3CAMX, we split the discrete nonlinear dynamics into a plant, and the rest (linear combinatorial logic) becomes the controller. The controller remains the same across the 3 benchmarks, but the plant varies. The mode selection logic is now part of the controller which takes in 8 inputs $w_1, \ldots, w_8$, where each $w_i \in [0, 100]$ and computes u. The 3 plants have discrete time nonlinear dynamics where the evolution is governed by $x^+ = f(x, u)$, where $f_i(x, u)$ comprises of polynomials of up to degree 3 and trigonometric functions in x. The falsification can only be found in the mode which is triggered when $\bigwedge_{i \in [1..4]} w_{2i}(t) > 90 \wedge w_{2i-1}(t) < 10$. The probability of triggering the mode is thus a meager 10^{-8}. Such a combinatorial search is not amenable to sampling-based searches, and both S-Taliro and S3CAM fail. On the other hand, S3CAMX can falsify the property in under a minute.

[4]http://www2.ece.ohio-state.edu/~passino/fuzzycontrol.html

7.7 Powertrain Control Benchmark

We use the most complex version of the abstract fuel control system benchmark (AFC) presented in [16]. It represents a complex closed loop control system modeling a plant with hybrid dynamics controlled by a PI controller. The original benchmark has both the plant and the controller implemented in Simulink™ . To test it using our approach, we use Embedded Coder™ to generate C code for the controller block, which is then hand-tuned to satisfy controller interface requirements. Due to the observability requirement discussed in Sec. 6, the plant model is modified by simplifying the variable transport delay block to a first order filter. The property checked is a modified form of the 'Worst-case excursions in the normal mode' property in [16], i.e., we try to falsify $\mu >= 0.02$ while $t \in [0, 1.0]$. The search is over the original parameters: pedal frequency, pedal amplitude and engine speed. Both S3CAMX and S3CAM take longer than S-Taliro to find the falsification due to the inefficient Matlab™ interface, as explained below.

In summary, symbolic execution being an expensive operation, increases the time taken by S3CAMX to find a falsification when compared with S3CAM. However, it also enables it to find falsifications where S3CAM completely fails. Specifically, in cases where the control program has non-robust paths and corner cases (hard to cover behaviors using a uniform random distribution) which lead to the violation, S3CAMX should perform better than a purely sampling based search like S3CAM. This is due to the discussed exhaustive exploration by symbolic execution of all possible control paths for a given set of plant states. This is exemplified by the DC Motor and MRS benchmarks. On the other hand, when the above is not the case, and controller paths leading to the violation can be exercised using uniform random sampling alone. This is evident by the benchmarks: SPI, Heat and FuzzyC.

S3CAM fares better than S-Taliro in all benchmarks except AFC (which involves a plant model in Simulink™ /Matlab™). This can be partly attributed to the inefficient interface between S3CAM/S3CAMX and Matlab™ – our tool has a few layers of communication and indirection to get the Python implementation to communicate with the simulation infrastructure in Simulink™ /Matlab™ . Part of the inefficiency can be attributed to the Simulink™ SIM function. Each call to SIMin Simulink™ has a setup time required for model preprocessing and compilation; this makes repeated simulations very expensive. This can be clearly seen in the amount of time taken for 100 random simulations of the AFC model. The latter issue has been recently addressed in a newer version of Simulink™ (R2015b) through the introduction of a feature *fast restart* which reduces the setup time to some extent.

8. CONCLUSIONS

In conclusion we presented a technique to falsify properties of control systems described by implementations of control software and models of physical systems (plant). A combination of *numerical simulations* to explore the implicit plant abstraction and *symbolic execution* to maximize path coverage on control code was used to find abstract error traces. These were then iteratively concretized to yield reproducible error traces.

Results on benchmarks, ranging from the simple to the complex ones implemented in Simulink™ were presented and compared with random testing, S-Taliro, and our previous, purely numerical technique S3CAM. We successfully demonstrated the effectiveness of symbolic execution in detecting corner cases in controller code. The implementation along with the benchmarks is made public at https://github.com/zutshi/S3CAMX.

Acknowledgements

We thank James Kapinski for countless useful discussions which helped shape this work. Zutshi and Sankaranarayanan were supported, in part, by the US National Science Foundation(NSF) under award number CNS-1319457 and, in part, by Toyota Engineering and Manufacturing North America(TEMA). All opinions are those of the authors and not necessarily of the NSF or TEMA.

9. REFERENCES

[1] Y. Annapureddy, C. Liu, G. Fainekos, and S. Sankaranarayanan. S-taliro: A tool for temporal logic falsification for hybrid systems. *Proc. TACAS*, pages 254–257, 2011.

[2] A. Bhatia and E. Frazzoli. Incremental search methods for reachability analysis of continuous and hybrid systems. *Proc. of HSCC*, pages 451–471, 2004.

[3] C. Cadar, D. Dunbar, and D. R. Engler. Klee: Unassisted and automatic generation of high-coverage tests for complex systems programs. In *OSDI*, volume 8, pages 209–224, 2008.

[4] C. Cadar, P. Godefroid, S. Khurshid, C. S. Păsăreanu, K. Sen, N. Tillmann, and W. Visser. Symbolic execution for software testing in practice: preliminary assessment. In *Proceedings of the 33rd International Conference on Software Engineering*, pages 1066–1071. ACM, 2011.

[5] C. Cadar and K. Sen. Symbolic execution for software testing: three decades later. *Communications of the ACM*, 56(2):82–90, 2013.

[6] E. Clarke, A. Fehnker, Z. Han, B. Krogh, J. Ouaknine, O. Stursberg, and M. Theobald. Abstraction and counterexample-guided refinement in model checking of hybrid systems. *International Journal of Foundations of Computer Science*, 14(04):583–604, 2003.

[7] P. Cousot and R. Cousot. Abstract interpretation: a unified lattice model for static analysis of programs by construction or approximation of fixpoints. In *Conference Record of the Fourth Annual ACM SIGPLAN-SIGACT Symposium on Principles of Programming Languages*, pages 238–252, Los Angeles, California, 1977. ACM Press, New York, NY.

[8] L. De Moura and N. Bjørner. Z3: An efficient smt solver. In *Tools and Algorithms for the Construction and Analysis of Systems*, pages 337–340. Springer, 2008.

[9] J. Deshmukh, X. Jin, J. Kapinski, and O. Maler. Stochastic local search for falsification of hybrid systems. In *Automated Technology for Verification and Analysis*, pages 500–517. Springer, 2015.

[10] A. Donzé. Breach, a toolbox for verification and parameter synthesis of hybrid systems. In *Proc. CAV*, pages 167–170, 2010.

[11] T. Dreossi, T. Dang, A. Donzé, J. Kapinski, X. Jin, and J. V. Deshmukh. Efficient guiding strategies for testing of temporal properties of hybrid systems. In *NASA Formal Methods*, pages 127–142. Springer, 2015.

[12] A. Fehnker and F. Ivančić. Benchmarks for hybrid systems verification. In *Proc. of HSCC*, volume 2993, pages 326–341, 2004.

[13] D. Giannakopoulou and K. Havelund. Automata-based verification of temporal properties on running programs. In *Automated Software Engineering, 2001.(ASE 2001). Proceedings. 16th Annual International Conference on*, pages 412–416. IEEE, 2001.

[14] K. Havelund and G. Roşu. Monitoring programs using rewriting. In *Automated Software Engineering, 2001.(ASE 2001). Proceedings. 16th Annual International Conference on*, pages 135–143. IEEE, 2001.

[15] K. Havelund and G. Roşu. Synthesizing monitors for safety properties. In *Tools and Algorithms for the Construction and Analysis of Systems*, pages 342–356. Springer, 2002.

[16] X. Jin, J. V. Deshmukh, J. Kapinski, K. Ueda, and K. Butts. Powertrain control verification benchmark. In *Proceedings of the 17th international conference on Hybrid systems: computation and control*, pages 253–262. ACM, 2014.

[17] J. Kim, J. M. Esposito, and V. Kumar. An RRT-based algorithm for testing and validating multi-robot controllers. Technical report, DTIC Document, 2005.

[18] J. C. King. Symbolic execution and program testing. *Communications of the ACM*, 19(7):385–394, 1976.

[19] S. M. LaValle. Rapidly-exploring random trees a new tool for path planning. Technical Report TR 98-11, Computer Science Dept., Iowa State University, Ames, Iowa, 1998.

[20] F. Lerda, J. Kapinski, E. Clarke, and B. Krogh. Verification of supervisory control software using state proximity and merging. *Hybrid Systems: Computation and Control*, pages 344–357, 2008.

[21] F. Lerda, J. Kapinski, H. Maka, E. M. Clarke, and B. H. Krogh. Model checking in-the-loop: Finding counterexamples by systematic simulation. In *American Control Conference, 2008*, pages 2734–2740. IEEE, 2008.

[22] R. Majumdar, I. Saha, K. Shashidhar, and Z. Wang. Clse: Closed-loop symbolic execution. In *NASA Formal Methods*, pages 356–370. Springer, 2012.

[23] T. Nahhal and T. Dang. Test coverage for continuous and hybrid systems. In *Computer Aided Verification*, pages 449–462, 2007.

[24] T. Nghiem, S. Sankaranarayanan, G. Fainekos, F. Ivancić, A. Gupta, and G. J. Pappas. Monte-carlo techniques for falsification of temporal properties of non-linear hybrid systems. In *Proceedings of the 13th ACM international conference on Hybrid systems: computation and control*, pages 211–220. ACM, 2010.

[25] K. M. Passino, S. Yurkovich, and M. Reinfrank. *Fuzzy control*, volume 42. Citeseer, 1998.

[26] J. Robinson. *The collected works of Julia Robinson*, volume 6. American Mathematical Soc., 1996.

[27] J. Schimpf and K. Shen. Ecl i ps e–from lp to clp. *Theory and Practice of Logic Programming*, 12(1-2):127–156, 2012.

[28] K. Sen, D. Marinov, and G. Agha. *CUTE: a concolic unit testing engine for C*, volume 30. ACM, 2005.

[29] N. Williams, B. Marre, P. Mouy, and M. Roger. Pathcrawler: Automatic generation of path tests by combining static and dynamic analysis. In *Dependable Computing-EDCC 5*, pages 281–292. Springer, 2005.

[30] A. Zutshi, S. Sankaranarayanan, J. V. Deshmukh, and J. Kapinski. Multiple shooting, cegar-based falsification for hybrid systems. In *Proceedings of the 14th International Conference on Embedded Software*, page 5. ACM, 2014.

SMT-Based Analysis of Virtually Synchronous Distributed Hybrid Systems*

Kyungmin Bae
SRI International

Peter Csaba Ölveczky
University of Oslo

Soonho Kong
Carnegie Mellon University

Sicun Gao
MIT CSAIL

Edmund M. Clarke
Carnegie Mellon University

ABSTRACT

This paper presents general techniques for verifying virtually synchronous distributed control systems with *interconnected* physical environments. Such cyber-physical systems (CPSs) are notoriously hard to verify, due to their combination of nontrivial continuous dynamics, network delays, imprecise local clocks, asynchronous communication, etc. To simplify their analysis, we first extend the PALS methodology—that allows to abstract from the timing of events, asynchronous communication, network delays, and imprecise clocks, as long as the infrastructure guarantees bounds on the network delays and clock skews—from real-time to hybrid systems. We prove a bisimulation equivalence between Hybrid PALS synchronous and asynchronous models. We then show how various verification problems for synchronous Hybrid PALS models can be reduced to SMT solving over nonlinear theories of the real numbers. We illustrate the Hybrid PALS modeling and verification methodology on a number of CPSs, including a control system for turning an airplane.

Keywords

Distributed hybrid systems; SMT; synchronizers; PALS

1. INTRODUCTION

Virtually synchronous distributed hybrid systems consist of a number of *distributed* controllers—where each controller may interact with its physical environment having continuous dynamics which, furthermore, can be correlated—that should logically behave in a synchronous way. This class of cyber-physical systems (CPSs) includes avionics, robotics, automotive, and medical systems. Designing and analyzing such systems is difficult because of the interrelated continuous behaviors combined with clock skews, network delays, execution times, and so on.

*This work was partially supported by ONR Grant N000141310090, NSF CPS-1330014 and CPS-1446675, and Air Force STTR Grant F14A-T06-0230.

HSCC'16, April 12-14, 2016, Vienna, Austria

© 2016 ACM. ISBN 978-1-4503-3955-1/16/04...$15.00

DOI: http://dx.doi.org/10.1145/2883817.2883849

A key step towards achieving manageable modeling and verification techniques for this complex class of CPSs is to extend the *PALS* framework to distributed hybrid systems. The PALS (physically asynchronous, logically synchronous) methodology [1, 3, 15] was developed to reduce the design and analysis of a virtually synchronous distributed *real-time system* (i.e., one without continuous behaviors) to the much simpler tasks of designing and analyzing the underlying *synchronous* models, provided that the network infrastructure can guarantee bounds on computation times, network delays, and imprecision of the local clocks. In this paper we introduce *Hybrid PALS* for virtually synchronous distributed hybrid systems. Hybrid PALS extends the approach in [5] to achieve a bisimulation equivalence between Hybrid PALS synchronous models and their asynchronous counterparts.

This means that verifying a virtually synchronous distributed hybrid system reduces to verifying its underlying synchronous model. Hybrid PALS allows us to abstract from asynchronous communication, network delays, message buffering, etc. However, the times at which physical states are sampled or actuator commands are sent to the environment cannot be abstracted away. Since these events are triggered by imprecise local clocks, we must also take into account those clocks. Furthermore, the physical environments of different components are often *tightly coupled*, so that the continuous dynamics of the entire system becomes *nonlinear*. For these reasons, analysis techniques for event-based systems (such as hybrid automata) or linear systems cannot be easily used to analyze Hybrid PALS models.

This paper presents SMT solving techniques to address the challenges of analyzing Hybrid PALS models. The verification of a synchronous Hybrid PALS model, which involves (nonlinear) ordinary differential equations (ODEs) and clock skews, is reduced to checking the satisfiability of SMT formulas over the real numbers, which is decidable up to any user-given precision [8, 10]. We show how standard verification problems for hybrid systems, such as bounded reachability, unbounded time inductive reasoning, and compositional assume-guarantee reasoning, can be encoded as SMT formulas for synchronous Hybrid PALS models.

We have applied our techniques on a range of non-trivial nonlinear systems, including: a control system for turning an airplane, a networked controller for physically connected water tanks, and a networked thermostat controller for interconnected adjacent rooms. These case studies involve nonlinear ODEs and continuous connections between different components, and take into account network delays, clock skews, asynchronous communication, execution times, etc.

To summarize, the new contributions in this paper (also compared to [5]) are: (i) more refined and complete Hybrid PALS models; (ii) a bisimulation result between synchronous and asynchronous Hybrid PALS models; (iii) general SMT techniques for analyzing synchronous Hybrid PALS models (as opposed to showing only concrete analysis of toy examples in [5]); and (iv) illustrating the effectiveness of Hybrid PALS and the proposed verification methodology on complex examples and hybrid systems benchmarks.

The rest of the paper is organized as follows. Section 2 discusses related work. Section 3 gives a background on PALS. Section 4 introduces Hybrid PALS. Section 5 shows SMT encodings for Hybrid PALS models and their analysis. Section 6 gives an overview of the Hybrid PALS case studies. Finally, Section 7 gives some concluding remarks.

2. RELATED WORK

PALS [1, 3, 15] targets distributed *real-time* systems, whose absence of continuous behaviors means that the timing of events, and hence local clocks, can be abstracted away in the synchronous models, which can therefore be verified by standard model checking techniques. In contrast, (synchronous) Hybrid PALS models must take both continuous behaviors and clock skews into account and therefore cannot be analyzed using such techniques for discrete systems.

The initial steps towards a hybrid extension of PALS were taken in [5]. However, the formal models of Hybrid PALS in [5] are very different from the models in this work, so that a bisimulation equivalence could not be provided in [5]. In this paper, Hybrid PALS models are significantly redefined to obtain a bisimulation between synchronous and distributed hybrid models, and to allow more general sampling and response times of sensors and actuators. For example, components in the same synchronous state may have different local times in [5], but those times are synchronized in this paper to properly model the continuous behavior for *tightly coupled* environments. Furthermore, [5] shows that two interconnected thermostats can be verified using dReal, but does *not* present general SMT techniques for analyzing synchronous Hybrid PALS models.

Our case studies on networks of identical hybrid systems are related to symmetry-reduction approaches for networks of timed or hybrid automata (e.g., [6, 11, 13]), and their compositional analysis for any number of identical processes is related to [12]. Such work uses hybrid or timed automata where communication is specified using joint synchronous actions, whereas our work focuses on time-triggered systems with nonlinear dynamics where communication is governed by real-time constraints, taking into account network delays, execution times, and clock skews, and where the local environments of tightly coupled components *continuously* interact with each other. In addition, Hybrid PALS considers general virtually synchronous distributed hybrid systems (e.g., the airplane example in our paper), besides symmetric distributed hybrid systems.

3. PRELIMINARIES ON PALS

PALS transforms a multirate *synchronous design SD* into a distributed real-time system $\mathcal{MA}(SD, \Gamma)$ that satisfies the same temporal logic properties, provided that the underlying infrastructure assures bounds $\Gamma = (\epsilon, \alpha_{\min}, \alpha_{\max}, \mu_{\min}, \mu_{\max})$ with: (i) $\epsilon \geq 0$ the maximal skew of any local clock with respect to the global clock, (ii) $[\alpha_{\min}, \alpha_{\max}]$ time bounds for executing a transition, and (iii) $[\mu_{\min}, \mu_{\max}]$ time bounds for the network transmission delay. This section overviews the synchronous models *SD*, the distributed models $\mathcal{MA}(SD, \Gamma)$, and their relationship (we refer to [3, 15] for details).

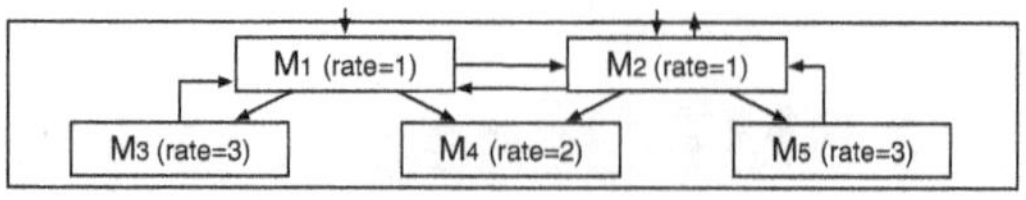

Figure 1: A multirate ensemble $\mathcal{E}_T$.

3.1 Discrete Synchronous Models

The synchronous model *SD* is specified as an *ensemble* of (nondeterministic) state machines with input and output ports. In each iteration, a machine performs a transition based on its current state and its inputs, proceeds to the next state, and generates new outputs for the next iteration.

Definition 1. A *typed machine* $M = (D_i, S, D_o, \delta_M)$ is composed of: (i) $D_i = D_{i_1} \times \cdots \times D_{i_n}$ an input set (a value to the k-th *input port* is an element of D_{i_k}), (ii) S a set of states, (iii) $D_o = D_{o_1} \times \cdots \times D_{o_m}$ an output set, and (iv) $\delta_M \subseteq (D_i \times S) \times (S \times D_o)$ a total transition relation.

A collection $\{M_j\}_{j \in J_S \cup J_F}$ of state machines with different rates can be composed into a *multirate ensemble* $\mathcal{E}_T$ with global period T, as illustrated in Fig. 1, where the period of a slow typed machine $s \in J_S$ (with $rate(s) = 1$) is k times the period of a fast machine $f \in J_F$ with $rate(f) = k > 1$. A *wiring diagram* connects the input and output ports, so that there are no connections between two fast machines.

In each round of $\mathcal{E}_T$, all components perform a transition *in lockstep*. A fast machine f is *slowed down* and performs $k = rate(f)$ *internal* transitions in one global synchronous step. Since a fast machine produces k-tuples of outputs in one step, *input adaptors* are used to generate single values (e.g., the last value, or the average of the k values) for a slow machine. Likewise, a single output from a slow machine is adapted to a k-tuple of inputs for a fast machine.

This *synchronous composition* of an ensemble $\mathcal{E}_T$ is thus equivalent to one machine $M_{\mathcal{E}_T} = (D_i^{\mathcal{E}_T}, S^{\mathcal{E}_T}, D_o^{\mathcal{E}_T}, \delta_{M_{\mathcal{E}_T}})$. If a machine in $\mathcal{E}_T$ has a feedback wire connected to itself or to another component, then the output becomes an input of the destination in the next iteration. That is, $M_{\mathcal{E}_T}$'s states $S^{\mathcal{E}_T}$ consist of the states of its subcomponents M_j and the "feedback" outputs. For example, $M_{\mathcal{E}_T}$ of the ensemble $\mathcal{E}_T$ in Fig. 1 is the machine given by the outer box.

Definition 2. The transition system for $M_{\mathcal{E}_T}$ is a tuple $ts(M_{\mathcal{E}_T}) = (S^{\mathcal{E}_T} \times D_i^{\mathcal{E}_T}, \longrightarrow_{\mathcal{E}_T})$, where $(\vec{s}_1, \vec{i}_1) \longrightarrow_{\mathcal{E}_T} (\vec{s}_2, \vec{i}_2)$ iff an ensemble in state $\vec{s}_1$ with input $\vec{i}_1$ from the interface has a transition to state $\vec{s}_2$ (i.e., $\exists \vec{o}\ ((\vec{i}_1, \vec{s}_1), (\vec{s}_2, \vec{o})) \in \delta_{M_{\mathcal{E}_T}}$).

3.2 PALS Distributed Real-Time Models

Each component in the distributed model $\mathcal{MA}(\mathcal{E}_T, \Gamma)$ is composed of a machine in $\mathcal{E}_T$ and *wrappers* around it, as depicted in Fig. 2. In $\mathcal{MA}(\mathcal{E}_T, \Gamma)$, each machine performs transitions at its own rate according to its local clock. At the beginning of its period, it reads input from the layer above, performs a transition, and then generates output.

A wrapper has I/O buffers, timers, and access to the local clock of the machine. A PALS wrapper has the same period

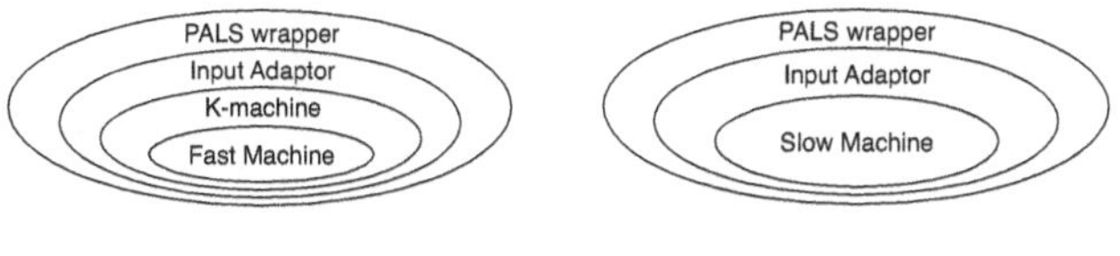

Figure 2: The wrapper hierarchies in $\mathcal{MA}(\mathcal{E}_T, \Gamma)$.

T and stores received inputs in its input buffer. When its i-th round begins (at some time in $(iT-\epsilon, iT+\epsilon)$), it delivers the contents of its input buffer to its input adaptor wrapper, and sets its *backoff timer* to $2\epsilon - \mu_{min}$. When the execution of the inner components ends *and* the backoff timer expires, the contents of the output buffer are sent out.

An input adaptor wrapper receives the inputs from the PALS wrapper and applies input adaptors for each period T. A k-machine wrapper extracts each value from the k-tuple input and delivers it to the enclosed fast machine at each fast period T/k, and delivers the *k-tuples* from the outputs of the fast machine to its outer layer at a global period T.

Notice that a fast machine M_f may *not* be able to finish all of its k transitions in a global round, but only k' transitions *before* the outputs must be sent. If $k' < k$, then the k-machine wrapper only sends the first k' values. The input adaptor of each input port whose source is M_f must be $(k'+1)$-*oblivious*: that is, it ignores the last $k - k'$ values $v_{k'+1}, \ldots, v_k$ in a k-tuple $(v_1, \ldots, v_k)$.

Stable states of $\mathcal{MA}(\mathcal{E}_T, \Gamma)$ are snapshots of the system at times $iT - \epsilon$, just before the components in $\mathcal{MA}(\mathcal{E}_T, \Gamma)$ start performing local machine transitions [15]. In $\mathcal{MA}(\mathcal{E}_T, \Gamma)$, network transmission can happen only in the interval $(iT + \epsilon, (i+1)T - \epsilon)$. In stable states at times $iT - \epsilon$, the input buffers of the PALS wrappers are full, and the other input and output buffers are empty. The function *sync* maps stable states to the corresponding states of $M_{\mathcal{E}_T}$.

Definition 3. For a stable state C of $\mathcal{MA}(\mathcal{E}_T, \Gamma)$, $sync(C)$ is a pair $(\{s_j, \vec{f_j}\}_{j \in J_S \cup J_F}, \vec{i}) \in S^{\mathcal{E}_T} \times D_{\vec{i}}^{\mathcal{E}_T}$ such that: (i) the machine states in C give the states $\{s_j\}_{j \in J_S \cup J_F}$ in $M_{\mathcal{E}_T}$; and (ii) the values in the input buffers of the PALS wrappers in C give the values $\{\vec{f_j}\}_{j \in J_S \cup J_F}$ in the feedback wires and the input $\vec{i}$ from the ensemble interface in $M_{\mathcal{E}_T}$.

Big-step transitions $\longrightarrow_{st}$ are defined between two stable states, and they are related to single synchronous steps of $M_{\mathcal{E}_T}$. Because of $(k'+1)$-obliviousness of the input adaptors, two stable states are related by $C_1 \sim_{obl} C_2$ iff their machine states are identical and their associated input buffer contents *cannot* be distinguished by input adaptors.

THEOREM 1. *[3] The binary relation $(\sim_{obl}; sync)$ is a* bisimulation *between the transition system $ts(M_{\mathcal{E}_T})$ and the big-step transition system $(Stable(\mathcal{MA}(\mathcal{E}_T, \Gamma)), \longrightarrow_{st})$.*

4. HYBRID PALS

This section introduces *Hybrid PALS*, which extends PALS to distributed hybrid systems. In PALS, the time when an event takes place does not matter, as long as it happens within a certain time interval. However, in hybrid systems, we cannot abstract from the time when a continuous value is read or an actuator command is given (both of which depend on a component's local clock), and thus those times are also included in the *synchronous* Hybrid PALS models.

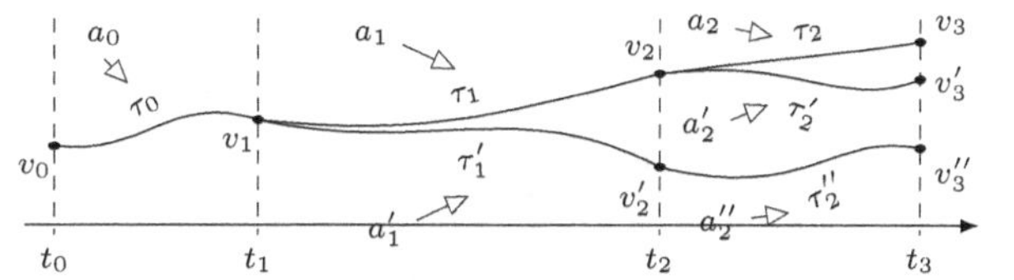

Figure 3: A controlled physical environment; e.g., $((a_1, v_1, t_2 - t_1), \tau_1) \in \Lambda$, $((a_1', v_1, t_2 - t_1), \tau_1') \in \Lambda$, etc.

In Hybrid PALS, the standard PALS models $\mathcal{MA}(\mathcal{E}_T, \Gamma)$ and $\mathcal{E}_T$ are *nondeterministic models* defined for *all possible* environment behaviors. For a physical environment E, the *environment restrictions* $\mathcal{MA}(\mathcal{E}_T, \Gamma) \upharpoonright E$ and $\mathcal{E}_T \upharpoonright E$ define the behavior of the models constrained by E. Section 4.5 gives a *bisimulation equivalence* between $\mathcal{MA}(\mathcal{E}_T, \Gamma) \upharpoonright E$ and $\mathcal{E}_T \upharpoonright E$ (we refer to the longer report [4] for more details on the definitions and the proof).

4.1 Controlled Physical Environments

A state of a physical environment of machine M is given by a tuple $\vec{v} = (v_1, \ldots, v_l) \in \mathbb{R}^l$ of its physical parameters $\vec{x} = (x_1, \ldots, x_l)$. The behavior of $\vec{x}$ can be modeled by ODEs that specify *trajectories* $\tau_1, \ldots, \tau_l$ of $\vec{x}$ over time. A trajectory of duration T is a function $\tau : [0, T] \to \mathbb{R}$ [14]. The *prefix* of τ at time $u \in [0, T]$ is denoted by $\tau \trianglelefteq u$, and the *suffix* of τ at time u is denoted by $\tau \trianglerighteq u$ (that is, $(\tau \trianglelefteq u)(t) = \tau(t)$ for $t \in [0, u]$, and $(\tau \trianglerighteq u)(t) = \tau(t + u)$ for $t \in [0, T - u]$). Let $\mathcal{T}$ denote the set of all trajectories.

A physical environment E_M of machine M is specified as a *controlled physical environment*, defining any possible trajectory of its parameters $\vec{x}$ for the control commands from M. For a state $\vec{v} \in \mathbb{R}^l$, a control command a, and a duration $t \in \mathbb{R}$, a physical environment E_M gives a trajectory $\vec{\tau} \in \mathcal{T}^l$ of its parameters $\vec{x}$ of duration t, as illustrated in Fig. 3.

Definition 4. A *controlled physical environment* is a tuple $E_M = (C, \vec{x}, \Lambda)$, where: (i) C is a set of *control commands*; (ii) $\vec{x} = (x_1, \ldots, x_l)$ is a vector of real number variables; and (iii) $\Lambda \subseteq (C \times \mathbb{R}^l \times \mathbb{R}_{\geq 0}) \times \mathcal{T}^l$ is a *physical transition relation* such that $((a, \vec{v}, t), \vec{\tau}) \in \Lambda$ iff for a control command $a \in C$ that lasts for duration t, E_M's physical state $\vec{x}$ follows the trajectory $\vec{\tau} \in \mathcal{T}^l$ from state $\vec{\tau}(0) = \vec{v} \in \mathbb{R}^l$.

Many physical environments can be physically correlated, and one local environment may immediately affect another environment. Such correlations are naturally expressed as *time-invariant constraints* $\forall t. \psi$ of physical parameters over time t. For example, if parameter x_1 of E_{M_1} must be equal to parameter x_2 of E_{M_2}, then the time-invariant constraint is the formula $\forall t.\ x_1(t) = x_2(t)$ with t a variable over time.

Example 1. Consider a distributed CPS controller to roll an airplane by moving its *ailerons* (flaps attached to the end of the left or the right wing), illustrated in Fig. 4. Each aileron subcontroller moves the corresponding aileron towards the goal angle given by the main controller. The subcontrollers and the main controller operate at different rates. The objective of the main controller is to roll the aircraft toward the goal angle specified by the pilot.

The physical environment E_M of each subcontroller M specifies the dynamics of the aileron angle x_M according to the moving rate r_M (the control command from M) by the

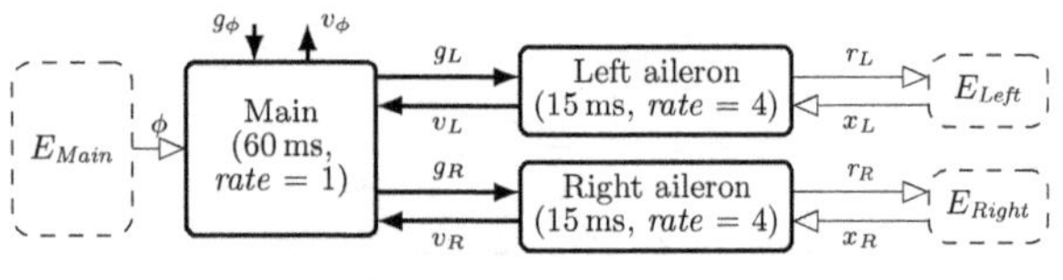

Figure 4: The simple distributed CPS controller.

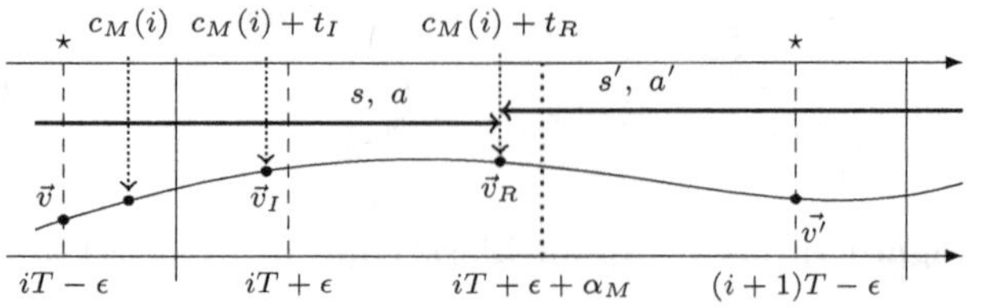

Figure 5: Timeline for an environment-restricted controller with a local clock c_M, where the curved line represents the state of E_M, and the thick straight lines represent the discrete states of M.

ODE $\dot{x}_M = r_M$. The controlled physical environment is given by $E_M = (\mathbb{R}, x_M, \Lambda_M)$, with $\mathbb{R}$ the domain of r_M, and $\Lambda_M \subseteq (\mathbb{R} \times \mathbb{R} \times \mathbb{R}_{\geq 0}) \times \mathcal{T}$ such that $((r_M, v_M, 15), \tau) \in \Lambda_M$ iff $\forall t \in [0, 15].\ \tau(t) = v_M + \int_0^t r_M \, \mathrm{d}t$.

The physical environment E_{Main} of the main controller specifies the dynamics of the roll angle ϕ using the ODEs $\dot{\phi} = p$ and $\dot{p} = c(\zeta_R - \zeta_L)$, disregarding the yawing effect caused by the rolling, where p is the rolling moment, and ζ_R and ζ_L are the angles of respective ailerons. The controlled physical environment is $E_{Main} = (\{*\}, (\phi, p, \zeta_L, \zeta_R), \Lambda_{Main})$, with the singleton $\{*\}$, indicating that E_{Main} has no control command, and $\Lambda_{Main} \subseteq (\{*\} \times \mathbb{R}^4 \times \mathbb{R}_{\geq 0}) \times \mathcal{T}^4$ such that $((*, (v_\phi, v_p, v_{\zeta_L}, v_{\zeta_R}), 60), (\tau_\phi, \tau_p, \tau_{\zeta_L}, \tau_{\zeta_R})) \in \Lambda_{Main}$ iff:

$$\forall t \in [0, 60].\ \begin{bmatrix} \tau_\phi \\ \tau_p \end{bmatrix}(t) = \begin{bmatrix} v_\phi \\ v_p \end{bmatrix} + \int_0^t \begin{bmatrix} \tau_p(t) \\ c(\tau_{\zeta_R}(t) - \tau_{\zeta_L}(t)) \end{bmatrix} \mathrm{d}t.$$

The control angles ζ_L and ζ_R must always be the same as the respective aileron angles x_L and x_R of the subcontrollers. However, since the main controller and the subcontrollers have *different periods with local clock skews*, the ODEs of the subcontrollers cannot be "plugged" into E_{Main}. Instead, their physical correlations are specified by the time-invariant constraint: $\forall t.\ (\zeta_L(t) = x_L(t)) \wedge (\zeta_R(t) = x_R(t))$. ■

4.2 Sampling and Response Timing

A controller M interacts with its physical environment E_M according to its local clock, which may differ from the global time by up to the maximal clock skew $\epsilon > 0$. Let $c_M : \mathbb{N} \to \mathbb{R}_{>0}$ denote the *global time* $c_M(i)$ at the beginning of the $(i+1)$-th period according to M's local clock.

Fig. 5 depicts the behavior of M with respect to E_M in a PALS distributed model for an interval $[iT - \epsilon, (i+1)T - \epsilon]$ for its period T. The $(i+1)$-th period of M begins at time $c_M(i) \in (iT - \epsilon, iT + \epsilon)$. Because of PALS bounds, M has already received all the inputs $\vec{i}$ before time $iT - \epsilon$. Next, the physical state $\vec{v}_I$ of E_M is read at time $c_M(i) + t_I$ for some sampling time t_I. M then executes its transition based on the inputs $\vec{i}$, the sampled state $\vec{v}_I$, and the machine state s. After the execution, the machine state changes to s', and the new controller command a is sent to E_M at time $c_M(i) + t_R$ for some response time t_R for the execution and the actuator processing. The new outputs $\vec{o}$ from M are delivered to their destinations for the next round before time $(i+1)T - \epsilon$.

We assume that a control command from M to E_M only depends on M's current state s. In Fig. 5, a current control command a (by state s) remains effective until the execution of M ends at time $u_R = c_M(i) + t_R$, and then a new control command a' (by state s') takes effect. That is, E_M defines trajectories $\vec{\tau}$ of its physical parameters $\vec{x}$ in a time interval $[iT - \epsilon, (i+1)T - \epsilon]$ of duration T with respect to (a, a', u_R).

Definition 5. Trajectories $\vec{\tau}$ of duration T are *realizable* with respect to commands $a, a' \in C$ and a response duration $u \in \mathbb{R}$ for E_M, denoted by $\vec{\tau} \in \mathcal{R}^T_{E_M}(a, a', u)$, iff $((a, \vec{\tau}(0), u), \vec{\tau} \trianglelefteq u) \in \Lambda$ and $((a', \vec{\tau}(u), T - u), \vec{\tau} \trianglerighteq u) \in \Lambda$.

In practice, the sampling and response times depend on the machine instructions of a controller M to perform these tasks, which are expressed as state transitions in our model. Therefore, we assume that the sampling times of M depend on its state s, and the response times depend on its state s and input $\vec{i}$. To compose M with its physical environment E_M, we define the "interface" between them.

Definition 6. The *interface* of controller M is defined by the projection functions $\pi = (\pi_C, \pi_T, \pi_R, \pi_I)$, for state s and input $\vec{i}$: (i) $\pi_C(s) \in C$ the control command of M to E_M; (ii) $\pi_T(s) \in \mathbb{N}$ a round number; (iii) $\pi_R(s, \vec{i}) \in \mathbb{R}$ a response time; and (iv) $\pi_I(s) \in \mathbb{R}$ a sampling time ($\pi_I(s) \leq \pi_R(s, \vec{i})$).

4.3 Environment-Restricted Controllers

A controller M is basically a *nondeterministic* machine parameterized by any behavior of its environment E_M. A controller M has a state space of the form $S \times \mathbb{R}^m$, where $\mathbb{R}^m$ denotes the m physical parameters that M can *observe*. Likewise, E_M has a state space of the form $\mathbb{R}^l = \mathbb{R}^m \times \mathbb{R}^n$, where $\mathbb{R}^m$ is the *observable* part of $\mathbb{R}^l$. For state $\vec{v} \in \mathbb{R}^l$ of E_M, let $\pi_O(\vec{v}) \in \mathbb{R}^m$ denote the observable part of $\vec{v}$.

The *environment restriction* $M \upharpoonright E_M$ is a normal machine (see Def. 1) with a combined state space $S \times \mathbb{R}^l$, recording "snapshots" of E_M's states at times $iT - \epsilon$. A transition of $M \upharpoonright E_M$ from state $(s, \vec{v})$ to $(s', \vec{v}')$ corresponds to *realizable trajectories* $\vec{\tau}$ for its period T with respect to $\pi_C(s)$ and $\pi_C(s')$ and the response duration $u_R = (c_M(i) + \pi_R(s)) - (iT - \epsilon)$. The controller M performs a transition based on the observable physical state $\pi_O(\vec{\tau}(u_I))$ of E_M sampled after the sampling duration $u_I = (c_M(i) + \pi_I(s)) - (iT - \epsilon)$.

Definition 7. The *environment restriction* of M by E_M with an interface π is $M \upharpoonright_\pi E_M = (D_i, S \times \mathbb{R}^l, D_o, \delta_{M \upharpoonright_\pi E_M})$, where $((\vec{i}, (s, \vec{v})), ((s', \vec{v}'), \vec{o})) \in \delta_{M \upharpoonright_\pi E_M}$ iff for the round numbers $i = \pi_T(s)$ and $\pi_T(s') = i+1$, the sampling duration $u_I = (c_M(i) + \pi_I(s)) - (iT - \epsilon)$, and the response duration $u_R = (c_M(i) + \pi_R(s)) - (iT - \epsilon)$: (i) $\vec{\tau}(0) = \vec{v}$ and $\vec{\tau}(T) = \vec{v}'$ for some realizable trajectories $\vec{\tau} \in \mathcal{R}^T_{E_M}(\pi_C(s), u_R, \pi_C(s'))$, and (ii) $((\vec{i}, (s, \pi_O(\vec{\tau}(u_I)))), ((s', \pi_O(\vec{v}')), \vec{o})) \in \delta_M$.

Example 2. Consider a subcontroller M in Example 1 to move an aileron toward the specified angle. In each 15 ms round, beginning at time $c_M(i) \in (i \cdot 15\,\mathrm{ms} - \epsilon, i \cdot 15\,\mathrm{ms} + \epsilon)$, M receives a goal angle g_M, sets a new moving rate r'_M based on g_M and the observed angle v_M, and sends back v_M. M is specified as the machine $(\mathbb{R}, \mathbb{N} \times \mathbb{R}^2, \mathbb{R}, \delta_M)$, where $((g_M, (i, r_M, v_M)), ((i', r'_M, v'_M), o)) \in \delta_M$ holds iff $i' = i+1$, $r'_M = (g_M - v_M)/15$, and $o = v_m$.

The interface π_M is defined by the projection functions: (i) $\pi_C(i, r_M, v_M) = r_M$; (ii) $\pi_T(i, r_M, v_M) = i$ (the round number); (iii) $\pi_I(i, r_M, v_M) = 1\,\text{ms}$ (the sampling time); and (iv) $\pi_R((i, r_M, v_M), g_M) = 2\,\text{ms}$ (the response time). Thus, the sampling duration is $u_I = (c_M(i)+1) - (i \cdot 15 - \epsilon)$ and the response duration is $u_R = (c_M(i) + 2) - (i \cdot 15 - \epsilon)$ for each round. For $E_M = (\mathbb{R}, x_M, \Lambda_M)$ in Example 1, its observable state is given by the function $\pi_O(x_M) = x_M$.

The environment restriction of M by E_M is then defined as the machine $M \upharpoonright_{\pi_M} E_M = (\mathbb{R}, \mathbb{N} \times \mathbb{R}^2, \mathbb{R}, \delta_{M \upharpoonright_{\pi_M} E_M})$, where $((g_M, (i, r_M, v_M)), ((i', r'_M, v'_M), v_M)) \in \delta_{M \upharpoonright_{\pi_M} E_M}$ holds iff: (i) for some realizable trajectory $\tau \in \mathcal{R}^{15\,\text{ms}}_{E_M}(r_M, r'_M, u_R)$, $v_M = \tau(0)$ and $v'_M = \tau(15)$; and (ii) an M's transition $((g_M, (i, r_M, \tau(u_I))), ((i', r'_M, v'_M), v_M)) \in \delta_M$ holds. ■

Example 3. Consider the main controller M_{Main} to roll the aircraft toward the specified angle in Example 1. In each 60 ms round, beginning at $c_{Main}(i) \in (i \cdot 60\,\text{ms} - \epsilon, i \cdot 60\,\text{ms} + \epsilon)$, M_{Main} receives a desired roll angle g_ϕ and the aileron angles (v_L, v_R), and sends the new goal angles (g_L, g_R). M_{Main} is specified as the typed machine $(\mathbb{R}^3, \mathbb{N} \times \mathbb{R}^2, \mathbb{R}^3, \delta_{Main})$, where $(((g_\phi, v_L, v_R), (i, v_\phi)), ((i', v'_\phi), (o, g_L, g_R))) \in \delta_{Main}$ holds iff: $g_R = 0.3(g_\phi - v_\phi)$, $g_L = -g_R$, $o = v_\phi$, and $i' = i + 1$.

The interface π_{Main} is defined by the projection functions: (i) $\pi_C(i, v_\phi) = *$ (no control commands); (ii) $\pi_T(i, v_\phi) = i$; (iii) $\pi_I(i, v_\phi) = 3\,\text{ms}$; and (iv) $\pi_R((i, v_\phi), \vec{i}) = 10\,\text{ms}$. The sampling duration is $u_I = (c_{Main}(i) + 3\,\text{ms}) - (i \cdot 60\,\text{ms} - \epsilon)$ for each round (the response duration is not important). For E_{Main} in Example 1, since M_{Main} can only observe the roll angle ϕ, its observable state is $\pi_O(\phi, p, \zeta_L, \zeta_R) = \phi$.

The environment restriction of M_{Main} by E_{Main} is then $M_{Main} \upharpoonright_{\pi_{Main}} E_{Main} = (\mathbb{R}^3, \mathbb{N} \times \mathbb{R}^4, \mathbb{R}^3, \delta_{M_{Main} \upharpoonright_{\pi_{Main}} E_{Main}})$. For states $\vec{v} = (v_\phi, v_p, v_{\zeta_L}, v_{\zeta_R})$ and $\vec{v}' = (v'_\phi, v'_p, v'_{\zeta_L}, v'_{\zeta_R})$, a transition $(((g_\phi, v_L, v_R), (i, \vec{v})), ((i', \vec{v}'), (v_\phi, g_L, g_R)))$ holds iff: (i) $\vec{v} = \vec{\tau}(0)$ and $\vec{v}' = \vec{\tau}(60)$ for realizable trajectories $\vec{\tau} \in \mathcal{R}^{60\,\text{ms}}_{E_{Main}}(*, *, 10\,\text{ms})$, and (ii) for $\vec{\tau} = (\tau_\phi, \tau_p, \tau_{\zeta_L}, \tau_{\zeta_R})$, $(((g_\phi, v_L, v_R), (i, \tau_\phi(u_I))), ((i', v'_\phi), (v_\phi, g_L, g_R))) \in \delta_{Main}$. ■

4.4 Hybrid PALS Synchronous Models

The synchronous model in Hybrid PALS is specified as a multirate ensemble $\mathcal{E}_T$ and the physical environments of subcomponents, where physical correlations between those environments are specified as time-invariant constraints.

Definition 8. A *hybrid multirate ensemble* $\mathcal{E}_T \upharpoonright_\Pi E$ is composed of: (i) $\mathcal{E}_T$ a multirate ensemble, (ii) a family of interface functions $\Pi = \{\pi_j\}_{j \in J_S \cup J_F}$, and (iii) a family of local physical environments $E = \langle \{E_{M_j}\}_{j \in J_S \cup J_F}, (\forall t)\, \psi \rangle$ with $(\forall t)\, \psi$ the time-invariant constraints (shown in Fig. 6).

Example 4. For the simple CPS controller in Example 1, $\mathcal{E}_{60}$ is a multirate ensemble of the main controller M_{Main} and the subcontrollers M_L and M_R, where $rate(Main) = 1$ and $rate(L) = rate(R) = 4$. The machines $\{M_{Main}, M_L, M_R\}$, interfaces $\Pi = \{\pi_{Main}, \pi_L, \pi_R\}$, and physical environments $\{E_{Main}, E_L, E_R\}$ are defined in Examples 2–3. The network connections are shown in Fig. 4. The time-invariant constraint $(\forall t)\, \psi \equiv (\forall t)\, (\zeta_L(t) = x_L(t)) \wedge (\zeta_R(t) = x_R(t))$ specifies the continuous physical connections. ■

A hybrid ensemble $\mathcal{E}_T \upharpoonright_\Pi E$ induces a normal multirate ensemble $\overline{\mathcal{E}_T \upharpoonright_\Pi E}$ composed of the environment restrictions $\{M_j \upharpoonright_\pi E_{M_j}\}_{j \in J_S \cup J_F}$, which disregards the time-invariant constraints $(\forall t)\, \psi$. The behaviors of $\mathcal{E}_T \upharpoonright_\Pi E$ are a *subset* of the behaviors of $\overline{\mathcal{E}_T \upharpoonright_\Pi E}$, namely, the behaviors restricted by $(\forall t)\, \psi$. As mentioned, a transition of a (decelerated) environment-restricted machine $M_j \upharpoonright_\pi E_{M_j}$ corresponds to realizable trajectories $\vec{\tau}$ in a time interval $[iT - \epsilon, (i+1)T - \epsilon]$ for a global period T. Hence, a lockstep composition of such transitions *whose realizable trajectories $\vec{\tau}$ also satisfy the time-invariant constraints* $(\forall t)\, \psi$ gives a transition of the synchronous composition $M_{\mathcal{E}_T \upharpoonright_\Pi E}$.

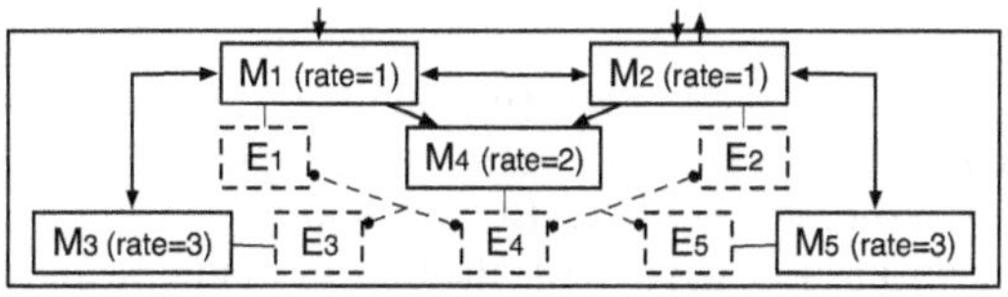

Figure 6: A hybrid multirate ensemble $\mathcal{E}_T \upharpoonright_\Pi E$, where (E_1, E_3, E_4) and (E_2, E_4, E_5) are connected by time-invariant constraints, denoted by dashed lines.

4.5 Hybrid PALS Distributed Models

Hybrid PALS maps a hybrid ensemble $\mathcal{E}_T \upharpoonright_\Pi E$ to the distributed hybrid system $\mathcal{MA}(\mathcal{E}_T, \Gamma) \upharpoonright_\Pi E$, together with PALS bounds Γ; i.e., $(\mathcal{E}_T \upharpoonright_\Pi E, \Gamma) \mapsto \mathcal{MA}(\mathcal{E}_T, \Gamma) \upharpoonright_\Pi E$. The distributed components in $\mathcal{MA}(\mathcal{E}_T, \Gamma) \upharpoonright_\Pi E$ are exactly the same as the wrapper hierarchies of Fig. 2 in $\mathcal{MA}(\mathcal{E}_T, \Gamma)$. But the controllers in $\mathcal{MA}(\mathcal{E}_T, \Gamma) \upharpoonright_\Pi E$ also interact with their physical environments in E, according to the sampling and response timing policy Π to determine sensor sampling timing t_I and actuator response timing t_R.

The behaviors of the Hybrid PALS distributed system $\mathcal{MA}(\mathcal{E}_T, \Gamma) \upharpoonright_\Pi E$ are the subset of those of the PALS distributed system $\mathcal{MA}(\mathcal{E}_T, \Gamma)$, restricted by the physical environments and the time-invariant constraints in E. The continuous dynamics of $\mathcal{MA}(\mathcal{E}_T, \Gamma) \upharpoonright_\Pi E$ is "completely" decided by the controllers, their physical environments, the timing policies, and the local clocks of the controllers.

More precisely, consider a normal ensemble $\overline{\mathcal{E}_T \upharpoonright_\Pi E}$ above, induced by a hybrid ensemble $\mathcal{E}_T \upharpoonright_\Pi E$, and composed of the environment-restricted controllers $\{M_j \upharpoonright_\pi E_{M_j}\}_{j \in J_S \cup J_F}$. A *big-step transition* is defined from one stable state at time $iT - \epsilon$ to another stable state at $(i+1)T - \epsilon$ for the system $\mathcal{MA}(\overline{\mathcal{E}_T \upharpoonright_\Pi E}, \Gamma)$, as explained in Section 3.2. For such time intervals $[iT - \epsilon, (i+1)T - \epsilon]$, each $M_j \upharpoonright_\pi E_{M_j}$ provides (k-step) realizable trajectories $\vec{\tau}_j$, based on round numbers, control commands, sampling timings, and response timings. The behaviors of $\mathcal{MA}(\mathcal{E}_T, \Gamma) \upharpoonright_\Pi E$ are the behaviors of $\mathcal{MA}(\overline{\mathcal{E}_T \upharpoonright_\Pi E}, \Gamma)$ that are restricted by the time-invariant constraints. Big-step transitions of $\mathcal{MA}(\mathcal{E}_T, \Gamma) \upharpoonright_\Pi E$ are therefore exactly those of $\mathcal{MA}(\overline{\mathcal{E}_T \upharpoonright_\Pi E}, \Gamma)$ whose associated trajectories $\vec{\tau}_j$ satisfy the time-invariant constraints $(\forall t)\, \psi$.

The correctness of Hybrid PALS follows from the fact that each physical measurement and physical activation *happens at the same time* in both $\mathcal{E}_T \upharpoonright_\Pi E$ and $\mathcal{MA}(\mathcal{E}_T, \Gamma) \upharpoonright_\Pi E$ with the *same timing policies* Π (see [4] for more details).

THEOREM 2. *The relation $(\sim_{obi}; sync)$ is a bisimulation between the transition system $ts(M_{\mathcal{E}_T \upharpoonright_\Pi E})$ and the big-step transition system induced by $\mathcal{MA}(\mathcal{E}_T, \Gamma) \upharpoonright_\Pi E$, exhibiting the exactly same set of realizable trajectories.*

PROOF SKETCH. Suppose that there exists a transition $s \longrightarrow_{\mathcal{E}_T \upharpoonright_\Pi E} s'$ of $M_{\mathcal{E}_T \upharpoonright_\Pi E}$ and $s\ (\sim_{obi}; sync)\ C$ for a stable state C of $\mathcal{MA}(\mathcal{E}_T, \Gamma) \upharpoonright_\Pi E$. By definition, there exists $s \longrightarrow_{\overline{\mathcal{E}_T \upharpoonright_\Pi E}} s'$ of $M_{\overline{\mathcal{E}_T \upharpoonright_\Pi E}}$ with some realizable trajectories $\vec{\tau}$ that satisfy the time-invariant constraints $(\forall t)\, \psi$ for the induced ensemble $\overline{\mathcal{E}_T \upharpoonright_\Pi E}$. By Theorem 1, $(\sim_{obi}\, ;\, sync)$ is a bisimulation between the transition systems $ts(M_{\overline{\mathcal{E}_T \upharpoonright_\Pi E}})$ and $(\mathit{Stable}(\mathcal{MA}(\overline{\mathcal{E}_T \upharpoonright_\Pi E}, \Gamma)), \longrightarrow_{st})$. Therefore, for some stable state C', there is a big-step transition $C \longrightarrow_{st} C'$ in $\mathcal{MA}(\overline{\mathcal{E}_T \upharpoonright_\Pi E}, \Gamma)$ such that $s'\ (\sim_{obi}\, ;\, sync)\ C'$, where both $s \longrightarrow_{\overline{\mathcal{E}_T \upharpoonright_\Pi E}} s'$ and $C \longrightarrow_{st} C'$ involve exactly the same machine states and inputs. By construction, round numbers, control commands, sampling timings, and response timings all depend on machine states and inputs. Therefore, the trajectories $\vec{\tau}$, which satisfy $(\forall t)\, \psi$, are also realizable for $C \longrightarrow_{st} C'$, and there exists a big-step transition $C \longrightarrow_{st} C'$ by $\mathcal{MA}(\mathcal{E}_T, \Gamma) \upharpoonright_\Pi E$. The other direction is similar. □

5. HYBRID PALS MODELS IN SMT

Theorem 2 implies that analyzing $\mathcal{MA}(\mathcal{E}_T, \Gamma) \upharpoonright_\Pi E$ can be reduced to the much simpler problem of analyzing $M_{\mathcal{E}_T \upharpoonright_\Pi E}$, which abstracts from asynchronous communication, network delays, execution times, message buffering, etc. This section shows how analysis problems for a hybrid ensemble $\mathcal{E}_T \upharpoonright_\Pi E$ can be encoded as formulas over the real numbers and ODEs. We symbolically encode *all possible local clocks* to deal with clock skews. Standard formal analysis problems for hybrid systems, such as bounded reachability, inductive reasoning, and compositional assume-guarantee reasoning, are encoded as logical formulas. The satisfiability of such formulas can be decided by δ-complete SMT solving [8, 10] up to a given precision $\delta > 0$. δ-complete SMT solving for a formula ϕ returns false if ϕ is unsatisfiable, and returns true if its *syntactic numerical perturbation* of ϕ by δ is satisfiable.[1]

5.1 Encoding Hybrid PALS Models

5.1.1 Encoding Environment-Restricted Controllers

A controller M can be expressed as a formula of the form $\phi_M(\vec{i}, \vec{y} \mid \vec{y}', \vec{o})$, with variables $\vec{i}$, $\vec{y}$, $\vec{y}'$, and $\vec{o}$ denoting input, the current state, the next state, and output, respectively, in such a way that $\phi_M(\vec{i}, s \mid s', \vec{o}) \iff ((\vec{i}, s), (s', \vec{o})) \in \delta_M$.

Example 5. For an aileron subcontroller M in Example 2, the formula is $\phi_M(y_{g_M}, y_i, y_{r_M}, y_{v_M} \mid y_i', y_{r_M}', y_{v_M}', y_o) \equiv (y_{r_M}' = (y_{g_M} - y_{v_M})/15 \wedge y_o = y_{v_M} \wedge y_i' = y_i + 1)$. Likewise, the formula for the main controller M_{Main} in Example 3 is $\phi_{Main}(y_{g_\phi}, y_{v_L}, y_{v_R}, y_i, y_{v_\phi} \mid y_i', y_{v_\phi}', y_o, y_{g_L}, y_{g_R}) \equiv (y_{g_R} = 0.3(y_{g_\phi} - y_{v_\phi}) \wedge y_{g_L} = -y_{g_R} \wedge y_o = y_{v_\phi} \wedge y_i' = y_i + 1)$. ■

A physical environment E_M is encoded as a formula of the form $\phi_{E_M}(\vec{a}, \vec{v}, u_0, u_t \mid \vec{\tau})$, with: *unary function symbols* $\vec{\tau}$ denoting the trajectories of E_M's physical parameters $\vec{x}$, and *variables* $\vec{a}$, $\vec{v}$, u_0, and u_t denoting, respectively, control commands, the initial values of $\vec{\tau}$ at time u_0, the times at the beginning and the end of the trajectory duration, where $\phi_{E_M}(\vec{a}, \vec{v}, u_0, u_t \mid \vec{\tau}) \iff ((\vec{a}, \vec{v}, u_t - u_0), \vec{\tau} \trianglerighteq u_0) \in \Lambda$.

If the continuous dynamics of $\vec{x}$ is specified as a system of ODEs $\frac{d\vec{x}}{dt} = F_{\vec{a}}(\vec{x}, t)$ for a control command $\vec{a}$ and an interval $[u_0, u_t]$, then ϕ_{E_M} includes universal quantification over time along with solutions of the ODEs, for example: $\bigvee \big(\mathit{guard}(\vec{a}) \rightarrow \forall t \in [u_0, u_t].\ \vec{\tau}(t) = \vec{v} + \int_0^{t-u_0} F_{\vec{a}}(\vec{x}, t)\, dt\big)$.

[1]If $\phi \equiv (x > 3) \wedge (y = z)$, then its syntactic numerical perturbation by δ is $(x - 3 > -\delta) \wedge (y - z \geq -\delta) \wedge (z - y \geq -\delta)$.

Example 6. For an aileron subcontroller M in Example 1, the formula $\phi_{E_M}(y_{r_M}, y_{v_M}, y_{u_0}, y_{u_t} \mid \tau_M)$ is defined by:

$$\forall t \in [y_{u_0}, y_{u_t}].\ \tau_M(t) = y_{v_M} + \int_0^{t - y_{u_0}} y_{r_M}\, dt.$$

For the main controller *Main*, if $y_{u_0} = 0$, then the formula $\phi_{E_{Main}}(y_{v_\phi}, y_{v_p}, y_{v_{\zeta_L}}, y_{v_{\zeta_R}}, 0, y_{u_t} \mid \tau_\phi, \tau_p, \tau_{\zeta_L}, \tau_{\zeta_R})$ is:

$$\forall t \in [0, y_{u_t}].\ \begin{bmatrix} \tau_\phi(t) \\ \tau_p(t) \end{bmatrix} = \begin{bmatrix} y_{v_\phi} \\ y_{v_p} \end{bmatrix} + \int_0^t \begin{bmatrix} \tau_p(t) \\ c(\tau_{\zeta_R}(t) - \tau_{\zeta_L}(t)) \end{bmatrix} dt,$$

where τ_{ζ_R} and τ_{ζ_L} are given by the subcontrollers using the time-invariant constraints. ■

The encoding of an environment restriction $M \upharpoonright_\pi E_M$ has the form $\phi^{T,i}_{M \upharpoonright_\pi E_M}(\vec{i}, \vec{y}, \vec{v} \mid \vec{y}', \vec{v}', \vec{o} \mid \vec{\tau})$, with unary function symbols $\vec{\tau}$ denoting E_M's trajectories, and variables: (i) $\vec{i}$ denoting input, (ii) $(\vec{y}, \vec{v})$ denoting a state at the beginning of the round (at time $iT - \epsilon$), (iii) $(\vec{y}', \vec{v}')$ denoting a state at the end of the round (at time $(i+1)T - \epsilon$), and (iv) $\vec{o}$ denoting output, given a period T and a round number i.

The values of sampling duration $u_I = (c_M(i) + t_I) - (iT - \epsilon)$ and response duration $u_R = (c_M(i) + t_R) - (iT - \epsilon)$ are unknown, due to clock skews. Since $iT - \epsilon < c_M(i) < iT + \epsilon$, we represent those times as formulas $t_I < u_I < t_I + 2\epsilon$ and $t_R < u_R < t_R + 2\epsilon$, so that $\phi_{M \upharpoonright_\pi E_M}(\vec{i}, s, \vec{v} \mid s', \vec{v}', \vec{o})$ iff $((\vec{i}, (s, \vec{v})), ((s', \vec{v}'), \vec{o})) \in \delta_{M \upharpoonright_\pi E_M}$ for *some* local clock c_M.

For an environment restriction $M \upharpoonright_\pi E_M$, the formula $\phi^{T,i}_{M \upharpoonright_\pi E_M}(\vec{i}, \vec{y}, \vec{v} \mid \vec{y}', \vec{v}', \vec{o} \mid \vec{\tau})$ is defined as follows (from the formal definitions of $M \upharpoonright_\pi E_M$ in Definitions 5–7):

$$\begin{aligned}(\exists \vec{a}, \vec{a}', u_I, u_R, \vec{v}_I, \vec{v}_R)\ & \vec{a} = \pi_C(\vec{y}) \ \wedge\ \vec{a}' = \pi_C(\vec{y}') \ \wedge \\ & \pi_I(\vec{y}) < u_I < \pi_I(\vec{y}) + 2\epsilon \ \wedge\ \vec{v}_I = \vec{\tau}(u_I) \ \wedge \\ & \pi_R(\vec{y}, \vec{i}) < u_R < \pi_R(\vec{y}, \vec{i}) + 2\epsilon \ \wedge\ \vec{v}_R = \vec{\tau}(u_R) \ \wedge \\ & \phi_{E_M}(\vec{a}, \vec{v}, iT, iT + u_R \mid \vec{\tau}) \ \wedge\ \vec{v} = \vec{\tau}(0) \ \wedge \\ & \phi_{E_M}(\vec{a}', \vec{v}_R, iT + u_R, (i+1)T, \mid \vec{\tau}) \ \wedge\ \vec{v}' = \vec{\tau}(T) \ \wedge \\ & \phi_M(\vec{i}, \langle \vec{y}, \pi_O(\vec{\tau}(u_I)) \rangle \mid \langle \vec{y}', \pi_O(\vec{v}') \rangle, \vec{o}).\end{aligned}$$

Example 7. For $M \upharpoonright_\pi E_M$ in Example 2, the formula $\phi^{15,0}_{M \upharpoonright_\pi E_M}(y_{g_M}, y_i, y_{r_M}, y_{v_M} \mid y_i', y_{r_M}', y_{v_M}', y_o \mid \tau_M)$ is given by: $\exists u_I, u_R, v_I, v_R.\ (1 < u_I < 1 + 2\epsilon) \wedge (2 < u_R < 2 + 2\epsilon) \wedge v_I = \tau_M(u_I) \wedge v_R = \tau_M(u_R) \wedge \phi_{E_M}(y_{r_M}, y_{v_M}, 0, u_R \mid \tau_M) \wedge \phi_{E_M}(y_{r_M}', v_R, u_R, 15, \mid \tau_M) \wedge y_{v_M} = \tau_M(0) \wedge y_{v_M}' = \tau_M(15) \wedge \phi_M(y_{g_M}, y_i, y_{r_M}, v_I \mid y_i', y_{r_M}', y_{v_M}', y_o)$. ■

5.1.2 Encoding Hybrid Ensembles

Recall that all machines in a synchronous composition $M_{\mathcal{E}_T}$ perform their transitions in lockstep; for a fast machine f, $k = \mathit{rate}(f)$ transitions in a global round. The encoding $\phi^{T,i}_{(M \upharpoonright_\pi E_M)\times k}$ of the k-step *deceleration* of an environment restriction $M \upharpoonright_\pi E_M$ is given by sequentially composing the k formulas $\phi^{T/k, ik}_{M \upharpoonright_\pi E_M}, \ldots, \phi^{T/k, (ik+k-1)}_{M \upharpoonright_\pi E_M}$ for the k *subintervals* $[(ik + n - 1)T/k - \epsilon, (ik + n)T/k - \epsilon]$ for $n = 1, \ldots, k$.

The encoding ϕ_{wire} of $\mathcal{E}_T$'s wiring diagram is a conjunction of equalities between variables for input and output ports. Each equality corresponds to a connection in $\mathcal{E}_T$ (together with an input adaptor for machines with different rates). Since feedback outputs becomes input of their destinations in the next step, we use a separate set of variables for such output ports connected to machines in $\mathcal{E}_T$.

A hybrid ensemble $\mathcal{E}_T \upharpoonright_\Pi E$ of typed machines $\{M_j\}_{j \in J}$, physical environments $\{E_{M_j}\}_{j \in J}$, for $J = J_S \cup J_F$, and the time-invariant constraint $(\forall t.\ \psi)$ is encoded as a formula $\phi_{\mathcal{E}_T \upharpoonright_\Pi E}(\vec{i}, \{\vec{y_j}, \vec{v_j}, \vec{f_j}\}_{j \in J} \mid \{\vec{y'_j}, \vec{v'_j}, \vec{f'_j}\}_{j \in J}, \vec{o} \mid \{\vec{\tau}_j\}_{j \in J})$ is:

$$\exists \{\vec{i_j}, \vec{o_j}\}_{j \in J}.\ \bigwedge_{s \in J_S} (\phi^{T,0}_{M_s \upharpoonright_{\pi_s} E_{M_s}}(\vec{i_s}, \vec{y_s}, \vec{v_s} \mid \vec{y'_s}, \vec{v'_s}, \vec{o}_s \mid \vec{\tau}_s))$$
$$\wedge \bigwedge_{f \in J_F} (\phi^{T,0}_{(M_f \upharpoonright_{\pi_f} E_{M_f})^{\times rate(f)}}(\vec{i_f}, \vec{y_f}, \vec{v_f} \mid \vec{y'_f}, \vec{v'_f}, \vec{o}_f \mid \vec{\tau}_f))$$
$$\wedge\, \phi_{wire}(\vec{i}, \vec{o}, \{\vec{i_j}, \vec{o_j}, \vec{f_j}, \vec{f'_j}\}_{j \in J}) \ \wedge\ (\forall t.\ \psi),$$

with unary function symbols $\vec{\tau}_j$ denoting trajectories for E_{M_j}, and variables $(\vec{y_j}, \vec{v_j})$, $\vec{f_j}$, $(\vec{y'_j}, \vec{v'_j})$, and $\vec{f'_j}$ denoting, respectively, the state of $M_j \upharpoonright_{\pi_j} E_{M_j}$ at the beginning of the round, the feedback outputs from the previous round, the state of $M_j \upharpoonright_{\pi_j} E_{M_j}$ at the end of the round, and the feedback outputs for the next round. The variable $\vec{i}$ denotes ensemble inputs, and $\vec{o}$ denotes ensemble outputs.

By construction, a formula $\phi_{\mathcal{E}_T \upharpoonright_\Pi E}$ is satisfiable iff there is a corresponding transition of the synchronous composition $M_{\mathcal{E}_T \upharpoonright_\Pi E}$ from $iT - \epsilon$ to $(i+1)T - \epsilon$ for *some* local clocks. Hence, by the bisimulation equivalence (Theorem 2):

THEOREM 3. *The formula $\phi_{\mathcal{E}_T \upharpoonright_\Pi E}$ is satisfiable iff there exists a corresponding stable transition for some local clocks in a distributed hybrid system $\mathcal{MA}(\mathcal{E}_T, \Gamma) \upharpoonright_\Pi E$.*

Example 8. The hybrid ensemble $\mathcal{E}_{60} \upharpoonright_\Pi E$ in Example 4 is encoded as the formula $\phi_{\mathcal{E}_{60} \upharpoonright_\Pi E}$, the conjunction of the following formulas: (i) for the main controller:

$$\phi^{60,0}_{M_M \upharpoonright_{\pi_M} E_M}(y^M_{g_\phi}, y^M_{v_L}, y^M_{v_R}, y_i, \vec{y} \mid y'_i, \vec{y}', y^M_o, y^M_{g_L}, y^M_{g_R} \mid \vec{\tau})$$

with $\vec{y} = (y_{v_\phi}, y_{v_p}, y_{v_{\zeta_L}}, y_{v_{\zeta_R}})$, $\vec{y}' = (y'_{v_\phi}, y'_{v_p}, y'_{v_{\zeta_L}}, y'_{v_{\zeta_R}})$, and $\vec{\tau} = (\tau_\phi, \tau_p, \tau_{\zeta_L}, \tau_{\zeta_R})$; (ii) for the subcontrollers:

$$\phi^{60,0}_{(M_L \upharpoonright_\pi E_L)^{\times 4}}(\vec{y}_{g_L}, \vec{y}^L_0, y^0_{v_L} \mid \vec{y}^L_4, y^4_{v_L}, \vec{y}_{o_L} \mid \tau_L)$$
$$\wedge\, \phi^{60,0}_{(M_R \upharpoonright_\pi E_R)^{\times 4}}(\vec{y}_{g_R}, \vec{y}^R_0, y^0_{v_R} \mid \vec{y}^R_4, y^4_{v_R}, \vec{y}_{o_R} \mid \tau_R)$$

with $\vec{y}_{g_m} = (y^1_{g_m}, \ldots, y^4_{g_m})$, $\vec{y}_{o_m} = (y^1_{o_m}, \ldots, y^4_{o_m})$, and for $m \in \{L, R\}$, $\vec{y}^m_n = (y^n_{i_m}, y^n_{r_m})$; (iii) for the wiring diagram:

$$(y^M_{v_L} = f^4_{o_L} \wedge f^{4\prime}_{o_L} = y^4_{o_L}) \wedge (\textstyle\bigwedge_{i=1}^4 y^i_{g_L} = f^M_{g_L} \wedge f^{M\,\prime}_{g_L} = y^M_{g_L})$$
$$\wedge\, (y^M_{v_R} = f^4_{o_R} \wedge f^{4\prime}_{o_R} = y^4_{o_R}) \wedge (\textstyle\bigwedge_{i=1}^4 y^i_{g_R} = f^M_{g_R} \wedge f^{M\,\prime}_{g_R} = y^M_{g_R})$$

with variables f_{port} denoting a feedback output from the previous step, and f'_{port} denoting one for the next step; and, finally, (iv) for the time-invariant equality constraint $(\forall t.\ \tau_{\zeta_L}(t) = \tau_L(t) \ \wedge\ \tau_{\zeta_R}(t) = \tau_R(t))$. ■

5.2 Encoding Verification Problems

Our goal is to verify safety properties of a distributed hybrid model $\mathcal{MA}(\mathcal{E}_T, \Gamma) \upharpoonright_\Pi E$, expressed as formulas of the form $safe(\vec{y}, \vec{\tau}(t))$ for *state variables* $\vec{y}$, *trajectories* $\vec{\tau}$, and time variable t. We exploit the bisimulation equivalence $M_{\mathcal{E}_T \upharpoonright_\Pi E} \approx \mathcal{MA}(\mathcal{E}_T, \Gamma) \upharpoonright_\Pi E$ to verify $\mathcal{MA}(\mathcal{E}_T, \Gamma) \upharpoonright_\Pi E$ using the simpler synchronous hybrid model $M_{\mathcal{E}_T \upharpoonright_\Pi E}$.

5.2.1 Bounded Reachability

To verify a safety property up to a given bound $n \in \mathbb{N}$ (i.e., for the time interval $[-\epsilon, nT - \epsilon]$), we encode its *bounded counterexamples* for the synchronous hybrid model $M_{\mathcal{E}_T \upharpoonright_\Pi E}$. If the formula is unsatisfiable (that is, no counterexample exists), then, by Theorem 3, the system satisfies the safety property in $[-\epsilon, nT - \epsilon]$ *for any local clocks.*

Definition 9. Bounded reachability of $M_{\mathcal{E}_T \upharpoonright_\Pi E}$ *up to n rounds* for a safety property $safe(\vec{y}, \vec{\tau}(t))$, an initial condition $init(\vec{y})$, and an input constraint $in(\vec{i})$ is encoded by:

$$\exists \vec{y}_0, \{\vec{y}_k, \vec{i}_k, \vec{o}_k, t_k\}_{k=1}^n.\ init(\vec{y}_0) \ \wedge\ \textstyle\bigvee_{k=1}^n \neg safe(\vec{y}_k, \vec{\tau}_k(t_k))$$
$$\wedge\ \textstyle\bigwedge_{k=1}^n (\phi_{\mathcal{E}_T \upharpoonright_\Pi E}(\vec{i}_k, \vec{y}_{k-1} \mid \vec{y}_k, \vec{o}_k \mid \vec{\tau}_k) \wedge in(\vec{i}_k)).$$

Some initial state $\vec{y}_0$ satisfies the *init* condition, and then $M_{\mathcal{E}_T \upharpoonright_\Pi E}$ performs n steps of synchronous transitions, each of which is from some state $\vec{y}_{k-1}$ to $\vec{y}_k$ using trajectories $\vec{\tau}_k$ of duration T with some input $\vec{i}_k$ satisfying the input constraint *in*. $M_{\mathcal{E}_T \upharpoonright_\Pi E}$ has bounded counterexamples if some state $(\vec{y}_k, \vec{\tau}_k(t_k))$ at some time t_k violates the safety *safe*.

5.2.2 Inductive Reasoning

For *unbounded* time verification, we encode an inductive proof of a safety property $safe(\vec{y}, \vec{\tau}(t))$ as a logical formula by using an inductive condition for $M_{\mathcal{E}_T \upharpoonright_\Pi E}$'s synchronous transitions, which implies the safety property. An inductive invariant consists of two formulas: $ind_d(\vec{y})$ for state variables $\vec{y}$, and $\forall t \in [0, T].\ ind_c(\vec{\tau}(t))$ for trajectories $\vec{\tau}$.[2]

Definition 10. Inductive reasoning of $M_{\mathcal{E}_T \upharpoonright_\Pi E}$ for a safety property $safe(\vec{y}, \vec{\tau}(t))$, an initial condition $init(\vec{y})$, and an input constraint $in(\vec{i})$, using an inductive invariant condition $(ind_d(\vec{y}) \ \wedge\ \forall t \in [0, T].\ ind_c(\vec{\tau}(t)))$ is encoded by:

- $\forall \vec{y}.\ init(\vec{y}) \implies ind_d(\vec{y})$
- $\forall \vec{y}, \vec{y}', \vec{i}, \vec{o}.\ (ind_d(\vec{y}) \ \wedge\ \phi_{\mathcal{E}_T \upharpoonright_\Pi E}(\vec{i}, \vec{y} \mid \vec{y}', \vec{o} \mid \vec{\tau}) \ \wedge\ in(\vec{i}))$ $\implies (ind_d(\vec{y}') \ \wedge\ \forall t \in [0, T].\ ind_c(\vec{\tau}(t)))$
- $\forall \vec{y}, \forall t \in [0, T].\ ind_d(\vec{y}) \wedge ind_c(\vec{\tau}(t)) \implies safe(\vec{y}, \vec{\tau}(t))$

The *init* condition implies the ind_d condition for any state variables $\vec{y}$. If a transition of $M_{\mathcal{E}_T \upharpoonright_\Pi E}$ is taken from state $\vec{y}$ satisfying the ind_d condition, then the ind_d condition again holds for any next state $\vec{y}'$, and in the meantime the ind_c condition holds for trajectories $\vec{\tau}$. The inductive condition $ind_d(\vec{y}) \wedge ind_c(\vec{\tau}(t))$ implies the safety property $safe(\vec{y}, \vec{\tau}(t))$ for one round. By proving these conditions, we show that the safety property holds for unbounded time with unbounded number of transitions. These formulas can be proved by checking the unsatisfiability of their *negated versions.*

5.2.3 Compositional Reasoning

We encode a divide-and-conquer proof to verify a safety property using standard assume-guarantee reasoning. It is very useful for dealing with the state explosion problem. In $M_{\mathcal{E}_T \upharpoonright_\Pi E}$, each component $M_j \upharpoonright_{\pi_j} E_{M_j}$ performs a transition based on its input $\vec{i}_j$ and trajectories $\vec{\tau}_j$ that are restricted by time-invariant constraints. Hence, we use an input condition $c^j_{in}(\vec{i}_j, \vec{\tau}_j(t))$ and an output condition $c^j_{out}(\vec{o}_j, \vec{\tau}_j(t))$, which satisfy necessary constraints for compositional reasoning: (i) assuming an input condition $c^j_{in}(\vec{i}_j, \vec{\tau}_j(t))$, if a transition is taken, then the output condition $c^j_{out}(\vec{o}_j, \vec{\tau}_j(t))$ holds; and (ii) the collection of the output conditions $\{c^j_{out}(\vec{o}, \vec{\tau}_j(t))\}_j$ implies each input condition $c^j_{in}(\vec{i}_j, \vec{\tau}_j(t))$. Let $\overline{M}_j$ denote its decelerated version $(M_j \upharpoonright_{\pi_j} E_{M_j})^{\times rate(j)}$.

[2] A key problem is finding such an inductive invariant for $M_{\mathcal{E}_T \upharpoonright_\Pi E}$, but providing general solutions for this problem is beyond the scope of this paper.

Definition 11. For each component j in a hybrid ensemble $\mathcal{E}_T \restriction_\Pi E$, consider a safety property $safe_j(\vec{y}_j, \vec{\tau}_j(t))$, an input constraint $in_j(\vec{i}_j)$ for input from $\mathcal{E}_T$'s interface, and an initial condition $init_j(\vec{y}_j)$. *I/O conditions* are given by:

$$\forall t.\ c^j_{in}(\vec{i}_j, \vec{\tau}_j(t)) \equiv (c^j_{in,d}(\vec{i}_j) \wedge \forall t \in [0,T].\ c^j_{in,c}(\vec{\tau}_j(t)))$$
$$\forall t.\ c^j_{out}(\vec{o}_j, \vec{\tau}_j(t)) \equiv (c^j_{out,d}(\vec{i}_j) \wedge \forall t \in [0,T].\ c^j_{out,c}(\vec{\tau}_j(t)))$$

that satisfy the necessary constraints for a compositional reasoning of the synchronous composition $M_{\mathcal{E}_T \restriction_\Pi E}$:

- $\forall \vec{i}_j, \vec{o}_j, \vec{y}_j, \vec{y}'_j.\ (\forall t \in [0,T].\ c^j_{in}(\vec{i}_j, \vec{\tau}_j(t)) \wedge \phi^{T,0}_{M_j}(\vec{i}_j, \vec{y}_j \mid \vec{y}'_j, \vec{o}_j \mid \vec{\tau}_j)) \implies \forall t \in [0,T].\ c^j_{out}(\vec{o}_j, \vec{\tau}_j(t))$
- $\forall t \in [0,T].\ \bigwedge_j c^j_{out}(\vec{o}, \vec{\tau}_j(t)) \implies \bigwedge_j c^j_{in}(\vec{i}_j, \vec{\tau}_j(t))$

Both bounded reachability and inductive reasoning can then be separately performed for each component by also assuming input conditions for individual components.[3] A compositional bounded reachability problem up to $n \in \mathbb{N}$ rounds for component j is encoded by:

$$\exists \vec{y}^j_0, \{\vec{y}^j_k, \vec{i}^j_k, \vec{o}^j_k, t^j_k\}^n_{k=1}.\ init_j(\vec{y}^j_0) \wedge \bigvee_{k=1}^{n} \neg safe_j(\vec{y}^j_k, \vec{\tau}^j_k(t_k))$$
$$\wedge \bigwedge_{k=1}^{n} \begin{bmatrix} \phi^T_{M_j}(\vec{i}^j_k, \vec{y}^j_{k-1} \mid \vec{y}^j_k, \vec{o}^j_k \mid \vec{\tau}^j_k) \wedge in_j(\vec{i}^j_k) \\ \wedge \forall t \in [0,T].\ c^j_{in}(\vec{i}^j_k, \vec{\tau}^j_k(t)) \end{bmatrix}$$

where the input condition $\forall t \in [0,T].\ c^j_{in}(\vec{i}^j_k, \vec{\tau}^j_k(t))$ is also assumed for each step in addition to Definition 9.

Likewise, a compositional inductive reasoning problem of $safe_j(\vec{y}_j, \vec{\tau}_j(t))$ for component j with an inductive condition $ind^j_d(\vec{y}_j) \wedge \forall t \in [0,T].\ ind^j_c(\vec{\tau}_j(t))$ can be encoded by:

- $\forall \vec{y}_j.\ init_j(\vec{y}_j) \implies ind^j_d(\vec{y}_j)$
- $\forall \vec{y}_j, \vec{y}'_j, \vec{i}_j, \vec{o}_j.\ \begin{bmatrix} ind^j_d(\vec{y}_j) \wedge \phi^{T,0}_{M_j}(\vec{i}_j, \vec{y}_j \mid \vec{y}'_j, \vec{o}_j \mid \vec{\tau}_j) \wedge \\ in_j(\vec{i}_j) \wedge \forall t \in [0,T].\ c^j_{in}(\vec{i}_j, \vec{\tau}_j(t)) \end{bmatrix}$
  $\implies (ind^j_d(\vec{y}'_j) \wedge \forall t \in [0,T].\ ind^j_c(\vec{\tau}_j(t)))$
- $\forall \vec{y}_j, \forall t.\ ind^j_d(\vec{y}_j) \wedge ind^j_c(\vec{\tau}_j(t)) \implies safe_j(\vec{y}_j, \vec{\tau}_j(t))$

The formulas for compositional reasoning can also be proved by checking the unsatisfiability of their *negated versions*.

5.3 Removing Universal Quantification

The formulas encoding Hybrid PALS models may contain universal quantification over *uninterpreted functions on the real numbers*, such as time-invariant constraints ($\forall t.\ \psi$) or formulas of the form $\forall t \in [u_0, u_t].\ \vec{\tau}(t) = \vec{v} + \int_0^{t-u_0} F_{\vec{a}}(\vec{x}, t)\, dt$, which are not directly supported by current state-of-the-art SMT techniques. This section explains how such universal quantification can be removed from the formulas.

We restrict our attention to time-invariant constraints with only *equality* terms, since continuous correlations typically can be expressed using only equalities (e.g., Example 1). Equality constraints, such as $x_1(t) = x_2(t)$, can be removed from the formula by replacing one side with the other, e.g., by replacing each function symbol x_1 with x_2. From now on we assume that time-invariant equality constraints have been removed from the formula in this way.

[3]Providing general solutions for how to find I/O conditions for $M_{\mathcal{E}_T \restriction_\Pi E}$ is beyond the scope of this paper.

Now consider universally quantified formulas of the form $\forall t \in [u_0, u_t].\ \vec{\tau}(t) = \vec{v} + \int_0^{t-u_0} F_{\vec{a}}(\vec{x}, t)\, dt$. Recall that the term $F_{\vec{a}}(\vec{x}, t)$ may include "uninterpreted" functions whose meaning is defined by other components. We *assign* to a time interval $[u_j, u'_j]$ in a global round such a "partial" ODE system $\frac{d\vec{x}_j}{dt} = F^j_{\vec{a}_j}(\vec{x}_j, t)$. If every component j assigns its partial ODE system $\frac{d\vec{x}_j}{dt} = F^j_{\vec{a}_j}(\vec{x}_j, t)$ to its interval $[u_j, u'_j]$, then a *complete ODE system* $\{\frac{d\vec{x}_j}{dt} = F^j_{\vec{a}_j}(\vec{x}_j, t)\}_j$, which contains no uninterpreted functions, can be constructed for the common interval $\bigcap_j [u_j, u'_j]$, provided that variables are renamed by the equality time-invariant constraints.

Example 9. The physical environment E_{Main} of the main controller in Example 1 involves the formula

$$\forall t \in [0, 60].\ \begin{bmatrix} \tau_\phi(t) \\ \tau_P(t) \end{bmatrix} = \begin{bmatrix} v_\phi \\ v_P \end{bmatrix} + \int_0^t \begin{bmatrix} \tau_P(t) \\ c(\tau_{\zeta_R}(t) - \tau_{\zeta_L}(t)) \end{bmatrix} dt.$$

including two uninterpreted function symbols τ_{ζ_L} and τ_{ζ_R}. Consider two logical formulas: for the left subcontroller, $\forall t \in [0, u^L_R].\ \tau_L(t) = v_L + \int_0^t rate^i_L\, dt$, and for the right subcontroller, $\forall t \in [u^R_R, 15].\ \tau(t) = v_R + \int_0^t rate^r_R\, dt$. For the common interval $[u^R_R, u^L_R]$, the complete ODE system is:

$$\begin{bmatrix} \tau_\phi(u^L_R) \\ \tau_P(u^L_R) \\ \tau_L(u^L_R) \\ \tau_R(u^L_R) \end{bmatrix} = \begin{bmatrix} \tau_\phi(u^R_R) \\ \tau_P(u^R_R) \\ \tau_L(u^R_R) \\ v_R \end{bmatrix} + \int_0^{u^L_R - u^R_R} \begin{bmatrix} \tau_P(t) \\ c(\tau_{\zeta_R}(t) - \tau_{\zeta_L}(t)) \\ rate^i_L \\ rate^r_R \end{bmatrix} dt.$$

This system indicates a period that the right subcontroller has responded (with the new rate $rate^r_R$) but the left one has not responded yet (due to the clock skews). ■

More precisely, a global period $[0, T]$ for one round of an ensemble $\mathcal{E}_T \restriction_\Pi E$ is divided into N contiguous subintervals $[0, t_1], [t_1, t_2], [t_2, t_3], \ldots, [t_{N-1}, T]$. Each interval denotes a single time segment to which a complete system of ODEs is assigned. The number N is determined by the total number of interval assignments in one round, namely, a number of ODE subformulas $\forall t \in [u_0, u_t].\ \vec{x}(t) = \vec{v} + \int_0^{t-u_0} F_{\vec{a}}(\vec{x}, t)\, dt$ in the formula $\phi_{\mathcal{E}_T \restriction_\Pi E}$. Finally, we can syntactically build a complete ODE system for each time segment by enumerating all possible combinations of partial ODE systems.

6. CASE STUDIES

This section gives an overview of some case studies that use our methodology to verify virtually synchronous distributed hybrid systems. All the case studies involve nonlinear ODEs and *continuous* interactions between distributed components. They also take into account asynchronous communication, network delays, clock skews, execution times, etc. Owing to the bisimulation equivalence, we can analyze the simpler synchronous models $\mathcal{E}_T \restriction_\Pi E$ instead of analyzing the distributed hybrid models $\mathcal{MA}(\mathcal{E}_T, \Gamma) \restriction_\Pi E$.

We have verified safety properties using inductive and compositional SMT encodings for *any possible* set of local clocks with maximal clock skew ϵ. We have applied the dReal SMT solver [9] to check the satisfiability of the SMT formulas up to a given precision $\delta > 0$ (which is decidable for nonlinear hybrid systems [8, 10]). All experiments were conducted on an Intel Xeon 2.0 GHz with 64 GB memory. The case studies and the experimental results are available at http://dreal.github.io/benchmarks/networks.

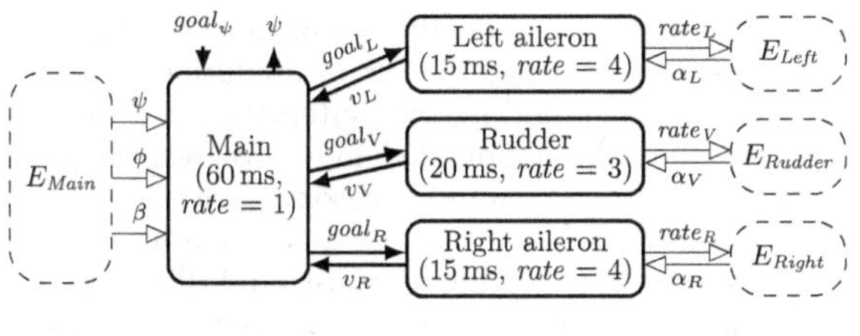

Figure 7: The controllers for turning an airplane.

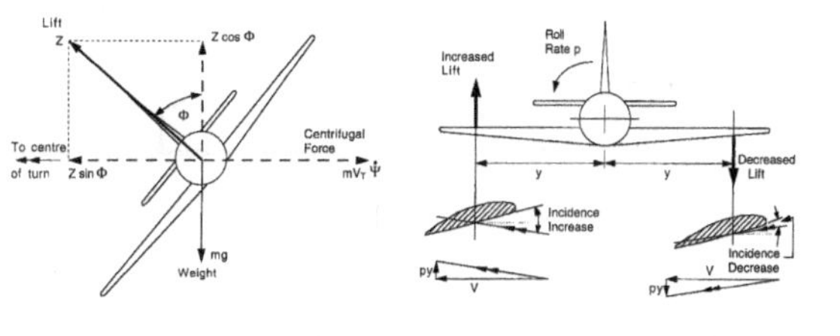

Figure 8: Forces acting in a turn of an aircraft [7].

6.1 Turning an Airplane

We consider a multirate virtually synchronous distributed controller to turn an airplane (adapted from [2]). This is a more elaborate version of Example 1. To make a turn, an aircraft rolls towards the direction of the turn by moving its ailerons. The rolling causes a yawing moment in the opposite direction, called *adverse yaw*, which is countered by using its *rudder* (a flap attached to the vertical stabilizer). The subcontrollers for the ailerons and the rudder operate at different rates, and the main controller orchestrates them to achieve a smooth turn, as illustrated in Fig. 7. The desired safety property is that the yaw angle β is always close to 0.

Each subcontroller M gradually moves its surface towards the goal angle $goal_M$ specified by the main controller M_{Main}, as explained in Example 1. In each round, M receives $goal_M$ from M_{Main}, determines the moving rate $rate_M$ based on $goal_M$ and the current sampled value v_M of the angle α_M, and sends back v_M to M_{Main}.[4] The local environment E_M specifies the dynamics of α_M by the ODE $\dot{\alpha_M} = rate_M$.

The main controller M_{Main} determines the goal angles for the subcontrollers to make a coordinated turn. In each round, M_{Main} receives a desired direction $goal_\psi$ (from the pilot) and the angles (v_L, v_V, v_R) from the subcontrollers, and sends back the new goals $(goal_L, goal_V, goal_R)$, based on the current sampled *position* values $(v_\psi, v_\phi, v_\beta)$ of the direction angle ψ, the roll angle ϕ, and the yaw angle β. We use a simple control logic to decide the new goal angles based on the current position angles, namely, by using some function $(goal_L, goal_V, goal_R) = f_{Main}(v_\psi, v_\phi, v_\beta)$.

The environment E_{Main} specifies the lateral dynamics of an aircraft as the nonlinear ODEs (depicted in Fig. 8):

$$\dot{\beta} = Y_{\zeta_L,\zeta_V,\zeta_R,\beta}/mV - r + (g/V)\cos\beta\sin\phi,$$
$$\dot{\phi} = p, \qquad \dot{\psi} = (g/V)\tan\phi,$$
$$\dot{p} = (c_1 r + c_2 p)\cdot r\tan\phi + c_3 L_{\zeta_L,\zeta_V,\zeta_R,\beta} + c_4 N_{\zeta_L,\zeta_V,\zeta_R,\beta},$$
$$\dot{r} = (c_8 p - c_2 r)\cdot r\tan\phi + c_4 L_{\zeta_L,\zeta_V,\zeta_R,\beta} + c_9 N_{\zeta_L,\zeta_V,\zeta_R,\beta}.$$

where p is the rolling moment, r is the yawing moment, and $Y_{\zeta_L,\zeta_V,\zeta_R,\beta}$, $L_{\zeta_L,\zeta_V,\zeta_R,\beta}$, and $N_{\zeta_L,\zeta_V,\zeta_R,\beta}$ are (linear) functions of the control angles $(\zeta_L, \zeta_V, \zeta_R)$ and β.

The physical environment E_{Main} clearly depends on the subcontrollers's physical environments. Each control angle ζ_M in E_{Main} must be the same as the corresponding surface angle α_M, but the ODEs of the subcontrollers cannot be directly "plugged" into E_{Main}, because the main controller and the subcontrollers have *different periods with local clock skews*. The continuous connections between the physical environments are specified by the time-invariant constraint: $\forall t.\,(\zeta_L(t) = \alpha_L(t)) \wedge (\zeta_V(t) = \alpha_V(t)) \wedge (\zeta_R(t) = \alpha_R(t))$.

[4]For example, the new value of $rate_M$ can be given by $\mathrm{sign}(goal_M - v_M)\cdot\min(\mathrm{abs}(goal_M - v_M)/T, max_M)$.

We first performed bounded reachability analysis to verify the safety property $\forall t.\,\mathrm{abs}(\beta(t)) < 0.2$, where all state variables are initially 0° and the goal direction from the pilot is fixed (e.g., 30°). In the analysis, we assume the sampling time $t_I = 0$ ms for every controller, the response time $t_R = 3$ ms for every subcontroller (the main controller has no actuator), and the maximal clock skew $\epsilon = 0.2$ ms. For bound $k = 10$, the analysis took 16 hours using dReal with precision $\delta = 0.001$, which is quite slow due to complex nonlinear ODEs, nontrivial discrete controls, etc.

Therefore, we have applied compositional reasoning to conduct a bounded reachability analysis in a compositional way. We first show that each subcontroller cannot abruptly change its surface angle towards its goal direction in one round, so that the change is always less than a certain value.[5] Next, assuming that a subcontroller cannot abruptly move its surface, we perform a bounded reachability analysis only for the main controller using the same initial condition. For bound $k = 20$, using dReal with precision $\delta = 0.0001$, the compositional bounded reachability analysis for the safety property $\forall t.\,\mathrm{abs}(\beta(t)) < 0.2$ took 2 minutes.

6.2 Networked Water Tank Controllers

In this benchmark, adapted from [16], a number of water tanks are connected by pipes as shown in Fig. 9. The water level in each tank is controlled by a pump in the tank, and depends on the pump's mode $m \in \{m_{\mathtt{on}}, m_{\mathtt{off}}\}$ and the water level of the input tank. The water level x_i of tank i changes according to the nonlinear ODEs:

$$A_i\dot{x}_i = \begin{cases} (q_i + a\sqrt{2g}\sqrt{x_{i-1}}) - b\sqrt{2g}\sqrt{x_i} & \text{if } m_i = m_{\mathtt{on}}, \\ a\sqrt{2g}\sqrt{x_{i-1}} - b\sqrt{2g}\sqrt{x_i} & \text{if } m_i = m_{\mathtt{off}}, \end{cases}$$

We set $x_0 = 0$ for the leftmost tank 1. Each pipe controller performs its transitions according to its local clock and sets the pump to `on` if $x_i \leq L_m$ and to `off` if $x_i > L_M$. The desired safety property is that each water level x_i is in the range $I = [L_m - \eta, L_M + \eta]$, expressed as $(\forall t)\, x_i(t) \in I$.

We have verified the safety property for *any number* of connected water tanks for unbounded time *with respect to clock skews* using compositional inductive reasoning. First, assuming that the input water level x_{i-1} is in I, we show that x_i is in a tighter range $I' = [L_m - \eta', L_M + \eta']$ with $\eta' < \eta$ during one round $[0, T]$.[6] Next, assuming that the input level x_{i-1} is in I, we show that $(\forall t)\, x_i(t) \in I$ is an inductive condition for one round (that is, $x_i(0) \in I$, $\phi_{\mathcal{E}_T \restriction_\Pi E}$, and $\forall t \in [0,T].\, c_{in}^{i-1}(x_{i-1}(t))$ implies $\forall t \in [0,T].\, x_i(t) \in I$).

[5]E.g., the output condition for the left subcontroller is $c_{out}^L(v_L, \alpha_L(t)) \equiv \forall t \in [0,T].\,\mathrm{abs}(\alpha_L(t) - v_L) < \gamma$.
[6]I/O conditions are $c_{in}^i(x_{i-1}(t)) \equiv (\forall t \in [0,T].\, x_{i-1}(t) \in I)$ and $c_{out}^i(x_i(t)) \equiv (\forall t \in [0,T].\, x_i(t) \in I')$.

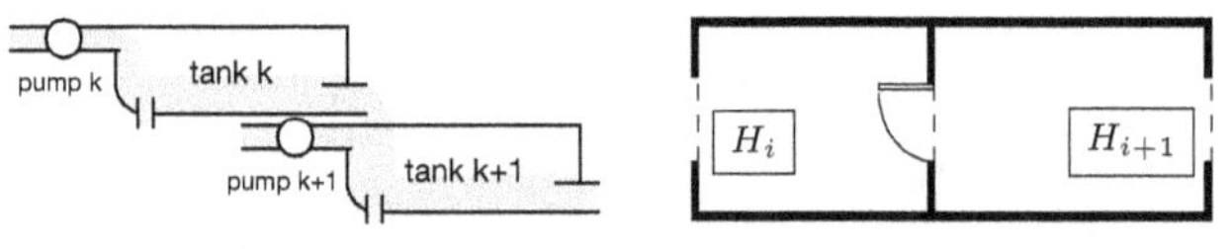

Figure 9: Connected water tanks, and rooms.

We have proved this compositional safety property for maximal clock skew $\epsilon = 30\,\mathrm{ms}$, sampling time $t_I = 20\,\mathrm{ms}$, and response time $t_R = 100\,\mathrm{ms}$, with precision $\delta = 0.001$ using dReal (the analysis took 4.3 seconds). However, if $\epsilon = 150\,\mathrm{ms}$, then the inductive condition $(\forall t)\, x_i(t) \in I$ is violated because the water level can increase up to extra 300 ms (the analysis took 1.46 seconds).

6.3 Networked Thermostat Controllers

A number of rooms are interconnected by open doors, as shown in Fig. 9. The temperature x_i of each room i is separately controlled by its own thermostat controller that turns the heater on and off. That is, x_i depends on the heater's mode $m \in \{m_{\mathtt{on}}, m_{\mathtt{off}}\}$ and the temperatures of the connected rooms, and changes according to the ODEs:

$$\dot{x}_i = \begin{cases} K_i(h_i - ((1-2c)x_i + cx_{i-1} + cx_{i+1})) & \text{if } m_i = m_{\mathtt{on}} \\ -K_i((1-2c)x_i + cx_{i-1} + cx_{i+1}) & \text{if } m_i = m_{\mathtt{off}} \end{cases}$$

In each transition, a controller of room i turns on the heater if $x_i \leq T_m$, and turns it off if $x_i > T_M$. The safety property is that the temperature x_i of each room is in a certain range $I = [T_m - \eta, T_M + \eta]$, expressed as $(\forall t)\, x_i(t) \in I$.

We have verified the desired safety property $(\forall t)\, x_i(t) \in I$ for *any number* of interconnected thermostat controllers for unbounded time, taking into account clock skews, by compositional inductive reasoning. Provided that both temperatures x_{i-1} and x_{i+1} of the connected rooms are in I, we show that x_i is in a tighter range $I' = [T_m - \eta', T_M + \eta'] \subseteq I$ with $\eta' < \eta$ during one round. Then, assuming that both x_{i-1} and x_{i+1} are in I, we show that $(\forall t)\, x_i(t) \in I$ is an inductive condition for one round in a similar way to Section 6.2.

We have proved the safety property for any number of thermostats for maximal clock skew $\epsilon = 2\,\mathrm{ms}$, sampling time $t_I = 10\,\mathrm{ms}$, and response time $t_R = 200\,\mathrm{ms}$, using dReal with precision $\delta = 0.001$ (the analysis took 2.6 seconds). However, if $\epsilon = 20\,\mathrm{ms}$, then the compositional inductive condition $(\forall t)\, x_i(t) \in I$ is violated because the temperature rises for extra 20 ms and thus $x_i \notin I$ at the end of the round (the analysis took 0.56 seconds).

7. CONCLUDING REMARKS

We have presented general techniques for verifying virtually synchronous distributed hybrid systems, with asynchronous communication, imprecise local clocks, network delays, etc., where each component has a local physical environment that can be correlated with other local environments. To make the verification of such systems feasible, we have extended the PALS methodology to hybrid systems, and have given a bisimulation equivalence between the distributed model and the much simpler "synchronous" model, which abstracts from message exchange (and the resulting interleavings), network delays, execution times, etc. However, Hybrid PALS cannot abstract from imprecise local clocks and the timing of sensing and actuating.

We have shown that verification problems for Hybrid PALS synchronous models (and, by our bisimulation result, the corresponding distributed hybrid systems) such as bounded reachability analysis, unbounded inductive reasoning, and compositional assume-guarantee reasoning, can be expressed as SMT formulas over the real numbers. We have verified safety properties of a number of non-trivial distributed hybrid systems, with nonlinear ODEs and continuous physical connections between different components, using dReal.

Future work should develop SMT techniques for finding inductive invariant and compositional I/O conditions for nonlinear distributed hybrid systems.

8. REFERENCES

[1] A. Al-Nayeem, M. Sun, X. Qiu, L. Sha, S. P. Miller, and D. D. Cofer. A formal architecture pattern for real-time distributed systems. In *IEEE RTSS*, 2009.

[2] K. Bae, J. Krisiloff, J. Meseguer, and P. C. Ölveczky. Designing and verifying distributed cyber-physical systems using Multirate PALS: An airplane turning control system case study. *Sci. Comp. Prog.*, 103, 2015.

[3] K. Bae, J. Meseguer, and P. C. Ölveczky. Formal patterns for multirate distributed real-time systems. *Sci. Comp. Program.*, 91:3–44, 2014.

[4] K. Bae, P. Ölveczky, S. Kong, and S. Gao. SMT-based analysis of virtually synchronous hybrid systems. http://kquine.github.io/vsdh/techrep.pdf.

[5] K. Bae and P. C. Ölveczky. Hybrid Multirate PALS. In *Logic, Rewriting, and Concurrency*, volume 9200 of *LNCS*. Springer, 2015.

[6] S. Bogomolov, C. Herrera, M. Muñiz, B. Westphal, and A. Podelski. Quasi-dependent variables in hybrid automata. In *HSCC*. ACM, 2014.

[7] R. P. Collinson. *Introduction to avionics systems.* Springer, 2013.

[8] S. Gao, J. Avigad, and E. M. Clarke. δ-complete decision procedures for satisfiability over the reals. In *IJCAR*, volume 7364 of *LNCS*. Springer, 2012.

[9] S. Gao, S. Kong, and E. M. Clarke. dReal: An SMT solver for nonlinear theories over the reals. In *CADE*, volume 7898 of *LNCS*. Springer, 2013.

[10] S. Gao, S. Kong, and E. M. Clarke. Satisfiability modulo ODEs. In *FMCAD*. IEEE, 2013.

[11] M. Hendriks, G. Behrmann, K. G. Larsen, P. Niebert, and F. W. Vaandrager. Adding symmetry reduction to Uppaal. In *FORMATS*, volume 2791 of *LNCS*, 2003.

[12] T. T. Johnson and S. Mitra. A small model theorem for rectangular hybrid automata networks. In *FMOODS/FORTE*. LNCS 7273, Springer, 2012.

[13] T. T. Johnson and S. Mitra. Anonymized reachability of hybrid automata networks. In *FORMATS*, volume 8711 of *LNCS*. Springer, 2014.

[14] N. Lynch, R. Segala, and F. Vaandrager. Hybrid I/O automata. *Infor. and Comput.*, 185(1), 2003.

[15] J. Meseguer and P. C. Ölveczky. Formalization and correctness of the PALS architectural pattern for distributed real-time systems. *Theoretical Computer Science*, 451:1–37, 2012.

[16] J. Raisch, E. Klein, S. O'Young, C. Meder, and A. Itigin. Approximating automata and discrete control for continuous systems. In *Hybrid Systems V*, volume 1567 of *LNCS*. Springer, 1999.

Scalable Static Hybridization Methods for Analysis of Nonlinear Systems*

Stanley Bak
Air Force Research Laboratory
Information Directorate, USA

Sergiy Bogomolov
IST Austria

Thomas A. Henzinger
IST Austria

Taylor T. Johnson
University of Texas at Arlington, USA

Pradyot Prakash
IIT Bombay, India

ABSTRACT

Hybridization methods enable the analysis of hybrid automata with complex, nonlinear dynamics through a sound abstraction process. Complex dynamics are converted to simpler ones with added noise, and then analysis is done using a reachability method for the simpler dynamics. Several such recent approaches advocate that only "dynamic" hybridization techniques—i.e., those where the dynamics are abstracted on-the-fly during a reachability computation—are effective. In this paper, we demonstrate this is not the case, and create static hybridization methods that are more scalable than earlier approaches.

The main insight in our approach is that quick, numeric simulations can be used to guide the process, eliminating the need for an exponential number of hybridization domains. Transitions between domains are generally time-triggered, avoiding accumulated error from geometric intersections. We enhance our static technique by combining time-triggered transitions with occasional space-triggered transitions, and demonstrate the benefits of the combined approach in what we call mixed-triggered hybridization. Finally, error modes are inserted to confirm that the reachable states stay within the hybridized regions.

The developed techniques can scale to higher dimensions than previous static approaches, while enabling the parallelization of the main performance bottleneck for many dynamic hybridization approaches: the nonlinear optimization required for sound dynamics abstraction. We implement our method as a model transformation pass in the HYST tool, and perform reachability analysis and evaluation using an unmodified version of SpaceEx on nonlinear models with up to six dimensions.

*DISTRIBUTION A. Approved for public release; Distribution unlimited. (Approval AFRL PA #88ABW-2016-0181, 28 JAN 2016)

HSCC'16, April 12 - 14, 2016, Vienna, Austria

ACM ISBN 978-1-4503-3955-1/16/04...$15.00
DOI: http://dx.doi.org/10.1145/2883817.2883837

1. INTRODUCTION

A hybrid automaton [7] is an expressive mathematical model useful for describing complex dynamic processes involving both continuous and discrete states and their evolution. Efficient algorithms and analysis tools for linear and affine systems have recently emerged [24]. However, the behaviour of many real-world systems can only be modeled with nonlinear differential equations.

Hybridization methods attempt to address this issue, enabling the application of existing algorithms for simpler dynamics (such as constant or affine dynamics) on the analysis of hybrid automata with nonlinear differential equations. Alternative recent approaches for analyzing nonlinear systems include simulation-based verification [22] or using efficient representations such as Taylor models [17]. Most hybridization methods work by dividing the state space into a set of domains. In each domain, the nonlinear dynamics are then converted to simpler ones with added noise to account for the abstraction error within the domain. Hybridization is also known as *conservative approximation* [8], which illustrates that it is a sound (or conservative) abstraction. Hybridization has been used to verify properties for several types of systems, from analog/mixed-signal circuits [19] to autonomous satellite maneuvers in space [14, 31].

We classify existing hybridization approaches along two axes as shown in Table 1: static versus dynamic, and space-triggered versus time-triggered. *Static* hybridization approaches use a fixed partitioning, and can make use unmodified, off-the-shelf analysis tools. In contrast, *dynamic* methods exploit runtime information to perform hybridization, and therefore must be tightly integrated within an analysis tool. On the other axis, *space-triggered* techniques perform geometric intersections along hybridization domain boundaries. Time-triggered hybridization, on the other hand, avoids this operation by creating a series of overlapping domains, and switches between them at specific points in time.

Based on this classification, a gap exists in existing research: no methods exist that perform static, time-triggered hybridization. The main contribution of this paper is the investigation of this category, and demonstrating that such methods can overcome some of the drawbacks of existing hybridization methods. Notably, the new hybridization methods are more scalable than existing space-triggered approaches. Furthermore, the expensive dynamics abstraction step, which is generally a global optimization problem, is easily parallelizable, which is not the case in dynamic

	Space-Triggered	Time-Triggered	Mixed-Triggered
Static	[8,10,29,31]	this paper	this paper
Dynamic	[8,9]	[1–3,5,20,28]	none

Table 1: Breakdown of hybridization approaches into static versus dynamic, and space-triggered versus time-triggered, as well as combinations thereof (mixed-triggered).

approaches. We further enhance our static technique by combining time-triggered transitions with occasional space-triggered transitions, and demonstrate the benefits of the combined approach in what we call *mixed-triggered hybridization*.

The static mixed-triggered hybridization approach works by hybridizing only a part of the state space. We use quick numeric simulations to guide the partitioning process. In this way, we mitigate the problem of exponential growth in the number of partitions. In addition, we generally use time-triggered guards in the transitions between partitions. This prevents costly geometric intersection computations which typically add overapproximation error to the result. We ensure the soundness of the constructed abstraction by adding *error modes* to guarantee that the computed reachable states remain within the hybridized region (which is constructed from simulations that may be imprecise).

We implement the hybridization method described in this paper as a model transformation pass in the HYST source-to-source translation tool. Since it is a static approach, we can use unmodified reachability tools on the hybridized models. We create affine abstractions of nonlinear dynamics, and use to perform reachability analysis.

Contributions and Paper Organization. The main contribution of this paper is the development of the first static time-triggered and mixed-triggered hybridization methods. Of critical importance in the proposed approaches is the choice of hybridization parameters, and a second contribution is an algorithm which uses simulations to generate these values. This algorithm is implemented in the HYST [12] model transformation tool, which allows it to quickly be applied to new systems and with new simulation parameters. Finally, we validate our claims that the method is more scalable than existing static approaches by evaluating it on nonlinear models, including a six-dimensional water tank model, and then using an unmodified version of SpaceEx [13, 15, 24], which does not natively support nonlinear dynamics, to compute the set of reachable states.

This paper first reviews and classifies existing hybridization methods in Section 2. Section 3 then presents mathematical background and formalisms, which are used in Section 4 to give formal descriptions and correctness arguments for several hybrid automaton transformations. A simulation-based algorithm to create the hybridization parameters used by the transformations is described next in Section 5. Section 6 discusses the implementation in HYST and experimental reachability results in SpaceEx, followed by a conclusion in Section 7.

2. HYBRIDIZATION METHODS

In this section, we discuss and classify previous research on hybridization. Hybridiziation is the process of using simple dynamics with noise to create an abstraction of a system with more complicated, usually nonlinear, dynamics. This is done to enable the analysis of systems with the more complicated dynamics by methods which work exclusively on the simpler ones.

This process is typically targeted for flow-pipe construction methods, where the set of reachable states is iteratively computed or overapproximated at monotonically increasing instances in time, starting from an initial set of states. Computational approaches maintain some representation of the set of states at each time instances, which we informally refer to as the *currently-tracked* set of states.

Static Space-Triggered Hybridization. Early hybridization methods were both static and space-triggered [29]. In these approaches, the state space is partitioned using a (typically uniform) grid or mesh, and transitions are added along the partition boundaries, resulting in state-dependent switching. The advantage of this approach is that existing termination checking techniques can be used, which is particularly useful in the case of periodic systems where linearizing a bounded subset of the state-space is reasonable [31].

There are, however, three main drawbacks. First, static mesh construction is traditionally done without knowledge of the reachable states. Therefore, it requires computing the mesh over the entire state space (or bounded subset thereof), which scales exponentially with the number of continuous dimensions in the system. Second, the geometric intersections required by space-triggered approaches may introduce error during reachability computation [4, 17]. This is because such intersections can require tools to convert from precise internal representations such as zonotopes [25], support functions [27], or Taylor models [17], to simpler representations where intersection operations can be computed, such as polytopes [6]. After intersection, the simpler representation is then converted back to the internal representation for subsequent computation [26]. These conversions can result in overapproximations of the original currently-tracked set of states, adding error each time they are performed. Since hybridization can be done more accurately when domains are small, many intersection operations may be necessary and this can quickly lead to error explosion, as well as an explosion in the number of modes of the hybrid automaton. Third, the currently-tracked set of reachable states may leave a hybridization domain along multiple facets, requiring splitting and, later, possibly remerging the set of reachable states, which can be both computationally expensive and inaccurate [20].

Dynamic Space-Triggered Hybridization. In order to help increase scalability, methods were developed that perform hybridization during reachability analysis [8]. This results in dynamic methods where the domain construction and the abstraction process is performed on-the-fly and only on states that are reachable [9]. Although dynamic space-triggered methods scale better into higher dimensions, they still suffer from the other two problems mentioned above: error accumulation due to many geometric intersections, and the splitting of the currently-tracked set of states along multiple facets.

Dynamic Time-Triggered Hybridization. To address the other two drawbacks, dynamic time-triggered approaches were developed [5, 20, 28]. These methods avoid geometric intersections by choosing hybridization domains around the currently-tracked set of states. As time is advanced, the hybridization domains are updated to be near the new position of the currently-tracked set of states, without requiring an intersection operation. This can be done at each step [28], or whenever the currently-tracked set of states leaves the hybridization domain [20]. This can be viewed as the mode of the abstract hybrid automaton changing at specific instances in time to a mode with new dynamics, which corresponds to a time-triggered transition.

Although dynamic time-triggered methods perform well, they also suffer from certain drawbacks. The most important drawback is that, in the earlier static approaches, performing the dynamics abstraction step was an embarrassingly parallel problem, so parallelism could be leveraged to reduce total runtime (or equivalently, increase precision for a fixed runtime). In dynamic methods, the bounds of each new abstraction domain depend on the set of reachable states in the previous domain, forcing this expensive step to be performed serially. For example, abstracting nonlinear dynamics using polynomial differential inclusions can yield an accurate hybridization, but it requires bounding the Lagrange remainder of the dynamics' Taylor expansion [1]. In previous work, this step was reported to take 1121 out of 1180 seconds on a nine-dimensional biological aging model (about 95% of the runtime), and 1155 out of 1296 seconds on hybrid variant of the same model (about 89%), although it was mentioned that some implementation optimizations were possible [1]. Some parallelization of reachability computation was considered to enable online reachability of car manoeuvres [2,3]. However, the crucial step of dynamics abstraction (computing the linearization errors) was still performed serially because the overapproximation of the Lagrange remainders of the Taylor expansions of the dynamics at each step was based on the Lagrange remainders at the previous step. This serial step dominated the reported runtime of the technique.

A second drawback of time-triggered approaches is that, if the currently-tracked set of states becomes large (which can be a property of the system regardless of the method used), the domains over which dynamics abstraction is performed also become large. This, in turn, increases the dynamics approximation error that must be added to the simpler dynamics to result in a sound abstraction, increasing error in the overapproximation of the set of reachable states. This can be overcome by splitting the set of reachable states [21], although this may yield an exponential number of sets that need to be tracked, and possibly redundant computation. This problem can be partially mitigated through extra tracking to perform cancellation of redundant sets of reachable states, which requires (expensive and error-introducing) intersection operations on the internal representations [5]. Space-triggered approaches do not suffer from this problem. In fact, introducing *occasional* artificial space-triggered transitions can serve to reduce the size and complexity of the currently-tracked set of reachable states [11].

Novel Hybridization Approaches. A classification of existing hybridization research is shown in Table 1. A research gap is noticeable in the static time-triggered category. This paper attempts to fill this gap by developing, to the best of the authors' knowledge, the first static time-triggered hybridization method. The approach is static, and therefore can perform the bottleneck step of dynamics abstraction in a parallel fashion. Since the approach is time-triggered, it can scale to larger numbers of dimensions while avoiding the accumulation of intersection error. Additionally, as the method is static and modifies the model directly, it can work with unmodified reachability tools, yielding immediate benefit of its application using the latest reachability methods.

There are also no fundamental reasons why a method could not use both time-triggered and space-triggered transitions during analysis. We develop such a *mixed-triggered* hybridization approach, which generally uses time-triggered transitions, but occasionally performs a state-triggered transition to attempt to reduce the size and complexity of the currently-tracked set of states. In our review of existing research, no such approaches currently exist.

Other Hybridization Factors. Research in hybridization also explores other aspects that are important, but less critical to the methods developed in this paper. One choice when performing hybridization is the shape of space-triggered domains. Rectangular domains are simple to reason about, although manual region selection [29], simplexes [9, 21, 31], and nonuniform meshes [8,10,31] have been considered. The sound and tight abstraction of dynamics within each domain is critical to control error when performing hybridization. The main reason to consider alternative domains is in order to reduce this error. For general nonlinear dynamics, this often requires solving constrained nonlinear optimization problems, which can be impossible in theory and expensive in practice. For rectangular domains, interval analysis [30] can be used to provide guaranteed bounds for this problem. For other types of domains, the success of the method depends on the system being analyzed. For example, to perform the nonlinear optimization step for simplicial domains, one can use knowledge of the system's Lipschitz constant (which will be sound but inaccurate), or compute bounds on the second partial derivatives (the elements of the Hessian matrix) [8, 9, 21]. In general, this is a nonlinear optimization problem with linear constraints, but for specific cases it can be efficiently solved. For example, for quadratic dynamics [20, 21], the Hessian matrix is constant. The choice of domains is not critical to the methods being developed in this paper, so for simplicity, we considered rectangular domains.

A second choice when performing hybridization is the type of 'simpler' dynamics. Choices range from constant bounds [16, 29, 31, 32], linear and affine bounds [9, 21, 31], to polynomial bounds [1, 18]. In this paper, we target an unmodified implementation of the SpaceEx tool [24], and therefore simplify from nonlinear dynamics to affine dynamics.

3. PRELIMINARIES

In order to define and justify the soundness of the model transformation steps used in our approach, we need to first precisely define the syntax and semantics of hybrid automata.

Definition 1. A *hybrid automaton* $\mathcal{H}$ is defined by a tuple $\mathcal{H} \triangleq (Modes, Var, Init, Flow, Trans, Inv)$, where: (a) *Modes* is a finite set of modes. (b) $Var = \{x_1, \ldots, x_n\}$ is a set of real-valued variables. (c) $Init(m) \subseteq \mathbb{R}^n$ is the set of initial values for $x_1, \ldots, x_n$ for each mode $m \in Modes$. (d) For each $m \in Modes$, the flow relation $Flow(m)$ is a relation over the variables in x and their derivatives $\dot{x} = f_m(x)$, where $x(t) \in \mathbb{R}^n$ and $f : \mathbb{R}^n \to 2^{\mathbb{R}^n}$, i.e., differential inclusions are allowed. (e) *Trans* is a set of discrete transitions $t = (m, g, v, m')$, where m and m' are the source and the target modes, g is the guard of t, and v is the update of t. (f) $Inv(m) \subseteq \mathbb{R}^n$ is an invariant for each mode $m \in Modes$.

For a time interval T, we define a *trajectory* of $\mathcal{H}$ from state $s = (m, \mathbf{x})$ to state $s' = (m', \mathbf{x}')$ as a tuple $(L, \mathbf{X})$. In this tuple, the function $L : T \to Modes$ and $\mathbf{X} : T \to \mathbb{R}^n$ are functions that define for each time point in T the mode and values of the continuous variables, respectively.

A state s' is *reachable from a state* s if there exists a trajectory starting with s and ending with s'. A state s' is *reachable* if s' is reachable from a state s where s is an initial state. We denote the set of states reachable from the set X in mode m by $\text{Reach}_{\mathcal{H}}(m, X)$. $\text{Reach}(\mathcal{H})$ of $\mathcal{H}$ is defined as the set of states that are reachable from the set of initial states. We use $\text{Reach}^c_{\mathcal{H}}(m, X)$ and $\text{Reach}^c(\mathcal{H})$ to denote the versions of the these operators that return only the *continuous* part of the computed state space. We refer to $\text{Reach}^c(\mathcal{H})$ as the *continuous reachable state space* of $\mathcal{H}$. We denote the projection of the set $R \subseteq \mathbb{R}^n$ over variables Var to the subset $Var' \subseteq Var$ by $R\downarrow_{Var'}$. Throughout the paper, we always refer to time-bounded reachability, i.e., we consider trajectories which evolve up to the time horizon T_{max}. In order to simplify notations, we implicitly take this assumption for granted in our reasoning. Finally, given a mode m of the automaton $\mathcal{H}$, we refer to the set of *outgoing* transitions as $Trans_{\mathcal{H}}(m)$.

4. TRANSFORMATIONS

We are interested in methods to compute an overapproximation of the time-bounded set of reachable states, which produce tight overapproximations, yet are feasible from the computational point of view. The proposed approaches rely on several hybrid automaton transformations. A source-to-source *transformation* takes as input a hybrid automaton $\mathcal{H}$, a mode $m \in Modes$,[1] possibly some additional parameters, and returns as output another hybrid automaton $\theta(\mathcal{H})$. The four described transformations are (1) *time-triggered splitting*, (2) *space-triggered splitting*, (3) *domain contraction*, and (4) *dynamics abstraction*. In time-triggered splitting, a given mode of $\mathcal{H}$ is split into possibly multiple modes via a time-triggered splitting of the modes. Similarly, in space-triggered splitting, a mode is split by augmenting the mode invariant with a constraint induced by a *space trigger function*. Domain contraction adds auxiliary invariants called *contraction domains* to a mode by intersecting them with the existing invariants of the mode. Dynamics abstraction overapproximates the dynamics in a mode of the automaton, which in this paper, abstracts nonlinear differential equations by linear differential inclusions, in particular a linear differential equation with an additive set-valued (interval vector) input.

As hybridization of the *continuous dynamics* of hybrid automata is the most challenging part of the hybridization process, we focus on the continuous dynamics of hybrid systems in the rest of the paper and assume that an input hybrid automaton has only *one* mode. Our approach *overapproximates* the behavior of the original system by a hybrid automata consisting of *multiple* modes. Therefore, only reachable *continuous states* are relevant for the soundness of the transformations. This fact allows us to to conclude that the inclusion of the original *continuous* reachable state space into the transformed one is enough to show soundness of our transformations. Note, however, that although the input hybrid automaton for the whole hybridization approach is assumed to be a singleton, our transformations are defined in terms of general hybrid automata.

In this section, each of these four transformations is precisely defined. After, these will be combined in order to perform static time-triggered and mixed-triggered hybridization.

4.1 Time-Triggered Splitting

The time-triggered splitting transformation, informally, separates the handling of system behavior in the first τ time units, and the rest of the trajectory up to the time horizon. In order to achieve this goal, the transformation splits a given mode of a hybrid automaton into two and imposes constraints that guarantee that the system dwells in the first mode for τ time units and proceeds to the second one once the time threshold has been reached.

Definition 2. A *time-triggered splitting* is a transformation θ_{tt} of a hybrid automaton $\mathcal{H}$, that takes as input an automaton $\mathcal{H}$, a mode $m \in Modes$ that has no outgoing transitions[2], and a real positive time τ, a *time-trigger threshold.* The hybrid automaton $\mathcal{H}_{tt} \triangleq \theta_{tt}(\mathcal{H})$ is defined as: (a) $Modes_{\mathcal{H}_{tt}} \triangleq Modes_{\mathcal{H}} \cup \{m_{tt}\}$, where m_{tt} is a fresh (i.e., unique) mode name, (b) $Var_{\mathcal{H}_{tt}} \triangleq Var_{\mathcal{H}} \cup \{t\}$, where t is known as the *time-trigger* variable and is fresh, i.e., assume without loss of generality that t is a unique variable name,[3] (c) the initial states are copied; in addition, if $Init_{\mathcal{H}}(m)$ is not the empty set (i.e., m is an initial mode), then $Init_{\mathcal{H}_{tt}}(m) \triangleq Init_{\mathcal{H}}(m) \wedge t = \tau$, and otherwise $Init_{\mathcal{H}_{tt}}(m) \triangleq Init_{\mathcal{H}}(m)$; $Init_{\mathcal{H}_{tt}}(m_{tt}) \triangleq \emptyset$, (d) the flows are copied, and $Flow_{\mathcal{H}_{tt}}(m_{tt}) \triangleq Flow_{\mathcal{H}}(m)$, so mode m_{tt} copies the original dynamics of m, and in m, $\dot{t} = -1$, and in all modes other than m, $\dot{t} = 0$, (e) the transitions are copied; in addition, $Trans_{\mathcal{H}_{tt}}(m_{tt}) \triangleq Trans_{\mathcal{H}}(m)$, with an additional transition created from m to m_{tt} with the guard $t = 0$; moreover, every incoming transition to m has the reset $t := \tau$ added, (f) the invariants are copied; in addition $t \geq 0$ is added to $Inv_{\mathcal{H}_{tt}}(m)$ and $Inv_{\mathcal{H}_{tt}}(m_{tt}) \triangleq Inv_{\mathcal{H}}(m)$ (m_{tt} copied the original invariant of m).

Figure 1 illustrates the time-triggered splitting for a single mode. A *time-triggered transition* corresponds to any transition with guard $t = 0$ taken when the time-trigger variable

[1]For simplicity of presentation, each transformation is defined for a given mode of the hybrid automaton $\mathcal{H}$, and their application to multiple modes of $\mathcal{H}$ is straightforward by iterating over each element of *Modes*.

[2]In order to make the presentation of our transformation clearer, we consider a mode with no outgoing transitions. Our construction can be easily generalized to also accommodate this feature.

[3] If the time-triggered splitting transformation θ_{tt} is applied to an automaton multiple times, the time-trigger variable may be reused in each splitting, as it needs only to be fresh on the first application of the transformation. This optimization is done in our implementation.

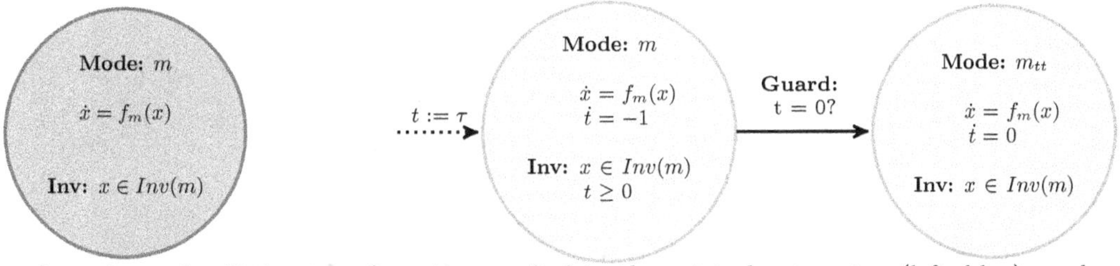

Figure 1: The time-triggered splitting transformation applied to the original automaton (left, blue) produces the output automaton (right, yellow). An additional time-trigger variable t is added that counts down to zero from an initial time τ.

$t = 0$. In contrast to general guards, the reachability along time-triggered transitions can be computed computationally efficient as many reachability algorithms automatically capture *time dependencies* as part of their workflow. For example, the STC scenario [23] of the hybrid model checker SpaceEx computes *time-dependent* piecewise-linear approximations of the support functions evolution.

The following lemma connects the time-triggered splitting transformation with the original hybrid automaton.

LEMMA 4.1. *Let $\mathcal{H}$ be a hybrid automaton with a set of continuous variables Var, $m \in$ Modes be a mode without outgoing transitions, and $\tau \in \mathbb{R}_{>0}$ be a time-trigger threshold. Then it holds that* $\text{Reach}^c(\mathcal{H}) \subseteq \text{Reach}^c(\theta_{tt}(\mathcal{H})) \downarrow_{Var}$.

Here, we note that we need to project away the auxiliary variable t in order to ensure that the sets of reachable states of $\mathcal{H}$ and $\theta_{tt}(\mathcal{H})$ can be compared.

4.2 Space-Triggered Splitting

Space-triggered splitting, similar to time-triggered splitting, breaks a given mode into several modes. However, in contrast to the time-triggered transformation, it uses a *space-trigger function* to define criteria for mode splitting.

Definition 3. A *space-triggered splitting* is a transformation θ_{st} of a hybrid automaton $\mathcal{H}$, that takes as input an automaton $\mathcal{H}$, a mode $m \in$ *Modes* that has no outgoing transitions, and a function $\pi : \mathbb{R}^n \to \mathbb{R}$ called the *space-trigger* function. The function π must satisfy the condition that upon entering mode m, $\pi(x) \geq 0$, where x is the current state. This means that if m is an initial mode, for all states $x \in Init(m)$, $\pi(x) \geq 0$. The hybrid automaton $\mathcal{H}_{st} \triangleq \theta_{st}(\mathcal{H})$ defined as: (a) $Modes_{\mathcal{H}_{st}} \triangleq Modes_{\mathcal{H}} \cup \{m_{st}\}$, where m_{st} is a fresh (i.e., unique) mode name, (b) $Var_{\mathcal{H}_{st}} \triangleq Var_{\mathcal{H}}$, (c) the initial states are copied; $Init_{\mathcal{H}_{st}}(m_{st}) \triangleq \emptyset$, (d) the flows are copied; in addition, $Flow_{\mathcal{H}_{st}}(m_{st}) \triangleq Flow_{\mathcal{H}}(m)$, (e) the transitions are copied; in addition, $Trans_{\mathcal{H}_{st}}(m_{st}) \triangleq Trans_{\mathcal{H}}(m)$; moreover, an additional transition created from m to m_{st} with the guard $\pi(x) = 0$, and (f) the invariants are copied, with $\pi(x) \geq 0$ added to $Inv_{\mathcal{H}_{st}}(m)$ and $Inv_{\mathcal{H}_{st}}(m_{st}) \triangleq Inv_{\mathcal{H}}(m)$ (m_{st} copied the original invariant of m).

The space-triggered splitting transformation adapts the idea of pseudo-invariants [11] to the hybridization setting. In our setting, a space-trigger function π basically plays a role of a pseudo-invariant.

The resulting automaton overapproximates the continuous reachable state space of the original one which is formally stated in the following lemma.

LEMMA 4.2. *Let $\mathcal{H}$ be a hybrid automaton, $m \in$ Modes be a mode without outgoing transitions, and $\pi : \mathbb{R}^n \to \mathbb{R}$ be a function satisfying the assumptions in Definition 3. Then* $\text{Reach}^c(\mathcal{H}) \subseteq \text{Reach}^c(\theta_{st}(\mathcal{H}))$.

4.3 Domain Contraction

Domain contraction adds auxiliary invariants known as *contraction domains* that should contain the set of reachable states. Given a set D and a mode m of a hybrid automaton $\mathcal{H}$ where $\dot{x} = f_m(x)$, if $\text{Reach}_{\mathcal{H}}(m, X) \subseteq D$ for $X \subseteq Inv(m)$, i.e. the set of reachable states from mode m starting from a subset $X \subseteq Inv(m)$ is contained in D, then D may safely be added as an invariant of m. Of course, the set of reachable states is not available and is what is being computed or approximated, so error modes known as *domain contraction error modes* (DCEMs) are used to maintain soundness if the system leaves the states represented by these auxiliary invariants.

Definition 4. A *domain contraction* is a transformation θ_{dc} of a hybrid automaton $\mathcal{H}$, that takes as input an automaton $\mathcal{H}$, a mode $m \in$ *Modes*, and a set $D \subseteq \mathbb{R}^n$ called the *contraction domain* auxiliary invariant.

The transformed hybrid automaton $\mathcal{H}_{dc} \triangleq \theta_{dc}(\mathcal{H})$ is defined as: (a) $Modes_{\mathcal{H}_{dc}} \triangleq Modes_{\mathcal{H}} \cup \{err\}$, the modes are the copied, with a new *domain contraction error mode* (DCEM) err added, (b) $Var_{\mathcal{H}_{dc}} \triangleq Var_{\mathcal{H}}$, (c) the initial states are copied; additionally, if m is an initial mode, and $Init(m)$ is not entirely contained in D, then add the err DCEM to the initial states; in this way, we capture a degenerate case if the initial set has states outside of the contraction domain. (d) the flows are copied; additionally, $Flow_{\mathcal{H}_{dc}}(err)$ of the form $\dot{x} = 0$ are added, (e) the transitions are copied, with additional transformations of the following form: given an incoming transition $d = (n, g, v, m)$ to mode m in $\mathcal{H}$, (1) augment the guard of the transition d with $x \in D$, and (2) add an additional transition $d' = (n, g \wedge x \in cl(\bar{D}), err)$ with an extra condition $x \in cl(\bar{D})$ on the guard and leading to the DCEM err, where $\bar{D}$ denotes the complement of D and $cl(\cdot)$ stands for topological closure and (3) add an additional transition $d'' = (m, x \in cl(\bar{D}), err)$, (f) the invariants are copied, except for the invariant $Inv_{\mathcal{H}_{dc}}(m) \triangleq Inv_{\mathcal{H}}(m) \cap x \in D$.

A visualization of the domain contraction transformation is given in Figure 2.

The conditions to enter a DCEM together ensure that regardless of the choice of the contraction domain, if the DCEM err is not reached, then the overapproximation of the reachable states is sound. Additionally, the condition that the dynamics are zero in the DCEM err ensures that during

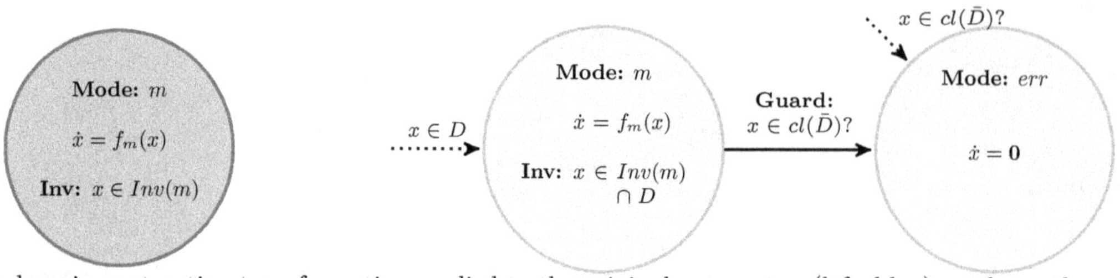

Figure 2: The domain contraction transformation applied to the original automaton (left, blue) produces the output automaton (right, yellow). The contraction domain D is added to the invariant, with DCEM *err* inserted to detect if the reachable set of states leaves D.

a reachability computation, the exploration of the *err* will terminate and be a dead-end in the exploration of the state-space. Note that the notion of topological closure is required to ensure that the intersection of guard and invariant is non-empty.

LEMMA 4.3. *Let $\mathcal{H}$ be a hybrid automaton, $m \in Modes$ be a mode, and $D \subseteq \mathbb{R}^n$ be a contraction domain. Then, if no DCEM is reachable,* $\text{Reach}^c(\mathcal{H}) \subseteq \text{Reach}^c(\theta_{dc}(\mathcal{H}))$.

The contraction domain auxiliary invariants may be arbitrary and may be determined using any method, so they may not actually contain the set of reachable states. To maintain soundness, the DCEMs are added such that if the contraction domains *do not* contain the set of reachable states, transitions to the DCEMs *may* be taken.[4] If no DCEMs are reached, then the domain contraction transformation is sound, but otherwise, if a DCEM is reached, the resultant set of set of reachable states may not be subset of the original automaton's set of reachable states. If it is known that the set of reachable states will not leave the contraction domain by some other analysis, then the DCEMs are not necessary and the invariants may simply be augmented (conjuncted) with the contraction domain. In summary, if the contraction domains do not contain the set of reachable states for a given mode, then a state with a mode equal to the DCEM will be reached.

4.4 Dynamics Abstraction

Continuous dynamics are abstracted by transforming the flows of the original hybrid automaton into flows with increased nondeterminism. In this paper, nonlinear differential inclusions are overapproximated using linear differential inclusions, specifically linear ODEs with an additive set-valued input.

Definition 5. A *dynamics abstraction* is a transformation θ_{da} of a hybrid automaton $\mathcal{H}$, that takes as input an automaton $\mathcal{H}$, a mode $m \in Modes$, and a set-valued function $g : \mathbb{R}^n \to 2^{\mathbb{R}^n}$ called the *abstract dynamics*, where, for the flow $\dot{x} = f_m(x)$ of mode m with invariant $Inv(m)$, $g_m(x)$ is such that $\forall x \in Inv(m)$: $f_m(x) \subseteq g_m(x)$. The hybrid automaton $\mathcal{H}_{da} \triangleq \theta_{da}(\mathcal{H})$ is defined as: (a) $Modes_{\mathcal{H}_{da}} \triangleq Modes_{\mathcal{H}}$, (b) $Var_{\mathcal{H}_{da}} \triangleq Var_{\mathcal{H}}$, (c) the initial states are copied, (d) the flows are copied, except for $Flow_{\mathcal{H}_{da}}(m)$ which is set to $\dot{x} = g(x)$, (e) the transitions are copied, (f) the invariants are copied.

[4]Since the semantics of hybrid automata defined do not support urgency or *must* transitions, we exploit the fact that the reachability computation explores all paths to ensure soundness.

Similarly to other transformations we have considered, we formulate a lemma relating the original and transformed systems.

LEMMA 4.4. *Let $\mathcal{H}$ be a hybrid automaton, $m \in Modes$ be a mode, $g : \mathbb{R}^n \to 2^{\mathbb{R}}$ be a set-valued function satisfying the assumptions in Definition 5. Then it holds that* $\text{Reach}^c(\mathcal{H}) \subseteq \text{Reach}^c(\theta_{da}(\mathcal{H}))$.

5. MIXED-TRIGGERED HYBRIDIZATION

Now we present the central result of the paper, a static mixed-triggered hybridization that combines the four transformations we have introduced.

Definition 6. A static *mixed-triggered hybridization* is a transformation θ_{mt} of a hybrid automaton $\mathcal{H}$ and has the following input:

- a single-mode automaton $\mathcal{H}$,
- a list of splitting elements $E_1 \ldots E_{n-1}$, where each element E_i is either a real number to be used for time-triggered splitting, or a π function to be used for space-triggered splitting (list 1),
- $D_1, \ldots, D_n$ are the contraction domains (sets) for each new location (list 2), and
- $g_1, \ldots, g_n$ are the dynamics abstraction functions for each location (list 3).

The mixed-triggered hybridization transformation consists of the following three steps:

- Apply either time-triggered splitting or space-triggered splitting based on the list $E_1 \ldots E_{n-1}$. We apply each transformation to the most-recently constructed mode, which has no outgoing transitions. The result of this step is a chain of modes.
- For each mode in the chain, apply N domain contractions based on the list $D_1, \ldots, D_n$.
- For each mode in the chain, apply N dynamics abstractions based on the list $g_1, \ldots, g_n$.

If the list of splitting elements (list 1) contains only time-triggered splitting elements (and no space-triggered splitting elements), then it is a *static time-triggered hybridization.*

The following theorem establishes the soundness of the mixed-triggered hybridization.

THEOREM 5.1. *For hybrid automaton $\mathcal{H}$, if no DCEM are reachable, then the continuous reachable state space of the mixed-triggered transformation $\theta_{mt}(\mathcal{H})$ overapproximates the continuous reachable state space of the original automaton:* $\text{Reach}^c(\mathcal{H}) \subseteq \text{Reach}^c(\theta_{mt}(\mathcal{H}))$.

PROOF. The proof follows by a straight-forward application of Lemmas 4.1, 4.2, 4.3, and 4.4. □

We observe that the mixed-triggered hybridization approach contains a number of parameters which must be carefully chosen in order to guarantee a sound abstraction, which is ensured when no error modes (DCEMs) are reachable. If the contraction domains are too small, then the set of reachable states will exit the domain and the DCEM will be reached. If the contraction domains are too large, then the dynamics abstraction will be a large overapproximation, and the set of reachable states will become both large and inaccurate. In modes copied during time-triggered splitting, whenever the time-triggered variable t reaches zero, the set of reachable states at each mode must be contained in the domains (invariants) of both the source and target locations. Space-triggered splitting requires as input the π functions which determine the splitting structure.

In the following, we describe an approach to generate the parameters for proposed hybridization approach in a way that will satisfy the above requirements. Again, the approach is described assuming a single-location hybrid automaton, where the initial set of states is a rectangle, although generalizations are not difficult.

5.1 Parameter Selection Algorithm

In order to construct the three lists to be used as hybridization parameters, an algorithm is proposed which uses numerical simulations. The proposed approach has its own user-provided parameters:

- T is the maximum time,
- $\mathcal{S}$ a simulation strategy, one of {POINT, STAR, STARCORNERS}
- δ_{tt} is the simulation time in a time-triggered transformation step,
- n_{pi} is the number of space-triggered transformation steps to use,
- δ_{pi} is the maximum simulation time when performing a space-triggered transformation step,
- ϵ is a bloating term to account for the difference between the simulated points the set of reachable states.

The algorithm first selects a finite set of simulation points sampled from the initial set of states. If $\mathcal{S}$ is POINT, only the center of the initial rectangle is used. If $\mathcal{S}$ is STAR, the center is used, as well as the center of every face of the rectangle, $1 + 2n$ points, where n is the number of variables. If $\mathcal{S}$ is STARCORNERS, the center is used, as well as the centers of every face, as well as the corners of the initial rectangle, $1 + 2n + 2^n$ points. Selecting more points may permit a smaller ϵ, but since the number of points is exponential, the STARCORNERS strategy may not always be practical. The collection of points are stored in a variable, `sims`.

The algorithm proceeds in iterations, at each iteration doing either a *space-triggered step*, or a *time-triggered step*. The three parameter lists (the output) are initially empty. A current time variable `ct`, initially zero, is maintained which tracks the amount of time elapsed during time-triggered steps (space-triggered steps do not add to `ct`). A second variable `next_st` tracks the time at which to insert the next space-triggered value. If $n_{pi} > 0$, `next_st` is initialized to 0, otherwise it is set to ∞.

At each iteration, if the current time `ct` variable is greater than or equal to next space-triggered time variable `next_st`, a space-triggered step is *attempted* and `next_st` is increased by $\frac{T}{n_{pi}}$. Otherwise, a time-triggered transition is performed and `ct` is increased by δ_{tt}. The process completes when `ct` exceeds the maximum time T.

A **time-triggered step** adds δ_{tt} to output list 1. Then, it computes the bounding box of `sims`, bloats it by ϵ, and stores it in `start`. Each point in `sims` is numerically simulated for δ_{tt} time. The bounding box of `sims` is computed again, bloated by ϵ, and stored in `end`. The bounding box of `start` and `end` is then computed, and put into output list 2 (contraction domains).

A visualization of two consecutive time-triggered steps is shown in Figure 3. Here, $\mathcal{S}$ = POINT, so `sims` is just a single point. Initially, `sims` is α. After δ_{tt} time, the point β is reached; after δ_{tt} further time, the simulation reaches γ. The modification of the output lists after these two steps would be the time-triggered value δ_{tt} twice inserted into list 1, the red rectangle set inserted into list 2, followed by the green rectangle set inserted into list 2.

A **space-triggered step** attempts to use numerical simulations to find a function π for space-triggered splitting, but may, in certain cases, be aborted without modifying the output lists. First, the bounding box of `sims` is computed, bloated by ϵ, and stored in `start`. The center point in `sims`, which we call **p**, is numerically simulated until either, (1) the plane induced by the point lies entirely on one side of `start`, or (2) the space-triggered time limit δ_{pi} is reached. If condition (2) occurs, the space-triggered step returns without modifying the output lists, and reverts the status of `sims`. For condition (1), the plane induced by a point **p** is a hyperplane that both contains **p** and is orthogonal to the gradient at **p**. The function π is created from the equation of the hyperplane, where π is zero along the plane and positive on the side of `start` (in the opposite direction of the gradient at **p**). Forcing transitions along hyperplanes orthogonal to the gradient was previously shown as effective in reducing the size of the currently-tracked set of reachable states in the context of pseudo-invariants [11, 12]. Each of the other points in `sims` are then numerically simulated until either (1) they reach a point along the constructed hyperplane where π evaluates to zero, or (2) they are simulated for the space-triggered time limit δ_{pi}. If for any point condition (2) occurs, again, the space-triggered step aborts without modifying the output lists, and reverts the status of `sims`. If condition (1) occurs for every point in `sims`, the bounding box of all the points in `sims` (which are all along the hyperplane) is taken, bloated by ϵ, and assigned to `end`. The bounding box of `start` and `end` is then computed, and put into output list 2 (contraction domains). The hyperplane function π is put into output list 1.

At the end of the iterative construction, output list 3 is created by performing linearization in each of the contraction domains in list 2, and then solving for the difference between the nonlinear dynamics function and its linearization. This is, in general, a global optimization problem, although guaranteed bounds can be computed using, for example, interval arithmetic. This is also an embarrassingly parallel problem, which can be exploited to speed up this computationally expensive step.

Finally, the last element of list 1 is removed, so that the last mode in the constructed chain will not be split. This process results in three lists, the first of size $N - 1$, and the

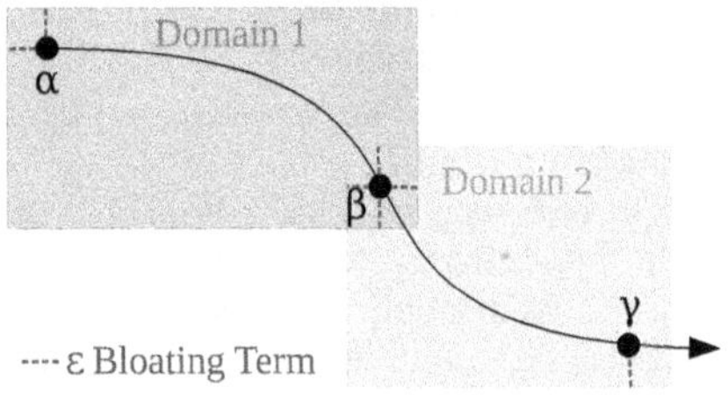

Figure 3: Two time-triggered steps use numerical simulations to create two contraction domains.

other two of size N, as is needed by the proposed mixed-triggered hybridization approach.

5.2 Generalizations

The proposed construction approach is simple in that only a small number of user-parameters are required. However, fine-tuning is possible which can create more precise abstractions, at the cost of requiring more input from the user.

First, the time step δ_{tt} could be changed for each domain. In Figure 3 this would correspond to the case where the difference in simulation times between points α and β is not the same as the difference between β and γ. Next, a per-domain bloating term ϵ is possible. Furthermore, each domain's bloating term could be further parameterized based on the face of the rectangular domain.

The domains need not be rectangles aligned to axes. Domains which are rotated rectangles, aligned with the direction of the flow, could reduce the error in the dynamics abstraction step. As with other hybridization work [21], domains which are triangles (simplices), or rotated variants could also be used. The complication with these approaches is that the global optimization step of domain abstraction, which is necessary for soundness, can become more complicated. For example, the simplex-based approach requires optimizing the Hessian matrix of the dynamics in a simplex domain, which may be difficult depending on the specific location's dynamics.

6. EVALUATION

As stated by Theorem 5.1, in order to soundly reason about the set of reachable states of the original automaton, the output automaton from the mixed-triggered hybridization process must not reach any DCEMs. The main purpose of the evaluation, therefore, is (1) to demonstrate that the hybridization parameters derived from simulations can result in models where DCEMs are not reached during reachability analysis of the output automaton. Additionally, we aim to (2) demonstrate the benefits of occasional space-triggered transitions compared with a pure time-triggered approach. Finally, we (3) demonstrate improved scalability by running our developed static approach on a higher dimensional model, at a granularity that would be impossible for existing static approaches. The evaluation was performed with these three goals in mind.

The proposed hybridization method was implemented in the HYST model translation and transformation tool [12][5]. The developed transformation pass implements the algorithm described in Section 5 leveraging the transformations of Section 4. We target the latest version of the SpaceEx tool, which supports time-triggered transitions using the `map-zero-duration-jump-sets` flag. In order to derive the dynamics abstraction function, we use a global optimization routine from the `scipy.optimize` library. Other options are possible, for example interval arithmetic, interval arithmetic with grid-paving, SMT solvers, or combinations of these methods. Since the optimizations in each domain are run in parallel, more effort can be taken to derive tighter bounds without significant effects on overall runtime. The reported times were measured on a computer with an Intel Core 2 Quad CPU (Q9650) at 3.00 GHz with 4 GB RAM.

[5]SpaceEx model files for the examples evaluated, both before and after hybridization, are available at: http://verivital.com/hyst/pass-hybridization/.

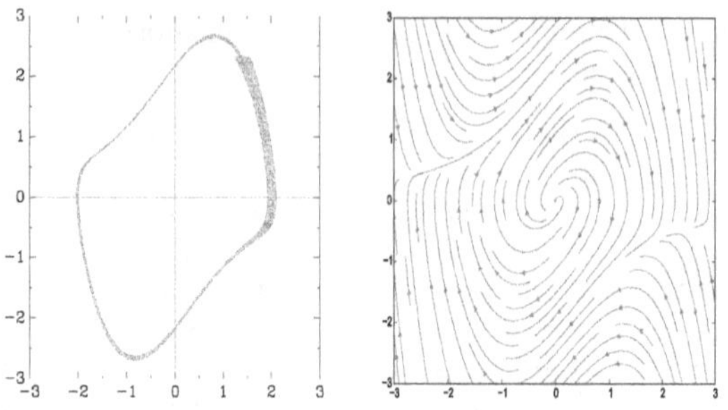

(a) Computed reachability (b) Streamplot

Figure 4: The limit cycle for the Van der Pol system was computed with SpaceEx using our hybridization approach.

6.1 Van der Pol Oscillator

The first set of experiments consider a Van der Pol oscillator, which is a two-dimensional system with the following nonlinear dynamics:

$$\dot{x} = y$$
$$\dot{y} = (1 - x^2) * y - x$$

We use the same initial states as evaluated in other hybridization approaches [1], $(x, y) \in [1.25, 1.55] \times [2.28, 2.32]$. A maximum time of 5.5 was used, which is sufficient to complete one cycle of the oscillator, as in the earlier work.

We used numerical simulations based on the $\mathcal{S}$ = STAR strategy, a time-triggered step of $\delta_{tt} = 0.05$, a bloating term of $\epsilon = 0.05$, a number of space-triggered transformation steps of $n_{pi} = 31$, and a maximum simulation time in a space-triggered transformation step of $\delta_{pi} = 1$. Analyzing the generated model with SpaceEx resulted in no DCEMs being reached, which means that the set of reachable states overapproximates the set of reachable states in the the original automaton. This demonstrates goal (1) of the evaluation. The combined hybridization and computation process took 10.3 seconds. A visualization of the resultant set of reachable states produced by SpaceEx is given in Figure 4a, and can be compared to a streamplot of the dynamics given in Figure 4b.

It is insightful to examine the bounding box of the numerical simulations upon entering each mode, and compare it to the bounding box of the set of reachable states at the same times. In particular, by looking at the maximum width in any dimension of the bounding box of `sims` and comparing it with the maximum width of bounding box of the set of reachable states, we can estimate how close the set of reachable states was to the boundaries of the contraction domains where a DCEM would be reached. A plot of these widths upon entering each mode is shown in Figure 5.

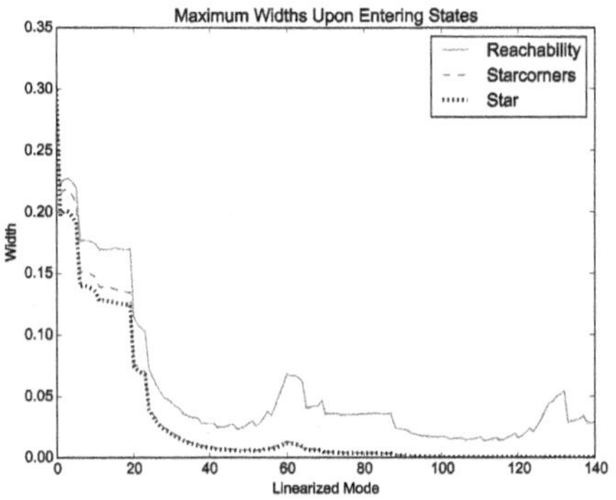

Figure 5: The maximum width of the bounding boxes of the reachable states and simulations upon entering each mode remains within $2 * \epsilon = 0.1$, which is necessary to avoid entering a DCEM.

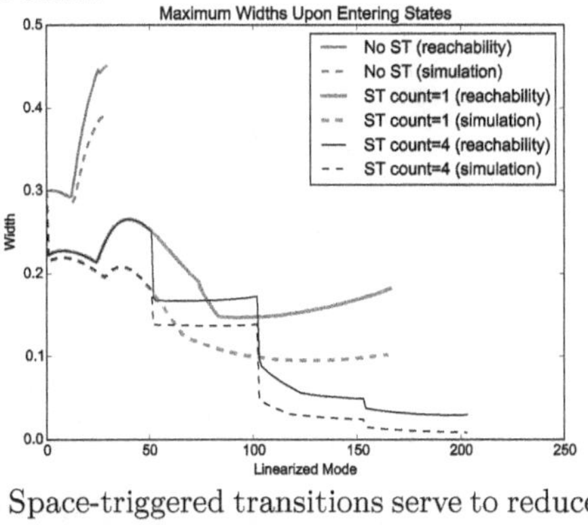

Figure 6: Space-triggered transitions serve to reduce the size of the tracked set of states.

Since we used a bloating term of $\epsilon = 0.05$, it is necessary that maximum width of the simulated states plus $2 * \epsilon = 0.1$ is greater than the maximum width of the set of reachable states at all times, otherwise, an error state will be reached. Additionally, from the plot we can see that the STARCORNERS strategy has slightly better tracking of widths of the set of reachable states near the start of the computation, although it makes less of a difference later on.

In order to show the effect of space-triggered transitions, we consider the same system using a shorter time bound of 2.0, a time step of $\delta_{tt} = 0.01$, and the same value of $\epsilon = 0.05$. We run the system with no space-triggered transitions, a single space-triggered transition at the start, and four space-triggered transitions. The widths of the tracked set of reachable states, and the bounding box of the simulated points is shown in Figure 6. Without space-triggered transitions, the width of the set of reachable states quickly gets larger than the simulated bounding box, and around time 0.29, a DCEM is reached. With a single space-triggered transition at the start, the tracked set of states is smaller, and a DCEM is not reached until around time 1.66. With four space-triggered transitions, the full 2.0 seconds is computed without reaching a DCEM. Furthermore, the decrease in the size of the tracked states is apparent at the space-triggered times 0.0 (mode #0), 0.5 (mode #51), 1.0 (mode #102), and 1.5 (mode #153). This demonstrates the effectiveness of space-triggered transitions in reducing the size of the currently-tracked set of states, goal (2) of the evaluation.

6.2 Nonlinear Water Tank

The next model we consider is a nonlinear tank model [5]. This model is parameterized on the number of tanks, n,

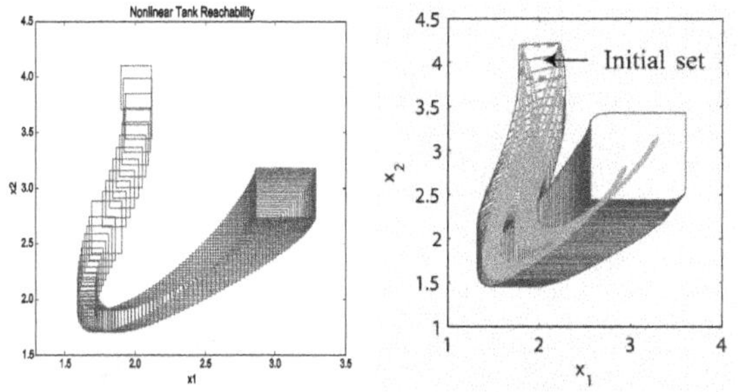

(a) Computed Reachability (b) Result from [5] (includes input disturbances)

Figure 7: A plot of a projection of the computed reachable states for x_1 and x_2 for the 6-D non-linear tank model.

where we use $n = 6$. Each tank i adds a single variable x_i to the model, which represents the height of the water in the tank. The input to the first tank is based on the level of the last tank, x_n. We analyze a deterministic version of the model, with no disturbance input and fixed tank parameters. The dynamics for x_1 and every other $x_{i>1}$ are:

$$\dot{x}_1 = 0.1 + 0.01(4 - x_n) + 0.015\sqrt{2gx_1}$$
$$\dot{x}_i = 0.015\sqrt{2gx_{i-1}} - 0.015\sqrt{2gx_i}$$

We used the same initial set of states as the earlier work, $x_1 \in [1.9, 2.1]$, $x_2 \in [3.9, 4.1]$, $x_3 \in [3.9, 4.1]$, $x_4 \in [1.9, 2.1]$, $x_5 \in [9.9, 10.1]$, and $x_6 \in [3.9, 4.1]$. Using the simulation strategy $\mathcal{S}$ = STARCORNERS, a maximum time of $T = 400$, a step size of $\delta_{tt} = 4$, a bloating term value of $\epsilon = 0.2$, a number of space-triggered transformation steps of $n_{pi} = 10$, and a maximum simulation time in a space-triggered transformation step of $\delta_{pi} = 10$, the hybridized model was created. SpaceEx was used to analyze this model, and indicated that no DCEMs were reached. The whole process took about 430 seconds. Figure 7 shows a projection of the set of reachable states onto x_1 and x_2, as well as a result from the earlier hybridization work.

This demonstrates goal (3) of the evaluation, that static-based hybridization approaches can scale to higher dimensions. Although only a six-dimensional model was considered, this is higher than we could find for any published static hybridization method.

7. CONCLUSION

In this paper, we developed the first static time-triggered and mixed-triggered hybridization approaches. The developed methods use simulations to guide the hybridization process and modify an input model for analysis with off-the-shelf verification tools, unlike dynamic hybridization methods that require tool modification. Additionally, we can perform the expensive dynamics abstraction (linearization) step for each mode in parallel, which can improve the speed of the method. We have shown the effectiveness of the method by hybridizing example nonlinear systems and computing the set of reachable states using SpaceEx, a tool that is only capable of reasoning with linear and affine systems.

Since this is the first paper investigating this category of hybridization techniques, we believe significant further optimization is possible. Extending the approach from single-mode input automata to multiple-mode systems would be a straightforward enhancement, and has been done in other hybridization approaches [1]. Dynamic mixed-triggered approaches, have also yet to be investigated. Parameter selection for the approach can also be challenging and could be further automated, perhaps by using a CEGAR-like approach to detect when DCEMs (error modes) are reached, and performing additional simulations from violation regions. Finally, the simulation-based parameter construction algorithm does not track the set of reachable states well when nondeterminism or disturbances are present, and other approaches from hybrid automaton falsification may work better in these cases.

Acknowledgment

The material presented in this paper is based upon work supported by the Air Force Office of Scientific Research (AFOSR), in part under contract number FA9550-15-1-0258 and the Summer Faculty Fellowship Program (SFFP), by AFRL through contract number FA8750-15-1-0105, and by the National Science Foundation (NSF) under grant numbers CNS 1464311 and CCF 1527398. Furthermore, this research was supported in part by the European Research Council (ERC) under grant 267989 (QUAREM) and by the Austrian Science Fund (FWF) under grant numbers S11402-N23 (RiSE) and Z211-N23 (Wittgenstein Award). Any opinions, findings, and conclusions or recommendations expressed in this publication are those of the authors and do not necessarily reflect the views of AFRL, AFOSR, or NSF.

8. REFERENCES

[1] M. Althoff. Reachability analysis of nonlinear systems using conservative polynomialization and non-convex sets. In *Proceedings of the 16th International Conference on Hybrid Systems: Computation and Control*, HSCC '13, pages 173–182, New York, NY, USA, 2013. ACM.

[2] M. Althoff and J. Dolan. Set-based computation of vehicle behaviors for the online verification of autonomous vehicles. In *Intelligent Transportation Systems (ITSC), 2011 14th International IEEE Conference on*, Oct 2011.

[3] M. Althoff and J. Dolan. Online verification of automated road vehicles using reachability analysis. *Robotics, IEEE Transactions on*, 30(4):903–918, Aug 2014.

[4] M. Althoff and B. H. Krogh. Avoiding geometric intersection operations in reachability analysis of hybrid systems. In *Hybrid Systems: Computation and Control, HSCC'12, Beijing, China, April 17-19, 2012*, pages 45–54, 2012.

[5] M. Althoff, O. Stursberg, and M. Buss. Reachability analysis of nonlinear systems with uncertain parameters using conservative linearization. In *47th IEEE Conference on Decision and Control (CDC)*, pages 4042–4048, Dec. 2008.

[6] M. Althoff, O. Stursberg, and M. Buss. Computing reachable sets of hybrid systems using a combination of zonotopes and polytopes. *Nonlinear Analysis: Hybrid Systems*, 4(2), 2010.

[7] R. Alur, C. Courcoubetis, N. Halbwachs, T. A. Henzinger, P.-H. Ho, X. Nicollin, A. Olivero, J. Sifakis, and S. Yovine. The algorithmic analysis of hybrid systems. *Theoretical Computer Science*, 138(1):3–34, 1995.

[8] E. Asarin, T. Dang, and A. Girard. Reachability analysis of nonlinear systems using conservative approximation. In *Hybrid Systems: Computation and Control*, volume 2623 of *LNCS*, pages 20–35. Springer, 2003.

[9] E. Asarin, T. Dang, and A. Girard. Hybridization methods for the analysis of nonlinear systems. *Acta Informatica*, 43:451–476, 2007.

[10] S.-i. Azuma, J.-i. Imura, and T. Sugie. Lebesgue piecewise affine approximation of nonlinear systems. *Nonlinear Analysis: Hybrid Systems*, 4(1):92–102, 2010.

[11] S. Bak. Reducing the wrapping effect in flowpipe construction using pseudo-invariants. In *4th ACM SIGBED International Workshop on Design, Modeling, and Evaluation of Cyber-Physical Systems (CyPhy 2014)*, pages 40–43, 2014.

[12] S. Bak, S. Bogomolov, and T. T. Johnson. HyST: A source transformation and translation tool for hybrid automaton models. In *Proc. of the 18th Intl. Conf. on Hybrid Systems: Computation and Control (HSCC)*. ACM, 2015.

[13] S. Bogomolov, A. Donzé, G. Frehse, R. Grosu, T. T. Johnson, H. Ladan, A. Podelski, and M. Wehrle. Abstraction-based guided search for hybrid systems. In E. Bartocci and C. R. Ramakrishnan, editors, *International SPIN Symposium on Model Checking of Software 2013*, LNCS. Springer, 2013.

[14] S. Bogomolov, A. Donze, G. Frehse, R. Grosu, T. T. Johnson, H. Ladan, A. Podelski, and M. Wehrle. Guided search for hybrid systems based on coarse-grained space abstractions. *Software Tools for Technology Transfer (STTT)*, Aug. 2015.

[15] S. Bogomolov, G. Frehse, M. Greitschus, R. Grosu, C. S. Pasareanu, A. Podelski, and T. Strump. Assume-guarantee abstraction refinement meets hybrid systems. In *10th International Haifa Verification Conference (HVC 2014)*, volume 8855 of *LNCS*, pages 116–131. Springer, 2014.

[16] S. Bogomolov, C. Schilling, E. Bartocci, G. Batt, H. Kong, and R. Grosu. Abstraction-based parameter synthesis for multiaffine systems. In *11th International Haifa Verification Conference (HVC 2015)*, volume 9434 of *LNCS*, pages 19–35. Springer, 2015.

[17] X. Chen, E. Abraham, and S. Sankaranarayanan. Taylor model flowpipe construction for non-linear hybrid systems. *2013 IEEE 34th Real-Time Systems Symposium*, 0:183–192, 2012.

[18] T. Dang. Approximate reachability computation for polynomial systems. In J. Hespanha and A. Tiwari, editors, *Hybrid Systems: Computation and Control*, Lecture Notes in Computer Science. Springer Berlin Heidelberg, 2006.

[19] T. Dang, A. Donze, and O. Maler. Verification of analog and mixed-signal circuits using hybrid system techniques. In A. Hu and A. Martin, editors, *Formal Methods in Computer-Aided Design*, volume 3312 of *LNCS*, pages 21–36. Springer, 2004.

[20] T. Dang, C. Le Guernic, and O. Maler. Computing reachable states for nonlinear biological models. In *Computational Methods in Systems Biology*, pages 126–141. Springer, 2009.

[21] T. Dang, O. Maler, and R. Testylier. Accurate hybridization of nonlinear systems. In *Hybrid Systems: Computation and Control (HSCC)*, pages 11–20, New York, NY, 2010. ACM.

[22] P. Duggirala, S. Mitra, M. Viswanathan, and M. Potok. C2e2: A verification tool for stateflow models. In C. Baier and C. Tinelli, editors, *Tools and Algorithms for the Construction and Analysis of Systems*, LNCS, pages 68–82. Springer, 2015.

[23] G. Frehse, R. Kateja, and C. Le Guernic. Flowpipe approximation and clustering in space-time. In *Hybrid Systems: Computation and Control (HSCC'13)*, pages 203–212. ACM, 2013.

[24] G. Frehse, C. Le Guernic, A. Donzé, S. Cotton, R. Ray, O. Lebeltel, R. Ripado, A. Girard, T. Dang, and O. Maler. SpaceEx: Scalable verification of hybrid systems. In *Computer Aided Verification (CAV)*, LNCS. Springer, 2011.

[25] A. Girard. Reachability of uncertain linear systems using zonotopes. In M. Morari and L. Thiele, editors, *Hybrid Systems: Computation and Control*, LNCS. Springer, 2005.

[26] A. Girard and C. Le Guernic. Zonotope/hyperplane intersection for hybrid systems reachability analysis. In M. Egerstedt and B. Mishra, editors, *Hybrid Systems: Computation and Control*, volume 4981 of *LNCS*, pages 215–228. Springer, 2008.

[27] A. Girard, C. Le Guernic, et al. Efficient reachability analysis for linear systems using support functions. In *Proc. of the 17th IFAC World Congress*, pages 8966–8971, 2008.

[28] Z. Han and B. Krogh. Reachability analysis of nonlinear systems using trajectory piecewise linearized models. In *American Control Conference, 2006*, pages 6 pp.–, June 2006.

[29] T. Henzinger, P.-H. Ho, H. Wong-Toi, et al. Algorithmic analysis of nonlinear hybrid systems. *IEEE Transactions on Automatic Control*, 43(4):540–554, 1998.

[30] L. Jaulin, M. Kieffer, and O. Didrit. *Applied interval analysis : with examples in parameter and state estimation, robust control and robotics*. Springer, London, 2001.

[31] T. T. Johnson, J. Green, S. Mitra, R. Dudley, and R. S. Erwin. Satellite rendezvous and conjunction avoidance: Case studies in verification of nonlinear hybrid systems. In D. Giannakopoulou and D. Méry, editors, *Proceedings of the 18th International Conference on Formal Methods (FM 2012)*, pages 252–266. Springer, Paris, France, Aug. 2012.

[32] A. Puri and P. Varaiya. Verification of hybrid systems using abstractions. In *Hybrid Systems II*, LNCS, pages 359–369. Springer, 1994.

Adaptive Decentralized MAC for Event-Triggered Networked Control Systems

Mikhail Vilgelm
Chair of Communication Networks
Technical University of Munich
Munich, Germany
mikhail.vilgelm@tum.de

Mohammad H. Mamduhi
Chair of Information-oriented Control
Technical University of Munich
Munich, Germany
mh.mamduhi@tum.de

Wolfgang Kellerer
Chair of Communication Networks
Technical University of Munich
Munich, Germany
wolfgang.kellerer@tum.de

Sandra Hirche
Chair of Information-oriented Control
Technical University of Munich
Munich, Germany
hirche@tum.de

ABSTRACT

Control over shared communication networks is a key challenge in design and analysis of cyber-physical systems. The quality of control in such systems might be degraded due to the congestion while accessing the scarce communication resources. In this paper, we consider a multiple-loop networked control system (NCS), where all control loops share a communication network. Medium Access Control (MAC) is performed in contention-based fashion using a multi-channel slotted ALOHA protocol, where each control loop decides locally whether to attempt a transmission based on some error thresholds. We further introduce a local event-based resource-aware scheduling design with an adaptive choice of the error thresholds for a transmission. This leads to a hybrid channel access mechanism where the control loops are deterministically categorized into two sets of eligible and ineligible sub-systems for transmission in an event-based fashion, before a random process to select the available channels. In addition, employing the introduced policy, we show the stability of the resulting NCS in terms of Lyapunov stability in probability. We illustrate numerically the efficiency of our proposed approach in terms of reducing the average networked-induced error variance, and show the superiority of the adaptive event-based scheduler compared to the scheduling design with non-adaptive thresholds.

Keywords

Networked Control Systems; Medium Access Control; Slotted ALOHA; Scheduler Design;

HSCC'16, April 12-14, 2016, Vienna, Austria

© 2016 ACM. ISBN 978-1-4503-3955-1/16/04…$15.00

DOI: http://dx.doi.org/10.1145/2883817.2883829

1. INTRODUCTION

Traditional digital control systems are characterized by collocated sensors, actuators and controllers as well as by time-triggered control schemes with periodic sampling. With the advent of new technologies, the parts of control systems are becoming spatially distributed and their interaction is being increasingly supported by shared communication networks, which usually impose energy and capacity limitations [22]. In the context of wireless communication, distributed control systems form a specific subset of applications known as Machine-to-Machine (M2M) communication [31]. Smart grids or industrial automation are common examples of M2M use cases.

Control over shared communication resources imposes various challenges, such as congestion due to bandwidth limitation, collisions, and time delays, that compromise the control performance and can even lead to instability. In order to utilize the limited communication and energy resources efficiently, event-triggered control and scheduling schemes have been proposed recently [6,10,19,20,27,28]. These aforecited works suggest that it is usually more beneficial to transmit the sampled data upon the occurrence of certain events rather than at periodic time instants. This is even more so in case of large-scale networked control systems due to the sheer amount of data that needs to be exchanged.

In the event-based paradigm, events are typically triggered by either deterministic [23,30], or stochastic policies [7, 18, 24, 26]. Deterministic event-based policies award the channel to the entity with the highest priority. Try-Once-Discard (TOD) is a basic event-based deterministic protocol that awards the medium access to the system with the largest estimation error and consequently discards the other transmission requests [30]. However, TOD is prone to system noise and can cope with collisions only with a given pre-defined priority order, and hence is not convenient for practical realizations [5]. Therefore, an efficient event-based policy for dealing with collisions is still an open research topic.

Due to the non-deterministic transmission patterns of event-based control systems, and typically long idle periods between consecutive transmissions, it is not possible to reserve radio resources for event-based control applications. Thus, it makes them prone to the notorious problem of existing wireless standards, namely, congestion during the connection establishment phase [8,9,14].

The problem has been extensively studied in the context of Long Term Evolution (LTE) Random Access (RA) procedure, where it is commonly modeled as a multi-channel slotted ALOHA system [29]. Many results exist which propose improvements for the LTE RA procedure [1,12,16,17] for general class of M2M devices, however, significantly less contributions can be found in coupling the control system properties and efficient network resource allocation. In [2,3] authors compare the event-based and periodic control via single channel ALOHA for a network of homogeneous integrator sub-systems. Additionally, Cervin *et. al.* [4] compare different MAC strategies for event-based NCS, however, their assumption about the collision resolution time is basically diminishing the effect of collisions, which is non-negligible for most of the scenarios. In [21] the authors investigate an adaptive price-based scheduling mechanism for multiple loop NCSs with shared communication resource. In this approach distributed optimization method and adaptive Markov decision process are employed to develop distributed self-regulating event-triggers which are capable of adapting their transmission request rate in order to fulfill a global resource constraint.

In this paper, we analyze the behavior of the multi-channel slotted ALOHA medium access, considering an event-based networked control system consisting of multiple linear time-invariant (LTI) control sub-systems as the communication endpoints. First, we describe our local threshold-based scheduler which determines whether a sub-system is eligible for a transmission attempt. Stability of the resulting NCS over the multi-channel slotted ALOHA is then discussed in terms of Lyapunov stability in probability (LSP). We evaluate the performance of the event-based scheduler, and further propose an improvement to it, an adaptive scheduler. In the new scheduler design, network and control systems are coupled via the knowledge of the network state: each local scheduler adapts its threshold based on the available network resources. Numerically, we demonstrate that an adaptive choice of the transmission threshold is beneficiary compared to the non-adaptive static design.

The remainder of this paper is structured as follows. We start by introducing the problem statement and preliminaries in Section 2. Stochastic stability of the resulting NCS design in discussed in Section 3. Section 4 is dedicated to the numerical performance evaluation and divided into two parts: Subsection 4.1 illustrates the performance of the static scheduler, and in Subsection 4.2 we demonstrate the benefits of using an adaptive scheduler.

2. PROBLEM STATEMENT

In this paper, we consider an NCS consisting of N physically isolated LTI control sub-systems which are coupled through a shared communication network. A control sub-system i is composed of a linear plant $\mathcal{P}_i$ and a controller $\mathcal{C}_i$. The feedback loop from the plant to the controller is closed via the shared communication network and the decision of whether to attempt the access to the network is taken by the local scheduler $\mathcal{S}_i$. The plant process is subject to system noise and can be described with the following stochastic difference equation:

$$x^i_{k+1} = A_i x^i_k + B_i u^i_k + w^i_k, \tag{1}$$

where $x^i_k \in \mathbb{R}^{n_i}$ denotes the ith system state at time-step k, $u^i_k \in \mathbb{R}^{d_i}$ describes the control input at time-step k. The constant matrices $A_i \in \mathbb{R}^{n_i \times n_i}$, $B_i \in \mathbb{R}^{n_i \times d_i}$ describe system and input matrices, respectively. The noise sequence w^i_k is considered to be an independent and identically distributed (i.i.d) vector distributed according to a zero-mean Gaussian distribution with the covariance matrix W_i. Independent of the noise variables w^i_k, the initial state x^i_0 can be considered to be a random variable of any arbitrary symmetric distribution with bounded second moment. At each time-step k, the binary variable $\delta^i_k \in \{0,1\}$ represents the decision of the local scheduler $\mathcal{S}_i$ for sub-system i as follows:

$$\delta^i_k = \begin{cases} 1, & x^i_k \text{ sent through the channel} \\ 0, & x^i_k \text{ blocked.} \end{cases}$$

Assume that the communication network has M available transmission channels at each time-step (see Fig. 2). According to the multi-channel slotted ALOHA protocol, each sub-system which is eligible for transmission, selects one of the M transmission channels randomly to send its own data packet. We denote number of available channels M as a **network state**.

A collision would occur if two or more sub-systems select the same channel at a certain sample time k. Consequently, none of those sub-systems transmit at k and have to try for transmission at the next time-step $k+1$. (6) A successful transmission (i.e., the scheduled packet is not collided) is confirmed by the binary variable $\gamma^i_k \in \{0,1\}$ as follows:

$$\gamma^i_k = \begin{cases} 1, & x^i_k \text{ successfully received} \\ 0, & x^i_k \text{ collided.} \end{cases}$$

Accordingly, the received signal z^i_k at the controller side of the sub-system i is given as a function of scheduling variable δ^i_k and collision indicator γ^i_k as follows:

$$z^i_k = \begin{cases} x^i_k, & \theta^i_k = 1 \\ \varnothing, & \text{otherwise,} \end{cases}$$

where, $\theta^i_k = \delta^i_k \gamma^i_k$. Each sub-system is assumed to be controlled by a state-feedback controller which is updated at every time-step k by either the true state values x^i_k (in case sub-system i successfully transmits, i.e. $\delta^i_k = 1$ and $\gamma^i_k = 1$)

Table 1: Summary of most-used notations

x^i_k	system state of a sub-system i at time-step k
e^i_k	error state of a sub-system i at time-step k
w^i_k	system noise of a sub-system i at time-step k
A_i	system matrix of sub-system i
δ^i_k	scheduling variable
θ^i_k	transmission indicator
$\lVert\cdot\rVert$	Euclidean norm
$\mathsf{E}[\cdot\vert\cdot]$	conditional expectation operator
Λ_i	error threshold for sub-system i
Λ'	global error threshold for all sub-systems
N	total number of control sub-systems
M	network state: number of available channels per slot

or by the state estimates $\mathsf{E}\left[x_k^i\right]$ (in case sub-system i is blocked by the scheduler, i.e. $\delta_k^i = 0$ or a collision occurs, i.e. $\gamma_k^i = 0$). It is assumed that the sensor and controller of the ith sub-system merely have local knowledge, i.e., of A_i, B_i, W_i and the distribution of x_0^i. Therefore, we assume that the control law ϑ^i is described by measurable and causal mapping of the past observations:

$$u_k^i = \vartheta_k^i(Z_k^i) = -L_i\mathsf{E}\left[x_k^i|Z_k^i\right], \quad (2)$$

where $Z_k^i = \{z_0^i, \ldots, z_k^i\}$ is the ith controller observation history, and L_i is an arbitrary stabilizing feedback gain. In case a transmission fails, either due to a blocking by the scheduler (i.e. $\delta_k^i = 0$) or collision (i.e. $\gamma_k^i = 0$), the estimate of system state x_k^i is computed by a model-based estimator as follows:

$$\mathsf{E}\left[x_k^i|Z_k^i\right] = (A_i - B_iL_i)\mathsf{E}\left[x_{k-1}^i|Z_{k-1}^i\right], \quad (3)$$

with the initial condition $\mathsf{E}\left[x_0^i|Z_0^i\right] = 0$. The estimate (3) is well-behaved only if a stabilizing gain L_i exists to ensure that the closed-loop matrix $(A_i - B_iL_i)$ is Hurwitz. Accordingly, the network-induced estimation error $e_k^i \in \mathbb{R}^{n_i}$ is defined as the difference between the actual and estimated values of the system state, i.e.

$$e_k^i := x_k^i - \mathsf{E}\left[x_k^i|Z_k^i\right]. \quad (4)$$

Having the definition (4) and employing (1)-(3), we can derive the dynamics of the networked-induced error state e_k^i. Assume that a sub-system i successfully transmits at time-step k, i.e. $\theta_k^i = 1$. Therefore, $z_k^i = x_k^i$ and subsequently $u_k^i = -L_ix_k^i$. Thus, the error at the next time-step can be calculated as:

$$\begin{aligned}
e_{k+1}^i &= x_{k+1}^i - \mathsf{E}\left[x_{k+1}^i|Z_{k+1}^i\right] \\
&= A_ix_k^i - B_iL_ix_k^i + w_k^i - \mathsf{E}\left[A_ix_k^i - B_iL_ix_k^i + w_k^i|x_k^i\right] \\
&= (A_i - B_iL_i)x_k^i + w_k^i - (A_i - B_iL_i)x_k^i \\
&= w_k^i.
\end{aligned}$$

On the other hand, if the sub-system i does not successfully transmit at time-step k, i.e. $\theta_k^i = 0$, then $z_k^i = \varnothing$ and the controller will be updated by the estimated value of x_k^i, i.e. $u_k^i = -L_i\mathsf{E}\left[x_k^i|Z_k^i\right]$. In this case, we have

$$\begin{aligned}
e_{k+1}^i &= A_ix_k^i - B_iL_i\mathsf{E}\left[x_k^i|Z_k^i\right] + w_k^i \\
&\quad - \mathsf{E}\left[A_ix_k^i - B_iL_i\mathsf{E}\left[x_k^i|Z_k^i\right] + w_k^i|Z_k^i\right] \\
&= A_ix_k^i - B_iL_i\mathsf{E}\left[x_k^i|Z_k^i\right] + w_k^i - A_i\mathsf{E}\left[x_k^i|Z_k^i\right] + B_iL_i\mathsf{E}\left[x_k^i|Z_k^i\right] \\
&= A_i(x_k^i - \mathsf{E}\left[x_k^i|Z_k^i\right]) + w_k^i \\
&= A_ie_k^i + w_k^i.
\end{aligned}$$

Rewriting the error dynamics for the general θ_k^i, we obtain the following form:

$$e_{k+1}^i = (1 - \theta_k^i)A_ie_k^i + w_k^i. \quad (5)$$

The decision whether to attempt a transmission or not is taken by the scheduler $\mathcal{S}_i$ described in the next Subsec. 2.1.

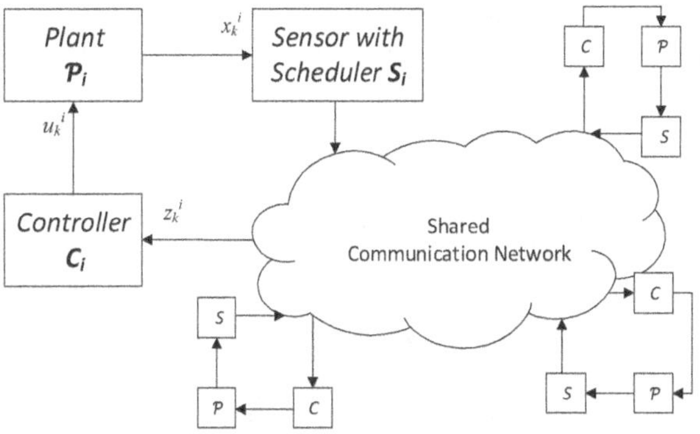

Figure 1: A multi-loop NCS with a shared communication channel and local scheduling mechanism.

2.1 Local threshold-based scheduler

The local scheduler situated at each local control loop decides to access the medium at every time-step k only if the following threshold inequality holds:

$$\|e_k^i\| > \Lambda_i, \quad (6)$$

where, Λ_i is the local error threshold for sub-system i. Therefore, if (6) is satisfied at some time-step k, then the corresponding sub-system is eligible for transmission at the next time-step $k+1$. Otherwise, it is deterministically excluded from the channel access, i.e.

$$\mathsf{P}[\delta_{k+1}^i = 1|e_k^i] = \begin{cases} 0, & \text{if } \|e_k^i\| \leq \Lambda_i \\ 1, & \text{otherwise.} \end{cases} \quad (7)$$

Note that the deployed scheduling policy (7) is not explicitly dependent on the whether the transmission has been successful or it has collided, therefore, channel sensing of acknowledgements are not necessary for the policy's realization.

The communication network model is restricted to the Media Access Layer (MAC) and is represented by a multi-channel slotted ALOHA protocol [25], see Fig. 2. As the most common practical example, we can refer to LTE-based system and its Random Access Channel [9], while mappings to different single-hop wireless or even bus systems can also be imagined. In every time slot, there are several non-overlapping transmission channels available. We denote the number of available channels as M. As we investigate the multi-channel model in this paper, we assume $M \geq 2$.

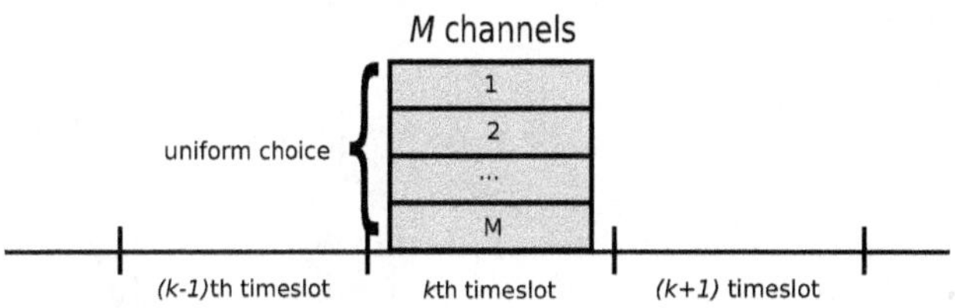

Figure 2: Communication system model: multi-channel slotted ALOHA. One time slot is assumed equal to a control period of any sub-system. A channel can represent a frequency, code [29] or time domain transmission opportunity, depending on the communication technology in use.

The information about the available number of channels is assumed to be known for all sub-systems in the beginning of each time slot.

For the sake of simplicity, we assume that the communication time slots are equal in duration to the control sampling periods, and that all sub-systems' control periods are synchronized. Thus, in every control period we have M available transmission channels, meaning:

$$\sum_{i=1}^{N} \theta_k^i \leq M \tag{8}$$

According to the slotted ALOHA protocol, if a packet is scheduled for transmission, it will be sent through one of M channels, randomly chosen. Thus, if we denote a set of sub-systems which are eligible for transmission at time-step k as $\mathcal{G}_k$, then the probability of successful transmission for a given eligible sub-system in the k timestep is calculated as:

$$\mathsf{P}[\gamma_{k+1}^i = 1 \| \|e_k^i\| > \Lambda_i] = \left(\frac{M-1}{M}\right)^{g_k}, \tag{9}$$

where g_k is the cardinality of the set $\mathcal{G}_k$.

The transmission threshold Λ_i is influencing directly both the error of the sub-system, and the arrival rate of the requests for network access. Since the network is modeled by slotted ALOHA mechanism, too high arrival rate of requests will result in a high collision rate and consequently degrades the performance of the overall networked system, significantly. Following this observation, our hypothesis is that adapting Λ_i to network state, can be beneficial for the control performance.

3. STABILITY ANALYSIS

In this section, we study stability of multiple-loop NCSs with shared multi-channel communication networks subject to the constraint (8), and the introduced threshold-based decentralized scheduling policy (7). We show stochastic stability of the overall networked system by the notion of Lyapunov stability in probability (LSP). Before introducing the notion of LSP, we will describe the overall network state at some time-step k by the aggregation of the system states x_k^i from all sub-systems $i \in \{1, \ldots, N\}$ and error states e_k^i from all sub-systems $i \in \{1, \ldots, N\}$, i.e. $[x_k^\mathsf{T}, e_k^\mathsf{T}]^\mathsf{T}$, where $x_k = \left[x_k^{1^\mathsf{T}}, \ldots, x_k^{N^\mathsf{T}}\right]^\mathsf{T}$ and $e_k = \left[e_k^{1^\mathsf{T}}, \ldots, e_k^{N^\mathsf{T}}\right]^\mathsf{T}$. From (1)-(3), together with the definition of the estimation error e_k^i in (4), it is straightforward to see that the individual aggregate networked state $\left[x_k^{i^\mathsf{T}}, e_k^{i^\mathsf{T}}\right]^\mathsf{T}$ within each sub-system i has triangular dynamics as follows:

$$\begin{bmatrix} x_{k+1}^i \\ e_{k+1}^i \end{bmatrix} = \begin{bmatrix} A_i - B_i L_i & (1-\theta_k^i) B_i L_i \\ 0 & (1-\theta_k^i) A_i \end{bmatrix} \begin{bmatrix} x_k^i \\ e_k^i \end{bmatrix} + \begin{bmatrix} w_k^i \\ w_k^i \end{bmatrix}. \tag{10}$$

This implies that the evolution of the error state e_k^i is in fact independent of the system state x_k^i. We employ an emulation-based control design to stabilize the control subsystems in case their corresponding loops are closed, i.e. the controllers are updated with their own true state values. This incurs that, assuming each pair (A_i, B_i) is stabilizable, there exists stabilizing feedback gain L_i such that the closed-loop matrix $(A_i - B_i L_i)$ is Hurwitz, and consequently the system state x_k^i is asymptotically stable. It should however be noted that existence of stabilizing control laws u_k^i's does not guarantee the stability of overall networked system with the introduced networked state $\left[x_k^{i^\mathsf{T}}, e_k^{i^\mathsf{T}}\right]^\mathsf{T}$, since the evolution of the error state is independent of the control laws. This statement is clear from (10), which illustrates that if a sub-system does not transmit at a certain time-step, stabilizing gain L_i guarantees the stability only if error state e_k^i is stable. Now we are ready to introduce the concept of stability, i.e. LSP, considered in this paper.

Definition 1. *(Lyapunov Stability in Probability (LSP), [13]) A linear system with state vector x_k possesses LSP if given $\varepsilon, \varepsilon' > 0$, exists $\rho(\varepsilon, \varepsilon') > 0$ such that $|x_0| < \rho$ implies*

$$\lim_{k\to\infty} \sup \mathsf{P}\left[x_k^T x_k \geq \varepsilon'\right] \leq \varepsilon. \tag{11}$$

The following lemma shows the LSP is achievable by solely considering the error state e_k in our NCS of interest.

Lemma 1. *For an NCS described by (1)-(5), the condition in (11) is equivalent to*

$$\lim_{k\to\infty} \sup \mathsf{P}\left[e_k^T e_k \geq \xi'\right] \leq \xi, \tag{12}$$

where $\xi' > 0$ and the constant ξ fulfills $0 \leq \xi \leq \varepsilon$.

Proof. As already stated, the system state x_k^i for each control loop i evolves as

$$x_{k+1}^i = (A_i - B_i L_i) x_k^i + (1-\theta_k^i) B_i L_i e_k^i + w_k^i. \tag{13}$$

As already discussed, the evolution of the error e_k^i is independent of the system state x_k^i within each individual control loop. Furthermore, by assuming the emulative control law (2), the closed-loop matrix $(A_i - B_i L_i)$ is ensured to be Hurwitz. Together with the assumption that x_0^i has a symmetric bounded variance distribution, it follows that the system state x_k^i is converging with any stabilizing feedback gain L_i. In addition, the disturbance process w_k^i is i.i.d. according to $\mathcal{N}(0, I)$, and is bounded in probability. Thus, showing $\lim_{k\to\infty} \sup \mathsf{P}\left[e_k^{i^\mathsf{T}} e_k^i \geq \xi_i'\right] \leq \xi_i$ ensures existence of constants ε_i and $\varepsilon_i' > 0$ such that $\lim_{k\to\infty} \sup \mathsf{P}\left[x_k^{i^\mathsf{T}} x_k^i \geq \varepsilon_i'\right] \leq \varepsilon_i$, where $\xi_i \leq \varepsilon_i$. As individual loops operate independently, we take the aggregate NCS state (x_k, e_k). Then, the existence of ξ and $\xi' > 0$ such that $\lim_{k\to\infty} \sup \mathsf{P}\left[e_k^T e_k \geq \xi'\right] \leq \xi$, implies existence of ε and $\varepsilon' > 0$ such that $\lim_{k\to\infty} \sup \mathsf{P}\left[x_k^T x_k \geq \varepsilon'\right] \leq \varepsilon$ for $\xi \leq \varepsilon$, and the proof readily follows. □

This lemma enables us to study stability of the overall networked system only by looking at the error state e_k, considering that stabilizing feedback gains L_i are designed.

As expected values are more straightforward in pursuing further analysis than probabilities, we employ the following inequality for $\xi' > 0$ as

$$\mathsf{P}\left[e_k^\mathsf{T} e_k \geq \xi'\right] \leq \frac{\mathsf{E}\left[e_k^\mathsf{T} e_k\right]}{\xi'}. \tag{14}$$

The above expression is derived using *Markov's inequality*. This confirms that showing the error is uniformly bounded in expectation ensures finding appropriate ξ and $\xi' > 0$ such that (12) is satisfied for arbitrary $\rho(\xi', \xi)$. Therefore, we focus on deriving an upper bound for the expectation of quadratic error norm, i.e.

$$\mathsf{E}\left[e_k^\mathsf{T} e_k\right] = \sum_{i=1}^{N} \mathsf{E}\left[e_k^{i^\mathsf{T}} e_k^i\right] = \sum_{i=1}^{N} \mathsf{E}\left[\|e_k^i\|^2\right] \tag{15}$$

This modifies the condition (12) as follows:

$$\lim_{k\to\infty} \sup \mathsf{P}\left[e_k^\mathsf{T} e_k \geq \bar{\xi}'\right] \leq \bar{\xi}. \tag{16}$$

Due to the nature of the multi-channel communication network with capacity constraint (8), and threshold-based scheduler policy (7), the boundedness of (15) cannot always be shown over one time-step transition, i.e. $k \to k+1$. This observation is discussed in the following illustrative example:

Illustrative example Consider an NCS consisting of three identical scalar unstable sub-systems with systems matrices $A_1 = A_2 = A_3 = A > 1$, competing for two available transmission channels at each time slot over a shared multi-channel communication network. For simplicity, assume $\Lambda_1 = \Lambda_2 = \Lambda_3 = \bar{\Lambda}$, and $e_k^1 = e_k^2 = e_k^3 = \bar{e}_k$. In addition, consider that the condition (6) is fulfilled, i.e. all three sub-systems are eligible for channel access at time-step $k+1$. Each sub-system selects each of the two available transmission channels by probability of $\frac{1}{2}$. Two scenarios are viable: 1) one successful transmission occurs from one of the sub-systems, and the other two will inevitably collide. It is straightforward to calculate that this scenario happens with the probability of $\frac{3}{4}$; 2) all three sub-systems choose the same transmission channel and consequently all three will collide, which means no successful transmission is occurred, where this scenario occurs with probability of $\frac{1}{4}$. As the sub-systems are identical, and for the sake of illustrative purposes, assume a realization for the first scenario that e.g. sub-system 1 transmits and sub-systems 2 and 3 are collided. Employing (5), we calculate the error expectation in (15) for one step transition, as follows:

$$\begin{aligned}
&\sum\nolimits_{i=1}^{3} \mathsf{E}\left[\|e_{k+1}^i\|^2 | e_k\right] = \sum\nolimits_{i=1}^{3} \mathsf{E}\left[\|\left(1-\theta_k^i\right) A e_k^i + w_k^i\|^2\right] \\
&= \frac{1}{4}\sum\nolimits_{i=1}^{3} \mathsf{E}[\|A\bar{e}_k + w_k^i | \bar{e}_k\|^2] \\
&+ \frac{3}{4}\left(\mathsf{E}[\|A\bar{e}_k + w_k^2|\bar{e}_k\|^2] + \mathsf{E}[\|A\bar{e}_k + w_k^3|\bar{e}_k\|^2] + \mathsf{E}[\|w_k^1\|^2]\right) \\
&= \frac{1}{4}\sum\nolimits_{i=1}^{3} \|A\bar{e}_k\|^2 + \mathsf{E}[\|w_k^i\|^2] \\
&+ \frac{3}{4}\left(2\|A\bar{e}_k\|^2 + \sum\nolimits_{i=1}^{3} \mathsf{E}[\|w_k^i\|^2]\right) \\
&= \frac{1}{4}\left(3\|A\bar{e}_k\|^2 + 3\right) + \frac{3}{4}\left(2\|A\bar{e}_k\|^2 + 3\right) \\
&= 3 + 2.25\|A\bar{e}_k\|^2,
\end{aligned}$$

which is not uniformly bounded for arbitrary $\bar{e}_k$ and system matrix A. Intuitively, between two consecutive transmissions of each sub-system, they operate in open loop. Hence, in general, the respective local errors are expected to grow. Thus to obtain boundedness of error state, we need to look at an interval of time-steps rather than only one transition step such that, given the channel capacity constraint (8), all sub-systems have non-zero chances of transmission. Therefore, one can infer that an interval of length $\left\lfloor \frac{N}{M-1} \right\rfloor$ provides enough transmission possibilities for an NCS of N sub-systems and M available transmission channels per time-step. It should be reminded that the linearity of our sub-systems guarantees the boundedness over any finite longer horizons.

For stability analysis, we assume the worst case scenario by considering the minimum number of available transmission channels, i.e. only two transmission channels at each time-step. This yields that the minimum length of the interval over which LSP is investigated equals N.

THEOREM 1. *Consider an NCS with N heterogeneous LTI control sub-systems, with the plants given by (1), sharing a multi-channel communication network with two available transmission channels per time-step. Given the control law (2) and threshold policy (7), the NCS of interest is Lyapunov stable in probability if the MAC employs slotted ALOHA protocol.*

PROOF. See Appendix A. □

REMARK 1. *The notion of stability considered in this paper, i.e., LSP, determines the probability that the overall NCS state remain bounded. This probability is not one due to the fact that there exists a non-zero probability, though might be very close-to-zero, such that at all time-steps the NCS is operating all the transmissions fail due to successive collisions. This is the structural property of the decentralized MAC we are considering in this paper and in case such a scenario occurs, it means all control loops, either stable or unstable, operate in open-loop which consequently lead to instability of the overall NCS due to the presence of unstable plants.*

4. PERFORMANCE EVALUATION

In this section, we evaluate the performance of a threshold-based scheduler over multi-channel slotted aloha. Both communication and control-related aspects are investigated.

For the simulations, we consider an evaluation setup as follows. An NCS in consideration is composed of two heterogeneous classes of scalar control loops: class one including multiple homogeneous stable plants with the system matrix $A_1 = 0.75$ and class two consisting of unstable plants with $A_2 = 1.25$. The plants within each group are homogeneous, and all sub-systems are influenced by the i.i.d. noise processes randomly chosen from the standard normal distribution, i.e. $w_k^i \sim \mathcal{N}(0,1)$ for all time-steps k. The input matrices for both groups are $B_1 = B_2 = 1$. For the plants' stabilization, deadbeat control law $L_i = A_i$ is employed. We consider the total amount of sub-systems to be N, while each group of control loops has $N/2$ sub-systems. The number of transmission channels in each slot, unless stated otherwise, is considered to be $M = 10$. It is worth mentioning that not only stability or instability of a plant determines the urge of a transmission, but also system noise influences the threshold-based policy. Therefore, it is not guaranteed that if a plant is stable, then it is asymptotically stable even if no transmission is associated with that sub-system. Due to presence of noise, a sub-system with stable plant might become in more urgent situation for transmission than a sub-system with unstable plant.

For a control performance evaluation, we study the average error variance among N sub-systems:

$$\Sigma = \frac{1}{N}\sum_{i=1}^{N} \mathsf{var}[e_k^i] \tag{17}$$

From the communication point of view, we use two metrics. First one is average channel utilization, commonly known as throughput T, defined as:

$$T = \frac{\mathsf{E}[n_p^s]}{M}, \tag{18}$$

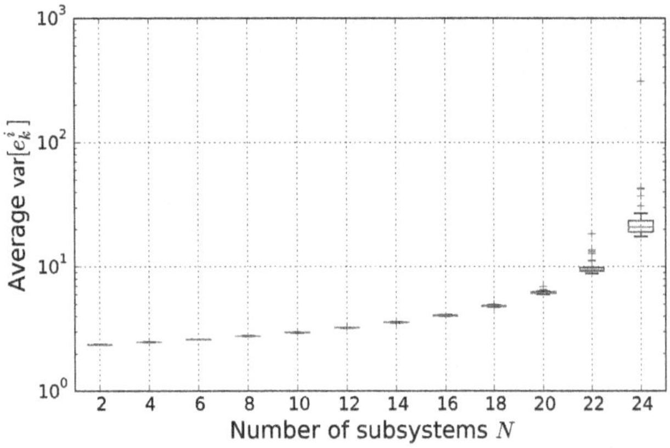

Figure 3: Average error variance var$[e_k^i]$ vs. number of sub-systems N (30 runs): $M = 10$, $\Lambda' = 2$.

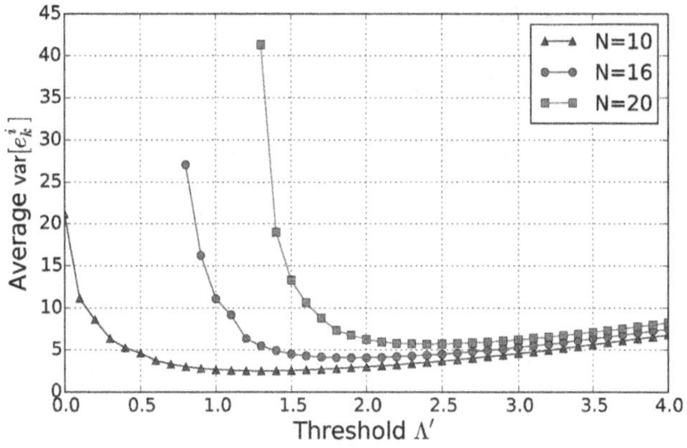

Figure 4: Average error variance var$[e_k^i]$ vs. Λ'. Parameters: $M = 10$.

where $\mathsf{E}[n_p^s]$ is expected number of successful transmissions per slot. Ratio of collided packets is used as the second performance metric. It is defined as:

$$r_{coll} = \frac{\mathsf{E}[n_p^c]}{\mathsf{E}[n_p^c] + \mathsf{E}[n_p^s]}, \tag{19}$$

where $\mathsf{E}[n_p^c]$ is expected number of collided transmissions per slot.

The transmission threshold Λ_i is considered homogeneous for all N sub-systems throughout the simulation:

$$\Lambda_i = \Lambda_j, \quad \forall i, j \in N. \tag{20}$$

To simplify the notations, we denote it by Λ'.

4.1 Static Threshold Scheduler

For the first setup we consider a scheduler, where the transmission threshold is chosen arbitrary and is independent of the number of transmission channels M.

Fig. 3 demonstrates the evolution of the average error variance with the increasing number of sub-systems. We observe a non-linear growth of the error variance, and, on the same time, higher variation of the resulting variance over multiple runs. The growth of the error variance can be explained by looking at Fig. 5: with the increasing number of sub-systems we see an increase in collision rate. Since for the unstable systems, the error accumulates exponentially with every collision, linear increase in collisions results in a non-linear increase in the variance of the error.

In Fig. 5, we observe that the shape of the plot for throughput corresponds to the commonly known dependency for multi- and single-channel slotted aloha with Poisson distribution arrival rate [29]. The highest value $T \approx 1/e \approx 0.368$ is achieved at $N = 26$.

Fig. 4 shows how the error variance depends on the transmission threshold Λ'. As we observe, and it is inline with the hypothesis we have stated in the Section 2, the dependency is a convex function. With the values of Λ' close to 0, the transmission is attempted every time, thus, causing many collisions and shifting the throughput T operating region as in 5 to the right. The collisions, in turn, further increase the $\|e_k^i\|$ for all unstable systems with $A_i > 1$, thus, further increasing the amount of access attempts. As expected, the error variance among all sub-systems grows. If, however,

Table 2: Optimal $\Lambda' = f(N, M)$.

	N						
	4	6	8	10	12	14	16
$M = 5$	1.0	1.5	2.0	2.4	3.5	5.2	8.1
$M = 10$	0.6	0.8	1.0	1.2	1.4	1.6	1.8

the Λ' is chosen too high, the increase in the error variance is caused by the underutilized communication medium (throughput T low). Thus, it is observed that there exists an optimal value for Λ' in a given NCS scenario defined by N, M.

4.2 Scheduler with Threshold Adaptation

Following the observation about the existence of an optimal Λ', we propose an improvement to the threshold design defined in (21). Namely, we use a knowledge about the network state M and the number of present sub-systems N, in order to choose the Λ' for the optimal performance:

$$\Lambda' = f(M), \tag{21}$$

where higher number of channels results in a higher Λ'.

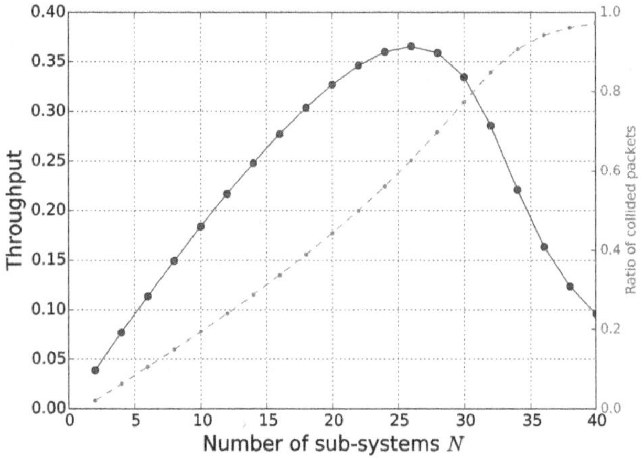

Figure 5: Average throughput and collision rate vs. number of sub-systems N. Parameters: $M = 10$.

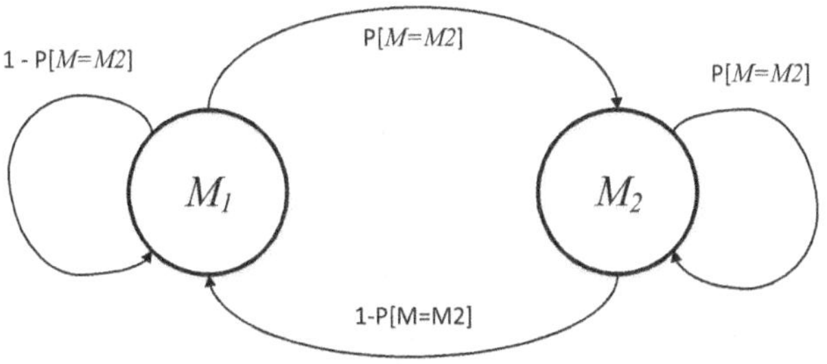

Figure 6: Model of number of channels M variations.

Numerically obtained values for Λ' for M and N choices we use for evaluation are summarized in Table 2.

The benefits of this approach can be seen for the case of the varying number of available channels M. For simplicity, we model the number of channels as a random variable with two possible values $M \in \{M_1, M_2\}$, $M_1 < M_2$, with:

$$\mathsf{P}[M = M1] = 1 - \mathsf{P}[M = M2]. \tag{22}$$

The model is depicted in Fig. 6. These two states can represent presence or absence of a background traffic with reserved channels, for example, as described in [11, 15]. Although we consider only two states for M, it has to be noted that the proposed scheduler design is extendable for a more general case of multiple states. In the evaluation scenario $M_1 = 5$ and $M_2 = 10$, and $\mathsf{P}[M = M1] = 0.5$ are used.

For comparison, we consider two choices of Λ' for static scheduler: **(A)** first, where Λ' is statically set to minimize the error variance for $M = M_1$, and **(B)** second to minimize the error variance for $M = M_2$ for a given number of sub-systems in the simulation N. The comparison results are presented in Fig. 7. It is observed, that the error variance with the adaptive scheduler is always lower or equal than for non-adaptive. It is further observed, that the first static scheduler **(A)**, optimizing the threshold for the lower number of channels M_2 is performing noticeably better than the scheduler **(B)**, optimizing the threshold for the higher number of channels M_1. The effect is supported by the observations from Fig. 4 that the slope on the left from the optimal point is much higher than on the right from it, thus, over-utilization is more harmful for the error variance than underutilization.

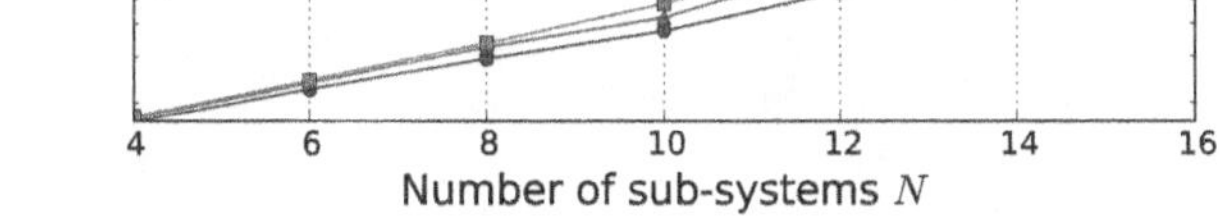

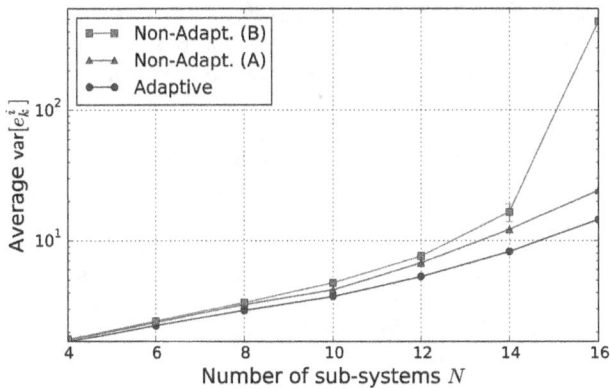

Figure 7: Average error variance vs. number of sub-systems N for three cases: Adaptive Λ', Non-Adaptive (Λ' optimal for $M1$ channels), Non-Adaptive (Λ' optimal for $M2$ channels). Parameters: $M_1 = 5$, $M_2 = 10$, $\mathsf{P}[M = M_2] = 0.5$.

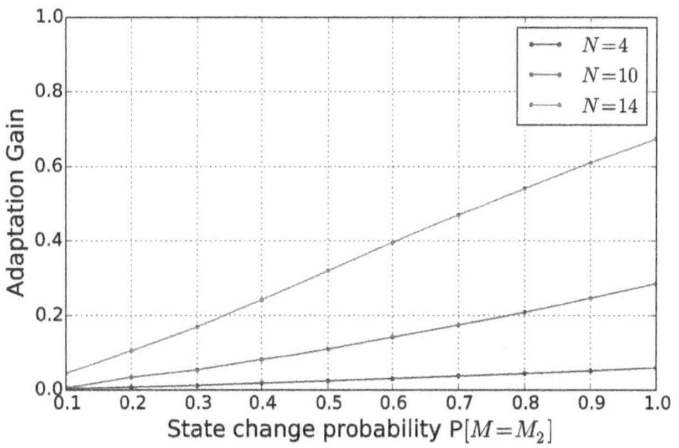

Figure 8: Adaptation gain G_{adap} vs. Probability of the "good" channel $\mathsf{P}[M = M2]$ for $N \in \{4, 10, 14\}$. Parameters: $M_1 = 5$, $M_2 = 10$.

To evaluate how the probability of a network state change $\mathsf{P}[M = M_2]$ influences the performance gain from the adaptive scheduler, we use the reduction of the average error variance as a metric for adaptation gain:

$$G_{adap} = \frac{\Sigma_{na} - \Sigma_a}{\Sigma_{na}}, \tag{23}$$

where Σ_{na} and Σ_a represent the average error variances for static (non-adaptive) and adaptive schedulers, respectively.

The resulting dependency is depicted in Fig. 8. The parameter $\mathsf{P}[M = M2]$ is in this case a measure of how frequently the network state is changing. For $\mathsf{P}[M = M2] = 0.1$ almost no changes are there, hence, both schedulers are close to optimal. On the other hand, for $\mathsf{P}[M = M2] = 1$, although also no changes are present, the default state of the channel is $M = M2$, thus, the static scheduler is not optimal in any time-slot. For the network state changing every second time, the adaptive scheduler is able to reduce the error variance by up to 30%.

5. CONCLUSIONS

In this paper, we propose a decentralized threshold-based scheduling policy for an NCS composed of multiple heterogeneous LTI control loops operating via a multi-channel shared communication medium. The Medium Access Control (MAC) is assumed to be performed in contentious fashion using a multi-channel slotted ALOHA protocol. The analysis in the paper proves stochastic stability of such NCSs.

After demonstrating that there exists an global threshold value minimizing the average error variance, we further introduce a local resource-aware scheduler design with an adaptive choice of the error threshold based on knowledge of the network state, and numerically demonstrate that by deploying it instead of the static threshold choice, we can significantly increase the control performance. Future work aims at finding the exact relation or a close approximation of the relation between the network state and the optimal transmission threshold.

6. ACKNOWLEDGMENTS

This work has been in parts supported by TUM Institute for Advanced Study.

7. REFERENCES

[1] 3GPP. Technical Report 37.868: Study on RAN Improvements for Machine-type Communications (Release 11). Technical report, 3GPP Technical Specification Group Radio Access Network, 2011.

[2] R. Blind and F. Allgöwer. Analysis of Networked Event-Based Control with a Shared Communication Medium: Part I-Pure ALOHA. *Jeb*, 1:2, 2011.

[3] R. Blind and F. Allgöwer. Analysis of networked event-based control with a shared communication medium: Part II-Slotted ALOHA. In *IFAC World Congress*, pages 8830–8835, 2011.

[4] A. Cervin and T. Henningsson. Scheduling of event-triggered controllers on a shared network. In *Decision and Control, 2008. CDC 2008. 47th IEEE Conference on*, pages 3601–3606, Dec 2008.

[5] D. Christmann, R. Gotzhein, S. Siegmund, and F. Wirth. Realization of Try-Once-Discard in wireless multihop networks. *IEEE Transactions on Industrial Informatics*, 10(1):17–26, Feb 2014.

[6] D. Dimarogonas and K. Johansson. Event-triggered control for multi-agent systems. In *Decision and Control, held jointly with the 28th Chinese Control Conference. CDC/CCC 2009. Proceedings of the 48th IEEE Conference on*, pages 7131–7136, Dec 2009.

[7] M. Donkers, W. Heemels, D. Bernardini, A. Bemporad, and V. Shneer. Stability analysis of stochastic networked control systems. *Automatica*, 48(5):917–925, 2012.

[8] M. Gerasimenko, V. Petrov, O. Galinina, S. Andreev, and Y. Koucheryavy. Impact of machine-type communications on energy and delay performance of random access channel in LTE-advanced. *Trans. Emerging Telecommun. Techn.*, 24(4):366–377, 2013.

[9] M. Hasan, E. Hossain, and D. Niyato. Random access for machine-to-machine communication in LTE-advanced networks: issues and approaches. *IEEE Commun. Mag.*, 51(6):86–93, June 2013.

[10] W. P. M. H. Heemels, J. H. Sandee, and P. P. J. Van Den Bosch. Analysis of event-driven controllers for linear systems. *International Journal of Control*, 81(4):571–590, 2008.

[11] D. Kim, W. Kim, and S. An. Adaptive random access preamble split in LTE. In *Proc. Int. Wireless Commun. and Mobile Computing Conf. (IWCMC)*, pages 814–819, July 2013.

[12] K. S. Ko, M. J. Kim, K. Y. Bae, D. K. Sung, J. H. Kim, and J. Y. Ahn. A Novel Random Access for Fixed-Location Machine-to-Machine Communications in OFDMA Based Systems. *IEEE Commun. Letters*, 16(9):1428–1431, September 2012.

[13] F. Kozin. A survey of stability of stochastic systems. *Automatica*, 5(1):95–112, Jan. 1969.

[14] A. Laya, L. Alonso, and J. Alonso-Zarate. Is the Random Access Channel of LTE and LTE-A Suitable for M2M Communications? A Survey of Alternatives. *IEEE Commun. Surveys & Tut.*, 16(1):4–16, First Qu. 2014.

[15] K.-D. Lee, S. Kim, and B. Yi. Throughput comparison of random access methods for M2M service over LTE networks. In *GLOBECOM Workshops (GC Wkshps), 2011 IEEE*, pages 373–377, Dec 2011.

[16] S.-Y. Lien, T.-H. Liau, C.-Y. Kao, and K.-C. Chen. Cooperative Access Class Barring for Machine-to-Machine Communications. *IEEE Trans. Wireless Commun.*, 11(1):27–32, January 2012.

[17] G. Madueno, S. Stefanovic, and P. Popovski. Efficient LTE access with collision resolution for massive M2M communications. In *Proc. IEEE Globecom Workshops*, pages 1433–1438, Dec 2014.

[18] M. Mamduhi, A. Molin, and S. Hirche. Event-based scheduling of multi-loop stochastic systems over shared communication channels. In *21st International Symposium on Mathematical Theory of Networks and Systems (MTNS)*, pages 266–273, Jul 2014.

[19] A. Molin and S. Hirche. On the optimality of certainty equivalence for event-triggered control systems. *Automatic Control, IEEE Transactions on*, 58(2):470 –474, 2013.

[20] A. Molin and S. Hirche. A bi-level approach for the design of event-triggered control systems over a shared network. *Discrete Event Dynamic Systems*, 24(2):153–171, 2014.

[21] A. Molin and S. Hirche. Price-based adaptive scheduling in multi-loop control systems with resource constraints. *Automatic Control, IEEE Transactions*, pages 3282 – 3295, 2014.

[22] R. Murray, K. Astrom, S. Boyd, R. Brockett, and G. Stein. Future directions in control in an information-rich world. *Control Systems, IEEE*, 23(2):20–33, Apr 2003.

[23] D. Nesic and A. Teel. Input-output stability properties of networked control systems. *Automatic Control, IEEE Transactions on*, 49(10):1650–1667, 2004.

[24] C. Ramesh, H. Sandberg, and K. Johansson. Stability analysis of multiple state-based schedulers with CSMA. In *Decision and Control (CDC), 2012 IEEE 51st Annual Conference on*, pages 7205–7211, 2012.

[25] R. Rom and M. Sidi. *Multiple Access Protocols: Performance and Analysis*. Springer-Verlag New York, Inc., New York, NY, USA, 1990.

[26] M. Tabbara and D. Nesic. Input–output stability of networked control systems with stochastic protocols and channels. *Automatic Control, IEEE Transactions on*, 53(5):1160–1175, 2008.

[27] P. Tabuada. Event-triggered real-time scheduling of stabilizing control tasks. *Automatic Control, IEEE Transactions on*, 52(9):1680 –1685, 2007.

[28] D. Tolić and R. Fierro. Decentralized output synchronization of heterogeneous linear systems with fixed and switching topology via self-triggered communication. In *American Control Conference*, pages 4655–4660, June 2013.

[29] R. Tyagi, F. Aurzada, K.-D. Lee, S. Kim, and M. Reisslein. Impact of Retransmission Limit on Preamble Contention in LTE-Advanced Network. *Systems Journal, IEEE*, 9(3):752–765, Sept 2015.

[30] G. C. Walsh, H. Ye, and L. G. Bushnell. Stability analysis of networked control systems. *Control*

Systems Technology, IEEE Transactions on, 10(3):438–446, 2002.

[31] G. Wu, S. Talwar, K. Johnsson, N. Himayat, and K. Johnson. M2M: From mobile to embedded Internet. *IEEE Commun. Mag.*, 49(4):36–43, April 2011.

APPENDIX

A. PROOF OF THEOREM 1

PROOF (*Theorem 1*). : To show LSP, let the NCS of interest operate over the interval $[k, k{+}N]$ of length N, starting from time-step k with arbitrary initial state e_k. We assume that the NCS freely operates from the initial time k until $k{+}N-1$ and we predict the error evolution considering all the possible scenarios under the introduced threshold-based scheduling policy over the interval $[k, k{+}N{-}1]$. Then, looking at the final time-step $k{+}N$, we show the aggregate error state e_{k+N} fulfills (15). Depending on whether the condition (6) is satisfied at every time-step k', we divide the sub-systems $i \in \{1, \dots, N\}$ into two complementary and disjoint sets as follows:

$$i \in \begin{cases} \mathcal{G}_{k'} & \|e^i_{k'}\| > \Lambda_i \\ \bar{\mathcal{G}}_{k'} & \|e^i_{k'}\| \le \Lambda_i, \end{cases} \tag{24}$$

where $\mathcal{G}_{k'} \cup \bar{\mathcal{G}}_{k'} = N$. According to (6), sub-systems belonging to $\mathcal{G}_{k'}$ are eligible for transmission at time-step $k'{+}1$. In accordance with the slotted ALOHA policy, if a sub-system i is eligible for transmission at some time $k'+1$, i.e. $\|e^i_{k'}\| > \Lambda_i$, then i selects one of the available transmission channels in uniform random fashion. If no other transmission-eligible sub-system $j \neq i$ selects that certain transmission channel, then sub-system i successfully transmits. Otherwise, a collision occurs and both collided packets are dropped and the corresponding sub-systems will have to wait until the next time-step, i.e. $k'+2$, to transmit, only if the inequality (6) is satisfied. To take this into account, we discern four complementary and mutually exclusive cases, covering the entire state space the error state e_k evolves until time-step $k{+}N{-}1$ as follows:

Sub-system i:

c_1: has either successfully transmitted or not within the past $N{-}1$ time-steps, and is in set $\bar{\mathcal{G}}_{k+N-1}$, i.e.
$$i \in \bar{\mathcal{G}}_{k+N-1} \quad \Rightarrow \quad \|e^i_{k+N-1}\| \le \Lambda_i,$$

c_2: has successfully transmitted at least once within the past $N{-}1$ time-steps, and is in set $\mathcal{G}_{k+N-1}$, i.e.
$$\exists k' \in [k, k{+}N{-}1] : \theta^i_{k'} = 1 \text{ and } \|e^i_{k+N-1}\| > \Lambda_i,$$

c_3: has not successfully transmitted within the past $N{-}1$ time-steps, and is in the set $\mathcal{G}_{k+N-1}$, but has been in the set $\bar{\mathcal{G}}_{k'}$ at least once at some time-step $k' \in [k, k + N - 2]$, i.e.
$$\forall k' \in [k, k{+}N{-}1] : \theta^i_{k'} = 0 \text{ and } \|e^i_{k'}\| \le \Lambda_i.$$

c_4: has not successfully transmitted within the past $N{-}1$ time-steps, and has always been in the set $\mathcal{G}_{k'}$ for all time-steps $k' \in [k, k{+}N{-}1]$, i.e.
$$\forall k' \in [k, k{+}N{-}1] : \theta^i_{k'} = 0 \text{ and } \|e^i_{k'}\| > \Lambda_i.$$

Introducing the above cases, we study the boundedness of error norm expectation over the interval $[k, k{+}N]$ for cases c_1-c_4. Since, the cases are complementary and mutually exclusive, i.e. each sub-system belongs exactly to one of the cases c_1-c_4, we can express (15) as

$$\sum_{i=1}^{N} \mathsf{E}\left[\|e^i_{k+N}\|^2\right] = \sum_{i\in c_l}^{l=1,2,3,4} \mathsf{E}\left[\|e^i_{k+N}\|^2 | c_l\right]. \tag{25}$$

Suppose that some sub-systems i belong to c_1, i.e. those sub-systems have never attempted for transmission. Since $i \in \bar{\mathcal{G}}_{k+N-1}$, it follows from (24) that $\|e^i_{k+N-1}\| \le \Lambda_i$. Thus, those sub-systems are not eligible for transmission at time-step $k + N$, i.e. $\theta^i_{k+N} = 0$. Then, it follows from (5) and (25) that

$$\begin{aligned} \sum_{i\in c_1} \mathsf{E}\left[\|e^i_{k+N}\|^2 | e_k\right] &= \sum_{i\in c_1} \mathsf{E}\left[\|A_i e^i_{k+N-1} + w^i_{k+N-1}\|^2 | e_k\right] \\ &\le \sum_{c_1} \|A_i\|_2^2 \mathsf{E}\left[\|e^i_{k+N-1}\|^2 | e_k\right] + \mathsf{E}\left[\|w^i_{k+N-1}\|^2\right] \\ &\le \sum_{c_1} \Lambda_i^2 \|A_i\|_2^2 + \mathsf{E}\left[\|w^i_{k+N-1}\|^2\right]. \end{aligned} \tag{26}$$

This fulfills the condition (16) with $\bar{\xi}' > \sum_{c_1} \Lambda_i^2 \|A_i\|_2^2 + \mathsf{E}\left[\|w^i_{k+N-1}\|^2\right]$, and $\bar{\xi} = \frac{\sum_{c_1} \mathsf{E}[\|e^i_{k+N}\|^2 | e_k]}{\bar{\xi}'} < 1$.

For some $i \in c_2$, let a successful transmission occur at time-step $k{+}r_i$, where $r_i \in [1, N{-}1]$, i.e. $\theta^i_{k+r_i} = 1$. We express e^i_{k+N} as a function of the error at time $k{+}r_i{-}1$ as

$$\begin{aligned} e^i_{k+N} = &\prod_{j=r_i}^{N} \left(1 - \theta^i_{k+j}\right) A_i^{N-r_i+1} e^i_{k+r_i-1} \\ &+ \sum_{r=r_i}^{N} \left[\prod_{j=r+1}^{N} \left(1 - \theta^i_{k+j}\right) A_i^{N-r} w^i_{k+r-1}\right], \end{aligned} \tag{27}$$

where we define $\prod_{N+1}^{N}(1 - \theta^i_{k+j}) := 1$. The first term of the above equality vanishes as $\theta^i_{k+r_i} = 1$. By statistical independence of w^i_{k+r-1} and θ^i_{k+j}, it follows from (27)

$$\begin{aligned} &\sum_{i\in c_2} \mathsf{E}\left[\|e^i_{k+N}\|^2 | e_k\right] \\ &= \sum_{c_2} \mathsf{E}\left[\|\sum_{r=r_i'}^{N} \prod_{j=r+1}^{N} \left[1 - \theta^i_{k+j}\right] A_i^{N-r} w^i_{k+r-1}\|^2\right] \\ &\le \sum_{c_2} \sum_{r=r_i'}^{N} \mathsf{E}\left[\|A_i^{N-r} w^i_{k+r-1}\|^2\right]. \end{aligned} \tag{28}$$

Hence, the condition (16) is satisfied considering $\bar{\xi}'$ chosen to be larger than (28), and $\bar{\xi} = \frac{\sum_{c_2} \mathsf{E}[\|e^i_{k+N}\|^2 | e_k]}{\bar{\xi}'} < 1$. Note that we assume to have only two transmission channels per time slot in this proof, therefore if the number of sub-systems which are eligible for transmission is greater than two, and one sub-system belongs to c_2, then the rest of the transmission eligible sub-systems belong to either set c_3 or c_4. This means that, one successful transmission occurs through one of the two available channels, while the other sub-systems which attempt to access the channel will not successfully transmit as they simultaneously select the second channel and eventually their corresponding data packet are collided.

For the case c_3, assume that the $k + r_i$ is the last time-step for sub-systems $i \in c_3$ that $i \in \bar{\mathcal{G}}_{k+r_i}$, which in turn implies that $\|e^i_{k+r_i}\| \le \Lambda_i$. Recall that the sub-systems $i \in c_3$ belong to $\mathcal{G}_{k+N-1}$. Knowing that $\theta^i_{k'} = 0$ for $i \in c_3$ for all $k' \in [k, k + N - 1]$, we reach

$$\begin{aligned} &\sum_{c_3} \mathsf{E}\left[\|e^i_{k+N}\|^2 | e_k\right] \le \\ &\sum_{c_3} \left[\Lambda_i^2 \|A_i^{N-r_i}\|_2^2 + \sum_{r=r_i}^{N-1} \mathsf{E}\left[\|A_i^{N-r-1} w^i_{k+r}\|^2\right]\right]. \end{aligned} \tag{29}$$

The condition (16) is met by choosing $\bar{\xi}'$ larger than the uniform upper bound (29), and $\bar{\xi} = \frac{\sum_{c_3} \mathsf{E}[\|e^i_{k+N}\|^2 | e_k]}{\bar{\xi}'} < 1$.

The sub-systems $i \in c_4$ have always been candidates for channel access, i.e. $i \in \mathcal{G}_{[k,k+N-1]}$, but they have never transmitted, which means that every single attempt from those sub-systems ended up with a collision. Hence, $\|e^i_{k'}\| > \Lambda_j$ for all $k' \in [k, k+N-1]$ while $\theta^i_{k'} = 0$. To show LSP in this case, we consider the worst case scenario by assuming every sub-system $i \in \{1, \ldots, N\}$ belongs to the set c_4, which instead ensures having successive collisions over the entire interval $[k, k+N]$. Indeed, we assume that every attempts to access one of the two available channels results in collisions and consequently no successful transmission would happen over the entire period. Generally, the probability that such a scenario happens for M available transmission channels can be calculated as follows:

$$\mathsf{P}_{fail} = \prod_{i=k}^{k+N} \mathsf{P}^i_{fail}, \tag{30}$$

where P^k_{fail} is the probability that all sub-systems collide in a given slot k with M channels. In general, the number of sub-systems eligible for transmission in a given slot k is $g_k = |\mathcal{G}_k|$. Thus, the probability P^k_{fail} can be derived as:

$$\mathsf{P}^k_{fail} = \frac{M^{g_k} - m_{1s}}{M^{g_k}}, \tag{31}$$

where M^{g_k} is the total number of possible channel choices for all transmitting sub-systems for a given slot, and m_{1s} is the number of outcomes with at least one successful transmission.

The probability of one specific sub-system to succeed is given in (9). As it can be any of g_k sub-systems, and they can be successful with any channel, total number of such outcomes is defined as:

$$g_k M \left(\frac{M-1}{M}\right)^{g_k} \tag{32}$$

Now, by Inclusion-Exclusion principle, the probabilities of two successful transmissions in the slot k are counted in (32) twice. There are exactly 2! ways for two success matches, and they can occur in for any pair channels for any pair of sub-systems, resulting in

$$2! \binom{M}{2} \binom{g_k}{2} (M-2)^{g_k-2} \tag{33}$$

possible outcomes. Following the Inclusion-Exclusion principle, we need to subtract the number of outcomes with three successes, and so forth.

Thus, at the end, we can derive m_{1s} as follows:

$$m_{1s} = \sum_{j=1}^{min(g_k,M)} (-1)^{j+1} \cdot j! \binom{M}{j} \binom{g_k}{j} (M-j)^{g_k-j}. \tag{34}$$

Using expression (34) in (31), we get the probability of all transmissions fail in one slot:

$$\mathsf{P}^k_{fail} = \frac{M^{g_k} + \sum_{j=1}^{min(g_k,M)} (-1)^j \cdot j! \binom{M}{j} \binom{g_k}{j} (M-j)^{g_k-j}}{M^{g_k}}, \tag{35}$$

Note that for any given slot, maximum number of eligible for transmission sub-systems is at most N, thus, $g_k \leq N$. Therefore, we can derive the upper bound on the P_{fail} as:

$$\mathsf{P}_{fail} \leq (\mathsf{P}^k_{fail})^N, \tag{36}$$

with:

$$\mathsf{P}^k_{fail} \leq \frac{M^N + \sum_{j=1}^{min(N,M)} (-1)^j \cdot j! \binom{M}{j} \binom{N}{j} (M-j)^{N-j}}{M^N}. \tag{37}$$

From (27), if no sub-system transmits over the N-step horizon, we can choose $\bar{\xi}' = \sum_{i=1}^N \|A_i^N e^i_k + \sum_{r=1}^N A_i^{N-r} w^i_{k+r-1}\|^2 > 0$. Therefore, we have

$$\sup_{e_k} \mathsf{P}\left[\sum_{i=1}^N \|e^i_{k+N}\|^2 \geq \bar{\xi}'\right] < \mathsf{P}_{fail}, \tag{38}$$

for an arbitrary $\rho(\bar{\xi}', \bar{\xi})$ such that $\sum_{i=1}^N \|e^i_k\|^2 < \rho$ and LSP of the overall NCS is readily obtained according to (16). □

Remark 2. *It should be noted that P_{fail} depends on the system parameters Λ_i and A_i and the noise covariance W_i via the variable g_k. In fact, inclusion or exclusion of a sub-system i in the set $\mathcal{G}_k$ does not only depend on the transmission history, but also on the system parameters and noise variables.*

Event-Separation Properties and Asymptotic Behaviour of Hybrid Event-Based Control Systems

Tobias Noesselt
IAV GmbH
Rockwellstr. 16
38518 Gifhorn, Germany
Tobias.Noesselt@iav.de

Matthias Schultalbers
IAV GmbH
Rockwellstr. 16
38518 Gifhorn, Germany
Matthias.Schultalbers@iav.de

Jan Lunze
Institute of Automation and Computer Control
Ruhr-University Bochum
44780 Bochum, Germany
Lunze@atp.rub.de

ABSTRACT

In hybrid event-based control (HEBC) systems the controller influences a continuous plant G through two input signals with different characteristics. A continuous input is used to attenuate disturbances and to force the plant to follow a reference signal, whereas a discrete-valued input is determined by an event-based component of the controller in order to adjust the operation point of the plant. HEBC systems have typical characteristics of hybrid dynamical systems including state jumps and switching dynamics.

This paper analyses HEBC systems with linear components. It derives bounds on the event threshold in order to avoid Zeno behaviour and to guarantee a minimum inter-event time. The main result is a condition under which the closed-loop system is asymptotically stable and has an asymptotic set-point tracking behaviour. An application example illustrates the results.

1. INTRODUCTION

Hybrid event-based control (HEBC) systems consist of a plant with multiple inputs, where the discrete-valued input u_2 is used to adjust the operation point of the plant and the continuous input u_1 is used by the controller K_1 to attenuate disturbances and to force the plant to follow a command signal r (Fig. 1). The input u_2 is generated by an event-based controller with the aim to shift the state of the plant into a new operation point before the input u_1 reaches its limits. The event generator E determines the time instants at which the component K_2 of the controller has to be active.

The resulting control loop is a hybrid dynamical system with state jumps and switches of the dynamics. Hence, the analysis of the closed-loop system poses the typical problems of hybrid systems with respect to stability of the closed-loop system, Zeno behaviour, and performance of the system in response to the disturbance d and the command signal r.

HSCC'16, April 12-14, 2016, Vienna, Austria

DOI: http://dx.doi.org/10.1145/2883817.2883835

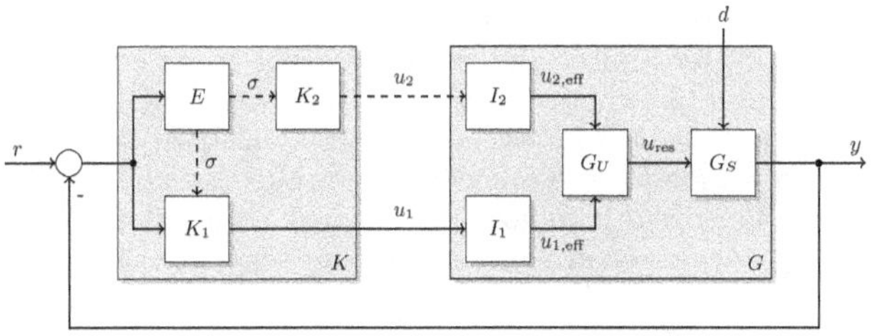

Figure 1: Structure of hybrid event-based control systems

Fields of application. As the following examples show, there are numerous applications, in which continuous control is combined with event-based switching in the sense of HEBC. They can be classified by the way in which the input signals interact.

- In HEBC systems with multiplicative control inputs ($u_{\text{res}} = u_{1,\text{eff}} \cdot u_{2,\text{eff}}$) the discrete input signal u_2 determines the gain of the continuous input signal u_1. Examples of this kind of systems include **speed control of vehicles** with an automatic gearbox and **terminal voltage control** of electrical power plants. In the latter example the transformation ratio between the bus voltage and the terminal voltage is switched in order to hold the continuous bus voltage controller within its limited operation region.

- In HEBC systems with additive control inputs ($u_{\text{res}} = u_{1,\text{eff}} + u_{2,\text{eff}}$) the controller has two complementary ways of affecting the plant like, for example, in **hybrid positioning systems**. Another example are **multistage pumping systems** where a number of parallel pumps simultaneously feed a load. Here the discrete control input signal u_2 switches the pumps on and off, whereas an additional pump with input u_1 is used to continuously adjust the pumping power to the changing load.

As this classification shows, HEBC systems appear in many application areas, but they have usually been designed by heuristic rules while ignoring their hybrid character. This paper describes systematic ways to analyse and to design such systems taking into account the hybrid behaviour of the closed-loop system.

Literature. In the literature on hybrid systems, e. g. [3, 4, 7, 9], it has been shown that it is important to restrict the class of systems under consideration in order to obtain efficient methods and results. For HEBC systems, the authors have shown in [11] that under certain conditions the behaviour of the hybrid closed-loop system can be approximated by a linear model and the hybrid controller can be derived from the corresponding linear controller. This paper deals with the same class of systems and extends the analysis by proving conditions under which the closed-loop system is asymptotically stable and tracks a constant reference signal.

From a second viewpoint, HEBC systems can be considered as a specific class of event-based control loops, where the feedback loop is closed only at time instants that are determined by an event generator in dependence upon the plant state [8]. Between these time instants the plant input is determined by an input generator in an open-loop manner. The typical motivation of event-based control is to minimize the communication effort between sensors, controller, and actuators (see e.g. [1, 5, 10]). In HEBC systems, the motivation for the event-based working principle is different. The event-based component of the controller is used to shift the operation point of the plant so as to ensure that the continuous control loop does not reach its limits. In many event-based control systems it is important to maintain a lower bound on the inter-event times. This problem is analysed in [2] for general event-based control systems. In Section 5 an analytical expression for the minimum inter-event time of HEBC systems is proved.

Structure of the paper. Sections 2 – 4 give a definition of the system class under investigation, describe a systematic way to design a hybrid controller and analyse the stability of the closed-loop system using a linear approximation. The main results of the paper are presented in Sections 5 and 6. The influence of the event threshold on the event-separation properties of the hybrid closed-loop system is analysed in Section 5 and rules for the proper choice of the threshold are derived. Section 6 shows under what conditions the closed-loop system asymptotically tracks constant command signals. Finally, an example is presented in Section 7 to illustrate the results.

2. HEBC SYSTEMS WITH ADDITIVE INPUT SIGNALS

Figure 1 shows the structure of HEBC systems. The solid arrows represent continuous signals whereas the dashed arrows indicate that the corresponding signals are activated only at event time instants. The components of the control loop are described in detail in this section.

In the application examples mentioned above, G_{U} is a static system representing either a multiplication or a summation of the control input signals. This paper concentrates on HEBC systems with linear components and additive control input signals.

2.1 Model of the plant dynamics

The plant G has two control input signals. The first input $u_1(t)$ has a continuous domain limited by

$$|u_1(t)| \le \bar{u}_1 \tag{1}$$

with a given threshold $\bar{u}_1$. The second input $u_2(t)$ is discrete-valued with a constant quantisation

$$u_2(t) \in \mathcal{U}_2 = \{u_{2,\min}, u_{2,\min} + \Delta u_2, \ldots, u_{2,\max}\}. \tag{2}$$

The effect of the input signals is described by the state-space models of the input dynamics

$$I_1: \left\{ \begin{array}{rcl} \dot{\boldsymbol{x}}_{\mathrm{I}1}(t) &=& \boldsymbol{A}_{\mathrm{I}1}\boldsymbol{x}_{\mathrm{I}1}(t) + \boldsymbol{b}_{\mathrm{I}1}u_{1,\mathrm{sat}}(t) \\ u_{1,\mathrm{sat}}(t) &=& \begin{cases} \bar{u}_1 & \text{if } u_1(t) \ge \bar{u}_1 \\ u_1(t) & \text{if } |u_1(t)| < \bar{u}_1 \\ -\bar{u}_1 & \text{if } u_1(t) \le -\bar{u}_1 \end{cases} \\ u_{1,\mathrm{eff}}(t) &=& \boldsymbol{c}_{\mathrm{I}1}^{\mathrm{T}}\boldsymbol{x}_{\mathrm{I}1}(t) \end{array} \right. \tag{3}$$

and

$$I_2: \left\{ \begin{array}{rcl} \dot{\boldsymbol{x}}_{\mathrm{I}2}(t) &=& \boldsymbol{A}_{\mathrm{I}2}\boldsymbol{x}_{\mathrm{I}2}(t) + \boldsymbol{b}_{\mathrm{I}2}u_2(t) \\ u_{2,\mathrm{eff}}(t) &=& \boldsymbol{c}_{\mathrm{I}2}^{\mathrm{T}}\boldsymbol{x}_{\mathrm{I}2}(t) \end{array} \right. \tag{4}$$

and by the additive coupling $u_{\mathrm{res}}(t) = u_{1,\mathrm{eff}}(t) + u_{2,\mathrm{eff}}(t)$. The internal plant dynamics are represented by

$$G_{\mathrm{S}}: \left\{ \begin{array}{rcl} \dot{\boldsymbol{x}}_{\mathrm{GS}}(t) &=& \boldsymbol{A}_{\mathrm{GS}}\boldsymbol{x}_{\mathrm{GS}}(t) + \boldsymbol{b}_{\mathrm{u}}u_{\mathrm{res}}(t) + \boldsymbol{b}_{\mathrm{d}}d(t) \\ y(t) &=& \boldsymbol{c}_{\mathrm{GS}}^{\mathrm{T}}\boldsymbol{x}_{\mathrm{GS}}(t). \end{array} \right. \tag{5}$$

By combining eqs. (3) – (5) and assuming that $u_1(t)$ stays within the interval $[-\bar{u}_1, \bar{u}_1]$ a linear representation of the overall plant G is obtained:

$$G: \left\{ \begin{array}{rcl} \begin{pmatrix} \dot{\boldsymbol{x}}_{\mathrm{GS}}(t) \\ \dot{\boldsymbol{x}}_{\mathrm{I}1}(t) \\ \dot{\boldsymbol{x}}_{\mathrm{I}2}(t) \end{pmatrix} &=& \underbrace{\begin{pmatrix} \boldsymbol{A}_{\mathrm{GS}} & \boldsymbol{b}_{\mathrm{u}}\boldsymbol{c}_{\mathrm{I}1}^{\mathrm{T}} & \boldsymbol{b}_{\mathrm{u}}\boldsymbol{c}_{\mathrm{I}2}^{\mathrm{T}} \\ \boldsymbol{O} & \boldsymbol{A}_{\mathrm{I}1} & \boldsymbol{O} \\ \boldsymbol{O} & \boldsymbol{O} & \boldsymbol{A}_{\mathrm{I}2} \end{pmatrix}}_{\boldsymbol{A}_{\mathrm{G}}} \underbrace{\begin{pmatrix} \boldsymbol{x}_{\mathrm{GS}}(t) \\ \boldsymbol{x}_{\mathrm{I}1}(t) \\ \boldsymbol{x}_{\mathrm{I}2}(t) \end{pmatrix}}_{\boldsymbol{x}_{\mathrm{G}}} \\ && + \underbrace{\begin{pmatrix} \boldsymbol{0} & \boldsymbol{0} & \boldsymbol{b}_{\mathrm{d}} \\ \boldsymbol{b}_{\mathrm{I}1} & \boldsymbol{0} & \boldsymbol{0} \\ \boldsymbol{0} & \boldsymbol{b}_{\mathrm{I}2} & \boldsymbol{0} \end{pmatrix}}_{\boldsymbol{B}_{\mathrm{G}} = (\boldsymbol{b}_1\ \boldsymbol{b}_2\ \boldsymbol{b}_3)} \begin{pmatrix} u_1(t) \\ u_2(t) \\ d(t) \end{pmatrix} \\ y(t) &=& \underbrace{\begin{pmatrix} \boldsymbol{c}_{\mathrm{GS}}^{\mathrm{T}} & \boldsymbol{0}^{\mathrm{T}} & \boldsymbol{0}^{\mathrm{T}} \end{pmatrix}}_{\boldsymbol{c}_{\mathrm{G}}^{\mathrm{T}}} \begin{pmatrix} \boldsymbol{x}_{\mathrm{GS}}(t) \\ \boldsymbol{x}_{\mathrm{I}1}(t) \\ \boldsymbol{x}_{\mathrm{I}2}(t) \end{pmatrix}. \end{array} \right. \tag{6}$$

2.2 Hybrid controller

The hybrid controller consists of three components: the event generator E, the continuous controller K_1 and the discrete controller K_2. In order to satisfy the input limitations (1) and (2), the hybrid controller has to shift the control effort from the input u_1 towards u_2 whenever u_1 reaches a given threshold $\bar{e}$. Consequently, the event generator E supervises the input u_1 and generates an event according to the following rules:

$$E: \left\{ \begin{array}{rcl} t_0 &=& 0 \\ t_k &=& \min\{t \ge t_{k-1} : |u_1(t)| \ge \bar{e}\},\ k \ge 1 \\ e_k &=& \mathrm{sgn}(u_1(t_k)) \cdot \Delta u_2. \end{array} \right. \tag{7}$$

The input $u_2(t)$ is generated as the output of an integrator with jumping state

$$K_2: \left\{ \begin{array}{rcl} \dot{x}_{\mathrm{s}2}(t) &=& 0, \quad x_{\mathrm{s}2}(0) = x_{\mathrm{s}2,0} \\ x_{\mathrm{s}2}(t_k^+) &=& x_{\mathrm{s}2}(t_k^-) + e_k \\ u_2(t) &=& x_{\mathrm{s}2}(t), \end{array} \right. \tag{8}$$

where the state increment e_k is generated by the event generator at time t_k.

The continuous input u_1 is generated by the continuous controller

$$K_1 : \begin{cases} \begin{pmatrix} \dot{\boldsymbol{x}}_{\mathrm{K}}(t) \\ \dot{x}_{\mathrm{s1}}(t) \end{pmatrix} = \begin{pmatrix} \boldsymbol{A}_{\mathrm{K}} & \boldsymbol{0}^{\mathrm{T}} \\ \boldsymbol{0} & 0 \end{pmatrix} \begin{pmatrix} \boldsymbol{x}_{\mathrm{K}}(t) \\ x_{\mathrm{s1}}(t) \end{pmatrix} \\ \qquad\qquad + \begin{pmatrix} \boldsymbol{b}_{\mathrm{K}} \\ 0 \end{pmatrix} (r(t) - y(t)) \\ \begin{pmatrix} \boldsymbol{x}_{\mathrm{K}}(t_k^+) \\ x_{\mathrm{s1}}(t_k^+) \end{pmatrix} = \begin{pmatrix} \boldsymbol{x}_{\mathrm{K}}(t_k^-) \\ x_{\mathrm{s1}}(t_k^-) + e_k \end{pmatrix} \\ u_1(t) = \begin{pmatrix} \boldsymbol{c}_{\mathrm{K}}^{\mathrm{T}}, & -1 \end{pmatrix} \begin{pmatrix} \boldsymbol{x}_{\mathrm{K}}(t) \\ x_{\mathrm{s1}}(t) \end{pmatrix} + d_{\mathrm{K}}(r(t) - y(t)), \end{cases} \tag{9}$$

consisting of the continuous controller $(\boldsymbol{A}_{\mathrm{K}}, \boldsymbol{b}_{\mathrm{K}}, \boldsymbol{c}_{\mathrm{K}}^{\mathrm{T}}, d_{\mathrm{k}})$ that is introduced later in eqn. (15) and an integrator. By choosing appropriate initial values, the two integrator states coincide (cf. Section 3):

$$x_{\mathrm{s1}}(t) = x_{\mathrm{s2}}(t) = x_{\mathrm{s}}(t) \; \forall t \geq 0. \tag{10}$$

2.3 Hybrid event-based control loop

The overall system consisting of the plant (6) and the hybrid controller (7) – (9) is a hybrid dynamical system, which is represented by the following model:

$$\begin{pmatrix} \dot{\boldsymbol{x}}_{\mathrm{K}}(t) \\ \dot{\boldsymbol{x}}_{\mathrm{G}}(t) \end{pmatrix} = \underbrace{\begin{pmatrix} \boldsymbol{A}_{\mathrm{K}} & -\boldsymbol{b}_{\mathrm{K}}\boldsymbol{c}_{\mathrm{G}}^{\mathrm{T}} \\ \boldsymbol{b}_1\boldsymbol{c}_{\mathrm{K}}^{\mathrm{T}} & \boldsymbol{A}_{\mathrm{G}} - \boldsymbol{b}_1 d_{\mathrm{K}}\boldsymbol{c}_{\mathrm{G}}^{\mathrm{T}} \end{pmatrix}}_{\boldsymbol{A}_{\mathrm{b}}} \underbrace{\begin{pmatrix} \boldsymbol{x}_{\mathrm{K}}(t) \\ \boldsymbol{x}_{\mathrm{G}}(t) \end{pmatrix}}_{\boldsymbol{x}_{\mathrm{C}}(t)} \tag{11}$$

$$+ \underbrace{\begin{pmatrix} \boldsymbol{b}_{\mathrm{K}} & \boldsymbol{0} \\ \boldsymbol{b}_1 d_{\mathrm{K}} & \boldsymbol{b}_3 \end{pmatrix}}_{\boldsymbol{B}_{\mathrm{b}}} \begin{pmatrix} r(t) \\ d(t) \end{pmatrix} - \underbrace{\begin{pmatrix} \boldsymbol{0} \\ \boldsymbol{b}_1 - \boldsymbol{b}_2 \end{pmatrix}}_{\boldsymbol{b}_{\Delta}} x_{\mathrm{s}}(t)$$

$$y(t) = \boldsymbol{c}_y^{\mathrm{T}} \boldsymbol{x}_{\mathrm{C}}(t)$$
$$\dot{x}_{\mathrm{s}}(t) = 0, \; t \neq t_k.$$

At the event time instants t_k the system performs the following discrete state jumps

$$\begin{pmatrix} \boldsymbol{x}_{\mathrm{K}}(t_k^+) \\ \boldsymbol{x}_{\mathrm{G}}(t_k^+) \\ x_{\mathrm{s}}(t_k^+) \end{pmatrix} = \begin{pmatrix} \boldsymbol{x}_{\mathrm{K}}(t_k^-) \\ \boldsymbol{x}_{\mathrm{G}}(t_k^-) \\ x_{\mathrm{s}}(t_k^-) + e_k \end{pmatrix}, \; t = t_k \tag{12}$$

with t_k and e_k being determined by (7) and (9). The input u_1 does not reach its limits, because the event generator invokes a change of u_1 and u_2 whenever the input u_1 reaches the limit $\bar{e}$. Hence, the restriction (1) as well as the discrete quantisation of u_2 is satisfied by construction. Furthermore it is assumed that the upper and lower limit $u_{2,\mathrm{min}}$, $u_{2,\mathrm{max}}$ are small and large enough not to restrict the performance of the control loop in practice.

Definition 2.1. *A* hybrid event-based control system with additive input signals *is a system with the structure shown in Fig. 1 consisting of the plant G described by (6) with $u_{\mathrm{res}}(t) = u_{1,\mathrm{eff}}(t) + u_{2,\mathrm{eff}}(t)$ and the controller K described by (7) – (9).*

In the following, such systems will be referred to as *HEBC systems* for short.

3. DESIGN OF THE HYBRID CONTROLLER

3.1 Control aim

The controller K of the HEBC system should be designed so that the overall system satisfies the following requirements:

(i) **Asymptotic stability:** The closed-loop system is asymptotically stable.

(ii) **Set-point following:** For a constant reference signal $r(t) = \bar{r}$, the output of the overall system satisfies the relation

$$\lim_{t \to \infty} |y(t) - \bar{r}| = 0. \tag{13}$$

(iii) **Disturbance attenuation:** Bounded disturbances only lead to bounded deviations of the system state. Furthermore, equation 13 still holds for nonzero constant disturbances $d(t) = \bar{d} \neq 0$.

(iv) **Event-separation:** The hybrid closed-loop system maintains a lower bound on the inter-event times and no Zeno-behaviour occurs.

3.2 Controller design

This section gives a brief summary of a design method for the hybrid controller, which has been proposed in [11]. The main idea is to first design a linear controller K' for a linear approximate model of the hybrid plant and to replace the controller K' by a hybrid controller (7) – (9).

In the first step, a simplified single-input single-output plant G' is obtained when using only the second control input $u_2(t) = u'(t)$ and assuming that this input has a continuous domain:

$$G' : \begin{cases} \dot{\hat{\boldsymbol{x}}}_{\mathrm{G}}(t) &= \boldsymbol{A}_{\mathrm{G}}\hat{\boldsymbol{x}}_{\mathrm{G}}(t) + \boldsymbol{b}_2 u'(t) \\ y(t) &= \boldsymbol{c}_{\mathrm{G}}^{\mathrm{T}}\hat{\boldsymbol{x}}_{\mathrm{G}}(t) \end{cases} \tag{14}$$

Then a linear controller

$$K' : \begin{cases} \dot{\boldsymbol{x}}_{\mathrm{K}}(t) &= \boldsymbol{A}_{\mathrm{K}}\boldsymbol{x}_{\mathrm{K}}(t) + \boldsymbol{b}_{\mathrm{K}}(r(t) - y(t)) \\ u'(t) &= \boldsymbol{c}_{\mathrm{K}}^{\mathrm{T}}\boldsymbol{x}_{\mathrm{K}}(t) + d_{\mathrm{K}}(r(t) - y(t)) \end{cases} \tag{15}$$

can be designed using methods from linear control theory such that the closed-loop system (14), (15) meets the requirements (i) – (iii). The resulting closed-loop system is called the *continuous reference system* and represented by

$$\dot{\hat{\boldsymbol{x}}}(t) = \underbrace{\begin{pmatrix} \boldsymbol{A}_{\mathrm{K}} & -\boldsymbol{b}_{\mathrm{K}}\boldsymbol{c}_{\mathrm{G}}^{\mathrm{T}} \\ \boldsymbol{b}_2\boldsymbol{c}_{\mathrm{K}}^{\mathrm{T}} & \boldsymbol{A}_{\mathrm{G}} - \boldsymbol{b}_2 d_{\mathrm{K}}\boldsymbol{c}_{\mathrm{G}}^{\mathrm{T}} \end{pmatrix}}_{\boldsymbol{A}_{\mathrm{a}}} \hat{\boldsymbol{x}}(t)$$

$$+ \underbrace{\begin{pmatrix} \boldsymbol{b}_{\mathrm{K}} & \boldsymbol{0} \\ \boldsymbol{b}_2 d_{\mathrm{K}} & \boldsymbol{b}_3 \end{pmatrix}}_{\boldsymbol{B}_{\mathrm{a}}} \begin{pmatrix} r(t) \\ d(t) \end{pmatrix} \tag{16}$$

$$\hat{y}(t) = \underbrace{\begin{pmatrix} \boldsymbol{0}^{\mathrm{T}} & \boldsymbol{c}_{\mathrm{G}}^{\mathrm{T}} \end{pmatrix}}_{\boldsymbol{c}_y^{\mathrm{T}}} \hat{\boldsymbol{x}}(t)$$

with the state $\hat{\boldsymbol{x}}(t) = (\hat{\boldsymbol{x}}_{\mathrm{K}}^{\mathrm{T}}(t) \; \hat{\boldsymbol{x}}_{\mathrm{G}}^{\mathrm{T}}(t))$. The output of the controller K' is now given by

$$u'(t) = \underbrace{\begin{pmatrix} \boldsymbol{c}_{\mathrm{K}}^{\mathrm{T}} & -d_{\mathrm{K}}\boldsymbol{c}_{\mathrm{G}}^{\mathrm{T}} \end{pmatrix}}_{\boldsymbol{c}_{u'}^{\mathrm{T}}} \hat{\boldsymbol{x}}(t) + d_{\mathrm{K}} r(t).$$

The aim of the second step is to derive a hybrid controller K from K' that determines the control input signals $u_1(t)$ and $u_2(t)$ such that

$$u_1(t) + u_2(t) = u'(t),$$

while at the same time the constraints represented by eqns. (1) and (2) are met. The controller parameters $(\boldsymbol{A}_\mathrm{K}, \boldsymbol{b}_\mathrm{K}, \boldsymbol{c}_\mathrm{K}^\mathrm{T}, d_\mathrm{k})$ of the reference controller K' can be directly used as the parameters of the component K_1 of the hybrid controller. Assuming that the additional integrators $x_{\mathrm{s}1}(t)$ and $x_{\mathrm{s}2}(t)$ are initialised with the same value $x_{\mathrm{s}1}(0) = x_{\mathrm{s}2}(0)$ it follows that the hybrid controller tracks the output of the reference controller by

$$u_1(t) + u_2(t) = u'(t) \;\; \forall t \geq 0$$

with

$$|u_1(t)| \leq \bar{e} \tag{17}$$

and

$$u_2(t) = n \cdot \Delta u_2, \; n \in \mathbb{Z}.$$

Hence, condition (1) is satisfied if the event threshold meets the inequality $\bar{e} < \bar{u}_1$.

4. PRACTICAL STABILITY OF HEBC SYSTEMS

This section proves a necessary and sufficient condition for practical stability of an HEBC system. This result is an extension of the results of [11] where it was proved that the difference between the output $\hat{y}(t)$ of the continuous reference system and the output $y(t)$ of the HEBC system is bounded if the continuous reference system is asymptotically stable (i.e. the matrix $\boldsymbol{A}_\mathrm{a}$ is Hurwitz). The idea of the subsequent analysis is to first derive a linear approximate model of the overall system and second to investigate under what condition this system and the original system are practically stable.

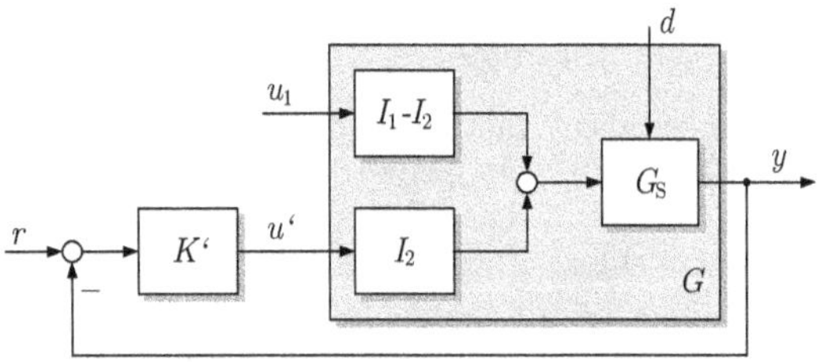

Figure 2: Structure of the linear approximate system

The system (11) – (12) can be approximated by

$$\dot{\boldsymbol{x}}_\mathrm{C}(t) = \boldsymbol{A}_\mathrm{a}\boldsymbol{x}_\mathrm{C}(t) + \boldsymbol{B}_\mathrm{a}\begin{pmatrix} r(t) \\ d(t) \end{pmatrix} + \boldsymbol{b}_\Delta u_1(t) \tag{18}$$

where the nonlinearities of the system are represented by the bounded signal $|u_1(t)| \leq \bar{e}$. Figure 2 shows the structure of the linear approximate system.

Definition 4.1. *An HEBC system subject to bounded reference and disturbance signals $|r(t)| \leq \bar{r}$, $|d(t)| \leq \bar{d}$, is called* practically stable *(bounded), if for every $\delta > 0$ there exists $x_{\mathrm{C,max}} > 0$ and $x_{\mathrm{s,max}} > 0$ such that the following condition holds: If the initial state $\boldsymbol{x}_\mathrm{C}(0)$ is bounded by*

$$\left\|\boldsymbol{x}_\mathrm{C}(0)\right\|_\infty < \delta,$$

the state $\boldsymbol{x}_\mathrm{C}(t)$ is bounded for all $t \geq 0$ by

$$\left\|\boldsymbol{x}_\mathrm{C}(t)\right\|_\infty < x_{\mathrm{C,max}}$$

and the discrete state $x_\mathrm{s}(t)$ is bounded by

$$|x_\mathrm{s}(t)| \leq x_{\mathrm{s,max}}.$$

According to the following theorem, practical stability of the HEBC system can be deduced from the asymptotical stability of the continuous reference system (18).

Theorem 1. *An HEBC system (11) – (12) is practically stable in the sense of Definition 4.1, if and only if the continuous reference system (16) is asymptotically stable.*

Proof. The hybrid closed-loop system (11) – (12) can be described by the continuous reference system (18) extended with the bounded signal $u_1(t)$ taken as an external input signal. Asymptotic stability of the reference system implies that the eigenvalues of $\boldsymbol{A}_\mathrm{a}$ have negative real parts. Hence, boundedness of the input signals $r(t)$, $d(t)$ and $u_1(t)$ imply boundedness of the state $\boldsymbol{x}_\mathrm{C}(t)$

$$|r(t)| \leq \bar{r}, \; |d(t)| \leq \bar{d}, \; |u_1(t)| \leq \bar{e} \;\; \Rightarrow \|\boldsymbol{x}_\mathrm{C}(t)\|_\infty \leq x_{\mathrm{C,max}}.$$

Vice versa, with $\boldsymbol{A}_\mathrm{a}$ being unstable no bound on $\|\boldsymbol{x}_\mathrm{C}(t)\|_\infty$ can be given for large t.

In the second step it has to be shown that boundedness of $\boldsymbol{x}_\mathrm{C}(t)$ implies boundedness of the discrete state $x_\mathrm{s}(t)$ of the hybrid system. The continuous control input is

$$u_1(t) = u'(t) - u_2(t) = u'(t) - x_\mathrm{s}(t)$$

with

$$u'(t) = \boldsymbol{c}_{u'}^\mathrm{T}\boldsymbol{x}_\mathrm{C}(t) + d_\mathrm{K} r(t).$$

Hence, $x_\mathrm{s}(t)$ is bounded by

$$|x_\mathrm{s}(t)| \leq \|\boldsymbol{c}_{u'}^\mathrm{T}\|_\infty x_{\mathrm{C,max}} + d_\mathrm{K}\bar{r} + \bar{e} = x_{\mathrm{s,max}}. \;\square$$

5. EVENT-SEPARATION PROPERTIES

This section derives conditions on the event threshold in order to ensure that the hybrid control loop, subject to arbitrary bounded reference and disturbance signals, does not exhibit Zeno behaviour. It further gives a lower bound on the minimum inter-event time that serves as a basis for the choice of the event threshold.

5.1 Exclusion of Zeno behaviour

Assuming that $u_{2,\mathrm{min}}$ and $u_{2,\mathrm{max}}$ are small and large enough, the hybrid controller K has to be able to generate arbitrary resulting control input signals $u_\mathrm{res}(t) = \bar{u}_\mathrm{res} \in [u_{2,\mathrm{min}}, u_{2,\mathrm{max}}]$ in order to compensate an arbitrary disturbance $d(t) = \bar{d}$. In other words the domain of $u_1(t) + u_2(t)$ subject to (1) and (2)

$$u_1(t) + u_2(t) = n \cdot \Delta u_2 + m \cdot \bar{e}, \; n \in \mathbb{Z}, \; m \in [-1, 1]$$

has to cover the complete interval $[u_{2,\mathrm{min}}, u_{2,\mathrm{max}}]$.

Since the quantisation Δu_2 is a physical constraint, the event threshold $\bar{e}$ has to be chosen properly. The event threshold determines the domain of the continuous control input signal $u_1(t)$. Hence, if $\bar{e}$ is small and the quantisation Δu_2 is large, there might be values within $[u_{2,\min}, u_{2,\max}]$ which cannot be represented as a sum $u_1(t) + u_2(t)$. On the other hand, if $\bar{e}$ is large and Δu_2 is small, more than one combination of $u_1(t)$ and $u_2(t)$ exist for the same value of $u_{\text{res}}(t)$.

Figure 3 visualises this correlation. The vertical lines represent discrete values of control input u_2, while the grey areas mark the reachable values of $\bar{u}_{\text{res}}$ centered around the values of u_2. Hence, the distance between two neighbouring vertical lines is Δu_2 and the width of the grey areas is $2 \cdot \bar{e}$.

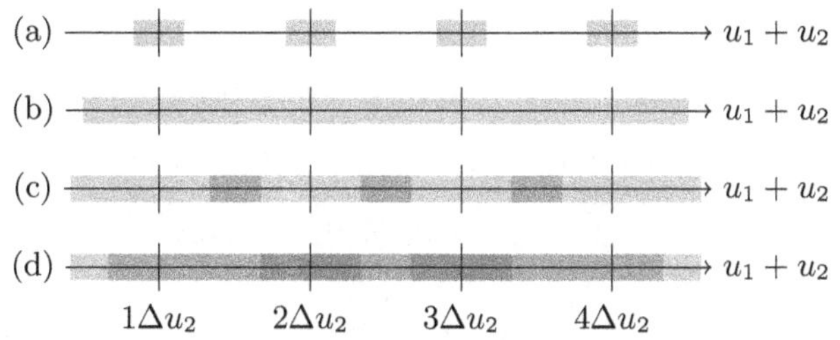

Figure 3: Visualisation of the control input overlap

Different cases can be distinguished:

- Diagram (a) of Fig. 3: If the event threshold is

$$\bar{e} < \frac{\Delta u_2}{2},$$

the domain of $u_1(t)+u_2(t)$ does not cover the complete interval $[u_{2,\min}, u_{2,\max}]$.

- Diagram (b): An event threshold of

$$\bar{e} = \frac{\Delta u_2}{2},$$

represents the limit case, where the domain of $u_1(t) + u_2(t)$ covers the complete interval $[u_{2,\min}, u_{2,\max}]$, but the behaviour of the system is not robust with respect to small deviations of Δu_2.

- Diagrams (c) and (d): If the threshold is

$$\bar{e} > \frac{\Delta u_2}{2},$$

multiple feasible combinations of $u_1(t)$ and $u_2(t)$ exist for a given value of $\bar{u}_{\text{res}}$.

THEOREM 2. *Consider a practically stable HEBC system subject to a reference signal $|r(t)| \leq \bar{r}$ with bounded rate $|\dot{r}(t)| \leq \dot{r}_{\max}(t)$ and a bounded disturbance signal $|d(t)| \leq \bar{d}$. The inequality*

$$\bar{e} \geq \frac{\Delta u_2}{2} \tag{19}$$

is a necessary condition for the exclusion of Zeno behaviour. The inequality

$$\bar{e} > \frac{\Delta u_2}{2} \tag{20}$$

is even sufficient.

Proof. The necessity of condition (19) is proved by contradiction. If the threshold is $\bar{e} < \frac{\Delta u_2}{2}$, the hybrid controller K cannot generate arbitrary control signals $u_{\text{res}}(t)$. Assuming the event threshold $u_1(t_k^-) = \bar{e}$ is reached at time $t = t_k$, a state jump leads to

$$u_1(t_k^+) = u_1(t_k^-) - \Delta u_2 = \bar{e} - \Delta u_2 \leq -\bar{e},$$

because Δu_2 is assumed to satisfy the inequality

$$\Delta u_2 \leq 2 \cdot \bar{e}.$$

Consequently, the event condition (7) is satisfied

$$|u_1(t_k^+)| \geq \bar{e}$$

and the next event is generated immediately with $t_{k+1} = t_k$. Obviously, the repetition of this sequence generates an infinite number of events at the same instant of time $t_k = t_{k+1} = t_{k+2} = ...$ (Zeno behaviour), which proves the necessity of (19).

In order to prove the sufficiency of (20), it is shown in the following that the discrete events are separated in time. The event threshold $|u_1(t_k)| \geq \bar{e}$ can be reached on two different ways. At $t = 0$ the initial values of the system states can be such that $u_1(0) > \bar{e}$. In this case a finite number m of events are generated at the same instant of time

$$t_0 = t_1 = ... = t_{m-1}.$$

This event sequence does not imply Zeno behaviour, because the number of events

$$m = \min\{j \in \mathbb{N} : |u_1(t_0^-)| - j \cdot \Delta u_2 < \bar{e}\} \tag{21}$$

is finite. The number of events is determined by the event generator such that the sum of the state jumps leads to the violation of the event condition

$$|u_1(t_{m-1}^+)| < \bar{e}.$$

On the other hand, the event threshold can be reached by continuous evolution. In this case only one event is generated with

$$|u_1(t_k^-)| = \bar{e} \Rightarrow |u_1(t_k^+)| = |\bar{e} - \Delta u_2| < \bar{e}.$$

It can be concluded that a sequence of one or more discrete events will always be followed by a time period with continuous evolution of the system state. During these time periods, the behaviour of the closed-loop system is determined by the continuous dynamics (11). The first control input signal is given by

$$u_1(t) = \boldsymbol{c}_{u'}^{\mathrm{T}} \boldsymbol{x}_{\mathrm{C}}(t) + d_{\mathrm{K}} r(t) - x_{\mathrm{s}}(t). \tag{22}$$

Hence, $u_1(t)$ can be interpreted as the output signal of the continuous dynamical system (11), (22). Because of the continuous dynamics (which are stable by assumption) and the bounded rate of $r(t)$, there is a minimum time span $T > 0$ before the next discrete event can occur:

$$|u_1(t_k^+)| < \bar{e} \Rightarrow \exists T > 0 : |u_1(t_k + \tau)| < \bar{e} \, \forall \tau < T.$$

Therefore, Zeno behaviour is excluded. □

5.2 Minimum inter-event time

The minimum inter-event time represents the minimum time span between two consecutive events. It is an important property of hybrid systems. Many methods for stability and performance analysis of hybrid systems are based on the fact that the system holds a certain minimum inter-event time (see e.g. [6]). By extending the results of Section 5.1, Theorem 3 gives a lower bound for the minimum inter-event time of an HEBC system.

THEOREM 3. *Consider an HEBC system subject to a reference signal* $|r(t)| \leq \bar{r}$ *with bounded rate* $|\dot{r}(t)| \leq \dot{r}_{\max}(t)$ *and a bounded disturbance signal* $|d(t)| \leq \bar{d}$. *There is a minimum inter-event time*

$$T_{\text{MIET}} = \frac{\bar{e} - |\bar{e} - \Delta u_2|}{\dot{u}_{1,\max}}, \tag{23}$$

such that

$$t_{k+1} - t_k \geq T_{\text{MIET}},$$
$$\forall k \geq m = \min\{j \in \mathbb{N} : |u_1(0)| - j \cdot \Delta u_2 < \bar{e}\} \tag{24}$$

with

$$\dot{u}_{1,\max} = \|\boldsymbol{c}_{\text{u}'}^{\text{T}} \boldsymbol{A}_{\text{b}}\|_\infty x_{\text{C},\max} + \|\boldsymbol{c}_{\text{u}'}^{\text{T}} \begin{pmatrix} \boldsymbol{b}_{\text{K}} \\ \boldsymbol{b}_1 d_{\text{K}} \end{pmatrix}\|_\infty \bar{r} \tag{25}$$
$$+ \|\boldsymbol{c}_{\text{u}'}^{\text{T}} \begin{pmatrix} \boldsymbol{0} \\ \boldsymbol{b}_3 \end{pmatrix}\|_\infty \bar{d} + \|\boldsymbol{c}_{\text{u}'} \boldsymbol{b}_\Delta\|_\infty x_{\text{s},\max} + |d_{\text{K}}| \dot{r}_{\max}.$$

Proof. Differentiating equation (22) gives an expression for the rate of change of the continuous control input signal

$$\dot{u}_1(t) = \boldsymbol{c}_{\text{u}'}^{\text{T}} \dot{\boldsymbol{x}}_{\text{C}}(t) + d_{\text{K}} \dot{r}(t) \tag{26}$$
$$= \boldsymbol{c}_{\text{u}'}^{\text{T}} \left[\boldsymbol{A}_{\text{b}} \boldsymbol{x}_{\text{C}}(t) + \boldsymbol{B}_{\text{b}} \begin{pmatrix} r(t) \\ d(t) \end{pmatrix} - \boldsymbol{b}_\Delta x_{\text{s}}(t) \right] + d_{\text{K}} \dot{r}(t) \tag{27}$$

which is bounded by[1]

$$|\dot{u}_1(t)| \leq \|\boldsymbol{c}_{\text{u}'}^{\text{T}} \boldsymbol{A}_{\text{b}}\|_\infty x_{\text{C},\max} + \|\boldsymbol{c}_{\text{u}'}^{\text{T}} \begin{pmatrix} \boldsymbol{b}_{\text{K}} \\ \boldsymbol{b}_1 d_{\text{K}} \end{pmatrix}\|_\infty \bar{r} \tag{28}$$
$$+ \|\boldsymbol{c}_{\text{u}'}^{\text{T}} \begin{pmatrix} \boldsymbol{0} \\ \boldsymbol{b}_3 \end{pmatrix}\|_\infty \bar{d} + \|\boldsymbol{c}_{\text{u}'} \boldsymbol{b}_\Delta\|_\infty x_{\text{s},\max} + |d_{\text{K}}| \dot{r}_{\max}.$$

Hence, regarding a time span without discrete events it holds

$$|u_1(t_1) - u_1(t_0)| \leq \int_{t_0}^{t_1} |\dot{u}_1(\tau)| \mathrm{d}\tau \leq \dot{u}_{1,\max} \cdot (t_1 - t_0). \tag{29}$$

Using (29) the evolution of $u_1(t)$ starting at the time instant t_k of a discrete event can be approximated by

$$|u_1(t_k + \tau) - u_1(t_k^+)| \leq \dot{u}_{1,\max} \cdot \tau.$$

With $\bar{e}$ satisfying (19) the absolute value of $u_1(t_k^+)$ after a discrete event is

$$|u_1(t_k^+)| = |\bar{e} - \Delta u_2|.$$

It can be concluded that

$$|u_1(t_k^+ + \tau)| < \bar{e} \ \forall \tau < T_{\text{MIET}},$$

i.e. the control signal $u_1(t)$ cannot reach the event threshold before the time span T_{MIET} has elapsed. □

[1]The following definition of the infinity norm of a matrix $\boldsymbol{A} \in \mathbb{R}^{n \times m}$ is used:

$$\|\boldsymbol{A}\|_\infty = \sqrt{nm} \cdot \max_{ij} |a_{ij}|.$$

Remark. As analysed in Section 5.1 the initial values of the system states can trigger an initial sequence of m discrete events. Due to the uncertainty of the inital states, the value of $u_1(t_{m-1}^+)$ after this sequence of events is not exactly known. That is the reason why the minimum inter-event time T_{MIET} is only guaranteed for all events t_k with $k \geq m$. □

5.3 Choice of the event threshold

This section analyses how to properly choose the event threshold $\bar{e}$. In order to avoid Zeno behaviour, Theorem 2 has given a lower bound on $\bar{e}$. A second constraint on $\bar{e}$ follows from the need of the hybrid controller to satisfy (1) in order to keep $u_1(t)$ in the linear region:

$$\bar{e} \leq \bar{u}_1 \ \Rightarrow \ |u_1(t)| \leq \bar{u}_1 \ \forall t \geq 0.$$

It can be concluded that the following condition on the constraints of the control input signals $u_1(t)$ and $u_2(t)$ is necessary for the applicability of the design approach described in Section 3:

$$\Delta u_2 < 2 \cdot \bar{u}_1. \tag{30}$$

With (30) being satisfied, the event threshold can be chosen to take any value of the interval $\bar{e} \in]\frac{\Delta u_2}{2}, \bar{u}_1]$.

ASSUMPTION 5.1. *In the remainder of the paper the event threshold* $\bar{e}$ *is assumed to be*

$$\bar{e} = \Delta u_2.$$

It follows from (23) that the largest minimum inter-event time can be guaranteed for $\bar{e} = \Delta u_2$. This is because it implies that $u_1(t)$ is reset to zero at the time instants of the discrete events.

6. ASYMPTOTIC BEHAVIOUR

In the previous sections the behaviour of HEBC systems has been analysed for arbitrary bounded reference and disturbance signals. This section is dedicated to the asymptotic behaviour of HEBC systems for constant reference and disturbance signals.

If the differences between the input dynamics I_1 and I_2 are too large, practical stability of the closed-loop system does not imply that the system converges to an equilibrium as illustrated by the application example in Section 7.2. Therefore, sufficient conditions ensuring that the system asymptotically converges to an equilibrium and tracks a constant reference signal are derived in this section.

6.1 Finite number of discrete events

In order to prove that the system converges to an asymptotically stable equilibrium, it has to be guaranteed that the switching of the discrete control input signal u_2 stops for sufficiently large t.

LEMMA 1. *If there is a time instant* t_s *such that the difference between the reference control input signal* $u'(t)$ *and an arbitrary constant value* u_c *is bounded for all* $t > t_s$ *by*

$$|u'(t) - u_c| < \frac{1}{2}\bar{e}, \ \ \forall t > t_s, \tag{31}$$

not more than one discrete event will occur for $t > t_s$.

Proof. The proof is done by case-by-case analysis. Based on the fact that the derivatives of u' and u_1 are identical for $t \neq t_k$ and assuming that $u'(t)$ enters the region around u_c from above

$$u'(t_s) - u_c = \frac{\bar{e}}{2}$$

the set of values that $u_1(t)$ can reach by continuous evolution is constrained by

$$u_1(t)\Big|_{t>t_s} \in \left]u_1(t_s) - \bar{e},\, u_1(t_s)\right[.$$

It can be concluded that no discret event can occur for $t > t_s$ if $u_1(t_s) \geq 0$. If $u_1(t_s) < 0$ the event threshold can be reached by $u_1(t_k^-) = -\bar{e}$. Consequently, the interval that can be reached by u_1 is shifted by $\bar{e}$

$$u_1(t)\Big|_{t>t_k} \in \left]u_1(t_s),\, u_1(t_s) + \bar{e}\right[,$$

such that no more event can be triggered for $t > t_k$.

Similar considerations hold if $u'(t)$ enters the region around u_c from below

$$u'(t_s) - u_c = -\frac{\bar{e}}{2}.$$

In this case the set of values that $u_1(t)$ can reach by continuous evolution is constrained by

$$u_1(t)\Big|_{t>t_s} \in \left]u_1(t_s),\, u_1(t_s) + \bar{e}\right[.$$

Hence, no more event can occur if $u_1(t_s) \leq 0$, while $u_1(t_s) > 0$ can lead to one more event $t_k > t_s$ before the switching stops. □

Based on Lemma 1 the following Theorem gives a sufficient condition on the system dynamics ensuring that the switching of u_2 stops for sufficiently large t.

THEOREM 4. *Consider an HEBC system subject to constant reference and disturbance signals $r(t) = \bar{r}$, $d(t) = \bar{d}$. The switching of the discrete control input signal $u_2(t)$ stops for sufficiently large t, if the following inequality holds:*

$$\int_0^\infty \left| \boldsymbol{c}_{u'}^{\mathrm{T}} e^{\boldsymbol{A}_{\mathrm{a}}\tau} \boldsymbol{b}_\Delta \right| \mathrm{d}\tau < \frac{1}{2} \tag{32}$$

Proof. Similar to the proof of Theorem 1 the linear approximation (18) is applied with $|u_1(t)| \leq \bar{e}$ representing the nonlinearities. Hence, the trajectory of the reference control input signal $u'(t)$ is determined by

$$u'(t) = \boldsymbol{c}_{u'}^{\mathrm{T}} e^{\boldsymbol{A}_{\mathrm{a}}t} \boldsymbol{x}_{\mathrm{C}}(0) + \int_0^t \boldsymbol{c}_{u'}^{\mathrm{T}} e^{\boldsymbol{A}_{\mathrm{a}}(t-\tau)} \boldsymbol{B}_{\mathrm{a}} \begin{pmatrix} \bar{r} \\ \bar{d} \end{pmatrix} \mathrm{d}\tau + \int_0^t \boldsymbol{c}_{u'}^{\mathrm{T}} e^{\boldsymbol{A}_{\mathrm{a}}(t-\tau)} \boldsymbol{b}_\Delta u_1(t) \mathrm{d}\tau + d_{\mathrm{K}}\bar{r}. \tag{33}$$

The zero-input response converges to zero, because the matrix $\boldsymbol{A}_{\mathrm{a}}$ is assumed to be Hurwitz. Furthermore the value u_c is defined by

$$u_c = \int_0^\infty \boldsymbol{c}_{u'}^{\mathrm{T}} e^{\boldsymbol{A}_{\mathrm{a}}\tau} \boldsymbol{B}_{\mathrm{a}} \begin{pmatrix} \bar{r} \\ \bar{d} \end{pmatrix} \mathrm{d}\tau + d_{\mathrm{K}}\bar{r}.$$

Consequently, for sufficiently large t the following expression for $u'(t)$ holds

$$u'(t) = u_c + \int_0^t \boldsymbol{c}_{u'}^{\mathrm{T}} e^{\boldsymbol{A}_{\mathrm{a}}(t-\tau)} \boldsymbol{b}_\Delta u_1(t) \mathrm{d}\tau, \quad t \gg 0$$

which is bounded by

$$|u'(t) - u_c| \leq \int_0^\infty \left| \boldsymbol{c}_{u'}^{\mathrm{T}} e^{\boldsymbol{A}_{\mathrm{a}}\tau} \boldsymbol{b}_\Delta \right| \mathrm{d}\tau \cdot \bar{e}, \quad t \gg 0$$

It follows that inequality (32) leads to

$$|u'(t) - u_c| < \frac{\bar{e}}{2}, \quad t \gg 0$$

for sufficiently large t and Lemma 1 can be applied. □

6.2 Asymptotic set-point tracking

A different approximation of the hybrid closed-loop system can be used to derive a condition ensuring the requirement (ii) on asymptotic set-point tracking:

$$\begin{aligned} \dot{\boldsymbol{x}}_{\mathrm{C}}(t) &= \boldsymbol{A}_{\mathrm{b}} \boldsymbol{x}_{\mathrm{C}}(t) + \boldsymbol{B}_{\mathrm{b}} \begin{pmatrix} r(t) \\ d(t) \end{pmatrix} - \boldsymbol{b}_\Delta u_2(t) \\ y(t) &= \boldsymbol{c}_y^{\mathrm{T}} \boldsymbol{x}_{\mathrm{C}}(t) \end{aligned} \tag{34}$$

Instead of using $u_1(t)$ to represent the nonlinearities of the system, eqn. (34) takes the discrete control input signal $u_2(t)$ as an external input signal, which is constant if the switching has stopped. Figure 4 shows the structure of the corresponding linear approximate model.

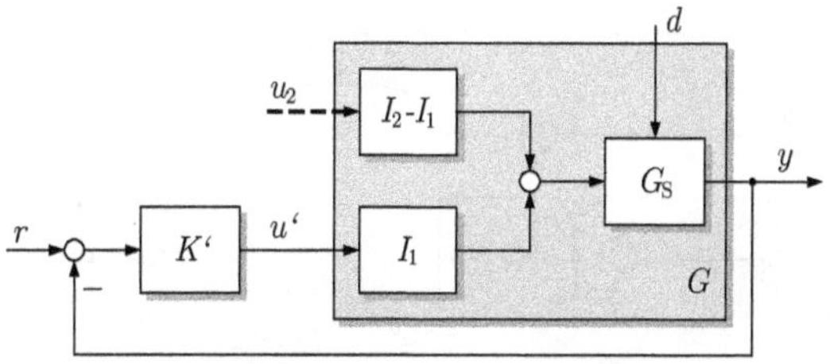

Figure 4: Structure of the second linear approximate model

The linear model can be analysed in the frequency domain with $I_1(s)$, $I_2(s)$, $K'(s)$, $G_{\mathrm{S}}(s)$ representing the transfer functions of the corresponding subsystems. The transfer function $G_{u2}(s) = \frac{Y(s)}{U_2(s)}$ is determined by

$$G_{u2}(s) = \frac{(I_2(s) - I_1(s))G_{\mathrm{S}}(s)}{1 + K'(s)I_1(s)G_{\mathrm{S}}(s)}.$$

It is assumed that the input dynamics I_1 and I_2 have the same DC gain: $I_1(0) = I_2(0)$. Hence, $G_{u2}(0)$ is zero for arbitrary controllers K'. The disturbance transfer function

$$G_d(s) = \frac{Y(s)}{D(s)} = \frac{G_{\mathrm{S}}(s)}{1 + K'(s)I_1(s)G_{\mathrm{S}}(s)}$$

and the reference transfer function

$$G_r(s) = \frac{Y(s)}{R(s)} = \frac{K'(s)I_1(s)G_{\mathrm{S}}(s)}{1 + K'(s)I_1(s)G_{\mathrm{S}}(s)}$$

show that asymptotic tracking behaviour is achieved, if K' contains an integrator and all the poles of $G_r(s)$ have a negative real part (or equivalently the matrix $\boldsymbol{A}_{\mathrm{b}}$ is Hurwitz). This fact leads to the following Theorem:

THEOREM 5. *An HEBC system subject to a constant disturbance signal $d(t) = \bar{d}$ asymptotically tracks a constant reference signal $r(t) = \bar{r}$ if the following conditions are met:*

1. *The matrices $\boldsymbol{A}_\mathrm{a}$ and $\boldsymbol{A}_\mathrm{b}$ are Hurwitz.*
2. *The inequality*

$$\int_0^\infty \left| \boldsymbol{c}_{u'}^\mathrm{T} e^{\boldsymbol{A}_\mathrm{a}\tau} \boldsymbol{b}_\Delta \right| \mathrm{d}\tau < \frac{1}{2}$$

   holds.

3. *The continuous reference controller K' (and thereby the continuous controller K_1) contains an integrator.*

Proof. Conditions 1 and 2 ensure that the switching of u_2 stops for sufficiently large t and the system converges to an asymptotically stable equilibrium. Condition 3 guarantees that the output of the system in the equilibrium is equal to the reference signal $\bar{y} = \bar{r}$. □

7. APPLICATION EXAMPLE

7.1 Multistage pumping system

This section illustrates the results of this paper for a multistage pumping system (Fig. 5) taken from [11]. The aim

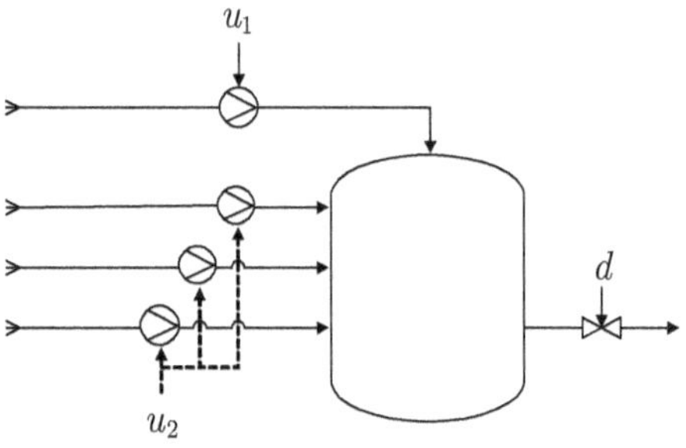

Figure 5: Multistage pumping system

is to control the liquid level of a tank that is fed by several pumps with fixed power and an additional pump with flexible power. The fixed-power pumps can be switched on and off via u_2 with I_2 representing the turn-on and turn-off delays. The power of the flexible pump can be adjusted continuously via u_1, where I_1 represents the dynamics of the pump. The drain is considered as a disturbance input. With I_1 and I_2 modeled as first-order lags with time constants T_1 and T_2 and G_S as an integrator with time constant T_3, the plant can be described by (6) with

$$\boldsymbol{A}_\mathrm{G} = \begin{pmatrix} 0 & \frac{1}{T_3} & \frac{1}{T_3} \\ 0 & -\frac{1}{T_1} & 0 \\ 0 & 0 & -\frac{1}{T_2} \end{pmatrix}, \; \boldsymbol{b}_1 = \begin{pmatrix} 0 \\ \frac{1}{T_1} \\ 0 \end{pmatrix}, \; \boldsymbol{b}_2 = \begin{pmatrix} 0 \\ 0 \\ \frac{1}{T_2} \end{pmatrix}$$

$$\boldsymbol{c}_\mathrm{G}^\mathrm{T} = \begin{pmatrix} 1 & 0 & 0 \end{pmatrix}, \; \boldsymbol{b}_3 = \begin{pmatrix} \frac{1}{T_3} \\ 0 \\ 0 \end{pmatrix}. \tag{35}$$

The reference controller is designed to be a PI controller with

$$\boldsymbol{A}_\mathrm{K} = 0, \; \boldsymbol{b}_K = \frac{k}{T_K}, \; \boldsymbol{c}_\mathrm{K}^\mathrm{T} = 1, \; d_\mathrm{K} = k$$

and the event threshold is chosen to be $\bar{e} = \Delta u_2$. Hence, Zeno behaviour is excluded due to Theorem 2. The matrices $\boldsymbol{A}_\mathrm{a}$ and $\boldsymbol{A}_\mathrm{b}$ are

$$\boldsymbol{A}_\mathrm{a} = \begin{pmatrix} 0 & -\frac{1}{T_k} & 0 & 0 \\ 0 & 0 & \frac{1}{T_3} & \frac{1}{T_3} \\ 0 & 0 & -\frac{1}{T_1} & 0 \\ \frac{1}{T_2} & -\frac{k}{T_2} & 0 & -\frac{1}{T_2} \end{pmatrix} \tag{36}$$

$$\boldsymbol{A}_\mathrm{b} = \begin{pmatrix} 0 & -\frac{1}{T_k} & 0 & 0 \\ 0 & 0 & \frac{1}{T_3} & \frac{1}{T_3} \\ \frac{1}{T_1} & -\frac{k}{T_1} & -\frac{1}{T_1} & 0 \\ 0 & 0 & 0 & -\frac{1}{T_2} \end{pmatrix}. \tag{37}$$

For the parameters from Table 1 the matrices $\boldsymbol{A}_\mathrm{a}$ and $\boldsymbol{A}_\mathrm{b}$ are Hurwitz. Therefore, the HEBC system is practically stable

Table 1: Simulation parameters

Parameter	T_1	T_2	T_3	Δu_2	k	T_K	$\bar{e}$
Value	0.2	1	1.5	1	0.5	9	1

(Theorem 1).

Asymptotic tracking of the reference signal can be proven by Theorem 5, where conditions 1 and 3 are already checked and condition 2 is met because

$$\int_0^\infty \left| \boldsymbol{c}_{u'}^\mathrm{T} e^{\boldsymbol{A}_\mathrm{a}\tau} \boldsymbol{b}_\Delta \right| \mathrm{d}\tau = 0.46 < \frac{1}{2}.$$

Figure 6 shows the system behaviour. The top diagram depicts the output signal $y(t)$ (solid line) following the dashed reference signal $r(t)$. There is a jump of the disturbance signal at $t = 40$. The grey band marks the maximum deviation $|y(t) - \hat{y}(t)|$. The second diagram shows the continuous control input signal $u_1(t)$. Every time $u_1(t)$ reaches the event threshold, a discrete event is triggered (third diagram). Consequently u_1 is reset to zero and u_2 (fourth diagram) is switched to the next quantisation level. The bottom diagram shows the reference control input signal $u'(t) = u_1(t) + u_2(t)$. The horizontal lines mark the region around u_c indicating that the switching is going to stop. The value of u_c depends on the disturbance signal $d(t)$. Hence, the jump of $d(t)$ leads to a jump of u_c with

$$u_c = \begin{cases} 0, & t < 40 \\ 1.4, & t \geq 40. \end{cases}$$

At $t = t_s$ the reference control signal enters this region from below and one discrete event is triggered after t_s before the switching stops.

7.2 HEBC system with a limit cycle

Figure 7 shows the behaviour of the multistage pumping system as described in the previous section, where the input dynamics I_1 are replaced by a second-order filter with a resonance frequency of $\omega_0 = 0.75$ and a damping coefficient of $D = 0.2$. Theorem 1 is still satisfied ensuring that the closed-loop system is practically stable in the sense of Definition 4.1. However, the system does not converge to an equilibrium. This is due to the large differences between the input dynamics I_1 and I_2. Instead of converging to an equilibrium the system reaches a limit cycle with periodic discrete events.

Obviously, a weakly dampened second order filter is not a realistic model for the dynamics of a pump. However, this

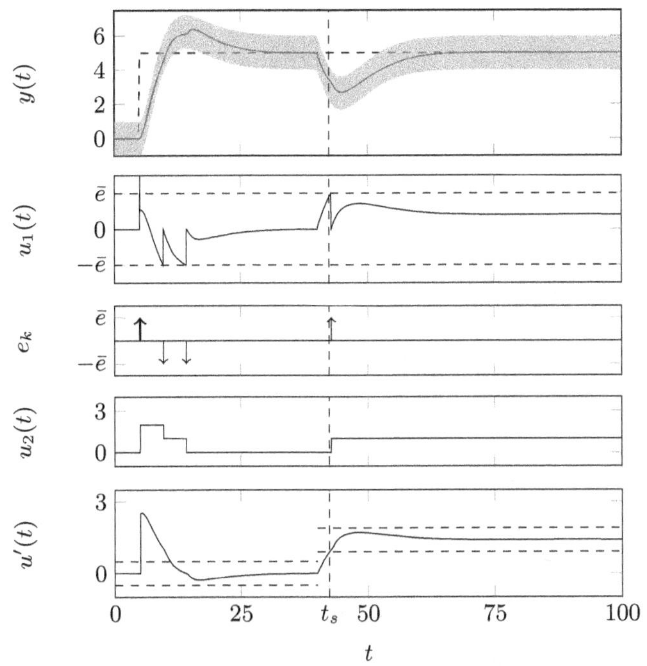

Figure 6: Behaviour of the pumping system

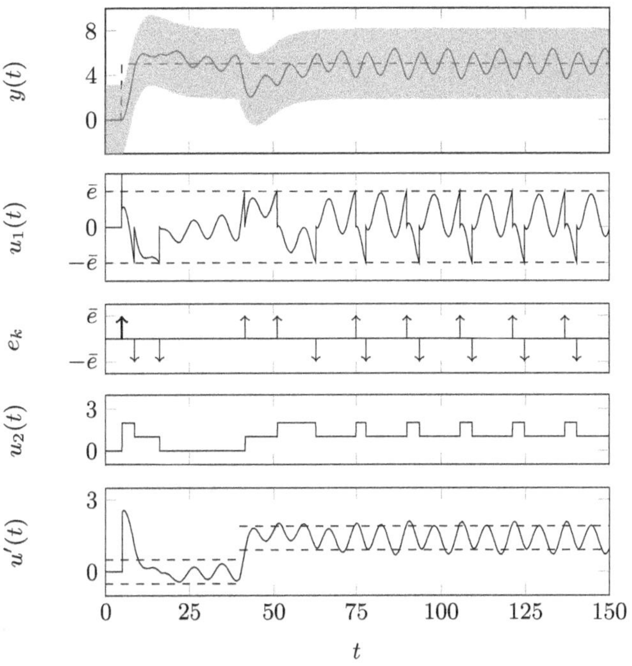

Figure 7: HEBC system with a limit cycle

example shows that the stability condition of Theorem 1 does not imply asymptotic tracking of a set-point, but further conditions are needed as described in Section 6.

8. CONCLUSIONS

The class of HEBC systems has been introduced in [11] as an interesting class of hybrid control systems and a method to design the hybrid controller for HEBC systems with additive control input signals has been proposed. This paper has given a detailed analysis of the resulting hybrid closed-loop system. It proves necessary and sufficient conditions concerning the event-separation properties of the system, which imply the exclusion of Zeno behaviour. Based on the analysis, rules on the proper choice of the event threshold could be derived. Furthermore it has been analysed which conditions the continuous reference system has to meet such that the resulting hybrid system asymptotically tracks the reference signal.

Future work will concentrate on a generalisation of the results. In order to cover a wide spread of applications, systems with multiplicative control input signals have to be included. In this extension, switches of the controller dynamics are necessary to adapt the continuous controller to the changing gain of its control input signal. By that, the hybrid character of the system is strengthened even more.

9. REFERENCES

[1] K. J. Aström. Event based control. *Analysis and Design of Nonlinear Control Systems*, pp. 127–147. Springer, 2008.

[2] D. Borgers and W. Heemels. Event-separation properties of event-triggered control systems. *IEEE Trans. on Automatic Control*, 59(10):2644–2656, 2014.

[3] R. Goebel, R. G. Sanfelic, and A. R. Teel. Hybrid dynamical systems. *IEEE Control Systems*, 29(2):28–93, April 2009.

[4] W. M. Haddad, V. Chellaboina, and S. G. Nersesov. *Impulsive and Hybrid Dynamical Systems: Stability, Dissipativity, and Control.* Princeton University Press, 2006.

[5] W. Heemels, J. Sandee, and P. Van Den Bosch. Analysis of event-driven controllers for linear systems. *Intern. J. of Contr.*, 81(4):571–590, 2008.

[6] J. P. Hespanha and A. S. Morse. Stability of switched systems with average dwell-time. In *IEEE Conf. on Decision and Control*, 1999. pp. 2655–2660.

[7] D. Liberzon. *Switching in Systems and Control.* Birkhäuser, 2003.

[8] J. Lunze. Event-based control: a tutorial introduction. *J. of the Society of Instrument and Control Engineers*, 49(11):783–788, 2010.

[9] J. Lunze and F. Lamnabhi-Lagarrigue. *Handbook of Hybrid Systems Control.* Cambridge University Press, 2009.

[10] J. Lunze and D. Lehmann. A state-feedback approach to event-based control. *Automatica*, 46(1):211–215, 2010.

[11] T. Noesselt, M. Schultalbers, and J. Lunze. A design method for hybrid event-based control systems. *IFAC Conf. on Analysis and Design of Hybrid Systems*, 48(27):135 - 140, 2015.

Semi-autonomous Intersection Collision Avoidance through Job-shop Scheduling

Heejin Ahn
Massachusetts Institute of Technology
77 Massachusetts Avenue
Cambridge, MA, 02139
hjahn@mit.edu

Domitilla Del Vecchio
Massachusetts Institute of Technology
77 Massachusetts Avenue
Cambridge, MA, 02139
ddv@mit.edu

ABSTRACT

In this paper, we design a supervisor to prevent vehicle collisions at intersections. An intersection is modeled as an area containing multiple conflict points where vehicle paths cross in the future. At every time step, the supervisor determines whether there will be more than one vehicle in the vicinity of a conflict point at the same time. If there is, then an impending collision is detected, and the supervisor overrides the drivers to avoid collision. A major challenge in the design of a supervisor as opposed to an autonomous vehicle controller is to verify whether future collisions will occur based on the current drivers choices. This verification problem is particularly hard due to the large number of vehicles often involved in intersection collision, to the multitude of conflict points, and to the vehicles dynamics. In order to solve the verification problem, we translate the problem to a job-shop scheduling problem that yields equivalent answers. The job-shop scheduling problem can, in turn, be transformed into a mixed-integer linear program when the vehicle dynamics are first-order dynamics, and can thus be solved by using a commercial solver.

Keywords

Intersection collision avoidance; multi-vehicle control; supervisory control; collision detection; verification; scheduling

1. INTRODUCTION

In the United States, 33,561 people lost their lives in vehicle crashes in 2012, and 26 % of them occurred at or near intersections [26]. This raises the need for improved safety systems that actively prevent collisions at intersections. For example, a centralized controller could be implemented on the infrastructure to coordinate vehicles near an intersection so as to prevent collisions. However, since a large number of vehicles are often involved in intersection collisions and vehicles are dynamic agents, the design of such systems faces challenges in terms of computational complexity. An additional substantial complication is that the system should override the drivers only when their driving will certainly cause a collision. That is, override actions should be minimally restrictive. This allows drivers to be in control of the vehicle unless unable to handle a dangerous situation. This supervisor can also be used as a safety guard for future fully autonomous vehicles driving in complex environment.

In this paper, we design a supervisor, which can be implemented on an infrastructure, communicating with human-driven vehicles near an intersection as shown in Figure 1. The most important and challenging part in the design is to determine whether vehicles' current driving will cause collisions at some future time. This is important because the exact collision detection, called the *verification problem*, makes the supervisor least restrictive. This problem is not scalable with respect to the number of vehicles near an intersection yet their future safety must be verified ev-

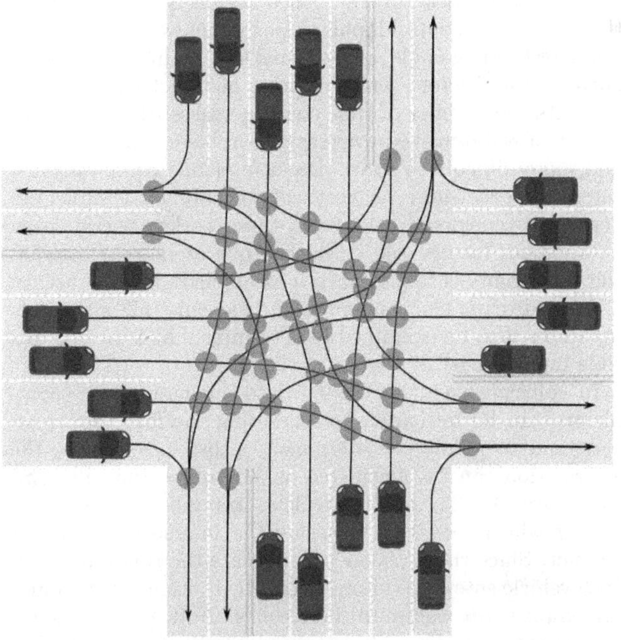

Figure 1: General intersection scenario, taken from [25] to encompass the most dangerous intersections in Massachusetts, USA. This intersection contains forty eight conflict areas (small red circles). The supervisor designed in this paper can prevent collisions at the conflict areas by minimally overriding the vehicles.

HSCC'16, April 12-14, 2016, Vienna, Austria

DOI: http://dx.doi.org/10.1145/2883817.2883830

ery τ seconds, where τ is usually 100 ms [21]. To solve the verification problem in real-time, we formulate a job-shop scheduling problem, and prove that this is equivalent to the former problem. Although the job-shop scheduling problem is NP-hard [15], we can solve this problem using a commercial solver by converting it into a mixed-integer linear programming problem.

Mixed integer programming can handle both discrete and continuous aspects of a system. For example, collision avoidance can be formulated using discrete variables while the dynamic behaviors of vehicles, such as position and speed, are represented by continuous variables. Thus, mixed-integer programming has been employed in various collision avoidance applications such as air traffic control [4, 8, 28] and multi-robot control [13, 18]. Since the decision variables of these works are control inputs, for example, velocity, acceleration, or heading angle, at each time step within a finite time horizon, the discrete-time dynamics of vehicles are considered. As the number of time steps increases, the discretization error is diminished whereas the problem becomes larger and more difficult to solve. Because of this computational complexity, real-time verification is usually not feasible and hence not considered. Moreover, these works are cast in an autonomous framework in which if one input that satisfies the constraints is found, then it is applied. In contrast, in a semi-autonomous framework, such as ours, all admissible inputs need to be examined to determine if at least one feasible input exists.

In collision avoidance confined to an intersection, complexity can be mitigated by exploiting the fact that vehicles tend to follow predetermined paths. Given this, the intersection can be considered as a resource that all vehicles share. In [23, 24, 30], vehicles are assigned time slots during which they can be inside the intersection without conflict. Since the decision variables are the times at which each vehicle enters the intersection, the continuous dynamics are employed to compute these times. Notice that this approach considers $O(n)$ decision variables if n is the number of vehicles, whereas the approach in the previous paragraph considers at least $n * N$ decision variables if N is the number of time steps on a finite time horizon. Because of the significantly smaller number of decision variables, the scheduling approach is computationally more efficient. The above works also assume full autonomy, which is not applicable to the scenarios considered in this paper. A detailed review of autonomous intersection management can be found in [7].

A semi-autonomous framework with the scheduling approach is considered in [10, 11] by proving the equivalence between the verification problem and the scheduling problem. In these works, the authors design a least restrictive supervisor and restrict their attention to a special intersection scenario where all paths of vehicles intersect at one conflict area as indicated by the dashed region in Figure 2. While maintaining the same structure of the supervisor as in [10, 11], we formulate a *job-shop scheduling problem* to account for general scenarios of an intersection, where the paths of vehicles intersect at multiple points as in Figure 1. Considering multiple conflict points enables us to design a less conservative verification problem, but makes it more difficult to translate the problem to a job-shop scheduling problem. In this paper, we prove that our job-shop scheduling problem is equivalent to the verification problem with multiple conflict points. By virtue of this proof, we can solve

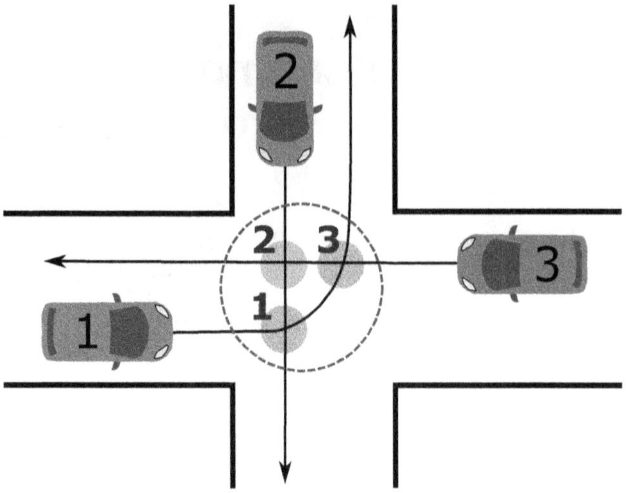

Figure 2: Example of three vehicles with three conflict areas. The dashed circle represents the intersection model used in [10, 11]. In this paper, the intersection is modeled as multiple conflict areas as represented by the three shaded circles.

the verification problem by solving the job-shop scheduling problem, which is computationally tractable. The job-shop scheduling problem is then transformed into a mixed-integer linear programming problem by assuming the single integrator dynamics of vehicles. Although a mixed-integer linear programming problem is NP-hard [15], it can be solved by commercial solvers such as CPLEX [22] or Gurobi [19].

The rest of this paper is organized as follows. In Section 2, we introduce the intersection model and the dynamic model of vehicles. In Section 3, we formally state the verification problem and the supervisor-design problem. The verification problem can be solved by formulating and solving a job-shop scheduling problem, which plays the most important role in the design of the supervisor. We then transform the job-shop scheduling problem into a mixed-integer linear programming problem to solve the job-shop scheduling problem using a commercial solver. These solutions will be given in Section 4. We conclude this paper by presenting the results of computer simulations in Section 5 and conclusions in Section 6.

2. SYSTEM DEFINITION

Let us consider n vehicles approaching an intersection. The vehicles follow their predetermined paths, and a point at which at least two of the paths intersect is defined as a *conflict point.* Around a conflict point, we define a *conflict area* to account for the size of vehicles. The intersection is modeled as a set of m conflict areas as in Figures 1 and 2. Throughout this paper, vehicles and conflict areas are distinguished by integer indexes $1, \ldots, n$ and $1, \ldots, m$, respectively. In order to focus only on intersection collision, we assume that there is only one vehicle per road.

To model the longitudinal dynamics of vehicles, let $x_j \in X_j$ be the dynamic state of vehicle j. Let $u_j \in U_j \subset \mathbb{R}$ the control input of vehicle j. Then, the longitudinal dynamics are as follows:

$$\dot{x}_j = f_j(x_j, u_j), \qquad y_j = h_j(x_j). \tag{1}$$

The output of the system is the position $y_j \in Y_j$ along the path. Here, u_j is in a compact set, e.g., $u_j \in U_j := [u_{j,min}, u_{j,max}]$. With abuse of notation, let u_j denote the input signal as well as the input value in $\mathbb{R}$. The input signal $u_j \in \mathcal{U}_j$ is a function of time defined as $\{u_j(t) : u_j(t) \in U_j \text{ for } t \geq 0\}$. We assume that the output y_j continuously depends on the input $u_j \in \mathcal{U}_j$ and $\mathcal{U}_j$ is path-connected.

Let $x_j(t, u_j, x_j(0))$ denote the state reached after time t with input signal u_j starting from $x_j(0)$, where $x_j(0)$ is an initial state at $t = 0$. Similarly, let $y_j(t, u_j, x_j(0))$ denote the position reached after time t with input signal u_j starting from $x_j(0)$. The aggregate state, output, input, and input signal are denoted by $\mathbf{x} \in \mathbf{X}, \mathbf{y} \in \mathbf{Y}, \mathbf{u} \in \mathbf{U}$, and $\mathbf{u} \in \mathcal{U}$, respectively.

One of the most important properties of the dynamic model (1) is the order-preserving property. That is, for $u_j(t) \leq u'_j(t)$ for all t, we have $x_j(t, u_j, x_j(0)) \leq x_j(t, u'_j, x_j(0))$ and $y_j(t, u_j, x_j(0)) \leq y_j(t, u'_j, x_j(0))$ for all $t \geq 0$. We will exploit this property in the design of the supervisor, particularly in formulating the job-shop scheduling problem.

3. PROBLEM STATEMENT

Let $(\alpha_{ij}, \beta_{ij}) \subset \mathbb{R}$ denote the location of conflict area i along the longitudinal path of vehicle j. A conflict area is defined around a conflict point such that a collision occurs if more than one vehicle stay in a conflict area at the same time. That is, a collision occurs if $\mathbf{y} \in B$ where

$$B := \{\mathbf{y} \in Y : \text{ for some } j \text{ and } j', \\ y_j \in (\alpha_{ij}, \beta_{ij}) \text{ and } y_{j'} \in (\alpha_{ij'}, \beta_{ij'})\}. \tag{2}$$

This set B is called the *bad set*, and if $\mathbf{y}(t) \notin B$ for all $t \geq 0$, we consider the system *safe*.

The verification problem is to determine if collisions at an intersection can be prevented at all future times given an initial state. We formally state this problem using the bad set (2) as follows.

PROBLEM 1 (VERIFICATION). *Given $\mathbf{x}(0)$, determine if there exists $\mathbf{u} \in \mathcal{U}$ such that $\mathbf{y}(t, \mathbf{u}, \mathbf{x}(0)) \notin B$ for all $t \geq 0$.*

Now, we design a supervisor as follows. Every time τ, the supervisor receives the measurements of current states of vehicles and drivers' inputs. Based on the measurements, the supervisor determines whether it must override the vehicles at this time step because otherwise there will be no admissible input to avoid collisions at the next time step. This decision can be made by solving the verification problem.

The supervisor-design problem is formulated as follows.

PROBLEM 2 (SUPERVISOR-DESIGN). *At time $k\tau$, given state $\mathbf{x}(k\tau)$ and drivers' input $\mathbf{u}^k_{driver} \in U$, design a supervisor that satisfies the following specifications.*

Spec 1. *For time $[k\tau, (k+1)\tau)$, it returns $\mathbf{u}^k_{driver}$ if there exists $\mathbf{u} \in \mathcal{U}$ such that for all $t \geq 0$*

$$\mathbf{y}(t, \mathbf{u}, \mathbf{x}(\tau, \mathbf{u}^k_{driver}, \mathbf{x}(k\tau))) \notin B,$$

or returns $\mathbf{u}^k_{safe} \in \mathcal{U}$ otherwise. Here, $\mathbf{u}^k_{safe}$ is defined as the safe input that guarantees the existence of $\mathbf{u}' \in \mathcal{U}$ such that for all $t \geq 0$,

$$\mathbf{y}(t, \mathbf{u}', \mathbf{x}(\tau, \mathbf{u}^k_{safe}, \mathbf{x}(k\tau))) \notin B. \tag{3}$$

Spec 2. *It is non-blocking, that is, $\mathbf{u}^k_{safe}$ must exist for any $k > 0$ if $\mathbf{u}^0_{safe}$ exists.*

In Problem 2, Spec 1 guarantees that the supervisor is least restrictive, and Spec 2 guarantees that the supervisor always has an input to override vehicles to ensure safety.

4. PROBLEM SOLUTION

In this section, we solve the two problems: the verification problem (Problem 1) and the supervisor-design problem (Problem 2). As a main result, we formulate a job-shop scheduling problem and prove that this problem is equivalent to Problem 1. Before formulating the job-shop scheduling problem in Section 4.2, we introduce classical job-shop scheduling in Section 4.1. In Section 4.2, we also convert the job-shop scheduling problem into a mixed-integer linear programming problem with the assumption of first-order vehicle dynamics. In Section 4.3, the supervisor algorithm satisfying the specifications of Problem 2 is given.

4.1 Classical job-shop scheduling

In classical job-shop scheduling [27], n jobs are processed on m machines subject to the constraints that (a) each job has its own prescribed sequence of machines to follow, and (b) each machine can process at most one job at a time. This can be represented by a disjunctive graph with a set of nodes $\mathcal{N}$ and two sets of arcs $\mathcal{C}$ and $\mathcal{D}$. Here, the sets are defined as follows.

$$\mathcal{N} := \{(i,j) : (i,j) \text{ is the process of job } j \text{ on machine } i \\ \text{for all } j \in \{1, \dots, n\}\},$$

$$\mathcal{C} := \{(i,j) \to (i',j) : \text{job } j \text{ must be processed on machine } i \\ \text{and then on machine } i' \text{ for all } j \in \{1, \dots, n\}\},$$

$$\mathcal{D} := \{(i,j) \leftrightarrow (i,j') : \text{two jobs } j \text{ and } j' \text{ are to be processed} \\ \text{on machine } i \text{ for all } i \in \{1, \dots, m\}\}.$$

The arcs in $\mathcal{C}$, called the conjunctive arcs, represent the routes of the jobs, and the arcs in $\mathcal{D}$, called the disjunctive arcs, connect two operations processed on a same machine.

Let $\mathcal{F} \subseteq \mathcal{N}$ denote a set of the first operations of jobs, and $\mathcal{L} \subseteq \mathcal{N}$ denote a set of the last operations of jobs. If each job has only one operation on its route, $\mathcal{N} = \mathcal{F} = \mathcal{L}$.

The scenario in Section 2 can be described in job-shop scheduling by considering vehicles as jobs and conflict areas as machines. For instance, each vehicle in Figure 2 has its own prescribed route. Vehicle 1 crosses conflict area 1 first and then conflict area 3. At most one vehicle can be inside each conflict area at a time, because otherwise collisions occur. The corresponding disjunctive graph is shown in Figure 3.

Example 1. The disjunctive graph in Figure 3 consists of the set of nodes

$$\mathcal{N} = \{(1,1), (3,1), (2,2), (1,2), (3,3), (2,3)\},$$

and the sets of conjunctive and disjunctive arcs

$$\mathcal{C} = \{(1,1) \to (3,1), (2,2) \to (1,2), (3,3) \to (2,3)\},$$
$$\mathcal{D} = \{(1,1) \leftrightarrow (1,2), (2,2) \leftrightarrow (2,3), (3,3) \leftrightarrow (3,1)\},$$

respectively.

The sets of the first and the last operations are $\mathcal{F} = \{(1,1), (2,2), (3,3)\}$ and $\mathcal{L} = \{(3,1), (1,2), (2,3)\}$, respectively.

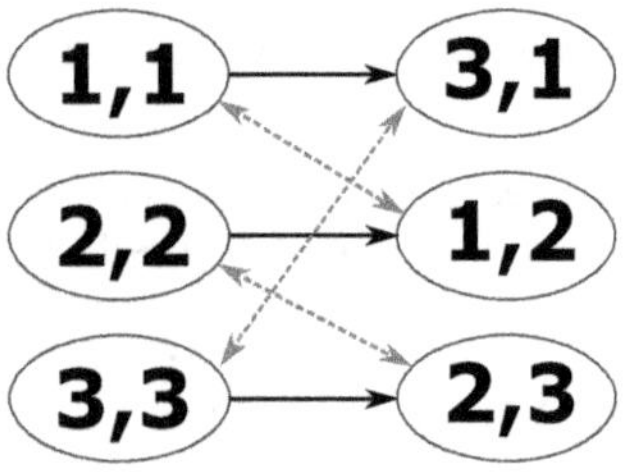

Figure 3: Disjunctive graph of the example in Figure 2. The black solid lines are the conjunctive arcs, and the red dotted lines are the disjunctive arcs.

In [3], as a variant of job-shop scheduling, release times and deadlines are considered such that jobs must start after given release times and be finished before given deadlines. The release time r_j and the deadline d_j are defined for each job j, not for each operation (i, j). The process time p_j is a constant for all operations of job j independent of the machines. Then, the classical job-shop scheduling problem with deadline is formulated as follows.

PROBLEM 3 (CLASSICAL JOB-SHOP). *Given the release times r_j, the deadlines d_j, and the process time p_j, determine if there exists the operation starting times t_{ij} for all $(i, j) \in \mathcal{N}$ such that*

$$\begin{aligned} &\textit{for all } (i,j) \in \mathcal{F}, && r_j \le t_{ij}, \\ &\textit{for all } (i,j) \in \mathcal{L}, && t_{ij} + p_j \le d_j, \\ &\textit{for all } (i,j) \to (i',j) \in \mathcal{C}, && t_{ij} + p_j \le t_{i'j}, \\ &\textit{for all } (i,j) \leftrightarrow (i,j') \in \mathcal{D}, && t_{ij} \le t_{ij'} \Rightarrow t_{ij} + p_j \le t_{ij'}. \end{aligned}$$

In the next section, a new job-shop scheduling problem similar to Problem 3 is formulated to solve Problem 1.

4.2 Solution of Problem 1

4.2.1 Job-shop scheduling

In contrast to classical job-shop scheduling, our problem must account for the dynamic model of vehicles (1). Thus, process times, release times, and deadlines are not initially given and not constant with operation starting times. Also, they are defined for each operation, that is, depending on the jobs and the machines as follows.

Definition 1. Given initial condition $\mathbf{x}(0)$ and schedule $\mathbf{T} := \{T_{ij} \in \mathbb{R} : y_j(T_{ij}, u_j, x_j(0)) = \alpha_{ij}$ for some $u_j \in \mathcal{U}_j,\ \forall (i,j) \in \mathcal{N}\}$, process time P_{ij} is defined for operation $(i, j) \in \mathcal{N}$ as follows.

- If $(i, j) \in \mathcal{L}$, for $h_j(x_j(0)) = y_j(0) < \alpha_{ij}$,

$$P_{ij} := \min_{u_j \in \mathcal{U}_j} \{t : y_j(t, u_j, x_j(0)) = \beta_{ij} \text{ with constraint } y_j(T_{ij}, u_j, x_j(0)) = \alpha_{ij}\}. \tag{4}$$

For $\alpha_{ij} \le y_j(0) < \beta_{ij}$, set $P_{ij} := \min_{u_j}\{t : y_j(t, u_j, x_j(0)) = \beta_{ij}\}$. For $\beta_{ij} \le y_j(0)$, set $P_{ij} = 0$. If the constraint is not satisfied, set $P_{ij} = \infty$.

- If $(i, j) \notin \mathcal{L}$, that is, $\exists (i', j)$ such that $(i, j) \to (i', j) \in \mathcal{C}$, for $y_j(0) < \alpha_{ij}$,

$$P_{ij} := \min_{u_j \in \mathcal{U}_j} \{t : y_j(t, u_j, x_j(0)) = \beta_{ij} \text{ with constraint } y_j(T_{ij}, u_j, x_j(0)) = \alpha_{ij} \text{ and } y_j(T_{i'j}, u_j, x_j(0)) = \alpha_{i'j}\}. \tag{5}$$

For $\alpha_{ij} \le y_j(0) < \beta_{ij}$, set $P_{ij} := \min_{u_j}\{t : y_j(t, u_j, y_j(0)) = \beta_{ij}$ with constraint $y_j(T_{i'j}, u_j, x_j(0)) = \alpha_{i'j}\}$. For $\beta_{ij} \le y_j(0)$, set $P_{ij} = 0$. If the constraints are not satisfied, set $P_{ij} = \infty$.

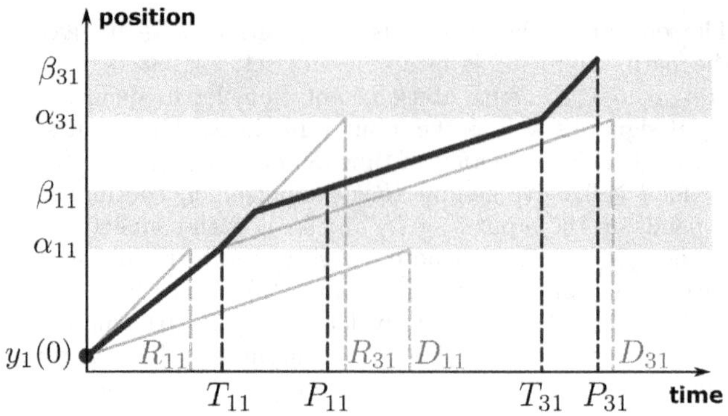

Figure 4: Process time, release time, and deadline of vehicle 1 in the example in Figure 2. The thick blue line represents the position of vehicle 1 on its longitudinal path with the schedules T_{11} and T_{31}. For $(1, 1) \notin \mathcal{L}$, P_{11} is a function of T_{11} and T_{31}, while for $(3, 1) \in \mathcal{L}$, P_{31} is a function of T_{31} only. Also, for $(3, 1) \notin \mathcal{F}$, R_{31} and D_{31} are functions of T_{11}.

By the above definition, process time P_{ij} is the earliest time at which vehicle j can exit conflict area i.

Definition 2. Given initial condition $\mathbf{x}(0)$ and schedule $\mathbf{T} := \{T_{ij} \in \mathbb{R} : y_j(T_{ij}, u_j, x_j(0)) = \alpha_{ij}$ for some $u_j \in \mathcal{U}_j,\ \forall (i,j) \in \mathcal{N}\}$, release time R_{ij} and deadline D_{ij} are defined for operation $(i, j) \in \mathcal{N}$ as follows.

- If $(i, j) \in \mathcal{F}$, for $y_j(0) < \alpha_{ij}$,

$$\begin{aligned} R_{ij} &:= \min_{u_j \in \mathcal{U}_j} \{t : y_j(t, u_j, x_j(0)) = \alpha_{ij}\}, \\ D_{ij} &:= \max_{u_j \in \mathcal{U}_j} \{t : y_j(t, u_j, x_j(0)) = \alpha_{ij}\}. \end{aligned} \tag{6}$$

For $\alpha_{ij} \le y_j(0)$, set $R_{ij} = 0$ and $D_{ij} = 0$.

- If $(i, j) \notin \mathcal{F}$, that is, $\exists (i', j)$ such that $(i', j) \to (i, j) \in \mathcal{C}$, for $y_j(0) < \alpha_{ij}$,

$$\begin{aligned} R_{ij} &:= \min_{u_j \in \mathcal{U}_j} \{t : y_j(t, u_j, x_j(0)) = \alpha_{ij} \text{ with constraint } y_j(T_{i'j}, u_j, x_j(0)) = \alpha_{i'j}\}, \\ D_{ij} &:= \max_{u_j \in \mathcal{U}_j} \{t : y_j(t, u_j, x_j(0)) = \alpha_{ij} \text{ with constraint } y_j(T_{i'j}, u_j, x_j(0)) = \alpha_{i'j}\}. \end{aligned} \tag{7}$$

For $\alpha_{ij} \le y_j(0)$, set $R_{ij} = 0$ and $D_{ij} = 0$. If the constraint cannot be satisfied by any $u_j \in \mathcal{U}_j$, set $R_{ij} = \infty$ and $D_{ij} = -\infty$.

By definition, release time R_{ij} is the earliest time at which vehicle j can enter conflict area i, and deadline D_{ij} is the latest such time.

If an intersection is modeled as a single conflict point as in [10, 11], the process time is defined by (4), and the release time and deadline by (6). This is because each vehicle has a single operation so that $\mathcal{F} = \mathcal{L} = \mathcal{N}$. As for multiple conflict points, we have to include the effect of preceding and succeeding operations in the definition. Notice that the process time P_{ij} in (5) depends on the schedules T_{ij} and $T_{i'j}$ where (i', j) is the succeeding operation of (i, j), and the release time R_{ij} and deadline D_{ij} in (7) depend on $T_{i'j}$ where (i', j) is the preceding operation of (i, j). An example of these definitions is illustrated in Figure 4.

Using the above definitions, we formulate the job-shop scheduling problem as follows.

PROBLEM 4 (JOB-SHOP SCHEDULING). *Given* $\mathbf{x}(0)$, *determine the existence of a schedule* $\mathbf{T} := \{T_{ij} : (i,j) \in \mathcal{N}\} \in \mathbb{R}_+^{|\mathcal{N}|}$ *that satisfies the following constraints.*

$$\text{for all } (i,j) \in \mathcal{N}, \qquad R_{ij} \leq T_{ij} \leq D_{ij}, \tag{8}$$

$$\text{for all } (i,j) \leftrightarrow (i,j') \in \mathcal{D}, \quad T_{ij} \leq T_{ij'} \Rightarrow P_{ij} \leq T_{ij'}. \tag{9}$$

Constraint (9) implies avoidance of intersection collisions between vehicles j and j' by ensuring that vehicle j must exit conflict area i before vehicle j' enters it.

We now prove that Problem 1 is equivalent to Problem 4. Before this, we introduce the formal definition of the equivalence between two problems, and prove a lemma that relates constraint (8) to the existence of an input u_j such that $y_j(T_{ij}, u_j, x_j(0)) = \alpha_{ij}$ and $y_j(P_{ij}, u_j, x_j(0)) = \beta_{ij}$ for $(i, j) \in \mathcal{N}$.

Definition 3. [12] An instance I_A of Problem A is the information required to solve the problem. If I_A satisfies Problem A, we write $I_A \in$ Problem A.

Problem A is reducible to Problem B if for any instance I_A of Problem A, an instance I_B of Problem B can be constructed in polynomial time, and $I_A \in$ Problem A if and only if $I_B \in$ Problem B. If Problem A is reducible to Problem B, and Problem B is reducible to Problem A, then Problem A is equivalent to Problem B.

LEMMA 1. *If* $R_{ij} \leq T_{ij} \leq D_{ij}$ *for all* $(i,j) \in \mathcal{N}$ *with* $y_j(0) < \alpha_{ij}$, *there exists* $u_j \in \mathcal{U}_j$ *such that* $y_j(T_{ij}, u_j, x_j(0)) = \alpha_{ij}$ *and* $y_j(P_{ij}, u_j, x_j(0)) = \beta_{ij}$.

PROOF. By the definitions of R_{ij} and D_{ij} in (6), for the first operation (i_1, j) on the route of vehicle j, there exists an input signal u_j such that $y_j(T_{i_1j}, u_j, x_j(0)) = \alpha_{i_1j}$. This is because the input space is path-connected, and the output y_j continuously depends on u_j. Then, for the next operation (i_2, j), that is, $(i_1, j) \rightarrow (i_2, j) \in \mathcal{C}$, since the constraint in definition (7) is satisfied by the input signal u_j, there is an input signal u_j such that $y_j(T_{i_2j}, u_j, x_j(0)) = \alpha_{i_2j}$. By induction on the sequence of operations, for all $(i, j) \in \mathcal{N}$, there exists an input signal u_j such that $y_j(T_{ij}, u_j, y_j(0)) = \alpha_{ij}$.

This input signal u_j satisfies the constraints in the definition of P_{ij} in (4) and (5). Since there exists at least one input signal that satisfies the constraints, an input signal u_j exists such that $y_j(P_{ij}, u_j, x_j(0)) = \beta_{ij}$ for all $(i, j) \in \mathcal{N}$. □

THEOREM 1. *Problem 1 is equivalent to Problem 4.*

PROOF. An instance of Problem 1 is $\{\mathbf{x}(0), \Theta\}$, where $\Theta = \{\{\alpha_{ij}, \beta_{ij} : \forall (i,j) \in \mathcal{N}\}, d, X, Y, U, \mathcal{U}, \mathcal{N}, \mathcal{F}, \mathcal{L}, \mathcal{C}, \mathcal{D}\}$. Notice that an instance of Problem 4 is $\{\mathbf{x}(0), \Theta\}$, which is identical to an instance of Problem 1. Thus, the construction of an instance takes $O(1)$ time. All we have to show is that given $I = \{\mathbf{x}(0), \Theta\}$, $I \in$ Problem 1 if and only if $I \in$ Problem 4.

Suppose $I \in$ Problem 1. Then, there exists $\tilde{\mathbf{u}} \in \mathcal{U}$ such that $\mathbf{y}(t, \tilde{\mathbf{u}}, \mathbf{x}(0)) \notin B$ for all $t \geq 0$. In this proof, we assume $y_j(0) < \alpha_{ij}$. For all $(i,j) \in \mathcal{N}$, let $\tilde{T}_{ij} = \{t : y_j(t, \tilde{u}_j, x_j(0)) = \alpha_{ij}\}$ and $\tilde{P}_{ij} = \{t : y_j(t, \tilde{u}_j, x_j(0)) = \beta_{ij}\}$. We will show that $\{\tilde{T}_{ij} : (i,j) \in \mathcal{N}\}$ satisfies the constraints in Problem 4 so that $\{\mathbf{x}(0), \Theta\} \in$ Problem 4.

By the definitions of R_{ij} and D_{ij}, we have $R_{ij} \leq \tilde{T}_{ij} \leq D_{ij}$ (constraint (8)). For all $(i,j) \leftrightarrow (i,j') \in \mathcal{D}$, assume without loss of generality vehicle j enters conflict area i before vehicle j'. Then we know that at $t = \tilde{P}_{ij}$, since $y_j(t, \tilde{u}_j, x_j(0)) = \beta_{ij}$, we have $y_{j'}(t, \tilde{u}_j, x_j(0)) \leq \alpha_{ij'}$. That is, $\tilde{P}_{ij} \leq \tilde{T}_{ij'}$. Since $\tilde{u}_j$ satisfies all the constraints given in the definitions of P_{ij}, we have $P_{ij} \leq \tilde{P}_{ij}$. Therefore, $P_{ij} \leq \tilde{T}_{ij'}$ (constraint (9)).

Suppose $I \in$ Problem 4. Then, there exists $\hat{\mathbf{T}}$ satisfying the constraints in Problem 4. By Lemma 1, there exists $\hat{\mathbf{u}}$ that satisfies $y_j(\hat{T}_{ij}, \hat{u}_j, x_j(0)) = \alpha_{ij}$ and $y_j(P_{ij}, \hat{u}_j, x_j(0)) = \beta_{ij}$ for all $(i,j) \in \mathcal{N}$. In constraint (9), for all $(i,j) \leftrightarrow (i,j') \in \mathcal{D}$, we have $P_{ij} \leq \hat{T}_{ij'}$ if $\hat{T}_{ij} \leq \hat{T}_{ij'}$. Then, at $t = P_{ij'}$, we have $y_j(t, \hat{u}_j, x_j(0)) = \beta_{ij}$ while $y_{j'}(t, \hat{u}_{j'}, x_{j'}(0)) \leq \alpha_{i'j}$. This implies that any two vehicles never meet inside a conflict area, that is, $\mathbf{y}(t, \hat{\mathbf{u}}, \mathbf{x}(0)) \notin B$ for all $t \geq 0$.

Therefore, there exists $\hat{\mathbf{u}}$ such that $\mathbf{y}(t, \hat{\mathbf{u}}, \mathbf{x}(0)) \notin B$ for all $t \geq 0$. □

By Theorem 1, we can solve Problem 1 by solving Problem 4. One may notice that Problem 4 is similar to the classical job-shop scheduling problem (Problem 3) if $D_{ij} = d_j - p_j$ and $P_{ij} = t_{ij} + p_j$. However, in Problem 4, the release times, deadlines, and process times are defined for each operation as functions of the schedules. The fact that they vary depending on the schedules significantly complicates the problem. We thus cannot directly employ the solutions from the scheduling literature. Instead, we have to formulate a mixed-integer linear programming problem, which is proved to yield the equivalent answers to Problem 4 by assuming that the vehicle dynamics are single integrator dynamics.

4.2.2 Mixed-integer programming

Problem 4 can be transformed into a mixed-integer programming problem, which is an optimization problem subject to equality and inequality constraints in the presence of continuous and discrete variables. Notice that constraint (8) is already an inequality constraint. However, constraint (9) contains a disjunctive constraint, which can be converted into linear inequalities by introducing a binary variable $k_{ijj'} \in \{0, 1\}$ and using the big-M method [17]. In particular, define

$$k_{ijj'} := \begin{cases} 1 & \text{if vehicle } j \text{ crosses conflict area } i \\ & \qquad\qquad\qquad \text{before vehicle } j', \\ 0 & \text{otherwise.} \end{cases}$$

Also, let M be a large positive constant in $\mathbb{R}$. Then constraint (9) can be rewritten as follows:

$$\begin{aligned} &\text{for all } (i,j) \leftrightarrow (i,j') \in \mathcal{D}, \\ &\quad k_{ijj'} + k_{ij'j} = 1, \quad k_{ijj'}, k_{ij'j} \in \{0,1\} \\ &\quad P_{ij} \leq T_{ij'} + M(1 - k_{ijj'}), \\ &\quad P_{ij'} \leq T_{ij} + M(1 - k_{ij'j}), \end{aligned} \tag{10}$$

for M sufficiently larger than T_{ij} and P_{ij} for all $(i,j) \in \mathcal{N}$. If $k_{ijj'} = 1$ and $k_{ij'j} = 0$, vehicle j crosses conflict area i before vehicle j' so that $T_{ij} \leq T_{ij'}$. Then, $P_{ij} \leq T_{ij'}$ is imposed while $P_{ij'} \leq T_{ij} + M$ is automatically satisfied because of a sufficiently large M. Thus, (10) encodes the same constraint as (9).

Notice that because R_{ij}, D_{ij}, and P_{ij} are functions of variable T_{ij}, Problem 4 with constraint (8) and (10) is a general mixed-integer program (MIP). Due to its high complexity, this formulation is usually difficult to solve [6]. If the constraints can be expressed in a linear function of variables, the problem becomes a mixed-integer linear program (MILP). Although MILP are combinatorial, several algorithmic approaches are available to solve medium to large size application problems [14].

To this end, we assume that the longitudinal dynamics of vehicles are modeled as a single integrator as follows. For vehicle j,

$$\dot{x}_j = u_j, \qquad y_j = x_j. \tag{11}$$

Notice that the dynamic state $x_j \in X_j \subseteq \mathbb{R}$ is the position, and the control input $u_j \in U_j$ is the speed. Since vehicles do not go in reverse, we let $u_{j,min} > 0$. Although this simplification does not fully represent the complex dynamics of vehicles, its control law can be extended to the complex system by employing abstraction as in [9, 16]. Thus, this paper focuses on designing the supervisor for these simple dynamics.

With the first order dynamic model (11), we can transform Problem 4 into a mixed-integer linear programming problem. Let us write $P_{ij} = T_{ij} + \min_{u_j}\{t : y_j(t, u_j, \alpha_{ij}) = \beta_{ij}\}$ so that the constraint that $y_j(T_{ij}, u_j, x_j(0)) = \alpha_{ij}$ is automatically satisfied. By defining

$$p_{ij} := \{t : y_j(t, u_j, \alpha_{ij}) = \beta_{ij}\},$$

p_{ij} corresponds to the time spent inside conflict area i, independent of T_{ij}. Then, the variables for the mixed-integer linear programming problem are as follows:

- T_{ij} for $(i,j) \in \mathcal{N}$, continuous variables,
- p_{ij} for $(i,j) \notin \mathcal{L}$, continuous variables,
- $k_{ijj'}$ and $k_{ij'j}$ for $(i,j) \leftrightarrow (i,j') \in \mathcal{D}$, binary variables.

Notice that p_{ij} for $(i,j) \in \mathcal{L}$ is excluded from the variables because we can set $p_{ij} = (\beta_{ij} - \alpha_{ij})/u_{max}$. This is possible because $P_{ij} = T_{ij} + (\beta_{ij} - \alpha_{ij})/u_{max}$ by definition (4), and the minimum p_{ij} is most likely to satisfy the problem formulated in the following paragraph.

Given the single integrator dynamics, we formulate the mixed-integer linear programming problem as follows.

PROBLEM 5. *Given $\mathbf{x}(0)$, determine if there exists a feasible solution subject to the following constraints.*

A. *If $(i,j) \in \mathcal{F}$, for $y_j(0) < \alpha_{ij}$*

$$\frac{\alpha_{ij} - y_j(0)}{u_{j,max}} \leq T_{ij} \leq \frac{\alpha_{ij} - y_j(0)}{u_{j,min}}.$$

For $\alpha_{ij} \leq y_j(0)$, consider $T_{ij} = 0$.

B. *If $(i,j) \notin \mathcal{F}$, that is $\exists (i',j)$ such that $(i',j) \rightarrow (i,j) \in \mathcal{C}$,*

$$T_{i'j} + p_{i'j} + \frac{\alpha_{ij} - \beta_{i'j}}{u_{j,max}} \leq T_{ij} \leq T_{i'j} + p_{i'j} + \frac{\alpha_{ij} - \beta_{i'j}}{u_{j,min}}.$$

C. *If $(i,j) \notin \mathcal{L}$, for $y_j(0) < \alpha_{ij}$,*

$$\frac{\beta_{ij} - \alpha_{ij}}{u_{j,max}} \leq p_{ij} \leq \frac{\beta_{ij} - \alpha_{ij}}{u_{j,min}}.$$

For $\alpha_{ij} \leq y_j(0)$, consider instead $\frac{\beta_{ij} - y_j(0)}{u_{j,max}} \leq p_{ij} \leq \frac{\beta_{ij} - y_j(0)}{u_{j,min}}$. If $\beta_{ij} \leq y_j(0)$, the schedule of operation (i,j) is not of interest.

D. *For all $(i,j) \leftrightarrow (i,j') \in \mathcal{D}$, with a large number $M \in \mathbb{R}_+$,*

$$\begin{aligned} &T_{ij} + p_{ij} \leq T_{ij'} + M(1 - k_{ijj'}), \\ &T_{ij'} + p_{ij'} \leq T_{ij} + M(1 - k_{ij'j}), \\ &k_{ijj'} + k_{ij'j} = 1. \end{aligned}$$

Problem 5 yields equivalent answers to the job-shop scheduling problem (Problem 4) with the first-order dynamics. Constraints A,B, and C are imposed by the bounded inputs, and constraint D implies collision avoidance of vehicles j and j' at conflict area i. More formally, these constraints are explained in the following proof by discussing their relations with constraints (8) and (10).

THEOREM 2. *If the vehicle dynamics (1) are modeled as (11), Problem 4 is equivalent to Problem 5.*

PROOF. Problem 4 and Problem 5 have an identical instance $I = \{\mathbf{x}(0), \Theta\}$. Thus, we need to show that $I \in$ Problem 4 if and only if $I \in$ Problem 5. We will prove that $I \in$ Problem 4 if $I \in$ Problem 5, and $I \notin$ Problem 4 if $I \notin$ Problem 5.

Suppose $I \in$ Problem 5. Then there exist a feasible solution $(\tilde{\mathbf{T}}, \tilde{\mathbf{p}}, \tilde{\mathbf{k}})$ where $\tilde{\mathbf{T}} = \{\tilde{T}_{ij} : \forall (i,j) \in \mathcal{N}\}$, $\tilde{\mathbf{p}} = \{\tilde{p}_{ij} : \forall (i,j) \notin \mathcal{L}\}$, and $\tilde{\mathbf{k}} = \{\tilde{k}_{ijj'}, \tilde{k}_{ij'j} : \forall (i,j) \leftrightarrow (i,j') \in \mathcal{D}\}$.

For $(i,j) \in \mathcal{F}$, $R_{ij} = (\alpha_{ij} - y_j(0))/u_{j,max}$ and $D_{ij} = (\alpha_{ij} - y_j(0))/u_{j,min}$ by definition (6). For $(i,j) \notin \mathcal{F}$, that is, $\exists (i',j) \rightarrow (i,j) \in \mathcal{C}$, there is the constraint in definition (7) that $y_j(\tilde{T}_{i'j}) = \alpha_{i'j}$. Thus, R_{ij} and D_{ij} are as follows.

$$\begin{aligned} R_{ij} &= \tilde{T}_{i'j} + \frac{\alpha_{ij} - \alpha_{i'j}}{u_{j,max}} = \tilde{T}_{i'j} + \tilde{p}_{i'j} + \frac{\alpha_{ij} - \beta_{i'j}}{u_{j,max}}, \\ D_{ij} &= \tilde{T}_{i'j} + \frac{\alpha_{ij} - \alpha_{i'j}}{u_{j,min}} = \tilde{T}_{i'j} + \tilde{p}_{i'j} + \frac{\alpha_{ij} - \beta_{i'j}}{u_{j,min}}. \end{aligned}$$

The second equalities in both equations result from constraint C. Therefore, constraints A and B imply $R_{ij} \leq \tilde{T}_{ij} \leq D_{ij}$ for all $(i,j) \in \mathcal{N}$ (constraint (8)).

In constraint D, we have $P_{ij} \leq \tilde{T}_{ij} + \tilde{p}_{ij}$ because P_{ij} is the minimum time to reach β_{ij}. Therefore, we have $P_{ij} \leq \tilde{T}_{ij} + \tilde{p}_{ij} \leq \tilde{T}_{ij'} + M(1 - \tilde{k}_{ijj'})$. Similarly, $P_{ij'} \leq \tilde{T}_{ij'} + \tilde{p}_{ij'} \leq \tilde{T}_{ij} + M(1 - \tilde{k}_{ij'j})$ (constraint (10)).

Thus, $\tilde{\mathbf{T}}$ satisfies the constraints in Problem 4. That is, $I \in$ Problem 4.

Suppose $I \notin$ Problem 5. Notice that if constraint C is ignored and let $p_{ij} = 0$, the problem is always feasible because for $(i_1, j) \in \mathcal{F}$ and $(i_1, j) \to (i_2, j), \ldots, (i_{d-1}, j) \to (i_d, j) \in \mathcal{C}$,

$$T_{i_1,j} = \frac{\alpha_{i_1 j} - y_j(0)}{u_{j,max}}, \; T_{i_2 j} = T_{i_1 j} + \frac{\alpha_{i_2 j} - \beta_{i_1 j}}{u_{j,max}}, \; \ldots, \; T_{i_d j} = T_{i_{d-1} j} + \frac{\alpha_{i_d j} - \beta_{i_{d-1} j}}{u_{j,max}}$$

becomes a feasible solution for any j. Constraint D is also satisfied because either $T_{ij} \leq T_{i'j}$ or $T_{i'j} \leq T_{ij}$ is always true. We can thus find the maximum process time that is a feasible solution for the problem without constraint C. Since $I \notin$ Problem 5, this solution violates constraint C. Thus, there is no $p_{ij} \geq (\beta_{ij} - \alpha_{ij})/u_{j,max}$ for any $(i,j) \notin \mathcal{L}$ such that constraints A, B, and D are satisfied. This, in turn, implies that given the definition $P_{ij} = T_{ij} + \min p_{ij}$, there is no $P_{ij} \geq T_{ij} + (\beta_{ij} - \alpha_{ij})/u_{j,max}$ such that the constraints in Problem 4 are satisfied. Since P_{ij} is not feasible, neither are T_{ij} and $k_{ijj'}$. Thus, $I \notin$ Problem 4. □

We solve Problem 5 using CPLEX. The procedure that solves Problem 5 given an instance $I = \{\mathbf{x}(0), \Theta\}$ is referred to as $\texttt{Jobshop}(I)$. If $I \in$ Problem 5, that is, $I \in$ Problem 1 by Theorems 1 and 2, $\texttt{Jobshop}(I)$ returns $\{\mathbf{T}, \mathbf{p}, yes\}$. Otherwise, it returns $\{\emptyset, \emptyset, no\}$.

4.3 Solution of Problem 2

The supervisor runs in discrete time with a time step τ. At time $k\tau$ where $k > 0$, it receives the measurements of the states $\mathbf{x}(k\tau)$ and drivers' inputs $\mathbf{u}^k_{driver} \in \mathbf{U}$ of the vehicles near an intersection. By assuming that $\mathbf{u}^k_{driver}$ is constant for time $[k\tau, (k+1)\tau)$, we predict a state at the next time step, called a state prediction and denoted by $\hat{\mathbf{x}}(\mathbf{u}^k_{driver})$, as follows.

$$\hat{\mathbf{x}}(\mathbf{u}^k_{driver}) = \mathbf{x}(\tau, \mathbf{u}^k_{driver}, \mathbf{x}(k\tau)).$$

Notice that $\texttt{Jobshop}(\hat{\mathbf{x}}(\mathbf{u}^k_{driver}), \Theta)$ determines whether or not collisions can be avoided at all future times given the state prediction. If it returns $\{\mathbf{T}, \mathbf{p}, yes\}$, then the supervisor allows the vehicles to drive with input $\mathbf{u}^k_{driver}$ for time $[k\tau, (k+1)\tau)$. The schedule $\mathbf{T}$ and the process time $\mathbf{p}$ are used to generate a safe input signal $\mathbf{u}^{k+1,\infty}_{safe}$, defined on time $[(k+1)\tau, \infty)$. We define a safe input operator $\sigma(\hat{\mathbf{x}}(\mathbf{u}^k_{driver}), \mathbf{T}, \mathbf{p})$ as follows.

$$\begin{aligned} &\sigma(\hat{\mathbf{x}}(\mathbf{u}^k_{driver}), \mathbf{T}, \mathbf{p}) \\ &\in \{(u_1, \ldots, u_n) \in \mathcal{U} : y_j(T_{ij}, u_j, \hat{x}_j(u^k_{driver,j})) = \alpha_{ij} \\ &\qquad \text{and } y_j(p_{ij}, u_j, \alpha_{ij}) = \beta_{ij} \; \forall (i,j) \in \mathcal{N}\}, \end{aligned} \tag{12}$$

where $u^k_{driver,j}$ is the jth entry of $\mathbf{u}^k_{driver}$, and $\hat{x}_j(u^k_{driver,j})$ is the jth entry of $\hat{\mathbf{x}}(\mathbf{u}^k_{driver})$. This safe input signal is stored for possible uses at the next time step.

If $\texttt{Jobshop}(\hat{\mathbf{x}}(\mathbf{u}^k_{driver}), \Theta)$ returns $\{\emptyset, \emptyset, no\}$, then the supervisor overrides the vehicles using the safe input signal stored at the previous step, $\mathbf{u}^{k,\infty}_{safe}$. Since $\mathbf{u}^{k,\infty}_{safe}$ is defined on time $[k\tau, \infty)$, let $\mathbf{u}^k_{safe} \in \mathcal{U}$ be $\mathbf{u}^{k,\infty}_{safe}$ restricted to time $[k\tau, (k+1)\tau)$. The supervisor blocks the drivers' inputs $\mathbf{u}^k_{driver}$ and returns the safe input $\mathbf{u}^k_{safe}$ for time $[k\tau, (k+1)\tau)$ to prevent future collisions.

This procedure is written as an algorithm as follows.

Algorithm 1 $\texttt{Supervisor}(\mathbf{x}(k\tau), \mathbf{u}^k_{driver})$

1: $\{\mathbf{T}_1, \mathbf{p}_1, answer_1\} = \texttt{Jobshop}(\hat{\mathbf{x}}(\mathbf{u}^k_{driver}), \Theta)$
2: **if** $answer_1 = yes$ **then**
3: $\quad \mathbf{u}^{k+1,\infty} \leftarrow \sigma(\hat{\mathbf{x}}(\mathbf{u}^k_{driver}), \mathbf{T}_1, \mathbf{p}_1)$
4: $\quad \mathbf{u}^{k+1}_{safe} \leftarrow \mathbf{u}^{k+1,\infty}(t)$ for $t \in [(k+1)\tau, (k+2)\tau)$
5: $\quad$ **return** $\mathbf{u}^k_{driver}$
6: **else**
7: $\quad \{\mathbf{T}_2, \mathbf{p}_2, answer_2\} = \texttt{Jobshop}(\hat{\mathbf{x}}(\mathbf{u}^k_{safe}), \Theta)$
8: $\quad \mathbf{u}^{k+1,\infty} \leftarrow \sigma(\hat{\mathbf{x}}(\mathbf{u}^k_{safe}), \mathbf{T}_2, \mathbf{p}_2)$
9: $\quad \mathbf{u}^{k+1}_{safe} \leftarrow \mathbf{u}^{k+1,\infty}(t)$ for $t \in [(k+1)\tau, (k+2)\tau)$
10: $\quad$ **return** $\mathbf{u}^k_{safe}$
11: **end if**

If $answer_1 = yes$, then the supervisor generates and stores the safe input $\mathbf{u}^{k+1}_{safe}$ in lines 3-4, and does not intervene in line 5. If $answer_1 = no$, the supervisor solves the verification problem in line 7 given the state predicted with the safe input $\mathbf{u}^k_{safe}$. It will be proved in the following theorem that $answer_2$ is always yes, which implies the non-blocking property of the supervisor. Based on $\mathbf{T}_2$ and $\mathbf{p}_2$, the supervisor generates and stores the safe input $\mathbf{u}^{k+1}_{safe}$ in lines 8-9, and overrides the vehicles in line 10.

THEOREM 3. *Algorithm 1 solves Problem 2.*

PROOF. To prove that Algorithm 1 is a solution of Problem 2, we check if the algorithm satisfies the specifications in Problem 2.

Specification 1 is met by the design of the algorithm. If there exists $\mathbf{u} \in \mathcal{U}$ such that $\mathbf{y}(t, \mathbf{u}, \hat{\mathbf{x}}(\mathbf{u}^k_{driver})) \notin B$ for all $t \geq 0$, then $\texttt{Jobshop}(\hat{\mathbf{x}}(\mathbf{u}^k_{driver}), \Theta)$ returns *yes*. In this case, the supervisor returns $\mathbf{u}^k_{driver}$. Otherwise, it returns $\mathbf{u}^k_{safe} \in \mathcal{U}$. The fact that this input makes $\texttt{Jobshop}(\hat{\mathbf{x}}(\mathbf{u}^k_{safe}), \Theta)$ return *yes* will be clear in the proof of the non-blocking property.

To prove the non-blocking property, we use mathematical induction on k where $t = k\tau$. At $t = 0$, we assume $\mathbf{u}^0_{safe} \neq \emptyset$. At $t = (k-1)\tau$, suppose there exists $\mathbf{u}^{k-1}_{safe}$. That is, by definition, there exists $\mathbf{u}' \in \mathcal{U}$ such that $\mathbf{y}(t, \mathbf{u}', \hat{\mathbf{x}}(\mathbf{u}^{k-1}_{safe})) \notin B$ for all $t \geq 0$. If $\texttt{Jobshop}(\hat{\mathbf{x}}(\mathbf{u}^{k-1}_{driver}), \Theta)$ returns *yes*, then then there exists $\mathbf{u} \in \mathcal{U}$ such that $\mathbf{y}(t, \mathbf{u}, \hat{\mathbf{x}}(\mathbf{u}^{k-1}_{driver})) \notin B$ for all $t \geq 0$ by Problem 1.

Now at $t = k\tau$, we want to prove that there exists $\mathbf{u}^k_{safe}$. Notice that $\mathbf{x}(k\tau)$ is either $\hat{\mathbf{x}}(\mathbf{u}^{k-1}_{driver})$ or $\hat{\mathbf{x}}(\mathbf{u}^{k-1}_{safe})$. In the former case, let $\mathbf{u}^k$ be $\mathbf{u}$ restricted to time $[k\tau, (k+1)\tau)$, and $\mathbf{u}^{k+1,\infty}$ be $\mathbf{u}$ restricted to time $[(k+1)\tau, \infty)$. Then, we have

$$\mathbf{y}(t, \mathbf{u}^{k+1,\infty}, \mathbf{x}(\tau, \mathbf{u}^k, \hat{\mathbf{x}}(\mathbf{u}^{k-1}_{driver}))) \notin B.$$

Thus there exists $\mathbf{u}^k_{safe} = \mathbf{u}^k$. Similarly for the latter case, let $\mathbf{u}'^k$ be $\mathbf{u}'$ restricted to time $[k\tau, (k+1)\tau)$, and $\mathbf{u}'^{k+1,\infty}$ be $\mathbf{u}'$ restricted to time $[(k+1)\tau, \infty)$. Then, we have

$$\mathbf{y}(t, \mathbf{u}'^{k+1,\infty}, \mathbf{x}(\tau, \mathbf{u}'^k, \hat{\mathbf{x}}(\mathbf{u}^{k-1}_{safe}))) \notin B.$$

Thus there exists $\mathbf{u}^k_{safe} = \mathbf{u}'^k$. Therefore, in any case, there exists a safe input $\mathbf{u}^k_{safe}$.

If $\mathbf{u}^0_{safe}$ exists, there exists $\mathbf{u}^k_{safe}$ for any $k > 0$. The supervisor is thus, non-blocking. □

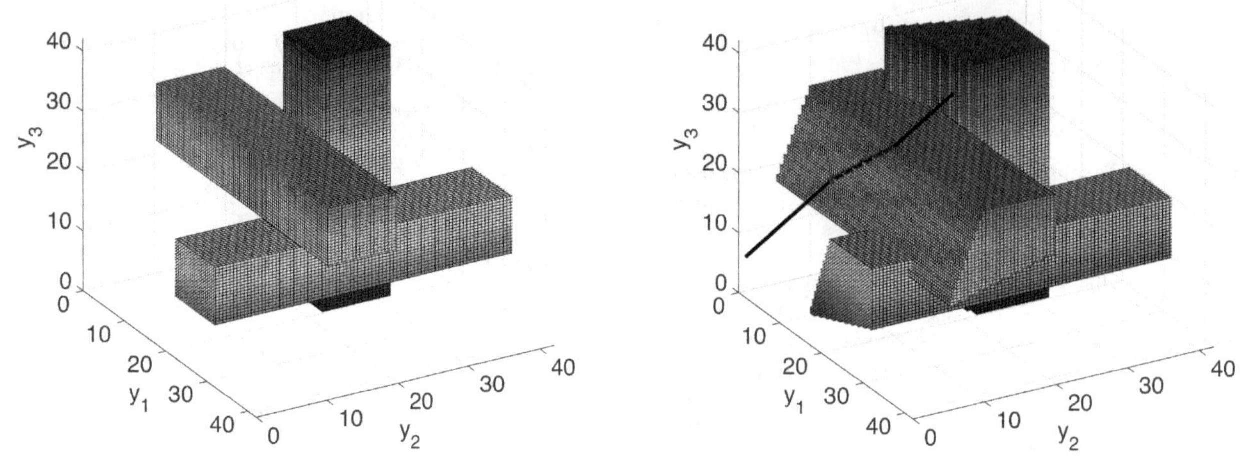

(a) Bad set

(b) Capture set

Figure 5: Position space of the three vehicles in the scenario of Figure 2. Subfigure (a) shows the bad set defined in (2), and subfigure (b) shows the resulting capture set defined in (13). In (b), the black line is the trajectory of the system, and the blue thick line highlights the positions at times when the supervisor overrides the vehicles. Notice that the supervisor prevents them from entering the capture set, thereby averting collision.

5. SIMULATION RESULTS

This section presents simulation results of the supervisor. In particular, considering the intersection scenarios illustrated in Figures 1 and 2, we validate that the supervisor prevents impending collisions by minimally overridng vehicles. Also, the simulations illustrate that for a system with a large number of vehicles, the computation time required for the supervisor algorithm (Algorithm 1) at each step is within the allotted 100 ms.

We implement Algorithm 1 using MATLAB, in which mixed-integer programming in Problem 5 is solved by using CPLEX. To speed up the process of generating the constraints of the problem, MATLAB Coder^{TM}[29] is used to replace the code written in MATLAB with the C code and compile it into a MATLAB executable function. Simulations are performed on a personal computer, which runs Windows 7 Home Premium and consists of an Intel Core i7-3770s processor at 3.10 GHz and 8 GB random-access memory.

Consider first Figure 2, in which three vehicles are approaching the intersection containing three conflict points. The parameters used in the simulations are τ =0.1, $U_j = [0.1, 0.3]$ for all $j \in \{1, \dots, n\}$, $(\alpha_{ij}, \beta_{ij})$ =(10,20) for $(i,j) \in \mathcal{F}$, and $(\alpha_{ij}, \beta_{ij}) = (\alpha_{i'j} + 22, \alpha_{ij} + 10)$ for $(i,j) \notin \mathcal{F}$, where $(i',j) \to (i,j) \in \mathcal{C}$.

To solve the verification problem (Problem 1), the work in [20] considers the set of initial states such that no input exists to avoid a collision. This subset of the state space is called the *capture set* and defined as follows.

$$\mathcal{CS} := \{\mathbf{x} \in \mathbf{X} : \forall \mathbf{u} \in \mathcal{U}, \ \exists t \text{ such that } \mathbf{y}(t, \mathbf{u}, \mathbf{x}) \in B\}. \tag{13}$$

The capture set resulting from the bad set in Figure 5(a) is shown in Figure 5(b). Given an instance $I = \{\mathbf{x}(0), \Theta\}$ of Problem 1, $I \notin$ Problem 1 if and only if $\mathbf{x}(0) \in \mathcal{CS}$ by definition. By Theorems 1 and 2, if $\mathbf{x}(0) \in \mathcal{CS}$, $I \notin$ Problems 4 and 5.

In Figure 5(b), the black line represents the trajectory of the system given an initial condition $\mathbf{x}(0)$ =(-2.8,-3.7,-1.2). When the supervisor overrides the vehicles, the trajectory is shown in blue. The drivers' inputs are set to be $\mathbf{u}^k_{driver} = (0.15, 0.11, 0.25)$ and constant for all $k \geq 0$ where $t = k\tau$, so that without override actions of the supervisor, the trajectory would enter the bad set in Figure 5(a). Notice that the supervisor overrides the vehicles right before the trajectory enters the capture set and makes the trajectory ride on the boundary of the capture set. The drivers regain the control of their vehicles once the dangerous situation is resolved. This confirms that the supervisor is least restrictive because it intervenes only when the state prediction $\hat{\mathbf{x}}(\mathbf{u}^k_{driver})$ enters the capture set. The computation of the supervisor algorithm (Algorithm 1) takes less than 4 ms per iteration in the worst case.

We then run Algorithm 1 for the intersection instance shown in Figure 1, which contains twenty vehicles and forty eight conflict points. Then, we inserted additional vehicles per road (far enough so to ensure that rear-end collsions do not occur) to determine how many vehicles the supervisor can handle within the 100 ms. In Figure 6, the computation time required for one iteration of Algorithm 1 is shown with respect to the number of vehicles. Notice that as the number of vehicles increases, the computation time increases exponentially. Although the problem is not scalable, about twenty five vehicles can be managed by the supervisor within the 100 ms even in the complicated intersection scenario.

The intersection scenario of Figure 1 is created from the top 20 crash intersection locations in the report of the Massachusetts Department of Transportation [25] such that it can represent each intersection topology by removing or com-

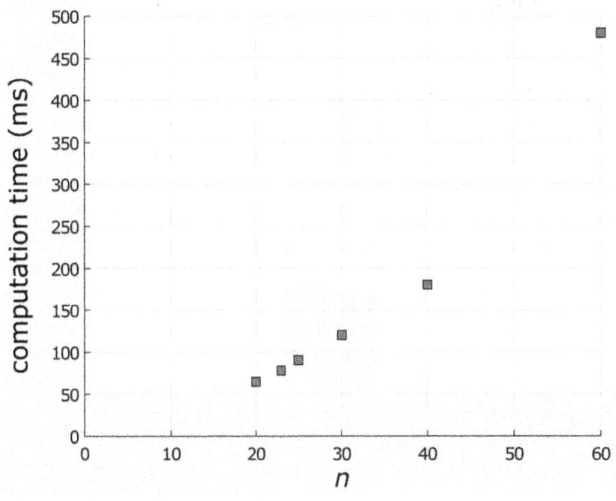

Figure 6: Computation time for one iteration of Algorithm 1 in the worst case with respect to the number of vehicles.

bining its lanes. That is, this intersection scenario consisting of twenty lanes and forty eight conflict points is more complicated than the twenty most dangerous intersections in Massachusetts. If we do not consider rear-end collisions and assume that there is only one vehicle per road, the number of vehicles in typical intersection scenarios usually does not exceed twenty. We can thus conclude that this supervisor is practical for typical intersection scenarios. How accounting for rear-end collisions affects computational complexity will be investigated in future work. It is shown in [11] that additional vehicles on the same lane increase computational complexity less than those on different lanes due to precedence constraints. Since in Figure 6, we did not consider these precedence constraints, we expect that the computation time will be lower than that shown in Figure 6.

6. CONCLUSIONS

We have designed a supervisor that overrides human-driven vehicles only when a future collision is detected and has a non-blocking property. To this end, we have formulated the verification problem and the job-shop scheduling problem and proved that they are equivalent. To solve the job-shop scheduling problem, we have converted it into a mixed-integer linear programming problem by assuming the single integrator vehicle dynamics. The computer simulations confirm that the supervisor guarantees safety while overriding vehicles only when a future collision is unavoidable otherwise. Also, the computational studies show that despite the combinatorial complexity of the verification problem, the supervisor can deal with a complicated intersection scenario as in Figure 1 within the allotted 100 ms per iteration.

While this paper considers a general intersection model in terms of conflict areas, the inclusion of rear-end collisions in the scenario makes it more practical. Moreover, to account for more realistic dynamic behaviors of vehicles, a nonlinear second-order model will be considered. In particular, for second-order linear dynamics, the job-shop scheduling problem may be reformulated as a mixed-integer quadratic programming problem. Also, as considered in [5, 1, 2] in which an intersection is modeled as a single conflict area, measurement and process uncertainty and the presence of unequipped vehicles will be investigated in future work. Undetermined routes of vehicles will also be investigated by considering possible decisions of steering inputs.

7. ACKNOWLEDGMENTS

The authors would like to thank Alessandro Colombo and Gabriel Campos at Politecnico di Milano for the helpful discussions and suggestions. This work was in part supported by NSF CPS Award No. 1239182.

8. REFERENCES

[1] H. Ahn, A. Colombo, and D. Del Vecchio. Supervisory control for intersection collision avoidance in the presence of uncontrolled vehicles. In *American Control Conference (ACC)*, June 2014.

[2] H. Ahn, A. Rizzi, A. Colombo, and D. Del Vecchio. Experimental testing of a semi-autonomous multi-vehicle collision avoidance algorithm at an intersection testbed. In *IEEE/RSJ International Conference on Intelligent Robots and Systems (IROS)*, 2015.

[3] E. Balas, G. Lancia, P. Serafini, and A. Vazacopoulos. Job shop scheduling with deadlines. *Journal of Combinatorial Optimization*, 1(4):329–353, 1998.

[4] F. Borrelli, D. Subramanian, A. Raghunathan, and L. Biegler. MILP and NLP techniques for centralized trajectory planning of multiple unmanned air vehicles. In *American Control Conference (ACC)*, 2006.

[5] L. Bruni, A. Colombo, and D. Del Vecchio. Robust multi-agent collision avoidance through scheduling. In *IEEE Conference on Decision and Control (CDC)*, Dec. 2013.

[6] M. R. Bussieck and S. Vigerske. MINLP Solver Software. In *Wiley Encyclopedia of Operations Research and Management Science*. John Wiley & Sons, Inc., 2010.

[7] L. Chen and C. Englund. Cooperative Intersection Management: A survey. *IEEE Transactions on Intelligent Transportation Systems*, 2015.

[8] M. Christodoulou and S. Kodaxakis. Automatic commercial aircraft-collision avoidance in free flight: the three-dimensional problem. *IEEE Transactions on Intelligent Transportation Systems*, 7(2):242–249, 2006.

[9] A. Colombo and D. Del Vecchio. Supervisory control of differentially flat systems based on abstraction. In *IEEE Conference on Decision and Control and European Control Conference (CDC-ECC)*, 2011.

[10] A. Colombo and D. Del Vecchio. Efficient algorithms for collision avoidance at intersections. In *Hybrid Systems: Computation and Control (HSCC)*, 2012.

[11] A. Colombo and D. Del Vecchio. Least restrictive supervisors for intersection collision avoidance: A scheduling approach. *IEEE Transactions on Automatic Control*, 2014.

[12] T. H. Cormen. *Introduction to algorithms*. MIT Press, 2009.

[13] M. Earl and R. D'Andrea. Modeling and control of a multi-agent system using mixed integer linear programming. In *IEEE Conference on Decision and Control (CDC)*, 2002.

[14] C. A. Floudas. *Nonlinear and mixed-integer optimization: fundamentals and applications.* Oxford University Press, 1995.

[15] M. R. Garey and D. S. Johnson. *Computers and Intractability: A Guide to the Theory of NP-Completeness.* W. H. Freeman and Company, San Francisco, 1979.

[16] A. Girard and G. J. Pappas. Hierarchical control system design using approximate simulation. *Automatica*, 45(2):566–571, 2009.

[17] I. E. Grossmann and J. P. Ruiz. Generalized disjunctive programming: A framework for formulation and alternative algorithms for MINLP optimization. In *Mixed Integer Nonlinear Programming*, volume 154 of *The IMA Volumes in Mathematics and its Applications*, pages 93–115. Springer New York, 2012.

[18] E. I. Grotli and T. A. Johansen. Path planning for UAVs under communication constraints using SPLAT! and MILP. *Journal of Intelligent and Robotic Systems*, 65(1-4):265–282, 2011.

[19] Gurobi Optimization, Inc. Gurobi optimizer reference manual. http://www.gurobi.com/documentation/6.0/refman/, 2014.

[20] M. Hafner, D. Cunningham, L. Caminiti, and D. Del Vecchio. Cooperative Collision Avoidance at Intersections: Algorithms and Experiments. *IEEE Transactions on Intelligent Transportation Systems*, 14(3):1162–1175, 2013.

[21] Intellient Tranportation Systems, Joint Program Office, U.S. Department of Transportation. ITS Strategic plan 2015-2019. http://www.its.dot.gov/strategicplan.pdf, 2014.

[22] International Business Machines Corporation. IBM ILOG CPLEX V12.1: Users manual for CPLEX. ftp://public.dhe.ibm.com/software/websphere/ilog/docs/optimization/cplex/ps_usrmancplex.pdf, 2009.

[23] H. Kowshik, D. Caveney, and P. Kumar. Provable systemwide safety in intelligent intersections. *IEEE Transactions on Vehicular Technology*, 60(3):804–818, 2011.

[24] J. Lee and B. Park. Development and Evaluation of a Cooperative Vehicle Intersection Control Algorithm Under the Connected Vehicles Environment. *IEEE Transactions on Intelligent Transportation Systems*, 13(1):81–90, 2012.

[25] Massachusetts Department of Transportation. 2012 Top Crash Locations Report. https://www.massdot.state.ma.us/Portals/8/docs/traffic/CrashData/12TopCrashLocationsRpt.pdf, 2014.

[26] National Highway Traffic Safety Administration, U.S. Department of Transportation. 2012 Motor Vehicle Crashes: Overview, Traffic Safety Facts. http://www-nrd.nhtsa.dot.gov/Pubs/811856.pdf, 2013.

[27] M. Pinedo. *Scheduling theory, algorithms, and systems.* Springer, 4th edition, 2012.

[28] A. Richards, T. Schouwenaars, J. P. How, and E. Feron. Spacecraft trajectory planning with avoidance constraints using mixed-integer linear programming. *Journal of Guidance, Control, and Dynamics*, 25(4):755–764, 2002.

[29] The MathWorks, Inc. MATLAB Coder™User's Guide. http://de.mathworks.com/help/pdf_doc/coder/coder_ug.pdf, 2015.

[30] F. Yan, M. Dridi, and A. El Moudni. Autonomous vehicle sequencing algorithm at isolated intersections. In *IEEE International Conference on Intelligent Transportation Systems (ITSC)*, 2009.

Building Power Consumption Models from Executable Timed I/O Automata Specifications

Benoît Barbot*, Marta Kwiatkowska, Alexandru Mereacre and Nicola Paoletti
Department of Computer Science, University of Oxford, UK
{benoit.barbot, marta.kwiatkowska, alexandru.mereacre, nicola.paoletti}@cs.ox.ac.uk

ABSTRACT

We develop a novel model-based hardware-in-the-loop (HIL) framework for optimising energy consumption of embedded software controllers. Controller and plant models are specified as networks of parameterised timed input/output automata and translated into executable code. The controller is encoded into the target embedded hardware, which is connected to a power monitor and interacts with the simulation of the plant model. The framework then generates a power consumption model that maps controller transitions to distributions over power measurements, and is used to optimise the timing parameters of the controller, without compromising a given safety requirement. The novelty of our approach is that we measure the real power consumption of the controller and use thus obtained data for energy optimisation. We employ timed Petri nets as an intermediate representation of the executable specification, which facilitates efficient code generation and fast simulations. Our framework uniquely combines the advantages of rigorous specifications with accurate power measurements and methods for online model estimation, thus enabling automated design of correct and energy-efficient controllers.

1. INTRODUCTION

Embedded devices are at the core of numerous safety-critical applications in areas such as avionics, automotive and biomedical. One of the main challenges in the design and implementation of embedded devices is to ensure that their behaviour meets design-time requirements while, at the same time, consuming the least amount of energy possible.

These contrasting aspects are typically addressed in two separate phases: requirements are enforced through developing formal models of the system and analysing their correctness using formal verification methods, whereas energy efficiency through selecting low-power hardware components and tuning the physical device to reduce consumption. An established approach to deal with this separation is to employ integrated design and analysis of software and hardware components, called hardware/software co-design, and in particular *hardware-in-the-loop (HIL) optimization*. This involves automated optimisation of hardware based on evaluating its behaviour in interaction with the simulation of the plant model, a method known as *HIL simulation* [3]. Since the device under test works in real-time, effective HIL simulation approaches must enable real-time simulations, as well as synchronisation and data transfer between hardware and software. However, existing HIL optimisation approaches are ad hoc and lack automated support that incorporates formal verification and synthesis methods.

In this paper, we develop a comprehensive and fully automated model-based framework for hardware-in-the-loop energy optimization of embedded devices that, for the first time, integrates rigorous specifications with data-driven energy optimisation and online estimation of power models. At the system-design level, we adopt the widely used MATLAB Stateflow modelling formalism. We support hybrid systems specified as networks of parameterised timed I/O automata and encoded in Stateflow, and employ parameter synthesis methods to restrict the search to the device parameters that guarantee a given safety property. At the HIL optimisation level, we implement a novel method to generate executable code from the Stateflow diagrams by resorting to an intermediate representation as timed Petri nets, which is compact and event-driven, and thus facilitates fast real-time simulations and hardware/software synchronisation. The novelty of our approach is that we derive predictive power consumption models from actual power measurement data, and query these models to find the device parameters that maximise battery lifetime. Our framework is sufficiently general to synthesise energy-efficient embedded software for a variety of applications, which we demonstrate through the evaluation on a temperature controller and a cardiac pacemaker.

1.1 Overview of the framework

The purpose of our framework is twofold. First, we aim to *estimate* detailed power consumption models for enabling the design of energy-efficient embedded software. Second, we aim to *parameterise* the device in order to optimise power consumption and prolong battery life, such that the correct functioning of the device is not compromised. Figure 1 shows the high-level structure of our framework. We consider systems characterised by a *controller* that acts on a *plant*.

At the system design level, the specifications for the plant and controller are given as *timed input/output automata with data (TIOA)* [26]. This formalism (described in Section

*Now in LACL, Université Paris Est Créteil, France

HSCC'16, April 12-14, 2016, Vienna, Austria

DOI: http://dx.doi.org/10.1145/2883817.2883844

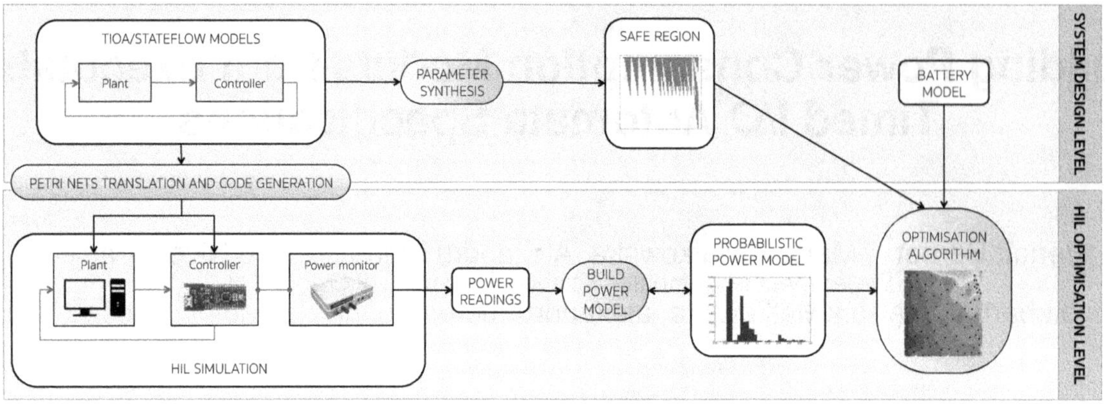

Figure 1: Modelling, hardware-in-the-loop optimisation and power model estimation framework

2.1) is able to represent networked systems with real-time constraints and discrete control actions (suitable to model the controller), as well as hybrid dynamics through continuous variables and non-linear update functions (to model the plant). Importantly, the framework supports the use of MATLAB Stateflow for specifying TIOA models. At this level, we additionally focus on guaranteeing correctness, which we achieve by excluding the region of controller parameter values that violate a given *safety* requirement. Such parameters describe, for instance, the switching frequency of the device from the active to the idle modes, or the frequency of data capture and processing. This phase is described in Section 2.2 and builds on a *parameter synthesis* method implemented using Satisfiability Modulo Theory (SMT) techniques. In order to optimise the battery lifetime, we also need a *battery model*, given, in our case, as a system of ordinary differential equations (ODEs) (see Section 2.3).

At the HIL optimisation level, HIL simulation has the role of executing the controller code, which is embedded in programmable hardware (e.g. a microcontroller or FPGA), in combination with the plant simulation, running on a computer system. The generation of executable code for HIL simulations from formal TIOA specifications leverages an intermediate representation in terms of timed Petri nets (TPNs), which enables real-time simulations as well as fast event scheduling and hardware-software synchronisation. In Section 3.1, we describe the translation from TIOAs into TPNs, the generation of executable code and the HIL simulation algorithm. The controller unit is attached to a *power monitor* that measures the power consumption of the device. In particular, we are interested in the amount of energy consumed by the controller when performing specific transitions, which is used to build the probabilistic power consumption model, as illustrated in Section 3.2. By taking consumption data from multiple HIL simulations, this step produces a *probabilistic power model* with the same structure as the controller TIOA, but annotated with rewards that describe, for transition t and energy value e, the probability that the device consumes an amount of energy equal to e when performing t. Finally, the optimisation algorithm uses the battery and consumption models to optimise the battery lifetime. This objective is evaluated by simulating the plant, controller and power consumption models on the computer until the battery runs out. Note that, in this case, a real-time HIL simulation would take an excessive amount of time. Here, we speed up this task through pure software simulation that nevertheless utilises real power readings through the estimated power consumption model. Specifically, we follow a Gaussian process optimisation scheme (see Section 3.3), which has the additional advantage of deriving a statistical model of the objective function with respect to controller parameters. To avoid sampling unsafe parameters, the optimisation algorithm also requires the safe region synthesised at the system design level.

1.2 Related work

In recent years, a number of approaches have been proposed for the design of energy-efficient systems. Benini et.al. [9] provide a comprehensive survey, examining techniques for optimizing energy at different levels: modelling, system design and runtime management. The review by Unsal et.al. [31] focuses on techniques enabling low-power design for real-time systems, covering the whole span of architectural levels, from hardware to operating systems and computer networks. HIL simulation has been successfully employed in a number of industrial applications, including the testing of automotive control systems [20], power electronics [12], avionics [24] and biomedical devices [11, 18, 21]. HIL optimisation approaches are relatively more recent and have been used to optimise, e.g., the performance of wireless networks [28], or the speed of humanoid robots [19]. Despite much research on energy-aware design and combined hardware/software testing, our work is the first to seamlessly integrate, in a fully automated framework based on the widely used Simulink Stateflow notation, rigorous design methods, specifically parameter synthesis, with HIL optimisation and the generation of data-driven power consumption models from real hardware measurements.

In our previous work [8], we introduced a HIL optimisation approach for the energy consumption of cardiac pacemakers, using the Simulink code generation capabilities and evaluating the safety of the pacemaker parameters at HIL simulation time. In contrast, the framework presented in this paper supports general system specifications – even if we also evaluate the pacemaker case study, see Section 4.2 – and provides numerous improvements and novelties, including the derivation of probabilistic consumption models, optimisation of battery lifetime and the formal synthesis of safe controller parameters. Importantly, here we implement a dedicated code generation method in place of the one provided by Simulink. Indeed, the code generated through the latter method is not suitable for accurate energy consumption measurements because it keeps the device running, and thus consuming energy, even when the controller is inactive, e.g. waiting for events from the plant. On the other hand, our code and scheduling algorithm use the power saving modes of the embedded system when the controller is idle. In this way, energy readings consistently reflect the controller activity, at the same time improving energy efficiency of the code. Other approaches exist for generating executable code from timed automata and Petri nets specifications, to mention [2, 29, 5].

The method for synthesising safe parameters has been adapted from our previous work [26]. There, we consider the problem of maximising the robustness of parameters with respect to a given safety property, which we could solve without exploring the full parameter space. In contrast, in this work we have to synthesise the full safe region, and thus cannot exclude any parameter region from the analysis. Parameter synthesis for TIOA models was first considered in [16] and solved by combining parameter sampling and constraint solving.

2. SYSTEM DESIGN LEVEL

2.1 Timed I/O automata with data

We consider a set of variables $V = \mathcal{X} \cup \mathcal{D}$, where $\mathcal{X}$ and $\mathcal{D}$ are the set of *clocks* and *data*, respectively. A variable valuation $\eta : V \to \mathbb{R}$ is a function that maps data variables to the reals and clocks to the non-negative reals. We also consider a set of real-valued *parameters* Γ and valuation functions $\gamma : \Gamma \to \mathbb{R}$. For a set $\mathcal{Y}$, we denote with $\mathcal{V}(\mathcal{Y})$ the set of all valuations over $\mathcal{Y}$. The *update* of a set of variables $V' \subseteq V$ is a real-valued function $r : V' \times \mathcal{V}(V) \times \mathcal{V}(\Gamma) \to \mathbb{R}$. Given valuations η and γ, η is updated by reset r to the valuation $\eta[r] = \{v \mapsto r(v, \eta, \gamma) \mid v \in V'\} \cup \{v \mapsto \eta(v) \mid v \notin V'\}$ that applies the reset r to the variables in V' and leaves the others unchanged. We denote with $\mathcal{R}$ the set of update functions. We consider guard constraints of the form $g = \bigwedge_i v_i \bowtie_i f_i$, where $v_i \in \mathcal{X}$ is a clock, $\bowtie_i \in \{<, \leqslant, >, \geqslant\}$ and f_i is a real-valued function over data variables and parameter valuations. We denote with $\mathcal{B}(V)$ the set of guard constraints over V.

In the following, we introduce our main modelling language, which extends [25] with priorities, data variables and parameters.

DEFINITION 1 (TIOA). *A deterministic timed I/O automaton (TIOA) with priority and data* $\mathcal{A} = (\mathcal{X}, \Gamma, \mathcal{D}, Q, q_0, \Sigma_{\text{in}}, \Sigma_{\text{out}}, \to)$ *consists of:*

- *A finite set of clocks* $\mathcal{X}$*, data variables* $\mathcal{D}$ *and parameters* Γ.
- *A finite set of locations* Q*, with initial location* $q_0 \in Q$.
- *Finite sets of input* Σ_{in} *and output* Σ_{out} *actions.*
- *A finite set of edges* $\to \subseteq Q \times (\Sigma_{\text{in}} \cup \Sigma_{\text{out}}) \times \mathbb{N} \times \mathcal{B}(V) \times \mathcal{R} \times Q$. *Each edge* $e = (q, a, pr, g, r, q')$ *is described by a source location* q*, an action* a*, a priority* pr*, a guard* g*, an update* r *and a target* q'.

TIOAs are able to express hybrid dynamics, since they support data variables and arbitrary functions in the right-hand side of guards and updates. Continuous flows, i.e. the update of variables through differential equations, cannot be expressed directly, but can be modelled with update functions using the explicit solution of the equations. Therefore, TIOAs can express any hybrid automata whose flows admit explicit solutions that can be effectively computed.

We require that priorities define a total ordering of the edges out of any location, and that output actions have higher priority than input actions. To facilitate modular designs, TIOAs are able to synchronise on matching input and output actions, thus forming *networks of communicating automata*. We say that an output edge is *enabled* when the associated guard holds. On the other hand, an input edge is enabled when both its guard holds and it can synchronise with a matching output action fired by another component of the network. Note that, unlike input edges, output edges can fire even without synchronising with a matching input action. A component of a network of TIOAs is enabled if, from its current location, there is at least one outgoing edge enabled. Also, we assume that output edges are *urgent*, meaning that they are taken as soon as they become enabled. As shown in [16], priority and urgency imply that *the TIOA is deterministic.*

DEFINITION 2 (NETWORK OF TIOAS). *A network of TIOAs with m components is a tuple* $\mathcal{N} = (\{\mathcal{A}^1, \ldots, \mathcal{A}^m\}, \mathcal{X}, \Gamma, \mathcal{D}, \Sigma_{\text{in}}, \Sigma_{\text{out}})$ *of TIOAs, where*

- *for* $j = 1, \ldots, m$, $\mathcal{A}^j = (\mathcal{X}, \Gamma, \mathcal{D}, Q^j, q_0^j, \Sigma_{\text{in}}, \Sigma_{\text{out}}, \to^j)$ *is a TIOA,*
- $\mathcal{X}$, Γ, $\mathcal{D}$, Σ_{in} *and* Σ_{out} *are the common sets of clocks, parameters, data variables, input and output actions, respectively.*

We define the set of network modes by $\vec{Q} = Q^1 \times \cdots \times Q^m$*, with initial mode* $\vec{q_0} = (q_0^1, \ldots, q_0^m)$ *and the initial variable valuation* η_0*. A state of the network is a pair* $(\vec{q}, \eta)$*, where* $\vec{q} \in \vec{Q}$ *is the vector of active locations and* $\eta \in \mathcal{V}(V)$ *is the variable valuation.*

A *parametric network of TIOAs* is a network where the parameter valuation is unknown. $\mathcal{N}(\gamma)$ denotes the concrete network obtained by instantiating the valuation γ.

The execution of a network $\mathcal{N}(\gamma)$ of TIOAs is described by a path $\rho = (\vec{q_0}, \eta_0) \xrightarrow{t_0} (\vec{q_1}, \eta_1) \xrightarrow{t_1} \cdots$, where, for each i, $\rho[i] = (\vec{q_i}, \eta_i)$ is a state of the network and t_i is the time spent in that state. A step in the path occurs as soon as at least one component is enabled. In this case, each enabled component fires the enabled edge with maximum priority, moving to the corresponding target location. The new variable valuation reflects the updates of the fired edges and time spent in the previous state. For a detailed account of the formal semantics of TIOA networks, see [26].

EXAMPLE 1. *Consider the TIOAs* $\mathcal{A}_1$*,* $\mathcal{A}_2$ *and* $\mathcal{A}_3$ *from Fig. 2. The automata model the bang-bang temperature control system given in [1]. The controller switches the boiler on or off depending on the current temperature (variable t) and on a predefined* threshold θ*. Automaton* $\mathcal{A}_1$ *has the role of controlling the boiler, while* $\mathcal{A}_2$ *models the led light that notifies the user when the boiler is heating or switched off. The boiler automaton* $\mathcal{A}_3$ *changes the room temperature. Parameters are:* T_{on}*, which describes the minimum time before the controller switches on the boiler, if the temperature (variable t) is below the threshold* θ*;* T_{P}*, which defines the*

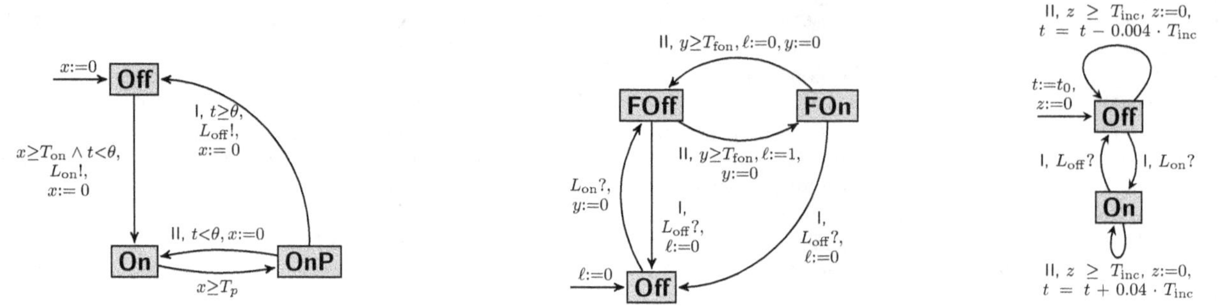

(a) Temperature controller, $\mathcal{A}_1$ (b) Led controller, $\mathcal{A}_2$ (c) Boiler (plant), $\mathcal{A}_3$

Figure 2: TIOA network for the bang-bang temperature control example [1]. Roman numbers indicate edge priorities. Symbols "!" and "?" denote output and input actions, respectively.

polling period of the temperature sensor; the switching frequency T_{fon} *for the led, whose state is given by variable* ℓ*; and* T_{inc}*, the time step for updating the temperature in the boiler automaton. Starting from the initial temperature* t_0*,* t *increases by* $0.04°$C *per milliseconds when the heater is on, while it decreases by* $0.004°$C *when it is off.*

The automata $\mathcal{A}_1$*,* $\mathcal{A}_2$ *and* $\mathcal{A}_3$ *can be composed to form a network. Call this* $\mathcal{N}$*. The states of* $\mathcal{N}$ *are of the form* $((q_{\mathcal{A}_1}, q_{\mathcal{A}_2}, q_{\mathcal{A}_3}), \eta)$ *where, for* $i = 1, 2, 3$, $q_{\mathcal{A}_i}$ *is the active location in* $\mathcal{A}_i$ *and* $\eta = (\eta(x), \eta(\ell), \eta(y), \eta(t), \eta(z))$ *is the variable valuation. Network components communicate with each other by means of actions* L_{on} *and* L_{off}*. By instantiating the set of parameters* T_{on}*,* T_{p}*,* θ*,* t_0 *and* T_{inc}*,* $\mathcal{N}$ *induces an execution* ρ*, for instance:*

$$\rho = ((\mathbf{Off}, \mathbf{Off}, \mathbf{Off}), (0, 0, 0, t_0, 0)) \xrightarrow{T_{\text{inc}}}$$
$$((\mathbf{Off}, \mathbf{Off}, \mathbf{Off}), (T_{\text{inc}}, 0, T_{\text{inc}}, t_0 - 0.004 \cdot T_{\text{inc}}, 0)) \xrightarrow{T_{\text{on}} - T_{\text{inc}}}$$
$$((\mathbf{On}, \mathbf{FOff}, \mathbf{On}), (0, 0, 0, t_0 - 0.004 \cdot T_{\text{inc}}, T_{\text{on}} - T_{\text{inc}})) \cdots$$

We now define the model of TIOAs with rewards labelling the transitions, which we will use to describe the power consumption model.

Definition 3 (TIOAs with rewards). *A deterministic timed I/O automaton (TIOA) with rewards is a tuple* $\mathcal{A}_r = (\mathcal{X}, \Gamma, \mathcal{D}, Q, q_0, \Sigma_{\text{in}}, \Sigma_{\text{out}}, \rightarrow_r)$*, where* $\mathcal{X}, \Gamma, \mathcal{D}, Q, q_0, \Sigma_{\text{in}}$*, and* Σ_{out} *are defined as in Def. 1 and* $\rightarrow_r \subseteq Q \times (\Sigma_{\text{in}} \cup \Sigma_{\text{out}}) \times \mathbb{N} \times \mathcal{B}(V) \times \mathcal{R} \times Distr(\mathbb{Q}_{\geq 0}) \times Q$*.*

In the above definition, $Distr(\mathbb{Q}_{\geq 0})$ is the set of all probability distribution functions with finite support over the set of positive rational numbers. For instance, we can associate to an edge $e \in \rightarrow_r$ the function $Prob \in Distr(\mathbb{Q}_{\geq 0})$ that assigns $Prob(23) = \frac{1}{3}$ and $Prob(\frac{1}{4}) = \frac{2}{3}$. We let rewards accumulate over executions of $\mathcal{A}_r$. For example, when the total reward accumulated so far is c and $\mathcal{A}_r$ takes the edge e, c will be increased by 23 with probability $\frac{1}{3}$ and by $\frac{1}{4}$ with probability $\frac{2}{3}$. The definition of network of TIOAs with rewards follows from Definitions 2 and 3.

Encoding in Stateflow. TIOA models can be expressed as MATLAB Stateflow diagrams, which are generally richer than TIOAs. Our framework only supports the TIOA fragment of the Stateflow language, thus excluding features like hierarchical components and continuous flows. However, unlike TIOAs, Stateflow diagrams do not support the definition of arbitrary clocks and clock updates. In particular, each Stateflow component only possesses an implicit clock, which is reset to 0 whenever an edge is taken, and guards are specified through Stateflow temporal operators. Specifically, we use the operator after(t) in place of the guard $x \geq t$, before(t) for $x \leq t$ and at(t) for $x = t$, where x is the implicit clock and t is a time value that can be specified as a function over data variables and parameters.

2.2 Computation of safe region

We compute the set of parameter valuations such that the TIOA network meets a given safety property using a method adapted from [26] and based on satisfiability modulo theory (SMT) solving [14]. For a path ρ of length k, we focus on bounded safety properties of the form $\phi = \bigwedge_{i=0}^{k-1} f_i(\rho[0], \ldots, \rho[i])$, where f_i is a predicate over the states of the network up to position i. Then, for property ϕ, we seek to compute the set $\mathcal{S}$ of safe parameter valuations, defined as $\mathcal{S} = \{\gamma \in \mathcal{V}(\Gamma) \mid \rho(\gamma) \models \phi\}$.

The algorithm for computing the set $\mathcal{S}$ (described in the technical report [7]) relies on a symbolic SMT-based encoding of the network and the property, and works by exhaustively exploring bounded counter-examples to safety, which amounts to finding valuations such that $\neg\phi$ holds at some point in the path. To ensure decidability, we provide a discrete encoding in the theory of bit-vectors (SMT UF_BV), where non-integer values and non-linear functions are expressed in a sound way through a conservative interval-based abstraction. We remark that the framework can be generalised to support more general path properties, see [26].

2.3 Kinetik battery model

Using a battery model, one can describe the state of the battery over time, which in our framework enables the development of power usage models and the optimisation of battery lifetime. We consider the Kinetik Battery Model, which describes variations of the battery capacity as a function of charge and discharge currents [27]. The model is given by the following system of ODEs:

$$\frac{dy_1(t)}{dt} = -i(t) + k\left(\frac{y_2(t)}{1-c} - \frac{y_1(t)}{c}\right) \quad (1)$$
$$\frac{dy_2(t)}{dt} = -k\left(\frac{y_2(t)}{1-c} - \frac{y_1(t)}{c}\right)$$

The battery charge is distributed in two wells: available charge $y_1(t)$ and bound charge $y_2(t)$. The function $i(t)$ denotes the current applied to the battery. When the value of $i(t)$ is zero the battery enters the recovery mode, where the energy flows from the bound-charge well to the available-charge well. However, when the current $i(t)$ is not zero, both $y_1(t)$ and $y_2(t)$ decrease over time. If C [Ah] (ampere-hour) is the initial total capacity of the battery then $y_1(0) = c \cdot C$ and $y_2(0) = (1 - c) \cdot C$, where c is a fraction of the total capacity. The conduction parameter k represents the flow rate of charge from the bound-charge well to the available-charge well. The battery is considered to be empty when $y_1(t) = 0$. As explained in Section 3.3, integration with the TIOA power consumption model results in a piecewise constant $i(t)$, and thus in a hybrid battery model.

2.4 Timed Petri nets

Petri nets are a well known formalism for modelling the control flow of concurrent systems [15]. They have an intuitive semantics and are ideally suited to generating event based executable code. We use them as an intermediate model in the process of generating code from networks of TIOAs. The main advantage of the Petri net formalism compared to TIOAs is the ability to compute in advance the synchronisation event between different transitions, which is central to the real-time scheduling algorithm for HIL simulation, as we will explain in Section 3.1.

Definition 4 (Petri net). *A Petri net or Place/Transition net is a tuple* $\mathcal{O} = (P, T, W^-, W^+, W^0, m_0)$ *with* $P \cap T = \varnothing$ *where*

- P *is a finite set of places.*
- T *is a finite set of transitions.*
- $W^- : P \times T \to \mathbb{N}$ *is the* pre incidence matrix.
- $W^+ : P \times T \to \mathbb{N}$ *is the* post incidence matrix.
- $W^0 : P \times T \to \mathbb{N}$ *is the* inhibitor incidence matrix.
- $m_0 \in \mathbb{N}^P$ *is the initial marking.*

We call a *marking* $m \in \mathbb{N}^P$ of a Petri net $\mathcal{N}$ a vector assigning an integer to each place of the net. A transition $\mathbf{t} \in T$ is enabled in a marking m if $\forall p \in P.\ m(p) - W^-(p, \mathbf{t}) \geq 0 \wedge m(p) - W^0(p, \mathbf{t}) < 0$. The firing of an enabled transition $\mathbf{t}$ from a marking m leads to marking m', denoted $m \xrightarrow{t} m'$, where m' is defined, for each $p \in P$, as $m'(p) = m(p) - W^-(p, \mathbf{t}) + W^+(p, \mathbf{t})$.

Timed behaviours are introduced in Petri nets by adding time constraints on transitions [10]. We denote by $\mathcal{R}^d$ the set of update functions defined as in the case of TIOAs, except that we restrict the functions only to data variables.

Definition 5 (TPN). *A timed Petri net (TPN) with priority and data is a tuple* $\mathcal{O} = (P, T, W^-, W^+, W^0, m_0, \mathcal{D}, \alpha, \beta, Pr, up)$ *with* $P \cap T = \varnothing$ *where*

- $(P, T, W^-, W^+, W^0, m_0)$ *is a Petri net with inhibitor arcs.*
- $\mathcal{D}$ *is a finite set of data variables.*
- $\alpha : T \to (\mathbb{R}^+ \cup \infty)$ *is a function assigning to each transition its earliest firing time.*
- $\beta : T \to (\mathbb{R}^+ \cup \infty)$ *is a function assigning to each transition its latest firing time.*
- $\forall \mathbf{t} \in T.\ \alpha(\mathbf{t}) \leq \beta(\mathbf{t})$.

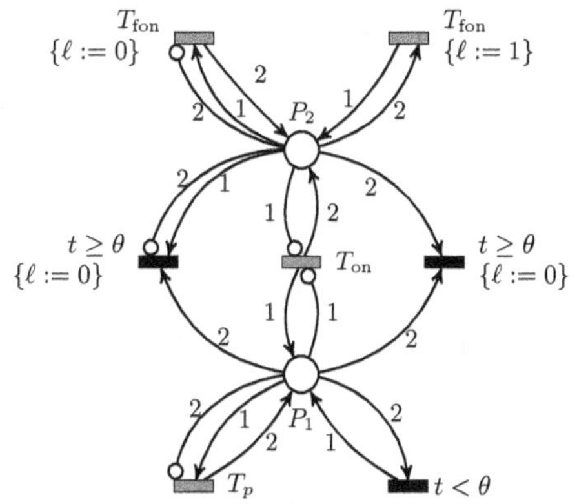

Figure 3: Petri net for the bang-bang controller of Fig. 2. Arcs with arrowheads are input and output arcs. Arcs ending with a circle are inhibitor arcs. Each arc is labelled by its valuation. Transitions in grey are timed; transition in black, instantaneous. Updates of data variables are enclosed in brackets.

- $Pr : T \to \mathbb{N}$ *is a function assigning to each transition a priority.*
- $up : T \to \mathcal{R}^d$ *mapping transitions to update functions over data variables.*

An implicit clock is associated with each transition $\mathbf{t}$ of the net. The clock is reset when the transition becomes enabled. The transition is *enabled* when the clock valuation lies between the earliest ($\alpha(\mathbf{t})$) and latest ($\beta(\mathbf{t})$) firing times. A transition can fire only if no transition with higher priority is enabled. In our setting we work with TPNs for which the timed behaviour is *deterministic*, that is, for any transition $\mathbf{t}$, $\alpha(\mathbf{t}) = \beta(\mathbf{t})$ and all transitions have different priorities.

From TIOA networks to TPNs. For our purposes, we only need to consider the subset of TIOAs derived from Stateflow diagrams. As explained in Section 2.1, this corresponds to having, for each TIOA $\mathcal{A}$, exactly one clock $x_{\mathcal{A}}$, which is reset every time an edge is taken.

For each automaton $\mathcal{A}^j = (\mathcal{X}, \Gamma, \mathcal{D}, Q^j, q_0^j, \Sigma_{\text{in}}, \Sigma_{\text{out}}, \to^j)$ of a network $\mathcal{N}$, we build a TPN $\mathcal{O}_j = (\{p_j\}, T_j, W_j^-, W_j^+, W_j^0, m_{0,j}, \mathcal{D}, \alpha_j, \beta_j, Pr_j, up_j)$. We define an injective function $f_j : Q^j \to \mathbb{N}$ that allows encoding each location $q \in Q^j$ of the automaton as a marking of the place p_j. For each edge $(q, a, pr, g, r, q') \in \to^j$ of $\mathcal{A}^j$, a transition $\mathbf{t}$ is added to the TPN $\mathcal{O}_j$. Three arcs are added between p_j and $\mathbf{t}$: an input arc with valuation $f_j(q)$, an inhibitor arc with valuation $f_j(q) + 1$ and an output arc with valuation $f_j(q')$. The update function is defined such that $up_j(\mathbf{t}) = r$. The firing time of the transition is set to the smallest time satisfying the guard g. A temporary labelling function $\Lambda(\mathbf{t}) = a$ keeps the action of $\mathbf{t}$. Pr_j reflects the priorities in the original automaton. The algorithm for composing all TPNs $\mathcal{O}_1, \ldots, \mathcal{O}_j$ obtained from $\mathcal{N}$ into a single TPN $\hat{\mathcal{O}}$ is described in the technical report [7]. The resulting TPN is of the same order of magnitude as the input TIOA and, thus is very compact and facilitates efficient code generation. It can be shown that deterministic delays and the structure of W_j^-, W_j^+ and W_j^0 imply that such a derived TPN preserves the determinism of the input TIOA.

Example 2. *In Fig. 3 we depict the composed TPN* $\hat{\mathcal{O}}$ *obtained from the network of automata* $\mathcal{A}_1$ *and* $\mathcal{A}_2$ *from Example 1. Locations of* $\mathcal{A}_1$ *and* $\mathcal{A}_2$ *are encoded as markings* *of the net $\hat{O}$ as follows. Place P_1 encodes the locations of $\mathcal{A}_1$ with the function $f_1 = \{\mathbf{Off} \mapsto 0, \mathbf{On} \mapsto 1, \mathbf{OnP} \mapsto 2\}$ that maps each locations of the automaton to the corresponding number of tokens. The function $f_2 = \{\mathbf{Off} \mapsto 0, \mathbf{FOn} \mapsto 1, \mathbf{FOff} \mapsto 2\}$ encodes the locations of $\mathcal{A}_2$ in P_2. Automata edges that do not synchronise with other components are translated into transitions that are connected to only one place (visible at the top and bottom of Fig. 3). For example, the edge from* **On** *to* **OnP** *in $\mathcal{A}_1$ corresponds to the TPN transition on the bottom-left corner. Given the weights on the connected arcs, this transition can be fired when P_1 contains exactly 1 token and, after firing, puts 2 tokens back in place P_1. Each possible synchronisation between automata edges is translated into a single TPN transition, which is connected to all places encoding for the automata involved in the synchronisation. An example is the transition in the centre of the figure between P_1 and P_2. Edges with a time guard are translated into timed transitions in $\hat{O}$ (depicted in grey and labelled with the delay). Edges without time guards are translated into immediate transitions (depicted in black).*

3. HIL OPTIMISATION LEVEL

3.1 Code generation for HIL simulation

In this step, we generate executable C code from the TPN translation of the TIOA network. Importantly, the generated code facilitates cross-platform deployment, since it uses the same simulation and event scheduling algorithm for the plant and the controller, which are run on two separate hardware platforms. In this way, the HIL simulation algorithm can execute the plant code and the controller code as if they were two TIOAs in a network, except that the actions are sent and received using hardware communication protocols (serial, Ethernet, Bluetooth, etc). The only platform-dependent aspects are related to the functions used for handling simulation time and data communication, which may vary depending on the target architecture.

We implemented the code generation procedures as an extension of the Cosmos tool [4], which already provides features for encoding TPN models into C code.

The executable code consists of two main parts, responsible for encoding the structure of the TPN and for simulating the execution of the TPN, respectively. The main challenge is scheduling the execution of the next transition/event in a very short amount of time, which is crucial to ensure real-time HIL simulations. Importantly, by analysing the structure of the TPN, we can pre-compute both the maximum number n of transitions enabled for scheduling and, for each transition **t**, the set of transitions that might become enabled or disabled after firing **t**. This significantly increases the speed of simulation because it restricts the number of transitions to test, thus enabling fast HIL simulations.

The algorithm for simulating a TPN relies on a heap data structure to store the scheduled events. This structure guarantees the removal and insertion in $O(\log(n))$. Each event is of the form $e = (\mathsf{id}, \mathsf{time}, \mathsf{transition})$, where id is the identifier of e, time is the firing time and transition the corresponding TPN transition. The memory consumption of the heap is constant and equals $n \cdot (2s_{id} + s_{float})$ bits, where s_{id} is the number of bits required to store the identifier of an event, and s_{float} is the number of bits required to store the floating point representation of the firing time. The code for simulation and scheduling is presented in Algorithm 1. The main functions used by the algorithm are as follows:

initialEventHeap() - computes the event heap in the initial state of the simulator.

realTime() - returns the current simulation time.

sleep(t) - enters the idle mode and waits for t milliseconds. If an event is received, the wait period is interrupted.

IsDataAvailable() - returns true if there is new data on the hardware communication link. The data transferred between plant and controller correspond to the identifiers of the fired transitions.

readData() - receives and reads data, and updates the state of the TPN accordingly.

fire(**t**) - fires transition **t**, updating both the marking of the net and the value of the variables related to **t**.

update(EQ) - updates the event queue according to the new state. A naive implementation of this function is to examine each transition **t** and check if it is enabled; if so, add **t** to the event queue together with the minimal time for which **t** can fire. Our implementation is more involved, but much faster, because it exploits the precomputed information about the enabled transitions, as discussed above.

Algorithm 1: HIL Simulation Algorithm

```
Function Simulate()
    EQ := initialEventHeap()
    ctime := realTime()
    while EQ ≠ ∅ do
        e := min(EQ)
        if e.time > ctime then
            sleep(e.time - ctime)
            ctime := RealTime()
            if IsDataAvailable() then
                readData()
                update(EQ)
        else
            ctime := e.time
            fire(e.transition)
            update(EQ)
```

The algorithm iterates over the elements of the heap and picks the transitions with the minimal absolute firing time. If this is greater than the current simulation time (ctime), the algorithm stays in the idle mode for time e.time − ctime. If there is an event available, which is tested through function IsDataAvailable(), the algorithm wakes up. We remark that, at soon as an event is received, the algorithm exits the sleep mode and processes the event, which implies a deterministic waiting time. When the sleep function is called by the plant, we just pause its execution. When it is called by the controller, the hardware platform that embeds the controller code enters the power saving mode. In this way, the algorithm optimises the power consumption of the device by changing its power states only when transitions are enabled.

3.2 Power model builder

The controller unit is attached to a power monitor device that measures the consumption of the unit in order to build the probabilistic power model for the controller. This process takes in the readings from the power monitor, corresponding to measurements of the electric current consumed by the controller at each instant of time. Note that we can equate power and current consumption in our setting, because the voltage applied by the power monitor to the hardware is constant, and thus power consumption is proportional to current consumption.

As output, the process produces a TIOA network with the same structure as the controller network, but annotated with rewards that characterise the consumption of each transition. Given that the actual power consumption depends on many physical parameters that we cannot control or model, we choose to construct a probabilistic model through multiple executions of the HIL simulator. In this way, each controller transition is mapped to a probability distribution (see Definition 3) which is built from the power measurements recorded for that transition. When, instead, the controller is idle, we assign a constant current in the model, taken as the average of the readings obtained in the idle mode.

3.3 Optimisation of battery lifetime

We aim to find the controller parameters that maximise the expected battery lifetime, that is, the time T at which the available charge is depleted in the battery model: $y_1(T) = 0$ (see Eq. (1)).

As explained in Section 1.1, the objective function is evaluated by simulating the plant and the controller on the computer until the battery runs out. With a sufficiently large number of simulations, this provides a good estimate of the expected battery lifetime under the current parameters. Clearly, this step cannot be performed through HIL simulation (real-time) due to the excessive time needed to deplete the battery. To incorporate real measurements in the simulation, we integrate the battery model with the power consumption model as follows. For each transition performed by the controller during a simulation, we sample an electrical current value r from the corresponding probability distribution in the power consumption model. Then, r is used to update the current function $i(t)$ applied to the battery model (see Eq. (1)). Therefore, $i(t)$ is a piecewise constant function. Finally, the battery lifetime T is computed by deriving the analytical solution for $y_1(t)$ at each sub-domain of $i(t)$.

The objective function T is maximized with respect to the set $\mathcal{S}$ of safe parameters (computed as per Section 2.2) by running the optimisation algorithm described below.

Optimisation algorithm. We use a black-box optimisation method known as *Gaussian process optimisation (GPO)*. The main advantage of GPO is that, together with a sub-optimal solution to the optimisation problem, it provides a statistical model of the (unknown) response function f, corresponding in our case to the battery lifetime T. As new samples are evaluated, these are used to improve *online* the accuracy of the statistical model, which, in turn, is queried to draw new samples. The algorithm is based on [23] and consists of the following steps:

i) select n initial samples (by e.g. Latin hypercube) from $\mathcal{S}$ and compute their objective values; ii) estimate a statistical model from the current samples;

iii) use the model to predict the point $x^* \in \mathcal{S}$ that maximises the expected improvement and obtain the objective value $f(x^*)$;

iv) add $(x^*, f(x^*))$ to the set of samples and go to step ii).

The algorithm terminates after performing steps ii-iv) for a given number of iterations. The statistical model is built following the *Gaussian process regression (GPR)* method [30], which can be seen as a stochastic generalisation of classical regression. Given n samples $x_1, \ldots, x_n$ and their respective objective function values $f(x_1), \ldots, f(x_n)$, the method assumes that they are drawn from a model of the form:

$$f(x_i) = \vec{g}(x_i)^T \cdot \vec{\beta} + \epsilon(x_i) \quad i = 1, 2, \ldots, n \tag{2}$$

$\vec{g}(x_i)^T \cdot \vec{\beta}$ is called the *regression part*, where $\vec{g}(x_i)$ is the vector of basis functions and $\vec{\beta}$ is the vector of unknown coefficients estimated through classical regression techniques. ϵ is normally distributed with zero mean and correlation dependent on a weighted Euclidean distance of the n samples. Such weights are the parameters of the statistical model, and are estimated by maximising the likelihood function. For a point x^*, GPR is able to predict both an approximate value for $f(x^*)$, assuming it is randomly distributed according to Eq. (2), and an estimate of the prediction standard error.

4. THE SETUP AND CASE STUDIES

The hardware setup for the case studies consists of three main components: a desktop computer, Arduino board containing AVR microcontroller, and Monsoon^{TM} power monitor. The controller model runs on the AVR board and communicates with the computer through a USB to serial converter. The USB link between the computer and the USB to serial converter has been altered to ensure that no energy flows through it. We use two transistors and two resistors controlled by the microcontroller to simulate the energy consumed by the controller unit. For instance, in the pacemaker case study (see Section 4.2), these act as the leads of the pacemaker. The power monitor supplies the circuit with a voltage while monitoring power consumption.

For the software setup, we use Stateflow to specify TIOA models, the Z3 theorem prover [13] to compute the safe region, the MATLAB-based SUMO toolbox [17] to perform GPO, and the Cosmos tool [4] to generate code and perform simulations. Specifically, we implemented conversion procedures from Stateflow diagrams to TPNs and extended Cosmos in order to generate code for the AVR microcontroller. Finally, we have consolidated and integrated each software component into a single script that realises the full HIL loop. Stateflow diagrams and corresponding Petri net translations are available at http://www.veriware.org/heart_pm_methods.php#HIL.

4.1 Temperature Controller

In our experimental evaluation, we aim to find values for parameters T_{on} and T_{p} that maximise the battery lifetime. Figure 6 summarises the results of the safe region computation and optimisation. We set the temperature threshold θ to 24°C and define a safety property ensuring that the room temperature is always within 23.6°C and 24.4°C.

In the computation of the safe region (depicted in Fig. 6a), we consider $T_{\text{on}} \in [1, 200]$ ms, $T_{\text{p}} \in [1, 200]$ ms and a path length of 50. However, we find safe parameters only in the region $T_{\text{on}} \in [1, 110]$ ms and $T_{\text{p}} \in [1, 20]$ ms, which we use as the parameter space in the optimisation loop. We also observe that, with $T_{\text{p}} > 11$ ms, the property cannot be guaranteed in a robust way, that is, several unsafe parameter values exist. This suggests that a relatively high polling

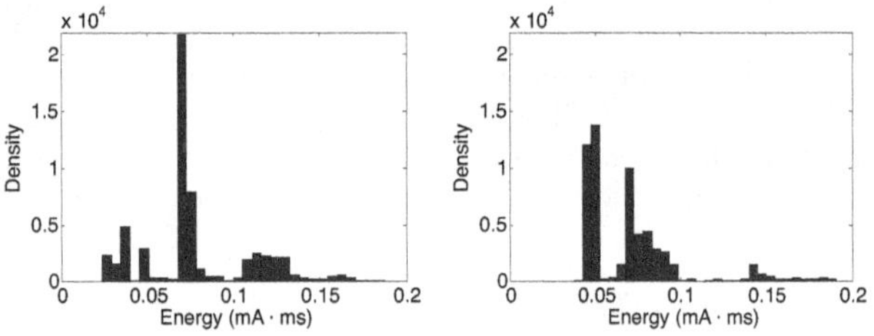

(a) **Off → On** (b) **On → OnP**

Figure 4: Power model for the temperature controller. Plots show the distributions over the energy consumed by controller actions for: switching the boiler on (a) and polling the sensor (b).

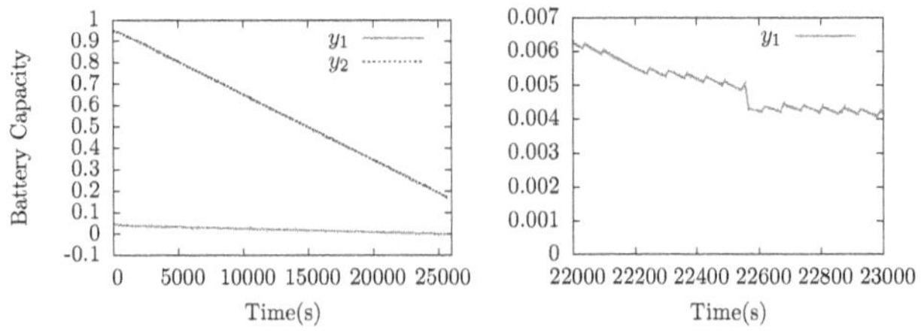

(a) (b)

Figure 5: (a) Evolution of battery capacity during one simulation. y_1 (red) is the available charge. y_2 (blue) is the bound charge. (b) Zoom of the available capacity.

frequency is necessary to keep the temperature within tight bounds.

Figure 4 shows the synthesised power model for the temperature controller. The model associates controller's actions with the discrete probability distributions over the energy measurements. In particular, we report the electric charge (measured in mA·ms) that, under fixed voltage, is proportional to the electric energy. As regards the action of switching the boiler on (Fig. 4a), the most likely energy value is around 0.07 mA·ms, whereas for the action of polling the sensor (Fig. 4b) it is around 0.05 mA·ms. In general, we observe that the shapes of the two histograms cannot by adequately approximated with an analytical distribution (e.g. Gaussian), which supports our choice of using discrete distributions for the power model.

Figure 5 illustrates the evolution of the battery capacity along a simulation trace, up to the point where the available charge is depleted. In Figure 5b, we zoom into a shorter time window, to show the detailed evolution of the available capacity. The effects of the periodic polling of the sensor are clearly visible, as well as the activation of the heater in the middle of the graph.

In this case study, we employ 5000 simulations for each evaluation of the expected battery lifetime, that is, the function we seek to optimise. The optimisation algorithm returns a statistical model of the objective function (Figures 6b and 6c) together with the maximising parameters, in this case being: $T_p = 16$ ms and $T_{on} = 104$ ms. However, we notice that all the simulated parameters (black dots in Fig. 6b) yield similar objective function values. This results in "almost uniform" sampling strategy by the GPO algorithm, with a slightly higher number of sampled parameters around the optimal one. Thus, the standard deviation (SD) of the estimation is "almost constant" (see Fig. 6c). Due to the regression algorithm, SD values tend to decrease in proximity of sampled parameters. Indeed, we detect higher SD values only for high T_p, where many parameters are unsafe and thus excluded from the search. The analysis of the standard deviation is crucial because we generally aim to derive parameters that not just yield (sub-)optimal mean values, but also with low uncertainty.

4.2 Heart and Pacemaker

To demonstrate the versatility of our framework, we consider a system composed of a cardiac pacemaker (the controller) and the heart (the plant). The heart model is used to reproduce the propagation of the cardiac action potential from the atrium to the ventricle. The pacemaker has the role of maintaining the synchronisation between the two chambers, by delivering impulses that establish correct heart rhythm. We consider the TIOA model for the heart recently presented in [6]. The pacemaker model is a TIOA adaptation of the model in [22]. The heart-pacemaker TIOA network comprises 14 components, 38 locations and 75 edges, leading to more than 1 billion reachable states. The TPN translation resulted in 21 places, 95 transitions and 427 arcs, which is less than an order of magnitude larger than the automaton and, thus provides evidence of a very efficient representation.

We consider the following two parameters: TAVI, which mimics the conduction time from the atrium to the ventricle, and TURI, which sets an upper bound on the heart rate. In particular, TURI is the amount of time that the pacemaker waits before pacing the ventricle, after an impulse from the atrium has occurred and TAVI elapsed. The nominal values as suggested by pacemaker manufacturers are TAVI $= 150$ ms and TURI $= 500$. The safe region (Fig. 7a) is constructed by considering TAVI $\in [1, 2000]$ ms, TURI $\in [1, 2000]$, a path length of 25 and a safety property requiring that the time between two consecutive beats in the ventricle is always within the range $[500, 1000]$ ms, which implies a heart rate between 60 and 120 BPM. The algorithm is able to find safe parameters only in the interval TAVI $\in [1, 620]$ ms and TURI $\in [1, 1000]$ ms, used as the search space in the optimisation algorithm.

In the first experiment, we aim to minimise the total electric current during 1 minute of HIL simulation. In this alternative configuration of our framework, we bypass the construction of the power model and feed the measurements directly into the optimisation algorithm, which, in turn, sends the parameters to evaluate to the HIL simulator. Results indicate that the optimal parameters overestimate the nominal ones and are obtained at TAVI $= 208$ ms and TURI $= 778$ ms, but we can achieve similar consumption values for most of the simulated points (see Fig. 7b). In the region approximately given by TAVI $\in [300, 600]$ ms and TURI $\in [600, 800]$ ms, we observe much higher consumption values. However, these are just estimations by the GP regression algorithm, since no parameters are actually simulated in this region. High standard deviation values are registered in this region (see Fig. 7c) and, more prominently, in the unsafe half-plane of the parameter space. As explained in Section 4.1, unsafe parameters are excluded from the optimisation, resulting in high uncertainty in their statistical estimation.

Second, we maximise the expected battery lifetime, thus running the default HIL optimisation loop. Results are reported in Fig. 7d and 7e. In this case, the optimal param-

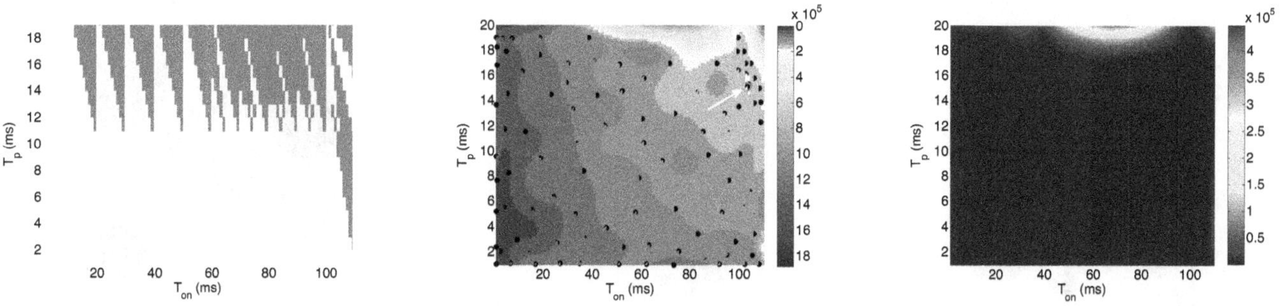

(a) Safe region (b) Mean (c) SD

Figure 6: Battery lifetime optimisation results for the temperature controller. Parameters are T_{on} (x-axis) and T_p (y-axis). (a) depicts the safe (white) and the unsafe (red) parameters. (b) The heat map shows the mean values of the estimated Gaussian process (red: short battery life, blue: long battery life). In this case, the colour scale is not linear. Black dots indicate the simulated samples, the red dot the optimal sample (indicated also by a white arrow). (c) Standard deviation (blue: low, red: high). Max expected battery lifetime: 177193 ms at $T_p = 16$ ms and $T_{on} = 104$ ms (white arrow in plot b).

eters underestimate the nominal ones and are: TAVI = 64 ms and TURI = 205 ms. The other simulated parameters give comparable objective function values (all above 89% of the optimal lifetime), except for the parameters TAVI = 207 ms and TURI = 382 ms, which yield a lifetime 44% lower than the optimal. This can be ascribed to the probabilistic nature of the power model. By regression, we register a red area (low lifetime) around this point (plot 7d), and a high standard deviation in its surroundings (plot 7e).

We highlight the strengths of our approach, which is not limited to the evaluation of the single optimal parameter valuation, but also allows for a detailed analysis of the whole parameter space, in terms of correctness (through parameter synthesis) and energy efficiency (through the statistical estimation by GPO). These aspects are crucial for the design of safety-critical systems like cardiac pacemakers.

5. CONCLUSION

We presented a framework for optimising energy consumption of embedded software and estimating consumption models from measurement data, which supports hybrid systems specified as parametric timed automata with data, and encoded in MATLAB Stateflow. We implemented this framework through a fully automated workflow, employing a wide range of methods, including SMT-based parameter synthesis, embedded code generation from Petri nets, real energy measurements and Gaussian process optimisation. Our approach is the first to integrate HIL optimisation with rigorous design methods, parameter synthesis and online power model construction, thus providing, in addition to the optimised parameters, a wealth of information on the design space of the system. The evaluation on the temperature controller and cardiac pacemaker case studies demonstrates the versatility and effectiveness of the approach, which ultimately enables the synthesis of embedded controllers that are both *correct-by-design* and *energy-efficient-by-design* for a wide variety of embedded systems. As future work, we aim at extending our framework to support probabilistic plant models and the synthesis of controller code and components.

Acknowledgements. This work is supported by the ERC AdG VERIWARE, ERC PoC VERIPACE and the Institute for the Future of Computing, Oxford Martin School.

6. REFERENCES

[1] Bang-bang control using temporal logic. http://tinyurl.com/ngp4epu.

[2] T. Amnell, E. Fersman, P. Pettersson, H. Sun, and W. Yi. Code synthesis for timed automata. *Nord. J. Comput.*, 9(4):269–300, 2002.

[3] M. Bacic. On hardware-in-the-loop simulation. In *CDC-ECC*, pages 3194–3198. IEEE, 2005.

[4] P. Ballarini, B. Barbot, M. Duflot, S. Haddad, and N. Pekergin. HASL: A new approach for performance evaluation and model checking from concepts to experimentation. *Performance Evaluation*, 2015.

[5] V. Bandur, W. Kahl, and A. Wassyng. Microcontroller assembly synthesis from timed automaton task specifications. In *Formal Methods for Industrial Critical Systems*, pages 63–77. Springer, 2012.

[6] B. Barbot et al. Estimation and verification of hybrid heart models for personalised medical and wearable devices. In *CMSB*, pages 3–7, 2015.

[7] B. Barbot et al. Building Power Consumption Models from Executable Timed I/O Automata Specifications. Technical Report CS-RR-16-01, Dept of Computer Science, University of Oxford, 2016.

[8] C. Barker et al. Hardware-in-the-loop simulation and energy optimization of cardiac pacemakers. In *EMBC*, pages 7188–7191. IEEE, 2015.

[9] L. Benini and G. d. Micheli. System-level power optimization: techniques and tools. *ACM TODAES*, 5(2):115–192, 2000.

[10] B. Berthomieu and M. Diaz. Modeling and verification of time dependent systems using time Petri nets. *IEEE TSE*, 17(3):259–273, 1991.

[11] E. Dassau et al. In silico evaluation platform for artificial pancreatic β-cell development-a dynamic simulator for closed-loop control with hardware-in-the-loop. *Diabetes technology & therapeutics*, 11(3):187–194, 2009.

[12] E. de Jong et al. European white book on real-time power hardware in the loop testing: Derlab report no. r-005.0. 2012.

[13] L. De Moura and N. Bjørner. Z3: An efficient SMT solver. In *TACAS*, pages 337–340. Springer, 2008.

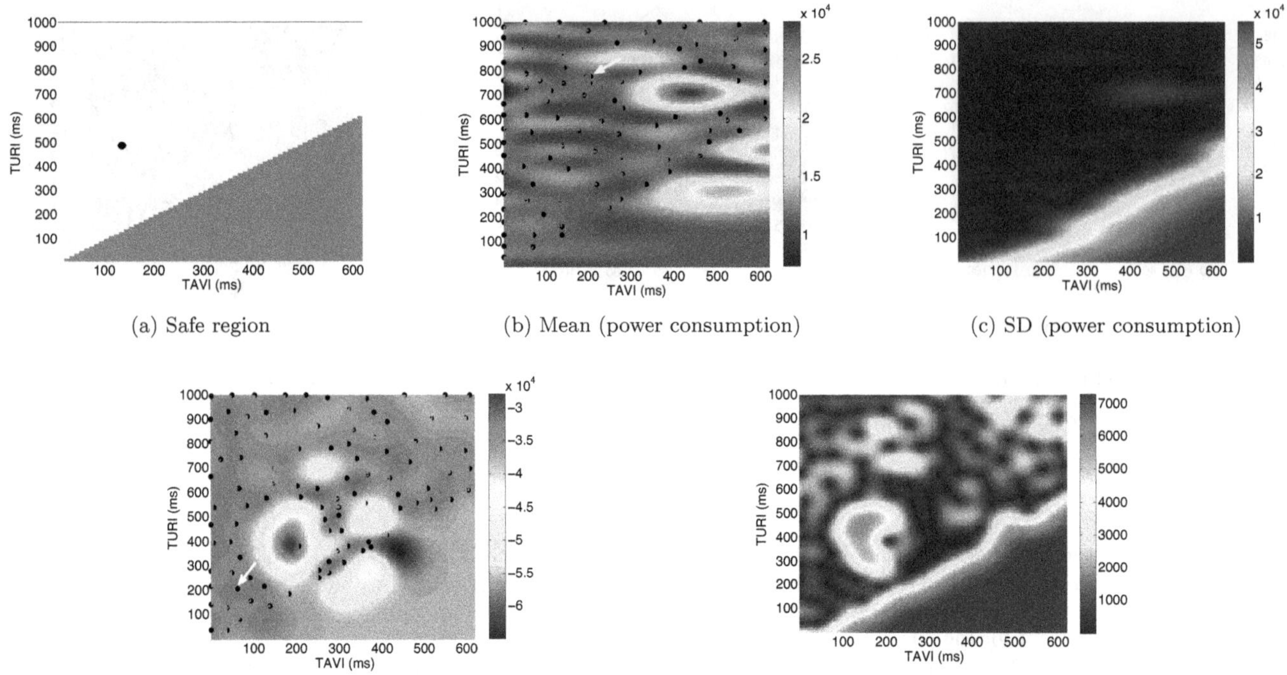

(a) Safe region (b) Mean (power consumption) (c) SD (power consumption)

(d) Mean (battery lifetime) (e) SD (battery lifetime)

Figure 7: Optimisation of the total power consumption (b,c) and battery lifetime (d,e) of the pacemaker. Legend is as in Fig. 6. The black dot in plot (a) indicates the default pacemaker parameters. (b) Mean value of the Gaussian process for min current: 11803 mA at TAVI = 208 ms and TURI = 778 ms (red: high consumption, blue: low consumption). (d) Max expected battery lifetime: 58303 ms at TAVI=64 ms and TURI=205 ms.

[14] L. De Moura and N. Bjørner. Satisfiability modulo theories: An appetizer. In *SBMF*, volume 5902 of *LNCS*, pages 23–36. Springer, 2009.

[15] M. Diaz. *Petri Nets: Fundamental models, verification and applications.* Wiley, 2010.

[16] M. Diciolla, C. H. P. Kim, M. Kwiatkowska, and A. Mereacre. Synthesising Optimal Timing Delays for Timed I/O Automata. In *EMSOFT*. ACM, 2014.

[17] D. Gorissen et al. A surrogate modeling and adaptive sampling toolbox for computer based design. *Journal of Machine Learning Research*, 11:2051–2055, 2010.

[18] B. Hanson, M. Levesley, K. Watterson, and P. Walker. Hardware-in-the-loop-simulation of the cardiovascular system, with assist device testing application. *Medical engineering & physics*, 29(3):367–374, 2007.

[19] T. Hemker et al. Hardware-in-the-loop optimization of the walking speed of a humanoid robot. In *Proc. of CLAWAR*, 2006.

[20] R. Isermann et al. Hardware-in-the-loop simulation for the design and testing of engine-control systems. *Control Engineering Practice*, 7(5):643–653, 1999.

[21] Z. Jiang et al. Cyber–physical modeling of implantable cardiac medical devices. *Proc. of the IEEE*, 100(1):122–137, 2012.

[22] Z. Jiang et al. Modeling and verification of a dual chamber implantable pacemaker. In *TACAS*, pages 188–203. Springer, 2012.

[23] D. R. Jones, M. Schonlau, and W. J. Welch. Efficient global optimization of expensive black-box functions. *Journal of Global optimization*, 13(4):455–492, 1998.

[24] D. Jung and P. Tsiotras. Modeling and hardware-in-the-loop simulation for a small unmanned aerial vehicle. *AIAA Infotech at Aerospace, AIAA*, pages 07–2763, 2007.

[25] D. Kaynar et al. The theory of timed I/O automata. *Synthesis Lectures on Distributed Computing Theory*, 1(1):1–137, 2010.

[26] M. Kwiatkowska, A. Mereacre, N. Paoletti, and A. Patanè. Synthesising robust and optimal parameters for cardiac pacemakers using symbolic and evolutionary computation techniques. In *HSB*, 2015.

[27] J. F. Manwell and J. G. McGowan. Lead acid battery storage model for hybrid energy systems. *Solar Energy*, 50(5):399–405, 1993.

[28] M. Mehari et al. Efficient multi-objective optimization of wireless network problems on wireless testbeds. In *CNSM*, pages 212–217. IEEE, 2014.

[29] S. Philippi. Automatic code generation from high-level petri-nets for model driven systems engineering. *Journal of Systems and Software*, 79(10), 2006.

[30] C. E. Rasmussen. *Gaussian processes for machine learning.* MIT press, 2006.

[31] O. S. Unsal and I. Koren. System-level power-aware design techniques in real-time systems. *Proc. of the IEEE*, 91(7):1055–1069, 2003.

Control Synthesis for Large Collections of Systems with Mode-Counting Constraints

Petter Nilsson
Dept. of Electrical Engineering and Computer Science
University of Michigan
Ann Arbor, MI
pettni@umich.edu

Necmiye Ozay
Dept. of Electrical Engineering and Computer Science
University of Michigan
Ann Arbor, MI
necmiye@umich.edu

ABSTRACT

Given a large homogeneous collection of switched systems, we consider a novel class of safety constraints, called mode-counting constraints, that impose restrictions on the number of systems that are in a particular mode. We propose an approach for synthesizing correct-by-construction switching protocols to enforce such constraints over time. Our approach starts by constructing an approximately bisimilar abstraction of the individual system model. Then, we show that the aggregate behavior of the collection can be represented by a linear system, whose system matrices are induced by the transition graph of the abstraction. Finally, the control synthesis problem with mode-counting constraints is reduced to a cycle assignment problem on the transition graph. One salient feature of the proposed approach is its scalability; the computational complexity is independent of the number of systems involved. We illustrate this approach on the problem of coordinating a large collection of thermostatically controlled loads while ensuring a bound on the number of loads that are extracting power from the electricity grid at any given time.

Keywords

Control synthesis; Control of switched systems; Abstraction; Energy applications

1. INTRODUCTION

Formal methods-based correct-by-construction control synthesis has attracted considerable attention in recent years as a principled means to ensure that the closed-loop behavior of a dynamical system satisfies certain high-level specifications [23]. This synthesis paradigm is particularly convenient to incorporate state and input constraints, and to handle continuous as well as hybrid systems in a unified manner. Unfortunately, many correct-by-construction control synthesis methods suffer from the curse of dimensionality. Therefore, it is crucial to take into account the special structure of the problem at hand to improve scalability, as demonstrated in recent work in the context of synthesis [20, 3, 5, 4] and in the context of verification [10].

In this paper, we consider the problem of synthesizing controllers to coordinate a collection of N identical switched systems subject to a novel class of safety constraints, called mode-counting constraints. Mode-counting constraints impose restrictions on the number of systems that are in a particular mode at any given time. Although the individual systems are dynamically decoupled, coordination among them is required to ensure that the mode-counting constraints are not violated. In order to address this problem, we first construct an ϵ-approximately bisimilar finite abstraction for an individual system. Then, we construct a linear system that models the dynamics of the population of systems on the nodes of a graph that the abstraction induces. Finally, by restricting the controllers to have a prefix-suffix form, we reduce the control synthesis problem to an (integer) linear program, constraints of which are determined by the abstraction graph, the population dynamics, and the mode-counting constraints. Tightness and complexity of the approach and its various relaxations are discussed. One salient feature of the approach is that its complexity is almost independent of the number of systems N. Examples are provided where N is in the order of tens of thousands.

The motivation for this problem comes from coordination of thermostatically controlled loads (TCLs) to help improve power grid operations [12, 26, 15, 21]. Thermostatically controlled loads include air conditioners, water heaters, refrigerators, etc., that operate within a desired temperature range. The idea in TCL coordination is to use the flexibility within these temperature ranges to track a power signal by appropriately turning the loads on and off. Aggregate TCL population models based on state-space partitioning are proposed in [12, 26, 21], which are similar to the abstractions that we develop in this paper. Yet, the relation between the actual and aggregate models has not been quantified formally in the earlier works as is done in this paper, except in a stochastic setting in [6]. Moreover, in all of these papers, aggregate models are used for control design with the objective to track a power signal. The more traditional control design techniques that are used do not take into account any hard constraints on overall power consumption. Nevertheless, it is well-known that if all air conditioners are turned on at the same time, for instance during some transient phase, it can result in distribution line overload [18]. Similarly, it might be desirable to have at least a certain

HSCC'16, April 12-14, 2016, Vienna, Austria

DOI: http://dx.doi.org/10.1145/2883817.2883831

amount of loads on at any given time to utilize the TCL collection as a "battery" that stores energy from renewable resources [12]. Motivated by these types of requirements or hard constraints, which can be precisely captured by mode-counting constraints, we propose a novel control synthesis approach for enforcing them.

This paper is structured in the following way. The subsequent Section 2 introduces notation, along with the bisimilarity notion for a general class of transition systems. We proceed with our problem statement in Section 3, followed by a solution approach in Section 4. To motivate the applicability of this approach, two synthesis examples are provided in Section 5. There are several possible extensions of varying difficulty, which we outline in Section 6, before the paper is concluded in Section 7.

2. PRELIMINARIES

In the following paragraphs we introduce some notation that is used throughout the paper. To express a finite set of positive integers, we write $[N] = \{1, \ldots, N\}$. The indicator function of a set A is denoted $\mathbb{1}_A(x)$ and is equal to 1 if $x \in A$ and 0 otherwise. The identity function is written as Id. For two sets A and B, we write $A \oplus B = \{a + b : a \in A, b \in B\}$, and $A \ominus B$ is the largest (w.r.t. inclusion) solution to $X \oplus B = A$.

To denote the floor of a number, $\lfloor \cdot \rfloor$ is used. We use the same notation for vectors, where the floor operation is performed component-wise. We write the infinity norm as $\| \cdot \|$, and the ϵ-ball centered at the point x is denoted as $\mathcal{B}(x, \epsilon) = \{y : \|y - x\| \le \epsilon\}$. The vector of all 1's is written as $\mathbf{1}$.

Given an ODE $\dot{x} = f_m(x)$, the corresponding flow operator is denoted by $\phi_t^m(x)$ and has the properties that $\phi_0^m(x) = x$, $\frac{\mathrm{d}}{\mathrm{d}t}\phi_t^m(x) = f_m(\phi_t^m(x))$. So called $\mathcal{KL}$-functions are related to nonlinear stability theory and are functions $\beta : \mathbb{R}^+ \times \mathbb{R}^+ \to \mathbb{R}^+$ that are strictly increasing from 0 in the first argument and decreasingly converging to 0 in the second argument.

We also employ the following definition for a *transition system*, which captures systems with both continuous and discrete state spaces.

Definition 1. A **transition system** is a tuple $(Q, U, \longrightarrow, Y)$, where Q is a set of states, U a set of actions, $\longrightarrow \subset Q \times U \times Q$ a transition relation, and $Y : Q \longrightarrow \mathbb{R}^n$ an output function.

As an intuitive notation for transitions, we write $q_1 \xrightarrow{u} q_2$ to indicate that $(q_1, u, q_2) \in \longrightarrow$. When we speak about trajectories of a transition system, we mean a sequence $q_1, q_2, \ldots$ of states in Q, with the property that $q_i \xrightarrow{u_i} q_{i+1}$ for some $u_i \in U$.

We adopt the notion of approximate bisimilarity of transition systems from [23].

Definition 2. Two transition systems $(Q_1, U_1, \underset{1}{\longrightarrow}, Y_1)$ and $(Q_2, U_2, \underset{2}{\longrightarrow}, Y_2)$ are **ϵ-approximately bisimilar** if there exists a relation $R \subset Q_1 \times Q_2$ such that for all $(q_1, q_2) \in R$,

- $\|Y_1(q_1) - Y_2(q_2)\| \le \epsilon$,
- if $q_1 \xrightarrow[1]{u_1} p_1$, there exists $q_2 \xrightarrow[2]{u_2} p_2$ s.t $(p_1, p_2) \in R$,
- if $q_2 \xrightarrow[2]{u_2} p_2$, there exists $q_1 \xrightarrow[1]{u_1} p_1$ s.t $(p_1, p_2) \in R$.

3. PROBLEM STATEMENT

We consider a family of identical switched individual systems. The state x_i of system number i obeys the switched differential equation

$$\Sigma : \dot{x}_i(t) = f_{\sigma_i(t)}(x_i(t)), \quad \sigma_i : \mathbb{R} \mapsto [M], \qquad (1)$$

where $\sigma_i(t)$ is the mode for system i at time t. We restrict attention to a compact domain of interest $\mathcal{D}^d \subset \mathbb{R}^d$. The *time-sampled* analogue of (1) on $\mathcal{D}^d$, Σ_τ, is defined as the transition system

$$\Sigma_\tau = (\mathcal{D}^d, [M], \underset{\tau}{\longrightarrow}, \mathrm{Id}_{\mathbb{R}^d}), \qquad (2)$$

where $x_1 \xrightarrow[\tau]{m} x_2$ if and only if $\phi_\tau^m(x_1) = x_2$.

For a time-sampled system, we define the *mode-counting problem with mode safety constraints* as follows.

Problem 1. Given a family of N plants with states $\{x_i\}_{i \in [N]}$ obeying the dynamics of (2), mode-specific unsafe sets $\{\mathcal{U}_m\}_{m \in [M]}$, and mode-counting bounds $\{\underline{K}_m, \overline{K}_m\}_{m \in [M]}$, synthesize an aggregate switching policy $\{\sigma_i\}_{i \in [N]}$, such that for all $m \in [M]$ and all trajectories $x_i(0), x_i(1), \ldots$

$$(x_i(s), \sigma_i(s)) \notin \mathcal{U}_m \times \{m\} \quad \forall\, i \in [N], s \in \mathbb{N}, \qquad (3)$$

$$\underline{K}_m \le \sum_{i=1}^{N} \mathbb{1}_{\{m\}}(\sigma_i(s)) \le \overline{K}_m \quad \forall\, s \in \mathbb{N}. \qquad (4)$$

An instance of this problem is referred to with the tuple $(N, \Sigma_\tau, \{(\mathcal{U}_m, \underline{K}_m, \overline{K}_m)\}_{m \in [M]})$.

An analogous problem could easily be defined for the continuous-time system (1). The difference is that in the time-sampled system, mode switches can only happen at the sampling instants. Furthermore, a solution where mode safety constraints are violated in between samplings (but satisfied at sample instants) is still a valid solution to Problem 1. If such inter-sample safety violations are unacceptable, the unsafe sets can be expanded by some margin determined by the dynamics to ensure safety satisfaction for all $t \in \mathbb{R}$.

In order to leverage the bisimulation theory presented below, we make the following assumption.

Assumption 1. The system $\dot{x} = f_m(x)$ is forward complete and incrementally stable for all $m \in [M]$. That is, there exist $\mathcal{KL}$-functions β_m for $m \in [M]$, such that

$$\|\phi_t^m(x) - \phi_t^m(y)\| \le \beta_m(\|x - y\|, t)\,. \qquad (5)$$

4. SOLUTION APPROACH

We propose an abstraction-based solution to Problem 1. In Section 4.1, we describe how the dynamics can be abstracted so that the time-sampled system (2) is ϵ-approximately bisimilar to the abstraction. We can then define the discrete analogue to Problem 1, and show that existence of a solution on the abstraction is equivalent to existence of a solution for the time-sampled system, up to an error margin ϵ.

We then proceed by presenting a way to solve the discrete mode-counting problem. Our method relies on reasoning about the discrete transition graph, we derive some properties of this graph in Section 4.2. Subsequently, in Section 4.3 we give a linear program from which, if feasible, a solution can be extracted. We analyze some aspects of our approach in Section 4.4.

4.1 Abstractions and aggregation

Let Σ be a system of the form (1). For a parameter $\eta > 0$ we define an abstraction function $\alpha_\eta : \mathcal{D}^d \to \mathcal{D}^d \oplus \mathcal{B}(0, \eta/2)$ as

$$\alpha_\eta(x) = \eta \cdot \left\lfloor \frac{x}{\eta} \right\rfloor + \frac{\eta}{2}\mathbf{1}. \quad (6)$$

This function takes a finite number of values (since $\mathcal{D}^d$ is compact) and is constant on hyper boxes of side η. Using this function, we define a transition system $\Sigma_{\tau,\eta} = (Q_\eta, U, \underset{\tau,\eta}{\longrightarrow}, Y)$, in the following referred to as the *time-state abstraction* of Σ, as follows:

1. $Q_\eta = \alpha_\eta(\mathcal{D}^d)$,
2. $U = [M]$,
3. $q_1 \underset{\tau,\eta}{\overset{m}{\longrightarrow}} q_2$ if and only if $\alpha_\eta(\phi_\tau^m(q_1)) = q_2$,
4. $Y(q) = q$.

In essence, the domain is partitioned into uniform boxes, and every mode is simulated during time τ starting at the center of each box in order to determine transition relations.

Remark 1. The transition system $\Sigma_{\tau,\eta}$ is deterministic. That is, for each state q_1 and action m there exists (at most) one successor state q_2. In the event that the ODE solution starting in q_1 for mode m exits the domain, i.e. $\phi_\tau^m(q_1) \notin \mathcal{D}^d$, the action m is disabled at the discrete state q_1.

Using a result from [17], it follows that an abstraction constructed in this way is bisimilar to the time-sampled system (2) if a certain inequality holds.

THEOREM 1 ([17]). *Suppose Assumption 1 holds and let β_m be $\mathcal{KL}$-functions satisfying* (5) *for $m \in [M]$. If the inequality $\beta_m(\epsilon, \tau) \le \epsilon - \eta/2$ holds for all $m \in [M]$, then Σ_τ and $\Sigma_{\tau,\eta}$ are ϵ-approximately bisimilar.*

It is known that the trajectories of ϵ-approximately bisimilar systems remain within distance ϵ of each other, when "similar" control actions are chosen at each time instant (c.f. Definition 2) [8]. This fact is the key to establishing relations between existence of solutions for Σ_τ and existence of solutions for $\Sigma_{\tau,\epsilon}$ later in the text.

Aggregation dynamics:.

The abstraction constructed above can be viewed as a graph $G = (V, E)$, where the edges are labeled according to the mode. In the following, we take an arbitrary such *mode-transition graph* (not necessarily obtained from an abstraction) and define a linear system that represents the aggregate dynamics on such a graph.

To this end, we assume that there are N systems which simultaneously move around on G. Assume that the number of nodes in the graph is K, i.e., $|V| = K$, and that they are labeled ν_k for $k \in [K]$. Furthermore, assume that there are M different mode-labels numbered from 1 to M, and let $l_E : E \to [M]$ be the function which assigns a mode to each edge.

We then introduce $K \times M$ aggregate states labeled w_k^m for $k \in [K], m \in [M]$, that describe the number of individual systems that are *at node ν_k and in mode m*. By also introducing control actions $r_k^{m_1,m_2}$ that represent the number of systems *at node ν_k that switch from mode m_1 to mode m_2*, the aggregate dynamics $\Sigma_{\tau,\eta}^N$ can be written as

$$(w_k^{m_1})^+ = \sum_{j \in \mathcal{N}_k^{m_1}} \left(w_j^{m_1} + \sum_{m_2 \in [M]\setminus\{m_1\}} (r_j^{m_2,m_1} - r_j^{m_1,m_2}) \right), \quad (7)$$

for $k \in [K]$, $m_1 \in [M]$, where $\mathcal{N}_k^m$ is the set of predecessors of the k'th node under the action m. That is,

$$\mathcal{N}_k^m = \{i \in [K] : (\nu_i, \nu_k) \in E,\ l_E(\nu_i, \nu_k) = m\}.$$

We constrain the control actions $r_k^{m_1,m_2}$ so that for all $m_1 \in [M]$,

$$0 \le \sum_{m_2} r_k^{m_1,m_2} \le w_k^{m_1}, \quad (8)$$

which ensures the continued positivity of the states. That is, $(w_k^m)^+ \ge 0$ for $k \in [K]$, $m \in [M]$. Furthermore, we have the invariant $\sum_k \sum_m w_k^m = N$ over time, where N is the number of individual systems. In the following, we use the compact notation

$$\mathbf{w}^+ = A\mathbf{w} + B\mathbf{r}, \quad (9)$$

where $\mathbf{w}_i = w_k^m$ if $i = K(m-1) + k$, to denote this system. Here A and B are composed of the incidence matrices of the mode-transition graph for each mode. If $A_1, \ldots, A_M$ are the incidence matrices, then A is the block-diagonal matrix with block diagonal given by $[A_1, \ldots, A_M]$, and B is a block matrix composed by the same A_m's. The state space $\mathcal{W}$ and admissible control space $\mathcal{R}$ of this system are

$$\mathcal{W} = \left\{ \mathbf{w} \in \mathbb{N}^{KM} : \sum \mathbf{w} = N \right\},$$

$$\mathcal{R} = \left\{ \mathbf{r} \in \mathbb{N}^{M(M-1)K} : \text{(8) holds for } (\mathbf{w}, \mathbf{r}) \right\}.$$

For a given state $\mathbf{w} \in \mathbb{N}^{MK}$ of (7), we can define a *condensed state* $\lambda \in \mathbb{N}^K$ as $\lambda_k = \sum_m w_k^m$, which counts the number of systems at node ν_k irrespective of mode. We introduce a mapping Λ that takes $\mathbf{w}$ to its condensed counterpart, $\mathbf{w} \overset{\Lambda}{\mapsto} [\sum_m w_1^m, \ldots, \sum_m w_K^m] \in \mathbb{N}^K$.

We are now in a position to define the discrete analogue of Problem 1.

Problem 2. Given a discrete-time linear system Γ of the aggregate form (9) built from a mode-transition graph, an initial condensed state λ_0, unsafe subsets $\{U_m\}_{m \in [M]}$ of $[K]$, and mode-counting bounds $\{\underline{K}_m, \overline{K}_m\}_{m \in [M]}$, synthesize an initial mode assignment $\mathbf{w}(0)$ such that $\Lambda(\mathbf{w}(0)) = \lambda_0$, and a controller $\mathbf{r} : \mathcal{W}^* \to \mathcal{R}$, such that for all $m \in [M]$ and all $s \in \mathbb{N}$,

$$w_k^m(s) = 0 \quad \forall k \in U_m, \quad (10)$$

$$\underline{K}_m \le \sum_{i \in [N]} w_i^m(s) \le \overline{K}_m. \quad (11)$$

We will refer to an instance of this problem as $(N, \Gamma, \{(U_m, \underline{K}_m, \overline{K}_m)\}_{m \in [M]})$.

Since no disturbance is included in this formulation, it is enough to consider open-loop controllers. In the following, we will denote such controllers with $\mathbf{r}(s)$ for $s = 0, 1, \ldots$. Now, using the approximate bisimilarity between Σ_τ and $\Sigma_{\tau,\eta}$ we can state the following results.

THEOREM 2. *Let Σ_τ, $\Sigma_{\tau,\eta}$ be the time-sampled and time-state abstracted dynamics of a system Σ of the form (1), such that Σ_τ and $\Sigma_{\tau,\eta}$ are ϵ-approximately bisimilar. Let α_η be the abstraction function for $\Sigma_{\tau,\eta}$. Furthermore, let $\Sigma_{\tau,\eta}^N$ be the aggregate sampled dynamics of the form (9) obtained from the mode-transition graph of $\Sigma_{\tau,\eta}$.*

Then, if there exists a solution to the instance $\left(N, \Sigma_{\tau,\eta}^N, \{(\alpha_\eta(\mathcal{U}_m \oplus \mathcal{B}(0,\epsilon)), \underline{K}_m, \overline{K}_m)\}_{m\in[M]}\right)$ of Problem 2, there exists a solution to the instance $(N, \Sigma_\tau, \{(\mathcal{U}_m, \underline{K}_m, \overline{K}_m)\}_{m\in[M]})$ of Problem 1.

PROOF. Assume that a controller $\mathbf{r}(s)$ constitutes a solution to Problem 2, i.e. produces a closed-loop trajectory $\mathbf{w}(s)$ of $\Sigma_{\tau,\eta}^N$ that satisfies (10) - (11). Then we can extract N individual trajectories $\xi_i(0), \xi_i(1), \dots,$ of $\Sigma_{\tau,\eta}$. By implementing switching protocols $\{\sigma_i\}_{i\in[N]}$ on the continuous level that agree with the modes of the individual trajectories, it immediately follows that (4) is satisfied also for the resulting trajectories $x_i(0), x_i(1), \dots,$ of Σ_τ with the same bounds $\{\underline{K}_m, \overline{K}_m\}_{m\in[M]}$. Furthermore, since $\Sigma_{\tau,\eta}$ and Σ_τ are ϵ-approximately bisimilar, it holds that for all $s \in \mathbb{N}$, $\|\xi_i(s) - x_i(s)\| \le \epsilon$, therefore $\xi_i(s) \notin \alpha_\eta(\mathcal{U}_m \oplus \mathcal{B}(0,\epsilon))$ implies that $x_i(s) \notin \mathcal{U}_m$ so (3) also holds. □

Theorem 2 ensures that if a discrete-state solution exists for unsafe sets with an added ϵ-margin, then it can be implemented on the continuous-state level while preserving correctness. Conversely, we can show that within an $(\epsilon + \eta/2)$-margin, existence of a discrete-state solution is also a necessary condition.

THEOREM 3. *Under the same assumptions as in Theorem 2, if there is no solution to the instance $\left(N, \Sigma_{\tau,\eta}^N, \{(\alpha_\eta(\mathcal{U}_m \ominus \mathcal{B}(0,\epsilon+\eta/2)), \underline{K}_m, \overline{K}_m)\}_{m\in[M]}\right)$ of Problem 2, there is no solution to the instance $(N, \Sigma_\tau, \{(\mathcal{U}_m, \underline{K}_m, \overline{K}_m)\}_{m\in[M]})$ of Problem 1.*

PROOF. Assume that a solution exists to the instance $(N, \Sigma_\tau, \{(\mathcal{U}_m, \underline{K}_m, \overline{K}_m)\}_{m\in[M]})$ of Problem 1, but that no solution exists to the instance $\left(N, \Sigma_{\tau,\eta}^N, \{(\alpha_\eta(\mathcal{U}_m \ominus \mathcal{B}(0,\epsilon+\eta/2)), \underline{K}_m, \overline{K}_m)\}_{m\in[M]}\right)$ of Problem 2.

Like in the previous result, the continuous-state switching protocol can be implemented on the discrete-state system, and the resulting trajectories will deviate at most ϵ due to approximate bisimilarity. Thus a continuous-state solution with unsafe sets $\mathcal{U}_m$ can be implemented on the discrete-state system and will be correct for unsafe sets $\mathcal{U}_m \ominus \mathcal{B}(0,\epsilon) \supset \alpha_\eta\left(\mathcal{U}_m \ominus \mathcal{B}(0,\epsilon+\eta/2)\right)$, which is a contradiction. □

4.2 Mode-transition graph properties

We now state some results that connect the properties of the underlying mode-transition graph to the aggregate dynamics. Let a system Γ of the form (9) obtained from a mode-transition graph $G = (V, E)$ with M different modes be given, such that every node $\nu \in V$ has at most[1] M outgoing edges. We proceed by stating some results about this graph. Assume that the nodes are labeled with integers 1 through K, i.e., $V = \{\nu_k : k \in [K]\}$.

We recall some standard definitions from graph theory. A *path* in G is a list of edges $(\nu_1, \nu_2), (\nu_2, \nu_3), \dots, (\nu_{J-1}, \nu_J)$. If the first and last nodes are equal, i.e. $\nu_J = \nu_1$, the path is a *cycle*. A cycle is *simple* if it visits every node at most one time. For a subset of nodes $D \subset V$ (or the corresponding subgraph, which we use interchangeably), it is said to be *strongly connected* if for each pair $v_1, v_2 \in D$, there exists a path from v_1 to v_2. Any directed graph can be decomposed into strongly connected components. The *period* of a subgraph D is the greatest common divisor of all cycles in D. A subgraph D is called *aperiodic* if it has period one.

To ensure infinite horizon correctness we will focus on solution trajectories that consist of a finite prefix phase, and a periodic suffix phase defined on cycles. The purpose of the prefix phase is to steer the system to a "nice" state from which there is a periodic solution. Before explaining such solutions, we first define a concept of controllability on a subset of nodes D for the aggregate dynamics Γ. Similarly as for controllability of linear systems on a subspace, controllability of Γ on D means that the system can be steered between any two aggregate states with support on D.

Definition 3. A subset of nodes $D \subset V$ is **completely controllable** for Γ if for any two condensed states λ^1, λ^2 with support[2] on D such that $\sum \lambda^1 = \sum \lambda^2$, there exists a finite horizon T, controls $\{\mathbf{r}(s)\}_{s=0}^{T-1}$, and states $\{\mathbf{w}(s)\}_{s=0}^{T}$ such that $\Lambda(\mathbf{w}(0)) = \lambda^1, \Lambda(\mathbf{w}(T)) = \lambda^2$, and $\mathbf{w}(s+1) = A\mathbf{w}(s) + B\mathbf{r}(s)$ for $s = 0, \dots, T-1$.

As the following result shows, the aggregate system Γ of the form (9) has a lot of "control freedom" on strongly connected, aperiodic components.

THEOREM 4. *If a strongly connected component D is aperiodic, it is completely controllable for Γ.*

PROOF. It is known that the incidence matrix A_D of an aperiodic, strongly connected graph D is primitive [22], i.e., there exists an integer T such that all entries of A_D^T are positive. This means that for each vertex pair (ν_j, ν_l), there exists a path of length T that connects them. Thus, by sending p_{jl} systems along paths $\nu_j \to \nu_l$ such that $\sum_l p_{jl} = \lambda_j^1$ and $\sum_j p_{jl} = \lambda_l^2$, the condensed state at time T will be equal to λ^2. We can define a control $\mathbf{r}(s)$ that realizes these paths by switching the correct number of systems at each node over time. □

In the case of periodicity, it is not possible to reach every condensed state. In fact, the periodicity will preserve the parity structure of the initial state. However, within this restriction, the system is still controllable in the following sense. If a strongly connected component D has period P, its nodes can be labeled with a function $L_P : D \to \{0, 1, \dots, P-1\}$ such that a node ν_1 with $L_P(\nu_1) = p$ only has edges to nodes ν_2 with $L_P(\nu_2) = i + 1 \ (mod\ P)$. Let $D_0, \dots, D_{P-1}$ be the subsets of nodes induced by the equivalence relation $\nu_1 \sim \nu_2$ iff $L_P(\nu_1) = L_P(\nu_2)$.

COROLLARY 1. *The subsets of nodes D_i as constructed above are completely controllable for Γ.*

PROOF. We can connect the nodes in D_i with edges that correspond to paths of length P in D. By construction, the resulting graphs are aperiodic, so the previous result applies. □

[1]Some modes can be disabled at certain nodes.

[2]That a condensed state λ has support on D means that $\lambda_k = 0$ for $\nu_k \notin D$.

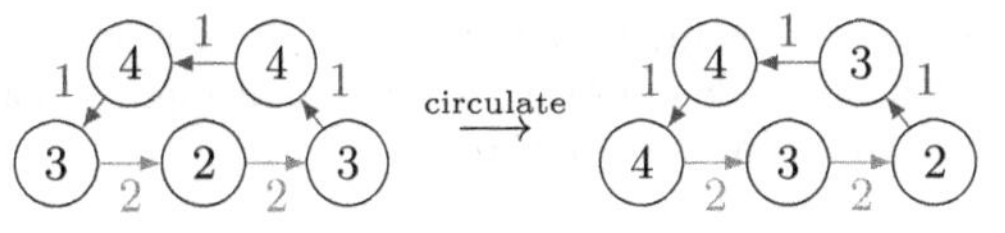

Figure 1: Illustration of the assignment $\alpha = [3, 2, 3, 4, 4]$ on a cycle C of length 5, with two modes 1 (blue) and 2 (red). On the left, the mode-1-count is 3+4+4 = 11, while the mode-2-count is 3+2=5. After circulating the assignment one step, as displayed to the right, the mode-1-count is 2+3+4 = 9 and the mode-2-count is 4+3 = 7. Over all possible circulations, the minimal mode-1-count is 8, and the maximal mode-1-count is 11, so $\overline{\Psi}^1(C, \alpha) = 11$ and $\underline{\Psi}^1(C, \alpha) = 8$. Similarly, $\overline{\Psi}^2(C, \alpha) = 8$ and $\underline{\Psi}^2(C, \alpha) = 5$.

In order to treat the periodic suffix part of a solution, we introduce the following notation pertaining to a cycle $C = (\nu_1, \nu_2), \ldots, (\nu_{J-1}, \nu_1)$ of length given by $|C| = J - 1$.

Definition 4. The **outgoing mode** $\Xi_C(\nu_j)$ is the mode of the outgoing edge at ν_j, that is,

$$\Xi_C(\nu_j) = \begin{cases} l_E(\nu_j, \nu_1) & \text{if } j = |C|, \\ l_E(\nu_j, \nu_{(j+1)}) & \text{otherwise}. \end{cases}$$

Definition 5. An **assignment** to a cycle C is a function $\alpha : [|C|] \to \mathbb{R}^+$.

Definition 6. An **integer assignment** to a cycle C is an assignment α to C such that $\alpha(j)$ is an integer for $j \in [|C|]$.

Definition 7. The **maximal mode-m-count** for a cycle C with assignment α is

$$\overline{\Psi}^m(C, \alpha) = \max_{k \in [|C|]} \sum_{i:\, \Xi_C(v_i) = m} \alpha\left((k + i) \mod |C|\right).$$

For a given assignment, the maximal mode-m-count denotes the maximal number of systems that are simultaneously in mode m when the assignment α circulates around C.

Definition 8. The **minimal mode-m-count** for a cycle C with assignment α is

$$\underline{\Psi}^m(C, \alpha) = \min_{k \in [|C|]} \sum_{i:\, \Xi_C(v_i) = m} \alpha\left((k + i) \mod |C|\right).$$

These functions are illustrated in Figure 1 for an example cycle-assignment pair. Finally, we define a function $\Phi_C : \mathbb{R}^{|C|} \to \mathbb{R}^{|V|}$ that for a cycle C maps the values of a cycle assignment α to the corresponding nodes in the graph.

$$\Phi_C(\alpha)_k = \begin{cases} \alpha(j) & \text{if } \nu_j \text{ in } C \text{ corresponds to } \nu_k \text{ in } V, \\ 0 & \text{otherwise}. \end{cases}$$

4.3 Prefix-suffix strategies as a linear program

We are now ready to define the type of strategies that we consider in this paper.

Definition 9. A control strategy for a condensed initial state λ_0 is of **prefix-suffix** type if it consists of an initial mode assignment $\mathbf{w}(0)$ s.t. $\Lambda(\mathbf{w}(0)) = \lambda_0$, a finite number of inputs $\mathbf{r}(0), \ldots, \mathbf{r}(T-1)$, and a set of cycles $\{C_j\}_{j \in J}$ with assignments $\{\alpha_j\}_{j \in J}$ such that the cycles are populated with their respective cycle assignments at time T.

For given initial positions $\lambda_0 \in \mathbb{N}^K$, mode-counting bounds $\{\underline{K}_m, \overline{K}_m\}_{m \in [M]}$, a given set of cycles $\{C_j\}_{j \in J}$, and a horizon T, the following linear feasibility program searches for a prefix-suffix control strategy that solves Problem 2.

$$\begin{aligned}
\text{find} \quad & \alpha_1, \ldots, \alpha_J \text{ cycle assignments}, \\
& \mathbf{r}(0), \ldots, \mathbf{r}(T-1), \\
& \mathbf{w}(0), \ldots, \mathbf{w}(T), \\
\text{s.t.} \quad & \underline{K}_m \leq \sum_{k \in [K]} w_k^m(s) \leq \overline{K}_m, \quad s = 0, \ldots, T, && \text{(12a)} \\
& \underline{K}_m \leq \sum_j \underline{\Psi}^m(C_j, \alpha_j), && \text{(12b)} \\
& \sum_j \overline{\Psi}^m(C_j, \alpha_j) \leq \overline{K}^m, && \text{(12c)} \\
& \Lambda(\mathbf{w}(T)) = \sum_j \Phi_{C_j}(\alpha_j), && \text{(12d)} \\
& \mathbf{w}(s+1) = A\mathbf{w}(s) + B\mathbf{r}(s), \quad s = 0, \ldots, T-1, && \text{(12e)} \\
& \Lambda(\mathbf{w}(0)) = \lambda_0, && \text{(12f)} \\
& \sum_{m_2} r_j^{m_1, m_2} = w_j^{m_1} \text{ for all } j \in \bigcup_{i \in U_{m_1}} \mathcal{N}_i^{m_1}, && \text{(12g)} \\
& r_j^{m_2, m_1} = 0 \text{ for all } m_2 \in [M], j \in U_{m_1}, && \text{(12h)} \\
& \text{control constraints (8)}. && \text{(12i)}
\end{aligned}$$

We briefly describe the purpose of each constraint. Firstly, (12a) assures that mode-counting constraints are satisfied in the prefix phase, i.e., up to time T. Similarly, (12b)-(12c) restrict mode-counting in the suffix phase by ensuring that the sums of maximal and minimal mode-counts over all cycles are within the bounds. Eq. (12d) connects the prefix phase to the suffix phase by ensuring that the condensed state at time T agrees with the sum of all cycle assignments, while (12e) propagates the dynamics up to time T, and (12f) implies that the initial state $\mathbf{w}(0)$ must condense to the given initial condition λ_0. The mode-safety constraints are taken care of through (12g)-(12h).

The maximal and minimal mode-counts for a given assignment α to a cycle C can be represented by the maximal and minimal entries of the product $Y_C^m \alpha$, where Y_C^m is the circulant $(0, 1)$-matrix s.t.

$$[Y_C^m]_{ij} = \begin{cases} 1, & \text{if } \Xi_C(\nu_{j-(i-1) \mod |C|}) = m, \\ 0, & \text{otherwise}. \end{cases}$$

To illustrate, the cycle C in Figure 1 has matrices

$$Y_C^1 = \begin{bmatrix} 0&0&1&1&1 \\ 1&0&0&1&1 \\ 1&1&0&0&1 \\ 1&1&1&0&0 \\ 0&1&1&1&0 \end{bmatrix}, \quad Y_C^2 = \begin{bmatrix} 1&1&0&0&0 \\ 0&1&1&0&0 \\ 0&0&1&1&0 \\ 0&0&0&1&1 \\ 1&0&0&0&1 \end{bmatrix}.$$

Thus, the constraints $\underline{\Psi}^m(C, \alpha) \geq \underline{K}_m$, $\overline{\Psi}^m(C, \alpha) \leq \overline{K}_m$, can be enforced by the linear vector inequalities

$$\underline{K}_m \mathbf{1} \leq Y_C^m \alpha \leq \overline{K}_m \mathbf{1}.$$

The feasibility program (12) can be solved either as a normal linear program (LP) feasibility problem or as an integer linear program (ILP) feasibility problem. Since the size of it can be large in practice (for instance due to a fine-grained abstraction, see paragraph on complexity below), the ILP version may be impractical. Furthermore, the number of individual systems N may affect the difficulty of the ILP, since a larger N increases the number of possible integer points. In the next section we discuss how feasible solutions to the ILP are related to feasible solutions of the LP. By construction, the following result holds.

PROPOSITION 1. *If a feasible integer solution of* (12) *exists, a solution to Problem 2 can be extracted.*

The formulation of (12) can be altered to capture different requirements. For instance, if the counts of certain modes are not important for the application, they can be omitted. An objective function can also be added to search for the tightest possible bounds, but in practice ILP solvers are typically more efficient in finding feasible points than in proving optimality.

How to select the cycle set.

The number of cycles in a graph is infinite, so in order to provide a finite number of cycles as input to (12), a selection must be made. As shown in Section 4.4 below, it is enough to consider the set of simple cycles in the LP case, whereas non-simple cycles may enable tighter bounds in the ILP case. However, even the number of simple cycles can be exponential in the size of the graph. For this reason, some randomized cycle selection is a reasonable choice in practice.

How to select the horizon T.

If mode-counting constraints during the prefix phase are disregarded, Theorem 4 implies the existence of a time T in which any assignment can be achieved. This time is upper bounded by a quadratic polynomial for general graphs, although more specialized bounds exist [13]. However, mode-counting constraints may exacerbate the upper bounds, so there is a trade-off between a short prefix horizon T and tight mode-counting constraints during the prefix phase.

Complexity of linear program.

The number of variables and constraints in the linear program above are

$$\mathcal{O}\left(M^2KT + \sum_{j\in J}|C_j|\right), \quad \mathcal{O}\left(MKT + \sum_{j\in J}|C_j|^2\right),$$

respectively. Taking the abstraction step into account, $K = \mathcal{O}\left((1/\eta)^d\right)$, where η is the state discretization parameter and d the state-space dimension for an individual system. Notably, the complexity does not depend on the number of systems N, which makes our approach attractive for large collections of relatively simple homogeneous systems.

4.4 Analysis

We now give sufficient conditions for the existence of a feasible solution to (12).

THEOREM 5. *If there exists an (integer) solution to Problem 2, then there exists a finite horizon T such that the LP version of* (12) *is feasible when solved for the cycle set consisting of all simple cycles.*

The proof of this result is divided into two parts. First, we show in Lemma 1 that it is sufficient to consider solutions consisting of a transient and a periodic (i.e., cyclic) part. Secondly, we show in Lemma 2 that an assignment for a non-simple cycle can be decomposed into (non-integer) assignments for simple cycles, while preserving the same bounds. Together, these results constitute a proof to Theorem 5.

We also give a result that bounds the maximal deviation in suffix phase mode-counting when a non-integer solution is rounded to an integer solution.

LEMMA 1. *Suppose that a correct strategy $\mathbf{r}^*$ induces a behavior such that there are times T_1 and $T_2 > T_1$ for which $\Lambda(\mathbf{w}(T_1)) = \Lambda(\mathbf{w}(T_2))$. Then there is a prefix-suffix strategy that achieves the same performance.*

In particular, if $\mathbf{r}^*$ is an integer strategy the lemma applies, since it will necessarily result in a behavior that satisfies the assumptions in this lemma due to the finiteness of the number of possible condensed states.

PROOF. We show that the graph flows induced by $\mathbf{r}^*$ on the time interval $[T_1, T_2]$ can be achieved with cycle assignments. To this end, we define a static flow on a graph in a higher dimension, decompose it into cyclic flows, and project the cyclic flow onto the original graph.

Let $G = (V, E)$ be the system graph, and define a new graph $H = (V_H, E_H)$. The node set $V_H = \underbrace{V \times V \times \ldots \times V}_{T_2 - T_1 \text{ times}}$ contains $T_2 - T_1$ copies of each vertex in V, and copies of $\nu \in V$ are labeled ν_t for $t \in [T_1, T_2]$. The set of edges is defined as

$$E_H = \{(\nu_t, \tilde{\nu}_{t+1}) : t \in \{T_1, \ldots, T_2 - 1\},\ (\nu, \tilde{\nu}) \in E\} \bigcup \{(\nu_{T_2}, \nu_{T_1}) : \nu \in V\}.$$

A static flow is induced on H by $\mathbf{r}^*$, obtained by letting the flow along $(\nu_t, \tilde{\nu}_{t+1})$ be the number that traverses the edge $(\nu, \tilde{\nu}) \in E$ at time t, and letting the flow along (ν_{T_2}, ν_{T_1}) be equal to the number of systems at ν at time T_1. By construction, this flow is balanced at each node (i.e. inflows equal outflows).

By the flow decomposition theorem [1, Theorem 3.5], we can then find cycles in H that achieve the static edge flow. By projecting these cycles onto a single copy of V, we obtain cycles and assignments that when circulated mimic the performance of $\mathbf{r}^*$ on the interval $[T_1, T_2]$.

We can therefore define a prefix-suffix strategy by taking as the prefix part inputs $\mathbf{r}^*(s)$ up to time $s = T_1 - 1$, together with a suffix part consisting of the cycles and assignments found above. □

The preceding result implies the following convergence statement, which provides a converse result to Proposition 1.

COROLLARY 2. *Suppose Problem 2 has an (integer) solution. Then, there exists an integer $L < \infty$ and a finite horizon T such that the ILP version of* (12) *formulated with the set of all cycles of length smaller than or equal to L, has a feasible solution.*

Next, we show that it is sufficient to consider simple cycles, but this comes at the cost of possible non-integer assignments. In the integer case, it is in fact *not* sufficient to consider simple cycles only, as the example in Figure 2 shows.

LEMMA 2. *Suppose $C = C_1 \cup C_2$ is a cycle that visits a node ν_1 twice, so that it can be decomposed into two cycles $C_1 = (\nu_1, \nu_2), \ldots, (\nu_{J_1}, \nu_1)$ and $C_2 = (\nu_1, \nu_{i+1}) \ldots, (\nu_{J_2}, \nu_1)$.*
Let α be an assignment to C. If α satisfies

$$\underline{K}_m \leq \underline{\Psi}^m(C, \alpha), \quad \overline{\Psi}^m(C, \alpha) \leq \overline{K}^m, \tag{13}$$

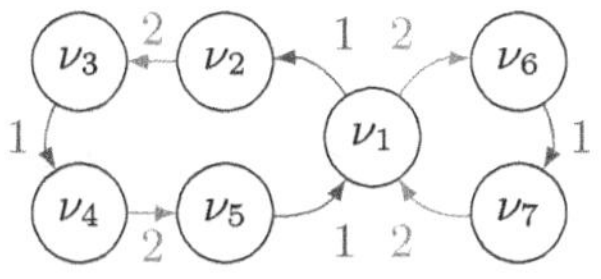

Figure 2: Illustration showing how simple cycles may fail to realize mode-counting bounds that are possible with non-simple cycles. Considering $(\nu_1, \nu_2, \nu_3, \nu_4, \nu_5, \nu_1, \nu_6, \nu_7)$ as a single (non-simple) cycle, it can be assigned $[1,1,1,1,0,0,0,0]$ to achieve a constant mode-count of 4 for both mode 1 (blue) and mode 2 (red). However, there is no way to create separate integer assignments for the simple cycles $(\nu_1, \nu_2, \nu_3, \nu_4, \nu_5)$ and (ν_1, ν_6, ν_7), which achieve the same constant mode-counting over time.

then there exist assignments α_1, α_2 (not necessarily integral) for C_1, C_2 such that

$$\sum_{i\in[|C_1|]} \alpha_1(i) + \sum_{i\in[|C_2|]} \alpha_2(i) = \sum_{i\in[|C|]} \alpha(i), \tag{14}$$

$$\underline{K}_m \leq \underline{\Psi}^m(C_1, \alpha_1) + \underline{\Psi}^m(C_2, \alpha_2), \tag{15}$$

$$\overline{\Psi}^m(C_1, \alpha_1) + \overline{\Psi}^m(C_2, \alpha_2) \leq \overline{K}_m. \tag{16}$$

PROOF. Note that (13) implies that for $k \in [|C|]$,

$$\underline{K}_m \leq \sum_{i:\, \Xi_C(\nu_i)=m} \alpha((k+i) \mod |C|) \leq \overline{K}_m.$$

Summing these inequalities over $k = 1, \ldots, |C|$ yields, since each $\alpha(i)$ will appear exactly $|C|_m := |\{\nu_i \in C : \Xi_C(\nu_i) = m\}|$ times,

$$|C|\underline{K}_m \leq |C|_m \sum_{i\in[|C|]} \alpha(i) \leq |C|\overline{K}_m. \tag{17}$$

Now consider the constant "averaging" assignments

$$\alpha_1(i) = \alpha_2(j) = \frac{\sum_{i\in[|C|]} \alpha(i)}{|C|}.$$

We obviously have

$$\sum_{i\in[|C_1|]} \alpha_1(i) + \sum_{i\in[|C_2|]} \alpha_2(i) = \underbrace{\frac{|C_1| + |C_2|}{|C|}}_{=1} \sum_{i\in[|C|]} \alpha(i),$$

so (14) is satisfied. Furthermore, for any k_1, k_2,

$$\begin{aligned} &\sum_{i:\, \Xi_{C_1}(\nu_i)=m} \alpha_1((i+k_1) \mod |C_1|) \\ &\quad + \sum_{j:\, \Xi_{C_2}(\nu_j)=m} \alpha_2((j+k_2) \mod |C_2|) \\ &= \underbrace{(|C_1|_m + |C_2|_m)}_{=|C|_m} \frac{\sum_{i\in[|C|]} \alpha(i)}{|C|}. \end{aligned}$$

From (17) we can conclude that this expression is in the interval $[\underline{K}_m, \overline{K}_m]$. It follows that

$$\begin{aligned} \underline{K}_m &\leq \underline{\Psi}^m(C_1, \alpha_1) + \underline{\Psi}^m(C_2, \alpha_2) \\ &= \overline{\Psi}^m(C_1, \alpha_1) + \overline{\Psi}^m(C_2, \alpha_2) \leq \overline{K}_m, \end{aligned}$$

so (15)-(16) hold. □

The next result shows how the mode-counting bounds are affected when the suffix part of a non-integer strategy is rounded to integer cycle assignments. A proof can be found in the Appendix.

PROPOSITION 2. *For any integer N_C and a cycle C, there exists an integer assignment α_{int}, with $\sum_i \alpha_{int}(i) = N_C$, such that for the average assignment $\alpha_{avg}(i) := N_C/|C|$,*

$$\begin{aligned} \underline{\Psi}^m(C, \alpha_{int}) &\geq \underline{\Psi}^m(C, \alpha_{avg}) \\ &\quad - \min\left(\frac{|C|_m}{|C|} z, \left(1 - \frac{|C|_m}{|C|}\right)(|C| - z)\right), \\ \overline{\Psi}^m(C, \alpha_{int}) &\leq \underline{\Psi}^m(C, \alpha_{avg}) \\ &\quad + \min\left(\frac{|C|_m}{|C|}(|C| - z), \left(1 - \frac{|C|_m}{|C|}\right) z\right), \end{aligned}$$

where $z = N_C \mod |C|$ and $|C|_m := |\{\nu_i \in C : \Xi_C(\nu_i) = m\}|$.

Remark 2. Looser, but less cumbersome, bounds can be obtained by noting that

$$\begin{aligned} &\min\left(\frac{|C|_m}{|C|} z, \left(1 - \frac{|C|_m}{|C|}\right)(|C| - z)\right) \\ &= |C| \min\left(\frac{|C|_m}{|C|} \frac{z}{|C|}, \left(1 - \frac{|C|_m}{|C|}\right)\left(1 - \frac{z}{|C|}\right)\right) \\ &\leq \frac{|C|}{4}, \end{aligned}$$

since $\max_{a,b\in[0,1]} \min(ab, (1-a)(1-b)) = 1/4$. The same bound holds for the second inequality due to symmetry.

We conjecture that the bounds in Proposition 2 can be tightened substantially by a clever integer assignment algorithm, as opposed to the worst-case analysis used to obtain the bounds above. This question, together with the issue of rounding also the prefix part of a non-integer strategy, will be subject to future research.

5. EXAMPLES

We provide two examples, one numerical example where the individual systems have two states, and one that applies the method to a scheduling problem of thermostatically controlled loads. In both examples, we use the Gurobi solver [9] to obtain LP and ILP solutions of (12)[3].

5.1 Numerical example

As a first example, consider the aggregate dynamics where the state of each individual system is governed by the switched two-dimensional nonlinear ODE $\dot{x}_i(t) = f_{\sigma_i(t)}(x_i(t))$, where for $j = 1, 2$,

$$f_j : \begin{bmatrix} x_1 \\ x_2 \end{bmatrix} \mapsto \begin{bmatrix} -(x_1 - \bar{x}_1^j) + x_2 \\ -(x_1 - \bar{x}_1^j) - x_2 - x_2^3 \end{bmatrix}, \quad \begin{aligned} \bar{x}_1^1 &= 1, \\ \bar{x}_1^2 &= -1. \end{aligned} \tag{18}$$

We want to solve Problem 1 with $N = 10000$ systems with a desired mode-1-count of exactly 6750 systems, without having systems enter an unsafe set $\mathcal{U}_1 = \mathcal{U}_2 = [-0.3, 0.3] \times [-0.2, 0.2] \subset \mathbb{R}^2$.

Using abstraction parameters $\tau = 0.5, \eta = 0.05$ on the domain $\{(x, y) : -2 \leq x \leq 2, -1 \leq y \leq 1\}$, we obtain

[3]Our software is available at github.com/pettni/mode-count.

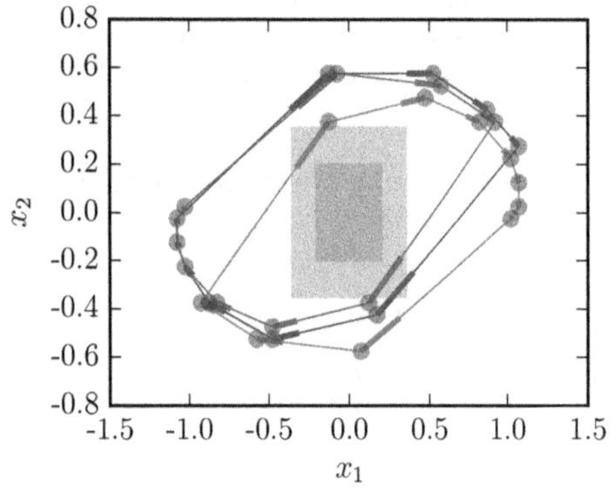

Figure 3: Illustration of the suffix part of the solution of (12) for (18). The cycles found by the synthesis procedure are highlighted in different colors. The unsafe set is shown in red, with an added margin to compensate for bisimulation approximation errors.

an abstraction with 3483 states that is 0.15-approximately bisimilar to its time-sampled counterpart. Consequently, we need to add a margin of 0.15 to the unsafe set to ensure safety[4]. With a horizon of 10τ (i.e., $T = 10$) and using 100 randomly generated cycles, an ILP solution can be found in about 16 seconds on a 3.4 GHz iMac. The suffix part of the solution consists of three cycle assignments, and the mode-1-count is guaranteed to be exactly 6750 over time. Figure 3 shows a visualization of the cycles found by the solver.

The cycles have the following mode-profiles:

$$C_1 : 1, 1, 1, 1, 1, 1, 2, 2, 2, 1,$$
$$C_2 : 2, 1, 1, 1, 2, 2, 2, 2, 2, 2,$$
$$C_3 : 2, 2, 2, 1, 1, 1, 1, 2, 2, 2,$$

and the corresponding cycle assignments found by the solver are

$$\alpha_1 = [917, 917, 917, 917, 917, 917, 917, 917, 917, 917],$$
$$\alpha_2 = [1, 1, 1, 1, 1, 1, 1, 1, 1, 1],$$
$$\alpha_3 = [0, 164, 0, 164, 0, 164, 0, 164, 0, 164].$$

It follows that the mode-1-count is constant for all three cycles, and is equal to 6419, 3, and 328, respectively.

5.2 Application example

Next, we apply the proposed algorithm to a TCL coordination problem, where the objective is to control the aggregate load of a family of domestic air condition units. The dynamics of a single unit are

$$\dot{\theta}_i = -a(\theta_i - \theta_a) - bP_i^m,$$

where $P_i^m = 0$ when unit i is `off` and $P_i^m = 5.6$ when unit i is `on`. The parameters[5] are taken from [15].

We assume that all units are set to the desired temperature $\theta_0 = 22.5°\text{C}$, and that deviations up to 1°C are tolerated (larger deviations constitute unsafe states). The objective is to control the aggregate load, i.e. the number of TCL's that are on, while simultaneously guaranteeing that the state θ_i of every TCL will remain in the interval $[21.5, 23.5]$.

[4]Safety is guaranteed only at sample instants.
[5]$\theta_a = 32°\text{C}$, $a = 0.25$, $b = 1.25$

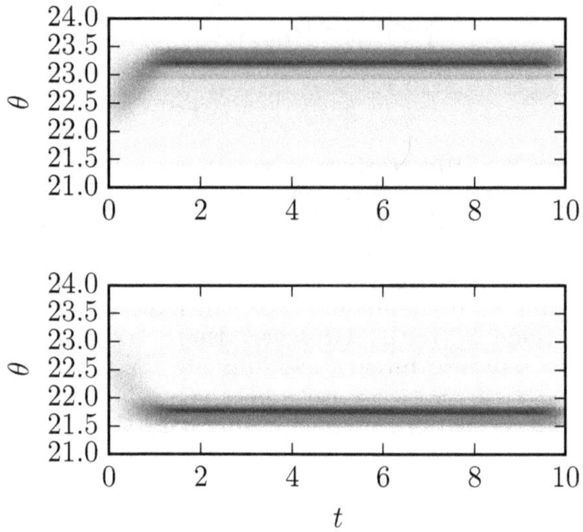

Figure 4: Densities (kernel-smoothened for visualization) of TCL populations over time for the desired mode-on-count 3600 (upper) and 3200 (lower). Red color indicates that a larger number of TCL's are in that interval. In the initial phases, control is being applied to place the TCL's on cycles. After this is achieved at $t = 1$, the TCL's circulate in their respective cycles which results in a more regular behavior. As can be seen, when the desired mode-on-count is higher, the temperatures group in the lower part of the allowed temperature range. The reason is that when the temperature difference is large, the room is warmed up at a higher rate, thus the air condition units can be turned on during a larger percentage of the time, on average.

For this example, we created an abstraction with parameters $\tau = 0.05$, $\eta = 0.0195$, which is approximately bisimilar to the original system with accuracy $\epsilon = 0.1$. We then solve (12) for a population of 10000 TCL's with randomized initial states, using a set of 100 randomized cycles and horizon $T = 20$. Since the number of variables in the linear program is quite large, we utilize a two-step approach to obtain an integer solution. First, (12) is solved as a non-integer linear program, which results in non-integer assignments. Secondly, these assignments are rounded to integer assignments and controls needed to reach these integer assignments are found by solving (12) as an ILP with fixed assignments. This reduces the number of variables and constraints which makes the ILP more tractable, however, the rounding of cycle assignments may lead to bound violations, as alluded to in Proposition 2.

We synthesized control strategies for two sets of desired mode-on-count bounds, one around 3600 (high) and another one around 3200 (low), using the same randomized initial

Table 1: Guaranteed mode-on-counting bounds for the TCL application.

Desired mode-count	low	high
Prefix phase bounds	$[2500, 2564]$	$[3696, 4300]$
Suffix phase bounds	$[3180, 3217]$	$[3595, 3604]$

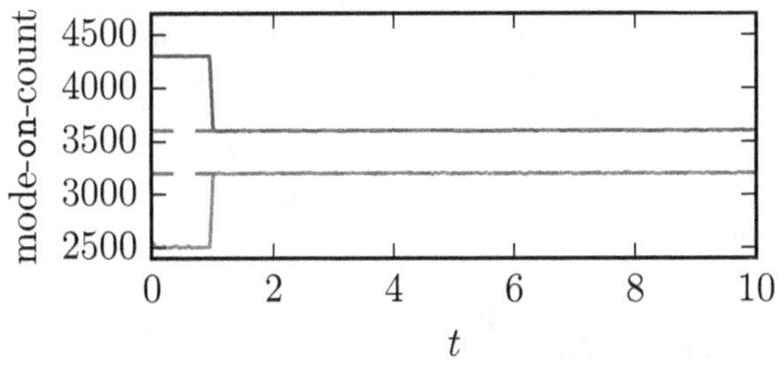

Figure 5: mode-on-count over time for desired mode-on-count 3600 (red) and 3200 (blue). As can be seen, the mode-on-counts are close to the desired values in the suffix phase.

conditions. To allow more flexibility, we relaxed the mode-counting constraints during the prefix phase. With this setup, we obtained control strategies satisfying the bounds in Table 1. In Figure 4, the densities of TCL's in the temperature spectrum are shown over time for both desired mode-on-counts. These densities are of continuous-state trajectories, which are guaranteed to stay within 0.1-distance of their discrete counterparts. Figure 5 shows mode-on-counts over time for both solutions.

6. DISCUSSION AND EXTENSIONS

In this section we discuss possible extensions of the proposed framework and potential application areas where mode-counting like constraints can be relevant.

Our approach can be readily applied to a "heterogeneous" collection of systems if there is a limited number of types of systems and the systems are still homogeneous within each type. This is for instance the case with TCLs where one can categorize air conditioners or refrigerators as different types [6]. This will require computing an ϵ-approximate state-time abstraction and an aggregate linear system of the form (9) per type. The resulting feasibility problem will contain these different abstractions and aggregate dynamics as constraints, together with additional mode-counting constraints that couple them. Another straightforward extension is to include state-dependent mode-counting constraints or mode-counting like constraints, where mode is not necessarily the switching signal but a region of the state-space, and mode-counting like constraints restrict the number of systems in these regions of the state-space over time. Such mode-counting like constraints are relevant in application areas like air traffic control or swarm robotics. Another interesting extension is to consider richer constraints on the mode-counts beyond a bound, for instance to synthesize controllers that enforce a linear temporal logic (LTL) property defined on the mode-counts. Such constraints can be incorporated in the proposed framework using mixed integer programming encodings of LTL [11, 24].

There are some limitations of the proposed framework that require less trivial extensions. For instance, there could be small deviations from the model (1) between individual systems that will lead to an uncertain system model. Similarly, all the states might not be available for measurement, or state measurements might be noisy or delayed [15]. Also, the individual system dynamics might not be incrementally stable. Although there are techniques for constructing abstractions that take into account such imperfections [25, 16, 14], the resulting abstract transition system is usually non-deterministic. Therefore, such an extension will require feedback control strategies for which one can potentially use reactive synthesis or a robust ILP formulation [19]. However, the resulting reactive synthesis problem is challenging to solve due to the size of the aggregate (uncertain in this case) linear system (9). A better characterization of the trade-offs between solving the problem (12) as a linear program versus an integer linear program is also important to explore, in order to enable some of these extensions in a computationally tractable way.

Considering the structural properties of the problem, what enables massive aggregation of individual dynamics is the permutation invariance of dynamics due to homogeneity and the permutation invariance of mode-counting constraints. Therefore, it will be interesting to consider other classes of systems with symmetries (see, e.g., [7]) where one can utilize techniques similar to those proposed in this paper to achieve scalability.

Finally, our work is also related to scheduling based methods used in intersection collision avoidance [4] and air traffic control [2]. A crucial difference is that these works consider finite-horizon objectives, whereas we require control strategies that are valid on an infinite horizon. Therefore, we believe the proposed work can be used in these application domains when infinite horizon guarantees are required.

7. CONCLUSIONS

We have considered a new class of constraints, called mode-counting constraints, and proposed an approach to synthesize controllers that can enforce this type of constraints for a homogeneous collection of switched systems. The proposed approach utilizes the particular structure of the problem, the specific form of the control objective and the homogeneity of the systems, in a way that allows handling very large collections of systems. The efficacy of the approach has been demonstrated both with a numerical example and with an application to a TCL coordination problem that involves ten thousand systems.

As discussed in Section 6, there is a wide range of possibilities for future directions; both in terms of potential application areas where mode-counting like constraints are relevant, and in terms of extensions to the type of systems that can be handled or the type of mode-counting constraints that can be enforced. We will explore these directions as part of our future work.

Acknowledgments

The authors would like to thank Johanna Mathieu for enlightening discussions on the TCL coordination problem that motivated this research. The work of PN is supported by NSF grant CNS-1239037 and the work of NO is supported in part by NSF grant CNS-1446298.

8. REFERENCES

[1] R. K. Ahuja, T. L. Magnanti, and J. B. Orlin. *Network flows*. Prentice Hall, 1993.

[2] A. Bayen, C. Tomlin, Y. Ye, and J. Zhang. Milp formulation and polynomial time algorithm for an aircraft scheduling problem. In *Proc. of IEEE CDC*, pages 5003–5010, 2003.

[3] A. Borri, D. V. Dimarogonas, K. H. Johansson, M. D. Di Benedetto, and G. Pola. Decentralized symbolic control of interconnected systems with application to vehicle platooning. In *4th IFAC Workshop on Distributed Estimation and Control in Networked Systems*, pages 285–292, 2013.

[4] A. Colombo and D. Del Vecchio. Least restrictive supervisors for intersection collision avoidance: A scheduling approach. *IEEE Trans. on Automatic Control*, 60(6):1515–1527, June 2015.

[5] S. Coogan and M. Arcak. Efficient finite abstraction of mixed monotone systems. In *Proc. of HSCC*, pages 58–67, 2015.

[6] S. Esmaeil Zadeh Soudjani and A. Abate. Aggregation and control of populations of thermostatically controlled loads by formal abstractions. *IEEE Trans. on Control Systems Technology*, 23(3):975–990, 2015.

[7] E. Frazzoli, M. Dahleh, and E. Feron. Maneuver-based motion planning for nonlinear systems with symmetries. *IEEE Trans. on Robotics*, 21(6):1077–1091, 2005.

[8] A. Girard and G. J. Pappas. Approximation Metrics for Discrete and Continuous Systems. *IEEE Trans. on Automatic Control*, 52(5):782–798, 2007.

[9] Gurobi Optimization, Inc. Gurobi optimizer reference manual, 2015.

[10] T. T. Johnson and S. Mitra. A small model theorem for rectangular hybrid automata networks. In *FMOODS/FORTE*, pages 18–34. Springer, 2012.

[11] S. Karaman, R. G. Sanfelice, and E. Frazzoli. Optimal control of mixed logical dynamical systems with linear temporal logic specifications. In *Proc. of IEEE CDC*, pages 2117–2122, 2008.

[12] S. Koch, J. L. Mathieu, and D. S. Callaway. Modeling and control of aggregated heterogeneous thermostatically controlled loads for ancillary services. In *Proc. of PSCC*, pages 1–7, 2011.

[13] M. Lewin. On exponents of primitive matrices. *Numerische Mathematik*, 18(2):154–161, 1971.

[14] J. Liu and N. Ozay. Abstraction, discretization, and robustness in temporal logic control of dynamical systems. In *Proc. of HSCC*, 2014.

[15] J. L. Mathieu, S. Koch, and D. S. Callaway. State estimation and control of electric loads to manage real-time energy imbalance. *IEEE Trans. on Power Systems*, 28(1):430–440, 2013.

[16] O. Mickelin, N. Ozay, and R. M. Murray. Synthesis of correct-by-construction control protocols for hybrid systems using partial state information. In *Proc. of ACC*, 2014.

[17] G. Pola and P. Tabuada. Symbolic Models for Nonlinear Control Systems: Alternating Approximate Bisimulations. *SIAM J. Control Optim.*, 48(2):719–733, 2009.

[18] P. Pourbeik, P. S. Kundur, and C. W. Taylor. The anatomy of a power grid blackout. *IEEE Power and Energy Magazine*, 4(5):22–29, 2006.

[19] V. Raman, A. Donzé, D. Sadigh, R. M. Murray, and S. A. Seshia. Reactive synthesis from signal temporal logic specifications. In *Proc. of HSCC*, pages 239–248, 2015.

[20] M. Rungger, M. Mazo Jr, and P. Tabuada. Specification-guided controller synthesis for linear systems and safe linear-time temporal logic. In *Proc. of HSCC*, pages 333–342, 2013.

[21] B. M. Sanandaji, H. Hao, and K. Poolla. Fast regulation service provision via aggregation of thermostatically controlled loads. In *Proc. of HICSS*, pages 2388–2397, 2014.

[22] E. Seneta. *Non-negative matrices and Markov chains*. Springer, 2006.

[23] P. Tabuada. *Verification and control of hybrid systems: a symbolic approach*. Springer, 2009.

[24] E. M. Wolff, U. Topcu, and R. M. Murray. Optimization-based trajectory generation with linear temporal logic specifications. In *Proc. of ICRA*, pages 5319–5325, 2014.

[25] M. Zamani, G. Pola, M. Mazo Jr, and P. Tabuada. Symbolic models for nonlinear control systems without stability assumptions. *IEEE Trans. on Automatic Control*, 57:1804–1809, 2012.

[26] W. Zhang, K. Kalsi, J. Fuller, M. Elizondo, and D. Chassin. Aggregate model for heterogeneous thermostatically controlled loads with demand response. In *Proc. of PES General Meeting*, pages 1–8, 2012.

APPENDIX

PROOF OF PROPOSITION 2. Let $N_C = |C| \times r + z$, where $0 \le z < |C|$. Consider the assignment α_{int} such that

$$\alpha_{int} = \begin{cases} r+1, & i = 1, \dots, z, \\ r, & i = z+1, \dots, |C|. \end{cases}$$

Then $\sum_i \alpha_{int}(i) = r|C| + z = N_C$. From a worst-case analysis, it follows that the max- and min-counts satisfy:

$$\begin{aligned} \underline{\Psi}(C, \alpha_{int}) &\ge r \min\left(|C|_m, |C| - z\right) \\ &\quad + (r+1) \max\left(0, |C|_m - (|C| - z)\right) \\ &= r|C|_m + \max\left(0, |C|_m - (|C| - z)\right), \\ \overline{\Psi}(C, \alpha_{int}) &\le (r+1) \min\left(|C|_m, z\right) + r \max(0, |C|_m - z) \\ &= r|C|_m + \min(|C|_m, z). \end{aligned}$$

It follows that,

$$\begin{aligned} &\underline{\Psi}\left(C, \alpha_{avg}\right) - \underline{\Psi}\left(C, \alpha_{int}\right) \\ &\le |C|_m \frac{N_C}{|C|} - \left(r|C|_m + \max\left(0, |C|_m - (|C| - z)\right)\right) \\ &= |C|_m \left(\frac{|C|r + z}{|C|}\right) - \left(r|C|_m + \max\left(0, |C|_m - (|C| - z)\right)\right) \\ &= |C|_m \frac{z}{|C|} - \max\left(0, |C|_m - (|C| - z)\right) \\ &= \min\left(\frac{|C|_m}{|C|} z, \left(1 - \frac{|C|_m}{|C|}\right)(|C| - z)\right). \end{aligned}$$

Similarly,

$$\begin{aligned} \overline{\Psi}(C,\alpha_{int}) - \overline{\Psi}(C, \alpha_{avg}) &\le |C|_m r + \min(|C|_m, z) - |C|_m \frac{N_C}{|C|} \\ &= |C|_m r + \min(|C|_m, z) - |C|_m r - |C|_m \frac{z}{|C|} \\ &= \min\left(\frac{|C|_m}{|C|}(|C| - z), \left(1 - \frac{|C|_m}{|C|}\right) z\right). \end{aligned}$$

□

Compositional Synthesis with Parametric Reactive Controllers

Rajeev Alur
University of Pennsylvania
alur@seas.upenn.edu

Salar Moarref
University of Pennsylvania
moarref@seas.upenn.edu

Ufuk Topcu
University of Texas at Austin
utopcu@utexas.edu

ABSTRACT

Reactive synthesis with the ambitious goal of automatically synthesizing correct-by-construction controllers from high-level specifications, has recently attracted significant attention in system design and control. In practice, complex systems are often not constructed from scratch but from a set of existing building blocks. For example in robot motion planning, a robot usually has a number of predefined motion primitives that can be selected and composed to enforce a high-level objective. In this paper, we propose a novel framework for synthesis from a library of parametric and reactive controllers. Parameters allow us to take advantage of the symmetry in many synthesis problems. Reactivity of the controllers takes into account that the environment may be dynamic and potentially adversarial. We first show how these controllers can be automatically constructed from parametric objectives specified by the user to form a library of parametric and reactive controllers. We then give a synthesis algorithm that selects and instantiates controllers from the library in order to satisfy a given linear temporal logic objective. We implement our algorithms symbolically and illustrate the potential of our method by applying it to an autonomous vehicle case study.

1. INTRODUCTION

Reactive synthesis with the ambitious goal of automatically synthesizing correct-by-construction controllers from high-level specifications, has recently attracted significant attention in system design and control. Recent advances in this growing research area have enabled automatic synthesis of interesting real-world systems [4], indicating the potential of the synthesis algorithms for solving realistic problems.

Although automatic synthesis of realistic systems with large state spaces seems to be unattainable for now, in practice, complex systems are often not constructed from scratch (an implicit assumption in many of the related works,) but from a set of existing building blocks. For example in robot motion planning, a robot usually has a number of predefined motion primitives that can be selected and composed to enforce a high-level objective [7]. Intuitively, a compositional approach that solves smaller and more manageable subproblems, and hierarchically composes the solutions to implement more complicated behaviors seems to be a more plausible way to synthesize complex systems.

To this end, we propose a compositional and hierarchical framework for synthesis from a library of *parametric* and *reactive* controllers. Parameters allow us to take advantage of the symmetry in many synthesis problems, e.g., in motion planning for autonomous robots and vehicles. Reactivity of the controllers takes into account that the environment may be dynamic and potentially adversarial. We first show how these controllers can be synthesized from parametric objectives specified by the user to form a library of parametric and reactive controllers. We then give a synthesis algorithm that selects and instantiates controllers from the library in order to satisfy a given safety and reachability objective.

Consider an autonomous vehicle V_1 that starting from an initial location s_0 needs to navigate safely through streets and intersections to reach a final destination d, as shown in Figure 1. Safe navigation means that the vehicle must follow the traffic rules (e.g., moving in specific directions of streets), and besides avoid collision with other vehicles. In this example, V_1 can cross both intersections I_1 and I_2 on its way toward the location d. One can observe that although intersections I_1 and I_2 are located in different positions, V_1 can safely cross them in a similar way. In other words, V_1 can employ a controller to cross the intersection I_1 and employ the same controller to cross I_2. To take advantage of such *symmetry* in synthesis problems, we introduce *parametric* controllers. Let (x, y) be the location of V_1 at any time step. Assume a, b are two parameters. We would like to synthesize a controller that starting from a parametric location $(x, y) = (a, b)$, guarantees to eventually move two steps forward horizontally, i.e., eventually $(x, y) = (a+2, b)$, while avoiding collision with other vehicles. To this end, the parametric controller must also be reactive, i.e., it must react to other vehicles' movements to avoid collision. Once such parametric reactive controller is obtained, it can be instantiated by assigning values to parameters. For example, the same parametric controller can be instantiated based on the current location of the vehicle and be used to advance the vehicle in different locations. Note that in many application domains, systems may have task-specific controllers that are designed and verified a priori, e.g., an autonomous vehicle can have specialized controllers for different scenarios such as crossing intersections, making U-turns, switching lanes, etc.

HSCC'16, April 12-14, 2016, Vienna, Austria

DOI: http://dx.doi.org/10.1145/2883817.2883842

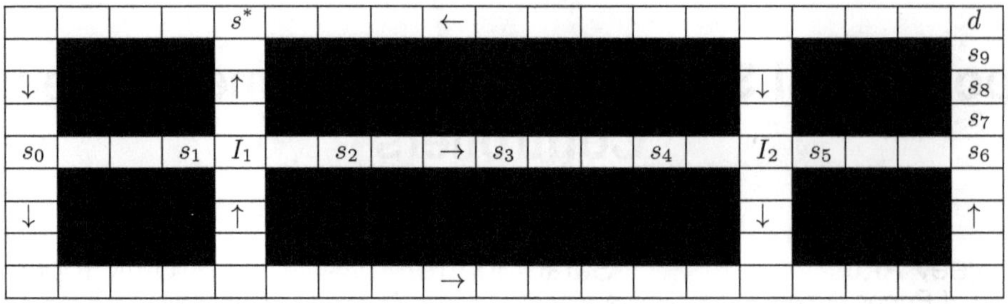

Figure 1: One-way streets connected by intersections.

Such controllers can be defined parametrically and instantiated and composed to perform more complicated tasks.

The proposed framework has two layers, parametric controller synthesis (bottom layer) and synthesis from a library of parametric controllers (top layer). In the bottom layer, a set of parametric controllers are synthesized from parametric objectives specified by the user. Here, unlike other related works [7,12,14], we do not assume that the controllers are a priori given, but we let the user specify them and synthesis is done automatically. This facilitates the design process and makes it more flexible, allowing the user to utilize her insight into the system being designed to construct different libraries. Furthermore, the user may not know the range of the parameter values that guarantees correct behavior of the controller. We allow the user to provide a parametric specification and the set of acceptable parameter values are discovered automatically. On the other hand, the high-level composer does not necessarily need to know *how* controllers enforce their objectives. Thus a *controller interface* that hides the controller's specific implementation while providing information on possible outcomes of the controller is synthesized for each parametric controller. A library of parametric controllers can be reused to realize more complex behaviors. In the top layer of the framework, given a library of parametric controllers and a high-level objective for the system, a *control strategy* that selects and instantiates parametric controllers from the library such that their composition enforces the objective is synthesized.

Note that adding parameters increases the size of the state space and can add to the complexity of the problem. Therefore, how parameters are handled is crucial. We provide *symbolic* algorithms that efficiently explore the parametric space. Besides, we show that the upper bound on the number of symbolic steps, i.e., pre-image or post-image computations, performed by the symbolic algorithm is independent from the parameters. Nevertheless, this does not mean that adding parameters has no cost as it increases the complexity of the symbolic steps. The main advantages of the introduced framework are *i)* *reusability of controllers* (parametric controllers are computed once and can be reused in different compositions to achieve higher level objectives,) *ii)* *separation of concerns* (design of controllers is separated from their composition which can also lead to strategies that are defined hierarchically and are easier to understand).

One of the main motivations for our work is the growing interest in controller synthesis for autonomous robots and vehicles from high-level temporal logic specifications (e.g., [8,9,11,18]). A common theme is based on first computing a discrete controller satisfying the LTL specification over a discrete abstraction of the system, which is then used to synthesize continuous or hybrid controllers guaranteed to fulfill the high-level specification. In this paper, we assume that a finite-state abstraction of the system is given and we present a compositional algorithm for synthesizing a discrete controller. The computed controller can then be refined to a controller enforcing the specification over the original system using the techniques in the literature [16].

The concept of *motion primitives* is popular and widely used in robotics and control literature, since they can be designed by one group, e.g., the robot designer, and then be used by other groups of people such as the end-users to implement higher level objectives. The end-user only needs to have an understanding of what a specific motion primitive does through a provided interface, and the actual implementation is encapsulated and hidden from the end-user. A compositional motion planning framework for multi-robot systems is presented in [14] where given a library of motion primitives, the motion planning problem is reduced to solving a satisfiability modulo theories problem. A similar approach to ours is considered in [7] for solving motion-planning problems for time-invariant dynamical control systems with symmetries, such as mobile robots and autonomous vehicles, where motion plans are described as concatenation of a number of motion-primitives chosen from a finite library. The main difference of our work with [7,14] is that our motion primitives are *reactive*, i.e., the controllers also takes the ongoing interaction between system and environment into account. To the best of our knowledge, we are the first to study the problem of synthesizing controllers from a library of parametric and reactive controllers.

The problem of LTL synthesis from a library of reusable components is considered in [12]. Sequential composition of controllers considered in this paper is similar to control-flow composition in [12] and is inspired by software systems. In the software context, when a function is called, the function gains the control over the machine and the computation proceeds according to the function until it calls another function or returns. Similarly, the controllers in our framework gain and relinquish control over computations of the system. The controllers have a designated set of final states. Intuitively, a reactive controller receives the control by entering an initial state and returns the control when reaching a final state. The goal of the composer is to decide which controller will gain control when the control is returned from the controller currently in charge. Although by enumerating the parameter values and instantiating parametric controllers to obtain a library of non-parametric controllers our problem can be reduced to the one considered in [12], such naive enumeration may lead to an exponentially larger number of controllers in the library, making the method infeasible in practice. Our algorithms *symbolically* explore the parametric space, thus avoiding the excessive explicit enumeration. To the best of our knowledge, there is no implementation of the methods proposed in [12]. Compositional reactive synthesis from LTL specifications is also considered in some recent works [1, 2, 6, 10, 15] where a strategy is synthesized compositionally by treating parts of the given LTL specification separately and combining the solutions. The setting considered in this paper is different as we are interested in synthesizing from a library of controllers that can be reused.

Contributions. The main contributions of this paper are as follows. We give an algorithm for synthesizing a control strategy that reactively chooses and instantiates controllers from a given library of controllers to enforce a high-level safety and reachability objective for the system. We show how a designer can simply specify parametric controllers and then a controller and its interface along with admissible parameter values are synthesized automatically. We implement our algorithms symbolically using binary decision diagrams and apply them to an autonomous vehicle case study to show the potential of our approach.

2. PRELIMINARIES

In this section we present the notation and terminology used in the rest of the paper. Let $\mathbb{Z}$ be the set of integers. For $a, b \in \mathbb{Z}$, let $[a..b] = \{x \in \mathbb{Z} \mid a \leq x \leq b\}$. Let $\mathcal{V} = \{v_1, \cdots, v_n\}$ be a set of variables where each variable $v \in \mathcal{V}$ is defined over a finite domain Σ_v. We define $\Sigma_\mathcal{V} = \Sigma_{v_1} \times \cdots \times \Sigma_{v_n}$ to be the collective domain of the variables. Let $\mathcal{P} = \{p_1, \cdots, p_k\}$ be a set of parameters where each parameter $p \in \mathcal{P}$ is defined over a finite domain Σ_p. Let $\Sigma_\mathcal{P} = \Sigma_{p_1} \times \cdots \times \Sigma_{p_k}$. A valuation s over variables $\mathcal{V}$ is a value assignment to the variables in $\mathcal{V}$, i.e., $s \in \Sigma_\mathcal{V}$. For a subset $\mathcal{X} \subseteq \mathcal{V}$ of variables and a valuation $s \in \Sigma_\mathcal{V}$, we denote by $s_{|\mathcal{X}}$ the projection of s to $\mathcal{X}$.

Without loss of generality and to simplify the specification language, in the rest of the paper, we assume that all variables and parameters are defined over bounded integer domains. Boolean variables are special case where the domain is $\{0, 1\}$. Note that since the domains of variables and parameters are finite, they can be encoded using Boolean variables. Ordered binary decision diagrams (OBDDs) can be used for obtaining concise representations of sets and relations over finite domain [5]. Let $\mathcal{X} \subseteq \mathcal{V} \cup \mathcal{P}$. A predicate ϕ over $\mathcal{X}$ is a Boolean expression generated by the grammar $\phi ::= e \sim 0 \mid \phi \wedge \phi \mid \neg\phi$, where e is generated by the grammar $e ::= k \mid k \times v \mid e + e \mid e - e$, for $k \in \mathbb{Z}$ and $v \in \mathcal{V}$, and $\sim \in \{<, \leq, =, >, \geq\}$. We will use $v \neq k$ as a shorthand for $\neg(v = k)$. Other logical operators are defined in their standard manner. Let $\mathcal{X}_1, \cdots, \mathcal{X}_n$ be disjoint sets of variables defined over finite domains $\Sigma_{\mathcal{X}_i}$ for $i = 1..n$, and let ϕ be a predicate over $\mathcal{X}_1 \cup \cdots \cup \mathcal{X}_n$. A valuation $s = (s_1, \cdots, s_n) \in \Sigma_{\mathcal{X}_1} \times \cdots \times \Sigma_{\mathcal{X}_n}$ satisfies ϕ, denoted by $s \models \phi$, if replacing the variables in ϕ by their corresponding value in s makes ϕ true. For a predicate ϕ, let $\mathcal{VP}(\phi)$ be the set of variables and parameters that appear in the predicate's formula. We say ϕ is a *parametric* predicate, if $\mathcal{VP}(\phi) \cap \mathcal{P} \neq \emptyset$, i.e., there is at least one parameter in the predicate's formula. Otherwise we say ϕ is non-parametric. For a predicate ϕ over $\mathcal{X}$, we let $[\![\phi]\!]$ be the set of valuations over $\mathcal{X}$ that make ϕ true, that is, $[\![\phi]\!] = \{s \in \Sigma_\mathcal{X} \mid s \models \phi\}$. Given a parametric predicate ϕ over $\mathcal{V} \cup \mathcal{P}$ and a valuation $p \in \Sigma_\mathcal{P}$ over parameters, restriction of ϕ by p is a non-parametric predicate $\phi_{\downarrow p}$ obtained by replacing each parameter with its corresponding value. Given a parametric set $\Pi = \Sigma_\mathcal{V} \times \Sigma_\mathcal{P}$ and a parameter value $p \in \Sigma_\mathcal{P}$, projection of Π by p, denoted by $\Pi_{\downarrow p}$, is the set $\{s \in \Sigma_\mathcal{V} \mid (s, p) \in \Pi\}$.

2.1 Linear Temporal Logic (LTL)

We use LTL to specify system objectives. LTL is a formal specification language with two types of operators: logical connectives ($\neg$ (negation), $\vee$ (disjunction), $\wedge$ (conjunction), and $\rightarrow$ (implication)) and temporal operators (e.g., $\bigcirc$ (next), $\mathcal{U}$ (until), $\diamond$ (eventually), and $\Box$ (always)). The set of *atomic formulas AP* consists of any predicate over the variables $\mathcal{V}$. An LTL formula over variables $\mathcal{V}$ is interpreted over infinite words $w \in (\Sigma_\mathcal{V})^\omega$. The language of an LTL formula Φ, denoted by $\mathcal{L}(\Phi)$, is the set of infinite words that satisfy Φ, i.e., $\mathcal{L}(\Phi) = \{w \in (\Sigma_\mathcal{V})^\omega \mid w \models \Phi\}$. We assume some familiarity of the reader with LTL. An LTL specification over the set of variables $\mathcal{V} \cup \mathcal{P}$ is called a *parametric* LTL specification. Parametric LTL formulas are similar to non-parametric ones, except that their formulas are interpreted over infinite words $w \in (\Sigma_\mathcal{V} \times \Sigma_\mathcal{P})^\omega$.

EXAMPLE 1. *Let $x, y \in [0..3]$ be two integer variables. Let $a \in [0..3]$ be an integer parameter. LTL formula $\Phi = \Box(x > y) \wedge \diamond(x = y+1)$ requires that x must always be greater than y and that eventually x is equivalent to $y+1$. The infinite word $w = (x = 2, y = 0), (x = 2, y = 1)^\omega$ satisfies Φ, i.e., $w \models \Phi$. The parametric formula $\Phi_\mathcal{P} = \Box(x > y) \wedge \diamond(x = y+a)$ is an example of parametric LTL specification. Satisfaction of a parametric LTL formula also depends on parameter values. For example, by setting $a = 1$ in $\Phi_\mathcal{P}$, we have $w \models \Phi_{\mathcal{P}_{\downarrow a=1}}$.*

2.2 Symbolic Turn-Based Game Structures

Game structures provide a formalism for modeling possible executions of a system interacting with its environment. Let $\mathcal{V}$ be a set of variables defined over a finite domain $\Sigma_\mathcal{V}$, and $\mathcal{V}'$ be a primed copy of the variables in $\mathcal{V}$, used to represent the next values of variables after a transition. Assume there exists a special variable $t \in \mathcal{V}$ with domain $\Sigma_t = \{1, 2\}$ representing which player's turn it is during a game. Let Λ be a finite set of actions. A symbolic turn-based game structure $\mathcal{G}$ defined over the set of variables $\mathcal{V}$ and the set of actions Λ is a tuple $\mathcal{G} = (\mathcal{V}, \Lambda, \tau)$ where τ is a transition relation given as a predicate over $\mathcal{V} \cup \Lambda \cup \mathcal{V}'$. We denote by $\Sigma^i_\mathcal{V} = \{s \in \Sigma_\mathcal{V} \mid s_{|t} = i\}$ the set of player-i states for $i = 1, 2$. At any state $s \in \Sigma^i_\mathcal{V}$, the player-$i$ chooses an action $\ell \in \Lambda$ such that there exists a successor state $s' \in \Sigma_{\mathcal{V}'}$ where $(s, \ell, s') \models \tau$. Intuitively, at a player-i state, she chooses an available action according to the transition relation τ and the next state of the system is chosen from the possible successor states. For every state $s \in \Sigma_\mathcal{V}$, we define $\Gamma(s) = \{\ell \in \Lambda \mid \exists s' \in \Sigma_{\mathcal{V}'}.\ (s, \ell, s') \models \tau\}$ to be the set of available actions at that state. A *run* $s_0 s_1 s_2 \cdots$ of a game structure is a sequence of states $s_i \in \Sigma_\mathcal{V}$ such that for all $i > 0$ there is an action $\ell \in \Lambda$ with $(s_{i-1}, \ell, s'_i) \models \tau$, where s'_i is obtained by replacing the variables in s_i by their primed copies. A run π is maximal if either it is infinite or it ends in a state $s \in \Sigma_\mathcal{V}$ where $\Gamma(s) = \emptyset$.

Strategies. A strategy of player-i is a partial function $f_i : (\Sigma_\mathcal{V})^*.\Sigma^i_\mathcal{V} \rightarrow \Lambda$ such that for every sequence of states $r.s \in (\Sigma_\mathcal{V})^*$ ending in a player-i's state $s \in \Sigma^i_\mathcal{V}$, if s has a successor, then $f_i(r.s)$ is defined, and $(s, f_i(r.s), u) \models \tau$ for some $u \in \Sigma_{\mathcal{V}'}$. Given two strategies f_1 and f_2 for players 1 and 2, the *possible outcomes* $\Omega_{f_1,f_2}(s)$ from a state $s \in \Sigma_\mathcal{V}$ are runs: a run $s_0s_1s_2\cdots$ belongs to $\Omega_{f_1,f_2}(s)$ iff $s_0 = s$ and for all $j \geq 0$, either s_j has no successor, or $s_j \in \Sigma^i_\mathcal{V}$ and $(s_j, f_i(s_0\cdots s_j), s'_{j+1}) \models \tau$. Strategies may need memory to remember the history of a game. Let M be a finite set called memory. A finite-memory strategy $\mathcal{S} = (m_0, f_M, f_\Lambda)$ for player-i is defined as an initial memory $m_0 \in M$ along with a pair of functions: a memory-update function $f_M : M \times \Sigma_\mathcal{V} \rightarrow M$, which given the current state of the game and the memory, updates the memory, and a next-action function $f_\Lambda : M \times \Sigma^i_\mathcal{V} \rightarrow \Lambda$, which given the current player-i state and the memory, suggests the next action for the player. A strategy $\mathcal{S}$ is memory-less (a.k.a. positional) if the memory M is a singleton, i.e., $|M| = 1$. A memory-less strategy is independent of the history of the game and only depends on the current state. Thus, a memory-less strategy for player-i can be represented as a function $\mathcal{S} : \Sigma^i_\mathcal{V} \rightarrow \Lambda$.

Winning condition. A game $(\mathcal{G}, \phi_{init}, \Phi)$ consists of a game structure $\mathcal{G}$, a predicate ϕ_{init} over $\mathcal{V}$ specifying a set of initial states, and an objective Φ for player-2 given as an LTL formula. A run $\pi = s_0s_1\cdots$ is winning for player-2 if it is infinite and $\pi \in \mathcal{L}(\Phi)$. Let Π_1 be the set of runs that are winning for player-2. A strategy f_2 is winning for player-2 if for all strategies f_1 of player-1 and all states $s \models \phi_{init}$, we have $\Omega_{f_1,f_2}(s) \subseteq \Pi_1$, i.e., all possible outcomes are winning for player-2. The set of winning states $\mathcal{W}^\Phi$ for player-2 and for objective Φ in the game structure $\mathcal{G}$ is the set of states from which player-2 has a winning strategy. We say an objective Φ is enforceable over a game structure $\mathcal{G}$ from any initial state $s \models \phi_{init}$ if and only if player-2 has a winning strategy in the game $(\mathcal{G}, \phi_{init}, \Phi)$, in which case we also say $(\mathcal{G}, \phi_{init}, \Phi)$ is realizable. A game structure $\mathcal{G}$ defined over variables $\mathcal{V}$ and action Λ is deterministic iff for any state $s_1 \in \Sigma_\mathcal{V}$ and any actions $\ell \in \Lambda$, the set $Succ(s_1, \ell) = \{s_2 \in \Sigma_{\mathcal{V}'} \mid (s_1, \ell, s_2) \models \tau\}$ of successor states has at most one element, i.e., $\forall s_1 \in \Sigma_\mathcal{V}\ \forall \ell \in \Lambda.\ |Succ(s_1, \ell)| \leq 1$. Note that we allow non-determinism in our definition of game structures and we assume that the nondeterminism is always on player-1's side.

All the definitions can be extended to parametric versions in a straightforward manner by replacing $\mathcal{V}$ by $\mathcal{V}\cup\mathcal{P}$ and $\Sigma_\mathcal{V}$ by $\Sigma_\mathcal{V}\times\Sigma_\mathcal{P}$. For example, a parametric finite memory strategy $\mathcal{S}^\mathcal{P} = (m_0, f^\mathcal{P}_M, f^\mathcal{P}_\Lambda)$ for player-2 is defined by a memory-update function $f^\mathcal{P}_M : M \times \Sigma_\mathcal{V} \times \Sigma_\mathcal{P} \rightarrow M$ and next-action function $f^\mathcal{P}_\Lambda : M \times \Sigma^2_\mathcal{V} \times \Sigma_\mathcal{P} \rightarrow \Lambda$. For a parametric strategy $\mathcal{S}^\mathcal{P}$ and a parameters valuation $p \in \Sigma_\mathcal{P}$, *instantiation* of $\mathcal{S}^\mathcal{P}$ by p, denoted by $\mathcal{S}^\mathcal{P}_{\downarrow p}$, is a non-parametric finite-memory strategy $\mathcal{S}^\mathcal{P}_{\downarrow p} = (m_0, f_M, f_\Lambda)$ where for all $m \in M$ and $s \in \Sigma_\mathcal{V}$, $f_M(m, s) = f^\mathcal{P}_M(m, s, p)$ and $f_\Lambda(m, s) = f^\mathcal{P}_\Lambda(m, s, p)$.

Solving games. Symbolic algorithms for solving the realizability and synthesis problems are based on the *controllable predecessor* operator [13]. The (player-2) controllable predecessor operator $CPre : 2^{\Sigma_\mathcal{V}} \rightarrow 2^{\Sigma_\mathcal{V}}$ maps a set $Z \subseteq \Sigma_\mathcal{V}$ of states to the states from which player-2 can force the game into Z in one step. Player-2 can force the game into Z from a state $s \in \Sigma^1_\mathcal{V}$ iff for all available moves ℓ, all ℓ-successors of s are in Z, and she can force the game into Z from a state $s \in \Sigma^2_\mathcal{V}$ iff there is *some* available action ℓ such that all ℓ-successors of v are in Z. For example, the set of states from which player-2 can avoid a set $[\![\Phi_{err}]\!] \subseteq \Sigma_\mathcal{V}$ of states is the greatest fixed point $\nu Z.[\![\neg\Phi_{err}]\!] \cap CPre(Z)$ (safety objective,) and the set of states from which player-2 can reach a set of states $[\![\Phi_{reach}]\!] \subseteq \Sigma_\mathcal{V}$ is the least fixed point $\mu Z.[\![\Phi_{reach}]\!] \cup CPre(Z)$ (reachability objective).

2.3 Controllers and Controller Interfaces

Controller. We refer to memory-less strategies for player-2 with a designated set of final states as *finite-horizon reactive controllers* (or *controllers* for short). In our setting, controllers become active for a finite number of steps and interact with environment until reaching a desirable target state while avoiding some specified error states. Formally, a controller $\mathcal{C}$ is a pair $(\mathcal{S}, \mathcal{F})$ where $\mathcal{S} : \Sigma_\mathcal{V} \rightarrow \Lambda$ is a memory-less strategy and $\mathcal{F} \subseteq \Sigma_\mathcal{V}$ is a designated set of final states. At any time-step, if current state $s \in \Sigma_\mathcal{V}$ is a final state, i.e., $s \in \mathcal{F}$, the controller has reached the end of its computation. Note that we only consider controllers with reachability and safety objectives for which memory-less strategies suffice. A parametric reactive controller is a controller whose strategy and set of final states are parametric. Given a parameter valuation $p \in \Sigma_p$ and a parametric controller $\mathcal{C} = (\mathcal{S}, \mathcal{F})$, instantiation of $\mathcal{C}$ with $p \in \mathcal{P}$ is the controller $\mathcal{C}_{\downarrow p} = (\mathcal{S}_{\downarrow p}, \mathcal{F}_{\downarrow p})$ obtained by instantiating the strategy and projecting the set of final states by p.

Controller interface. A controller interface abstracts a controller by providing high-level information about its behavior while hiding its actual implementation. Formally, a controller interface $\mathcal{I}_\mathcal{C} = (\phi_{init_\mathcal{C}}, \phi_{inv_\mathcal{C}}, \phi_{f_\mathcal{C}})$ for a controller $\mathcal{C}$ is a tuple where $\phi_{init_\mathcal{C}}$ is a set of initial valuations over variables (and parameters), $\phi_{inv_\mathcal{C}}$ is an invariant that holds over all possible runs of $\mathcal{C}$ while it has the control, $\phi_{f_\mathcal{C}}$ is a possible set of valuations over variables (and parameters) once $\mathcal{C}$ reaches a final state. A controller $\mathcal{C} = (\mathcal{S}, \mathcal{F})$ over a game structure $\mathcal{G}$ *realizes* a controller interface $\mathcal{I}_\mathcal{C}$ if $\mathcal{S}$ is a winning strategy for the game $(\mathcal{G}, \phi_{init_\mathcal{C}}, \Psi)$ where $\Psi = \phi_{inv_\mathcal{C}}\ \mathcal{U}\ (\phi_{inv_\mathcal{C}} \wedge \phi_{f_\mathcal{C}})$ and $\mathcal{F} \subseteq [\![\phi_{f_\mathcal{C}}]\!]$, i.e., starting from any initial state $s \models \phi_{init_\mathcal{C}}$, the controller $\mathcal{C}$ guarantees that eventually a final state $s_f \models \phi_{f_\mathcal{C}}$ is visited and besides all the visited states along any possible outcome satisfy $\phi_{inv_\mathcal{C}}$, i.e., only safe states are visited. Instantiation of a controller interafce $\mathcal{I}_\mathcal{C}$ by $p \in \Sigma_\mathcal{P}$ is the non-parametric controller interface $\mathcal{I}_{\mathcal{C}_{\downarrow p}} = (\phi_{init_{\mathcal{C}_{\downarrow p}}}, \phi_{inv_{\mathcal{C}_{\downarrow p}}}, \phi_{f_{\mathcal{C}_{\downarrow p}}})$. A parameter valuation $p \in \Sigma_\mathcal{P}$ is *admissible* for controller $\mathcal{C}$ with interface $\mathcal{I}_\mathcal{C}$ over a game structure $\mathcal{G}$ iff the instantiation of $\mathcal{C}$ by p, $\mathcal{C}_{\downarrow p}$, realizes the non-parametric interface $\mathcal{I}_{\mathcal{C}_{\downarrow p}}$. Intuitively, a parametric controller can be instantiated by any admissible parameter value, and enforce its safety and reachability objectives, provided that its execution starts from a valid initial state. A set $\Sigma^a_\mathcal{P} \subseteq \Sigma_\mathcal{P}$ of admissible parameter values is maximal, if for any parameter valuation $p \in \Sigma_\mathcal{P}\backslash\Sigma^a_\mathcal{P}$, $\mathcal{C}_{\downarrow p}$ does *not* realize $\mathcal{I}_{\mathcal{C}_{\downarrow p}}$. A controller interface $\mathcal{I}_1 = (\phi_{init_1}, \phi_{inv_1}, \phi_{f_1})$ *respects* a controller interface $\mathcal{I}_2 = (\phi_{init_2}, \phi_{inv_2}, \phi_{f_2})$ if $\phi_{init_1} \rightarrow \phi_{init_2}$, $\phi_{inv_1} \rightarrow \phi_{inv_2}$, and $\phi_{f_1} \rightarrow \phi_{f_2}$. Note that any controller that realizes $\mathcal{I}_1$, also realizes the restricted interface $\mathcal{I}'_2 = (\phi_{init_1}, \phi_{inv_2}, \phi_{f_2})$, where $\mathcal{I}'_2$ is obtained from the interface $\mathcal{I}_2$ by restricting its initial states to $[\![\phi_{init_1}]\!] \subseteq [\![\phi_{init_2}]\!]$. In our setting, the designer can specify a parametric interface for the controllers without knowing for what parameter valuations the controller can enforce its safety and reachability objectives. A parametric controller, a maximal set of admissible parameter values, and an interface that respects the user-specified interface are then synthesized automatically.

2.4 Composing Controllers

Let $\mathcal{G} = (\mathcal{V}, \Lambda, \tau)$ be a game structure, and $\Gamma_\mathcal{C} = \{\mathcal{C}_1, \cdots \mathcal{C}_n\}$ be a set of parametric controllers. For a given set of initial states ϕ_{init} and objective Φ, the goal of the composer is to iteratively select a parametric controller and instantiate it with a parameter valuation, delegate the control to the instantiated controller until it enters a final state and relinquishes the control, upon which the composer selects the next controller and the next parameter valuation, and the process is repeated such that the objective Φ is enforced starting from any initial state $s_{init} \models \phi_{init}$. A *control strategy* $\mathcal{S}^\mathcal{C} : \Sigma_\mathcal{V} \to \Sigma_\mathcal{P} \times \Gamma_\mathcal{C}$ is a (partial) function that maps states of the game to a controller and a parameter valuation (note that we do not consider memory for the control strategy since it is not needed for safety and reachability objectives). A control strategy $\mathcal{S}^\mathcal{C}$ induces a finite-memory strategy $\mathcal{S} = (m_0, f_M, f_\Lambda)$ obtained by *sequentially* composing instantiated controllers according to $\mathcal{S}^\mathcal{C}$ as follows. Let $M \subseteq \Sigma_\mathcal{P} \times \Gamma_\mathcal{C} \cup \{\bot\}$ be the memory of the strategy where $m_0 = \bot$ and $\bot$ is a special symbol indicating the initial memory where a controller and a parameter valuation is yet to be selected. Intuitively, the memory of the strategy keeps track of the controller that currently has the control and the parameter valuation used to instantiate it. The memory-update function $f_M : M \times \Sigma_\mathcal{V} \to M$ and the next-action function $f_\Lambda : M \times \Sigma^2_\mathcal{V} \to \Lambda$ are defined as

$$f_M(m, s) = \begin{cases} m & \text{if } m \neq \bot \wedge s \notin \mathcal{F}_{\mathcal{C}_m} \\ \mathcal{S}^\mathcal{C}(s) & \text{otherwise} \end{cases}$$

$$f_\Lambda(m, s) = \begin{cases} \mathcal{S}_{\mathcal{C}_m}(s) & \text{if } m \neq \bot \wedge s \notin \mathcal{F}_{\mathcal{C}_m} \\ \mathcal{S}_{\mathcal{C}_{next}}(s) & \text{otherwise} \end{cases}$$

where $\mathcal{C}_m = (\mathcal{S}_{\mathcal{C}_m}, \mathcal{F}_{\mathcal{C}_m}) = \mathcal{C}_{i\downarrow p}$ is the instantiated controller for the memory $m = (p, \mathcal{C}_i)$, and $\mathcal{C}_{next} = (\mathcal{S}_{\mathcal{C}_{next}}, \mathcal{F}_{\mathcal{C}_{next}}) = \mathcal{C}^{next}_{\downarrow p^{next}}$ with $\mathcal{S}^\mathcal{C}(s) = (p^{next}, \mathcal{C}^{next})$ is the next controller chosen by the control strategy. Intuitively, when a final state of the currently active controller is reached or initially when no controller is selected, the next controller and the next parameter valuation are chosen according to the control strategy and the memory is updated to reflect this selection. The selected and instantiated controller then becomes active and guides the actions of the system while the memory stays unchanged, until the active controller enters a final state, upon which the control strategy decides the next action and the process is repeated. Note that in practice, the induced strategy $\mathcal{S}$ from $\mathcal{S}^\mathcal{C}$ is not computed explicitly, and the controllers can be dynamically fetched, instantiated and executed according to the control strategy.

3. PROBLEM STATEMENTS AND OVERVIEW

In this section we formally define the problems we consider in this paper and give an overview of our solution approach. Let $\mathcal{V}$ and $\mathcal{P}$ be sets of variables and parameters defined over finite domains $\Sigma_\mathcal{V}$ and $\Sigma_\mathcal{P}$, respectively, Λ be a finite set of actions, and $\mathcal{G}$ be a game structure over $\mathcal{V}$ and Λ. We are interested in how a parametric controller can be synthesized from a given parametric controller interface. Formally,

Problem Statement 1. *(Synthesis of Parametric Reactive Controllers.) Given a game structure $\mathcal{G}$ and a parametric controller interface $\mathcal{I} = (\phi_{init}, \phi_{inv}, \phi_f)$, synthesize a parametric reactive controller $\mathcal{C}$, its corresponding interface $\mathcal{I}_\mathcal{C}$, and a maximal set $\Sigma^a_\mathcal{P} \subseteq \Sigma_\mathcal{P}$ of admissible parameter valuations such that $\mathcal{I}_\mathcal{C}$ respects $\mathcal{I}$, and for any admissible parameter valuation $p \in \Sigma^a_\mathcal{P}$ for $\mathcal{C}$, instantiation of $\mathcal{C}$ by p, $\mathcal{C}_{\downarrow p}$, realizes the instantiated controller interface $\mathcal{I}_{\mathcal{C}_{\downarrow p}}$.*

(0,0)	(1,0)	(2,0)	(3,0)	(4,0)	(5,0)	(6,0)	(7,0)
(0,1)	(1,1)	(2,1)	(3,1)	(4,1)	(5,1)	(6,1)	(7,1)

Figure 2: Part of a road divided into grids.

A designer can specify a set of parametric controller interfaces. The synthesis algorithm then automatically computes the set of controllers, their corresponding interfaces and admissible parameter values. Once the parametric controllers are computed, they can be reused in different compositions to synthesize control strategies for different objectives.

Once a library of parametric controllers and their corresponding interfaces are obtained, the next natural question is how they can be composed to enforce high-level objectives. Let ϕ_{init} be a non-parametric predicate specifying initial states of the game, Φ be a non-parametric LTL objective over $\mathcal{V}$, $\Gamma_\mathcal{C} = \{\mathcal{C}_1, \cdots, \mathcal{C}_n\}$ be a set of parametric controllers, and $\Gamma_{\mathcal{I}_\mathcal{C}} = \{\mathcal{I}_{\mathcal{C}_1}, \cdots, \mathcal{I}_{\mathcal{C}_n}\}$ be the set of corresponding controller interfaces. Our goal is to synthesize a control strategy $\mathcal{S}^\mathcal{C}$ that instantiates and composes controllers from $\Gamma_\mathcal{C}$ using the information provided through interfaces $\Gamma_{\mathcal{I}_\mathcal{C}}$ such that its induced strategy enforces the global objective Φ in the game $(\mathcal{G}, \phi_{init}, \Phi)$. Formally,

Problem Statement 2. *(Synthesis with Parametric Reactive Controllers.) Given a game structure $\mathcal{G}$, a set of initial states specified by a non-parametric predicate ϕ_{init}, a non-parametric LTL objective Φ, and a set of parametric controllers $\Gamma_\mathcal{C}$ and their corresponding interfaces $\Gamma_{\mathcal{I}_\mathcal{C}}$, compute a control strategy $\mathcal{S}^\mathcal{C}$, if one exists, such that its induced strategy $\mathcal{S}$ is winning in the game $(\mathcal{G}, \phi_{init}, \Phi)$.*

We assume that Φ is given as a safety and/or reachability objective. We illustrate the methods with a simple example.

Example 2. *Consider a block of a double-lane road divided into grids each identified by a tuple (x, y) as shown in Figure 2. Assume there is a controlled vehicle V_1 initially at $(x_1, y_1) = (0, 1)$ moving from left to right. Moreover, assume there is an uncontrolled vehicle V_2 initially at $(x_2, y_2) = (7, 1)$ moving from right to left while staying on the same lane at all times, i.e., always $y_2 = 1$. Formally, let $\phi_{init} = (x_1 = 0 \wedge y_1 = 1 \wedge x_2 = 7 \wedge y_2 = 1)$ be the predicate specifying the initial state of the system. Assume V_1 has two actions: move-forward action, ℓ_1, that moves the vehicle one step ahead by incrementing x_1 while keeping it on the same lane, and lane-switch action, ℓ_2, that moves the vehicle one step forward and changes the lane at the same time. Our goal is to synthesize a controller that guides V_1 from the starting point to the other end of the road without colliding with V_2. This objective can be specified with the formula $\Phi = \phi_1\ \mathcal{U}\ (\phi_1 \wedge \phi_2)$ where $\phi_1 = (x_1 \neq x_2 \vee y_1 \neq y_2)$ (no collision) and $\phi_2 = (x_1 = 7)$ (reaching the other end.)*

Let a and b be two parameters. Assume the designer specifies a parametric controller interface $\mathcal{I} = (\phi_{init}, \phi_{inv}, \phi_f)$ where $\phi_{init} = (x_1 = a) \wedge (y_1 = b)$, $\phi_{inv} = (x_1 \neq x_2) \vee (y_1 \neq$

y_2), and $\phi_f = (x_1 = a+1)$, i.e., starting from initial parametric state $(x_1, y_1) = (a, b)$, V_1 must move one step forward (to satisfy ϕ_f) while avoiding collision with V_2 (thus satisfying ϕ_{inv}). A parametric controller $\mathcal{C} = (\mathcal{S}, \mathcal{F})$ is then synthesized with a memory-less strategy $\mathcal{S}$ defined as

$$\mathcal{S}(x_1, y_1, x_2, y_2, a, b) = \begin{cases} \ell_2 & \textit{if} \quad 0 \le a \le 6 \wedge x_1 = a \wedge y_1 = b \\ & \quad \wedge y_1 = y_2 \wedge x_2 = a+1 \\ \ell_1 & \textit{if} \quad 0 \le a \le 6 \wedge x_1 = a \wedge y_1 = b \wedge \\ & \quad (x_1 \ne x_2 \vee (y_2 \ne b \wedge y_2 \ne b+1)) \end{cases}$$

Intuitively, the controller $\mathcal{C}$ switches the current lane of the vehicle V_1 by taking lane-switch action ℓ_2 if the other vehicle V_2 is on the same lane and one cell ahead of V_1, and otherwise keeps moving forward by taking move-forward action ℓ_1. This way the controller $\mathcal{C}$ ensures that V_1 eventually makes progress by incrementing x_1 while avoiding collision with the other vehicle. For the set of final states of $\mathcal{C}$ we have $\mathcal{F} = (0 \le a \le 6 \wedge x_1 = a+1 \wedge ((x_1 \ne x_2) \vee (y_1 \ne y_2)))$, i.e., once the controller reaches a final state, V_1 has moved one step forward and does not occupy the same grid with V_2. Besides, correct behavior of the controller is guaranteed for the parameter values $0 \le a \le 6$. A potential controller interface $\mathcal{I}_\mathcal{C}$ for $\mathcal{C}$ is $(\phi'_{init}, \phi_{inv}, \phi_f)$ where $\phi'_{init} = \phi_{init} \wedge 0 \le a \le 6$. Note that $\mathcal{I}_\mathcal{C}$ respects $\mathcal{I}$ and $\mathcal{C}$ realizes $\mathcal{I}_\mathcal{C}$.

Once the parametric controllers are synthesized and a library is formed, the next step is to instantiate right parametric controllers and compose them to enforce a given system objective. In the above example, the controller $\mathcal{C}$ can be instantiated and composed sequentially in order to enforce the objective Φ according to the memory-less control strategy $\mathcal{S}^\mathcal{C}(x_1, y_1, x_2, y_2) = ((x_1, y_1), \mathcal{C})$ if $0 \le x_1 \le 6$. Intuitively, while V_1 has not reached the end of the road (i.e., $x_1 \ne 7$), the control strategy selects $\mathcal{C}$ and instantiates it with $(a = x_1, b = y_1)$, i.e., V_1's current location. To enforce the objective Φ, the parametric controller $\mathcal{C}$ is instantiated and composed 7 times, where each controller moves the vehicle one step forward without colliding with the other vehicle.

4. SYNTHESIZING PARAMETRIC REACTIVE CONTROLLERS

In this section we describe our solution for Problem 1 stated in Section 3. Let $\mathcal{G} = (\mathcal{V}, \Lambda, \tau)$ be a game structure, and $\mathcal{I} = (\phi_{init}, \phi_{inv}, \phi_f)$ be the user-specified controller interface. Our goal is to synthesize a controller $\mathcal{C}$ and its corresponding controller interface $\mathcal{I}_\mathcal{C} = (\phi_{init_\mathcal{C}}, \phi_{inv_\mathcal{C}}, \phi_{f_\mathcal{C}})$ and a set $\Sigma^a_\mathcal{P}$ of admissible parameter values such that for any $p \in \Sigma^a_\mathcal{P}$, $\mathcal{C}_{\downarrow p}$ realizes $\mathcal{I}_{\mathcal{C}_{\downarrow p}}$ and $\mathcal{I}_\mathcal{C}$ respects $\mathcal{I}$.

To this end, we first obtain a *parametric* game structure $\mathcal{G}^\mathcal{P}$ from $\mathcal{G}$. The idea is to treat parameters as special variables that have unknown initial value in a bounded set, but their value stays constant over the transitions of the game structure. Formally, let $\mathcal{P}'$ be a primed copy of parameters, and assume $same(\mathcal{P}, \mathcal{P}')$ is a predicate stating that the value of parameters stay unchanged. The parametric game structure $\mathcal{G}^\mathcal{P}$ is defined as $(\mathcal{V} \cup \mathcal{P}, \Lambda, \tau^\mathcal{P})$ where $\tau^\mathcal{P} = \tau \wedge same(\mathcal{P}, \mathcal{P}')$.

For example, Figure 3a shows a game structure where player-1 (player-2) states are depicted by ovals (boxes, respectively.) Each state is labeled by a state name q_i and a valuation over a variable x with domain $\Sigma_x = [0..3]$. At each player-i state for $i = 1, 2$, the player can choose one of

---

Algorithm 1: Parametric controller synthesis

Input: Game structure $\mathcal{G} = (\mathcal{V}, \Lambda, \tau)$, controller interface $\mathcal{I} = (\phi_{init}, \phi_{inv}, \phi_f)$ and parameters $\mathcal{P}$

Output: Parametric controller $\mathcal{C}$, controller interface $\mathcal{I}_\mathcal{C}$, and admissible parameter values $\Sigma^a_\mathcal{P}$ s.t. $\mathcal{I}_\mathcal{C}$ respects $\mathcal{I}$ and $\forall p \in \Sigma^a_\mathcal{P}.\ \mathcal{C}_{\downarrow p}$ realizes $\mathcal{I}_{\mathcal{C}_{\downarrow p}}$.

$\tau^\mathcal{P} := \tau \wedge same(\mathcal{P}, \mathcal{P}')$;
$\mathcal{G}^\mathcal{P} := (\mathcal{V} \cup \mathcal{P}, \Lambda, \tau^\mathcal{P})$;
$\Phi_\mathcal{I} := \phi_{inv}\ \mathcal{U}\ (\phi_{inv} \wedge \phi_f)$;
Let $[\![\phi_\mathcal{W}]\!]$ be the set of winning states in $\mathcal{G}^\mathcal{P}$ with respect to $\Phi_\mathcal{I}$;
$\phi_{init_\mathcal{C}} := \phi_{init} \wedge \phi_\mathcal{W}$;
$\phi^a_\mathcal{P} := \exists \mathcal{V}.\ \phi_{init_\mathcal{C}}$;
$\Sigma^a_\mathcal{P} := [\![\phi^a_\mathcal{P}]\!]$;
Let $\mathcal{S}$ be a parametric winning strategy in the game $(\mathcal{G}^\mathcal{P}, \phi_{init_\mathcal{C}}, \Phi_\mathcal{I})$;
$\phi_\mathcal{R} :=$ **Reachable**$(\mathcal{G}^\mathcal{P}, \phi_{init_\mathcal{C}}, \mathcal{S})$;
$\mathcal{F} := [\![\phi_f \wedge \phi_\mathcal{R}]\!]$;
$\mathcal{C} := (\mathcal{S}, \mathcal{F})$;
$\phi_{inv_\mathcal{C}} := \phi_\mathcal{R}$;
$\phi_{f_\mathcal{C}} := \phi_f \wedge \phi_\mathcal{R}$;
$\mathcal{I}_\mathcal{C} = (\phi_{init_\mathcal{C}}, \phi_{inv_\mathcal{C}}, \phi_{f_\mathcal{C}})$;
return $(\mathcal{C}, \mathcal{I}_\mathcal{C}, \Sigma^a_\mathcal{P})$;

---

the actions *inc* or *dec* (if available,) to increment or decrement x, respectively. Assume p is a parameter with domain $\Sigma_p = [0..2]$. Figure 3b shows the parametric game structure obtained from the game structure in Figure 3a. Each state is labeled with a state name q^j_i and a valuation over x and p. Each state q^j_i in the parametric game structure $\mathcal{G}^\mathcal{P}$ correspond to the state q_i in the game structure $\mathcal{G}$. Intuitively, the parametric game structure has parallel copies of the non-parametric game structure for different values of the parameters and moreover, there is no transition between different copies. Note that explicit-state representations of (parametric) game structures are *not* constructed in practice, and they are represented and manipulated symbolically, thus avoiding the explicit enumeration of the parameters.

Algorithm 1 shows how a parametric controller is synthesized for a given game structure $\mathcal{G}$ and specified interface $\mathcal{I}$. Once the parametric game structure $\mathcal{G}^\mathcal{P}$ is obtained, the game $(\mathcal{G}^\mathcal{P}, \phi_{init}, \Phi_\mathcal{I})$ where $\Phi_\mathcal{I} = \phi_{inv}\ \mathcal{U}\ (\phi_{inv} \wedge \phi_f)$ can be solved by standard realizability and synthesis algorithms and a set of winning states can be computed [13]. Let $\mathcal{W} \subseteq \Sigma_\mathcal{V} \times \Sigma_\mathcal{P}$ be the set of winning states in $\mathcal{G}^\mathcal{P}$ with respect to objective $\Phi_\mathcal{I}$, and let $\phi_\mathcal{W}$ be a predicate specifying $\mathcal{W}$, i.e., $[\![\phi_\mathcal{W}]\!] = \mathcal{W}$. We define $\phi_{init_\mathcal{C}} = \phi_{init} \wedge \phi_\mathcal{W}$ as the intersection of set of parametric initial states specified by the user and set of winning states where player-2 can enforce the objective $\Phi_\mathcal{I}$. The set $[\![\phi_{init_\mathcal{C}}]\!]$ includes all the parametric initial states from which player-2 can win the game $(\mathcal{G}^\mathcal{P}, \phi_{init_\mathcal{C}}, \Phi_\mathcal{I})$ and hence, it contains all the admissible parameter valuations. The set $\Sigma^a_\mathcal{P}$ of admissible parameter values can be computed by existentially quantifying the variables from $\phi_{init_\mathcal{C}}$, i.e., $\Sigma^a_\mathcal{P} = \exists \mathcal{V}.\ \phi_{init_\mathcal{C}}$. Algorithm 1 then computes a parametric winning strategy over the game $(\mathcal{G}^\mathcal{P}, \phi_{init_\mathcal{C}}, \Phi_\mathcal{I})$ using a game solver. Let $\phi_\mathcal{R} =$ **Reachable**$(\mathcal{G}^\mathcal{P}, \phi_{init_\mathcal{C}}, \mathcal{S})$ be a predicate specifying the set $[\![\phi_\mathcal{R}]\!] \subseteq \Sigma_\mathcal{V} \times \Sigma_\mathcal{P}$ of reachable states in the parametric game structure $\mathcal{G}^\mathcal{P}$ starting from any initial state $s \models \phi_{init_\mathcal{C}}$

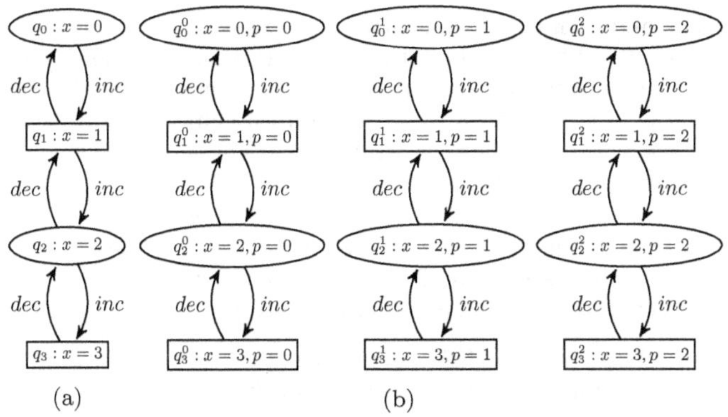

Figure 3: (a) A game structure $\mathcal{G}$ defined over a variable $x \in [0..3]$, and (b) A parametric game structure $\mathcal{G}^{\mathcal{P}}$ obtained from $\mathcal{G}$ with parameter $p \in [0..2]$.

when player-2 actions are chosen according to the strategy $\mathcal{S}$. We define $\mathcal{I}_{\mathcal{C}} = (\phi_{init_{\mathcal{C}}}, \phi_{inv_{\mathcal{C}}}, \phi_{f_{\mathcal{C}}})$ as the controller interface for $\mathcal{C}$ where $\phi_{inv_{\mathcal{C}}} = \phi_{\mathcal{R}}$ and $\phi_{f_{\mathcal{C}}} = \phi_f \wedge \phi_{\mathcal{R}}$. Intuitively, $\phi_{inv_{\mathcal{C}}}$ specifies the set of states that may be visited during the game when player-2 behaves according to the controller $\mathcal{C}$, and serves as the invariant of the computed controller interface. Similarly, $\phi_{f_{\mathcal{C}}}$ specifies a set of reachable final states when $\mathcal{C}$ is active. The following theorem states that Algorithm 1 can correctly synthesize a parametric controller, if one exists, and that it computes the controller with effort $O(|\Sigma_{\mathcal{V}}|)$, where effort is measured in symbolic steps, i.e., in the number of pre-image or post-image computation [3]. Due to the lack of space, the proofs of theorems are omitted and can be found in the technical report.

THEOREM 1. *Algorithm 1 is sound and complete. It performs $O(|\Sigma_{\mathcal{V}}|)$ symbolic steps in the worst case.*

The number of symbolic steps is not the only factor determining the time taken by the symbolic algorithm, however, it is an important measure of difficulty since image and preimage computations are typically the most expensive operations [3]. Intuitively, the number of symbolic steps in Algorithm 1 is independent of the parameters because the symbolic algorithm for computing the set of winning states can manipulate the parallel copies in the parametric game structure simultaneously, and that each copy is of size $O(|\Sigma_{\mathcal{V}}|)$ (the parametric game structure can be viewed as $|\Sigma_{\mathcal{P}}|$ copies of the original game structure.) As an example, consider the parametric game structure in Figure 3b. Observe that each copy for each parameter valuation is of the same size of the non-parametric game structure shown in Figure 3a. Let $\Phi = (X = p)$ be a parametric predicate. It is easy to see that states q_0^0, q_1^1, and q_2^2 in the parametric game structure satisfy Φ. The pre-image of these states (states that can reach them in one step) is the set $\{q_0^1, q_1^0, q_2^1, q_1^2, q_3^2\}$ that is computed by the symbolic algorithm in one step. Note that although the number of symbolic steps in Algorithm 1 is independent of the parameters, it does not mean that adding parameters has no additional cost as they may increase the complexity of the symbolic steps. However, transitions over parameters have a special structure that may be utilized for efficient implementation of the symbolic steps, which is subject to our future research.

5. SYNTHESIS OF CONTROL STRATEGY WITH PARAMETRIC CONTROLLERS

In this section we describe our solution for Problem 2 stated in Section 3. Our goal is to synthesize a control strategy $\mathcal{S}^{\mathcal{C}}$ such that its induced strategy is winning in the game $(\mathcal{G}, \phi_{init}, \Phi)$. To this end, we first obtain a *control game structure* $\mathcal{G}^{\mathcal{C}}$ using the set of controller interfaces $\Gamma_{\mathcal{I}_{\mathcal{C}}}$. Intuitively, $\mathcal{G}^{\mathcal{C}}$ models what controllers and parameter valuations the system can choose at any state, possible states that may be visited while the selected controller is active, and potential final states that may be reached once the controller is done. From the standpoint of the composer, each instantiated controller that becomes active goes through three steps: *initialization* (the controller starts its execution from a valid initial state), *execution* (the state of the system evolves according to the controller), and *termination* (the controller enters a final state and returns the control).

Formally, let $\gamma_{\mathcal{C}} \notin \mathcal{V}$ defined over the domain $\Sigma_{\gamma_{\mathcal{C}}} = [1..n]$ be a variable representing the controllers, i.e., $\gamma_{\mathcal{C}} = i$ corresponds to the controller $\mathcal{C}_i \in \Gamma_{\mathcal{C}}$ for $i = 1, \cdots, n$. Let $t_c \notin \mathcal{V}$ defined over $\Sigma_{t_c} = \{1, 2\}$ be a variable indicating which player's turn it is in the control game structure. Moreover, let $t_e \notin \mathcal{V}$ defined over $\Sigma_{t_e} = \{1, 2\}$ be an additional variable that player-1 uses to distinguish a controller's possible initial states from *intermediate* states that may be visited during the execution of the controller. A control game structure $\mathcal{G}^{\mathcal{C}}$ is a tuple $(\mathcal{V}^{\mathcal{C}}, \Lambda^{\mathcal{C}}, \tau^{\mathcal{C}})$ where $\mathcal{V}^{\mathcal{C}} = \mathcal{V} \cup \{t_c, t_e, \gamma_{\mathcal{C}}\} \cup \mathcal{P}$ is a set of variables defined over the domain $\Sigma_{\mathcal{V}^{\mathcal{C}}} = \Sigma_{\mathcal{V}} \times \Sigma_{t_c} \times \Sigma_{t_e} \times \Sigma_{\gamma_{\mathcal{C}}} \times \Sigma_{\mathcal{P}}$, $\Lambda^{\mathcal{C}} = \Sigma_{\mathcal{P}'} \times \Sigma_{\gamma'_{\mathcal{C}}}$ is a set of actions, and $\tau^{\mathcal{C}}$ is symbolically defined as $\tau^{\mathcal{C}} = \bigvee_{i=1}^{n} (\tau_s^{\mathcal{C}_i} \vee \tau_{e1}^{\mathcal{C}_i} \vee \tau_{e2}^{\mathcal{C}_i})$ where

$$\tau_s^{\mathcal{C}_i} := t_c = 2 \wedge same(\mathcal{V}, \mathcal{V}') \wedge t'_c = 1 \wedge t'_e = 1 \wedge \gamma'_c = i \wedge \phi'_{init_{\mathcal{C}_i}},$$

$$\tau_{e1}^{\mathcal{C}_i} := t_c = 1 \wedge \gamma_c = i \wedge t_e = 1 \wedge t'_c = 1 \wedge t'_e = 2 \wedge \phi'_{inv_{\mathcal{C}_i}} \wedge same(\mathcal{P}, \mathcal{P}') \wedge same(\gamma_c, \gamma'_c), \text{ and}$$

$$\tau_{e2}^{\mathcal{C}_i} := t_c = 1 \wedge t_e = 2 \wedge \gamma_c = i \wedge t'_c = 2 \wedge \phi'_{f_{\mathcal{C}_i}} \wedge same(\mathcal{P}, \mathcal{P}') \wedge same(\gamma_c, \gamma'_c)$$

where $\gamma'_{\mathcal{C}}$ is a primed copy of $\gamma_{\mathcal{C}}$, and ϕ' is obtained by replacing variables in ϕ by their primed copies. Note that the primed copies of the parameters and $\gamma_{\mathcal{C}}$ encode the actions $\Lambda^{\mathcal{C}}$ of the control game structure to indicate that the composer (player-2 in $\mathcal{G}^{\mathcal{C}}$) selects the parameter valuation and the parametric controller when it is her turn, and also to avoid introducing additional variables. We denote by $\Sigma^i_{\mathcal{V}^{\mathcal{C}}} = \{v^{\mathcal{C}} \in \Sigma_{\mathcal{V}^{\mathcal{C}}} \mid v^{\mathcal{C}}_{|t_c} = i\}$ the set of player-i states in the control game structure for $i = 1, 2$.

At any player-2 state in the control game structure, the composer must choose a controller $\mathcal{C} \in \Gamma_{\mathcal{C}}$ and an admissible parameter valuation $p \in \Sigma_{\mathcal{P}}$, if one exists. Furthermore, the composer must ensure that the selected controller starts from a valid initial state, i.e., the state where the instantiated controller $\mathcal{C}_{\downarrow}p$ receives the control satisfies the predicate $\phi_{init_{\mathcal{C}_{\downarrow p}}}$. This is captured in the predicate $\tau_s^{\mathcal{C}_i}$ of $\tau^{\mathcal{C}}$ for each controller $\mathcal{C}_i$. According to $\tau_s^{\mathcal{C}_i}$ at any state $(v, t_c = 2, t_e, \gamma_{\mathcal{C}}, p) \in \Sigma^2_{\mathcal{V}^{\mathcal{C}}}$, the controller $\mathcal{C}_i$ can be chosen by selecting $\gamma'_{\mathcal{C}} = i$ if there exists a parameter valuation $p' \in \Sigma_{\mathcal{P}'}$ such that the initial condition of the controller is satisfied, i.e., $(v', p') \models \phi'_{init_{\mathcal{C}_i}}$ where v' is obtained by replacing variables in v by their primed copies. $t'_c = 1$ means that it is player-1 state in the next turn, and $t'_e = 1$ means that player-1 states in the next turn satisfy the initial condition of the controller. Intuitively, each predicate $\tau_s^{\mathcal{C}_i}$ for $i = 1..n$ models initialization of a controller $\mathcal{C}_i$.

Once a controller $\mathcal{C}_i$ and a parameter valuation $p \in \Sigma_\mathcal{P}$ are selected by the composer, the control is transferred to the instantiated controller $\mathcal{C}_{i_{\downarrow p}}$, and the controller and parameter valuation are fixed until the control is returned to the composer. This is captured in $\tau_{e_1}^{\mathcal{C}_i}$ and $\tau_{e_2}^{\mathcal{C}_i}$ by $same(\mathcal{P}, \mathcal{P}') \wedge same(\gamma_\mathcal{C}, \gamma'_\mathcal{C})$. Player-1 states with $t_e = 1$ ($t_e = 2$) and $\gamma_{\mathcal{C}_i} = i$ in $\mathcal{G}^\mathcal{C}$ represent initial (intermediate) states where the predicate $\phi_{init_{\mathcal{C}_{i_{\downarrow p}}}}$ ($\phi_{inv_{\mathcal{C}_{i_{\downarrow p}}}}$, respectively) of the instantiated controller interface $\mathcal{I}_{\mathcal{C}_{i_{\downarrow p}}}$ is satisfied. Intuitively, each predicate $\tau_{e_1}^{\mathcal{C}_i}$ captures transitions from controller's initial state to its intermediate states (representing the execution of the controller), and $\tau_{e_2}^{\mathcal{C}_i}$ shows the transition from intermediate states to final states (modeling termination) where the controller has reached a final state and control is returned to the composer. We illustrate the ideas with a simple example.

Example 3. *Let $x \in [0..2]$ be a variable, and $p \in [0..2]$ be a parameter. Consider two controllers $\mathcal{C}_1$ and $\mathcal{C}_2$ with controller interfaces $\mathcal{I}_{\mathcal{C}_1} = (\phi_{init_{\mathcal{C}_1}}, \phi_{inv_{\mathcal{C}_1}}, \phi_{f_{\mathcal{C}_1}})$ and $\mathcal{I}_{\mathcal{C}_2} = (\phi_{init_{\mathcal{C}_2}}, \phi_{inv_{\mathcal{C}_2}}, \phi_{f_{\mathcal{C}_2}})$ defined as follows: $\phi_{init_{\mathcal{C}_1}} = (\phi_{\mathcal{P}_1} \wedge x = p)$, $\phi_{f_{\mathcal{C}_1}} = (\phi_{\mathcal{P}_1} \wedge (x = p+1))$, $\phi_{inv_{\mathcal{C}_1}} = \phi_{init_1} \vee \phi_{f_{\mathcal{C}_1}}$, $\phi_{init_{\mathcal{C}_2}} = (\phi_{\mathcal{P}_2} \wedge x = p)$, $\phi_{f_{\mathcal{C}_2}} = (\phi_{\mathcal{P}_2} \wedge (x = p - 1))$, and $\phi_{inv_{\mathcal{C}_2}} = \phi_{init_2} \vee \phi_{f_{\mathcal{C}_2}}$, where $\phi_{\mathcal{P}_1} = (0 \leq p \leq 1)$ and $\phi_{\mathcal{P}_2} = (1 \leq p \leq 2)$. Intuitively, $\mathcal{C}_1$ eventually increments the value of x by 1, while $\mathcal{C}_2$ eventually decrements it by 1. Furthermore, $\phi_{inv_{\mathcal{C}_i}} = \phi_{init_i} \vee \phi_{f_{\mathcal{C}_i}}$, for $i = 1, 2$, indicates that the set of states that are possibly visited during execution of controller $\mathcal{C}_i$ is the union of initial states and final states. Figure 4 shows the control game structure for this example where player-2 (player-1) states are depicted by boxes (ovals, respectively) and player-2 states are grouped together based on their valuations over x for a compact representation. Each node of the graph in Figure 4 is labeled with a name q_j and a set of predicates that hold in those states. For example, node q_0 represents all player-2 states in the control game structure for which $x = 1$. Nodes q_7 and q_{11} can be interpreted in a similar way. Outgoing edges from player-2 states are labeled by an instantiated controller that the composer can select at those states, e.g., at q_0, the composer can select either the instantiated controller $\mathcal{C}_{1_{\downarrow 1}}$ (corresponding to the action ($p' = 1, \gamma'_\mathcal{C} = 1$),) or the instantiated controller $\mathcal{C}_{2_{\downarrow 1}}$. If the composer chooses $\mathcal{C}_{2_{\downarrow}1}$, then the control of the system is transferred to $\mathcal{C}_{2_{\downarrow}1}$, and q_4 is visited next in the control game structure. Note that the controller and parameter valuations are selected by the composer and they do not change in player-1 states. Once the controller is initialized, any intermediate state that satisfies the invariant of the instantiated controller can be visited in the control game structure (nodes q_5 and q_6 in Figure 4,) and at the next step, a final state of the instantiated controller is visited (represented by q_{11}), indicating the execution of the controller is over and the composer must decide the next action.*

Once the control game structure is obtained, we solve the *control game* $(\mathcal{G}^\mathcal{C}, \phi_{init}^\mathcal{C}, \Phi)$ where $\phi_{init}^\mathcal{C} = (t_c = 2 \wedge \phi_{init})$, i.e., the control game starts from a player-2 state so that the composer can initially select a controller and a parameter valuations. If player-2 has a winning strategy in the control game, we synthesize a winning strategy $\mathcal{S}^\Phi$ of special form that only depends on the valuation over variables $\mathcal{V}$ and then extract a control strategy $\mathcal{S}^\mathcal{C}$ from it. Formally, let $\Upsilon = \mathcal{V}^\mathcal{C} \backslash \mathcal{V}$ be the set of parameters and additional variables introduced for the control game structure. We say a player-2 strategy $\mathcal{S}^\Phi$ in the control game structure is Υ-*independent* if there exists a partial function $f^\mathcal{C} : \Sigma_\mathcal{V} \to \Lambda^\mathcal{C}$ such that for any player-2 state $v^\mathcal{C} = (v, 2, i, j, p) \in \Sigma^2_{\mathcal{V}^\mathcal{C}}$, $\mathcal{S}^\Phi(v, 2, i, j, p) = f^\mathcal{C}(v)$. Intuitively, it means that $\mathcal{S}^\Phi$ only depends on the valuation over variables $\mathcal{V}$. The following theorem states that if player-2 can win the control game, then a Υ-independent winning strategy can be synthesized.

Theorem 2. *If the control game is realizable, then there exists a Υ-independent winning strategy for player-2.*

The main reason is that the predicates $\tau_s^{\mathcal{C}_i}$ in the transition relation $\tau^\mathcal{C}$ of $\mathcal{G}^\mathcal{C}$ do not depend on the variables $t_e, \gamma_\mathcal{C}$ or parameters (though depending on their primed copies,) and the value of $t_c = 2$ is fixed. Intuitively, it means the composer can select the next controller and parameter valuations only based on the current valuation over $\mathcal{V}$ and regardless of current values of parameters, t_e and $\gamma_\mathcal{C}$. A control strategy $\mathcal{S}^\mathcal{C} : \Sigma_\mathcal{V} \to \Sigma_\mathcal{P} \times \Gamma_\mathcal{C}$ is extracted from $\mathcal{S}^\Phi$ using the function $f^\mathcal{C}$ as follows. For any $v \in \Sigma_\mathcal{V}$ such that $f^\mathcal{C}(v)$ is defined and $f^\mathcal{C}(v) = (p', i) \in \Sigma_{\mathcal{P}'} \times \Sigma_{\gamma'_\mathcal{C}}$, we let $\mathcal{S}^\mathcal{C}(v) = (p, \mathcal{C}_i)$ where p is obtained by replacing primed copies of parameters in p' by their unprimed versions. Algorithm 2 summarizes the steps for computing $\mathcal{S}^\mathcal{C}$. The following theorem establishes the correctness and the complexity of Algorithm 2.

Theorem 3. *Algorithm 2 is sound. For reachability and safety objectives, it performs $O(|\Sigma_\mathcal{V}|)$ symbolic steps.*

Note that the upper-bound on the number of symbolic steps in Algorithm 2 is independent from the variables $\mathcal{V}^\mathcal{C} \backslash \mathcal{V}$. This is partly because transitions from player-2 states in the control game structure do not depend on the current valuation over variables $t_e, \gamma_\mathcal{C}$, and $\mathcal{P}$. Thus, if a player-2 state with the valuation $v \in \Sigma_\mathcal{V}$ over variables $\mathcal{V}$ is winning, then *all* player-2 states with the same valuation v over $\mathcal{V}$ are winning. Roughly speaking, the symbolic algorithm for computing the set of winning states manipulates the set of player-2 states based on their valuations over $\mathcal{V}$. Note that there are only $|\Sigma_\mathcal{V}|$ player-2 states with different valuations over $\mathcal{V}$ in $\mathcal{G}^\mathcal{C}$. Besides, any infinite run in $\mathcal{G}^\mathcal{C}$ starting from a player-2 state has a special form where every player-2 state is followed by two player-1 states and then a player-2 state is visited, and this pattern repeats infinitely. Due to this special form, with every three symbolic steps, either the symbolic algorithm terminates by reaching a fix point that characterize the set of winning states, or a new set of player-2 states with some valuation v over $\mathcal{V}$ are discovered to be winning (or losing) by the symbolic algorithm. Hence, the number of symbolic steps is bounded by $O(3|\Sigma_\mathcal{V}|) = O(|\Sigma_\mathcal{V}|)$.

Example 4. *Consider the setting in Example 3. Let $\phi_{init} = (x = 0)$ be a set of initial states, and $\Phi = \Box(x \neq 2) \wedge \Diamond(x = 1)$ be the objective. A control strategy enforcing the objective Φ is shown in Figure 4 by solid edges at player-2 states. Initially, at q_{11}, the composer chooses controller $\mathcal{C}_1$ with parameter value $p = 0$. Once $\mathcal{C}_{1_{\downarrow 0}}$ reaches a final state, the control is returned to the composer, and based on the current valuation over x, $x = 1$ in this example, the next controller, $\mathcal{C}_2$, and the next parameter valuation, $p = 1$, are chosen by the composer. Intuitively, at states with $x = 0$, the composer increments x by selecting $\mathcal{C}_1$ and at states with $x = 1$, it decrements x by choosing $\mathcal{C}_2$.*

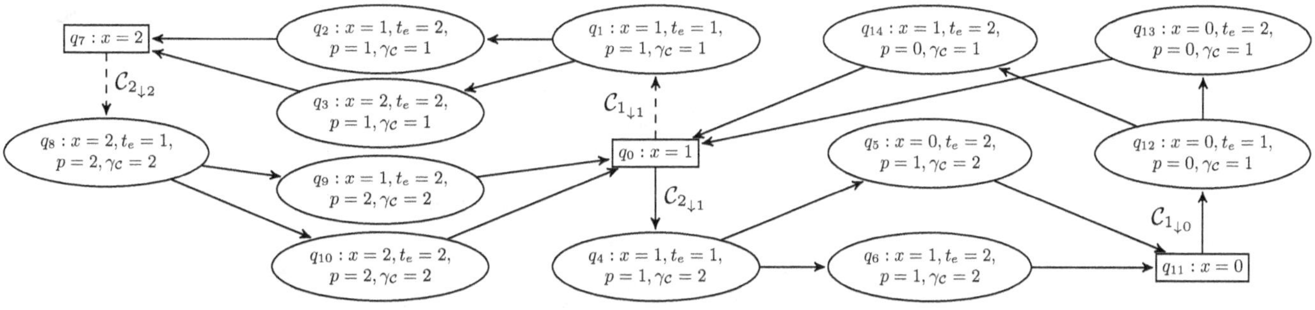

Figure 4: Control game structure for Example 3 where player-2 states are grouped together for a compact representation. Outgoing edges from player-2 states are labeled by an instantiated controller that the composer can choose at those states. A Control strategy for objective $\Phi = \Box(x \neq 2) \wedge \Diamond(x = 1)$ is to choose solid edges at player-2 states.

Algorithm 2: Control Strategy Synthesis

Input: A predicate ϕ_{init} specifying a set of initial states, a non-parametric safety and reachability objective Φ, a set $\Gamma_{\mathcal{I}_\mathcal{C}}$ of controller interfaces

Output: A control strategy $\mathcal{S}^\mathcal{C}$ s.t. its induced strategy is winning in the game $(\mathcal{G}, \phi_{init}, \Phi)$

Obtain the control game structure $\mathcal{G}^\mathcal{C}$ using $\Gamma_{\mathcal{I}_\mathcal{C}}$;

$\phi^\mathcal{C}_{init} := t_c = 2 \wedge \phi_{init}$;

Synthesize a $\mathcal{V}^\mathcal{C} \backslash \mathcal{V}$-independent winning strategy $\mathcal{S}^\Phi$ by solving the game $(\mathcal{G}^\mathcal{C}, \phi^\mathcal{C}_{init}, \Phi)$;

Extract and return a control strategy $\mathcal{S}^\mathcal{C}$ from $\mathcal{S}^\Phi$;

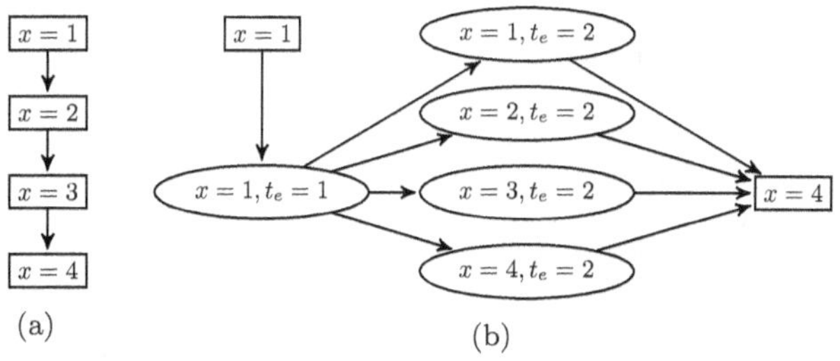

Figure 5: (a) Part of a run in a game structure where the controller takes the control at a state with $x = 1$ and increments x by 3. (b) Part of a control game structure capturing execution of the controller from a state with $x = 1$.

Completeness. Note that Algorithm 2 is not complete as the interfaces provide an abstraction of the controllers and they might lack some information on the *sequence* of states that will be visited during the execution of the controller. As an example consider a game structure $\mathcal{G}$ with an integer variable x. Consider a controller $\mathcal{C}$ that starting from a state $x = p$ where p is a parameter, increments x by three, i.e., eventually $x = p+3$. Assume that the controller does this by incrementing x one by one in three consecutive steps. Figure 5a shows a part of a run of $\mathcal{G}$ starting from a state where $x = 1$ and applying the controller $\mathcal{C}_{\downarrow p=1}$. For simplicity, we assume that all states in $\mathcal{G}$ are player-2 states (represented by boxes). The interface $\mathcal{I}_\mathcal{C}$ of the controller $\mathcal{C}$ is defined as $\mathcal{I}_\mathcal{C} = (\phi_{init_\mathcal{C}}, \phi_{inv_\mathcal{C}}, \phi_{f_\mathcal{C}})$ where $\phi_{init_\mathcal{C}} = (x = p)$, $\phi_{inv_\mathcal{C}} = \bigvee_{i=p}^{p+3} x = i$, and $\phi_{f_\mathcal{C}} = (x = p+3)$. That is, starting from a parametric state $x = p$ and using the controller $\mathcal{C}$, any state $x \in [p..p+3]$ can be visited, and eventually x is incremented by 3. Note that here we removed the constraints concerning the set of admissible parameter values from the interface to keep the example simple. Figure 5b shows part of a control game structure obtained from $\mathcal{I}_\mathcal{C}$ from any state with $x = 1$. To keep the figure simple, we removed the parameters and variables corresponding to the controllers, and similar to Example 3, player-2 states are grouped together based on their valuations over x. Let $\phi_{init} = (x = 1)$ and $\Phi = \Diamond(x = 3)$ specify the initial state and the objective of the system, respectively. It is easy to see that using controller $\mathcal{C}$ guarantees visiting the state $x = 3$ on its path to the final state $x = 4$. However, there is no control strategy over the control game structure that guarantees visiting $x = 3$ as player-1 can avoid the state with $x = 3$ in the control game structure. Intuitively, the sequence of states $(x = 1)(x = 2)(x = 3)(x = 4)$ is "lost" in the control game structure. This loss of information is the cost paid for having a simpler control game structure.

For a given objective Φ, completeness of the framework can be achieved by analyzing the controllers and enriching the interfaces, or in the extreme case by having interfaces that exactly capture the possible outcomes of applying corresponding controllers. However, our main emphasis is on simplicity and separating the two design layers, the parametric controller synthesis and synthesis from a library of parametric controllers. Controllers in our framework can be viewed as *black-boxes* where their input-output behavior is provided through their simple interfaces. An alternative view is to see the controllers as *white-boxes* and extract more information from them. The trade-off is that the former approach is simpler and more computationally efficient as the control game structure is simpler and requires less number of symbolic steps, while the latter guarantees completeness.

6. CASE STUDY

In this section we apply the methods developed in Sections 4 and 5 to an autonomous vehicle case study. Consider a network of one-way streets connected via intersections as shown in Figure 1. Assume there is a controlled autonomous vehicle V_1 initially positioned in the grid marked with s_0. Also assume there is an uncontrolled vehicle V_2 initially at the grid-cell s^*. Each vehicle has actions move-forward, backup, turn-left, turn-right, and stop that moves it one step forward, backward, to the left, to the right, and leaves its position unchanged, respectively. The goal is to synthesize a controller for V_1 that can guide it from the initial position

s to the final destination d while obeying the traffic laws (e.g., moving in the specified directions of streets, no stopping inside an intersection, etc.) and avoiding collision with V_2 and static obstacles. We assume that the uncontrolled vehicle respects traffic laws by always moving in the specified directions for the streets. We implemented our algorithms symbolically in Java and using BDD package JDD [17]. We first specify and synthesize a set of parametric reactive controllers that guarantee advancing the vehicle in north, south, west, and east directions while avoiding collision with static obstacles and the other vehicle. We then synthesize a control strategy that instantiates and composes these controllers to navigate V_1 safely from initial position to the destination.

Synthesis of Parametric Controllers. We denote the location of the vehicle V_i at any time-step with (x_i, y_i) for $i = 1, 2$. We specify four parametric controllers that can move the car in different directions: Controller $\mathcal{C}_1$ ($\mathcal{C}_2$) with specified controller interface $\mathcal{I}_1$ ($\mathcal{I}_2$) that moves the car three steps toward east (west, respectively), and controller $\mathcal{C}_3$ ($\mathcal{C}_4$) with specified controller interface $\mathcal{I}_3$ ($\mathcal{I}_4$) that advance the car one step toward north (south, respectively.) More specifically, let a, b be two parameters. Let $\phi_{init} = (x_1 = a \wedge y_1 = b)$ be the parametric initial state. Let $\phi_{inv} = (x_1 \neq x_2 \vee y_1 \neq y_2)$, i.e., no collision between vehicles. Finally, let $\phi_{f_1} = (x = a + 3, y = b)$, $\phi_{f_2} = (x = a - 3, y = b)$, $\phi_{f_3} = (x = a, y = b + 1)$, and $\phi_{f_4} = (x = a, y = b - 1)$ specify moving in different directions. Controllers are specified by interfaces $\mathcal{I}_{\mathcal{C}_i} = (\phi_{init}, \phi_{inv}, \phi_{f_i})$. Algorithm 1 is then used to synthesize parametric controllers, their corresponding interfaces and the set of admissible parameter values.

Synthesis of Control Strategy. Once a library of parametric reactive controllers $\Gamma_{\mathcal{C}}$ and their corresponding interfaces $\Gamma_{\mathcal{I}_{\mathcal{C}}}$ are formed, Algorithm 2 is used to synthesize a control strategy for the controlled vehicle. A synthesized control strategy instantiates and applies the controller $\mathcal{C}_1$ consecutively to advance the vehicle toward east and finally bring it to the position marked by s_6, from which controller $\mathcal{C}_3$ is instantiated and employed consecutively to take the vehicle to its destination. More specifically, at any position marked by s_i for $i = 0, \cdots, 5$, controller $\mathcal{C}_1$ is instantiated and becomes active, and it guarantees to eventually advance the controlled vehicle to the next position s_{i+1}. Similarly, at any position marked by s_i for $i = 6, \cdots, 9$, controller $\mathcal{C}_3$ is instantiated and becomes active, and it eventually navigates the controlled vehicle to the next position s_{i+1} where $s_{10} = d$ is the final destination. The control strategy sets the parameters a and b according to the current state of the vehicle, i.e., if the current position of V_1 is $(x_1 = i, y_1 = j)$, the control strategy instantiates the controllers $\mathcal{C}_1$ and $\mathcal{C}_3$ by parameter valuation $(a, b) = (i, j)$.

7. CONCLUSION AND FUTURE WORK

We presented a framework for symbolic synthesis from a library of parametric and reactive controllers. We also showed how these controllers can be synthesized from parametric objectives specified by the user. In this paper, we assumed that the controllers have perfect information about the state of the system at any time-step. However, in practice, this assumption might be unrealistic, e.g., due to the imperfection and limitations of the sensors of the system. In future, we plan to investigate how our approach can be generalized to synthesize strategies for systems from a library of controllers with *partial* information.

Acknowledgement

This research was partially supported by awards NSF Expeditions in Computing CCF 1138996, AFRL $FA8650$-15-C-2546, ONR $N000141310778$, ARO $W911NF$-15-1-0592, NSF 1550212 and DARPA $W911NF$-16-1-0001.

8. REFERENCES

[1] R. Alur, S. Moarref, and U. Topcu. Pattern-based refinement of assume-guarantee specifications in reactive synthesis. *TACAS*, 2015.

[2] C. Baier, J. Klein, and S. Klüppelholz. A compositional framework for controller synthesis. In *Concurrency Theory*. 2011.

[3] R. Bloem, H. N. Gabow, and F. Somenzi. An algorithm for strongly connected component analysis in n log n symbolic steps. *FMSD*, 2006.

[4] R. Bloem, B. Jobstmann, N. Piterman, A. Pnueli, and Y. Sa'ar. Synthesis of reactive (1) designs. *Journal of Computer and System Sciences*, 2012.

[5] E. M. Clarke, O. Grumberg, and D. Peled. *Model checking*. MIT press, 1999.

[6] E. Filiot, N. Jin, and J.-F. Raskin. Antichains and compositional algorithms for LTL synthesis. *FMSD*, 2011.

[7] E. Frazzoli, M. Dahleh, and E. Feron. Maneuver-based motion planning for nonlinear systems with symmetries. *IEEE Transactions on Robotics*, 2005.

[8] H. Kress-Gazit, G. E. Fainekos, and G. J. Pappas. Temporal-logic-based reactive mission and motion planning. *IEEE Transactions on Robotics*, 2009.

[9] H. Kress-gazit, T. Wongpiromsarn, and U. Topcu. Correct, reactive robot control from abstraction and temporal logic specifications.

[10] O. Kupferman, N. Piterman, and M. Vardi. Safraless compositional synthesis. In *CAV 2006*, 2006.

[11] J. Liu, N. Ozay, U. Topcu, and R. M. Murray. Synthesis of reactive switching protocols from temporal logic specifications. *IEEE Transactions on Automatic Control*, 58(7), 2013.

[12] Y. Lustig and M. Y. Vardi. Synthesis from component libraries. In *Foundations of Software Science and Computational Structures*. Springer, 2009.

[13] O. Maler, A. Pnueli, and J. Sifakis. On the synthesis of discrete controllers for timed systems. In *Symposium on Theoretical Aspects of Computer Science*, pages 229–242, 1995.

[14] I. Saha, R. Ramaithitima, V. Kumar, G. J. Pappas, and S. A. Seshia. Automated composition of motion primitives for multi-robot systems from safe LTL specifications. In *IROS*, 2014.

[15] S. Sohail and F. Somenzi. Safety first: A two-stage algorithm for LTL games. In *FMCAD*, 2009.

[16] P. Tabuada. *Verification and control of hybrid systems: a symbolic approach.* Springer Science & Business Media, 2009.

[17] A. Vahidi. Jdd. http://javaddlib.sourceforge.net/jdd/index.html.

[18] T. Wongpiromsarn, U. Topcu, and R. M. Murray. Receding horizon temporal logic planning. *AC*, 2012.

Nonlinear Controller Synthesis and Automatic Workspace Partitioning for Reactive High-Level Behaviors

Jonathan A. DeCastro
Sibley School of Mechanical and Aerospace Engineering
Cornell University
Ithaca, NY, USA
jad455@cornell.edu

Hadas Kress-Gazit
Sibley School of Mechanical and Aerospace Engineering
Cornell University
Ithaca, NY, USA
hadaskg@cornell.edu

ABSTRACT

Motivated by the provably-correct execution of complex reactive tasks for robots with nonlinear, under-actuated dynamics, our focus is on the synthesis of a library of low-level controllers that implements the behaviors of a high-level controller. The synthesized controllers should allow the robot to react to its environment whenever dynamically feasible given the geometry of the workspace. For any behaviors that cannot guarantee the task given the dynamics, such behaviors should be transformed into dynamically-informative revisions to the high-level task. We therefore propose a framework for synthesizing such low-level controllers and, moreover, offer an approach for re-partitioning and abstracting the system based on the synthesized controller library.

We accomplish these goals by introducing a synthesis approach that we call *conforming funnels*, in which controllers are synthesized with respect to the given high-level behaviors, the geometrical constraints of the workspace, and a robot dynamics model. Our approach computes controllers using a verification approach that optimizes over a wide range of possible controllers to guarantee the geometrical constraints are satisfied. We also devise an algorithm that uses the controllers to re-partition the workspace and automatically adapt the high-level specification with a new discrete abstraction generated on these new partitions. We demonstrate the controllers generated by our synthesis framework in an experimental setting with a KUKA youBot executing a box transportation task.

Keywords

motion planning, controller synthesis, nonlinear systems, verification, barrier certificates

1. INTRODUCTION

Reactive synthesis frameworks have shown promise for robotics applications requiring guaranteed behaviors in unpredictable environments [27, 14]. From a high-level specification, a controller is automatically synthesized, without needing to code each behavior by hand. This enables sensor-rich systems to execute tasks in a provably-correct manner. For the workspace shown in Fig. 1, reactive synthesis addresses tasks such as: "If you see a box, move to the pick-up location. If you are carrying a box, then visit a requested drop-off location. Always avoid people."

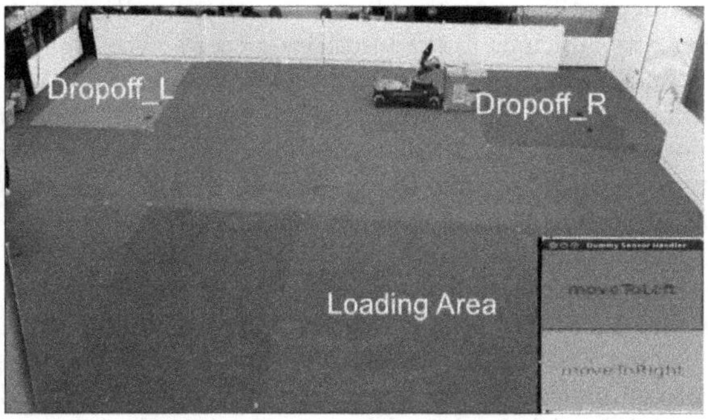

Figure 1: A robot executing a user-assisted warehouse supply task.

The existence of such hybrid (mixed discrete- and continuous-state) controllers relies on the the ability to extend high-level guarantees (on a discrete abstraction of the system) to the low-level (continuous) dynamical system. While recent activity toward this end has focused on frameworks that use a combination of on-line and off-line approaches for correct-by-construction controller synthesis for nonlinear systems (e.g. [18, 26, 16, 27, 2, 9]), we aim to provide *a-priori* guarantees (i.e. at synthesis time) that the task is implementable on the physical system.

One of the goals of this work is an approach that synthesizes continuous controllers for a dynamical system to implement the behaviors of a finite state machine in response to a dynamic environment (factors outside the robot's control) given the geometrical constraints of the workspace. We build on an existing framework that implements high-level behaviors and verifies the resulting controllers over a wide range of possible states, given a pre-defined low-level controller [9]. A high-level behavior consists of atomic actions that implement the transitions of a state machine, possibly in reaction to sensor events (e.g. motion between certain regions of the workspace, while avoiding other regions). To address the potential for conservatism of existing approaches that return a verified set of system states given a specific con-

HSCC'16, April 12–14, 2016, Vienna, Austria

DOI: http://dx.doi.org/10.1145/2883817.2883832

troller and system model (e.g. [9]), we aim for an approach that accepts a workspace, trajectory and nonlinear system model, and returns a feedback controller in addition to a verified set of continuous states.

If no such controllers can be found, there are a number of ways to revise the task in such a way that low-level controllers can be computed. For instance, if the synthesized controllers are unable to verify the act of moving to the pick-up location and avoid collisions with a person, then the statement "A person should never appear in the environment" could be added to the specification. However, guarantees without environment reactivity may be overly conservative on the part of the robot. Therefore, our second goal is to generate dynamically-informative revisions to the high-level task, alerting the user to any conditions – specifically, assumptions on what the environment is allowed to do – that are sufficient for the task to succeed. We aim for a framework that is able to automatically compute partitions in a manner that is consistent with the dynamics, resulting in more specific user feedback such as "When heading to a drop-off location, assume that a person will not appear when within 1 meter of the drop-off location".

The first main contribution of this paper is a new reachability-based controller design procedure, termed *conforming funnels* that takes into consideration a high-level behavior and the geometrical constraints of a workspace, providing a certificate (funnel) that the controller will implement the desired high-level behavior. We do so by introducing a new synthesis algorithm that combines the advantages of the invariant funnels approach [22] for nonlinear system verification and control barrier functions [20] to provide the ability to "shape" the feedback controller, and hence the resulting funnel, according to the workspace geometry. We provide a computational framework for automating the generation of such controllers as part of a library of controllers that are composed together to execute a high-level task. The resulting funnel conforms tightly to geometrical constraints where necessary, enabling the system to appropriately react to the environment while guaranteeing that the dynamical system adheres to all required high-level behaviors (e.g. collision avoidance). We do not address the challenge of finding optimal trajectories; hence we do not claim completeness in the sense that the framework will not necessarily find controllers wherever dynamically feasible.

Our second main contribution is a technique for generating a finer partitioning of the existing workspace based on an existing low-level controller that cannot implement a particular high-level behavior. New workspace regions that result from such a partitioning carry with them information concerning the verified behaviors of the dynamical system when the synthesized low-level controllers are executed at runtime. For instance, a partitioning may be created if, in the above example, a controller cannot verify collision-free motion for all trajectories that execute a robot's motion to the drop-off location. The new region for this case may indicate the set of states where the robot is unable to respond the appearance of a person when activating a certain low-level controller. We contribute a method for reasoning about such partitions via incremental changes to a discrete abstraction to make it consistent with the verified low-level controllers. In the context of a scheme developed recently for automatically synthesizing revisions to reactive specifications, [8], our proposed approach to finding revisions to the high-level specification may be viewed as a generalization when the underlying discrete abstraction depends on the result of low-level controller synthesis.

The dynamics-based partitioning approach can be displayed visually to users as an aid in explaining the implications of such revisions on the allowed environment behaviors. In this work, we do this by way of a labeled workspace map, which visually complements verbal statements explaining the revisions, which is demonstrated via both simulated and physical experiments on an actual robot. We also note that the creation of such abstractions (and hence revisions) is uniquely tied to our approach to low-level synthesis. With our proposed conforming funnels approach, we generate controllers that ensure that reactive behaviors are dynamically feasible. We evaluate for a specific example, the proposed synthesis framework against an existing approach to low-level controller synthesis. Through physical experiments on a KUKA youBot, we furthermore show that the trajectories generated by the physical platform remain within the funnels computed using our approach.

2. RELATED WORK

Numerous works have studied approaches to high-level planning that explicitly take into consideration the dynamics of an arbitrary nonlinear system. For static environments, Wolff, Topcu and Murray [26] synthesize a trajectory of control inputs by solving a constrained reachability problem that satisfies a given specification. Bhatia, et. al. [3] and Maly, et. al. [18] introduce two variants of a multi-layered synthesis paradigm applicable to nonlinear dynamics. In those approaches, obstacles that are unaccounted for at synthesis time are addressed by updating the planner when such obstacles are encountered at runtime. An abstraction-based approach is introduced in Wongpiromsarn, Topcu and Murray [27] that deals with nonlinear dynamics by formulating the synthesis task as a receding-horizon control problem. Our approach differs in that we rely on controllers constructed ahead of time with guarantees that the controllers can be executed over a wide range of continuous states. Rather than updating the controller on-the-fly to account for dynamics, in our approach we identify any necessary changes to the abstraction at synthesis time, providing an ability to alert the user to any necessary revisions to the specification.

A number of existing works address the reachability-based controller design problem for nonlinear systems. Works such as Tomlin, Lygeros and Sastry [23] and Mitchell, Bayen and Tomlin [19] are among those that solve the reach-avoid problem in a resolution-complete manner, while Burridge, Rizzi and Koditschek [5], Tedrake, et. al. [22] and Maidens and Arcak [17] offer methods that are generally not complete, but for which a solution can be found quickly for reasonable state dimensions. While those in the former category generally treat systems up to degree four, we opt for the trajectory-based approaches in the latter category that are capable of handling larger state dimensions. Specifically, our controller synthesis procedure is based on the invariant funnels method introduced in [22]. The general approach has been shown to verify a variety of nonlinear systems, including those having up to 12 states. Conner, Rizzi and Choset [7] introduce an approach for sequencing together a set of verified motion primitives satisfying the transitions of a state machine encoding a non-reactive task. To accommodate *reactive* tasks, DeCastro and Kress-Gazit [9] introduce an algorithm for generating a library of atomic (low-level) controllers for a wide range of nonlinear systems satisfying the transitions of a finite state machine. The synthesis step can be repeated an arbitrary number of times in order to add to the verified space. Compared with grid-based reach-avoid methods, e.g. [19, 23], the funnels-based approach scales favorably with the order of the model, at the expense of completeness.

Our proposed conforming funnels approach is closely related to the control barrier functions (CBF) approach introduced by Wieland and Allgower [25]. The CBF approach uses synthesized functions known as barrier functions [20] to construct a controller for a nonlinear system that yields trajectories that avoid unsafe regions of the state space. The approach was later unified with control Lyapunov functions (CLF) by Romdlony and Jayawardhan [21] by extending the properties of such controllers to assure asymptotic convergence to a stabilizing point in addition to having guarantees for safety. We use these basic constructions in our work to locally modify a funnel by first computing regions of attraction to points along a trajectory without consideration to the problem constraints, and then compute a CBF to assemble a low-level controller that can guarantee invariance to any unsafe regions with respect to a specified initial set.

Our framework for computing partitions of given workspace map departs from existing works (e.g. Kloetzer and Belta [13]) in that we deal with tasks that are reactive in nature, whereas existing works generally do not consider reactive environments at synthesis time. The workspace partitioning scheme developed in this work can be used in conjunction with existing abstraction update procedures in the literature (e.g. Clarke [6] and Liu and Ozay [15]), and hence can be seen as complementary to those works. The main difference is that our abstractions are defined on coarse partitions based on continuous rather than on a uniform grid, which reduces complexity. Automatic generation of discrete abstractions have also been introduced recently in DeCastro, Raman and Kress-Gazit [10]. In the proposed approach, we specifically focus on the problem of adding dynamics-informed partitions, whereas in that work, the existing partitioning was used as the basis for constructing a new abstraction. When used for reactive synthesis, our dynamically-feasible synthesis framework may be viewed as an instance of *counterexample-guided inductive synthesis* (CEGIS) [1], where an abstraction is synthesized on the basis of the computed atomic controllers and their reachable sets (the counterexample).

3. PRELIMINARIES

We define several basic concepts that lay the foundation for the remainder of this paper: the finite state machine, trajectory stabilizing controller, and the invariant funnels method.

In this paper, we consider systems of the control-affine form

$$\dot{x} = f(x) + g(x)u, \tag{1}$$

where $x \in \mathbb{R}^n$ is the continuous state of the robot, $u \in \mathbb{R}^m$ the command input of the robot at time $t \in \mathbb{R}_{\geq 0}$ and f and g are smooth, continuous vector fields with respect to x. Note that a wide variety of robot dynamics (mobile robots, manipulators, walking robots) fit within this system class.

Notation: Given some $T \in \mathbb{R}_{\geq 0}$ and a function $\mathcal{L}(t) \subset \mathbb{R}^n$ defined for all $t \in [0, T]$, denote the set cover by $\mathcal{L}(t)$ for all $t \in [0, T]$ as $[\mathcal{L}]$. In particular, $[\mathcal{L}] = \{x \mid \exists t \in [0, T] \text{ s.t. } x \in \mathcal{L}(t)\}$.

3.1 Finite State Machine

For the purposes of our discussion, we assume in this work we are given a finite-state machine $\mathcal{A} = (AP_e, AP_s, S, S_0, \delta)$, where AP_e and AP_s are sets of atomic propositions corresponding, respectively, to the *environment* (sensed events that the robot must react to) and *system* (the actions of the robot); S is the set of (discrete) states; $S_0 \subseteq S$ is the set of initial states; and $\delta \subseteq S \times 2^{AP_e} \times S$ represents a state transition relation of the current state, the current value of the environment input, and the successor state, respectively.

For each state $s_i \in S$, let $X_i \subset \mathbb{R}^n$ be a continuous set in a space of dimension n associated with s_i. Also, denote ∂X_i to be the boundary of X_i.

3.2 Trajectory-Stabilizing Control

Given an initial state $x(0) \in X_0 \subset \mathbb{R}^n$, where X_0 is the initial set and a time horizon $T > 0$, denote $\xi : [0, T] \to \mathbb{R}^n$ as a continuous finite-time trajectory of states under $\dot{x} = f(x) + g(x)\mu(t)$. Here, $\mu : [0, T] \to \mathbb{R}^m$ is a trajectory of control inputs. To generate the trajectory $\xi(t)$ and determine the final time T, we use a feedback linearization-based control strategy to drive the system to a point in Cartesian space. Trajectories may also be found using trajectory optimization.

About $\xi(t)$, take the linearization of (1) to be $\dot{\tilde{x}} = A_\xi(t)\tilde{x}(t) + B_\xi(t)\tilde{u}(t)$, where $\tilde{x}(t) = x(t) - \xi(t)$ and $\tilde{u}(t) = u(t) - \mu(t)$. For a given trajectory and a linearization of the system, our task is to design a trajectory-stabilizing controller. We do so by solving the time-varying LQR problem [12] for the linearized system, whose result yields the full-state feedback control input $u(t) = K(t)(x(t) - \xi(t)) + \mu(t)$. Under this feedback, we denote the closed-loop system as

$$\dot{x} = f(x) + g(x)\left[K(t)(x(t) - \xi(t)) + \mu(t)\right] = \hat{f}(x, t), \tag{2}$$

where the closed-loop system $\hat{f}(x, t)$ is defined for all $t \in [0, T]$.

3.3 Invariant Funnels

We now summarize the invariant funnels method of [22], which takes as input a trajectory and stabilizing controller introduced in Section 3.2. Define a Lyapunov function for (2) to be a positive-definite function $V(x, t)$ with $\dot{V}(x, t) = \frac{\partial V(x,t)}{\partial x}\hat{f}(x, t) < 0$. For some $t \in [0, T]$ and $\rho : [0, T] \to \mathbb{R}_{\geq 0}$, define the *$\rho$-sub-level set* of $V(x, t)$ as

$$\mathcal{L}(t) = \{x \mid V(x, t) \leq \rho(t)\}.$$

Let $X_i, X_j \subset \mathbb{R}^n$ be regions in the configuration space where the regions are adjacent. Consider a trajectory ξ whose initial value is $\xi(0) \in X_i$ and final value is $\xi(T) \in X_j$ and at every time instant stays in $X_i \cup X_j$. The problem of computing an *invariant funnel* is one where we verify the largest set of states about ξ that satisfy the same properties as ξ; namely, reachability from X_i to X_j and invariance to $X_i \cup X_j$ (safety from entering/colliding with the complement of $X_i \cup X_j$). Such a set is found via the following maximization problem:

$$\max_{\rho(t) \geq 0} \rho(t), \qquad t \in [0, T] \tag{3}$$

$$\text{s.t.} \quad V(x,t) \le \rho(t) \implies \dot{V}(x,t) \le \dot{\rho}(t), \quad \forall t \in [0,T], (4)$$

$$\mathcal{L}_{ij}(T) = \{x \mid V(x,T) \le \rho(T)\} \subseteq G, \quad (5)$$

for a goal set $G \subseteq X_j$. Computational tools such as the semidefinite programming solvers SeDUMI and MOSEK can solve a time-discretized form of the above problem, when expressed as a sums-of-squares program. Such tools apply to systems that are expressed as differential equations that are polynomial in their arguments; for this reason, we assume system models of this form throughout this paper. In [9], additional constraints are introduced to compute *bounded funnels* that are guaranteed to stay within an invariant $X_i \cup X_j$,

$$\mathcal{L}_{ij}(t) = \{x \mid V(x,t) \le \rho(t)\} \subseteq X_i \cup X_j, \quad (6)$$

for all $t \in [0,T]$. We denote any bounded funnel $\mathcal{L}_{ij}(t)$ as a *transition funnel* if $i \neq j$ and any bounded funnel $\mathcal{L}_i(t) = \mathcal{L}_{ii}(t)$ as an *inward-facing funnel*.

We briefly summarize the algorithm in [9], which provides a twofold procedure for constructing a library of controllers for all transitions in a state machine $\mathcal{A}$. First, let I_i be the index set of successors to state s_i; i.e. $I_i = \{k \mid \exists \sigma \in 2^{AP_e} : (s_k, \sigma, s_i) \in \delta\}$. For a particular $s_i \in S$ and $j \in I_i$, construct a controller and label the associated funnels $\mathcal{L}_{ij}$.

Next, if I_i contains two or more elements, additional controllers must be created to fulfill *reactive behaviors* of $\mathcal{A}$; that is, behaviors that ensure, for all time instants along any trajectory in $\mathcal{L}_{ij}$ enabling the transition from X_i to X_j, the system is able to react to sensor inputs and move instead to X_k, $k \in I_i$, $k \neq j$. In this case, denote the *reactive-composition* (RC) set as the set in which any outgoing transition from the current region to successor regions is possible, i.e. $\bigcap_{k \in I_i} [\mathcal{L}_{ik}]$. For each $\mathcal{L}_{ij}$ and $\mathcal{L}_i$, compute a new inward-facing funnel $\mathcal{L}_i$ whose initial set is taken from $\mathcal{L}_{ij}$ such that $[\mathcal{L}_{ij}] \cap \partial X_i \subseteq [\mathcal{L}_i]$ and whose final set $G = \bigcap_{j \in I_j} [\mathcal{L}_{ij}]$, each time storing them into the library. The composition requirement $[\mathcal{L}_{ij}] \cap \partial X_i \subseteq [\mathcal{L}_i]$ assures that the system can react to the environment regardless of which trajectory is used in $\mathcal{L}_{ij}$, up to the time at which it leaves X_i. More precisely, for all times t for which $\xi(t) \in [\mathcal{L}_{ij}] \cap X_i$, there exists a time $t' \ge t$ for which $\xi(t') \in [\mathcal{L}_i]$.

For example, consider a unicycle model consisting of three continuous states (x, y, θ): two Cartesian displacements and an orientation angle and whose command input is its angular rate, ω. The unicycle is assumed able to turn but with turning radius limited to remain below a fixed threshold and may only move in the forward direction with fixed velocity. For the example shown in Fig. 2, a controller and funnel $\mathcal{L}_{12}$ is constructed to implement movement between regions X_1 to X_2 using an under-actuated unicycle model. With $\mathcal{L}_{12}$, another controller and funnel $\mathcal{L}_1$ is computed to implement the transition keeping the system in X_1. The intersection of $[\mathcal{L}_{12}]$ and $[\mathcal{L}_1]$ (the RC set) indicates the states in which both transitions (s_1,`True`, s_2) and (s_1,`False`, s_1) can be achieved. Note that the maximization in (3) helps us to achieve a maximal set with respect to the given trajectory. Finally, the goal set G is determined from composition requirements. In particular, the set G when computing $\mathcal{L}_{12}$ is X_2, while G for $\mathcal{L}_1$ is the computed funnel $\mathcal{L}_{12}$. For the remainder of this paper, we assume funnels are computed in this manner.

Note that that above algorithm can fail at finding such an inward-facing funnel $\mathcal{L}_i$ in certain cases. For example, consider the unconstrained funnel shown in Fig. 2b. The funnel shown satisfies the reactivity requirement $[\mathcal{L}_{12}] \cap \partial X_1 \subseteq [\mathcal{L}_1]$, but not the invariance condition $[\mathcal{L}_1] \subseteq X_1$. If the funnel were smaller, it could satisfy invariance, but at the expense of reactivity for all trajectories in $\mathcal{L}_{12}$. The proposed approach outlined in the next section directly addresses this issue by finding a controller and funnel for a given trajectory that satisfies both the reactivity condition and the invariance condition.

4. PROBLEM STATEMENT

In this paper, we address the following two problems.

Problem 1 (Fulfillment of a reactive behavior for $s_i \in S$). *Given the dynamics f and g, a transition funnel $\mathcal{L}_{ij}$, region X_i, a goal set $G \subseteq X_i$, find a trajectory ξ, μ where $\xi(t) \in X_i$ for all $t \in [0,T]$ and synthesize a low-level controller $u(t)$ stabilizing the system to ξ and a funnel $\mathcal{B}(t) \subseteq X_i$ such that $[\mathcal{L}_{ij}] \cap X_i \subseteq [\mathcal{B}]$.*

Problem 2 (Partial fulfillment of a reactive behavior for $s_i \in S$, refining the workspace partitions). *If Problem 1 fails to be solved, given the dynamics f and g, a transition funnel $\mathcal{L}_{ij}$, region X_i, a goal set $G \subseteq X_i$, find a trajectory ξ, μ where $\xi(t) \in X_i$ for all $t \in [0,T]$ and synthesize a low-level controller $u(t)$ and a funnel $\mathcal{B}(t) \subseteq X_i$. Compute a new region X_{ij} defining the portion of the controller $\mathcal{L}_{ij}$ for which reactive behaviors cannot be attained, updating the mission specification accordingly.*

Note that Problem 1 does limit the discussion to inward-facing funnels. We may find *transition* funnels for $(s_\ell, \cdot, s_i)$ by setting a goal $G \subseteq X_j$, replacing the invariant X_i with $X_i \cup X_j$, and relaxing the composition requirement to $\mathcal{L}_{\ell i}(T) \subseteq [\mathcal{B}]$, provided we are given $\mathcal{L}_{\ell i}$ such that $\mathcal{L}_{\ell i}(T) \subseteq X_i$.

5. CONFORMING FUNNELS

In this section, we introduce an approach that attempts to compute a bounded funnel when the procedure outlined in Section 3.3 fails to do so. We do this by making use of the notion of control barrier functions; functions whose parameters can be tailored to achieve a certificate of safety with respect to an unsafe set. Such functions parameterize a nonlinear feedback control law that is executed by the system for the certificate to hold. In our case, for a given trajectory, we generate a sequence of certificates and feedback controllers for the system, giving rise to a funnel that conforms to the required invariant set.

In more precise terms, given trajectories ξ, μ, and controller K, the problem is to find controller parameters that verify the largest set of states that satisfies the invariance and reachability properties of ξ with respect to an invariant set. The controller leverages the proven idea of unified control barrier functions and control Lyapunov functions, which is extended in this section to the case of time-varying trajectory stabilization. While the developments in this section are largely inspired by the work of [25, 21], they are complementary to those works as we also offer a computational framework through sums-of-squares optimization to numerically compute such barrier functions and controllers.

5.1 Using Control Barrier Functions to Satisfy State Constraints

Suppose we extend the control input as $u(t) = K(t)(x(t) - \xi(t)) - \mu(t) + \bar{u}(t) = U(t) + \bar{u}(t)$. We then obtain the following

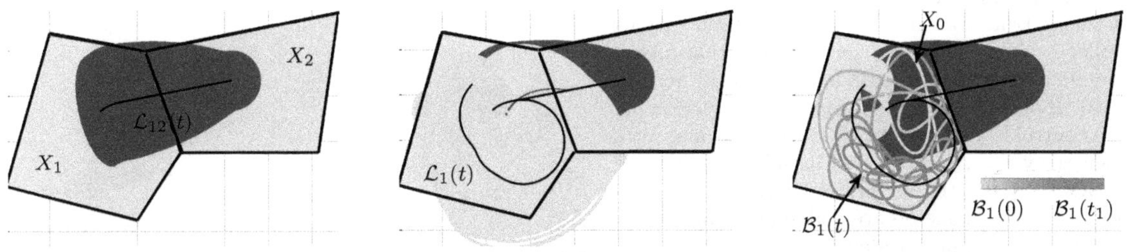

(a) (b) (c)

Figure 2: Constructing conforming funnels for a state machine: $S = \{s_1, s_2\}$ with transitions $\{(s_1,\texttt{True}, s_2), (s_1,\texttt{False}, s_1)\}$. (a) shows a funnel $\mathcal{L}_{12}$ computed for a three-state unicycle model (the funnel shown is a projection onto $\mathbb{R}^2$) for a low-level controller satisfying the transition. (b) shows a funnel $\mathcal{L}_1$ (green) that violates the invariant preventing it from entering X_2. (c) shows a conforming funnel $\mathcal{B}_1(t)$ that satisfies the transition of staying in X_1. $\mathcal{B}_1(t)$ consists of a segment of $\mathcal{L}_1$ (green), and a barrier whose zero-level set is shown at specific time instants.

augmented system

$$\dot{x} = \hat{f}(x,t) + g(x)\bar{u}, \qquad t \in [0,T]. \tag{7}$$

The authors of [25] show that there exists a control $\bar{u}(x)$ yielding a control barrier function (CBF) that ensures safety of trajectories within a nonlinear system. In this case, the CBF provides a certificate of *safety*, but in general does not guarantee convergence, which we require in order to ensure reachability of trajectories from an initial set to a goal set. Theorem 3 in [21] remedies this by expressing a set of conditions to construct a unified CBF and control Lyapunov function (CLF) to ensure safety of a time-invariant system whose static equilibrium lies in the interior of the barrier.

In this work, we extend this to the time-varying case for systems of the form of (7), where the problem is to find a controller that stabilizes to a *trajectory* rather than a static equilibrium.

Consider a function $B(x,t)$ defined over an interval $t \in [0,T]$ and let $a(x,t) = \frac{\partial B(x,t)}{\partial x}\hat{f}(x,t) + \frac{\partial B(x,t)}{\partial t}$, $b^T(x) = \frac{\partial B(x,t)}{\partial x}g(x)$, and X_u denote the unsafe set. The conditions for the time-varying problem assert that, if $B(x,t)$ can be found that satisfies the following conditions:

$$x \in X_u \implies B(x,t) \geq 0 \tag{8}$$

$$\frac{\partial B(x,t)}{\partial x}g(x) = 0 \implies \frac{\partial B(x,t)}{\partial x}\hat{f}(x,t) + \frac{\partial B(x,t)}{\partial t} < 0 \tag{9}$$

$$x \in X_0 \implies B(x,t) \leq 0 \tag{10}$$

then the control law:

$$\bar{u} = \begin{cases} -\frac{a+\sqrt{a^2+\gamma^2 b^T b}}{b^T b} b \text{ for } b \neq 0 \\ 0 \text{ for } b = 0 \end{cases} \tag{11}$$

ensures the safety of the system with respect to the initial conditions X_0, where $\gamma > 0$ is a tunable parameter. If found, $B(x,t)$ is a *time-varying control barrier function* (TV-CBF). In words, for a given $t \in [0,t_1]$, with $0 < t_1 \leq T$, the level set $B(x,t) = 0$ certifies a safety bound where $B(x,t)$ is strictly positive inside X_u, and strictly negative within the initial set X_0, provided that the control input $\bar{u}$ is applied for all x on the barrier certificate (i.e. in the set $\{x \mid B(x,t) = 0\}$).

In similar fashion to [21], we also show that the control law $\bar{u}$ (namely (11)), when applied in the interior of the barrier ($B(\xi(t),t) \leq 0$) simultaneously stabilizes the system to the trajectory and keeps the system safe within the barrier. The following provides a statement on the safety and reachability properties if the above conditions hold true:

Proposition 1. *Given the trajectory-stabilizing feedback system (2), an unsafe set X_u, and some initial set $X_0 \subset \mathbb{R}^n \backslash X_u$, then a feasible solution to (8)–(10) yields a safe trajectory with respect to X_u and guarantees trajectory convergence if $u(t) = U(t) + \bar{u}(t)$, with $\bar{u}(t)$ satisfying (11).*

Proof. To show that $\bar{u}(t)$ satisfying (11) gives rise to a trajectory stabilizing controller follows by showing that $B(x,t)$ is smooth (as per Lemma 3.6 in [11]), and that it results in a system that is a control Lyapunov function. Smoothness follows trivially by construction of $B(x,t)$. When $\frac{\partial B(x,t)}{\partial x}g(x) \neq 0$, then

$$\frac{\partial B(x,t)}{\partial x}\hat{f}(x,t) + \frac{\partial B(x,t)}{\partial x}g(x)\bar{u}(t) = -\sqrt{\left\|\frac{\partial B(x,t)}{\partial x}\hat{f}(x,t)\right\|^2 + \gamma\left\|\frac{\partial B(x,t)}{\partial x}g(x)\right\|^2} < 0.$$

for $\gamma > 0$ and $t \in [0,t_1]$. Otherwise (when $\frac{\partial B(x,t)}{\partial x}g(x) = 0$), $\frac{\partial B(x,t)}{\partial x}\hat{f}(x,t) + \frac{\partial B(x,t)}{\partial t} < 0$ holds, by construction, from condition (9). As $u(t) = U(t) + \bar{u}(t)$ is applied whenever $B(x,t) \leq 0$, and, for a given $t \in [0,T]$, then $B(x,t) = \min_x B(x,t)$ precisely when $x = \xi(t)$, the system is attractive to the trajectory.

We must also show that such controllers guarantee invariance to the barrier. If (8)–(10) is feasible for X_0 then, by construction, there exists a $B(x,t)$ for which $B(x,t) = 0$ separates X_u and X_0 for any given $t \in [0,t_1]$. □

Notice that the problem of finding the TV-CBF in (8)–(10) is within the sums-of-squares class of problems for cases where the system and constraint sets are polynomial in x and t. We have encoded this as such and adopt the package MOSEK in this work as the solver. Note also that the problem of trajectory stabilization generalizes many aspects of robotics in the case where there is no single global equilibrium; for example, the under-actuated unicycle model introduced in the previous section. For problems where it is possible to find a sufficiently large region of attraction about a static equilibrium, the time-invariant counterpart of Proposition 1 will suffice (Theorem 3 of [21]).

To summarize the result, assume we have an augmented system of the form (7) that is stable about a neighborhood of a nominal trajectory ξ, μ over a finite time horizon $t \in [0, T]$ (recall that this is true because u subsumes a time-varying LQR controller). Solve for a barrier function that meets state constraints (required invariants for the funnel) according to (8)–(10). If one is found, then this barrier function parameterizes a control law of the form (11) that, when applied to the augmented system, ensures that, for all states starting in the set $\{B(x,t) \leq 0\}$, the system is guaranteed to converge to the trajectory (make progress along the trajectory) and remain invariant to the zero-level set of $B(x,t)$ for all $t \in [0,T]$. The resulting set $\mathcal{B}(t) : \mathbb{R}_{\geq 0} \to \{x \mid B(x,t) \leq 0\}$ is a conforming funnel for the feedback-controlled system.

5.2 Computational Approach

As opposed to the funnel formulation of Section 3.3 in which the objective is to search for a $\rho(t)$ for a function with fixed parameterization, the TV-CBF conditions search directly for a barrier that is a function of x. This generally requires a larger number of decision variables, giving rise to a greater number of computations. We therefore outline a procedure for computing funnels using the TV-CBF objectives with small computational expense by bootstrapping it with an unconstrained funnel.

The procedure is as follows. As pictured in Fig. 3a–3b, compute first an unconstrained funnel according to the conditions (3) (i.e. without the addition of (6)). If this happens to satisfy the constraints (6), then we accept this funnel and return. Otherwise, as illustrated in Fig. 3c, select t_1 as the minimum time where $X_i \cup X_j$ contains the portion of $\mathcal{L}(t)$ for $t \in [t_1, T]$. On the interval $(t_1, T]$, we let $\mathcal{L}_{suff} = \{\mathcal{L}(t) \mid t \in (t_1, T]\}$ be a *suffix* of the original funnel that is safe with respect to the invariants over for all $t \in (t_1, T]$. We then set the initial condition as $X_0 = \mathcal{L}_{ij}(t^*)$ (where t^* will be introduced in Sec. 6.1). In order to enforce composability of $\mathcal{B}(t)$ with the suffix funnel, we ensure that $\mathcal{B}$ is contained inside $\mathcal{L}$ at time t_1. Therefore, we take the unsafe set X_u to be $\mathcal{L}(t_1)$ at time $t = t_1$; at all prior times $t = [0, t_1)$, we set $X_u = \mathbb{R}^n \backslash X_i$. We also set the constraint that $[\mathcal{L}_{ij}] \cap X_i \implies B(x,t) = 0$. This constraint ensures that the generated funnel is valid with respect to the reactivity condition for all trajectories in $\mathcal{L}_{ij}$.

We then proceed to compute a $\mathcal{B}(t)$ according to (8) as per Proposition 1 over the interval $[0, t_1]$. The computed conforming funnel and suffix funnel combine to form an aggregate funnel that verifies reachability to the goal set G and safety with respect to X_u for a well-defined neighborhood about the trajectory:

$$\mathcal{B}(t) = \begin{cases} \{x \mid B(x,t) = 0\} & \text{for } 0 \leq t \leq t_1 \\ \mathcal{L}_{suff}(t) & \text{for } t_1 < t \leq T \end{cases}$$

Note that $\mathcal{B}(t)$ is merely $\mathcal{L}(t)$ for the case where the TV-CBF computations are not necessary.

Observe that we do not preserve the portion of the funnel *before* it leaves the invariant set because the barrier computations require an over-approximation to the initial set in order to guarantee composition of funnels. At such time instants, this imposes tight constraints on the resulting barrier (the barrier would have to be larger than the last non-red ellipse shown in Fig. 3b, but smaller than the boundary). In practice, this has rendered the optimization problem infeasible in the majority of cases tested. Note that this controller will not exhibit Zeno behavior, since the the barrier function is smooth by construction and the control law involves no state-dependent switching.

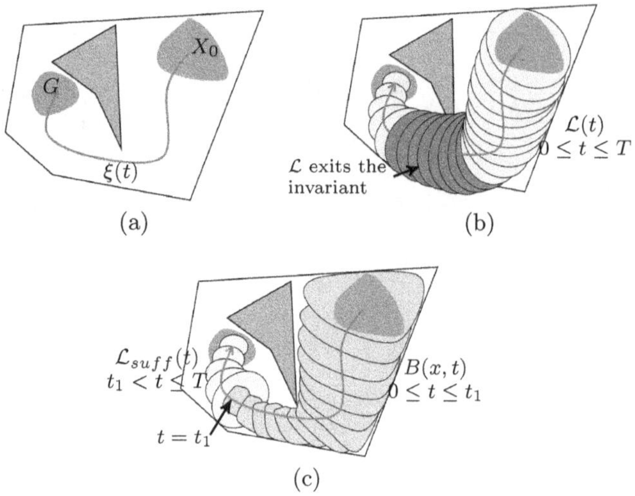

Figure 3: Generating conforming funnels. (a) A trajectory is created steering the system from the start set X_0 to G. (b) A fixed-parameter funnel is created, and checked for collisions. (c) $\mathcal{L}$ exits the invariant up to $t = t_1$; therefore a conforming funnel is computed respecting the invariant up to t_1.

6. WORKSPACE RE-PARTITIONING AND ABSTRACTION GENERATION

In the case where conforming funnels cannot be created for the high-level behavior (for the choice of trajectory), we may use controllers that do not verify the behavior exactly to create new workspace partitions, and update the discrete abstraction of the system on those partitions. In this vein, we introduce the second main contribution of this paper: an algorithm for constructing controllers and partitions in the case that a controller has not been found to satisfy a particular high-level behavior. We furthermore introduce a procedure for updating a specification written as linear temporal logic based on the results of the partitioning. The approach to partitioning lends well to automatic generation of intuitive explanations to users in the case where no satisfying finite state machine can be found; we discuss these implications via a case study.

6.1 Partial Fulfillment of High-Level Behaviors

Our goal is to find inward funnels for the entirety of the time the system spends in X_i. Notice that if, for a particular transition funnel $\mathcal{L}_{ij}$, a funnel $\mathcal{B}_i$ is found according to the criteria set forth in the Sec. 5, the system is reactive all the way up to the boundary; i.e. $[\mathcal{L}_{ij}] \cap \partial X_i \subseteq [\mathcal{B}_i]$. This means the transition $(s_i, \cdot, s_j)$ in $\mathcal{A}$ has been implemented exactly.

Otherwise, there exists a gap between the inward funnel and the region boundary where the robot may no longer reach the RC set without first crossing the boundary. We call such a gap a *reactivity gap* which is nonzero whenever there exist trajectories in $\mathcal{L}_{ij}$ that do not intersect with the set $\mathcal{B}_i$ up to the point at which it leaves X_i, i.e. $[\mathcal{L}_{ij}] \cap \partial X_i \not\subseteq [\mathcal{B}_i]$. Strictly speaking, this would result in failure to generate low-level controllers that satisfy $\mathcal{A}$, or else necessitate searching for new transition funnels $\mathcal{L}_{ij}$ that result in zero reactivity gap, a potentially expensive process with no termination guarantees.

In order to proceed with generating controllers in the case where such a transition cannot be fulfilled, we modify the original specification via a re-partitioned workspace given the existing set of low-level controllers. We do so with an approach that minimizes the reactivity gap modulo the given $\mathcal{L}_{ij}$. This translates into the problem of searching for a trajectory and funnel that is able to guarantee reactive composition and invariance to the region as late as possible along the transition funnel $\mathcal{L}_{ij}$; i.e. find a $\mathcal{B}_i^*$ as the argument for which

$$t^* = \max_{\mathcal{B}_i \text{ s.t. (8)–(10)}} \{t \mid \mathcal{L}_{ij}(t) \cap X_i \subset [\mathcal{B}_i]\}. \tag{12}$$

Given $\mathcal{B}_i^*$, the reactivity gap for $\mathcal{L}_{ij}$ is defined as a new region

$$X_{ij} = \{\mathcal{L}_{ij}(t) \mid t \in [t^*, T]\} \backslash [\mathcal{B}_i^*] \cap X_i. \tag{13}$$

For visualization purposes, we can over-approximate X_{ij} via a polytope projection onto, for example, a 2-D workspace map. With this new region defined, a procedure for updating the discrete abstraction in the context of linear temporal logic specifications is provided in the next section.

6.2 Robot Abstractions for Linear Temporal Logic Specifications

Reactive tasks may be expressed as linear temporal logic (LTL) specifications. LTL formulas are defined over the set AP of atomic (Boolean) propositions by the recursive grammar $\varphi ::= \pi \in AP \mid \varphi_1 \wedge \varphi_2 \mid \neg\varphi \mid \bigcirc\varphi \mid \varphi_1 \,\mathcal{U}\, \varphi_2$. The following operators are derived from the Boolean operators $\wedge$ "conjunction" and $\neg$ "negation", and the temporal operators $\bigcirc$ "next" and $\mathcal{U}$ "until": "disjunction" $\vee$, "implication" $\Rightarrow$, "equivalence" $\Leftrightarrow$, "always" $\Box$, and "eventually" $\Diamond$. For a description of the semantics of LTL, we refer the reader to [24].

Letting $\pi \in AP_e \cup AP_s$ represent a binary proposition, a mission specification is expressed as an LTL formula of the form:

$$\varphi := \varphi^e \implies \varphi^s,$$

where φ^e and φ^s are defined over $AP_e \cup AP_s \cup \bigcirc AP_e \cup \bigcirc AP_s$, and are further decomposed into formulas for initial conditions, safety conditions to be satisfied always, and goals to be satisfied infinitely often. Considering specifications of this form allows us to take advantage of efficient algorithms for synthesizing a finite-state machine $\mathcal{A}$ that satisfying the specification [4].

In the context of LTL mission specifications, a *discrete abstraction* is a set of LTL formulas that model the discrete behavior of the underlying continuous system. We encode discrete abstractions using the LTL encoding of [10], which takes into account actions with arbitrary completion times, allowing for a rich set of behaviors to occur concurrently. Under this encoding, let $\pi_{a\ell} \in AP_s$ denote the proposition that is `True` when activating a transition to some region X_ℓ, and $\pi_\ell \in AP_e$ denote the proposition that is `True` when motion to X_ℓ has been completed.

If $\mathcal{B}_i^*$ is computed such that there is a nonempty reactivity gap, i.e. $[\mathcal{L}_{ij}] \cap \partial X_i \not\subseteq [\mathcal{B}_i^*]$, we update the abstraction as follows. The first step is to compute a reactivity gap, as the set according to (13), then extend the set of propositions AP_e with a new region proposition π_{ij} that is `True` when the system is in X_{ij}. We then append the following formula to the formula for environment assumptions φ^e:

$$\begin{aligned}
&\Box\,(\pi_{ai} \wedge \pi_i \wedge \bigcirc\,\pi_i \wedge \neg\pi_{ij} \implies \bigcirc\,\neg\pi_{ij}) \wedge \\
&\Box\,(\pi_{aj} \wedge \pi_i \wedge \neg\pi_{ij} \implies \bigcirc\,\pi_i) \wedge \\
&\Box\,(\pi_{aj} \wedge \pi_i \wedge \pi_{ij} \implies \bigcirc\,\pi_{ij} \vee \bigcirc\,\pi_j) \wedge \\
&\Box\,(\bigcirc\,\neg\pi_i \implies \bigcirc\,\neg\pi_{ij}).
\end{aligned} \tag{14}$$

The first condition enforces that, if the system is commanded to remain in X_i, it must not enter X_{ij}. The second and third conditions enforce that if the robot is commanded to enter X_j when in X_i, it cannot do so without first entering X_{ij}. The last condition encodes the fact that X_{ij} is a subset of X_i.

6.3 Putting It All Together: Low-Level Controller Synthesis

We now describe an algorithm for constructing verified atomic controllers satisfying the reactive composition property according to criterion (12) for a transition from a state i to another state j. In line 8 of Algorithm 1, the optimization problem (8)–(10) is solved with the additional criteria where the resulting barrier conforms *precisely* for the portion of the invariant that intersects with the transition $\mathcal{L}_{ij}$. If this problem has a solution, this means that for any controlled trajectory from X_i to X_j, the system is verified to be able to react to the environment and move instead to any X_k, $k \in I_i$, $k \neq j$. For instance, if the robot may be represented by a fully-actuated (e.g. holonomic) model where the robot can move instantaneously in any direction, then the algorithm will be able to create controllers that satisfy a transition that exploits this property to its fullest. If this does not succeed, then line 10 solves the optimization again without this restriction. If successful, the abstraction is updated in line 12, and the funnel is returned in line 22. Otherwise, the time t_{init} is reduced in line 19 and the process repeats. Note that line 2 is a restatement of (12) that finds a suboptimal t^*, t_{init}, by iterating backward in time a fixed amount τ.

Upon returning from the algorithm, a decision is made to synthesize another finite state machine (if necessary with the aid of any LTL-based revisions as explained in [8]). If the abstraction has changed after constructing controllers for each transition, then synthesis takes place; otherwise it does not. If this new finite state machine is simulated by the old one, i.e. the new one contains a subset of the behaviors of the old one, then the existing library of low-level controllers is deemed sufficient for the finite state machine. Otherwise, new low-level controllers are generated in a manner that re-uses as much of the existing library as possible.

The overall synthesis approach is sound. Prior work [9] showed that the library of low-level controllers guarantees a given specification from which those controllers were generated. This, in conjunction with the fact that the abstraction is updated such that it simulates the continuous behaviors under the computed controllers, proves that our approach is sound under the repartitioned problem. While not complete in general, our approach refines the workspace partitions whenever an FSM cannot be implemented. Because the optimization problem of (8)–(10) yields a control law, if one exists, our approach is complete under the given choices of trajectories and feedback controller parameters.

Algorithm 1 Computing an inward-facing funnel $\mathcal{B}_i$ for s_i to implement a change from successor state s_j to s_k, $j, k \in I_i, j \neq k$.

procedure REACTIVECOMPOSITION($\mathcal{L}_{ij}$,X_i,X_j,τ)
  $t_{init} \leftarrow \arg\max_t\{t \mid \mathcal{L}_{ij}(t) \cap X_i \neq \emptyset\}$
  while $t_{init} \geq 0$ and not feasible **do**
    create a trajectory from $\mathcal{L}_{ij}(t_{init})$ to the RC set for state i
    $\mathcal{L}_i$, feasible $\leftarrow$ solution to (3)
    if feasible and $[\mathcal{L}_i] \not\subseteq X_i$ **then**
      $t_1 \leftarrow \arg\max_t\{t \mid \mathcal{L}_i(t) \cap (\mathbb{R}^n \backslash X_i) \neq \emptyset\}$
      $\mathcal{B}_i$, feasible $\leftarrow$ solution to (8)–(10) with additional constraints $[\mathcal{L}_{ij}] \cap X_i \implies \mathcal{B}_i(x, t) = 0$
      if not feasible **then**
        $\mathcal{B}_i$, feasible $\leftarrow$ solution to (8)–(10)
        if feasible **then**
          compute X_{ij} and update the abstraction as (14)
        end if
      end if
    else if feasible **then**
      $\mathcal{B}_i \leftarrow \mathcal{L}_i$
    end if
    if not feasible **then**
      $t_{init} = t_{init} - \tau$
    end if
  end while
  return $\mathcal{B}_i$
end procedure

7. EXAMPLE: A BOX TRANSPORTATION TASK

In this human-interactive problem domain, the task is to move packages from a pick-up area to one of two drop-off locations, as pictured in Fig. 1. Formally, "Visit the loading area. If push_box is active and go_to_left is requested, visit dropoff_L. If push_box is active and go_to_right is requested, visit dropoff_R. Activate push_box when in pickup and deactivate push_box when in dropoff_L or dropoff_R." We employ a KUKA youBot to perform the task, which operates on an omnidirectional base whose position and orientation is measured in real time. Packages are moved by way of pushing them along the ground using the robot's front fender. There is one action (treated as a system variable) in this scenario, push_box, which is `True` whenever the robot is moving a package and `False` otherwise.

In our discrete abstraction of the problem, we do not explicitly model the dynamics of the box, but rather we impose certain conditions that are required of the dynamics in order to assure that the box always maintains contact with the robot. We therefore impose the dynamics of a *unicycle* that is capable of forward velocities up to a certain forward velocity and within a given range of turning radii. Suitable maximum linear and angular velocities were determined experimentally in order to ensure the box is always in contact with the robot. In order to disengage the box, we impose holonomic (fully-actuated) dynamics with negative forward velocity. When push_box is `False`, the holonomic model is put into effect; otherwise, the unicycle model is used. We use the proposed approach to design controllers for this example.

7.1 Synthesis and Workspace Re-Partitioning

We express the task as a mission specification (linear temporal logic formulas), from which we synthesized a high-level state machine using the slugs synthesis tool[1]. Our state machine consists of 6 states and 9 transitions. Controllers were synthesized using the proposed conforming funnels approach and Algorithm 1. Our approach was coded as a set of MATLAB routines; with our implementation, each reactive funnel took on average 5.2 minutes to compute on a laptop with Intel Core i7 2.8GHz processor and 8GB of RAM. The original specification and dynamics necessitated an update to the abstraction that, in turn, required an update to the original specification.

Based on the abstraction update, a new finite state machine could not be synthesized without additional environment assumptions. Using the revisions approach algorithm in [8], we automatically generated environment assumptions that restrict its behavior in the newly-generated reactive gap regions. Specifically, given the regions $X_{middle,L}$ and $X_{middle,R}$, additional assumptions were generated in the form of LTL formulas added to the environment subformula. In natural language, the formulas state the following: "If the robot is in region middle,L, heading to dropoff_L and activating push_box do not issue the request go_to_right," and "If the robot is in middle,L, heading to dropoff_R and activating push_box do not issue the request go_to_left." With this new controller (10 states and 9 transitions), the low-level controller synthesis process continued for the new state machine.

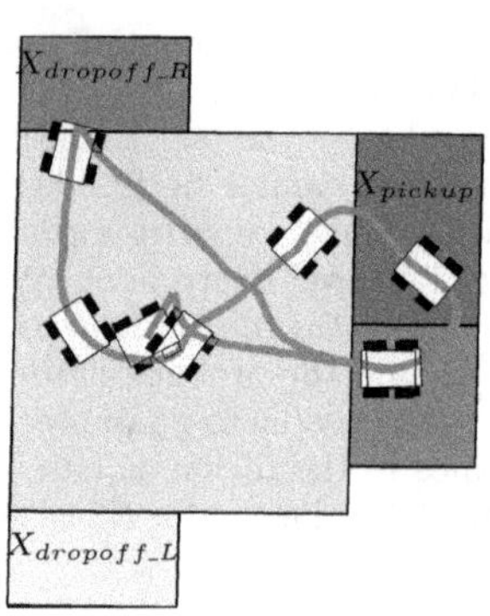

Figure 4: A trajectory for the box-transport example for the case where the environment is continually issuing the request go_to_right.

7.2 Execution of the Conforming Funnels

The proposed approach was evaluated in a set of laboratory experiments. The hybrid controller was executed on a laptop computer connected wirelessly to the youBot using the Robot Operating System (ROS) as the communication layer. The controller ran at a rate of approximately 5 Hz and the robot pose was obtained via a motion capture system.

A trajectory showing the execution of the controller on the youBot is pictured in Fig. 4 for the case where the environment is static. Notice that, when push_box is `True`, the robot executes the unicycle model and hence makes gradual turns; otherwise the holonomic model is active and the robot follows straight paths. An example of the robot reacting to the environment is depicted in Fig. 5. In Fig. 5c, the robot is executing a conforming funnel in order to fulfill a changing request just before the robot enters dropoff_L. The robot's resulting motion is smooth, remains within the funnel, and

[1]http://github.com/LTLMoP/slugs

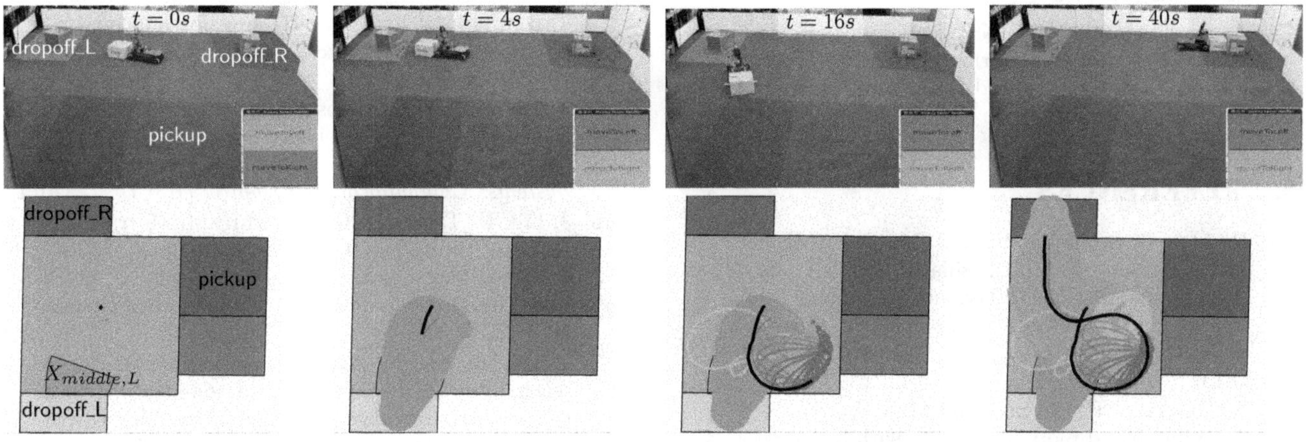

(a) (b) (c) (d)

Figure 5: Experimental results for the box-transportation scenario under a dynamic environment, a sequence of images captures taken from the video available at: `https://youtu.be/1XEVOGa3UEY`. (a)–(d), top, show the robot at several time instants as it delivers a box, with the inset showing the sensor values go_to_left, go_to_right. The map is diplayed at bottom of each subfigure, along with the robot's trajectory (black), the activated funnels, and the nominal trajectory for each funnel (magenta). The pink region in (a) is the reactivity gap region $X_{middle,L}$. Note that the sensor value changes from go_to_left to go_to_right at the time instant shown in (b).

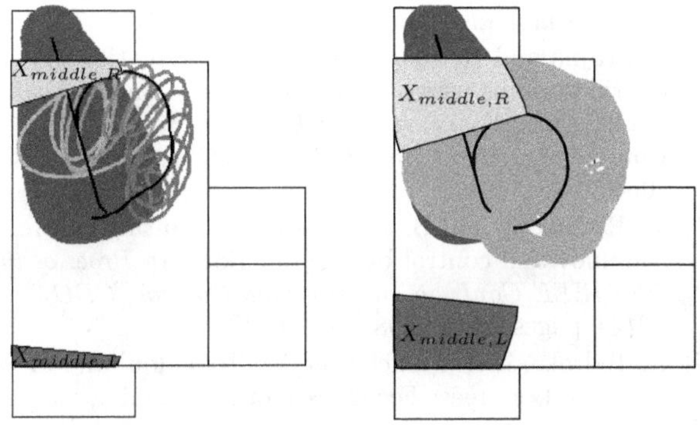

(a) (b)

Figure 6: Evaluation of the reactivity of the system to changes in the environment for the box-transport problem. (a) and (b) show reactivity gap regions computed using, respectively, the conforming funnels approach and funnels approach from [9].

can be seen to converge to the nominal trajectory. A complete video demonstrating the controllers is available at: `https://youtu.be/1XEVOGa3UEY`.

The conforming funnels approach was compared against funnels generated using the approach from [9]. As can be seen in Fig. 6a, the reactivity gap regions generated with the proposed approach are considerably smaller than those computed in the formulation of [9] in Fig. 6b. This is due to the fact that such a conforming funnel can be computed using a trajectory starting close to the drop-off region and inside the transition funnel yet still also able to verify the set of states in the transition funnel. The implication of this improvement is a greater responsiveness to the environment when the robot is in close proximity to the drop-off areas.

8. CONCLUSIONS

In this paper, we address two problems: (1) synthesizing hybrid controllers that allow a robot to react to its environment whenever dynamically feasible given the geometry of the workspace, and (2) an automated approach for transforming dynamically-informative revisions into changes to the specification, in the case that a controller cannot be obtained for a high-level behavior. To address the first, we contribute a method for synthesizing correct-by-construction controllers with respect to given high-level behaviors, the geometrical constraints of the workspace, and a robot dynamics model. Our approach generalizes existing techniques for nonlinear system verification using fixed-parameter funnels. In situations where the high-level behaviors cannot be fulfilled strictly, we also contribute an algorithm that uses the controllers to re-partition the workspace and automatically adapt the high-level specification with a new discrete abstraction generated on these new partitions. The approach is general; it is intended for a finite state machine synthesized from any reactive specification and any system model provided it can be expressed in terms of polynomial ODEs.

In the future, we will extend the approach to be more complete so that controllers can be generated over a wider portion of the state space. To address this challenge, it will become necessary to explore the possibility of optimizing among trajectories that both fulfill the high-level behavior and result in funnels that are maximal. Future work also includes exploring the significance of parameter adaptation in the construction of TV-CBF-based controllers; for example, the order of the polynomials used to parameterize the barrier function. Using the TV-CBF method, we intend to explore the computation of robust motion primitives that admit controllers that are provably correct over a wide array of parameters for the system model. Lastly, we intend to use these primitives as an aid for performing synthesis when unknown changes to the system model occur during execution.

Acknowledgement

This work was supported by NSF Expeditions in Computer Augmented Program Engineering (ExCAPE). The authors thank Prof. Ross Knepper and Prof. Alex Vladimirsky for valuable discussions leading to the formation of this work.

9. REFERENCES

[1] R. Alur, R. Bodík, G. Juniwal, M. M. K. Martin, M. Raghothaman, S. A. Seshia, R. Singh, A. Solar-Lezama, E. Torlak, and A. Udupa. Syntax-guided synthesis. In *Formal Methods in Computer-Aided Design (FMCAD 2013)*, pages 1–8, 2013.

[2] A. Bhatia, L. E. Kavraki, and M. Y. Vardi. Sampling-based motion planning with temporal goals. In *Proc. of the IEEE Int. Conf. on Robotics and Automation (ICRA 2010)*, pages 2689–2696, 2010.

[3] A. Bhatia, M. Maly, L. Kavraki, and M. Vardi. Motion planning with complex goals. *Robotics Automation Magazine, IEEE*, 18(3):55 –64, sept. 2011.

[4] R. Bloem, B. Jobstmann, N. Piterman, A. Pnueli, and Y. Sa'ar. Synthesis of reactive (1) designs. *Journal of Computer and System Sciences*, 78(3):911–938, 2012.

[5] R. Burridge, A. Rizzi, and D. Koditschek. Sequential composition of dynamically dexterous robot behaviors. *The International Journal of Robotics Research*, 18:534–555, 1999.

[6] E. Clarke. Counterexample-guided abstraction refinement. In *10th International Symposium on Temporal Representation and Reasoning / 4th International Conference on Temporal Logic (TIME-ICTL 2003)*, page 7, 2003.

[7] D. C. Conner, A. Rizzi, and H. Choset. Composition of local potential functions for global robot control and navigation. In *Proc. of 2003 IEEE/RSJ Int. Conf. on Intelligent Robots and Systems (IROS 2003)*, volume 4, pages 3546– 3551, 2003.

[8] J. A. DeCastro, R. Ehlers, M. Rungger, A. Balkan, P. Tabuada, and H. Kress-Gazit. Dynamics-based reactive synthesis and automated revisions for high-level robot control. *CoRR*, abs/1410.6375, 2014.

[9] J. A. DeCastro and H. Kress-Gazit. Synthesis of nonlinear continuous controllers for verifiably-correct high-level, reactive behaviors. *The International Journal of Robotics Research*, 34(3):378–394, 2015.

[10] J. A. DeCastro, V. Raman, and H. Kress-Gazit. Dynamics-driven adaptive abstraction for reactive high-level mission and motion planning. In *Proc. of the IEEE Int. Conf. on Robotics and Automation (ICRA 2015)*, pages 369 – 376, Seattle, WA, 2015.

[11] Z. Jiang, Y. Lin, and Y. Wang. Stabilization of nonlinear time-varying systems: a control lyapunov function approach. *J. Systems Science & Complexity*, 22(4):683–696, 2009.

[12] D. Kirk. *Optimal Control Theory: An Introduction.* Prentice-Hall, 1976.

[13] M. Kloetzer and C. Belta. A fully automated framework for control of linear systems from ltl specifications. In *Proc. of the 9th Int. Conf. on Hybrid Systems: Computation and Control (HSCC'06)*, pages 333–347, Berlin, Heidelberg, 2006. Springer-Verlag.

[14] H. Kress-Gazit, G. E. Fainekos, and G. J. Pappas. Temporal logic based reactive mission and motion planning. *IEEE Transactions on Robotics*, 25(6):1370–1381, 2009.

[15] J. Liu and N. Ozay. Abstraction, discretization, and robustness in temporal logic control of dynamical systems. In *Proc. of the 17th Int. Conf. on Hybrid Systems: Computation and Control (HSCC'14)*, 2014.

[16] J. Liu, U. Topcu, N. Ozay, and R. M. Murray. Reactive controllers for differentially flat systems with temporal logic constraints. In *Proc. of the 51st IEEE Conf. on Decision and Control (CDC 2012)*, pages 7664–7670, 2012.

[17] J. Maidens and M. Arcak. Trajectory-based reachability analysis of switched nonlinear systems using matrix measures. In *Proc. of the 53rd IEEE Conf. on Decision and Control (CDC 2014)*, pages 6358–6364, Dec 2014.

[18] M. R. Maly, M. Lahijanian, L. E. Kavraki, H. Kress-Gazit, and M. Y. Vardi. Iterative temporal motion planning for hybrid systems in partially unknown environments. In *Proc. of the 16th Int. Conf. on Hybrid Systems: Computation and Control (HSCC'13)*, pages 353–362, Philadelphia, PA, 2013.

[19] I. M. Mitchell, A. M. Bayen, and C. J. Tomlin. A time-dependent hamilton-jacobi formulation of reachable sets for continuous dynamic games. *IEEE Trans. Automat. Contr.*, 50(7):947–957, 2005.

[20] S. Prajna and A. Jadbabaie. Safety verification of hybrid systems using barrier certificates. In *Proc. of the 4th Int. Workshop on Hybrid Systems: Computation and Control (HSCC'04)*, pages 477–492, 2004.

[21] M. Romdlony and B. Jayawardhana. Uniting control lyapunov and control barrier functions. In *Proc. of the 53rd IEEE Conf. on Decision and Control (CDC 2014)*, pages 2293–2298, Dec 2014.

[22] R. Tedrake, I. R. Manchester, M. Tobenkin, and J. W. Roberts. Lqr-trees: Feedback motion planning via sums-of-squares verification. *the International Journal of Robotics Research*, 29(8):1038–1052, 2010.

[23] C. J. Tomlin, J. Lygeros, and S. Sastry. A game theoretic approach to controller design for hybrid systems. *Proceedings of IEEE*, 88:949–969, July 2000.

[24] M. Y. Vardi. An automata-theoretic approach to linear temporal logic. In *Logics for concurrency*, pages 238–266. Springer, 1996.

[25] P. Wieland and F. Allgower. Constructive safety using control barrier functions. In *Proc. of the 7th IFAC Symposium on Nonlinear Control Systems*, pages 473–478, 2007.

[26] E. Wolff, U. Topcu, and R. Murray. Automaton-guided controller synthesis for nonlinear systems with temporal logic. In *Proc. of the IEEE/RSJ Int. Conf. on Intelligent Robots and Systems (IROS 2013)*, pages 4332–4339, 2013.

[27] T. Wongpiromsarn, U. Topcu, and R. Murray. Receding horizon temporal logic planning. *Automatic Control, IEEE Transactions on*, 57(11):2817–2830, 2012.

Robust Asymptotic Stabilization of Hybrid Systems using Control Lyapunov Functions

Ricardo G. Sanfelice *
Computer Engineering Department
University of California
Santa Cruz, California, USA
ricardo@ucsc.edu

ABSTRACT

We propose tools for the study of robust stabilizability and the design of robustly stabilizing feedback laws for a wide class of hybrid systems given in terms of hybrid inclusions with inputs and disturbances. We introduce notions of robust uniform global stabilizability and stabilization that capture the case when disturbances can be fully rejected, practically rejected, and when they induce a residual set that can be stabilized. Robust control Lyapunov functions are employed to determine when stabilizing static state-feedback laws are available and also to synthesize robustly stabilizing feedback laws with minimum pointwise norm. Sufficient conditions on the data of the hybrid system as well as on the control Lyapunov function are proposed for the said properties to hold. An example illustrates the results throughout the paper.

CCS Concepts

•**Theory of computation** → **Timed and hybrid models;** •**Computing methodologies** → **Control methods;** •**Hardware** → *Process variations;*

Keywords

Hybrid systems; Robust stability; Control Lyapunov functions

1. INTRODUCTION

Recent advances in the theory of hybrid dynamical systems have provided powerful tools for the study of robustness of asymptotic stability. One of the main results in [7], which is for hybrid systems modeled as hybrid inclusions, is that asymptotic stability of a compact set is nominally robust when the objects defining the hybrid system satisfy mild regularity properties – by nominal robustness we mean that the stability property is be preserved semiglobally and practically for small enough perturbations. The importance of this result for control design is significant, as it highlights structural properties that the interconnection between the plant and the controller (both potentially hybrid) should satisfy so that, after a perturbation-free design, the behavior of the closed-loop system does not change much when small perturbations are present (even when those perturbations may affect the times at which flows and jumps occur). The case of large disturbances in hybrid systems was studied in [1] using the notion of input-to-state stability (ISS). While the results therein involving ISS Lyapunov functions can certainly be used for design, constructive design tools that guarantee robustness of asymptotic stability to large disturbances are not yet available.

Control Lyapunov functions have been shown to be very useful in constructively designing feedback control algorithms [14, 3, 13, 6]. In particular, in [6], tools for the design of robustly stabilizing feedback controllers are proposed for continuous-time systems for which a robust control Lyapunov function exists. A salient feature of using robust control Lyapunov functions is that, even under the presence of large disturbances, an asymptotic stability of a set, typically defined by a residual neighborhood around the desired equilibrium, can be guaranteed. Recently, the concept of control Lyapunov function was extended to different classes of hybrid systems without disturbances, see [11] for results for hybrid inclusions and [4] for results for discrete-time systems with continuous and discrete states.

Motivated by the constructive design tools for robust stability in [6], in this paper, we propose tools for the study of robust stabilizability and the design of robustly stabilizing feedback laws that employ control Lyapunov functions for hybrid systems with disturbances. For a wide class of hybrid systems given in terms of hybrid inclusions with inputs and disturbances, we introduce notions of robust uniform global stabilizability and stabilization that capture the case when disturbances can be fully rejected, practically rejected, and when they induce a residual set that can be stabilized. Building from results in [11], we propose conditions guaranteeing the existence of a continuous robust stabilizing static state-feedback law. We show that, under further conditions, continuous state-feedback laws with minimum pointwise norm can be constructed.

*Research partially supported by the National Science Foundation under CAREER Grant no. ECCS-1450484 and Grant no. CNS-1544396, and by the Air Force Office of Scientific Research under YIP Grant no. FA9550-12-1-0366 and Grant no. FA9550-16-1-0015.

HSCC'16, April 12-14, 2016, Vienna, Austria

DOI: http://dx.doi.org/10.1145/2883817.2883848

The remainder of this paper is organized as follows. In Section 2, we introduce the hybrid system model and related notions. The notions of robust stability, stabilizability, and control Lyapunov functions are introduced in Section 3. Conditions guaranteeing the existence of stabilizing feedback laws are given in Section 4, while the constructive design tools are in Section 5. Due to space constraints, the proof of the results are not included but will be published elsewhere.

Notation: $\mathbb{R}^n$ denotes n-dimensional Euclidean space. $\mathbb{R}$ denotes the real numbers. $\mathbb{R}_{\geq 0}$ denotes the nonnegative real numbers, i.e., $\mathbb{R}_{\geq 0} = [0, \infty)$. $\mathbb{N}$ denotes the natural numbers including 0, i.e., $\mathbb{N} = \{0, 1, \ldots\}$. $\mathbb{B}$ denotes the closed unit ball in a Euclidean space. Given a set K, $\overline{K}$ denotes its closure. Given a set S, ∂S denotes its boundary. Given $x \in \mathbb{R}^n$, $|x|$ denotes the Euclidean vector norm. Given a closed set $K \subset \mathbb{R}^n$ and $x \in \mathbb{R}^n$, $|x|_K := \inf_{y \in K} |x - y|$. Given vectors x and y, $\langle x, y \rangle$ denotes their inner product and, at times, we write $[x^\top y^\top]^\top$ simply as (x, y). A function $\rho : \mathbb{R}^n \to \mathbb{R}_{\geq 0}$ is positive definite with respect to a set S if $\rho(x) = 0$ for each $x \in S$ and $\rho(x) > 0$ for each $x \in \mathbb{R}^n \setminus S$. A function $\alpha : \mathbb{R}_{\geq 0} \to \mathbb{R}_{\geq 0}$ is said to belong to class-$\mathcal{K}$ if it is continuous, zero at zero, and strictly increasing. A function $\alpha : \mathbb{R}_{\geq 0} \to \mathbb{R}_{\geq 0}$ is said to belong to class-$\mathcal{K}_\infty$ if it is an unbounded class-$\mathcal{K}$ function. A function $\beta : \mathbb{R}_{\geq 0} \times \mathbb{R}_{\geq 0} \to \mathbb{R}_{\geq 0}$ is a class-$\mathcal{KL}$ function, also written $\beta \in \mathcal{KL}$, if it is nondecreasing in its first argument, nonincreasing in its second argument, $\lim_{r \to 0^+} \beta(r, s) = 0$ for each $s \in \mathbb{R}_{\geq 0}$, and $\lim_{s \to \infty} \beta(r, s) = 0$ for each $r \in \mathbb{R}_{\geq 0}$. Given a locally Lipschitz function $V : \mathbb{R}^n \to \mathbb{R}_{\geq 0}$, $V^\circ(x; \xi)$ denotes the Clarke generalized derivative of V at x in the direction of ξ; see [2]. Given a map f, its graph is denoted by gph(f). Given a set $S \subset \mathbb{R}_{\geq 0} \times \mathbb{N}$, $\sup_t S := \sup\{t \, : \, (t, j) \in S\}$ and $\sup_j S := \sup\{j \, : \, (t, j) \in S\}$.

2. HYBRID SYSTEMS WITH INPUTS AND DISTURBANCES

A hybrid system $\mathcal{H}_{u,w}$ with state x, control input $u = (u_c, u_d)$, and disturbance input $w = (w_c, w_d)$ is given by

$$\mathcal{H}_{u,w} \begin{cases} \dot{x} & \in & F(x, u_c, w_c) & (x, u_c, w_c) \in C \\ x^+ & \in & G(x, u_d, w_d) & (x, u_d, w_d) \in D \end{cases} \tag{1}$$

The space for the state x is $\mathbb{R}^n$, the space for the input $u = (u_c, u_d)$ is $\mathcal{U} = \mathcal{U}_c \times \mathcal{U}_d$, where $\mathcal{U}_c \subset \mathbb{R}^{m_c}$ and $\mathcal{U}_d \subset \mathbb{R}^{m_d}$, and the space for the disturbance $w = (w_c, w_d)$ is $\mathcal{W} = \mathcal{W}_c \times \mathcal{W}_d$, where $\mathcal{W}_c \subset \mathbb{R}^{d_c}$ and $\mathcal{W}_d \subset \mathbb{R}^{d_d}$. The data defining $\mathcal{H}_{u,w}$ is as follows:

- The set $C \subset \mathbb{R}^n \times \mathcal{U}_c \times \mathcal{W}_c$ is the *flow set*;
- The set-valued map $F : \mathbb{R}^n \times \mathbb{R}^{m_c} \times \mathbb{R}^{d_c} \rightrightarrows \mathbb{R}^n$ is the *flow map*;
- The set $D \subset \mathbb{R}^n \times \mathcal{U}_d \times \mathcal{W}_d$ is the *jump set*;
- The set-valued map $G : \mathbb{R}^n \times \mathbb{R}^{m_d} \times \mathbb{R}^{d_d} \rightrightarrows \mathbb{R}^n$ is the *jump map*.

The sets C and D in the definition of $\mathcal{H}_{u,w}$ define conditions that x, u, and w should satisfy for flows or jumps to occur. Throughout this paper, we assume that these sets impose conditions on u that only depend on x and conditions on w that only depend on x.

The state x of the hybrid system can include multiple logic variables, timers, memory states as well as physical (continuous) states, e.g., $x = (q, \tau, \xi)$ is a state vector with a state component given by a logic variable q taking values from a discrete set $\mathcal{Q}$, a state component given by a timer τ taking values from the interval $[0, \tau^*]$, where $\tau^* > 0$ is the maximum allowed value for the timer, and with a state component $\xi \in \mathbb{R}^{n_p}$ representing the continuously varying state – note that in such a case, $\mathcal{Q} \times [0, \tau^*] \times \mathbb{R}^{n_p}$ can be embedded in $\mathbb{R}^n$ for $n = 1 + 1 + n_p$.

Given a set $K \subset \mathbb{R}^n \times \mathcal{U}_\star \times \mathcal{W}_\star$ with $\star$ being either c or d, $\mathcal{U}_\star \subset \mathbb{R}^{m_\star}$, $\mathcal{W}_\star \subset \mathbb{R}^{d_\star}$, $V : \mathbb{R}^n \to \mathbb{R}_{\geq 0}$, and $r \geq 0$, we define

- $\mathcal{I}(r) := \{x \in \mathbb{R}^n \, : \, V(x) \geq r\}$
- The projector onto the state space
$$\Pi_\star(K) := \{x \, : \, \exists (u_\star, w_\star) \text{ s.t. } (x, u_\star, w_\star) \in K\}$$
- The projector onto the state and input space
$$\Delta_\star(r, K) := \Big\{(x, u_\star) \, : \, \exists w_\star \text{ s.t. } (x, u_\star, w_\star) \in K \cap (\mathcal{I}(r) \times \mathbb{R}^{m_\star} \times \mathbb{R}^{d_\star})\Big\}$$
- The projector onto the input and disturbance space
$$\widetilde{\Psi}^u_\star(x, K) := \{u'_\star \, : \, \exists w'_\star \text{ s.t. } (x, u'_\star, w'_\star) \in K\}$$
and
$$\widetilde{\Psi}^w_\star(x, K) := \{w'_\star \, : \, \exists u'_\star \text{ s.t. } (x, u'_\star, w'_\star) \in K\}$$
for each $x \in \mathbb{R}^n$, respectively;
- The projector onto the flow input, flow disturbance, jump input, and jump disturbance space
$$\Psi^u_c(x) := \widetilde{\Psi}^u_c(x, C), \quad \Psi^w_c(x) := \widetilde{\Psi}^w_c(x, C)$$
$$\Psi^u_d(x) := \widetilde{\Psi}^u_d(x, D), \quad \Psi^w_d(x) := \widetilde{\Psi}^w_d(x, D)$$
for each $x \in \mathbb{R}^n$, respectively.

That is, given a set K, $\Pi_\star(K)$ denotes the "projection" of K onto $\mathbb{R}^n$, $\Delta_\star(r, K)$ denotes the "projection" of K onto $(\mathbb{R}^n \cap \mathcal{I}(r)) \times \mathbb{R}^{m_\star}$, while, given x, $\widetilde{\Psi}^u_\star(x, K)$ denotes the set of values $u_\star$ such that $(x, u_\star, w_\star) \in K$; similarly for $\widetilde{\Psi}^w_\star(x, K)$.

Solutions to hybrid systems $\mathcal{H}_{u,w}$ are given in terms of hybrid arcs, hybrid disturbances, and hybrid inputs on hybrid time domains. A set $\mathcal{E} \subset \mathbb{R}_{\geq 0} \times \mathbb{N}$ is a compact hybrid time domain if

$$\mathcal{E} = \bigcup_{j=0}^{J-1} ([t_j, t_{j+1}], j)$$

for some finite sequence of times $0 = t_0 \leq t_1 \leq t_2 \leq \ldots \leq t_J$. It is a hybrid time domain if for all $(T, J) \in \mathcal{E}$,

$$\mathcal{E} \cap ([0, T] \times \{0, 1, \ldots, J\})$$

is a compact hybrid time domain.[1] A hybrid arc ϕ is a function on a hybrid time domain that, for each $j \in \mathbb{N}$,

[1]This property is to hold at each $(T, J) \in \mathcal{E}$, but $\mathcal{E}$ can be unbounded.

$t \mapsto \phi(t,j)$ is absolutely continuous on the interval

$$\{t \; : \; (t,j) \in \operatorname{dom}\phi \}$$

where $\operatorname{dom}\phi$ denotes the hybrid time domain of ϕ.

Hybrid disturbances w are functions of hybrid time that will be generated by some hybrid exosystem $\mathcal{H}_e$ of the form

$$\mathcal{H}_e \left\{ \begin{array}{lcll} \dot{w} & \in & F_e(w) & w \in C_e \\ w^+ & \in & G_e(w) & w \in D_e \end{array} \right. \tag{2}$$

with state (and output) $w = (w_c, w_d) \in \mathcal{W}$. A disturbance generated by a hybrid exosystem of the form (2) that, for given state trajectory and input, satisfies the dynamics of the hybrid system $\mathcal{H}_{u,w}$ is said to be admissible. For instance, the hybrid exosystem with data

$$C_e = D_e = \mathcal{W}_c \times \mathcal{W}_d, \quad G_e \equiv \mathcal{W}_c \times \mathcal{W}_d, \quad F_e \equiv c\mathbb{B}$$

where $c \geq 0$ is a constant, generates disturbances that remain in $\mathcal{W}$ and that are Lipschitz continuous during flows (with Lipschitz constant c), but not necessarily differentiable; see [9] for constructions of hybrid exosystems generating square and triangular signals.

Similarly, control inputs u are functions of hybrid time, i.e., $u : \operatorname{dom} u \to \mathcal{U}$ with $\operatorname{dom} u$ being a hybrid time domain, with the property that, for each j, $t \mapsto u(t,j)$ is Lebesgue measurable and locally essentially bounded on the interval $\{t \; : \; (t,j) \in \operatorname{dom} u \}$. A control input satisfying these properties and, for given state trajectory and disturbance, satisfies the dynamics of the hybrid system $\mathcal{H}_{u,w}$ is said to be admissible.

A solution to the hybrid system $\mathcal{H}_{u,w}$ in (1) is given by (ϕ, u, w), $u = (u_c, u_d)$, $w = (w_c, w_d)$, with $\operatorname{dom}\phi = \operatorname{dom} u = \operatorname{dom} w (= \operatorname{dom}(\phi, u, w))$ and satisfying the dynamics of $\mathcal{H}_{u,w}$, where ϕ is a hybrid arc, u is a hybrid input, and w is a hybrid disturbance. A solution (ϕ, u, w) to $\mathcal{H}_{u,w}$ is said to be *complete* if $\operatorname{dom}(\phi, u, w)$ is unbounded, and is said to be *maximal* if there does not exist another pair $(\phi, u, w)'$ such that (ϕ, u, w) is a truncation of $(\phi, u, w)'$ to some proper subset of $\operatorname{dom}(\phi, u, w)'$. For more details about solutions to hybrid systems with inputs, see [11].

Next, we illustrate the modeling framework in a system that will be revisited throughout the paper. Being of second order, with jumps in both of its state variables, and exhibiting Zeno behavior for specific choices of its inputs, the system is rich enough, yet not overly complex, for the purposes of illustrating our ideas and results.

EXAMPLE 2.1. *(controlled pendulum with impacts) Consider a point-mass pendulum impacting on a controlled slanted surface. Denote the pendulum's angle (with respect to the vertical) by x_1, where $x_1 > 0$ corresponds to a displacement to the right of the vertical and $x_1 < 0$ to a displacement to the left of the vertical. The pendulum's velocity (positive when the pendulum rotates in the counterclockwise direction) is denoted by x_2. When $x_1 \geq \mu$ with μ denoting the angle of the surface, its continuous evolution is given by*

$$\begin{array}{rcl} \dot{x}_1 & = & x_2 \\ \dot{x}_2 & = & -a \sin x_1 - (b + w_{c,2})x_2 + \tau + w_{c,1} \end{array}$$

where $a > 0$, $b \geq 0$ capture the system constants (e.g., gravity, mass, length, and friction) and τ corresponds to torque actuation at the pendulum's end. For simplicity, we assume that $x_1 \in [-\frac{\pi}{2}, \frac{\pi}{2}]$ and $\mu \in [-\frac{\pi}{2}, 0]$. The disturbance $w_{c,1}$ represents actuator noise and unmodeled dynamics, while $w_{c,2}$ represents uncertainty in the damping constant b. Impacts between the pendulum and the surface occur when

$$x_1 \leq \mu, \quad x_2 \leq 0. \tag{3}$$

At such events, the jump map takes the form

$$\begin{array}{rcl} x_1^+ & = & x_1 + \widetilde{\rho}(\mu)x_1 \\ x_2^+ & = & -(e(\mu) + w_d)x_2 \end{array}$$

where the functions

$$\widetilde{\rho} : [-\pi/2, 0] \to (-1, 0)$$

and

$$e : [-\pi/2, 0] \to [e_0, e_1]$$

$0 < e_0 < e_1 < 1$, *are linear in μ and capture the effect of pendulum compression and restitution at impacts, respectively, as a function of μ. For simplicity, the function $\widetilde{\rho}$ is used to capture (much more complex) rapid displacements of the pendulum at collisions by guaranteeing that $x_1 + \widetilde{\rho}(\mu)x_1 > x_1$ at jumps – in this way, after impacts away from $x_1 = 0$, the pendulum is pushed away from the contact condition. The restitution coefficient function e models the effect of gravity on energy dissipation at impacts via the angle μ: when the surface is placed as far to the left as possible ($\mu = -\pi/2$), e is given by the minimum value $e(-\pi/2) = e_0$, while when the surface is at $\mu = 0$, e takes the maximum value $e(0) = e_1$. The disturbance w_d represents uncertainty in the restitution coefficient.*

The model above can be captured by the hybrid system $\mathcal{H}_{u,w}$ given by

$$\mathcal{H}_{u,w} \left\{ \begin{array}{l} \left. \begin{array}{rcl} \dot{x}_1 & = & x_2 \\ \dot{x}_2 & = & -a \sin x_1 - (b + w_{c,2})x_2 + u_{c,1} + w_{c,1} \end{array} \right\} \\ \hfill =: F(x, u_c, w_c) \\ \hfill (x, u_c, w_c) \in C, \\ \left. \begin{array}{rcl} x_1^+ & = & x_1 + \widetilde{\rho}(u_d)x_1 \\ x_2^+ & = & -(e(u_d) + w_d)x_2 \end{array} \right\} =: G(x, u_d, w_d) \\ \hfill (x, u_d, w_d) \in D, \end{array} \right.$$

where $u_c = [u_{c,1} \; u_{c,2}]^\top = [\tau \; \mu]^\top \in \mathbb{R} \times [-\frac{\pi}{2}, 0] =: \mathcal{U}_c$, $u_d = \mu \in [-\frac{\pi}{2}, 0] =: \mathcal{U}_d$, $w_c = (w_{c,1}, w_{c,2}) \in \mathcal{W}_c := [0, \overline{w}_1] \times [0, \overline{w}_2]$ with $\overline{w}_1, \overline{w}_2 \in \mathbb{R}_{\geq 0}$, $w_d \in \mathcal{W}_d := [0, e_1 - e_0]$,

$$C := \left\{ (x, u_c, w_c) \in \left[-\frac{\pi}{2}, \frac{\pi}{2}\right] \times \mathbb{R} \times \mathcal{U}_c \times \mathcal{W}_c \; : \; x_1 \geq u_{c,2} \right\},$$

$$D \;:=\; \Big\{ (x, u_d, w_d) \in \left[-\frac{\pi}{2}, \frac{\pi}{2}\right] \times \mathbb{R} \times \mathcal{U}_d \times \mathcal{W}_d \; : \; x_1 \leq u_d, x_2 \leq 0 \Big\}$$

Note that the definitions of C and D impose state constraints on the inputs that only depend on the state x. $\triangle$

The following mild conditions on the data of $\mathcal{H}_{u,w}$ will be imposed in some of our results.

DEFINITION 2.2. *(hybrid basic conditions) A hybrid system $\mathcal{H}_{u,w}$ is said to satisfy the* hybrid basic conditions *if its data satisfies*

(A1) C and D are closed subsets of $\mathbb{R}^n \times \mathcal{U}_c \times \mathcal{W}_c$ and $\mathbb{R}^n \times \mathcal{U}_d \times \mathcal{W}_d$, respectively;

(A2) $F : \mathbb{R}^n \times \mathbb{R}^{m_c} \times \mathbb{R}^{d_c} \rightrightarrows \mathbb{R}^n$ *is outer semicontinuous relative to* C *and locally bounded*[2] *, and for all* $(x, u_c, w_c) \in C$, $F(x, u_c, w_c)$ *is nonempty and convex;*

(A3) $G : \mathbb{R}^n \times \mathbb{R}^{m_d} \times \mathbb{R}^{d_d} \rightrightarrows \mathbb{R}^n$ *is outer semicontinuous relative to* D *and locally bounded, and for all* $(x, u_d, w_d) \in D$, $G(x, u_d, w_d)$ *is nonempty.*

When F is single valued, (A2) reduces to F being continuous. Similarly, when G is single valued, (A3) reduces to G being continuous.

In the sections to follow, we will design state-feedback laws to control the hybrid system $\mathcal{H}_{u,w}$. The resulting closed-loop system under the effect of the control pair (κ_c, κ_d) is given by

$$\mathcal{H}_{cl} \begin{cases} \dot{x} \in F_{cl}(x, w_c) := F(x, \kappa_c(x), w_c) & (x, w_c) \in C_{cl} \\ x^+ \in G_{cl}(x, w_d) := G(x, \kappa_d(x), w_d) & (x, w_d) \in D_{cl} \end{cases} \tag{4}$$

with

$$C_{cl} := \{(x, w_c) \in \mathbb{R}^n \times \mathcal{W}_c \; : \; (x, \kappa_c(x), w_c) \in C\}$$

and

$$D_{cl} := \{(x, w_d) \in \mathbb{R}^n \times \mathcal{W}_d \; : \; (x, \kappa_d(x), w_d) \in D\}.$$

Note that when the components of u_c and u_d correspond to the same physical input, like μ in Example 2.1, such components of the feedback law pair (κ_c, κ_d) have to be identical – see the revisited version of Example 2.1 in Example 5.4.

REMARK 2.3. *When* $\mathcal{H}_{u,w}$ *satisfies the hybrid basic conditions and the state-feedback pair* (κ_c, κ_d) *is continuous, the hybrid closed-loop system* $\mathcal{H}_{cl}$ *satisfies the hybrid basic conditions. An important consequence of* $\mathcal{H}_{cl}$ *satisfying the hybrid basic conditions is that asymptotic stability of a compact set for* $\mathcal{H}_{u,w}$ *(with* $w \equiv 0$*) is automatically nominally robust, in the sense that the asymptotic stability property is preserved (semiglobally and practically) under the presence of small enough perturbations.*

3. ROBUST STABILITY, STABILIZABILITY, AND CONTROL LYAPUNOV FUNCTIONS

This section introduces the stability, stabilizability, and control Lyapunov function notions for $\mathcal{H}_{u,w}$ employed throughout the paper. Nominal versions of these notions can be found in [7] and [11].

First, we introduce a stability property of closed sets capturing robustness with respect to all admissible disturbances w. For simplicity, we write the global version, but, though more involved, a local version can certainly be formulated.

[2]A set-valued map $S : \mathbb{R}^n \rightrightarrows \mathbb{R}^m$ is *outer semicontinuous* at $x \in \mathbb{R}^n$ if for each sequence $\{x_i\}_{i=1}^{\infty}$ converging to a point $x \in \mathbb{R}^n$ and each sequence $y_i \in S(x_i)$ converging to a point y, it holds that $y \in S(x)$; see [10, Definition 5.4]. Given a set $X \subset \mathbb{R}^n$, it is *outer semicontinuous relative to* X if the set-valued mapping from $\mathbb{R}^n$ to $\mathbb{R}^m$ defined by $S(x)$ for $x \in X$ and $\emptyset$ for $x \notin X$ is outer semicontinuous at each $x \in X$. It is *locally bounded* if for each compact set $K \subset \mathbb{R}^n$ there exists a compact set $K' \subset \mathbb{R}^n$ such that $S(K) := \cup_{x \in K} S(x) \subset K'$.

DEFINITION 3.1. *(w-robust uniform global asymptotic stability) Given a control* u*, and closed sets* $\mathcal{A}$ *and* $\widetilde{\mathcal{A}}$ *subsets of* $\mathbb{R}^n$*, the set* $\widetilde{\mathcal{A}}$ *is said to be* w-robustly uniformly globally asymptotically stable relative to $\mathcal{A}$ *for the hybrid system* $\mathcal{H}_{u,w}$ *if*

$$\mathcal{A} \subset \widetilde{\mathcal{A}} \tag{5}$$

and there exists $\beta \in \mathcal{KL}$ *such that, for each admissible disturbance* w*, every solution* ϕ *to* $\mathcal{H}_{u,w}$ *using the given control* u *satisfies*

$$|\phi(t,j)|_{\widetilde{\mathcal{A}}} \le \beta(|\phi(0,0)|_{\widetilde{\mathcal{A}}}, t+j) \qquad \forall (t,j) \in \operatorname{dom} \phi \tag{6}$$

REMARK 3.2. *When the property in Definition 3.1 holds for* $\widetilde{\mathcal{A}} = \mathcal{A}$*, in which case we will drop "relative to* $\mathcal{A}$*," the notion resembles [7, Definition 3.6] with the addition that the property holds for every possible admissible disturbance. When* $\mathcal{A} \neq \widetilde{\mathcal{A}}$*, the set* $\widetilde{\mathcal{A}}$ *is a* residual set *relative to* $\mathcal{A}$*, meaning that complete solutions would converge to* $\widetilde{\mathcal{A}}$ *but may not converge to* $\mathcal{A}$*. A particular such situation is when* $\mathcal{A}$ *is the origin and the set* $\widetilde{\mathcal{A}}$ *is a small neighborhood around it. Finally, note that the property in Definition 3.1, and the ones introduced below, may hold for a large enough residual (e.g.,* $\widetilde{\mathcal{A}} = \mathbb{R}^n$*), though one is typically interested in having* $\widetilde{\mathcal{A}}$ *to be some small neighborhood of* $\mathcal{A}$*.*

REMARK 3.3. *The property in Definition 3.1 differs from input-to-state stability (ISS) with respect to* w *as the* $\mathcal{KL}$ *bound defining ISS involves the distance from the state trajectory to a set (like* $\mathcal{A}$*), rather than to a residual set (like* $\widetilde{\mathcal{A}}$*), and includes an additive offset that is a function of a norm of* w*; see [1] for a definition of ISS for hybrid systems as in (1). A key difference is that ISS guarantees attractivity of a neighborhood of a set (of size depending on a norm of the disturbance), while our* w*-robust notion guarantees an asymptotic stability of a residual set that is uniform over all admissible disturbances.*

The existence of some control u, perhaps (hybrid) time dependent, stabilizing a point or a set is known as *stabilizability*. Next, we introduce this notion for the case of hybrid systems under disturbances.

DEFINITION 3.4. *(robust stabilizability) Given a hybrid system* $\mathcal{H}_{u,w}$*, a closed set* $\mathcal{A} \subset \mathbb{R}^n$ *is said to be*

1) w-robustly uniformly globally asymptotically stabilizable *for* $\mathcal{H}_{u,w}$ *if there exists an admissible control* u *such that the set* $\mathcal{A}$ *is* w*-robustly uniformly globally asymptotically stable for* $\mathcal{H}_{u,w}$*;*
2) w-robustly practically uniformly globally asymptotically stabilizable *for* $\mathcal{H}_{u,w}$ *if for every* $\varepsilon > 0$ *there exist an admissible control* u *and a closed set* $\widetilde{\mathcal{A}}$ *satisfying*

$$\mathcal{A} \subset \widetilde{\mathcal{A}} \subset \mathcal{A} + \varepsilon\mathbb{B}$$

such that the set $\widetilde{\mathcal{A}}$ *is* w*-robustly uniformly globally asymptotically stable for* $\mathcal{H}_{u,w}$ *relative to* $\mathcal{A}$*;*

3) w-robustly uniformly globally asymptotically stabilizable with residual $\widetilde{\mathcal{A}}$ *for* $\mathcal{H}_{u,w}$ *with* $\widetilde{\mathcal{A}}$ *closed,* $\mathcal{A} \subsetneq \widetilde{\mathcal{A}}$*, if there exists an admissible control* u *such that the set* $\widetilde{\mathcal{A}}$ *is* w*-robustly uniformly globally asymptotically stable relative to* $\mathcal{A}$ *for* $\mathcal{H}_{u,w}$*.*

REMARK 3.5. *The notion in item 1) in Definition 3.4 captures the situation when the effect of the disturbances can be overcome and the desired set $\mathcal{A}$ rendered asymptotically stable by some control u. For the hybrid system in Example 2.1, for which the desired set $\mathcal{A}$ is naturally the origin, this set being w-robustly uniformly globally asymptotically stabilizable requires the existence of a control that renders the origin uniformly globally asymptotically stable for any disturbance (w_c, w_d); see Example 5.4. The practical notion in item 2) corresponds to the situation when the asymptotically stable residual set $\widetilde{\mathcal{A}}$ can be made arbitrarily close to the set $\mathcal{A}$ by some control u. Finally, item 3) captures the situation when only a residual set can be stabilized.*

Methods for synthesis of feedback control laws that induce the properties introduced above will employ control Lyapunov functions. For the nominal case, a control Lyapunov function for a hybrid system is a function that, for each value of the state, there exist control input values that make the function decrease during flows and jumps [11, Definition 2.1]. Following the construction in [6, Definition 3.8] for continuous-time systems, we introduce the following robust control Lyapunov function notion for $\mathcal{H}_{u,w}$.

DEFINITION 3.6. *(robust control Lyapunov function) Given a closed set $\mathcal{A} \subset \mathbb{R}^n$, sets $\mathcal{U}_c \subset \mathbb{R}^{m_c}$ and $\mathcal{U}_d \subset \mathbb{R}^{m_d}$, and sets $\mathcal{W}_c \subset \mathbb{R}^{d_c}$ and $\mathcal{W}_d \subset \mathbb{R}^{d_d}$, a continuous function $V : \mathbb{R}^n \to \mathbb{R}$ that is locally Lipschitz on an open set containing $\overline{\Pi_c(C)}$ is a* robust control Lyapunov function (RCLF) with $\mathcal{U}$ controls for $\mathcal{H}_{u,w}$ *if there exist[3] $r^* \geq 0$, $\alpha_1, \alpha_2 \in \mathcal{K}_\infty$, and a positive definite function α_3 such that*

$$\alpha_1(|x|_{\mathcal{A}}) \leq V(x) \leq \alpha_2(|x|_{\mathcal{A}}) \quad \forall x \in \Pi_c(C) \cup \Pi_d(D) \cup G(D), \quad (7)$$

$$\inf_{u_c \in \Psi_c^u(x)} \sup_{w_c \in \Psi_c^w(x)} \sup_{\xi \in F(x,u_c,w_c)} V^\circ(x;\xi) \leq -\alpha_3(|x|_{\mathcal{A}}) \quad \forall x \in \Pi_c(C) \cap \mathcal{I}(r),\ r \geq r^*, \quad (8)$$

$$\inf_{u_d \in \Psi_d^u(x)} \sup_{w_d \in \Psi_d^w(x)} \sup_{\xi \in G(x,u_d,w_d)} V(\xi) - V(x) \leq -\alpha_3(|x|_{\mathcal{A}}) \quad \forall x \in \Pi_d(D) \cap \mathcal{I}(r),\ r \geq r^*. \quad (9)$$

EXAMPLE 3.7. *(controlled pendulum with impacts (revisited)) For the hybrid system in Example 2.1, let $\mathcal{A} = \{(0,0)\}$ and consider the candidate robust control Lyapunov function with $\mathcal{U}$ controls for $\mathcal{H}_{u,w}$ given by*

$$V(x) = x^\top P x, \qquad P = \begin{bmatrix} 2 & 1 \\ 1 & 1 \end{bmatrix}. \quad (10)$$

Condition (7) holds trivially. During flows, we have that

$$\langle \nabla V(x), F(x,u_c,w_c)\rangle = 4x_1x_2 + 2x_2^2 + 2(-a\sin x_1 - (b + w_{c,2})x_2 + u_{c,1} + w_{c,1})(x_2 + x_1)$$

for all $(x, u_c, w_c) \in C$. It follows that (8) is satisfied with α_3 defined as $\alpha_3(s) := s^2$ for all $s \geq 0$. In fact, note that, for each $x \in \mathbb{R}^2$,

$$\Psi_c^u(x) = \begin{cases} \mathbb{R} \times [-\frac{\pi}{2}, \min\{x_1, 0\}] & \text{if } x_1 \in [-\frac{\pi}{2}, \frac{\pi}{2}] \\ \emptyset & \text{if } x_1 \notin [-\frac{\pi}{2}, \frac{\pi}{2}] \end{cases}$$

$$\Psi_c^w(x) = \begin{cases} \mathcal{W}_c & \text{if } x_1 \in [-\frac{\pi}{2}, \frac{\pi}{2}] \\ \emptyset & \text{if } x_1 \notin [-\frac{\pi}{2}, \frac{\pi}{2}] \end{cases}$$

and that $\Pi_c(C) = [-\frac{\pi}{2}, \frac{\pi}{2}] \times \mathbb{R}$. Then

$$\inf_{u_c \in \Psi_c^u(x)} \sup_{w_c \in \Psi_c^w(x)} \langle \nabla V(x), F(x,u_c,w_c)\rangle = -x^\top x$$

for all $x \in \Pi_c(C)$ such that $x_1 + x_2 = 0$, while when $x_1 + x_2 \neq 0$, we have

$$\inf_{u_c \in \Psi_c^u(x)} \sup_{w_c \in \Psi_c^w(x)} \langle \nabla V(x), F(x,u_c,w_c)\rangle = -\infty.$$

For each $x \in \mathbb{R}^2$, we have

$$\Psi_d^u(x) = \begin{cases} [x_1, 0] & \text{if } x_1 \in [-\frac{\pi}{2}, 0], x_2 \leq 0 \\ \emptyset & \text{otherwise}, \end{cases}$$

$$\Psi_d^w(x) = \begin{cases} \mathcal{W}_d & \text{if } x_1 \in [-\frac{\pi}{2}, 0], x_2 \leq 0 \\ \emptyset & \text{otherwise}, \end{cases}$$

and that $\Pi_d(D) = [-\frac{\pi}{2}, 0] \times (-\infty, 0]$. Then, at jumps, we have

$$\inf_{u_d \in \Psi_d^u(x)} \sup_{w_d \in \Psi_d^w(x)} V(G(x,u_d,w_d)) - V(x) \leq -\lambda x^\top x$$

for all $x \in \Pi_d(D)$, where

$$\lambda := \min_{\eta_1 \in [-\frac{\pi}{2}, 0]} \{2(1 - (1 + \widetilde{\rho}(\eta_1))^2), 1 - (e(\eta_1) + e_1 - e_0)^2\}$$

which, by the properties of $\widetilde{\rho}$ and e, is positive. Then, condition (9) is satisfied with α_3 defined as $\alpha_3(s) := \lambda s^2$ for all $s \geq 0$.

It follows that both (8) and (9) hold with this choice of α_3. △

4. ROBUST STABILIZABILITY VIA STATIC STATE-FEEDBACK LAWS

In this section, we provide conditions guaranteeing the existence of a robustly stabilizing control u inducing some of the properties introduced in Section 3. Our interest is in control laws that are of (static) state-feedback type and continuous, which, as argued in Remark 2.3, when $\mathcal{H}_{u,w}$ satisfies the hybrid basic conditions, would lead to a closed-loop system $\mathcal{H}_{cl}$ (without u) as in (4) satisfying the hybrid basic conditions.

Given the compact set $\mathcal{A}$ and a robust control Lyapunov function V satisfying Definition 3.6 with positive definite function α_3 and $r^* \geq 0$, define, for each $(x, u_c, w_c) \in \mathbb{R}^n \times \mathbb{R}^{m_c} \times \mathbb{R}^{d_c}$ and $r \geq r^*$, the function

$$\Gamma_c(x,u_c,r) := \begin{cases} \sup_{w_c \in \Psi_c^w(x)} \sup_{\xi \in F(x,u_c,w_c)} \langle \nabla V(x), \xi\rangle + \frac{1}{2}\alpha_3(|x|_{\mathcal{A}}) & \text{if } (x,u_c) \in \Delta_c(r,C), \\ -\infty & \text{otherwise} \end{cases}$$

[3]When $\mathcal{H}_{u,w}$ has purely continuous dynamics, i.e., it does not exhibit jumps, then $r \geq r^*$ can be replaced by $r > r^*$. In fact, in such a case, when $r^* = 0$ solutions cannot flow out of $\mathcal{A}$. However, when the system has jumps, if (9) only holds for each $r > r^* = 0$, there could still be solutions that jump outside of $\mathcal{A}$.

and, for each $(x, u_d, w_d) \in \mathbb{R}^n \times \mathbb{R}^{m_d} \times \mathbb{R}^{d_d}$ and $r \geq r^*$, the function

$$\Gamma_d(x, u_d, r) := \begin{cases} \sup\limits_{w_d \in \Psi_d^w(x)} \sup\limits_{\xi \in G(x,u_d,w_d)} V(\xi) - V(x) \\ \qquad + \frac{1}{2}\alpha_3(|x|_{\mathcal{A}}) \\ \qquad \text{if } (x, u_d) \in \Delta_d(r, D), \\ -\infty \qquad \text{otherwise.} \end{cases}$$

When these functions and the system satisfy further properties introduced below, the existence of a w-robustly stabilizing feedback law is guaranteed.

THEOREM 4.1. *Given a compact set $\mathcal{A} \subset \mathbb{R}^n$ and a hybrid system $\mathcal{H} = (C, F, D, G)$ satisfying the hybrid basic conditions, suppose there exists a robust control Lyapunov function V with $\mathcal{U}$ controls for $\mathcal{H}_{u,w}$ that is continuously differentiable on a neighborhood of $\Pi_c(C) \cap \mathcal{I}(r^*)$, where r^* comes from Definition 3.6. Furthermore, suppose the following conditions hold:*

R1) The set-valued maps Ψ_c^u and Ψ_d^u are lower semicontinuous[4] with convex values.

R2) For every $r > r^*$ and for every $x \in \Pi_c(C) \cap \mathcal{I}(r)$, the function $u_c \mapsto \Gamma_c(x, u_c, r)$ is convex on $\Psi_c^u(x)$ and, for every $r > r^*$ and every $x \in \Pi_d(D) \cap \mathcal{I}(r)$, the function $u_d \mapsto \Gamma_d(x, u_d, r)$ is convex on $\Psi_d^u(x)$.

R3) The set $\mathcal{W}$ is closed and the set-valued maps Ψ_c^w and Ψ_d^w are outer semicontinuous, locally bounded, and nonempty for each $x \in \Pi_c(C) \cap \mathcal{I}(r^*)$ and each $x \in \Pi_d(D) \cap \mathcal{I}(r^*)$, respectively.

Then, for each $r > r^*$, the set $\mathcal{A}$ is w-robustly uniformly globally asymptotically stabilizable with residual

$$\widetilde{\mathcal{A}} = \{x \in \mathbb{R}^n \; : \; V(x) \leq r\} \tag{11}$$

for $\mathcal{H}_{u,w}^{\mathcal{I}}$ by a state-feedback law (κ_c, κ_d) that is continuous on $(\Pi_c(C) \cap \mathcal{I}(r)) \times (\Pi_d(D) \cap \mathcal{I}(r))$, where $\mathcal{H}_{u,w}^{\mathcal{I}}$ is the restriction of $\mathcal{H}_{u,w}$ to $\mathcal{I}(r)$ given by

$$\mathcal{H}_{u,w}^{\mathcal{I}} \begin{cases} \dot{x} \in F(x, u_c, w_c) \\ \qquad (x, u_c, w_c) \in C \cap (\mathcal{I}(r) \times \mathbb{R}^{m_c} \times \mathbb{R}^{d_c}), \\ x^+ \in G(x, u_d, w_d) \\ \qquad (x, u_d, w_d) \in D \cap (\mathcal{I}(r) \times \mathbb{R}^{m_d} \times \mathbb{R}^{d_d}). \end{cases}$$

In particular, for each $r > r^*$, there exists a state-feedback law (κ_c, κ_d) with κ_c continuous on $\Pi_c(C) \cap \mathcal{I}(r)$ and κ_d continuous on $\Pi_d(D) \cap \mathcal{I}(r)$ defining an admissible control $u = (\kappa_c, \kappa_d)$ that renders the compact set $\widetilde{\mathcal{A}}$ in (11) w-robustly uniformly globally asymptotically stable relative to $\mathcal{A}$ for $\mathcal{H}_{u,w}^{\mathcal{I}}$.

EXAMPLE 4.2. *(controlled pendulum with impacts (revisited)) A robust control Lyapunov function satisfying the conditions in Theorem 4.1 was constructed in Example 3.7. Conditions R1) and R3) immediately hold from the constructions therein. The definition of Γ_c above gives, for each $r \geq 0$,*

$$\Gamma_c(x, u_c, r) = \begin{cases} \sup\limits_{w_c \in \Psi_c^w(x)} \big[4x_1x_2 + 2x_2^2 + 2(-a\sin x_1 \\ \quad -(b + w_{c,2})x_2 + u_{c,1} + w_{c,1})(x_2 + x_1) \\ \quad +\alpha_3(|x|_{\mathcal{A}})\big] \\ \qquad \textit{if } (x, u_c) \in \Delta_c(r, C), \\ -\infty \qquad \textit{otherwise} \end{cases}$$

while the definition of Γ_d above gives, for each $r \geq 0$,

$$\Gamma_d(x, u_d, r) = \begin{cases} \sup\limits_{w_d \in \Psi_d^w(x)} \big[-2x_1^2(1 - (1 + \widetilde{\rho}(u_d))^2) \\ \quad -x_2^2(1 - (e(u_d) + w_d)^2) \\ \quad -2x_1x_2(1 + (1 + \widetilde{\rho}(u_d))(e(u_d) + w_d)) \\ \quad +\alpha_3(|x|_{\mathcal{A}})\big] \\ \qquad \textit{if } (x, u_d) \in \Delta_d(r, D), \\ -\infty \qquad \textit{otherwise} \end{cases}$$

Then, R2) holds. Hence, since $r^* = 0$, according to Theorem 4.1, the hybrid system in Example 2.1 has its origin w-robustly practically uniformly globally asymptotically stabilizable. We will see in Example 5.4 that a non-practical property already holds and that a stabilizing state-feedback law can actually be synthesized. △

The result above guarantees a robust stabilizability property that either has a residual or is practical. For robust stabilizability of a compact set, extra conditions are required to hold nearby the compact set. For continuous-time systems, such conditions correspond to the so-called *small control property* [14, 6, 8]. To that end, given a compact set $\mathcal{A}$ and a robust control Lyapunov function V as in Definition 3.6, define, for each $(x, r) \in \mathbb{R}^n \times \mathbb{R}_{\geq 0}$, the set-valued map[5]

$$\widehat{S}_c(x, r) := \begin{cases} S_c(x, r) & \text{if } r > 0, \\ \kappa_{c,0}(x) & \text{if } r = 0, \end{cases} \qquad \widehat{S}_d(x, r) := \begin{cases} S_d(x, r) & \text{if } r > 0, \\ \kappa_{d,0}(x) & \text{if } r = 0, \end{cases} \tag{12}$$

where $\kappa_{c,0} : \mathbb{R}^n \to \mathcal{U}_c$ and $\kappa_{d,0} : \mathbb{R}^n \to \mathcal{U}_d$ induce forward invariance of $\mathcal{A}$ for $\mathcal{H}_{u,w}$, that is,

R4) Every maximal solution (ϕ, w_c) to

$$\dot{x} \in F(x, \kappa_{c,0}(x), w_c) \quad (x, \kappa_{c,0}(x), w_c) \in C$$

from $\mathcal{A}$ is such that the ϕ component satisfies $|\phi(t, 0)|_{\mathcal{A}} = 0$ for all $(t, 0) \in \operatorname{dom}(\phi, w_c)$.

R5) Every maximal solution (ϕ, w_d) to

$$x^+ \in G(x, \kappa_{d,0}(x), w_d) \quad (x, \kappa_{d,0}(x), w_d) \in D$$

from $\mathcal{A}$ is such that the ϕ component satisfies $|\phi(0, j)|_{\mathcal{A}} = 0$ for all $(0, j) \in \operatorname{dom}(\phi, w_d)$.

[4]A set-valued map $S : \mathbb{R}^n \rightrightarrows \mathbb{R}^m$ is lower semicontinuous if for each $x \in \mathbb{R}^n$ one has that $\liminf_{x_i \to x} S(x_i) \supset S(x)$, where $\liminf_{x_i \to x} S(x_i) = \{z : \forall x_i \to x, \exists z_i \to z \text{ s.t. } z_i \in S(x_i)\}$ is the *inner limit* of S (see [10, Chapter 5.B]). By lower semicontinuity of a set-valued map S with not open $\operatorname{dom} S$ we mean that the trivial extension of S proposed in [11, Lemma 4.2] is lower semicontinuous.

[5]Note that if either $\Pi_c(C)$ or $\Pi_d(D)$ do not intersect the compact set $\mathcal{A}$, then neither the existence of the functions $\kappa_{c,0}$ or $\kappa_{d,0}$, respectively, nor lower semicontinuity at $r = 0$ are needed, since R4) and R5) would hold for free.

Under the conditions in Theorem 4.1, with $r^* = 0$, the maps in (12) are lower semicontinuous for every $r > 0$. To be able to make continuous selections at $\mathcal{A}$, these maps are further required to be lower semicontinuous for $r = 0$. These conditions resemble those already reported in [6] for continuous-time systems.

THEOREM 4.3. *Under the conditions of Theorem 4.1 and when $r^* = 0$, if there exist continuous functions $\kappa_{c,0} : \mathbb{R}^n \to \mathcal{U}_c$ and $\kappa_{d,0} : \mathbb{R}^n \to \mathcal{U}_d$ such that conditions R4) and R5) hold, and*

R6) The set-valued map $\widehat{S}_c$ is lower semicontinuous at each $x \in \Pi_c(C) \cap \mathcal{I}(0)$;

R7) The set-valued map $\widehat{S}_d$ is lower semicontinuous at each $x \in \Pi_d(D) \cap \mathcal{I}(0)$;

R8) The hybrid exosystem $\mathcal{H}_e$ in (2) satisfies the hybrid basic conditions;

then $\mathcal{A}$ is w-robustly uniformly globally asymptotically stabilizable for $\mathcal{H}_{u,w}$ by a continuous state-feedback pair (κ_c, κ_d).

5. CONSTRUCTIVE DESIGN OF ROBUSTLY STABILIZING FEEDBACK LAWS

We show that, under further conditions, the results in Section 4 lead to a constructive design procedure of state-feedback control laws that induce w-robust asymptotic stability. The key idea is to define a selection from the "regulation map" that can be synthesized (or computed) for given system data and RCLF.

Recalling the construction of Γ_c and Γ_d in Section 4, we evaluate these functions at points (x, u_c, r) and (x, u_d, r) with $r = V(x)$ to define the functions

$$\begin{aligned}(x, u_c) &\mapsto \Upsilon_c(x, u_c) := \Gamma_c(x, u_c, V(x)),\\ (x, u_d) &\mapsto \Upsilon_d(x, u_d) := \Gamma_d(x, u_d, V(x))\end{aligned} \qquad (13)$$

and the set-valued maps

$$\begin{aligned}\mathcal{T}_c(x) &:= \Psi_c^u(x) \cap \{u_c \in \mathcal{U}_c \ : \ \Upsilon_c(x, u_c) \le 0\},\\ \mathcal{T}_d(x) &:= \Psi_d^u(x) \cap \{u_d \in \mathcal{U}_d \ : \ \Upsilon_d(x, u_d) \le 0\}.\end{aligned} \qquad (14)$$

Furthermore, define

$$R_c := \Pi_c(C) \cap \{x \in \mathbb{R}^n \ : \ V(x) > 0\} \qquad (15)$$

and

$$R_d := \Pi_d(D) \cap \{x \in \mathbb{R}^n \ : \ V(x) > 0\}. \qquad (16)$$

When, for each x, the functions $u_c \mapsto \Upsilon_c(x, u_c)$ and $u_d \mapsto \Upsilon_d(x, u_c)$ are convex, and the set-valued maps Ψ_c^u and Ψ_d^u have nonempty closed convex values on R_c and R_d, respectively, we have that $\mathcal{T}_c$ and $\mathcal{T}_d$ have nonempty convex closed values on (15) and on (16), respectively; this property follows from [5, Proposition 4.4]. Then, $\mathcal{T}_c$ and $\mathcal{T}_d$ have unique elements of minimum norm on R_c and R_d, respectively, and their minimal selections

$$\rho_c : R_c \to \mathcal{U}_c, \qquad \rho_d : R_d \to \mathcal{U}_d$$

are given by

$$\rho_c(x) := \arg\min\{|u_c| \ : \ u_c \in \mathcal{T}_c(x)\} \qquad (17)$$

$$\rho_d(x) := \arg\min\{|u_d| \ : \ u_d \in \mathcal{T}_d(x)\} \qquad (18)$$

Moreover, as the following result states, these selections are continuous under further properties of Ψ_c^u and Ψ_d^u.

THEOREM 5.1. *Given a compact set $\mathcal{A} \subset \mathbb{R}^n$ and a hybrid system $\mathcal{H}_{u,w} = (C, F, D, G)$ satisfying the hybrid basic conditions, suppose there exists a robust control Lyapunov function V with $\mathcal{U}$ controls for $\mathcal{H}_{u,w}$ that is continuously differentiable on a neighborhood of $\Pi_c(C) \cap \mathcal{I}(r^*)$, where r^* comes from Definition 3.6. Furthermore, suppose conditions R1)-R3) in Theorem 4.1 hold. Then, for each $r > r^*$, the state-feedback law pair*

$$\rho_c : R_c \cap \mathcal{I}(r) \to \mathcal{U}_c, \qquad \rho_d : R_d \cap \mathcal{I}(r) \to \mathcal{U}_d$$

defined as

$$\rho_c(x) \ := \ \arg\min\{|u_c| \ : \ u_c \in \mathcal{T}_c(x)\} \quad \forall x \in R_c \cap \mathcal{I}(r) \qquad (19)$$

$$\rho_d(x) \ := \ \arg\min\{|u_d| \ : \ u_d \in \mathcal{T}_d(x)\} \quad \forall x \in R_d \cap \mathcal{I}(r) \qquad (20)$$

renders the compact set

$$\widetilde{\mathcal{A}} = \{x \in \mathbb{R}^n \ : \ V(x) \le r\}$$

w-robustly uniformly globally asymptotically stable for $\mathcal{H}_{u,w}^{\mathcal{I}}$ relative to $\mathcal{A}$, where $\mathcal{H}_{u,w}^{\mathcal{I}}$ is the restriction of $\mathcal{H}_{u,w}$ to $\mathcal{I}(r)$ given as in Theorem 4.1.

Furthemore, if the set-valued maps Ψ_c^u and Ψ_d^u have closed graph then ρ_c and ρ_d are continuous.

REMARK 5.2. *When bounds (8) and (9) hold for functions $\alpha_{3,c}$ and $\alpha_{3,d}$, respectively, the expressions of the pointwise minimum norm control laws (17) and (18) can be rewritten in terms of those functions (instead of a common function α_3) by defining, respectively, $\mathcal{T}_c$ and $\mathcal{T}_d$ using $\alpha_{3,c}$ and $\alpha_{3,d}$ in place of α_3.*

The state-feedback law (19)-(20) asymptotically stabilizes $\widetilde{\mathcal{A}}$ for $\mathcal{H}_{u,w}^{\mathcal{I}}$, but not necessarily for $\mathcal{H}_{u,w}$, as without an appropriate extension of these laws to $\Pi_c(C)$ and $\Pi_d(D)$, respectively, there could exist solutions to the closed-loop system that jump out of $\widetilde{\mathcal{A}}$. This point motivates the (non-practical, and stronger) result that we present next.

Following the ideas behind Theorem 4.3, we extend the pointwise minimum norm state-feedback control law in Theorem 5.1 so as to w-robustly globally asymptotically stabilize a compact set $\mathcal{A}$. To that end, given a compact set $\mathcal{A}$ and a robust control Lyapunov function V satisfying Definition 3.6, for each $x \in \mathbb{R}^n$, define

$$\mathcal{T}_c'(x) \ := \ \Psi_c^u(x) \cap S_c'(x, V(x)), \qquad (21)$$

$$\mathcal{T}_d'(x) \ := \ \Psi_d^u(x) \cap S_d'(x, V(x)), \qquad (22)$$

where, for each $x \in \mathbb{R}^n$ and each $r \ge 0$,

$$\begin{aligned} S_c'(x, r) &:= \begin{cases} S_c^\circ(x, r) & \text{if } r > 0,\\ \rho_{c,0}(x) & \text{if } r = 0,\end{cases}\\ S_d'(x, r) &:= \begin{cases} S_d^\circ(x, r) & \text{if } r > 0,\\ \rho_{d,0}(x) & \text{if } r = 0,\end{cases}\end{aligned} \qquad (23)$$

$$S_c^\circ(x,r) = \begin{cases} \{u_c \in \mathcal{U}_c \ : \ \Gamma_c(x,u_c,r) \le 0 \} \\ \qquad\qquad \text{if } x \in \Pi_c(C) \cap \mathcal{I}(r), \\ \mathbb{R}^{m_c} \qquad\qquad \text{otherwise,} \end{cases}$$

$$S_d^\circ(x,r) = \begin{cases} \{u_d \in \mathcal{U}_d \ : \ \Gamma_d(x,u_d,r) \le 0 \} \\ \qquad\qquad \text{if } x \in \Pi_d(D) \cap \mathcal{I}(r), \\ \mathbb{R}^{m_d} \qquad\qquad \text{otherwise,} \end{cases}$$

and the feedback law pair

$$\rho_{c,0} : \mathbb{R}^n \to \mathcal{U}_c$$

$$\rho_{d,0} : \mathbb{R}^n \to \mathcal{U}_d$$

induces (strong) forward invariance of $\mathcal{A}$ as stated in R4) (with $\kappa_{c,0} = \rho_{c,0}$) and R5) (with $\kappa_{d,0} = \rho_{d,0}$) in Section 4. Note that under the conditions in Theorem 5.1, the maps in (12) are lower semicontinuous for every $r > 0$. To be able to make continuous selections at $\mathcal{A}$, these maps are further required to be lower semicontinuous for $r = 0$.

THEOREM 5.3. *Under the conditions of Theorem 5.1 and when $r^* = 0$, if there exists a feedback law pair ($\rho_{c,0} : \mathbb{R}^n \to \mathcal{U}_c$, $\rho_{d,0} : \mathbb{R}^n \to \mathcal{U}_d$) such that R4) and R5) in Section 4 hold*[6]*, and*

M1) The set-valued map $\mathcal{T}_c'$ in (21) is lower semicontinuous at each $x \in \Pi_c(C) \cap \mathcal{I}(0)$;

M2) The set-valued map $\mathcal{T}_d'$ in (22) is lower semicontinuous at each $x \in \Pi_d(D) \cap \mathcal{I}(0)$;

hold, then the state-feedback law pair

$$\rho_c : \Pi_c(C) \to \mathcal{U}_c, \qquad \rho_d : \Pi_d(D) \to \mathcal{U}_d$$

defined as

$$\rho_c(x) := \arg\min \left\{ |u_c| \ : \ u_c \in \mathcal{T}_c'(x) \right\} \quad \forall x \in \Pi_c(C) \quad (24)$$

$$\rho_d(x) := \arg\min \left\{ |u_d| \ : \ u_d \in \mathcal{T}_d'(x) \right\} \quad \forall x \in \Pi_d(D) \quad (25)$$

renders the compact set $\mathcal{A}$ w-robustly uniformly globally asymptotically stable for $\mathcal{H}_{u,w}$. Furthermore, if the set-valued maps Ψ_c and Ψ_d have closed graph and $(\rho_{c,0}, \rho_{d,0})(\mathcal{A}) = 0$, then ρ_c and ρ_d are continuous.

We revisit our running example and synthesize a stabilizing feedback. Simulations validate the results.

EXAMPLE 5.4. *(controlled pendulum with impacts (revisited)) From the constructions of Γ_c and Γ_d in Example 4.2, the set-valued map $\mathcal{T}_c$ is given by*

$$\begin{aligned} \Big\{ u_c \in \mathbb{R} \times \Big[-\frac{\pi}{2}, \min\{x_1, 0\}\Big] \ : \ & 4x_1x_2 + 2x_2^2 \\ & + 2(-a \sin x_1 - bx_2 + u_{c,1})(x_2 + x_1) + \lambda x^\top x \\ & + 2|x_2 + x_1|(\overline{w}_{c,2}|x_2| + \overline{w}_{c,1}) \le 0 \Big\} \end{aligned} \quad (26)$$

for each $x \in \Pi_c(C) \cap \{ x \in \mathbb{R}^2 \ : \ V(x) > 0 \}$.

Proceeding in the same way, the set-valued map $\mathcal{T}_d$ is given by

$$\begin{aligned} \{ u_d \in [x_1, 0] \ : \ & -2x_1^2(1 - (1 + \widetilde{\rho}(u_d))^2) \\ & -x_2^2(1 - (e(u_d) + e_1 - e_0)^2) + \lambda x^\top x \le 0 \Big\} \end{aligned}$$

for each $x \in \Pi_d(D) \cap \{ x \in \mathbb{R}^2 \ : \ V(x) > 0 \}$, where we dropped the term $-2x_1x_2(1 + (1 + \widetilde{\rho}(u_d))(e(u_d) + w_d))$ since on D we have that $x_1x_2 \ge 0$.

Now, we synthesize the control law using Theorem 5.3. Defining $\psi_0(x) := 4x_1x_2 + 2x_2^2 + 2(-a \sin x_1 - bx_2)(x_2 + x_1) + \lambda x^\top x$, $\psi_0^w(x) := 2|x_2 + x_1|(\overline{w}_{c,2}|x_2| + \overline{w}_{c,1})$, and $\psi_1(x) := 2(x_1 + x_2)$, the map in (26) can be rewritten as

$$\begin{aligned} \mathcal{T}_c(x) = \Big\{ & u_c \in \mathbb{R} \times \Big[-\frac{\pi}{2}, \min\{x_1, 0\}\Big] \ : \\ & \psi_0(x) + \psi_0^w(x) + \psi_1(x)u_{c,1} \le 0 \Big\} \end{aligned}$$

for each $x \in \Pi_c(C) \cap \{ x \in \mathbb{R}^2 \ : \ V(x) > 0 \}$. To determine the pointwise minimum norm control selection according to (17), note that, when $\psi_0(x) + \psi_0^w(x) \le 0$, the pointwise minimum norm control selection is $u_{c,1} = 0$ and that, when $\psi_0(x) + \psi_0^w(x) > 0$, is given by

$$-\frac{(\psi_0(x) + \psi_0^w(x))\psi_1(x)}{\psi_1^2(x)} = -\frac{\psi_0(x) + \psi_0^w(x)}{\psi_1(x)}$$

which leads to $\psi_0(x) + \psi_0^w(x) + \psi_1(x)u_{c,1} = 0$. Then, the pointwise minimum norm control selection is given by[7]

$$\begin{aligned} \rho_{c,1}(x) &:= \begin{cases} -\frac{\psi_0(x) + \psi_0^w(x)}{\psi_1(x)} & \psi_0(x) + \psi_0^w(x) > 0 \\ 0 & \psi_0(x) + \psi_0^w(x) \le 0 \end{cases} \\ \rho_{c,2}(x) &:= 0 \end{aligned}$$

on $\Pi_c(C) \cap \{ x \in \mathbb{R}^2 \ : \ V(x) > 0 \}$. Note that there is no division by zero in the construction of $\rho_{c,1}$ since, when $\psi_1(x) = 0$ we have that $\mathcal{T}_c(x)$ implies that $\psi_0(x) + \psi_0^w(x) \le 0$, in which case, $\rho_{c,1}$ is defined as zero.

Next, we design the state-feedback law to be used at jumps. According to (18), since $\widetilde{\rho}$ maps to $(-1, 0)$, e to (e_0, e_1), and $w_d \in [0, e_1 - e_0]$, the pointwise minimum norm control selection is given by

$$\rho_d(x) := 0.$$

for each $x \in \Pi_d(D) \cap \{ x \in \mathbb{R}^2 \ : \ V(x) > 0 \}$. Since $\rho_{c,2} = \rho_d$, the selection above uniquely defines the input μ.

Figures 1-4 show closed-loop trajectories using the designed pointwise minimum norm control law $((\rho_{c,1}, \rho_{c,2}), \rho_d)$. The restitution function used is linear with $e_0 = \frac{1}{3}$ and $e_1 = \frac{2}{3}$, and the function $\widetilde{\rho}$ is constant and equal to $-\frac{1}{20}$. The simulation results show convergence to the set $\mathcal{A} = \{(0,0)\}$, even under the presence of perturbations. For simplicity, the simulations are performed under constant disturbances (w_c, w_d), for different values of w_c and w_d.

The plots in Figure 1 and Figure 2 correspond to solutions for different values of w_c and with $w_d = 0$. The velocity component jumps at the impact time and then rapidly gets close to nearby zero. The larger the disturbance, the longer it takes for the solutions to converge. While not being part of the design procedure, the control law ρ_c steers the solutions to the origin from within the flow set. In fact, as the solutions approach a neighborhood of $\mathcal{A}$, they evolve nearby the manifold $x_1 + x_2 = 0$, which leads to large input values.

The plots in Figure 3 and Figure 4 correspond to solutions for different values of w_d and with $w_c = 0$. Since the disturbance w_d is positive and captures the uncertainty in the restitution coefficient function, large values of the disturbance cause large peaks after every jump as well as more jumps during the transient, when compared to the results in

[6]With $\kappa_{c,0} = \rho_{c,0}$ and $\kappa_{d,0} = \rho_{d,0}$.

[7]See [6, Chapter 4].

Figure 1 and Figure 2. After a few jumps, the solutions approach a neighborhood of $\mathcal{A}$ along the manifold $x_1 + x_2 = 0$.

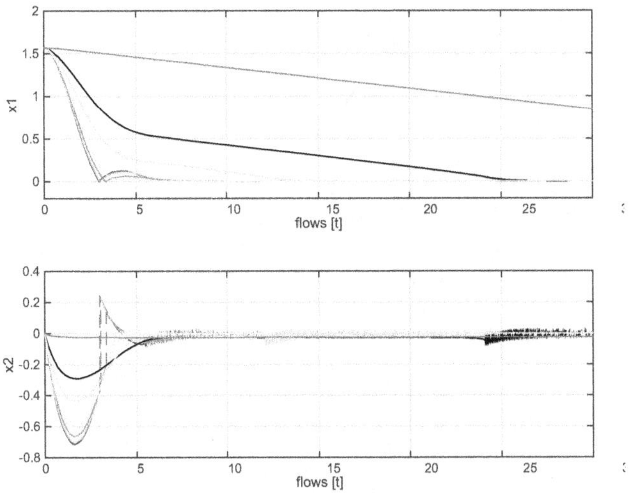

Figure 1: *Closed-loop trajectories as a function of flow time t to the system in Example 5.4 starting from $\phi(0,0) = (1.5707, 0)$ (marked with $\star$). The disturbances used are constant and with the following values: for each $i \in \{1,2\}$, $w_{c,i} = 0$ (blue), $w_{c,i} = 0.01$ (green), $w_{c,i} = 0.05$ (magenta), $w_{c,i} = 0.1$ (yellow), $w_{c,i} = 0.3$ (cyan), $w_{c,i} = 0.5$ (black), $w_{c,i} = 1$ (red); $w_d = 0$ (all simulations).*

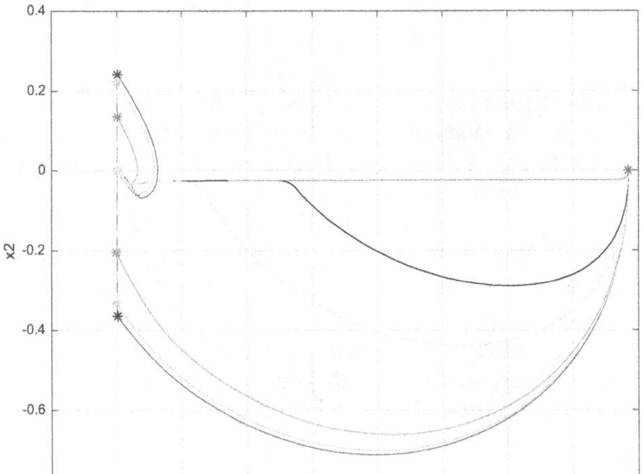

Figure 2: *Closed-loop trajectories on the plane to the system in Example 5.4 starting from $\phi(0,0) = (1.5707, 0)$ (marked with $\star$). The disturbances used are constant and with the following values: for each $i \in \{1,2\}$, $w_{c,i} = 0$ (blue), $w_{c,i} = 0.01$ (green), $w_{c,i} = 0.05$ (magenta), $w_{c,i} = 0.1$ (yellow), $w_{c,i} = 0.3$ (cyan), $w_{c,i} = 0.5$ (black), $w_{c,i} = 1$ (red); $w_d = 0$ (all simulations). The $\star$'s after the initial interval of flow in the plot of the solutions denote the values of the solution before and after the jump.*

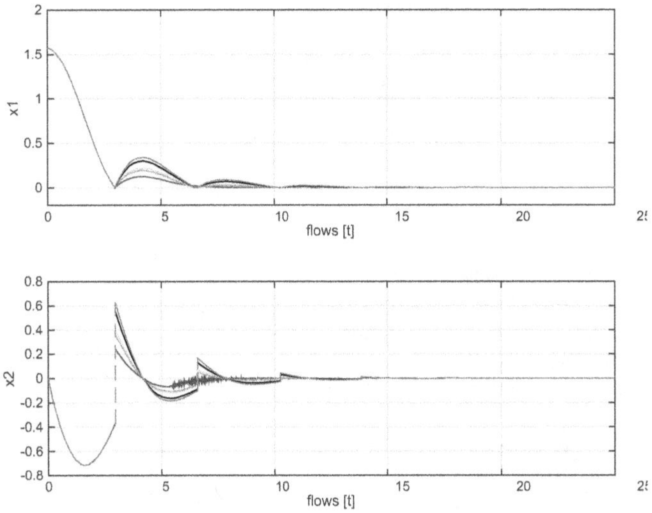

Figure 3: *Closed-loop trajectories as a function of flow time t to the system in Example 5.4 starting from $\phi(0,0) = (1.5707, 0)$ (marked with $\star$). The disturbances used are constant and with the following values: for each $i \in \{1,2\}$, $w_{c,i} = 0$ (all simulations); $w_d = 0$; (blue), $w_d = 0.3$ (magenta), $w_d = 0.4$ (green), $w_d = 0.8$ (black), $w_d = 1$ (red).*

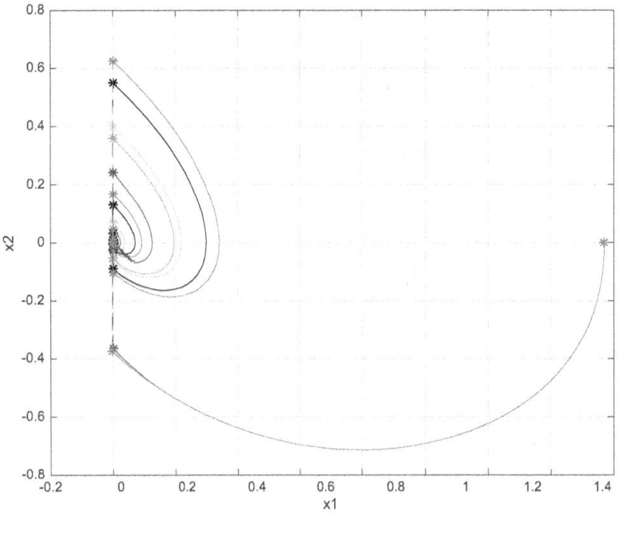

Figure 4: *Closed-loop trajectories on the plane to the system in Example 5.4 starting from $\phi(0,0) = (1.5707, 0)$ (marked with $\star$). The disturbances used are constant and with the following values: for each $i \in \{1,2\}$, $w_{c,i} = 0$ (all simulations); $w_d = 0$; (blue), $w_d = 0.3$ (magenta), $w_d = 0.4$ (green), $w_d = 0.8$ (black), $w_d = 1$ (red). The $\star$'s after the initial interval of flow in the plot of the solutions denote the values of the solution before and after the jump.*

6. CONCLUSION

For a wide class of hybrid systems given in terms of hybrid inclusions with inputs and disturbances, we presented CLF-based results to guarantee the existence of stabilizing state-feedback controllers and to constructively design them. When a CLF is available and the required conditions hold, a state-feedback law with pointwise minimum norm can be constructed to asymptotically stabilize a compact set with robustness to disturbances. A remarkable feature of this controller construction is that it guarantees w-robust asymptotic stability of the closed-loop system for any admissible disturbance taking values from (the w components of) points in the flow set or jump set. Such disturbances can indeed be large, unlike the disturbances allowed in our previous nominal robustness results in [7], and, as a difference to input-to-state stability-based results (see [1]), at times can be fully rejected.

The implementation of the proposed feedback laws requires careful treatment to allow for computation in realistic systems. In particular, the computations involved in determining the minimizers in the state-feedback laws (17) and (18) require a nonzero amount of time to terminate. A sample-and-hold or event-triggered implementation of such laws would require variables that trigger the computation events, allow the computations to terminate, and upon termination of the computations, update the inputs to the hybrid system under control. Recent results suggest that, as long as the time for the computations to terminate can be made sufficiently small, it is possible to implement such laws while preserving the stability properties semiglobally and practically [12]. Handling the challenges in performing such computations is part of current research efforts.

Finally, the proposed state-feedback law with pointwise minimum norm is expected to also induce an optimality property of the closed-loop system. Using inverse optimality ideas, the robust stabilization problem solved in this paper can be recast as a two-player zero-sum hybrid dynamical game. Under appropriate assumptions, we conjecture that the proposed control law suboptimally solves such hybrid game with a meaningful cost function.

7. REFERENCES

[1] C. Cai and A. R. Teel. Characterizations of input-to-state stability for hybrid systems. *Syst. & Cont. Letters*, 58:47–53, 2009.

[2] F. Clarke. *Optimization and Nonsmooth Analysis.* SIAM's Classic in Applied Mathematics, Philadelphia, 1990.

[3] F. Clarke, Y. S. Ledyaev, L. Rifford, and R. Stern. Feedback stabilization and Lyapunov functions. *SIAM: Journal of Control and Optimization*, 39(1):25–48, 2000.

[4] S. Di Cairano, W. M. H. Heemels, M. Lazar, and A. Bemporad. Stabilizing dynamic controllers for hybrid systems: a hybrid control Lyapunov function approach. *IEEE Transactions on Automatic Control*, 59(10):2629–2643, 2014.

[5] R. Freeman and P. Kokotovic. Inverse optimality in robust stabilization. *SIAM Journal of Control and Optimization*, 34:1365–1391, 1996.

[6] R. A. Freeman and P. V. Kokotovic. *Robust Nonlinear Control Design: State-Space and Lyapunov Techniques.* Birkhauser, 1996.

[7] R. Goebel, R. G. Sanfelice, and A. R. Teel. *Hybrid Dynamical Systems: Modeling, Stability, and Robustness.* Princeton University Press, New Jersey, 2012.

[8] M. Krstic and H. Deng. *Stabilization of nonlinear uncertain systems.* Springer-Verlag New York, 1998.

[9] M. Robles and R. G. Sanfelice. Hybrid controllers for tracking of impulsive reference trajectories: A hybrid exosystem approach. In *Proc. 14th International Conference Hybrid Systems: Control and Computation*, pages 231–240, 2011.

[10] R. Rockafellar and R. J.-B. Wets. *Variational Analysis.* Springer, Berlin Heidelberg, 1998.

[11] R. G. Sanfelice. On the existence of control Lyapunov functions and state-feedback laws for hybrid systems. *IEEE Transactions on Automatic Control*, 58(12):3242–3248, December 2013.

[12] R. G. Sanfelice. Computationally tractable implementations of pointwise minimum norm state-feedback laws for hybrid systems. In *Proceedings of the American Control Conference (to appear)*, 2016.

[13] E. Sontag and H. Sussmann. General classes of control-Lyapunov functions. In *Stability theory: Hurwitz Centenary Conference, Centro Stefano Franscini, Ascona, 1995.* 1996.

[14] E. D. Sontag. A 'universal' construction of Artstein's theorem on nonlinear stabilization. *Systems and Control Letters*, 13:117–123, 1989.

Optimal Co-Design of Scheduling and Control for Networked Systems

Sandra Hirche
Technical University of Munich

Abstract

Robots using distributed sensors in smart environments and smart infrastructure systems such as traffic and power systems are examples of networked cyber-physical systems where communication and/or computational resources are constrained. The scientific challenge is to design scheduling and control schemes taking into account such resource constraints and to preferably include fair resource sharing mechanisms among different control applications. In this talk we present a novel framework for the optimal co-design of scheduling and control for networked systems with resource constraints. In particular we consider multiple control loops, which transmit their measurements over a shared communication channel. Only a limited number of those control loops may close their feedback loop at a time. As a result the dynamics of the individual control loops are coupled through the resource constraint. The scientific question is, when a control loop should schedule the transmission of a measurement and what is the appropriate control law. We approach the problem from an optimality point of view with the scheduling and control policies being the optimization variables. We derive an efficient and tractable decomposition, which allows a distributed solution for control and scheduling decisions coordinated by a price-based mechanism. It turns out that an event-triggered control scheme is optimal and that certainty equivalence holds. In fact, our scheme exploits the adaptation ability of event-triggered control in terms of communication traffic elasticity. Furthermore, we provide stability results linking the resource constraints with the system dynamics.

Bio

Sandra Hirche holds the TUM Liesel Beckmann Distinguished Professorship and heads the Chair of Information-oriented Control in the Department of Electrical and Computer Engineering at Technical University of Munich, Germany (since 2013). She received the diploma engineer degree in Aeronautical and Aerospace Engineering in 2002 from the Technical University Berlin, Germany, and the Doctor of Engineering degree in Electrical and Computer Engineering in 2005 from Technical University of Munich, Germany. From 2005-2007 she has been a PostDoc fellow of the Japanese Society for the Promotion of Science at the Fujita Laboratory at Tokyo Institute of Technology, Japan. Prior to her present appointment she has been an associate professor at Technical University of Munich. Her main research interests include networked dynamical systems, cooperative and distributed control, and event-triggered control with applications in human-in-the-loop systems, robotics, and infrastructure systems. She has published more than 150 papers in international journals, books, and refereed conferences. Dr. Hirche has served or is serving on the Editorial Boards of the IEEE Transactions on Control Systems Technology, the IEEE Transactions on Haptics, and the IFAC journal Nonlinear Analysis: Hybrid Systems. She has received multiple awards such as the Rohde & Schwarz Award for her Ph.D. thesis in 2005, the IFAC World Congress Best Poster Award in 2005, together with students Best Paper Awards of IEEE Worldhaptics and IFAC Conference of Manoeuvring and Control of Marine Craft in 2009, and the prestigious ERC Starting Grant. Sandra Hirche is senior member of IEEE and serves as Vice-President for Member Activities in the IEEE Control System Society (CSS) since 2015.

HSCC'16, April 12–14, 2016, Vienna, Austria.
ACM 978-1-4503-3955-1/16/04.
DOI: http://dx.doi.org/10.1145/2883817.2883818

Entropy and Minimal Data Rates for State Estimation and Model Detection*

Daniel Liberzon Sayan Mitra

{liberzon, mitras}@illinois.edu
Coordinate Science Laboratory
University of Illinois at Urbana Champaign
Urbana, IL 61801

ABSTRACT

We investigate the problem of constructing exponentially converging estimates of the state of a continuous-time system from state measurements transmitted via a limited-data-rate communication channel, so that only quantized and sampled measurements of continuous signals are available to the estimator. Following prior work on topological entropy of dynamical systems, we introduce a notion of *estimation entropy* which captures this data rate in terms of the number of system trajectories that approximate all other trajectories with desired accuracy. We also propose a novel alternative definition of estimation entropy which uses approximating functions that are not necessarily trajectories of the system. We show that the two entropy notions are actually equivalent. We establish an upper bound for the estimation entropy in terms of the sum of the system's Lipschitz constant and the desired convergence rate, multiplied by the system dimension. We propose an iterative procedure that uses quantized and sampled state measurements to generate state estimates that converge to the true state at the desired exponential rate. The average bit rate utilized by this procedure matches the derived upper bound on the estimation entropy. We also show that no other estimator (based on iterative quantized measurements) can perform the same estimation task with bit rates lower than the estimation entropy. Finally, we develop an application of the estimation procedure in determining, from the quantized state measurements, which of two competing models of a dynamical system is the true model. We show that under a mild assumption of *exponential separation* of the candidate models, detection is always possible in finite time. Our numerical experiments with randomly generated affine dynamical systems suggest that in practice the algorithm always works.

*D. Liberzon's research was supported in part by the NSF grants CNS-1217811 and ECCS-1231196. S. Mitra's research was supported in part by the NSF grants CCF-1422798 and CNS-1338726.

HSCC'16, April 12-14, 2016, Vienna, Austria

© 2016 ACM. ISBN 978-1-4503-3955-1/16/04...$15.00

DOI: http://dx.doi.org/10.1145/2883817.2883820

Keywords

topological entropy, estimation, monitoring, detection, quantization

1. INTRODUCTION

Entropy is a fundamental notion in the theory of dynamical systems. Roughly speaking, it describes the rate at which the uncertainty about the system's state grows as time evolves. One can think of this alternatively as the exponential growth rate of the number of system trajectories distinguishable with finite precision, or in terms of the growth rate of the size of reachable sets. Different entropy definitions (notably, topological and measure-theoretic ones) and relationships between them are studied in detail in the book [10] and in many other sources, and continue to be a subject of active research in the dynamical systems community. The concept of entropy of course also plays a central role in thermodynamics and in information theory, as discussed, e.g., in [5].

In the context of control theory, if entropy describes the rate at which uncertainty is generated by the system (when no measurements are taken), then it should also correspond to the rate at which information about the system should be collected by the controller in order to induce a desired behavior (such as invariance or stabilization). This link has been recognized in the control community, and suitable entropy definitions for control systems have been proposed and related to minimal data rates necessary for controlling the system over a communication channel. The first such result was obtained by Nair et al. in [15], where topological feedback entropy for discrete-time systems was defined in terms of cardinality of open covers in the state space. An alternative definition was proposed later by Colonius and Kawan in [3], who instead counted the number of "spanning" open-loop control functions. The paper [4] summarized the two notions and established an equivalence between them. Colonius subsequently extended the formulation of [3] from discrete-time to continuous-time dynamics and from invariance to exponential stabilization in [2]. The survey paper [16] provides a broader overview of control under data rate constraints.

In this work we are concerned with the problem of estimating the state of a continuous-time system when state measurements are transmitted via a limited-data-rate communication channel, which means that only quantized and sampled measurements of continuous signals are available to the estimator. We do not address control problems here, although such observation problems and control problems are known to be closely related (through duality and the fact that state estimates can be used to close a feedback loop). Observability over finite-data-rate channels and its connection to topological entropy has been studied, most notably by Savkin [17]. Our point of departure in this paper is a synergy of ideas from Savkin [17] and Colonius [2]. As in [17], we focus on state estimation rather than control. However, we follow [2] in that we consider continuous-time dynamics and require that state estimates converge at a prescribed exponential rate. As a result, our definition of *estimation entropy* combines some features of the definitions used in [17] and [2]. We also propose a novel alternative definition of entropy which uses approximating functions that are not necessarily trajectories of the system. We show that, somewhat surprisingly, the two entropy notions turn out to be equivalent (Theorem 1). We proceed to establish an upper bound of $(L+\alpha)n/\ln 2$ for the estimation entropy of an n-dimensional nonlinear dynamical system with Lipschitz constant L, when the desired exponential convergence rate of the estimate is α (Proposition 2).

State estimation and monitoring of continuously evolving processes over data networks arise in a variety of engineering applications ranging from power grids to vehicular embedded control systems. Typically these estimation algorithms share a communication bus with many other competing protocols, and therefore, a principled approach to bandwidth allocation is necessary. One of the goals of this work is to develop algorithms for state estimation of continuous system behavior that are optimal with respect to sensing and communication data rates. To this end, we propose an iterative procedure that uses quantized and sampled state measurements to generate state estimates that converge to the true state at the desired exponential rate. The main idea in the algorithm, which borrows some elements from [13] and earlier work cited therein, is to exponentially increase the resolution of the quantizer while keeping the number of bits sent in each round constant. This is achieved by using the quantized state measurement of each round to compute a bounding box for the state of the system for the next round. Then, at the beginning of the next round, this bounding box is partitioned to make a new and more precise quantized measurement of the state. We show that the bounding box is exponentially shrinking in time at a rate α when the average bit rate utilized by this procedure matches the upper bound $(L+\alpha)n/\ln 2$ on the estimation entropy (Theorem 3 and Proposition 4). We also show that no other algorithm that performs state estimation based on iterative quantized measurements can perform the same estimation task with bit rates lower than the estimation entropy (Proposition 5). In other words, the "efficiency gap" of our estimation procedure is at most as large as the gap between the estimation entropy of the dynamical system and the above upper bound on it.

In the last part of the paper, we show an application of the estimation procedure in solving model detection problems. Suppose we are given two competing candidate models of a dynamical system and from the quantized state measurements we would like to determine which one is the true model. For example, the different models may arise from different parameter values or they could model "nominal" and "failure" operating modes of the system. This can be viewed as a variant of the standard system identification or model (in)validation problem (see, e.g., [9, 18]) except, unlike in classical results which rely on input/output data, here we use quantized state measurements and do not apply a probing input to the system. We show that under a mild assumption of *exponential separation* of the candidate models' trajectories, a modified version of our estimation procedure can always definitively detect the true model in finite time (Theorem 6). Our experiments with an implementation of this model detection procedure on randomly generated affine dynamical systems suggest that the model detection algorithm always works in practice.

1.1 Notation and terminology

By default, the base of all logarithms is 2 (when we use the natural logarithm we write ln). We denote by $|\cdot|$ some chosen norm in $\mathbb{R}^n$. In general definitions and results this norm can be arbitrary, but in specific quantized algorithm implementations we will find it convenient to use the ∞-norm $\|x\|_\infty := \max_{1\le i\le n}|x_i|$; in those places, the choice of the ∞-norm will be explicitly declared. For any $x\in\mathbb{R}^n$ and $\delta>0$, $B(x,\delta)\subseteq\mathbb{R}^n$ is the closed ball of radius δ centered at x, that is, $B(x,\delta)=\{y\in\mathbb{R}^n : |x-y|\le\delta\}$; for the ∞-norm this is a hypercube. For a bounded set $S\subseteq\mathbb{R}^n$ and $\delta>0$, a *δ-cover* is a finite collection of points[1] $C=\{x_i\}$ such that $\cup_{x_i\in C}B(x_i,\delta)\supseteq S$. For a hyperrectangle $S\subseteq\mathbb{R}^n$ and $\delta>0$, a *δ-grid* is a special type of δ-cover of S by hypercubes centered at points along axis-parallel planes that are 2δ apart. The boundaries of the δ-hypercubes centered at adjacent δ-grid points overlap. For a given set S, there are many possible ways of constructing specific δ-grids. We can choose any strategy for constructing them without changing the results in this paper. For example, we can construct a special grid on, say, the unit interval. Then, when working with a general interval I (a cross-section of S in any given dimension), we map I to the unit interval, mark the chosen grid on it, and then map it back to I. We denote the δ-grid on S by *grid*(S,δ).

2. ESTIMATION ENTROPY

Consider the (continuous-time) system model

$$\dot{x}=f(x),\qquad x\in\mathbb{R}^n \tag{1}$$

where f is a Lipschitz continuous function.[2] Let $\xi:\mathbb{R}^n\times\mathbb{R}_{\ge 0}\to\mathbb{R}^n$ denote the trajectories or solutions of (1), i.e., for $x\in\mathbb{R}^n$, $\xi(x,\cdot)$ denotes the solution from the initial point x. We assume that these solutions are defined globally in time. Suppose that initial states of the system live in a known compact set $K\subset\mathbb{R}^n$. Let there be given a time horizon $T>0$ and a desired convergence rate $\alpha\ge 0$.

For each $\varepsilon>0$, we say that a finite set of functions $\hat{X}=\{\hat{x}_1(\cdot),\ldots,\hat{x}_N(\cdot)\}$ from $[0,T]$ to $\mathbb{R}^n$ is (T,ε,α,K)-*approximating* if for every initial state $x\in K$ there exists some function $\hat{x}_i(\cdot)\in\hat{X}$ such that

$$|\xi(x,t)-\hat{x}_i(t)|<\varepsilon e^{-\alpha t}\qquad\forall\,t\in[0,T]. \tag{2}$$

[1]With a slight abuse of terminology, we take the elements of a cover to be the centers of the balls covering S and not the balls themselves.

[2]The Lipschitz continuity assumption is quite standard in nonlinear systems theory; in particular, it is needed to ensure the system's well-posedness (existence of unique solutions) [11].

Let $s_{\text{est}}(T, \varepsilon, \alpha, K)$ denote the minimal cardinality of such a $(T, \varepsilon, \alpha, K)$-approximating set. We define *estimation entropy* as

$$h_{\text{est}}(\alpha, K) := \lim_{\varepsilon \searrow 0} \limsup_{T \to \infty} \frac{1}{T} \log s_{\text{est}}(T, \varepsilon, \alpha, K).$$

It is easy to see that instead of $\lim_{\varepsilon \searrow 0}$ we could equivalently write $\sup_{\varepsilon > 0}$, because $s_{\text{est}}(T, \varepsilon, \alpha, K)$ grows as $\varepsilon \to 0$ for fixed T, α, K. Intuitively, since s_{est} corresponds to the minimal number of functions needed to approximate the state with desired accuracy, h_{est} is the average number of bits needed to identify these approximating functions. The inner lim sup extracts the base-2 exponential growth rate of s_{est} with time and the outer limit computes the worst case over $\varepsilon > 0$.

As a special case, further considered below, we can define the $\hat{x}_i(\cdot)$'s to be trajectories $\xi(x, \cdot)$ of the system from different initial states. Then, s_{est} corresponds to the number of different quantization points needed to identify the initial states, and h_{est} gives a measure of the long-term bit rate needed for communicating sensor measurements to the estimator. We pursue this connection in more detail in Section 3. We note that the norm in the above definition can be arbitrary.

2.1 Alternative entropy notion

In the above definition, the functions $\hat{x}_i(\cdot)$ are arbitrary functions of time and not necessarily trajectories of the system (1). If we insist on using system trajectories, then we obtain the following alternative definition: a finite set of points $S = \{x_1, \dots, x_N\} \subset K$ is $(T, \varepsilon, \alpha, K)$*-spanning* if for every initial state $x \in K$ there exists some point $x_i \in S$ such that the corresponding solutions satisfy

$$|\xi(x, t) - \xi(x_i, t)| < \varepsilon e^{-\alpha t} \qquad \forall t \in [0, T]. \tag{3}$$

Letting $s^*_{\text{est}}(T, \varepsilon, \alpha, K)$ denote the minimal cardinality of such a $(T, \varepsilon, \alpha, K)$-spanning set, we could define estimation entropy differently as

$$h^*_{\text{est}}(\alpha, K) := \lim_{\varepsilon \searrow 0} \limsup_{T \to \infty} \frac{1}{T} \log s^*_{\text{est}}(T, \varepsilon, \alpha, K).$$

Since every $(T, \varepsilon, \alpha, K)$-spanning set gives rise to a $(T, \varepsilon, \alpha, K)$-approximating set via $\hat{x}_i(t) := \xi(x_i, t)$, and since entropy is determined by the minimal cardinality of such a set, it is clear that

$$s_{\text{est}}(T, \varepsilon, \alpha, K) \le s^*_{\text{est}}(T, \varepsilon, \alpha, K) \qquad \forall T, \varepsilon, \alpha, K \tag{4}$$

and therefore

$$h_{\text{est}}(\alpha, K) \le h^*_{\text{est}}(\alpha, K) \qquad \forall \alpha, K.$$

We will now show that, interestingly, this last inequality is actually always equality. In other words, there is no advantage—as far as estimation entropy is concerned—in using any approximating functions (even possibly discontinuous ones) other than system trajectories.

Theorem 1 *For every $\alpha \ge 0$ and every compact set K we have $h_{est}(\alpha, K) = h^*_{est}(\alpha, K)$.*

To prove this, we bring in the notion of separated sets. The arguments that follow are along the lines of [10, Section 3.1.b], see also Lemma III.1 of [17]. With T, ε, α, K given as before, let us call a finite set of points $E = \{x_1, \dots, x_N\} \subset K$ a $(T, \varepsilon, \alpha, K)$*-separated* set if for every pair of points $x_1, x_2 \in E$ the solutions of (1) with these points as initial states have the property that

$$|\xi(x_1, t) - \xi(x_2, t)| \ge \varepsilon e^{-\alpha t} \qquad \text{for some } t \in [0, T]. \tag{5}$$

Let $n^*_{\text{est}}(T, \varepsilon, \alpha, K)$ denote the *maximal* cardinality of such a $(T, \varepsilon, \alpha, K)$-separated set. The next two lemmas relate n^*_{est} to the previously defined quantities s^*_{est} and s_{est}, respectively.[3]

Lemma 1 *For all T, ε, α, K we have*

$$s^*_{est}(T, \varepsilon, \alpha, K) \le n^*_{est}(T, \varepsilon, \alpha, K). \tag{6}$$

PROOF. The inequality (6) follows immediately from the observation that every maximal $(T, \varepsilon, \alpha, K)$-separated set E is also $(T, \varepsilon, \alpha, K)$-spanning; indeed, if E is not $(T, \varepsilon, \alpha, K)$-spanning then there exists an $x \in K$ such that for every $x_i \in E$ the inequality (3) is violated at least for some t, but then we can add this x to E and the separation property will still hold, contradicting maximality. □

Lemma 2 *For all T, ε, α, K we have*

$$n^*_{est}(T, 2\varepsilon, \alpha, K) \le s_{est}(T, \varepsilon, \alpha, K).$$

PROOF. Let $\hat{X} = \{\hat{x}_1(\cdot), \dots, \hat{x}_N(\cdot)\}$ be an arbitrary $(T, \varepsilon, \alpha, K)$-approximating set of functions, and let $E = \{x_1, \dots, x_M\}$ be an arbitrary $(T, 2\varepsilon, \alpha, K)$-separated set of points in K. We claim that $M \le N$ which would prove the lemma. By the approximating property of $\hat{X}$, for every $x \in K$ there exists some $\hat{x}_i(\cdot) \in \hat{X}$ such that (2) holds. Suppose that $M > N$. Then, for at least one function $\hat{x}_i(\cdot) \in \hat{X}$ we can find (at least) two points $x_p, x_q \in E$ such that (2) holds both with $x = x_p$ and with $x = x_q$. By the triangle inequality, this implies $|\xi(x_p, t) - \xi(x_q, t)| < 2\varepsilon e^{-\alpha t}$ for all $t \in [0, T]$. But this contradicts the $(T, 2\varepsilon, \alpha, K)$-separating property of E, and the claim is established. □

PROOF OF THEOREM 1. Combining Lemmas 1 and 2 and (4), we obtain for all $T, \varepsilon, \alpha, K$

$$\begin{aligned} n^*_{\text{est}}(T, 2\varepsilon, \alpha, K) &\le s_{\text{est}}(T, \varepsilon, \alpha, K) \\ &\le s^*_{\text{est}}(T, \varepsilon, \alpha, K) \le n^*_{\text{est}}(T, \varepsilon, \alpha, K) \end{aligned}$$

This implies that

$$\begin{aligned} \limsup_{T \to \infty} \frac{1}{T} \log n^*_{\text{est}}(T, 2\varepsilon, \alpha, K) &\le \limsup_{T \to \infty} \frac{1}{T} \log s_{\text{est}}(T, \varepsilon, \alpha, K) \\ &\le \limsup_{T \to \infty} \frac{1}{T} \log s^*_{\text{est}}(T, \varepsilon, \alpha, K) \\ &\le \limsup_{T \to \infty} \frac{1}{T} \log n^*_{\text{est}}(T, \varepsilon, \alpha, K) \end{aligned} \tag{7}$$

for all $T, \varepsilon, \alpha, K$. We can now take the limit as $\varepsilon \to 0$ in (7). This limit always exists (but may be infinite) because all quantities in (7) are monotonically non-decreasing as $\varepsilon \to 0$ (so taking the limit is actually equivalent to taking the supremum over $\varepsilon > 0$). The difference between 2ε in the first term and ε in the last term disappears as we pass to the limit, hence all inequalities become equalities. This proves that $h_{\text{est}}(\alpha, K) = h^*_{\text{est}}(\alpha, K)$ as claimed in Theorem 1. □

[3]We do not define a quantity n_{est} corresponding to separation between arbitrary curves (not necessarily system trajectories) as such a notion does not seem to be useful here.

Remark 1 The above proof shows, in addition, that the two entropy quantities appearing in the statement of Theorem 1 are also equal to

$$\lim_{\varepsilon\searrow 0}\limsup_{T\to\infty}\frac{1}{T}\log n^*_{\text{est}}(T,\varepsilon,\alpha,K).$$

By compactness of K and by the property of continuous dependence of solutions of (1) on initial conditions (see, e.g., [11]), for given ε,α,T there exists a $\delta>0$ such that (3) holds whenever x and x_i satisfy $|x-x_i|<\delta$. From this it immediately follows that $s^*_{\text{est}}(T,\varepsilon,\alpha,K)$, and hence also $s_{\text{est}}(T,\varepsilon,\alpha,K)$, is finite for every $\varepsilon>0$. This does not in principle preclude $h^*_{\text{est}}(\alpha,K)$ and $h_{\text{est}}(\alpha,K)$ from being infinite (the supremum over positive ε could still be ∞). However, we will see next that this does not happen because the system's right-hand side is Lipschitz.

2.2 Entropy bounds

In this section, we establish an upper bound on the estimation entropy of nonlinear systems. This bound is in terms of the *global* Lipschitz constant L of the system's right-hand side f. In case the system trajectories are confined to a compact invariant set, the result holds for a local Lipschitz constant over that set. We will also see that the entropy bound is independent of the choice of the initial set K; without significant loss of generality, we assume in the sequel that K is a set of positive measure and "regular" shape, such as a hypercube, large enough to contain all initial conditions of interest.

Proposition 2 *For the system* (1)*, the estimation entropy $h_{est}(\alpha,K)$ is finite and does not exceed $(L+\alpha)n/\ln 2$ where L is the Lipschitz constant of f.*

PROOF. This proceeds along the lines of the proof of Theorem 3.3 in [2] (see also [1] and the references therein for earlier results along similar lines). We fix the convergence parameters $\varepsilon,\alpha>0$, the initial set K, and the time horizon $T>0$, and try to come up with a bound on $s_{\text{est}}(T,\varepsilon,\alpha,K)$. Let us consider an open cover C of K with balls of radii $\varepsilon e^{-(L+\alpha)T}$ centered at points $x_1,\dots,x_N$; N is the cardinality of the set C.

Consider any initial state $x\in K$. By the construction of C, we know that there exists an $x_i\in C$ such that $|x-x_i|\le \varepsilon e^{-(L+\alpha)T}$. For any $t\le T$,

$$\begin{aligned}|\xi(x,t)-\xi(x_i,t)| &\le |x-x_i|+\int_0^t|f(\xi(x,s))-f(\xi(x_i,s))|ds\\ &\le |x-x_i|+L\int_0^t|\xi(x,s)-\xi(x_i,s)|ds\end{aligned}$$

using the Lipschitz constant of f. By the Bellman-Gronwall inequality (see, e.g., [11]), this implies

$$\begin{aligned}|\xi(x,t)-\xi(x_i,t)| &\le |x-x_i|e^{Lt}\le \varepsilon e^{-(L+\alpha)T}e^{Lt}\\ &\le \varepsilon e^{-(L+\alpha)t}e^{Lt}=\varepsilon e^{-\alpha t}.\end{aligned}$$

It follows that the cover $C=\{x_1,\dots,x_N\}$ defines a (T,ε,α,K)-approximating set: $\hat{X}=\{\xi(x_1,\cdot),\dots,\xi(x_N,\cdot)\}$. That is, $s_{\text{est}}(T,\varepsilon,\alpha,K)$ is upper bounded by N which is the minimum cardinality of the cover of $K\subseteq\mathbb{R}^n$ with balls of radii $\varepsilon e^{-(L+\alpha)T}$. Let $c(\delta,S)$ denote the minimal cardinality of a cover of a set S with balls of radius δ. Then we can write that $s_{\text{est}}(T,\varepsilon,\alpha,K)\le c(\varepsilon e^{-(L+\alpha)T},K)$. Next we proceed to compute a bound on h_{est} as follows:

$$\begin{aligned}&\limsup_{T\to\infty}\frac{1}{T}\log s_{\text{est}}(T,\epsilon,\alpha,K)\\ &\le \limsup_{T\to\infty}\frac{1}{T}\log c(\varepsilon e^{-(L+\alpha)T},K)\\ &=(L+\alpha)\limsup_{T\to\infty}\frac{\log c(\varepsilon e^{-(L+\alpha)T},K)}{T(L+\alpha)}\\ &=\frac{(L+\alpha)}{\ln 2}\limsup_{T\to\infty}\frac{\ln c(\varepsilon e^{-(L+\alpha)T},K)}{\ln(e^{(L+\alpha)T}/\varepsilon)+\ln\varepsilon}\\ &=\frac{(L+\alpha)}{\ln 2}\limsup_{T\to\infty}\frac{\ln c(\varepsilon e^{-(L+\alpha)T},K)}{\ln(e^{(L+\alpha)T}/\varepsilon)}\\ &\text{[constant does not affect lim sup]}\\ &=\frac{(L+\alpha)}{\ln 2}\limsup_{\delta\searrow 0}\frac{\ln c(\delta,K)}{\ln(1/\delta)}\\ &\text{[defining } \delta=\varepsilon e^{-(L+\alpha)T}\text{]}\\ &\le\frac{(L+\alpha)n}{\ln 2}.\end{aligned}$$

The last step follows from the fact that for any $K\subseteq\mathbb{R}^n$, the quantity $\limsup_{\delta\searrow 0}\frac{\ln c(\delta,K)}{\ln(1/\delta)}$, also called the upper box dimension of K, is no larger than (and typically equal to) n; cf. [10, Section 3.2.f]. By taking the limit $\varepsilon\to 0$, we obtain the result $h_{\text{est}}(\alpha,K)\le(L+\alpha)n/\ln 2$. □

Remark 2 In the case when (1) is a linear system

$$\dot{x}=Ax \tag{8}$$

the result of Proposition 2 can be sharpened. Namely, in this case one can show that the exact expression (not just an upper bound) for the estimation entropy is

$$1/(\ln 2)\sum_{\operatorname{Re}\lambda_i(A+\alpha I)>0}\operatorname{Re}\lambda_i(A+\alpha I)=1/(\ln 2)\sum_{\operatorname{Re}\lambda_i(A)>-\alpha}(\operatorname{Re}\lambda_i(A)+\alpha) \tag{9}$$

where $\operatorname{Re}\lambda_i(A)$ are the real parts of the eigenvalues of A. This follows from results that are essentially well known, although not well documented in the literature (especially for continuous-time systems); for discrete-time systems this is shown, e.g., in [17]. Namely, since the flow is $\xi(x,t)=e^{At}x$, the volume of the reachable set at time T from the initial set K is $\det(e^{AT})\text{vol}(K)$ which by Liouville's trace formula equals $e^{(\text{tr}A)T}\text{vol}(K)$. The decaying factor $e^{-\alpha t}$ on the right-hand side of (2) can be canceled by multiplying by $e^{\alpha t}$ on both sides; the effect of doing this on the left-hand side is that of replacing solutions of $\dot{x}=Ax$ by solutions of $\dot{x}=(A+\alpha I)x$, and suitably modifying the approximating functions. Projecting onto the unstable subspace of $A+\alpha I$, we can refine the trace to be the sum of only unstable eigenvalues of this matrix. The number of approximating functions must be at least proportional to the above volume (since the ε-balls around their endpoints must have enough volume to cover the reachable set), and after taking the logarithm, dividing by T, and letting $T\to 0$ we obtain (9) as the lower bound. The upper bound is obtained by reducing A to Jordan normal form followed by an argument similar to the proof of Proposition 2 above applied to each Jordan block (with the corresponding eigenvalue replacing the Lipschitz constant L), and ends up giving the same expression (9).

3. ESTIMATION OVER INFINITE HORIZON

We will first describe a procedure for state estimation of the system (1) over infinite time horizon. Next, we will show that the output from this estimation procedure exponentially converges to the actual state of the system. Finally, we will prove a bound on the bit rate that is sufficient to achieve this convergence. This is a measure of the rate at which information has to be communicated from the sensors of the plant to the estimator.

3.1 Estimation procedure

From this point on in this section, we will discuss a specific estimation procedure based on quantized state measurements. The norm used here will be the infinity norm $\|\cdot\|_\infty$. Accordingly, the $B(x,\delta)$ balls will be the hypercubes and the grids will be sets of hypercubes. We will treat all previous definitions and results related to entropy in terms of the infinity norm.

The estimation procedure computes a function $v : [0,\infty) \to \mathbb{R}^n$ and an exponentially shrinking envelope around $v(t)$ such that the actual state of the system $\xi(x,t)$ is guaranteed to be within this envelope. It has several inputs: (1) a sampling period $T_p > 0$, (2) a desired exponential convergence rate $\alpha > 0$, (3) an initial set K and an initial partition size $d_0 > 0$, and (4) the Lipschitz constant L of the function f in (1), and (5) a subroutine for computing solutions of the differential equation (1). In this paper we do not distinguish between this subroutine for computing solutions and the actual solutions $\xi(\cdot,\cdot)$. The procedure works in rounds $i = 1, 2, ...$ and each round lasts T_p time units. In each round, a new state measurement q is obtained and the values of three state variables S, δ, C are updated. We denote these updated values in the ith round as q_i, δ_i, S_i, and C_i. Roughly, $S_i \subseteq \mathbb{R}^n$ is a hypercubic over-approximation of the state estimate, δ_i is the radius of the set S_i, and C_i is a grid on S_i which defines the set of possible state measurements q_{i+1} for the next round. We think of the quantized state measurements q_i as being transmitted from the sensors to the estimator via a finite-data-rate communication channel, while the variables δ_i, S_i, and C_i are generated independently and synchronously on both sides of the channel.

The initial values of these state variables are: $\delta_0 = d_0$; S_0 is a hypercube with center, say x_c, and radius $r_c = \frac{diam(K)}{2}$, such that $K \subseteq B(x_c, r_c)$; and $C_0 = grid(S_0, \delta_0 e^{-(L+\alpha)T_p})$. Recall the definition of a grid cover from Section 1.1: C_0 is a specific collection of points in $\mathbb{R}^n$ such that $S_0 \subseteq \cup_{x \in C_0} B(x, \delta_0 e^{-(L+\alpha)T_p})$.

At the beginning of the ith round, the algorithm takes as input (from the sensors) a measurement q_i of the current state of the system with respect to the cover C_{i-1} computed in the previous round. The measurement q_i is obtained by choosing a grid point $c \in C_{i-1}$ such that the corresponding $\delta_{i-1}e^{-(L+\alpha)T_p}$-ball $B(c, \delta_{i-1}e^{-(L+\alpha)T_p})$ contains the current state $\xi(x, iT_p)$ of the system. (If there are multiple grid points satisfying this condition—and this may happen as C_{i-1} is a cover with closed sets having overlapping boundaries—then one is chosen arbitrarily.) Using this measurement, the algorithm computes the following: (1) $v_i : [0, T_p] \to \mathbb{R}^n$, which is an approximation function for the state over the interval spanning this round, defined as the solution of the system (1) from q_i, (2) δ_i is updated as $e^{-\alpha T_p}\delta_{i-1}$, (3) $S_i \subseteq \mathbb{R}^n$ is an estimate of the state after T_p time, that is, at the beginning of round $i+1$, and (4) C_i is a $\delta_i e^{-(L+\alpha)T_p}$-grid on S_i, where L is the Lipschitz constant of f. Specifically, S_i is computed by first evaluating the solution $v_i(T_p) = \xi(q_i, T_p)$ of the system starting from q_i after time T_p, and then constructing the hypercube $B(v_i(T_p), \delta_i)$. Note that the size of this hypercube decays geometrically at the rate $e^{-\alpha T_p}$ with each successive round. Recall Section 1.1 where we defined grids and provided examples of specific ways of constructing them. For what follows, the specific construction is less important than the fact that each C_i can be computed from q_i by translating and scaling C_{i-1}.

Consider the beginning of the ith round for some $i > 0$. From the algorithm it follows that if the current state x is contained in the estimate S_{i-1} computed in the last iteration, then the measurement q_i is one of the points in the cover C_{i-1} computed in the last iteration, and further, the error in the measurement $|q_i - x|$ is at most the precision of the cover which is $\delta_{i-1}e^{-(L+\alpha)T_p}$. This property will be used in the analysis below.

```
1  input: T_p, α, K, d_0, L, ξ(·,·)
2  i = 0;
3  δ_0 ← d_0;
4  S_0 ← B(x_c, r_c);   // x_c is the center of K
5  C_0 ← grid(S_0, δ_0 e^{-(L+α)T_p});
6  while (true)
   // at i^th round, i>0
7    i++;
8    input q_i ∈ C_{i-1};
9    // measurement of current state
10   v_i(·) ← ξ(q_i, ·)|[0, T_p];
11   δ_i ← e^{-αT_p} δ_{i-1};
12   S_i ← B(v_i(T_p), δ_i);
13   C_i ← grid(S_i, δ_i e^{-(L+α)T_p});
14   output S_i ⊆ R^n, C_i, v_i : [0, T_p] → R^n;
15   wait(T_p);
```

Figure 1: Estimation procedure.

Remark 3 Line 10 of the estimation procedure uses a subroutine for computing numerical solutions of the differential equation (1) from a given quantized initial state q_i over a fixed time horizon T_p. In this paper, we assume that these computations are precise. Extending the algorithms and results to accommodate numerical imprecisions would proceed along the lines of the techniques used in numerical reachability computations (for example, in [6, 12]). The present case, however, is significantly simpler as the solutions have to be computed from a single initial state and up to a fixed time horizon.

In order to analyze the accuracy of this estimation procedure, we define a piecewise continuous estimation function $v : [0,\infty) \to \mathbb{R}^n$ by $v(0) := v_1(0)$ and

$$v(t) = v_i(t-(i-1)T_p) \text{ for all } t \in ((i-1)T_p, iT_p],\ i = 1, 2, \ldots \quad (10)$$

The following theorem establishes an exponentially decaying upper bound on the error between the actual state of the system and the approximating function computed by the procedure.

Theorem 3 *For any choice of the parameters $\alpha, d_0, T_p > 0$, the procedure in Figure 1 has the following properties: for $i = 0, 1, 2, \ldots$ and for any initial state $x \in K$,*

(a) for any $t = iT_p, \xi(x,t) \in S_i$, and

(b) for any $t \in [iT_p, (i+1)T_p)$, $\|\xi(x,t) - v(t)\|_\infty \leq d_0 e^{-\alpha t}$.

PROOF. Part (a): We fix $x \in K$ and proceed to prove the statement by induction on the iteration index i. The base case: $i = 0$, that is, $t = 0$ and $\xi(x, 0) = x$. The required condition follows since $x \in K \subseteq B(x_c, r_c) = S_0$.

For the inductive step, we assume that $\xi(x, iT_p) \in S_i$ and have to show that $\xi(x, (i+1)T_p) \in S_{i+1}$. We proceed by establishing an upper bound on the distance between the actual trajectory of the system at $t = (i+1)T_p$ and the computed approximation $v(t)$:

$$\begin{aligned}
&\|\xi(x,(i+1)T) - v((i+1)T_p)\|_\infty \\
&= \|\xi(\xi(x,iT_p),T_p) - v_{i+1}(T_p)\|_\infty \\
&\qquad \text{[From Equation (10) defining } v(t)] \\
&= \|\xi(\xi(x,iT_p),T_p) - \xi(q_{i+1},T_p)\|_\infty \qquad (11)\\
&\qquad \text{[From Line 10 } v_{i+1}(T_p) = \xi(q_{i+1},T_p)] \\
&\leq e^{LT_p}\|\xi(x,iT_p) - q_{i+1}\|_\infty. \qquad (12)\\
&\qquad \text{[Bellman-Gronwall inequality]}
\end{aligned}$$

The measurement q_{i+1} is the input received at the beginning of round $i+1$ for the actual state $\xi(x, iT_p)$ with respect to the cover C_i of S_i. From the induction hypothesis we know that $\xi(x, iT_p) \in S_i$, and therefore, $q_{i+1} \in C_i$. Since C_i is a $\delta_i e^{-(L+\alpha)T_p}$-cover of S_i, it follows that

$$\|\xi(x,iT_p) - q_{i+1}\|_\infty \leq \delta_i e^{-(L+\alpha)T_p}. \qquad (13)$$

We have $\|\xi(x,(i+1)T_p) - v((i+1)T_p)\|_\infty$

$$\begin{aligned}
&\leq \delta_i e^{-(L+\alpha)T_p} e^{LT_p} \\
&= \delta_i e^{-\alpha T_p} \\
&= \delta_{i+1}. \quad \text{[Using definition of } \delta_{i+1}]
\end{aligned}$$

Thus, it follows that $\xi(x, (i+1)T_p) \in B(v((i+1)T_p), \delta_{i+1}) = S_{i+1}$.

Part (b): We fix an iteration index $i \geq 0$ and an initial state $x \in K$. If $t = iT_p$ then the result follows from Part (a) because $\delta_i = d_0 e^{-\alpha i T_p}$. For any $t \in (iT_p, (i+1)T_p)$, we establish an upper bound on the distance between the actual trajectory $\xi(x,t)$ of the system at time t and the computed approximation $v(t)$:

$$\begin{aligned}
\|\xi(x,t) - v(t)\|_\infty &= \|\xi(\xi(x,iT_p),t-iT_p) - v_{i+1}(t-iT_p)\|_\infty \\
&\qquad \text{[From equation (10) defining } v(t)] \\
&= \|\xi(\xi(x,iT_p),t-iT_p) - \xi(q_{i+1},t-iT_p)\|_\infty \\
&\qquad \text{[From } v_{i+1}(t) = \xi(q_{i+1},t)] \\
&\leq \|\xi(x,iT_p) - q_{i+1}\|_\infty e^{L(t-iT_p)} \\
&\qquad \text{[Bellman-Gronwall inequality]} \\
&\leq \delta_i e^{-(L+\alpha)T_p} e^{L(t-iT_p)} \\
&\qquad \text{[From (13)]} \\
&= d_0 e^{-\alpha i T_p} e^{-(L+\alpha)T_p} e^{L(t-iT_p)} \\
&\qquad [\delta_i = d_0 e^{-\alpha i T_p}] \\
&= d_0 e^{-\alpha(i+1)T_p} e^{L(t-(i+1)T_p)} \\
&\leq d_0 e^{-\alpha t}. \text{[Since } iT_p \leq t \leq (i+1)T_p]
\end{aligned}$$

□

3.2 Bit rate of estimation scheme and its relation to entropy

Now we estimate the communication bit rate needed by the estimation procedure in Figure 1. As the states S_{i-1} and C_{i-1} are maintained and updated by the algorithm in each round, the only information that is communicated from the system to the estimation procedure in each round is the measurement q_i. The number of bits needed for that is $\log(\#C_i)$, where $\#$ stands for the cardinality of a set. The long-term average bit rate of the algorithm is given by

$$b_r(\alpha, d_0, T_p) := \limsup_{j \to \infty} \frac{1}{jT_p} \sum_{i=1}^{j} \log(\#C_{i-1}).$$

We proceed to characterize this quantity from the description of the estimation procedure in Figure 1. We calculate $\#C_0 = \lceil \frac{diam(K)}{2d_0 e^{-(L+\alpha)T_p}} \rceil^n$. For each successive iteration i, $\#C_i = \lceil \frac{\delta_i}{\delta_i e^{-(L+\alpha)T_p}} \rceil^n = \lceil e^{(L+\alpha)T_p} \rceil^n$. Thus, $b_r(\alpha, d_0, T_p) = \lim_{i\to\infty} \frac{1}{T_p} \log(\#C_i) = (L+\alpha)n/\ln 2$ is the bit rate utilized by the procedure for any d_0 and T_p. Since it is independent of d_0 and T_p, we write it as $b_r(\alpha)$ from now on. We state our conclusion as follows.

Proposition 4 *The average bit rate used by the estimation procedure in Figure 1 is $(L+\alpha)n/\ln 2$.*

By Proposition 2, the bit rate $(L+\alpha)n/\ln 2$ used by the above algorithm is an upper bound on the entropy $h_{\text{est}}(\alpha, K)$. We now establish that no other similar algorithm can perform the same task with a bit rate lower than the entropy $h_{\text{est}}(\alpha, K)$. In other words, the "efficiency gap" of the algorithm is at most as large as the gap between the entropy and its upper bound known from Proposition 2. (Incidentally, combining this result with Proposition 4 we can arrive at an alternative proof of Proposition 2.) The lower bound in terms of entropy is proved below for an algorithm that uses a constant number of bits at each round; since in the above algorithm $\#C_0$ may be higher than $\#C_i$ for $i \geq 1$, we can think of this comparison as being valid once the algorithm has reached "steady state." Instead of giving a more formalized description of the class of algorithms to which Proposition 5 applies, we refer the reader to [17, Section 2] and the references therein for these details (which are by now quite standard).

Proposition 5 *Consider an algorithm of the above type with an arbitrary choice of the cover C_i but such that at each step i the set C_i has the same number of elements: $\#C_i = N\ \forall i$ (i.e., the coding alphabet is of fixed size). If this algorithm achieves the properties listed in Theorem 3 for an arbitrary $d_0 > 0$, then its bit rate cannot be smaller than $h_{est}(\alpha, K)$.*

PROOF. This proof follows along the same lines as the proof of Statement 1 of Theorem III.1 in [17]. Here the choice of norm does not matter so we revert to an arbitrary norm $|\cdot|$ on $\mathbb{R}^n$. Seeking a contradiction, suppose that an algorithm achieves the properties listed in Theorem 3 and has a bit rate smaller than $h_{\text{est}}(\alpha, K)$. Recall (see the proof of Lemma 2 and Remark 1) that

$$\begin{aligned} h_{\text{est}}(\alpha, K) &= \lim_{\varepsilon \searrow 0} \limsup_{T\to\infty} \frac{1}{T} \log n^*_{\text{est}}(T, 2\varepsilon, \alpha, K) \\ &= \sup_{\varepsilon>0} \limsup_{T\to\infty} \frac{1}{T} \log n^*_{\text{est}}(T, 2\varepsilon, \alpha, K). \end{aligned}$$

Thus for some $\varepsilon > 0$ small enough we have

$$b_r(\alpha) < \limsup_{T\to\infty} \frac{1}{T} \log n^*_{\text{est}}(T, 2\varepsilon, \alpha, K).$$

Let d_0 be equal to this ε. Next, for a sufficiently large fixed integer j we must have

$$b_r(\alpha) < \frac{1}{jT_p} \log n^*_{\text{est}}(jT_p, 2\varepsilon, \alpha, K)$$

where T_p is the sampling period in the algorithm. Since the average bit rate is given by

$$b_r(\alpha) = \frac{1}{T_p} \log N$$

we obtain

$$N^j < n^*_{\text{est}}(jT_p, 2\varepsilon, \alpha, K)$$

The left-hand side of the above inequality is the number of possible sequences of codewords $\{q_i\}$ that can be produced by the algorithm over j rounds, while the right-hand side is the cardinality of a maximal $(jT_p, 2\varepsilon, \alpha, K)$-separated set. This means that there must exist two different initial conditions x_1, x_2 in this $(jT_p, 2\varepsilon, \alpha, K)$-separated set such that the corresponding solutions $\xi(x_1, t), \xi(x_2, t)$ will produce the same sequence of q_i's, and hence will be approximated within $\varepsilon e^{-\alpha t}$ by the same approximating function $v(t)$:

$$|\xi(x_i, t) - v(t)| < \varepsilon e^{-\alpha t} \qquad \forall\, t \in [0, jT_p], \quad i = 1, 2. \tag{14}$$

On the other hand, by the definition of a $(jT_p, 2\varepsilon, \alpha, K)$-separated set it must hold that

$$|\xi(x_1, t) - \xi(x_2, t)| \geq 2\varepsilon e^{-\alpha t} \qquad \text{for some } t \in [0, jT_p]$$

which contradicts (14) in view of the triangle inequality. □

We note that the algorithm described in [17] performs a similar estimation task (with $\alpha = 0$ and in discrete time) and operates at an arbitrary bit rate above the entropy. However, that algorithm is quite abstract, since it relies on the existence of a suitable spanning set and does block coding over a sufficiently large time window using sequences from this spanning set. By contrast, our algorithm given in Section 3.1 is constructive in that it utilizes a specific quantization procedure and works with an arbitrary fixed sampling period.

Remark 4 For the case of a linear system (8), the algorithm of Section 3.1 can be modified so that its average bit rate equals the entropy of the linear system given by the formula (9). This can be achieved by aligning the grids C_i used in the algorithm with eigenvectors of the matrix A and replacing the Lipschitz constant L with eigenvalues of A (i.e., using a different number of quantization points for each dimension). Constructions of this type for linear systems are well established in the literature; see, e.g., [8, 19].

4. MODEL DETECTION

In this section, we show that the estimation algorithm of Figure 1 can be used to distinguish two system models, provided they are in some sense adequately different.

Consider two continuous-time system models:

$$\dot{x} = f_1(x), \quad x \in \mathbb{R}^n, \tag{15}$$

$$\dot{x} = f_2(x), \quad x \in \mathbb{R}^n \tag{16}$$

where the initial state is in the known compact set $K \subset \mathbb{R}^n$ and f_1 and f_2 are Lipschitz functions with Lipschitz constants L_1 and L_2. Here we assume that these are *global* Lipschitz constants; in case the system trajectories are confined to a compact invariant set, the result holds for local Lipschitz constants over that set. We denote the trajectories of the systems (15) and (16) by $\xi_1 : \mathbb{R}^n \times \mathbb{R}_{\geq 0} \to \mathbb{R}^n$ and $\xi_2 : \mathbb{R}^n \times \mathbb{R}_{\geq 0} \to \mathbb{R}^n$, respectively. From runtime data, we are interested in distinguishing whether the true dynamics of the system is f_1 or f_2. For example, if f_1 and f_2 correspond to models with different sets of parameter values, then solutions to this problem could be used for model parameter identification. As another example application, consider a scenario where f_1 captures the nominal dynamics of the system and f_2 models a known aberration or failure mode. Then, solution to the above detection problem can be used for failure detection. It is straightforward to generalize the solution proposed below to handle multiple competing models.

For $L_s, T_s > 0$ we say that the two models are (L_s, T_s)-*exponentially separated* if there exists a constant $\varepsilon_{\min} > 0$ such that for any $\varepsilon \leq \varepsilon_{\min}$, for any two states $x_1, x_2 \in \mathbb{R}^n$ with $|x_1 - x_2| \leq \varepsilon$,

$$|\xi_1(x_1, T_s) - \xi_2(x_2, T_s)| > \varepsilon e^{L_s T_s}.$$

Remark 5 The exponential separation property can be shown to hold if there exist constants $\alpha_{\min} \in (0, 2\pi)$ and $v_{\min} > 0$ such that the two models satisfy the following two conditions at each $x \in \mathbb{R}^n$ (or at each x reachable from K): (1) the two vector fields have a separation angle of at least $\alpha_{\min}$ (here we are assuming $n \geq 2$), and (2) at least one of them has a velocity of at least $v_{\min}$ (in particular, they have no common equilibria). Under these conditions, trajectories of the two systems with nearby initial conditions diverge from each other at the rate of at least $a := v_{\min} \sin(\alpha_{\min})$. Since for every $L > 0$ and every $T > 0$ we have $aT - \varepsilon > \varepsilon e^{LT}$ if $\varepsilon > 0$ is small enough, the exponential separation property follows (with arbitrary L_s, T_s). If the above transversality condition (1) fails, we may still be able to establish exponential separation for L_s small enough. We also believe that conditions (1) and (2) are "generic" in the sense that we expect them to hold for almost all pairs of systems; for example, for affine systems this claim can be made precise and is confirmed by the numerical experiments discussed below.

4.1 Distinguishing algorithm

In the above definition of exponential separation the norm can be arbitrary, but in the algorithm below we work with the infinity norm. With some modifications, the procedure in Figure 1 can detect models using observations. In Figure 2, we show the procedure for detecting models. First of all, before taking the measurement in each round (T_p time) it makes an additional check. If the current state is not in the set S_i (line 8) computed from the previous round, then the procedure immediately halts by detecting model 2. If the current state is in S_i, then it proceeds as before and records a measurement q_i of the current state as one of the points in the cover C_i. Secondly, the function v_i (line 13) is now computed as a solution $\xi_1(q_i, \cdot)$ of the system given by (15). Finally, in computing the radius of the elements in the cover C_i (line 16), the Lipschitz constant L_1 of the system (15) is used.

```
1    input: T_p, α, K, d_0, L_1, ξ_1(·,·)
2    i = 0;
3    δ_0 ← d_0;
4    S_0 ← B(x_c, r_c);
5    C_0 ← grid(S_0, δ_0 e^{-(L_1+α)T_p});
6    while (true)   // at i^th round, i > 0
7        i++;
8        if current state ∉ S_{i-1}
9            output ''second model'';
10           break;
11       else
12           input q_i ∈ C_{i-1};
13           v_i(·) ← ξ_1(q_i, ·)|[0, T_p];
14           δ_i ← e^{-αT_p} δ_{i-1};
15           S_i ← B(v_i(T_p), δ_i);
16           C_i ← grid(S_i, δ_i e^{-(L_1+α)T_p});
17       wait(T_p);
```

Figure 2: Procedure for detecting models.

Theorem 6 *Suppose that the true system model is either equation (15) or (16) and that the two models are (L_1, T_p)-exponentially separated. Then the procedure in Figure 2 outputs "second model" if and only if the system model is (16).*

PROOF. For the "if" part, assume that the true model is the second model, that is, given by equation (16). Fixing an initial state of the system x_0, we have the true trajectory $\xi_2(x_0, \cdot)$. Let us also fix the parameters T_p, d_0, α of the detection algorithm. Since the value of the program variable $\delta_i = d_0 e^{-\alpha i T_p}$ decays geometrically in each iteration, there exists an i^* such that for any iteration $k-1 \geq i^*$, $\delta_{k-1} e^{-(L_1+\alpha)T_p} \leq \varepsilon_{\min}$. We consider the execution of the algorithm at one such iteration $k-1$ and show that the condition in line 8 will be satisfied at the next iteration k.

We denote the actual state of the system at the beginning of the $(k-1)^{st}$ iteration as $x_2 = \xi_2(x_0, (k-1)T_p)$. Assume that the condition in line 8 is not satisfied, i.e., $x_2 \in S_{k-1}$; otherwise, the algorithm would have already produced the correct "second model" output. The measurement q_k of x_2 obtained in this iteration is an element of C_{k-1}. Thus, $\|x_2 - q_k\|_\infty \leq \delta_{k-1} e^{-(L_1+\alpha)T_p} \leq \varepsilon_{\min}$. By the (L_1, T_p)-separation with the infinity norm, it follows that

$$\|\xi_2(x_2, T_p) - \xi_1(q_k, T_p)\|_\infty > \delta_{k-1} e^{-(L_1+\alpha)T_p} e^{L_1 T_p} \quad (17)$$
$$= \delta_{k-1} e^{-\alpha T_p} = \delta_k.$$

As $v_k(\cdot) = \xi_1(q_k, \cdot)$, from the above strict inequality it follows that $\xi_2(x_0, kT_p) = \xi_2(x_2, T_p) \notin B(v_k(T_p), \delta_k) = S_k$. Thus, at the beginning of the kth iteration, the condition in line 8 will hold.

For the "only-if" part, assume that the true model is not the second (equation (16)). Let us fix an initial state of the system x_0. From the hypothesis we know that the true model is the first model and the true trajectory of the system is $\xi_1(x_0, t)$. From Theorem 3, it follows that at every iteration i, the state of the system at that round $\xi_1(x_0, iT_p) \in S_i$. Thus the **if**-condition in Line 8 is not satisfied at any iteration and consequently the algorithm never outputs "second model." □

Remark 6 The definition of exponential separation does not imply that the value of the upper bound $\varepsilon_{\min}$ is known, and short of that we cannot conclude for sure that the true model is the first model even if the state measurements conform with the constructed bound S_i in every round. However, if we know such an upper bound $\varepsilon_{\min}$ for which the models are (L_1, T_p)-exponentially separated, then with one extra conditional, the above algorithm can be made to decisively halt with the output "first model." For this, the conditional statement

```
else if δ_i e^{-L_1 T_p} < ε_min
    output ''first model''; break;
```

is to be inserted after line 10. This branch is executed by the algorithm at the ith round only if we had $\delta_{i-1} e^{-(L_1+\alpha)T_p} \leq \varepsilon_{\min}$ at the $(i-1)^{st}$ round and the measured state was in S_j for each of the preceding rounds $j < i$. At this point the algorithm can soundly infer "first model" because, according to the above proof of Theorem 6, the second model would have already triggered line 8 in the current round or one of the earlier rounds.

Remark 7 It is possible to run two versions of the detection algorithm, one with each of the candidate models, in parallel. While this may speed up detection in practice, in the worst case the two versions would take the same amount of time to reach a decision. This would also double the data rate without guaranteeing faster model detection. We thus opted for an approach which, while "asymmetric," works with the minimal needed data rate.

4.2 Experimental evaluation of detection algorithm

We have implemented the detection algorithm of Figure 2 in Python[4]. In this section, we discuss certain details about this implementation and numerical simulation-based results.

All sets in $\mathbb{R}^n$ in the implementation, including the initial set K and the S_i's, are n-dimensional hyperrectangles

[4]Available at https://bitbucket.org/mitras/detection.

and they are represented either by two corner points or by a center point and a radius. The choice of this representation has implications on the efficiency of the algorithms. It enables the implementation of all the necessary operations such as testing membership in S, computing a grid on S, and quantizing a point with respect to a grid, in time that is linear in the number of dimensions n. Specifically, the $grid(S, \delta)$ function computes n lists of points in $\mathbb{R}$ where the ith list is generated by uniformly partitioning the ith dimension of S into intervals of length 2δ. This list representation of $grid(S, \delta)$ is adequate for quantizing a state with respect to it. The detection algorithm has to compute solutions $\xi_1(\cdot, \cdot)$ of the system (15) over $[0, T_p]$. Moreover, in order to simulate the algorithm we have to compute the actual trajectories $\xi_2(\cdot, \cdot)$ of the system (16). For affine models $\dot{x} = Ax + b$, considered below, the analytic solution is given by

$$\xi(x,t) = e^{At}(x + A^{-1}b) - A^{-1}b$$

(provided A is invertible). Our implementation can handle more general models using the Python ODE solvers.

We generate pairs of random affine dynamical systems sys1 : $\dot{x} = A_1x + b_1$, sys2 : $\dot{x} = A_2x + b_2$, and then sys1 is used as the input model for the algorithm while sys2 is used as the true model of the system. With this set-up we performed many experiments to arrive at the following empirical conclusions. First of all, the detection algorithm always works (unless we deliberately choose $A_2 = A_1$ and $b_2 = b_1$). The detection time depends on several factors. As is expected from the algorithm, it increases with smaller values of α and T. If A_2 and b_2 are generated by perturbing A_1 and b_1 (not independently at random) then the detection time increases with smaller perturbations. Finally, on the average, the detection time increases with smaller-dimensional systems. This is possibly because with increasing n, there is a higher probability of having a larger separation in at least one of the eigenvalues of the models, and therefore, a faster detection.

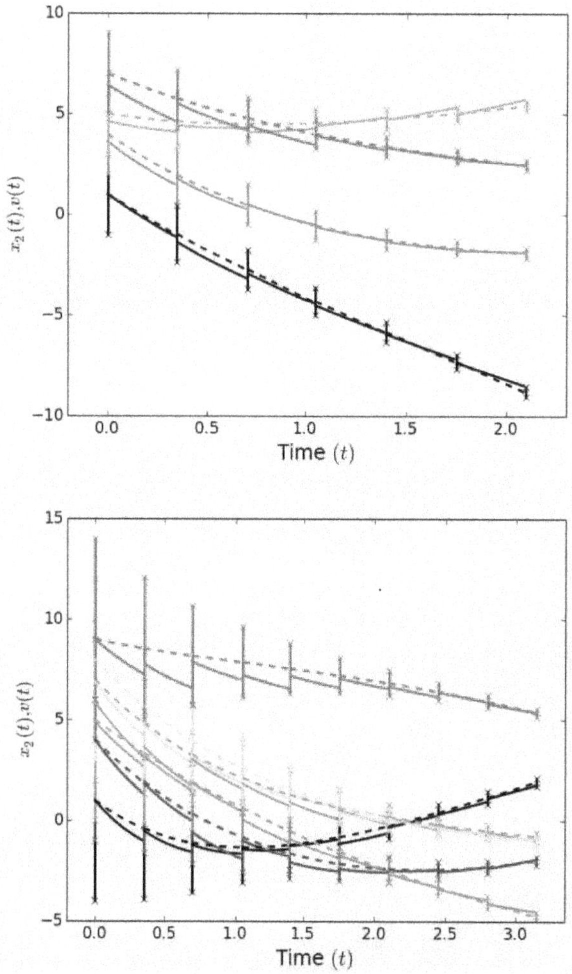

Figure 3: **Two sample executions of the detection algorithm for four- and six-dimensional systems ($n = 4, 6$) from initial state to the detection of second model. The dashed lines (−−) show the trajectories of the four (six) state variables of the actual system, sys2, and the solid lines show the estimates computed by the detection algorithm, $v(t)$. The vertical segments show the exponentially decaying envelope defined by $diam(S_i)$ in each round. Any one of the state components falling outside of S_i triggers detection.**

5. CONCLUSIONS AND FUTURE DIRECTIONS

This paper proposed a framework for studying state estimation algorithms that have guaranteed efficiency with respect to sensing and communication data rates. We introduced two different notions of *estimation entropy* and established their equivalence. We derived an upper bound of $(L + \alpha)n/\ln 2$ for the estimation entropy of an n-dimensional nonlinear dynamical system with Lipschitz constant L, when the desired exponential convergence rate of the estimate is α. We developed an iterative procedure whose average bit rate matches this upper bound on the entropy. We showed that no other iterative estimation algorithm can work with bit rates lower than the entropy. Finally, we presented an application of the estimation procedure in picking out one from a pair of candidate models using measurement data. We showed that under a mild assumption of *exponential separation*—which holds almost surely for randomly chosen model pairs—the algorithm can always detect the true model in finite time.

This work suggests several avenues for future investigations. First of all, the bounds given in this paper using Lipschitz constants could be refined to bounds using suitable matrix norms of the Jacobian matrix, following the results in [1, 7, 14]. Second, it would be desirable to have more rigorous and readily checkable versions of the sufficient conditions for exponential separation, building on what is described in Remark 5. Third, it would be interesting to establish a lower bound on the estimation entropy for the general nonlinear case; this result would parallel Theorem 3.2 of [2] which gives a lower bound for the control version of entropy. Finally, while here the digital communication channel was assumed to be error-free, it would be of interest to incorporate packet losses, delays, noise, etc.

6. REFERENCES

[1] V. A. Boichenko and G. A. Leonov. Lyapunov's direct method in estimates of topological entropy. *J. Math. Sci.*, 91:3370–3379, 1998.

[2] F. Colonius. Minimal bit rates and entropy for exponential stabilization. *SIAM J. Control Optim.*, 50:2988–3010, 2012.

[3] F. Colonius and C. Kawan. Invariance entropy for control systems. *SIAM J. Control Optim.*, 48:1701–1721, 2009.

[4] F. Colonius, C. Kawan, and G. Nair. A note on topological feedback entropy and invariance entropy. *Systems Control Lett.*, 62:377–381, 2013.

[5] T. M. Cover and J. A. Thomas. *Elements of Information Theory.* Wiley, New York, 1991.

[6] P. S. Duggirala, S. Mitra, and M. Viswanathan. Verification of annotated models from executions. In *Proceedings of the International Conference on Embedded Software, EMSOFT 2013, Montreal, QC, Canada, September 29 - Oct. 4, 2013*, pages 1–10. IEEE, 2013.

[7] C. Fan and S. Mitra. Bounded verification with on-the-fly discrepancy computation. In *Automated Technology for Verification and Analysis - 13th International Symposium, ATVA 2015, Shanghai, China*, volume 9364 of *LNCS*, pages 446–463. Springer, 2015.

[8] J. P. Hespanha, A. Ortega, and L. Vasudevan. Towards the control of linear systems with minimum bit-rate. In *Proc. 15th Int. Symp. on Mathematical Theory of Networks and Systems (MTNS)*, 2002.

[9] P. A. Ioannou and J. Sun. *Robust Adaptive Control.* Prentice Hall, New Jersey, 1996.

[10] A. Katok and B. Hasselblatt. *Introduction to the Modern Theory of Dynamical Systems.* Cambridge University Press, 1995.

[11] H. K. Khalil. *Nonlinear Systems.* Prentice Hall, New Jersey, 3rd edition, 2002.

[12] K.-D. Kim, S. Mitra, and P. R. Kumar. Computing bounded epsilon-reach set with finite precision computations for a class of linear hybrid automata. In *Proceedings of Hybrid Systems: Computation and Control (HSCC 2011)*, 2011.

[13] D. Liberzon and J. P. Hespanha. Stabilization of nonlinear systems with limited information feedback. *IEEE Trans. Automat. Control*, 50:910–915, 2005.

[14] J. Maidens and M. Arcak. Reachability analysis of nonlinear systems using matrix measures. *IEEE Trans. Automat. Control*, 60:265–270, 2015.

[15] G. N. Nair, R. J. Evans, I. M. Y. Mareels, and W. Moran. Topological feedback entropy and nonlinear stabilization. *IEEE Trans. Automat. Control*, 49:1585–1597, 2004.

[16] G. N. Nair, F. Fagnani, S. Zampieri, and R. J. Evans. Feedback control under data rate constraints: An overview. *Proc. IEEE*, 95:108–137, 2007.

[17] A. V. Savkin. Analysis and synthesis of networked control systems: Topological entropy, observability, robustness and optimal control. *Automatica*, 42:51–62, 2006.

[18] R. S. Smith and J. C. Doyle. Model validation: a connection between robust control and identification. *IEEE Trans. Automat. Control*, 37:942–952, 1992.

[19] S. Tatikonda and S. K. Mitter. Control under communication constraints. *IEEE Trans. Automat. Control*, 49:1056–1068, 2004.

Safety Verification of Piecewise-Deterministic Markov Processes

Rafael Wisniewski
Section for Automation & Control
Aalborg University, Denmark
raf@es.aau.dk

Christoffer Sloth
Section for Automation & Control
Aalborg University, Denmark
ces@es.aau.dk

Manuela Bujorianu
Department of Computer Science
University of Leicester
lb312@le.ac.uk

Nir Piterman
Department of Computer Science
University of Leicester
nir.piterman@le.ac.uk

ABSTRACT

We consider the safety problem of piecewise-deterministic Markov processes (PDMP). These are systems that have deterministic dynamics and stochastic jumps, where both the time and the destination of the jumps are stochastic. Specifically, we solve a p-safety problem, where we identify the set of initial states from which the probability to reach designated unsafe states is at most $1 - p$. Based on the knowledge of the full generator of the PDMP, we are able to develop a system of partial differential equations describing the connection between unsafe and initial states. We then show that by using the moment method, we can translate the infinite-dimensional optimisation problem searching for the largest set of p-safe states to a finite dimensional polynomial optimisation problem. We have implemented this technique on top of GloptiPoly and show how to apply it to a numerical example.

Keywords

Hybrid Systems; Verification; Sum of Squares; piecewise-deterministic Markov processes; Optimisation

1. INTRODUCTION

In this paper, we develop a method for safety verification of a class of hybrid systems. Specifically, we study piecewise deterministic Markov processes [5]. In a nutshell, a piecewise deterministic Markov process, for short PDMP, consists of deterministic dynamics that alternate with random discrete transitions. Randomness of the discrete transitions (jumps) is characterised by stochastic time of jumps, and stochastic jump-destinations. More formally, each jump time has associated 1) a survivor function, which defines the probability

HSCC'16, April 12 - 14, 2016, Vienna, Austria

ⓒ 2016 Copyright held by the owner/author(s). Publication rights licensed to ACM.
ISBN 978-1-4503-3955-1/16/04...$15.00

DOI: http://dx.doi.org/10.1145/2883817.2883836

of a jump time, and 2) a stochastic kernel, which defines the probability of a post jump location. We find PDMPs sufficiently general to represent hybrid systems and at the same time regular enough to develop a numerically tractable algorithm for computation of stochastic safety of hybrid systems. More general randomized models of hybrid systems have been studied in [2], where the continuous dynamics is generalised to stochastic differential equations, and in [24], where deterministic dynamics is generalised to differential inclusions.

Commonly, a system is said to be safe if it does not violate any system constraints. However, when considering stochastic systems this notion of safety must be relaxed, and a system is said to be p-safe if it does not violate system constraints with a probability of at least p. To this end, we address methods for safety verification, i.e., methods demonstrating that a system will not violate system constraints with a probability of at least p.

To develop an algorithm for safety verification, we use the observation that a PDMP is a Markov process for which the full generator is known. The full generator is an integro-differential operator defined on appropriate space of functions. Using the expression of the generator, we are able to relate the final states with initial states of the process in terms of a partial differential equation. Consequently, we are able to show how to compute the largest set of initial conditions such that a given stochastic system is safe with probability p.

To describe the initial states, final states and the states that are visited by realisations on the way from the initial to final states, we use the concepts of initial measure, hitting distribution, and occupation measure. To compute the initial measure, we rely on the moment method [14], which allows translation of an infinite dimensional optimization problem on measures to a polynomial optimization problem. By Haviland's theorem, the measures are characterised by infinite sequences of moments. Subsequently, these sequences are truncated (relaxed) to formulate a finite dimensional polynomial optimisation.

Much work has been conducted in relation to safety verification of control systems [6]. Methods for safety verification of dynamical systems include reachability methods [16] and the barrier certificate method [18]. Especially the barrier certificate method has attracted much attention, due to its simple computation.

The barrier certificate method has been used for verification [19], for estimation of operating envelope [26], for safe control [25], and has been combined with control barrier functions to include constraints [1, 22].

Work on stochastic safety verification was presented in [18] where a super martingale was used as a stochastic barrier certificate, and easy computational conditions were derived based on Doob's martingale inequality [17]. Also [2] thoroughly covers the subject of reachability of hybrid systems. It introduces a formal definition of stochastic reachability. The expected occupation measure and hitting distribution, also employed in this paper are introduced for the purpose of reachability. Reachability estimations in terms of hitting times, transition-operators semi-groups, Martin capacities, and martingale theory are discussed in [2].

The methodology exploited in this work is inspired by [11, 8], which computes regions of attraction for deterministic systems via solving convex programming problems. The problems are infinite dimensional; thus, finite dimensional truncations are used for the actual computations via the hierarchy of relaxations [13]. Note that for safety verification, it is imperative to obtain inner approximations of the set of safe initial states. In particular, the method developed in this paper provides an inner approximation. Our work is an extension of safety verification of diffusion processes in [23] to PDMPs.

The final part of the paper is devoted to a numerical example. The solution to the safety verification is found by solving a polynomial optimisation problem using GloptiPoly [9].

The outline of the paper is as follows. The definition of p-safety is provided in Section 2. In Section 3 we define the initial measure, the hitting distribution, and the occupation measure. Subsequently, we use them in Section 4 to formulate the safety problem in an optimisation framework. In Section 5, we recall the definition of a PDMP and illustrate expressiveness of PDMPs. The p-safety for a polynomial PDMP and semi-algebraic state space and semi-algebraic set of unsafe states is formulated as a linear optimisation problem in Section 6. Finally, an illustration of the method for computing p-safety is found in Section 7.

2. P-SAFETY

In short, the aim of this paper is to compute the largest set of initial states for which a process is safe with probability at least p. Specifically, we formulate the problem of p-safety for a Markov process[1]. Later in the paper, we will solve the problem for a specific class of Markov processes namely a PDMP.

We consider a Markov process (X_t, P^y) on the probability space $(\Omega, \mathcal{F}, P)$ with values in a state space E. We use the notation $X_t^y : \Omega \to E$ to indicate the solution that starts at y, that is, $P[X_0^y = y] = 1$. We denote by $P_t(y, A)$ the transition probabilities for the process X_t, i.e., $P_t(y, A) \equiv P^y[X_t \in A]$,[2] where P^y is the law of X_t^y, that is $P^y[X_t \in A] \equiv P[X_t^y \in A]$.

In the paper, we adopt the convention that whenever the initial state of the studied process is not specified, we use the notation X_t.

We make a technical assumption on the Markov process X_t:

1. E is a Borel space (E is a Borel subset of a complete separable metric space).
2. P-almost all sample functions of X_t are continuous from the right.

In the last part of the paper, the space E will be more concrete - a subset of $\bigcup_{v \in K}\{v\} \times \mathbb{R}^{d(v)}$, where K corresponds to the set of discrete states; whereas $\mathbb{R}^{d(v)}$ is the "continuous" state space - the Euclidean space of dimension $d(v)$ - corresponding to the mode v.

DEFINITION 2.1. *A* system *is the tuple*

$$\Gamma = (X_t, P^y, U, U_0, U_u),$$

where (X_t, P^y) is a Markov process, and $U \subseteq E$, $U_0 \subseteq U$, $U_u \subset U$ are Borel sets.

We think about E as the state space being continuous, discrete, or a combination of these, U as the set where the process lives on, U_0 as the subset of initial states, and U_u as the subset consisting of unsafe states.

We say that a system Γ is p-safe if the probability of the realisations initialised in the set U_0 that are contained in the set U and that reach the unsafe set U_u is less than $1 - p$.

The notion of p-safety of a system Γ is formalised in Definition 2.2. To this end, we employ the following stopping time. For a subset $V \subseteq E$, we define $\tau^y_{V,T}$ as the first time X_t^y hits V before reaching time T

$$\tau^y_{V,T} \equiv \inf(\{t \in \mathbb{R}_+ |\ X_t^y \in V\} \cup \{T\}), \tag{1}$$

where $\mathbb{R}_+$ is the set of nonnegative reals.

The function $\tau^y_{V,T}$ is indeed a stopping time with respect to the filtration generated by X_t^y, for details see Example 9.17 and Lemma 9.18 in [10]. We consider an event D^y - a subset of Ω containing all the realisations of X_t^y that hit U_u before hitting the complement of U

$$D^y \equiv D^y_T \equiv \left[\tau^y_{U^c,T} - \tau^y_{U_u,T} > 0\right],$$

where U^c is the complement of U in E.

We define

$$R(y) \equiv R_T(y) \equiv P(D^y). \tag{2}$$

It is the probability that X_t^y hits U_u before leaving U.

Suppose that a priori knowledge about the probability distribution of initial states is given in terms of a probability measure ν_0 on U. Consequently, the set of the states reaching U_u with probability no less than $1-p$ is $\{y \in U|\ R(y) \geq 1 - p\}$, and the probability that these states are initial is

$$\nu_0(\{y \in U|\ R(y) \geq 1 - p\}).$$

The reason for imposing the initial distribution is as follows. Suppose that there is a single trajectory that is not p-safe, then in normal condition the system will never follow "precisely" this trajectory; thus, it is p-safe. On the contrary,

[1]More formally, we study a family of Markov processes parameterised by the initial values.

[2]For a random variable $Z : (\Omega, \mathcal{F}) \to (Y, \mathcal{Y})$, where $(Y, \mathcal{Y})$ is a measurable space, and a set $B \in \mathcal{Y}$, we write $[Z \in B] \equiv \{\omega \in \Omega|\ Z(\omega) \in B\}$.

if the same system is initiated such that it actually follows this trajectory, then the p-safety is violated.

We are now ready to formalise the definition of p-safety.

DEFINITION 2.2 (p-SAFETY). *We say that the system $\Gamma = (X_t, P^y, U, U_0, U_u)$ is p-safe with respect to a measure ν_0 if*

$$\nu_0(\{y \in U_0 | \; R(y) \geq 1 - p\}) = 0. \quad (3)$$

REMARK 2.1. *If $E = \mathbb{R}^n$ and the initial states are uniformly distributed in a bounded set U_0. The formulation of p-safety in (3) reads*

$$l(\{x \in U_0 | \; R(x) \geq 1 - p\}) = 0, \quad (4)$$

where l is the Lebesgue measure on $\mathbb{R}^n$. In (4), one evaluates the volume of the sets of the points that reach the unsafe set with probability no less than $1 - p$. Notice that if there is a single trajectory γ such that for $x \in \gamma$, $R(x) \geq 1 - p$, then the system is still p-safe. From the practical point of view, the point x will not be "visible".

In this work, the set of initial states U_0 is not fixed, on the contrary, we strive to find the largest set of initial conditions for which a system is p-safe. The following definitions will be instrumental in formulating in which sense U_0 is to be the largest.

- On the set $\mathcal{P}(U)$ of all subsets of U,[3] we define the equivalence relation $\backsim_{\nu_0}$: For $U_1, U_2 \in \mathcal{P}(U)$, $U_1 \backsim_{\nu_0} U_2$ if and only if $\nu_0(U_1 \Delta U_2) = 0$, where Δ is the symmetric difference[4]. The equivalence class of U_1 will be denoted by $[U_1] \equiv \{v \in \mathcal{P}(U) | \; v \backsim_{\nu_0} U_1\}$, and the set of all equivalence classes by $\mathcal{P}(U)/\backsim_{\nu_0}$.
- On the set $\mathcal{P}(U)/\backsim_{\nu_0}$, we define a partial order $\preceq \equiv \preceq_{\nu_0}$ by: for two sets $[U_1]$ and $[U_2]$ in $\mathcal{P}(U)/\backsim_{\nu_0}$

$$[U_1] \preceq [U_2] \text{ if and only if } \nu_0(U_1) \leq \nu_0(U_2)$$
$$\text{for any } U_1 \in [U_1] \text{ and } U_2 \in [U_2].$$

PROBLEM 2.1 (p-SAFETY PROBLEM). *Given a Markov family (X_t, P^y), a number $p \in [0, 1]$, two subsets U and U_u, and a measure ν_0. Find a set U_0 such that $U_0 \subseteq U$, and $[U_0]$ is largest with respect to $\preceq$ such that $\Gamma = (X_t, P^y, U, U_0, U_u)$ is p-safe with respect to ν_0.*

A solution to the p-safety problem is provided in Section 4. Next, we exemplify the p-safety problem for a Markov chain. This will be the only instance of discrete-time stochastic process. The rest of the exposition addresses exclusively continuous -time Markov processes.

EXAMPLE 2.1. *Consider the graphical representation of a Markov chain in Figure 1, where the edges are labeled by the transition probabilities. The state space is*

$$U = \{A, B, C, D, E, F\}.$$

Suppose that the unsafe set $U_u = \{E\}$, and initial states are uniformly distributed on U. Then the states $\{A, D, F\}$ are 0.6-safe; specifically, $P^A(X_n = E) = 0.3 \cdot 1 + 0.2 \cdot 0.1 < 0.4$ Whereas, $P^B(X_n = E) = 0.5 \sum_{i=0}^{\infty} 0.5^i = 1$. Suppose now that the measure ν_0 is such that $\nu_0(B) = 0$, then the states $\{A, B, D, F\}$ are 0.6-safe. But $\{A, B, D, F\} \backsim_{\nu_0} \{A, D, F\}$, since the probability of the initial state at B is 0 the two sets $\{A, B, D, F\}$ and $\{A, D, F\}$ are regarded the same.

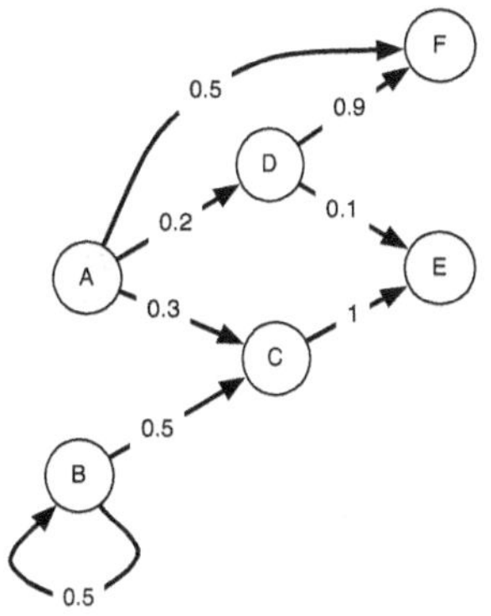

Figure 1: If E is the only unsafe state and the initial states are uniformly distributed then the states $\{A, D, F\}$ are 0.6-safe.

[3]For a set A, $\mathcal{P}(A)$ is the power set of A, i.e., the set of all subsets of A.

[4]$U_1 \Delta U_2 = U_1 \setminus U_2 \cup U_2 \setminus U_1$

3. MARKOV PROCESSES

We strive to reformulate the problem of p-safety in Definition 2.2 as an abstract optimisation problem. It will be effective for an arbitrary Markov proces. To this end, we will make use of two concepts: 1) a full generator and 2) an occupation measure, which together describe how much the process "occupies" in the state space. Subsequently, the abstract optimisation problem will be applied to an optimisation framework over polynomials for PDMPs. We will characterise the occupation measure by linear conditions satisfied by its moments. To numerically solve the optimisation problem for p-safety, it is relaxed by considering only a finite number of moments.

3.1 Full Generator

We follow the definition in Section 11.1.4 of [21] of the *full generator* of the process X_t. Let $M(E)$ denote the linear space of measurable functions on E over $\mathbb{R}$.

DEFINITION 3.1 (FULL GENERATOR). *A full generator of a Markov process (X_t, P^y) is a subset $\mathcal{A} \subseteq M(E) \times M(E)$ that satisfies the following conditions*

1. *If $(f, \tilde{f})$ and $(g, \tilde{g})$ are in $\mathcal{A}$ then $(af + bg, a\tilde{f} + b\tilde{g}) \in \mathcal{A}$ for any a, $b \in \mathbb{R}$.*
2. *For any $(f, \tilde{f}) \in \mathcal{A}$,*
   - *the function $t \mapsto \tilde{f}(X_t)$ is almost surely integrable with respect P^y for any initial state $y \in E$, and*
   - *the proces*

$$C_t^f = f(X_t) - f(X_0) - \int_0^t \tilde{f}(X_s) ds \quad (5)$$

is an $\mathcal{F}_t$-martingale, where $\mathcal{F}_t$ is the filtration generated by X_t, $\mathcal{F}_t = \sigma(X_s | \; 0 \leq s \leq t)$.[5]

[5]$\mathcal{F}_t$ is the σ-algebra generated by the past and the present of X_t.

Let $D(\mathcal{A}) \equiv \pi_1(\mathcal{A})$, where $\pi_1 : (f, \tilde{f}) \mapsto f$ is the projection, be the domain of the full generator $\mathcal{A}$. We will call a function $f \in D(\mathcal{A})$ a test function. Any function $\mathcal{U} : D(\mathcal{A}) \to M(E)$, such that $(f, \mathcal{U}(f)) \in \mathcal{A}$ will be called a selector for the full generator $\mathcal{A}$, or for short a selector (for $\mathcal{A}$).

The full generator of a PDMP will be discussed in Section 5.

REMARK 3.1. *For the space of bounded measurable functions $B(E)$, the operator*

$$P_t : B(E) \to B(E),\ f \mapsto P_t f(y) = E^y f(X_t),$$

where E^y is the expected value calculated with respect to P^y, has the semigroup property $P_t P_s = P_{t+s}$. We associate to P_t a strong generator

$$\mathcal{U}f(y) \equiv \lim_{t \downarrow 0} \frac{P_t f(y) - f(y)}{t} \tag{6}$$

with the domain $D(\mathcal{U})$ of $\mathcal{U}$.[6] *If almost all realisations of the process are right continuous then $P^y(X_t \in A)$ is uniquely defined by $\mathcal{U}$.*

By Proposition 14.13 in [5],

$$C_t^f = f(X_t) - f(X_0) - \int_0^t \mathcal{U}(X_s) ds$$

is an $\mathcal{F}_t$-martingale on $(\Omega, \mathcal{F}, \mathcal{F}_t, P^y)$. Hence, the strong generator is a selector for a full generator. In conclusion, the Kolmogorov backward equation, Proposition 14.10 in [5], is satisfied

$$E^y f(X_t) = f(y) + E^y \int_0^t \mathcal{U}f(X_s) ds, \text{ for } f \in D(\mathcal{U}). \tag{7}$$

This equation is fundamental for this work.

EXAMPLE 3.1. *A Poisson process $N_t : \Omega \to E = \{0, 1, 2, \dots\}$ with intensity $\lambda > 0$ has the strong generator $\mathcal{L}$ defined by*

$$\mathcal{L}(f)(v) = \lambda(f(v+1) - f(v)),$$

for test functions $f : \{0, 1, 2, \dots\} \to \mathbb{R}$.

The solution X_t of a dynamical system on $E = \mathbb{R}^n$, $\dot{x} = \xi(x)$, $X_0 = y$ is a Markov process with the generator ξ defined by[7]

$$\xi(f)(x) = \sum \xi_i(x) \frac{\partial f(x)}{\partial x_i}$$

for smooth functions $f : \mathbb{R}^n \to \mathbb{R}$.

We assume that for the studied Markov process X_t, the process C_t^f is uniformly integrable. In short, we need uniform integrability and martingale property of C_t^f to be able to substitute time t by an arbitrary stopping time using optional sampling theorem, Theorem 13.7 in [5].

To study the stopping time $\tau \equiv \tau_{V,T}^y$, we augment the selector $\mathcal{U}$ of a full generator $\mathcal{A}$ with a time component. To this end, motivated by [7], we introduce the *time-space selector* $\hat{\mathcal{U}}$ for the selector $\mathcal{U}$

$$\hat{\mathcal{U}}(\gamma f)(t, y) = \gamma(t)\mathcal{U}f(y) + \frac{\partial}{\partial t}\gamma(t) f(y)$$

for $f \in D(\mathcal{U})$ and $\gamma \in C_0^1(\mathbb{R}_+)$, where $C_0^1(\mathbb{R}_+)$ denotes the set of C^1-smooth functions with compact support.

Consequently,

$$\hat{C}_t^f \equiv \gamma(t) f(X_t) - \gamma(0) f(X_0) - \int_0^t \hat{\mathcal{U}}(\gamma f)(s, X_s) ds \tag{8}$$

is an $\mathcal{F}_t$-martingale. Specifically,

$$E^y \hat{C}_t^f = \hat{C}_0^f = 0. \tag{9}$$

REMARK 3.2. *We can construct a time-space selector by computing a selector for the full generator of X_t extended by an extra state corresponding to the deterministic process T_t representing the time, $P[T_t = t] = 1$.*

Since C_t^f is assumed to be uniformly integrable and the process X_t is right continuous, by the optional stopping theorem, (9) is still true if one substitutes time t by any finite stopping time τ

$$E^y \left[\gamma(\tau) f(X_\tau) - \gamma(0) f(y) - \int_0^\tau \hat{\mathcal{U}}(\gamma f)(s, X_s) ds \right] = 0,$$

and hence

$$E^y[\hat{f}(\tau, X_\tau)] = \hat{f}(0, y) + E^y \left[\int_0^\tau \hat{\mathcal{U}}(\hat{f})(s, X_s) ds \right], \tag{10}$$

where $\hat{f} \equiv \gamma f$.

Equation (10) lays the foundations for the development of p-safety algorithm in this paper. It describes how the expected value of a test function evaluated at a current state of the process develops in time.

3.2 Occupation Measures

This subsection details the evolution of a set of initial states subject to the time-space selector $\hat{\mathcal{U}}$.

Let $\mathcal{B}(E)$ denote the Borel σ-algebra on E. We start by defining the *hitting kernel* ν (also called the exit distribution in [7]), which gives the probability for process X_t reaching a subset $C \in \mathcal{B}(E)$ at time τ in a subset $B \in \mathcal{B}([0, T])$ (Borel σ-algebra on the interval [0, T]). The hitting kernel is defined as

$$\nu(y, B \times C) \equiv E^y(1_{B \times C}(\tau, X_\tau)) = P^y[(\tau, X_\tau) \in B \times C], \tag{11}$$

where $1_{B \times C} : \mathbb{R}_+ \times E \to \{0, 1\}$ is the indicator function of subset $B \times C$ in $\mathbb{R}_+ \times E$. Consequently, the left hand side of (10) can be written as

$$E^y[\hat{f}(\tau, X_\tau)] = \int_{[0,T] \times E} \hat{f}(t, z) \nu(y, dtdz).$$

Next, we define the expected *occupation kernel*

$$\begin{aligned} \mu(y, B \times C) &\equiv E^y \left[\int_{[0,\tau] \cap B} 1_C(X_s) ds \right] \\ &= \int_C \int_{[0,\tau] \cap B} P_t(y, dz) dt. \end{aligned}$$

Consequently, the second summand of the right hand side of (10) is expressed as

$$E^y \left[\int_0^\tau \hat{\mathcal{U}}(\hat{f})(s, X_s) ds \right] = \int_{[0,T] \times E} \hat{\mathcal{U}}(\hat{f})(t, z) \mu(y, dtdz).$$

[6] $t \downarrow 0$ in (6) is the right limit in the supremum norm.

[7] Note that a vector field $\xi = \sum \xi_i(x) \frac{\partial}{\partial x_i}$ acts on a differentiable functions as a directional derivative.

As the result, (10) reads

$$\int_{[0,T]\times E} \hat{f}(t,z)\nu(y,dtdz) \quad (12)$$

$$= \hat{f}(0,y) + \int_{[0,T]\times E} \hat{\mathcal{U}}\hat{f}(t,z)\mu(y,dtdz).$$

Equation (12) describes the time evolution of the initial condition, $X_0 = y$. A natural question arises: Suppose the pair of kernels $(\nu(y,\cdot,\cdot), \mu(y,\cdot,\cdot))$ are given. Are these in fact the hitting- and the occupation-kernels for the Markov process (X_t, P^y) (whose time-space selector is $\hat{\mathcal{U}}$). The answer to this question is given in the next proposition. Its proof follows from [12] shown for the situation with control.

PROPOSITION 3.1. *Suppose that $\mathcal{A}$ is the full generator of the transition semigroup of operators. Let E be partitioned into two regions V and its complement V^c. Let $\nu(y,\cdot,\cdot)$, $\mu(y,\cdot,\cdot)$ be positive measures on $[0,T]\times E$ with supports* supp $\nu(y,\cdot,\cdot) \subseteq [0,T]\times V^c$ *and* supp $\mu(y,\cdot,\cdot) \subseteq [0,T]\times V$ *such that (12) is satisfied. Then there is a process X_t giving rise to a selector $\mathcal{U}$ for $\mathcal{A}$ and stopping time $\tau = \tau^y_{V^c,T}$ for which (10) is satisfied.*

Let μ_0 be an initial probability measure on $(E, \mathcal{B}(E))$. It defines a distribution of initial states. Then the *hitting distribution* is defined as

$$\nu(B\times C) \equiv \int_U \nu(y, B\times C)\mu_0(dy) \quad (13)$$

for $B\in\mathcal{B}([0,T])$ and $C\in\mathcal{B}(E)$. The *occupation measure* is

$$\mu(B\times C) \equiv \int_U \mu(y, B\times C)\mu_0(dy). \quad (14)$$

Furthermore, integrating both sides of (12) with respect to μ_0 gives

$$\int_{[0,T]\times E} \hat{f}(t,z)\nu(dtdz) \quad (15)$$

$$= \int_E \hat{f}(0,y)\mu_0(dy) + \int_{[0,T]\times E} \hat{\mathcal{U}}\hat{f}(t,z)\mu(dtdz).$$

This equation will be used in the next section to formulate an abstract optimisation problem for p-safety.

4. SAFETY VERIFICATION FOR MARKOV PROCESSES

In this section, we come back to the problem of p-safety. When studying the p-safety algorithm in Section 6, it will be crucial to assume that U is compact and U_u is open. These two assumption will be effective in the rest of the paper.

To formulate the optimisation problem, we identify $\bar{\mu}_0$ with $\delta_0\otimes\mu_0$, where δ_0 is the Dirac measure at 0, and $\otimes$ is the product of measures.[8] Consequently, all the measures μ, ν, and $\bar{\mu}_0$ are defined on $[0,T]\times E$.

To address the problem of p-safety, we explicitly impose constraints on the supports of the initial measure, the hitting distributions and the occupation measure in (12). The supports of the measures μ and $\bar{\mu}_0$ are: supp $\mu \subseteq [0,T]\times(U\setminus U_u)$ and supp $\bar{\mu}_0 \subseteq \{0\}\times(U\setminus U_u)$. Furthermore, the measure $\nu = \nu_1+\nu_2$, where supp $\nu_1 \subseteq [0,T]\times(U\setminus U_u)$, and supp $\nu_2 \subseteq [0,T]\times\partial U_u$. Intuitively, ν_2 corresponds to the unsafe realisations, i.e., those which reach the unsafe set ∂U_u. Whereas, ν_1 corresponds to both the safe and the unsafe realisations, since supp $\nu_2 \subset$ supp ν_1.

[8] $\delta_0\otimes\mu_0(B\times C) = \delta_0(B)\mu_0(C)$.

The main result of this work is Theorem 4.1 in this section and its application to PDMP in the next section. Fix a measure ν_0 on $(E,\mathcal{B}(E))$. This is the measure according to which we have defined p-safety in Definition 2.2. Theorem 4.1 formulates an optimisation problem, which characterises the largest set U_0 of initial states with respect to $\preceq$ such that $\Gamma = (X_t, P^y, U, U_0, U_u)$ is p-safe with respect to a measure ν_0.

In the following, we write $\mu\geq 0$ to indicate that μ is a positive measure. To compress the notation, we denote the complement of U_u in U by $U_c \equiv U\setminus U_u$. Furthermore, we use the shorthand notations $\int$ for $\int_{[0,T]\times E}$, and $\forall\hat{f}$ for $\forall\hat{f}\in C_0^1(\mathbb{R}_+)\times D(\mathcal{U})$.

THEOREM 4.1. *The optimal value q^* of linear programming problem*

$$\begin{array}{rll} q^* = & \sup & \mu_0(E) \\ & s.t.\forall\hat{f} & \int\hat{f}d\nu_1 + \int\hat{f}d\nu_2 - \int\hat{f}d\bar{\mu}_0 = \int\hat{\mathcal{U}}\hat{f}d\mu \\ & & \int d\nu_2 \geq (1-p)\int d\bar{\mu}_0 \\ & & \nu_0\geq\mu_0\geq 0, \\ & & \bar{\mu}_0 = \delta_0\otimes\mu_0,\ \mu\geq 0,\ \nu_1\geq 0,\ \nu_2\geq 0, \\ & & \text{supp } \mu_0\subseteq U_c, \text{supp } \mu\subseteq[0,T]\times U_c, \\ & & \text{supp } \nu_1\subseteq[0,T]\times U_c, \\ & & \text{supp } \nu_2\subseteq[0,T]\times\partial U_u. \end{array} \quad (16)$$

is equal to

$$q^* = \nu_0(\text{supp } \mu_0^*),$$

where the quadruple $(\mu_0^*, \nu_1^*, \nu_2^*, \mu^*)$ is the solution of (16).

Furthermore, the set of initial states U_0 solving the p-safety for the system $\Gamma = (X_t, P^y, U, U_0, U_u)$, i.e., the largest set U_0 with respect to $\preceq$ such that the system Γ is p-safe, is

$$U_0 = (\text{supp } \mu_0^*)^c.$$

As announced, the optimisation problem (16) is linear, but infinite dimensional.

PROOF. Since the optimisation of μ_0 searches for the supremum of positive measures bounded by the measure ν_0, we conclude that there is a set W such that $\mu_0^* = \nu_0|_W$, i.e., supp $\mu_0\subseteq W$ and μ_0 is equal to ν_0 on $\mathcal{B}(W)$.

We will prove that $U_0 = (\text{supp } \mu_0^*)^c$. Recall the definition of $R(y)$ in (2). We will show that there is no nonempty set $A\subseteq U_c$ such that $A\cap\text{supp } \mu_0^* = \emptyset$, and for all $y\in A$, $R(y)\geq 1-p$ and $\nu_0(A)>0$. We will prove this claim by a contradiction. For this purpose, we suppose that there is such a set A. At the outset, we make two observations. By Proposition 3.1,

$$\int_{[0,T]\times\partial U_c} \nu(y; dtdz) = R(y), \text{ with } \nu = \nu_1+\nu_2.$$

Furthermore, by the second constraint and the cost functional in (16), $\nu_1^*|_{[0,T]\times\partial U_c} = 0$.

We define a new initial measure $\hat{\mu}_0 = \mu_0^* + \nu_0|_A$ and compute ν_1, ν_2, and μ such that

- they satisfy all the constraints of (16) but the second constraint (after replacing μ_0 with $\hat{\mu}_0$), and

- $\nu_1|_{[0,T]\times\partial U_c} = 0$.

Combining the above observations, we have

$$\int_{[0,T]\times\partial U_c} \nu_2(y; dtdz) = R(y).$$

Subsequently, we check if the optimisation constraints are satisfied for $\hat{\mu}_0$. To this end, we verify whether $\int d\nu_2 \geq (1-p)\int d\hat{\mu}_0$:

$$\begin{aligned}
&\int_{[0,T]\times\partial U_c} \nu_2(dtdz) = \int_E \int_{[0,T]\times\partial U_c} \nu_2(y, dtdz)\hat{\mu}_0(dy) \\
&= \int_{\text{supp } \mu_0^*\cup A} \int_{[0,T]\times\partial U_c} \nu_2(y, dtdz)\nu_0(dy) \\
&= \int_{\text{supp } \mu_0^*} \int_{[0,T]\times\partial U_c} \nu_2(y, dtdz)\nu_0(dy) \\
&+ \int_A \int_{[0,T]\times\partial U_c} \nu_2(y, dtdz)\nu_0(dy) \\
&\geq (1-p)\int_{[0,T]\times \text{supp } \mu_0^*} \delta_0 \otimes \nu_0(dtdy) + \int_A R(y)\nu_0(dy) \\
&\geq (1-p)\int_{[0,T]\times \text{supp } \mu_0^*} \delta_0 \otimes \nu_0(dtdy) + (1-p)\int_A \nu_0(dy) \\
&= (1-p)\int_{[0,T]\times(\text{supp } \mu_0^*\cup A)} d\nu_0 = (1-p)\int_{[0,T]\times E} d\hat{\mu}_0
\end{aligned}$$

A a consequence, the measure $\hat{\mu}_0$ satisfies the optimisation constraints, but $\int_E d\hat{\mu}_0 > q^*$. Hence, we arrive at a contradiction. In conclusion, $U_0 = (\text{supp } \mu_0^*)^c$. □

5. PIECEWISE-DETERMINISTIC MARKOV PROCESSES

Piecewise-deterministic Markov processes (PDMP) were introduced by Davis in 1984 [5]. They are nonlinear continuous time stochastic hybrid processes, whose dynamics represent alternation of continuous dynamics triggered by deterministic differential equations with stochastic jumps (discrete transitions). They are the class of stochastic hybrid systems, which shows non-diffusion phenomena. PDMPs involve a hybrid state space, i.e., with both continuous and discrete states. Only in the discrete transitions exhibit randomness. Between two consecutive discrete transitions the continuous state evolves according to ordinary differential equations. Discrete transitions occur either when the state hits the state space boundary or according to a generalised Poisson process in the interior of the state space. Whenever such a transition occurs, a post jump location is chosen according to a probabilistic kernel, which depends also on the hybrid state before the transition.

Formally, we introduce PDMPs following the notation of [21] and [3]. Let K be a countable set of discrete states (also called modes), and let $d : K \to \mathbb{N}$, and let $\mathcal{X} : K \to \bigcup_{v\in K} \{v\}\times\mathcal{P}(\mathbb{R}^{d(v)})$ be a multivalued map assigning to each discrete state $v \in K$ an open subset of $\{v\}\times\mathbb{R}^{d(v)}$. We call the set

$$\mathcal{S}(K, d, \mathcal{X}) \equiv \bigcup_{v\in K} \mathcal{X}(v) = \{(v, x) \in \mathcal{X}(v)|\ v \in K\}$$

a *(PDMP) hybrid state space* and

$$y = (v, x) \in \mathcal{S}(K, d, \mathcal{X})$$

the *hybrid state*. We define the boundary of the hybrid state space as

$$\partial\mathcal{S}(K, d, \mathcal{X}) \equiv \bigcup_{v\in K} \partial\mathcal{X}(v).$$

A vector field ξ on the hybrid state space $\mathcal{S}(K, d, \mathcal{X})$ is a map

$$\xi : \mathcal{S}(K, d, \mathcal{X}) \to \bigcup_{v\in K} \{v\}\times\mathbb{R}^{d(v)}$$

with the section property $\pi_1\xi = \text{id}$, where $\pi_1(v, x) = v$, and id is the identity map on K. In other words, ξ assigns to each hybrid state $y = (v, x)$ a vector $\xi(y) \in \{v\}\times\mathbb{R}^{d(v)}$. For an open interval $(-\epsilon, \epsilon) \subset \mathbb{R}$ the flow of ξ is a map

$$\phi : (-\epsilon, \epsilon)\times\mathcal{S}(K, d, \mathcal{X}) \to \mathcal{S}(K, d, \mathcal{X})$$

such that $\phi(0, y) = y$

$$\frac{d}{dt}\phi(t, y) = \xi(\phi(t, y)), \quad \text{for } t \in (-\epsilon, \epsilon). \tag{17}$$

To interpret (17), we define the maps ϕ_v and ξ_v by the following equalities

$$(v, \xi_v(x) = \xi(v, x))$$
$$(v, \phi_v(t, x)) = \phi((v, x), t).$$

Then the interpretation of (17) is

$$\frac{d}{dt}\phi_v(t, y) = \xi_v(\phi_v(t, y)).$$

Let

$$\Gamma(K, d, \mathcal{X}; \xi) \equiv \{y \in \partial\mathcal{S}(K, d, \mathcal{X})|\ \exists(y', t) \in \mathcal{S}(K, d, \mathcal{X})\times\mathbb{R}^+, y = \phi(y', t)\}$$

be the *active boundary*, and

$$\overline{\mathcal{S}}(K, d, \mathcal{X}; \xi) \equiv \mathcal{S}(K, d, \mathcal{X}) \cup \Gamma(K, d, \mathcal{X}; \xi).$$

In other words, the active boundary is the disjoint union of the open sets in $\mathbb{R}^{d(v)}$ together with the point of its boundary which are reached by the flow of ξ.

The hybrid state space $\mathcal{S}(K, d, \mathcal{X})$ plays the role of the state space E, which was discussed in the previous sections. Since $\mathcal{E} \equiv \bigcup_{v\in K}\{v\}\times\mathbb{R}^{d(v)}$ is a complete metric space and $\mathcal{S}(K, d, \mathcal{X}) \in \mathcal{B}(\mathcal{E})$, the state space $E \equiv \mathcal{S}(K, d, \mathcal{X})$ is a Borel space. The Borel sets $A \in \mathcal{B}(E)$ are characterised by $A = \bigcup_{v\in K}\{v\}\times A_v$, where $A_v \in \mathcal{B}(\mathbb{R}^{d(v)})$.

We can now introduce the definition of a piecewise deterministic Markov process.

Definition 5.1 (PDMP). *A piecewise-deterministic Markov process is a collection*

$$H = ((K, d, \mathcal{X}), \xi, \nu_0, \lambda, Q)$$

where:

- K *is a countable set of discrete variables;*
- $d : K \to \mathbb{N}$ *is a map defining the dimensions of the continuous state spaces.*
- $\mathcal{X} : K \to \bigcup_{v\in K}\{v\}\times\mathcal{P}(\mathbb{R}^{d(v)})$ *maps each* $v \in K$ *into an open subset* $\mathcal{X}(v)$ *of* $\{v\}\times\mathbb{R}^{d(v)}$.

- $\xi : \mathcal{S}(K, d, \mathcal{X}) \to \bigcup_{v \in K} \{v\} \times \mathbb{R}^{d(v)}$ *is a vector field.*
- $\nu_0 : \mathcal{B}(\mathcal{S}(K, d, \mathcal{X})) \to [0, 1]$ *is an initial probability measure on the measurable space* $(E, \mathcal{B}(E))$.
- $\lambda : \mathcal{S}(K, d, \mathcal{X}) \to \mathbb{R}^+$ *is a jump rate that gives the survivor function* F *of the ith jump after the jump at time* T_{i-1} *from the hybrid state* y_{i-1} *as follows*

$$F(y_{i-1}, t) = \begin{cases} \exp\left(-\int_0^t \lambda(\phi(y_{i-1}, \tau))d\tau\right) & \text{if } t < t^*(\mathbf{x}) \\ 0 & \text{if } t \geq t^*(\mathbf{x}), \end{cases}$$

where $t^* : \mathcal{S}(K, d, \mathcal{X}) \to \mathbb{R}^+ \cup \{\infty\}$ *is the exit time defined by*

$$t^*(y) = \inf\{t > 0 : \phi(y, t) \notin \mathcal{S}(K, d, \mathcal{X})\}.$$

- $Q : \mathcal{B}(\mathcal{S}(K, d, \mathcal{X})) \times \overline{\mathcal{S}}(K, d, \mathcal{X}; \xi) \to [0, 1]$ *is a transition measure. At any point* $y \in \mathcal{S}(K, d, \mathcal{X})$, $Q(A, y)$ *is the probability that the jump is onto the set* A.

In short, a realisation of a PDMP consists of a deterministic process X_t corresponding to the solution of ODE starting at y_{i-1}, alternating with stochastic jumps at time T_i defined by the survivor function $F(y_{i-1}, t)$. The post-jump location y_i is described by the transition measure $Q(dy_i, y_{i-1})$. Figure 2 illustrates the realisations of PDMPs.

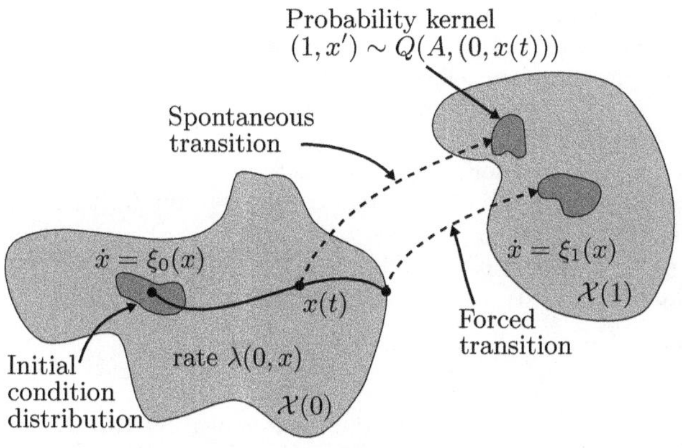

Figure 2: Realisations of PDMPs.

To ensure the process is well-defined, the following assumption is introduced in [5]. We will use the notation $\xi_v(x) \equiv \xi(v, x)$ for the vector field corresponding to the mode v evaluated at x.

ASSUMPTION 5.1.
(i) For all $v \in K$, ξ_v *is globally Lipschitz continuous.*
(ii) The transition rate function

$$\lambda : \mathcal{S}(Q, d, \mathcal{X}) \to \mathbb{R}^+$$

is measurable.
(iii) For all $y \in \mathcal{S}(K, d, \mathcal{X})$, *there exists* $\varepsilon > 0$ *such that the function* $t \to \lambda(\phi(y, t))$ *is integrable for all* $t \in [0, \varepsilon)$.
(iv) For all $A \in \mathcal{B}(\mathcal{S}(K, d, \mathcal{X}))$, $Q(A, \cdot)$ *is measurable.*

Additionally, to exclude Zeno executions the following assumption is also enforced.

ASSUMPTION 5.2. *Let*

$$N_t = \sum_i I_{(t \geq T_i)},$$

where T_i *is the time of* i^{th} *jump, be the number of jumps in* $[0, t]$. *Then* $E^y[N_t] < \infty$ *for all* $t \geq 0$ *and all initial states* y.

Under Assumptions 5.1 and 5.2, PDMPs are (strong) Markov processes [5].

5.1 Full Generator of PDMP

Theorem 11.2.2 in [21] provides a characterisation of the full generator for a PDMP. We use the shorthand notation $\mathcal{S} \equiv \mathcal{S}(Q, d, \mathcal{X})$ and $\overline{\mathcal{S}} \equiv \overline{\mathcal{S}}(K, d, \mathcal{X}; \xi)$.

THEOREM 5.1. *Let* $((K, d, \mathcal{X}), \xi, \nu_0, \lambda, Q)$ *be a PDMP. The restriction* $f|_{\mathcal{S}}$ *of a measurable function* $f : \overline{\mathcal{S}} \to \mathbb{R}$ *to* $\mathcal{S}$ *belongs to the domain* $D(\mathcal{A})$ *of the full generator* $\mathcal{A}$ *if*
(i) For each $y \in \mathcal{S}$, *the function* $t \mapsto f(\phi(t, y))$ *is absolutely continuous on the open interval* $]0, t^*(y)[$.
(ii) For each y *in the active boundary* Γ,

$$f(y) = \int_{\mathcal{S}} f(z)Q(dz; y). \tag{18}$$

(iii) For each $y \in \mathcal{S}$, *and* $t \geq 0$,

$$E^y\left[\sum_{i \in N_t} |f(X_{T_i}) - f(X_{T_{i-}})|\right] < \infty, \tag{19}$$

where $X^y_{T_{i-}}$ *is the limit* $\lim_{t \uparrow T_i} X^y_t$ *from the left.*
Furthermore, let $\mathcal{U}f$ *be defined by*

$$\mathcal{U}f(y) = \xi(f)(y) + \lambda(y)\int_{\mathcal{S}}(f(z) - f(y))Q(dz; y), \tag{20}$$

where ξf *is the action of the vector field* ξ *on a test function* f *defined by*

$$\xi(f)(y) = \xi(f)(v, x) = \xi_v(f_v)(x).$$

then $(f, \mathcal{U}f) \in \mathcal{A}$.

EXAMPLE 5.1. *Consider a PDMP with two modes* $K = \mathbb{Z}_2$. *Firstly, denote the open box* $]-1, 1[\times]-1, 1[\subset \mathbb{R}^2$ *by* $\overset{\circ}{\square}$, *and its closure in* $\mathbb{R}^2$ *by* $\square$. *Suppose that* $d : \mathbb{Z}_2 \to \{2\}$, *and* $\mathcal{X} : \mathbb{Z}_2 \to \{\overset{\circ}{\square}\}$. *As a consequence, the hybrid state space is* $\mathcal{S} = \mathbb{Z}_2 \times \overset{\circ}{\square}$.
Let the vector field on $\mathcal{S}$ *be denoted by*

$$\xi_0(x) \equiv \xi(0, x) \quad \text{and} \quad \xi_1(x) \equiv \xi(1, x).$$

Suppose that the jump rate is $\lambda(v, x) = \lambda_v$ *(*λ_0 *and* λ_1 *are constant on the continuous states). Consider deterministic jumps from the mode* v *to* $v + 1 \mod 2$ *defined by maps* $h_v : \square \to \overset{\circ}{\square}$. *Subsequently, the transition measure is*

$$Q(dy'; y) = Q(dv'dx'; v, x)$$
$$= \left(\delta_{h_0(x)}(dx')I_{\{v=0\}} + \delta_{h_1(x)}(dx')I_{\{v=1\}}\right)\delta_{(v+1 \bmod 2)}(dv').$$

Finally, suppose that the initial measure is concentrated at a point $(v_0, \bar{x}_0) \in \mathcal{S}$, $\nu_0 = \delta_{(v_0, \bar{x}_0)}$.
The realisations of the PDMP $((K, d, \mathcal{X}), \xi, \nu_0, \lambda, Q)$ *for the initial state* $(v_0, \bar{x}_0)$ *are of the form*

$$x_t(\omega) = (v, \phi_v(t, \bar{x}_i)) \text{ for } T_{i-1}(\omega) \leq t < T_i(\omega),$$

where ϕ_v is the flow map of the vector field ξ_v. At each time T_i, there is a jump from $(v, \phi_v(T_i(\omega), x_i))$ to

$$(v + 1 \bmod 2, h_v(\phi_v(T_i(\omega), x_i))).$$

The time of the ith jump is

$$T_0(\omega) = 0$$
$$T_i(\omega) = T_{i-1}(\omega) + S_i(\omega), \ i \in \mathbb{N}$$

where S_i are independent random variables of exponential distribution with the intensity $\lambda_{(i \bmod 2)}$.

In the following, we specialise the results of Section 4 to a PDMP. Using the notation $f_v(x) \equiv f(v, x)$, the selector in (20) is expressed as

$$\begin{aligned}\mathcal{U}f(v,x) &= \frac{\partial f_0}{\partial x}(x)\xi_0\delta_0(v) + \frac{\partial f_1}{\partial x}(x)\xi_1\delta_1(v)\\ &+ \lambda_v\left(f_1 \circ h_0(x)I_{\{v=0\}} + f_0 \circ h_1(x)I_{\{v=1\}} - f_v(x)\right).\end{aligned}$$

We use the time extension of the selector $\mathcal{U}$ as in Section 4 and formulate

$$\hat{\mathcal{U}}(\hat{f})(t; v, x) \equiv \hat{\mathcal{U}}(\gamma f)(t; v, x) = \mathcal{U}\hat{f}_t(v, x) + \frac{\partial \hat{f}(t; v, x)}{\partial t}. \tag{21}$$

In (21), we have used the notation $\hat{f}_t(v, x) \equiv \hat{f}(t; v, x)$ to indicate that the variable t is seen as a parameter.

Consequently, noticing that the occupation measure takes the form

$$\begin{aligned}\mu(z, dtdy) &= \mu(z, dtdvdx)\\ &= \mu^0(z, dtdx)\delta_0(dv) + \mu^1(z, dtdx)\delta_1(dv),\end{aligned}$$

the term in (15) that involves the generator in the optimisation formulation takes the form

$$\begin{aligned}&\int_{[0,T]\times\mathcal{S}} \hat{\mathcal{U}}(\hat{f})(t; v, x)\mu(dtdvdx) \qquad (22)\\ &= \int_{[0,T]\times\overset{\circ}{\square}} \left(\frac{\partial \hat{f}_0}{\partial t} + \frac{\partial \hat{f}_0}{\partial x}\xi_0 + \lambda_0(\hat{f}_1 \circ \mathrm{id} \times h_0 - \hat{f}_0)\right)\mu^0(dtdx)\\ &+ \int_{[0,T]\times\overset{\circ}{\square}} \left(\frac{\partial \hat{f}_1}{\partial t} + \frac{\partial \hat{f}_1}{\partial x}\xi_1 + \lambda_1(\hat{f}_0 \circ \mathrm{id} \times h_1 - \hat{f}_1)\right)\mu^1(dtdx).\end{aligned}$$

In (22), we have suppressed the arguments (t, x) and denoted $\hat{f}_v(t, h_w(x))$ by $(\hat{f}_v \circ \mathrm{id} \times h_w)(t, x)$, $w \in \mathbb{Z}_2$.

Notice that if $\lambda_0 = \lambda_1 = 0$, $\xi_1 = 0$, and $p = 1$. The p-safety verification of this PDMP corresponds to the verification of the dynamical system $\dot{x} = \xi_0(x)$; whereas, if the continuous state space is $\mathbb{R}$, $\lambda_0 = \lambda_1$, $\xi_0 = \xi_1 = 0$, and $h_0(x) = h_1(x) = x + 1$, it corresponds to p-safety verification of a Poisson process with intensity λ_0.

Finally, (18) takes the form: For any $x \in \Gamma \subset \partial\square$ and any $t \in \mathbb{R}_+$

$$f_0(t, x) = f_1(t, h_0(x))$$
$$f_1(t, x) = f_0(t, h_1(x)),$$

where Γ in plain words is the subset of the boundary of $\mathcal{S}$ that is reached by the realisations.

6. OPTIMISATION FORMULATION

This section provides a solution to Problem 2.1 in terms of an optimisation problem based on the evolution of a set of initial conditions given in (15). The presentation is motivated by [11, 8] that address the estimation of the region of attraction of a deterministic system.

To develop an algorithm for computing a solution of the safety problem, we restrict our study to polynomials, i.e., the state space, the set of initial states, and the set of unsafe states will be semi-algebraic sets (characterised by polynomials), and test functions will be polynomial.

PROBLEM 6.1 (POLYNOMIAL p-SAFETY FOR PDMP). *Let $H = ((K, d, \mathcal{X}), \xi, \nu_0, \lambda, Q)$ be a PDMP giving rise to a Markov family (X_t, P^y). For a number $p \in [0, 1]$, two basic semi-algebraic sets $U \subseteq E = \mathcal{S}(K, d, \mathcal{X}) \subseteq \bigcup_{v\in K}\{v\}\times\mathbb{R}^{d(v)}$, and $U_u \subset U$*

$$U = \{(v, x) \in E |\ g^U_{(v,i)}(x) \geq 0, \ (v, i) \in K_s\} \tag{23a}$$
$$U_u = \{(v, x) \in E |\ g^{U_u}_{(v,i)}(x) > 0, \ (v, i) \in K_u\}, \tag{23b}$$

where K_s and K_u are finite index sets with $\pi_1(K_s) = \pi_1(K_u) = K$, and $\pi_1 : (v, x) \mapsto v$ is the projection. Furthermore, $g^U_{(v,i)} \in \mathbb{R}[x]$, $g^{U_u}_{(v,i)} \in \mathbb{R}[x]$, and $U_u \subseteq U$. Suppose that U is compact (notice that U_u is open).

Find the largest set $U_0 \subseteq U$ (with respect to the partial order $\preceq$ defined in Section 2) such that (X_t, P^y, U, U_0, U_u) is p-safe with respect to the measure ν_0.

For the p-safety problem, we will formulate an optimisation problem that involves (15), where a time-space selector $\hat{\mathcal{U}}$ and test functions are given by Theorem 5.1. The objective is to find the hitting distribution, the initial and occupation measures satisfying certain linear constraints. This optimisation problem is linear but infinite dimensional. To this end, we will employ moment matching problem of [13], which leans on Haviland's theorem, see Chapter 3 in [15]. The theorem states that for any linear function $L : \mathbb{R}[x] \to \mathbb{R}$ such that $L(g) \geq 0$ for all $g \in \mathbb{R}[x]$ with $g \geq 0$ on K, there is a Borel measure μ_L on a closed subset $C \subseteq \mathbb{R}^n$ such that $L(g) = \int_C g(x)\mu_L(dx)$ for all $g \in \mathbb{R}[x]$. Specifically, for a sequence $\{M_\alpha |\ \alpha \in \mathbb{N}^n\} \subset \mathbb{R}$, we define a function L by

$$L : \sum_\alpha a_\alpha x^\alpha \mapsto \sum_\alpha a_\alpha M_\alpha,$$

where $x^\alpha \equiv x^{\alpha_1} \ldots x^{\alpha_n}$ are the monomials. By Haviland's theorem, if $\sum_\alpha a_\alpha M_\alpha \geq 0$ for any $f = \sum_\alpha a_\alpha x^\alpha \geq 0$ on C. Then there is a Borel measure μ_L on C such that M_α are α-moments of μ_L, i.e., $M_\alpha = \int_C x^\alpha \mu_L(dx)$. Consequently, the infinite optimisation with respect to measures is relaxed by considering only a finite number of moments.

In our set up, the unknown measures in Theorem 4.1 are defined on compact sets of the hybrid state space $\mathcal{S} \equiv \mathcal{S}(K, d, \mathcal{X}) \subseteq \bigcup_{v\in K}\{v\} \times \mathbb{R}^{d(v)}$. Specifically, C is a compact set in $\mathcal{S}$ if and only if $C_v \equiv C \cap \{v\} \times \mathbb{R}^{d(v)}$ are compact sets. To determine the positivity of the test function $f : \mathcal{S} \to \mathbb{R}$, we certify the positivity of the polynomial functions f_v, where $f_v(x) \equiv f(v, x)$, on C_v. To this end, we exploit Lasserre's hierarchy [13] making use of Putinar's Positivstellensatz [20].

7. EXAMPLE

This section provides a numerical computation of the largest set of p-safe initial states for a PDMP.

Similarly to Example 5.1, we consider a PDMP with two modes $K = \mathbb{Z}_2$, hybrid state space $S = \mathbb{Z}_2 \times \mathbb{R}^2$, and the vector field $\xi(v, x) = (i, \xi_v)$ with

$$\xi_0(x) = \begin{bmatrix} 2x_1 - x_2^2 + 2 \\ x_2 \end{bmatrix} \quad \text{and} \quad \xi_1(x) = \begin{bmatrix} x_1 \\ x_2 \end{bmatrix},$$

where $x = (x_1, x_2)$.

The set U, where the system lives on, is $U = \{0,1\} \times \square$, where $\square = [-1,1] \times [-1,1] \subset \mathbb{R}^2$. The jump rates are chosen to be constant on the continuous states

$$\lambda(0, x) = \lambda(1, x) = \lambda.$$

We will examine two cases: very big λ (the spontaneous jumps happen very often) and very small λ (the spontaneous jumps happen very seldom). Finally, the jump maps are chosen to be the identity, i.e., $h_0(x) = h_1(x) = x$ and $T = 10$.

To analyze the p-safety of the system, we assign $p = 0.1$ and define a set of unsafe states as

$$U_{\text{u}} = \{0,1\} \times \Delta_{\text{u}},$$

where $\Delta_{\text{u}} = \{x \in \square \mid x_1 + x_2 - 1.7 > 0\}$.

For this particular instance of a PDMP, the optimization problem (16) can be formulated as follows: For all $\hat{f}_0, \hat{f}_1 \in \mathbb{R}[t, x]$

$$\begin{array}{ll} \sup & \int d\mu_0^0 + \int d\mu_0^1 \\ & \int \hat{f}_0 d\nu_1^0 + \int \hat{f}_1 d\nu_1^1 + \int \hat{f}_0 d\nu_2^0 + \int \hat{f}_1 d\nu_2^1 - \int \hat{f}_0 d\bar{\mu}_0^0 \\ & - \int \hat{f}_1 d\bar{\mu}_0^1 = \int \hat{\mathcal{U}}^0 \hat{f}_0 d\mu^0 + \int \hat{\mathcal{U}}^1 \hat{f}_1 d\mu^1 \\ & \int d\nu_2^0 + \int d\nu_2^1 \geq (1-p)(\int d\bar{\mu}_0^0 + \int d\bar{\mu}_0^1) \\ & \lambda \geq \mu_0^0 \geq 0,\ \lambda \geq \mu_0^1 \geq 0 \\ & \bar{\mu}_0^0 = \delta_0 \otimes \mu_0^0,\ \mu^0 \geq 0,\ \bar{\mu}_0^1 = \delta_0 \otimes \mu_0^1,\ \mu^1 \geq 0, \\ & \nu_1^0 \geq 0,\ \nu_1^1 \geq 0,\ \nu_2^0 \geq 0,\ \nu_2^1 \geq 0, \\ & \text{supp}\ \mu_0^0 \subseteq U_{\text{c}}, \text{supp}\ \mu_0^1 \subseteq U_{\text{c}}, \\ & \text{supp}\ \mu^0 \subseteq [0,T] \times U_{\text{c}}, \text{supp}\ \mu^1 \subseteq [0,T] \times U_{\text{c}}, \\ & \text{supp}\ \nu_1^0 \subseteq [0,T] \times U_{\text{c}}, \text{supp}\ \nu_1^1 \subseteq [0,T] \times U_{\text{c}}, \\ & \text{supp}\ \nu_2^0 \subseteq [0,T] \times \partial U_{\text{u}}, \text{supp}\ \nu_2^1 \subseteq [0,T] \times \partial U_{\text{u}}. \end{array} \tag{24}$$

where

$$\int \hat{\mathcal{U}}^0 \hat{f}_0 d\mu^0 = \int \left(\frac{\partial \hat{f}_0}{\partial t} + \frac{\partial \hat{f}_0}{\partial x} \xi_0 + \lambda_0 (\hat{f}_1 - \hat{f}_0) \right) d\mu^0$$

$$\int \hat{\mathcal{U}}^1 \hat{f}_1 d\mu^1 = \int \left(\frac{\partial \hat{f}_1}{\partial t} + \frac{\partial \hat{f}_1}{\partial x} \xi_1 + \lambda_1 (\hat{f}_0 - \hat{f}_1) \right) d\mu^1$$

and with the following boundary constraints imposed on the test functions (see Example 5.1)

$$\hat{f}_0(t, x) = \hat{f}_1(t, x) \quad \forall x \in \Gamma.$$

The optimization problem is solved using GloptiPoly 3 [9], with polynomials truncated at degree 10.

REMARK 7.1. *To illustrate how the optimization problem is solved, we consider an example of a constraint*

$$\int f_0 d\nu_1^0 + \int f_1 d\nu_1^1 + \int (f_0 - f_1) d\mu = 0 \tag{25}$$

for all f_0, f_1. Let f_0 and f_1 be polynomials

$$f_0 = \sum_{\alpha \in \mathbb{N}^n} p_\alpha^0 z^\alpha \text{ and } f_1 = \sum_{\alpha \in \mathbb{N}^n} p_\alpha^1 z^\alpha,$$

where the monomials $z^\alpha = x_1^{\alpha_1} \cdots x_n^{\alpha_n} t^{\alpha_{n+1}}$. Then the constraint (25) can be written as

$$\int \sum_\alpha p_\alpha^0 z^\alpha d\nu_1^0 + \int \sum_\alpha p_\alpha^1 z^\alpha d\nu_1^1 + \int \sum_\alpha (p_\alpha^0 - p_\alpha^1) z^\alpha d\mu = 0$$

for all $p_\alpha^0, p_\alpha^1 \in \mathbb{R}$. As the consequence, the constraints for the moments are

$$\int z^\alpha d\nu_1^0 + \int z^\alpha d\mu = 0 \text{ and } \int z^\alpha d\nu_1^1 - \int z^\alpha d\mu = 0$$

for each $\alpha \in \mathbb{N}^{n+1}$. A solution to the set of constraints may be found by truncating $\alpha \in \mathbb{N}^{n+1}$ such that $|\alpha| \leq d$. Subsequently, a solution may be found as explained in Section 6.

Fig. 3 shows an inner approximation of the safe initial states for mode 0 on the left and for mode 1 on the right, which corresponds to a very big value of λ ($\lambda = 1000$). From Fig. 3, it is seen that the set of safe initial conditions (green

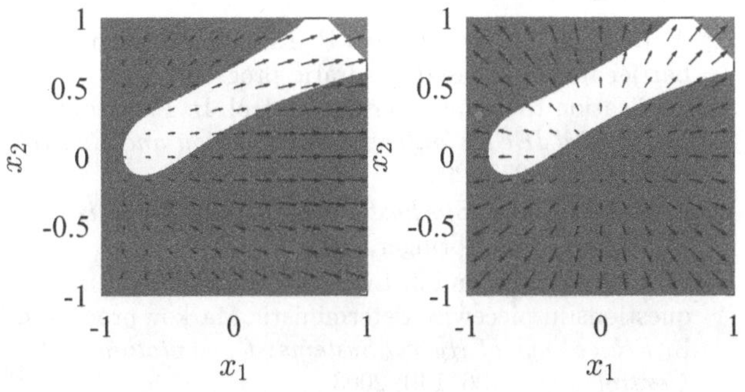

Figure 3: Phase plot (blue arrows) of the two vector fields. The red area is the set of unsafe states U_{u}, the green area is the approximated set of safe initial conditions, with $p = 0.1$ and $\lambda = 1000$.

Fig. 4 illustrates inner approximation of 0.1-safe initial states for a small λ ($\lambda = 0$). For this particular value of λ, there will be no switching between the two modes of the system. From Fig. 4 it is seen that the estimate of the safe initial states is conservative, i.e., some realisations initialised in the white area of the state space will not reach U_{u}.

An implementation of the example can be found here [4].

8. CONCLUSION

In this paper, a method was presented for finding the largest set of initial conditions such that a Markov process is safe with probability p. The method was based on formulating the safety problem as an optimisation problem on measures. The full generator for PDMPs is known; thus, the optimisation problem is solvable for this class of systems. We solve the optimisation problem by relaxing the solution and only considering a finite number of moments, which results in a finite dimensional convex optimisation problem.

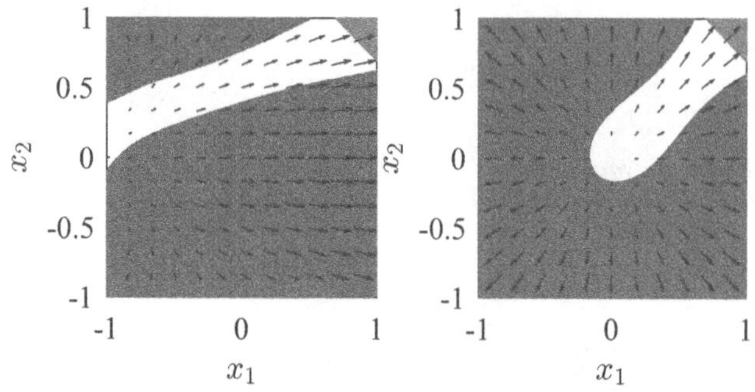

Figure 4: Phase plot (blue arrows) of the two vector fields. The red area is the set of unsafe states U_u, the green area is the approximated set of 0.1-safe initial states, with $p = 0.1$ and $\lambda = 0$.

Acknowledgements

The work of R. Wisniewski and C. Sloth is supported by the Danish Council for Independent Research under grant number DFF - 4005-00452 in the project CodeMe. The work of Piterman and Bujorianu is funded by the EPSRC project EP/L007177/1.

9. REFERENCES

[1] A. D. Ames, J. Grizzle, and P. Tabuada. Control barrier function based quadratic programs with application to adaptive cruise control. In *Proceedings of the 53rd IEEE Conference on Decision and Control*, pages 6271–6278, 2014.

[2] L. M. Bujorianu. *Stochastic Reachability Analysis of Hybrid Systems*. Springer, 2012.

[3] L. M. Bujorianu and J. Lygeros. Reachability questions in piecewise deterministic Markov processes. In *Proceedings of Hybrid Systems: Computation and Control*, pages 126–140, 2003.

[4] CodeMe. CodeMe - software. http://kom.aau.dk/project/CodeMe/software.html, 2015.

[5] M. H. A. Davis. *Markov models and optimization*, volume 49 of *Monographs on Statistics and Applied Probability*. Chapman & Hall, London, 1993.

[6] H. Guéguen, M.-A. Lefebvre, J. Zaytoon, and O. Nasri. Safety verification and reachability analysis for hybrid systems. *Annual Reviews in Control*, 33(1):25–36, 2009.

[7] K. Helmes, S. Röhl, and R. H. Stockbridge. Computing moments of the exit time distribution for Markov processes by linear programming. *Operations Research*, 49(4):516–530, 2001.

[8] D. Henrion and M. Korda. Convex computation of the region of attraction of polynomial control systems. *IEEE Transactions on Automatic Control*, 59(2):297–312, February 2014.

[9] D. Henrion, J. B. Lasserre, and J. Loefberg. GloptiPoly 3: moments, optimization and semidefinite programming. *Optimization Methods and Software*, 24(4-5):761–779, 2009.

[10] A. Klenke. *Probability theory : a comprehensive course*. Springer, London, 2008.

[11] M. Korda, D. Henrion, and C. N. Jones. Inner approximations of the region of attraction for polynomial dynamical systems. In *Proceedings of the 9th IFAC Symposium on Nonlinear Control Systems*, pages 534–539, 2013.

[12] T. G. Kurtz and R. H. Stockbridge. Existence of Markov controls and characterization of optimal Markov controls. *SIAM Journal on Control and Optimization*, 36(2):609–653, 1998.

[13] J. B. Lasserre. Global optimization with polynomials and the problem of moments. *SIAM Journal on Optimization*, 11(3):796–817, Mar. 2001.

[14] J. B. Lasserre. *Moments, Positive Polynomials and Their Applications*, volume 1 of *Imperial College Press Optimization Series*. Imperial Collage Press, 2010.

[15] M. Marshall. *Positive Polynomials and Sums of Squares*, volume 146. American Mathematical Society, 2008.

[16] I. Mitchell, A. Bayen, and C. Tomlin. A time-dependent Hamilton-Jacobi formulation of reachable sets for continuous dynamic games. *IEEE Transactions on Automatic Control*, 50(7):947–957, 2005.

[17] B. Øksendal. *Stochastic Differential Equations: An Introduction with Applications*. Springer-Verlag, 5th edition, 2000.

[18] S. Prajna, A. Jadbabaie, and G. J. Pappas. A framework for worst-case and stochastic safety verification using barrier certificates. *IEEE Transactions on Automatic Control*, 52(8):1415–1428, August 2007.

[19] S. Prajna and A. Rantzer. Convex programs for temporal verification of nonlinear dynamical systems. *SIAM Journal on Control and Optimization*, 46(3):999–1021, 2007.

[20] M. Putinar. Positive polynomials on compact semi-algebraic sets. *Indiana Univ. Math. J.*, 42(3):969–984, 1993.

[21] T. Rolski, H. Schmidli, V. Schmidt, and J. Teugels. *Stochastic processes for insurance and finance*. Wiley Series in Probability and Statistics. John Wiley & Sons, Ltd., Chichester, 1999.

[22] M. Romdlony and B. Jayawardhana. Uniting control Lyapunov and control barrier functions. In *Proceedings of the 53rd IEEE Conference on Decision and Control*, pages 2293–2298, 2014.

[23] C. Sloth and R. Wisniewski. Safety analysis of stochastic dynamical systems. In *Proceedings of the IFAC Conference on Analysis and Design of Hybrid Systems*, pages 62–67, 2015.

[24] A. Teel. Lyapunov conditions certifying stability and recurrence for a class of stochastic hybrid systems. *Annual Reviews In Control*, 37(1):1–24, Apr 2013.

[25] P. Wieland and F. Allgöwer. Constructive safety using control barrier functions. In *Proceedings of the 7th IFAC Symposium on Nonlinear Control Systems*, pages 462–467, 2007.

[26] R. Wisniewski, M. Svenstrup, A. S. Pedersen, and C. S. Steiniche. Certificate for safe emergency shutdown of wind turbines. In *Proceedings of American Control Conference*, pages 3667–3672, 2013.

Computing Distances between Reach Flowpipes *

Rupak Majumdar
MPI-SWS
rupak@mpi-sws.org

Vinayak S. Prabhu
MPI-SWS, and University of Porto
vinayak@mpi-sws.org

ABSTRACT

We investigate quantifying the difference between two hybrid dynamical systems under noise and initial-state uncertainty. While the set of traces for these systems is infinite, it is possible to symbolically approximate trace sets using *reachpipes* that compute upper and lower bounds on the evolution of the reachable sets with time. We estimate distances between corresponding sets of trajectories of two systems in terms of distances between the reachpipes.

In case of two individual traces, the Skorokhod distance has been proposed as a robust and efficient notion of distance which captures both value and timing distortions. In this paper, we extend the computation of the Skorokhod distance to reachpipes, and provide algorithms to compute upper and lower bounds on the distance between two sets of traces. Our algorithms use new geometric insights that are used to compute the worst-case and best-case distances between two polyhedral sets evolving with time.

1. INTRODUCTION

The quantitative conformance problem between two dynamical systems asks how close the traces of the two systems are under a given metric on hybrid traces [1, 2, 9]. If the systems are deterministic and start from unique initial conditions, each has exactly one trace, and the quantitative conformance problem computes the distance between these two traces. In this case, we have shown in previous work that the *Skorokhod metric* between traces provides a robust and efficiently computable distance that captures the intuitive notion of closeness of two systems [18, 9]. However, if there is uncertainty in the initial states and noise in the inputs, each system defines not just a single trace but a set of traces. In this work, we investigate algorithms to compute distances between sets of trajectories of two dynamical systems under initial state and input uncertainties.

Given two sets F_1, F_2 of trajectories of two dynamical systems, the natural generalization of the Skorokhod distance between traces is to ask what is the farthest a trajectory in one set can be from a trajectory in the other, *i.e.*, to compute

$$\mathcal{D}_{\mathsf{var}}(F_1, F_2) = \sup_{f_1, f_2} \mathcal{D}_{\mathsf{tr}}(f_1, f_2)$$

where $\mathcal{D}_{\mathsf{tr}}$ is the given Skorokhod metric on traces[1].

Unfortunately, due to the continuous nature of systems, trace sets F_1 and F_2 are not available in closed form for most kinds of systems. Instead, given a trace set F, one approximates it using a *reachpipe*, a function $R : [0, T] \to 2^{\mathbb{R}^d}$, such that $R(t) = \cup_{f \in F}\{f(t)\}$, *i.e.*, $R(t)$ is the set of all trace values that can be observed at time t. A reachpipe R can be viewed as an approximation $\mathsf{Fp}(R)$ to the original set of traces, the approximation $\mathsf{Fp}(R)$ includes every trace f such that $f(t) \in R(t)$, not just those allowed by the dynamics. In practice, even the reachpipe may not have an exact representation, and instead, one computes over- or under-approximations to the reachpipe by computing a sequence of *reach set* samples at discrete timepoints $t_0, t_1, \ldots$. Indeed, there are several techniques to compute such approximations of reach sets [7, 17, 11, 13, 15, 10, 21, 8, 6], differing in the quality of the approximation, the efficiency of computation, or the representation of the reach set approximations.

We consider the problem of estimating trajectory set distances when we only have the sampled sequences of over- and under-approximations of reach sets. As a first step, we define a lower and an upper bound on the distance between F_1 and F_2 based on the reach set approximations.

Second, we show how to compute these bounds. To compute the distance, we re-formulate reachpipes as set-valued traces, *i.e.*, as traces over the time interval $[0, T]$ where the trace value at time t is the set $R(t) \subseteq \mathbb{R}^d$. This alternative viewpoint allows us to define trace distances $\mathcal{D}^\dagger$ between reachpipes by viewing them as set-valued traces. We derive relationships between the distances $\mathcal{D}^\dagger$ under this alternative viewpoint, and distances bounding the trace set distance (obtained using approximations to the reachpipes).

Finally, we derive algorithms to compute the $\mathcal{D}^\dagger$ distances between reachpipes in case the underlying metric on traces is given by the Skorokhod distance and the reach set sequences are given as polytopes in $\mathbb{R}^d$. The Skorokhod distance on traces takes into account both timing distortions and value differences; our algorithms lift the metric to reach sets viewed as time-varying polytopes. The algorithms allows for timing distortions, and generalize the Skorokhod

*This research was funded in part by a Humboldt foundation grant, FCT grant SFRHBPD902672012, and by a contract from Toyota Motors.

HSCC '16, April 12–14, 2016, Vienna, Austria.

ISBN 978-1-4503-3955-1/16/04...$15.00

DOI: http://dx.doi.org/10.1145/2883817.2883850

[1]In comparing sets, we use the term "distance" for similarity/dissimilarity functions $\mathcal{D}_{\mathsf{var}}$ satisfying the triangle inequality; these functions are not necessarily metrics, as $\mathcal{D}_{\mathsf{var}}(F, F)$ need not be zero.

distance algorithm over polygonal lines to polytopes which vary with time. The main technical constructions in our algorithms are two novel geometric routines in a core part of the Skorokhod distance algorithm which allow us to move to the domain of time-varying polytopes for the set distances under consideration.

Putting everything together, we obtain polynomial time algorithms which compute bounds on traceset distances where the tracesets are observed only as reachset sample-polytopes at discrete timepoints.

Outline of the Paper. In Section 2, we recall the Skorokhod trace metric, and the related Fréchet metric. In Section 3, we formally present tracepipes and reachpipes, distances between trace sets, and bounds on these set distances. In Section 4 we explore the alternative viewpoint of reachpipes being set valued traces, and relate distances under this viewpoint and distances between reachpipes viewed as trace sets. In Section 5, we solve for the distance decision problems between reachpipes viewed as time-varying polytopes of $\mathbb{R}^d$. In Section 6 we put everything together and present various algorithms to compute bounds on Skorokhod traceset distances. Detailed proofs that were omitted due to lack of space can be found in the associated technical report [19].

2. PRELIMINARIES: TRACE METRICS

A (finite) *trace* $f : [T_i, T_e] \to \mathbb{R}^d$ is a continuous mapping from a finite closed interval $[T_i, T_e]$ of $\mathbb{R}_+$, with $0 \le T_i < T_e$, to $\mathbb{R}^d$.

2.1 The Skorokhod Trace Metric

We define a metric on the space of traces corresponding to a given metric on $\mathbb{R}^d$. A *retiming* $\mathsf{r} : I \mapsto I'$, for closed intervals I, I' of $\mathbb{R}_+$, is an order-preserving (i.e., monotone) continuous bijective function from I to I'; thus if $t < t'$ then $\mathsf{r}(t) < \mathsf{r}(t')$. Let $\mathsf{R}_{I \mapsto I'}$ be the class of retiming functions from I to I' and let id be the identity retiming. Given a trace $f : I_f \to \mathbb{R}^d$, and a retiming $\mathsf{r} : I \mapsto I_f$; the function $f \circ \mathsf{r}$ is another trace from I to $\mathbb{R}^d$.

Definition 1 (Skorokhod Metric)**.** Given a retiming $\mathsf{r} : I \mapsto I'$, define

$$|| \mathsf{r} - \mathsf{id} ||_{\sup} := \sup_{t \in I} | \mathsf{r}(t) - t|.$$

Given two traces $f : I_f \mapsto \mathbb{R}^d$ and $f' : I_{f'} \mapsto \mathbb{R}^d$, a norm L on $\mathbb{R}^d$, and a retiming $\mathsf{r} : I_f \mapsto I_{f'}$, define

$$\left\| f - f' \circ \mathsf{r} \right\|_{\sup} := \sup_{t \in I_f} \left\| f(t) - f'(\mathsf{r}(t)) \right\|_L.$$

The *Skorokhod metric*[2] between the traces f and f' is defined to be:

$$\mathcal{D}_{\mathcal{S}}(f, f') := \inf_{r \in \mathsf{R}_{I_f \mapsto I_{f'}}} \max\left(\|\mathsf{r} - \mathsf{id}\|_{\sup}, \left\|f - f' \circ \mathsf{r}\right\|_{\sup} \right). \quad \square$$

Intuitively, the Skorokhod metric incorporates two components: the first component quantifies the *timing discrepancy* of the timing distortion required to "match" the two traces, and the second quantifies the *value mismatch* (in the vector space $(\mathbb{R}^d, \|\cdot\|_L)$) of the values under the timing distortion. In the retimed trace $f \circ \mathsf{r}$, we see exactly the same values as in f, in exactly the same order, but the times at which the values are seen can be different.

[2]The two components of the Skorokhod metric (the retiming, and the value difference components) can be weighed with different weights – this simply corresponds to a change of scale.

2.2 The Fréchet Trace Metric

We showed in [18] that the Skorokhod metric is related to another metric, the Fréchet metric, over traces. We recall the definition and the relationship.

Definition 2 (Fréchet metric)**.** Let $\mathsf{C}_1 : I_1 \to \mathbb{R}^d$ and $\mathsf{C}_2 : I_2 \to \mathbb{R}^d$ be traces. The Fréchet metric between the two traces $\mathsf{C}_1, \mathsf{C}_2$ (given a norm L on $\mathbb{R}^d$) is defined to be

$$\mathcal{D}_{\mathcal{F}}(\mathsf{C}_1, \mathsf{C}_2) := \inf_{\substack{\alpha_1 : [0,1] \to I_1 \\ \alpha_2 : [0,1] \to I_2}} \max_{0 \le \theta \le 1} \left\| \mathsf{C}_1(\alpha_1(\theta)) - \mathsf{C}_2(\alpha_2(\theta)) \right\|_L$$

where α_1, α_2 range over continuous and strictly increasing bijective functions onto I_1 and I_2, respectively. $\square$

Intuitively, the *reparameterizations* α_1, α_2 control the "speed" of traversal along the two traces by two entities. The positions of the two entities in the two traces at "time" θ is given by $\alpha_1(\theta)$ and $\alpha_2(\theta)$ respectively; with the value of the traces at those positions being $\mathsf{C}_1(\alpha_1(\theta))$, and $\mathsf{C}_2(\alpha_2(\theta))$. The two entities always have a speed strictly greater than 0.

Given a trace $f : [T_i, T_e] \to \mathbb{R}^d$, we define the *time-explicit trace* $\mathsf{C}_f : [T_i, T_e] \to \mathbb{R}^d \times \mathbb{R}$ where we add the time value as an extra dimension, that is, $\mathsf{C}_f(t) = (f(t), t)$ for all $t \in [T_i, T_e]$. Given a value $\langle \boldsymbol{p}, t \rangle \in \mathbb{R}^d \times \mathbb{R}$, and a a norm L over $\mathbb{R}^d$, define the norm

$$\|\langle \boldsymbol{p}, t\rangle\|_{L^{\max}} = \max\left(\|\boldsymbol{p}\|_L, |t|\right). \quad (1)$$

Proposition 1 (From Skorokhod to Fréchet [18])**.** *Let $f : [T_i^f, T_e^f] \to \mathbb{R}^d$ and $g : [T_i^g, T_e^g] \to \mathbb{R}^d$ be two continuous traces. Consider the corresponding time-explicit traces $C_f : [T_i^f, T_e^f] \to \mathbb{R}^{d+1}$ and $C_g : [T_i^g, T_e^g] \to \mathbb{R}^{d+1}$. Consider the Skorokhod distance $\mathcal{D}_{\mathcal{S}}(f, g)$ with respect to a given norm L over $\mathbb{R}^d$. We have*

$$\mathcal{D}_{\mathcal{S}}(f, g) = \mathcal{D}_{\mathcal{F}}(\mathsf{C}_f, \mathsf{C}_g),$$

where the Fréchet distance $\mathcal{D}_{\mathcal{F}}(\mathsf{C}_f, \mathsf{C}_g)$ is with respect to the norm $L^{\max}$ over $\mathbb{R}^{d+1}$. $\square$

3. PIPES & PIPE-VARIATION DISTANCES

3.1 Tracepipes, Reachpipes and Set Distances

A *tracepipe* F is a nonempty collection of traces over some closed interval $[T_i, T_e]$. A *reachpipe* $R : [T_i, T_e] \to 2^{\mathbb{R}^d} \setminus \emptyset$ maps a finite closed interval $[T_i, T_e]$ of $\mathbb{R}_+$, denoted $\mathsf{tdom}(R)$, to non-empty subsets of $\mathbb{R}^d$. To a reachpipe R, we associate a tracepipe $\mathsf{Fp}(R)$ consisting of all continuous traces f over $\mathsf{tdom}(R)$ such that $f(t) \in R(t)$ for all $t \in \mathsf{tdom}(R)$. Dually, corresponding to each tracepipe F, we associate the reachpipe $\mathsf{Rp}(F)$, over the same time-domain, defined by $\mathsf{Rp}(F)(t) = \cup_{f \in F}\{f(t)\}$. Note that $F \subseteq \mathsf{Fp}(\mathsf{Rp}(F))$, but equality need not hold: $\mathsf{Fp}(\mathsf{Rp}(F))$ may contain more traces than F.

A reachpipe $R' : [T_i, T_e] \to 2^{\mathbb{R}^d}$ is an *over-approximation* (respectively, *under-approximation*) of a reachpipe $R : [T_i, T_e] \to 2^{\mathbb{R}^d}$ if for each $t \in [T_i, T_e]$, we have $R(t) \subseteq R'(t)$ (respectively, $R'(t) \subseteq R(t)$).

Example 1. Consider a linear dynamical system in $\mathbb{R}$ described by $\dot{x} = ax$, for $a > 0$ with initial state $x_0 \in [0, 0.1]$ over the time interval $[0, 10]$. For a fixed value of x_0, we get a trace $x_0 e^{at}$. Let $F = \{f_{x_0} \mid x_0 \in [0, 0.1]$ and $f_{x_0}(t) = x_0 e^{at}$ for $t \in [0, 10]\}$ be a tracepipe. The reachpipe $\mathsf{Rp}(F)$ corresponding to the tracepipe F is given by $\mathsf{Rp}(F)(t) = [0, 0.1e^{at}]$ for $t \in [0, 10]$. Observe that $\mathsf{Fp}(\mathsf{Rp}(F))$ contains the more traces than F, for instance, the constant trace $f(t) = 0.1$. $\square$

Let $\mathcal{D}_{\mathsf{tr}}$ be a given metric on traces. We define the *variation distance* $\mathcal{D}_{\mathsf{var}}(F_1, F_2)$ between two tracepipes F_1 and F_2 corresponding to the trace metric $\mathcal{D}_{\mathsf{tr}}$ as

$$\mathcal{D}_{\mathsf{var}}(F_1, F_2) := \sup_{f_1 \in F_1, f_2 \in F_2} \mathcal{D}_{\mathsf{tr}}(f_1, f_2) \tag{2}$$

The value $\mathcal{D}_{\mathsf{var}}(F_1, F_2)$ gives us the maximum possible inter-trace distance if one trace is from F_1 and the other from F_2. Notice that for all tracepipes F_1, F_2, F_3, we have that

1. $\mathcal{D}_{\mathsf{var}}(F_1, F_2) \geq 0$;
2. $\mathcal{D}_{\mathsf{var}}(F_1, F_2) = \mathcal{D}_{\mathsf{var}}(F_2, F_1)$; and
3. $\mathcal{D}_{\mathsf{var}}(F_1, F_3) \leq \mathcal{D}_{\mathsf{var}}(F_1, F_2) + \mathcal{D}_{\mathsf{var}}(F_2, F_3)$.

We may however have $\mathcal{D}_{\mathsf{var}}(F, F) > 0$, thus, $\mathcal{D}_{\mathsf{var}}$ need not be a metric over tracepipes. The value $\mathcal{D}_{\mathsf{var}}(F, F)$ gives us the maximum distance amongst traces in F according to the original trace metric $\mathcal{D}_{\mathsf{tr}}$.

Tracepipes cannot be constructed for most dynamical systems. However, *reachpipe* sets can be over/under-approximated at desired timepoints using analytic techniques. In the next subsection, we present a framework for bounding the tracepipe distance $\mathcal{D}_{\mathsf{var}}(F_1, F_2)$ using over/under-approximated reachpipes.

3.2 Approximating the Variation Distance

Let F_1 and F_2 be tracepipes. Since $F \subseteq \mathsf{Fp}(\mathsf{Rp}(F))$ for any tracepipe F, and Rp, Fp, and the variation distance $\mathcal{D}_{\mathsf{var}}$ are all monotonic, we have that

$$\mathcal{D}_{\mathsf{var}}(F_1, F_2) \leq \mathcal{D}_{\mathsf{var}}\big(\mathsf{Fp}\left(\lceil \mathsf{Rp}\left(F_1\right)\rceil\right), \mathsf{Fp}\left(\lceil \mathsf{Rp}\left(F_2\right)\rceil\right)\big) \tag{3}$$

for any over-approximations $\lceil \mathsf{Rp}(F_1) \rceil$ and $\lceil \mathsf{Rp}(F_2) \rceil$ of the reachpipes $\mathsf{Rp}(F_1)$ and $\mathsf{Rp}(F_2)$. Thus, in order to get an upper bound on $\mathcal{D}_{\mathsf{var}}(F_1, F_2)$ we can use over-approximations of the corresponding reachpipes.

Define the *minimum set distance*:

$$\mathcal{D}_{\min}(F_1, F_2) := \inf_{f_1 \in F_1, f_2 \in F_2} \mathcal{D}(f_1, f_2) \tag{4}$$

For this distance, it is clear that

$$\mathcal{D}_{\min}\big(\mathsf{Fp}\left(\mathsf{Rp}(F_1)\right), \mathsf{Fp}\left(\mathsf{Rp}(F_2)\right)\big) \leq \mathcal{D}_{\mathsf{var}}(F_1, F_2)$$

Combining this with Equation (3), we get the following Proposition for bounding the variation distance.

Proposition 2 (Tracepipe Variation Distance Bounds). *Let F_1 and F_2 be tracepipes, and let $\lceil \mathsf{Rp}(F_1) \rceil$ and $\lceil \mathsf{Rp}(F_2) \rceil$ be over-approximations of the reachpipes $\mathsf{Rp}(F_1)$ and $\mathsf{Rp}(F_2)$. We have*

$$\mathcal{D}_{\min}\Big(\mathsf{Fp}\left(\lceil \mathsf{Rp}(F_1)\rceil\right), \mathsf{Fp}\left(\lceil \mathsf{Rp}(F_2)\rceil\right)\Big) \leq \mathcal{D}_{\mathsf{var}}(F_1, F_2)$$

$$\mathcal{D}_{\mathsf{var}}(F_1, F_2) \leq \mathcal{D}_{\mathsf{var}}\Big(\mathsf{Fp}\left(\lceil \mathsf{Rp}(F_1)\rceil\right), \mathsf{Fp}\left(\lceil \mathsf{Rp}(F_2)\rceil\right)\Big) \quad \square$$

Remark: Hausdorff Metric. A natural candidate for under-approximating the variation distance is the *Hausdorff* set metric, defined as:

$$\mathcal{D}_H(F_1, F_2) = \max\left\{ \sup_{f_1 \in F_1} \inf_{f_2 \in F_2} \mathcal{D}(f_1, f_2),\ \sup_{f_2 \in F_2} \inf_{f_1 \in F_1} \mathcal{D}(f_1, f_2) \right\} \tag{5}$$

Intuitively, if $\sup_{f_1 \in F_1} \inf_{f_2 \in F_2} \mathcal{D}(f_1, f_2)$ is less than δ, then given any trace $f_1 \in F_1$, there exists a trace $f_2 \in F_2$ such that $\mathcal{D}(f_1, f_2) < \delta$. Note that $\sup_{f_1 \in F_1} \inf_{f_2 \in F_2} \mathcal{D}(f_1, f_2) \leq \mathcal{D}_{\mathsf{var}}(F_1, F_2)$ and also $\sup_{f_2 \in F_2} \inf_{f_1 \in F_1} \mathcal{D}(f_1, f_2) \leq \mathcal{D}_{\mathsf{var}}(F_1, F_2)$, thus, we have

$$\mathcal{D}_H(F_1, F_2) \leq \mathcal{D}_{\mathsf{var}}(F_1, F_2) \tag{6}$$

Thus, on first glance, the Hausdorff metric appears to be a good candidate for under-approximating the variation distance. As mentioned earlier, obtaining tracepipe sets is usually not possible; we have to work with over or under-approximations obtained by way of reachpipes. Unfortunately, there is no obvious relationship between $\mathcal{D}_H(A, B)$ and $\mathcal{D}_H(A', B')$ for $A \subseteq A'$ and $B \subseteq B'$. This can be seen pictorially in Figure 1. The sets A, B, A', B' are subsets of the interval $[0, 10]$. In the first case, we have $\mathcal{D}_H(A, B) > \mathcal{D}_H(A', B')$ and in the second, $\mathcal{D}_H(A, B) < \mathcal{D}_H(A', B')$.

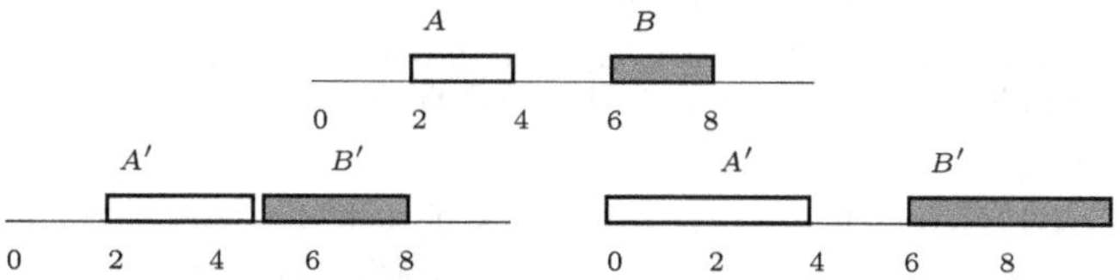

Figure 1: Sets A, B, and two cases of $A \subseteq A'$, $B \subseteq B'$

Thus, we cannot use the reachpipe over-approximations $\lceil \mathsf{Rp}(F_1) \rceil$ and $\lceil \mathsf{Rp}(F_2) \rceil$ to get a lower (or upper) bound on $\mathcal{D}_H(F_1, F_2)$. This problem occurs even even in the case of exact reachpipes $\mathsf{Rp}(F_1), \mathsf{Rp}(F_2)$ as we may have $F_1 \subsetneq \mathsf{Fp}\left(\mathsf{Rp}(F_1)\right)$ and $F_2 \subsetneq \mathsf{Fp}\left(\mathsf{Rp}(F_2)\right)$

For the special case where $F_1 = \{f_1\}$ is a singleton set, we have

$$\mathcal{D}_H(\{f_1\}, F_2) = \mathcal{D}_{\mathsf{var}}(\{f_1\}, F_2) \tag{7}$$

Thus, in case of a singleton $F_1 = \{f_1\}$, the value $\mathcal{D}_H\big(\mathsf{Fp}\left(\mathsf{Rp}(F_1)\right), \mathsf{Fp}\left(\mathsf{Rp}(F_2)\right)\big)$ is equal to the RHS of Equation (3), and hence only gives an upper bound on $\mathcal{D}_{\mathsf{var}}(F_1, F_2)$.

We note that even if we under-approximate the reach sets to obtain $\mathsf{Fp}\left(\lfloor \mathsf{Rp}(F_1) \rfloor\right)$, and $\mathsf{Fp}\left(\lfloor \mathsf{Rp}(F_2) \rfloor\right)$, we still do not have a lower bound for the Hausdorff distance as we cannot tell in which direction the distance changes on taking subsets (Figure 1). In addition, we may have $F \subsetneq \mathsf{Fp}\left(\lfloor \mathsf{Rp}(F) \rfloor\right)$ as for a traceset F, as $\mathsf{Fp}\left(\mathsf{Rp}(F)\right)$ over-approximate F, and competes with the fact that $\lfloor \mathsf{Rp}(F) \rfloor$ under-approximates $\mathsf{Rp}(F)$.

3.3 Constructing Reachpipes

For most dynamical systems, one cannot get a closed-form representation for the set of all traces. However, reachpipe sets can be over/under-approximated at desired timepoints using analytic techniques [7, 17, 11, 13, 15, 10, 21, 8, 6]. The procedure for bounding the tracepipe variation distance in this paper operates on reachpipes (the bounding quantities are as in Proposition 2). As a result it is necessary to choose an appropriate representation of reachpipes so that the distance computation procedure remains tractable.

Reachpipe Completion. Typically, reachset computation tools give us reach sets at sampled time-points, *i.e.*, the tools give us reachpipe samples $R(t_0), \ldots, R(t_m)$ at discrete time-points $t_0, \ldots, t_m$. We need to "complete" the reachpipes for intermediate time values. We do this completion by generalizing linear interpolation using scaling and Minkowski sums. Specifically, we define an over-approximated completion of R in between t_k, t_{k+1} as follows for $t_k \leq t \leq t_{k+1}$:

$$\lceil R \rceil(t) = \left\{ \boldsymbol{p} + \frac{t - t_k}{t_{k+1} - t_k} \cdot (\boldsymbol{q} - \boldsymbol{p}) \;\middle|\; \boldsymbol{p} \in R(t_k) \text{ and } \boldsymbol{q} \in R(t_{k+1}) \right\}.$$

For a set $A \subseteq \mathbb{R}^d$, given $\lambda \in \mathbb{R}$, let $\lambda \cdot A$ denote $\{\lambda \cdot \boldsymbol{p} \mid \boldsymbol{p} \in A\}$. The Minkowski sum of two sets A, B is defined as

$A+B = \{\boldsymbol{p}+\boldsymbol{q} \mid \boldsymbol{p} \in A \text{ and } \boldsymbol{q} \in B\}$. We also denote $-1 \cdot A$ by $-A$. Under this notation, we have

$$\lceil R \rceil(t) = R(t_k) + \frac{t - t_k}{t_{k+1} - t_k} \cdot (R(t_{k+1}) - R(t_k)) . \quad (8)$$

Alternately, one can observe individual traces of the system at discrete times and complete the trace by linear interpolation at intermediate points. That is, suppose we observe a trace f at discrete points t_k and t_{k+1}: $f(t_k) = \boldsymbol{p}$ and $f(t_{k+1}) = \boldsymbol{p}'$ and complete the trace as $f(t) = \boldsymbol{p} + \frac{t-t_k}{t_{k+1}-t_k}(\boldsymbol{p}' - \boldsymbol{p})$ for all points $t_k \leq t \leq t_{k+1}$. We explain why Equation (8) is an over-approximation for linearly interpolated completions of observed trace samples. Recall that

$R(t) = \{\boldsymbol{p} \mid \text{ there exists some trace } f \text{ such that } f(t) = \boldsymbol{p}\}$.

Under linear interpolation completion of traces, this set is

$$R(t) = \left\{ \boldsymbol{p} + \frac{t - t_k}{t_{k+1} - t_k} \cdot (\boldsymbol{q} - \boldsymbol{p}) \;\middle|\; \begin{array}{l} \text{there exists a trace } f \\ \text{such that } f(t_k) = \boldsymbol{p} \text{ and} \\ f(t_{k+1}) = \boldsymbol{q} \end{array} \right\} \quad (9)$$

In general $R(t)$ as defined in Equation (9) can be a strict subset of $\lceil R \rceil(t)$ as defined in Equation (8). For an example,

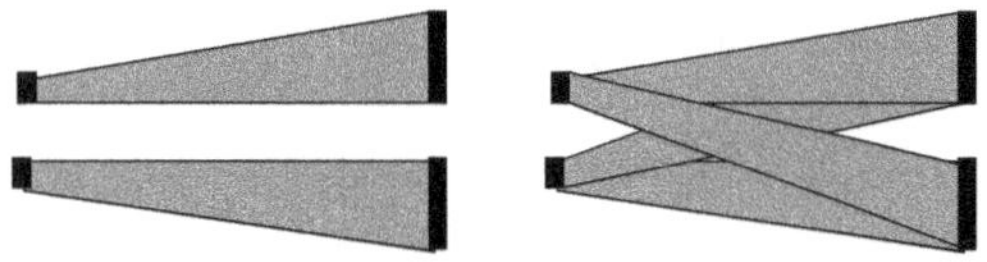

Figure 2: Reachpipe Completion (i) $R(t)$; (ii) $\lceil R \rceil(t)$

see Figure 2, where $R(t_k) \subseteq \mathbb{R}$ and $R(t_{k+1}) \subseteq \mathbb{R}$ are the disjoint black line segments at the ends, and the shaded portions are the completions for $t \in (t_k, t_{k+1})$. The left side shows $R(t)$. The traces evolve from the top (resp. bottom) left black bars to the top (resp. bottom) right black bars. The figure on the right shows that $\lceil R \rceil$ over-approximates by assuming traces from the top left black bar to the bottom right black bar (and similarly from the bottom left bar). The strict inclusion can hold even if $R(t_k)$ and $R(t_{k+1})$ are convex sets.

Reachpipe Sample Sets. We now look at choosing appropriate forms of reachpipe sample sets $R(t_k)$. In hybrid systems literature the common forms of reach sets are (i) ellipsoids [17], (ii) support functions [15], (iii) zonotopes [11, 12], (iv) polyhedra and polytopes [10, 16, 7, 21, 21, 8], (v) polynomial approximations [20, 6].

In this work we use convex polytopes as reachpipe sample sets. A *polyhedron* is specified as: $A \cdot \boldsymbol{x} \leq \boldsymbol{b}$, where A is a $n \times d$ real-valued matrix, $\boldsymbol{x} = [x_1, \ldots, x_d]^\mathsf{T}$ is a column vector of d variables, $\boldsymbol{b} = [b_1, \ldots, b_d]^\mathsf{T}$ is a column vector with $b_k \in \mathbb{R}$ for every k, and "$\cdot$" denotes the standard matrix product. The polyhedron $A \cdot \boldsymbol{x} \leq \boldsymbol{b}$ consists of all points $(p_1, \ldots, p_d) \in \mathbb{R}^d$ such that for all $1 \leq i \leq n$, we have $\sum_{k=1}^{d} A_{i,k} \cdot p_k \leq b_k$. A polyhedron is thus the intersection of n halfspaces, namely, the halfspaces $\sum_{k=1}^{d} A_{i,k} \cdot x_k \leq b_k$ for $1 \leq i \leq n$. We use $\boldsymbol{a}_i \cdot \boldsymbol{x} \leq b_i$ as a shorthand to denote the i-th halfspace, where $\boldsymbol{a}_i$ is the i-th row vector of A. A *polytope* is a bounded polyhedron. Polytopes can also be specified as convex hulls of a finite set of points [14] (unfortunately, polynomial time algorithms are not known to obtain one representation from the other [4]). We use the halfspace representation as it has been shown to be amenable to computing over-approximations of reach sets of hybrid systems using the template polyhedra approach [16, 7, 21, 21, 8], in which the reachsets at sampled timepoints are over-approximated by polytopes by varying the constants in $\boldsymbol{b}$ (the matrix A stays unchanged). Zonotopes are special forms of polytopes, the algorithms developed in this work are also applicable for these special polytopes.

We note the property that if $R(t_k)$ and $R(t_{k+1})$ are polytopes (resp. zonotopes) in Equation (8), the completions $\lceil R \rceil(t)$ for every t are also polytopes (resp. zonotopes). This follows from the facts that for P_1 and P_2 polytopes (resp. zonotopes), (i) $\lambda \cdot P_1$ and $\lambda \cdot P_2$ are polytopes (resp. zonotopes) for λ a constant; and (ii) the Minkowski sum $P_1 + P_2$ is also a polytope (resp. zonotope) [14].

Polygonal Polytope-Reachpipe (PPR). A *polygonal polytope-reachpipe* (PPR) is a reachpipe specified by reachpipe time-samples $R(0), \ldots R(m)$, such that for $k \in \{0, 1, \ldots m-1\}$ (a) each $R(k)$ is a polytope in $\mathbb{R}^{d+1}$; and (b) $R(t)$ for $k < t < k+1$ is taken to be the linear interpolation as specified in Equation (8). Note that we take the reachpipe samples to occur at integer parameter values, this is WLOG as the actual time value can be added as an extra dimension as discussed in Subsection 2.2 with a slight modification: for a polygonal trace f consisting of affine segments starting at times $t_0, t_1, \ldots$, we let the corresponding (polygonal) time-explicit trace C be such that $C(k) = (f(t_k), t_k)$ for $k \in \{0, 1, \ldots m\}$ (for non-integer $\rho \in [0, m]$, the trace C is specified by linear interpolation of the integer endpoints). Next, we study the variation distance between time-explicit PPRs with respect to the Fréchet trace metric in order to bound the Skorokhod distance between the corresponding tracepipes.

4. FRÉCHET DISTANCES BETWEEN POLYTOPE-REACHPIPES

We now investigate computing the pipe variation distance bounds given in Proposition 2 in the case of the Skorokhod trace metric. As a first step, we show it suffices to consider the Fréchet metric as the trace metric in the pipe variation distance.

Consider the setting of Subsection 3.3, which presented linear interpolation completion of sampled trace values. The traces so obtained by completion are continuous. We can define corresponding time-explicit traces $C_f : [T_i^f, T_e^f] \to \mathbb{R}^d \times \mathbb{R}$ for the traces $f : [T_i^f, T_e^f] \to \mathbb{R}^d$ obtained by completing the time sampled traces by linear interpolation. This makes Proposition 1 applicable. Corresponding to a tracepipe F over $\mathbb{R}^d$, we can define a time-explicit tracepipe F^* over $\mathbb{R}^d \times \mathbb{R}$ with traces $f \in F$ corresponding to time-explicit traces C_f in F^*. We then have (referring to trace metrics $\mathcal{S}$ or $\mathcal{F}$ explicitly in the variation distance through the notation $\mathcal{D}_{\mathcal{S}\mathsf{var}}$ or $\mathcal{D}_{\mathcal{F}\mathsf{var}}$):

$$\begin{aligned} \mathcal{D}_{\mathcal{S}\mathsf{var}}(F_1, F_2) &= \sup_{f_1 \in F_1, f_2 \in F_2} \mathcal{D}_{\mathcal{S}}(f_1, f_2) \\ &= \sup_{\mathsf{C}_{f_1} \in F_1^*, \mathsf{C}_{f_2} \in F_2^*} \mathcal{D}_{\mathcal{F}}(\mathsf{C}_{f_1}, \mathsf{C}_{f_2}) \\ &= \mathcal{D}_{\mathcal{F}\mathsf{var}}(F_1^*, F_2^*) \end{aligned}$$

Thus we focus on computing the pipe variation distances with respect to the Fréchet trace metric.

In Section 3, we considered distances between *sets* of traces, and investigated bounding the variation distance between sets of traces (*i.e.*, between tracepipes) using over-approximate tracesets obtained through reachpipes. In the next two subsections, we define a notion of Fréchet distance *directly* on reachpipes, by viewing a reachpipe as a trace from $[0,T]$ to polytopes of $\mathbb{R}^{d+1}$.

Let R_1, R_2 be PPRs from $[0,m_1]$ and $[0,m_2]$ to polytopes over $\mathbb{R}^{d+1}$. Our objective is to bound the tracepipe variation distance with respect to the Fréchet trace metric. From Proposition 2, we need to compute (a) $\mathcal{D}_{\mathcal{F}_{\mathsf{var}}}(\mathsf{Fp}(R_1), \mathsf{Fp}(R_2))$ and (b) $\mathcal{D}_{\mathcal{F}_{\min}}(\mathsf{Fp}(R_1), \mathsf{Fp}(R_2))$.

4.1 Variation Distance on PPRs

In this subsection, we consider $\mathcal{D}_{\mathcal{F}_{\mathsf{var}}}(\mathsf{Fp}(R_1), \mathsf{Fp}(R_2))$. Recall that this value is defined as:

$$\mathcal{D}_{\mathcal{F}_{\mathsf{var}}}(\mathsf{Fp}(R_1), \mathsf{Fp}(R_2)) = \sup_{f_1 \in \mathsf{Fp}(R_1), f_2 \in \mathsf{Fp}(R_2)} \mathcal{D}_{\mathcal{F}}(f_1, f_2) \quad (10)$$

We define a new variation distance on reachpipes as follows.

Definition 3. Let R_1, R_2 be PPRs from $[0,m_1]$ and $[0,m_2]$ to polytopes over $\mathbb{R}^{d+1}$, and let L be a given norm on $\mathbb{R}^{d+1}$. The reachpipe variation distance $\mathcal{D}_{\mathcal{F}_{\mathsf{var}}}^{\dagger}(R_1, R_2)$ is defined as:

$$\inf_{\substack{\alpha_1:[0,1]\to[0,m_1]\\ \alpha_2:[0,1]\to[0,m_2]}} \max_{0\le\theta\le1} \max_{\substack{\mathbf{p}_1 \in R_1(\alpha_1(\theta))\\ \mathbf{p}_2 \in R_2(\alpha_2(\theta))}} \|\mathbf{p}_1 - \mathbf{p}_2\|_L \quad (11)$$

where α_1, α_2 range over continuous and strictly increasing bijective functions onto $[0,m_1]$ and $[0,m_2]$ respectively. □

Note that $\mathcal{D}_{\mathcal{F}_{\mathsf{var}}}^{\dagger}$ is defined over *reachpipes* R, as compared to $\mathcal{D}_{\mathcal{F}_{\mathsf{var}}}$ which is defined over tracepipes F or $\mathsf{Fp}(R)$. Also note that for any reparameterizations α_1, α_2, the sets $R_1(\alpha_1(\theta))$ and $R_2(\alpha_2(\theta))$ are closed and bounded. Thus, $\max_{\mathbf{p}_1 \in R_1(\alpha_1(\theta)),\, \mathbf{p}_2 \in R_2(\alpha_2(\theta))} \|\mathbf{p}_1 - \mathbf{p}_2\|_L$ is well defined. The function $\mathcal{D}_{\mathcal{F}_{\mathsf{var}}}^{\dagger}$, like the function $\mathcal{D}_{\mathcal{F}_{\mathsf{var}}}$, is not a metric (notably, we can have $\mathcal{D}_{\mathcal{F}_{\mathsf{var}}}^{\dagger}(R,R) > 0$).

Informally, we go along the PPRs R_1 and R_2 according to our chosen reparameterizations α_1, α_2, and compare the *polytopes* $R_1(\alpha_1(\theta))$ and $R_2(\alpha_2(\theta))$ for each value of $0 \le \theta \le 1$. If we view a PPR R as a mapping from $[0,m]$ to the set of polytopes of $\mathbb{R}^{d+1}$, then Definition 3 seems similar to the definition of the Fréchet distance over traces (Definition 2), where we use the following function to compare polytopes P_1, P_2:

$$\Phi_{\max}(P_1, P_2) = \max_{\mathbf{p}_1 \in P_1, \mathbf{p}_2 \in P_2} \|\mathbf{p}_1 - \mathbf{p}_2\|_L \quad (12)$$

Using $\Phi_{\max}$, Equation (11) can be written as:

$$\mathcal{D}_{\mathcal{F}_{\mathsf{var}}}^{\dagger}(R_1, R_2) = \inf_{\substack{\alpha_1:[0,1]\to[0,m_1]\\ \alpha_2:[0,1]\to[0,m_2]}} \max_{0\le\theta\le1} \Phi_{\max}\Big(R_1(\alpha_1(\theta))\,,\, R_2(\alpha_2(\theta))\Big) \quad (13)$$

The following theorem shows that $\mathcal{D}_{\mathcal{F}_{\mathsf{var}}}^{\dagger}(R_1, R_2)$ over-approximates the tracepipe distance $\mathcal{D}_{\mathcal{F}_{\mathsf{var}}}(\mathsf{Fp}(R_1), \mathsf{Fp}(R_2))$.

Theorem 1. *Let R_1, R_2 be PPRs from $[0,m_1]$ and $[0,m_2]$ to polytopes over $\mathbb{R}^{d+1}$, and let L be a given norm on $\mathbb{R}^{d+1}$. We have*

$$\mathcal{D}_{\mathcal{F}_{\mathsf{var}}}^{\dagger}(R_1, R_2) \;\ge\; \mathcal{D}_{\mathcal{F}_{\mathsf{var}}}\big(\mathsf{Fp}(R_1),\, \mathsf{Fp}(R_2)\big)$$

where the tracepipe distance $\mathcal{D}_{\mathcal{F}_{\mathsf{var}}}(\mathsf{Fp}(R_1), \mathsf{Fp}(R_2))$ is as defined in Equation (10), and the reachpipe distance $\mathcal{D}_{\mathcal{F}_{\mathsf{var}}}^{\dagger}(R_1, R_2)$ is as defined in Definition 3.

Proof. Consider any $f_1 \in \mathsf{Fp}(R_1)$, and any $f_2 \in \mathsf{Fp}(R_2)$. We have

$$\mathcal{D}_{\mathcal{F}}(f_1, f_2) = \inf_{\substack{\alpha_1:[0,1]\to[0,m_1]\\ \alpha_2:[0,1]\to[0,m_2]}} \max_{0\le\theta\le1} \|f_1(\alpha_1(\theta)) - f_2(\alpha_2(\theta))\|_L$$

Observe that $f_j(\alpha_j(\theta)) \in R_j(\alpha_j(\theta))$ for $j \in \{1,2\}$. Thus, for every $\alpha_1, \alpha_2, \theta$,

$$\|f_1(\alpha_1(\theta)) - f_2(\alpha_2(\theta))\|_L \le \Phi_{\max}(R_1(\alpha_1(\theta)), R_2(\alpha_2(\theta)))$$

Thus, we have

$$\mathcal{D}_{\mathcal{F}}(f_1, f_2) \le \inf_{\substack{\alpha_1:[0,1]\to[0,m_1]\\ \alpha_2:[0,1]\to[0,m_2]}} \max_{0\le\theta\le1} \Phi_{\max}\Big(R_1(\alpha_1(\theta))\,,\, R_2(\alpha_2(\theta))\Big)$$

That is, for every $f_1 \in \mathsf{Fp}(R_1)$ and $f_2 \in \mathsf{Fp}(R_2)$, we have $\mathcal{D}_{\mathcal{F}}(f_1, f_2) \le \mathcal{D}_{\mathcal{F}_{\mathsf{var}}}^{\dagger}(R_1, R_2)$. This implies that $\sup_{f_1 \in \mathsf{Fp}(R_1),\, f_2 \in \mathsf{Fp}(R_2)} \mathcal{D}_{\mathcal{F}}(f_1, f_2) \le \mathcal{D}_{\mathcal{F}_{\mathsf{var}}}^{\dagger}(R_1, R_2)$. □

The above theorem can be applied with $R_1 = \lceil \mathsf{Rp}(F_1) \rceil$ and $R_2 = \lceil \mathsf{Rp}(F_2) \rceil$ in order to obtain the upper bound in Proposition 2 using the reachpipe variation distance $\mathcal{D}_{\mathcal{F}_{\mathsf{var}}}^{\dagger}$ between $\lceil \mathsf{Rp}(F_1) \rceil$ and $\lceil \mathsf{Rp}(F_2) \rceil$. We next consider the lower bound.

4.2 Minimum Distance on PPRs

We now consider $\mathcal{D}_{\mathcal{F}_{\min}}(F^{R_1}, F^{R_2})$ for PPRs R_1, R_2 from $[0,m_1]$ and $[0,m_2]$ to polytopes over $\mathbb{R}^{d+1}$ respectively. This distance is defined as:

$$\mathcal{D}_{\mathcal{F}_{\min}}\big(\mathsf{Fp}(R_1),\, \mathsf{Fp}(R_2)\big) = \inf_{f_1 \in \mathsf{Fp}(R_1),\, f_2 \in \mathsf{Fp}(R_2)} \mathcal{D}_{\mathcal{F}}(f_1, f_2) \quad (14)$$

Analogous to the $\mathcal{D}_{\mathcal{F}_{\mathsf{var}}}$ function of Definition 3, we define a minimum set distance $\mathcal{D}_{\mathcal{F}_{\min}}$ over reachpipes. We use the following function to compare polytopes (given a norm L over $\mathbb{R}^{d+1}$):

$$\Phi_{\min}(P_1, P_2) = \min_{\mathbf{p}_1 \in P_1,\, \mathbf{p}_2 \in P_2} \|\mathbf{p}_1 - \mathbf{p}_2\|_L \quad (15)$$

Using this function, we define $\mathcal{D}_{\mathcal{F}_{\min}}$ as follows.

Definition 4. Let R_1, R_2 be PPRs from $[0,m_1]$ and $[0,m_2]$ to polytopes over $\mathbb{R}^{d+1}$, and let $\Phi_{\min}$ be the polytope comparison function as described previously. The reachpipe minimum set distance $\mathcal{D}_{\mathcal{F}_{\min}}^{\dagger}(R_1, R_2)$ is defined as:

$$\mathcal{D}_{\mathcal{F}_{\min}}^{\dagger}(R_1, R_2) = \inf_{\substack{\alpha_1:[0,1]\to[0,m_1]\\ \alpha_2:[0,1]\to[0,m_2]}} \max_{0\le\theta\le1} \Phi_{\min}\Big(R_1(\alpha_1(\theta))\,,\, R_2(\alpha_2(\theta))\Big) \quad (16)$$

where α_1, α_2 range over continuous and strictly increasing bijective functions onto $[0,m_1]$ and $[0,m_2]$ respectively. □

The following theorem shows that $\mathcal{D}_{\mathcal{F}_{\min}}^{\dagger}(R_1, R_2)$ is equal to the tracepipe distance $\mathcal{D}_{\mathcal{F}_{\min}}(\mathsf{Fp}(R_1), \mathsf{Fp}(R_2))$.

Theorem 2. *Let R_1, R_2 be PPRs from $[0,m_1]$ and $[0,m_2]$ to polytopes over $\mathbb{R}^{d+1}$, and let L be a given norm on $\mathbb{R}^{d+1}$. We have*

$$\mathcal{D}_{\mathcal{F}_{\min}}^{\dagger}(R_1, R_2) \;=\; \mathcal{D}_{\mathcal{F}_{\min}}\big(\mathsf{Fp}(R_1), \mathsf{Fp}(R_2)\big)$$

where the tracepipe distance $\mathcal{D}_{\mathcal{F}_{\min}}(\mathsf{Fp}(R_1), \mathsf{Fp}(R_2))$ is as defined in Equation (14), and the reachpipe distance $\mathcal{D}_{\mathcal{F}_{\min}}^{\dagger}(R_1, R_2)$ is as defined in Definition 4. □

Theorems 1 and 2 allow us to bound to the tracepipe variation distance $\mathcal{D}_{\mathcal{F}_{\mathsf{var}}}$ using the reachpipe distances $\mathcal{D}_{\mathcal{F}_{\mathsf{var}}}^{\dagger}$ and $\mathcal{D}_{\mathcal{F}_{\min}}^{\dagger}$ that were defined in the current section. In the next section we present algorithms for computing these two reachpipe distances over PPRs.

5. FRÉCHET DISTANCES BETWEEN POLYTOPE-TRACES

Theorems 1 and 2 show that the distance functions $\mathcal{D}_{\mathcal{F}_{\mathsf{var}}}^{\dagger}$ and $\mathcal{D}_{\mathcal{F}_{\min}}^{\dagger}$ over PPRs can be used to bound the tracepipe distances $\mathcal{D}_{\mathcal{F}_{\mathsf{var}}}$ and $\mathcal{D}_{\mathcal{F}_{\min}}$. We now present procedures for computing $\mathcal{D}_{\mathcal{F}_{\mathsf{var}}}^{\dagger}$ and $\mathcal{D}_{\mathcal{F}_{\min}}^{\dagger}$ as follows. In Subsection 5.1 we extend the geometric free space concept used in [3, 18] to compute the Fréchet distance between two traces to the case of PPRs, and show how the PPR distance decision problem can be reduced to a two-dimensional reachability problem. In Subsection 5.2 we present algorithms for the reachability problems corresponding to $\mathcal{D}_{\mathcal{F}_{\mathsf{var}}}^{\dagger}$ and $\mathcal{D}_{\mathcal{F}_{\min}}^{\dagger}$.

5.1 The Free Space for Polytope-Traces

Let $\mathsf{PTopes}(\mathbb{R}^{d+1})$ denote the set of all polytopes in $\mathbb{R}^{d+1}$. A PPR R defined over the time interval $[0, m]$ can be viewed as a polytope-trace, defined as a function from $[0, m]$ to $\mathsf{PTopes}(\mathbb{R}^{d+1})$. Recall that a PPR R is specified by reachpipe time-samples $R(0), \dots R(m)$, such that for $k \in \{0, 1, \dots m-1\}$ the portion of R in between $(k, k+1)$ is assumed to be completed according to linear interpolation using $R(k)$ and $R(k+1)$. We denote this portion of R between $R(k)$ and $R(k+1)$ as $R^{[k]}$, *i.e.*, the portion of R defined over $k \leq t \leq k+1$.

Alt and Godau introduced *free spaces* [3] to compute the Fréchet distance between piecewise affine and continuous curves in $\mathbb{R}^d$. We show free spaces can also be used to compute the functions $\mathcal{D}_{\mathcal{F}_{\mathsf{var}}}^{\dagger}$ and $\mathcal{D}_{\mathcal{F}_{\min}}^{\dagger}$. First, we show how to extend free spaces to the domain of PPRs.

Definition 5 (Free Space). Given PPRs $R_1 : [0, m_1] \rightarrow \mathsf{PTopes}(\mathbb{R}^{d+1})$ and $R_2 : [0, m_2] \rightarrow \mathsf{PTopes}(\mathbb{R}^{d+1})$, a real number $\delta \geq 0$, and a polytope comparison function $\Phi : \mathsf{PTopes}(\mathbb{R}^{d+1}) \times \mathsf{PTopes}(\mathbb{R}^{d+1}) \rightarrow \mathbb{R}_+$, the *$\delta$-Free Space* of R_1, R_2 with respect to Φ is defined as the set $\mathsf{Free}_\delta^\Phi(R_1, R_2) =$

$$\left\{(\rho_1, \rho_2) \in [0, m_1] \times [0, m_2] \;\middle|\; \Phi\Big(R_1(\rho_1), R_2(\rho_2)\Big) \leq \delta\right\} \quad \square$$

The free space for PPRs serves a similar role as in the case of the free space for traces. The tuples (ρ_1, ρ_1) belonging to $\mathsf{Free}_\delta^\Phi(R_1, R_2)$ denote the positions in the two reparameterizations such that the Φ value for those position pairs is at most δ. Thus $\mathsf{Free}_\delta^\Phi(R_1, R_2)$ collects the pairs (ρ_1, ρ_2) which could be used in valid reparameterizations of Definition 3 or 4. A pictorial representation of the free space is referred to as the *free space diagram.* The space $[0, m_1] \times [0, m_2]$ can be viewed as consisting of $m_1 m_2$ *cells*, with cell i, j being $[i, i+1] \times [j, j+1]$ for $0 \leq i < m_1$, and $0 \leq j < m_1$. Observe that $\mathsf{Free}_\delta^\Phi(R_1, R_2)$ intersected with cell i, j is just the free space corresponding to the PPR segments $R_1^{[i]}, R_2^{[j]}$; *i.e.*, the intersection of the cell i, j with $\mathsf{Free}_\delta^\Phi(R_1, R_2)$ is equal to $\mathsf{Free}_\delta^\Phi(R_1^{[i]}, R_2^{[j]})$.

Proposition 3 (Free Space & Reparameterizations). *Given two PPRs R_1, R_2 from $[0, m_1]$ and $[0, m_2]$ to $\mathsf{PTopes}(\mathbb{R}^{d+1})$, we have $\mathcal{D}_{\mathcal{F}_{\mathsf{var}}}^{\dagger}(R_1, R_2) \leq \delta$ (resp., $\mathcal{D}_{\mathcal{F}_{\min}}^{\dagger}(R_1, R_2) \leq \delta$) iff there is a non-decreasing (in both dimensions) curve $\alpha : [0, 1] \rightarrow [0, m_1] \times [0, m_2]$ in $\mathsf{Free}_\delta^{\Phi_{\max}}(R_1, R_2)$ (resp. $\mathsf{Free}_\delta^{\Phi_{\min}}(R_1, R_2)$) from $(0, 0)$ to (m_1, m_2).* $\square$

The curve α can be thought of as a pair of parameterized curves (α_1, α_2), with $\alpha_1 : [0, 1] \rightarrow [0, m_1]$ and $\alpha_2 : [0, 1] \rightarrow [0, m_2]$. The functions α_1, α_2 can be viewed

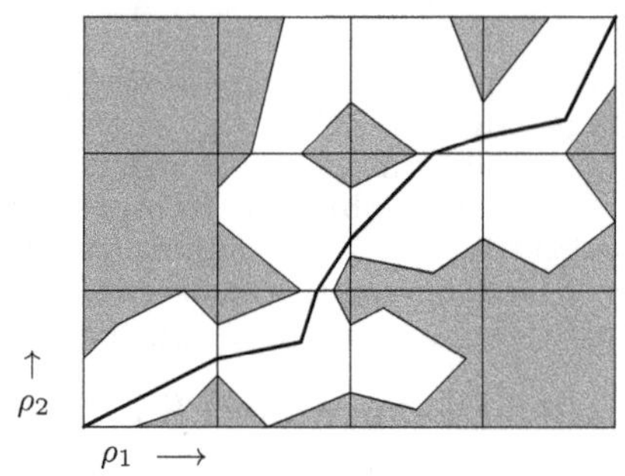

Figure 3: The Free Space $\mathsf{Free}_\delta^\Phi(R_1, R_2)$.

as the reparameterization functions in Definitions 3 and 4. The general shape of the free space for two PPRs is depicted in Figure 3. The unshaded portion is the free space. The figure also includes a continuous curve which is non-decreasing in both coordinates, from $(0, 0)$ to (m_1, m_2).

Note that the curve α (and hence also each of α_1, α_2) in Proposition 3 is non-decreasing; whereas the reparameterizations in Definitions 3 and 4 are strictly increasing. This is to account for the fact that optimal reparameterizations in Definitions 3 and 4 might not exist, as we have an "inf". It can be shown that $\mathcal{D}_{\mathcal{F}_{\min}}^{\dagger}$ and $\mathcal{D}_{\mathcal{F}_{\mathsf{var}}}^{\dagger}$ values do not change over PPRs if we allow non-decreasing reparameterizations since PPRs change smoothly due to the linear interpolation scheme. This issue also arises in the case of traces, and is discussed (for the case of traces) in more detail in [18]. We omit the technicalities, and henceforth assume that non-decreasing reparameterizations are allowed in Definitions 3 and 4.

5.2 The Polytope-Trace $\mathcal{D}^\dagger$ Decision Problems

In this section, we solve for the decision problems $\mathcal{D}_{\mathcal{F}_{\mathsf{var}}}^{\dagger}(R_1, R_2) \leq \delta$ and $\mathcal{D}_{\mathcal{F}_{\min}}^{\dagger}(R_1, R_2) \leq \delta$, given a $\delta \geq 0$ and PPRs R_1, R_2. We use the free space reduction of Proposition 3 for these decision problems. The first step in this procedure is to compute the free space. Towards this step, we first show that the free spaces for the polytope comparison functions $\Phi_{\min}$ and $\Phi_{\max}$ are convex in individual cells of the free space diagram. This is done in Subsection 5.2.1. Using this convexity property, we show in Subsection 5.2.2 that in order to obtain the free space of a cell, it suffices to obtain the free space at the cell boundaries. We obtain algorithms to compute the free space cell boundaries in Subsection 5.2.3 (for $\Phi_{\min}$), and in 5.2.4 (for $\Phi_{\max}$). The procedure of Subsection 5.2.4 has a high time complexity, we present a polynomial time algorithm which works in case the PPRs satisfy certain conditions in Subsection 5.2.5. The results of the section are summarized in Propositions 5, 6 and 8.

5.2.1 Convexity of Free Space

The following lemma proves that the free space in the first cell (over $[0, 1] \times [0, 1]$) is convex for both the set comparison functions $\Phi_{\min}$ and $\Phi_{\max}$. Other cells are translations and have a similar proof.

Lemma 1 (Convexity of Free Space of Individual Cells). *Let P_a^0, P_a^1, and P_b^0, P_b^1 be polytopes in $\mathbb{R}^{d+1}$. Let $R_a : [0, 1] \rightarrow \mathsf{PTopes}(\mathbb{R}^{d+1})$ and $R_b : [0, 1] \rightarrow \mathsf{PTopes}(\mathbb{R}^{d+1})$ be (single-segment) PPRs constructed from the polytopes P_a^0, P_a^1 and P_b^0, P_b^1 respectively, via linear interpolation (as described in Equation (8)), taking $P_a^0 = R_a(0)$ and $P_a^1 = R_a(1)$ and $P_b^0 = R_b(0)$ $P_b^1 = R_b(1)$, respectively.*

The free space of R_a, R_b given a $\delta \geq 0$ for both

$\Phi_{\min}$ *and* $\Phi_{\max}$ *is convex. That is,* $\mathsf{Free}_\delta^{\Phi_{\min}}(R_a, R_b)$ *and* $\mathsf{Free}_\delta^{\Phi_{\max}}(R_a, R_b)$ *are both convex sets.*

Proof. Let Φ be $\Phi_{\min}$ or $\Phi_{\max}$. Suppose two points (in $[0,1] \times [0,1]$) belong to $\mathsf{Free}_\delta^{\Phi}(R_a, R_b)$. Let these points be $\rho = (\rho_a, \rho_b)$ and $\rho' = (\rho'_a, \rho'_b)$. We show that for any $0 \le \lambda \le 1$, the point $\rho^* = \lambda \cdot \rho + (1-\lambda) \cdot \rho'$ also belongs to $\mathsf{Free}_\delta^{\Phi}(R_a, R_b)$. The point ρ^* is the tuple

$$(\rho^*_a, \rho^*_b) = \big(\lambda \cdot \rho_a + (1-\lambda) \cdot \rho'_a \ , \ \lambda \cdot \rho_b + (1-\lambda) \cdot \rho'_b\big). \quad (17)$$

To show $(\rho^*_a, \rho^*_b) \in \mathsf{Free}_\delta^{\Phi}(R_a, R_b)$, we need to show that

$$\Phi\big(R_a(\rho^*_a), R_b(\rho^*_b)\big) \le \delta \quad (18)$$

We show this individually for $\Phi_{\min}$ and $\Phi_{\max}$.

(1) $\Phi_{\min}$.
By the definition of $\Phi_{\min}$ (Equation (15)), and the facts that (ρ_a, ρ_b) and (ρ'_a, ρ'_b) are in $\mathsf{Free}_\delta^{\Phi_{\min}}(R_a, R_b)$, we have that:

- There exist points $\boldsymbol{p}_a \in R_a(\rho_a)$ and $\boldsymbol{p}_b \in R_b(\rho_b)$ such that $\|\boldsymbol{p}_a - \boldsymbol{p}_b\| \le \delta$.
- There exist points $\boldsymbol{p}'_a \in R_a(\rho'_a)$ and $\boldsymbol{p}'_b \in R_b(\rho'_b)$ such that $\|\boldsymbol{p}'_a - \boldsymbol{p}'_b\| \le \delta$.

Consider the points $\boldsymbol{p}^*_a = \lambda \cdot \boldsymbol{p}_a + (1-\lambda) \cdot \boldsymbol{p}'_a$; and $\boldsymbol{p}^*_b = \lambda \cdot \boldsymbol{p}_b + (1-\lambda) \cdot \boldsymbol{p}'_b$ (where λ is the same value as that used in Equation (17)). We have

$$\begin{aligned}
\|\boldsymbol{p}^*_a - \boldsymbol{p}^*_b\| &= \Big\| \big(\lambda \cdot \boldsymbol{p}_a + (1-\lambda) \cdot \boldsymbol{p}'_a\big) - \big(\lambda \cdot \boldsymbol{p}_b + (1-\lambda) \cdot \boldsymbol{p}'_b\big) \Big\| \\
&= \big\| \lambda \cdot (\boldsymbol{p}_a - \boldsymbol{p}_b) + (1-\lambda) \cdot (\boldsymbol{p}'_a - \boldsymbol{p}'_b) \big\| \\
&\le \lambda \cdot \|\boldsymbol{p}_a - \boldsymbol{p}_b\| + (1-\lambda) \cdot \|\boldsymbol{p}'_a - \boldsymbol{p}'_b\| \\
&\qquad\qquad \text{(by basic norm properties)} \\
&\le \lambda \cdot \delta + (1-\lambda) \cdot \delta \\
&= \delta
\end{aligned}$$

We now show $\boldsymbol{p}^*_a \in R_a(\rho^*_a)$, and $\boldsymbol{p}^*_b \in R_b(\rho^*_b)$ Observe that the polytope $R_a(\rho^*_a)$ which is defined to be the polytope

$$\begin{aligned}
&R_a(0) + \rho^*_a \cdot (R_a(0) - R_a(1)) \\
&= R_a(0) + \big(\lambda \cdot \rho_a + (1-\lambda) \cdot \rho'_a\big) \cdot (R_a(0) - R_a(1)) \\
&= \lambda \cdot (R_a(0) + \rho_a \cdot (R_a(0) - R_a(1))) \ + \\
&\qquad (1-\lambda) \cdot \big(R_a(0) + \rho'_a \cdot (R_a(0) - R_a(1))\big) \\
&= \lambda \cdot R_a(\rho_a) + (1-\lambda) \cdot R_a(\rho'_a)
\end{aligned} \quad (19)$$

Thus, $R_a(\rho^*_a)$ equals the polytope $\lambda \cdot R_a(\rho_a) + (1-\lambda) \cdot R_a(\rho'_a)$. Since $\boldsymbol{p}^*_a = \lambda \cdot \boldsymbol{p}_a + (1-\lambda) \cdot \boldsymbol{p}'_a$ for $\boldsymbol{p}_a \in R_a(\rho_a)$ and $\boldsymbol{p}'_a \in R_a(\rho'_a)$, this means that $\boldsymbol{p}^*_a \in R_a(\rho^*_a)$. Similarly, $\boldsymbol{p}^*_b \in R_b(\rho^*_b)$. Since we have demonstrated that $\|\boldsymbol{p}^*_a - \boldsymbol{p}^*_b\| \le \delta$, this means that $\Phi_{\min}\left(R_a(\rho^*_a), R_b(\rho^*_b)\right) \le \delta$. This shows that Equation (18) holds for $\Phi_{\min}$.

(2) $\Phi_{\max}$.
Now we show that Equation (18) holds for $\Phi_{\max}$. By the definition of $\Phi_{\max}$ (Equation (12)), and the facts that (ρ_a, ρ_b) and (ρ'_a, ρ'_b) are in $\mathsf{Free}_\delta^{\Phi_{\min}}(R_a, R_b)$, we have that:

- For all points $\boldsymbol{p}_a \in R_a(\rho_a)$ and $\boldsymbol{p}_b \in R_b(\rho_b)$ we have that $\|\boldsymbol{p}_a - \boldsymbol{p}_b\| \le \delta$.
- For all points $\boldsymbol{p}'_a \in R_a(\rho'_a)$ and $\boldsymbol{p}'_b \in R_b(\rho'_b)$ we have that $\|\boldsymbol{p}'_a - \boldsymbol{p}'_b\| \le \delta$.

Consider any point $\boldsymbol{p}^*_a$ which belongs to $R_a(\rho^*_a)$ and any point $\boldsymbol{p}^*_b$ which belongs to $R_b(\rho^*_b)$. By Equation (19), we have $R_a(\rho^*_a) = \lambda \cdot R_a(\rho_a) + (1-\lambda) \cdot R_a(\rho'_a)$; and similarly for $R_b(\rho^*_b)$ Thus, by definition,

- $\boldsymbol{p}^*_a = \lambda \cdot \boldsymbol{p}_a + (1-\lambda) \cdot \boldsymbol{p}'_a$ for some $\boldsymbol{p}_a \in R_a(\rho_a)$ and $\boldsymbol{p}'_a \in R_a(\rho'_a)$; and

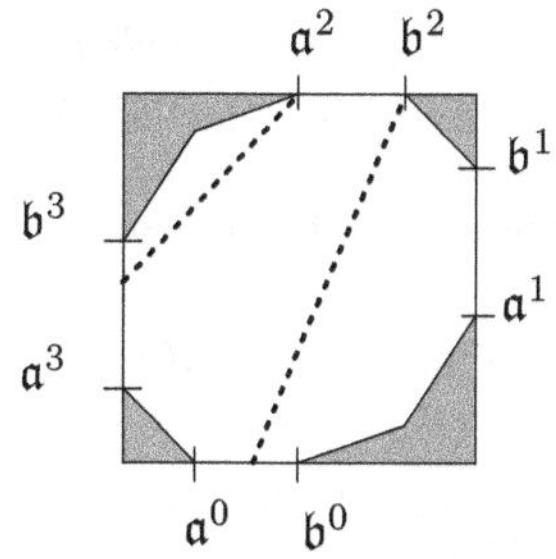

Figure 4: Cell Crossing with Non-Decreasing Curves.

- $\boldsymbol{p}^*_b = \lambda \cdot \boldsymbol{p}_b + (1-\lambda) \cdot \boldsymbol{p}'_b$ for some $\boldsymbol{p}_b \in R_a(\rho_b)$ and $\boldsymbol{p}'_b \in R_b(\rho'_b)$

It can be shown (as in the $\Phi_{\min}$ case) using the above two facts that $\|\boldsymbol{p}^*_a - \boldsymbol{p}^*_b\| \le \delta$. That is, we have that for any point $\boldsymbol{p}^*_a \in R_a(\rho^*_a)$, and any point $\boldsymbol{p}^*_b \in R_b(\rho^*_b)$, the value $\|\boldsymbol{p}^*_a - \boldsymbol{p}^*_b\|$ does not exceed δ. This means that

$$\sup_{\boldsymbol{p}^*_a \in R_a(\rho^*_a),\, \boldsymbol{p}^*_b \in R_b(\rho^*_b)} \|\boldsymbol{p}^*_a - \boldsymbol{p}^*_b\| \le \delta$$

Thus, $\Phi_{\max}\left(R_a(\rho^*_a), R_b(\rho^*_b)\right) \le \delta$. This shows that Equation (18) holds also for $\Phi_{\max}$ (in addition to $\Phi_{\min}$). □

5.2.2 Computing the Free Space

The convexity demonstrated by Lemma 1 simplifies the problem of computing a non-decreasing curve in the free space. As a result of the convexity of the free space for a cell, it suffices to only compute the free space boundaries at the cell boundaries. We refer to Figure 4. The dotted lines are example non-decreasing curves that cross the cell. As can be seen, to check if we can go from the left free space boundary to the top free space boundary of the cell, we only need the top free space boundary (and the precondition that the left free space boundary is non-empty). A similar situation arises for checking traversal from the bottom to top or bottom to right boundaries via non-decreasing curves. Convexity makes the internal shape of the free space inside a cell irrelevant. Invoking convexity again, we actually only need to compute the points $\mathfrak{a}^k, \mathfrak{b}^k$ for $k \in \{0,3\}$. We present the computation procedure next.

We compute the bottom free space boundaries of cells (the other boundaries have similar algorithmic solutions). We need to compute the points $\mathfrak{a}^0, \mathfrak{b}^0$ in Figure 4. We do this for the first cell (over $[0,1] \times [0,1]$), other cells are translations and are similar. The point $\mathfrak{a}^0 = \langle \lambda^{\min}, 0 \rangle$, and the point $\mathfrak{b}^0 = \langle \lambda^{\max}, 0 \rangle$ for some $\lambda^{\min}$ and $\lambda^{\max}$ in $[0,1]$. It hence suffices to compute $\lambda^{\min}$ and $\lambda^{\max}$. We solve for $\lambda^{\min}$ (the solution for $\lambda^{\max}$ is similar) . This value $\lambda^{\min}$ is the solution of the following optimization problem (where $R_1(0), R_1(1), R_2(0)$ are given polytope samples of PPRs R_1 and R_2) :

$$\begin{aligned}
&\text{minimize} \quad \lambda \\
&\text{subject to} \quad \Phi\left(R_1(\lambda), R_2(0)\right) \le \delta \\
&\qquad\qquad\quad 0 \le \lambda \le 1
\end{aligned}$$

Expanding $R_1(\lambda)$, we get:

$$\begin{aligned}
&\text{minimize} \quad \lambda \\
&\text{subject to} \quad \Phi\big(\lambda \cdot R_1(0) + (1-\lambda) \cdot R_1(1),\ R_2(0)\big) \le \delta \quad (20) \\
&\qquad\qquad\quad 0 \le \lambda \le 1
\end{aligned}$$

The solution to the above problem depends on the function Φ. We solve each case $\Phi_{\min}$ and $\Phi_{\max}$ individually.

5.2.3 Free Space Cell Boundaries for $\mathbf{\Phi}_{\min}$

In this subsection, we compute the bottom free space boundary of the first cell (over $[0,1] \times [0,1]$). The optimization problem (20) for $\Phi = \Phi_{\min}$ has the same solution as:

$$\begin{aligned} &\text{minimize} \quad \lambda \\ &\text{such that} \quad \begin{array}{l} \exists \text{ point } \boldsymbol{p} \in \lambda \cdot R_1(0) + (1-\lambda) \cdot R_1(1), \\ \exists \text{ point } \boldsymbol{q} \in R_2(0) \end{array} \\ &\qquad\qquad \text{s.t. } \|\boldsymbol{p} - \boldsymbol{q}\| \leq \delta \\ &\qquad 0 \leq \lambda \leq 1 \end{aligned}$$

Let $R_1(0)$ be the polytope $A_1^0 \cdot \boldsymbol{x} \leq \boldsymbol{b}_1^0$, $R_1(1)$ be the polytope $A_1^1 \cdot \boldsymbol{x} \leq \boldsymbol{b}_1^1$, and $R_2(0)$ be the polytope $A_2 \cdot \boldsymbol{x} \leq \boldsymbol{b}_2$; where the As are $n \times (d+1)$ matrices of given constants, and $\boldsymbol{b}$s are column vectors of size $d+1$ containing given constants; and $\boldsymbol{x}$s are column vectors of variables. The previous optimization problem can be stated using these polytopes as:

$$\begin{aligned} \text{minimize} \quad & \lambda \\ \text{subject to} \quad & \left\|\lambda \cdot \boldsymbol{x}^0 + (1-\lambda) \cdot \boldsymbol{x}^1 - \boldsymbol{y}\right\| \leq \delta \\ & A_1^0 \cdot \boldsymbol{x}^0 \leq \boldsymbol{b}_1^0 \\ & A_1^1 \cdot \boldsymbol{x}^1 \leq \boldsymbol{b}_1^1 \\ & A_2 \cdot \boldsymbol{y} \leq \boldsymbol{b}_2 \\ & 0 \leq \lambda \leq 1 \end{aligned} \tag{21}$$

The optimization above is over the variables $\lambda, \boldsymbol{x}^0, \boldsymbol{x}^1, \boldsymbol{y}$. The values for $A_1^0, A_1^1, A_2, \boldsymbol{b}_1^0, \boldsymbol{b}_1^1, \boldsymbol{b}_2, \delta$ are given. We would like to reduce the problem to Linear Programming (LP), however we note that, as stated, the problem is an instance of quadratic programming due to the multiplication of the parameter λ with parameter column vectors $\boldsymbol{x}^0$ and $\boldsymbol{x}^1$. We show that these multiplicative constraints can be removed. Towards this, we need the following lemma.

Lemma 2. *Suppose $A \cdot \boldsymbol{x} \leq \boldsymbol{b}$ is a non-empty polytope in $\mathbb{R}^{d+1}$ and $\boldsymbol{b} \neq \mathbf{0}$. Then $A \cdot \boldsymbol{x} \leq \mathbf{0}$ either has no solution, or contains the only point $\boldsymbol{x} = \mathbf{0}$.* □

Using the above lemma, the following result can be shown.

Lemma 3. *Let $A_1^0 \cdot \boldsymbol{x}^0 \leq \boldsymbol{b}_1^0$, and $A_1^1 \cdot \boldsymbol{x}^1 \leq \boldsymbol{b}_1^1$, and $A_2 \cdot \boldsymbol{y} \leq \boldsymbol{b}_2$ be non-empty polytopes in $\mathbb{R}^{d+1}$. The following optimization problem has the same solution as Problem (21).*

$$\begin{aligned} \textit{minimize} \quad & \lambda \\ \textit{subject to} \quad & \left\|\boldsymbol{z}^0 + \boldsymbol{z}^1 - \boldsymbol{y}\right\| \leq \delta \\ & A_1^0 \cdot \boldsymbol{z}^0 \leq \lambda \cdot \boldsymbol{b}_1^0 \\ & A_1^1 \cdot \boldsymbol{z}^1 \leq (1-\lambda) \cdot \boldsymbol{b}_1^1 \\ & A_2 \cdot \boldsymbol{y} \leq \boldsymbol{b}_2 \\ & 0 \leq \lambda \leq 1 \end{aligned} \tag{22}$$

□

We thus can take $\lambda_{\min}$ to be the solution of the optimization problem (22). Consider the norms $L_1^{\max}$ (recall the derived norms given in Equation (1)); or $L_\infty^{\max}$ (which is just the same as the L_∞ norm). Let us use any of these norms as the norm in $\left\|\boldsymbol{z}^0 + \boldsymbol{z}^1 - \boldsymbol{y}\right\|$. The optimization problem (22) as stated is not a LP instance. However, we showed in [18] how constraint problems involving the $L_1^{\max}$, or L_∞ norms can be framed as LP by doubling the number of variables. A similar approach works here, thus, Problem (22) can be solved using linear programming. We solved for the minimal λ. We can employ the same techniques for finding the maximal λ. This gives us the following result.

Proposition 4 (Free Space Cell Boundaries for $\Phi_{\min}$). *Given two PPRs R_1, R_2, the set $\mathsf{Free}_\delta^{\Phi_{\min}}(R_1, R_2)$ at cell-(i,k) boundaries can be computed in time $O\left(\mathsf{LP}\left(S_1^i + S_1^{i+1} + S_2^k + S_2^{k+1}\right)\right)$, where S_j^l denotes the halfspace representation size of polytope $R_j(l)$, and $\mathsf{LP}(\cdot)$ is the (polynomial time) upper bound for solving linear programming instances.* □

After computing the free space cell boundaries, we can employ a dynamic programming algorithm to check if there is a non-decreasing curve travelling through the free space from the point $(0,0)$ to (m_1, m_2).

Proposition 5 ($\mathcal{D}_{\mathcal{F}_{\min}^{\dagger}}$ Decision Problem). *Given PPRs R_1, R_2 represented as m_1, m_2 polytopes respectively, and a $\delta \geq 0$, we can decide the question $\mathcal{D}_{\mathcal{F}_{\min}^{\dagger}}(R_1, R_2) \leq \delta$ in time $O\left(m_1 \cdot m_2 \cdot \mathsf{LP}(S_{\max})\right)$ for both $L_1^{\max}$ and L_∞ norms on $\mathbb{R}^{d+1}$, where $S_{\max}$ is the maximum of the halfspace representation sizes of the given polytopes, and $\mathsf{LP}(\cdot)$ is the (polynomial time) upper bound for solving linear programming.* □

5.2.4 Free Space Cell Boundaries for $\mathbf{\Phi}_{\max}$

In this subsection, we compute the bottom free space boundary of the first cell (over $[0,1] \times [0,1]$). The optimization problem (20) for $\Phi = \Phi_{\max}$ has the same solution as:

$$\begin{aligned} &\text{minimize} \quad \lambda \\ &\text{such that} \quad \begin{array}{l} \forall \text{ points } \boldsymbol{p} \in \lambda \cdot R_1(0) + (1-\lambda) \cdot R_1(1), \\ \forall \text{ points } \boldsymbol{q} \in R_2(0) \end{array} \\ &\qquad\qquad \text{we have } \|\boldsymbol{p} - \boldsymbol{q}\| \leq \delta \\ &\qquad 0 \leq \lambda \leq 1 \end{aligned}$$

Unfortunately, this cannot be converted into an LP instance as in the $\Phi_{\min}$ case because of the "for all" quantifier in the constraints. The above optimization problem can be expressed in the theory of reals which is decidable [5]. This gives us a procedure to compute the free space cell boundaries for $\Phi_{\max}$. Once we have the free space boundaries, we can use a dynamic programming algorithm (as in the $\Phi_{\min}$ case) to obtain the following result.

Proposition 6 ($\mathcal{D}_{\mathcal{F}_{\mathsf{var}}^{\dagger}}$ Decision Problem). *Given PPRs R_1, R_2 represented as m_1, m_2 polytopes respectively, and a $\delta \geq 0$, it is decidable to check $\mathcal{D}_{\mathcal{F}_{\mathsf{var}}^{\dagger}}(R_1, R_2) \leq \delta$ for both $L_1^{\max}$ and L_∞ norms on $\mathbb{R}^{d+1}$.* □

The check in Proposition 6 uses the theory of reals and has a high complexity. We show in the next subsection that under certain assumptions on the PPRs, we can obtain a polynomial time procedure.

5.2.5 $\mathbf{\Phi}_{\max}$ Free Space: Polynomial Time Special Case

In this subsection, we obtain a polynomial time algorithm for computing the free space for $\mathbf{\Phi}_{\max}$, under mild conditions on the PPRs.

For a *fixed* λ, we can check if

$$\Phi_{\max}\Big(\lambda \cdot R_1(0) + (1-\lambda) \cdot R_1(1), R_2(0)\Big) \leq \delta.$$

This is done as follows. Consider the optimization problem

$$\begin{aligned} \text{maximize} \quad & \Delta \\ \text{such that} \quad & \left\|\lambda \cdot \boldsymbol{x}^0 + (1-\lambda) \cdot \boldsymbol{x}^1 - \boldsymbol{y}\right\| \geq \Delta \\ & A_1^0 \cdot \boldsymbol{x}^0 \leq \boldsymbol{b}_1^0 \\ & A_1^1 \cdot \boldsymbol{x}^1 \leq \boldsymbol{b}_1^1 \\ & A_2 \cdot \boldsymbol{y} \leq \boldsymbol{b}_2 \\ & 0 \leq \Delta \end{aligned} \tag{23}$$

The following cases arise.

- If the optimal Δ is strictly bigger than δ, then
$$\Phi_{\max}\big(\lambda \cdot R_1(0) + (1-\lambda) \cdot R_1(1),\, R_2(0)\big) > \delta$$
because in this case the constraints in (23) imply that there exist points $\boldsymbol{x}^0 \in R_1(0)$ and $\boldsymbol{x}^1 \in R_1(1)$ and $\boldsymbol{y} \in R_2(0)$ such that $\left\|\lambda \cdot \boldsymbol{x}^0 + (1-\lambda) \cdot \boldsymbol{x}^1 - \boldsymbol{y}\right\| \geq \Delta > \delta$. Hence $\langle\lambda, 0\rangle$ does not belong to the free space.
- If $\Delta \leq \delta$, it implies that $\Phi_{\max}\big(\lambda \cdot R_1(0) + (1-\lambda) \cdot R_1(1),\, R_2(0)\big) \leq \delta$. Hence $\langle\lambda, 0\rangle$ belongs to the free space.

Finally, note that the feasible region of (23) is never empty since for $\Delta = 0$ the variables $\boldsymbol{x}^0, \boldsymbol{x}^1, \boldsymbol{y}$ can range over values in $R_1(0), R_1(1), R_2(0)$ respectively; hence one of the above cases will hold. Problem (23) can be framed as an LP instance by adding additional variables using the same methods as in the case for $\Phi_{\min}$ for $L_1^{\max}$ or L_∞ norms.

If we can find *one* λ value such that $\Phi_{\max}\big(\lambda \cdot R_1(0) + (1-\lambda) \cdot R_1(1),\, R_2(0)\big) \leq \delta$, then we can do binary search over the interval $[0, \lambda]$ to get $\lambda^{\min}$ (and similarly for $\lambda^{\max}$). We next present a heuristic to do this in polynomial time. Fix an integer K, partition $[0,1]$ into K equal intervals, and check for $\lambda = 0, \frac{1}{K}, \frac{2}{K}, \ldots, 1$ whether $\langle\lambda, 0\rangle$ belongs to the free space.

Once the first $\lambda \in \{0, \frac{1}{K}, \frac{2}{K}, \ldots, 1\}$ is found such that $\langle\lambda, 0\rangle$ belongs to the free space, we perform a binary search around it over the interval $(\lambda - 1/K, \lambda]$ to obtain $\lambda^{\min}$ to a desired degree of accuracy (which we take to be less than 2^{-cK} for a constant c for convenience), and similarly for $\lambda^{\max}$. If the binary search fails to obtain a lower or upper boundary, we set the corresponding lower or upper boundary to λ. In total, we solve $O(K)$ instances of problem (23). Suppose that the actual free space interval at the bottom boundary of the cell is $[\lambda^{\min}, \lambda^{\max}] \times \{0\}$. If $\lambda^{\max} - \lambda^{\min} < 1/K$, we *may* find an empty subinterval. If $\lambda^{\max} - \lambda^{\min} \geq 1/K$, we are *guaranteed* to find the interval (to any desired degree of accuracy).

Observe that if the bottom boundary of cell i, j is $[\lambda^{\min}, \lambda^{\max}] \times \{j\}$, then it means that the set of *all* optimal reparameterizations α_1, α_2 in Equation (13) in addition satisfy $\big(\alpha_2(\theta) = j\big) \rightarrow \big(\alpha_1(\theta) \in [\lambda^{\min}, \lambda^{\max}]\big)$. In other words, the polytope at time $\alpha_2(\theta)$ in the PPR R_2 can only be mapped to R_1 polytopes in between times $[\lambda^{\min}, \lambda^{\max}]$. The smaller the interval $[\lambda^{\min}, \lambda^{\max}]$, the more restricted the allowable timing distortions which witness $\mathcal{D}_{\mathcal{F}_{\mathsf{var}}^{\dagger}}(R_1, R_2) \leq \delta$, and thus, the smaller the degree of freedom of time-distorting of the time-point j in R_2; which in turn means the less robust the possible reparameterizations..

Proposition 7 ($\Phi_{\max}$ Free Space in Polyomial time). *Given two* PPR*s R_1 and R_2, the set $\mathsf{Free}_{\delta}^{\Phi_{\max}}(R_1, R_2)$ at the boundaries of cell i, k can be computed to a precision of $O(K)$ bits in time $O\big(K \cdot \mathsf{LP}\,(S_1^i + S_1^{i+1} + S_2^k + S_2^{k+1})\big)$, provided the free space intervals at the cell boundaries, if non-empty, are of length at least $\frac{1}{K}$, where S_j^l denotes the halfspace representation size of polytope $R_j(l)$, and $\mathsf{LP}(\cdot)$ is the (polynomial time) upper bound for solving linear programming.* □

This gives us the following decision procedure using a dynamic programming algorithm, and improves Proposition 6 time complexity if the PPRs satisfy certain conditions.

Proposition 8 ($\mathcal{D}_{\mathcal{F}_{\mathsf{var}}^{\dagger}}$ Decision Problem in Polynomial Time). *Given* PPR*s R_1, R_2 represented by m_1, m_2 polytopes respectively, $\delta \geq 0$, and integer $K > 0$, we can decide the question $\mathcal{D}_{\mathcal{F}_{\mathsf{var}}^{\dagger}}(R_1, R_2) \leq \delta$ under the two conditions:*

1. *$\forall\, i \in \{0..m_1\}$, and $\forall\, j \in \{0..m_2 - 1\}$, either (a) there exists a sub-interval $[\lambda^{\min}, \lambda^{\max}] \subseteq [j, j+1]$, with $\lambda^{\max} - \lambda^{\min} \geq 1/K$, such that $\Phi_{\max}(R_1(i), R_2(t)) \leq \delta$ for all $t \in [\lambda^{\min}, \lambda^{\max}]$, or (b) for all $t \in [j, j+1]$, we have $\Phi_{\max}(R_1(i), R_2(t)) > \delta$; and*
2. *$\forall\, j \in \{0..m_2\}$, and $\forall\, i \in \{0..m_1 - 1\}$, either (a) there exists a sub-interval $[\lambda^{\min}, \lambda^{\max}] \subseteq [i, i+1]$, with $\lambda^{\max} - \lambda^{\min} \geq 1/K$, such that $\Phi_{\max}(R_1(t), R_2(j)) \leq \delta$ for all $t \in [\lambda^{\min}, \lambda^{\max}]$, or (b) for all $t \in [i, i+1]$, we have $\Phi_{\max}(R_1(t), R_2(j)) > \delta$*

in time $O(m_1 \cdot m_2 \cdot K \cdot \mathsf{LP}(S_{\max}))$ for both $L_1^{\max}$, L_∞ norms where $S_{\max}$ is the maximum of the halfspace representation sizes of the given polytopes, and $\mathsf{LP}()$ *is the (polynomial time) upper bound for solving linear programming.* □

An analysis of the dynamic programming reachability algorithm shows that the two conditions in Proposition 8 are only required for an i, j pair collection for which a cell-i, j from the collection occurs in *every* path from $0, 0$ to m_1, m_2 in the free space diagram of the two PPRs. As a result, for a sufficiently large K, we expect the algorithm of this subsection to work in all except for certain pathological cases.

Proposition 8 gives us a conservative procedure in case the validity of the two stated conditions is not known: if for a chosen $K > 0$, the procedure returns that the distance is less than or equal to δ, then indeed $\mathcal{D}_{\mathcal{F}_{\mathsf{var}}^{\dagger}}(R_1, R_2) \leq \delta$. Also note that as δ increases, the corresponding free space and the free space boundaries become larger, and when δ is increases enough, the PPR conditions are satisfied. Since we intend to use the $\mathcal{D}_{\mathcal{F}_{\mathsf{var}}^{\dagger}}$ distances of PPRs as over-approximations of tracepipes, the conservative nature of Proposition 8 does not break the over-approximation scheme.

6. VARIATION DISTANCE BOUNDS

We now put everything together, using the results of the preceding sections to obtain bounds on the variation distance $\mathcal{D}_{\mathcal{S}_{\mathsf{var}}}(F_1, F_2)$ for PPRs F_1 and F_2. From Propositions 2, 1, and Theorems 1, 2, and using binary search on the decision algorithms of Propositions 5 and 6 we get the following theorem.

Theorem 3. *Suppose tracepipes F_1 and F_2 correspond to sampled over-approximate reach set polytopes $\lceil\mathsf{Rp}(F_1)\rceil(t_1^1), \ldots, \lceil\mathsf{Rp}(F_1)\rceil(t_1^{m_1})$ at time-points $t_1^1, \ldots, t_1^{m_1}$, and $\lceil\mathsf{Rp}(F_2)\rceil(t_2^1), \ldots, \lceil\mathsf{Rp}(F_2)\rceil(t_2^{m_2})$ at time-points $t_2^1, \ldots, t_2^{m_2}$ respectively. Let $\lceil\mathsf{Rp}(F_1)\rceil$ and $\lceil\mathsf{Rp}(F_1)\rceil$ be corresponding reachpipe completions constructed by linear interpolation. We can compute $\beta_{\min}, \beta_{\max}$ with*

$$\beta_{\min} \leq \mathcal{D}_{\mathcal{S}_{\mathsf{var}}}(F_1, F_2) \leq \beta_{\max}$$

for the Skorokhod trace metric over L_1, L_∞ norms on $\mathbb{R}^d$ such that

- *$\beta_{\min} = \mathcal{D}_{\mathcal{S}_{\min}}\big(\mathsf{Fp}\,(\lceil\mathsf{Rp}(F_1)\rceil),\, \mathsf{Fp}\,(\lceil\mathsf{Rp}(F_2)\rceil)\big)$ and*
- *$\beta_{\max}$ is an upper-bound of the variation distance $\mathcal{D}_{\mathcal{S}_{\mathsf{var}}}\big(\mathsf{Fp}\,(\lceil\mathsf{Rp}(F_1)\rceil),\, \mathsf{Fp}\,(\lceil\mathsf{Rp}(F_2)\rceil)\big)$; and is equal to the the Skorokhod distance $\mathcal{D}_{\mathcal{S}_{\mathsf{var}}^{\dagger}}(\lceil\mathsf{Rp}(F_1)\rceil, \lceil\mathsf{Rp}(F_2)\rceil)$ between the reachpipes $\lceil\mathsf{Rp}(F_1)\rceil$ and $\lceil\mathsf{Rp}(F_2)\rceil$ (where $\mathcal{D}_{\mathcal{S}_{\mathsf{var}}^{\dagger}}$ is defined analogously to $\mathcal{D}_{\mathcal{F}_{\mathsf{var}}^{\dagger}}$).* □

In order to do binary searches on the decision procedures used in Theorem 3, we need an upper bound U on $\beta_{\max}$. This upper bound can be obtained as follows (in polynomial time). We pick one pair of reparameterizations and use these to get an upper bound U on $\mathcal{D}_{\mathcal{F}_{\mathsf{var}}^{\dagger}}(R_1, R_2)$ (and thus on $\mathcal{D}_{\mathcal{S}_{\mathsf{var}}^{\dagger}}(R_1, R_2)$) for $R_1 = \lceil\mathsf{Rp}(F_1)\rceil$, and $R_2 = \lceil\mathsf{Rp}(F_2)\rceil$.

Assume $m_2 \geq m_1$. Fix $\alpha_1 : [0,1] \to [0, m_1]$ to be any non-decreasing reparameterization such that $\alpha_1(\theta) = m_1$ for $\theta \geq 0.5$; and let $\alpha_2 : [0,1] \to [0, m_1]$ be a non-decreasing reparameterization such that $\alpha_2(\theta) = \alpha_1(\theta)$ for $\theta \leq 0.5$, and α_2 over $[0.5, 1]$ being non-decreasing to $[m_1, m_2]$. An upper bound of $\mathcal{D}_{\mathcal{F}^{\dagger}_{\text{var}}}(R_1, R_2)$ is

$$\max_{0 \leq \theta \leq 1} \Phi_{\max}\left(R_1(\alpha_1(\theta)),\, R_2(\alpha_2(\theta))\right) \tag{24}$$

The stated reparameterizations are such that $R_1(i)$ is compared to $R_2(i)$ for $0 \leq i \leq m_1$ in $\Phi_{\max}$, and $R_2(i)$ for $i > m_1$ is compared to $R_1(m_1)$. It can be shown that the value of Expression (24) is the maximum of $\max_{i \in \{0,1,\ldots,m_1\}} \Phi_{\max}(R_1(i), R_2(i))$ and $\max_{j \in \{m_1,\ldots,m_2\}} \Phi_{\max}(R_1(m_1), R_2(j))$. These two maximums can be computed in polynomial time by computing $\Phi_{\max}(R_1(i), R_2(j))$ for required i, j pairs using linear programming (see [19] for details). Once the upper bound U is obtained, we can compute $\beta_{\min}$ in $O((\lg(U) + B) \cdot m_1 \cdot m_2 \cdot \mathsf{LP}(S_{\max}))$ time, where B is the number of desired bits of the fractional part in $\beta_{\min}$, and $S_{\max}$ is the maximum of the halfspace representation sizes of the given polytopes, and $\mathsf{LP}(\cdot)$ is the (polynomial time) upper bound for solving linear programming.

Polynomial Time Case for $\beta_{\max}$. Theorem 3 uses the theory of reals to obtain $\beta_{\max}$. In case an upper bound U on $\beta_{\max}$ is given and the PPRs and $\delta < U$ are such that the conditions of Proposition 8 are satisfied, we can employ the polynomial time algorithm of the proposition in the decision question queries for obtaining $\beta_{\max}$. This procedure runs in $O((\lg(U) + B) \cdot m_1 \cdot m_2 \cdot K \cdot \mathsf{LP}(S_{\max}))$ time, where K is an integer governing the robustness of retiming functions (in the sense discussed above Proposition 7). Note that if the PPRs do not satisfy the the conditions of Proposition 8, then this procedure will still give an upper bound on $\mathcal{D}_{\text{var}}(\mathsf{Fp}(\lceil \mathsf{Rp}(F_1) \rceil), \mathsf{Fp}(\lceil \mathsf{Rp}(F_2) \rceil))$, but it may be larger than the Skorokhod distance $\mathcal{D}_{\mathcal{S}^{\dagger}_{\text{var}}}(\lceil \mathsf{Rp}(F_1) \rceil, \lceil \mathsf{Rp}(F_2) \rceil)$ between the reachpipes $\lceil \mathsf{Rp}(F_1) \rceil$ and $\lceil \mathsf{Rp}(F_2) \rceil$.

Using Sliding Windows. The Skorokhod metric allows matching an F_1 trace segment in between times t_1^0, t_1^1 to F_2 trace segments in between times $t_2^{m_2-1}, t_2^{m_2}$, *i.e.*, the retimings put no limit on the timing distortions. In practice, we have bounds on timing distortions. As a result, we can restrict the retimings to be in a window W: we require that trace segment j of one trace only be matched to portions of other traces consisting of segments $j - W$ though $j + W$. Under this restriction, the algorithm of Theorem 3 can be improved to run in time $O(((\lg(U) + B) \cdot m \cdot W \cdot K \cdot \mathsf{LP}(S_{\max}))$, where $m = \max(m_1, m_2)$. Usually W, B and K can be taken to be constants, thus we get a practical running time of $O(m \cdot \lg(U) \cdot \mathsf{LP}(S_{\max}))$, which is linear in the number of given polytope reachsets, and linear in the LP solving time involving the largest given polytope representation.

7. CONCLUSIONS

We have considered the problem of determining the distance between two tracepipes. Such problems arise in the analysis of dynamical systems under the presence of uncertainties and noise. Our starting point was the polynomial-time algorithm to compute the Skorokhod metric between individual traces [18]. Our algorithm takes as input discrete sequences of polyhedral approximations to the reach set, such as those provided by symbolic tools such as SpaceEx [13, 10]. Our main result shows polynomial time algorithms to approximate the distance from above and from below.

Acknowledgements. The authors thank Fernando Pereira for helpful discussions; and Raimund Seidel for pointing out the interpretation of reachpipes as set-valued traces for applying the free-space technique.

8. REFERENCES

[1] H. Abbas, B. Hoxha, G.E. Fainekos, J.V. Deshmukh, J. Kapinski, and K. Ueda. Conformance testing as falsification for cyber-physical systems. *CoRR*, abs/1401.5200, 2014.

[2] H. Abbas, H. D. Mittelmann, and G. E. Fainekos. Formal property verification in a conformance testing framework. In *MEMOCODE 2014*, pages 155–164. IEEE, 2014.

[3] H. Alt and M. Godau. Computing the Fréchet distance between two polygonal curves. *Int. J. Comput. Geometry Appl.*, 5:75–91, 1995.

[4] D. Avis, D. Bremner, and R. Seidel. How good are convex hull algorithms? *Comput. Geom.*, 7:265–301, 1997.

[5] S. Basu, R. Pollack, and M.F. Roy. *Algorithms in Real Algebraic Geometry.* Springer-Verlag, 2006.

[6] X. Chen, E. Ábrahám, and S. Sankaranarayanan. Taylor model flowpipe construction for non-linear hybrid systems. In *RTSS 2012*, pages 183–192. IEEE Computer Society, 2012.

[7] A. Chutinan and B. H. Krogh. Computational techniques for hybrid system verification. *IEEE Trans. Automat. Contr.*, 48(1):64–75, 2003.

[8] M. Colón and S. Sankaranarayanan. Generalizing the template polyhedral domain. In *ESOP 2011*, LNCS 6602, pages 176–195. Springer, 2011.

[9] J. V. Deshmukh, R. Majumdar, and V. S. Prabhu. Quantifying conformance using the Skorokhod metric. In *CAV 2015*, LNCS 9207, pages 234–250 Part(II). Springer, 2015.

[10] G. Frehse, C. Le Guernic, A. Donzé, S. Cotton, R. Ray, O. Lebeltel, R. Ripado, A. Girard, T. Dang, and O. Maler. Spaceex: Scalable verification of hybrid systems. In *CAV 2011*, LNCS 6806, pages 379–395. Springer, 2011.

[11] A. Girard. Reachability of uncertain linear systems using zonotopes. In *HSCC 2005*, LNCS 3414, pages 291–305. Springer, 2005.

[12] A. Girard and C. Le Guernic. Zonotope/hyperplane intersection for hybrid systems reachability analysis. In *HSCC*, LNCS 4981, pages 215–228. Springer, 2008.

[13] A. Girard, C. Le Guernic, and O. Maler. Efficient computation of reachable sets of linear time-invariant systems with inputs. In *HSCC 2006*, LNCS 3927, pages 257–271. Springer, 2006.

[14] G.M.Ziegler. *Lectures on Polytopes.* Springer, 1995.

[15] C. Le Guernic and A. Girard. Reachability analysis of linear systems using support functions. *Nonlinear Analysis: Hybrid Systems*, 4(2):250–262, 2010.

[16] Z. Han and B. H. Krogh. Reachability analysis of large-scale affine systems using low-dimensional polytopes. In *HSCC 2006*, LNCS 3927, pages 287–301. Springer, 2006.

[17] A. B. Kurzhanski and P. Varaiya. Ellipsoidal techniques for reachability under state constraints. *SIAM J. Contr. & Optim.*, 45(4):1369–1394, 2006.

[18] R. Majumdar and V. S. Prabhu. Computing the Skorokhod distance between polygonal traces. In *HSCC 2015*, pages 199–208. ACM, 2015.

[19] R. Majumdar and V.S. Prabhu. Computing distances between reach flowpipes. *CoRR*, 1602.03266, 2016.

[20] P. Prabhakar and M. Viswanathan. A dynamic algorithm for approximate flow computations. In *HSCC 2011*, pages 133–142. ACM, 2011.

[21] S. Sankaranarayanan, T. Dang, and F. Ivancic. A policy iteration technique for time elapse over template polyhedra. In *HSCC 2008*, LNCS 4981, pages 654–657. Springer, 2008.

Reachset Conformance Testing of Hybrid Automata

Hendrik Roehm, Jens Oehlerking, Matthias Woehrle
Robert Bosch GmbH, Corporate Research
Renningen, Germany
{firstname.lastname}@de.bosch.com

Matthias Althoff
Department of Informatics
Technische Universität München, Germany
althoff@in.tum.de

ABSTRACT

Industrial-sized hybrid systems are typically not amenable to formal verification techniques. For this reason, a common approach is to formally verify abstractions of (parts of) the original system. However, we need to show that this abstraction conforms to the actual system implementation including its physical dynamics. In particular, verified properties of the abstract system need to transfer to the implementation. To this end, we introduce a formal conformance relation, called reachset conformance, which guarantees transference of safety properties, while being a weaker relation than the existing trace inclusion conformance. Based on this formal relation, we present a conformance testing method which allows us to tune the trade-off between accuracy and computational load. Additionally, we present a test selection algorithm that uses a coverage measure to reduce the number of test cases for conformance testing. We experimentally show the benefits of our novel techniques based on an example from autonomous driving.

CCS Concepts

•Computing methodologies → Model verification and validation; •Software and its engineering → Software verification; Software safety; Software verification and validation; *Dynamic analysis;* **•Computer systems organization →** *Embedded systems;*

Keywords

Conformance; Testing; Reachability Analysis; Test Selection; Hybrid Automata

1. INTRODUCTION

Embedded software controls the evolution of the physical behaviour of systems through a perception-action loop. Typically, this software comes with safety-critical properties that should be verified. Since the software strongly interacts with the physical dynamics, the composed system has to be taken into account for typical verification tasks. Hybrid automata are a suitable modeling formalism for these systems that can be directly used to formally verify embedded software. However, formal verification is computationally expensive and becomes infeasible for larger models of embedded systems. For this reason, a common approach is to use abstractions that are amenable to formal verification [4, 9]. However, when properties are verified on an abstract model, we have to check that they also transfer to the real system, which is often ignored or done in a non-formal way. A formal conformance relation between the systems enables to transfer properties from the abstract model to the real system. Given a class of relevant properties, the conformance relation should be as permissive as possible, yet as strong as necessary to transfer these properties between systems. A major problem is that in practice the conformance between systems cannot be formally shown, because real systems and complex simulation models are typically not amenable to formal techniques. In contrast, conformance testing is possible, which means searching for counter-examples falsifying the considered relation. This is an important condition for the applicability of formal methods for industrial-sized problems, because it substantiates the confidence in the abstract model and the properties verified thereon. For (formal) conformance testing there are three main tasks: (*i*) formally defining the *conformance relation* and proving the *transference* of properties, (*ii*) establishing a sound *conformance check*, such that only true counter-examples are identified, (*iii*) selecting *test inputs*, which produce different be-

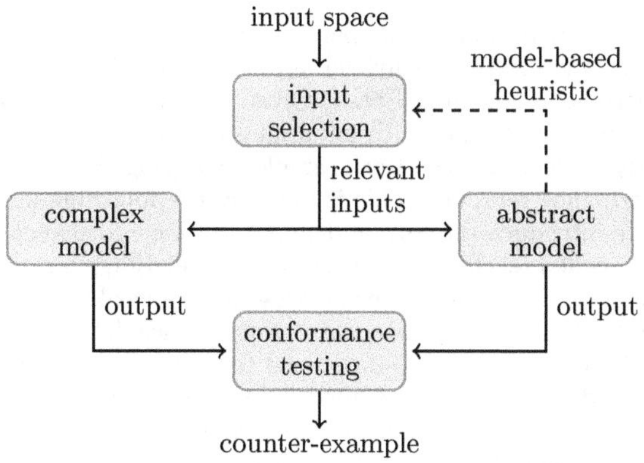

Figure 1: Overall structure of the proposed method.

HSCC'16, April 12 - 14, 2016, Vienna, Austria

ISBN 978-1-4503-3955-1/16/04...$15.00

DOI: http://dx.doi.org/10.1145/2883817.2883828

haviours, because only a limited, finite number of tests can be performed. In this work all three tasks are addressed.

It is essential that conformance testing is as formal as possible, e. g. to have a sound understanding which properties transfer with the given relation. The question in this paper is, which conformance relation should be used for safety properties and how conformance testing of this relation can be done.

Existing notions of conformance mainly determine if the traces of one system are contained in the set of traces of another, see Sec. 7. This is usually not an easy task and leads to very bloated and incomprehensible abstract models. Reachability analysis has been used for conformance testing, but the conformance relation has not been formally defined [4].

The contribution of this paper is a formal framework for conformance testing of hybrid automata considering safety properties, as shown in Fig. 1. Given a complex and an abstract model together with an input space, our method efficiently searches for counter-examples falsifying the reachset conformance relation. This is done by the following steps: (*i*) We introduce the formal definition of a conformance relation, called reachset conformance. The relation guarantees the transference of safety properties and is a weaker relation than the already existing trace conformance (cf. Sec. 3). (*ii*) We formalize the conformance testing approach of Althoff and Dolan [4] and extend it by using tighter overapproximations for inclusion checking and prove the soundness of the presented method. Therefore the trade-off between accuracy and computational load can be freely adapted and errors of simulations and measurements can be considered. (*iii*) We present a model-based input selection algorithm based on a reachset coverage measure. It can be used to reduce the number of tests for a given set of test cases. One benefit of the framework is the possibility to use measurements of a real system directly for falsification of the reachset conformance relation. Finally, we experimentally show that we are able to falsify more conformance relations between systems than the previous work by Althoff and Dolan [4].

In Sec. 2 we give basic definitions, such as hybrid automata, traces, and reachable sets. In Sec. 3 we introduce the formal definition of reachset conformance. We prove the transference of safety properties and the weakness compared to trace conformance. A method for reachset conformance testing for a given input is presented in Sec. 4. For the selection of relevant inputs, an algorithm is introduced in Sec. 5. The results of an autonomous driving example are shown in Sec. 6. Finally, we review the related work in Sec. 7 and give a conclusion in Sec. 8.

2. MODEL AND DEFINITIONS

We model hybrid systems as hybrid automata with inputs and outputs. Let $\|g\|_2$ be the Euclidean vector norm of a vector g and g^T be the transpose of a vector. We use $u(.)$ as a notation for an input trajectory and $u(t)$ as an input at time t.

Our definition of a *hybrid automaton* is a finite automaton whose discrete states are annotated with differential inclusions that define the evolution of the continuous states. Due to non-deterministic modeling, we use differential inclusions for the continuous flow resulting in infinitely many solutions for a given initial state. The initially possible states are given by the initial set and according to the continuous evolution and the input, the system can switch its discrete state. Here, we consider hybrid automata that take continuous input functions $u(.) : \mathbb{R}^+ \to \mathbb{R}^d$ from a set $U(.)$ of input functions to influence the evolution. For a more precise definition of hybrid automata, defining invariant sets, guard conditions, and reset maps, we refer to the work of Mitchell [18]. For simplicity, we assume that all hybrid automata are non-zeno and non-blocking and for every input there exists at least one solution.

A (state) solution x of the hybrid automaton S under a given input $u(.) \in U(.)$ is a trajectory that has the form

$$x = (q_0, x_0(.))(q_1, x_1(.)) \dots$$

where q_i are discrete states and $x_i : [t_i, t_{i+1}] \to \mathbb{R}^n$ is the continuous evolution between t_i and t_{i+1} with $t_0 = 0$ and $t_{i+1} \geq t_i$.

For one solution x, the output trace that is the mapping of the state solution onto the observable output space, is defined as $\tau : \mathbb{R}^+ \to \mathbb{R}^m$, where

$$\forall i \; \forall t \in [t_i, t_{i+1}) : \quad \tau(t) = O(q_i, x_i(t))$$

holds, where O is the output mapping. The set of all output traces under an input $u(.)$ is denoted by $\mathit{Traces}(S, u(.))$. If $\mathit{Traces}(S, u(.))$ has one element only for every $u(.)$, the system S is called deterministic. For a finite subset of time instances $T \subset \mathbb{R}^+$, the sampled trace of τ is the restriction to the preimage T

$$\tau_T : T \to \mathbb{R}^m, t \mapsto \tau(t).$$

For one point in time t, the reachable set of S at time t is defined as

$$\mathit{Reach}_t(S, u(.)) = \{\tau(t) \mid \tau \in \mathit{Traces}(S, u(.))\}$$

for a given input trajectory $u(.)$.

The elements of *Traces* are functions over time, whereas the set Reach_t consists of output states for one point in time t. Note that we define both in the output space, but not in the state space as done in other works (cf. [4]). We also consider a set of initial states but do not annotate this with a subscript. In the following, when we talk about systems, we assume they are modelled as hybrid automata.

3. REACHSET CONFORMANCE

Throughout the paper we use two systems S_r and S_a. The system S_r represents a real system or a complex simulation model that is not amenable to formal verification techniques. However, we can obtain measurements of executions or simulation runs for a given input. The system S_a is an abstract model that is simple enough to be used for formal verification. The main question here is if S_r conforms to S_a and which properties transfer.

First, we discuss the existing *trace conformance* relation used in [7]. Although it is a very strong relation that enables the transference of all properties which are ∀-quantified over the traces, it is also difficult to generate an abstract model S_a where it holds. If the focus is on the transference of safety properties, such as collision-free trajectories for autonomous vehicles, such a strong relation is not needed. Therefore, we define the weaker *reachset conformance* relation that is able to transfer such properties. This enables us to transfer safety properties between systems where the trace conformance does not hold.

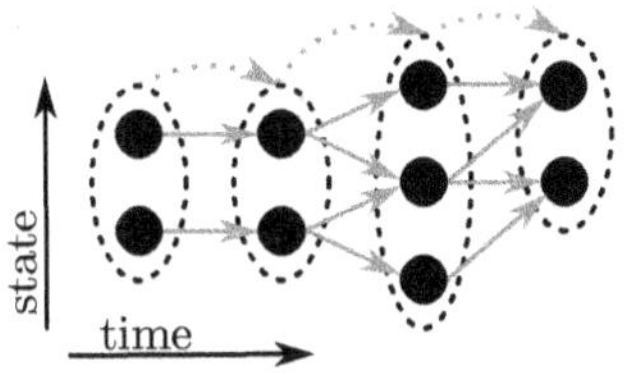

Figure 2: The reachable sets do not maintain the individual state transitions. Solid: States and transitions, dotted: Reachable sets and their transitions.

3.1 Trace conformance

In this subsection, we discuss the conformance relation used for instance by Dang [7] (cf. Sec. 7).

DEFINITION 1 (TRACE CONFORMANCE). *Let S_r and S_a be two systems with the same input set and output space, then S_r is trace conformant to S_a, denoted by $S_r \preceq_{Tr} S_a$, iff*

$$Traces(S_r, u(.)) \subseteq Traces(S_a, u(.))$$

holds for all $u(.) \in U(.)$.

The trace conformance reflects the conventional notion of conformance of discrete automata where traces of one system also have to be traces of the other. When the trace conformance does hold, all properties with an $\forall$-quantifier over traces, such as Metric Temporal Logic formulas, transfer (cf. [1]). However, considering safety properties only, for the trace conformance check of nondeterministic hybrid systems, we have to deal with two problems: (1) We have to check a relation that transfers more properties than we are interested in. Therefore we can relate less systems without any benefit. (2) For conformance testing we have to sample not only the input space but also the nondeterminism of the system leading to more traces needed for a test coverage. In the following subsection we define the reachset conformance relation to overcome the mentioned problems.

3.2 Reachset conformance

We now introduce the formal definition of a reachset conformance relation which is able to preserve safety properties, such as non-intersection with unsafe states. It is weaker than trace conformance and can be checked by applying the whole range of methods from reachability analysis.

Inspired by Althoff and Dolan [4], we formally define a new notion of conformance that focuses not on the set of traces, but on the set of reachable states.

DEFINITION 2 (REACHSET CONFORMANCE). *Let S_r and S_a be two systems with the same input set and output space, then S_r is reachset conformant to S_a, denoted by $S_r \preceq_R S_a$, iff*

$$Reach_t(S_r, u(.)) \subseteq Reach_t(S_a, u(.)) \quad (1)$$

holds for all $u(.) \in U(.)$ and $t \geq 0$.

The proposed reachset conformance allows the transference of safety properties from S_a to S_r:

PROPOSITION 1. *Let two systems S_r and S_a be given with $S_r \preceq_R S_a$. For any input trajectory $u(.)$ and any unsafe set B_t the following transference holds for every t:*

$$Reach_t(S_a, u(.)) \cap B_t = \emptyset \Rightarrow Reach_t(S_r, u(.)) \cap B_t = \emptyset.$$

Since the relation considers only reachsets, we do not have to maintain the individual dependences of each reachable state for one time instance to another as depicted in Fig. 2. Since trace conformance considers the entire signals, it is a stronger relation.

PROPOSITION 2. *Let S_r and S_a be two systems with the same input set and output space, then*

$$S_r \preceq_{Tr} S_a \quad \Rightarrow \quad S_r \preceq_R S_a \quad (2)$$

holds. The converse holds if the system S_a is deterministic.

PROOF. Let $u(.)$ be an input trajectory, t a point in time, and $y \in Reach_t(S_r, u(.))$ and $S_r \preceq_{Tr} S_a$. Then, there is a $\tau \in Traces(S_r, u(.))$ with $\tau(t) = y$. From $S_r \preceq_{Tr} S_a$ it follows, that τ is also a trace of S_a and $y \in Reach_t(S_a, u(.))$. The proposition follows, because the aforementioned implication holds for all y, t, and $u(.)$. When the system S_a is deterministic, there is only one trace in $Traces(S_a, u(.))$ and the reachable sets consist of only one state. Hence S_r has the same trace and is also deterministic. □

The main difference between trace and reachset conformance consists in the handling of nondeterminism. In the following, we present an example to give a better understanding of the conformance notions and to show that the reverse implication of Eq. (2) does not hold in general.

EXAMPLE 1. *For the sake of simplicity, we pick two continuous systems without inputs. Let S_r be a 2-dim. system with $F((x_1, x_2)^T) = (x_2, -x_1)^T$, output map $O((x_1, x_2)^T) = x_1$, and initial set*

$$A = \{(x_1, x_2)^T \mid x_1^2 + x_2^2 = 0.5\}.$$

Then the set of traces is

$$Traces(S_r) = \{0.5 \sin(t + c) \mid c \in [-\pi, \pi)\}$$

and the reachable set is the time-invariant set

$$Reach_t(S_r) = [-0.5, 0.5] \quad \forall t \geq 0.$$

Let S_a be a 1-dim. abstract system with $F(x) = 0$, initial set $A = [-1, 1]$, and output map $O(x) = x$. Then the set of traces is

$$Traces(S_a) = \{x(t) \mid \exists c \in [-1, 1] \, \forall t : x(t) = c\}$$

and the reachable set is $Reach_t(S_a) = [-1, 1]$ for all $t \geq 0$.

Since both reachable sets are constant over time, it is easy to see that S_r is reachset conformant to S_a. However, all traces of S_a are constant traces, so none *of the sine traces of S_r is contained in S_a and S_r is not trace conformant to S_a. In Fig. 3 the reachable sets and some traces are shown. Although we use non-determinism only for the initial set, we also could use non-deterministic flow to design a similar example.*

Even though the system traces could be very different, we can nevertheless reason about safety properties of the system S_r with the abstract system S_a. A key point for applicability is an implementable conformance checking framework. Therefore, in the rest of the paper we are dealing with how to check reachset conformance.

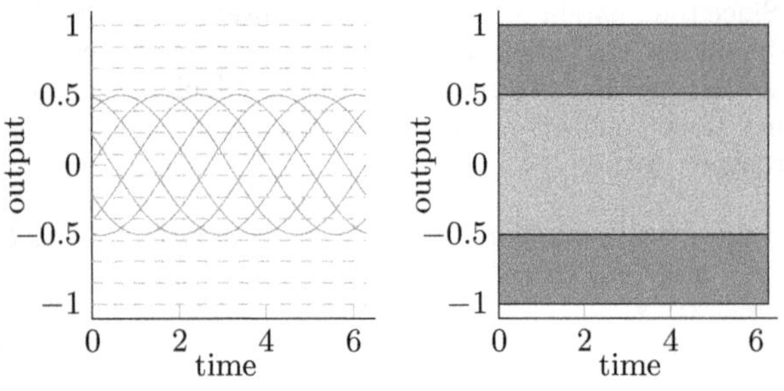

(a) some traces (b) reachable sets

Figure 3: Systems S_r (solid, light gray) and S_a (dashed, dark gray) of Example 1.

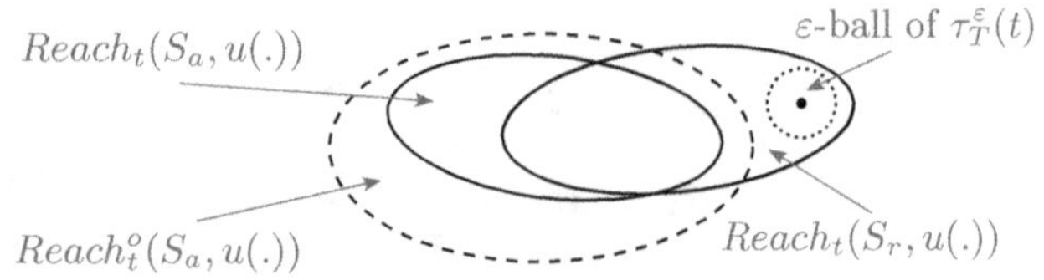

Figure 4: A counter-example falsifying the reachset conformance, because overapproximation (dashed) and ε-ball (dotted) are disjoint.

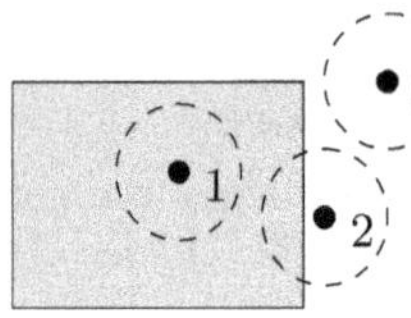

Figure 5: Error aware inclusion check: The true point is somewhere in the ball around the erroneous point, thus only point 3 is a non-spurious counter-example.

4. REACHSET CONFORMANCE TESTING

In practice, it is hard to show that Eq. (1) holds for two systems S_r and S_a, because the system S_r is too complex and high-dimensional for formal methods, such as reachable set computations. However, falsification is possible by providing a counter-example proving the negation of Eq. (1):

$$\exists u(.) \in U(.) \exists t \geq 0 \, Reach_t(S_r, u(.)) \not\subseteq Reach_t(S_a, u(.)) \quad (3)$$

A practical approach is to use simulation runs or real data measurements as underapproximations of the reachable sets $Reach_t(S_r, u(.))$. Since neither the simulations nor the measurements provide exact data, we have to consider numerical errors or measurement errors. Therefore, we have to deal with an error bound ε and an approximation τ_T^ε of the true timed trace τ_T with

$$\max_{t \in T} \|\tau_T^\varepsilon(t) - \tau_T(t)\|_2 \leq \varepsilon. \quad (4)$$

Note that many other norms can be used, although the Euclidean norm is used here for the ease of presentation (cf. [17]). An overapproximation of the reachable set of S_a and an erroneous trace of S_r can be used to prove that S_r is not reachset conformant to S_a as depicted in Fig. 4.

PROPOSITION 3 (COUNTER-EXAMPLE). *A counter-example, falsifying the conformance relation $S_r \preceq_R S_a$ consists of*

1. *An input trajectory $u(.) \in U(.)$,*
2. *A point in time t,*
3. *An overapproximation $Reach_t^o(S_a, u(.))$ of the reachable set of S_a,*
4. *A sampled, erroneous trace $\tau_T^\varepsilon(.)$ of system S_r under input $u(.)$ with $t \in T$,*

where all elements x of the output space with $\|x - \tau_T^\varepsilon(t)\|_2 \leq \varepsilon$ are not contained in $Reach_t^o(S_a, u(.))$. This implies $S_r \not\preceq_R S_a$.

PROOF. Using Eq. (4), $\tau_T(t) = \tau(t)$ is also not contained in $Reach_t^o(S_a, u(.))$ which proves Eq. (3) and thus Eq. (1) cannot hold. □

An example is depicted in Fig. 5. If we check the erroneous sampled trace without considering the error, we get the points 2 and 3 as counter-examples. However, the true point 2 could possibly be contained in the box and we cannot be sure that it is not. By considering the error we are able to find the non-spurious counter-example point 3 only.

One advantage of this approach is that the sampled trace does not have to be a simulation. Erroneous measurements of the real system can be used also to falsify abstract models, which plays an important role for the applicability of model-based design. In the following we describe how to check for counter-examples.

4.1 Fixed input conformance testing

In this subsection, the conformance testing method as introduced by Althoff and Dolan [4] is described. In the following subsection we develop this method further and take the error bound ε for trace errors into account. This will lead to sound counter-examples and to more system pairs where the non-conformance can be proven.

The goal is to check if the non-conformance $S_r \not\preceq_R S_a$ can be shown by a counter-example for a given input $u(.)$. The test consists of 3 steps:

1. Compute an underapproximation $Reach_t^u(S_r, u(.))$ of the reachable states of S_r for any time t within a finite set T of points in time.
2. Compute an overapproximation $Reach_t^o(S_a, u(.))$ of the reachable set of S_a for each $t \in T$.
3. If $Reach_t^u(S_r, u(.)) \not\subseteq Reach_t^o(S_a, u(.))$ holds for any $t \in T$, at least one counter-example is found.

Rapidly-exploring random trees (RRTs) can be used to underapproximate $Reach_t(S_r, u(.))$, as described in [4]. They provide an efficient way of estimating the reachable set for complex systems by simulations and can also be used for black-box models, of which the dynamics are not known. As mentioned above, the first step could also be replaced by real measurements of a system.

The overapproximation of S_a can be efficiently computed using reachability analysis. Here, we consider the reachability tool CORA [3], where reachable set overapproximations are represented by zonotopes. Zonotopes are special convex set representations for efficient linear transformations and Minkowski addition (cf. [5]).

DEFINITION 3 (ZONOTOPE). *A n-dimensional zonotope Z in generator representation (G-representation) is the set*

$$Z = z(c, \langle g_1, \dots, g_m \rangle) := \left\{ c + \sum_{i=1}^{m} \lambda_i g_i \middle| \lambda_i \in [-1, 1] \right\},$$

where $c \in \mathbb{R}^n$ is the center and $g_1, \dots, g_m \in \mathbb{R}^n$ are the generators of Z.

Zonotopes are special, point symmetric polytopes:

DEFINITION 4 (POLYTOPE). *A n-dimensional polytope P in halfspace representation (H-representation) is the set*

$$P = p(H, k) := \{x \in \mathbb{R}^n \mid H \cdot x \leq k\}$$

with $H \in \mathbb{R}^{m \times n}$, $k \in \mathbb{R}^m$, also called a m-polytope.

The inclusion check by Althoff and Dolan [4] is done by abstracting from the zonotope and the samples to axis-aligned bounding boxes. Let v be the vector representing the box size in each dimension, then $v = 2\sum_{i=1}^{m} |g_i|$ holds. Although the inclusion check is very fast, it introduces a very coarse overapproximation which leads to a conservative falsification result found with less counter-examples found. This problem actually increases with the number of output dimensions. Therefore we introduce a new approach for inclusion checking.

4.2 A configurable inclusion check with error-awareness

In this subsection we introduce a new inclusion check for points in a zonotope which leads to more counter-examples and a less conservative falsification result as later demonstrated in Sec. 6.3. We achieve this by reducing the error introduced by the transformation of the zonotope to an easily checkable representation. A useful approximation should give the possibility to configure the trade-off between accuracy and computational time, while providing an estimation of the approximation error. With the following inclusion check the trade-off can be freely adapted.

Reachability analysis for nonlinear dynamics with high accuracy needs a lot of generators, sometimes more than 1000. Because of scaling problems, methods that are only usable for a small number of generators are not directly applicable. Therefore, we are using overapproximations of zonotopes for the inclusion check.

In the following, let Z be a n-dimensional zonotope with center c and generators $g_1, \dots, g_m$. For a polytope P in H-representation, a point x is contained in P, iff all inequalities $H \cdot x \leq k$ hold. This can be efficiently computed. Since zonotopes are special polytopes, they can be transformed to H-representation by using one inequality for every facet. However, Althoff et al. [5] showed that for a zonotope in dimension n with m independent generators the number of facets is $2\begin{pmatrix} m \\ n-1 \end{pmatrix}$. Hence, the exact transformation approach does not scale, especially for $m \geq 1000$ and $n \geq 3$. However, by using support functions, described by Girard et al. [11, 17], the zonotope can be tightly overapproximated.

DEFINITION 5 (SUPPORT FUNCTION). *Let a zonotope Z be given. Then for $d \in \mathbb{R}^n$ the support function of Z is*

$$\rho_Z(d) = \max_{x \in Z} d^T \cdot x = d^T \cdot c + \sum_{i=1}^{m} |d^T \cdot g_i|.$$

Since the resulting overapproximation is a polytope, the H-representation can be used for inclusion checking. The zonotope is point symmetric to its center. Therefore, the directions d and $-d$ can be easily checked together. Hence, the inclusion in a $2l$-polytope can be checked with l directions.

PROPOSITION 4 (OVERAPPROXIMATION). *Let a finite set of directions $D \subset \mathbb{R}^n$ and a zonotope Z be given. Then*

$$Z \subseteq \bigcap_{d \in D} H_d$$

holds, where H_d are the halfspaces

$$H_d = \{x \in \mathbb{R}^n \mid d^T \cdot x \leq \rho_Z(d)\}.$$

A point $x \in \mathbb{R}^n$ is contained in $H_d \cap H_{-d}$, iff

$$|d^T \cdot x - d^T \cdot c| \leq \rho_Z(d) - d^T \cdot c$$

holds [10].

Using this polytope, the inclusion can be checked for the approximation τ_T^{ε} using the error bound ε as shown next.

PROPOSITION 5 (INCLUSION CHECK). *Let τ_T^{ε} and an overapproximation Z of the reachable set $Reach_t(S_a, u(.))$ be given. The inequality*

$$|d^T \cdot \tau_T^{\varepsilon}(t) - d^T \cdot c| > \rho_Z(d) - d^T \cdot c + \varepsilon \|d\|_2 \quad (5)$$

for any d implies that the real state $\tau(t)$ is not contained in $Reach_t(S_a, u(.))$.

PROOF. If the center c of the zonotope is not the origin, we can translate the zonotope and the point with $-c$. Therefore, without loss of generality $c = 0$ and $\|d\|_2 = 1$ holds. Let us assume the real state $\tau(t)$ is contained in the zonotope Z and Eq. (5) holds. This leads to the equation

$$|d^T \cdot \tau_T^{\varepsilon}(t)| > \rho_Z(d) + \varepsilon \geq |d^T \cdot \tau(t)| + \varepsilon. \quad (6)$$

However Eq. (4) and the triangle inequality lead to

$$|d^T \cdot \tau_T^{\varepsilon}(t)| \leq |d^T \cdot \tau(t)| + |d^T \cdot (\tau_T^{\varepsilon}(t) - \tau(t))| \leq |d^T \cdot \tau(t)| + \varepsilon,$$

which is a contradiction to Eq. (6) □

The directions remain as free parameters, so that we can tune the accuracy and computational cost with their selection. For example, when selecting the directions e_i, where the e_i are the canonical basis vectors, the aforementioned box overapproximation used by Althoff and Dolan [4] is obtained. Hence, it is a special case of the presented method.

Since a priori there is no knowledge about the zonotope generators, the selected directions should be evenly distributed over the space of possible directions or evenly distributed over one halfspace of $\mathbb{R}^n$ considering the symmetry of the zonotope. While optimization-based direction generation methods iteratively improve their solution, explicit methods have the advantage of directly generating good directions. In 2 dimensions, l evenly distributed directions $d_1, \dots, d_l$ are

$$d_i = \left(\cos\left(\frac{i\pi}{l}\right), \sin\left(\frac{i\pi}{l}\right) \right)^T. \quad (7)$$

In 3 dimensions, the Fibonacci lattice can be used, as described by González [13]. The directions $d_1, \dots, d_l$ are generated via

$$d_i = (\sin(lat_i)\cos(lon_i), \sin(lat_i)\sin(lon_i), \cos(lat_i))^T, \quad (8)$$

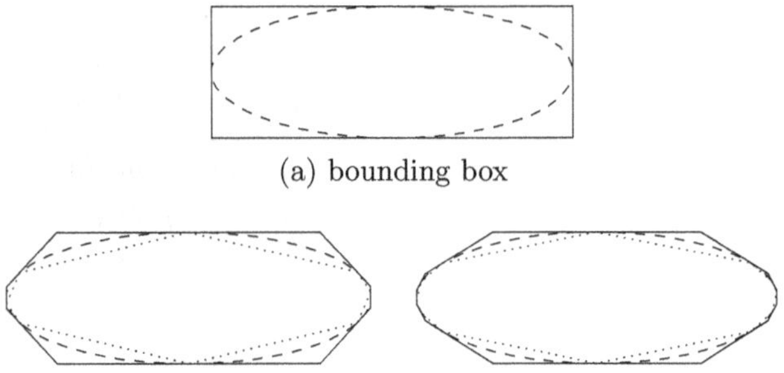

(a) bounding box

(b) 4 directions (c) 6 directions

Figure 6: Example of overapproximations (solid) and underapproximations (dotted) of a zonotope (dashed).

where the angles are

$$lat_i = \arcsin\left(\frac{2(i-1)}{2l-1}\right) \text{ and } lon_i = \pi(i-1)(\sqrt{5}-1)$$

As far as we know, there is no applicable explicit method in higher dimensions, hence in this case we use an optimization-based direction generation method. Since we are generating evenly distributed directions in a preprocessing step and use the same set for every inclusion check over time, the computational load of the direction generation is independent of the number of inclusion checks.

To generate good directions by optimization, a simple method by Frehse et al. [9] is used. First, m directions are randomly generated. Then, a direction d is randomly generated and the nearest direction is replaced by d if the distribution of the other directions with d is more uniform. This can be done as long as a termination condition on the uniformity is not fulfilled.

EXAMPLE 2 (ELLIPSE). *In Fig. 6, an 2D example is presented. The considered zonotope $Z = z(0, \langle g_1, \dots, g_{20}\rangle)$ has 20 generators*

$$g_i = \left(3\sin\left(\frac{\pi i}{20}\right), \cos\left(\frac{\pi i}{20}\right)\right)^T$$

and is very close to an ellipse. The overapproximations are generated via Eq. (7). While the box overapproximation is very coarse, the configurable approximation consisting of 4 respectively 6 directions that approximate the zonotope more tightly. With more or less directions the accuracy and computational time can be tuned. Note that with l directions the used overapproximation is a $2l$-polytope.

In Fig. 6 one can see that the overapproximation is not very tight if different dimensions have different scales. Therefore we normalize the directions according to the axis-aligned bounding box of the zonotope to produce a tighter overapproximation. Let $W = diag(v_1, \dots, v_n)$ be the diagonal matrix consisting of the box size of each dimension of the bounding box. Then a direction d is normalized to

$$d' := W^{-1}d. \tag{9}$$

EXAMPLE 3. *Considering the normalization with $W = diag(3,1)$ for the ellipse of Example 2, the approximation is tighter as depicted in Fig. 7.*

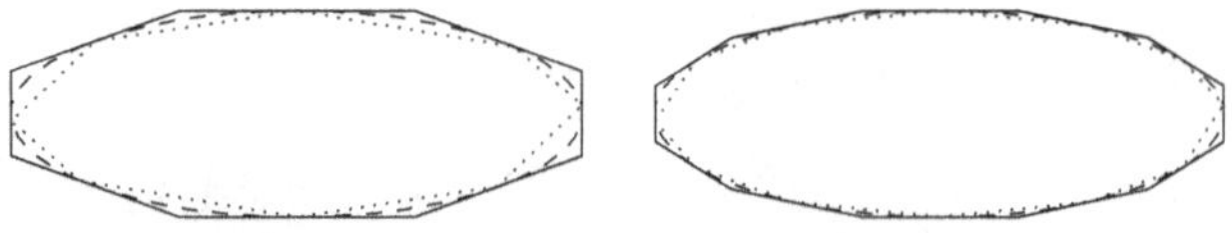

(a) 4 directions (b) 6 directions

Figure 7: Example of overapproximations (solid) and underapproximations (dotted) of a zonotope (dashed) with normalized directions.

With Eq. (9) and (5) the inclusion check for a overapproximation Z, a set of directions D, and a set of points M with maximum error ε, can be implemented. If a counterexample is found, it will be returned. Otherwise, false will be returned. For a practical example and comparison of the introduced method, see Sec. 6.3.

4.3 Quality of the zonotope overapproximation

Since overapproximations of zonotopes are used for the inclusion check, the non-inclusion of some points cannot be seen. Therefore, we want to quantify the error introduced by the overapproximation, e.g. to decide if more directions are needed. Althoff et al. [5] introduced a relative quality measure $\Theta := \sqrt[n]{\frac{vol(W\cdot Z^o)}{vol(W\cdot Z)}}$ for the overapproximation Z^o of a n-dimensional zonotope Z. The volume vol in $\mathbb{R}^n$ is defined as the Lebesgue measure and the matrix W is a normalization matrix. Since the exact volume of the zonotope Z cannot be computed easily, the quality measure is not directly applicable here. Therefore we present a method to bound the overapproximation error.

Every support function $\rho_Z(d)$ comes with an extremal point

$$p_d := c + \sum_{i=1}^{m} sign(d^T \cdot g_i) g_i$$

of the zonotope and the convex hull of these points forms an underapproximation of the zonotope, as shown in [12]. Thus, this can be used to get a bound for the approximation error.

PROPOSITION 6. *The measure $\Theta_* := \sqrt[n]{\frac{vol(W\cdot Z^o)}{vol(W\cdot Z^u)}}$ with $Z^u := convexhull(\{p_d \mid d \in D\})$ is an upper bound for the relative error and $vol(W\cdot Z^o) \leq \Theta_*^n vol(W\cdot Z)$ holds.*

Since the approximating polytopes have less facets than the original zonotope, it is faster to compute the volumes.

EXAMPLE 4. *In the 2-dimensional Example 2 the relative size of the configurable approximation can be bounded by $\Theta_* = 1.161$ respectively $\Theta_* = 1.098$, whereas with normalization in Example 3 the bounds are $\Theta_* = 1.079$ respectively $\Theta_* = 1.036$.*

5. INPUT SELECTION AND COVERAGE

In the previous section we describe how to check conformance for a given input. However, we have not yet discussed how to select the inputs. This is an important step, because when inputs are selected such that they nearly generate the same output, the conformance check might miss behaviours which are non-conformant. Hence, we are interested in selecting the inputs that produce different outputs. Furthermore, we are interested in a small number of

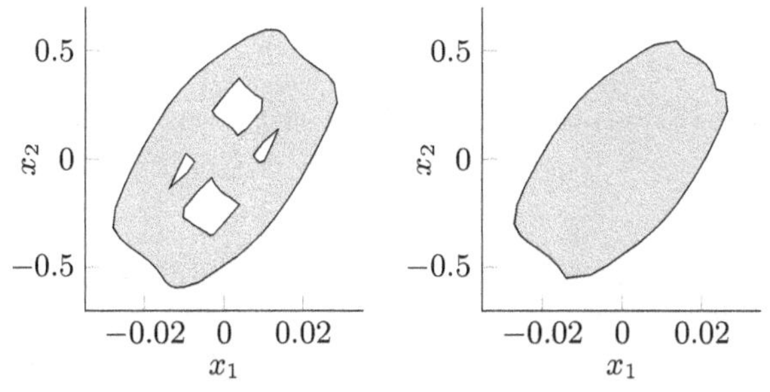

Figure 8: Example of the covered state space (gray) for different inputs.

test cases, because simulation results of a complex system and real measurements are costly to obtain. Therefore we present a method to reduce the number of test cases from a generated finite test set.

Since we are focusing on non-deterministic models for S_a in this paper, we assume that the reachable sets have a volume greater than zero. Otherwise, one has to consider only the spanned dimensions. Due to non-determinism, these dimensions are time-invariant and can be selected offline.

To speed up the process, we introduce a method to preselect input trajectories without computing the output of both systems and without conformance checking. In literature, different methods for input sampling have been introduced, such as Monte Carlo sampling. Another method presented by Dang [7] generates input samples based on rapidly-exploring random trees such that the reachable space is approximately covered. However, not all of the generated inputs can be performed on the original model, because this is too costly. Assuming a finite set of test cases U_1 is generated by the aforementioned methods, we present a method to select an input subset U_2. The method compares different inputs by comparing the reachsets of S_a under the inputs. Therefore, input trajectories whose output can be also achieved by another input trajectory with non-determinism can be removed. The assumption is that inputs reaching the same states on system S_a are less interesting for conformance testing than other inputs that reach new states for S_a.

Hence, we are interested in an input set that covers the reachable set of the system S_a. Although a priori the overall reachable set is not known, we are able to use the reachable sets $Reach_t(S_a, u(.))$ to define a coverage measure and select a relevant subset U_2 of an input set U_1.

DEFINITION 6 (COVERAGE MEASURE). *Let a system S and an input set U be given. Then the covered state space is*

$$Reach(S,U) = \bigcup_{u(.)\in U} \bigcup_{t\geq 0} Reach_t(S,u(.))$$

and a coverage measure is $vol(W \cdot Reach(S,U))$, where W is a normalization matrix similar to the one in Eq. (9).

Since exact reachable set comparison and volume computation is typically not possible for nonlinear dynamics and complex geometric sets, we evaluate it in an overapproximative way, denoted by $Reach^o$. This can be used as a heuristic to iteratively pick the input that increases the state space coverage the most. For example in Fig. 8 the right input covers a bigger part of the state space than the left one and thus should be selected. The covered space of the selected inputs is compared to the initial covered space by the input set U_1.

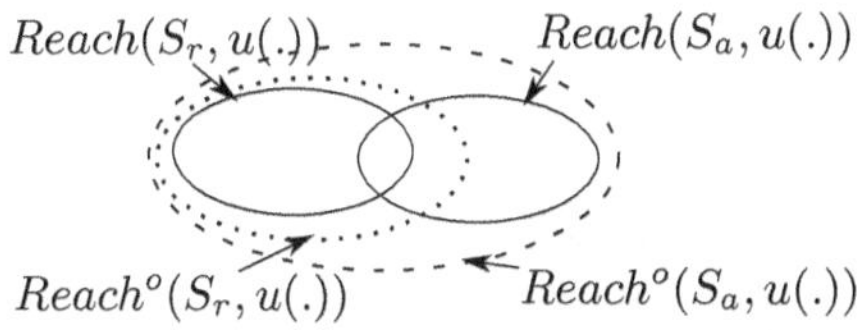

Figure 9: Comparison of the overapproximation does not lead to a non-spurious statement of the reachable sets.

DEFINITION 7 (RELATIVE COVERAGE). *Let two sets of inputs U_1 and U_2 with $U_2 \subseteq U_1$ for a system S be given. Then the relative covered state space is*

$$rcov(S, U_1, U_2) = \frac{vol_2}{vol_1},$$

where the vol_i are computed as the volumes of $Reach(S, U_i)$ as defined in Def. 6.

A greedy input selection algorithm can be implemented by iteratively choosing the input which increases the coverage measure the most. With a given parameter ϵ for the relative coverage needed, we can adapt the trade-off between reaching the whole covered state space of U_1 and the size of the input set U_2. If the dimensions have different scales, a normalization for the volume computation could be applied via W to get a better representation of small scale dimensions.

If we compare the overapproximation for two input trajectories, we cannot formally argue about inclusions. As depicted in Fig. 9, the overapprox. $Reach^o(S_r, u(.))$ of system S_r is enclosed by the overapproximation $Reach^o(S_a, u(.))$, although the covered state space $Reach(S_r, u(.))$ is not contained in $Reach(S_a, u(.))$. To prove that $Reach(S_r, u(.))$ is contained in $Reach(S_a, u(.))$ we would need an underapproximation. Since, as far as the authors know, tools that compute tight underapproximations do not exist yet, especially for nonlinear dynamics, $Reach^o$ is used as a heuristic only and does not give formal bounds. Often, the overapproximation is relatively close to the exact reachable set and therefore the heuristic is also close to the theoretically intended measure.

6. EXPERIMENTS

In this section the presented methods are evaluated on an example from the domain of autonomous driving. We first describe which models we use, how the inputs are selected, and then how the directions are chosen for conformance testing. Finally, we show and discuss the numerical results.

6.1 Models

We consider the setup and the two models used by Althoff and Dolan [4] with the friction coefficient $\mu = 0.9$. The systems S_r and S_a are models of an autonomous car that follows a planned trajectory. The model S_a is a 6-dimensional continuous bicycle model which models: The 2-dimensional position of the center of mass x and y, the heading angle ψ, the yaw rate $\dot{\psi}$, the velocity v, and the slip angle β. The model S_r published by Allen et al. [2, Appendix A] is a more complex model with 28 continuous variables and bounded actuators, thus it has some simple hybrid behaviour. The output of S_r is the projection of its states onto the state space of S_a and thus 6-dimensional. The non-determinism of both systems models sensor inaccuracies, such as disturbances in the position perception.

Since the bicycle model has simplified dynamics and especially simplifies the estimation of slip angle β and the friction influence on v, additional non-determinism of the bicycle model flow is introduced for β and v

$$\dot{\beta} \in F_\beta(.) + [-d_\beta, d_\beta], \quad \dot{v} \in F_v(.) + [-2d_v, 0],$$

where $F_\beta(.)$ and $F_v(.)$ are the differential equations of β and v without non-determinism and d_β, d_v are the parametric bounds of the non-determinism.

The input space of the models consists of trajectories of the x- and y-position, the heading angle, the yaw rate, and the velocity $(x, y, \psi, \dot{\psi}, v)$ with initial state $(0, 0, 0, 0, 15)$ and evolutions bounded by

$$\|(a_x, a_y)^T\|_2 < 7[m/s^2] \text{ and } \|(\dot{a}_x, \dot{a}_y)^T\|_2 < 50[m/s^3]$$

where $a_.$ is the x- respectively y-acceleration of the vehicle. Furthermore, we fix the velocity to $15[m/s]$ for simplicity of presentation.

6.2 Input selection

The input space is randomly sampled by input trajectories, where the lateral acceleration is constant for 0.2 seconds respectively approaches the choosen acceleration with maximum acceleration rate. Therefore, we get a set of inputs U_1 with 5000 driving maneuvers of 2 seconds length.

Since vehicle dynamics are invariant with respect to position x, y and heading angle ψ, we do not consider these state variables for the coverage measure and thus project the reachable set to the other state variables. The method described in Sec. 5 is used to choose the set of inputs U_2 with $\varepsilon = 0.96$. The resulting four input trajectories are compared to other sets of inputs that are random selections of the same size. Since the coverage computation and the input selection took only slightly more time compared to one full inclusion check, it successfully speeded up the conformance test.

6.3 Inclusion check

We discretized the time into around 3500 points. For every point in time, the RRT-algorithm generated 70 samples from the reachable set of S_r and the zonotope overapproximation of the reachable set of S_a is generated. The inclusion check with normalized directions is done as described in Sec. 4 using 4 different direction selection methods: (i) Axis-aligned bounding boxes, (ii) overapproximations on every 2D projection on two state dimensions, (iii) overapproximations on every 3D projection on three state dimensions, (iv) overapproximation with evenly distributed directions in 6D. For the 2D and 3D projections we consider all possible projections and select the directions according to Eq. (7) and Eq. (8) in Sec. 4. The evenly distributed directions in 6D are obtained by the optimization method, described in Sec. 4. Consider that we use the same amount of directions for all methods, except for the box check, as shown in Table 1.

6.4 Results

The results for the four directions selections and 257 sampled values for each parameter d_β and d_v of the abstract

boxes	2D proj.	3D proj.	evenly in 6D
6	$15 \cdot 40$	$20 \cdot 30$	600

Table 1: Number of directions used for each method.

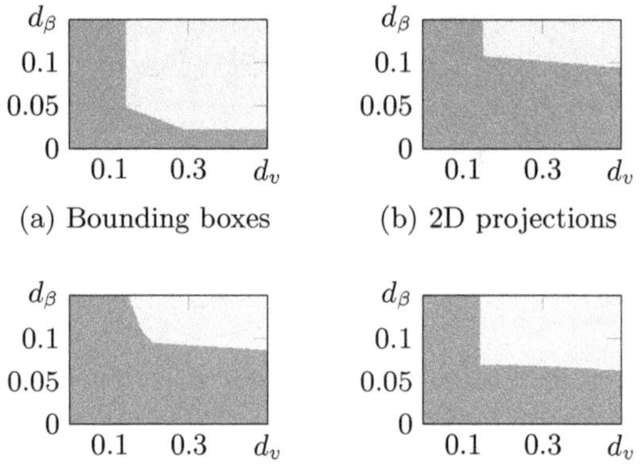

(a) Bounding boxes (b) 2D projections (c) 3d projections (d) evenly in 6d

Figure 10: Inclusion check for different parameter combinations. Dark gray: $S_r \not\preceq_R S_a$ proven, light gray: no counter-example found.

system S_a are visualized for one input trajectory in Fig. 10. Parameter combinations are colored dark gray if the conformance test found a counter-example. As one can see, our direction choices lead to more parameter combinations, where $S_r \not\preceq_R S_a$ can be proven. Clearly, the choice of the directions directly influences the falsification result.

The dark gray area in Fig. 10 can be used to compare the falsification results of different set of inputs. Therefore we use the ratio of the dark gray area to the whole considered area as a falsification measure. A high falsification measure states that the method is able to falsify many parameter combinations, which is good for a falsification method. We compare the ratio for our selected set of inputs against several randomly chosen ones. The set of inputs U_2 gives a good falsification result for all four methods, see Fig. 11. However, there is one input set that gives a better result than our selected set of inputs. This cannot be shown by the already existing bounding box check, but with our new method. Since there are no formal guarantees that our algorithm picks the best set of inputs, some inputs can lead to better results depending on the dynamics of the real model S_r that are not used for selection. Note that in our case we get similar results for evenly distributed directions in 6D, 2D and 3D projections. Possibly, this is due to the considered systems dynamics and the relation of the state variables therein. Depending on the resulting shape of the reachable set, it can be more accurate to check projections rather than the exact set giving a fixed number of directions. Nevertheless, in this particular example there is significantly more falsification possible with our new approach.

7. RELATED WORK

While we focus on reachset conformance in this paper, we also relate it to trace conformance (cf. Sec. 3). Therefore we briefly discuss trace conformance for a comprehensive overview. There are various conformance relations for differ-

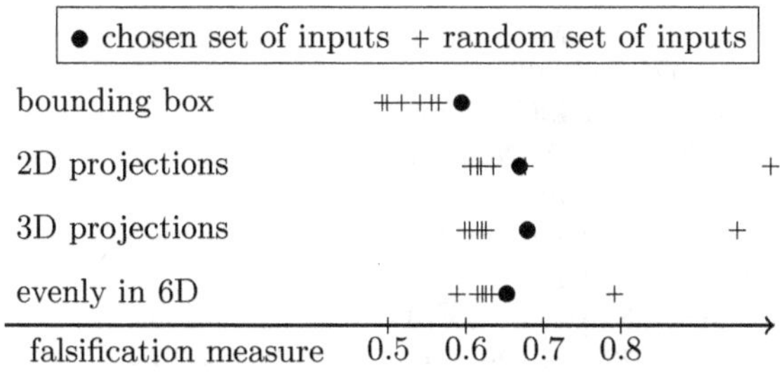

Figure 11: Falsification measure for different input sets.

ent types of models. The IO conformance (IOCO) is a formal approach to conformance testing of purely discrete models (labelled transition systems) by Tretmans [22]. IOCO has been extended to timed systems with subtle differences, see work by Schmaltz et al. for an overview [20]. Note, in the overview [20] the same wording "reachable set" is used, although input and output actions are considered together as transitions, leading to a different meaning. IOCO was also extended to hybrid systems conformance by van Osch [23] based on hybrid transition systems. A similar notion of hybrid conformance based on hybrid automata is described by Dang [7]. Approximate simulation relations are used by Tabuada [21] to verify models based on abstractions. Abbas et al. [1] use (τ, ε)-conformance, where the traces of the two systems only have to be close to each other. They prove that if their conformance relation $S_r \preceq_{(\tau,\varepsilon)} S_a$ holds, only a transformed version of the properties of S_a holds on S_r. A comparison between Hybrid Input-Output Conformance, Approximate Simulation, and (τ, ε)-conformance is done by Khakpour and Mousavi [16]. All of the above mentioned conformance relations are basically trace conformance relations.

There are different strategies in literature for overapproximating a zonotope with a simplified representation. Girard et al. [10] and Althoff et al. [5] present methods to reduce the number of generators of a zonotope. While the reduction to a small number of generators helps to scale the inclusion check, there is a significant penalty in accuracy of the inclusion check as the simplified zonotope is close to the box approximation. Girard [12] use zonotope approximations to check if the zonotope intersects with a guard of a hybrid automaton. Guibas et al. [14] describe an exact inclusion check for zonotopes that is limited to 3 dimensions only. The inclusion check presented in this paper is based on support function that are used e. g. in SpaceEx for reachable set computations [9]. While SpaceEx could also be leveraged for our approach, it is restricted to affine hybrid system models. Similarly, C2E2 [8] could be possibly leveraged for conformance testing, however it requires to annotate the model with certificates called discrepancy functions. If these certificates are given, Mitra provide a conformance checking procedure for continuous systems without inputs that particularly focus on security [19]. In this work we consider CORA [3] for the reachable set computation for the following reasons: (*i*) it supports non-linear hybrid systems, (*ii*) it allows us to easily incorporate our new reachset conformance, (*iii*) it provides a useful zonotope representation for reachable sets and (*iv*) allows us to compare our results to previous conformance testing on the autonomous vehicle models by Althoff and Dolan [4]. Kanade et al. [15] have done a reachable set underapproximation of Simulink models restricted to linear transformations. However, since their method takes a trace and builds a reachset around it, it does not consider different discrete behaviour. Generally, for verification purposes we would also need set-based underapproximation techniques for non-linear hybrid systems, that are still missing. Backward reachability for example is not usable because of ill-conditioning, as outlined by Mitchell [18].

For test generation of discrete systems there are several methods for test generation, such as transition coverage for finite automata. However, these methods do not work well for hybrid systems because they do not consider any continuous flow. A test generation method is proposed by van Osch [23] that has a non-deterministic selection process. Since it has no selection heuristic, it does not use knowledge about the system in contrast to our method. A RRT-based test generation process was introduced by Branicki et al. [6]. Dang [7] further developed the approach by using a statistical measure called star discrepancy to guide the simulations to unreached parts of the state space. However, there are typically too many inputs in the resulting input set to apply them all on a complex model.

8. CONCLUSIONS

We introduce the formal definition of reachset conformance and prove the transference of safety properties. Since the reachset conformance is weaker than trace conformance it can be used to relate more systems and therefore properties transfer between more systems. We present a formal reachset conformance testing, which is based on reachable set computations and overapproximations with support functions and considers the error of simulation runs or real measurements. The trade-off between accuracy and computational load can be tuned by an appropriate choice of the directions for the overapproximations. We introduce an input selection algorithm to reduce the size of an input set, generated by existing sampling methods. It uses a coverage measure based on the reachable sets of the abstract system. The example shows that the selected inputs are reasonable and that the conformance testing method can falsify more relations than the state of the art.

ACKNOWLEDGMENT

The authors would like to thank the anonymous reviewers as well as Christoph Gladisch, Thomas Heinz and Christian Heinzemann for their valuable comments and suggestions to improve the quality of the paper. Jens Oehlerking, Matthias Woehrle and Matthias Althoff gratefully acknowledge financial support by the European Commission project UnCoVerCPS under grant number 643921.

9. REFERENCES

[1] H. Abbas, H. D. Mittelmann, and G. E. Fainekos. Formal property verification in a conformance testing framework. In *ACM/IEEE MEMOCODE*, pages 155–164, 2014.

[2] R. W. Allen, H. T. Szostak, D. H. Klyde, T. J. Rosenthal, and K. J. Owens. Vehicle dynamic stability and rollover. Technical report, U.S. Department of Transportation, Final Report DOT HS 807 956, 1992.

[3] M. Althoff. An introduction to CORA 2015. In *Proc. of the Workshop on Applied Verification for Continuous and Hybrid Systems*, pages 120–151, 2015.

[4] M. Althoff and J. M. Dolan. Reachability computation of low-order models for the safety verification of high-order road vehicle models. In *American Control Conference*, pages 3559–3566. IEEE, 2012.

[5] M. Althoff, O. Stursberg, and M. Buss. Computing reachable sets of hybrid systems using a combination of zonotopes and polytopes. *Nonlinear Analysis: Hybrid Systems*, 4(2):233–249, 2010.

[6] M. S. Branicky, M. M. Curtiss, J. Levine, and S. B. Morgan. RRTs for nonlinear, discrete, and hybrid planning and control. In *Decision and Control*, volume 1, pages 657–663. IEEE, 2003.

[7] T. Dang. Model-based testing of hybrid systems. In *Model-Based Testing for Embedded Systems*, chapter 14, pages 383–424. CRC Press, Inc., 2011.

[8] P. S. Duggirala, S. Mitra, M. Viswanathan, and M. Potok. C2E2: A verification tool for Stateflow models. In *Tools and Algorithms for the Construction and Analysis of Systems*, pages 68–82. 2015.

[9] G. Frehse, C. L. Guernic, A. Donzé, S. Cotton, R. Ray, O. Lebeltel, R. Ripado, A. Girard, T. Dang, and O. Maler. SpaceEx: Scalable verification of hybrid systems. In *Computer Aided Verification*, pages 379–395, 2011.

[10] A. Girard. Reachability of uncertain linear systems using zonotopes. In *Hybrid Systems: Computation and Control*, pages 291–305. 2005.

[11] A. Girard and C. L. Guernic. Zonotope/hyperplane intersection for hybrid systems reachability analysis. In *Hybrid Systems: Computation and Control*, pages 215–228. 2008.

[12] A. Girard, C. L. Guernic, and O. Maler. Efficient computation of reachable sets of linear time-invariant systems with inputs. In *Hybrid Systems: Computation and Control*, pages 257–271. 2006.

[13] Á. González. Measurement of areas on a sphere using fibonacci and latitude–longitude lattices. *Mathematical Geosciences*, 42(1):49–64, 2010.

[14] L. J. Guibas, A. Nguyen, and L. Zhang. Zonotopes as bounding volumes. In *Proc. of the ACM-SIAM Symposium on Discrete Algorithms*, pages 803–812, 2003.

[15] A. Kanade, R. Alur, F. Ivancic, S. Ramesh, S. Sankaranarayanan, and K. C. Shashidhar. Generating and analyzing symbolic traces of Simulink/Stateflow models. In *Computer Aided Verification*, pages 430–445, 2009.

[16] N. Khakpour and M. R. Mousavi. Notions of Conformance Testing for Cyber-Physical Systems: Overview and Roadmap. In *Int. Conf. on Concurrency Theory*, volume 42 of *LIPIcs*, pages 18–40, 2015.

[17] C. Le Guernic, A. Girard, C. L. Guernic, and A. Girard. Reachability analysis of hybrid systems using support functions. In *Computer Aided Verification*, pages 540–554, 2009.

[18] I. M. Mitchell. Comparing forward and backward reachability as tools for safety analysis. In *Hybrid Systems: Computation and Control*, pages 428–443. 2007.

[19] S. Mitra. Proving abstractions of dynamical systems through numerical simulations. In *Proc. of the Symposium and Bootcamp on the Science of Security*, page 12, 2014.

[20] J. Schmaltz and J. Tretmans. On conformance testing for timed systems. In *Formal Modeling and Analysis of Timed Systems*, pages 250–264. 2008.

[21] P. Tabuada. *Verification and Control of Hybrid Systems - A Symbolic Approach.* Springer, 2009.

[22] G. J. Tretmans. *A formal approach to conformance testing.* PhD thesis, Universiteit Twente, 1992.

[23] M. P. W. J. van Osch. *Automated model-based testing of hybrid systems.* PhD thesis, Eindhoven University of Technology, 2009.

From Simulation Models to Hybrid Automata Using Urgency and Relaxation *

Stefano Minopoli
Univ. Grenoble Alpes, VERIMAG
Centre Équation - 2, avenue de Vignate
38610 GIÉRES
stefano.minopoli@imag.fr

Goran Frehse
Univ. Grenoble Alpes, VERIMAG
Centre Équation - 2, avenue de Vignate
38610 GIÉRES
goran.frehse@imag.fr

ABSTRACT

We consider the problem of translating a deterministic *simulation model* (like Matlab-Simunk, Modelica or Ptolemy models) into a *verification model* expressed by a network of hybrid automata. The goal is to verify safety using reachability analysis on the verification model. Simulation models typically use transitions with urgent semantics, which must be taken as soon as possible. Urgent transitions also make it possible to decompose systems that would otherwise need to be modeled with a monolithic hybrid automaton. In this paper, we include urgent transitions in our verification models and propose a suitable adaptation of our reachability algorithm. However, the simulation model, due to its imperfections, may be unsafe even though the corresponding hybrid automata are safe. Conversely, set-based reachability may not be able to show safety of an ideal formal model, since complex dynamics necessarily entail overapproximations. Taken as a whole, the formal modeling and verification process can both falsely claim safety and fail to show safety of the concrete system.

We address this inconsistency by relaxing the model as follows. The standard semantics of hybrid automata is a mathematical idealization, where reactions are considered to be instantaneous and physical measurements infinitely precise. We propose semantics that relax these assumptions, where guard conditions are sampled in discrete time and admit measurement errors. The relaxed semantics can be translated to an equivalent relaxed model in standard semantics. The relaxed model is realistic in the sense that it can be implemented on hardware fast and precise enough, and in a way that safety is preserved. Finally, we show that overapproximative reachability analysis can show safety of relaxed models, which is not the case in general.

*The authors gratefully acknowledge financial support by the European Commission project UnCoVerCPS under grant number 643921.

HSCC'16, April 12 - 14, 2016, Vienna, Austria

ISBN 978-1-4503-3955-1/16/04...$15.00

DOI: http://dx.doi.org/10.1145/2883817.2883825

Keywords

Hybrid Systems, Hybrid Automata, Reachability Analysis, Numerical Analysis, Urgency

1. INTRODUCTION

A hybrid system describes the interaction of both discrete and continuous components over time. This combination can quickly lead to complex behaviors that are difficult to predict and control. The model based design of hybrid systems is commonly based on *simulation models* for tools like Matlab/Simulink [16], Modelica [17], Ptolemy [5], and many more. It is very hard to exhaustively test models using numerical simulation, so critical behaviors may go undetected. Set-based verification methods, on the other hand, can cover all possible behaviors in a single analysis. But they require a *verification model*, typically in the form of a *Hybrid Automaton* (HA) [12]. Hybrid Automata extend traditional state machines with continuous variables, governed by differential equations for modeling the continuous evolution of physical activities. We assume that verification models are used to verify safety or bounded liveness properties using approximative, set-based reachability algorithms, which are applicable to systems with piecewise-affine dynamics and hundreds of continuous variables [8, 7]. In this paper, we propose a relaxation of hybrid automata such that they are conservative abstractions of simulation models, and show how standard reachability techniques can be applied without necessarily compromising the computational cost of the analysis.

In the standard semantics of hybrid automata, transitions are nondeterministic: The system may take a transition when it satisfies the guard condition of a transition or remain in the same discrete state as long as the invariant (staying condition) holds. Simulation models are typically deterministic, since the simulator needs to be able to compute what happens in the next step. Simulation models therefore use urgent semantics, where a transition is taken as soon as the guard condition is satisfied. Urgent transitions make it possible to decompose systems that would otherwise need to be modeled with a monolithic hybrid automaton. This greatly facilitates the translation from deterministic models to hybrid automata, since it can be done component-wise. This is important in practice, since the structure of the model has a profound impact on several aspects of safety-critical model development, see [25]. Urgent semantics are not covered by standard reachability algorithms, since the computation of the states reachable by time elapse is more complex. In addition, instantaneous reactions can not be guaranteed by combining invariants and transitions guards. For example when the variables in the guard condition have a derivative equal to zero, the system may remain forever on the border between invariant and guard and this is in contrast with the instantaneous reaction requirement. We fill this gap by generalizing the urgent time elapse operator in [19] from piecewise constant dynamics to piecewise affine dynamics. We show that the time elapse computation with urgency can be reduced to time elapse with a nonconvex invariant. Since the standard reachability algorithms work on convex invariants, we propose a a time elapse operator for nonconvex invariants. The idea is to consider a coverage of the invariant, where the elements are convex and closed. Then the standard time elapse is applied recursively on each of the elements.

The introduction of urgency in hybrid automata allows us a relatively straightforward translation from simulation models, e.g. the translation tool *SL2SX* [21, 18]. But the obtained hybrid automata are a mathematical idealization, where reactions (the effects of discrete events) are considered to be instantaneous and the variables have infinite precision. Clearly this is not the case for simulation, which computes an approximation of the state while taking discrete time steps. When the safety of a verification model relies on the assumption of instantaneous reaction, it can not be always implemented by a simulation model. In other words, the safety of the ideal hybrid automaton does not prove the safety of the corresponding simulation model. This should not be simply dismissed as a defect of the simulation model. In industrial practice, simulation models are developed over years and finely tuned up to the point that the simulator output is considered a faithful reflection of reality [9]. Furthermore, if the system can not be simulated numerically, it stands to reason that it can also not be implemented on a digital controller.

We illustrate the point with a variation of a *DC-to-DC switched-mode power converter* from [23], implemented in Simulink/Stateflow. The state variables are currents and voltages whose continuous dynamics are specified by switched linear ordinary differential equations. We add an urgent transition to change the dynamics when the voltage reaches the value $x = 15$ exactly. In the Simulink output shown in Fig. 1(a), the simulator does not detect any of the three crossings of $x = 15$. This could be considered a bug in the model, since we could have used one of Simulink's special blocks for detecting zero crossings. It could also point to a bug in the controller design, since an implementation of the system with a digital controller may miss the crossing just like the simulator. Either way, one should hope to detect this behavior using formal verification.

We convert the simulink model to a hybrid automaton using the translator *SL2SX* [21, 18], and run the verification tool SpaceEx [8]. In the hybrid automaton model, the urgent transition is always and instantaneously fired when the guard $x = 15$ is satisfied, as shown in Fig. 1(b). As a consequence, the reachability set is different and can not be used to prove safety of the simulation model. In the following we propose a relaxed hybrid automaton, which is an abstraction of the simulation model and therefore contains both behaviors, as shown in Fig. 1(c). Usually this is achieved by conservative abstraction, in the sense that it covers all behaviors. But in practice this is often overly conservative, such that the analysis either returns false negatives or becomes infeasible due to state explosion. The mathematical reason for this is that in numerical simulation the approximation errors may cancel each other out, while in set-based reachability they accumulate. Our approach can deal with the simulation model without adding overly conservative error terms. This makes it applicable to more complex systems and properties. Since this approach does not add any additional variables, locations or transitions to the model, it therefore does not fundamentally change scalability compared to standard HA models.

In this paper, we propose to relax the semantics of the hybrid automaton to capture that the simulated system

(*i*) may check guard conditions at discrete time points, assuming a bound $\Delta \geq 0$ on the time step, and

(*ii*) may check guard conditions with a precision error ϵ.

Point (*i*) is the relaxation of the instantaneous reaction assumption and point (*ii*) is the relaxation of the infinite precision assumption. For $\Delta = 0$ and $\varepsilon = 0$, we obtain the standard semantics. We show that the behaviors generated by relaxed semantics are equivalent to a relaxed model with standard semantics. The relaxation consists of enlarging the guards and shrinking urgent guard conditions accordingly. Our reachability algorithm can then be applied on the relaxed model.

Notice that our assumptions (see also Sec. 3.2) cover all simulation runs with a time step of Δ or smaller. Even zero crossing detection is covered by these assumptions since it amounts to reducing the time step for particular sections of a trajectory. If one has enough confidence in the zero crossing detection algorithm to be sure that no zeros are missed above some time step Δ^* (e.g., the minimal step size of the zero detection algorithm), then one can substitute Δ^* for Δ.

The relaxed semantics with urgency have additional interesting properties, some of them similar to *almost asap semantics* from [26]. First, *fast is better*, meaning that if the relaxed model with sampling time Δ and precision error ϵ is safe, then it is also safe for any smaller sampling time Δ' using the same precision error ϵ. Second, *precision is quality*, meaning that if the relaxed model with sampling time Δ and error ϵ is safe, then it is also safe for Δ and any smaller precision error ϵ'. Third, relaxed models are realistic in the sense that they can be implemented on hardware *fast and precise enough*, and in a way that safety is preserved. Indeed, our approach compensates for time discretization and approximation errors incurred in numerical simulation. Controllers implemented in digital hardware suffer from exactly the same flaws, if we consider measurement errors part of the approximation error. Safety of the simulation model therefore implies safety of a hardware system with high enough overall accuracy (including computation and measurement errors).

Moreover, we show that overapproximative reachability analysis can show safety of relaxed models, which is not the case in general.

For lack of space, some proofs were omitted from this paper; they can be found in [20].

Related Work.

Time-elapse computations for nonconvex invariants have already been tackled for hybrid automata with piecewise

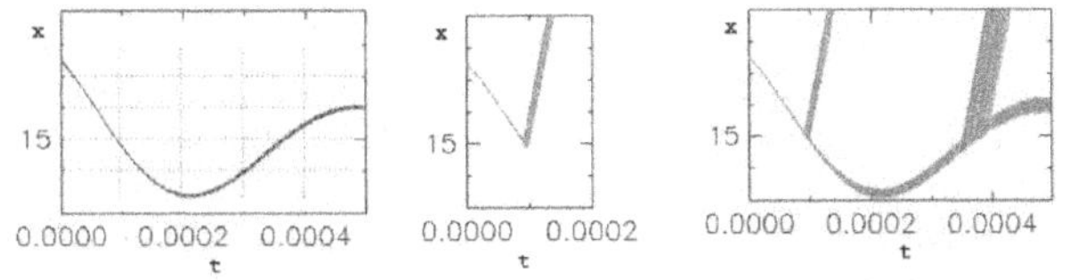

(a) Simulink (b) ideal HA (c) relaxed HA

Figure 1: The simulation model may differ from an idealized hybrid automata model; a relaxed hybrid automaton can capture all cases

constant dynamics (LHA). The technique proposed by [14, 4] consist of modeling the nonconvex invariant by splitting locations, each one with a single convex component of the invariant. The technique in [19] is similar, but skips the construction of auxiliary locations by iterating over a convex cover of the invariant. It also resolves technicalities arising from strict inequalities. We follows this last approach, extending the results to piecewise affine dynamics.

A detailed and formal discussion of urgency can be found in [10] and the references therein. A general class of hybrid automata with urgency conditions is described in [24]. Urgency conditions are also part of the *Computational Interchange Format for Hybrid Systems (CIF)* [3], and a restricted class of urgent guard conditions can be handled by the classic reachability tool HyTech [13]. Computing the reachable states for the general case of urgency is not trivial. An algorithm for an effective computation of the time-elapse for HA with urgency was proposed for linear hybrid automata (LHA) in [19]. This time elapse computation with urgency is reduced to time-elapse with nonconvex invariants. We follows a similar approach, extending the algorithm to piecewise affine dynamics.

Our timed relaxation is closely related to [26], which introduces a parametric semantics for timed controllers called *Almost ASAP semantics (AASAP)*. These semantics relax the assumption of instantaneous reaction by imposing the controller to react within Δ time units when an urgent action takes place. Similar to our case, the AASAP semantics is such that faster is better and such that any controller proven to be correct for some $\Delta > 0$ can be implemented. Our semantics can be seen as an extension of the this semantics from timed to hybrid automata with finite precision on the measurements.

The formalism of *Lazy Hybrid Automata* [2, 1, 15] also relaxes the ideal assumptions. It refers to HA whose dynamics is governed by a vector of constants rates, and where the plant state evolves continuously while the controller samples the plant state and changes the control state discretely at specific sampling times T_i. The relaxation of the instantaneous reaction hypothesis is done by distinguishing the delays δ_h on sensors and δ_g on actuators, while the finite precision is modeled by considering neighborhood of the guards. Transition may be fired when guards are satisfied at least one time in intervals, next to sampling points, of length δ_h. This does not ensure that transitions are fired also with smaller sensors delay (i.e. by setting $\delta'_h < \delta_h$) and then the property faster is better is not valid for lazy HA. The analysis of the behavior of lazy HA is based on state discretization, which may compromise scalability.

2. REACHABILITY FOR HYBRID AUTOMATA WITH URGENCY

In this section, we give our definition of *Hybrid Automata (HA)* with urgency. They include in each location an urgency condition represented by a nonconvex polyhedron. As in [19], we also include non-convex invariants.

2.1 Hybrid Automata with Urgency

We first need to define some notation. A *convex polyhedron* is a subset of $\mathbb{R}^n$ that is the intersection of a finite number of strict and non-strict affine half-spaces. A *polyhedron* is a subset of $\mathbb{R}^n$ that is the union of a finite number of convex polyhedra. For clarity, we write $\widehat{P}$ if P is convex. For a general (i.e., not necessarily convex) polyhedron $G \subseteq \mathbb{R}^n$, we denote by $[\![G]\!] \subseteq 2^{\mathbb{R}^n}$ its representation as a (minimal) finite union of convex polyhedra. The topological closure of P is denoted by $cl(P)$. Given an ordered set $X = \{x_1, \ldots, x_n\}$ of variables, a *valuation* is a function $v : X \to \mathbb{R}$. Let $Val(X)$ denote the set of valuations over X. There is an obvious bijection between $Val(X)$ and $\mathbb{R}^n$, allowing us to extend the notion of (convex) polyhedron to sets of valuations. We denote by $CPoly(X)$ (resp., $Poly(X)$) the set of convex polyhedra (resp., polyhedra) on X. Moreover, we denote by $SPoly(X)$ the subset of $\mathbb{R}^X$ that can be obtained by finite disjunction of closed convex polyhedra.

We use $\dot{X}$ to denote the set $\{\dot{x}_1, \ldots, \dot{x}_n\}$ of dotted variables, used to represent the first derivatives, and X' to denote the set $\{x'_1, \ldots, x'_n\}$ of primed variables, used to represent the new values of variables after a discrete transition. Arithmetic operations on valuations are defined in the straightforward way. An *activity* over X is a function $f : \mathbb{R}^{\geq 0} \to Val(X)$ that is continuous on its domain and differentiable except for a finite set of points. Let $Acts(X)$ denote the set of activities over X. The *derivative* $\dot{f}$ of an activity f is defined in the standard way and it is a partial function $\dot{f} : \mathbb{R}^{\geq 0} \to Val(\dot{X})$.

Formally, a hybrid automaton

$$H = (Loc, X, Lab, Inv, Urg, Flow, Trans, Init)$$

consists of the following components:

- a finite set *Loc* of *locations*;
- a finite set $X = \{x_1, \ldots, x_n\}$ of real-valued *variables*. A *state* is a pair $\langle \ell, v \rangle$ of a location ℓ and a valuation $v \in Val(X)$;
- a finite set of labels *Lab*;
- a set $Inv \subseteq Loc \times \mathbb{R}^n$, called the *invariant*. The system may only remain in a location ℓ as long as the state is inside its *invariant* $Inv(\ell)$.
- a set $Urg \subseteq Loc \times \mathbb{R}^n$, called the *urgency condition*. The urgency condition impedes time elapse, i.e., no continuous activities in a location ℓ continue from a valuation that satisfies the condition $Urg(\ell)$;
- a set $Flow \subseteq Loc \times \mathbb{R}^n \times \mathbb{R}^n$, defined over the first derivative of the variables, which determines how variables can change over time.
- a finite set *Trans* of *discrete transitions* that describes instantaneous changes of locations, in the course of

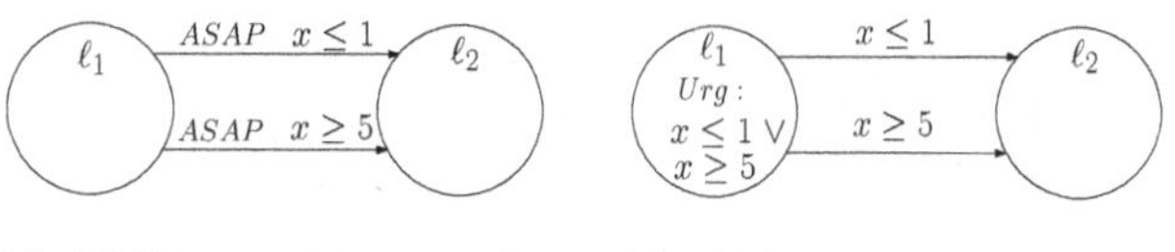

(a) ASAP transitions explicitly modeled

(b) ASAP transitions modeled by urgent condition

Figure 2: ASAP transitions modeled by urgent

which variables may change their value. Each transition $(\ell, \alpha, \mathcal{G}, Asgn, \ell') \in Trans$ consists of a *source location* ℓ, a *target location* ℓ', a label $\alpha \in Lab$, a *guard* $\mathcal{G} \subseteq \mathbb{R}^n$ and an *assignment* $Asgn : \mathbb{R}^n \to 2^{\mathbb{R}^n}$. A state $\langle \ell, v \rangle$ can jump to $\langle \ell', v' \rangle$ if $v \in \mathcal{G}$ and $v' \in Asgn(v)$.

- a set $Init \subseteq Loc \times \mathbb{R}^n$, contained in the invariant, defining the *initial states* of the automaton. All behavior originates from these states.

The set of states of H is $S = Loc \times Val(X)$. Given a set of states A and a location ℓ, we denote by $A\downharpoonright_\ell$ the projection of A on ℓ, i.e. $A\downharpoonright_\ell = \{v \in Val(X) \mid \langle \ell, v \rangle \in A\}$.

The kind of dynamics modeled by the component *Flow* determines the special class of Hybrid Automata. When *Flow* is expressed by polyhedral inclusion, i.e. $Flow : Loc \to CPoly(\dot{X})$, we are talking about the subclass of *Linear Hybrid Automata*. Otherwise, the subclass of *Affine Hybrid Automata* is defined by affine continuous dynamics with uncertain inputs of the form

$$\dot{x}(t) = Ax(t) + u(t), u \in \mathcal{U},$$

where $x(t) \in \mathbb{R}^n$, A is a real-valued $n \times n$ matrix and $\mathcal{U} \subseteq \mathbb{R}^n$ is a closed and bounded convex set.

In both subclasses, the transition assignments *Asgn* are of the form $x' = Rx + w, w \in \mathcal{W}$, where R is a real-valued $n \times n$ matrix, and $\mathcal{W} \subset \mathbb{R}^n$ is a closed and bounded set of nondeterministic inputs.

Urgent Conditions and ASAP Transitions.

Urgency is used to model the so-called *must semantics* where, unlike the *may semantics* of standard HA, transitions must be taken immediately when associated guards are satisfied. Because urgent conditions impede elapsing of time, they can be satisfied only in a single time point. This point is the exact moment when the urgency is met (i.e. the frontier of the urgent condition).

In our definition, the urgency condition is defined for each location. An alternative approach, popular mainly because of its syntactical simplicity, is to designate each discrete transition as urgent or not. This is also referred to as *as-soon-as-possible (ASAP) transitions.* As shown by Fig. 2, urgent transitions can easily be translated to an urgency condition: let $Trans_U \subseteq Trans$ be the set of urgent transitions. Then the equivalent urgency condition is the union of the outgoing guards,

$$Urg(\ell) = \bigcup \{\mathcal{G} \mid (\ell, \alpha, \mathcal{G}, Asgn, \ell') \in Trans_U\}.$$

2.2 Parallel Composition

One attractive feature of urgency is that a model can be decomposed for cases where this is not possible without urgency. Consider the example of an automaton for the plant and an automaton for the controller. Without urgency, the controller automaton can in general not prevent time elapse in the plant automaton, unless an additional clock is introduced and that clock is sampled periodically.

We give a brief formal definition of parallel composition with urgency for the case where both automata range over the same variables. The key here is that the urgency condition of the composition is the union of the urgency conditions of the operands. Given a hybrid automata H_1, H_2 with $H_i = (Loc_i, X, Lab_i, Inv_i, Urg_i, Flow_i, Trans_i, Init_i)$, their *parallel composition* is the HA $H = (Loc_1 \times Loc_2, X, Lab_1 \cup Lab_2, Edg, Flow, Inv, Urg, Init)$, written as $H = H_1 \| H_2$, where $Flow(l_1, l_2) = Flow_1(l_1) \cap Flow_2(l_2)$; $Inv(l_1, l_2) = Inv_1(l_1) \cap Inv_2(l_2)$; $Urg(l_1, l_2) = Urg_1(l_1) \cup Urg_2(l_2)$; $Init(l_1, l_2) = Init_1(l_1) \cap Init_2(l_2)$ and transitions $((l_1, l_2), \alpha, \mathcal{G}, Asgn, (l'_2, l'_2)) \in Edg$ iff

- $\alpha \in Lab_1 \cap Lab_2$, for $i = 1, 2$, $(l_i, \alpha, \mathcal{G}_i, Asgn_i, l'_i) \in Edg_i$, $\mathcal{G} = \mathcal{G}_1 \cap \mathcal{G}_2$, $Asgn = Asgn_1 \cap Asgn_2$, or
- $\alpha \notin Lab_1$, $l'_2 = l_2$, $(l_1, \alpha, \mathcal{G}, Asgn, l'_1) \in Edg_1$, or
- $\alpha \notin Lab_2$, $l'_1 = l_1$, $(l_2, \alpha, \mathcal{G}, Asgn, l'_2) \in Edg_2$.

2.3 Run Semantics

The behavior of a HA is based on two types of steps: *discrete* steps correspond to the *Trans* component, and produce an instantaneous change in both the location and the variable valuation; *timed* steps describe the change of the variables over time in accordance with the *Flow* component.

Definition 1 (Discrete Step). Given two states s, s', and a transition $e = (loc(s), \alpha, \mathcal{G}, Asgn, loc(s')) \in Trans$, there is a *discrete step* $s \xrightarrow{e} s'$ with *source* s and *target* s' iff

(i) $s, s' \in Inv$,

(ii) $val(s) \in \mathcal{G}$, and

(iii) $val(s') = Asgn(val(s))$.

Whenever (ii) holds, we say that e is *enabled* in s. Given a state $s = \langle \ell, v \rangle$, let $loc(s) = \ell$ and $val(s) = v$. An activity $f \in Acts(X)$ is called *admissible from* s if (i) $f(0) = v$ and (ii) for all $\delta \geq 0$, if $\dot{f}(\delta)$ is defined then $\dot{f}(\delta) \in Flow(\ell)$. We denote by $Adm(s)$ the set of activities that are admissible from s.

To take into account the urgency condition, which affects timed steps, we need to know the maximum amount of time δ such that the system, by following an activity f, is allowed to remain in a give location ℓ. Formally we define, for an activity $f \in Adm(s)$, the *Switching Time* of f in ℓ, denoted by $SwitchT(f, Urg(\ell))$, as the value $\delta \geq 0$ such that, for all $0 \leq \delta' < \delta$, $f(\delta') \notin Urg(\ell)$ and $f(\delta) \in Urg(\ell)$. When for all $\delta \geq 0$ it holds that $f(\delta) \notin Urg(\ell)$, we write $SwitchT(f, Urg(\ell)) = \infty$.

Definition 2 (Timed Step). Given two states s, s', there is a *timed step* $s \xrightarrow{\Delta, f} s'$ with *duration* $\Delta \in \mathbb{R}^{\geq 0}$ and activity $f \in Adm(s)$ iff

(i) for all $0 \leq \delta' \leq \Delta$, $(\langle \ell, f(\delta') \rangle) \in Inv$,

(ii) $s' = \langle loc(s), f(\Delta) \rangle$, and

(iii) $\Delta \leq SwitchT(f, Urg(loc(s)))$.

Conditions (i) says that the system always remains in the invariant $I = Inv(\ell)$ during the duration Δ of the step, while condition (iii) says that during this step the system can satisfy the urgency condition only at time Δ.

A *run* is a sequence

$$r = s_0 \xrightarrow{\delta_0, f_0} s'_0 \xrightarrow{e_0} s_1 \xrightarrow{\delta_1, f_1} s'_1 \xrightarrow{e_1} s_2 \cdots s_n \ldots \quad (1)$$

of alternating timed and discrete steps. If the run r is finite, we define $len(r) = n$ to be the length of the run, otherwise we set $len(r) = \infty$. The set $Runs(H)$ denotes the set of all runs of the automaton H.

Given a state $s \in S$ and a hybrid automaton H with initial set of states *Init*, s is said to be *reachable* in H if there exists a finite *run* $r = s_0 \xrightarrow{\delta_0, f_0} s'_0 \xrightarrow{e_0} s_1 \xrightarrow{\delta_1, f_1} s'_1 \xrightarrow{e_1} s_2 \cdots s_n$, such that $s_0 \in Init$ and $s_n = s$. We denote the set of reachable states by $Reach(H)$.

2.4 Reachability Computation

In this section we propose an extension of the algorithm proposed by [19] in order to compute the time-elapse operator for the class for automata with piecewise affine dynamics with urgent conditions. This problem is reduced to the computation of the time-elapse for non-convex invariants, for which so far no algorithm is available for piecewise affine dynamics.

2.4.1 Standard Post Operators

A classic algorithm to compute the set $Reach(H)$ is a fixed-point procedure based on a *continuous post operator* and on a *discrete post operator*: given a set of states $S' \subseteq S$, the continuous post is used to compute the states reachable from S' by following an admissible trajectory, while the discrete post is used to compute the states reachable from S' via discrete transitions.

Given a hybrid automaton H, a location $\ell \in Loc$, a set of valuations $P, I \subseteq Inv(\ell)$, $U = Urg(\ell)$, and a time horizon $T \geq 0$, the Δ-*timed horizon continuous post operator* $\Delta Post_\ell(P, I, T)$ contains the set of all valuations $v \in Val(X)$ reachable from some $u \in P$, within the time T by never leaving I:

$$\Delta Post_\ell(P, I, T) = \{v \in val(X) \mid \exists 0 \leq \delta \leq T, u \in P, \\ f \in Adm(\langle \ell, u \rangle) : \forall 0 \leq \delta' \leq \delta : f(\delta') \in I \\ \text{and } f(\delta) = v\}. \quad (2)$$

The standard *continuous post operator* $Post_\ell(P, I)$ contains the set of all valuations $v \in Val(X)$ reachable from some $u \in P$, without leaving I:

$$Post_\ell(P, I) = \bigcup_{\delta \geq 0} \Delta Post_\ell(P, I, \delta) \quad (3)$$

The *discrete post operator* $Post_e(P)$ contains the set of all valuations $v \in Val(X)$ reachable from some $u \in P$ by taking the discrete transition $e = (\ell, \mathcal{G}, Asgn, \ell')$:

$$Post_e(P) = \{v \in val(X) \mid \exists u \in P \cap \mathcal{G} \wedge v \in Inv(\ell')\}. \quad (4)$$

Notice that urgency does not affect discrete steps, hence the above definition of discrete post is still valid in case of urgency. From these operators on valuations we obtain the continuous and discrete post operators for a set of states S by iterating over all locations and transitions:

$$Post_c(S) = \bigcup_{\ell \in Loc} \{\ell\} \times Post_\ell(S\lfloor_\ell, Inv(\ell)), \quad (5)$$

$$Post_d(S) = \bigcup_{(\ell, \alpha, \mathcal{G}, Asgn, \ell') \in Trans} \{\ell'\} \times Post_{(\ell, \alpha, \mathcal{G}, Asgn, \ell')}(S\lfloor_\ell). \quad (6)$$

Note that definition (3) is valid regardless whether I is convex or not. For the sake of clarity, we will denote the continuous post with $Post_\ell(P, I)$ when I is convex, and with $ncPost_\ell(P, I)$ when I is nonconvex.

The reachable states $Reach(H)$ are computed as the smallest fixed point of the sequence $S_0 = Post_c(Init)$ and $S_{k+1} = S_k \cup Post_c(Post_d(S_k))$.

2.4.2 Computation of ncPost

We describe here an approach for computing the continuous post when the invariant I of a location is a non-convex and closed polyhedron. The technique is similar to the one proposed in [19] for piecewise constant dynamics. However, the proof differs since [19] relies entirely on straight-line trajectories.

We propose a characterization of $ncPost_\ell$ based on the standard $Post_\ell$ evaluated iteratively over a convex cover of I. Given an affine HA $\mathcal{H}$ and let $\ell \in Loc$, $I = Inv(\ell)$ and consider the initial set $P \subseteq I$. For each convex component $\widehat{I'} \in [\![I]\!]$, we apply the standard continuous post operator with $P \cap \widehat{I'}$ as initial set and $\widehat{I'}$ as invariant. The procedure is applied recursively by building a sequence $W_0 \subseteq W_1 \subseteq \ldots W_k$ of reachable valuations, with $W_0 = P$. Then $ncPost_\ell(P, I)$ is the fixed point of that sequence. This is formalized by the following theorem:

Theorem 1. Given a location $\ell \in Loc$ and let $I = Inv(\ell)$ be the invariant in location ℓ. For every set of valuations $P \subseteq I$ such that the sequence $W_0 = P$,

$$W_{k+1} = \bigcup_{\widehat{I'} \in [\![I]\!]} Post_\ell(W_k \cap \widehat{I'}, \widehat{I'})$$

satisfies $W_k = W_{k+1}$ for some k, then $ncPost_\ell(P, I) = W_k$.

PROOF. (Sketch – for a full proof see [20]). To show that $ncPost_\ell(P, I) \subseteq W_k$, we show that $v \in ncPost_\ell(P, I)$ implies that $v \in W_{i+1}$ for some $i \leq k$. Let u be a valuation in P. We proceed by induction over the number of crossings between convex components of I to get from u to v along some activity. Since the activities are analytic functions, the number of crossings is finite (analytic functions have isolated zeros).

The induction hypothesis is as follows: If $v_i \in W_i$ be reachable through $i-1$ crossings of convex components of I, then any valuation reachable from v_i by crossing one more convex component belongs to W_{i+1}. The base case for $i = 1$ is straightforward, since it refers to states reachable inside a single convex component of I, i.e., the classic convex post operation. Suppose that during a run leading from u to v, the last crossing involves the convex components $\widehat{I}_{i-1}, \widehat{I}_i \in I$. Hence there exists a valuation $u' \in \widehat{I}_{i-1} \cap \widehat{I}_i$ reachable with $i-1$ crossings and then by inductive hypothesis $u' \in W_i$. But since the last crossing is from $\widehat{I}_{i-1}$ to $\widehat{I}_i$, then from u' to v the system always remains inside $\widehat{I}_i$, meaning that $v \in Post_\ell(W_i \cap \widehat{I}_i, \widehat{I}_i) \subseteq W_{i+1}$.

We now show $W_k \subseteq ncPost_\ell(P, I)$. $v \in W_{i+1}$ means that there exists a convex component $\widehat{I'}$ and a valuation $u' \in W_i$ such that $v \in Post_\ell(W_i \cap \widehat{I'}, \widehat{I'})$. This means that v is reachable from some $u' \in W_i \cap \widehat{I'}$ and by inductive hypothesis $u' \in ncPost_\ell(P, I)$ and there exists a valuation $u \in P$ such that u' is reachable from u with $i-1$ crossings. Suppose that u' also belongs to another convex component $\widehat{I}''$, this means that in order to reach v from u' the system needs to complete a further crossing from $\widehat{I}''$ to $\widehat{I}'$ and hence $v \in ncPost_\ell(P, I)$ by performing i crossings. Otherwise v already belongs to W_i and then we can apply the inductive hypothesis to conclude the proof. □

Theorem 1 provides an effective way to compute an overapproximation of the post with non-convex invariants. Indeed several algorithms for computing overapproximation of the standard post with convex invariants are available, and they can be used to compute overapproximation of the sets W_i. The *overapproximative post operator*, whose error is bounded by the non-negative real number $v \geq 0$, is denoted by $Post_\ell^v$. The definition of the *overapproximative reachability set* denoted by $Reach^v$, is straightforward. The following result is a direct consequence of Theorem 1.

Corollary 1. Given a location $\ell \in Loc$ and let $I = Inv(\ell)$ be the non-convex invariant in location ℓ and $v \geq 0$ a non-negative number. For every set of valuations $P \subseteq I$ such that the sequence $W_0 = P$,

$$W_{k+1} \quad = \quad \bigcup_{\widehat{I}' \in [\![I]\!]} Post_\ell^v(W_k \cap \widehat{I}', \widehat{I}')$$

reaches fixed point in k iterations, then W_k is an overapproximation of $ncPost_\ell(P, I)$ with error kv.

2.4.3 Computation of UPost

We now define the continuous post operator under urgency conditions, and show that it can be approximated using the post operator for nonconvex invariants. The *urgent continuous post operator* is

$$\begin{aligned} UPost_\ell(P, I, U) = \{v \in val(X) \big| \exists \delta \geq 0, u \in P, \\ f \in Adm(\langle \ell, u \rangle) : \forall 0 \leq \delta' \leq \delta : f(\delta') \in I, \\ f(\delta) = v, \delta \leq SwitchT(f, U)\}. \quad (7) \end{aligned}$$

The intuition is that, since an urgent condition U blocks activities that inside U, the complement of U can be added to the invariant. This allows time-elapse only outside U. However, the system can reach the border of U, which is not included in the complement of U. Hence we include the topological closure of $\overline{U}$ in the invariant, at the price of including spurious behavior. The spurious behavior arises from admissible activities that continue after touching the border of the urgent condition, as illustrated in Figure 3. They are excluded if U is enlarged even slightly. Let the ε*-ball* of some norm $\|\cdot\|$ be $\mathcal{B}_\varepsilon = \{x \mid \|x\| \leq \varepsilon\}$.

Theorem 2. Given a location $\ell \in Loc$. Let P be a set of valuations, $I = Inv(\ell)$ be the invariant in location ℓ and $U = Urg(\ell)$ be the urgent condition of ℓ. The urgent post operator $UPost_\ell(P, I, U)$ can be overapproximated by

$$UPost_\ell(P, I, U) \subseteq ncPost_\ell(P, I \cap cl(\overline{U})),$$

and any $\varepsilon > 0$,

$$ncPost_\ell(P, I \cap cl(\overline{U \oplus \mathcal{B}_\varepsilon})) \subseteq UPost_\ell(P, I, U).$$

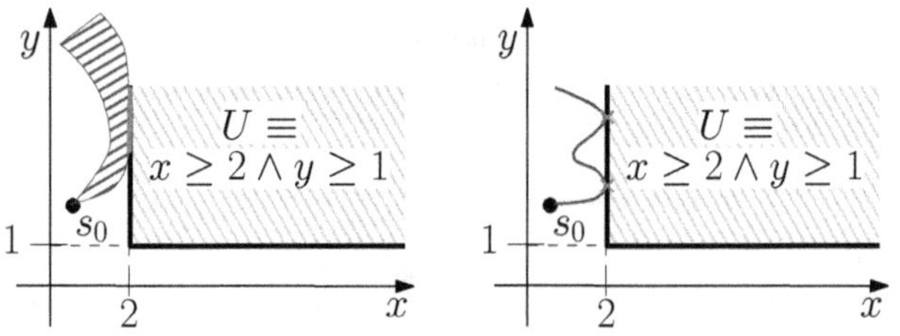

(a) the red line is computed but is not in $UPost_\ell$ (b) the red crosses are computed but are not in $UPost_\ell$

Figure 3: The two cases when the computation of $UPost_\ell$ is an approximation

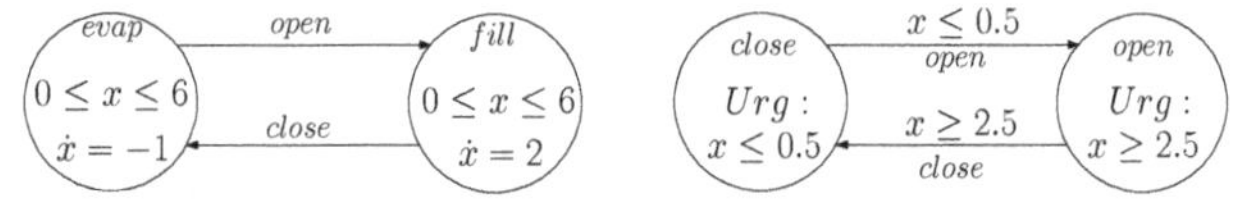

(a) tank (b) controller

Figure 4: Hybrid automata modeling the Water Tank Controller (WTC)

3. RELAXATIONS OF HYBRID AUTOMATA

The standard semantics of hybrid automata, as presented in Sect. 2, may be problematic if the goal is to verify a given simulation model. They are a mathematical idealization, while numerical simulation is based on time discretization and finite precision arithmetic.

ASSUMPTION 1. *An execution of the simulation model approximates each activity $f(t)$ at time points $t_0, t_1, \ldots$ with a sequence of valuations $v_0, v_1, \ldots$ such that for all $i = 0, 1, \ldots,$*

(i) $t_{i+1} - t_i \leq \Delta$ (bounded time step), and

(ii) $\|f(t_i) - v_i\| \leq \varepsilon$ (bounded precision).

For the purpose of this paper, assumption (i) can be relaxed so that it applies only to states within a neighborhood of the urgent guards. Assumption (ii) is satisfied by most ODE solvers, except that the global bound ε is usually not known in absolute terms. Instead, solvers guarantee convergence as the time step goes to zero, e.g., $\varepsilon = \mathcal{O}(\Delta^p)$, where p is the order of the solver. ODE solvers that guarantee global bounds are available [22], but convergence and scalability are more challenging when conservative error bounds are imposed.

Example 1. We use a simplification of the Water Tank Control (*WTC*) model reported in [11] to illustrate why a verification model can be safe while its simulation model can be instead unsafe. The WTC consists of a single tank with a valve that can be controlled to add water. The water is subject to natural evaporation. The level of the water inside the tank is monitored by a sensor. A verification model of the WTC is used to check whether, via a sequence of opening and closing of the valve, it is possible to maintain the level of the water within given bounds.

The verification model consists of the hybrid automata in Fig. 4. The tank model is shown in Fig. 4(a). A continuous variable x models the water level. Two locations are used

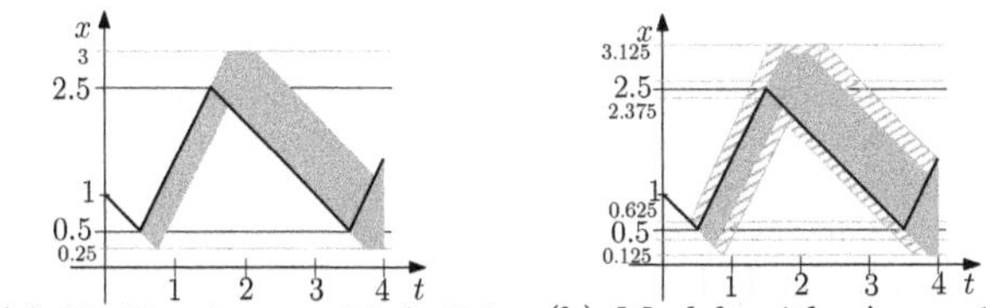

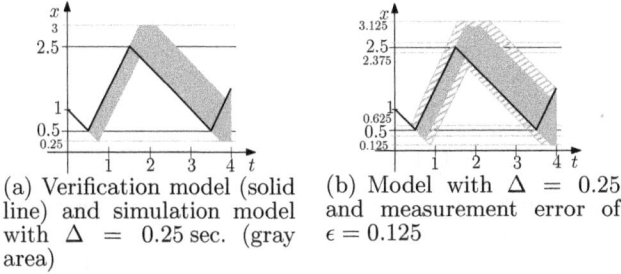

(a) Verification model (solid line) and simulation model with $\Delta = 0.25$ sec. (gray area)

(b) Model with $\Delta = 0.25$ and measurement error of $\epsilon = 0.125$

Figure 5: Reachability sets (over the first 4 sec.) for verification and simulation models for WTC

to model when x is decreasing (i.e. closed valve and evaporation) and increasing (i.e. open valve). The automaton for the controller is shown by Fig. 4(b). It has two locations for modeling the open and close commands for the valve. Since the desired safety property is to maintain x inside the interval $S = [0.5, 2.5]$, the urgent (ASAP) guards are $x \leq 0.5$ for opening and $x \geq 2.5$ for closing the value; the urgency conditions of the locations are the union of the urgent guard conditions.

The reachability analysis under standard semantics shows the safety of the verification model. The solid black line of Fig. 5(a) is a graphical representation of the reachability set from initial condition $x = 1$, over the first 4 sec., and it is easy to see that x never exceeds the limits 0.5 and 2.5.

A numerical simulation with an upper bound Δ on the time step may recognize an urgent guard condition during the next sample time, thus by delaying the reaction by Δ units of times. This delay leads the system to unsafe states, as shown the gray area of Fig. 5(a). For $\Delta = 0.25$ sec., the system may exceed the upper limit by 0.5 units by delaying the switch Δ extra time with flow $\dot{x} = 2$. Similarly, the lower limit may be exceeded by 0.25 units.

To capture the finite precision computation, let the approximate value be $\hat{x} = x + \epsilon'$, where $\epsilon' \in \varepsilon = [-\epsilon, +\epsilon]$. The guard check of the simulator evaluates $\hat{x} \in \mathcal{G}$. As a consequence, the resulting reachable set contains some extra valuations, as depicted in Fig. 5(b) by the tiled gray area for $\Delta = 0.25$ sec. and $\epsilon = 0.125$.

3.1 Relaxed Semantics

In this section we define relaxed semantics for hybrid automata. The semantics uses as parameters a bound Δ on the time step of the simulation model and a bound ϵ on the precision error, as defined in Assumption 1.

To formally define the relaxed semantics, we need some extra notation. Let P be a set of valuations and $\epsilon \geq 0$. The *ε-enlargement* of P is the set

$$\lceil P \rceil \varepsilon = \{w \mid \exists v \in P : \|v - w\| \leq \varepsilon\} = P \oplus \mathcal{B}_\varepsilon,$$

where $\oplus$ denotes the Minkowski sum and $\mathcal{B}_\varepsilon$ is the ball of size ε of the chosen norm. The *ε-shrinkage* of P is the set

$$\lfloor P \rfloor_\varepsilon = \bigcap_{b \in \mathcal{B}_\varepsilon} \{v - b \mid v \in P\} = P \ominus \mathcal{B}_\varepsilon.$$

We now define the relaxed semantics. Let $\Delta \geq 0$ be the bound on the time step and $\epsilon \geq 0$ be the precision error. A *discrete step* in relaxed semantics is obtained from a discrete step in standard semantics, Def. 1, by replacing condition (ii), the check of the guard condition, with the following condition that accounts for the precision error:

(ii)* $\exists e \in \mathcal{B}_\varepsilon$: $val(s) + e \in \mathcal{G}$.

To define a relaxed time step, we use a relaxed definition of the switching time, which takes into account that the urgent condition is checked only at discrete time points, and that the check is subjected to the precision error. First, time may elapse until the urgency condition U is satisfied even when taking into account all possible precision errors. Second, since the urgency condition is only checked at discrete time points, the urgency condition must be satisfied for at least Δ time to be sure that a check takes place. Both phenomena are captured by the following relaxation of the switching time. The *relaxed switching time* of an activity $f \in Adm(s)$ in location ℓ, denoted by $SwitchT_\varepsilon^\Delta(f, Urg(\ell))$, is the value $T + \Delta \geq 0$ such that, for all $0 \leq \delta' < T$, there exists some precision error $e \in \mathcal{B}_\varepsilon$ such that $f(\delta') + e \notin Urg(\ell)$, and for all $T \leq \delta' \leq T + \Delta$ and for all precision errors $e \in \mathcal{B}_\varepsilon$, $f(\delta') + e \in Urg(\ell)$. When such a value does not exists, we write $SwitchT_\varepsilon^\Delta(f, Urg(\ell)) = \infty$.

A *timed step* in relaxed semantics is obtained from a timed step in standard semantics, Def. 2, by replacing condition (iii), the check of the urgency condition via the switching time, with the relaxed switching time:

(iii)* $\delta \leq SwitchT_\varepsilon^\Delta(f, Urg(loc(s)))$.

The definition of a *relaxed run* is straightforward, as well as the resulting definition of reachability. We denote the set of the run under relaxed semantics by $Runs_\epsilon^\Delta(H)$ and the set of reachable states under relaxed semantics by $Reach_\epsilon^\Delta(H)$.

The following properties about relaxed semantics are intuitive, and the related proofs can be found in [20].

Property 1. [Faster is better] Let H be a hybrid automaton and given $\epsilon \geq 0$. For any $\Delta_1, \Delta_2 \in \mathbb{R}^{\geq 0}$ such that $\Delta_1 \leq \Delta_2$, it holds that $Reach_\varepsilon^{\Delta_1}(H) \subseteq Reach_\varepsilon^{\Delta_2}(H)$.

Property 2. [Precision is a quality] Let H be a hybrid automaton and given $\Delta \geq 0$. For any $\epsilon_1, \epsilon_2 \in \mathbb{R}^{\geq 0}$ such that $\epsilon_1 \leq \epsilon_2$, it holds that $Reach_{\varepsilon_1}^\Delta(H) \subseteq Reach_{\varepsilon_2}^\Delta(H)$.

Property 3. [Preserving Safety] Let H be a hybrid automaton, $\Delta' > 0$ be a bound on the sampling time and $\epsilon' > 0$ be a bound on the precision error. If H is safe in relaxed semantics, then there is a bound $0 < \Delta \leq \Delta'$ on the sampling time and a bound on the precision error $0 < \varepsilon \leq \varepsilon'$ such that all executions of the simulation model are safe under Assumption 1.

3.2 Relaxed Hybrid Automata

In this section we will show that the relaxed semantics can be translated to an equivalent relaxed model evaluated under standard semantics. The advantage of having this equivalence is that the correctness of a simulation model could be proved by using the standard reachability on the relaxed model.

We already show the reachability set $Reach_\epsilon^\Delta(H)$ for the WTC example obtained with a time step bounded by $\Delta = 0.25$ sec and a global error measurement bounded by $\epsilon = 0.125$ (see the gray area depicted by Fig. 5(b)).

Consider now another version of controller modeled by the linear hybrid automaton H', obtained from the by replacing guards and urgent conditions of automaton H depicted by Fig. 4(b). Now the urgent conditions are less restrictive (i.e. $x \leq 0.125$ and $x \geq 3.125$ for the two locations, respectively), as well as the guards (i.e. $x \leq 0.625$ and $x \geq 2.375$, respectively). The obtained relaxed model is such that, under the standard semantics, the model may perform a discrete transition when $x \in (0.125, 0.625]$ or $x \in [2.375, 3.125)$, while it must jump when $x = 0.125$ or 3.125. Accordingly the reachability set $\mathit{Reach}(H')$ of such a model is clearly bounded by the interval $\in [0.125, 3.125]$, and moreover is completely equivalent to the relaxed reachability set $\mathit{Reach}_\varepsilon^\Delta(H)$. In other words, the standard reachability set on the relaxed model is equal to the relaxed reachability set on the standard model. The key point behind this equivalence is that the relaxed automaton was obtained by properly relaxing urgent conditions and guards of transitions. In particular, guard are enlarged according to the interval error ε. Instead urgent condition are shrunk according to ε and in addition in a way that allows time-elapse for further Δ units of time, where Δ is the bound of the time step. The following definition is the formalization of the urgency relaxation.

Definition 3 (Urgency *Relaxation*). Given a location $\ell \in \mathit{Loc}$, and let $U = \mathit{Urg}(\ell)$ be the urgent condition location ℓ, $\Delta \geq 0$ and $\epsilon \geq 0$ be bounds on time step and precision error, respectively.

The *relaxation* of the urgency condition U is the set of valuations

$$\begin{aligned} \lfloor U \rfloor_\varepsilon^\Delta = \{p \in \lfloor U \rfloor_\varepsilon | p \notin \mathit{Post}_\ell(\overline{\lfloor U \rfloor_\varepsilon}, \mathbb{R}^n) \text{ or} \\ \exists u \in \overline{\lfloor U \rfloor_\varepsilon}, f \in \mathit{Adm}(\langle \ell, u \rangle), 0 < \delta_1 < \delta_2 \text{ with } \delta_2 \geq \delta_1 + \Delta : \\ \forall 0 \leq \delta' < \delta_1, f(\delta') \notin \lfloor U \rfloor_\varepsilon, \\ \forall \delta_1 \leq \delta' \leq \delta_2, f(\delta') \in \lfloor U \rfloor_\varepsilon, \text{ and} \\ f(\delta_2) = p\} \end{aligned} \quad (8)$$

There is an immediate relation between the relaxed switching time of an urgent condition U and the standard switching time of a corresponding relaxed condition, as stated by the following lemma.

Lemma 1. Given a location $\ell \in \mathit{Loc}$, and let $U = \mathit{Urg}(\ell)$ be a urgent condition, $\Delta, \epsilon \geq 0$ be upper bounds on time step and precision error, respectively. Then for all $u \in \lfloor U \rfloor_\varepsilon \cap$ and $f \in \mathit{Adm}(\langle \ell, u \rangle)$,

$$\mathit{SwitchT}(f, \lfloor U \rfloor_\varepsilon^\Delta) = \mathit{SwitchT}_\varepsilon^\Delta(f, U).$$

A proof of Lemma 1 can be found in [20].

Now we are ready to formalize the automaton relaxed by considering a reaction delay Δ and a global measurement error ϵ.

Definition 4 (Relaxed Hybrid Automaton). Let $\mathcal{H} = (\mathit{Loc}, X, \mathit{Lab}, \mathit{Inv}, \mathit{Urg}, \mathit{Flow}, \mathit{Trans}, \mathit{Init})$ be a hybrid automaton, $\Delta, \epsilon \geq 0$ be upper bounds on time step and error precision, respectively. Then the *relaxed hybrid automaton* $\mathcal{H}_\varepsilon^\Delta = (\mathit{Loc}, X, \mathit{Lab}, \mathit{Inv}, \mathit{Urg}', \mathit{Flow}, \mathit{Trans}', \mathit{Init})$ is such that:

- $\mathit{Urg}' = \{\langle \ell, \lfloor U \rfloor_\varepsilon^\Delta \rangle | \langle \ell, U \rangle \in \mathit{Urg}\}$
- $\mathit{Trans}' = \{\langle \ell_1, \alpha, \lceil \mathcal{G} \rceil_\varepsilon, \mathit{Asgn} \rangle \mid \langle \ell_1, \alpha, \mathcal{G}, \mathit{Asgn} \rangle \in \mathit{Trans}\}$

As already informal discussed, there is a direct relation that connects an automaton $\mathcal{H}$ evaluated under relaxed semantics and its relaxation $\mathcal{H}_\varepsilon^\Delta$ evaluated on standard semantics. As the intuition suggests, the corresponding sets of all the runs are equivalent, as formalized by the following theorem (the proof can be found in [20]).

Theorem 3. [Relaxed Semantics Equivalence] Given a hybrid automaton $\mathcal{H} = (\mathit{Loc}, X, \mathit{Lab}, \mathit{Inv}, \mathit{Urg}, \mathit{Flow}, \mathit{Trans}, \mathit{Init})$. Let $\Delta \geq 0$ be a reaction delay, and $\epsilon \geq 0$ be a global measurement error. The relaxed automaton $\mathcal{H}_\varepsilon^\Delta = (\mathit{Loc}, X, \mathit{Lab}, \mathit{Inv}, \mathit{Urg}', \mathit{Flow}, \mathit{Trans}', \mathit{Init})$ is such that

$$\mathit{Runs}_\epsilon^\Delta(\mathcal{H}) = \mathit{Runs}(\mathcal{H}_\varepsilon^\Delta).$$

From Theorem 3 directly follows the reachability equivalence, as stated by the following corollary

Corollary 2. Given a hybrid automaton $\mathcal{H} = (\mathit{Loc}, X, \mathit{Lab}, \mathit{Inv}, \mathit{Urg}, \mathit{Flow}, \mathit{Trans}, \mathit{Init})$. Let $\Delta \geq 0$ be a reaction delay, and $\epsilon \geq 0$ be a global measurement error. The relaxed automaton $\mathcal{H}_\varepsilon^\Delta = (\mathit{Loc}, X, \mathit{Lab}, \mathit{Inv}, \mathit{Urg}', \mathit{Flow}, \mathit{Trans}', \mathit{Init})$ is such that

$$\mathit{Reach}_\epsilon^\Delta(\mathcal{H}) = \mathit{Reach}(\mathcal{H}_\epsilon^\Delta).$$

Corollary 2 has a practice consequence on the task of proving safety w.r.t. a safe state S of a simulation model via reachability of a corresponding verification model H. Indeed, Prop. 3 says that this can by done by checking whether $\mathit{Reach}_\epsilon^\Delta(\mathcal{H}) \cap S$ is empty or not. But by Corollary 2 this is equivalent to check whether $\mathit{Reach}(\mathcal{H}_\varepsilon^\Delta) \cap S$ is empty or not. In other words, the safety of a simulation model can be proved via the standard reachability on the corresponding relaxed automaton as formalized by the following corollary

Corollary 3. Given a time step bounded by $\Delta > 0$, an error measurement bounded by $\epsilon > 0$ and a safe state S. Let $\mathcal{H}_\epsilon^\Delta$ be a relaxed automaton. Then there exists a safe implementation of $\mathcal{H}_\epsilon^\Delta$ by a simulation model with time step bounded by $0 < \Delta' \leq \Delta$ and an error measurement bounded by $0 < \epsilon' \leq \epsilon$ if and only if

$$\mathit{Reach}(\mathcal{H}_\epsilon^\Delta) \cap S = \emptyset.$$

Theorem 3 establishes the equivalence between relaxed semantics on ideal models and standard semantics on relaxed models. Now we present how to compute the corresponding relaxed automaton.

The following lemmas gives a way to compute the enlargement and shrinkage operators for the case of polyhedral sets. The exact solution would be of exponential complexity in the number of variables. To keep the computation scalable, we use conservative approximations.

Lemma 2. [Enlargement and Shrinkage] Given a convex polyhedron $P = \{x \in \mathbb{R}^n | \bigwedge_i a_i^T x \leq b_i\}$ and a real number $\epsilon \geq 0$,

$$\lceil P \rceil_\varepsilon \subseteq \{x \in \mathbb{R}^n \mid \bigwedge_i a_i^T x \leq b_i + \epsilon \|a_i\|\}, \text{ and}$$

$$\{x \in \mathbb{R}^n \mid \bigwedge_i a_i^T x \leq b_i - \epsilon \|a_i\|\} \subseteq \lfloor P \rfloor_\varepsilon.$$

While the enlargement and shrinkage operations on polyhedra in Lemma 2 are only approximative, the approximation error goes to zero as $\epsilon \to 0$. This is sufficient for the purposes of this paper and the results that follow. The next lemma establishes how to compute the relaxation of urgent conditions.

Lemma 3. [Computation for relaxed urgency] The relaxed urgency condition $\lfloor U \rfloor_{\varepsilon}^{\Delta}$ can be computed as:

$$\lfloor U \rfloor_{\varepsilon}^{\Delta} = \lfloor U \rfloor_{\epsilon} \setminus \Delta Post_{\ell}(\overline{\lfloor U \rfloor_{\varepsilon}}, \mathbb{R}^n, \Delta).$$

PROOF. [$\subseteq$] Let p be a valuation belonging to $\lfloor U \rfloor_{\varepsilon}^{\Delta}$. The definition of relaxation implies that $p \in \lfloor U \rfloor_{\varepsilon}$ and either (a) $p \notin Post_{\ell}(\overline{\lfloor U \rfloor_{\varepsilon}}, \mathbb{R}^n)$ or (b) there exists a valuation $u \in \overline{\lfloor U \rfloor_{\varepsilon}}$, an activity $f \in Adm(\langle \ell, u \rangle)$ and times $0 < \delta_1 < \delta_2$ with $\delta_2 \geq \delta_1 + \Delta$ such that for all $0 \leq \delta' < \delta_1$ it holds that $f(\delta') \notin \lfloor U \rfloor_{\varepsilon}$, for all $\delta_1 \leq \delta' \leq \delta_2$ it holds that $f(\delta') \in \lfloor U \rfloor_{\varepsilon}$, and $f(\delta_2) = p$.

Case (a) implies that $p \notin \Delta Post_{\ell}(\overline{\lfloor U \rfloor_{\varepsilon}}, \mathbb{R}^n, \Delta)$, and hence $p \in \lfloor U \rfloor_{\epsilon} \setminus \Delta Post_{\ell}(\overline{\lfloor U \rfloor_{\varepsilon}}, \mathbb{R}^n, \Delta)$. Otherwise, for case (b) suppose by contradiction that $p \in \Delta Post_{\ell}(\overline{\lfloor U \rfloor_{\varepsilon}}, \mathbb{R}^n, \Delta)$, that is there exists a valuation $u \in \overline{\lfloor U \rfloor_{\varepsilon}}$, an activity $f \in Adm(\langle \ell, u \rangle)$ and a time $\delta \leq \Delta$ such that $f(\delta) = p$. Hence, for reaching $p \in \lfloor U \rfloor_{\varepsilon}$ from $u \in \overline{\lfloor U \rfloor_{\varepsilon}}$ the system spends at most $\delta < \Delta$ time inside $\lfloor U \rfloor_{\varepsilon}$. The last would imply $p \notin \lfloor U \rfloor_{\varepsilon}^{\Delta}$, that is in contrast with the hypothesis $p \in \lfloor U \rfloor_{\varepsilon}^{\Delta}$. Hence $p \notin \Delta Post_{\ell}(\overline{\lfloor U \rfloor_{\varepsilon}}, \mathbb{R}^n, \Delta)$, and by recalling that $p \in \lfloor U \rfloor_{\varepsilon}$ we can write $p \in \lfloor U \rfloor_{\varepsilon} \setminus \Delta Post_{\ell}(\overline{\lfloor U \rfloor_{\varepsilon}}, \mathbb{R}^n, \Delta)$.

[$\supseteq$] Let p be a valuation belonging to $\lfloor U \rfloor_{\epsilon} \setminus \Delta Post_{\ell}(\overline{\lfloor U \rfloor_{\varepsilon}}, \mathbb{R}^n, \Delta)$. That is $p \in \lfloor U \rfloor_{\epsilon}$ and $p \notin \Delta Post_{\ell}(\overline{\lfloor U \rfloor_{\varepsilon}}, \mathbb{R}^n, \Delta)$. Last one condition means that either (a) $p \notin Post_{\ell}(\overline{\lfloor U \rfloor_{\varepsilon}}, \mathbb{R}^n)$ or (b) there exists a time $\Delta_1 > \Delta$ such that $p \in \Delta Post_{\ell}(\overline{\lfloor U \rfloor_{\varepsilon}}, \mathbb{R}^n, \Delta_1)$. By definition of relaxation of urgency, case (a) trivially implies that $p \in \lfloor U \rfloor_{\varepsilon}^{\Delta}$. Otherwise case (b) says that there exist a valuation $u \in \overline{\lfloor U \rfloor_{\varepsilon}}$, an activity $f \in Adm(\langle \ell, u \rangle)$ and a time δ with $\Delta < \delta \leq \Delta_1$, such that $f(\delta) = p$. On the trajectory leading from $u = f(0) \in \overline{\lfloor U \rfloor_{\varepsilon}}$ to $p = f(\delta) \in \lfloor U \rfloor_{\varepsilon}$ it is always possible to identify the last time δ^* with $\Delta < \delta^* \leq \delta$ such that for all $\delta^* \leq \delta' \leq \delta$ it holds that $f(\delta') \in \lfloor U \rfloor_{\varepsilon}$. If $\delta - \delta^* < \Delta$ then by definition $p \in \Delta Post_{\ell}(\overline{\lfloor U \rfloor_{\varepsilon}}, \mathbb{R}^n, \Delta)$ that contradicts the hypothesis. Hence $\delta - \delta^*$ must be at least equal to Δ and then by definition of relaxed urgency $p \in \lfloor U \rfloor_{\varepsilon}^{\Delta}$. □

3.3 Approximative Reachability

In general, the reachable states of a hybrid system with piecewise affine dynamics can only be computed approximatively. When checking safety properties, one can use conservative overapproximations to obtain soundness. But this may lead to false negatives, i.e., the analysis could indicate a violation of safety even if actually the system is safe. Concretely, if the reachability analysis indicates that the system is unsafe then it is not clear whether one should repeat the analysis with increased precision or whether one should conclude that the system is actually unsafe. It has long been argued, e.g., in [6], that real systems should robustly satisfy safety properties, and that including robustness assumptions in the semantics or the analysis can lead to decidability. A similar argument can be made for the relaxed semantics presented in this paper.

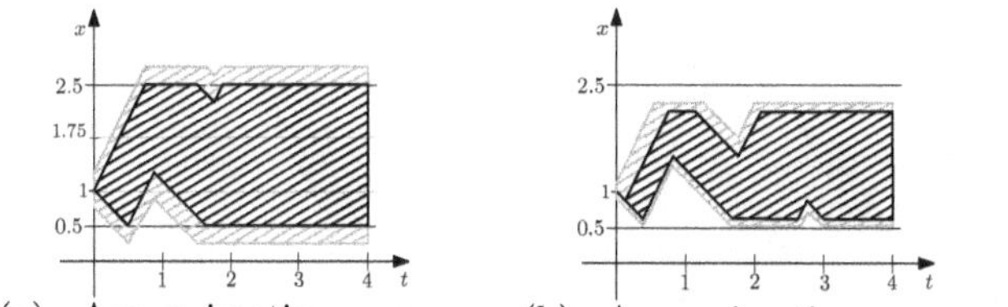

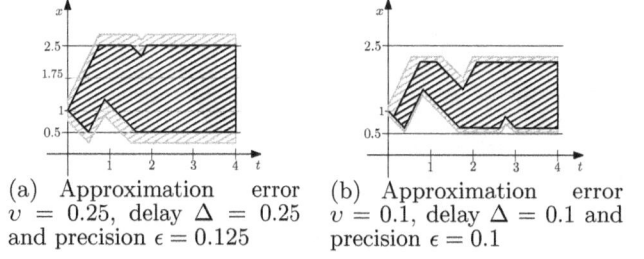

(a) Approximation error $\upsilon = 0.25$, delay $\Delta = 0.25$ and precision $\epsilon = 0.125$

(b) Approximation error $\upsilon = 0.1$, delay $\Delta = 0.1$ and precision $\epsilon = 0.1$

Figure 6: Reachability sets with different parameters for the relaxed WTC

For illustration, consider a safe relaxed hybrid automaton whose exact reachability set is depicted by the black area of Fig. 6(a). For this case, the reachability analysis with an approximation error of $\upsilon_1 = 0.25$ indicates a violation of safety even if the model is safe. A first possibility is to compute the reachability set with a smaller error, for example by setting $\upsilon' = 0.1$, but this may not be sufficient no matter how small υ'. In order to give more room to the approximation error, we can use smaller bound on the time step (for example $\Delta' = 0.1$ *sec*) and on the error measurement (for example $\epsilon' = 0.1$). With these parameters, the reachability analysis is now able to show the safety of the system, as shown by Fig. 6(b).

In order to formalize the feature described above, we introduce some extra notation. Let Loc be the set of locations, $S = \{\langle \ell, v \rangle \| \ell \in Loc, v \in Val(X)\}$ be a set of states and s be a state. With abuse of notation we use $bndry(s, S)$ to denote the boundary between the valuation of s and the set of valuations of S, that is $bndry(val(s), S\downarrow_{Loc})$.

The next assumption is enough to avoid false positive.

ASSUMPTION 2. *Let H_{ϵ}^{Δ} be a relaxed hybrid automaton with $\Delta > 0$ and $\epsilon > 0$, and S be a set of safe states. The reachability set of H_{ϵ}^{Δ} is such that each state $s \in Reach(H_{\epsilon}^{\Delta})$ with $bndry(s, \overline{S}) \neq \emptyset$ can only be reachable by a run $r = s_0 \xrightarrow{\delta_0, f_0} s_0' \xrightarrow{e_0} s_1 \xrightarrow{\delta_1, f_1} s_1' \xrightarrow{e_1} s_2 \cdots s_n' = s$ such that*

$$\exists \delta_i > 0 : \delta_i = SwitchT\Big(f_i, Urg\big(loc(s_i')\big)\Big).$$

Assumption 2 says that each reachable state s lying on the boundary with the unsafe set can be reachable only via a run where at least an urgent condition is satisfied after a non-zero elapsing of time. From a practical point of view we are assuming that critical behaviors of the systems are generated by those trajectories that at some point in time touch an urgent condition, and this is plausible if one considers that urgent conditions are used precisely in order to prevent unsafe behaviors. Moreover the condition of $\delta_i > 0$ implies that initial states do not belong to the unsafe state $\overline{S}$. And also this choice is plausible because initial states belonging to $\overline{S}$ make the system unsafe by definition.

Given a relaxed automaton H_{ϵ}^{Δ} and a set of safe states S, the practical sufficient condition to guarantee that H_{ϵ}^{Δ} satisfies Assumption 2 is the existence of an error location $err \in Loc$ accessible through urgent transitions, one from each location in the unsafe set. The urgent condition associated to these transitions is the topological closure of the unsafe set of valuations, that is $Z = cl(val(\overline{S}))$. Moreover, the set of initial valuations of H_{ϵ}^{Δ} must not belong to Z.

The following theorem is the formalization of the features described above, for a complete proof see [20].

Theorem 4. [Absorption of the overapproximation] Let H_ϵ^Δ be a relaxed hybrid automaton with $\Delta > 0$ and $\epsilon > 0$, and S be a set of safe states. If H_ϵ^Δ satisfies Assumption 2 and $Reach(H_\epsilon^\Delta) \cap \overline{S} = \emptyset$ then there exists an approximation error $\upsilon > 0$, a time step bound $0 < \Delta' < \Delta$ and a precision error bound $0 < \epsilon' < \epsilon$ such that $Reach^\upsilon(H_{\epsilon'}^{\Delta'}) \cap \overline{S} = \emptyset$.

4. REFERENCES

[1] M. Agrawal and P. Thiagarajan. Lazy rectangular hybrid automata. In R. Alur and G. Pappas, editors, *Hybrid Systems: Computation and Control*, volume 2993 of *Lecture Notes in Computer Science*, pages 1–15. Springer Berlin Heidelberg, 2004.

[2] M. Agrawal and P. Thiagarajan. The discrete time behavior of lazy linear hybrid automata. In M. Morari and L. Thiele, editors, *Hybrid Systems: Computation and Control*, volume 3414 of *Lecture Notes in Computer Science*, pages 55–69. Springer Berlin Heidelberg, 2005.

[3] D. Beek, M.A., Reniers, R.R.H., Schiffelers, and J. Rooda. Foundations of a compositional interchange format for hybrid systems. In *HSCC'07*, volume 4416 of *LNCS*, pages 587–600. Springer, 2007.

[4] S. Bogomolov, D. Magazzeni, S. Minopoli, and M. Wehrle. Pddl+ planning with hybrid automata: Foundations of translating must behavior. In *Proceedings International Conference on Automated Planning and Scheduling, ICAPS*, volume 2015-January, pages 42–46. AAAI Press, 2015.

[5] J. T. Buck, S. Ha, E. A. Lee, and D. G. Messerschmitt. *Ptolemy: A framework for simulating and prototyping heterogeneous systems.* Ablex Publishing Corporation, 1994.

[6] M. Fränzle. Analysis of hybrid systems: An ounce of realism can save an infinity of states. In *Computer Science Logic*, pages 126–139. Springer, 1999.

[7] G. Frehse. Reachability of hybrid systems in space-time. In *EMSOFT'15*, 2015.

[8] G. Frehse, C. L. Guernic, A. Donzé, S. Cotton, R. Ray, O. Lebeltel, R. Ripado, A. Girard, T. Dang, and O. Maler. Spaceex: Scalable verification of hybrid systems. In *CAV 11: Proc. of 23rd Conf. on Computer Aided Verification*, pages 379–395, 2011.

[9] G. Frehse and A. Paice. Optimal control of a gas compressor field. In *MTNS'00*, 2000.

[10] B. Gebremichael and F. Vaandrager. Specifying urgency in timed i/o automata. In *SEFM'05*, pages 64–74. IEEE Computer Society, 2005.

[11] W. Heemels, D. Lehmann, J. Lunze, and B. De Schutter. Introduction to hybrid systems. In *Handbook of Hybrid Systems Control – Theory, Tools, Applications*, pages 3–30. Cambridge University Press, Cambridge, UK, 2009.

[12] T. Henzinger. The theory of hybrid automata. In *11th IEEE Symp. Logic in Comp. Sci.*, pages 278–292, 1996.

[13] T. A. Henzinger, P.-H. Ho, and H. Wong-Toi. Hytech: the next generation. In *Proc. IEEE Real-Time Systems Symposium (RTSS '95)*, page 56. IEEE Computer Society, 1995.

[14] P.-H. Ho. *Automatic Analysis of Hybrid Systems.* PhD thesis, Cornell University, Aug. 1995. Technical Report CSD-TR95-1536.

[15] S. Jha, B. Brady, and S. Seshia. Symbolic reachability analysis of lazy linear hybrid automata. In J.-F. Raskin and P. Thiagarajan, editors, *Formal Modeling and Analysis of Timed Systems*, volume 4763 of *Lecture Notes in Computer Science*, pages 241–256. Springer Berlin Heidelberg, 2007.

[16] MathWorks. Mathworks simulink: Simulation et model-based design, Mar. 2014. www.mathworks.fr/products/simulink.

[17] S. E. Mattsson, H. Elmqvist, and M. Otter. Physical system modeling with modelica. *Control Engineering Practice*, 6(4):501–510, 1998.

[18] S. Minopoli and G. Frehse. SL2SX tool and case study. www-verimag.imag.fr/~minopoli/SL2SXdemo.zip.

[19] S. Minopoli and G. Frehse. Non-convex invariants and urgency conditions on linear hybrid automata. In *12th International Conference on Formal Modeling and Analysis of Timed Systems*, 2014.

[20] S. Minopoli and G. Frehse. From simulation models to hybrid automata using urgency and relaxation. Technical Report TR-2015-10, Verimag, October 2015.

[21] S. Minopoli and G. Frehse. SL2SX translator: From simulink to spaceex models. In *HSCC'16*, 2016.

[22] N. S. Nedialkov, K. R. Jackson, and G. F. Corliss. Validated solutions of initial value problems for ordinary differential equations. *Applied Mathematics and Computation*, 105(1):21–68, 1999.

[23] L. V. Nguyen and T. T. Johnson. Dc-to-dc switched-mode power converters. In *1st Workshop on Applied Verification for Continuous and Hybrid Systems (ARCH)*. http://cps-vo.org/node/12113, 2014.

[24] X. Nicollin, A. Olivero, J. Sifakis, and S. Yovine. An approach to the description and analysis of hybrid systems. In *Hybrid Systems*, pages 149–178. Springer, 1993.

[25] M. W. Whalen, A. Murugesan, S. Rayadurgam, and M. P. E. Heimdahl. Structuring simulink models for verification and reuse. In *Proceedings of the 6th International Workshop on Modeling in Software Engineering*, MiSE 2014, pages 19–24, New York, NY, USA, 2014. ACM.

[26] M. Wulf, L. Doyen, and J.-F. Raskin. Almost asap semantics: From timed models to timed implementations. In *HSCC'04*, volume 2993 of *LNCS*, pages 296–310. Springer, 2004.

Parallelotope Bundles for Polynomial Reachability*

Tommaso Dreossi
University of Udine
VERIMAG
2 Avenue de Vignate
38610 Gieres, France
tommaso.dreossi@imag.fr

Thao Dang
VERIMAG
2 Avenue de Vignate
38610 Gieres, France
thao.dang@imag.fr

Carla Piazza
University of Udine
via delle Scienze 206
33100 Udine, Italy
carla.piazza@uniud.it

ABSTRACT

In this work we present *parallelotope bundles*, i.e., sets of parallelotopes for a symbolic representation of polytopes. We define a compact representation of these objects and show that any polytope can be canonically expressed by a bundle. We propose efficient algorithms for the manipulation of bundles. Among these, we define techniques for computing tight over-approximations of polynomial transformations. We apply our framework, in combination with the Bernstein technique, to the reachability problem for polynomial dynamical systems. The accuracy and scalability of our approach are validated on a number of case studies.

Keywords

Reachability; dynamical system; parallelotope bundle; polytope

1. INTRODUCTION

In this paper we are concerned with polynomial image computation and its application to reachability analysis of dynamical systems. The image computation can be stated as follows: given a function $\mathbf{f} : D \to R$ and a set $X \subset D$, compute the image of X by $\mathbf{f}$, that is the set $Y = \{\mathbf{f}(\mathbf{x}) \mid \mathbf{x} \in X\}$. The function $\mathbf{f}$, commonly called *dynamics*, describes the flow of the system (or its approximation derived from the system vector field), where the sets D and R are typically $\mathbb{R}^n$ when the state variables of the dynamical system in question are real-valued. Set-based image computation is a central operation for many verification and synthesis procedures. A number of approaches in the verification of continuous and hybrid systems can be seen as extensions of numerical integration where the iterative numerical schemes are computed on sets. In addition, image computation finds applications in other problems such as control synthesis [22] or program verification through invariant computation via fixed-point iteration.

For affine functions, image computation can be efficiently computed using various set representations, such as polyhedra, ellipsoids, support functions, zonotopes (see, e.g., [10, 4, 29, 18, 23, 27, 24, 1, 15]). For nonlinear functions such as polynomials, the problem is more difficult since many properties of linear functions that facilitate image computation (such as convexity preservation) are no longer valid. One approach to handle nonlinearity is to use piecewise linear approximations [20, 5, 6, 2]. While this approach can be applied to a quite general class of flows and vector fields, other approaches focus on some special classes of functions and exploit their properties. Among these classes, polynomials have drawn a particular interest thanks to their applications in the modeling of biological processes, economic, and engineering systems.

In [13] we proposed a technique for polynomial systems using the Bernstein expansion, which allows one to efficiently approximate the image of a box domain by a polynomial. However, the box representation is restrictive in geometrical expressiveness and thus limited in approximation power. For better approximation accuracy, more general sets should be used. In [12] we introduced the idea of using parallelotopes as a trade-off between computational complexity and approximation accuracy. Indeed, using parallelotopes, the transformation to boxes can be done efficiently, and in addition, the choice of parallelotopic form can be used to fine tune the approximation. In this work, we generalize this idea to polytopes defining *parallelotope bundles* that allow one to represent polytopes as finite sets of parallelotopes. Intuitively, the strength of parallelotope bundles is that the images of the represented polytopes can be over-approximated by the intersection of the images of the parallelotopes that constitute the bundles. Hence, exploiting the transformations of single parallelotopes, thanks to parallelotope bundles we can tightly over-approximate the images of polytopes by polynomials.

Related to our work, in [8, 9], for a continuous system described by nonlinear ODEs, the flow is first approximated from an interval domain in a time interval by a Taylor polynomial around some point inside the domain. Then, this polynomial is bloated by an interval to account for the remainder terms. Taylor models support basic arithmetic operations using interval arithmetics techniques and can thus handle polynomials. Prior to this work, in [21] interval-based integration of ODEs was used for computing the reachable set of nonlinear hybrid systems. In [26] the reachable set

*This work has been partially supported by GNCS-INdAM and the ANR-INS project MALTHY.

HSCC '16, April 12–14, 2016, Vienna, Austria.
© 2016 ACM. ISBN 978-1-4503-3955-1/16/04. . . $15.00
DOI: http://dx.doi.org/10.1145/2883817.2883838

is also represented by box cells in a partition of the state space and the propagation of the system from one box to a neighboring one is conservatively determined by the flow constraints on their boundary. In terms of reachable set representation, all the above-mentioned methods use boxes. Parallelotopes have been used in [3] as domains for abstract interpretation and algorithms for linear operations, together with specific operations for program verification (assignment, union). Nevertheless, the abstract domain is defined by a single parallelotope and nonlinear operators are not yet considered. The use of zonotopes and template polyhedra adopted by [28, 27, 17, 1, 19] as set representations are also close to our work, but the box-domain requirement of the Bernstein technique makes this sets less convenient to handle, since their transformation to boxes are expensive.

The paper is organized as follows: in Section 2 we introduce basic definitions; Section 3 defines parallelotope bundles and operations on them; Section 4 is dedicated to the representation and the algorithmic manipulation of parallelotope bundles; in Section 5 a reachability algorithm based parallelotope bundles for polynomial dynamical systems is given; the proposed techniques are experimentally validated in Section 6; Section 7 ends the paper with some remarks. The proofs of this work are available at http://www-verimag.imag.fr/~dreossi/docs/papers/bundles_2015.pdf

2. PRELIMINARIES

A half-space h of $\mathbb{R}^n$ is a subset of $\mathbb{R}^n$ characterized by a linear inequality, i.e., $h = \{\mathbf{x} \in \mathbb{R}^n \mid \mathbf{dx} \leq c\}$, where $\mathbf{d} \in \mathbb{R}^n$ is a non-null vector also called *normal vector* and $c \in \mathbb{R}$ is an *offset*.

Definition 1 (Polytope). *A* polytope Q *is a bounded subset of* $\mathbb{R}^n$ *such that there is a finite set* $H = \{h_1, \dots, h_k\}$ *of half-spaces whose intersection is* Q, *i.e.,* $Q = \cap_{i=1}^k h_i$.

The linear constraints that generate the half-spaces can be organized in a matrix $D \in \mathbb{R}^{k \times n}$, called *direction matrix* (or *template*) and a vector $\mathbf{c} \in \mathbb{R}^k$, called *offset vector*. The i-th row D_i of D together with the i-th component $\mathbf{c}_i$ of $\mathbf{c}$ define the half-space $h_i \in H$, being its normal vector and offset, respectively. With a slight abuse of notation, we denote with $\langle D, \mathbf{c} \rangle$ the polytope generated by the direction matrix D the offset vector $\mathbf{c}$. Notice that polytopes are bounded subsets of $\mathbb{R}^n$, hence not all the pairs $\langle D, \mathbf{c} \rangle$ define a polytope.

A polytope Q can be represented as the intersection of different sets of half-spaces. For instance, adding to Q new half-spaces that do not affect the intersection, we get a new representation of Q. Moreover, even without adding new half-spaces, we can get a new representation by multiplying the i-th row of D and the i-th component of $\mathbf{c}$ by a positive constant. However, if needed, one can refer to the canonical representation in which all the half-spaces are necessary and the direction vectors are versors, i.e., vectors of norm one.

Parallelotopes are centrally symmetric polytopes of $\mathbb{R}^n$ having $2n$ pairwise parallel constraints.

Definition 2 (Parallelotope). *Let* $\langle \Lambda, \mathbf{c} \rangle$ *be a polytope in* $\mathbb{R}^n$ *with* $\Lambda \in \mathbb{R}^{2n \times n}$ *direction matrix such that* $\Lambda_i = -\Lambda_{i+n}$, *for* $i \in \{1, \dots, n\}$ *and* $\mathbf{c} \in \mathbb{R}^{2n}$ *offset vector. The* parallelotope P *generated by* Λ *and* $\mathbf{c}$ *is* $P = \langle \Lambda, \mathbf{c} \rangle$.

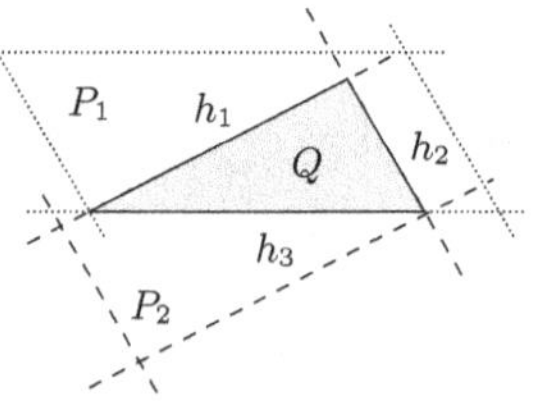

Figure 1: A polytope Q and a possible decomposing bundle $\{P_1, P_2\}$, i.e., $\{P_1, P_2\}^{\cap} = Q$.

3. PARALLELOTOPE BUNDLES

We now define *parallelotope bundles*, that are sets of parallelotopes whose intersections symbolically represent polytopes. Our definition and notation are inspired by [1].

Definition 3 (Parallelotope Bundle). *A* parallelotope bundle *is a finite set of parallelotopes* $\{P_1, \dots, P_b\}$ *whose* intersection, *denoted by* $\{P_1, \dots, P_b\}^{\cap} = \bigcap_{i=1}^b P_i$, *is the polytope generated by* $\langle D, \mathbf{c} \rangle$, *where* D *and* $\mathbf{c}$ *are the union of the templates and offsets of* P_i, *for* $i \in \{1, \dots, b\}$.

Two parallelotope bundles $\{P_1, \dots, P_b\}$ and $\{P'_1, \dots, P'_{b'}\}$ are *equivalent* if they denote the same polytope. A bundle $\{P_1, \dots, P_b\}$ allows us to symbolically represent a polytope $\{P_1, \dots, P_b\}^{\cap}$ without requiring the explicit computation of the intersection of the parallelotopes P_i. Since we are interested in bundles as symbolic representations of polytopes, we can always replace a bundle with an equivalent one, whenever this is convenient.

Lemma 1 (Polytope Decomposition). *Let* Q *be a polytope. There exists a finite set of parallelotopes* $\{P_1, \dots, P_b\}$ *such that* $Q = \{P_1, \dots, P_b\}^{\cap}$.

Lemma 2 (Decomposition Cardinality). $\lceil m/n \rceil$ *parallelotopes are sufficient to decompose a polytope* Q *defined by* m *constraints into a bundle.*

Lemma 1 states that any polytope can be represented by a parallelotope bundle while Lemma 2 fixes the maximum number of parallelotopes sufficient to decompose a polytope. Figure 1 shows a polytope Q together with a possible decomposition, i.e., a bundle $\{P_1, P_2\}$ such that $\{P_1, P_2\}^{\cap} = Q$. Here $m = 3$ and $n = 2$, so $\lceil 3/2 \rceil = 2$ parallelotopes are sufficient to decompose Q (in our case P_1 and P_2). In Section 5 we will describe an algorithm for decomposing a polytope into a bundle in view of accurate image approximation.

Definition 4 (Set Enclosure). *Let* $S \subset \mathbb{R}^n$ *be a compact set and* $Q = \langle D, \mathbf{c} \rangle \subset \mathbb{R}^n$ *be a polytope. The enclosure of* S *with respect to* Q *is defined as the polytope* $\odot(S, Q) = \langle D, \mathbf{c}' \rangle$, *where* $\mathbf{c}'_i = \max_{\mathbf{x} \in S} D_i \mathbf{x}$, *for* $i = 1, \dots, k$.

The enclosure of S with respect to Q can be seen as tight over-approximation of S obtained using the template of Q. The following properties of set enclosure can be easily proved.

Lemma 3. *Let* $S, S' \subset \mathbb{R}^n$ *be compact sets with* $S \subseteq S'$ *and* $Q = \langle D, \mathbf{c} \rangle$, $Q' = \langle D', \mathbf{c}' \rangle$ *be two polytopes such that* $D' \subseteq D$. *It holds that:*

(1) $S \subseteq \odot(S, Q)$;

(2) $\odot(S, Q) = \odot(S, \odot(S, Q)) = \odot(\odot(S, Q), Q)$;

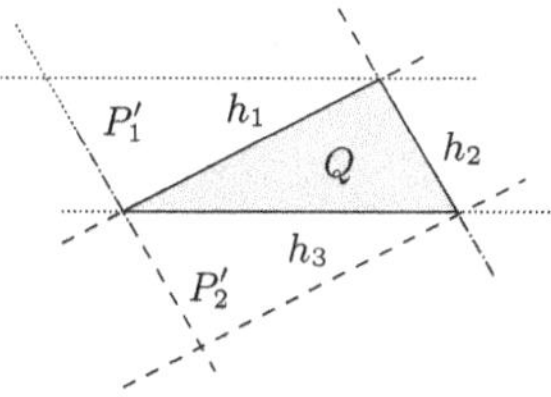

Figure 2: A polytope Q and a its set bundle enclosure with respect to $\{P_1, P_2\}$ of Figure 1: $\boxdot(Q, \{P_1, P_2\}) = \{P_1', P_2'\}$.

(3) $\odot(S, Q) \subseteq \odot(S', Q)$;

(4) $\odot(S, Q) \subseteq \odot(S, Q')$.

The notion of set enclosure can be extended to bundles.

Definition 5 (Set Bundle Enclosure). *Let $S \subset \mathbb{R}^n$ be a compact set and $\{P_1, \dots, P_b\}$ be a bundle. The enclosure of S with respect to the bundle $\{P_1, \dots, P_b\}$ is defined as $\boxdot(S, \{P_1, \dots, P_b\}) = \{P_1', \dots, P_b'\}$, where $P_i' = \odot(S, P_i)$, for $i = 1, \dots, b$.*

The set bundle enclosure surrounds S with the parallelotopes P_i, producing a bundle whose parallelotopes P_i' wrap S. The two operators are related by the following equality.

Lemma 4. $\boxdot(S, \{P_1, \dots, P_b\})^{\sqcap} = \odot(S, \{P_1, \dots, P_b\}^{\sqcap})$.

The set bundle enclosure of S with respect to the bundle $\{P_1, \dots, P_b\}$ coincides with the enclosure of S with respect to the polytope $\{P_1, \dots, P_b\}^{\sqcap}$. As a consequence, we get that $\odot(\cdot, \cdot)$ and $\boxdot(\cdot, \cdot)$ are equivalent, with the difference that $\odot(\cdot, \cdot)$ returns a polytope, while $\boxdot(\cdot, \cdot)$ returns a bundle. Figure 2 shows the set bundle enclosure of the polytope Q with respect to the bundle $\{P_1, P_2\}$ of Figure 1. The result of $\boxdot(S, \{P_1, P_2\})$ is the new bundle $\{P_1', P_2'\}$.

We say that $\{P_1', \dots, P_{b'}'\}$ is a *sub-bundle* of $\{P_1, \dots, P_b\}$ if $\{P_1', \dots, P_{b'}'\} \subseteq \{P_1, \dots, P_b\}$ and that two bundles are *strongly similar* if the set of normal vectors defining a parallelotope in one bundle is equal to the set of normal vectors defining a parallelotope in the other bundle. The following properties of the bundle enclosure operator immediately follow by definitions, Lemma 3, and Lemma 4.

Lemma 5. *Let $S, S' \subset \mathbb{R}^n$ be compact sets with $S \subseteq S'$, $\{P_1, \dots, P_b\}$ be a bundle, $\{P_1', \dots, P_{b'}'\}$ be one of its sub-bundles, and $\{P_1'', \dots, P_b''\}$ be a bundle strongly similar to $\{P_1, \dots, P_b\}$. It holds that:*

(1) $S \subseteq \boxdot(S, \{P_1, \dots, P_b\})^{\sqcap}$;

(2) $\boxdot(S, \{P_1, \dots, P_b\}) = \boxdot(S, \boxdot(S, \{P_1, \dots, P_b\})) = \boxdot(\boxdot(S, \{P_1, \dots, P_b\}), \{P_1, \dots, P_b\})$;

(3) $\boxdot(S, \{P_1, \dots, P_b\})^{\sqcap} \subseteq \boxdot(S', \{P_1, \dots, P_b\})^{\sqcap}$;

(4) $\boxdot(S, \{P_1', \dots, P_{b'}'\}) \subseteq \boxdot(S, \{P_1, \dots, P_b\})$ *and* $\boxdot(S, \{P_1, \dots, P_b\})^{\sqcap} \subseteq \boxdot(S, \{P_1', \dots, P_{b'}'\})^{\sqcap}$;

(5) $\boxdot(S, \{P_1, \dots, P_b\})$ *is strongly similar to* $\{P_1, \dots, P_b\}$;

(6) $\boxdot(S, \{P_1, \dots, P_b\}) = \boxdot(S, \{P_1'', \dots, P_b''\})$.

A bundle representing a polytope may not be "minimal" in the sense that one or more paralleloptopes can be shrunk while the resulting bundle still represents the same polytope. The shrinking process removes parts of parallelotopes that are not in the polytope and it is useful for many operations, in particular image over-approximation. As we will see later, the shrinking reduces the error when the image over-approximation is performed on shrunk parallelotopes. A bundle that remains unchanged after a shirking is said to be in *canonical form.*

Definition 6 (Bundle Canonical Form). *A bundle $\{P_1, \dots, P_b\}$ is in* canonical form *if and only if:*

$$\boxdot(\{P_1, \dots, P_b\}^{\sqcap}, \{P_1, \dots, P_b\}) = \{P_1, \dots, P_b\}.$$

Intuitively, a bundle $\{P_1, \dots, P_b\}$ is in canonical form if the enclosure of its symbolic polytope $P^{\sqcap} = \{P_1, \dots, P_b\}^{\sqcap}$ with respect to $\{P_1, \dots, P_b\}$ does not affect the parallelotopes P_i, for $i \in \{1, \dots, b\}$. The canonical form of a bundle $\{P_1, \dots, P_b\}$ can be obtained by enclosing its polytope $P^{\sqcap}$ with respect to its parallelotopes P_i. The bundle $\{P_1', P_2'\}$ of Figure 2 is in canonical form, since it is the result of the bundle enclosure $\boxdot(Q, \{P_1, P_2\}) = \{P_1', P_2'\}$ where $Q = \{P_1, P_2\}^{\sqcap}$. In virtue of Lemma 5 item *(2)*, the result of a bundle enclosure is always in canonical form. In other terms, the operator $\boxdot(\cdot, \cdot)$ can be exploited for canonizing bundles, as stated by the following result.

Lemma 6 (Canonization). *Let $\{P_1, \dots, P_b\}$ be a bundle. The bundle $\boxdot(\{P_1, \dots, P_b\}^{\sqcap}, \{P_1, \dots, P_b\})$ is in canonical form and it is equivalent to $\{P_1, \dots, P_b\}$.*

A bundle in canonical form is a "minimal" representation of the polytope with respect to a given set of parallelotope directions, since all the offsets are shifted towards the constraints of the polytope. The advantage of dealing with bundles in canonical form will become clearer on images approximation.

In the following we show the advantage of bundles in image approximation. We start by proving some inclusions that hold on the images of bundles by a continuous function. Note that these properties hold for all continuous functions, and in the case of polynomials, they are particularly useful for our image approximation problem, because we can indeed effectively enclose the image of a parallelotope.

Lemma 7 (Bundle Image). *Let $\{P_1, \dots, P_b\}$ be a bundle with $P^{\sqcap} = \{P_1, \dots, P_b\}^{\sqcap}$ and $\mathbf{f} : \mathbb{R}^n \to \mathbb{R}^n$ be a continuous function. The following inclusions hold:*

$$\begin{aligned} \mathbf{f}(P^{\sqcap}) \subseteq \boxdot(\mathbf{f}(P^{\sqcap}), \{P_1, \dots, P_b\})^{\sqcap} \subseteq \quad & (7.1)\\ \subseteq \bigcap_{i=1}^{b} \boxdot(\mathbf{f}(P_i), \{P_1, \dots, P_b\})^{\sqcap} \subseteq \quad & (7.2)\\ \subseteq \bigcap_{i=1}^{b} \boxdot(\mathbf{f}(P_i), \{P_i\})^{\sqcap} \quad & (7.3)\end{aligned}$$

Figure 3 shows the intersection of the enclosures of $\mathbf{f}(P_1)$ and $\mathbf{f}(P_2)$ with respect to $\{P_1, P_2\}$; Figure 4 shows the enclosure of $\mathbf{f}(P_1)$ with respect to P_1 intersected with the enclosure of $\mathbf{f}(P_2)$ with respect to P_2. Note how the over-approximation of the first method is tighter than the second one.

Intuitively Lemma 7 suggests us two possible ways of approximating the image of a polytope $P^{\sqcap}$ represented by a bundle $\{P_1, \dots, P_b\}$. In case (7.2), we can over-approximate $\mathbf{f}(P^{\sqcap})$ with the bundle enclosures of the transformed parallelotopes $\mathbf{f}(P_i)$ with respect to $\{P_1, \dots, P_b\}$. In case (7.3), we can consider the set enclosures of each parallelotope image $\mathbf{f}(P_i)$ with respect to its original directions. In both cases we only need to be able to compute the images of the parallelotopes and their enclosures.

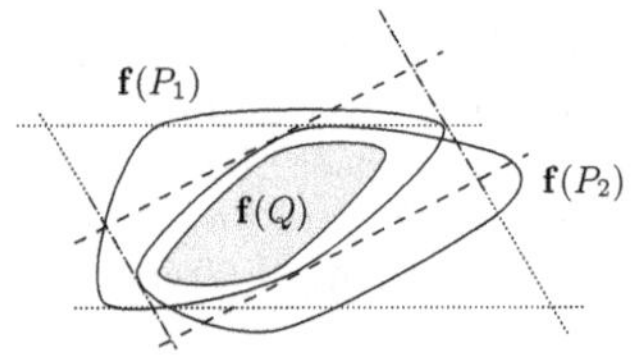

Figure 3: $\boxdot(\mathbf{f}(P_1), \{P_1, P_2\})^\sqcap \cap \boxdot(\mathbf{f}(P_2), \{P_1, P_2\})^\sqcap$.

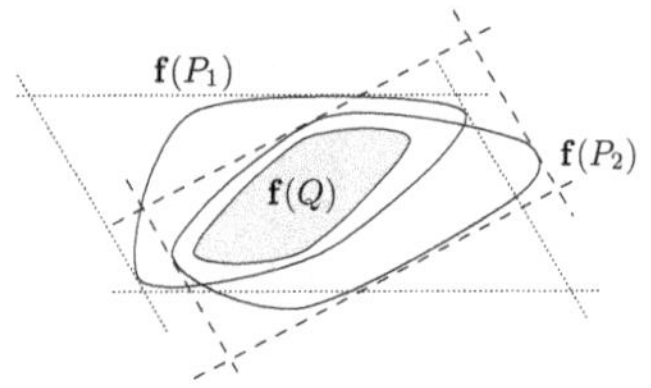

Figure 4: $\odot(\mathbf{f}(P_1), P_1) \cap \odot(\mathbf{f}(P_2), P_2)$.

Notice however that the bundle $\{P_1, \ldots, P_b\}$ may not be in canonical form. The following result shows that if we approximate the image of $\{P_1, \ldots, P_b\}^\sqcap$ exploiting Lemma 7 on the canonical bundle $\boxdot(\{P_1, \ldots, P_b\}^\sqcap, \{P_1, \ldots, P_b\})$ we get tighter approximations.

THEOREM 1 (CANONICAL BUNDLE IMAGE). *Let us consider a bundle $\{P_1, \ldots, P_b\}$, with $P^\sqcap = \{P_1, \ldots, P_b\}^\sqcap$, and a function $\mathbf{f} : \mathbb{R}^n \to \mathbb{R}^n$. Let also $\{P'_1, \ldots, P'_b\} = \boxdot(\{P_1, \ldots, P_b\}^\sqcap, \{P_1, \ldots, P_b\})$. The following relations hold among the over-approximations of $\mathbf{f}(P^\sqcap)$:*

$$\boxdot(\mathbf{f}(P^\sqcap), \{P'_1, \ldots, P'_b\})^\sqcap = \boxdot(\mathbf{f}(P^\sqcap), \{P_1, \ldots, P_b\})^\sqcap \subseteq$$

$$\bigcap_{i=1}^b \boxdot(\mathbf{f}(P'_i), \{P'_1, \ldots, P'_b\})^\sqcap \subseteq \bigcap_{i=1}^b \boxdot(\mathbf{f}(P_i), \{P_1, \ldots, P_b\})^\sqcap$$

$$\text{\rotatebox{90}{$\subseteq$}} \qquad\qquad \text{\rotatebox{90}{$\subseteq$}}$$

$$\bigcap_{i=1}^b \boxdot(\mathbf{f}(P'_i), \{P'_i\})^\sqcap \subseteq \bigcap_{i=1}^b \boxdot(\mathbf{f}(P_i), \{P_i\})^\sqcap$$

As a consequence, having to compute the image of a generic compact set S, one can first over approximate S through the bundle enclosure operator, which returns a bundle in canonical form, and then exploit the above results to over-approximate the image of S.

4. BUNDLE DATA STRUCTURE

In this section we define a data structure and some methods for the compact representation and transformation of bundles in canonical form.

A parallelotope bundle in canonical form can be compactly represented with the tuple $\langle L, \overline{\mathbf{d}}, \underline{\mathbf{d}}, T\rangle$ where:

- $L \in \mathbb{R}^{k \times n}$ is the *directions matrix* that contains the directions used to build the parallelotopes. The i-th row L_i of L represents a direction;
- $\overline{\mathbf{d}} \in \mathbb{R}^k$ is the *upper offsets vector*. The i-th element of $\overline{\mathbf{d}}$, associated with the i-th direction L_i, constitutes the half-space $L_i\mathbf{x} \leq \overline{\mathbf{d}}_i$;
- $\underline{\mathbf{d}} \in \mathbb{R}^k$ is the *lower offsets vector*. The i-th element of $\underline{\mathbf{d}}$, associated with the i-th direction L_i, constitutes the half-space $-L_i\mathbf{x} \leq \underline{\mathbf{d}}_i$;
- $T \in \{1, \ldots, k\}^{b \times n}$ is the *templates* matrix that represents the set of the parallelotope templates. Each element in T is a reference to a direction in L and offsets in $\overline{\mathbf{d}}$ and $\underline{\mathbf{d}}$. A row in T constitutes a set of half-spaces that generates a parallelotopes.

Consider for instance the bundle $\{P'_1, P'_2\}$ in canonical form of Figure 2 where $P'_1 = \langle \Lambda'_1, \mathbf{c}'_1\rangle$ and $P'_2 = \langle \Lambda'_2, \mathbf{c}'_2\rangle$ with:

$$\Lambda'_1 = \begin{pmatrix} 1.6 & 1 \\ 0 & 1 \\ -1.6 & -1 \\ 0 & -1 \end{pmatrix} \mathbf{c}'_1 = \begin{pmatrix} 10 \\ 3.1 \\ -1 \\ -1 \end{pmatrix} \Lambda'_2 = \begin{pmatrix} 1.6 & 1 \\ -0.5 & 1 \\ -1.6 & -1 \\ 0.5 & -1 \end{pmatrix} \mathbf{c}'_2 = \begin{pmatrix} 10 \\ 1 \\ -1 \\ 1.7 \end{pmatrix}$$

This bundle can be represented by the tuple $\langle L, \overline{\mathbf{d}}, \underline{\mathbf{d}}, T\rangle$ where:

$$L = \begin{pmatrix} 1.6 & 1 \\ 0 & 1 \\ -0.5 & 1 \end{pmatrix} \overline{\mathbf{d}} = \begin{pmatrix} 10 \\ 3.1 \\ 1 \end{pmatrix} \underline{\mathbf{d}} = \begin{pmatrix} -1 \\ -1 \\ 1.7 \end{pmatrix} T = \begin{pmatrix} 1 & 2 \\ 1 & 3 \end{pmatrix}.$$

With this representation we avoid the storage of redundant directions shared by different parallelotopes. In doing so, a single operation on an entry in the tuple, indirectly affects several parallelotopes in the bundle. Moreover, for each parallelotope we store only n directions against $2n$ constraints, since we know that parallel constraints can be obtained by reversing the signs of the normal vectors. Note that each direction L_i is associated with a unique upper and lower offset $\overline{\mathbf{d}}_i$ and $\underline{\mathbf{d}}_i$. This means that if two parallelotopes share a direction, the constraints defined by this direction coincide in the two parallelotopes. Hence, this data structure does not allow us to represent all the possible bundles (for instance the one shown in Figure 1), but it is expressive enough to capture all the canonical bundles (like the one of Figure 2).

We now show how the operations presented in Section 3 can be defined on our data structure $\langle L, \overline{\mathbf{d}}, \underline{\mathbf{d}}, T\rangle$. We begin with the decomposition of a polytope (see Definition 3).

METHOD 1 (POLYTOPE DECOMPOSITION). *Let $Q \subset \mathbb{R}^n$ be a polytope defined by m constraints. Let $L \in \mathbb{R}^{k \times n}$ be a matrix containing all the versors of Q without repetitions, i.e., the elements of L are pairwise linearly independent. To generate the i-th decomposing parallelotope, it is sufficient to pick n directions $L_{j_1}, \ldots, L_{j_n}$ from L and store their indices in the template matrix $T_i = (j_1, \ldots, j_n)$. By Lemmas 1 and 2, we have to generate at most $\lceil m/n \rceil$ parallelotopes such that the union of the picked directions is a cover of the constraints of Q. Finally, the offset vectors $\overline{\mathbf{d}}, \underline{\mathbf{d}} \in \mathbb{R}^k$ can be obtained by enclosing Q with respect to the constructed parallelotopes as described in Method 2.*

We now show how to compute the set bundle enclosure.

METHOD 2 (SET BUNDLE ENCLOSURE $\boxdot(\cdot, \cdot)$). *The enclosure of a bounded set $S \subset \mathbb{R}^n$ with respect to a canonical bundle $\{P_1, \ldots, P_b\}$ stored as $\langle L, \overline{\mathbf{d}}, \underline{\mathbf{d}}, T\rangle$ can be obtained by updating the upper and lower offset vector as $\overline{\mathbf{d}}_i = \max_{\mathbf{x} \in S} L_i\mathbf{x}$ and $\underline{\mathbf{d}}_i = \max_{\mathbf{x} \in S} -L_i\mathbf{x}$, for $i = 1, \ldots, k$.*

The described methods work only on canonical bundles and return a compact representation of a canonical bundle. The enclosure of a polytope with respect to a bundle requires the resolution of $2k$ linear programs. Thus, the canonization of a bundle can be done by solving a series of linear programs where only the offsets of the constraints that do not participate to the intersection are modified.

The transformation of a bundle through a continuous function can be rather difficult, depending on the transforming function. If the function is linear, it is possible to exactly compute the image of each parallelotope and then obtain the exact bundle transformation. Things are more complex when the function is nonlinear and the geometric properties of the parallelotopes are not preserved. We will now describe two methods based on Theorem 1, requiring only computations on single parallelotopes (besides being able to implement Method 2). As stated by Lemma 7 item *(3)*, an over-approximation of a bundle transformation $\mathbf{f}(P^{\cap})$, with $P^{\cap} = \{P_1, \ldots, P_b\}$, can be obtained by enclosing each image $\mathbf{f}(P_i)$ with $P'_i = \boxdot(\mathbf{f}(P_i), \{P_i\})^{\cap}$ and then considering the intersection $\bigcap_{i=1}^{b} P'_i$ (see (7.3)). We call this approximation *one-for-one (OFO)*, since each parallelotope in the bundle is independently approximated.

METHOD 3 (ONE-FOR-ONE IMAGE (OFO)). *The one-for-one approximation of the bundle $\langle L, \overline{\mathbf{d}}, \underline{\mathbf{d}}, T\rangle$ can be obtained by retrieving each parallelotope P_i, computing the enclosures $P'_i = \odot(\mathbf{f}(P_i), P_i)$, and then computing the canonization of $\{P'_1, \ldots, P'_b\}^{\cap} = P'^{\cap}$, that is $\boxdot(P'^{\cap}, \{P_1, \ldots, P_b\})$.*

The polytope provided by the OFO method corresponds to the polytope $\bigcap_{i=1}^{b} \boxdot(\mathbf{f}(P_i), \{P_i\})^{\cap}$ of Lemma 7 item *(3)*.

In order to obtain a finer over-approximation, it is possible to change the template in the approximation process, i.e., we can fix a new template to enclose $\mathbf{f}(P_i)$. As suggested by Lemma 7 item *(2)*, we can exploit all the directions of the bundle, i.e., instead of looking for a new template for each parallelotope, we can bound each set $\mathbf{f}(P_i)$ with all the directions of the transformed bundle. We call this approximation *all-for-one (AFO)* since all the directions of the bundle are used to approximate the image of a single parallelotope.

METHOD 4 (ALL-FOR-ONE IMAGE (AFO)). *The* all-for-one *approximation of the bundle $\langle L, \overline{\mathbf{d}}, \underline{\mathbf{d}}, T\rangle$ can be obtained by retrieving each parallelotope P_i, computing the set bundle enclosures $\{P'_{i1}, \ldots, P'_{ib}\} = \boxdot(\mathbf{f}(P_i), \{P_1, \ldots, P_b\})$, for $i = 1, \ldots, b$, and enclosing the polytope $\bigcap_{i=1}^{b}\{P'_{i1}, \ldots, P'_{ib}\}^{\cap}$ with respect to the transformed bundle, i.e., computing the bundle enclosure $\boxdot(\bigcap_{i=1}^{b}\{P'_{i1}, \ldots, P'_{ib}\}^{\cap}, \{P_1, \ldots, P_b\})$.*

The AFO transformation produces a bundle whose polytope corresponds to $\bigcap_{i=1}^{b} \boxdot(\mathbf{f}(P_i), \{P_1, \ldots, P_b\})^{\cap}$ of Lemma 7 item *(2)*. By Lemma 7, the AFO approximation is finer than the of OFO one. Clearly the precision has a cost: the OFO method requires $b(2n) + k$ optimizations against the $b(2k) + k$ optimizations of the AFO approach (recall that $k \geq n$).

Both the approximation methods are based on a series of enclosures. The offsets of the constraints necessary to obtain the enclosures can be attained by solving optimization problems of the form $\overline{\mathbf{d}}_j = \max_{\mathbf{x} \in \mathbf{f}(P_i)} L_j \mathbf{x}$. If the transformation function $\mathbf{f}$ is nonlinear, these optimization problems might be computationally expensive. In the next section we expose a method, based on the Bernstein coefficients, to efficiently deal with optimizations of polynomial functions.

5. POLYNOMIAL REACHABILITY

In this section we recall a technique to over-approximate the image of a parallelotope in the case of polynomial functions. The technique is based on Bernstein coefficients and has been described in our previous works [13, 14, 12]. Together with the methods defined in the previous section, this gives us an algorithm for the reachability computation of discrete-time polynomial dynamical systems.

A discrete-time polynomial dynamical system can be described by difference equations as follows:

$$\begin{aligned} \mathbf{x}_{k+1} &= \mathbf{f}(\mathbf{x}_k) \\ \mathbf{x}_0 &\in X_0 \end{aligned} \tag{1}$$

where $\mathbf{x} \in \mathbb{R}^n$ is the vector of state variables and $\mathbf{f} : \mathbb{R}^n \to \mathbb{R}^n$ is a vector of n multi-variate polynomials of the form $\mathbf{f}_i : \mathbb{R}^n \to \mathbb{R}$, for each $i \in \{1, \ldots, n\}$. The set $X_0 \subseteq \mathbb{R}^n$ is called the *initial set*.

Given an initial set X_0, we are interested in computing the bounded time *reachable set* of the dynamical system, i.e, the set of states visited by the dynamical system up to a fixed time horizon $K \in \mathbb{N}$. The reachable set can be obtained as the solution of the recursion $X_{i+1} = \{\mathbf{f}(\mathbf{x}) \mid \mathbf{x} \in X_i\}$, for $i = 0, \ldots, K$. In this approach, the computation of the reachable set can be reduced to a series of images of sets by the polynomial $\mathbf{f}$. This means that if we represent with a bundle the set X_i, we can reduce the single step evolution $X_{i+1} = \{\mathbf{f}(\mathbf{x}) \mid \mathbf{x} \in X_i\}$ to a bundle transformation.

Algorithm 1 shows our reachability algorithm based on parallelotope bundles. For brevity, the bundle $\{P_1, \ldots, P_b\}$ computed at the i-th iteration is abbreviated by $\mathcal{B}_i$.

Algorithm 1 Bundle Reachability

```
1: function REACH(X_0)                         ▷ X_0 polytope
2:     B_0 ←DECOMPOSE(X_0)                     ▷ Init. bundle
3:     for i = 1, ..., K do
4:         B_i ←TRANSFORM(f, B_{i-1})
5:         B_i ←DECOMPOSE(B_i)                 ▷ Optional
6:     end for
7: end function
```

The algorithm receives in input a polytope X_0 that is decomposed into the bundle $\mathcal{B}_0$ (Line 2). Then, it enters in a loop where at each iteration it over-approximates the set of states reachable at time i through the transformation of the bundle $\mathcal{B}_{i-1}$ with respect to the dynamics $\mathbf{f}$ (Line 4). The transformation performed by the function TRANSFORM can be either the OFO (see Method 3) or the AFO (see Method 4). In both cases, the transformation produces a bundle $\mathcal{B}_i$ in canonical form that over-approximates the states reachable by the dynamical system from $\mathcal{B}_{i-1}$. Finally, the symbolic polytope of the computed bundle $\mathcal{B}_i$ can be decomposed (Line 5), obtaining a new bundle whose parallelotopes combine the directions differently from $\mathcal{B}_{i-1}$. The decomposition is optional, but it might improve the precision in the over-approximation of the future transformations, since the over-approximating parallelotopes might be smaller than the ones produced by the transformation. In the following we will discuss in detail the functions TRANSFORM and DECOMPOSE. We begin with the polynomial transformation since, as we will discover later, the decomposition is strictly related to the way we transform the bundles.

Transformation. The operation at the basis of the transformation of a parallelotope P is the nonlinear optimization problem of the form $\mathbf{c}'_i = \max_{\mathbf{x} \in \mathbf{f}(P)} \Lambda_i \mathbf{x}$, or equivalently, $\mathbf{c}'_i = \max_{\mathbf{x} \in P} \Lambda_i \mathbf{f}(\mathbf{x})$, where $\Lambda_i \in \mathbb{R}^n$ is a generic direction. Solving this problem, or finding a tight upper-bound of $\mathbf{c}'_i$, means being able to find the offset of a constraint with normal vector Λ_i tangent or close to the set $\mathbf{f}(P)$. In our previous works [14, 12], inspired by [13], we developed a method to bound polynomials over boxes and parallelotopes. The method, based on a particular property of the Bernstein coefficients, is summarized in the following.

A polynomial $\pi : \mathbb{R}^n \to \mathbb{R}$ can be expressed in the common power basis as $\pi(\mathbf{x}) = \sum_{\mathbf{i} \in I} \mathbf{a}_\mathbf{i} \mathbf{x}^\mathbf{i}$, where $\mathbf{x} = (\mathbf{x}_1, \ldots, \mathbf{x}_n) \in \mathbb{R}^n$ is a vector or variables, $\mathbf{i} = (\mathbf{i}_1, \ldots, \mathbf{i}_n) \in \mathbb{N}^n$ is a multi-index, I is the multi-index set of π, and $\mathbf{a}_\mathbf{i} \in \mathbb{R}$ are the polynomial coefficients. In the following, we write $\mathbf{d}/\mathbf{i}$ for $(\mathbf{d}_1/\mathbf{i}_1, \ldots, \mathbf{d}_n/\mathbf{i}_n)$ and $\binom{\mathbf{d}}{\mathbf{i}}$ for the product $\binom{\mathbf{d}_1}{\mathbf{i}_1} \ldots \binom{\mathbf{d}_n}{\mathbf{i}_n}$. The same polynomial π can be represented using the Bernstein basis as $\pi(\mathbf{x}) = \sum_{\mathbf{i} \in I} \mathbf{b}_\mathbf{i} \mathcal{B}_{(\mathbf{d},\mathbf{i})}(\mathbf{x})$, where $\mathbf{d} \in \mathbb{N}^n$ is the degree of π, i.e., the multi-index that dominates the multi-indices in I, $\mathbf{b}_\mathbf{i} = \sum_{\mathbf{j} \leq \mathbf{i}} \binom{\mathbf{i}}{\mathbf{j}} / \binom{\mathbf{d}}{\mathbf{j}} \mathbf{a}_\mathbf{j}$ are the *Bernstein coefficients*, and $\mathcal{B}_{(\mathbf{d},\mathbf{i})}(\mathbf{x}) = \beta_{(\mathbf{d}_1,\mathbf{i}_1)}(\mathbf{x}_1) \ldots \beta_{(\mathbf{d}_n,\mathbf{i}_n)}(\mathbf{x}_n)$ is the $\mathbf{i}$-th *Bernstein basis* where $\beta_{(\mathbf{d}_j,\mathbf{i}_j)}(x) = \binom{\mathbf{d}_j}{\mathbf{i}_j} x^{\mathbf{i}_j}(1-x)^{\mathbf{d}_j - \mathbf{i}_j}$. The points $(\mathbf{i}/\mathbf{d}, \mathbf{b}_\mathbf{i}) \in \mathbb{R}^{n+1}$ are called *Bernstein control points*.

Bernstein coefficients own the useful *range enclosing property* stating that for all the $\mathbf{x} \in [0,1]^n$, $\min_{\mathbf{i} \in I} \mathbf{b}_i \leq \pi(\mathbf{x}) \leq \max_{\mathbf{i} \in I} \mathbf{b}_i$. This means that the image of the unit box $\pi([0,1]^n)$ is bounded by the minimum and maximum Bernstein coefficients. Hence, if we want to bound a polynomial over the unit box, instead of solving a nonlinear optimization problem, we can compute the Bernstein coefficients $\mathbf{b}_\mathbf{i}$ and take their maximum and minimum. The following lemma [13] bounds the distance between a polynomial and its Bernstein control points, or in other words, the error between the maximum and minimum of a polynomial and the bounds provided by its Bernstein coefficients. This lemma provides us a criterion for decomposing a bundle and for dividing sets in order to achieve better precision.

LEMMA 8. *[13] Let $C_\pi : \mathbb{R}^n \to \mathbb{R}$ be the piecewise linear function defined by the Bernstein control points of the polynomial $\pi : \mathbb{R}^n \to \mathbb{R}$, with respect to the box $[0,1]^n$. For all $\mathbf{x} \in [0,1]^n$*

$$| \pi(\mathbf{x}) - C_\pi(\mathbf{x}) | \leq \max_{\mathbf{x} \in [0,1]^n; i,j \in \{1,\ldots,n\}} | \partial_i \partial_j \pi(\mathbf{x}) | \qquad (2)$$

where $| \cdot |$ is the infinity norm on $\mathbb{R}^n$.

Several convergent subdivision procedures for reducing the gap between bounds and optimums have been proposed [16, 25]. Note that the range enclosing property works only on the unit-box domain. If we want to apply this property to a generic box or a parallelotope $X \subset \mathbb{R}^n$, we can define a linear transformation $\mathbf{v} : [0,1]^n \to X$ that maps the unit box to X, and exploit the Bernstein range enclosing property on the function $\pi(\mathbf{v}(\mathbf{x})) : [0,1]^n \to \mathbb{R}$. With this technique we can define a procedure BOUND(π,X) that receives in input a polynomial π and a box or parallelotope X, computes the linear transformation $\mathbf{v} : [0,1]^n \to X$, composes π with $\mathbf{v}$, computes the Bernstein coefficients of $\pi(\mathbf{v}(\mathbf{x}))$, and returns the maximum Bernstein coefficients $b^* \in \mathbb{R}$. By the range enclosing property, b^* is such that $b^* \geq \max_{\mathbf{x} \in X} \pi(\mathbf{x})$.

The function BOUND can be used to bound our optimization problem and compute the transformation of a bundle: given a parallelotope P, the determination of $\mathbf{c}'_i$ for a direction Λ_i such that $\Lambda_i \mathbf{x} \leq \mathbf{c}'_i \supseteq \mathbf{f}(P)$, can be obtained with the procedure $\mathbf{c}'_i = \text{BOUND}(\Lambda_i \mathbf{f}(\mathbf{x}), P)$.

We now take advantage of the function BOUND to define our bundle transformation methods. The OFO transformation of a bundle $\langle L, \overline{\mathbf{d}}, \underline{\mathbf{d}}, T \rangle$, as exposed in Method 3, can be obtained by retrieving each parallelotope $P_i = \langle \Lambda, \mathbf{c} \rangle$, for $i = 1, \ldots, b$, computing the new offsets $\mathbf{c}'_j = \text{BOUND}(\Lambda_j \mathbf{f}(\mathbf{x}), P_i)$, for $j = 1, \ldots, 2n$, and defining the over-approximating parallelotope $P'_i = \langle \Lambda, \mathbf{c}' \rangle \supseteq \mathbf{f}(P_i)$. Finally, the canonization of the transformed bundle $\{P'_1, \ldots, P'_b\}$ can be obtained by solving a family of linear programs of the form $\max_{\mathbf{x} \in P'^\sqcap} \Lambda_i \mathbf{x}$, where Λ_i belongs to the template matrices of P'_j and $P'^\sqcap = \{P'_1, \ldots, P'_b\}^\sqcap$ is the polytope of the computed bundle.

The AFO transformation of a bundle $\langle L, \overline{\mathbf{d}}, \underline{\mathbf{d}}, T \rangle$, as defined in Method 4, can be done as follows. For each parallelotope of the bundle P_i, for $i = 1, \ldots, b$, we have to compute the enclosure $\{P'_{i1}, \ldots, P'_{ib}\} = \boxdot(\mathbf{f}(P_i), \{P_1, \ldots, P_b\})$. An over-approximation of P'_{im}, with $m \in 1, \ldots, b$, is the parallelotope $\langle \Lambda, \mathbf{c}' \rangle$ where Λ is the template of P_{im} and $\mathbf{c}'_j = \text{BOUND}(\Lambda_j \mathbf{f}(\mathbf{x}), P_{im})$, for all $j = 1, \ldots, 2n$. Finally, the canonization $\boxdot(\bigcap_{i=1}^b \{P'_{i1}, \ldots, P'_{ib}\}^\sqcap, \{P_1, \ldots, P_b\})$ can be computed by solving a group of linear programs of the form $\max_{\mathbf{x} \in P'^\sqcap} \Lambda_j \mathbf{x}$, where Λ_j belongs to the template matrices of P'_{im} and $P'^\sqcap = \bigcap_{i=1}^b \{P'_{i1}, \ldots, P'_{ib}\}^\sqcap$ is the intersection of the polytopes represented by the computed bundles.

Decomposition. Since in our reachability algorithm we may be interested in decomposing a polytope in a bundle (see Algorithm 1), we define a function DECOMPOSE that receives in input a bundle in canonical form $\langle L, \overline{\mathbf{d}}, \underline{\mathbf{d}}, T \rangle$ (whose polytope $P^\sqcap$ has to be decomposed) and reorganizes the templates matrix T creating a new collection of parallelotopes around the polytope $P^\sqcap$. The goal of the decomposition is to create a set of small parallelotopes whose intersection is $P^\sqcap$. There are two reasons why we want small parallelotopes:

1. smaller parallelotopes P_i lead to a smaller bundle image $\{\mathbf{f}(P_1), \ldots, \mathbf{f}(P_d)\}$ and then to a more accurate over-approximation $\mathbf{f}(P^\sqcap)$ (see, e.g., Theorem 1);
2. the shorter the largest side length of P_i, the more accurate the over-approximation introduced by the Bernstein coefficients (see Lemma 8).

Hence, the aspects to take into account in the construction of the parallelotopes are the volume and the maximum side length. Moreover, we do not have to forget that the set of the parallelotope directions must cover the directions of polytope to be decomposed (see Definition 3). Finding the best decomposition in terms of volume and maximum length minimization is computationally expensive and might not be possible (recall that the set cover problem is NP-hard).

In order to efficiently find a good decomposition, we propose a heuristic technique that constructs the parallelotopes while trying to minimize the volumes and maximum side lengths. The proposed heuristic starts from a decomposition, applies a series of random changes to the templates matrix, and keeps only the best one accordingly to an evaluation function that we will soon define. The procedure is repeated until a fixed number of iterations is reached.

Given a bundle $P^\sqcap = \{P_1, \ldots, P_b\}$, the evaluation function should take into account the volumes and side lengths of the parallelotopes P_i, for $i \in \{1, \ldots, b\}$. The exact computation of the volume of a parallelotope is rather expensive, since it is equal to the determinant of a $n \times n$ matrix. To lighten the computation, we approximate the volume of $P = \langle \Lambda, \mathbf{c} \rangle$ with the product of the distances of its constraints:

$$\tilde{v}(P) = \prod_{i=1}^n \delta(\Lambda_i \mathbf{x} \leq \mathbf{d}_i, \Lambda_{i+n} \mathbf{x} \leq \mathbf{d}_{i+n}) \qquad (3)$$

where $\delta(\Lambda_i \mathbf{x} \leq \mathbf{d}_i, \Lambda_{i+n}\mathbf{x} \leq \mathbf{d}_{i+n}) = |\mathbf{d}_i - \mathbf{d}_{i+n}|/\|\Lambda_i\|$ and $\|\cdot\|$ is the Euclidean norm.

The computation of the side lengths of a parallelotope passes inevitably through the determination of its vertices, an operation that can be computationally expensive. Instead of calculating the exact lengths, we opt for a faster heuristic that guesses the lengths of a parallelotope from the angles of the directions of its constraints. Intuitively, in the two-dimensional case, having fixed two parallel lines, the lengths of the edges not lying on the two fixed lines are minimal when the added directions and the fixed ones are orthogonal. Thus, we define the notion of *orthogonal proximity* $\theta(\Lambda_i, \Lambda_j) = \widehat{\Lambda_i, \Lambda_j} \pmod{\pi/2}$, where $\widehat{\Lambda_i, \Lambda_j}$ is the angle between Λ_i and Λ_j, i.e., $\widehat{\Lambda_i, \Lambda_j} = \arccos \frac{\Lambda_i \Lambda_j}{\|\Lambda_i\|\|\Lambda_j\|}$. The orthogonal proximity of a parallelotope $P = \langle \Lambda, \mathbf{c} \rangle$ is defined as:

$$\Theta(P) = \max_{i,j \in \{1,\ldots,2n\}} \theta(\Lambda_i, \Lambda_j). \tag{4}$$

Exploiting the notions of approximated volume $\tilde{v}$ and orthogonal proximity Θ, we define the evaluation function w for a bundle as:

$$w(\{P_1, \ldots, P_b\}) = \max_{i \in \{1,\ldots,b\}} \alpha\tilde{v}(P_i) + (1-\alpha)\Theta(P_i) \tag{5}$$

where $\alpha \in [0,1]$ is a tunable parameter.

6. EXPERIMENTAL RESULTS

We implemented a C++ tool called *Sapo* that manipulates parallelotope bundles and computes the reachable set of polynomial dynamical systems. The tool is structured in three main blocks: the bundle handler that stores and works with bundles; the base converter that computes the Bernstein coefficients of polynomials (the coefficients are symbolically calculated using our improved matrix method [14]); the reachability layer, where a dynamical system is specified and its reachable set is computed. Our tool relies on the libraries GiNaC[1] for the symbolic manipulation of formulas and GLPK (GNU Linear Programming Kit)[2] for the resolution of linear programs.

In the following we present four case studies. All the experiments were carried out on a laptop computer Intel Core(TM) Duo (2.40 GHz, 4GB RAM) running Ubuntu 12.04. The tool and the full descriptions of the case study configurations can be found at the link https://github.com/tommasodreossi/sapo.

Test Model. Our first experiment is based on the following illustrative 2-dimensional dynamical system:

$$\begin{aligned} x_{k+1} &= x_k + (0.5x_k^2 - 0.5y_k^2)\Delta \\ y_{k+1} &= y_k + (2x_k y_k)\Delta \end{aligned} \tag{6}$$

The directions constituting the bundles are $L_0 = (1,0), L_1 = (0,1), L_2 = (-1,1), L_3 = (1,1)$, the initial set is a box with $x \in [0.05, 0.1]$ and $y \in [0.99, 1.00]$, and $\Delta = 0.01$. Figure 5 shows the reachable sets computed with the different techniques plotted over time up to 25 steps. Figure 5a shows the sets computed using the OFO and AFO transformations (in white and gray, respectively), without the bundle decomposition. In both cases the bundle is composed by two parallelotopes obtained by coupling L_0 with L_1 and L_2 with L_3, respectively. The picture shows that the AFO transformation is finer than the OFO one. The OFO computation took 0.14s, the AFO 0.21s. Figure 5b compares the sets computed using the AFO transformation with (in black) and without (in gray) the bundle decomposition. In the decomposition function, the parameter α is equal to 0.5 and the number of decompositions randomly generated at each step is 500. The computation without decomposition took 0.22s against 1.94s of the one with decomposition. Note how the black flow is always included in the gray one, meaning that decomposition, applied with the AFO transformation, is finer than non-decomposed AFO and OFO transformations. Finally, Figure 5c depicts the AFO transformation with decomposition for $\alpha = 0$ (in gray) and $\alpha = 1$ (in white), computed in 1.92s and 1.95s (also here 500 decompositions are generated at each step). This experimental evaluation shows how the parameter α affects the reachable set computation. In this case, it is difficult to establish which is the best technique, since there is not a strict inclusion. However, the areas of the sets computed with $\alpha = 0$ are smaller than the ones with $\alpha = 1$.

SIR Epidemic Model. The second case study we consider is a 3-dimensional dynamical system that shows the benefits of using multiple directions and parallelotopes. We study the classic SIR epidemic model, where a population of individuals is divided in three compartments: s, the healthy individuals but *susceptible* to the disease; i, the *infected* individuals; r the individuals *removed* from the system (e.g., recovered). Two parameters regulate the evolution of the system variables: β, the contraction rate and γ, where $1/\gamma$ is the mean infective period. Δ is the discretization step. The dynamics of the SIR model are the following:

$$\begin{aligned} s_{k+1} &= s_k - (\beta s_k i_k)\Delta \\ i_{k+1} &= i_k + (\beta s_k i_k - \gamma i_k)\Delta \\ r_{k+1} &= r_k + (\gamma i_k)\Delta \end{aligned} \tag{7}$$

For this case we applied the AFO transformation without bundle decomposition. First, we computed the reachable set using a single axis-aligned template. Then, we added 5 directions not aligned with the axis and grouped them in 4 different templates. In both cases we computed the reachable sets up to 60 steps. Figure 6 shows the computed results, i.e., the single template computation (in white) and the four templates one (in black). In both cases the population is normalized and the initial set is the box with $s \in [0.79, 0.80]$, $i \in [0.19, 0.20]$, and $r = 0.00$. The chosen parameter values are $\beta = 0.34$, $\gamma = 0.05$, and $\Delta = 0.5$. The single parallelotope computation required 0.05s against the 1.04s of the 4 parallelotopes one. From the figure we can observe that multiple templates lead to a much finer result: the black flow is always included in the white one.

Honeybees Site Choice. In our third case study, we analyze a model that describes the decision-making process mechanism adopted by a swarm of honeybees to choose one among two different nest-sites. In this model [7], a population of honeybees is divided in five groups: x, the neutral bees that have not chosen a site; y_1 and y_2, evangelic bees dancing for the first and second site, respectively; z_1 and z_2, non-evangelic bees that have been converted to the first

[1] http://www.ginac.de/

[2] http://www.gnu.org/software/glpk/glpk.html

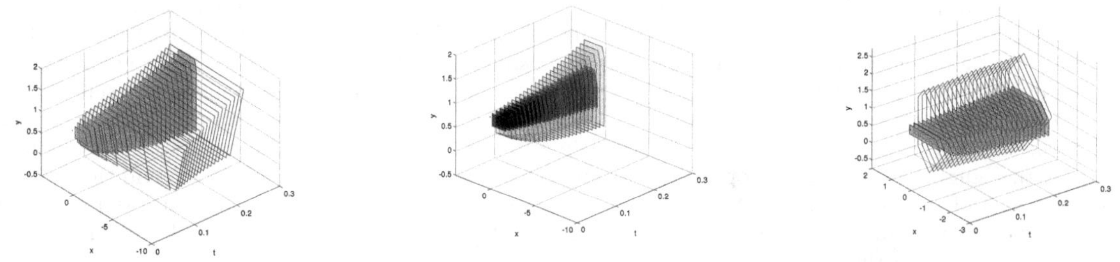

(a) OFO (white, 0.13s) and AFO (gray, 0.24s) transformations.

(b) AFO transformation without (gray, 0.24s) and with (black, 0.97s) decomposition ($\alpha = 0.5$).

(c) AFO transformation with decomposition. $\alpha = 0$ (gray, 0.95s) and $\alpha = 1$ (white, 0.98s).

Figure 5: Reachable set of a 2-dimensional test system.

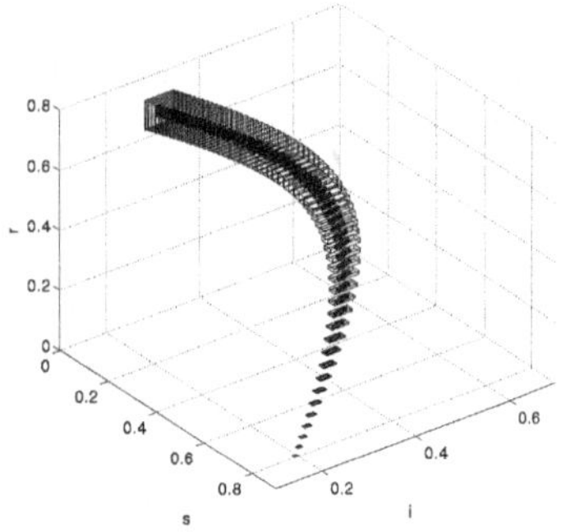

Figure 6: Reachable set of 3-dimensional SIR model. Sets have been computed with 1 temp/3 dirs (in white, 0.12s), and 4 temps/6 dirs (in black, 2.83s).

or second site, respectively, but who do not dance. The dynamics of the system are the following:

$$\begin{aligned}
x_{k+1} &= x_k + (-\beta_1 x_k y_{1_k} - \beta_2 x_k y_{2_k})\Delta \\
y_{1_{k+1}} &= y_{1_k} + (\beta_1 x_k y_{1_k} - \gamma y_{1_k} + \delta\beta_1 y_{1_k} z_{1_k} + \alpha\beta_1 y_{1_k} z_{2_k})\Delta \\
y_{2_{k+1}} &= y_{2_k} + (\beta_2 x_k y_{2_k} - \gamma y_{2_k} + \delta\beta_2 y_{2_k} z_{2_k} + \alpha\beta_2 y_{2_k} z_{1_k})\Delta \\
z_{1_{k+1}} &= z_{1_k} + (\gamma y_{1_k} - \delta\beta_1 y_{1_k} z_{1_k} - \alpha\beta_2 y_{2_k} z_{1_k})\Delta \\
z_{2_{k+1}} &= z_{2_k} + (\gamma y_{2_k} - \delta\beta_2 y_{2_k} z_{2_k} - \alpha\beta_1 y_{1_k} z_{2_k})\Delta
\end{aligned} \tag{8}$$

The parameters β_1 and β_2 are the persuasion parameters, i.e., how vigorously the evangelic bees y_1 and y_2 dance; δ is the per capita rate at which the bees spontaneously leave the neutral and non-dancing groups x, z_1, z_2 for the dancing classes y_1, y_2; γ is the per capita rate of ceasing to dance from the dancing classes y_1, y_2 to the non-dancing ones x_1, x_2; α is the proportionality of switching back spontaneously to the neutral state x; Δ is the discretization step. Similarly to the previous case study, the goal of this test is to study the scalability of our method in terms of number of directions and templates, and verify eventual improvements in the precision of the computed reachable set. For the simulation of this model we choose as initial set the box with $x_0 = 500, y_1 \in [390, 400], y_2 \in [90, 100], z_1 = z_2 = 0$. The parameter values are $\beta_1 = \beta_2 = 0.001, \gamma = 0.3, \delta = 0.5, \alpha = 0.7$, and $\Delta = 0.01$. Figure 7 shows the projections of the dancing bees y_1 and y_2 computed with three different configurations up to 1500 steps. The bundles have been transformed with

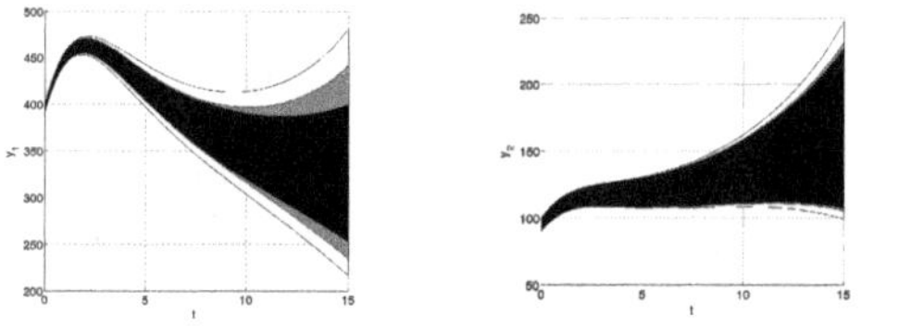

(a) Dancing bees y_1.

(b) Dancing bees y_2.

Figure 7: Projections of reachable set of 5-dimensional honeybees decision-making model. Sets have been computed with 1 temp/5 dirs (in white, 6.57s), 2 temps/6 dirs (in gray, 26.90s), and 3 temps/7 dirs (in black, 81.27s).

the AFO method and no decomposition. In the first configuration (in white), the computation has been carried out with a single template composed by 5 axis-aligned directions (6.57s); the second (in gray) involved 2 templates composed by 6 directions, some of which were not aligned with the x and y_1 axis (26.90s). In the third configuration we defined 3 templates composed by 7 directions, some of which not aligned with x, y_1, and y_2 axis (81.27s). From Figure 7 we can see how the precision of the computed reachable set increases with the addition of directions and templates.

Quadcopter. In our last study we focus on the scalability of our method in terms of system dimension. In this case, we consider the model of a quadrotor drone composed by 17 variables regulated by quadratic dynamics. The model consists of 13 dynamics that drive the drone itself, plus 4 dynamics modeling its controller. The state variables of the drone include the inertial position (p_n, p_e, h), linear velocity (u, v, w), Euler angles expressed using quaternions (q_0, q_1, q_2, q_3), and angular velocity (p, q, r), while the controller variables involve some parameters of position, speed, and angle (h_I, u_I, v_I, ψ_I). Given a reference height h_r, horizontal speeds u_r, v_r, and nose angle ψ_r, the goal of the controller is to bring the drone from its actual configuration to the one specified by the reference values. The detailed description of the model and its dynamics can be found in [11]. All the parameters (such as mass, axis moment of inertia, propeller masses, etc.) have been set accordingly with the real quadcopter CrazyFlie Nano by Bitcraze[3]. The chosen initial conditions are $h_0 \in [0.20, 0.21]$, $q_0 = 1$, and all

[3]https://www.bitcraze.io/

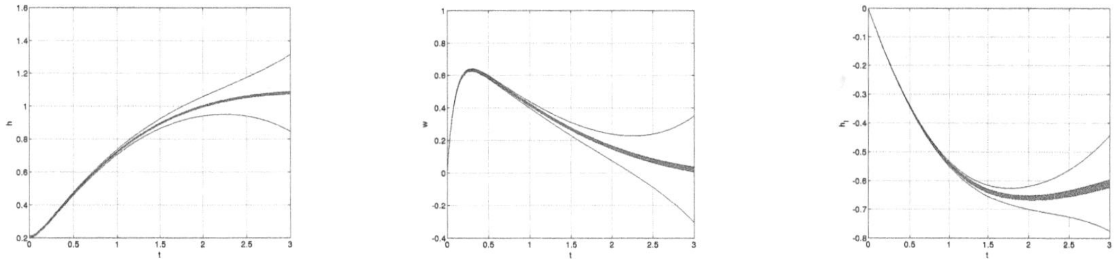

(a) Height (h). (b) Vertical speed (w). (c) Controller height (h_I).

Figure 8: Projections of reachable set of 17-dimensional quadcopter model. Sets have been computed with 1 temp/17 dirs (in white, 17.74s), 2 temps/18 dirs (in gray, 39.07s).

the other variables are set to zero. The reference height is $h_r = 1$, while speeds and angle are $u_r = v_r = \psi_r = 0$. We computed the reachable set up to 300 steps, corresponding to 3s of flight. We adopted 2 configurations, both based on AFO transformation without the bundle decomposition: the first consists in a single box template with axis-aligned constraints, the second has an additional parallelotope involving the dimensions that more vary during the flight (height, vertical speed, angle quaternions, and controller height). Figure 8 shows the projections of the computed reachable sets. The figure reports the evolutions over time of height h (Figure 8a), vertical speed w (Figure 8b), and the height computed by the controller h_I (Figure 8c), obtained with a single (in white) and two templates (in gray). The first technique took 9.40s of computations, the second 20.32s. Note how a single additional template sensibly improves the precision of the computed reachable set and avoids wrapping effects.

7. CONCLUSION

In this work we defined parallelotope bundles and a family of operations that allowed us to define a reachability algorithm for polynomial dynamical systems. We showed the effectiveness of our method studying four nontrivial systems with polynomial dynamics. The obtained data shown the significant precision improvements with respect to the single box/parallelotope inclusion methods.

This work lays the foundation for future developments. An almost direct extension can be towards the reachability analysis of parametric dynamical systems, where a set of parameter values is provided in input. A more complicated problem would be the parameter synthesis involving bundles. Here, it is asked to refine the given parameter set so that the system satisfies a specification. Finally, note that all the defined operations on bundles are easily parallelizable. It could be interesting to implement a parallel bundle manipulator and investigate on the scalability in terms of system dimension and reachable set precision.

8. REFERENCES

[1] M. Althoff and B. H. Krogh. Zonotope bundles for the efficient computation of reachable sets. In *Conference on Decision and Control and European Control Conference, CDC-ECC*, pages 6814–6821. IEEE, 2011.

[2] M. Althoff and B. H. Krogh. Reachability analysis of nonlinear differential-algebraic systems. *IEEE Trans. Automat. Contr.*, 59(2):371–383, 2014.

[3] G. Amato and F. Scozzari. The abstract domain of parallelotopes. *Electron. Notes Theor. Comput. Sci.*, 287:17–28, Nov. 2012.

[4] E. Asarin, O. Bournez, T. Dang, and O. Maler. Approximate reachability analysis of piecewise-linear dynamical systems. In *Hybrid Systems: Computation and Control, HSCC*, pages 20–31. Springer, 2000.

[5] E. Asarin, T. Dang, and A. Girard. Hybridization methods for the analysis of nonlinear systems. *Acta Inf.*, 43(7):451–476, 2007.

[6] E. Asarin, T. Dang, O. Maler, and R. Testylier. Using redundant constraints for refinement. In *Automated Technology for Verification and Analysis, ATVA*, pages 37–51, 2010.

[7] N. Britton, N. Franks, S. Pratt, and T. Seeley. Deciding on a new home: how do honeybees agree? *Royal Society of London B: Biological Sciences*, 269(1498):1383–1388, 2002.

[8] X. Chen, E. Abraham, and S. Sankaranarayanan. Taylor model flowpipe construction for non-linear hybrid systems. In *Real-Time Systems Symposium, RTSS*, pages 183–192. IEEE, 2012.

[9] X. Chen, E. Ábrahám, and S. Sankaranarayanan. Flow*: An analyzer for non-linear hybrid systems. In *Computer Aided Verification, CAV*, pages 258–263, 2013.

[10] A. Chutinan and B. H. Krogh. Computing polyhedral approximations to flow pipes for dynamic systems. In *Conference on Decision and Control, CDC*, volume 2, pages 2089–2094. IEEE, 1998.

[11] A. E. C. da Cunha. Benchmark: Quadrotor attitude control. In *Applied Verification for Continuous and Hybrid Systems, ARCH*, 2015.

[12] T. Dang, T. Dreossi, and C. Piazza. Parameter synthesis using parallelotopic enclosure and applications to epidemic models. In *Hybrid Systems and Biology, HSB*, pages 67–82, 2014.

[13] T. Dang and R. Testylier. Reachability analysis for polynomial dynamical systems using the Bernstein expansion. *Reliable Computing*, 17(2):128–152, 2012.

[14] T. Dreossi and T. Dang. Parameter synthesis for polynomial biological models. In *Hybrid Systems: Computation and Control, HSCC*, pages 233–242, 2014.

[15] G. Frehse, C. Le Guernic, A. Donzé, S. Cotton, R. Ray, O. Lebeltel, R. Ripado, A. Girard, T. Dang,

and O. Maler. Spaceex: Scalable verification of hybrid systems. In *Computer Aided Verification, CAV*, pages 379–395. Springer, 2011.

[16] J. Garloff and A. P. Smith. Investigation of a subdivision based algorithm for solving systems of polynomial equations. *Nonlinear Analysis: Theory, Methods & Applications*, 47(1):167–178, 2001.

[17] K. Ghorbal, E. Goubault, and S. Putot. The zonotope abstract domain taylor1+. In *Computer Aided Verification, CAV*, pages 627–633, 2009.

[18] A. Girard, C. Le Guernic, and O. Maler. Efficient computation of reachable sets of linear time-invariant systems with inputs. In *Hybrid Systems: Computation and Control, HSCC*, pages 257–271. Springer, 2006.

[19] E. Goubault. Static analysis by abstract interpretation of numerical programs and systems, and FLUCTUAT. In *Static Analysis Symposium, SAS*, pages 1–3, 2013.

[20] Z. Han and B. Krogh. Reachability analysis of nonlinear systems using trajectory piecewise linearized models. In *American Control Conference, ACC*, pages 6 pp.–, June 2006.

[21] T. A. Henzinger, B. Horowitz, R. Majumdar, and H. Wong-Toi. Beyond HYTECH: hybrid systems analysis using interval numerical methods. In *Hybrid Systems: Computation and Control, HSCC*, pages 130–144, 2000.

[22] E. K. Kostousovat. Control synthesis via parallelotopes: optimzation and parallel compuations. *Optimization Methods and Software*, 4(14):267–310, 1 2001.

[23] A. A. Kurzhanskiy, P. Varaiya, et al. Ellipsoidal toolbox. *EECS Department, University of California, Berkeley, Tech. Rep. UCB/EECS-2006-46*, 2006.

[24] C. Le Guernic and A. Girard. Reachability analysis of linear systems using support functions. *Nonlinear Analysis: Hybrid Systems*, 4(2):250–262, 2010.

[25] B. Mourrain and J. P. Pavone. Subdivision methods for solving polynomial equations. *J. Symb. Comput.*, 44(3):292–306, 2009.

[26] S. Ratschan and Z. She. Safety verification of hybrid systems by constraint propagation-based abstraction refinement. *ACM Trans. Embedded Comput. Syst.*, 6(1), 2007.

[27] S. Sankaranarayanan, T. Dang, and F. Ivančić. Symbolic model checking of hybrid systems using template polyhedra. In *Tools and Algorithms for the Construction and Analysis of Systems, TACAS*, pages 188–202. Springer, 2008.

[28] S. Sankaranarayanan, H. B. Sipma, and Z. Manna. Scalable analysis of linear systems using mathematical programming. In *Verification, Model Checking, and Abstract Interpretation, VMCAI*, pages 25–41, 2005.

[29] O. Stursberg and B. H. Krogh. Efficient representation and computation of reachable sets for hybrid systems. In *Hybrid Systems: Computation and Control, HSCC*, pages 482–497. Springer, 2003.

HSCC 2016 Posters and Demos

POSTERS

- A Scalable Method for Finding Flaws in the Design of Technical Systems that Are Modelled by Ordinary Differential Equations
  Jan Kuratko and Stefan Ratschan
- DynIBEX: A Differential Constraint Library for Studying Dynamical Systems
  Julien Alexandre Dit Sandretto and Alexandre Chapoutot
- CSiSAT: A Satisfiability Solver for SMT Formulae with Continuous Probability Distributions
  Yang Gao and Martin Franzle
- Temporal Logic Verification for Delay Differential Equations
  Peter Nazier Mosaad and Martin Franzle
- Statistical Verification of the Toyota Powertrain Control Verification Benchmark
  Nima Roohi, Yu Wang, Matthew West, Geir Dullerud and Mahesh Viswanathan
- Online Learning of STL Formulae for Signal Classification
  Giuseppe Bombara and Calin Belta

DEMOS

- Montre: A Tool for Monitoring Timed Regular Expressions
  Dogan Ulus
- System Testing with S-TaLiRo: Recent Functionality and Additions
  Bardh Hoxha, Adel Dokhanchi and Georgios Fainekos
- Hybrid Systems Model Transformations with HyST
  Stanley Bak, Sergiy Bogomolov and Taylor T Johnson

Author Index